MW01011649

Romans 9–16

CONCORDIA COMMENTARY

A Theological Exposition of Sacred Scripture

ROMANS 9–16

Michael P. Middendorf

Concordia Publishing House

Saint Louis

Library of Congress Cataloging-in-Publication Data

Library of Congress Cataloging-in-Publication Data

Middendorf, Michael Paul, 1959–
     Romans 1–8 / Michael P. Middendorf.
       pages   cm. — (Concordia commentary: a theological exposition of sacred scripture)
     Includes bibliographical references and indexes.
     ISBN 978-0-7586-3867-0
     1. Bible. N.T. Romans I–VIII—Commentaries. I. Title. II. Series.

     BS2665.53.M53   2013
     227'.1077—dc23

                                  2012032829

1 2 3 4 5 6 7 8 9 10   25 24 23 22 21 20 19 18 17 16

To my wife, Lana, in whom the Spirit produces
his fruit abundantly (Gal 5:22–23)

In memory of my father,
the Rev. Dr. Marvin Luther Middendorf (1927–2012),
who loved his students into Greek and, thereby, into the Word
of our loving Lord, in whom Marvin rejoices eternally (Phil 4:4)

Contents

Pages 1–802 are in *Romans 1–8*.

15:14–16:27 Wrapping Up the Letter

Editors' Preface

What may a reader expect from the Concordia Commentary: A Theological Exposition of Sacred Scripture?

The purpose of this series, simply put, is to assist pastors, missionaries, and teachers of the Scriptures to convey God's Word with greater clarity, understanding, and faithfulness to the divine intent of the text.

Since every interpreter approaches the exegetical task from a certain perspective, honesty calls for an outline of the presuppositions held by those who have shaped this commentary series. This also serves, then, as a description of the characteristics of the commentaries.

First in importance is the conviction that the content of the scriptural testimony is Jesus Christ. The Lord himself enunciated this when he said, "The Scriptures … testify to me" (Jn 5:39), words that have been incorporated into the logo of this series. The message of the Scriptures is the Good News of God's work to reconcile the world to himself through the life, death, resurrection, ascension, and everlasting session of Jesus Christ at the right hand of God the Father. Under the guidance of the same Spirit who inspired the writing of the Scriptures, these commentaries seek to find in every passage of every canonical book "that which promotes Christ" (as Luther's hermeneutic is often described). They are *Trinitarian*, Christ-centered, and *Christological* commentaries.

As they unfold the scriptural testimony to Jesus Christ, these commentaries expound Law and Gospel. This approach arises from a second conviction—that Law and Gospel are the overarching doctrines of the Bible itself and that to understand them in their proper distinction and relationship to each other is a key for understanding the self-revelation of God and his plan of salvation in Jesus Christ.

Now, Law and Gospel do not always appear in Scripture labeled as such. The palette of language in Scripture is multicolored, with many and rich hues. The dialectic of a pericope may be fallen creation and new creation, darkness and light, death and life, wandering and promised land, exile and return, ignorance and wisdom, demon possession and the kingdom of God, sickness and healing, being lost and found, guilt and righteousness, flesh and Spirit, fear and joy, hunger and feast, or Babylon and the new Jerusalem. But the common element is God's gracious work of restoring fallen humanity through the Gospel of his Son. Since the predominant characteristic of these commentaries is the proclamation of that Gospel, they are, in the proper sense of the term, *evangelical.*

A third, related conviction is that the Scriptures are God's vehicle for communicating the Gospel. The editors and authors accept without reservation that the canonical books of the Old and New Testaments are, in their entirety, the inspired, infallible, and inerrant Word of God. The triune God is the ultimate author of the Bible, and every word in the original Hebrew, Aramaic, and Greek is inspired by the Holy Spirit. Yet rather than mechanical dictation, in the mysterious process by which the Scriptures were divinely inspired (e.g., 2 Tim 3:16; 2 Pet 1:21), God made use of the human faculties, knowledge, interests, and styles of the biblical writers, whose individual books surely are marked by distinctive features. At the same time, the canon of Scripture has its own inner unity, and each passage must be understood in harmony with the larger context of the whole. This commentary series pays heed to the smallest of textual details because of its acceptance of *plenary and verbal inspiration* and interprets the text in light of the whole of Scripture, in accord with the analogy of faith, following the principle that *Scripture interprets Scripture.* The entirety of the Bible is God's Word, *sacred* Scripture, calling for *theological* exposition.

A fourth conviction is that, even as the God of the Gospel came into this world in Jesus Christ (the Word Incarnate), the scriptural Gospel has been given to and through the people of God, for the benefit of all humanity. God did not intend his Scriptures to have a life separated from the church. He gave them through servants of his choosing: prophets, sages, evangelists, and apostles. He gave them to the church and through the church, to be cherished in the church for admonition and comfort and to be used by the church for proclamation and catechesis. The living context of Scripture is ever the church, where the Lord's ministry of preaching, baptizing, forgiving sins, teaching, and celebrating the Lord's Supper continues. Aware of the way in which the incarnation of the Son of God has as a consequence the close union of Scripture and church, of Word and Sacraments, this commentary series features expositions that are *ecclesiological* and *sacramental.*

This Gospel Word of God, moreover, creates a unity among all those in whom it works the obedience of faith and who confess the truth of God revealed in it. This is the unity of the one holy Christian and apostolic church, which extends through world history. The church is to be found wherever the marks of the church are present: the Gospel in the Word and the Sacraments. These have been proclaimed, confessed, and celebrated in many different cultures and are in no way limited nor especially attached to any single culture or people. As this commentary series seeks to articulate the universal truth of the Gospel, it acknowledges and affirms the confession of the scriptural truth in all the many times and places where the one true church has been found. Aiming to promote *concord* in the confession of the one scriptural Gospel, these commentaries seek to be, in the best sense of the terms, *confessional, ecumenical,* and *catholic.*

All of those convictions and characteristics describe the theological heritage of Martin Luther and of the confessors who subscribe to the *Book of Concord* (1580)—those who have come to be known as Lutherans. The editors and authors forthrightly confess their subscription to the doctrinal exposition of Scripture in the *Book of Concord.* As the publishing arm of The Lutheran Church—Missouri Synod, Concordia Publishing House is bound to doctrinal agreement with the Scriptures and the Lutheran Confessions and seeks to herald the true Christian doctrine to the ends of the earth. To that end, the series has enlisted confessional Lutheran authors from other church bodies around the world who share the evangelical mission of promoting theological concord.

The authors and editors stand in the exegetical tradition of Martin Luther and the other Lutheran reformers, who in turn (as their writings took pains to demonstrate) stood in continuity with faithful exegesis by theologians of the early and medieval church, rooted in the hermeneutics of the Scriptures themselves (evident, for example, by how the New Testament interprets the Old). This hermeneutical method, practiced also by many non-Lutherans, includes (1) interpreting Scripture with Scripture according to the analogy of faith, that is, in harmony with the whole of Christian doctrine revealed in the Word; (2) giving utmost attention to the grammar (lexicography, phonetics, morphology, syntax, pragmatics) of the original language of the Hebrew, Aramaic, or Greek text; (3) seeking to discern the intended meaning of the text, the "plain" or "literal" sense, aware that the language of Scripture ranges from narrative to discourse, from formal prose to evocative poetry, from archaic to acrostic to apocalyptic, and it uses metaphor, type, parable, and other figures; (4) drawing on philology, linguistics, archaeology, literature, philosophy, history, and other fields in the quest for a better understanding of the text; (5) considering the history of the church's interpretation; (6) applying the text as authoritative also in the present milieu of the interpreter; and (7) above all, seeing the fulfillment and present application of the text in terms of Jesus Christ and his corporate church; upholding the Word, Baptism, and the Supper as the means through which Christ imparts salvation today; and affirming the inauguration, already now, of the eternal benefits of that salvation that is yet to come in the resurrection on the Last Day.

To be sure, the authors and editors do not feel bound to agree with every detail of the exegesis of our Lutheran forefathers. Nor do we imagine that the interpretations presented here are the final word about every crux and enigmatic passage. But the work has been done in harmony with the exegetical tradition that reaches back through the Lutheran confessors all the way to the biblical writers themselves, and in harmony with the confession of the church: grace alone, faith alone, Scripture alone, Christ alone.

The editors wish to acknowledge their debt of gratitude for all who have helped make possible this series. It was conceived at CPH in 1990, and a couple of years of planning and prayer to the Lord of the church preceded its formal launch on July 2, 1992. During that time, Dr. J. A. O. Preus II volunteered his enthusiasm for the project because, in his view, it would nurture and advance the faithful proclamation of the Christian faith as understood by the Lutheran church. The financial support that has underwritten the series was provided by a gracious donor who wished to remain anonymous. Those two faithful servants of God were called to heavenly rest not long after the series was inaugurated.

During the early years, former CPH presidents Dr. John W. Gerber and Dr. Stephen J. Carter had the foresight to recognize the potential benefit of such a landmark work for the church at large. CPH allowed Dr. Christopher W.

Mitchell to devote his time and energy to the conception and initial development of the project. Dr. Mitchell has remained the CPH editor and is also the Old Testament editor. Dr. Dean O. Wenthe has served on the project since its official start in 1992 and is the general editor, as well as a commentary author. Julene Gernant Dumit (M.A.R.) has been the CPH production editor for the entire series. Dr. Jeffrey A. Gibbs, author of the Matthew commentary volumes, served on the editorial board as the New Testament editor from 1999 into 2012. Dr. Curtis P. Giese, author of the commentary on 2 Peter and Jude, joined the board as interim assistant New Testament editor in 2011 and now serves as the New Testament editor.

CPH thanks all of the institutions that have enabled their faculty to serve as authors and editors. A particular debt of gratitude is owed to Concordia Theological Seminary, Fort Wayne, Indiana, for kindly allowing Dr. Dean O. Wenthe to serve as the general editor of the series and to dedicate a substantial portion of his time to it for many years. CPH also thanks Concordia Seminary, St. Louis, Missouri, for the dedication of Dr. Jeffrey A. Gibbs during his tenure as the New Testament editor. Moreover, Concordia University Texas is granting Dr. Curtis P. Giese a reduced load to enable him to carry on as the New Testament editor of the series. These institutions have thereby extended their ministries in selfless service for the benefit of the greater church.

The editors pray that the beneficence of their institutions may be reflected in this series by an evangelical orientation, a steadfast Christological perspective, an eschatological view toward the ultimate good of Christ's bride, and a concern that the wedding feast of the King's Son may be filled with all manner of guests (Mt 22:1–14).

> Now to him who is able to establish you by my Gospel and the preaching of Jesus Christ, by the revelation of the mystery kept secret for ages past but now revealed also through the prophetic Scriptures, made known to all the nations by order of the eternal God unto the obedience of faith—to the only wise God, through Jesus Christ, be the glory forever. Amen! (Rom 16:25–27)

Author's Preface

Volume 1 of this commentary concludes by describing Rom 8:31–39 as a majestic mountaintop "from which one can look back clearly over the terrain covered thus far and rejoice that a high point on the hike through Romans has been reached."[1] Hopefully, all who walk the first half of the Romans road will receive the Good News of God's saving righteousness (chapters 1–4) and rejoice in the life he bestows in and through Jesus Christ our Lord (chapters 5–8).

As this author looks back over his commentary on Romans 1–8, the trail taken thus far evokes a renewed sense of gratitude to God, as well as an encouraging sense of accomplishment which inspires one to march forward. It is satisfying to reaffirm the identification of the overall direction, emphases, and flow of Paul's line of argumentation in Romans 1–8.[2] It is also gratifying to endorse positions taken on disputed isagogical issues (e.g., the addressees[3]). Finally, this author continues to espouse specific interpretations articulated in volume 1. Potentially controversial stances include viewing νόμος ("law," "principle") as a consistent reference to the Mosaic Torah;[4] identifying Paul, past and then present, as the referent of the "I" in Romans 7;[5] and understanding ὑπακούω and ὑπακοή in the broader sense of "responsive hearing," rather than as always conveying active "obedience."[6]

At the same time, a glance backward reveals that occasionally a better or more accurate trajectory could have been followed. Two may be noted briefly. First, the main theme of Paul's argument revolves around the "righteousness of God" (δικαιοσύνη θεοῦ, 1:17). Therefore volume 1 properly recognizes the critical nature of 3:26.[7] The latter half of the verse asserts this fundamental conclusion about God: "with the result that he is righteous and declares righteous the one from faith of/[in] Jesus" (εἰς τὸ εἶναι αὐτὸν δίκαιον καὶ δικαιοῦντα

---

[1] Middendorf, *Romans 1–8*, 733.

[2] See Middendorf, *Romans 1–8*, 21–22, 28–31, 49–51, 377–80. In this volume, see "Much Has Been Said—Much Remains to Be Said" in the introduction to Romans 9–16.

[3] See Middendorf, *Romans 1–8*, 10–14, 17–21. In this volume, see "Who Are the 'Weak' and the 'Strong'? Addressees Again!" in the introduction to 14:1–15:13.

[4] See, for example, the commentary on 3:27; 7:21, 23; 8:2; 13:8–10, and the excursus "Paul and the Law" following the commentary on 13:8–14. Note also the general agreement presented convincingly in regard to "the Law of Christ" in Gal 6:2 and then applied throughout both Romans and Galatians by Das, *Galatians*, 607–12.

[5] See the excursuses "Who Is the 'I' in Romans 7:7–11? The Referent Question" following the commentary on 7:7–13 and "Who Is the 'I' in Romans 7:14–25? Christian or Non-Christian?" following the commentary on 7:14–25.

[6] See the note on 1:5 in *The Lutheran Study Bible*, 1908, which suggests "listening" for the use of ὑπακοή in that verse; see also 6:17. In this volume, see the commentary on 10:16–17; 15:18; 16:26.

[7] Middendorf, *Romans 1–8*, 289–93.

τὸν ἐκ πίστεως Ἰησοῦ, 3:26b).[8] The translation adopted in volume 1, however, could have better recognized the adverbial participle δικαιοῦντα and also conveyed the intensive force of the preceding καί (BDAG, 2 b). Thus Paul's thought is better communicated as "with the result that he is righteous *even while* declaring righteous the one from faith of/[in] Jesus."[9] This properly maintains God's righteousness. Yet it highlights even further the extent to which God went and the impact of what his righteousness also accomplished: the redemption of sinners by the atoning sacrifice of Jesus Christ (3:23–25).

Second, volume 1 extensively covers the use of the first person singular in Romans 7.[10] Rom 8:1–4 is then presented as "Paul's greatest hinge."[11] The argument and vocabulary of 8:1–4 demonstrate how these verses resolve the conundrum of 7:14–25 while *also* pointing ahead into the rest of Romans 8.[12] But if the former is the case, why does Paul drop the first person singular form of expression in Rom 8:1–4? The frustration expressed by Paul in 7:14–25 employs the first person singular to give *his own perspective* regarding himself, the Law, and sin.[13] "Whenever sin, the Law, and 'I' are the only participants in the drama, the failures of 7:14–23 will inevitably mount, and expressions of exasperation are bound to ensue."[14] But what really counts is *God's perspective*.[15] God's declaration regarding Paul's reality (and ours) remains: "nothing [is] condemnation for the ones in Christ Jesus" (8:1). This change of perspective explains *why Paul moves away from first person language* in 8:1–4 to speak authoritatively of God's view, rather than his/our own, and to detail what the triune God has accomplished for us.

As discussed in the author's preface to volume 1, numerous interpreters have already traversed the Romans road and sought to mark out its path for those who follow. All deserve commendation, and a few are worthy of special praise. For understanding the church fathers, the volume on Romans in the Ancient Christian Commentary on Scripture series edited by Bray provides many great insights. Among the plethora of more modern works consulted and cited along the way (see the bibliography), this author continues to find the commentaries of Cranfield, Dunn, and Moo particularly helpful. Each of them engages the Greek text proficiently, provides a survey of options based upon the work of previous scholars, and generally offers well-founded conclusions. Of course, on

---

[8] For the appropriate ambiguity of "faith of/[in] Jesus" at the end of the verse, see the excursus "πίστις Ἰησοῦ Χριστοῦ, 'Faith of/[in] Jesus Christ' " following the commentary on 3:21–31.

[9] Thanks here to my colleague Dr. Mark Brighton.

[10] See especially Middendorf, *Romans 1–8*, 543–52, 584–97.

[11] Middendorf, *Romans 1–8*, 601–15. A number of effective hinges appear in Romans 9–16 as well. See, for example, the commentary on 9:24; 10:4–5; 10:16–17; 15:7.

[12] Middendorf, *Romans 1–8*, 598–99.

[13] For further details, see the excursus "Paul and the Law" following the commentary on 13:8–14.

[14] Middendorf, *Romans 1–8*, 580 (emphasis removed).

[15] Middendorf, *Romans 1–8*, 49.

matters of interpretation they regularly differ among themselves, with a sizable number of the other referenced commentaries, and with my own understandings of the text. But these three repeatedly help to establish the parameters of the discussion and to invigorate one's own thinking. They have been my constant companions throughout this Romans pilgrimage.

In retrospect, one wonders whether doing exegetical work can actually be taught or if it more often must be caught by observing the diligence and passion with which others engage in the task. In this regard, the foundations for my motivation and ability reside largely with the exegetical faculty of Concordia Seminary, St. Louis. Worthy of special note are James Voelz (my *Doktorvater*), Paul Raabe, Louis Brighton, Horace Hummel, Jonathan Grothe, and Andrew Bartelt.

The words of gratitude conveyed in the author's preface to volume 1 deserve to be reinforced, but will not all be repeated here. However, thanks must again be expressed to Dr. Christopher Mitchell, Dr. Curtis Giese, and Julene Dumit, who substantially improved my work through their skillful editing. Additionally, leaders, colleagues, and students at Concordia University Irvine have graciously provided ongoing encouragement and support. Worthy of special praise are President Kurt Krueger, Provost Mary Scott, and Dr. Steven Mueller, the dean of Christ College, particularly for awarding me the Harry and Caroline Trembath Chair of Confessional Theology again in the fall of 2013 and for a research grant for fall 2014. Thanks also to Concordia Publishing House for giving me the added opportunity to expound on the inspired truths of Romans 9–16.

As another journey through Romans now stands complete, this author expresses his most profound gratitude to God the Father, whose righteousness found a way to declare us sinners righteous and to give us life "in Christ Jesus our Lord" (6:23; 8:39). One must also praise the Holy Spirit, who inspired Paul's words. The Holy Spirit and Paul surely form the greatest authorship team of all time! In the opinion of many, including this author, Romans provides the most magnificent evidence of their combined efforts. One could make this assessment purely on the basis of volume. Paul's thirteen letters contain a total of approximately 32,407 Greek words.[16] Romans, with over 7,100 of them,[17] occupies more than a fifth of the total (21.9 percent). Of course, the letter's greatest impact stems from its powerful, all-encompassing, and enduring Gospel message. No final words can eclipse those of Paul himself, who ascribes all praise "to [the] only, wise God, through Jesus Christ—to whom [is] the glory into the ages. Amen" (16:27).

June 29, 2015
Feast of St. Peter and St. Paul, Apostles

---

[16] http://catholic-resources.org/Bible/NT-Statistics-Greek.htm.

[17] See also Morris, *Romans*, 2.

Principal Abbreviations

Books of the Bible

Gen	2 Ki	Is	Nah	Rom	Titus
Ex	1 Chr	Jer	Hab	1 Cor	Philemon
Lev	2 Chr	Lam	Zeph	2 Cor	Heb
Num	Ezra	Ezek	Hag	Gal	James
Deut	Neh	Dan	Zech	Eph	1 Pet
Josh	Esth	Hos	Mal	Phil	2 Pet
Judg	Job	Joel	Mt	Col	1 Jn
Ruth	Ps (pl. Pss)	Amos	Mk	1 Thess	2 Jn
1 Sam	Prov	Obad	Lk	2 Thess	3 Jn
2 Sam	Eccl	Jonah	Jn	1 Tim	Jude
1 Ki	Song	Micah	Acts	2 Tim	Rev

Books of the Apocrypha and Other Noncanonical Books of the Septuagint

1–2 Esdras	1–2 Esdras
Tobit	Tobit
Judith	Judith
Add Esth	Additions to Esther
Wisdom	Wisdom of Solomon
Sirach	Sirach/Ecclesiasticus
Baruch	Baruch
Ep Jer	Epistle of Jeremiah
Azariah	Prayer of Azariah
Song of the Three	Song of the Three Young Men
Susanna	Susanna
Bel	Bel and the Dragon
Manasseh	Prayer of Manasseh
1–2 Macc	1–2 Maccabees
3–4 Macc	3–4 Maccabees
Ps 151	Psalm 151
Odes	Odes
Ps(s) Sol	Psalm(s) of Solomon

Reference Works and Scripture Versions

AC	Augsburg Confession
ACCS	Ancient Christian Commentary on Scripture
AE	*Luther's Works*. St. Louis: Concordia, and Philadelphia: Fortress, 1955– [American Edition]
Ap	Apology of the Augsburg Confession
BDAG	Bauer, W., F. W. Danker, W. F. Arndt, F. W. Gingrich. *A Greek-English Lexicon of the New Testament and Other Early Christian Literature*. 3d ed. Chicago: University of Chicago Press, 2000
BDB	Brown, F., S. R. Driver, and C. A. Briggs. *A Hebrew and English Lexicon of the Old Testament*. 1906. Repr., Oxford: Clarendon, 1979
BDF	Blass, F., A. Debrunner, and R. W. Funk. *A Greek Grammar of the New Testament and Other Early Christian Literature*. Chicago: University of Chicago Press, 1961
CBQ	*Catholic Biblical Quarterly*
CER	Origen. *Commentarii in Epistulam ad Romanos*. Edited by T. Heither. 6 vols. Freiburg im Breisgau, Germany: Herder, 1990–1999
CSEL	Corpus scriptorum ecclesiasticorum latinorum
DCH	*The Dictionary of Classical Hebrew*. Edited by D. J. A. Clines. 8 vols. Sheffield: Sheffield Academic Press, 1993–2011
DPL	*Dictionary of Paul and His Letters*. Edited by G. F. Hawthorne, R. P. Martin, and D. G. Reid. Downers Grove, Ill.: InterVarsity, 1993
ESV	English Standard Version of the Bible
ET	English translation
FC Ep	Formula of Concord, Epitome
FC SD	Formula of Concord, Solid Declaration
GNT	Good News Translation (of the Bible) in Today's English Version
HALOT	Koehler, L., W. Baumgartner, and J. J. Stamm. *The Hebrew and Aramaic Lexicon of the Old Testament*. Translated and edited under the supervision of M. E. J. Richardson. 5 vols. Leiden: Brill, 1994–2000
Joüon	Joüon, P. *A Grammar of Biblical Hebrew*. Translated and revised by T. Muraoka. 2 vols. Subsidia biblica 14/1–2. Rome: Editrice Pontificio Istituto Biblico, 1991
KJV	King James Version of the Bible

LC	Large Catechism of Martin Luther
LCL	Loeb Classical Library
LEH	Lust, J., E. Eynikel, and K. Hauspie. *Greek-English Lexicon of the Septuagint.* Rev. ed. Stuttgart: Deutsche Bibelgesellschaft, 2003
LSB	*Lutheran Service Book.* St. Louis: Concordia, 2006
LSJM	Liddell, H. G., R. Scott, H. S. Jones, and R. McKenzie. *A Greek-English Lexicon.* 9th ed. with rev. supplement. Oxford: Clarendon, 1996
LXX	Septuagint
MT	Masoretic Text of the Hebrew Bible
Muraoka	Muraoka, T. *A Greek-English Lexicon of the Septuagint.* Leuven, Belgium: Peeters, 2009
NA[27]	Nestle, E. and E., K. and B. Aland, et al. *Novum Testamentum Graece.* 27th ed. Stuttgart: Deutsche Bibelgesellschaft, 1993
NA[28]	Nestle, E. and E., K. and B. Aland, et al. *Novum Testamentum Graece.* 28th ed. Stuttgart: Deutsche Bibelgesellschaft, 2012
NASB	New American Standard Bible
NDBT	*New Dictionary of Biblical Theology.* Edited by T. Desmond Alexander and Brian S. Rosner. Downers Grove, Ill.: InterVarsity, 2000
NEB	New English Bible
NETS	*A New English Translation of the Septuagint and the Other Greek Translations Traditionally Included under That Title.* Edited by A. Pietersma and B. G. Wright. Oxford: Oxford University Press, 2007
NKJV	New King James Version of the Bible
NPNF[1]	*The Nicene and Post-Nicene Fathers.* Series 1. Edited by P. Schaff. 14 vols. Repr., Peabody, Mass.: Hendrickson, 1994
NRSV	New Revised Standard Version of the Bible
NT	New Testament
OED	*The Oxford English Dictionary.* Prepared by J. A. Simpson and E. S. C. Weiner. 2d ed. 20 vols. New York: Oxford University Press, 1989
OT	Old Testament
OTP	*The Old Testament Pseudepigrapha.* Edited by J. H. Charlesworth. 2 vols. Garden City, N.Y.: Doubleday, 1983, 1985

PG	Patrologia graeca. Edited by J.-P. Migne. 161 vols. Paris, 1857–1866
RSV	Revised Standard Version of the Bible
SC	Small Catechism of Martin Luther
Str-B	Strack, H. L., and P. Billerbeck. *Kommentar zum Neuen Testament aus Talmud und Midrasch.* 6 vols. in 7. Munich: Beck, 1922–1961
TDNT	*Theological Dictionary of the New Testament.* Edited by G. Kittel and G. Friedrich. Translated by G. W. Bromiley. 10 vols. Grand Rapids: Eerdmans, 1964–1976
WA DB	*D. Martin Luthers Werke: Kritische Gesamtausgabe. Die Deutsche Bibel.* 12 vols. in 15. Weimar: Böhlau, 1906–1961 [Weimarer Ausgabe Deutsche Bibel]

Icons

These icons are used in the margins of this commentary to highlight the following themes:

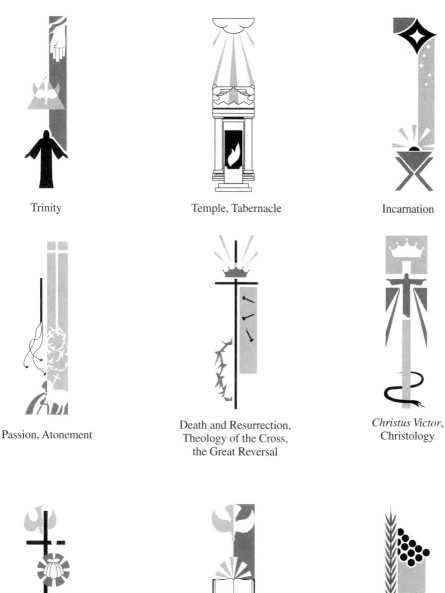

Trinity

Temple, Tabernacle

Incarnation

Passion, Atonement

Death and Resurrection,
Theology of the Cross,
the Great Reversal

Christus Victor,
Christology

Baptism

Catechesis,
Instruction, Revelation

Lord's Supper

Ministry of Word and Sacrament,
Office of the Keys

The Church,
Christian Marriage

Worship

Sin, Law Breaking,
Death

Hope of Heaven,
Eschatology

Justification

Bibliography

Achtemeier, Paul J. *Romans*. Interpretation: A Bible Commentary for Teaching and Preaching. Atlanta: John Knox, 1985.

Alford, Henry. *The Greek Testament*. 5th ed. 4 vols. Cambridge: Deighton, Bell, and Co., 1865.

Allen, Leslie C. "The Old Testament in Romans I–VIII." *Vox evangelica* 3 (1964): 6–41.

Althaus, Paul. *Der Brief an die Römer*. 10th ed. Das Neue Testament Deutsch 6. Göttingen: Vandenhoeck & Ruprecht, 1966.

———. *Paulus und Luther über den Menschen*. Gütersloh: Bertelsmann, 1938.

Astley, Nolan. "Morning People." *Concordia Pulpit Resources* 24/1 (December 1, 2013–March 2, 2014): 12–13.

Baker, David L. *Two Testaments: One Bible: The Theological Relationship between the Old and New Testaments*. 3d ed. Downers Grove, Ill.: IVP Academic, 2010.

Bandstra, Andrew John. *The Law and the Elements of the World: An Exegetical Study in Aspects of Paul's Teaching*. Kampen: Kok, 1964.

Barclay, William. *The Mind of St Paul*. New York: Harper, 1958.

Barrett, C. K. *A Commentary on the Epistle to the Romans*. Black's New Testament Commentaries. London: Black, 1957.

———. *Paul: An Introduction to His Thought*. Louisville, Ky.: Westminster John Knox, 1994.

Barth, Karl. *Church and State*. London: SCM, 1939.

———. *The Epistle to the Romans*. Translated by Edwyn C. Hoskyns. London: Oxford University Press, 1933.

Bassler, Jouette M. "Divine Impartiality in Paul's Letter to the Romans." *Novum Testamentum* 26 (1984): 43–58.

Beker, J. Christiaan. "The Faithfulness of God and the Priority of Israel in Paul's Letter to the Romans." Pages 327–32 in *The Romans Debate*. Edited by Karl P. Donfried. Rev. ed. Peabody, Mass.: Hendrickson, 1991.

———. *Paul the Apostle: The Triumph of God in Life and Thought*. Philadelphia: Fortress, 1980.

Bengel, Johann Albrecht. *Gnomon Novi Testamenti in quo ex native verborum vi simplicitas, profunditas, concinnitas, salubritas sensuum coelestium indicatur*. 3d ed. (1773). Stuttgart: Steinkopf, 1860.

Betz, Hans Dieter. "Christianity as Religion: Paul's Attempt at Definition in Romans." Pages 206–39 in *Paulinische Studien*. Tübingen: Mohr, 1994.

Bibliowicz, Abel Mordechai. *Jews and Gentiles in the Early Jesus Movement: An Unintended Journey*. New York: Palgrave Macmillan, 2013.

Black, Matthew. *Romans*. New Century Bible. London: Oliphants, 1973.

Blackwell, Ben C., John K. Goodrich, and Jason Maston, eds. *Reading Romans in Context: Paul and Second Temple Judaism*. Grand Rapids: Zondervan, 2015.

Bolling, Richard E. *Interpretation of Scripture according to the Word of God*. Bellevue, Neb.: Richard E. Bolling, 2008.

Bonhoeffer, Dietrich. *Life Together: A Discussion of Christian Fellowship*. New York: Harper, 1954.

Bornkamm, Günther. *Early Christian Experience*. Translated by Paul L. Hammer. London: SCM, 1969.

———. "The Letter to the Romans as Paul's Last Will and Testament." Pages 16–28 in *The Romans Debate*. Edited by Karl P. Donfried. Rev. ed. Peabody, Mass.: Hendrickson, 1991.

Bornkamm, Heinrich. *Luther's Doctrine of the Two Kingdoms*. Philadelphia, Fortress, 1966.

Bottorff, J. F. "The Relation of Justification and Ethics in the Pauline Epistles." *Scottish Journal of Theology* 26 (1973): 421–30.

Bowker, John. *The Targums and Rabbinic Literature: An Introduction to Jewish Interpretations of Scripture*. London: Cambridge University Press, 1969.

Bray, Gerald, ed. *Romans*. Ancient Christian Commentary on Scripture, New Testament 6. Downers Grove, Ill.: InterVarsity, 1998.

Brighton, Louis A. *Revelation*. Concordia Commentary. St. Louis: Concordia, 1999.

Bruce, F. F. *The Letter of Paul to the Romans: An Introduction and Commentary*. Rev. ed. Tyndale New Testament Commentaries. Grand Rapids: Eerdmans, 1985.

———. *Paul: Apostle of the Heart Set Free*. Grand Rapids: Eerdmans, 1977.

———. "The Romans Debate—Continued." Pages 175–94 in *The Romans Debate*. Edited by Karl P. Donfried. Rev. ed. Peabody, Mass.: Hendrickson, 1991.

Brunner, Emil. *The Letter to the Romans: A Commentary*. Philadelphia: Westminster, 1959.

Bultmann, Rudolf. *The Old and New Man in the Letters of Paul*. Translated by Keith R. Crim. Richmond, Va.: John Knox, 1967.

———. *Der Stil der paulinischen Predigt und die kynisch-stoische Diatribe*. Göttingen: Vandenhoeck & Ruprecht, 1910.

———. *Theology of the New Testament*. 2 vols. Translated by Kendrick Grobel. New York: Scribner, 1951–1955.

Burke, Trevor J., and Brian S. Rosner, eds. *Paul as Missionary: Identity, Activity, Theology, and Practice*. Library of New Testament Studies 420. New York: T&T Clark, 2011.

Byrne, Brendan. *"Sons of God"—"Seed of Abraham": A Study of the Idea of the Sonship of God of All Christians in Paul against the Jewish Background*. Rome: Biblical Institute, 1979.

Caird, G. B. *The Language and Imagery of the Bible*. London: Duckworth, 1980.

Calvin, John. *The Epistles of Paul the Apostle to the Romans and to the Thessalonians*. Translated by Ross Mackenzie. Grand Rapids: Eerdmans, 1961.

Campbell, Constantine R. *Paul and Union with Christ: An Exegetical and Theological Study*. Grand Rapids: Zondervan, 2012.

Campbell, William S. *Paul and the Creation of Christian Identity*. London: T&T Clark, 2006.

———. "Romans III as a Key to the Structure and Thought of the Letter." Pages 251–64 in *The Romans Debate*. Edited by Karl P. Donfried. Rev. ed. Peabody, Mass.: Hendrickson, 1991.

Capes, David B., Rodney Reeves, and E. Randolph Richards. *Rediscovering Paul: An Introduction to His World, Letters and Theology*. Downers Grove, Ill.: IVP Academic, 2007.

Carter, T. L. "The Irony of Romans 13." *Novum Testamentum* 46 (2004): 209–28.

Charles, R. H., ed. *The Apocrypha and Pseudepigrapha of the Old Testament in English*. 2 vols. Oxford: Clarendon, 1913.

Charlesworth, James H. *The Old Testament Pseudepigrapha and the New Testament: Prolegomena for the Study of Christian Origins*. Cambridge: Cambridge University Press, 1985.

Collins, John J. *Diakonia: Re-interpreting the Ancient Sources*. New York: Oxford University Press, 1990.

Commission on Theology and Church Relations of The Lutheran Church—Missouri Synod. *Biblical Revelation and Inclusive Language*. February 1998.

———. *The Charismatic Movement and Lutheran Theology*. January 1972.

———. *Gospel and Scripture: The Interrelationship of the Material and Formal Principles in Lutheran Theology*. November 1972.

———. *The Inspiration of Scripture*. March 1975.

———. *Racism and the Church*. February 1994.

———. *Render unto Caesar ... and unto God: A Lutheran View of Church and State*. September 1995.

———. *Response to* Human Sexuality: Gift and Trust. April 2012.

———. *Spiritual Gifts*. September 1994.

———. *Theology and Practice of Prayer: A Lutheran View*. November 2011.

———. *Together with All Creatures: Caring for God's Living Earth*. April 2010.

Conzelmann, Hans. *An Outline of the Theology of the New Testament*. Translated by John Bowden. London: SCM, 1969.

Cranfield, C. E. B. *A Critical and Exegetical Commentary on the Epistle to the Romans*. 2 vols. International Critical Commentary. Edinburgh: T&T Clark, 1975.

———. "St. Paul and the Law." *Scottish Journal of Theology* 17 (1964): 43–68.

Cullmann, Oscar. *Christ and Time: The Primitive Christian Conception of Time and History*. Translated by Floyd V. Filson. Rev. ed. London: SCM, 1962.

————. *The State in the New Testament*. New York: Harper, 1956.

Danby, Herbert, trans. *The Mishnah*. Oxford: Oxford University Press, 1933.

Das, A. Andrew. "Beyond Covenantal Nomism: Paul, Judaism, and Perfect Obedience." *Concordia Journal* 27 (2001): 234–52.

————. *Galatians*. Concordia Commentary. St. Louis: Concordia, 2014.

————. "The Gentile-Encoded Audience of Romans: The Church outside the Synagogue." Pages 29–46 in *Reading Paul's Letter to the Romans*. Edited by Jerry Sumney. Atlanta: Society of Biblical Literature, 2012.

————. "Paul of Tarshish: Isaiah 66.19 and the Spanish Mission of Romans 15.24, 28." *New Testament Studies* 54 (2008): 60–73.

————. *Paul, the Law, and the Covenant*. Peabody, Mass.: Hendrickson, 2001.

————. " 'Praise the Lord, All You Gentiles': The Encoded Audience of Romans 15.7–13." *Journal for the Study of the New Testament* 34 (2011): 90–110.

————. *Solving the Romans Debate*. Minneapolis: Fortress, 2007.

Daube, David. "Appended Note: Participle and Imperative in I Peter." Pages 467–88 in *The First Epistle of St. Peter: The Greek Text with Introduction, Notes and Essays* by Edward Gordon Selwyn. London: Macmillan, 1947.

Davidson, Richard M. *Typology in Scripture: A Study of Hermeneutical τύπος Structures*. Berrien Springs, Mich.: Andrews University Press, 1981.

Davies, W. D. *Paul and Rabbinic Judaism: Some Rabbinic Elements in Pauline Theology*. 4th ed. Philadelphia: Fortress, 1980 (1st ed.: London: SPCK, 1948).

Deissmann, Adolf. *St. Paul: A Study in Social and Religious History*. Translated by Lionel R. M. Strachan. London: Hodder & Stoughton, 1922.

Denney, James. "St. Paul's Epistle to the Romans." Pages 555–725 in vol. 2 of *The Expositor's Greek Testament*. Edited by W. Robertson Nicoll. Grand Rapids: Eerdmans, 1897.

Deterding, Paul E. *Colossians*. Concordia Commentary. St. Louis: Concordia, 2003.

Dodd, C. H. *The Apostolic Preaching and Its Developments: Three Lectures with an Appendix on Eschatology and History*. New York: Harper, 1964.

————. *The Epistle of Paul to the Romans*. Moffatt New Testament Commentary. New York: Harper, 1932.

Donaldson, Terence L. " 'Riches for the Gentiles' (Rom 11:12): Israel's Rejection and Paul's Gentile Mission." *Journal of Biblical Literature* 112 (1993): 81–98.

Donfried, Karl Paul. "False Presuppositions in the Study of Romans." Pages 102–25 in *The Romans Debate*. Edited by Karl P. Donfried. Rev. ed. Peabody, Mass.: Hendrickson, 1991.

————. "A Short Note on Romans 16." Pages 44–52 in *The Romans Debate*. Edited by Karl P. Donfried. Rev. ed. Peabody, Mass.: Hendrickson, 1991.

Donfried, Karl P., ed. *The Romans Debate*. Rev. ed. Peabody, Mass.: Hendrickson, 1991.

Dunn, James D. G. "The Formal and Theological Coherence of Romans." Pages 245–50 in *The Romans Debate*. Edited by Karl P. Donfried. Rev. ed. Peabody, Mass.: Hendrickson, 1991.

———. "The New Perspective on Paul." *Bulletin of the John Rylands University Library of Manchester* 65/2 (1982–1983): 95–122.

———. "Once More, ΠΙΣΤΙΣ ΧΡΙΣΤΟΥ." Pages 730–44 in *Society of Biblical Literature 1991 Seminar Papers*. Edited by Eugene H. Lovering, Jr. Atlanta: Scholars, 1991.

———. *Romans*. 2 vols. Word Biblical Commentary 38. Dallas: Word, 1988.

———. *The Theology of Paul the Apostle*. Grand Rapids: Eerdmans, 1997.

Edwards, James R. *Romans*. New International Biblical Commentary 6. Peabody, Mass.: Hendrickson, 1992.

Ehrensperger, Kathy, and R. Ward Holder, eds. *Reformation Readings of Romans*. Romans through History and Cultures Series 8. New York: T&T Clark, 2008.

Elliott, Neil. *The Arrogance of Nations: Reading Romans in the Shadow of Empire*. Minneapolis: Fortress, 2008.

Ellis, E. Earle. *Paul's Use of the Old Testament*. Edinburgh: Oliver and Boyd, 1957. Repr., Grand Rapids: Baker, 1981.

Fee, Gordon D., and Douglas Stuart. *How to Read the Bible for All Its Worth*. 4th ed. Grand Rapids: Zondervan, 2014.

Fitzmyer, Joseph A. *Romans: A New Translation with Introduction and Commentary*. Anchor Bible 33. New York: Doubleday, 1993.

Franzmann, Martin H. *Romans*. Concordia Commentary. St. Louis: Concordia, 1968.

Friedrich, Gerhard. "Das Gesetz des Glaubens Röm. 3, 27." *Theologische Zeitschrift* 10 (1954): 401–17.

Furnish, Victor Paul. "Living to God, Walking in Love: Theology and Ethics in Romans." Pages 187–202 in *Reading Paul's Letter to the Romans*. Edited by Jerry L. Sumney. Atlanta: Society of Biblical Literature, 2012.

Gaffin, Richard B. *The Centrality of the Resurrection: A Study in Paul's Soteriology*. Grand Rapids: Baker, 1978.

Gager, John G. *The Origins of Anti-Semitism: Attitudes toward Judaism in Pagan and Christian Antiquity*. New York: Oxford University Press, 1983.

Gagnon, Robert A. J. "Why the 'Weak' at Rome Cannot Be Non-Christian Jews." *Catholic Biblical Quarterly* 62 (2000): 64–82.

Gamble, Harry. *The Textual History of the Letter to the Romans: A Study in Textual and Literary Criticism*. Studies and Documents 42. Grand Rapids: Eerdmans, 1977.

Gaston, Lloyd. "Israel's Misstep in the Eyes of Paul." Pages 309–26 in *The Romans Debate*. Edited by Karl P. Donfried. Rev. ed. Peabody, Mass.: Hendrickson, 1991.

———. "Paul and the Torah." Pages 48–71 in *Anti-Semitism and the Foundations of Christianity*. Edited by Alan T. Davies. New York: Paulist, 1979.

———. *Paul and the Torah*. Vancouver: University of British Columbia Press, 1987.

Gaugler, Ernst. *Der Römerbrief*. 2 vols. Prophezei: Schweizerisches Bibelwerk für die Gemeinde. Zürich: Zwingli, 1945–1952.

Gerhard, Johann. *On Creation and Angels; On Providence; On Election and Reprobation; On the Image of God in Man before the Fall*. Theological Commonplaces 7–11. Translated by Richard J. Dinda. St. Louis: Concordia, 2013.

Gibbs, Jeffrey A. "Christ Is Risen, Indeed: Good News for Him, and for Us." *Concordia Journal* 40 (2014): 113–31.

———. "Filling in the Blanks on 'Witness': God Raised Jesus from the Dead." *Concordia Journal* 38 (2012): 112–14.

———. *Matthew 1:1–11:1*. Concordia Commentary. St. Louis: Concordia, 2006.

———. *Matthew 11:2–20:34*. Concordia Commentary. St. Louis: Concordia, 2010.

Giese, Curtis P. *2 Peter and Jude*. Concordia Commentary. St. Louis: Concordia, 2012.

Goppelt, Leonhard. *Typos: The Typological Interpretation of the Old Testament in the New*. Grand Rapids: Eerdmans, 1982.

Grafe, Eduard. *Die paulinische Lehre vom Gesetz nach den vier Hauptbriefen*. Tübingen, Mohr, 1884.

Grant, Michael. *Saint Paul*. London: Weidenfeld and Nicolson, 1976.

Greidanus, Sidney. *Preaching Christ from the Old Testament: A Contemporary Hermeneutical Method*. Grand Rapids: Eerdmans, 1999.

Grenholm, Cristina, and Daniel Patte, eds. *Reading Israel in Romans: Legitimacy and Plausibility of Divergent Interpretations*. Romans through History and Cultures Series 1. New York: T&T Clark, 2000.

Grieb, A. Katherine. "The Righteousness of God in Romans." Pages 65–78 in *Reading Paul's Letter to the Romans*. Edited by Jerry L. Sumney. Atlanta: Society of Biblical Literature, 2012.

———. *The Story of Romans: A Narrative Defense of God's Righteousness*. Louisville, Ky.: Westminster John Knox, 2002.

Guerra, Anthony J. *Romans and the Apologetic Tradition: The Purpose, Genre, and Audience of Paul's Letters*. Cambridge: Cambridge University Press, 1995.

Gundry, Robert H. "Grace, Works, and Staying Saved in Paul." *Biblica* 66 (1985): 1–38.

Guthrie, Donald. *New Testament Introduction*. 3d ed. Downers Grove, Ill.: InterVarsity, 1970.

Harrisville, Roy A. *Romans*. Augsburg Commentary on the New Testament. Augsburg: Minneapolis, 1980.

Harstad, Adolph L. *Joshua*. Concordia Commentary. St. Louis: Concordia, 2004.

Hays, Richard B. *Echoes of Scripture in the Letters of Paul.* New Haven, Conn.: Yale University Press, 1989.

———. *The Faith of Jesus Christ: An Investigation of the Narrative Substructure of Galatians 3:1–4:11.* Chico, Calif.: Scholars, 1983.

Hill, Andrew E., and John H. Walton. *A Survey of the Old Testament.* Grand Rapids: Zondervan, 1991.

Hill, David. *Greek Words and Hebrew Meanings: Studies in the Semantics of Soteriological Terms.* London: Cambridge University Press, 1967.

Hoerber, Robert George. *A Grammatical Study of Romans 16, 17.* Mankato, Minn.: Lutheran Synod Book Company, 1947.

Holladay, William L., ed. *A Concise Hebrew and Aramaic Lexicon of the Old Testament.* Grand Rapids: Eerdmans, 1971.

Holwerda, David E. *Jesus and Israel: One Covenant or Two?* Grand Rapids: Eerdmans, 1995.

Horsley, Richard A., ed. *Paul and the Roman Imperial Order.* Harrisburg, Pa.: Trinity Press International, 2004.

Hübner, Hans. *Law in Paul's Thought.* Translated by James C. G. Greig. Edinburgh: T&T Clark, 1984.

Hultgren, Arland J. *Paul's Letter to the Romans: A Commentary.* Grand Rapids: Eerdmans, 2011.

Hummel, Horace D. *The Word Becoming Flesh: An Introduction to the Origin, Purpose and Meaning of the Old Testament.* St. Louis: Concordia, 1979.

Jervell, Jacob. "The Letter to Jerusalem." Pages 53–64 in *The Romans Debate.* Edited by Karl P. Donfried. Rev. ed. Peabody, Mass.: Hendrickson, 1991.

Jewett, Robert. "Following the Argument of Romans." Pages 265–77 in *The Romans Debate.* Edited by Karl P. Donfried. Rev. ed. Peabody, Mass.: Hendrickson, 1991.

———. *Romans: A Commentary.* Hermeneia. Philadelphia: Fortress, 2007.

Johnson, E. Elizabeth. "God's Covenant Faithfulness to Israel." Pages 157–67 in *Reading Paul's Letter to the Romans.* Edited by Jerry L. Sumney. Atlanta: Society of Biblical Literature, 2012.

Johnson Hodge, Caroline. " 'A Light to the Nations': The Role of Israel in Romans 9–11." Pages 169–86 in *Reading Paul's Letter to the Romans.* Edited by Jerry L. Sumney. Atlanta: Society of Biblical Literature, 2012.

Johnston, J. Kirk. *Why Christians Sin: Avoiding the Dangers of an Uncommitted Life.* Grand Rapids: Discovery House, 1992.

Josephus. Translated by H. St. J. Thackeray et al. 13 vols. Loeb Classical Library. Cambridge, Mass.: Harvard University Press, 1926–1965.

Juel, Donald. *Luke-Acts: The Promise of History.* Atlanta: John Knox, 1983.

Just, Arthur A., Jr. *Luke 1:1–9:50.* Concordia Commentary. St. Louis: Concordia, 1996.

————. *Luke 9:51–24:53*. Concordia Commentary. St. Louis: Concordia, 1997.

Kaden, David A. "The Methodological Dilemma of Evaluating the Variation Unit in Romans 11:31: A Text Critical Study and a Suggestion about First Century Social History and Scribal Habits." *Novum Testamentum* 53 (2011): 165–82.

Kallas, James. "Romans xiii. 1–7: An Interpolation." *New Testament Studies* 11 (1964–1965): 365–74.

Karris, Robert J. "Romans 14:1–15:13 and the Occasion of Romans." Pages 65–84 in *The Romans Debate*. Edited by Karl P. Donfried. Rev. ed. Peabody, Mass.: Hendrickson, 1991.

Käsemann, Ernst. *Commentary on Romans*. Translated and edited by Geoffrey W. Bromiley. Grand Rapids: Eerdmans, 1980.

Keener, Craig S. *Romans*. New Covenant Commentary Series. Eugene, Oreg.: Cascade, 2009.

Keesmaat, Sylvia C. "Reading Romans in the Capital of the Empire." Pages 47–64 in *Reading Paul's Letter to the Romans*. Edited by Jerry L. Sumney. Atlanta: Society of Biblical Literature, 2012.

Kelly, J. N. D. *Early Christian Creeds*. 3d ed. Harlow: Longman, 1972.

Kim, Seyoon. *Paul and the New Perspective: Second Thoughts on the Origin of Paul's Gospel*. Grand Rapids: Eerdmans, 2002.

Kimball, Dan. *They Like Jesus but Not the Church: Insights from Emerging Generations*. Grand Rapids: Zondervan, 2007.

Kinnaman, David, and Gabe Lyons. *Unchristian: What a New Generation Really Thinks about Christianity—and Why It Matters*. Grand Rapids: Baker, 2007.

Klein, Günter. "Paul's Purpose in Writing the Epistle to the Romans." Pages 29–43 in *The Romans Debate*. Edited by Karl P. Donfried. Rev. ed. Peabody, Mass.: Hendrickson, 1991.

Kleinig, John W. *Leviticus*. Concordia Commentary. St. Louis: Concordia, 2003.

Kleinig, Vernon P. "Lutheran Liturgies from Martin Luther to Wilhelm Löhe." *Concordia Theological Quarterly* 62 (1998): 125–44.

Koch, Dietrich-Alex. *Die Schrift als Zeuge des Evangeliums: Untersuchungen zur Verwendung und zum Verständnis der Schrift bei Paulus*. Tübingen: Mohr, 1986.

Kruse, Colin G. *Paul's Letter to the Romans*. Pillar New Testament Commentary. Grand Rapids: Eerdmans, 2012.

Kümmel, Werner Georg. *Römer 7 und die Bekehrung des Paulus*. Leipzig: Hinrichs, 1929. Reprinted as *Römer 7 und das Bild des Menschen im Neuen Testament: Zwei Studien*. Munich: Kaiser, 1974.

Kuske, David P. *A Commentary on Romans 9–16*. Milwaukee: Northwestern, 2014.

Kuss, Otto. *Der Römerbrief*. 2d ed. 3 vols. Regensburg: Pustet, 1963–1978.

Lambrecht, Jan. *The Wretched "I" and Its Liberation: Paul in Romans 7 and 8*. Grand Rapids: Eerdmans, 1992.

Lampe, Peter. "The Roman Christians of Romans 16." Pages 216–30 in *The Romans Debate*. Edited by Karl P. Donfried. Rev. ed. Peabody, Mass.: Hendrickson, 1991.

Lang, Mabel. *Cure and Cult in Ancient Corinth: A Guide to the Asklepieion*. Princeton, N.J.: American School of Classical Studies at Athens, 1977.

Leenhardt, Franz J. *The Epistle to the Romans: A Commentary*. Translated by Harold Knight. London: Lutterworth, 1961.

Lenski, R. C. H. *The Interpretation of St. Paul's Epistle to the Romans*. Repr., Minneapolis: Augsburg, 1961.

———. *The Interpretation of St. Paul's First and Second Epistles to the Corinthians*. Repr., Minneapolis: Augsburg, 1963.

Lessing, R. Reed. *Isaiah 40–55*. Concordia Commentary. St. Louis: Concordia, 2011.

———. *Isaiah 56–66*. Concordia Commentary. St. Louis: Concordia, 2014.

Levy, Ian Christopher, Philip D. W. Krey, and Thomas Ryan, trans. and eds. *The Letter to the Romans*. The Bible in Medieval Tradition. Grand Rapids: Eerdmans, 2013.

Lincicum, David. *Paul and the Early Jewish Encounter with Deuteronomy*. Grand Rapids: Baker Academic, 2013.

Linder, Amnon, trans. and ed. *The Jews in Roman Imperial Legislation*. Detroit: Wayne State University Press, 1995.

Linebaugh, Jonathan A. *God, Grace, and Righteousness in Wisdom of Solomon and Paul's Letter to the Romans: Texts in Conversation*. Supplements to Novum Testamentum 152. Leiden: Brill, 2013.

Lloyd-Jones, D. M. *Romans: An Exposition of Chapter 6: The New Man*. Grand Rapids: Zondervan, 1972.

———. *Romans: An Exposition of Chapters 7.1–8.4: The Law, Its Functions and Limits*. Grand Rapids: Zondervan, 1973.

———. *Romans: An Exposition of Chapter 8.17–39: The Final Perseverance of the Saints*. Grand Rapids: Zondervan, 1975.

Loader, William R. G. "Paul and Judaism: Is He Fighting Strawmen?" *Colloquim* 16 (1984): 11–20.

Lockwood, Gregory J. *1 Corinthians*. Concordia Commentary. St. Louis: Concordia, 2000.

Loewenich, Walther von. *Luther's Theology of the Cross*. Translated by Herbert J. A. Bouman. Minneapolis: Augsburg, 1976.

Lohse, Eduard. "ὁ νόμος τοῦ πνεύματος τῆς ζωῆς: Exegetische Anmerkungen zu Röm 8,2." Pages 279–87 in *Neues Testament und christliche Existenz: Festschrift für Herbert Braun*. Edited by Hans Dieter Betz und Luise Schottroff. Tübingen: Mohr, 1973.

Longenecker, Richard N. *Galatians*. Word Biblical Commentary 41. Dallas: Word, 1990.

———. *Introducing Romans: Critical Issues in Paul's Most Famous Letter*. Grand Rapids: Eerdmans, 2011.

———. *Paul: Apostle of Liberty*. New York: Harper, 1964.

Luckritz Marquis, Timothy. *Transient Apostle: Paul, Travel, and the Rhetoric of Empire*. New Haven, Conn.: Yale University Press, 2013.

Lutheran Study Bible, The. Edited by Edward A. Engelbrecht et al. St. Louis: Concordia, 2009.

MacKenzie, Cameron A. "The Challenge of History: Luther's Two Kingdoms Theology as a Test Case." *Concordia Theological Quarterly* 71 (2007): 3–28.

Maier, Paul L. *In the Fullness of Time: A Historian Looks at Christmas, Easter, and the Early Church*. New York: Harper Collins, 1991.

Manson, T. W. "Romans." Pages 940–53 in *Peake's Commentary on the Bible*. Edited by Matthew Black and H. H. Rowley. New York: Nelson, 1962.

———. "St. Paul's Letter to the Romans—And Others." Pages 3–15 in *The Romans Debate*. Edited by Karl P. Donfried. Rev. ed. Peabody, Mass.: Hendrickson, 1991.

Maschke, Timothy. *Gathered Guests: A Guide to Worship in the Lutheran Church*. St. Louis: Concordia, 2003.

Matera, Frank J. *Romans*. Paideia: Commentaries on the New Testament. Grand Rapids: Baker Academic, 2010.

Mathew, Susan. *Women in the Greetings of Romans 16.1–16: A Study of Mutuality and Women's Ministry in the Letter to the Romans*. Library of New Testament Studies 471. London: Bloomsbury, 2013.

McCauley, Leo P., trans. *Funeral Orations by Saint Gregory Nazianzen and Saint Ambrose*. Fathers of the Church 22. New York: Fathers of the Church, 1953.

McGrath, Alister E. *Luther's Theology of the Cross*. New York: Blackwell, 1985.

McKnight, Scot, and Joseph B. Modica, eds. *Jesus Is Lord, Caesar Is Not: Evaluating Empire in New Testament Studies*. Downers Grove, Ill.: InterVarsity, 2013.

Meeks, James A. "The New Perspective on Paul: An Introduction for the Uninitiated." *Concordia Journal* 27 (2001): 208–33.

Meeks, Wayne A. *The First Urban Christians: The Social World of the Apostle Paul*. New Haven, Conn.: Yale University Press, 1983.

Mekilta de-Rabbi Ishmael. Translated by Jacob Lauterbach. 3 vols. Philadelphia: Jewish Publication Society of America, 1933–1935.

Melanchthon, Philip. *Commentary on Romans*. 2d English ed. Translated by Fred Kramer. St. Louis: Concordia, 2010.

Metzger, Bruce M. *A Textual Commentary on the Greek New Testament*. New York: United Bible Societies, 1971.

Michel, Otto. *Der Brief an die Römer*. Kritisch-exegetischer Kommentar über das Neue Testament. 13th ed. Göttingen: Vandenhoeck & Ruprecht, 1966.

———. *Paulus und seine Bibel*. 1929. Repr., Darmstadt: Wissenschaftliche Buchgesellschaft, 1972.

Middendorf, Michael P. "The Bud Has Flowered: Trinitarian Theology in the New Testament." *Concordia Theological Quarterly* 67 (2003): 295–307.

———. *The "I" in the Storm: A Study of Romans 7*. St. Louis: Concordia, 1997.

———. "The New Obedience: An Exegetical Glance at Article VI of the Augsburg Confession." *Concordia Journal* 41 (2015): 201–19.

———. *Romans 1–8*. Concordia Commentary. St. Louis: Concordia, 2013.

Middendorf, Michael P., and Mark Schuler. *Called by the Gospel: An Introduction to the New Testament*. Eugene, Oreg.: Wipf & Stock, 2007.

Mitchell, Christopher W. *The Meaning of* BRK *"To Bless" in the Old Testament*. Atlanta: Scholars Press, 1987.

———. *Our Suffering Savior: Exegetical Studies and Sermons for Ash Wednesday through Easter Based on Isaiah 52:13–53:12*. St. Louis: Concordia, 2003.

———. *The Song of Songs*. Concordia Commentary. St. Louis: Concordia, 2003.

Moe, Olaf. *The Apostle Paul*. Translated by L. A. Vigness. 2 vols. Minneapolis: Augsburg, 1950–1954.

Moffatt, James. *An Introduction to the Literature of the New Testament*. New York: Scribner, 1911.

———. *A New Translation of the Bible Containing the Old and New Testaments*. New York: Harper, 1935.

Montefiore, C. G. *Judaism and St. Paul: Two Essays*. London: Goschen, 1914. Repr., New York: Arno, 1973.

Moo, Douglas J. *The Epistle to the Romans*. New International Commentary on the New Testament. Grand Rapids: Eerdmans, 1996.

———. " 'Law,' 'Works of the Law,' and Legalism in Paul." *Westminster Theological Journal* 45 (1983): 73–100.

Morales, Rodrigo J. " 'Promised through His Prophets in the Holy Scriptures': The Role of Scripture in the Letter to the Romans." Pages 109–24 in *Reading Paul's Letter to the Romans*. Edited by Jerry L. Sumney. Atlanta: Society of Biblical Literature, 2012.

Morris, Leon. *The Apostolic Preaching of the Cross*. Grand Rapids: Eerdmans, 1956.

———. *The Gospel according to John*. New International Commentary on the New Testament. Grand Rapids: Eerdmans, 1971.

———. *The Epistle to the Romans*. Grand Rapids: Eerdmans, 1988.

———. "The Theme of Romans." Pages 249–63 in *Apostolic History and the Gospel: Biblical and Historical Essays Presented to F. F. Bruce on His 60th Birthday*. Edited by W. Ward Gasque and Ralph P. Martin. Grand Rapids: Eerdmans, 1970.

Moule, C. F. D. *An Idiom Book of New Testament Greek*. 2nd ed. Cambridge: Cambridge University Press, 1959.

Moulton, James Hope. *Prolegomena*. Vol. 1 of *A Grammar of New Testament Greek*. 3d ed. Repr., Edinburgh: T&T Clark, 1978.

Mounce, William D. *Basics of Biblical Greek: Grammar*. 2nd ed. Grand Rapids: Zondervan, 2003.

Mueller, John Theodore. *Christian Dogmatics: A Handbook of Doctrinal Theology for Pastors, Teachers, and Laymen*. St. Louis: Concordia, 1934.

Mueller, Steven P., ed. *Called to Believe, Teach, and Confess: An Introduction to Doctrinal Theology*. Eugene, Oreg.: Wipf & Stock, 2005.

Munck, Johannes. *Christ and Israel: An Interpretation of Romans 9–11*. Philadelphia: Fortress, 1967.

———. *Paul and the Salvation of Mankind*. Richmond, Va.: John Knox, 1959.

Murphy-O'Connor, Jerome. *Paul: A Critical Life*. Oxford: Clarendon, 1996.

———. *Paul: His Story*. New York: Oxford University Press, 2004.

———. *Paul the Letter-Writer: His World, His Options, His Skills*. Collegeville, Minn.: Liturgical Press, 1995.

Murray, John. *The Epistle to the Romans*. 2 vols. New International Commentary on the New Testament. Grand Rapids: Eerdmans, 1959–1965.

Nanos, Mark D. *The Mystery of Romans: The Jewish Context of Paul's Letter*. Minneapolis: Fortress, 1996.

———. "Romans 11 and Christian-Jewish Relations: Exegetical Options for Revisiting the Translation and Interpretations of This Central Text." *Criswell Theological Review* 9 (2012): 3–21.

———. "To the Churches within the Synagogues of Rome." Pages 11–28 in *Reading Paul's Letter to the Romans*. Edited by Jerry L. Sumney. Atlanta: Society of Biblical Literature, 2012.

Naselli, Andrew David. *From Typology to Doxology: Paul's Use of Isaiah and Job in Romans 11:34–35*. Eugene, Oreg.: Pickwick, 2012.

Neusner, Jacob. "Comparing Judaisms." *History of Religions* 18 (1978–1979): 177–91.

———. *Judaic Law from Jesus to the Mishnah: A Systematic Reply to Professor E. P. Sanders*. Atlanta: Scholars, 1993.

Newman, Barclay M., and Eugene A. Nida. *A Handbook on Paul's Letter to the Romans*. Helps for Translators 14. London: United Bible Societies, 1973.

Niebuhr, H. Richard. *Christ and Culture*. New York: Harper, 1956.

Nygren, Anders. *Commentary on Romans*. Translated by Carl C. Rasmussen. Philadelphia: Muhlenberg, 1949.

Panning, Armin J. *Romans*. People's Bible Commentary. St. Louis: Concordia, 2000.

Pate, C. Marvin. *The End of the Age Has Come: The Theology of Paul*. Grand Rapids: Zondervan, 1995.

Paulson, Steven D. *Lutheran Theology*. New York: T&T Clark, 2011.

Pieper, Francis. *Christian Dogmatics*. 4 vols. St. Louis: Concordia, 1950–1957.

Porter, Stanley E., and Christopher D. Land, eds. *Paul and His Social Relations*. Pauline Studies 7. Leiden: Brill, 2013.

Porter, Stanley E., and Christopher D. Stanley, eds. *As It Is Written: Studying Paul's Use of Scripture*. Society of Biblical Literature Symposium Series 50. Atlanta: Society of Biblical Literature, 2008.

Preus, Jacob A. O. *Just Words: Understanding the Fullness of the Gospel*. St. Louis: Concordia, 2000.

Preus, Robert D. *The Inspiration of Scripture: A Study of the Theology of the Seventeenth Century Lutheran Dogmaticians*. 2d ed. Edinburgh: Oliver and Boyd, 1957. Repr., St. Louis: Concordia, 1981 (Concordia Heritage Series) and 2003 (Concordia Classics).

Raabe, Paul R. "Deliberate Ambiguity in the Psalter." *Journal of Biblical Literature* 110 (1991): 213–27.

Raabe, Paul R., and James W. Voelz. "Why Exhort a Good Tree? Anthropology and Paraenesis in Romans." *Concordia Journal* 22 (1996): 154–63.

Rabens, Volker. *The Holy Spirit and Ethics in Paul: Transformation and Empowering for Religious-Ethical Life*. 2d ed. Wissenschaftliche Untersuchungen zum Neuen Testament 2/283. Tübingen: Mohr Siebeck, 2013.

Räisänen, Heikki. *Paul and the Law*. Tübingen: Mohr, 1983.

———. "Paul's Conversion and the Development of His View of the Law." *New Testament Studies* 33 (1987): 404–19.

Ramsay, William Mitchell. *St. Paul the Traveller and the Roman Citizen*. 3d ed. London: Hodder & Stoughton, 1897. Repr., Grand Rapids: Baker, 1962.

Reicke, Bo. "Paulus über das Gesetz." *Theologische Zeitschrift* 41 (1985): 237–57.

Ridderbos, Hermann. *Paul: An Outline of His Theology*. Translated by John Richard de Witt. Grand Rapids: Eerdmans, 1975.

Robertson, A. T. *A Grammar of the Greek New Testament in the Light of Historical Research*. Nashville: Broadman, 1934.

Robinson, John A. T. *The Body: A Study in Pauline Theology*. London: SCM, 1952.

———. *Wrestling with Romans*. Philadelphia: Westminster, 1979.

Rogers, Cleon L., Jr., and Cleon L. Rogers III. *The New Linguistic and Exegetical Key to the Greek New Testament*. Grand Rapids: Zondervan, 1988.

Rosner, Brian S. *Paul and the Law: Keeping the Commandments of God*. Downers Grove, Ill.: InterVarsity, 2013.

Saarnivaara, Uuras. *Luther Discovers the Gospel: New Light upon Luther's Way from Medieval Catholicism to Evangelical Faith*. St. Louis: Concordia, 1951.

Sanday, William, and Arthur C. Headlam. *A Critical and Exegetical Commentary on the Epistle to the Romans*. International Critical Commentary 32. New York: Scribner, 1902.

Sanders, E. P. *Paul and Palestinian Judaism: A Comparison of Patterns of Religion.* Philadelphia: Fortress, 1977.

———. *Paul, the Law, and the Jewish People.* Philadelphia: Fortress, 1983.

Schoberg, Gerry. *Perspectives of Jesus in the Writings of Paul: A Historical Examination of Shared Core Commitments with a View to Determining the Extent of Paul's Dependence on Jesus.* Princeton Theological Monograph Series 190. Eugene, Oreg.: Pickwick, 2013.

Schreiner, Thomas R. *Interpreting the Pauline Epistles.* 2d ed. Grand Rapids: Baker Academic, 2011.

———. *The Law and Its Fulfillment: A Pauline Theology of Law.* Grand Rapids: Baker, 1993.

———. *Romans.* Baker Exegetical Commentary on the New Testament 6. Grand Rapids: Baker, 1998.

Schuchard, Bruce G. *1–3 John.* Concordia Commentary. St. Louis: Concordia, 2012.

Schulz, Ray R. "Romans 16:7: Junia or Junias?" *Expository Times* 98 (1986–1987): 108–10.

Schweitzer, Albert. *The Mysticism of Paul the Apostle.* Translated by William Montgomery. New York: Seabury, 1968.

———. *Paul and His Interpreters: A Critical History.* Translated by William Montgomery. London: Black, 1912.

Smyth, Herbert Weir. *Greek Grammar.* Revised by Gordon M. Messing. Cambridge, Mass.: Harvard University Press, 1956, 1984.

Soderlund, Sven K., and N. T. Wright, eds. *Romans and the People of God: Essays in Honor of Gordon D. Fee on the Occasion of His 65th Birthday.* Grand Rapids: Eerdmans, 1999.

Soulen, Richard N. *Handbook of Biblical Criticism.* 2d ed. Atlanta: John Knox, 1981.

Sprinkle, Preston M. *Paul and Judaism Revisited: A Study of Divine and Human Agency in Salvation.* Downers Grove, Ill.: IVP Academic, 2013.

Stanley, Christopher D. *Paul and the Language of Scripture: Citation Technique in the Pauline Epistles and Contemporary Literature.* Cambridge: Cambridge University Press, 1992.

Stanley, Christopher D., ed. *Paul and Scripture: Extending the Conversation.* Early Christianity and Its Literature 9. Atlanta: Society of Biblical Literature, 2012.

Staples, Jason A. "What Do the Gentiles Have to Do with 'All Israel'? A Fresh Look at Romans 11:25–27." *Journal of Biblical Literature* 130 (2011): 371–90.

Steinmann, Andrew E. *Daniel.* Concordia Commentary. St. Louis: Concordia, 2008.

———. *Proverbs.* Concordia Commentary. St. Louis: Concordia, 2009.

Stendahl, Krister. "The Apostle Paul and the Introspective Conscience of the West." *Harvard Theological Review* 56 (1963): 199–215. Reprinted as pages 78–96 in *Paul among Jews and Gentiles, and Other Essays.* Philadelphia: Fortress, 1976.

———. "Paul among Jews and Gentiles." Pages 1–77 in *Paul among Jews and Gentiles, and Other Essays*. Philadelphia: Fortress, 1976.

Stephenson, John R. "The Two Governments and the Two Kingdoms in Luther's Thought." *Scottish Journal of Theology* 34 (1981): 321–37.

Stoeckhardt, George. *The Epistle to the Romans*. Translated by Erwin Koehlinger. Repr., Fort Wayne, Ind.: Concordia Theological Seminary Press, 1980.

Stowers, Stanley K. *The Diatribe and Paul's Letter to the Romans*. Chico, Calif.: Scholars, 1981.

_____. *A Rereading of Romans: Justice, Jews, and Gentiles*. New Haven, Conn.: Yale University Press, 1994.

Strack, H. L., and Günter Stemberger. *Introduction to the Talmud and Midrash*. Translated by Markus Bockmuehl. Minneapolis: Fortress, 1992.

Stuhlmacher, Peter. "The Purpose of Romans." Pages 231–42 in *The Romans Debate*. Edited by Karl P. Donfried. Rev. ed. Peabody, Mass.: Hendrickson, 1991.

———. *Paul's Letter to the Romans: A Commentary*. Translated by Scott J. Hafemann. Louisville, Ky.: Westminster/John Knox, 1994.

———. "The Theme of Romans." Pages 333–45 in *The Romans Debate*. Edited by Karl P. Donfried. Rev. ed. Peabody, Mass.: Hendrickson, 1991.

Sumney, Jerry L. "Reading the Letter to the Romans." Pages 1–9 in *Reading Paul's Letter to the Romans*. Edited by Jerry L. Sumney. Atlanta: Society of Biblical Literature, 2012.

Sumney, Jerry L., ed. *Reading Paul's Letter to the Romans*. Atlanta: Society of Biblical Literature, 2012.

Surburg, Mark P. "Rectify or Justify? A Response to J. Louis Martyn's Interpretation of Paul's Righteousness Language." *Concordia Theological Quarterly* 77 (2013): 45–77.

Swanson, Reuben J., ed. *New Testament Greek Manuscripts: Variant Readings Arranged in Horizontal Lines against Codex Vaticanus: Romans*. Wheaton, Ill.: Tyndale, 2001.

Talbert, Charles H. *Romans*. Smyth & Helwys Bible Commentary. Macon, Ga.: Smyth & Helwys, 2002.

Theissen, Gerd. *Psychological Aspects of Pauline Theology*. Translated by John P. Galvin. Philadelphia: Fortress, 1987.

Thielicke, Helmut. *The Waiting Father: Sermons on the Parables of Jesus*. Translated by John W. Doberstein. New York: Harper, 1959.

Thrall, Margaret E. "The Pauline Use of Συνείδησις." *New Testament Studies* 14 (1967–1968): 118–25.

Ticciati, Susannah. "The Nondivisive Difference of Election: A Reading of Romans 9–11." *Journal of Theological Interpretation* 6 (2012): 257–78.

Tobin, Thomas H. *Paul and Politics: Ekklesia, Israel, Imperium, Interpretation: Essays in Honor of Krister Stendahl*. Edited by Richard A. Horsley. Harrisburg, Pa.: Trinity Press International, 2000.

———. *Paul's Rhetoric in Its Contexts: The Argument of Romans*. Peabody, Mass.: Hendrickson, 2004.

Toon, Peter. *Our Triune God: A Biblical Portrayal of the Trinity*. Wheaton, Ill.: Victor, 1996.

Torrance, Thomas F. "One Aspect of the Biblical Conception of Faith." *Expository Times* 68 (1956–1957): 111–14.

Tov, Emanuel. *Textual Criticism of the Hebrew Bible*. 2d rev. ed. Minneapolis: Fortress, 2001.

Trench, Richard Chenevix. *Synonyms of the New Testament*. Grand Rapids: Baker, 1989.

Turner, Nigel. *Grammatical Insights into the New Testament*. Edinburgh: T&T Clark, 1965.

———. *Syntax*. Vol. 3 of *A Grammar of New Testament Greek* by James H. Moulton. Edinburgh: T&T Clark, 1963.

Twelftree, Graham H. *Paul and the Miraculous: A Historical Reconstruction*. Grand Rapids: Baker, 2013.

Tyson, Joseph B. " 'Works of Law' in Galatians." *Journal of Biblical Literature* 92 (1973): 423–31.

Urbach, Ephraim E. *The Sages: Their Concepts and Beliefs*. Translated by Israel Abrahams. 2 vols. Jerusalem: Magnes, 1975.

VanderKam, James C. *The Dead Sea Scrolls Today*. 2d ed. Grand Rapids: Eerdmans, 2010.

Veith, Gene Edward. *God at Work: Your Christian Vocation in All of Life*. Wheaton, Ill.: Crossway, 2002.

Vermes, Geza, trans. *The Dead Sea Scrolls in English*. 4th ed. Sheffield: Sheffield Academic Press, 1995.

Voelz, James W. "Biblical Hermeneutics: Where Are We Now? Where Are We Going?" Pages 235–57 in *Light for Our World: Essays Commemorating the 150th Anniversary of Concordia Seminary, St. Louis, Missouri*. Edited by John W. Klotz. St. Louis: Concordia Seminary, 1989.

———. *Fundamental Greek Grammar*. 3d rev. ed. St. Louis: Concordia, 2011.

———. *Mark 1:1–8:26*. Concordia Commentary. St. Louis: Concordia, 2013.

———. *What Does This Mean? Principles of Biblical Interpretation in the Post-Modern World*. 2d ed. St. Louis: Concordia, 1997.

Wallace, Daniel B. *The Basics of New Testament Syntax: An Intermediate Greek Grammar*. Grand Rapids: Zondervan, 2000.

———. *Greek Grammar beyond the Basics: An Exegetical Syntax of the New Testament*. Grand Rapids: Zondervan, 1996.

———. "Junia among the Apostles: The Double Identification Problem in Romans 16:7." June 24, 2004. https://bible.org/article/junia-among-apostles-double-identification-problem-romans-167 - _ftn1.

Walther, C. F. W. *The Proper Distinction between Law and Gospel: 39 Evening Lectures*. Reproduced from the German edition of 1897 by W. H. T. Dau. St. Louis: Concordia, 1986.

Watson, Francis. "The Law in Romans." Pages 93–107 in *Reading Paul's Letter to the Romans*. Edited by Jerry L. Sumney. Atlanta: Society of Biblical Literature, 2012.

———. *Paul and the Hermeneutics of Faith*. New York: T&T Clark, 2004.

———. *Paul, Judaism and the Gentiles: A Sociological Approach*. London: Cambridge University Press, 1986.

———. "The Two Roman Congregations: Romans 14:1–15:13." Pages 203–15 in *The Romans Debate*. Edited by Karl P. Donfried. Rev. ed. Peabody, Mass.: Hendrickson, 1991.

Webber, Robert E., ed. *The Biblical Foundations of Christian Worship*. Complete Library of Christian Worship 1. Peabody, Mass.: Hendrickson, 1993.

Wedderburn, A. J. M. "Paul and the Law." *Scottish Journal of Theology* 38 (1985): 613–22.

———. "The Purpose and Occasion of Romans Again." Pages 195–202 in *The Romans Debate*. Edited by Karl P. Donfried. Rev. ed. Peabody, Mass.: Hendrickson, 1991.

Weinrich, William C. *John 1:1–7:1*. Concordia Commentary. St. Louis: Concordia, 2015.

Westerholm, Stephen. *Israel's Law and the Church's Faith: Paul and His Recent Interpreters*. Grand Rapids: Eerdmans, 1988.

———. *Justification Reconsidered: Rethinking a Pauline Theme*. Grand Rapids: Eerdmans, 2013.

Whitson, William, trans. *The Works of Josephus*. Rev. ed. Peabody, Mass.: Hendrickson, 1987.

Wiefel, Wolfgang. "The Jewish Community in Ancient Rome and the Origins of Roman Christianity." Pages 85–101 in *The Romans Debate*. Edited by Karl P. Donfried. Rev. ed. Peabody, Mass.: Hendrickson, 1991.

Wilckens, Ulrich. *Der Brief an die Römer*. 3 vols. Evangelisch-Katholischer Kommentar zum Neuen Testament 6. Zürich: Benziger, 1978–1982.

Williamson, Clark M. "The New Testament Reconsidered: Recent Post-Holocaust Scholarship." *Quarterly Review* 4/4 (1984): 37–51.

Wilson, A. N. *Paul: The Mind of the Apostle*. New York: Norton, 1997.

Winger, Thomas M. *Ephesians*. Concordia Commentary. St. Louis: Concordia, 2015.

———. "*Simul justus et peccator*: Did Luther and the Confessions Get Paul Right?" *Lutheran Theological Review* 17 (2004–2005): 90–108.

Wingren, Gustaf. *Luther on Vocation*. Translated by Carl C. Rasmussen. Philadelphia: Muhlenberg, 1957.

Witherington, Ben, III. *The Paul Quest: The Renewed Search for the Jew of Tarsus*. Downers Grove, Ill.: InterVarsity, 1998.

———. *Paul's Letter to the Romans: A Socio-Rhetorical Commentary*. Grand Rapids: Eerdmans, 2004.

_____. *Paul's Narrative Thought World: The Tapestry of Tragedy and Triumph*. Louisville, Ky.: Westminster/John Knox, 1994.

Wolters, Al. "ΙΟΥΝΙΑΝ (Romans 16:7) and the Hebrew Name *Yĕḥunnī*." *Journal of Biblical Literature* 127 (2008): 397–408.

Wright, N. T. *The Climax of the Covenant: Christ and the Law in Pauline Theology*. Minneapolis: Fortress, 1992.

———. *Justification: God's Plan and Paul's Vision*. Downers Grove, Ill.: IVP Academic, 2009.

———. "The Letter to the Romans: Introduction, Commentary, and Reflections." Pages 393–770 in vol. 10 of *The New Interpreter's Bible*. Nashville: Abingdon, 2002.

_____. "Paul and Caesar: A New Reading of Romans." Pages 173–93 in *A Royal Priesthood? The Use of the Bible Ethically and Politically: A Dialogue with Oliver O'Donovan*. Edited by Craig Bartholomew. Grand Rapids: Zondervan, 2002.

_____. *Paul and the Faithfulness of God*. 2 vols. Minneapolis: Fortress, 2013.

———. *Paul: In Fresh Perspective*. Minneapolis: Fortress, 2005.

———. "Paul's Gospel and Caesar's Empire." Pages 160–83 in *Paul and Politics: Ekklesia, Israel, Imperium, Interpretation: Essays in Honor of Krister Stendahl*. Edited by Richard A. Horsley. Harrisburg, Pa.: Trinity Press International, 2000.

———. "Romans and the Theology of Paul." Pages 184–213 in *Society of Biblical Literature 1992 Seminar Papers*. Edited by Eugene H. Lovering, Jr. Atlanta: Scholars, 1992.

Wuellner, Wilhelm. "Paul's Rhetoric of Argumentation in Romans: An Alternative to the Donfried-Karris Debate over Romans." Pages 128–46 in *The Romans Debate*. Edited by Karl P. Donfried. Rev. ed. Peabody, Mass.: Hendrickson, 1991.

A Brief Introduction to Romans 9–16

Much Has Been Said—Much Remains to Be Said

"The righteous person will live from faith." Paul's thematic citation from Hab 2:4 in Rom 1:17 serves as the basis from which he launches into the careful development of thought in his most influential letter.[1] Thus far, Paul has thoroughly presented "the Good News of God ... concerning his Son" (1:1, 3). This Gospel reveals and affirms the "righteousness of God" (see 1:17; 3:21, 22).

Romans 1–4: The Righteousness of God

As volume 1 of this commentary emphasizes, Paul's focus in chapters 1–4 is *firmly set on God and his righteousness*. He concludes almost every section with fundamental assertions not about humanity, but about God himself (e.g., 1:17, 32; 2:11, 16, 29; 3:1–8, 19–20, 29–30; 4:5, 17, 21).[2] Lenski's claim that "the great theme of Romans is the Sinner's *Personal* Justification by Faith"[3] illustrates an individualistic and anthropocentric reading which is critiqued in the introduction to this commentary and throughout volume 1.[4] Along the same lines Wright calls us to rethink "those traditions of reading the letter that assume its central question to be that of Martin Luther: 'How can I find a gracious God?'" Wright maintains:

> The flow of thought through the letter as a whole makes far more sense if we understand the statement of the theme in 1:17 as being about God and God's covenant faithfulness and justice, rather than simply about "justification." ... Within this larger theme there is still all the room required for that which other readings have traditionally seen as the major subject—namely, the justification and salvation of individual human beings.[5]

This reordering of Paul's priorities maintains a proper and laudable focus upon God. However, two caveats should be made: First, Wright's emphasis on God's faithfulness[6] reflects an attribute of God that does *not* reside prominently within the actual text of Romans. Aside from 3:3 and perhaps the first

---

[1] For an exposition of the quotation from Habakkuk and its influence throughout the letter, see Middendorf, *Romans 1–8*, 27–31 and 98–109.

[2] For example, Middendorf, *Romans 1–8*, 21–22, 27, 29–30, 51, 144, 173–74, 188–89.

[3] Lenski, *Romans*, 84; emphasis original.

[4] Middendorf, *Romans 1–8*, 21–22, 27, 49–51; see also the commentary on the verses just referenced: 1:17, 32; 2:11, 16, 29; 3:1–8, 19–20, 29–30; 4:5, 17, 21. This author has titled his lectures on chapters 1–4 as "Romans: It's Not Really about You, and That's a Good Thing!"

[5] Wright, "Romans," 403–4. For an overview of Luther's experience with the letter, see Middendorf, *Romans 1–8*, 40–42.

[6] In addition to the quotation of Wright above, note also the title of Wright's two-volume work on Paul's theology: *Paul and the Faithfulness of God*. It was published in 2013, after the completion of the first draft of this commentary, and so it will not be engaged fully here.

ἐκ πίστεως ("from faith[fulness]") of 1:17,[7] Paul rarely dwells there. By way of contrast, the vital matter of *God's righteousness* permeates the letter thematically (e.g., 1:17; 3:5, 21, 22, 25, 26; 10:3; 14:17), and challenges to it are directly rebuffed (e.g., 3:5; 9:14).[8] To be sure, if God were shown to be unfaithful, that would bring his righteousness into question as well.

Second, Paul makes it abundantly clear that God's righteousness intersects with humanity *either* in terms of his wrath (1:18–3:20) *or* his salvation (1:16–17; 3:21–31). All people have sinned and rightly deserve to face his coming wrath (e.g., 2:5, 8; 3:5, 9, 23). But the Good News delivers God's saving power to all who are "declared righteous undeservedly by his grace through the redemption, the one in Christ Jesus" (3:24; see also 3:29–30); this eschatological verdict comes already now to "everyone who believes" (1:16), just as it did to father Abraham, who was declared righteous from faith in God's promise now fulfilled in Christ (Romans 4).

Romans 5–8: Life in and through Our Lord Jesus Christ

Romans 5–8 emphasizes that those who receive God's declaration of righteousness from faith (5:1) are thereby also graced with the *life* he bestows "in Christ Jesus our Lord" (6:23; 8:39; cf. 5:1, 11, 21; 7:25).[9] This thematic phrase with its *plural* pronoun "our" counters individualistic understandings of the faith as well. Jesus Christ is not simply "my personal Lord"; he is "our Lord," and he graciously grants us *life together*.[10]

Romans 5 shows how everything which sin and death brought into the world through Adam has been trumped by the overarching, triumphant work of Christ; through faith we presently receive peace, grace, hope, love, and reconciliation with God, along with the confident assurance that we will reign in *life* with Christ. Therefore, believers rejoice already "now," even in the midst of the numerous "not yet" realities addressed throughout Romans 6–8.[11]

- Romans 6 teaches that all those who were baptized into Christ Jesus are no longer slaves under sin's reign; therefore, Paul calls us to fully engage in an ongoing battle against sin and to walk, instead, in *life's* renewal.
- Rom 7:1–8:4 assures believers that we have been freed from the lordship of the Law with its resulting condemnation because God sent his Son to fulfill its righteous requirements; yet we still struggle to do the good the Law commands and to abstain from the evil it forbids.
- Finally, Romans 8 declares that those in Christ *live* by his Spirit and are now overwhelmingly victorious even over death itself; yet they remain in mortal bodies

---

[7] See Middendorf, *Romans 1–8*, 96–98.

[8] See "The Background and Meaning of 'Righteousness' Words" in Middendorf, *Romans 1–8*, 92–96, and a listing of all appearances of that word group throughout the letter in Middendorf, *Romans 1–8*, 106.

[9] Middendorf, *Romans 1–8*, 30, 51, 377–80.

[10] The italicized phrase comes from the seminal book *Life Together* by Dietrich Bonhoeffer.

[11] Middendorf, *Romans 1–8*, 441–42.

and so yearn, along with creation itself, to be redeemed from bondage to the decay sin has wrought.

What about the Second Half?

Romans 1–8 may be properly appraised as a comprehensive exposition of the righteousness of God and an all-encompassing application of Paul's theme as articulated in 1:16–17. But that theme surely encompasses Romans 9–16 as well. Indeed, the most critical realization to have upon arriving at the climactic pinnacle that concludes chapter 8 is one that inspires the reader to keep moving forward! Indeed, Paul has in no way "finished his main argument."[12] On the contrary, *he has only arrived at the halfway point* of his correspondence with the Roman Christians.[13] In fact, some of his richest theology resides in Romans 9–11 (see the separate introduction to Romans 9–11). Furthermore, it is surely a mistake to overlook the content of Paul's appeals for Christian living in chapters 12–15 or to miss the theological foundations which almost continuously undergird them (see the separate introduction to Romans 12–16). Finally, it is not until Romans 14–16 that we receive vital clues for identifying the original addressees of the letter and for discerning the overall purpose*s* (note the plural) for which Paul writes his most magnificent treatise.[14]

Those who give uneven treatment to the latter half of the letter make unwarranted assumptions regarding its content and improperly give Paul's inspired words in Romans 9–16 the short end of the stick. Nygren's commentary, for example, devotes over 300 pages to Romans 1–8 but handles Romans 9–16 in just over 100 pages.[15] Even though verse divisions are uneven and somewhat arbitrary, their numbers illustrate the point: Romans 1–8 has 225 verses, while Romans 9–16 contains 208, nearly as many. Paul surely intends for us to read and ponder *the entire letter with equal seriousness*. This is because he still has much to say—to the believers in Rome and to us.

Universal Application Has Contextual Implications

The fifty-four-page introduction in the first volume of this commentary gives its conclusion of how Romans is best viewed under the title "A Contextual Letter with Universal Application."[16] That section elucidates Paul's use of

---

[12] Asserted by Sanday and Headlam, *Romans*, 225.

[13] See Middendorf, *Romans 1–8*, 29–31, for a complete outline of the letter. That outline is fleshed out more fully in this commentary's table of contents, which covers both volumes.

[14] See especially Middendorf, *Romans 1–8*, 14–22, as well as the introduction to 14:1–15:13, the commentary on 15:22 and 15:23–24, and the concluding section in the commentary on 16:1–16 in this volume.

[15] Nygren, *Romans*, covers Romans 1–8 on pages 43–349 and Romans 9–16 on pages 353–457. Similarly, the commentaries of Barrett (160 pages versus 114), Lenski (550 versus 355), and Murray (408 versus 286); note also Paulson, *Lutheran Theology* (190 versus 66); see Middendorf, *Romans 1–8*, 47, including n. 220.

[16] Middendorf, *Romans 1–8*, 49–51.

numerous all-encompassing expressions in his letter. While he most characteristically emphasizes the equal standing of Jew and Gentile/Greek in Christ before God (e.g., 1:16; 2:9, 10; 3:9, 29; also 9:24; 10:12; 15:8–9), Paul also employs a variety of other inclusive terminology, including more than seventy uses of the Greek word πᾶς, "each, every, all."[17] In this way, Romans conveys truths applicable to people of all times and places. This surely stands as one factor which explains the tremendous impact the letter has had ever since it was first written. In the first half of Romans, Paul lays the foundational theological groundwork for what follows in Romans 9–16. In so doing, he conveys the gist of the Christian faith in a universal manner which has been cherished by believers and has challenged unbelievers, perhaps more so than any other biblical book, for two millennia.

In Rome

A proper recognition of the universal application of the letter, however, should not overshadow its original contextual purpose. In the latter half of the letter, Paul proceeds to articulate more specific implications of Romans 1–8 for his original recipients. The introduction in volume 1 of this commentary laid out the limited evidence available about the historical background of the Jewish and Christian presence in Rome, as well as the current state of knowledge about the various house churches to whom Paul specifically writes.[18] That he knows at least something of their situation is evidenced by the twenty-six people whom he greets by name in 16:1–16.[19] These names seem to reflect a Gentile majority, but *at least four* (Aquila, Andronicus, Junia[s], and Herodion), and perhaps as many as eight, are Jewish.[20] Therefore, whether or not that ratio is proportional to that of the members of the whole community of house churches, Paul's address "to all the ones in Rome [πᾶσιν τοῖς οὖσιν ἐν Ῥώμῃ] who are loved by God, to those called, holy" (1:7) certainly incorporates both Jews and Gentiles within the intended audience of the letter.[21] Although partially conjectural, this commentary agrees with the assessment of Talbert cited previously:

> A consensus seems to be building … that the main need in the Roman church addressed by Paul was that of resolving the disunity between Jews and

---

[17] Middendorf, *Romans 1–8*, 50.

[18] See Middendorf, *Romans 1–8*, 7–14, 17–18.

[19] Lampe, "The Roman Christians of Romans 16," 230, utilizes these verses to draw a picture of a fractured community with "at least seven separate groups." See "House Churches" in the conclusion to the commentary on 16:1–16.

[20] For a complete analysis, see "Jews and Gentiles" in the conclusion to the commentary on 16:1–16.

[21] In this volume, see "Who Are the 'Weak' and the 'Strong'? Addressees Again!" in the introduction to 14:1–15:13.

Gentiles. If so, then the spiritual gift Paul wanted to impart was his gospel, which was to be the basis of unity for the Roman congregations.[22]

Further evidence in support of this proposal comes via the process of "mirror reading" the letter.[23] It reveals how Paul hones in more specifically on the context of his addressees in the second half of Romans.

The argument of Romans 9–11 is firmly rooted in the theological exposition of the preceding chapters, especially Romans 2–4. As in those earlier chapters, Paul again highlights assertions about God.[a] But in chapters 9–11 Paul draws on those truths in a discussion of God's interaction with Israel throughout her history. He does so precisely in order to target the situation of divided groups of Jewish and Gentile believers within and among separate house churches in Rome.[24] Moo expounds further upon this line of thought:

(a) See, e.g., Rom 9:5, 11b–12a, 16, 22–24, 29; 10:21; 11:1–2, 32–36

> Paul's complex theologizing in chaps. 9–11 has a very practical purpose: to unite the squabbling Roman Christians behind his vision of the gospel and its implications for the relationship of Jew and Gentile. As so often in Romans, Paul's approach is balanced. He insists, against the presumption of many Gentiles in the community, that the gospel does not signal the abandonment of Israel (chap. 11, especially). But he also makes clear that Jews and Jewish Christians who think that they have an inalienable salvific birthright are in error (chaps. 9 and 10, especially). Paul therefore criticizes extremists from both sides, paving the way for his plea for reconciliation in chaps. 14–15.[25]

In between Romans 9–11 and chapters 14–15, Romans 12 calls more generally for daily sacrificial living in response to the mercies of God both within and outside the gathered body of Christ (cf. Mt 5:1–12; Ephesians 4–6). But the discussion of governing authorities in chapter 13, unparalleled elsewhere in Paul, reflects a subsidiary purpose, particularly relevant for those living in the imperial capital.[26]

In 14:1–15:7 Paul spells out the most immediate and specific implications of the Gospel to his Roman audience. Those whom Christ has "received … to himself" (15:7), whether categorized by Paul as "weak" or "strong," ought to exhibit the same attitude of acceptance instead of judgment toward one another (14:1; 15:1–3). Although the letter was directed to all the believers in Rome, Wiefel emphasizes that

---

22 Talbert, *Romans*, 12; similarly, Witherington, *Romans*, 21. See 1:11–15 and Middendorf, *Romans 1–8*, 19.

23 Longenecker, *Introducing Romans*, 55; see Middendorf, *Romans 1–8*, 8, which summarizes "mirror reading" as follows: "This term describes reading into, or behind, the *content* of a given letter to try to see a reflection of what is happening in the *context*."

24 See Middendorf, *Romans 1–8*, 12–14 and 17–18, as well as "Who Are the 'Weak' and the 'Strong'? Addressees Again!" in the introduction to 14:1–15:13, and the final portion of the commentary on 16:1–16 under the heading "What Can We Conclude?"

25 Moo, *Romans*, 552–53.

26 See Middendorf, *Romans 1–8*, 20.

it was written to assist the Gentile Christian majority, who are the primary addressees of the letter, to live together with the Jewish Christians in one congregation, thereby putting an end to their quarrels about status.[27]

Paul's practical plea stands firmly rooted in the all-sufficiency of "our Lord Jesus Christ" (15:6).

Rom 15:7–13 then contains Paul's climactic theological statement regarding Christ, the Servant who receives both Jews and Gentiles to himself (15:7–9a). He then buttresses this with foundational citations from the Torah, the Prophets, and the Psalms (15:9b–12) before offering a final blessing (15:13).

For Paul

Only after addressing the context in Rome does Paul turn to discuss his own situation and plans in 15:14–33. As Moo notes, numerous issues, within which Paul himself often resided "at the center," also contribute to the content of the letter:

> A decade of struggle to preserve the integrity and freedom of the gospel from a fatal mixture with [an improper Pharisaic/legalistic understanding of] the Jewish torah lies behind him; a critical encounter [in Jerusalem] with Jews and Jewish Christians suspicious of him because of his outspoken stance in this very struggle lies immediately ahead (cf. Rom. 15:30–33). And the Roman Christians themselves are caught up in this issue, divided over the degree to which, as Christians, they are to retain the Jewish heritage of their faith.[28]

Looking toward the future, Paul then hopes for a united partnership in the Gospel (cf. Phil 1:5) with the Roman Christians as he moves farther west (Rom 15:23–29). Thus Hultgren properly highlights "those passages written by Paul at the beginning and end of the letter in which he speaks of mutual edification upon his planned arrival in Rome and makes an appeal for his readers' support for a mission to Spain"[29] (i.e., 1:8–15; 15:14–33).

Conclusion

Chapters 9–16 reveal quite clearly that Romans is not a generic theological treatise. From his multifaceted vantage point, Paul addresses a specific context with specific purposes. In terms of its major emphases, his letter to Rome "wishes to argue for two things: total equality of Jew and Gentile within the church, and a mission to Gentiles which always includes Jews as well within its scope."[30] This understanding stands in concert with the more complete assessment of the setting and purpose of the letter articulated in the full introduction

---

[27] Wiefel, "The Jewish Community in Ancient Rome and the Origins of Roman Christianity," 96.

[28] Moo, *Romans*, 548; see also Middendorf, *Romans 1–8*, 16–17 and 19–20.

[29] Hultgren, *Romans*, x.

[30] Wright, *The Climax of the Covenant*, 234.

to this commentary.[31] It does not, however, in any way diminish the universal impact of the eternal, inspired theological truths Paul enunciates in Romans about God—how he interacts with people in his righteousness and how all those who have been empowered by the Holy Spirit to call him "Abba, Father" (8:15) are to relate to one another in and through *our* Lord Jesus Christ. To that end "may the God of hope fill you [with] all joy and peace while believing, so that you might have an abundance in hope by [the] power of [the] Holy Spirit" (15:13).

---

[31] See Middendorf, *Romans 1–8*, 18–22 and 49–51.

Romans 9:1–11:36

The Righteousness of God and Israel

Introduction to Romans 9–11

The Place and Purposes of Romans 9–11 in the Letter

Among Paul's thirteen epistles in the NT, "Romans is his longest letter, with about 7,100 words. Its length as well as the profundity of its subject matter marks it out as a most unusual letter."[1] Within the letter itself, the sheer length of the sustained argument of Romans 9–11 stands as an impressive testament to Paul's literary genius. Hultgren contends that, as a single unit, Romans 9–11 remains "unrivaled by its length in all the rest of Paul's undisputed letters."[2] Its 90 verses comprise over 20 percent of the 433 verses in Romans. A proper assessment of the role of these chapters within Romans, however, remains a disputed matter. This is due, in part, to the apparent "stand alone" character of Romans 9–11. As Käsemann states: "Apart from ch. 16, no part of the epistle is so self-contained as this. Hence none may be detached so easily or, as it seems, at so little risk."[3] Isolating these chapters from the rest of Romans leads some scholars to undermine their importance; conversely, it causes other interpreters to raise them high above what precedes and follows.

On one side of the spectrum are those who downplay the significance of Romans 9–11. For example, Murray asks and then responds: "But what of chapters 9 to 11? It might seem there is discontinuity in this portion of the epistle and its length appears to aggravate the question raised."[4] Dodd goes so far as to suggest that "the epistle could be read without any sense of a gap if these chapters were omitted."[5] Lloyd-Jones even calls Romans 9–11 "a kind of postscript."[6] A subsidiary aspect of this view postulates that Romans 9–11 represents a previously assembled unit of material which Paul inserted into the letter.[7] It is impossible to determine whether some or all of these chapters consist of preformed material. Even if it were so, that assessment does not diminish the content of Romans 9–11 or the place of these chapters within the letter, where they are neither a digression nor a "stand alone" piece. "Those who relegate

---

[1] Morris, *Romans*, 1–2; see Middendorf, *Romans 1–8*, 4.

[2] Hultgren, *Romans*, 347; the closest comparable section, 1 Cor 12:1–14:40, contains 84 verses.

[3] Käsemann, *Romans*, 253.

[4] Murray, *Romans*, 2:xii.

[5] Dodd, *Romans*, 149.

[6] Lloyd-Jones, *Romans: An Exposition of Chapter 8.17–39*, 367. Sanday and Headlam, *Romans*, 225, similarly conclude that by the end of Romans 8 "St. Paul has now finished his main argument."

[7] Dodd, *Romans*, 149, hypothesizes: "It is the kind of sermon that Paul must often have had occasion to deliver. ... It is quite possible that he kept by him a MS. of such a sermon, for use as occasion demanded, and inserted it here."

chaps. 9–11 to the periphery of Romans have misunderstood the purpose of Rom. 9–11, or of the letter, or of both."[8]

On the other side are those who contend that Paul intends Romans 9–11 to serve as the most important section of his letter. Stendahl identifies these chapters as "the real center of gravity in Romans."[9] Wright similarly concludes that they serve "as the intended major climax of the whole letter"[10] and contain "the climax of the theological argument."[11] These descriptions overstate the case in the opposite direction. Paul has carefully arranged the flow of his thought in Romans. As he moves forward in a definite progression, every section plays a vital role in his argument. Just as it is improper to claim that the letter peaks in Romans 1–4 or in Romans 8, so there remains a flaw in the view that it does so in chapters 9–11, implying that Romans 12–16 merely serve as some kind of ancillary epilogue.

A proper recognition of the role of Romans 9–11 remains a matter of proper balance. To disregard these three lengthy chapters as some type of subsidiary excursus is certainly most inaccurate. At the same time, to view them as the focal point of the letter also seems unwarranted. In both cases, interpreters downplay the contextual nature of the letter. Romans 9–11 stands as an integral unit within the flow of Paul's thought, but not as its culmination.

Looking Back on Romans 1–8

Romans 9–11 builds upon and applies what Paul has already articulated in Romans 1–8. Indeed, it reaches all the way back to the letter's thematic statement in 1:16–17. Cranfield even suggests that "the theme of Romans, as set forth in 1.16b–17, requires the inclusion in the epistle of a discussion of the relation of the nation of Israel to the gospel."[12] While he may be overstating the case, the key emphases on the righteousness of God and faith are evident. This is illustrated by the presence of the key thematic terms derived from the Habakkuk quotation (Hab 2:4) in Rom 1:17 in this section, as well as throughout the letter. The following word counts, reproduced from the commentary on 1:17,[13] provide the basis for points discussed more fully there:

---

[8] Moo, *Romans*, 548.

[9] Stendahl, "Paul among Jews and Gentiles," 28.

[10] Wright, "Romans," 403–4; he contends that if we start with questions such as "how can I find a gracious God?" then "Paul's discussion of Israel and its Torah either takes second place or, worse, is relegated to a more abstract and generalized discussion of the sin and salvation of humans in general, in which the question of Israel's fate is essentially a side issue" (403).

[11] Wright, *The Climax of the Covenant*, 234; Stendahl, "Paul among Jews and Gentiles," 4, and "The Apostle Paul and the Introspective Conscience of the West," 85, uses similar terminology.

[12] Cranfield, *Romans*, 446.

[13] See Middendorf, *Romans 1–8*, 106–7.

Romans	1–4	5–8	9–11	12–16	Total
"Righteous(ness)" word group	27	17	11	1	56
All "right-" terms*	39	22	12	4	77
"Faith"/"believe" word group	37	3	16	10	66
"Live"/"life" word group	3	27	3	8	41

*A word group includes cognate nouns, adjectives, and verbs. The wider group of "right-" terms also counts compound words such as δικαιοκρισία, "righteous judgment" (2:5), negated terms such as ἀδικία, "unrighteousness" (e.g., 1:18), and other related forms. For the complete list with references, see Middendorf, *Romans 1–8*, 106.

These statistics demonstrate the significance of "righteousness" terminology throughout Romans 1–11. The prominence of "faith"/"believe" words also returns in Romans 9–11, occurring sixteen times in these chapters. By way of contrast, "life" terms are used only three times. These word counts justify the conclusion that in these chapters Paul returns to address or, more correctly, apply aspects related to the main themes of Romans 1–4, primarily righteousness and faith.

The questions posed and addressed in 3:1–4 seem to pertain even more specifically to the issues discussed in chapters 9–11.[14] There Paul engages in this lively and profound dialogue:

> [1]Then what is the advantage of the Jew or what is the benefit of the circumcision? [2]Much in every way! Indeed, [it is] primarily that they were entrusted with the sayings of God. [3]What, then, if some were unfaithful? Their faithlessness will not make the faithfulness of God ineffective, will it? [4]May it never come to be! But let God be true and every person a liar, just as it stands written: "In order that you might be righteous in your words and you will overcome when you judge."

Right at the outset of the letter, Paul contended that what he calls "the sayings of God" in 3:2 were inscribed as "the Good News of God which he promised beforehand through his prophets in holy writings" (1:1–2). Such promises now stand fulfilled by virtue of the resurrection of God's Son and David's seed, "Jesus Christ our Lord" (1:4). In the face of the unbelief of *some* Jews (3:3), Paul has already emphatically reasserted the faithfulness of God, as well as affirmed that he is true and righteous in his judging (3:3–4). Paul hints in 3:1–4 that the unbelief of some in Israel provokes his own consternation as expressed in 9:1–5. This consternation becomes his more prominent concern as Romans 9–11 continues (e.g., 9:30–10:3; 10:16; 11:7, 22–23). At the same time, *Paul does not emphasize Israel's unbelief, but, rather, how God responds, even in the midst of it, with*

---

[14] Campbell, "Romans III as a Key to the Structure and Thought of the Letter," 257.

faithfulness, righteousness, and truth (e.g., 3:4; 10:19–21; 11:1–2). Thus one prevailing theme is that God's Word has not failed and is not fallen (9:6).

More immediate evidence for the connection of Romans 9–11 with what comes before stems from the linkage between Romans 8 and 9. On the one hand, it is true that "the tone shifts dramatically from celebration (8:31–39) to lamentation (9:1–3)."[15] But, as has been true throughout the letter, even Paul's most abrupt breaks are carefully linked with what preceded (see 1:18; 3:21; 5:1; 8:1–4). If one keeps the end of Romans 8 fresh in mind, both textual and thematic bridges reach into Romans 9. For example, Moo identifies the following:

> The theme of election (compare 8:26–30 and 9:6b–23), with its key words πρόθεσις ["purpose"] (8:28; 9:11) and κλητός/καλέω ["called"/"to call"] (8:28, 30; 9:7, 11 [Greek 9:12a], 24, 26); the issue of "sonship"/adoption (cf. υἱοθεσία ["adoption"/"sonship"] in 8:15, 23; cf. 9:4; τέκνα ["children"] in 8:16, 17, 21; cf. 9:7, 8; υἱός ["son"] in 8:14, 19; cf. 9:9, 26); and the hope for eschatological glory (cf. δόξα ["glory"] in 8:18, 21 [cf. (8:)30]; cf. 9:4, 23).[16]

All of this supports Barrett's assessment that "the connexion between chs. i–viii and chs. ix–xi is much closer than is sometimes recognized."[17]

Looking Ahead to Romans 12–16

At the same time, Romans 9–11 also points forward toward the letter's concluding emphases. As powerful as 8:31–39 is, Paul does not stop there. Similarly, regardless of the profound content contained in Romans 9–11, including its resounding concluding doxology (11:33–36), Paul utilizes these deep theological truths to move farther forward with them. Thus it is also improper to view Romans 12–16 as something of an addendum or to treat those chapters as if they were "only loosely connected with the first part" of Romans.[18] To do so fails to consider all of what Paul wrote, indeed to properly grasp the significance of the concluding chapters as the culmination of his magnificent treatise. Any careful reading of the letter reveals that it is far too well integrated for it to not be progressing toward a momentous climax. To ignore the movement of Paul's thought all the way through to the end of the letter surely makes just as much of a mistake as leaping over Romans 9–11. The intricate development of Paul's thought most certainly moves forward toward his specific concluding goals to be enunciated in Romans 12–16.

What then is the role of Romans 9–11 within the flow of his thought? Wright's appraisal coincides with the view of this commentary. He contends that by properly understanding Romans 9–11, "the Roman church will be on the one hand ready to support Paul fully in his own mission and on the other

---

[15] Moo, *Romans*, 555.

[16] Moo, *Romans*, 555, n. 2. The verb καλέω, "to call," also occurs in 9:25; note also its significance in 4:17.

[17] Barrett, *Romans*, 175.

[18] Kümmel, *Römer 7*, 5.

hand willing to unite across racial barriers in the way indicated (building on 9–11) in chs. 14–15."[19]

The Three Foci of Romans 9–11

The more general and corporate nature of Paul's discussion in Romans 9–11, particularly in regard to Israel, serves as one reason scholars are tempted to regard the chapters as tangential for NT Christians. Barrett aptly summarizes how that was not the case in Romans 1–8 and remains off target in chapters 9–11 as well:

> Chs. i–viii are not so much concerned with an "experience of salvation" as with the character and deeds of God who is the source of salvation, and chs. ix–xi are not at all concerned with Paul's patriotic sentiments but with the character and deeds of God who elected the Jews and now calls the Gentiles.[20]

In Romans 9–11 Paul expresses his arguments in terms of God's righteous involvement with people groups, as well as with individuals personally, in a manner fully consistent with his Word. Therefore the three major themes of these chapters revolve around God, God's Word, and God's people.[21]

God

The focus of Paul's teaching continues to be *primarily upon God, not people.*[22] For example, Paul uses the noun for "God" (θεός) twenty-six times in Romans 9–11. More importantly, his dominant assertions throughout the section state fundamental truths about God,[a] much as they did in the letter's opening chapters.[b]

Käsemann more specifically proposes that, in keeping with the "righteousness of God" of 1:17 (δικαιοσύνη θεοῦ; see also 3:5, 21, 22, 25, 26; 10:3), the dominant theme within Romans 9–11 continues to be God's righteousness:

> If salvation history is understood as suggested, God's righteousness is its center, [and] it is the worldwide dimension of this righteousness. In place of an alternative we thus have an indissoluble material relation [between chapters 1–8 and chapters 9–11]. In this framework, of course, the problem of Israel must be discussed and as the problem of God's faithfulness to his uttered word.[23]

(a) E.g., Rom 9:5, 11b–12a, 16, 22–24, 29; 10:21; 11:1–2, 32–36

(b) E.g., Rom 1:32; 2:11, 16, 29; 3:1–8, 19–20, 26, 29–30; 4:5, 17, 21

---

[19] Wright, *The Climax of the Covenant*, 236.

[20] Barrett, *Romans*, 175.

[21] Wright, *Paul and the Faithfulness of God*, 609–18, summarizes *all* of Paul's theology on the basis of three comparable themes, which he contends also served as "the three main elements of second-Temple Jewish 'theology,' namely, monotheism, election [of a people] and eschatology" (610). Wright's 2013 work was published after the draft of this commentary was completed and, therefore, will not be engaged further here.

[22] Middendorf, *Romans 1–8*, 21–22, 27, 51; similarly, Wright, "Romans," 403. See also the commentary on 1:17, 32; 2:11, 16, 29; 3:1–8, 19–20, 29–30; 4:5, 17, 21.

[23] Käsemann, *Romans*, 256.

Moo responds that the righteousness of God "cannot stand as the theme" here because of Paul's in-depth discussion of the Israelites.[24] Admittedly, Paul's use of righteousness terminology in Romans 9–11 is congregated exclusively in 9:30–10:10, where "right-" (δικ-) forms occur eleven times. Nevertheless, Paul's primary task in these chapters is to engage in an articulation of God's righteous dealings with his people, as he also defends challenges against those dealings (e.g., 9:14; 11:1). Only when one views the "righteousness of God" (δικαιοσύνη θεοῦ) as an inert characteristic of God does one overlook its vital significance within Romans 9–11. Matera points out:

> God's "righteousness" (*dikaiosynē*) is God's "salvation" (*sōtēria*). Righteousness, then, is not a static quality whereby God exercises justice but a dynamic quality whereby God effects salvation.[25]

Once one comprehends that his righteousness is *always active* in relationship with people, either in terms of wrath or salvation (something Paul aptly demonstrates in Romans 1–4), the influence of the "righteousness of God" continues to serve as the bedrock for these chapters as well. As a result, therefore, the Law/Gospel paradox systemic throughout chapters 1–8 remains. Thus we heed Paul's imperative to see *both* the "kindness" and the "severity" of God (οὖν χρηστότητα καὶ ἀποτομίαν θεοῦ, 11:22) and to hear his culminating theological assertion in 11:32: "indeed, God locked up all people into unpersuadedness in order that he might show mercy to all."

Paul presents God's righteousness in relationship with people in Romans 9–11 by employing a variety of other terminology as well.[26] In particular, Paul emphasizes that, in accordance with God's *gracious purpose* (9:11; 11:5–6; cf. 8:28), he *calls* (e.g., 9:7, 12, 24, 25, 26; cf. 8:28, 30) and shows *mercy* (e.g., 9:15, 18, 23; 11:30, 31, 32; cf. 12:1; 15:9). In this way, God's *salvation, that is, his righteousness in action* is presented repeatedly (e.g., 10:10).[27]

The text itself must be allowed to exclude other improper or, at least, inadequate assertions about God supposedly based upon this section. For example, Kruse represents those scholars who summarize Paul's teaching, particularly in Romans 9, as a kind of predestination to damnation: "He argues that the present exclusion of many Jews from the blessings of salvation is the result of God's own sovereign choice, the exercise of his prerogative as Creator."[28] As

---

[24] Moo, *Romans*, 548, n. 3.

[25] Matera, *Romans*, 35–36.

[26] For an explanation of Paul's use of various expressions, see the excursus "Paul's Gospel Metaphors" following the commentary on 4:1–12.

[27] For the use of Hebrew synonyms in the OT, see Middendorf, *Romans 1–8*, 92–94, including n. 47.

[28] Kruse, *Romans*, 367; similarly, also Dunn, *Romans*, 554; Matera, *Romans*, 232; Moo, *Romans*, 598, 601; Murray, *Romans*, 2:24–25; Keener, *Romans*, 119–20; see especially the commentary on 9:14–25.

a result, such commentators identify God's "freedom" as a dominant theme.[29] But such assessments do not coincide with Paul's terminology in reference to God throughout Romans 9–11; neither do they express a valid conclusion from his argument. The proof is in the exegesis of the actual text, which begins in the commentary below (see especially 9:14–24). As something of a preemptive strike, however, note that throughout Paul's discussion he does not use words we would or could translate as "sovereign" or "sovereignty." Neither is God's "freedom" ever spoken of directly; far less does Paul emphasize it thematically. *These can hardly be among Paul's dominant themes.* Instead, he speaks regularly of God with the salvific language referenced at the conclusion of the preceding paragraph.

Furthermore, it has "been customary since the Reformation … to give undue prominence in these chapters to the question of predestination."[30] Moo discusses how this approach goes back to Augustine, who viewed Romans 9–11 as an excursus on the doctrine of predestination.[31] While Paul uses the verb for God's relational foreknowledge in 8:29 (προγινώσκω, "know relationally beforehand"), it appears only once in Romans 9–11, where it speaks positively of God's past relationship with Israel and affirms its ongoing relevance (11:2). While the verb προορίζω, commonly translated as "predestine," occurs twice near the end of Romans 8 (in 8:29, 30, where it is rendered "appointed beforehand"), it is completely absent not only in Romans 9–11, but also throughout the rest of the letter.[32] To assert predestination as a dominant theme here will also lead one astray from Paul's main line of thought.[33]

God's Word

The theological assertion which launches Paul into the complex argument of Romans 9–11 comes in 9:6: "but by no means [is it] that God's Word has

---

[29] E.g., Cranfield, *Romans*, 483, 484, 492; Moo, *Romans*, 592, 594, 596; Matera, *Romans*, 228; Käsemann, *Romans*, 266.

[30] Käsemann, *Romans*, 253; see also Matera, *Romans*, 231–34.

[31] Moo, *Romans*, 547–48, nn. 1–2, citing for a discussion of Augustine's view Peter Gorday, *Principles of Patristic Exegesis: Romans 9–11 in Origen, John Chrysostom, and Augustine* (New York: Mellen, 1983), especially 1–3, 190–91, 232–33.

[32] As noted above, the noun πρόθεσις, "purpose," does link 8:28 and 9:11. Also the noun ἐκλογή, "choice," appears four times in Romans, all in chapters 9–11 (9:11; 11:5, 7, 28). However, see the commentary on those verses.

[33] For example, Murray, *Romans*, 2:37: "The predestinarian background cannot be denied"; also Moo, *Romans*, 598, who contends Rom 9:18, in particular, "provides important exegetical support for the controversial doctrine of 'double predestination'" (that God predestined some for salvation and others for damnation), which, according to Moo, "was given its classic expression in the theology of Calvin" (599, n. 56). For an analysis of the issue, see Matera, *Romans*, 231–34, who properly concludes: "It is doubtful that Paul sought to develop a 'doctrine' of predestination in Romans" (234). For a proper understanding of the topic, see the commentary on 8:29 and "Conclusion" in the commentary on 8:18–30 (Middendorf, *Romans 1–8*, 692–93, 698–99).

failed and remains fallen" (see also the introduction to 9:6–29 titled "God's Enduring Word"). As a result,

> the density of scriptural citation and allusion increases dramatically in these chapters, as Paul seeks to show that Israel's unbelief, though paradoxical, is neither unexpected nor final. … The purpose of Romans 9–11—as of the letter in its entirety—is to show that God's dealing with Israel and the nations in the present age is fully consistent with God's modus operandi in the past and with his declared purposes. Both the narrative of God's past action and his prophetic promises for the future are found in Scripture.[34]

The data regarding Paul's use of the OT in Romans 9–11 makes a significant impression in and of itself. Hultgren provides these statistics:

> Within its 90 verses are 35 direct quotations from the OT (39% of the verses) plus many more allusions and summaries of OT material. … That means that about 69 percent of the OT quotations within Romans are in chapters 9 through 11.[35]

Luther suggests that in writing Romans Paul wanted "to prepare an introduction to the entire Old Testament."[36] If so, these chapters establish a key interpretive methodology. At the very least, Paul establishes a Christian hermeneutic for understanding the OT in light of the coming of the promised Messiah. Paul also provides a most stimulating and, in many cases, surprising method of applying OT texts to the NT people of God.[37]

The recognition of Paul's move toward the present people of God is important. In Romans 9–11 Paul, for the most part, goes beyond proving that Jesus is the promised Messiah/Christ. Of course this was his customary opening argument, laid out, for example, in the synagogue in Thessalonica. There he reasoned "from the Scriptures" (ἀπὸ τῶν γραφῶν, Acts 17:2) that it was necessary for the Messiah to suffer and rise again before concluding, "The Jesus whom I am proclaiming to you, this one is the Messiah" (Acts 17:3; cf. also Acts 13:23, 27–33; 18:5; 20:21). Paul presumes an acceptance of this fact on the part of the believers in Rome and certainly elaborates on its significance earlier in the letter (e.g., Rom 3:21–26; 5:6–11, 15–21; 8:1–4). While Christocentric assertions are by no means absent from Romans 9–11 (especially 9:5; see also 9:33; 10:4, 9, 12–13, 17), Paul's emphasis remains upon how the Christ-event is playing itself out in the ongoing life of God's people on earth, now comprised of believers from both Israelites and Gentiles (9:24). The following assessment does apply specifically to Romans 9–11 quite well:

---

[34] Hays, *Echoes of Scripture in the Letters of Paul*, 64.

[35] Hultgren, *Romans*, 348. OT quotations are in Rom 9:7, 9, 12, 13, 15, 17, 20, 25, 26, 27, 28, 29, 33; 10:5, 6, 7, 8, 11, 13, 15, 16, 18, 19, 20, 21; 11:2, 3, 4, 8, 9, 10, 26, 27, 34, 35.

[36] Luther, "Preface to the Epistle of St. Paul to the Romans," AE 35:380.

[37] See the excursus "Paul's Use of the Old Testament in Romans" following the commentary on 15:7–13.

Because Paul sees the fulfillment of prophecy not primarily in events in the life of Jesus (as Matthew does) but in God's gathering of a church composed of Jews and Gentiles together, his hermeneutic is functionally ecclesiocentric rather than christocentric.[38]

While it is necessary to affirm that Paul does, in fact, see Jesus' death and resurrection as the culmination of God's OT promises,[c] one can also recognize how Hays' insight pertains particularly well to Romans 9–11. Here Paul does not cite OT passages primarily to speak about Israel's past or to prove the Messiahship of Jesus. Instead, he predominantly applies God's infallible Word (9:6) to the present situation of those within, as well as outside of, the NT people of God.

(c) E.g., Rom 1:2–4; 3:21–26; 4:22–25; 5:6–11; 10:4, 8–9, 16–17; 15:8–12

Nevertheless, as throughout Romans 1–8, Paul's primary focus is neither anthropocentric nor individualistic. His focus is still on God, his righteousness, and his efficacious Word. In a manner fully consistent with 1:16–17, this Word proclaims the Good News of the saving righteousness of God.

> Paul must, then, demonstrate that the God who chose and made promises to Israel is the same God who has opened the doors of salvation "to all who believe" [1:16]. To do so, Paul must prove that God has done nothing in the gospel that is inconsistent with his word of promise to Israel; that the gospel he preaches is not the negation but the affirmation of God's plan revealed in the OT (see, e.g., 1:2; 3:21).[39]

Paul insists this means that God's Word of mercy calls both Jews and Gentiles (e.g., 9:24; 10:16–17; 11:32) and unites all those who believe together in the olive tree of Israel (11:17–26; 15:5–12). This leads to a consideration of Paul's third theological focus.

God's People

In Romans 9–11 Paul specifically focuses our attention upon the interaction between God, his Word, and his people. Thus an examination of his relationship with Israel, past *and* present, becomes a dominant topic of concern. This is evident from the titles given to Romans 9–11 by various scholars, such as "Israel in God's Plan,"[40] "Problem of Israel's Unbelief,"[41] and "The Place of Israel."[42] While such titles might tend to stress an anthropocentric focus, others more properly identify the link between God's righteousness and Israel: "The

---

[38] Hays, *Echoes of Scripture in the Letters of Paul*, xiii.

[39] Moo, *Romans*, 550. Similarly, Hays, *Echoes of Scripture in the Letters of Paul*, 64, concludes: "Thus, Romans 9–11 is an extended demonstration of the congruity between God's word in Scripture and God's word in Paul's gospel. If there is no such congruity, then the word of God has 'fallen' (Rom. 9:6)."

[40] Hultgren, *Romans*, 347.

[41] Sanday and Headlam, *Romans*, xlix.

[42] Morris, *Romans*, 343.

Righteousness of God and the Problem of Israel,"[43] "God's Righteousness and the Destiny of Israel,"[44] and "God's Justice and Israel's Future."[45]

Even as God's relationship with "Israel" (as nuanced under "Israel" below) stands as Paul's dominant concern in Romans 9–11, he continues to state truths about God's righteousness and Word which stand applicable to *all people of all times and places* (e.g., πᾶς in 9:5; 10:4, 11, 12 [twice], 13; 11:32 [twice]). As indicated in the introduction, the content of what Paul writes in Romans can be characterized as a contextual letter with universal application.[46] This recognition leads to more inclusive titles being given to Romans 9–11 such as "Human Unbelief and Divine Grace,"[47] "The Unbelief of Men and the Faithfulness of God,"[48] and "The Divine Purpose in History."[49] These, however, seem overly generic. Schreiner captures Paul's emphases well with "God's Righteousness to Israel and the Gentiles."[50]

"Israel"

The outline of this commentary summarizes the content of Romans 9–11 with the description "the righteousness of God and Israel."[51] By no means, however, is "Israel" (Ἰσραήλ) to be understood exclusively in an ethnic or racial sense. To read it as such would be to miss one of the major points of Paul's theology. He uses the term eleven times in Romans and *all of them* are in chapters 9–11. Similarly, "Israelite" (Ἰσραηλίτης) occurs only in 9:4 and 11:1.

Kuhn asserts that an observable distinction exists in the Jewish literature of the intertestamental period and later:

> יִשְׂרָאֵל ["Israel"] is the name which the people uses for itself, whereas יְהוּדִים— Ἰουδαῖοι ["Jews"] is the non-Jewish name for it. Thus יִשְׂרָאֵל ["Israel"] always emphasizes the religious aspect, namely, that "we are God's chosen people."[52]

Moo notes "the tendency of some intertestamental books to use 'Israelite' or 'Israel' when speaking from the standpoint of the people's special religious position and 'Jew' when speaking from the standpoint of the people's national or political status … (e.g., in 1 Maccabees …)."[53] Specifically in regard to Romans, Dunn makes the following observation:

---

[43] Käsemann, *Romans*, 253.

[44] Matera, *Romans*, 211.

[45] Witherington, *Romans*, 236.

[46] Middendorf, *Romans 1–8*, 49–51.

[47] Bruce, *Romans*, 171.

[48] Cranfield, *Romans*, 445.

[49] Dodd, *Romans*, 148.

[50] Schreiner, *Romans*, 469.

[51] Middendorf, *Romans 1–8*, 31.

[52] K. G. Kuhn, "Ἰσραήλ," *TDNT* 3:360 (Hebrew vowel pointing added).

[53] Moo, *Romans*, 561, n 30.

"Israel" being the people's preferred name for itself (cf., e.g., Sir 17:17; *Jub.* 33.20; *Pss. Sol.* 14.5), while "Jew" was the name by which they were known to others. … Paul observes this distinction, having used Ἰουδαῖος ["Jew"] exclusively in the opening chapters where "the Jews'" sense of distinctiveness over against others was in question. … Now he turns to speak of his people's own view of themselves, as himself an insider rather than as one looking in from outside (9:6, 27, 31; 10:19, 21; 11:1, 2, 7, 25, 26; …); whereas Ἰουδαῖος ["Jew"] (9 times in chaps. 1–3) occurs here only twice (9:24 and 10:12).[54]

In response to claims of such a clear demarcation, Moo recognizes that "this evidence cannot be pushed too far because it does not hold for all intertestamental books (e.g., Sirach, Judith, Tobit, *Psalms of Solomon*) and because stylistic choice may sometimes play a role."[55] The strict separation of terms does not hold in Romans either. The presence of "Jew" (Ἰουδαῖος) in 9:24 and 10:12 means Paul does not exclusively switch terminology in Romans 9–11. Furthermore, 9:6 proves that the apostle uses "Israel" (Ἰσραήλ) in at least more than one sense. He also does not hesitate to use "Israel" (Ἰσραήλ) in negative characterizations (e.g., 9:31; 10:19, 21; 11:7). Thus *he does not adhere to a rigid distinction between the terms.* Nevertheless, it seems that "Israel" (Ἰσραήλ) and "Israelites" (Ἰσραηλῖται) generally reflect the "consciousness of being the people of God."[56]

But it is important to recognize that while Paul repeatedly refers to "Israel" (Ἰσραήλ) in Romans 9–11, he also consistently integrates "the Gentiles" into the discussion as well ([τὰ] ἔθνη, 9:24, 30; 11:11–13, 25; ἔθνος, "nation," 10:19). This enables Paul to assert his most profound truth about the people of God. Gentile believers are actually integrated or grafted into Israel itself (11:17–24)! For him, this is the inexplicable and unanticipated mystery of grace now revealed (e.g., 11:25; 16:25–27; Eph 3:2–6). For him, the term "Israel" (Ἰσραήλ) now serves predominantly as a term for all those united in Christ. Thus what Paul says of God's righteousness and Israel now encompasses "everyone who believes" (1:16; 10:4). As stated thematically already in 1:16–17, this is the extraordinary essence of the Good News of salvation received by all, Jew and Greek, through faith in our Lord Jesus Christ.

At the same time, Paul *never* uses the phrase "the new Israel,"[57] nor does the rest of the NT. That terminology is misleading and best avoided.[58] For example,

---

[54] Dunn, *Romans*, 526; he bases this conclusion in large part on the work of K. G. Kuhn, "Ἰσραήλ," *TDNT* 3:359–65. See also "God's Word and Israel's (9:6)" in the commentary on 9:6–13.

[55] Moo, *Romans*, 561, n. 30.

[56] Dunn, *Romans*, 460–61; see also K. G. Kuhn, "Ἰσραήλ," *TDNT* 3:360, and the third textual note on 9:6.

[57] As does Franzmann, *Romans*, 162, who titles the section "The Gospel Creates a New Israel out of Jew and Gentile." So, regretfully, did Middendorf, *Romans 1–8*, 105, in the first printings of volume 1.

[58] The NT does use other terminology for the church as the community of believing Jews and Gentiles: "one new man" (Eph 2:15); "a new creation" (Gal 6:15; cf. 2 Cor 5:17); "the Israel

in the analogy of 11:17–24, it would improperly convey that one olive tree was replaced by another, a "new" and different tree. That is emphatically *not* what Paul says.[59] Instead, the mystery now revealed (16:25–26) is that believing Gentiles are branches grafted into the already existing olive tree, that is, incorporated into God's one Israel, which means they are now included within the people of God in continuity with the patriarchs (11:18, 28; see also Romans 4).

Collective and Individual Applications

The controversies regarding Romans 9–11 have swirled most prominently around Paul's assertion in 11:26: "and thus all Israel will be saved." While the meaning of this clause must be heard after the flow of thought in the section has progressed to this point, a few preliminary thoughts are appropriate here. First, God's people have always existed as a corporate, communal, and congregational entity. The commentary on Romans 1–8 repeatedly emphasizes this in opposition to the largely Western tendency to hear the letter in individualistic terms. Reading Romans 9–11 with an individualistic approach once again leads one off the main track of Paul's argument.[60]

Romans 9–11 speaks mainly in general, communal, or corporate terms for both Israelites/Jews and Gentiles in Christ. In fact, Paul addresses this letter to just such an inclusive community, "to all the ones in Rome who are loved by God" (1:7). At the same time, he also speaks of many individuals within his discussion (e.g., Abraham, Sarah, Isaac, Rebekah, Jacob, Esau, the Pharaoh, Elijah, and Paul himself).[61] Thus Paul's generalities are just that. Many of his statements regarding Israel (or Gentiles for that matter) are not meant to be understood as applicable to each and every person in the group. In these cases, he does not intend for what he says to encompass every individual, universally and without exception. This observation simply recognizes what has been true *throughout Scripture.* God's gracious dealing with his beloved, chosen people Israel did not always encompass every Israelite, e.g., individuals such as Nadab and Abihu (Lev 10:1–5), Korah (Numbers 16), Zimri (Num 25:14), Achan (Joshua 7), Ahab (1 Kings 16–22), and Manasseh (2 Kings 21). Similarly, his actions against pagan nations did not necessarily exclude every individual Gentile from a place within the covenant community of Israel; see, e.g., Rahab the Canaanite (Joshua 6; Mt 1:5; Heb 11:31; James 2:25), Ruth the Moabitess (her eponymous book and Mt 1:5), and Uriah the Hittite (2 Samuel 11; Mt 1:6); see also the "mixed multitude" in Ex 12:38.

Paul's characterizations are similarly applicable in general terms to some/many of the persons within the group being described (e.g., note τινες, "some,"

---

of God" (Gal 6:16); cf. the "new covenant" (e.g., 1 Cor 11:25; 2 Cor 3:6) and the "new Jerusalem" (Rev 3:12; 21:2).

[59] Note also that in the parable of the Tenants (Mt 21:33–46) the tenants are replaced, but the *vineyard remains the same*; see Middendorf, *Romans 1–8*, 225–26.

[60] See also "God's Word" above in this introduction to Romans 9–11.

[61] Later, he sends greetings to twenty-six individuals in Rome by name as well (16:1–16).

in 3:3; 11:14, 17). But Paul does not always or even regularly intend to include every Israelite in his references to "Israel" or the "Jew." This is evident, for example, in 2:17–24 by the series of qualifications he makes regarding the "Jew" he addresses (see the commentary there). In Romans 9–11, Paul himself emphatically asserts this right at the outset: "For not all these from Israel are Israel" (9:6). Later, in 9:31 he speaks of "Israel" in a manner qualified by the description "while pursuing a Law of righteousness." This, then, is not every single Israelite, but only those doing what Paul characterizes. The same is true in 11:7: "Israel" sought earnestly and "the chosen obtained," but "the rest" who "did not obtain" were hardened.

In a comparable manner, Paul certainly does not include every Gentile or even most Gentiles when he speaks of those who attained righteousness in 9:30. The same is true when he announces that salvation has come to the Gentiles in 11:11. Neither does he mean to include every Gentile in Rome when he addresses the presumptive attitude of "you Gentiles" (11:13). Paul himself expresses both sides of these qualifications in 11:25. Israel's hardening is "in part"; not all Gentiles come in, but "the fullness of the Gentiles."

Moo tries to balance the communal nature of Paul's argument with its individual application:

> If some earlier expositors of Paul were too preoccupied with his teaching about the individual's relationship to God at the expense of his emphasis on the corporate relationship between Jews and Gentiles, many contemporary scholars are making the opposite mistake. Individual and corporate perspectives are intertwined in Paul.[62]

The point of Paul's generalizations, then, is that the place of individual Israelites or Jews remains intertwined with the salvation history of Israel as a people, but what he says of Israel does not automatically or universally apply to every individual Jewish person. More importantly, Israel's salvation history has reached its culmination in Jesus their Messiah, the Christ (9:5; 10:4, 17). Being *intertwined with him* though faith now stands as the decisive factor for both Jew and Gentile (cf. 1:16).

Furthermore, despite the categorical assertions about "Israel" by many commentators, Paul repeatedly utilizes qualifying terms like "some" (11:14, 17; cf. 3:3) and "not all" (10:16). Throughout Romans 9–11, then, one must continually keep in mind that *many Jews did believe the Good News*, starting with the Twelve and other disciples; the 120 in Acts 1:15; the three thousand added on Pentecost (Acts 2:41); the five thousand in Jerusalem, which included many priests (Acts 4:4; 6:7); and Paul himself (Acts 9). Furthermore, Acts repeatedly refers to the successes Paul had with Jews in the synagogues he visited.[d] There are certainly also Jewish Christians among the believers in Rome. This stands proven by the three whom Paul explicitly identifies as his "kinsmen,"

(d) E.g., Acts 13:43; 14:1; 17:4, 12; 18:4, 8; 19:8, 10; 28:17–24

---

62 Moo, *Romans*, 552.

Andronicus, Junia(s), and Herodion (Rom 16:7, 11), plus a fourth, Aquila (Rom 16:3), who is identified in Acts 18:2 as Jewish also. Additionally, it seems likely that as many as four of the other names in Rom 16:3–15 belong to Jews as well.[63]

Even more glorious, many believing Gentiles have also now become knit together with, or, as Paul says it, grafted into, Israel's family tree in and through the same Christ (9:24; 11:17–24). Thus Paul expresses the continuity of the people of God throughout Scripture.[64] Those in Christ stand, along "with ancient Israel, created by the promise: 'called,' 'saints,' 'children of Abraham,' 'servants,' 'sons of God,' 'those that love God,' 'the elect of God'—these can all be paralleled from the Old Testament."[65]

The fact that Romans 9–11 draws so extensively upon Israel's story means that "Israel's unbelief of the gospel is a matter of significance not only to the Roman Christians, or to first-century Christians generally, but to all Christians."[66] To overlook this aspect remains precarious. Indeed, Moo's very use of the phrase "Israel's unbelief" provides a great illustration of the points about generalities discussed above. As 9:24; 9:27; and 11:1–6 make abundantly clear, there always has been and now remains a faithful remnant among the Jewish people. The *general* rejection of the Messiah by many in Israel is by no means true of every Israelite, most notably Paul himself (11:1)! Most importantly, as he wrote earlier, "what, then, if *some* were unfaithful? Their faithlessness will not make the faithfulness of God ineffective, will it? May it never come to be!" (3:3–4). This is why 11:5 declares: "Thus therefore also in the present momentous time a remnant has come to be and still exists according to [God's] choice of grace." Cranfield suggests that "the very integrity and authenticity of [Paul's] apostleship to the Gentiles would be called in question, were he able to give up his fellow-Israelites, were he not to suffer grief so long as they continued in unbelief."[67] Romans 9–11 makes it abundantly clear that Paul has not given up on them. Thankfully, and of far greater significance, neither has God. "May it never come to be!" (μὴ γένοιτο, 11:1).

Outline and Interconnectedness

Prior to engaging the text, a final factor must be emphasized. The careful integration of Paul's thought perhaps becomes most evident in these chapters.

---

[63] For a complete analysis, see "Jews and Gentiles" in the conclusion to the commentary on 16:1–16.

[64] See J. G. Millar, "People of God," *NDBT*, 684–87.

[65] Franzmann, *Romans*, 163.

[66] Moo, *Romans*, 553. Munck's influential monograph, *Christ and Israel*, subtitled *An Interpretation of Romans 9–11*, makes much the same argument; see especially the foreword by Krister Stendahl, ix.

[67] Cranfield, *Romans*, 454.

This commentary's outline, detailed in the introduction, presents the structure of Romans 9–11 in this manner:[68]

Because of the intricate connections *within* these chapters, it is critical that they be considered in their entirety. Cranfield states:

> It is of the utmost importance to take these three chapters together as a whole, and not to come to conclusions about Paul's argument before one has heard it to the end; for chapter 9 will certainly be understood in an altogether un-Pauline sense, if it is understood in isolation from its sequel in chapters 10 and 11.[70]

For a brief example already presented in this commentary's treatment of 8:28–30,[71] Romans 9 insists upon God's initiative in election and the call of his grace, which accomplishes everything for his people's salvation, both in OT and NT times. But Romans 10, in keeping with Isaiah, also holds forth the reality of the resistibility of grace in both eras (e.g., 10:16–17, 20–21). Rather than being resolved, the implications and consequences of both divine monergism[72] in salvation and the human ability to reject grace need to be properly balanced

---

68 For the complete outline of the letter, see Middendorf, *Romans 1–8*, 29–31, and the table of contents in this volume.

69 Notice how the OT passages cited in 10:19–21 also function as a hinge. They express both Israel's attitude and God's action.

70 Cranfield, *Romans*, 447–48.

71 Middendorf, *Romans 1–8*, 689–90.

72 Divine monergism is the biblical teaching (-ism) that God (divine) alone (mono-) does all the work (-erg-) for our salvation. Neither human works nor human free will contribute to salvation in any way. For the topic, see further Article IV, "Justification," and Article XVIII, "Freedom of the Will," in both the Augsburg Confession and the Apology of the Augsburg Confession.

and the tensions between them maintained as one drives toward the conclusion Paul expresses in 11:32–36.

Conclusion

Paul, while announcing that the Good News of salvation in Christ is also for the Gentiles, insists on maintaining the special place of the Jewish people in God's plan of salvation. On the other hand, while proclaiming that Jesus is the Messiah who fulfills what was promised to Israel, Paul repeatedly declares that this Gospel is for all people. He articulates all of this under the umbrella of God's righteousness. Paradoxically, his righteousness places Jew and Gentile alike under his wrath (1:18–3:20), but it also now stands revealed in the Gospel as the power of God unto salvation for all who believe (1:16; 3:21–26; also 10:4, 11).

Romans 9–11 then functions as an integral component within the flow of Romans. Paul here presents God's saving righteousness in relationship with his Israel that now comprises both believing Jews together with Gentiles whom God has brought into the community of faith in Christ (e.g., 9:24; 10:12–13; 11:17). The very concise summary of 11:32 affirms that God remains the main actor throughout Romans 9–11, and it states what his righteousness means for Israelites and Gentiles alike: "God locked up all people [τοὺς πάντας] into unpersuadedness in order that he might show mercy to all [τοὺς πάντας]." This then drives all who receive his mercy forward to doxology (11:33–36) and then onward into Paul's description of living in response to the mercies of God (12:1–15:13).

In Romans 12–15 Paul presses on to explain how those who have been called and gathered in Jesus Christ ought to live together as his people in response to his mercies (12:1; see the introduction to Romans 12–16). Thus the major theme of Romans 5–8, life in and through our Lord Jesus Christ, returns to prominence in Romans 12–15 (cf. "our Lord Jesus Christ" in 15:6, 30).[73] *But it does so only in and through Romans 9–11.* As Paul nears the conclusion of his letter, his exhortations culminate in 15:7: "therefore, receive one another to yourselves, just as the Christ also received you to himself to [the] glory of God." As Paul makes clear in 15:8–12, Jesus' ministry was in service to both Jews and Gentiles, to all of God's Israel, "so that with the same purpose you [plural] might with one mouth glorify the God and Father of our Lord Jesus Christ" (15:6); "to him [is] the glory into the ages. Amen!" (11:36).

---

[73] See "Romans 5–8: Life in and through Jesus Christ Our Lord" in Middendorf, *Romans 1–8*, 377–80, as well as the introduction to Romans 12–16 in this volume.

Paul's Anguish and Israel's Advantage

Translation

9 ¹**I speak in Christ a truth; I am not lying, as my conscience is testifying together with me in [the] Holy Spirit, ²that for me there is great sorrow and unceasing anguish in my heart. ³For I would pray [that] I myself be cursed away from the Christ/Messiah in behalf of my brothers, [that is,] my kinsmen according to [the] flesh; ⁴such ones are Israelites, of whom are the adoption and the glory and the covenants, also the giving of the Law and the temple service and the promises, ⁵of whom [are] the fathers and from whom [is] the Christ/Messiah, that is, according to the flesh, the One being over all, blessed God into the ages. Amen!**

Textual Notes

9:1 ἀλήθειαν λέγω ἐν Χριστῷ—In 2 Cor 12:6 Paul similarly writes ἀλήθειαν γὰρ ἐρῶ. A grammatical question here concerns where to attach ἐν Χριστῷ, "in Christ." It is best connected with the verb λέγω, "I speak in Christ" (cf. 2 Cor 2:17; 12:19), rather than taken as an expression revealing "a truth in Christ." Cranfield describes the phrase as Paul's "implicit appeal to Christ as the ultimate guarantor of the truth" he proceeds to express.[1]

οὐ ψεύδομαι—The deponent verb ψεύδομαι means "to tell a falsehood, *lie*" (BDAG, 1). With the negative οὐ BDAG calls the clause "I am not lying" a "formula of affirmation" (BDAG, 1; as also in 2 Cor 11:31; Gal 1:20). Note 1 Tim 2:7, where Paul similarly states: ἀλήθειαν λέγω οὐ ψεύδομαι, "I speak a truth; I am not lying."

συμμαρτυρούσης μοι τῆς συνειδήσεώς μου—This clause comprises a genitive absolute.[2] The same noun and verb, "conscience" and "testify together," are used in the same construction and with the same general meaning in 2:15: συμμαρτυρούσης αὐτῶν τῆς συνειδήσεως (see the fifth textual note on 2:15). The present tense of the participle συμμαρτυρούσης expresses action "*contemporaneous* in time to the action of the main verb [ψεύδομαι]":[3] "as my conscience is testifying together with me." Moo suggests "to me" for μοι,[4] but the prefixed σύν on συμμαρτυρούσης supports "with me."

9:2 ὅτι … ἐστιν—The ὅτι which opens the verse is explanatory, "that … there is."

λύπη … μεγάλη καὶ ἀδιάλειπτος ὀδύνη—The feminine noun, λύπη, means "pain of mind or spirit, *grief, sorrow, affliction*" (BDAG). It is modified by μεγάλη as "great," and coupled with ἀδιάλειπτος ὀδύνη. The feminine noun ὀδύνη means "mental pain,

---

[1] Cranfield, *Romans*, 452.

[2] See Wallace, *Greek Grammar*, 654–55; Voelz, *Fundamental Greek Grammar*, 133–34.

[3] Wallace, *Greek Grammar*, 625.

[4] Moo, *Romans*, 555.

distress" (BDAG, 2); the translation "anguish" conveys the emotional duress. Paul modifies ὀδύνη with the adverb ἀδιάλειπτος, "unceasing."

9:3 ηὐχόμην γάρ—The conjunction γάρ, "for," introduces Paul's explanation for the previous statement. BDAG defines this use of γάρ as a "marker of clarification" which has an "explanatory function" (BDAG, 2). The verb ηὐχόμην (imperfect tense of εὔχομαι) raises two issues. The first is related to its definition; the second concerns its tense. Whereas the compound verb προσεύχομαι always means "to pray," the simple verb εὔχομαι can mean either "to speak to or to make requests of God, *pray*" (BDAG, 1) or, more simply, to "*wish*" (BDAG, 2). The former certainly stands as the dominant sense here, though Dunn merges the two by suggesting that " 'would to God' renders it nicely."[5] For further discussion and an explanation of the significance of the tense, see the commentary.

ἀνάθεμα—This technical Greek term, *anathema*, can express two seemingly antinomous ideas. First, it can refer to "that which is dedicated as a votive offering, *a votive offering* set up in a temple" (BDAG, 1; see the variant reading in Lk 21:5). "But in [the] LXX it is used to translate חֵרֶם, devoted to God to be destroyed, so that the sense 'accursed' becomes dominant (Lev 27:28; Deut 7:26; 13:17 [MT/LXX 13:18]; Zech 14:11; the episode of Achan obviously making a lasting impression [Josh 6:17–18; 7:1, 11–13; 22:20; 1 Chron 2:7])."[6]

ἀπὸ τοῦ Χριστοῦ—BDAG defines the prepositional phrase "in pregnant constr[uction] like ἀνάθεμα εἶναι ἀ[πὸ] τοῦ Χριστοῦ [as] *be separated fr[om] Christ by a curse*" (s.v. ἀπό, 1 e; cf. 2 Cor 11:3; Col 2:20). Here the phrase is rendered comparably, "be cursed away from the Christ/Messiah." Χριστός translates the Hebrew מָשִׁיחַ. Both the Hebrew and the Greek nouns serve as titles for the "Anointed One."

ὑπὲρ τῶν ἀδελφῶν μου—For the preposition ὑπέρ as *both* "in behalf of" *and* "in the place of," see the discussion of ὑπὲρ ἀσεβῶν in the third textual note on 5:6. The preposition is key to Paul's declaration that Christ died in our behalf in 5:6–8 (applicable also in 8:27, 32). It is true that ἀδελφός, "brother," is "in the Bible nearly always reserved for fellow-members of the elect community (Israel or the Church)."[7] In this context, however, the "simple" appositional phrase[8] to follow (see the next textual note) signals that Paul utilizes the term "brother" in an ethnic sense (see the commentary). In both usages the masculine noun functions generically, encompassing women as well.[9]

---

[5] Dunn, *Romans*, 524.

[6] Dunn, *Romans*, 524.

[7] Cranfield, *Romans*, 459.

[8] Wallace, *Greek Grammar*, draws a helpful distinction between a "genitive in simple apposition" and a "genitive of apposition" (94–100). Simple apposition is when "the two nouns are equivalent to a convertible proposition" (96). That is the case here: the two genitive phrases τῶν ἀδελφῶν μου and τῶν συγγενῶν μου could be rephrased as a proposition: "my brothers *are* my kinsmen" or "my kinsmen are my brothers."

[9] *Biblical Revelation and Inclusive Language*, a report of the Commission on Theology and Church Relations of The Lutheran Church—Missouri Synod, 37, concludes:

The plural *adelphoi* (ἀδελφοί, "brothers") sometimes may mean "brothers and sisters," and the translator should be sensitive to those instances where the context makes clear

τῶν συγγενῶν μου—The adjective συγγενής means "belonging to the same extended family or clan, *related, akin to*" or "belonging to the same people group, *compatriot, kin*" (BDAG, 1 and 2). Based upon the clarifications Paul makes here, his use is more in line with the second definition. But the term is not primarily political, as conveyed by definitions like "fellow-countrymen, members of the same nation."[10] Instead, it denotes being of the same ethnic group and here encompasses the Israelites or Jewish people, whatever their current national affiliation or location (as also in 16:7, 11, 21). "Kinsmen" conveys the sense (ESV), though it is somewhat archaic.

κατὰ σάρκα—Dunn contends that "according to flesh" here "contains its usual negative overtone for Paul"[11] as in, for example, 8:4, 5, 12, 13 (see σάρξ also in 7:5, 18, 25). However, the phrase occurs here, as in 1:3 and 9:5, in a neutral sense to denote a "relationship to someth[ing], *with respect to, in relation to* κ[ατὰ] σάρκα *w[ith] respect to the flesh, physically* of human descent" (BDAG, s.v. κατά, 6; see also the commentary on 1:3).

9:4 οἵτινές εἰσιν Ἰσραηλῖται—The relative pronoun οἵτινες is nominative plural. Here it may illustrate how "quite oft[en] ὅστις takes the place of the simple rel[ative] ὅς, ἥ, ὅ" (BDAG, s.v. ὅστις, 3). But it also serves to define more precisely those of whom Paul speaks as "belonging to a class or having a status" (BDAG, 2). Rom 9:4 contains the first of Paul's two uses of Ἰσραηλίτης, "Israelite," in the letter (also 11:1; see "God's People" in the introduction to Romans 9–11). Does the phrase οἵτινές εἰσιν Ἰσραηλῖται then provide further definition of τῶν συγγενῶν μου κατὰ σάρκα in 9:3, functioning as a heading for the list to follow in 9:4–5, or is it the first element in the list? It is best read appositionally, restating and, thereby, clarifying who the "brothers …" are in 9:3 (τῶν ἀδελφῶν μου τῶν συγγενῶν μου κατὰ σάρκα). The subsequent relative pronoun ὧν (see the next textual note) then signals the beginning of the list to follow.

ὧν—This genitive plural form of the relative pronoun ὅς, "who," expresses possession,[12] "of whom." Paul proceeds to list what belongs to the Israelites because of the blessings God entrusted to them. The same form occurs two times in 9:5.

ἡ υἱοθεσία—For the noun υἱοθεσία, "adoption (as a son)," see "Not a Spirit of Slavery, but the Spirit of Adoption (8:15)" in the commentary on 8:14–17 and the commentary below on 9:4.

αἱ διαθῆκαι—A textual variant has the singular, ἡ διαθήκη, "the covenant." Although the singular is well attested ($\mathfrak{P}^{46}$ B D), it is clearly the easier reading in light of its common usage in the NT. Aside from Gal 4:24 and Eph 2:12, the other thirty NT uses of διαθήκη, "covenant," are all singular, including Rom 11:27; 1 Cor 11:25; 2 Cor 3:6,

---

that the author is referring to both men and women. One such instance may be 1 Cor. 15:1: "Now I would remind you brethren (ἀδελφοί) in what terms I preached to you the gospel. …" Here the plural very likely refers to the Christians at Corinth quite apart from any intended gender differentiation. Therefore, the translation "I made known to you, brothers and sisters, the gospel which I preached to you" may better capture the meaning of the word.

[10] Cranfield, *Romans*, 459.

[11] Dunn, *Romans*, 525.

[12] See Wallace, *Greek Grammar*, 81–83.

14; Gal 3:15, 17. "Certainly there is no good reason why the singular, if original, should have been altered to the plural."[13] Furthermore, the poetic structure of this list points toward διαθῆκαι. The feminine plural ending -αι matches the ending of the final item in the corresponding list of three to follow, ἐπαγγελίαι, "promises." The plural, "covenants," is able to encompass all the covenants God made in the OT; see the commentary.

ἡ νομοθεσία—The noun νομοθεσία occurs in the NT only here. Cranfield notes that it, "like the English word 'legislation' … can denote both (i) the action of making or giving laws, and (ii) the made or given laws considered collectively."[14] While the two cannot be completely separated, the primary sense, the giving of the Law at Sinai, "has better lexical support" in extrabiblical Jewish literature and "fits Paul's argument better."[15] This clearly applies to the sense of the related verb νομοθετέω in Heb 7:11; 8:6 as well.

ἡ λατρεία—This Greek noun represents the technical use of the Hebrew noun עֲבוֹדָה, utilized in cultic contexts for the "service/worship (of God)" (BDAG). For the Hebrew noun, see, e.g., Ex 12:25–26; 13:5; Josh 22:27; 1 Chr 28:13; in all of those verses the LXX renders it by the Greek noun λατρεία, which has the same sense also in Heb 9:1, 6. Throughout the LXX and the NT, λατρεία focuses "on the Israelite sacrificial system,"[16] with one exception: Rom 12:2 (see also λατρεύω in 1:9).

αἱ ἐπαγγελίαι—For "the promises," see the second textual note on 4:13, which speaks of "the promise to Abraham."

9:5 ἐξ ὧν—This is the third of the three uses of the genitive plural relative pronoun ὧν in 9:4–5, but this final one is preceded by ἐξ, the form of the preposition ἐκ that is utilized before a vowel. Grammatically this signals that the list is drawing to a close. Theologically, "*from* whom" conveys "that the Messiah is not limited to nor under the control of Israel, even though he is descended from Israel."[17]

ὁ Χριστὸς τὸ κατὰ σάρκα—The first use of the article, ὁ, is masculine singular and conveys, as it often does, the title "*the* Messiah." The second article, τό, is neuter singular, expressing a qualification, "*that is*, according to the flesh."[18] The clarification points out that the Christ/Messiah comes from Israel "only in respect to that relationship which is strictly and narrowly human."[19] For κατὰ σάρκα, "according to the flesh," see 1:3 and 9:3. The matter of how to connect this phrase with the rest of the verse remains a matter of dispute. In terms of punctuation, does Paul intend a soft or hard break after

---

[13] Metzger, *A Textual Commentary on the Greek New Testament*, 519.

[14] Cranfield, *Romans*, 462–63.

[15] Moo, *Romans*, 564.

[16] Moo, *Romans*, 564; see the commentary.

[17] Schreiner, *Romans*, 486.

[18] Moo, *Romans*, 565, n. 56, citing BDF, § 266.2, notes that the disagreement in gender between ὁ and τό stresses "the limitation expressed in the prepositional phrase ['according to (the) flesh']."

[19] Moo, *Romans*, 565. Similarly, Lenski, *Romans*, 586, states that Christ "was only derived from them, and that as according to flesh, i.e., according to his human nature."

σάρκα? This, in large part, determines whether the following doxology refers to God the Father or to the Christ/Messiah. See the commentary.

ἀμήν—This is a Greek transliteration of the Hebrew adverb אָמֵן, *amen*, "truly, surely," which derives from the verb אָמַן, whose Hiphil means "to believe" (in God) and whose Niphal, "to be faithful, reliable," can refer to God.[20] BDAG notes that in the LXX ἀμήν occasionally represents אָמֵן, but that the Hebrew term is more often translated with γένοιτο. Here ἀμήν stands as an affirmation that what Paul *believes* is true.

Commentary

Paul's Anguish (9:1–2)

Paul begins this new section with an appeal to Jesus Christ. "I speak *in Christ*" (ἐν Χριστῷ, 9:1). This is in keeping with the dominant theme of Romans 5–8, which this commentary has titled "Life in and through Our Lord Jesus Christ."[21] Chapter 8 is framed by the assertions that "nothing [is] condemnation for the ones *in Christ* Jesus" (ἐν Χριστῷ, 8:1) and that nothing "will be able to separate us from God's love which is *in Christ* Jesus our Lord" (ἐν Χριστῷ, 8:39). But in 9:1 "the tone shifts dramatically from celebration (8:31–39) to lamentation (9:1–3)."[22] As Paul speaks of his own anguish, this opening statement reminds us that he does so "as one who is conscious of his dependence on the living Christ and on his authorization and approval."[23] He is Jesus' "called apostle" (1:1). From that vantage point, Paul speaks "truth" (ἀλήθεια, 9:1).

Paul then reiterates the validity of what follows with a negatively stated formula of affirmation, "I am not lying" (οὐ ψεύδομαι, 9:1). This echoes earlier words which connect directly with the subject matter Paul is introducing in 9:1–5. In Romans 3 he asks this regarding the Jewish people and then even more vehemently rejects the possibility of any falsehood: "What, then, if some were unfaithful? Their faithlessness will not make the faithfulness of God ineffective, will it? May it never come to be! But let God be true and every person a liar" (3:3–4). Gennadius of Constantinople suggests that Paul, as in 3:1–8, may be responding to accusations at this point of the letter as well:

> The Jews who opposed the [Jewish] apostles and their message said that one or another of the following propositions must be truth. Either the gospel is a lie, or God is a liar. … For God promised Abraham that he would bless his offspring [Gen 12:1–3; 22:17–18], but now he has shown favor to impure and foreign people, i.e., the Gentiles, instead of us. Now if your preaching is a way out of these promises, as you claim, then it is clear that God lied to our ancestors. On the other hand, if it is wrong to speak of God in this way, then you and your message are a lie.

---

[20] See "The Background and Meaning of 'Faith' Words" in the commentary on 1:16 (Middendorf, *Romans 1–8*, 88–90); " 'From Faith[fulness] into Faith' (1:17)" on 96–98; and also 106–7.

[21] See Middendorf, *Romans 1–8*, 377–80.

[22] Moo, *Romans*, 555.

[23] Dunn, *Romans*, 523.

It was to answer this kind of charge that the apostle Paul wanted to work out an alternative position and demonstrate both that the message of the gospel was true and that God was not lying.[24]

Paul then declares that his truthful speaking happens "as my conscience is testifying together with me in [the] Holy Spirit" (9:1). This is similar to the expression Paul employed previously in 2:15.[25] As indicated by the preposition "with" (σύν) on "testifying together" (συμμαρτυρούσης), Paul's conscience speaks "together with me [μοι]" and affirms what he stated immediately beforehand. There are not two Pauls here, any more than there are two "I"s in Rom 7:14–25. Instead, the key phrase is the final one: "in [the] Holy Spirit" (ἐν πνεύματι ἁγίῳ). Paul himself speaks emphatically in the first half of 9:1. Now his "conscience, enlightened by the Holy Spirit, bears witness" as well.[26]

Paul's certainty thus resides in the corroborative testimony (συμμαρτυρούσης) of the Spirit, who dwells within (8:9, 11) and informs the witness of Paul's conscience. Dunn elaborates this and points to numerous comparable expressions in Paul:

> This confidence is underlined by the ἐν πνεύματι ἁγίῳ ["in (the) Holy Spirit"], ... expressing a sense of basic inspiration informing and determining his conscience and the whole process of its witness bearing (cf. 2:29; 7:6; 8:9; 14:17; 15:16; 1 Cor 6:11; 12:3, 9, 13; 14:16; 2 Cor 6:6; Gal 6:1; Eph 2:18, 22; 3:5; 5:18; 6:18; Phil 1:27; 1 Thess 1:5; ...).[27]

The impact of Rom 9:1 drives forward to what Paul states in 9:2. But this should not diminish the manner in which "Paul's statement in v. 2 has been introduced with so much emphasis and solemnity."[28] In light of what follows, Paul likely relies upon the Spirit's work as he recently described it in 8:26: "And likewise, the Spirit is also alongside assisting [us] in our weakness. For we do not know what we should pray for as it is appropriate, but the Spirit himself pleads in our behalf with unspeakable groans."

Paul explicates the truth and the corroborated testimony of his Spirit-filled conscience (9:1) by revealing "that for me there is great sorrow and unceasing anguish in my heart" (9:2). The terms "sorrow" (ὀδύνη) and "anguish" (λύπη) depict emotional or mental pain of mind and spirit. It is intriguing that the few other places in Biblical Greek where the two words are associated include LXX Is 35:10 and 51:11: "In both verses [the] LXX renders 'sorrow' (יָגוֹן) by the double expression, ὀδύνη καὶ λύπη ['sorrow and anguish']."[29] The translation of a single Hebrew word by these same two Greek nouns is noteworthy, but the

---

24 Gennadius of Constantinople, *Romans* (Bray, *Romans*, ACCS NT 6:245).

25 See the third textual note on 9:1.

26 Franzmann, *Romans*, 166.

27 Dunn, *Romans*, 523.

28 Cranfield, *Romans*, 453.

29 Dunn, *Romans*, 523–24.

context in Isaiah seems too different for this to be anything but a distant echo.[30] At the same time, those passages support this broader observation:

> Such lament over Israel is a quite well-established motif in Jewish and apoc-
> alyptic literature, particularly in reference to the destruction of Jerusalem.[31]

Paul heightens the combined degree of "sorrow" and "anguish" in his heart with the modifiers "great" (μεγάλη) and "unceasing" (ἀδιάλειπτος, 9:2).

An Extraordinary Plea (9:3–4a)

The intensity of language continues to build. "For I would pray [that] I myself be cursed away from the Christ/Messiah in behalf of my brothers, [that is,] my kinsmen according to [the] flesh; such ones are Israelites" (9:3–4a). This statement contains a number of contested elements. The first concerns the meaning of the initial verb ηὐχόμην, rendered as "I would pray." Although numerous translations render the form of εὔχομαι here as "to wish" (e.g., ESV, KJV, NASB), "all other NT occurrences of the word denote a wish expressed to God (Acts 26:29; 27:29; 2 Cor. 13:7, 9; Jas. 5:16; 3 John 2) and, therefore, for all intents and purposes, a prayer."[32]

A second issue involving the verb concerns the force of its imperfect tense. Cranfield gives four options, which can be summarized as follows:

- It may express the way Paul *used* to pray in the past, but no longer does.

- It may have a conative sense in terms of *attempting* to pray, but unsuccessfully, "the meaning being that the idea of such a prayer … entered his mind, but was never actually accepted by him or made his own."

- It may convey a present kind of praying which contains some vagueness or indifference (equivalent to the Classical Greek optative mood with ἄν).

- It may describe something unattainable or impermissible (equivalent to the Classical Greek imperfect with ἄν).[33]

Cranfield adopts the final option, which he renders as "for I would pray (were it permissible for me so to pray and if the fulfilment of such a prayer could bene-fit them)."[34] This communicates the best meaning in this context. Paul selflessly wishes he could be condemned by God instead of his brother and sister Israelites.

Third, Paul's use of ἀνάθεμα, *anathema*, "cursed," introduces a powerful word with two seemingly opposite definitions. It can refer to an offering ded-icated to God (e.g., 2 Macc 2:13; Lk 21:5 [variant reading]; Acts 23:14). But it is used more commonly in the NT, including all five times Paul employs the

---

[30] Hays, *Echoes of Scripture in the Letters of Paul*, 29–32, discusses "seven tests" for discern-ing the presence of scriptural echoes, one of which he calls "volume" (30).

[31] Dunn, *Romans*, 524, citing, e.g., Jer 4:19; 14:17; Lamentations; Dan 9:3; *Testament of Judah* 23:1; *4 Ezra* 8:16; 10:24, 39; *2 Baruch* 10:5; 35:1–3; 81:2.

[32] Moo, *Romans*, 558, n. 16.

[33] Cranfield, *Romans*, 455–56.

[34] Cranfield, *Romans*, 456–57.

term (Rom 9:3; 1 Cor 12:3; 16:22; Gal 1:8, 9), for "that which has been cursed, *cursed, accursed*," in accord with its usage in the LXX, where, "as a rule," it renders the Hebrew noun חֵרֶם, and so "what is 'devoted to the divinity' can be either consecrated or accursed" (BDAG, 2). The extreme consequence of Paul's wish conveys the depth of his own anguish in regard to the matter at hand. "Here in Rom 9.3 ἀνάθεμα εἶναι ['to be cursed'] clearly means 'to forfeit final salvation.'"[35] Paul heightens the personal implications with "I myself" (αὐτὸς ἐγώ). The obvious personal reference of the emphatic phrase here, as well as in 15:14, makes it very unlikely that the same expression could refer to someone other than Paul in 7:25.[36]

Paul's situation calls to mind the role of Moses in Ex 32:30–32, where he finally prays, "But now, if you will forgive their sin—but if not, please blot me out from your book, which you have written" (Ex 32:32). Moo contends that "allusions to Moses' history and person elsewhere in Rom. 9–11 (e.g., 9:14–18; 10:19; 11:13–14) make it likely that Paul does see Moses as, to some extent, his own model."[37] While the roles are comparable, Paul does not identify himself with Moses exclusively. For example, in 11:1–6 he more directly portrays himself as a current-day Elijah.

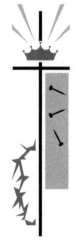

In spite of Moses' and Paul's extraordinary, self-sacrificial appeals to God, their comparable requests were not allowable. The exception, of course, stands in the case of the Son of God himself, who willingly offered himself as the substitutionary sacrifice for us and was forsaken by God in order to bear the curse of the Law for his estranged sisters and brothers (Mt 27:46; Mk 15:34; Rom 8:2–3; Gal 3:14–15). "For while we were still being weak, yet at the opportune moment, Christ died in behalf of the ungodly" (Rom 5:6; cf. Rom 5:8; 8:3; Gal 3:14–15). Paul's momentous offer, therefore, reminds us of what Christ did for us and also leads us to marvel at the extent of Paul's desire to imitate his Savior (e.g., 1 Cor 11:1; Phil 1:10–11). Origen captures this well:

> Why be surprised that the apostle desires to be cursed for his brethren's sake, when he who is in the form of God emptied himself and took on the form of a servant and was made a curse for us? Why be surprised if, when Christ became a curse for his servants, one of his servants should become a curse for his brethren?[38]

The precise reason why Paul remains so distraught has not been stated, though he certainly implies it. Moo proposes that "Paul's willingness to suffer such a fate himself makes sense only if those on behalf of whom he offers himself stand under that curse themselves."[39] The point becomes clearer as his

---

[35] Cranfield, *Romans*, 457.

[36] Middendorf, *The "I" in the Storm*, 148–57; see the excursus "Who Is the 'I' in Romans 7:14–25? Christian or Non-Christian?" following the commentary on 7:14–25.

[37] Moo, *Romans*, 559.

[38] Origen, *Romans* (Bray, *Romans*, ACCS NT 6:245).

[39] Moo, *Romans*, 557–58.

argument continues (e.g., 10:1; 11:1, 7, 14, 20, 22). This provides one piece of evidence against any two-covenant theory where Israel's place before God is secure apart from Christ.[40] Indeed, the phrase added to "cursed" (ἀνάθεμα) here, "away from the Christ/Messiah" (ἀπὸ τοῦ Χριστοῦ, 9:3), reinforces that specific point. To be apart "from the Christ" is to be separated from the promise now fulfilled in him as well. The phrase "away from the Christ/Messiah" (ἀπὸ τοῦ Χριστοῦ) also provides a striking contrast with 8:39. There Paul rejoiced that no created entity "will be able to *separate* us *from* God's love [ἀπὸ τῆς ἀγάπης τοῦ θεοῦ] which is in Christ Jesus our Lord!" Now the same Greek preposition, ἀπό, "away from," explains what it means to be "cursed" (ἀνάθεμα). It entails being "apart from the Christ." Understanding the phrase as "from the *Messiah*" better conveys the meaning within a Jewish context.[41] Thus "Paul's anguish, its reason not yet specified, is that God's people have failed to recognize their Messiah."[42]

Paul specifies those over whom he has such sorrow in the remainder of 9:3 and the initial clause of 9:4. His prayer is that he might be cursed away from the Christ "in behalf of my brothers, [that is,] my kinsmen according to [the] flesh; such ones are Israelites" (9:3–4a). The use of the Greek preposition ὑπέρ, "in behalf of," recalls earlier uses in 5:6–8; 8:27, 31–34. The preposition encompasses both "in the place of" and "in behalf of." The exchange image conveyed by it reinforces the interpretation that the current state of those Paul refers to as being "away from the Messiah" means they currently stand under a curse themselves (cf. Gal 3:13).

Initially, the object of the preposition is "my brothers" (τῶν ἀδελφῶν μου). Dunn notes that "elsewhere Paul always uses ἀδελφός ['brother'] for his fellow Christians."[43] This observation leads Cranfield to the following assertion:

> The clear implication of this is that for Paul—and this must be stated with emphasis, since it has often been forgotten by Christians—unbelieving Israel is within the elect community, not outside of it.[44]

However, just because the referent of "brother" is a fellow Christian everywhere else in Paul, this does not mean it *must* be so here. Furthermore, this is an exceptional case in any event since Paul would certainly not consider the unbelievers in Israel, whatever their place before God, as "fellow Christians." While the phrase "my brothers" (τῶν ἀδελφῶν μου) might initially lead us to assume Paul is speaking of the believers "within the elect community," the remainder

---

[40] A two-covenant theory is advocated by, for example, Stendahl, "Paul among Jews and Gentiles," 3–4; Gager, *The Origins of Anti-Semitism*, 251–61; Gaston, "Israel's Misstep in the Eyes of Paul," 323–25; Gaston, *Paul and the Torah*, 92–99, 135–50. See the commentary on 11:26.

[41] See the third textual note on 9:3.

[42] Dunn, *Romans*, 525.

[43] Dunn, *Romans*, 525.

[44] Cranfield, *Romans*, 459.

of the verse provides immediate clarification (see also the two different senses of "Israel" in 9:6). In apposition to "my brothers" (τῶν ἀδελφῶν μου) is "my kinsmen according to [the] flesh" (τῶν συγγενῶν μου κατὰ σάρκα). The second phrase defines his "brothers" in the ethnic sense of physical relationship. They belong to the same extended family as Paul; they are his "relatives" or "kinsmen."[45] Thus "my brothers" does not refer to fellow Christians in spiritual terms here. Instead, Paul himself clarifies the expression in terms of ethnicity. He reinforces this again with "according to [the] flesh" (κατὰ σάρκα), as well as by the further clarification provided in the initial words of what we call the next verse, 9:4. Unfortunately, the verse division is poorly placed.

Paul speaks of his "brothers" as those of his same ethnicity and then explicitly defines them: "such ones are Israelites" (9:4). "Israelite" (Ἰσραηλίτης) appears here for the first time in the letter, a term Paul utilizes once more in it, in 11:1. Note also that "Israel" (Ἰσραήλ) occurs a total of eleven times in the epistle, and it as well appears exclusively in chapters 9–11.[46]

Israel's Advantages (9:4b–5a)

The versification in this section continues to be disruptive. The remainder of 9:4 and the first half of 9:5 provide an extraordinary list. It is introduced by the relative pronoun "of whom" (ὧν), which indicates possession. The list to follow comprises things which "belong to" the Israelites. But they are so only because *God* entrusted them *to* Israel. These gifts have all been graciously bestowed, and they are blessings Paul himself shares (9:3; 11:1).

The items which follow elaborate upon a question asked, and only partially answered, in 3:1–2: "Then what is the advantage of the Jew or what is the benefit of the circumcision? Much in every way! Indeed, [it is] primarily they were entrusted with the sayings of God [τὰ λόγια τοῦ θεοῦ]." In addition to this primary advantage, Paul now adds these further blessings given to the Israelites: "of whom are the adoption and the glory and the covenants, also the giving of the Law and the temple service and the promises, of whom [are] the fathers and from whom [is] the Christ/Messiah" (9:4b–5a).

The six items listed in the remainder of 9:4 provide a good example of structured assonance. Together with six occurrences of feminine forms of the definite article (ἡ, *hey*, and αἱ, *hi*), "the elegant double sequence of feminine nouns ending in -θεσια [-*thesia*], -α [-*a*], -αι [-*ai*] would be pleasing to the ear."[47] The two sets with three corresponding feminine nouns each are υἱοθεσία, *huiothesia*; δόξα, *doxa*; διαθῆκαι, *diathekai*; followed by νομοθεσία, *nomothesia*; λατρεία, *latreia*; and ἐπαγγελίαι, *epangeliai*.

The *first* term, "the adoption" (ἡ υἱοθεσία), "is surprising, since it [υἱοθεσία] occurs nowhere in the LXX or in other Jewish writings of the

---

[45] See the fifth textual note on 9:3.

[46] See 9:6 and "God's People" in the introduction to Romans 9–11.

[47] Dunn, *Romans*, 522.

period."[48] However, Paul's use of it in 8:15 and 8:23 clearly leads to his continued focus upon God's adoption of his people into his family. Based upon the OT, the applicability to the Israelites is also most appropriate. They have become Yahweh's people because he chose them to be his own (e.g., Deut 7:6–11; 14:2; 1 Ki 3:8; Is 41:8–9; Ezek 20:5), something comparable to adopting. The OT then regularly describes *the resulting state*: the Israelites are God's (firstborn) "son" or "sons," and he is their "Father."[a] In fact, "the adoption" (ἡ υἱοθεσία) conveys "the acceptance of the nation of Israel as son of God" (BDAG, a) and is translated by some as "the adoption as sons" (NASB) or "the sonship" (RSV).

The *second* term, "the glory" (ἡ δόξα), also recalls earlier uses in Romans. The sense of this noun in 5:2; 8:18, 21 anticipates our future "glory" (see also 8:17, 30). But one need not separate the promise of eschatological fullness from the glimpses of God's glory experienced already in salvation history. "The reference is clearly to 'the glory of the Lord,' particularly, no doubt, to the theophanies which had been Israel's special privilege as God's people (Exod 16:10; 24:15–17; 40:34–35; Lev 9:23; Num 14:10)."[49] One may add NT theophanies of "glory" witnessed by Jesus' Israelite disciples as well (e.g., Lk 9:29–31; Acts 1:9; 1 Tim 3:16; 2 Pet 1:16–18). Unfortunately, in this context, a more distant echo of the "glory" exchanged is also relevant to Israel.[50] Interestingly, theophanic references to "the glory" are always accompanied by the divine name or a divine title in the OT and rabbinic literature,[51] as often in the NT too (e.g., "the glory of the Lord," Lk 2:9; 2 Cor 3:18; 8:19). Paul may have omitted such a reference here for stylistic reasons, simply to maintain the sequence of feminine nouns noted above.

The *third* term, the plural phrase "the covenants" (αἱ διαθῆκαι), likely represents the original reading (see the textual note). It encompasses the covenant with Abraham (Gen 15:18–21; 17:1–22), which, with its promises of blessing (Gen 12:1–3; 18:18; 22:17–18; 26:3–4; 28:14), was reiterated to Isaac and Jacob (Ex 2:24; 2 Ki 13:23; Ps 105:8–10), as well as the covenants at Sinai (Ex 19:5–6; 24:7–8), on the plains of Moab (Deuteronomy 29–31), at Ebal and Gerizim (Josh 8:30–35), and perhaps with David also (2 Chr 21:7; Ps 89:3 [MT 89:4]). Analogous uses of the plural occur in Sirach 44:12, 18; Wisdom 18:22; 2 Macc 8:15; *4 Ezra* 5:29.[52]

The *fourth* term, "the giving of the Law" (ἡ νομοθεσία), was a lofty privilege for Israel alone out of all the nations on earth (Deut 4:7–8; Ps 147:19–20). Yet "the *Law*" may not, at first, seem to belong among the *blessings* bestowed upon the Israelites by God. This is perhaps particularly true for Lutherans

(a) E.g., Ex 4:22–23; Deut 14:1–2; Is 43:6; 63:16; 64:8 (MT 64:7); Jer 31:9; Hos 1:10 (MT 2:1); 11:1

---

[48] Dunn, *Romans*, 526.

[49] Dunn, *Romans*, 526.

[50] See Jer 2:11 and the commentary on Rom 1:23, where humanity "exchanged the glory [ἤλλαξαν τὴν δόξαν] of the incorruptible God" for idolatrous images of people and animals.

[51] Moo, *Romans*, 563, n. 43.

[52] Dunn, *Romans*, 527.

accustomed to applying the Law's commands primarily in their sense of convicting all people of their sin (the second or proper use of the Law), based upon passages such as Rom 3:20; 4:15; 5:20; 7:5, 7–11, 23; 8:2b. While overstating the case in the other direction, Cranfield offers a balancing corrective about the positive nature of the Law. "The fact that ἡ νομοθεσία ['the giving of the Law'] is mentioned among the excellent privileges of Israel is clearly of the greatest significance for our understanding of Paul's view of the law."[53]

The broader sense of "Law" as referring to all the revelation given at Sinai applies here. Indeed, Yahweh's very first "word" there (cf. "the Ten *Words*," Ex 34:28; Deut 4:13; 10:4) reminded Israel that he was their God and that he had already rescued them from slavery (Ex 20:1–2); then followed the commandments, most of which are phrased as declarative statements (Ex 20:3–17).[54] Paul similarly asserts that the Torah given to Israel testifies to the righteousness of God through faith (Rom 3:21; cf. 3:27, 31; 8:2a) and then lays out the path toward a life full of further promised blessings from Yahweh himself (see the commentary on Rom 7:10; also Rom 10:5, citing Lev 18:5). Indeed, Paul has already referred to the Law as "the embodiment of the knowledge and the truth" (Rom 2:20) and described it as "holy" (7:12); even its commands are "holy and righteous and good" (7:12). Rom 13:8–10 then affirms the Law's ongoing, positive guidance for believers (see the excursus "Paul and the Law" following the commentary on 13:8–14).

A similar mishearing may take place with the *fifth* term, "the temple service" (ἡ λατρεία). In biblical use, this Greek noun refers almost exclusively to the sacrificial cultus at the tabernacle, which was then continued at the temple.[55] People tend to hear "temple service" in terms of what the Israelites did to serve God (e.g., sacrifices, offerings, praise). However, Leviticus repeatedly affirms that the tabernacle was a located place where Yahweh *served forgiveness* to Israel (e.g., Lev 4:20, 26, 31, 35; 5:10, 13, 16, 18). Solomon expands upon the abundant blessings promised by God when he dedicates the temple in 1 Kings 8. The temple primarily *served Israel* as the designated place where Yahweh promised to hear and respond to the needs of his people by delivering his gifts, both physical and spiritual, to them there (1 Ki 8:28–43). "The temple service" (ἡ λατρεία) conveys most appropriately what is meant by the phrase "Divine Service."[56] This is in keeping with the dominant sense of the German word *Gottesdienst* as the "service of God" *to* his people. In Rom 12:1 Paul uses the term *uniquely* for the other side, for the "service of God" *by* his people. He also extends the context beyond ritual worship in calling for those who have

---

[53] Cranfield, *Romans*, 463.

[54] Hummel, *The Word Becoming Flesh*, 74–75; Middendorf, *Romans 1–8*, 200.

[55] See the references in the sixth textual note on 9:4.

[56] See the explanation in *LSB*, viii, xxiv. "Divine Service" is the traditional Lutheran title for the chief worship service in the church (e.g., *LSB*, 151, 167, 184, 203, 213).

received the service of God's mercies to offer their entire lives in service back to God (τὴν λογικὴν λατρείαν ὑμῶν, Rom 12:1).[57]

The *sixth* and final term in 9:4 is "the promises" (αἱ ἐπαγγελίαι). In light of previous uses of the noun "promise" in 4:13, 14, 16, 20, the dominant reference is to the promises made to Abraham (compare Gal 3:16–29 to Gen 12:1–3; 15:3–6; 17:1–7; 18:18; 22:17–18). Of course, these and other promises were reiterated to Isaac and Jacob and applied repeatedly to all the Israelites.[b]

(b) E.g., Gen 26:3–4; 28:13–15; Ex 3:16–17; 2 Sam 7:12–16, 21; Ps 105:8–9, 42–45; Jer 29:10; 33:14–16

At the beginning of Rom 9:5, Paul signals that the end of his list is near by repeating its opening word, ὧν, "of whom." This relative pronoun states that "the fathers" (οἱ πατέρες) also belong to the Israelites. As in 11:28, the phrase "the fathers" refers to the patriarchs, Abraham, Isaac, Jacob, and Jacob's twelve sons. They are the "founding fathers" of the twelve tribes of Israel and, therefore, of all Israelites (e.g., Ex 3:13–16; Num 20:15; 26:55; Deut 1:8; 8:3, 16, 18; 9:5). All the blessings discussed previously were promised to and passed down through them.

Then, as promised, the Messiah came from these fathers: "from whom [is] the Christ/Messiah" (ἐξ ὧν ὁ Χριστός, Rom 9:5). Jesus himself similarly said, "Salvation is from the Jews" (ἡ σωτηρία ἐκ τῶν Ἰουδαίων ἐστίν, Jn 4:22). This promise too stretches all the way back to Abraham (Gen 12:3; 22:18), and even before (Gen 3:15). Paul immediately clarifies the phrase with "that is, according to the flesh" (τὸ κατὰ σάρκα). The neuter Greek article (τό) means that Paul is making a qualification regarding Jesus' *human descent*, rather than modifying the masculine title "the Christ" (ὁ Χριστός). Paul made the same point in regard to Jesus' earthly lineage from David at the very opening of the letter (Rom 1:3). In fulfillment of 2 Sam 7:12–16, the apostle defines God's Son as "the one who came from the seed of David according to flesh" (τοῦ γενομένου ἐκ σπέρματος Δαυὶδ κατὰ σάρκα, Rom 1:3).

This entire list defines elements which belonged to the Israelites. But, hearkening back to 3:1–2, these blessings were all bestowed upon them by God. Together with "the sayings of God" (3:2), they were entrusted to Israel and provided blessed advantages. At this point in Romans, one cannot but notice how Paul has already stated that Gentile believers now also partake in some of these same gracious gifts. "The blessings they share are Israel's blessings; particularly υἱοθεσία ['adoption'] (8:15, 23), δόξα ['glory'] (8:18, 21), and ἐπαγγελία ['promise'] (4:13–14, 16)."[58] Based upon 1 Cor 11:25 and Gal 3:29, we can add "the covenants" (αἱ διαθῆκαι, Rom 9:4) and "the fathers" (οἱ πατέρες, 9:5) to the list of blessings now given to Gentile believers as well. All of these are

---

[57] See also the discussion of λατρεύω, "to serve," in 1:9 in "Thanksgiving and Prayers (1:8–10)" in Middendorf, *Romans 1–8*, 75–76.

[58] Dunn, *Romans*, 522.

extended to them because of the Christ/Messiah, who came into this world in his human nature via the patriarchs of Israel (9:5).[59]

The Doxology of Romans 9:5b—To Jesus or Not to Jesus?

Various Options

The remainder of 9:5 provides one of the greatest interpretive puzzles in the NT.[60] The Greek states: ὁ ὢν ἐπὶ πάντων θεὸς εὐλογητὸς εἰς τοὺς αἰῶνας, ἀμήν. The semantic meaning of the words is not in dispute; the controversy is about the referent of "the One being over all ... God" (ὁ ὢν ἐπὶ πάντων ... θεός). Does it refer to God the Father or to Jesus, the Christ/Messiah? If the latter is the case, we have a clear declaration that *Jesus is God over all*. Punctuation in the Greek would, of course, resolve the controversy. A hard stop (e.g., a colon or period) after "flesh" (σάρκα) would, in all likelihood, mean the phrase utters a separate sentence, a doxology to God the Father. A comma would indicate that Paul proclaims the doxology directly to "the Christ" (ὁ Χριστός). Ambiguity stems from the sound assumption that punctuation was not included in the Greek autograph manuscripts which, of course, we do not have.[61] Metzger evaluates its presence in early extant texts of the NT as "sporadic and haphazard,"[62] but it became more common and uniform as copyists added it to later manuscripts.

> Since the earliest manuscripts of the New Testament are without systematic punctuation, editors and translators of the text must insert such marks of punctuation as seem to be appropriate to the syntax and meaning. The present passage has been the object of much discussion.[63]

Rom 9:5 provides perhaps the most significant example with which to illustrate that when inserted later, as is presumably the case, punctuation marks inevitably have an interpretive effect, as do chapter and verse divisions. While often quite helpful, such additions should not be regarded as inspired; occasionally, they can even be misleading.

---

[59] The genealogies in Matthew and Luke also stress the human lineage of Jesus as the son of Abraham, Isaac, Jacob, and Judah (Mt 1:1–2; Lk 3:33–34).

[60] For a more thorough discussion, see Sanday and Headlam, *Romans*, 233–38; see also Metzger, *A Textual Commentary on the Greek New Testament*, 520–23.

[61] Metzger, *A Textual Commentary on the Greek New Testament*, 521, states that punctuation "originated at a time subsequent to Paul's writing"; also Hultgren, *Romans*, 353. But see Robertson, *A Grammar of the Greek New Testament*, 242, for evidence of some use of punctuation in written texts prior to the NT.

[62] According to Metzger, *A Textual Commentary on the Greek New Testament*, 521, n. 2, "the presence of marks of punctuation in early manuscripts of the New Testament is so sporadic and haphazard that one cannot infer with confidence the construction given by the punctuator to the passage."

[63] Metzger, *A Textual Commentary on the Greek New Testament*, 520.

Cranfield lays out five possible options for how the statement ὁ ὢν ἐπὶ πάντων θεὸς εὐλογητὸς εἰς τοὺς αἰῶνας, ἀμήν in 9:5 may be interpreted. These can be summarized as follows:[64]

A. The entire expression refers to Christ and to him as God:

    1. "… from whom is the Christ, according to the flesh, [the Christ] who is God over all, blessed forever." Or

    2. "… from whom is the Christ, according to the flesh, [the Christ] who is over all, God blessed forever."

B. Only the first half refers to Christ, and not to him as God:

    3. "… from whom is the Christ, according to the flesh, [the Christ] who is over all. God [be] blessed forever."

C. None of the expression refers to Christ, and therefore not to him as God:

    4. "… from whom is the Christ, according to the flesh. God who is over all be blessed forever." Or

    5. "… from whom is the Christ, according to the flesh. He who is over all, God, be blessed forever."

Despite these enumerated options, only two camps essentially exist. The key division between them remains, of course, whether "God" is attributed to "Christ" (options 1 and 2) or not to "Christ" (options 3, 4, and 5).

The attestation from early church history supports both basic alternatives. *Interpreters* generally line up on the former side. For example, Origen asserts: "It is clear from this passage that Christ is the *God who is over all* [Rom 9:5]."[65] Ambrosiaster explains why he supports the same position:

> As there is no mention of the Father's name in this verse and Paul is talking about Christ, it cannot be disputed that he is called God here. For if Scripture is speaking about God the Father and adds the Son, it often calls the Father God and the Son Lord.[66]

On the other hand, *the evidence of punctuation added by scribes* tends to support the "not to Christ" understanding. Metzger summarizes both kinds of evidence and evaluates them in this way:

> Evidence from the Church Fathers, who were almost unanimous in understanding the passage as referring to ὁ Χριστός, is of relatively minor significance, as is also the opposing fact that four uncial manuscripts (A B C L) and at least twenty-six minuscule manuscripts have a point [the equivalent of "either a

---

[64] Cranfield, *Romans*, 465. Cranfield includes a sixth option that requires a conjectural emendation of the text, but his verdict is that the sixth option "is surely to be rejected" (466).

[65] Origen, *Romans* (Bray, *Romans*, ACCS NT 6:246).

[66] Ambrosiaster, *Romans* (Bray, *Romans*, ACCS NT 6:247). Passages in support of his final point include 1 Cor 1:3; 8:6; 2 Cor 1:2; Gal 1:3; Eph 1:2; 4:5–6; see Middendorf, "The Bud Has Flowered: Trinitarian Theology in the New Testament," 303; see also the commentary on 14:4.

colon or a full stop"] after σάρκα, either by the first hand or by subsequent correctors.[67]

Answering Arguments against Jesus as "God"

The main argument *against* taking all (or part) of 9:5b as a reference to Christ predominantly rests upon the assertion that Paul does not appear to refer to Jesus as "God" (θεός) elsewhere.[68] Dunn notes: "Where Paul elsewhere ascribes universal lordship to Christ there is a clear note of theological reserve."[69] He therefore argues that to apply this ascription of "God" (θεός) directly to Jesus "would imply that Paul had abandoned all his inhibitions and theological circumspection so carefully maintained elsewhere."[70] The majority of the committee that worked on *A Textual Commentary to the Greek New Testament* (1971) similarly concluded: "On the basis of the general tenor of his theology, it was considered tantamount to impossible that Paul would have expressed Christ's greatness by calling him God blessed for ever."[71] Dunn also cites "the *lack* of Christological focus in the matching doxological conclusion to this whole section (11:33–36)."[72]

There are some possible exceptions to the exclusive claim that Paul does not refer to Jesus as God elsewhere. 2 Thessalonians concludes with the phrase κατὰ τὴν χάριν τοῦ θεοῦ ἡμῶν καὶ κυρίου Ἰησοῦ Χριστοῦ (2 Thess 1:12). This could all be read as a reference to Jesus Christ, "according to the grace of our God and Lord, [namely, the 'God and Lord' who is] Jesus Christ." However, the phrase might refer to God the Father and then the Lord Jesus Christ separately, "the grace of our God and of [the] Lord Jesus Christ." In Titus 2:13 the situation is much the same. Paul speaks of the eschatological appearing "of the glory of the great God and our Savior Jesus Christ" (τῆς δόξης τοῦ μεγάλου θεοῦ καὶ σωτῆρος ἡμῶν Ἰησοῦ Χριστοῦ). Once again, the entire description could be read as applying to Jesus, "our great God and Savior Jesus Christ," or it could be intended to speak of both the Father and the Son. These passages do, however, challenge the certainty of the assertions in the preceding paragraph; thus "it may *not* be assumed that Paul *never* ascribes the title Θεός ['God'] to Christ."[73] One should also weigh the evidence of straightforward statements in Scripture outside of Paul's letters which do identify Jesus as "God" (θεός)

---

[67] Metzger, *A Textual Commentary on the Greek New Testament*, 520–21; for the bracketed insertion, see 520.

[68] Metzger, *A Textual Commentary on the Greek New Testament*, 522; similarly, Dodd, *Romans*, 152; Dunn, *Romans*, 529; Käsemann, *Romans*, 259–60.

[69] Dunn, *Romans*, 529.

[70] Dunn, *Romans*, 529.

[71] Metzger, *A Textual Commentary on the Greek New Testament*, 522.

[72] Dunn, *Romans*, 529.

[73] Murray, *Romans*, 2:247; emphasis added.

before proposing what is "tantamount to impossible"[74] for Paul to assert (e.g., Jn 1:1; "the only-begotten God," Jn 1:18; "my Lord and my God," Jn 20:28; "the righteousness from our God and Savior Jesus Christ," 2 Pet 1:1).[75] Finally, even if it is true that Paul does not explicitly refer to Jesus as "God" (θεός) anywhere else in his extant writings, this does not prove he did not do so here.

Moreover, Paul does, in fact, use several expressions elsewhere "which predicate of Jesus the fulness of deity. Perhaps most notable is Phil. 2:6—ἐν μορφῇ Θεοῦ ὑπάρχων ['being in the form of God']."[76] Col 2:9 also declares that in Jesus "all the fullness of the deity dwells bodily" (ὅτι ἐν αὐτῷ κατοικεῖ πᾶν τὸ πλήρωμα τῆς θεότητος σωματικῶς). Furthermore, the confessions of Jesus as "Lord" (κύριος) in the context of OT passages where the LXX uses that title to render the divine name, Yahweh (יהוה), are also quite explicit in their force. For example, both Acts 2 and Romans 10 cite the prophet Joel (2:32 [MT/LXX 3:5]) and, in the immediate context, identify Jesus as "Lord" (κύριος) (Acts 2:21, 36; Rom 10:9, 13). While the LXX of that passage has the title κύριος (LXX Joel 3:5), the original Hebrew is יהוה, Yahweh (MT Joel 3:5). In Phil 2:9–11 the Father gives Jesus "the name above every name" (τὸ ὄνομα τὸ ὑπὲρ πᾶν ὄνομα, Phil 2:9) in order that "every knee might bow ... and every tongue might confess" (πᾶν γόνυ κάμψῃ ... καὶ πᾶσα γλῶσσα ἐξομολογήσηται) that "Jesus Christ is Lord [κύριος]" (Phil 2:10–11). Here Paul loudly echoes Is 45:23, where Yahweh (יהוה, Is 45:21) ascribes the same worship to himself: "To *me* shall every knee bow and every tongue confess; 'Only in *Yahweh*,' it shall be said *to me*, 'is manifold righteousness and strength' " (Is 45:23–24). Paul's wording in Philippians 2 closely resembles the LXX translation of Is 45:23: "To *me* shall every knee bow, and every tongue shall confess *to God*" (ἐμοὶ κάμψει πᾶν γόνυ καὶ ἐξομολογήσεται πᾶσα γλῶσσα τῷ θεῷ).[77]

Paul also ascribes to Jesus actions which he would certainly view as limited to the purview of God himself. Examples include creating (Col 1:16), forgiving sins (Col 3:13; cf. Lk 5:20–26), giving grace (Rom 1:7), and judging sins (1 Cor 4:4–5; 2 Cor 5:10; 2 Thess 1:7–9).[78] All of this leads Murray to conclude: "The clause ὁ ὢν ἐπὶ πάντων ['the one being over all,' Rom 9:5] as an assertion of Christ's lordship is in accord with Paul's teaching elsewhere (*cf.* 1:4; 14:9; Eph. 1:20–23; Phil. 2:9–11; Col. 1:18, 19; for parallels *cf.* Matt. 28:18; John 3:35; Acts 2:36; Heb. 1:2–4; 8:1; I Pet. 3:22)."[79] The combined force of this evidence

---

[74] Cited above from Metzger, *A Textual Commentary on the Greek New Testament*, 522.

[75] The translation of 2 Pet 1:1 is that of Giese, *2 Peter and Jude*, 27. For his commentary on that verse, see 32–33.

[76] Murray, *Romans*, 2:247.

[77] See also 1 Cor 8:6; 12:3; 2 Cor 4:5. For a more complete discussion, see Middendorf, "The Bud Has Flowered: Trinitarian Theology in the New Testament," 299–303, and the commentary on 10:13.

[78] Moo, *Romans*, 568, n. 73.

[79] Murray, *Romans*, 2:248.

demonstrates beyond any reasonable doubt that "a Christ who is *only* 'according to the flesh' [Rom 9:5] is not the Christ of Paul."[80]

Arguments in Favor of Jesus as "God"

A couple substantial matters of style and structure also speak loudly *in favor of the view* that all or part of the statement "the One being over all, blessed God into the ages" (ὁ ὢν ἐπὶ πάντων θεὸς εὐλογητὸς εἰς τοὺς αἰῶνας) refers to Jesus.

First, Metzger points out the following:

> Pauline doxologies … are never asyndetic but always attach themselves to that which precedes: with ὅς ἐστιν ["who is"] (Ro 1.25); with ὁ ὤν ["the one being"] (2 Cor 11.31); with ᾧ ["to whom"] (Ga 1.5; 2 Tm 4.18; cf. He 13.21; 1 Pe 4.11); with αὐτῷ ["to him"] (Ro 11.36; Eph 3.21; cf. 1 Pe 5.11; 2 Pe 3.18); with τῷ δὲ θεῷ ["to God"] (Php 4.20; 1 Tm 1.17).[81]

Second, doxological structures elsewhere in Scripture indicate that Rom 9:5 is not, in all likelihood, a separate doxology to God the Father. Aside from one example, where εὐλογητός, "blessed," is the final word of LXX Ps 67:19, in all other independent doxologies in Scripture, the term blessed (Rom 9:5 has εὐλογητός) is always "the first word in the sentence."[82] In other words, the reference to God, in name or by a title, always *follows* the word for "blessed." Metzger even notes that in the one possible exception, LXX Ps 67:19, its final word, εὐλογητός, "blessed," has "no corresponding word in Hebrew and seems to be a double translation."[83] If Paul intends ὁ ὢν ἐπὶ πάντων θεὸς εὐλογητὸς εἰς τοὺς αἰῶνας (Rom 9:5) to serve as a separate doxology to God the Father, the *style* is unique among his writings; the *structure*, aside from one questionable exception, would also stand unique in all of Scripture! Since it is unlikely that this verse would be unique in both of these two respects, the statement surely pertains to Jesus the Messiah.

As a result of the (virtually) unanimous consistency on these two points, Cranfield concludes: "The superiority of the case for taking v. 5b to refer to

---

[80] Franzmann, *Romans*, 169; the phrase he quotes occurs in both 1:3 and 9:5.

[81] Metzger, *A Textual Commentary on the Greek New Testament*, 522. Similarly, Cranfield, *Romans*, 467, observes: "Pauline doxologies are generally either an integral part of the preceding sentence or else closely connected with it (the doxology referring to a person named in the preceding sentence)." See also Kuske, *Romans 9–16*, 24.

[82] Cranfield, *Romans*, 467. For example, in the NT, see either εὐλογημένος or εὐλογητός, both meaning "blessed," in Mt 21:9; 23:39; Mk 11:9; Lk 1:42, 68; 13:35; 19:38; Jn 12:13; 2 Cor 1:3; Eph 1:3; 1 Pet 1:3.

[83] Metzger, *A Textual Commentary on the Greek New Testament*, 522, n. 5. LXX Ps 67:19 ends with κύριος ὁ θεὸς εὐλογητός, "may the Lord God be blessed." The Hebrew verse, MT Ps 68:19 (ET 68:18), simply has יָהּ אֱלֹהִים, "Yahweh/the LORD God." Therefore εὐλογητός at the end of LXX Ps 67:19 may be a repetition of the first word of the next verse. The initial word in LXX Ps 67:20 is εὐλογητός, "blessed," which corresponds to the initial word of MT Ps 68:20 (ET 68:19), בָּרוּךְ, "blessed." Most English translations follow the MT and not the LXX because they have no word for "blessed" in Ps 68:18 (MT 68:19) but begin Ps 68:19 (MT 68:20) with "blessed."

Christ is so overwhelming as to warrant the assertion that it is very nearly certain that it ought to be accepted."[84] While "very nearly certain" may be overstated, his conclusion is sound. Though a bit more cautious, Sanday and Headlam reach the same conclusion as Cranfield and enunciate the position advocated by this commentary:

> Throughout there has been no argument which we have felt to be quite conclusive, but the result of our investigations into the grammar of the sentence and the drift of the argument is to incline us to the belief that the words would naturally refer to Christ, unless θεός ["God"] is so definitely a proper name that it would imply a contrast in itself. We have seen that that is not so. Even if St. Paul did not elsewhere use the word ["God"] of the Christ, yet it certainly was so used at a not much later period. St. Paul's phraseology is never fixed; he had no dogmatic reason against so using it. In these circumstances with some slight, but only slight, hesitation we adopt the first alternative ["placing a comma after σάρκα ('flesh') and referring the whole passage to Christ"] and translate, "Of whom is the Christ as concerning the flesh, who is over all, God blessed for ever. Amen."[85]

Moo concurs, noting that "connecting 'God' to 'Christ' is therefore exegetically preferable, theologically unobjectionable, and contextually appropriate."[86]

In this context, we have then a reference to Jesus *both* as the Messiah who came from the family tree of the patriarchs according to his human nature ("flesh") *and* as "the One being over all, blessed God into the ages" (9:5). Thus Paul "is drawing a distinction between the earthly descent of the Messiah and his exalted status, much as he does in Rom. 1:3–4."[87] Franzmann agrees with the parallel to the opening verses of the letter:

> As in 1:3, the phrase "according to the flesh" calls for a counterpart; that counterpart is there given in the phrase "according to the Spirit of holiness" (1:4) and is given here [9:5] in the words "God over all, blessed forever."[88]

The Formula of Concord, therefore, makes this appropriate Christological statement:

> We believe, teach, and confess that although the Son of God is a separate, distinct, and complete divine person and therefore has been from all eternity true, essential, and perfect God with the Father and the Holy Spirit, yet, when the time had fully come, he took the human nature into the unity of his person, not in such a manner that there are now two persons or two Christs, but in such a way that Christ Jesus is henceforth in *one* person simultaneously true eternal God, born of the Father from eternity, and also a true man,

---

[84] Cranfield, *Romans*, 468.

[85] Sanday and Headlam, *Romans*, 238; the bracketed insertion about the comma is quoted from 233.

[86] Moo, *Romans*, 568; similarly, Fitzmyer, *Romans*, 548–49, Murray, *Romans*, 2:245–48; Nygren, *Romans*, 358–59; Wright, "Romans," 629–31.

[87] Matera, *Romans*, 221–22.

[88] Franzmann, *Romans*, 169.

born of the most blessed virgin Mary, as it is written, "Of their race, according to the flesh, is the Christ, who is God over all, blessed for ever" (Rom. 9:5). (FC SD VIII 6)

Lenski aptly draws this discussion to a close and points ahead toward a proper response: "The exegesis is sound: Christ, an Israelite according to the flesh, is Lord of all, God blessed forever, to which we, like Paul, add an emphatic 'amen.' "[89]

Amen! (9:5)

In light of the preceding discussion, the concluding "amen" (ἀμήν) is worthy of comment. It represents a transliterated form of the Hebrew (see the third textual note on 9:5). After Paul describes the human and divine Messiah, his "amen" utters the voice of faith. This, then, points to the critical matter at hand in regard to the Good News. In 1:16–17, the relationship between the Gospel and faith was enunciated thematically. As Paul's argument continues in chapters 9–11, he engages the matter of human response more fully. Is the "amen" of faith spoken by those who hear the "Word of Christ" (10:17) regarding his person and saving work, as in 9:5 and 10:6–13? Or is the message heard and met with unbelief (e.g., 3:3; 10:16, 18, 21; 11:20)? How then does God react in response to those who do not "listen responsively to the Good News" (10:16; see 11:1–12, 22–23)?

The Way Forward (9:6–11:36)

Before dealing with those matters, Paul continues his argument by describing the merciful call of God through his Word in both the past and the present (9:6–29). He goes on to diagnose various human responses to God's call (9:30–10:21) and the divine reaction in the face of human unbelief (11:1–12). Paul then describes the current, ongoing, and future state of God's relationship with Israelites as well as with Gentiles (11:13–32). Finally, Romans 9–11 concludes with a resounding doxology (11:33–36) which beautifully forms a frame with the one which ends the initial segment of these three chapters (9:5). Paul thereby surrounds his discussion with praise to God the Father, who does all things for us (11:35–36) in "the Christ/Messiah, ... the One being over all, blessed God into the ages. Amen!" (9:5).

---

[89] Lenski, *Romans*, 589.

Introduction to Romans 9:6–29:
God's Enduring Word

Volume 1 of this commentary argues that Paul's emphasis throughout Romans is not anthropocentric, but, rather, centered upon on God, his righteousness (Romans 1–4), and life in our Lord Jesus Christ (Romans 5–8). These themes prevail in Romans 9–11 as well. This has significant implications for matters of interpretation in Romans 9. More fundamentally, it also affects how one identifies what the major issues at hand actually are prior to assessing what Paul teaches about them.[1]

An added component here involves the manner in which Paul goes about making his case. Two important points should be noted: "Paul writes for readers who know the Bible."[2] And he writes for those who also accept the Bible's inspired authority. This section, as well as those to follow, illustrates the validity of the first point and the importance of the second. In regard to the second, Paul begins with an assertion of long-range significance: "but by no means [is it] that God's Word has failed and remains fallen" (9:6).

Furthermore, Paul, in drawing support for his assertions from the OT narrative of Genesis, assumes that his hearers know the characters and incidents referred to without giving much explanation or detail. In 9:6–13, Paul proceeds to quote rapidly from the OT four times (9:7, 9, 12, 13). As Paul continues into the remainder of the chapter,

> the opening assertion that the word of God has not failed is documented by the series of OT quotations in the body of the paragraph (vv 7, 9, 12, 13, 15, 17, 20) and the concluding catena of four passages (vv 25–29). …
>
> The verse [9:6] is therefore thematic not only for the next paragraph or two … but for the whole section (chaps. 9–11), climaxing in 11:29.[3]

At the same time, the more general truths about God which Paul draws out from these OT accounts do not simply come to his readers out of the blue. The questions raised earlier in 3:1–4 remain relevant (see the introduction to Romans 9–11). Additionally, based upon the terminology Paul uses, "the strong echo of the argument in chap. 4 is no accident: ἐπαγγελία ['promise'] (4:13, 14, 16, 20; 9:4, 8, 9), λογίζεσθαι ['to credit, reckon, account'] (4:3–6, 8–11, 22–24; 9:8), σπέρμα ['seed'] (4:13, 16, 18; 9:7–8)."[4] Thus the account of Abraham and all that it reveals about the God who called him come to the fore again in a manner applicable to all his offspring.

[1] See further the introduction to Romans 9–16 and the introduction to Romans 9–11.

[2] Wilckens, *Römer*, 2:194, quoted in Dunn, *Romans*, 542.

[3] Dunn, *Romans*, 537, 539; similarly asserted by Cranfield, *Romans*, 473; Moo, *Romans*, 572.

[4] Dunn, *Romans*, 541.

Before entering 9:6–29, it is helpful to note that the detail with which Paul has crafted this section again reveals his masterful literary skill. That detail also serves to highlight the key terminology he wishes to emphasize. "Indicative of the careful composition of the paragraph is its chiastic structure":[5]

A **9:6–9:** "Word" (λόγος); "Israel" (Ἰσραήλ); "seed" (σπέρμα); "children (of God)" (τέκνα [τοῦ θεοῦ]); "to be called" (the passive of καλέω)

  B **9:10–13:** "to call" (καλέω); "to love" (ἀγαπάω)

    C **9:14–18:** "to show mercy" (ἐλεέω); "to will" (θέλω)

    C' **9:19–23:** "to will" (θέλω); "mercy" (ἔλεος)

  B' **9:24–25:** "to call" (καλέω); "to love" (ἀγαπάω)

A' **9:26–29:** "to be called" (the passive of καλέω); "sons (of God)" (υἱοὶ [θεοῦ]); "Israel" (Ἰσραήλ); "Word" (λόγος); "seed" (σπέρμα)

This analysis supports the titles for these sections as developed here: "God's Word of Promise and His Purposeful Call" (9:6–13); "God's Word of Mercy Calls Us" (9:14–24); and "God's Word Stands—for Both Jews and Gentiles" (9:24–29).

---

[5] Dunn, *Romans*, 537. The chiasm is adapted from Dunn.

God's Word of Promise
and His Purposeful Call

Translation

9 **⁶But by no means [is it] that God's Word has failed and remains fallen. For not all these from Israel are Israel. ⁷Neither [is it] that all children are seed of Abraham, but "in Isaac seed will be called for you." ⁸This is, the children of the flesh, these are not children of God, but the children of the promise are credited as seed. ⁹For the Word of promise is this: "According to this time I will come, and there will be a son belonging to Sarah."**

¹⁰And not only [this], but also Rebekah, having sexual intercourse from one man, Isaac our father— ¹¹indeed, when [they] were not yet born nor had practiced anything good or base (in order that the purpose of God in accordance with [his] choice might endure, ¹²not from works, but from the One who calls), it was spoken to her: "The older one will be a slave to the younger," ¹³just as it stands written: "Jacob I loved, but Esau I spurned."

Textual Notes

9:6 οὐχ οἷον δὲ ὅτι—The only uncommon term here is the relative pronoun οἷος, meaning "*of what sort (such)*" (BDAG). Yet Cranfield describes οὐχ οἷον ... ὅτι as "an unusual expression ... a mixture of two idioms."[1] It "is a mixture of οὐχ οἷον ... 'by no means'... and οὐχ ὅτι 'not as if' " (BDAG, s.v. οἷος, citing BDF, §§ 304, 480). Additionally, ἐστίν is assumed. All of this combines to form the translation "but by no means [is it] that."

ἐκπέπτωκεν—Paul uses the perfect indicative active of ἐκπίπτω, which "means 'fall,' 'fall away from' (in a physical sense: Acts 12:7; 27:17, 26, 29, 32: Jas. 1:11; 1 Pet. 1:24; in a metaphorical sense: Gal. 5:4; 2 Pet. 3:17). But it can also mean 'fail,' 'become weakened.' "[2] BDAG, 4, explains the latter meaning here as "become inadequate for some function, *fail, weaken.*" A well-known example of this sense is 1 Cor 13:8: "love never fails" (πίπτει or ἐκπίπτει; see also Sirach 34:7). "The force of the perfect tense is simply that it describes an event that, completed in the past ... has results existing in the present time."[3] This verb is rendered with the conjoining definitions "it has failed and remains fallen." But with the emphatic negation (see the preceding textual note),

---

[1] Cranfield, *Romans*, 472.

[2] Moo, *Romans*, 572, n. 13.

[3] Wallace, *Greek Grammar*, 573.

"Paul is saying that the completed action of this verb and the continuing result did not happen."[4] Cf. the use of πίπτω in 11:11.

ἐξ Ἰσραὴλ … Ἰσραήλ—These are the first two occurrences of the noun "Israel" in Romans. All eleven uses are in chapters 9–11. The key point here is that Paul utilizes Ἰσραήλ with two different, but overlapping, referents. See "God's People" in the introduction to Romans 9–11 and the commentary on this verse.

9:7   οὐδ' ὅτι—This phrase connects the thought of 9:6 with what follows and assumes another ἐστίν. The conjunction ὅτι serves as a "marker of explanatory clauses" (BDAG, 2), hence "neither [is it] that."

σπέρμα Ἀβραάμ—For σπέρμα, "seed," see the third textual note on 1:3, where it refers to the seed of David. See also 4:13, where, as here, it refers to that of Abraham.

πάντες τέκνα—For τέκνα, "children," as an equivalent of υἱοί, "sons," see the third textual note on 8:14, which has υἱοὶ θεοῦ, "sons of God," who are then called τέκνα θεοῦ, "children of God," in 8:16.

κληθήσεται—The verb καλέω, "call," is thematic in this chapter, occurring in 9:7, 12, 24, 25, 26; see the commentary on 8:30. In 9:7, "from the m[eanings] 'summon' and 'invite' there develops the extended sense **choose for receipt of a special benefit or experience, call**" (BDAG, 4). Dunn discusses how the context in Genesis points to the idiomatic use of the Hebrew and Greek verbs "to call" for giving names to people (see קָרָא in the MT, translated by καλέω in the LXX, in Gen 21:3, 12, as well as Gen 16:11, 15; 17:5, 15, 19; see also BDAG, 1 c). However, he concludes that consistently translating καλέω as "call" best highlights "the thematic function of the verb in this section."[5] The passive voice of the future tense κληθήσεται should be interpreted as a divine or theological passive.[6] "Seed will be called" by God.

σοι—The dative case of the second person singular pronoun expresses interest or advantage, "for you."[7]

9:8   τοῦτ' ἔστιν—It is important to read this clause as an explanation, rather than a more limiting clarification. Paul is "resuming someth[ing] previously mentioned, w[ith] special emphasis" (BDAG, s.v. οὗτος, 1 a ε; as in Rom 7:18; 10:6, 8; Philemon 12; Heb 2:14; 7:5; 9:11; 10:20; 11:16; 13:15). Moo suggests that the clause may be equivalent to the formula פִּשְׁרוֹ, "its interpretation [is]," used frequently in the *Pesharim* (Bible commentaries) among the Dead Sea Scrolls.[8] For a complete discussion, see the commentary on 10:6.

τὰ τέκνα τῆς ἐπαγγελίας—"The children of the promise" relates to "the promise to Abraham and to his seed;" for which, see the second textual note and the commentary on 4:13.

---

[4]   Kuske, *Romans 9–16*, 29.

[5]   Dunn, *Romans*, 541; see 540–41.

[6]   See Wallace, *Greek Grammar*, 437–38.

[7]   See Wallace, *Greek Grammar*, 142–44.

[8]   Moo, *Romans*, 576, n. 31.

λογίζεται εἰς σπέρμα—"Are credited as seed" reiterates other key terms from earlier in Romans. Paul utilizes λογίζομαι nineteen times in the letter, including eleven times in chapter 4; see especially 4:3 and 6:11. For σπέρμα, "seed," see 1:3 and 4:13. Under "Semitic influence," the preposition εἰς with the accusative σπέρμα functions together with the verb λογίζομαι as a predicate nominative (BDAG, s.v. εἰς, 8 and 8 a γ). The clause could mean "the children of the promise are *counted* as seed" in light of the *number* of offspring (see 4:18). But here λογίζεται as another divine passive[9] emphasizes that the children of the promise are "credited" as offspring by God's gracious call (see 9:9, 12; cf. 4:19–20).

9:9 κατὰ τὸν καιρὸν τοῦτον—This phrase is replicated from LXX Gen 18:10. The preposition κατά functions temporally here and provides a definite indication of time (BDAG, B 2 a), "according to this time."

ἐλεύσομαι—The future tense of ἔρχομαι, "I will come," is a synonym of the future ἥξω, "I will come," in LXX Gen 18:10 and might also reflect ἀναστρέψω, "I will return," in LXX Gen 18:14. Paul employs the verb to bridge his combination of quotations from Gen 18:10 (see the preceding textual note) and Gen 18:14 (see the following textual note). In this context, the first person singular may enhance the notion of divine activity, "*I* will come."

ἔσται τῇ Σάρρᾳ υἱός—This clause from LXX Gen 18:14 with the dative τῇ Σάρρᾳ literally reads "there will be to Sarah a son." To express possession, "the genitive is used when ... the emphasis is on the possessor ... and the dative [is used] when the object possessed is to be stressed" (BDF, § 189),[10] so the stress here is on Sarah's "son."

9:10 οὐ μόνον δέ, ἀλλὰ καί—Paul returns to the formulaic expression "not only ... but also," used extensively in Romans (see 4:12).[a]

ἐξ ἑνὸς κοίτην ἔχουσα—This clause literally means "having bed from one man." However,

> κοίτη, meaning originally "bed" (cf. Luke 11:7), came to refer especially to the "marriage bed" (e.g., Heb. 13:4) and hence to sexual intercourse (Lev. 15:21–26; Wis. 3:13, 16; Rom. 13:13; ...). It can also refer to the semen itself (Lev. 15:16–17, 32; 18:20; 22:4; Num. 5:20).[11]

Dunn suggests that "the idiom is quite close to our own: 'having sex with one man.'"[12] BDAG similarly translates: "*conceive children by one man*" (s.v. κοίτη, 2 b). But, as Dunn also notes, the point of ἐξ ἑνός here conveys an even more specific point, namely, "having conceived by the one act of sexual intercourse."[13]

Ἰσαὰκ τοῦ πατρός—As a transliteration of the Hebrew name יִצְחָק (Gen 17:19), the name Ἰσαάκ, "Isaac," does not decline in Greek. However, here its case is genitive, as shown by the appositional τοῦ πατρός, "(the) father." The case of both is determined by

(a) Also in Rom 1:32; 4:16, 23–24; 5:3, 11; 8:23; 9:24; 13:5; 16:4

---

[9] See Wallace, *Greek Grammar*, 437–38.

[10] For the dative of possession, see also Wallace, *Greek Grammar*, 149–51.

[11] Moo, *Romans*, 579, n. 46.

[12] Dunn, *Romans*, 542.

[13] Dunn, *Romans*, 542.

the preposition ἐξ (ἐκ, "from") in the preceding textual note, as they are further defining its object, ἑνός, "one man."

9:11 μήπω γὰρ γεννηθέντων μηδὲ πραξάντων τι—Paul inserts an incomplete genitive absolute. The assumed subject is αὐτῶν, "they," referring to the two sons Rebekah conceived, who will be named in 9:13. The finite controlling verb for both aorist participles (γεννηθέντων, "having been born," and πραξάντων, "having practiced") is the aorist indicative ἐρρέθη, "it was spoken," in 9:12. Since an aorist participle "usually denotes *antecedent* time to that of the controlling verb,"[14] both participles in this clause speak of what had "not yet" (μήπω) happened before "it was spoken." The clause is translated as "indeed, when [they] were not yet born nor had practiced anything good or base." For a discussion of the distinction, if any, between the verb πράσσω and the synonymous ποιέω, see the commentary on 7:15.

ἀγαθὸν ἢ φαῦλον—Rather than κακός, "bad, evil," which is the more familiar antonym of ἀγαθός, "good," Paul uses φαῦλος. He makes the same contrast in 2 Cor 5:10. BDAG suggests that φαῦλος pertains "to being low-grade or morally substandard, *base*." Thus it "allows a deeper note of 'good-for-nothingness.' "[15]

ἵνα … μένῃ—Paul arrives at his point with this purpose clause (ἵνα plus the subjunctive). For μένω, BDAG gives the intransitive meanings "to continue to exist, *remain, last, persist, continue to live*," later adding "*endure*," which fits well here (BDAG, 2 and 2 b; as in Ps 33:11 [LXX 32:11]; 2 Cor 3:11; 9:9; 1 Pet 1:23, 25). The verb μένω conveys "the sense of standing firm, being accomplished, not failing. As used here, it is the opposite to ἐκπίπτειν ['fail'] as used in v. 6."[16]

ἡ … πρόθεσις—For the divine "purpose," see the third textual note and the commentary on 8:28.

κατ᾽ ἐκλογήν—The preposition κατά with the accusative introduces "the norm which governs" something (BDAG, 5 a) and means "*in accordance w[ith]*" (BDAG, 5 a γ). For ἐκλογή, BDAG, 1, gives "a special choice, *selection, choice, election*," translating the sense of this passage as "*the purpose of God which operates by selection*." Moo may well overemphasize the sense of "election" when he summarizes the use and significance of ἐκλογή:

> ἐκλόγη, "election," is used in the NT elsewhere by Paul only in 1 Thess. 1:4; Rom. 11:5, 7, 28 (other NT occurrences are Acts 9:15 and 2 Pet. 1:10; it is not used in the LXX). The word can refer to the act "electing" (1 Thess. 1:4; Rom. 11:5, 28) or to those who are elected (Rom. 11:7). Two other words from the same root are important for Paul: ἐκλέγομαι, "choose" (1 Cor 1:27 [twice], 28; Eph. 1:4); ἐκλεκτός, "one chosen" (Rom. 8:33; 16:13; Col. 3:12; 1 Tim. 5:21; 2 Tim. 2:10; Tit. 1:1). Outside of Rom. 9–11, Paul always uses these terms of Christians (with the exception of 1 Tim. 5:21, where the reference is to angels).[17]

---

[14] Wallace, *Greek Grammar*, 614.

[15] Dunn, *Romans*, 542.

[16] Cranfield, *Romans*, 478.

[17] Moo, *Romans*, 581, n. 53.

9:12 ἐρρέθη … ὅτι—Paul introduces a Scripture quotation with the aorist passive of λέγω, as in 9:26. The divine passive implies that "it was spoken" by God.[18] Cf. the perfect passive of λέγω in 4:18 (κατὰ τὸ εἰρημένον). Cf. also the formula with γράφω in the first textual note on 9:13.

ὁ μείζων—Paul utilizes the comparative of μέγας, "*large, great*," in an expression of age, "*the older*" one (BDAG, 1 and 1 d).

δουλεύσει τῷ ἐλάσσονι—The verb δουλεύω, "to serve, be a slave," takes the dative case (here τῷ ἐλάσσονι), as in 6:6; 7:25 (cf. 7:6). The form ἐλάσσων is then "used as [a] comp[arative] of μικρός 'smaller' in age = *younger* (opp[osite] μείζων)" (BDAG, s.v. ἐλάσσων, 3).

9:13 καθὼς γέγραπται—Paul uses γέγραπται, the perfect passive of γράφω, "to write," to introduce Scripture quotations sixteen times in Romans; see the fourth textual note on 1:17.

τὸν Ἰακὼβ … τὸν δὲ Ἠσαῦ—The issue here is the referent. In Genesis, these names refer to Jacob and Esau (Gen 25:27–34). But in light of Mal 1:3b–5, the citation from Mal 1:2–3a here encompasses the nations descended from them, Israel and Edom, respectively. See the commentary.

ἐμίσησα—The verb μισέω typically is translated as "hate" (BDAG, 1; see the translation of this verse in ESV, KJV, NASB, RSV).[19] Moo observes: "Only here in the NT is God said to hate anyone; in the OT, see Ps. 5:6 [ET 5:5]; 11:5; Jer. 12:8."[20] In the LXX, μισέω is the antithesis of ἀγαπάω, "to love" (e.g., Deut 21:15; Judg 14:16; see also Prov 13:24; 15:32; cf. Deut 22:13; 24:3). But BDAG also gives "to be disinclined to, *disfavor, disregard*" (BDAG, 2). The latter notion is conveyed here by the translation "spurned." The sense of rejection stands within a contrast of favor given to another.

Commentary
Children of the Flesh and of the Promise (9:6–9)
God's Word and Israel's (9:6)

After the doxology which concludes 9:5, Paul clearly begins a new section. Though the initial phrase is awkward to translate, it is also redundantly emphatic (see the first textual note on 9:6). "But by no means [is it] that God's Word has failed and remains fallen" (ἐκπέπτωκεν, 9:6a). This half verse serves as a transition from 9:1–5, the introduction, into the main discourse of Romans 9–11. It also governs a large portion of Paul's argument which is concerned, once again, with declaring a truth about God. Whatever grieves Paul so much about the Israelites (9:2–5a), he immediately insists the fault does not reside with "God's Word" (ὁ λόγος τοῦ θεοῦ, 9:6a). Cranfield notes that the verb ἐκπίπτω here, "fall," frequently refers to flowers fading and falling (e.g., LXX Job 14:2; 15:30, 33; Is 28:1, 4; 40:7). They serve as a negative contrast for

---

18 See Wallace, *Greek Grammar*, 437–38.

19 See Murray, *Romans*, 2:21–24.

20 Moo, *Romans*, 587, n. 79.

the Word of God already in Isaiah 40: "Grass withers, a flower fades [LXX: ἐξέπεσεν], when Yahweh's Spirit blows upon it. Surely the people are grass. Grass withers, a flower fades, but the Word of our God endures [LXX: μένει] forever" (Is 40:7–8, quoted in 1 Pet 1:20–25; cf. James 1:11).[21] Paul's opening salvo similarly asserts there has been no failure on the part of the God whose Word endures eternally.[22]

Paul's initial explanation in the remainder of 9:6 appears contradictory. However, it establishes a principle which runs throughout chapters 9–11 and must be kept in mind when one finally arrives at the highly contested statement in 11:26 that "all Israel will be saved." The same Paul who insists upon that outcome also clearly employs the term "Israel" with two different referents here. In the second half of 9:6 he states: "For not all these from Israel are Israel."[23] The opening "not all" (οὐ … πάντες, Rom 9:6b) asserts that belonging to the larger set of people, "all these from Israel" in an ethnic sense, does not all-inclusively equate with being "Israel" in terms of their relationship with God.[24] His restatement in 9:8 provides further clarification of these two categories.

Paul hints at the reason *why* these two groups are not coterminous in 9:11–12. He then elaborates in detail beginning in 9:30 in a discussion which runs all the way through Romans 10. There another "not all" gives this concise explanation: "But they did not all [οὐ πάντες] listen responsively to the Good News. For Isaiah says: 'Lord, who believed our message?' " (Rom 10:16, quoting Is 53:1; cf. Rom 3:3). Instead of faith in the promise, some in Israel relied on their physical ancestry, as John the Baptist underscored when he warned them, "And do not begin to say within yourselves, 'We have Abraham as [our] father.' For I say to you that God is able from these stones to raise up children for Abraham" (Lk 3:8). But Paul focuses our attention on God, rather than on Abraham or Israel, as he engages in an ongoing defense of the divine Word.

Abraham and Sarah, Isaac and Ishmael (9:7–9)

As Paul proceeds, the verse divisions are again misplaced and disruptive. Furthermore, there are also grammatical difficulties:

> In vv 6–13 the most striking stylistic features are the broken syntax of vv 10–13, with v 10 left incomplete while vv 11–12a are brought in as a kind of parenthesis, and with v 12b serving syntactically as the completion of both. As so often with Paul the conclusion to a section (v 13) serves also as introduction to the next section.[25]

---

[21] The translation of Is 40:7–8 comes from Lessing, *Isaiah 40–55*, 103.

[22] See further "God's Word" in the introduction to Romans 9–11 and the introduction to 9:6–29, "God's Enduring Word."

[23] The Greek word order could be rendered a number of different ways. This translation follows the structure identified by Kuske, *Romans 9–16*, 27.

[24] For Paul's use of "Israel" in Romans, see also "God's People" in the introduction to Romans 9–11.

[25] Dunn, *Romans*, 538.

In a manner similar to the appositional restatements of "my brothers" in 9:3–4, Paul clarifies 9:6 by rephrasing his assertion in 9:7: "Neither [is it] that all children are seed of Abraham, but 'in Isaac seed will be called for you.' " Again, there is a subset within the larger group. Contrary to most translations (ESV, KJV, NASB, RSV), the "children" here are the broader category.[26] The "children," that is, the physical children of Abraham or, as Paul will soon say, "the children of the flesh" (9:8), are not all "true descendants" of Abraham (NRSV). Thus he employs "children" (τέκνα) differently than in Romans 8 (see 8:16, 17, 21). Here the term "children" refers to the biological children of Israel, that is, the ethnic Israelites in the OT and the Jewish people of Paul's own day. But Paul again speaks exclusively: not all of them are the "seed of Abraham" (9:7). As in Romans 4, "seed" (σπέρμα) *consistently remains the term of promise* (see 4:13, 16, 18; cf. Gal 3:16, 19, 29). As Paul will soon say, "The children of the promise are credited as seed" (9:8).

Genesis 21:12 in Romans 9:7

Paul then begins his OT citations. Sometime after the birth of Isaac in Gen 21:1–7, Sarah insists that Hagar and Ishmael be sent away (Gen 21:10). The LXX does not seem to specify any behavior on the part of Hagar or Ishmael to warrant the dismissal other than Sarah's insistence that Ishmael not share in Isaac's inheritance: "For the son of the slave woman will not inherit with my son, Isaac" (οὐ γὰρ κληρονομήσει ὁ υἱὸς τῆς παιδίσκης ταύτης μετὰ τοῦ υἱοῦ μου Ισαακ, LXX Gen 21:10). In the LXX, Sarah's declaration occurs after she sees Ishmael "playing" with Isaac (παίζοντα, LXX Gen 21:9). The MT, however, is more ambivalent. The Hebrew verb in Gen 21:9 (מְצַחֵק, Piel participle) makes a pun on the name "Isaac" (יִצְחָק), which was prophesied in Gen 17:19, 21 and bestowed in Gen 21:3. In the Qal (צָחַק), this verb means "to laugh," and the "laughing" of Abraham (Gen 17:17) and Sarah (Gen 18:12–15) at God's promise of a child figured into his naming. But in the Piel, the verb extends to "play" (Gen 26:8; Ex 32:6), "mock, ridicule" (Gen 39:14, 17), or "make sport of, cruelly make someone entertain" (Judg 16:25). Paul advances the negative sense in Gal 4:29, asserting that Ishmael, "the one who was born in accordance with flesh, was *persecuting* the one [born] in accordance with [the] Spirit" (ὁ κατὰ σάρκα γεννηθεὶς *ἐδίωκεν* τὸν κατὰ πνεῦμα).

Abraham was dismayed at Sarah's demand. "But God said to Abraham, 'Let it not be evil in your eyes regarding the boy [Ishmael] and your slave woman [Hagar]. All that Sarah says to you, listen to her voice, for *in Isaac seed will be called for you*' " (Gen 21:12). Paul reproduces the LXX exactly from the final part of Gen 21:12, ὅτι ἐν Ισαακ κληθήσεταί σοι σπέρμα. In Hebrew the cited portion is כִּי בְיִצְחָק יִקָּרֵא לְךָ זָרַע. The Niphal (passive) Hebrew verb יִקָּרֵא could convey "he will be named," as the Qal (active), קָרָא, can mean "to name" (see the fourth textual note on 9:7). But since Isaac has already been named in

---

[26] Matera, *Romans*, 222; Dunn, *Romans*, 540.

Gen 21:3, that nuance is less pronounced in Gen 21:12. Furthermore, Paul's five uses of καλέω in Romans 9 (9:7, 12, 24, 25, 26) should be translated consistently as "call." It carries with it the positive assurances of 8:28 and 8:30 as well. Even more emphatically, it recalls 4:17–21. In referring at least initially to the birth of Isaac, Paul describes God as the one who "calls [καλοῦντος] the things not being so that [they] are being" (4:17). Thus Paul articulates how this verb manifests a divine gift.

Paul does not even mention Ishmael here, but his use of Ishmael in Gal 4:21–31 to portray allegorically those in slavery to the Law is striking (Gal 4:21, 25). It supports the view that here also Ishmael (who is implied as the alternative to "Isaac" in Rom 9:7) "probably represents Jewish unbelievers."[27] At the same time, the episode in Genesis 21 does not exclude Ishmael from God's providential care. Note how God cared for his mother and for him (Gen 16:7–14; 21:15–21) and promised to bless him (Gen 17:20; 21:13, 18).[28]

Defining the Two Israels

Rom 9:8 then applies the verse from Genesis (21:12) and also restates the sense of Rom 9:6b and 9:7a. "This is, the children of the flesh, these are not children of God, but the children of the promise are credited as seed" (9:8). Now Paul has completed the thought which formed his seemingly contradictory categories in 9:6b. He envisions the following:

- An Israel which equates with the children of Abraham in 9:7; these are the physical or fleshly children
- An Israel whose members are children *both* of God *and* of the promise; these are "counted" or "credited as seed" (λογίζεται εἰς σπέρμα, 9:8), seed by God[29]

But this does not present us with some sort of platonic dichotomy. "Paul does not mean to imply that [these] children of God are not also children of the flesh ... but to indicate that the mere fact of being physically children of Abraham does not by itself make men children of God."[30] It must be emphasized that there are *not* two separate groups in Genesis that can be called "the children of the flesh" versus "the children of the promise." On the contrary, Isaac and Jacob were physical, fleshly descendants of Abraham. However they are "tied to Abraham by both natural descent *and* God's promise."[31] The key, as with Abraham in Romans 4, remains God's Word of promise. As it was received in faith by Abraham (see 4:13–16), so it is for "the children of the promise" (τὰ τέκνα τῆς ἐπαγγελίας, 9:8). The matter of whether or not the promise is received, and how, is taken up later (see 9:12, 16, 30–32; 10:16–21).

---

[27] Schreiner, *Romans*, 497; but see the commentary on 9:21.

[28] See Cranfield, *Romans*, 475.

[29] These same parallels and contrasts are laid out by Kuske, *Romans 9–16*, 27.

[30] Cranfield, *Romans*, 475.

[31] Moo, *Romans*, 576.

Paul's emphasis in this section is on God's action: (1) his calling (καλέω, 9:7) of Isaac as the one through whom he would fulfill his promise to Abraham and (2) his crediting their offspring as seed (λογίζεται εἰς σπέρμα, 9:8; see also 4:3–5). God's Word has not failed and is not fallen (9:6a). Instead, his Word of promise accomplishes what he promises, something as true now as it was then.

In 9:9, Paul reinforces his main theme about the enduring effect of God's Word (ὁ λόγος τοῦ θεοῦ, 9:6). The introductory clause, literally, "for *of promise* the Word is this" (ἐπαγγελίας γὰρ ὁ λόγος οὗτος), also reiterates the note of "promise" (ἐπαγγελία) from 9:8. The emphatic position of "promise" at the beginning of the clause further highlights the certainty of the divine Word. Paul then proceeds to state the specific promise under consideration. "For the Word of promise is this: 'According to this time I will come, and there will be a son belonging to Sarah' " (9:9).

Genesis 18:10, 14 in Romans 9:9

Paul's quotation appears to stitch together a phrase and a clause from Genesis 18.[32] The first half of LXX Gen 18:10 reads: "And he said, 'While returning I will come to you according to this time in spring, and Sarah, your wife, will have a son' " (εἶπεν δέ ἐπαναστρέφων ἥξω πρὸς σὲ κατὰ τὸν καιρὸν τοῦτον εἰς ὥρας καὶ ἕξει υἱὸν Σαρρα ἡ γυνή σου).[33] From this verse, Paul grabs "according to this time " (κατὰ τὸν καιρὸν τοῦτον). That phrase might also be rendered as "according to this *season*," since the following prepositional phrase in the LXX, εἰς ὥρας, may mean "in springtime" (cf. Muraoka, s.v. ὥρας, 5; also s.v. ὥρα, 2), although Paul in Rom 9:9 does not include εἰς ὥρας from LXX Gen 18:10. Paul then provides the verb "I will come" (ἐλεύσομαι). Though the Greek verb is not verbatim from either LXX Gen 18:10 or LXX Gen 18:14, it is synonymous with ἥξω in LXX Gen 18:10 and fits the context perfectly well (see the second textual note on Rom 9:9). In all three verses (LXX Gen 18:10, 14; Rom 9:9), the first person singular future tense verb, "*I* will … ," emphasizes God's initiative and action in fulfilling his promise.

The final clause of Rom 9:9 replicates the concluding clause of LXX Gen 18:14 exactly.[34] The entire verse reads: "A word is not impossible with God; at this time I will return to you, in spring, *and there will be a son belonging to Sarah*" (μὴ ἀδυνατεῖ παρὰ τῷ θεῷ ῥῆμα· εἰς τὸν καιρὸν τοῦτον ἀναστρέψω

---

[32] Dunn, *Romans*, 541–42; Cranfield, *Romans*, 476.

[33] The Hebrew reads:

וַיֹּאמֶר שׁוֹב אָשׁוּב אֵלֶיךָ כָּעֵת חַיָּה וְהִנֵּה־בֵן לְשָׂרָה

He [Yahweh] said, "I will surely return to you at the time of life [spring], and behold, a son for Sarah." (Gen 18:10a)

[34] One may readily simplify the matter of Paul's source for the quotation in Rom 9:9 if one assumes that all of it is adapted from LXX Gen 18:14. If so, Paul would have (1) altered the preposition εἰς to κατά, (2) replaced ἀναστρέψω with ἐλεύσομαι, and (3) omitted πρὸς σὲ εἰς ὥρας.

πρὸς σὲ εἰς ὥρας καὶ ἔσται τῇ Σαρρα υἱός, LXX Gen 18:14).[35] *As and when* promised, Sarah had Isaac (Gen 21:1–3). Thus Paul's point is established and illustrated by the inspired narrative. God's Word did not fail (cf. Rom 9:6a). Paul then jumps to the next generation for reaffirmation of its efficacy and reliability.

God's Purposeful Call (9:10–13)

Rebekah and Isaac (9:10)

Paul introduces 9:10 with an expression which appears eleven times in Romans, "not only ... but also" (see the first textual note on 9:10). At the same time, his sentence structure remains incomplete: "And not only [this], but also Rebekah, having sexual intercourse from one man, Isaac our father" (9:10). This implies that the reader must not only insert the proper grammatical assumptions but also be aware of the overall narrative of Genesis 15–25 in order to grasp Paul's point fully.

It is intriguing that Paul explicitly names and thereby highlights the comparable roles of the women who are mothers in the accounts. Moo notes:

> Rebecca, like Sarah, was barren; Rebecca's barrenness, like Sarah's, was overcome by divine intervention (Gen. 25:21); and, especially important for Paul's argument, Rebecca's son, like Sarah's, was called by God to become the heir of the covenant promises.[36]

At the same time, Paul also mentions Abraham in Rom 9:7 and refers to Isaac by name here in 9:10. Although Isaac receives much less attention in the OT than his father, Abraham, and his son Jacob/Israel,[37] he stands among the patriarchs as an integral link between them. Note that Paul calls Isaac "our father" (9:10). As illustrated by 4:1, "it is usually Abraham who is called 'our father,' not Isaac. But the line ran from Abraham through Isaac; thus the expression, though unusual, presents no problems."[38] Furthermore, as evident already from 9:3–4, "the use of *our* includes Paul with Israel; he is not separating himself from his fellow-Jews,"[39] something he explicitly emphasizes in 11:1.

The episode involving Rebekah introduced in 9:10 and then utilized in 9:11–13 sharpens Paul's argument. Isaac and Ishmael had the same father,

---

[35] The Hebrew reads:

הֲיִפָּלֵא מֵיְהוָה דָּבָר לַמּוֹעֵד אָשׁוּב אֵלֶיךָ כָּעֵת חַיָּה וּלְשָׂרָה בֵן׃

Can a word/matter be too miraculous for Yahweh [to do]? At the season I will return to you, at the time of life [spring], and there will be a son to Sarah. (Gen 18:14)

See the comments on the significance of the first half of Gen 18:14 in the discussion of "power" (δύναμις) in Rom 1:16 and "powerful" (δυνατός) in 4:21.

[36] Moo, *Romans*, 579.

[37] For example, Abraham occupies much of Gen 11:27–25:11, and Jacob/Israel is the main focus in Gen 25:19–35:29. Isaac overlaps both his father and his son in Genesis 21–35 but is largely in the background throughout most of that section.

[38] Morris, *Romans*, 355.

[39] Morris, *Romans*, 355.

Abraham, though different mothers, as Isaac was the son promised to Sarah, while Ishmael's mother, Hagar, was a slave girl (Genesis 16). However, Jacob and Esau not only shared the same mother (Rebekah) *and* father (Isaac), but Paul's idiomatic expression in Rom 9:10 emphasizes that they were also conceived at the same time (Gen 25:19–26). The beginning of Rom 9:11 adds other dimensions: "indeed, when [they] were not yet born nor had practiced anything good or base." God's upcoming declaration was spoken prior to birth and also prior to any work, whether good or evil, fair or foul, which Esau or Jacob had done. The divine pronouncement, however, does not come until midway through 9:12 beginning with "it was spoken to her."

Käsemann identifies 9:10 as an anacoluthon and then describes all of 9:11–12a as a parenthesis.[40] While this commentary takes only 9:11b–12a as parenthetical, Käsemann's keen insight readily applies: "The true point lies in the parenthesis."[41] Paul introduces the main conclusion to be drawn from 9:6–13 with a purpose (ἵνα) clause, "in order that …" (9:11). Unfortunately the significance is once again somewhat obscured by another poor verse division. Nevertheless, 9:11 concludes and 9:12 begins by affirming that all the events Paul refers to happened "in order that the purpose of God in accordance with [his] choice might endure, [12]not from works, but from the One who calls." An analysis of these words follows the treatment of 9:12b–13.

Jacob and Esau (9:12b–13)

After the parenthetical insertion of 9:11b–12a, the second half of what we call 9:12 and all of 9:13 return to complete the thought of 9:10–11a. Before Esau and Jacob were born or had done anything, "it was spoken to her, 'The older one will be a slave to the younger,' [13]just as it stands written: 'Jacob I loved, but Esau I spurned.'"

Genesis 25:23 in Romans 9:12

The initial Scripture citation from Gen 25:23 records the words spoken by Yahweh to Rebekah. Paul changes the introductory formula from the active "Yahweh/the Lord said to her" (MT/LXX Gen 25:23) to the divine passive "it was spoken to her" (ἐρρέθη αὐτῇ, Rom 9:12). Otherwise he quotes the conclusion of the verse as it appears in the LXX:[42]

---

[40] Käsemann, *Romans*, 263.

[41] Käsemann, *Romans*, 264.

[42] The Hebrew of Gen 25:23 is as follows:

וַיֹּאמֶר יְהוָה לָהּ שְׁנֵי גיים גוֹיִם בְּבִטְנֵךְ וּשְׁנֵי לְאֻמִּים מִמֵּעַיִךְ יִפָּרֵדוּ
וּלְאֹם מִלְאֹם יֶאֱמָץ וְרַב יַעֲבֹד צָעִיר׃

And Yahweh said to her, "Two nations [are] in your womb, and two peoples will be separated from your inner parts. And [one] people will be stronger than [the other] people and [the] greater/older will serve [the] lesser/younger."

καὶ εἶπεν κύριος αὐτῇ δύο ἔθνη ἐν τῇ γαστρί σού εἰσιν, καὶ δύο λαοὶ ἐκ τῆς κοιλίας σου διασταλήσονται· καὶ λαὸς λαοῦ ὑπερέξει, καὶ ὁ μείζων δουλεύσει τῷ ἐλάσσονι.

And the Lord said to her, "Two nations are in your belly, and two peoples will be set apart from your womb, and a people will be surpassed by a people, and the older one will be a slave to the younger one." (LXX Gen 25:23)

Paul's omission of the intervening prophecy regarding the "two nations" (δύο ἔθνη) and "two peoples" (δύο λαοί) indicates that his attention focuses on the two *individuals*, Jacob and Esau, rather than on the nations/peoples of Israel and Edom (see the discussion of Mal 1:2–3 below). We now have the same mother (Rebekah) and father (Isaac), the same act of conception, and a prophecy spoken prior to their birth, as well as before either had done any act. The final dimension introduced by this quotation is that one is older and the other younger, yet the Lord declared that the normal precedence in regard to birth order would be reversed.

Malachi 1:2–3 in Romans 9:13

Paul's next quotation is introduced with "as it stands written" (καθὼς γέγραπται, Rom 9:13). Paul slightly reorders the Greek wording of the LXX from the ending of Mal 1:2 and the beginning of Mal 1:3, which reads: "And I loved Jacob, but Esau I spurned" (καὶ ἠγάπησα τὸν Ιακωβ ³τὸν δὲ Ησαυ ἐμίσησα), which reflects the word order in the original Hebrew.[43]

Paul's main point in regard to Jacob and Esau remains. "The initiative is entirely God's, without any reference to Esau's (or Edom's) deeds."[44] Dunn references the insertion of Pseudo-Philo: "but he hated Esau *because of his deeds*" (Pseudo-Philo, 32.5).[45] But Pseudo-Philo certainly reads that into the text of both Genesis and Malachi. As with Isaac in Rom 9:7, Paul once again emphasizes the child of the promise. Jacob is the dominant character for him, the one whom Yahweh loved. "The idea of divine rejection (Ἡσαῦ ἐμίσησα ['Esau I spurned']) arises only as a corollary to the principal claim (Ἰακὼβ ἠγάπησα ['Jacob I loved']). … Its starting and central point is the sense of grace freely extended in an unexpected way to one who was wholly undeserving."[46]

Not "Hated," but "Spurned"

Once this has been properly affirmed, one can proceed to deal with the rejection of Esau. The underlying Hebrew verb שָׂנֵא, typically translated as "hate," is instructive. The narrative of Jacob from Genesis 29 provides valuable insight:

³⁰He [Jacob] went into Rachel also, and he loved also Rachel, more than Leah, and served with him [Laban] still for seven other years. ³¹Yahweh saw

---

[43] In Mal 1:2–3 Yahweh declares:

וָאֹהַב אֶת־יַעֲקֹב וְאֶת־עֵשָׂו שָׂנֵאתִי

[44] Dunn, *Romans*, 544.

[45] Dunn, *Romans*, 544.

[46] Dunn, *Romans*, 545.

that Leah was *hated* [שְׂנוּאָה; LXX: μισεῖται], and he opened her womb, but Rachel was barren. ³²And Leah conceived and birthed a son, and she called his name Reuben, for she said, "Surely Yahweh saw my affliction; surely now my husband will love me." ³³She conceived again and birthed a son and said, "Surely Yahweh heard that I am *hated* [שְׂנוּאָה; LXX: μισοῦμαι], and so he gave me this [son] also." And she called his name Simeon. (Gen 29:30–33)

It was in contrast to Jacob's greater love for Rachel that Leah was spurned (שָׂנֵא; LXX: μισέω). This does not mean that he "hated" Leah in the contemporary understanding of that word. The narrative explains that although Jacob certainly favored Rachel, he kept Leah as his wife and even had six sons with her (!), beginning with his firstborn, Reuben, and then Simeon as noted above. While his treatment of Rachel went beyond the proper bounds of mere favoritism, he did not, thereby, "hate" Leah. The translation "spurned" captures the sense here. This should be the understanding of μισέω in other difficult passages as well (e.g., for one of two wives in LXX Deut 21:15–17; in the NT, Lk 14:26; Jn 12:25; cf. Mt 6:24).

When we apply this understanding of Jacob's regard for his wife Leah to what God says of Jacob and Esau, three points need to be clarified: First, " 'love' and 'hate' are not here, then, emotions that God feels but actions that he carries out."[47] Second, as used by Malachi and then Paul, the terms cannot be viewed as predictive or in any way congruous with a statement about election and predestination to damnation, as if all the descendants of Jacob would be saved and all those of Esau would be consigned to hell. Cranfield mistakenly contends that "love" and "hate" should "be understood as denoting election and rejection respectively."[48] Malachi, however, records a statement from Yahweh reflecting back on his interaction with the patriarchs in historical events which *happened more than a millennium before*! The past tense verbs attest to this.[49]

Third, in regard to Yahweh's treatment of Esau, "it must be stressed that, as in the case of Ishmael, so also with Esau, the rejected one is still, according to the testimony of Scripture, an object of God's merciful care."[50] For example:

- Isaac also blesses Esau (Gen 27:39–40).
- Jacob and Esau are reunited in Genesis 33 and join together in burying their father (Gen 35:29).
- Genesis 36 records Esau's extensive genealogy as the founding father of the nation of Edom (see also 1 Chr 1:35–42).
- Yahweh himself later reminds the Israelites, "You shall not abhor [תְתַעֵב; LXX βδελύξῃ] an Edomite, for he is your brother" (Deut 23:7 ESV [MT/LXX 23:8]).

---

[47] Moo, *Romans*, 587.

[48] Cranfield, *Romans*, 480.

[49] Rom 9:13 and LXX Mal 1:2–3 use the aorist tense for both verbs. In the Hebrew of Mal 1:2–3 the first verb is an imperfect with *waw* consecutive, and the second is a perfect.

[50] Cranfield, *Romans*, 480.

Conclusions

As noted above, Paul's *omission* in Rom 9:12 of the phrases "two nations" and "two peoples" from Gen 25:23 signals that he is focusing on the two individuals in the narrative,[51] rather than on the future of the nations which spring forth from them. The distinction between "loved" and "spurned" (Rom 9:13), then, is a relational one and applied, in the context of Romans 9, to the choice of God in terms of the fulfillment of his "Word of promise" (9:9, 11). This means that for Jacob "it is election to privilege that is in mind."[52] As Moo observes: "Paul is not clearly asserting that Jacob and Isaac were saved while Esau and Ishmael were not."[53] The contrast Paul draws is, rather, between (1) Jacob as the one from whom the line of the promised seed descends through the covenant people of Israel and, ultimately, "from whom [is] the Christ/Messiah" (Rom 9:5; cf. Gen 12:3) and (2) those who, though blessed, are spurned in regard to that line of the promised seed. Thus, as 9:21 makes clear, we have vessels "meant for an honorable use" and those "for ordinary use" (see the commentary on 9:21). On what basis was this distinction made?

Paul's Point: God's Purposeful Call (9:11b–12a)

All this occurred "in order that the purpose of God in accordance with [his] choice might endure, not from works, but from the One who calls" (9:11b–12a). As indicated above, this parenthetical states the purpose for which Paul engages in the discussion recorded in 9:6–13 and forms its primary assertion. At the outset of this section, Paul states in *negative* terms: "*By no means* [is it] that God's Word has failed" (9:6a). In 9:11–12, he proceeds to articulate his thematic *positive* point by taking the same tack he does throughout Romans. Paul turns our attention away from the humans involved and focuses upon God.[54] Paul proposes, thereby, to articulate *God's* "purpose" (9:11).

He begins: "In order that the purpose of God in accordance with [his] choice might endure" (ἵνα ἡ κατ᾽ ἐκλογὴν πρόθεσις τοῦ θεοῦ μένῃ, 9:11b). The noun "purpose" (πρόθεσις)

---

[51] Moo, *Romans*, 585, against Morris, *Romans*, 356. Murray, *Romans* 2:16–18, argues for both alternatives; there is certainly truth in that position, especially in light of the Malachi quotation, but the emphasis is on the roles of the individuals, Jacob and Esau.

[52] Morris, *Romans*, 356; see also Bruce, *Romans*, 177–78.

[53] Moo, *Romans*, 586, though he adds: "But he is arguing that God in his own day is bringing into being a covenant people in the same way that he did in the days of the patriarchs: by choosing some and rejecting others." The idea that God is now "rejecting" anyone is contrary to, first of all, the universal atonement: the substitutionary sacrifice of Jesus atoned for the sins of all humanity (Jn 1:29; 1 Jn 2:2). It is also contrary to the universality of the Gospel call: God desires all people to be saved (1 Tim 2:4), and he sends out the saving Gospel message to call all to repent, believe, and be saved (Rom 10:8–18). See the full exposition of the biblical teaching on eternal foreknowledge and divine election in FC SD XI.

[54] See, e.g., Rom 1:32; 2:11, 16, 29; 3:19–20, 26, 29–30; 4:5, 17, 21; see Middendorf, *Romans 1–8*, 21, 27, 51.

is one of those many words that connect Paul's argument here with his teaching about the children of God in 8:18–39. … In 8:28, it denotes the "plan" or "design" according to which God calls people to belong to him, a plan whose steps Paul unfolds in [8:]29–30.[55]

Here God's purpose endures "in accordance with [his] choice" (9:11). Rather than "the purpose of God" being some abstract concept, "in accordance with [his] choice" shows us that it "takes concrete shape."[56] God deals with specific people within human history to accomplish his purpose. But on what basis does he do so?

The exclusion which follows in 9:12a, "not from works" (οὐκ ἐξ ἔργων), obviously also recalls phrases from earlier in Romans (e.g., 3:20, 28; 4:2, 6; cf. 9:32; 11:6). The fact that God's purpose and choice are "not from works" need not be understood exclusively as works in accord with the revealed Law of Moses (see 2:12–16), but it certainly encompasses them.[57] The point here is broader, particularly since the Law of Moses (Exodus 20–23) was not yet revealed to the cast of characters from Genesis cited in Rom 9:6–13 (see also 4:1–5, 13–16). In all cases, including that of Abraham, Sarah, Isaac, Rebekah, Jacob, and Esau, "the purpose of God in accordance with [his] choice" (9:11) was *not based upon any human activity*. What then was the reason for his choosing? In light of a whole string of passages (e.g., 1:17; 3:21–22, 28; 4:4–5), one might expect "not from works" (οὐκ ἐξ ἔργων, 9:12) to be countered by "from faith" (ἐκ πίστεως). Yet Paul's argument at this point in Romans 9–11 is not even about receptive faith (but see 9:30–10:15). Instead, Paul stresses God's intervening "purpose" (πρόθεσις, 9:11), which endures (μένω) because it depends solely upon his active call of specific people within salvation history. *At this point in Romans 9, it is all about God, his enduring purpose, his choice, and his call.*

The verb "call" (καλέω) in 9:12a reaches all the way back to the letter's introduction. Paul uses the cognate adjective "called" (κλητός) three times (1:1, 6, 7) in order to emphasize that he and those in Rome are "called" by God. Later, in 4:17, Paul describes how Abraham believed in the God who "calls the things not being so that [they] are being" (καλοῦντος τὰ μὴ ὄντα ὡς ὄντα, 4:17). Then "call" (καλέω) was one in the string of five verbs in 8:29–30 (ἐκάλεσεν, 8:30) that Paul uses to detail how God works "for the benefit of the ones who are called according to [his] purpose" (τοῖς κατὰ πρόθεσιν κλητοῖς οὖσιν, 8:28). The language and theology regarding God's purpose and call there stand comparable to 9:11–12. Now Paul literally describes God with a substantive participle as "the One who calls" (τοῦ καλοῦντος, 9:12). *"Call" (καλέω) then functions as the dominant term in Romans 9, occurring in 9:7, 12, 24, 25, 26.*

---

[55] Moo, *Romans*, 580.

[56] Käsemann, *Romans*, 264.

[57] Dunn, *Romans*, 543, though he oddly contends Paul is excluding "Israel's faithfulness to the law." See the excursus "The Background of 'Works of the Law'" following the commentary on 3:9–20.

Paul marvels at the fact that God's purpose endures (ἡ … πρόθεσις τοῦ θεοῦ μένη, 9:11) because his Word, rather than being fallen, stands forever (9:6a; see Is 40:8). Through it God actively calls according to his choice, not our works (οὐκ ἐξ ἔργων ἀλλ᾽ ἐκ τοῦ καλοῦντος, 9:12). Paul portrays this purely as an act of God's grace and initiative. By drawing on the OT narratives of Genesis, Paul demonstrates "precisely that God's dealings with man have the same character from start to finish."[58] It was so with God's "Word of promise" (9:9) to Abraham and Sarah, Isaac and Rebekah, and Jacob and his sons. It was so for those called in Rome (1:6–7). So it is for all those "whom he also called, [namely,] us, not only from Jews but also from Gentiles" (9:24).

Conclusion

What Paul Does *Not* Say

In wrapping up this section, it is important to make mention of what Paul does *not* say.[59] What does Paul not say about God's *call*? In keeping with previous uses in Romans, he does not focus upon God's call as if it extends only to some, but not to others. He does not speak about God's call being "effectual" to some, implying that his call is somehow "ineffectual" to others.[60] Nor does he say anything about God's call being "irresistible."[61] Rom 10:16–21 in particular dispels any and all such assertions (see the commentary there).

What does Paul *not* say about "the purpose of God in accordance with [his] choice" (9:11)? Moo improperly suggests: "God is free to 'narrow' the apparent boundaries of election by choosing only some Jews to be saved (vv. 6–13, 27–29)."[62] Paul never says anything even close to that. Cranfield more properly identifies how

> God distinguished, in the working out of His purpose, between Isaac and Ishmael and between Jacob and Esau. But this was a distinguishing inside the general area of election, since, although they were not Israelites, offspring of Jacob, Ishmael was a son of Abraham, "the friend of God," with whom the covenant had been established, and Esau was one of the twin sons of Isaac, that son of Abraham in whom Abraham's seed was to be reckoned.[63]

---

[58] Dunn, *Romans*, 544.

[59] See also "God" in "The Three Foci of Romans 9–11" in the introduction to Romans 9–11.

[60] Schreiner, *Romans*, 495, rightly states: "In this context in Romans it ['calling'] also bears its usual Pauline meaning, an effective call that creates what is desired." See also the discussion of God's call according to Rom 8:30 in "Within Time (8:30a)" in Middendorf, *Romans 1–8*, 695–96.

[61] Thus Moo, *Romans*, 582, is wrong when he asserts: "Highlighted again is the activity of the God of creation and history whose own word powerfully and *irresistibly* brings about what he chooses" (emphasis added).

[62] Moo, *Romans*, 569.

[63] Cranfield, *Romans*, 481, including n. 1, citing James 2:23 (cf. 2 Chr 20:7; Is 41:8) for Abraham as "the friend of God." However, he also speaks of a "selective" use of the term "Israel" (473), which would seem to imply that a non-selected portion of "Israel" also exists.

What about God's purpose and choice in dealing with the *specific people* mentioned in 9:6–13? Is Paul engaged in discussing predestination? Does what he say here support the notion of double predestination, some to salvation and some to damnation? Moo's approach to these questions serves as a representative of those scholars who answer affirmatively.[64] He proposes these three options regarding the aforementioned OT texts from Genesis and Malachi:

> (1) Paul sticks to their original meaning and applies them only to salvation-historical roles. (2) Paul disregards the original sense of the OT texts and sees them as containing "types" of God's salvific methods (e.g., Käsemann, [*Romans*,] 264). (3) Paul legitimately uses principles derived from OT texts that speak of God's formation of his people Israel to show how God operates to call out his true spiritual people.[65]

In response to the first option, Moo takes "issue with an increasingly large number of scholars who are convinced that Paul in this paragraph, and in the succeeding ones (9:14–18, 19–23), is implying nothing about the salvation of individuals."[66] Moo then contends that the third option is best. "It was God's will alone, and not natural capacity, religious devotion, or even faith that determined their respective destinies."[67] Matera's title for Romans 9–11, "God's Righteousness and the Destiny of Israel," reveals a similar approach.[68] But the term "destiny" is an odd word to use biblically. Even Moo concedes: "The OT verses Paul cites do not clearly refer to the eternal destiny of the individuals concerned."[69] Are, then, eternal destinies being determined by God, even apart from any mention of faith?

That whole notion underscores one problematic result of an anthropocentric and individualistic reading of the letter.[70] In many ways, Romans 9–11 provides a key filter for diagnosing the propriety of a person's understanding of all of Romans. *Indeed, one's overall approach to the entire letter is either undermined or supported here.* If one insists on reading the letter primarily in terms of what it says about "me," individual humans, or even humanity in general, the topic of predestination logically rises to the fore in Romans 9. But this entire commentary has endeavored to demonstrate how Paul's overall focus in the letter is on God and his righteousness.[71] This is particularly clear in Romans

---

[64] Moo, *Romans*, 571; with some qualification also Käsemann, *Romans*, 265, who contends: "Only here does Paul present double predestination"; and Schreiner, *Romans*, 501: "Does the text suggest double predestination? Apparently it does."

[65] Moo, *Romans*, 571, n. 10.

[66] Moo, *Romans*, 571.

[67] Moo, *Romans*, 578.

[68] Matera, *Romans*, 211.

[69] Moo, *Romans*, 571.

[70] See "Romans 1–4: The Righteousness of God" in the introduction to Romans 9–16.

[71] Middendorf, *Romans 1–8*, 21–22, 27, 49–51; in this volume, see "Romans 1–4: The Righteousness of God" in the introduction to Romans 9–16, as well as "God" in "The Three Foci of Romans 9–11" in the introduction to Romans 9–11.

1–4.[72] In regard to Romans 9, Matera conducts a brief summary of the history of interpretation before concluding:

> It is doubtful that Paul sought to develop a "doctrine" of predestination in Romans. His immediate purpose in Rom. 9 is to show that despite the failure of most of his contemporaries to believe in the Messiah, God's Word has not failed.[73]

Indeed, even the assertion that Paul's discussion is focused upon *Israel's unbelief* does not diminish the essentially *theo*logical (God-centered) nature of that topic.

> Paul makes clear that the problem of Israel is at the same time the problem of God's word and, ultimately, of God himself. ... Has God revoked these blessings and gone back on his word to Israel? ... For how could Christians trust such a God to fulfill his promises to them?[74]

What Paul *Does* Say

Paul's use of language reveals that even a focus upon Israel, including the patriarchs themselves, is misplaced. The purpose (ἵνα) clause in 9:11b–12a ("in order that the purpose of God ...") summarizes the main points to be taken from Paul's discussion in 9:6–13. Throughout the narrative of the patriarchs, Paul emphasizes how God's purpose in bringing their Messiah to and through them is accomplished in accordance with his choice; God is further defined as "the One who calls" (9:12). Paul also insists that God's purpose endures (9:11); his Word has not failed and is not fallen (9:6a). Therefore Paul's "starting and central point is the sense of grace freely extended in an unexpected way to one who was wholly undeserving."[75] *God's enduring purpose "in accordance with [his] choice" (9:11) is to extend such grace through the purposeful call of his Word (see 11:5–6).* On the basis of the OT narratives, this is the lesson Paul here teaches about God.

The relevant human questions are secondary to God's action. Indeed, in many and various ways, this section repeatedly reaffirms that God's call is *not* dependent on human parentage, birth order, merits, or "works" (9:12). Rom 9:21 will shortly resolve the matter of the specific area of God's calling under consideration in 9:6–13. There Paul concludes that the narrative of Genesis, as discussed above, reveals how God chooses "to make out of the same lump a vessel which is meant for an honorable use, on the one hand, and, on the other, [a vessel] which is for ordinary use" (9:21). All the people named in 9:9–13 belong to the same lump, the family of Abraham.

What then of "faith," which is emphasized so prominently in 1:17 and throughout chapters 1–4? Augustine states the applicable teaching at this point of Romans 9–11: "No one believes who is not called. God calls in his mercy

---

[72] See the commentary on 1:32; 2:11, 16, 29; 3:19–20, 26, 29–30; 4:21.

[73] Matera, *Romans*, 234; for his overview, see 231–34.

[74] Moo, *Romans*, 572; similarly, Hays, *Echoes of Scripture in the Letters of Paul*, 38, 64.

[75] Dunn, *Romans*, 545.

and not as rewarding the merits of faith. The merits of faith follow his calling; they do not precede it."[76] This explains why faith is not yet the focus in 9:6–13. But this does not dismiss the matter of faith entirely from Paul's purview. The earlier chapters of Romans clearly demonstrate faith's importance, but at this point Paul demonstrates that its role is secondary or, more appropriately, one that is always *responsive to and receptive of God's active call*. Faith will return more fully to the fore when Paul engages in his discussion of human responses to God's call in 9:30–10:21. Thus 9:6–13 illustrates how one cannot read Romans 9 and conclude that the whole matter is set in stone apart from hearing the entire discussion through the end of Romans 11, particularly that which ensues beginning in 9:30. As discussed in the introduction to Romans 9–11, these three chapters in particular must be read as a whole; their sections cannot be separated from one another or taken out of their larger context.[77] It is thus time to press on ahead and hear what Paul has to say about the *content* of God's purposeful call.

---

[76] Augustine, *To Simplician on Various Questions*, 1.2.1 (Bray, *Romans*, ACCS NT 6:251).

[77] See "Outline and Interconnectedness" in the introduction to Romans 9–11.

God's Word of Mercy Calls Us

Translation

9 **¹⁴What then will we say? There is not unrighteousness with God, is there? May it never come to be! ¹⁵For he says to Moses, "I will show mercy to whomever I show mercy, and I will have compassion on whomever I have compassion." ¹⁶Consequently then, [God's mercy is] not of the one willing nor of the one striving, but of the God who shows mercy. ¹⁷Indeed, the Scripture says to the Pharaoh, "For this very reason I raised you up in order that I might demonstrate in you my [saving] power and in order that my name might be announced in all the earth." ¹⁸Consequently then, [to] whom he wills he shows mercy and whom he wills he hardens.**

¹⁹You will therefore say to me, "Why then is he still finding fault? For who has set himself against and withstood his intention?" ²⁰O you human being! On the contrary, who are you to talk back to God? That which is formed will not say to the one who formed it, "Why did you make me this way?" will it? ²¹Or does not the potter have authority [over] the clay to make out of the same lump a vessel which is meant for an honorable use, on the one hand, and, on the other, [a vessel] which is for ordinary use?

²²And [who are you to talk back] if God, willing to demonstrate [his] wrath and to make known his [saving] power, bore with much patience vessels of wrath which have been fitted for and are headed toward destruction, ²³and in order to make known the abundance of his glory upon vessels of mercy which he prepared beforehand for glory, ²⁴whom he also called, [namely,] us, not only from Jews but also from Gentiles?

Textual Notes

9:14 τί οὖν ἐροῦμεν;—For "what will we say?" see the third textual note on 3:5, and for the identical question as here with οὖν, "then, therefore," see the first textual note on 6:1. The question τί (οὖν) ἐροῦμεν; occurs seven times in the NT, all in Romans. Paul uses it in 4:1 to introduce his discussion of Abraham. In 8:31 and 9:30 "what then will we say?" introduces Paul's conclusion. But in 3:5; 6:1; 7:7; and here, "Paul uses this formula at a point where he recognizes that a false conclusion could be drawn, instead of the true one, from what he has just been saying."[1] In these four instances, τί (οὖν) ἐροῦμεν is followed by a negative question and μὴ γένοιτο (see the second textual note below).

---

[1] Cranfield, *Romans*, 481.

μὴ ἀδικία παρὰ τῷ θεῷ—Normally μή negates non-indicative verb forms. But in interrogative sentences, as here, it indicates that a negative response is expected.[2] Therefore the translation concludes with "there is not unrighteousness with God, *is there?*" The preposition παρά with the dative (τῷ θεῷ) here connects "a quality or characteristic w[ith] a pers[on], *with*" (BDAG, B 4; cf. 2:11 and 2:13). Moo suggests the usage could reflect the Hebrew preposition עִם.[3]

μὴ γένοιτο—For "may it never come to be!" see the first textual note on 3:4.

9:15 ἐλεήσω … ἐλεῶ—Paul introduces a key thematic verb in Romans 9–11, "show mercy," by quoting LXX Ex 33:19. He uses ἐλεέω also in Rom 9:18; 11:30, 31, 32, as well as the synonymous ἐλεάω in 9:16; the cognate noun ἔλεος, "mercy," occurs in 9:23 and 11:31 (also 15:9). The verb ἐλεέω means "to be greatly concerned about someone in need, *have compassion/mercy/pity*" (BDAG). In the LXX, ἐλεέω translates the Hebrew חָנַן in Ex 33:19. Both of the verb forms here are first singular active forms of a contract verb. The first, ἐλεήσω, is future indicative; the second, ἐλεῶ, is present subjunctive.

ὃν ἄν—This is the masculine accusative singular form of the relative pronoun ὅς followed by the particle ἄν, which inserts an "aspect of contingency" (BDAG, s.v. ἄν I). It makes "a definite statement contingent upon something, e.g., changing 'who' to 'whoever.' "[4]

οἰκτιρήσω … οἰκτίρω—Drawn also from LXX Ex 33:19, οἰκτίρω occurs in parallelism with ἐλεέω (see the first textual note on 9:15) and similarly means "*have compassion*" (BDAG). The verb does not occur elsewhere in the NT, but note the presence of the cognate noun, οἰκτιρμός, "mercy," in 12:1. This verb translates the Hebrew רָחַם in Paul's citation of Ex 33:19.

9:16 ἄρα οὖν—For "consequently then," see the second textual note on 5:18 (also 7:3, 25; 8:12; 9:18; 14:12, 19; cf. ἄρα νῦν in 8:1). Typically, the expression marks "what follows as a significant conclusion."[5]

τοῦ τρέχοντος—This is an articular genitive singular substantival participle of τρέχω, "run." The verb literally describes forward motion, to "*rush, advance*" (BDAG, 1), as in its English derivative "trek." But the use here reflects the metaphorical sense, "to make an effort to advance spiritually or intellectually, *exert oneself*" (BDAG, 2).

τοῦ ἐλεῶντος θεοῦ—While BDAG identifies ἐλεῶντος as a form of ἐλεάω, which it distinguishes from the nearly identical contract verb ἐλεέω (see the first textual note on 9:15), no distinction in meaning is present. The active participle ἐλεῶντος is used adjectivally to modify θεοῦ, "God." Paul describes him as, literally, "the mercying God." Unfortunately, English lacks a single verb for this action (cf. the discussion of πιστεύω and δικαιόω in the commentary on 1:16–17). Thus translation requires

[2] Voelz, *Fundamental Greek Grammar*, 261.

[3] Moo, *Romans*, 591, n. 10.

[4] Mounce, *Basics of Biblical Greek*, 96.

[5] Moo, *Romans*, 472.

inserting some other verb, e.g., "does," "shows," or "has," followed by the noun "mercy." This combination produces the translation "the God who shows mercy."

9:17 τῷ Φαραώ—As BDAG points out, this is "actually the title of Egyptian kings" (cf. "the President"), rather than a personal name. The phrase is translated as "to the Pharaoh."

ὅτι—This conjunction serves as a "marker of narrative or discourse content" (BDAG, 1), which can be direct or indirect. Here it introduces words spoken directly from Yahweh to Moses, with which he is sent to confront the Pharaoh (Ex 9:13–19). The direct discourse is conveyed in translation here by the use of quotation marks.

εἰς αὐτὸ τοῦτο—The preposition εἰς, together with the demonstrative pronoun τοῦτο, expresses purpose, "*for this reason* or *purpose*" (BDAG, s.v. εἰς, 4 f). The reflexive pronoun αὐτός functions as an identical adjective.[6] BDAG translates αὐτὸ τοῦτο as "*just this, the very same thing*" (s.v. αὐτός, 1 g).

ἐξήγειρά σε—The aorist indicative of ἐξεγείρω literally means "I raised up." Dunn suggests the notion "cause to appear, bring into being,"[7] but that is too weak. BDAG more properly interprets this specific case as "give one higher status, *elevate*" (BDAG, 5). Sanday and Headlam point to "the almost technical meaning of the verb ἐξεγείρειν in the LXX. It is used of God calling up the actors on the stage of history" (e.g., LXX Hab 1:6; Zech 11:16; Jer 27:41 [MT/ET 50:41]).[8] All of this lies behind the translation "I raised up." See the commentary for the Hebrew and LXX being quoted.

ὅπως ἐνδείξωμαι—Paul uses ὅπως twice in this verse to convey the "purpose for an event or state, *(in order) that*" (BDAG, 2). Paul employs another compound verb, ἐνδείκνυμι (cf. ἐξεγείρω in the preceding textual note), which means "to direct attention to or cause someth[ing] to become known, *show, demonstrate*" (BDAG, 1; also 2:15; 9:22). Note especially the use of the cognate noun ἔνδειξις, translated as "proof," in 3:25 and 3:26. The conjunction ὅπως requires the verb to be in the subjunctive mood, ἐνδείξωμαι, which is also aorist and first person singular.

ἐν σοί—The phrase translates literally as "in you," but its meaning is influenced by the underlying Hebrew; see the commentary.

τὴν δύναμίν μου—For δύναμις as God's "*power ... into salvation*," see 1:16. The commentary below discusses how the impact of Paul's thematic statement in 1:16 influences his meaning here. Additionally, throughout his letters, Paul uses δύναμις predominantly as a reference to God's "*saving* power" (e.g., 1 Cor 1:18, 24; 2:5; 6:14; 2 Cor 4:7; 6:7; 13:4).[9] See also τὸ δυνατὸν αὐτοῦ, "his [saving] power," in the third textual note on Rom 9:22.

ὅπως διαγγελῇ—For the same construction, ὅπως with the subjunctive, see the fifth textual note on 9:17. The verb διαγγέλλω means "to make someth[ing] known far and

---

[6] Mounce, *Basics of Biblical Greek*, 103, including n. 9.

[7] Dunn, *Romans*, 554.

[8] Sanday and Headlam, *Romans*, 256.

[9] Cranfield, *Romans*, 487.

wide, *proclaim, spread the news concerning/about*" (BDAG, 1). διαγγελῇ is an irregular aorist passive third singular.

9:18 ἄρα οὖν—See the first textual note on 9:16.

ὃν θέλει ἐλεεῖ—The accusative masculine singular form, ὅν, of the relative pronoun ὅς conveys an indefinite sense here, "whom(ever)," comparable to ὃν ἄν in 9:15. The verb θέλω here means "to have someth[ing] in mind for oneself, of purpose, resolve, *will, wish, want*" (BDAG, 2; see the commentary on 7:18). For ἐλεεῖ, see the first textual note on 9:15.

σκληρύνει—According to BDAG, σκληρύνω means "to cause to be unyielding in resisting information, *harden* (LXX)." Dunn adds "make unresponsive."[10] The verb is used thirty-seven times in the LXX, but elsewhere in the NT only in Acts 19:9 and Hebrews (3:8, 13, 15; 4:7). Paul employs an active form (present indicative), most likely to refer to the key verse Ex 9:12, since LXX Ex 9:12 has the active (aorist) form ἐσκλήρυνεν (compared to the aorist passive form in LXX Ex 7:22; 8:15 [ET 8:19]; 9:35). See the commentary.

9:19 ἐρεῖς μοι οὖν—This lively interjection, "you will therefore say to me," anticipates and almost invites a response in diatribe style. See "Rhetorical and Epistolary Forms" in "Structure and Outline" in the commentary introduction; see also the introduction to Romans 2.[11] The verb ἐρεῖς is a future second singular form of λέγω. Its other future forms in this section are ἐροῦμεν in 9:14 and ἐρεῖ in 9:20.

τί [οὖν]—The neuter form of the pronoun τίς utters an "interrogative expression of reason for, *why?*" (BDAG, 2). The textual evidence favors the inclusion of οὖν (𝔓46 B D), but its absence would not substantially alter the meaning.

μέμφεται—This verb form looks like a perfect tense, but the root already contains the duplication (μέμ-) so the tense is present. The ending is middle/passive in form, but the verb is deponent in meaning. μέμφομαι means "*find fault with, blame*" (BDAG); for the use here, BDAG suggests "*why does he still find fault?* or *what fault can he still find?*" See the commentary.

τῷ γὰρ βουλήματι αὐτοῦ—The conjunction γάρ is explanatory. According to BDAG, βούλημα basically means "*intention*" but also conveys the ideas of "*will*," "*purpose*," and "*desire*." The noun occurs only twice in the LXX and three times in the NT (also Acts 27:43; 1 Pet 4:3).

τίς ἀνθέστηκεν;—The interrogative pronoun τίς often occurs "in questions to which the answer 'nobody' is expected" (BDAG, 1 a α ℵ). ἀνθίστημι literally expresses "to stand against." This leads to definitions such as "be in opposition to, *set oneself against, oppose*" (BDAG, 1), as well as "*resist*" (BDAG, 2). See the commentary for various understandings here, as well as for the significance of the perfect tense form ἀνθέστηκεν.

---

[10] Dunn, *Romans*, 554.

[11] Middendorf, *Romans 1–8*, 22–27, 151.

9:20 ὦ ἄνθρωπε—The interjection ὦ and the masculine singular vocative ἄνθρωπε express direct address.[12] Here Paul conveys his exasperated response to the previously stated or anticipated objections. As with the same expression in 2:1 and 2:3, the address should not be regarded as merely rhetorical.[13]

μενοῦνγε—This combination of particles (μέν + οὖν + γέ) occurs especially "in answers, to emphasize or correct … *on the contrary, who are you … ?* (or, *who in the world are you to [take issue with God]?)*" (BDAG, s.v. μενοῦν). Sanday and Headlam call it "a strong correction. The word seems to belong almost exclusively to N.T. Greek, and would be impossible at the beginning of a sentence in classical Greek."[14] Note its same emphatic sense in Rom 10:18 and Phil 3:8.

ὁ ἀνταποκρινόμενος τῷ θεῷ—For ἀνταποκρίνομαι, BDAG offers *"answer in turn"* and translates this substantival participial phrase as *"one who answers back to God."* Cranfield identifies parallels in LXX Job 16:8; 32:12; and Lk 14:6.[15] Dunn adds: "Paul obviously chooses the double compound form [ἀντί + ἀπό + κρίνομαι] to strengthen the implication that the reply is unwarranted, improperly contentious."[16] This validates the somewhat colloquial translation "to talk back to God."

μή—See the second textual note on 9:14.

τὸ πλάσμα τῷ πλάσαντι—The aorist participle πλάσαντι with article τῷ is used substantively,[17] "(to) the one who formed." The verb πλάσσω means "to manufacture someth[ing] by molding a soft substance," to *"form, mold"* (BDAG). The derived noun πλάσμα then refers to "that which is formed or molded, *image, figure"* (BDAG). "Forms in -μα … express the result of an action" (BDAG, s.v. δικαίωμα, 3; note the fourteen nouns with -μα in 5:15–21).

οὕτως—This is the adverb of οὗτος, "referring to what precedes, *in this manner, thus, so"* (BDAG, s.v. οὕτω/οὕτως, 1).

9:21 ἔχει ἐξουσίαν—The noun ἐξουσία describes "a state of control over someth[ing], *freedom of choice, right"* (BDAG, 1; as also in 1 Cor 7:37; 9:12, 18), hence "have authority."

ὁ κεραμεὺς τοῦ πηλοῦ—The noun κέραμος (Lk 5:19) means "clay," and so the noun κεραμεύς here denotes one who works with clay, a *"potter"* (BDAG). πηλός is another noun for "clay" or "mud."

ἐκ τοῦ αὐτοῦ φυράματος—The noun φύραμα originally referred to a mixed batch of bread dough (BDAG, 1; e.g., Rom 11:16; 1 Cor 5:6–7; Gal 5:9). Later it was applied to any "dough-like mixture," such as a lump of mixed clay (BDAG, 2).

ποιῆσαι—This is the aorist active infinitive of ποιέω, "to make."

---

[12] See Wallace, *Greek Grammar*, 67–69.

[13] Dunn, *Romans*, 556; see also the commentary, as well as Middendorf, *Romans 1–8*, 170–74.

[14] Sanday and Headlam, *Romans*, 259.

[15] Cranfield, *Romans*, 491.

[16] Dunn, *Romans*, 556.

[17] See Wallace, *Greek Grammar*, 619–21.

ὃ μὲν ... ὃ δέ—For "the one ... the other," see the first textual note on 2:7. BDAG lists this passage under a category where "the combination μὲν ... δέ does not emphasize a contrast, but separates one thought from another in a series, so that they may be easily distinguished" (s.v. μέν, 1 c).

εἰς τιμὴν σκεῦος ... εἰς ἀτιμίαν—The neuter noun σκεῦος, which is accusative singular here after εἰς, refers to "a container of any kind, *vessel, jar, dish*" (BDAG, 2). The preposition εἰς describes "the vocation, use, or end indicated *for, as*" and, in this verse, "*meant for*" (BDAG, s.v. εἰς, 4 d). The same expression appears in the parallel 2 Tim 2:21: σκεῦος εἰς τιμήν. The potter makes one clay pot "εἰς τιμήν *for honor* = to be honored" (BDAG, s.v. τιμή, 2 b). The other prepositional phrase, εἰς ἀτιμίαν, does not mean that another clay pot is created to be "dishonored"; it rather depicts "a vessel to which no special value is attached εἰς ἀ[τιμίαν] *for ordinary (use)*" (BDAG, s.v. ἀτιμία). Paul makes the same point of contrast even more clearly in 2 Tim 2:20, cited in the commentary.

Note the repeated use of paired terminology in Rom 9:13 ("loved ... spurned"); 9:18 ("shows mercy ... hardens"); 9:21 ("honorable use ... ordinary use"); and 9:22–23 ("vessels of wrath ... vessels of mercy").

9:22–23 For various explanations of the incomplete Greek syntax of 9:22–23, see the commentary.

9:22 εἰ δὲ θέλων ὁ θεὸς ἐνδείξασθαι—For ἐνδείκνυμι, "demonstrate," see the fifth textual note on 9:17. Its aorist functions here as a complementary infinitive of the participle θέλων, "willing."[18]

γνωρίσαι—The verb γνωρίζω, "make known," expresses the causative sense of γινώσκω, "know," and commonly reflects the Hiphil stem of the Hebrew verb יָדַע.[19] γνωρίσαι (like ἐνδείξασθαι) is an aorist complementary infinitive of the participle θέλων, "willing."[20]

τὸ δυνατὸν αὐτοῦ—This is the sole NT instance in which the neuter form of the adjective δυνατός, "capable, powerful," is used with the article (τό) as a substantive, "power." BDAG, s.v. δυνατός, 2 b, affirms that it is the equivalent of ἡ δύναμις (see the seventh textual note on 9:17) and translates it as "*God's power*."

ἤνεγκεν—The verb φέρω occurs here in its very irregular aorist indicative form. In this context, the verb means "to hold out in the face of difficulty, *bear patiently, endure, put up with*" (BDAG, 9).

ἐν πολλῇ μακροθυμίᾳ—The noun μακροθυμία denotes the "state of being able to bear up under provocation, *forbearance, patience* toward others" (BDAG, 2). Note the important parallel in 2:4. The adjective πολύς here denotes degree, "*much, great, strong, ... deep, profound*" (BDAG, 3 a α).

σκεύη ὀργῆς κατηρτισμένα εἰς ἀπώλειαν—For σκεῦος, "vessel," see the sixth textual note on 9:21. The form here, σκεύη, is neuter accusative plural. The genitive

---

[18] See Wallace, *Greek Grammar*, 598–99.

[19] R. Bultmann, "γνωρίζω," *TDNT* 1:718.

[20] See Wallace, *Greek Grammar*, 598–99.

ὀργῆς, "of wrath," might be understood as objective, attributive, or qualitative.[21] Wallace proposes that it could be a genitive of destination (or direction), wherein "the genitive substantive indicates where the head noun is going (or the direction it is 'moving' in),"[22] i.e., "vessels moving toward wrath," but the prepositional phrase εἰς ἀπώλειαν, "toward destruction," serves that purpose here. Rather, "of wrath" functions as a descriptive genitive which means the vessels are "characterized by, described by"[23] the noun "wrath." The neuter plural accusative κατηρτισμένα is a perfect participle of καταρτίζω modifying the "vessels [σκεύη] of wrath." καταρτίζω means "to prepare for a purpose, *prepare, make, create, outfit*" (BDAG, 2). The participle's voice could be middle or passive, but is more likely the latter. BDAG's suggestion for this specific passage, that the vessels of wrath are "*designed*" for destruction (BDAG, 2 a), is inadequate. The perfect tense participle connects with σκεύη ὀργῆς, not simply σκεύη. Paul's point is that vessels of, or under, God's wrath "have been fitted for and are headed toward destruction." See the commentary.

9:23 ἵνα γνωρίσῃ—The conjunction ἵνα takes the subjunctive and denotes "purpose, aim, or goal, *in order that, that*" (BDAG, 1).[24] For γνωρίζω, "make known," see the second textual note on 9:22. The form γνωρίσῃ is an aorist subjunctive active second singular.

τὸν πλοῦτον—The noun πλοῦτος denotes a "plentiful supply of someth[ing], *a wealth, abundance*" (BDAG, 2). See the second textual note on 2:4.[a] God is described with the cognate verb πλουτέω, "be rich," in 10:12.

ἐπὶ σκεύη ἐλέους—The prepositional phrase is translated as "upon vessels of mercy." For σκεῦος, "vessel," see the sixth textual note on 9:21. The noun ἔλεος is cognate to the verb ἐλεέω, for which, see the first textual note on 9:15. The sense of its genitive case in the phrase σκεύη ἐλέους is comparable to that of the genitive ὀργῆς in the phrase σκεύη ὀργῆς; see the sixth textual note on 9:22.

ἃ προητοίμασεν εἰς δόξαν—The neuter plural form ἅ, "which" (of the relative pronoun ὅς), agrees with its antecedent, the "*vessels* [σκεύη] of mercy." The verb προετοιμάζω means "prepare *beforehand*," and its active voice is used in Christian literature "only of God" (BDAG). It is used here with an "indication of the goal" (BDAG). The only other NT use is Eph 2:10. The goal here is expressed by εἰς δόξαν. Thus Paul speaks of those whom God "prepared beforehand for glory."

;—The punctuation NA[27] places at the end of 9:23 represents a question mark. However, placing a comma here and positioning the question mark at the end of 9:24 better conveys Paul's meaning (as in ESV and RSV).

(a) See also Rom 11:12, 33; 2 Cor 8:2; Eph 1:7, 18; 2:7; 3:8, 16; Phil 4:19; Col 1:27; 2:2

---

[21] An objective genitive is supported by Dunn, *Romans*, 559; Käsemann, *Romans*, 270. However, Lenski, *Romans*, 624, calls it attributive; see Wallace, *Greek Grammar*, 86–88. Moo, *Romans*, 607, n. 98, describes it as qualitative; see Turner, *Syntax*, 214; BDF, § 165; similarly, C. Maurer, "σκεῦος," *TDNT* 7:364, though it certainly cannot be, as Maurer suggests, vessels "through which God works out His wrath." Munck, *Christ and Israel*, 68, also considers the option of "agents who effect God's wrath."

[22] Wallace, *Greek Grammar*, 100–101; he cites this instance as a debatable example.

[23] See Wallace, *Greek Grammar*, 79; see 79–81.

[24] Wallace, *Greek Grammar*, 472, also calls this a "final" or "telic" ἵνα.

9:24 This hinge verse concludes this section (9:14–24) and introduces 9:25–29. Therefore it is included in both sections with commentary provided here below. See also "The Connection of Romans 9:24 with the Catena of Romans 9:25–29" in the commentary on 9:24–29.

οὓς καί—See the commentary for a discussion of why this relative pronoun and conjunction identify the thought to follow as an exposition of 9:23.

ἐκάλεσεν—For καλέω in reference to God "calling," see the fourth textual note on 9:7.

οὐ μόνον … ἀλλὰ καί—As in 9:10, Paul returns to a formulaic expression used extensively in Romans (see 4:12).[b]

(b) Also in Rom 1:32; 4:16, 23–24; 5:3, 11; 8:23; 9:24; 13:5; 16:4

Commentary

"The God Who Shows Mercy" (9:14–18)

Introduction and Overview: What Is the Topic at Hand?

This particular segment of Romans has been disparaged by scholars. Moo contends that "these verses [9:14–23] are a detour from the main road of Paul's argument."[25] Dodd suggests that "Paul takes [what] seems to be a false step" in 9:17–18 and that 9:20–21 stands as "the weakest point in the whole epistle."[26] These evaluations stem from reading the section anthropocentrically. Paul, on the other hand, has repeatedly focused our attention on what he is teaching about God. This was true throughout Romans 1–4, as well as in 9:6–13. Paul continues to fix our attention there.[27]

What then is Paul's main point about God in 9:14–24? A repeated proposal is that Paul seeks to assert God's "freedom."[28] Käsemann titles 9:14–23 "God's Free Power."[29] But this is misguided since Paul himself never uses words such as "free" or "freedom" in reference to God here or elsewhere in the letter. Thus it is tendentious, at best, to regard that as his main point. Matera's exposition of 9:1–29 seeks "to highlight what" he believes "is at stake: God's sovereignty."[30] Murray combines those two proposals to suggest that Paul's primary emphasis is on "accentuating God's free and sovereign choice."[31] But nowhere in this passage either does Paul utilize vocabulary for God as "sovereign."

It seems much more appropriate to identify Paul's theme *by drawing upon terminology which actually appears in the text*. That leads to the more fitting

---

[25] Moo, *Romans*, 589.

[26] Dodd, *Romans*, 157, 159.

[27] Middendorf, *Romans 1–8*, 21–22, 27, 49–51; in this volume, see "Romans 1–4: The Righteousness of God" in the introduction to Romans 9–16, as well as "God" in "The Three Foci of Romans 9–11" in the introduction to Romans 9–11.

[28] E.g., Cranfield, *Romans*, 483, 484, 492; Moo, *Romans*, 592, 594, 596; Matera, *Romans*, 228; see also "God" in "The Three Foci of Romans 9–11" in the introduction to Romans 9–11.

[29] Käsemann, *Romans*, 266.

[30] Matera, *Romans*, 232; see also Murray, *Romans*, 2:24–25.

[31] Murray, *Romans*, 2:25.

assessment that "the leading motif is God's *mercy*" (ἐλεέω, ἐλεάω, or ἔλεος, 9:15, 16, 18, 23).[32] Paul makes this particularly evident by references to God "showing mercy" (ἐλεέω) in the conclusions he draws in 9:16 and 9:18, both of which begin with "consequently then" (ἄρα οὖν). Paul then defends these assertions in 9:19–23. When 9:24 is included as the climactic resolution of this section, all of which responds to 9:6–13, one arrives at the theme identified by this commentary's title for the pericope: "God's Word of Mercy Calls Us." The inclusion of "calls" is warranted by the verb "call" (καλέω) in 9:24 (also 9:7, 12, 25, 26). Thus Paul's emphasis resides with neither God's freedom nor his sovereignty, though, properly understood, both are valid biblical truths. Instead, Paul exalts in the astonishing fact that God's Word of *mercy* calls out to anyone and everyone who hears it, which means that "he also called … us" (9:24). Already in the letter's introduction, Paul describes himself, as well as his addressees in Rome, as "called" (κλητός in 1:1, 6, 7). God's merciful call continues to summon all those who hear the compassionate invitation of his enduring Word.

The interactive nature of this section is clearly evident from its structure. The suggestion posed in 9:14 reacts to 9:6–13. This then leads into Paul's responses in 9:15–18, which are largely based upon statements of God himself cited from the Scriptures. These are followed by Paul drawing out the consequences in 9:16 and 9:18. The further challenge of 9:19 produces a series of rhetorical questions in 9:20–24. Thus, in a manner reminiscent of Romans 2 and 3:1–8, the format becomes highly dialogical. Indeed, Paul's engaging diatribe style reaches its most intense point in 9:14–23.[33] For example, Paul himself begins: "What then will we say?" (9:14). Later, 9:19 expects a rebuttal by suggesting, "You will therefore say to me." In 9:20, Paul directly confronts "you" who would dare to "talk back to God." All of this interaction no doubt reflects the importance and sensitivity of the topic at hand.

A Challenge to God's Righteousness Rebuked (9:14)

Rom 9:14 returns to the supposition of 3:5 in both format and topic. There the issue posed and rejected was "but if our unrighteousness demonstrates God's righteousness, what will we say? God, the one who brings wrath, is not unrighteous, is he? (I am speaking in a human way.) May it never come to be!" (3:5–6a). Now Paul similarly suggests and rejects this notion about "unrighteousness": "What then will we say? There is not unrighteousness with God, is there? May it never come to be!" (9:14). The wording of the question itself expects a negative response ("there is not … , is there?"), and the notion is further rebuked by "may it never come to be!" (μὴ γένοιτο, 9:14; see also 3:5–6; 6:1–2; 7:7; cf. 11:1, 11).

---

[32] Dunn, *Romans*, 551 (emphasis added).

[33] For comments on the diatribe, see "Rhetorical and Epistolary Forms" in "Structure and Outline" in the commentary introduction and the introduction to Romans 2 (Middendorf, *Romans 1–8*, 24–27, 151).

"Unrighteousness [ἀδικία] with God" (9:14)? Who could feasibly entertain any such notion? At this stage of the letter, the challenge is probably best regarded as Paul's own "reflective question."[34] But Käsemann goes too far in concluding that "there is no trace of concrete opponents or missionary experiences" that could have elicited the question.[35] Matera enunciates the issue of contention this way: "Is not God's elective purpose arbitrary and a manifestation of 'injustice' (*adikia*) on God's part—an objection that echoes the charge in 3:5?"[36] As in 3:5–8, Paul recognizes that this conclusion may be an allegation made against him or may well arise as a challenge based upon what he has just stated. Whatever the source on the human side of things, Käsemann properly grounds the reality of Paul's discussion in enunciations like those just made in 9:6–13. He points out that Paul is not engaged in some abstract discussion of theodicy, but dealing with the implications and ramifications of "God in his concrete acts" in history.[37]

Murray suggests the issue at hand is "the ultimate and decisive question of justice."[38] The objection of 9:14 then accuses Paul of attributing "injustice" to God (ESV, NASB, RSV) or portraying God as acting in an "unfair" or "partial" manner (cf. "no partiality" in 2:11). As discussed in this commentary's introduction, notions of "fairness" and "equal justice" obscure the *coram Deo* depth of the matters Paul grapples with and tends to reduce them to human levels of behavior.[39] Furthermore, Paul has ably proven that any notion of seeking "fairness" from God would end in utter ruin (1:18–3:20; especially 3:9–20). Questioning the impartiality of God at least raises a fundamental theological matter, but one which Paul has already answered and refuted (e.g., 2:6–11; see also 3:29–31).

More pertinent throughout Romans, ever since 1:17, is the recognition that "Paul also uses 'righteousness' language to refer to God's faithfulness to his own person and character."[40] Although "unrighteousness" (ἀδικία, 9:14) occurs in reference to God only three times in the LXX (God is declared not to be "unrighteousness" in LXX Deut 32:4; 2 Chr 19:7; Ps 91:16 [MT 92:16; ET 92:15]), the challenge to God's integrity and character is at stake here. Thus the translation "unrighteousness" (Rom 9:14 KJV, NKJV) accurately conveys what is being contested. Paul already felt the need to affirm God's righteousness, faithfulness,

---

[34] Cranfield, *Romans*, 482.

[35] Käsemann, *Romans*, 267.

[36] Matera, *Romans*, 224.

[37] Käsemann, *Romans*, 267.

[38] Murray, *Romans*, 2:25; similarly, Elliot, *The Arrogance of Nations*, 75.

[39] Middendorf, *Romans 1–8*, 47–48; see also "The Background and Meaning of 'Righteousness' Words" in the commentary on 1:17 (Middendorf, *Romans 1–8*, 92–96; see also 106–7). In this volume, see "Righteousness Returns" and "Righteousness Defined" in the introduction to 9:30–10:15.

[40] Moo, *Romans*, 591.

and truth in 3:1–8 and also 3:26 (see the commentary on those passages). The matter resurfaces here and must be refuted again.

God's Mercy Affirmed (Ex 33:19 in Rom 9:15)

Paul responds most appropriately by letting God speak for himself with two quotations from the OT. As a result, the issue of whether God's Word has itself failed or fallen (9:6) also remains at the heart of the matter. Paul introduces his initial evidence that there is no "unrighteousness" (ἀδικία, 9:14) with God by an explanatory γάρ, "*for* he says to Moses, 'I will show mercy to whomever I show mercy, and I will have compassion on whomever I have compassion'" (9:15).

This remarkable double blessing comes from the direct words of Yahweh to Moses in Ex 33:19. The significance of the setting should not be overlooked. Immediately after the golden calf episode (Ex 32:1–6), Yahweh intends to destroy the Israelites (Ex 32:10). But Moses intercedes in Israel's behalf and Yahweh relents (Ex 32:11–14). Then Moses seeks assurance that God's presence will go with him and the people (Ex 33:15–16). Yahweh provides that assurance. The entire verse from MT Ex 33:19 is as follows:

וַיֹּאמֶר אֲנִי אַעֲבִיר כָּל־טוּבִי עַל־פָּנֶיךָ וְקָרָאתִי בְשֵׁם יְהוָה לְפָנֶיךָ
וְחַנֹּתִי אֶת־אֲשֶׁר אָחֹן וְרִחַמְתִּי אֶת־אֲשֶׁר אֲרַחֵם:

> And he said, "I myself will cause to cross over upon your face all my goodness. And I will call out with the name of 'Yahweh' before you. And I will be gracious to whomever I will be gracious, and I will show compassion to whomever I will show compassion."

Paul cites the latter half of the verse exactly as it appears in the LXX. There the entire verse reads:

> καὶ εἶπεν ἐγὼ παρελεύσομαι πρότερός σου τῇ δόξῃ μου καὶ καλέσω ἐπὶ τῷ ὀνόματί μου κύριος ἐναντίον σου· καὶ ἐλεήσω ὃν ἂν ἐλεῶ, καὶ οἰκτιρήσω ὃν ἂν οἰκτίρω.

> And he said, "I will pass by before you in my glory, and I will call upon my name, 'Lord,' in front of you, and I will show mercy to whomever I show mercy, and I will have compassion on whomever I have compassion."

Except for one interesting change, the LXX represents the Hebrew literally. In the first half of the verse, the LXX changes Yahweh's reference from his "goodness" to that of his own "glory" (δόξα). The context in Exodus, then, aligns with Rom 1:23, where people exchanged God's "glory" (δόξα) for the worship of idols.

Paul cites the most significant, latter portion of the verse. The text itself thereby identifies the key component at issue through "the emphatic double repetition of the idea of mercy."[41] The passage is well chosen, then, to emphasize *the dominant, essential nature of God's character, that is, his graciousness, compassion, and mercy.* Dunn suggests that Paul draws on "an exceptional unveiling of God, of his glory and his name (Exod 33:18–19). That is, God in

---

[41] Cranfield, *Romans*, 483.

his fullest self-disclosure … , God in the fullest extent to which he could be known by man—his glory."[42] Note, however, that nothing is said about God's freedom or sovereignty.

God's Mercy Reaffirmed (9:16)

Paul himself then signals the conclusion he intends to be drawn from the citation by continuing with "consequently then" (ἄρα οὖν, as also in 9:18): "consequently then, [God's mercy is] not of the one willing nor of the one striving, but of the God who shows mercy" (9:16). The present tense of the participles causes this verse to read "like a general principle."[43] At the same time, the sentence lacks a subject and a main verb. But in light of the emphasis of the quotation in the previous verse (9:15), the topic at hand is "God's bestowal of mercy."[44] Cranfield conveys the thought as "God's mercy is not a matter of (or perhaps 'does not depend on') man's willing or activity."[45]

Essentially, 9:16 repeats or at least parallels the content of 9:11b–12a. The phrase "not from works" there (οὐκ ἐξ ἔργων, 9:12) stands equivalent to what Paul states here, "not of the one willing nor of the one striving." Thus the "not *from* works" of 9:12 indicates that the two negated genitive participles in 9:16, each translated with "of," should similarly be understood as expressing source.[46] The first, "not *of* the one willing" (οὐ τοῦ θέλοντος), manifests the "contrast between man's willing (v 16) and God's (vv 16, 18, 22), which alone is decisive."[47] The second negated participle, "nor *of* the one striving" (οὐδὲ τοῦ τρέχοντος), introduces the picture of athletics[48] (see 1 Cor 9:24, 26; Gal 2:2; 5:7; Phil 2:16). The verb τρέχω, often literally "to run" (e.g., Mk 5:6; Jn 20:2, 4), does not simply function "as a more intense form of περιπατέω ('walk') in the sense of 'conduct oneself.' "[49] Instead, the two participles combine to "sum

---

[42] Dunn, *Romans*, 552. (Dunn refers to "God in his fullest self-disclosure *prior to Christ*," but the words here italicized are replaced by an ellipsis in the quotation above, because the personal appearances of Yahweh's "glory" in the OT are theophanies of the preincarnate Christ himself; compare, e.g., Ezek 1:26–27 to Rev 1:12–16 and cf. Jn 1:14; 8:56; 17:4; 1 Cor 10:4.) Dunn suggests that this points to

> an intended link with the repetition and development of Exod 33:19 in 34:6, since the latter is one of the most cited and echoed passages in the OT and postbiblical Jewish literature (Num 14:18; Neh 9:17; Pss 86 [LXX 85]:15; 103 [LXX 102]:8; 145 [LXX 144]:8; Joel 2:13; Jonah 4:2; Nah 1:3).

H. Bietenhard, "ὄνομα," *TDNT* 5:272, similarly discusses the NT linking of God's name with his glory.

[43] Moo, *Romans*, 593.

[44] Moo, *Romans*, 593; other suggestions he notes are "salvation" and "God's purpose in election" (9:11).

[45] Cranfield, *Romans*, 484–85.

[46] Wallace, *Greek Grammar*, 110, lists 9:16 under this category; see 109–10, also 371; Moo, *Romans*, 593, n. 27.

[47] Dunn, *Romans*, 553.

[48] Cranfield, *Romans*, 485.

[49] Dunn, *Romans*, 553.

up the totality of man's capacity."[50] Therefore, in regard to the issue at hand, neither the willing nor the striving of people has any effect on God's mercy. There is nothing determinative, or even of influence, going from humanity toward God; instead, the actions that matter come exclusively from God toward us (as in 3:19–26; 4:4–5; 9:30–10:15).

The parallel passage of 9:12 places the emphasis upon God: "from the One who calls" (ἐκ τοῦ καλοῦντος). Here, based upon the Exodus citation in 9:15, Paul adds a characteristic action which defines the God who calls: literally, he is "the God who *mercies*" (τοῦ ἐλεῶντος θεοῦ, 9:16). While this verb may technically be a form of ἐλεάω (see the third textual note on 9:16), it is synonymous with the nearly identical thematic verb ἐλεέω, "show mercy," in 9:15, which appears again in 9:18. The cognate noun ἔλεος, "mercy," occurs in 9:23 (also 11:31; 15:9). Unfortunately, English is deficient at this point because it lacks a simple cognate verb.[51] The biblical terms convey an action, not simply an emotion or feeling. This is reflected at the end of the parable of the Good Samaritan: he was "the one who did mercy" (ὁ ποιήσας τὸ ἔλεος, Lk 10:37). Similarly, God actively "does mercy" or "shows mercy" to whomever he desires. The same is true with the other verb in 9:15b, οἰκτίρω, "have compassion." Rather than merely having compassion in his heart, God "does compassion" or "acts compassionately." The granting of his mercy and compassion also then bestows the numerous other blessings which accompany them.

Thus the primary actor on stage throughout Rom 9:6–29 is God. The only activities of consequence remain his Word of promise (9:9), his choosing (9:11), his active call (9:12), and now his acts of mercy and compassion (9:16). On what basis, then, does the mercy-ing God act? Apollinaris of Laodicea echoes Paul well: God "does not dispense mercy according to human standards, but according to the wisdom of God. For we are shown mercy not because of our own works but because of God, who has the power to show mercy."[52] 1 Cor 1:24 elaborates further, explicitly identifying Christ as the wisdom and power of God. Christ also provides the basis upon which God shows mercy to us (1 Tim 1:16; 1 Pet 1:3; Jude 21). The emphasis on God's mercy stands validated when Paul finally arrives at the culminating theological assertions of Romans 9–11. In 11:30–32, the verb "show mercy" (ἐλεέω) appears three times. But one cannot skip over the intervening verses on the way there.

Moo rejects the notion that God's mercy merely chooses different persons or nations in the outworking of his salvific plan within human history. Instead, commenting on 9:16, Moo insists that "Paul's use of OT examples of

---

[50] Dunn, *Romans*, 553.

[51] English also lacks readily recognizable verbs for the thematic nouns of Romans, "faith" and "righteousness." This leads many translations to utilize "believe" and "justify," respectively, obscuring the connection between the Greek verbs, nouns, and adjectives. See Middendorf, *Romans 1–8*, 88 and 92.

[52] Apollinaris of Laodicea, *Romans* (Bray, *Romans*, ACCS NT, 6:255).

God's choosing and rejecting develop a principle that he applies to the salvation of individual Jews and Gentiles in his own day."[53] The obvious rebuttal at this point is that neither Paul in 9:14–16 (but cf. 9:13) nor the Exodus passage cited in Rom 9:15 mentions anything about rejecting. But one has to deal with another negative action of God very shortly.

Is This Fair to the Pharaoh? (9:17–18)

Some scholars contend that 9:17–18 serves as an additional response to the soundly rejected assertion of "unrighteousness with God" in 9:14. Cranfield suggests that the opening "for, indeed" (γάρ) in 9:17 connects with 9:14, just as the "for" (γάρ) of 9:15 does.[54] Moo agrees that the two scriptural citations in 9:15 and 9:17 both support the "may it never come to be!" (μὴ γένοιτο) which concludes 9:14. If so, 9:17–18 offers a second, emphatic denunciation of any notion that God could be unrighteous.[55] But simple redundancy seems unlikely. These verses surely mark a development in Paul's argument flowing from 9:16.[56] If so, it might initially appear that the essence of 9:17–18 is to articulate the negative side of the argument: the introduction of the Pharaoh from the Exodus narrative would then reinforce what happened with Ishmael (versus Isaac in 9:7) and Esau (versus Jacob in 9:13). But a wholly negative appraisal overlooks the reiteration of mercy when Paul draws his conclusion in 9:18, as well as the original location and force of Paul's quotation in 9:17.

In 9:15, Paul introduces his quote from Ex 33:19 in terms of what God "says" (λέγει) to Moses. The subject of the third singular verb comes from the object of the prepositional phrase in 9:14, "with God" (παρὰ τῷ θεῷ). Later, in the parallel statement in 9:17, Paul personifies the Scripture itself as speaking (λέγει γὰρ ἡ γραφή). This provides "a graphic illustration that Paul thinks of scripture as the Word of God (cf. Gal 3:8; 4:30)."[57] Indeed, God actually speaks directly *to Moses* in Ex 9:16. But it is still God speaking through Moses when he delivers this message to the Pharaoh. And it is still God speaking whenever the now-written words of Scripture are read or heard (note the present tense of λέγει, "says," in 9:17).

Exodus 9:16 in Romans 9:17

Unlike the exact replication of the LXX Ex 33:19 in Rom 9:15, the complexities involved in Paul's quotation of Ex 9:16 in Rom 9:17 are substantial. They involve differences in the underlying text, as well as the manner in which the message of the words is meant to be heard. Paul's citation of Ex 9:16, introduced by ὅτι (translated by quotation marks, as in, e.g., Rom 8:36 and 1 Cor 14:21; see the second textual note on Rom 9:17), quotes words God initially

---

[53] Moo, *Romans*, 593.

[54] Cranfield, *Romans*, 485.

[55] Moo, *Romans*, 594.

[56] Dunn, *Romans*, 553.

[57] Dunn, *Romans*, 553.

spoke to Moses in the midst of the plagues. The context of this episode, there-fore, stands prior to the exodus redemption itself and means these words occur much earlier in the narrative than the quote in Rom 9:15 from Exodus 33 (after the crossing of the Red Sea and the covenant at Sinai). This supports the notion that Rom 9:17–18 is not simply a return to 9:14. Paul could have simply fol-lowed the order of the Exodus verses in the narrative. The fact that he reverses track here to an earlier point in the account indicates there is a deliberate *non*-chronological sequencing of the substance he intends to convey.

In 9:17, Paul records the Scripture (Ex 9:16) speaking to the Pharaoh. For comparison, the text of Romans, the LXX, and the underlying Hebrew appear below.

εἰς αὐτὸ τοῦτο ἐξήγειρά σε ὅπως ἐνδείξωμαι ἐν σοὶ τὴν δύναμίν μου καὶ ὅπως διαγγελῇ τὸ ὄνομά μου ἐν πάσῃ τῇ γῇ.

For this very reason I raised you up in order that I might demonstrate in you my [saving] power and in order that my name might be announced in all the earth. (Rom 9:17)

καὶ ἕνεκεν τούτου διετηρήθης, ἵνα ἐνδείξωμαι ἐν σοὶ τὴν ἰσχύν μου, καὶ ὅπως διαγγελῇ τὸ ὄνομά μου ἐν πάσῃ τῇ γῇ.

And on account of this you were kept in order that I might demonstrate in you my strength and in order that my name might be proclaimed in all the earth. (LXX Ex 9:16)

וְאוּלָם בַּעֲבוּר זֹאת הֶעֱמַדְתִּיךָ בַּעֲבוּר הַרְאֹתְךָ אֶת־כֹּחִי וּלְמַעַן סַפֵּר שְׁמִי בְּכָל־הָאָרֶץ׃

But for the sake of this I caused you to stand, for the sake to cause you to see my strength, in order to proclaim my name in all the earth. (MT Ex 9:16)

The LXX represents the MT accurately in form and meaning. One minor note is that the object suffix of the Hiphil infinitive construct הַרְאֹתְךָ, "to cause you to see," is rendered with the prepositional phrase ἐν σοί, "*in* you," by the LXX and in Rom 9:17. Their Greek clause ἐνδείξωμαι ἐν σοί, "that I might demon-strate in you," is comparable to the Hebrew infinitive, and in neither the Hebrew nor the Greek does God say "*against* you."[58]

A number of differences between the LXX and Romans exist. Two of these seem inconsequential. In Romans the quote begins with εἰς αὐτὸ τοῦτο, "for this very reason," rather than καὶ ἕνεκεν τούτου, "and on account of this" (LXX). Both of the initial clauses that begin with those prepositional phrases express purpose; they explain *why* God did something. In the second purpose clause, in place of the ἵνα of the LXX Paul has ὅπως; both are translated "in order that." Thus Paul has two consecutive ὅπως clauses, which make the two pur-pose clauses appear even more synonymous than they already are in the LXX. (Like Paul, the Hebrew has the identical preposition, בַּעֲבוּר, in both purpose

---

[58] As rightly pointed out by Lenski, *Romans*, 614.

clauses.) This also heightens the notion that Paul intends for the two clauses to be read as equivalent.

The text of Romans reveals two more substantial changes from the LXX. First, Paul uses ἐξήγειρά σε, "I raised you up," instead of the LXX's διετηρήθης, "you were kept." Cranfield suggests that the LXX verb conveys the more general "sense of keeping alive."[59] The thought of the LXX is that, up to this point in the narrative, the Pharaoh has been "preserved" or "spared" by God. But from what? The immediate meaning could be that God has kept the Pharaoh safe from the most recent plague of boils (Ex 9:8–12), as well as the other plagues thus far (Ex 7:14–9:7). The LXX rendering with "keep" (διατηρέω), therefore, seems to convey the general idea of "kept alive up until now."

In any case, Sanday and Headlam respond: "The passage as quoted by St. Paul could not be so interpreted."[60] Paul's use of ἐξήγειρά σε, "I raised you up," better reflects the Hiphil stem, the active voice, and the object suffix of the Hebrew, הֶעֱמַדְתִּיךָ, "I caused you to stand."[61] The sense, then, is that Yahweh raised him up, but not in some general sense. Instead, the Pharaoh was *granted an exalted position*. Paul's divergence from the LXX also serves to emphasize God's involvement in elevating the Pharaoh "to the Egyptian throne during the period in which the exodus of Israel was to take place."[62] But, as we will see below, the matter of controversy concerns what happened after God granted this particular Pharaoh such a powerful role.

Second, Paul alters the LXX's "my strength" (τὴν ἰσχύν μου) to "my power" (τὴν δύναμίν μου). In general meaning, the nouns may be roughly equivalent. But, in the context of Romans, the switch is not merely "stylistic";[63] neither can it be "explained as simply the substitution of a word in common use [δύναμις] for one [ἰσχύς], which, while of frequent occurrence in the LXX, is relatively rare in Greek usage generally."[64] Instead, the switch in terminology readily recalls the thematic assertion of 1:16: the Good News Paul proclaims is the "power of God" (δύναμις θεοῦ). With the lone exception of 1:20, Paul's use of the noun "power" (δύναμις) consistently carries with it the connotation present in 1:16, that of God's "*saving* power."[c] Paul's *insertion* of the word into the context of the exodus reinforces the notion that for him δύναμις is "power directed toward the deliverance of God's people."[65] Then, as now, Paul contends

(c) As also in 1 Cor 1:18, 24; 4:20; 6:14; 2 Cor 4:7; 6:7; 13:4; Eph 1:19; 3:7, 20; 2 Tim 1:8

---

[59] Cranfield, *Romans*, 486.

[60] Sanday and Headlam, *Romans*, 256.

[61] The Hiphil of עָמַד can mean "to station, place, appoint" someone to a royal or religious office such as a prince or priest (e.g., 2 Chr 11:15, 22).

[62] Lenski, *Romans*, 614. Cranfield, *Romans*, 486, notes that God "caused him to appear on the stage of history, for this purpose." Similarly, Moo, *Romans*, 595; Sanday and Headlam, *Romans*, 256.

[63] As Moo, *Romans*, 594, n. 37, maintains.

[64] Cranfield, *Romans*, 486.

[65] Cranfield, *Romans*, 487.

that "it is [the] power of God into salvation for everyone who believes, to Jew first and also to Greek" (1:16). The *inclusion of Gentiles* was also true in the time of the exodus. Notice, for example, that "a mixed multitude also went up" (וְגַם־עֵרֶב רַב עָלָה) with the Israelites as they left Egypt together (Ex 12:38; LXX: καὶ ἐπίμικτος πολὺς συνανέβη; cf. Ex 12:48).[66]

In Paul's citation, "my power" (τὴν δύναμίν μου) is paralleled with "my name" (τὸ ὄνομά μου). Particularly in Exodus, the name "Yahweh" is God's self-revelation in contexts of salvation (e.g., in the context of the upcoming redemption of Israel in Ex 3:14–16; in the context of Yahweh's gracious compassion in Ex 33:19). Thus Yahweh's saving power stands synonymous with his name. Lenski points out:

> "My Name" is a gospel term; [it is] the revelation of who and what God really is in his love, mercy, grace, and saving power. God's purpose in the way in which he delivered Israel went far beyond Israel. All Egypt was to know this God.[67]

Even more broadly, Ex 9:16 asserts that Yahweh's saving name would be proclaimed "in all the earth." Paul quotes this when he declares: "Indeed, the Scripture says to the Pharaoh, 'For this very reason I raised you up in order that I might demonstrate in you my [saving] power and in order that my name might be announced in all the earth" (Rom 9:17).

It was to accomplish his saving purpose for Israel that Yahweh, the God of the nations, raised up the Pharaoh. His exalted position of earthly power and influence was a blessing from God. He stood in a position comparable to that of King Cyrus of Persia centuries later (Is 45:1–13; Ezra 1:1–4). The citation of Is 45:9 almost immediately in Rom 9:20 reinforces the connection. Just as with Cyrus, so it is "in" the Pharaoh ("in you," ἐν σοί) that Yahweh's saving "power" (δύναμις) would be made evident (Rom 9:17).

But how would the Pharaoh respond to being raised up by Yahweh for this purpose? As with Cyrus, the point with the Pharaoh is *not* that God raised him up in order to smash him down or to harden him. Nothing in the text of Exodus or of Romans suggests this (nor does the text of Is 44:28–45:13 for Cyrus). Moo's contention that "God 'raised up' Pharaoh with a negative rather than a positive purpose"[68] does not stand. God's purpose (cf. Rom 9:11) in elevating this Pharaoh is both God-focused and positive according to Paul. God's saving power will be shown and his name, Yahweh, will be announced in all the world. In light of what follows, one appropriately observes that "by resisting God's will

---

[66] This is not the only OT example of the inclusion of believing Gentiles. See, for example, individuals such as Ruth the Moabitess (the book of Ruth) and Uriah the Hittite (2 Samuel 11). The large-scale conversion and inclusion of Gentiles was envisioned by the prophets; see, for example, Is 2:1–4; 11:1–16; 19:18–25; 56:6–8; 60:1–11; 66:18–23; Ezek 16:53–63; Amos 9:11–12; Micah 4:1–3; Zeph 3:9–10; Zech 2:11 (MT 2:15); 14:16.

[67] Lenski, *Romans*, 615.

[68] Moo, *Romans*, 595.

to deliver his people from bondage, Pharaoh caused that deliverance to assume a more spectacular aspect than it would have otherwise."[69]

Hardening

On this basis, Paul then utters one of his most thought-provoking conclusions: "Consequently then, [to] whom he wills he shows mercy and whom he wills he hardens" (9:18). At this point, Cranfield's wise advice cited in the introduction to Romans 9–11 is worth repeating:

> It is of the utmost importance to take these three chapters together as a whole, and not to come to conclusions about Paul's argument before one has heard it to the end; for chapter 9 will certainly be understood in an altogether un-Pauline sense, if it is understood in isolation from its sequel in chapters 10 and 11.[70]

Indeed, one can easily refer to 11:32 for the answer to the question of whom it is that God desires to grant mercy: *his will is to show mercy to all* (ἵνα τοὺς πάντας ἐλεήσῃ, 11:32). But it is best to follow Paul's example and let both sides of God's will remain in tension for now, uncomfortable as that might be. Jumping too far ahead too readily avoids the necessary challenge of wrestling with what the intervening verses have to say. Furthermore, engaging fully in what Paul has to say from 9:17 up until 11:32 enables one to discern who it is that God wills to harden. In fact, the entire matter of which side of Paul's dramatic assertion in 9:18 applies to "whom" becomes answerable quite decisively.

Nothing was said about hardening in either of Paul's quotations from Exodus (Rom 9:15, 17). But the introduction of the Pharaoh leads Paul readily there. The concept of God's hardening stands "particularly prominent" in the section of the Exodus narrative in which Moses interacts with the Pharaoh.[71] For example, in LXX Exodus 4–14, the verb Paul uses in Rom 9:18 for "to harden," σκληρύνω, occurs fourteen times. In addition, various other Greek words depict the same action (see below).

Dunn asserts that "to look for reasons for God's hardening in Pharaoh's 'evil disposition' or previous self-hardening … is a rationalizing expediency."[72] But, as we will see, a sequence of events, of actions and reactions, forms the essence of Paul's entire argument as he moves on from here through Romans 10 and on to the end of Romans 11 (e.g., 10:16–21; 11:7, 25). As 9:1–13 has already demonstrated, Paul assumes a considerable amount of OT knowledge on the part of his hearers. Thus when one follows the Exodus narrative and locates Paul's quote appropriately, "the history of this hardening certainly speaks for itself."[73] It may be helpful to follow the progression of the narrative of the Pharaoh's

---

[69] Moo, *Romans*, 595–96.

[70] Cranfield, *Romans*, 447–48.

[71] Dunn, *Romans*, 554.

[72] Dunn, *Romans*, 555.

[73] Lenski, *Romans*, 617.

hardening, particularly up until Ex 9:16. The Hebrew verb forms are particularly relevant.

The Sequence of Hardening in the Exodus Narrative

Ex 4:21 and Ex 7:3 contain two predictive statements by Yahweh telling Moses how things will turn out for the Pharaoh in the end. "I myself will strengthen/harden his heart" (וַאֲנִי אֲחַזֵּק אֶת־לִבּוֹ, Ex 4:21) and "I myself will cause the heart of the Pharaoh to be hard" (וַאֲנִי אַקְשֶׁה אֶת־לֵב פַּרְעֹה, Ex 7:3). Although the Hebrew verbs are different, both times the LXX uses the same verb Paul does, σκληρύνω. However, both times the Greek verb is accented as *future* tense, which reflects the Hebrew imperfect verbs. The LXX renderings are ἐγὼ δὲ σκληρυνῶ τὴν καρδίαν αὐτοῦ (Ex 4:21) and ἐγὼ δὲ σκληρυνῶ τὴν καρδίαν Φαραω (Ex 7:3). *One cannot simply ignore the tenses.* The fact that "the Lord tells Moses the final outcome"[74] does not "imply that Pharaoh's hardening of his own heart was the result of God's prior act of hardening."[75] Indeed, these texts do not say that any such event has yet occurred, but that it will in the future. The Hebrew verbs are not prophetic perfects,[76] but Hebrew imperfects rendered properly as Greek future tenses by the LXX. Furthermore, although Moo suggests that God is the implied subject of passive verbs in LXX Ex 7:13 (sic), 14, 22; 8:11, 15 (ET 8:15, 19),[77] as if God performed the hardening, the Hebrew text of those verses actually contains stative verbs, that is, verbs that describe a state of being without ascribing any agency to God (see below).

With that introduction, the narrative of Exodus contains these relevant texts:

- Ex 7:13: After the Pharaoh's magicians replicated the signs of Moses, the Hebrew uses a stative (active, intransitive) verb in the Qal stem to assert: "and the heart of Pharaoh was strong/hard" (וַיֶּחֱזַק לֵב פַּרְעֹה). The LXX rendering is comparable: "and the heart of Pharaoh was strong/hard" (καὶ κατίσχυσεν ἡ καρδία Φαραω).

- Ex 7:14: This reiterates the idea of the preceding verse (Ex 7:13), and its verb, while different, has a similar sense. The MT has another stative verb in the Qal stem, a perfect: "the heart of Pharaoh was heavy/dull/unresponsive" (כָּבֵד לֵב פַּרְעֹה, Ex 7:14). The LXX too switches to a different verb, βαρέω (related to βαρύνω), but with a similar meaning. It translates with a perfect passive: βεβάρηται ἡ καρδία Φαραω, literally, "the heart of Pharaoh was heavy." Although middle/passive in form, this Greek verb has an intransitive (cf. stative) meaning. In both Classical Greek and the LXX, passive forms of βαρέω and βαρύνω generally have intransitive meanings, e.g., in Classical Greek, "be heavy" (see LSJM, svv. βαρέω, II,

---

[74] Lenski, *Romans*, 617.

[75] Moo, *Romans*, 598.

[76] In the Hebrew OT, particularly the prophets, prophecies about the future are commonly phrased with perfect verbs, as if to imply that since God has spoken, the future actions most certainly will take place and can even be considered as already accomplished.

[77] Moo, *Romans*, 598, n. 53; however, the bullet point in the text that quotes Ex 7:13 demonstrates that in that verse neither the MT nor the LXX has the verb in the passive voice.

and βαρύνω, I 1), or in the LXX, "become unfavorably disposed" (Muraoka, s.v. βαρύνω, 5, citing Ex 7:14).[78]

- Ex 7:22: The same statement as in Ex 7:13 is made during the plague of blood: "and the heart of Pharaoh was strong/hard" (וַיֶּחֱזַק לֵב־פַּרְעֹה, Ex 7:22). The LXX employs σκληρύνω, an active form of which Paul uses in Rom 9:18. Its passive form in Ex 7:22 (also Ex 8:15; 9:35) is comparable in meaning to the Hebrew and Greek verbs in Ex 7:13, 14: "and the heart of Pharaoh became hard" (καὶ ἐσκληρύνθη ἡ καρδία Φαραω, Ex 7:22). As with the passive forms of βαρέω in Ex 7:14 and of βαρύνω in Ex 8:15 (LXX 8:11); 9:7, the passive of σκληρύνω in the LXX has an "intr[ansitive] force" (Muraoka), thus "be or become hard."[79]

- Ex 8:15 (MT/LXX 8:11): After the plague of frogs ended, Pharaoh "caused his heart to be heavy" (וְהַכְבֵּד אֶת־לִבּוֹ). The verb is the Hiphil stem, with a causative meaning, of the verb whose Qal, with a stative meaning, was in Ex 7:14; see above. (Somewhat unusual is the use of the infinitive absolute form הַכְבֵּד in place of a perfect or imperfect form, but the meaning is unaffected.) Although the Hiphil is transitive and takes a direct object ("his heart"), the subject—the one who performs the action—is, in the MT, Pharaoh himself. The LXX has no direct object and uses an aorist passive to state that "his heart became heavy" (ἐβαρύνθη ἡ καρδία αὐτοῦ). For the intransitive meaning of this Greek passive form of βαρύνω, see the point above on Ex 7:14.

- Ex 8:19 (MT/LXX 8:15): When the plague of gnats ended, the MT reverted to the same statement as in Ex 7:13 and Ex 7:22: "and the heart of Pharaoh was strong/ hard" (וַיֶּחֱזַק לֵב־פַּרְעֹה, Ex 8:19 [MT 8:15]). The LXX replicates its rendering from Ex 7:22: "and the heart of Pharaoh became hard" (καὶ ἐσκληρύνθη ἡ καρδία Φαραω, Ex 8:19 [LXX 8:15]).

- Ex 8:32 (MT/LXX 8:28): Following the fourth plague, that of flies, the report of Ex 8:15 (MT 8:11) is essentially repeated with the same causative Hiphil verb (but here in a usual form, an imperfect with *waw* consecutive): "and Pharaoh made his heart heavy" (וַיַּכְבֵּד פַּרְעֹה אֶת־לִבּוֹ, Ex 8:32 [MT 8:28]). As in Ex 8:15 (MT/LXX 8:11), it is noteworthy that the subject of the transitive verb is Pharaoh himself. The LXX employs the verb βαρύνω, as in Ex 8:15 (LXX 8:11); 9:7, 34. Whereas aorist passive forms appear in Ex 8:15 (LXX 8:11) and Ex 9:7, here (and in Ex 9:34) the aorist is active voice: "and Pharaoh made his heart heavy" (καὶ ἐβάρυνεν Φαραω τὴν καρδίαν αὐτοῦ, Ex 8:28).

- Ex 9:7: When the plague strikes the livestock of the Egyptians, the Hebrew restates the stative Qal verb used in Ex 7:14 as an equivalent imperfect with *waw* consecutive: "and the heart of Pharaoh was heavy" (וַיִּכְבַּד לֵב פַּרְעֹה, Ex 9:7). The aorist passive verb form used in Ex 8:15 (LXX 8:11) is repeated here: "the heart of Pharaoh became heavy" (ἐβαρύνθη ἡ καρδία Φαραω, Ex 9:7).

---

[78] Muraoka treats βεβάρηται in Ex 7:14 as a form of βαρύνω and has no separate entry for βαρέω. Instead of "become unfavorably disposed," a more appropriate meaning for this verse may be "to be unreceptive, unresponsive"; for active forms, Muraoka, 3, gives "to make unreceptive, unresponsive."

[79] The English "to harden" is acceptable here if understood intransitively, as in, for example, "as the molten metal cooled, it hardened."

The assertions thus far all contend that it is *the nature or state of Pharaoh's heart to be hard or that Pharaoh himself hardens his own heart* against Yahweh's will as spoken to him repeatedly through Moses.

It is at this point that Paul quotes from the narrative of Exodus. Yahweh has been particularly patient with the Pharaoh up through five plagues, a point Paul asserts in general terms in Rom 9:22. He is, after all, the God whom Paul specifically identifies as "the God who shows mercy" (9:16).

Then a momentous change occurs. During the sixth plague, of boils, *for the very first time* the text says: "and Yahweh made the heart of Pharaoh strong/hard" (וַיְחַזֵּק יְהוָה אֶת־לֵב פַּרְעֹה, Ex 9:12). Now the verb form is not a stative Qal (as it was in Ex 7:13, 22, 8:19 [MT 8:15], which have חָזַק, and Ex 7:14; 9:7, which have כָּבֵד), but a Piel, which gives חָזַק a causative sense (BDB). The LXX expresses the same meaning by translating with an active, transitive verb, with Yahweh as its subject: "and the Lord hardened the heart of Pharaoh" (ἐσκλήρυνεν δὲ κύριος τὴν καρδίαν Φαραω, Ex 9:12). Similar terminology reflects the same action of Yahweh upon the Pharaoh's heart in Ex 10:20, 27; 11:10; 14:4, 8, as well as upon the Egyptians generally in Ex 14:17. Interestingly, Ex 9:34 reports that Pharaoh and his officials hardened their own hearts (וַיַּכְבֵּד לִבּוֹ הוּא וַעֲבָדָיו; LXX: καὶ ἐβάρυνεν αὐτοῦ τὴν καρδίαν καὶ τῶν θεραπόντων αὐτοῦ). Finally, in Ex 9:35 the text again reports that the Pharaoh's heart "was strong/hard" (וַיֶּחֱזַק לֵב פַּרְעֹה). The LXX corresponds: "and the heart of Pharaoh was hard" (καὶ ἐσκληρύνθη ἡ καρδία Φαραω).

As a result, the inspired Hebrew text (corroborated by the LXX) supports the view that the Pharaoh whom God had raised up for his saving purposes was free to let Israel go at any time, at least up until Yahweh's hardening of his heart. If Pharaoh had, in fact, freed his many Israelite slaves in humble submission to the God in whose name Moses spoke, Yahweh's saving power and name would have been announced throughout the land of Egypt and, ultimately, "in all the earth" (Rom 9:17). As 10:12–13 will soon make clear on the basis of Joel 2, "everyone" who, that is, "whoever" (πᾶς ... ὃς ἄν), calls on the name of the Lord will be saved (Joel 2:32 [MT 3:5]). Using Joel 2 as his text, Peter boldly proclaims the same truth on Pentecost (Acts 2:21, 38–39). Thus "everyone" means "everyone." There are no exceptions to "all," and God wills to show mercy to "all" (πάντας, Rom 11:32), including the Pharaoh.

But the flow of the narrative also makes it plainly evident that "Pharaoh wanted none of the mercy for himself and for his own nation and with all his might intended to block the plans of that mercy with regard to Israel."[80] The point to be drawn from the narrative is that God's hardening of Pharaoh in Exodus 9 was a *response* to his hardened nature and his repeated self-hardening against God's recurrently revealed will for him, expressed in Yahweh's call to let Israel go. The overall context of the quote from Ex 9:16 in Rom 9:17,

---

[80] Lenski, *Romans*, 617.

therefore, *does not convey a predetermined judgment against the Pharaoh or that he was predestined not to believe the divine Word*. The text seems very careful expressly *not* to say this.[81]

Hardening Elsewhere in the New Testament

The other uses of the verb σκληρύνω, "to harden," in the NT also speak *against* the idea that it carries with it the notion of a predetermined decision of God. In Acts 19, after Paul spoke the Gospel boldly for three months in the synagogue at Ephesus (Acts 19:8), "some became hardened and were unpersuaded" (τινες ἐσκληρύνοντο καὶ ἠπείθουν, Acts 19:9). One could read the imperfect verb ἐσκληρύνοντο as a middle voice, "they were hardening themselves," or as a passive, "they were being hardened." Even if the latter were the case, the active voice of the second verb in Acts 19:9, ἠπείθουν, "were unpersuaded,"[82] indicates that the passive ἐσκληρύνοντο should be understood in an active but intransitive sense,[83] just like the passive forms of σκληρύνω in LXX Ex 7:22; 8:15 (ET 8:19); 9:35; and the Hebrew stative verbs in the verses from Exodus cited above. Furthermore, both the three months in Acts 19:8 and the imperfect tenses in Acts 19:9 express a *process* of (self-)hardening against the Word of God which resembles the narrative regarding Pharaoh presented above.

All the other NT uses of σκληρύνω, "harden," are in Hebrews (3:8, 13, 15; 4:7). Each of these passages uses it in a prohibition by which the author of Hebrews applies the warning of Ps 95:8 (LXX Ps 94:8), "do not harden your hearts" (in Heb 3:8, 15; 4:7 the author cites the LXX: μὴ σκληρύνητε τὰς καρδίας ὑμῶν). This warning was originally given to the Israelites in the wilderness. The first half of the psalm speaks to those whose Creator and Shepherd is Yahweh (Ps 95:6–7). The second half (Ps 95:8–11) then issues a stern warning against hardening their own hearts specifically against the call to worship the One who is their God (Ps 95:1–2, 6). The author of Hebrews repeatedly reissues the same warning to his believing hearers (apparently Jewish Christians). In Heb 3:8, 15; 4:7, the negated aorist subjunctive σκληρύνητε "is used to forbid the occurrence of an action."[84] The Jewish Christians apparently were being

---

[81] The contexts of the earlier declarations by Yahweh that "I will strengthen/harden his heart" (Ex 4:21; 7:3), spoken before Pharaoh had heard the first plea to let his people go, imply that those declarations refer to this subsequent hardening that began in Ex 9:12 after Pharaoh had repeatedly rejected the divine Word. Anyone who rejects the Word of God hardens his or her heart against it, and God foreknew that unbelieving Pharaoh would do this. However, God's foreknowledge, which is part of his omniscience, is not to be equated with a divine predetermination. Knowing in advance how someone will react is not the same as causing a person to react in that manner; see FC Ep XI 1–4 and FC SD XI 4. See further the discussion of Pharaoh in FC SD XI 83–86.

[82] See ἀπειθέω, "to be unpersuaded" (by the Christian faith), in Rom 2:8; 10:21; 11:30–31; 15:31.

[83] See Voelz, *Fundamental Greek Grammar*, 144–46.

[84] Wallace, *Greek Grammar*, 469, who calls this construction a prohibitive subjunctive. Technically, the form could also be a present subjunctive, but an aorist makes better sense contextually with the nuance of not beginning to harden oneself.

tempted to revert to Judaism, but had not yet turned away from Christ. *The contexts of Psalm 95 and Hebrews certainly do not portray people who have been predetermined to harden themselves or to be hardened by their God.* In other words, God is not pushing them away from himself or toward evil (see Rom 11:1). Instead, the Jewish-Christian believers, like the Israelites in the wilderness, who hear the repeated warning are called to repentance and renewed faith, instilled by the Word of God. They could choose to respond with hardening, but God's gracious will is for their repentant returning to the Good News, his promise of eternal rest (Heb 4:1–2).

This interpretation of hardening also fits Paul's use of the cognate noun σκληρότης, "hardness, callousness," in Rom 2:5. First Paul warns "you, the person who is judging" (2:3), against scorning "the abundance of his kindness and forbearance and patience [μακροθυμία], while ignoring that the kindness of God is leading you into repentance" (2:4). If they do scorn it, then, he charges that "according to your callousness [σκληρότης] and [your] unrepentant heart, you are storing up for yourself wrath" (2:5). The significant reappearance of God's "patience" (μακροθυμία) in 9:22 will be discussed further below, but its applicability to the Pharaoh comes across clearly in the Exodus narrative. As Origen observes: "Although Pharaoh's wickedness was enormous, God in his patience did not withdraw the possibility of conversion from him."[85] Instead of recognizing God's repeated merciful callings, Pharaoh responded according to the callousness of his own unrepentant heart and, therefore, received the "wrath" Paul mentions in Rom 2:5. In 2:4–5 Paul warns those who judge others not to follow such an example, for it only results in doom.

Conclusions to Romans 9:14–18

So whom does God will to harden (9:18)? Calvin contends: "Paul's purpose is to make us accept the fact that it has seemed good to God to enlighten some in order that they may be saved, and blind others in order that they may be destroyed."[86] Moo similarly asserts:

> The "hardening" Paul portrays here, then, is a sovereign act of God that is not *caused* by anything in those individuals who are hardened. And 9:22–23 and 11:7 suggest that the outcome of hardening is damnation. It seems, then, that this text, in its context, provides important exegetical support for the controversial doctrine of "double predestination"; just as God decides, on the basis of nothing but his own sovereign pleasure, to bestow his grace and so save some individuals, so he also decides, on the basis of nothing but his own sovereign pleasure, to pass over others and so to damn them.[87]

But the Exodus narrative and the review of Scripture's use of the term σκληρύνω, "harden," conducted above, lead to the conclusion that the assertions

---

[85] Origen, *Romans* (Bray, *Romans*, ACCS NT 6:258).

[86] Calvin, *Romans*, 207.

[87] Moo, *Romans*, 598.

of Calvin and Moo must be rejected. First of all, the hardening of Pharaoh was not immediate, much less already accomplished before hearing the Word of God. Second, at least throughout the first five plagues, Pharaoh's hardening was also not final; indeed, Yahweh's hardening of him had not yet even begun! Finally, Exodus demonstrates how God was incredibly patient with the Pharaoh, a point Paul reiterates in general terms (Rom 9:22), prior to any hardening of him. More true to the witness of Scripture, therefore, is Lenski's observation that "the only objects of this hardening are men who have first hardened themselves against all God's mercy."[88]

While necessary in light of theological misunderstandings, this extended discussion of hardening poses the danger of leading one off the main track of Romans. *It is tangential to Paul's repeated emphasis upon God's mercy.* It also provides a clear illustration regarding how too many discussions about Romans emphasize the wrong actor. In 9:17–18 Paul's focus is not on humanity, the Pharaoh,[89] or Israel, but is squarely fixed upon God.

> The thought is not so much of judgment directed against Pharaoh but of God's covenant mercy to Israel. … The whole argument is mounted from a Jewish perspective: it is as a Jew that Paul makes a point in relation to his fellow Jews; Pharaoh serves as a foil to the central point held in common—that is, God's choice of Israel as an expression of his sovereign mercy.[90]

Yet Dunn's insertion of "sovereign" to describe God's "mercy" remains unwarranted. This is not at all to dismiss the sovereignty or absolute freedom of God, but Paul does not use such terminology, and his emphasis does not reside there. Instead, in the Exodus narrative referenced by Paul, we observe God in action,

> fulfilling his mercy on [Israel] in great pity when they were being crushed and ground to nothing by a fierce tyrant. Israel saw that God's power alone carried out the promises and the mercy. This is not mere omnipotence or omnipotence set over against mercy but omnipotence serving mercy.[91]

Mercy then remains the dominant note which resounds throughout 9:14–18. "Show mercy" occurs in the OT quotation cited in 9:15, recurs in 9:16, and is replayed again in 9:18. Paul's quotation of Ex 9:16 in Rom 9:17 introduces the context in which God speaks to the Pharaoh. Paul thus provides historical evidence that *God's saving power and name will prevail* as it did in the exodus. Precisely how God's saving will worked itself out in relationship to this Pharaoh was the result of Pharaoh's sinful, impenitent will. How did he respond to God's call of mercy for Israel? "Pharaoh did what Pharaoh willed to do; he opposed the Word of God that Moses brought to him."[92] After continued obstinate and

---

[88] Lenski, *Romans*, 616.

[89] Lenski, *Romans*, 614, contends that "Pharaoh is a minor figure, a side issue," but this may overstate the matter in the opposite direction.

[90] Dunn, *Romans*, 554.

[91] Lenski, *Romans*, 614.

[92] Franzmann, *Romans*, 176.

stubborn refusals, God responded by confirming the Pharaoh in his own hardened state. The question at hand in Paul's day is "how will Israel respond?" Paul engages in and analyzes the matter from 9:30 through 10:21.

Paul's emphasis on God's mercy in 9:14–18 resides within a larger context. Paul is engaged in rebuking the assertion that God might in any way be "*unrighteous*" (9:14; see also 3:5–6). *This would, however, surely be the case if he doled out his mercy arbitrarily as in the doctrine of double predestination.* It would also be so if he reached out in reaction to human "works" (9:12) or human "willing" or "striving" (9:16) instead of persistently calling all by his universal mercy (11:32).

Finally, these verses reiterate the major point introduced in 9:6. God's Word to Pharaoh did not fail; God's Word to Israel is not fallen. The following foundational truths run throughout Romans and are especially critical for a proper understanding of chapters 9–11:[93]

1. The OT is the Word of God, an efficacious disclosure of God's being, his universal mercy, and his will to save all people.[94]

2. God himself, as disclosed in his Word, is the standard of righteousness. Paul is not *proving* that God is righteous by applying to his deeds an abstract standard of righteousness; he is illustrating the righteousness of God by pointing to God's righteous words and merciful, salvific deeds of old.

Why, then, the extended discussion of hardening? The narrative of Exodus reveals what Paul reluctantly affirms later in Romans 10–11. With great irony, those who now most closely resemble the Pharaoh are contemporary Israelites, descended from those whom Yahweh redeemed from Egypt with a mighty demonstration of his saving power (ἐνδείξωμαι … τὴν δύναμίν μου, 9:17; cf. Ps 95:8). As God dealt with that Pharaoh, Paul observes, so he deals with "some" in Israel (3:3; 11:14; the "not all" in 10:16), namely, those who similarly do not believe the Good News of God's saving power (1:16; 10:16), now fully revealed "through the redemption, the one in Christ Jesus" (3:24), an even greater "proof" of his righteousness (ἔνδειξις in 3:25, 26). The verb σκληρύνω, "harden," in 9:18 has "exactly the same sense" as the verb πωρόω, "harden," and its cognate noun πώρωσις, "hardening," which will be used of unbelieving Israel in 11:7 and 11:25 respectively.[95] *God, therefore, hardens those who obstinately choose to persist in unbelief* (3:3; 10:16, 20, 23).[96]

---

[93] The following two points are adapted from Franzmann, *Romans*, 177.

[94] Starting with Chrysostom in the early church, theologians have distinguished between God's "first" or "antecedent" will to save all people and his "second" or "consequent" will to condemn those who reject his mercy (see Chrysostom, *Homilies on Ephesians*, 1 [*NPNF*[1] 13:52]). This distinction is evident in Scripture in, e.g., Jn 3:17–18. See the discussion in Gerhard, *On Election and Reprobation* (commonplace 10), §§ 78–80 (pp. 152–53). See also Pieper, *Christian Dogmatics*, 1:454–55.

[95] K. L. Schmidt and M. A. Schmidt, "σκληρύνω," *TDNT* 5:1030.

[96] Thus FC SD XI 40 states that God "has also ordained in his counsel that he would harden, reject, and condemn all who, when they are called through the Word, spurn the Word and persistently resist the Holy Spirit who wants to work efficaciously in them through the Word."

All of this explains Paul's anguish and his ardent pleas in behalf of ethnic Israel (e.g., 9:2; 10:1). But, just as God was patient with the Pharaoh, *how much more so* is he patient with the portion of Israel that persists in unbelief (see 11:23). His hardening of this people is by no means permanent (e.g., 10:21; 11:14–15, 23–24). Instead, his hands are stretched out to them (10:21), and his merciful call is to all people. Such is the God who shows mercy (9:16).

Thou Art the Potter; We All Are like Clay (9:19–21)[97]

No Talking Back! (9:19–20a)

The Source of the Challenge (9:19)

Rom 9:14 began with a rhetorical question couched in the first person plural: "what then will we say?" In 9:19, Paul heightens the interaction by engaging in direct conversation. He inserts a possible retort which is introduced by "you [singular] will therefore say to me." The second person singular recalls Paul's comparable use throughout much of Romans 2 (e.g., 2:1–5, 17–27).[98] The level of intensity in the diatribe increases even further here with repeated follow up questions bantering back and forth in 9:19–23. Who is the singular "you" for and to whom Paul speaks? Augustine and (Pseudo-)Constantius go so far as to propose that Paul assumes the role of "devil's advocate."[99] Moo more plausibly suggests that "Paul's 'opponent' may … be a Pharisaic Jew who criticizes Paul's doctrine for not leaving enough room for human free will."[100] This is improperly based, at least in part, upon Moo's exclusion of any human free will based upon his advocacy of unconditional double predestination as discussed above. Free will is hardly the focus of the conversation in Romans 9.[101] But the assumption of the viewpoint of a Pharisee or Pharisaic-minded Christian (e.g., Acts 15:5; cf. Acts 11:2–3) seems most plausible. If so, the parties in the second person singular conversation would essentially be the same as those engaged in Rom 2:17–27.

The speaker in 9:19 offers a provocative rebuttal to 9:14–18 and to 9:18 in particular: "Why then is he still finding fault? For who has set himself against and withstood his intention?" (9:19). Dunn poses the essence of the challenge in

---

[97] Note the comparable song lyrics from stanza 1 of "Have Thine Own Way" by Adelaide A. Pollard (first published in the *Northfield Hymnal* with Alexander's Supplement [1907]; public domain):

Have Thine own way, Lord! Have Thine own way! Thou art the Potter, I am the clay. Mold me and make me after Thy will, While I am waiting, yielded and still.

[98] See "Rhetorical and Epistolary Forms" in "Structure and Outline" in the commentary introduction; see also the introduction to Romans 2 and the commentary on 2:17.

[99] (Pseudo-)Constantius, *Romans*; Augustine, *Commentary on Statements in Romans*, 62 (Bray, *Romans*, ACCS NT 6:256 and 6:259, respectively).

[100] Moo, *Romans*, 600, n. 60. He references the discussion of Josephus in *Antiquities*, 13.171–73, where the Pharisees are characterized as advocating "that certain events are the work of Fate, but not all; as to other events, it depends upon ourselves whether they shall take place or not" (13.172 [LCL]).

[101] For the topic, see AC XVIII, "Free Will," and Ap XVIII, "Free Will."

this way: "Yet if *God's* act is the *effective* cause of *human* hardness, what room is left for *human* responsibility?"[102] But this once again betrays an anthropocentric view. Paul places his emphasis upon the challenge that *God* is unrighteous (9:14) in finding fault with humanity.

Though the basis for the assertion is not the same, the comparable dialogue in 3:5–6 should be kept in mind: "But if our unrighteousness demonstrates God's righteousness, what will we say? God, the one who brings wrath, is not unrighteous, is he? (I am speaking in a human way.) May it never come to be! If so, how will God judge the world?" In Romans 3, the challenge proposes that if our unrighteousness merely serves, by way of contrast, to provide further evidence for God's righteousness, then God would be *unrighteous* in imposing his wrath upon us for our unrighteousness. Paul rejects that hypothesis (3:6) and affirms the condemnation of those who make it (3:8). In Romans 9, however, the assertion rests on a different supposition. Here the claim that God improperly finds fault rests on the assumption of the second question in 9:19. It implies that no one can oppose *God's* intention. If it is impossible to resist God, then why can he find fault with any of us?

Who Can Stand against God's Intention and Prevail? (9:19)

The key to understanding this verse properly resides in recognizing *both* components of the perfect tense verb ἀνθέστηκεν, "has set himself against *and* withstood." For example, ignoring the past action ("has") leads to the assertion that "the perfect tense has no past-referring significance here; it is a 'gnomic' perfect, used like the present tense to state a general truth."[103] It is similarly improper to read the indicative like a deliberative subjunctive by inserting "can" into the statement: "who can resist?"[104] Another odd summation suggests: "The point is not that it is impossible for men to resist, but that no man does, as a matter of fact, resist."[105] All these interpretations reveal the fallacy of considering only the past impact of the perfect, "who *has* set himself against his [God's] intention?" The rather obvious answer to that questions remains *"everyone has and everyone does!"* The facts of history illustrate that, ever since the fall, people have continually and consistently resisted God's intention. For example, on the basis of Ps 14:2–3, Rom 3:11–12 asserts: "There is not one who understands; there is not one who seeks out God. All turned away; together they became worthless."

Indeed, God's forbearance has at least temporarily allowed *all people* to oppose his intention, plan, and will in the hope that his patience would lead them to repentance (2:4–5; see also 9:22–23). This is exemplified in the past by the

---

[102] Dunn, *Romans*, 555.

[103] Moo, *Romans*, 600, n. 62.

[104] So RSV; NEB; Barrett, *Romans*, 184, 187; for a discussion of deliberative subjunctives, see Wallace, *Greek Grammar*, 465–68.

[105] Cranfield, *Romans*, 490.

case of the Pharaoh who "set himself against" God's call to let his people go during the first five plagues (Pharaoh hardened his *own* heart [Ex 8:15, 32 (MT/LXX 8:11, 28); 9:34]). He provides a profound example of the "past-referring significance"[106] of the Greek verb ἀνθέστηκεν (Rom 9:19). The Pharaoh was able to "set himself against" God's intention repeatedly up to a certain point. This is because

> God's power is patience, and it is a very great power indeed. For who would not be overawed by the enormous patience of God? For he says that it is for this reason that he has agreed to let Pharaoh rule, that it may be shown how patient he is.[107]

But the additional *present implication* of the Greek perfect tense here means that he was not able to *withstand* Yahweh's intent to display his saving power to free his people (see 9:17). In other words, the resistant Pharaoh *did not prevail.* Understood in this way, the perfect tense of ἀνθέστηκεν makes "perfect" sense!

LXX Job 9:19 uses the future tense of the same verb (ἀνθίστημι) to emphasize the same eventual outcome. Job is agonizing over his inability to render himself righteous and withstand God's overwhelming power (Job 9:1–18): "for because he prevails by force, who therefore will withstand his judgment?" (ὅτι μὲν γὰρ ἰσχύι κρατεῖ· τίς οὖν κρίματι αὐτοῦ ἀντιστήσεται, LXX Job 9:19). With the same verb and in language very similar to the final clause of Rom 9:19, Wisdom likewise affirms that no one will be able to stand against God's judgment: "For who will say, 'What did you do?' or who will withstand your judgment?" (τίς γὰρ ἐρεῖ τί ἐποίησας; ἢ τίς ἀντιστήσεται τῷ κρίματί σου; Wisdom 12:12). As 3:6 affirms, God will rightly judge the world. *On that day*, no one will withstand God's judgment!

Similarly, when the Pharaoh repeatedly set himself against God's saving intention, eventually he was not able to withstand it. In Paul's day, many in Israel had been resistant up to the present (e.g., 3:3; 10:1, 16–21; 11:20), but such resistance will not ultimately prevail against God's coming judgment (e.g., 2:8–9, 12, 16; 3:19–20). Prior to that final day, however, Paul contends that there is no unrighteousness with God *in showing mercy based upon who he is* and not based upon our willing or striving (9:16). Indeed, all too often our willing and striving are contrary to his will and resistant to his mercy.

Paul's Retort (9:20a)

However, to deride God for finding fault with those who presently set themselves against his saving intention prompts exasperation from Paul:[108] "O you human being! On the contrary, who are you to talk back to God?" (9:20a). While

---

[106] Moo, *Romans*, 600, n. 62.

[107] Oecumenius, *Romans* (Bray, *Romans*, ACCS NT 6:258).

[108] Although one might question his characterization of the opponent being engaged, Bruce, *Romans*, 179, eloquently captures the level of consternation: "Paul has been misunderstood and unfairly criticized through failure to recognize that it is the God-defying rebel and not the bewildered seeker after God whose mouth he so peremptorily shuts."

Paul's retort is not accusatory in a completely derogatory sense, Barrett's rendition of ὦ ἄνθρωπε as "my dear sir" makes it overly polite.[109] In light of what follows, the vocative ἄνθρωπε, "O man," highlights the status of the addressee as a created human being.[110] The μενοῦνγε, "on the contrary," which follows is more corrective than condemnatory. As in Phil 3:8, it conveys a "heightening" in the tone of the argument and, as in 10:18, it begins to sharpen the contrast between Creator and created.[111]

"Who are you to talk back to God?" (9:20a). The emphatic presence and placement of "you" (σύ, singular) establishes an adversarial stance, but also one of active engagement in dialogue (as in 2:17–27). The notion of talking back (cf. ἀντιλέγοντα in 10:21) presumes God has said something first. In this context, one can presume the talking back is a reply most directly to the words of God in Ex 33:19 and Ex 9:16, cited in Rom 9:15 and 9:17, respectively. It might also signal that the whole exposition of God's Word since 9:6 is also coming to a head in a manner which culminates in 9:24.

Vessels for God's Use: Some Honorable—Others Ordinary (9:20b–21)

Paul's reply draws, once again, upon the Scriptures. The verse division would go better between 9:20a and 9:20b, allowing the remainder of 9:20 to flow into 9:21. The *final* question in 9:20, expecting a negative reply, responds most immediately to the presumptive attempt to talk back to God (9:20a). The form of the question in 9:21 signals a positive answer and conveys a more general response to the larger issue at hand.

> That which is formed will not say to the one who formed it, "Why did you make me this way?" will it? [21]Or does not the potter have authority [over] the clay to make out of the same lump a vessel which is meant for an honorable use, on the one hand, and, on the other, [a vessel] which is for ordinary use? (9:20b–21)

The Background and Use of the Potter and Clay Image

(d) E.g., Job 10:9; 38:14; Ps 2:9; Is 29:16; 41:25; 45:9–10; 64:8–9 (MT 64:7–8); Jer 18:1–12; see also Wisdom 15:7–17; Sirach 27:5; 33:13; 38:29–30

The picture of the potter and the clay occurs repeatedly in the OT.[d] In these diverse contexts,

> various applications are made of the potter-vessel relationship; it can depict man's accountability to his Maker (Is. 29:16), or the impiety of man in questioning the ways of God (Is. 45:9), or the humility of an appeal made by a sinful people to the mercy of the God who created them (Is. 64:8 [MT 64:7]), or God's freedom to visit wrath or mercy on a nation according to His will, even if the nation is His chosen people (Jer. 18:6). Basic to all is the idea of God's unquestionable authority over the history of His creature, man.[112]

---

[109] Barrett, *Romans*, 184.

[110] Moo, *Romans*, 601; Cranfield, *Romans*, 490; Dunn, *Romans*, 556.

[111] Cranfield, *Romans*, 490–91.

[112] Franzmann, *Romans*, 179.

The language of Rom 9:20 draws most closely on Is 29:16, which reads as follows in the LXX:[113]

μὴ ἐρεῖ τὸ πλάσμα τῷ πλάσαντι οὐ σύ με ἔπλασας; ἢ τὸ ποίημα τῷ ποιήσαντι οὐ συνετῶς με ἐποίησας;

That which is formed will not say to the one who formed it, "You did not form me." Neither [will] that which was made [say] to the one who made [it], "You did not wisely make me."

The initial part of Paul's quotation in 9:20b follows the LXX exactly (μὴ ἐρεῖ τὸ πλάσμα τῷ πλάσαντι, "that which is formed will not say to the one who formed it"). As far as talking back to God, this settles the matter. Of course the clay *never* talks back to the potter! But humans challenge God nevertheless. Paul cites only one challenge. It is not the initial one in Isaiah, "you did not form me." It leans closer to Isaiah's second, "you did not wisely make me."

In Rom 9:20b, the assertion becomes a provocative question: "*why* did you make me this way?" This language aligns well with a portion of Is 45:9 in the LXX which reads: "The clay will not say to the potter, 'What are you making?'" (μὴ ἐρεῖ ὁ πηλὸς τῷ κεραμεῖ τί ποιεῖς, LXX Is 45:9). Wisdom 12:12 has similar wording and is relevant as it employs the same verb as Paul in Rom 9:19 (ἀνθίστημι, "set against and withstand"): "For who will say, 'What did you do?' or who will withstand your judgment?" (τίς γὰρ ἐρεῖ τί ἐποίησας; ἢ τίς ἀντιστήσεται τῷ κρίματί σου;); see also Wisdom 15:7, cited below.

What theological background stands most prominently behind Paul's truncated quotation? Dunn identifies one possible location: "The use of πλάσσειν ['to form'] in Gen 2:7–8, 15 [God's creation of Adam from clay] was quite often taken up in Jewish thought in talk of God's creative activity."[114] But that connotation seems a bit off the track in the context of the Isaiah references and, more importantly, with regard to the force of Paul's argument. He is hardly engaged in a debate over the creative work of God. More relevant is Dunn's second observation "that πλάσσειν ['to form'] is used also of God's election of Israel."[115] This ties in particularly well with the extended use of the potter analogy in Jeremiah 18, where Yahweh's actions in relationship with the apostate "house of Israel" are explicitly under consideration (e.g., Jer 18:6, 11).

---

[113] The MT conveys the same underlying thoughts, but expresses them in a different manner and basically in reverse order:

הַפְכְּכֶם אִם־כְּחֹמֶר הַיֹּצֵר יֵחָשֵׁב כִּי־יֹאמַר מַעֲשֶׂה לְעֹשֵׂהוּ
לֹא עָשָׂנִי וְיֵצֶר אָמַר לְיוֹצְרוֹ לֹא הֵבִין׃

You turn things upside down! Shall the potter be regarded as the clay, that the thing made should say of its maker, "He did not make me"; or the thing formed say of him who formed it, "He has no understanding"? (Is 29:16 ESV)

[114] Dunn, *Romans*, 556, citing as examples Job 10:8–9; Ps 33:15 (LXX 32:15); 2 Macc 7:23; *Sibylline Oracles* 3:24–25; Josephus, *Antiquities*, 1.32, 34; 1QS 11:22. Dunn notes that in Philo πλάσσω is used exclusively of God.

[115] Dunn, *Romans*, 557, citing, e.g., Is 43:1, 7; 44:2, 21, 24; cf. Is 49:5; 53:11.

The Same Clay, Different Uses (9:21)

The clay's presumptive question in Rom 9:20b, "why did you make me this way?" points ahead to Paul's follow-up question in 9:21. It expresses the reasons *why* the potter forms vessels in different ways: "or does not the potter have authority [over] the clay [πηλός] to make out of the same lump a vessel which is meant for an honorable use, on the one hand, and, on the other, [a vessel] which is for ordinary use?" (9:21).

Dunn again points to the image of a potter creating with "clay" (πηλός).[116] However, Paul's discussion of God's relations with Israel in this context means the language regarding vessels is more appropriately rooted specifically in Is 45:9 and Jer 18:6–10. Dunn himself acknowledges: "The more natural sense of the metaphor is of vessels put to differing uses within history."[117] However, Paul is not defending God's prerogative "to use the nation [Israel] in a negative way in salvation history."[118] That problematic interpretation stems from two faulty assumptions.

First, while nations are the primary focus of the potter and clay imagery in Jeremiah 18 (e.g., Jer 18:7–10), Paul is not discussing various nations in Romans 9. As discussed in the introduction to Romans 9–11 (see "God's People"), Paul's uses of "Israel" and "Israelites" are primarily religious descriptions which emphasize the spiritual status of God's people. Even Paul's treatment of the Pharaoh in 9:17–18 does not bring the nation of Egypt into the discussion. The notion of political nations rising and falling is completely absent.

Second, it misreads in a negative way Paul's phrase εἰς ἀτιμίαν, "for ordinary use," as if it meant "for *dishonorable* use." Paul is not contrasting vessels of honor with vessels that are made for dishonor or, even worse, predestined to destruction. Paul speaks of "vessels of wrath" in 9:22, but one cannot use what he says there to contend that already in 9:21 the "ordinary" vessels are made for the purpose of wrath and destruction. That parallel simply does not work. Neither does it make any sense; what potter would go to the work and expense of making vessels only to smash them?

In fact, Wisdom 15:7 uses all three of the terms Paul employs in Rom 9:21, "potter" (κεραμεύς), "clay" (πηλός), and "vessel" (σκεῦος) in order to make the same type of contrasts Paul does:

> For when a potter [κεραμεύς] kneads the soft earth and laboriously molds each vessel for our service, he fashions out of the same clay [ἐκ τοῦ αὐτοῦ πηλοῦ] both the vessels [σκεύη] that serve clean uses [τῶν καθαρῶν ἔργων] and those for contrary uses, making all in like manner; but which shall be the use of each of these the worker in clay decides. (RSV)[119]

---

[116] Dunn, *Romans*, 557, citing Ps 2:9; Is 29:16; 41:25; 45:9; Jer 18:1–6; Sirach 33:13; *Testament of Naphtali* 2:2, 4; 1QS 11:22; 1QH.

[117] Dunn, *Romans*, 557, citing Rom 9:17 and its close parallel, 2 Tim 2:20; cf. 1 Thess 4:4; 1 Pet 3:7; and in the OT cf. especially Jer 22:28; Hos 8:8.

[118] Moo, *Romans*, 602.

[119] For a comprehensive study, see Linebaugh, *God, Grace, and Righteousness in Wisdom of Solomon and Paul's Letter to the Romans*.

The Jewish terminology of "clean" (καθαρός) in Wisdom 15:7 indicates that the "contrary" use is not for evil or destruction, but rather for the realm of the common and ordinary things of life.[120] The main point, both in Wisdom 15:7 and in Rom 9:21, conveys the potter's authority to make clay pots for varying good purposes, all from the same clay. The production results in "some vessels for noble, and some for menial, uses."[121]

Even more relevant, *Paul himself uses the same analogy with the same terminology in 2 Tim 2:20* in a manner which strongly affirms this as his understanding:

ἐν μεγάλῃ δὲ οἰκίᾳ οὐκ ἔστιν μόνον σκεύη χρυσᾶ καὶ ἀργυρᾶ ἀλλὰ καὶ ξύλινα καὶ ὀστράκινα, καὶ ἃ μὲν εἰς τιμὴν ἃ δὲ εἰς ἀτιμίαν.

But in a great house there are not only vessels of gold and silver but also wooden and clay [vessels], namely, [those] which [are], on the one hand, meant for honorable use and [those] which [are], on the other hand, meant for ordinary use.

Again, *all the vessels* are made to be used, and *all* are made for a beneficial purpose, though the dignity of their intended uses varies considerably.[122] A comparable contemporary distinction would be between the fine china we may bring out for meals on special occasions and the everyday dishes that serve adequately for most meals. A contrast can also be made regarding a large championship bowl placed up on the mantel versus one utilized more commonly (in both senses of the term) as a dishpan or even a bedpan. It bears reemphasizing, however, that in none of these instances are vessels made for no use or to be abused. *It is all the more unwarranted to contend that any are made in order to be smashed and destroyed. What artisan would take pleasure in utilizing his sovereign authority over the clay for that (cf. Ezek 18:23, 32; 33:11)?*

In the context of Romans 9, then, Paul's reference to "the same lump" (9:21) asserts that "Moses and Pharaoh, the obdurate Jews and the believing Christians, were of the same human clay."[123] Furthermore, God uses them all for "various functions in the on-going course of salvation-history for the sake of the fulfilment of His over-all purpose."[124] Thus the analogy reaches back to encompass the entire chapter thus far and explains the essence of God's call

---

[120] See the textual notes and the commentary on Mk 7:1–23 in Voelz, *Mark 1:1–8:26*, 448–74, especially 452–54.

[121] Cranfield, *Romans*, 492; he also states: "The thought of the differences in dignity among the vessels is also expressed" (491).

[122] Bruce, *Romans*, 184, recognizes the similarities between the two passages and their meaning by commenting on Rom 9:21 as follows:

One vessel for beauty and another for menial use. Cf. 2 Timothy 2:20, where, however, the vessels are made of various materials, and those which are for "ignoble" use are designed for less ornamental (but not necessarily less serviceable) purposes than those which are "for noble use."

[123] Lenski, *Romans*, 621.

[124] Cranfield, *Romans*, 492.

in 9:6–13. He calls some people to serve in various roles, including Abraham, Sarah, Isaac, Rebekah, Jacob, and Moses, but also Ishmael, Esau, and even the Pharaoh. Though some are privileged to have a more honored role than others (e.g., Isaac more than Ishmael in 9:7; Jacob more than Esau in 9:11–12), the Scriptures demonstrate that all have a role. More importantly, none are predetermined for rejection and wrath.

Two statements from the church fathers aptly draw together Paul's use of the potter and clay imagery in the context of 9:20b–21. Theodore of Mopsuestia utilizes questions as Paul does in asking: "Whoever heard of a clay pot made for menial use blaming the potter for the way it was made and demanding to be remolded for some better purpose?"[125] (Pseudo-)Constantius insightfully applies the analogy within the wider interrogative context of 9:19–21:

> There is no difference in the clay which the potter molds in his hand. He can make whatever kind of vessel he wants to, and the vessel cannot answer back and say how it would prefer to be made. But here, in words like *resist* and *find fault with God's will* [9:19], he shows the free will of the one who dares to draw back from the will of God.[126]

Vessels of Wrath and Vessels of Mercy (9:22–23)

Rom 9:22–23 forms an incomplete sentence. Essentially, Paul begins with the "if" clause of a conditional sentence (protasis), but never completes the "then" portion (apodosis).[127] The "ellipsis of the apodosis of a conditional sentence is fairly common in classical Greek and occurs several times in the NT."[128] That it occurs in one of Paul's letters, therefore, is not surprising, and, despite the grammatical omission, one readily gets his point. If the "if" clause anticipates a response, it could be something like this: "what is that to you?" A better solution entails retrieving a previous assertion from 9:20a. There Paul asks, "Who are you to talk back to God?" The same presumptive assertion serves well here also. In light of Paul's transition into 9:24, the phrase from 9:20 is inserted in brackets at the beginning of 9:22 in order to fill out Paul's thought as follows:

> [22]And [who are you to talk back] if God, willing to demonstrate [his] wrath and to make known his [saving] power, bore with much patience vessels of wrath which have been fitted for and are headed toward destruction, [23]and in order to make known the abundance of his glory upon vessels of mercy which he prepared beforehand for glory, [24]whom … ?

---

[125] Theodore of Mopsuestia, *Romans* (Bray, *Romans*, ACCS NT 6:262).

[126] (Pseudo-)Constantius, *Romans* (Bray, *Romans*, ACCS NT 6:260). As his quote implies, fallen people do have "free will" in the sense that they are able to choose to reject God and disbelieve the Good News of Christ. Yet sinful people do not have "free will" in the sense of being able to decide to believe and be saved. Faith is a gift worked entirely by God through his Word, and salvation is by grace alone, apart from any human works. See further AC XVIII, "Free Will," and Ap XVIII, "Free Will."

[127] Moo, *Romans*, 604; he also lays out other possibilities (604, n. 86).

[128] Cranfield, *Romans*, 492; he references Jn 6:62 and Acts 23:9: "what if … ?"; and Lk 19:42: "if only … !" (492–93).

The "and if" (εἰ δέ) which opens 9:22 does *not* simply restate the thought of 9:20–21. Instead, it introduces Paul's final response to the assertions of 9:14, "There is not unrighteousness with God, is there?" and 9:19, "Why then is he still finding fault? For who has set himself against and withstood his intention?" Paul's focus remains firmly *upon God* and, though he begins with "if" (εἰ), "the conditional clause states what Paul believes to be true—it is not hypothetical."[129]

God's Willing (9:22)

Scholars have debated the force of "willing" (the adverbial participle θέλων). It is said to have either a concessive ("although")[130] or causal force ("because").[131] But this presents a false alternative and also strives to separate imposed grammatical categories too narrowly.[132] A better understanding recognizes that "the participle is ambiguous and would probably be read simply as a relative … , describing what is always true of God."[133] What follows θέλων in 9:22 describes God's "willing," which exerts itself in two ways, *both* "to demonstrate [his] wrath" (ἐνδείξασθαι τὴν ὀργήν) *and* also "to make known his [saving] power" (γνωρίσαι τὸ δυνατὸν αὐτοῦ).

These two dimensions stand fully consistent with the "righteousness of God" (δικαιοσύνη … θεοῦ) of 1:17, which Paul elaborates upon extensively in Romans 1–4. First, Paul delineates and defends God's righteous wrath upon all human unrighteousness in 1:18–3:20. Then, in 3:21–4:25, the Good News of his saving power in Jesus Christ also reveals and even proves God's righteousness (e.g., 3:21–26). The use of the noun "proof/demonstration" (ἔνδειξις) in 3:25 and 3:26 parallels the presence of the cognate verb "demonstrate" (ἐνδείκνυμι), along with "my power" (τὴν δύναμίν μου), in 9:17. The latter also stands synonymous with the cognate adjective in the expression "his [saving] power" (τὸ δυνατὸν αὐτοῦ) in 9:22.[134] It further recalls what Abraham believed about God in 4:21, "he is powerful [δυνατός ἐστιν] also to do," and extends all the way back to the theme in 1:16: "for I am not ashamed of the Good News, because it is [the] power of God [δύναμις … θεοῦ] into salvation for everyone who believes."[135] The specific implications of "his [saving] power" (τὸ δυνατὸν αὐτοῦ, 9:22) in this context are explained more fully in 9:23–24.

God's Patience (9:22)

Rather than reflecting any kind of predetermined or eternal decision, Paul's whole discussion since 9:6 has been describing how God interacts with

---

[129] Cranfield, *Romans*, 493.

[130] So Sanday and Headlam, *Romans*, 261; similarly, Cranfield, *Romans*, 493–94; Lenski, *Romans*, 622.

[131] Moo, *Romans*, 605.

[132] See Middendorf, *Romans 1–8*, 53–54.

[133] Dunn, *Romans*, 558.

[134] See the commentary on 9:17.

[135] Middendorf, *Romans 1–8*, 86–87.

humanity *within history*. Here Paul first summarizes how "God deals with recalcitrant humanity."[136] He "bore with much patience [ἤνεγκεν ἐν πολλῇ μακροθυμίᾳ] vessels of wrath which have been fitted for and are headed toward destruction" (9:22).

In contrast with how God deals with Israel, 2 Macc 6:14 claims God's patience with Gentiles has a punitive function: "for in the case of other nations the Lord waits patiently [ἀναμένει μακροθυμῶν] to punish them until they have reached the full measure of their sins" (RSV). In Maccabees, the purpose is "to punish" (κολάσαι). But Paul has already revealed the purpose of God's "patience" (μακροθυμία) in Rom 2:4: "or do you think scornfully of the abundance of his kindness and forbearance and patience, while ignoring that the kindness of God is leading you into repentance?" Moo concedes: "On two other occasions Paul ascribes 'patience' (*makrothymia*) to God, and both assume a positive purpose for that patience: allowing an opportunity for repentance (Rom. 2:4; 1 Tim. 1:16)."[137] As 2 Macc 6:15–16 goes on to state, this positive purpose was *expected* in the case of Israel. Indeed, "God's patience with his chosen people was one of Israel's most common refrains."[138]

Paul's climactic affirmation in Rom 2:11 asserts that God's "patience" (μακροθυμία, 2:4) aims to benefit *both* Jews *and* Greeks since "there is no partiality in the presence of God" (2:11; cf. also 1:16; 2:6–10; 3:29–30). This is in keeping with the OT, which also demonstrates the goodness of God's patience as he interacts with the nations (e.g., Jonah 4:2; Ps 145:8–9 [LXX 144:8–9]). As the case of repentant Nineveh, saved from destruction and brought to faith in the true God by the reluctant preaching of recalcitrant Jonah (Jonah 3), exemplifies so beautifully, the purpose for God's patience can hardly be "to allow the rebellion of his creation to gain force and intensity so that his consequent victory is all the more glorious."[139] On the contrary, Chrysostom expresses Paul's understanding of God's impartial patience in its proper and positive function, which applies both to Israel and the Pharaoh:

> God, being very good, shows the same kindness to both. For it was not only to those who were saved that God showed kindness but to Pharaoh also. … For both Pharaoh and God's people had the advantage of God's patience. And if Pharaoh was not saved it was because of his own will, since God had done as much for him as he had done for those who were saved.[140]

---

[136] Dunn, *Romans*, 558.

[137] Moo, *Romans*, 606.

[138] Dunn, *Romans*, 558, citing Ex 34:6.

[139] As Moo, *Romans*, 606, maintains.

[140] Chrysostom, *Homilies on Romans*, 16 (Bray, *Romans*, ACCS NT 6:264). Lenski, *Romans*, 622–23, similarly affirms:

> Foolish men may think that his threats of judgment are not serious; God is willing to run that risk. Displaying his grace is supreme to him. …

> God should have destroyed them long ago but delayed and delayed. Although they are intolerable to him, he tolerated them. …

> We at once think of Pharaoh.

Vessels of Wrath and Destruction (9:22)

Due to his abundant patience, God did not simply endure; he actually "bore with much patience" those whom Paul depicts as "vessels of wrath" (σκεύη ὀργῆς, 9:22). Among the possible grammatical alternatives for the meaning of this construction,[141] the objective genitive may seem most reasonable: the phrase depicts "vessels which are objects of God's wrath now."[142] Paul states the *present* impact already in 1:18: "indeed, [the] wrath of God is being revealed [ἀποκαλύπτεται γὰρ ὀργὴ θεοῦ] from heaven upon every [πᾶσαν] ungodliness and unrighteousness of people." However, if forced to choose a specific grammatical category, a simple descriptive genitive may be the best option: "vessels characterized/described by wrath."[143]

These vessels "of" or "under" wrath are further described as vessels "which have been fitted for and are headed toward destruction" (κατηρτισμένα εἰς ἀπώλειαν, 9:22).[144] The implied actor who so "fitted" them must surely be God and not Satan.[145] The divine passive participle (κατηρτισμένα) is also in the perfect tense, which refers to a past action whose effects remain in the present. Both time components of the participle's action (past and present), as well as the direction indicated by the preposition εἰς ("for; toward"), are conveyed by the translation "have been fitted for and are headed toward destruction" (9:22).

The object of the preposition εἰς is the noun ἀπώλεια, "destruction," which typically refers to condemnation at the final judgment (see Phil 1:28; 3:19; 2 Thess 2:3; 1 Tim 6:9; as does the cognate verb ἀπόλλυμι, "destroy," in Rom 2:12; 1 Cor 1:18; 2 Cor 2:15; 4:3). While consensus on that point generally exists in regard to the noun ἀπώλεια, "destruction," in Rom 9:22, the meaning of the verb καταρτίζω, "to prepare, fit," remains disputed. First, it must be noted that Paul chooses a different verb in 9:23 (προητοίμασεν, "prepared"; see below). Thus it seems improper to render them synonymously by importing the notion of "prepared" from 9:23 already back into 9:22. Paul, therefore, does *not* describe " 'vessels on whom God's wrath rests' as prepared by God himself for eternal condemnation."[146] Neither does the Greek participle κατηρτισμένα, "having been fitted," begin with the preposition προ-, "before(hand)," which would express an action of God "prior" to the beginning of time; therefore, a translation such as " 'to foreordain' (for destruction)"[147] is unjustified. On the other hand, it is pushing too far in the other direction to view κατηρτισμένα as

[141] See the sixth textual note on 9:22. See also Middendorf, *Romans 1–8*, 53, for the somewhat arbitrary and overly interpretive process involved here.

[142] Dunn, *Romans*, 559.

[143] See further the sixth textual note on 9:22.

[144] Again, see the sixth textual note on 9:22.

[145] So Moo, *Romans*, 607. Satan is suggested by Lenski, *Romans*, 624.

[146] This incorrect statement is from Moo, *Romans*, 607.

[147] That improper translation is given in G. Delling, "ἄρτιος," *TDNT* 1:476.

meaning "ripe" or "ready" for destruction because the wickedness of these vessels has finally exceeded the limit of God's patience.[148] Instead,

> the implication is of an action performed on something already to hand in order that it might be put in proper order. This is certainly how Paul uses it [καταρτίζω, "to prepare, fit"] elsewhere (1 Cor 1:10; 2 Cor 13:11; Gal 6:1; 1 Thess 3:10; cf. 2 Cor 13:9; Eph 4:12; 1 Pet 5:10).[149]

What, then, has God put in order or seen fit to ordain? The most significant observation regards what Paul does *not* state. He does not assert that certain vessels are predetermined for wrath and destruction in contrast to the others, soon to be depicted in 9:23, which are prepared beforehand for mercy and glory. Suggesting that this is, in fact, what Paul does teach, leads to the following erroneous assertion: "One cannot by exegetical means rescue God from willing the fate of the vessels of wrath. This too was part of his plan, and thus double predestination cannot be averted."[150] What Paul does affirm in 9:22 is that vessels of wrath "have been fitted for and are headed toward destruction." His point is that all vessels *of wrath* will get destruction. This is the manner in which God will put things in proper order.

The second half of 1 Pet 2:8 presents a similar reading. Peter writes: "Those who are unpersuaded by the Word are stumbling, into which also they were placed" (οἳ προσκόπτουσιν τῷ λόγῳ ἀπειθοῦντες εἰς ὃ καὶ ἐτέθησαν). The verse would be misinterpreted if read as asserting that certain ones are "destined" to "disobey the word" (ESV). But Peter asserts that something else is set in place, namely, that those who refuse to be persuaded by the Word (ἀπειθέω, "to be unpersuaded," as in Rom 10:21; 11:30–31) will "stumble" as a result (προσκόπτω, as in Rom 9:32; cf. πταίω, "fall," in 11:11).

Who Are "Vessels of Wrath" (9:22)?

The remaining question, then, is how do we know which people Paul refers to when he speaks of "vessels of wrath"? One need not rehearse all of 1:18–3:20 to reach the simple conclusion that, apart from the intervention of God's mercy, *all people* are under divine wrath and are headed toward destruction at the final judgment. Paul repeatedly asserts that all are under sin (e.g., 3:9, 23), that, with or without the Law, all sinners will perish at the final judgment (2:12, 16), and that no one is righteous before God (3:10–11, 20). This includes Jew and Gentile (2:8–9), Israel and the Pharaoh. This side of God's righteousness (apart from Christ) condemns and dooms everyone (1:18, 32; 2:8–9; 3:9, 19–20). Elsewhere Paul describes everyone as follows: "we all ... and we were children of wrath by nature, as also [are] the rest" (ἡμεῖς πάντες ... καὶ ἤμεθα τέκνα φύσει ὀργῆς ὡς

---

[148] As maintained by Lenski, *Romans*, 622–23, and suggested also by Franzmann, *Romans*, 179. That definition is noted but properly rejected by G. Delling, "ἄρτιος," *TDNT* 1:476, n. 2, who contends that it has "no philological justification," as well as by Schreiner, *Romans*, 522.

[149] Dunn, *Romans*, 559.

[150] Schreiner, *Romans*, 522.

καὶ οἱ λοιποί, Eph 2:3). Apart from divine intervention, all people are encompassed by the description "vessels of wrath" (9:22; cf. 1:18; 2:8).

Therefore, regardless of any excuse or protestation which might be offered (e.g., 9:14, 19), here Paul reiterates a point he already made in 3:5–6:

> But if our unrighteousness demonstrates God's righteousness, what will we say? God, the one who brings wrath, is not unrighteous, is he? (I am speaking in a human way.) May it never come to be! If so, how will God judge the world?

There is no unrighteousness with God (9:14) in carrying out his wrath against such vessels and, ultimately, bringing about their eternal destruction. All those under God's wrath are surely headed there.

The extraordinary thing in 9:22 is that God bears with these vessels of wrath, which are headed toward destruction, with much patience, with the goal that his kindness will lead them to repentance (2:4; 9:22). The goal of moving them to repentance also explains the primary reason why a partial measure of his wrath is already being poured out (Rom 1:18; cf. Rev 16:1, 9, 11). In other words, the ominous fact that they "are indeed objects of God's wrath at the time in question, does not imply that they must always remain such. … That they are worthy of destruction is clearly implied, but not that they will necessarily be destroyed."[151]

Vessels of Mercy (9:23)

Even more extraordinary is the assertion of 9:23. God not only wishes to demonstrate his wrath (9:22), but he also wills "to make known the abundance of his glory upon vessels of mercy which he prepared beforehand for glory" (9:23). The phrase "abundance of his glory" uses the same noun (πλοῦτος, literally, "wealth") Paul employed in 2:4 to speak of "the abundance of his kindness and forbearance and patience." This corroborates the interpretation that, just as in 2:4, God's "patience" in 9:22 similarly wills (θέλω) to lead vessels of wrath toward repentance and salvation instead of destruction. This is so that they might share in the complete "abundance of his glory" (9:23), which will be made fully known at the eschaton as well (see "glory" or "glorify" in 8:17, 18, 30; cf. 2:10; 5:2).

To whom will God "make known the abundance of his glory" (9:23)? Now Paul refers to "vessels of mercy" (9:23). The noun "mercy" (ἔλεος) appears here for the first time in Romans, but the cognate verb "show mercy" conveys one of the driving themes of this section (ἐλεέω, 9:15 [twice], 18; also ἐλεάω in 9:16). The force of the genitive in this phrase ("vessels of mercy"), however it is precisely to be categorized, surely remains the same as in the "vessels of wrath" (σκεύη ὀργῆς) in 9:22 (see above). These "vessels of mercy" are vessels on whom God's mercy now rests. Such vessels can be certain that they are also depicted as headed for glory (e.g., 8:17, 18, 21, 30).

---

[151] Cranfield, *Romans*, 495–96.

Unlike the participle "fitted" (κατηρτισμένα) in 9:22, the compound indicative verb "he prepared beforehand" (προητοίμασεν) in 9:23 does indeed have the Greek prefixed preposition προ-, indicating time "beforehand." Any notion of "predestination" fits only in this verse, if here at all; the Lutheran tradition prefers to speak of "election."[152] The only other place where the compound verb προετοιμάζω occurs in the NT is Eph 2:10, where it describes the "good works which God *prepared beforehand*" (ἔργοις ἀγαθοῖς οἷς προητοίμασεν ὁ θεός) for his people to walk in them. The sense there hardly conveys predeterminism. While God prepares the works, he certainly does not force his people to do them. They often are wont to not walk in them and, therefore, fail to do so despite and contrary to God's will (see the discussion of ἀνθέστηκεν, "has set himself against and withstood," in 9:19). For better or for worse, we are not like puppets manipulated into doing the good works God has prepared beforehand for us to do.

Similarly, God does *not* prepare beforehand that some vessels are vessels of wrath irretrievably headed toward destruction, while other vessels are unalterably locked into receiving the abundance of his glory.[153] Neither does he say that *any* vessels are prepared "beforehand" for destruction. What Paul actually asserts is that God has prepared beforehand, even before time, that vessels of mercy are headed for glory, indeed, the abundance of his glory.[154] The verb "he prepared beforehand" (προητοίμασεν, 9:23) provides assurance in only one direction, an election to grace. As the Formula of Concord observes:

> Concerning "the vessels of mercy" he says specifically that the Lord himself "has prepared them unto glory" [9:23]. He does not say this of the damned, whom God has not prepared but who have prepared themselves to be vessels of damnation.[155]

The Implications of Romans 9:22–23

As the beginning of 9:22 states, Paul here reveals to us what God wills ("God, willing," θέλων ὁ θεός, 9:22). Thus these two verses have great significance. Although God's proper work and primary purpose remain gracious (9:11),[156] one must reckon with both 9:22 and 9:23. They need to be held together in spite of the paradoxical tension between God's wrath and his mercy. "Paul is clear here, as he is elsewhere: some people receive God's mercy and are saved,

---

[152] See, e.g., FC SD XI, "Eternal Foreknowledge and Divine Election."

[153] If this falsehood were true, it would appear to support the unbiblical notions of unconditional double predestination, irresistible grace, and "once saved, always saved."

[154] Thus Moo, *Romans*, 608, properly observes that "prepared beforehand" in 9:23 does refer to "the same thing as the word 'predestine' in 8:29."

[155] FC SD XI 82. The phrase "election to grace" or "gracious election" appears in FC Ep XI 13, 16 and FC SD XI 90–91.

[156] Cranfield, *Romans*, 496, overstates this by speaking of "one ultimate gracious purpose of God."

while others do not receive that mercy and so are eternally condemned."[157] "Thereby God displays the full range of his attributes: both his powerful wrath and the sunshine of his mercy."[158] This seems as simple as the "and" (καί) which opens 9:23 and has surely been demonstrated sufficiently thus far in Romans. Paul's overarching theme is to demonstrate how God's righteousness *both* justly pronounces condemnation (1:18–3:20) *and* also offers his saving declaration of life (e.g., 1:16–17; 3:19–26).

Why, then, will some end up facing destruction while others bask in the abundance of eternal glory? Moo places the onus on God by contending that Paul is teaching "about the unconstrained freedom of God in making choices that determine people's lives. Paul also makes even clearer that the choices he is talking about have to do not just with historical roles but with eternal destinies."[159] Moo also contends:

> His mercy is in this context clearly discriminating rather than universal: some receive mercy (v. 18), those "vessels" of mercy whom God chooses (vv. 15–16); others, vessels of wrath, are hardened (v. 18). Therefore we must not allow the preeminence of God's purpose in bestowing mercy *on some* to cancel out the reality and finality of his wrath *on others*.[160]

It might initially seem in concert with the theocentric emphasis of this commentary to agree, since Moo properly focuses upon God.[161] But are God's overriding characteristics freedom, sovereignty, and an unalterable choice to predetermine which people receive wrath versus who gets mercy? Paul does not say so. Instead, he here emphasizes God's "mercy" (9:15 [twice], 16, 18, 23). In discussing 9:18, this commentary pointed ahead to 11:32. God's determined will ("willing," θέλων, 9:22) is that "he might show mercy to all" (τοὺς πάντας ἐλεήσῃ, 11:32). This is even more powerful (cf. δυνατόν, "[saving] power," 9:22) than the fact that *all* are disobedient sinners (3:9), justifiably objects of God's wrath and headed toward destruction apart from his mercy (9:22).

But 11:32 does not teach universalism, asserting that *everyone* is a vessel of mercy and, therefore, that all people are headed toward glory. Any such suggestion disregards a major point discussed beginning in 9:30 and running throughout Romans 10. In other words, one cannot read Romans 9 by itself without some cognizance of what comes in between this chapter and 11:32. God's merciful call has gone out into the whole world (10:18; cf. 9:12, 15, 16, 24). But Paul reveals that vessels to whom God wills to show mercy can, unfortunately, forfeit his mercy by pursing it improperly through works (9:30–32; cf. 11:7) or rejecting it in unbelief or unfaith (9:32; 10:16; 11:20). The same

---

[157] Moo, *Romans*, 608.

[158] Schreiner, *Romans*, 523.

[159] Moo, *Romans*, 609.

[160] Moo, *Romans*, 608.

[161] Middendorf, *Romans 1–8*, 21–22, 27, 29–30, 51; see also "God" in "The Three Foci of Romans 9–11" in the introduction to Romans 9–11.

point was made regarding "some" in Israel already in 3:2–3. The fact that God's mercy is resistible means that predeterminism on the part of God ought to be rejected, along with any notion of irresistible grace. This reality applies not only to "vessels of mercy" (9:23) but also to "vessels of wrath" (9:22). On that basis, 9:22–23 serves "to allow the possibility and hope that the 'vessels of wrath' (redefined to include unbelieving Israel) will become 'vessels of mercy' (cf. Isa 54:16–17 LXX …)."[162] This is most certainly Paul's fervent plea and goal (Rom 10:11; 11:14; 15:20).

Above all, God wills (θέλων ὁ θεός, 9:22) to make known his *saving* "power" (δύναμις, 1:16; 9:17; τό δυνατόν in 9:22) "in all the earth" (9:17). This is the whole point of the letter and Paul's exposition of the Gospel. God's righteousness is revealed therein for Jew and Gentile (1:16–17; 3:27–31; 9:24) by One who mercifully deigns to declare godless, headed-for-wrath vessels righteous on account of Christ (4:6; 9:15–16, 22). This same God also wills to make known the abundance of glory which he prepared beforehand for the vessels of his mercy (9:23). How, then, can we know that his mercy is *ours*?

God Called Us: A Conclusive Hinge (9:24)

Paul proceeds by retrieving the thematic word he uses to depict God's characteristic activity in 9:6–13. There he describes God as "the One who calls" (τοῦ καλοῦντος, 9:12). The vessels of mercy in 9:23 are defined by 9:24 as those "whom he also called [ἐκάλεσεν], [namely,] us, not only from Jews but also from Gentiles" (9:24).

Structural Matters

As in 9:5, the insertion of punctuation becomes a significant interpretive matter. NA[27] places a question mark after 9:23 and a comma after 9:24. This would indicate that 9:23 concludes a thought and that 9:24 leads forward into a new section. Moo similarly contends that, after the "excursus" of 9:14–23, Paul returns to the thought of 9:6–13; thus 9:24 marks the "beginning of a new sentence (and, indeed, a new paragraph)."[163] On the one hand, it is true that 9:24–29 shares "the characteristic vocabulary of that earlier paragraph: 'sons of God' (v. 26; cf. v. 8); 'seed' (v. 29; cf. vv. 7 and 8); and, especially, 'call' (vv. 24 and 26; cf. vv. 7 and 12)."[164]

But if Paul intends to begin a new section with 9:24, he starts quite oddly with the relative pronoun "whom" (οὕς). It is followed by the conjunction καί (usually "and"), which carries a connective sense, "also." As a result, Schreiner observes that "syntactically verse 24 is joined with verse 23."[165] Therefore Cranfield, along with Matera, the ESV, RSV, and NRSV, properly takes "the

---

[162] Dunn, *Romans*, 560.
[163] Moo, *Romans*, 611; see also 610.
[164] Moo, *Romans*, 610.
[165] Schreiner, *Romans*, 525.

whole verse [9:24] as a relative clause dependent on σκεύη ἐλέους ['vessels of mercy'] in v. 23."[166] Furthermore, the presence of "he called" (ἐκάλεσεν) in 9:24 does not pertain merely to 9:6–13. It also draws upon Paul's use of the identical verb in 8:30 (ἐκάλεσεν, "he called"; cf. 4:17). Those "vessels of mercy which he prepared beforehand for glory" (9:23) are the same as those "whom he appointed beforehand, these he also called" (οὓς δὲ προώρισεν, τούτους καὶ ἐκάλεσεν, 8:30). Similarly, "he prepared beforehand" (προητοίμασεν) in 9:23 leads directly into "he called" (ἐκάλεσεν) in 9:24. Therefore both the grammar and content of 9:24 serve to corroborate its close attachment to 9:23.

As exemplified by 8:1–4, Paul regularly uses a hinge to link sections together as he moves along.[e] Rom 9:24 is best viewed in this manner. The fact that the God who shows mercy (9:16) called *us* to be vessels of his mercy connects the thought of 9:24 with 9:23. "Us" (ἡμᾶς, 9:24) is then further defined as being "not only from Jews but also from Gentiles" (9:24). The last half of the verse points ahead to the conclusions Paul draws out of the Scripture citations to follow in 9:25–29. Further evidence that Paul's argument steadily progresses forward comes from the sources of his scriptural references. In 9:7–13 he utilizes people from the Genesis narrative, quoting from that book three times, along with Malachi's later words regarding Jacob and Esau. In 9:14–18 his citations are drawn from Exodus. In 9:20 and 9:25–29 he draws from the Prophets. Therefore 9:24 serves very nicely as a pivot. In this commentary, it ends this section and also introduces the next.

Our "Not Only … But Also" God

The latter half of 9:24 also contains a favorite formula of Paul which occurs repeatedly throughout Romans: "not only … but also" (see 4:12).[f] Throughout the letter, Paul makes the point that the God who calls (9:12) and who shows mercy (9:16) is a "not only … but also" God. This conception of God permeates this entire section: not only mercy, but also compassion (9:15); not only mercy, but also hardening (9:18); not only honorable use, but also ordinary use (9:21); not only wrath, but also saving power (9:22); not only vessels of wrath headed toward destruction, but also vessels of mercy prepared beforehand for the abundance of glory (9:22–23). Now he calls "us," who are not only from Jews but also from Gentiles (9:24). This conveys a recurrent theme of the letter (3:29; 9:24; similarly, "Jew(s)" and "Greek(s)" in 1:16; 2:9, 10; 3:9; 10:12; see also 15:7–9). Based upon Ex 12:38, Pelagius observes how this is no recent innovation: "Since even then some of the Egyptians left with the children of Israel … so too now God has called not only Jews but also Gentiles to faith."[167] As it was in the days of the exodus, so it is also proclaimed by the OT prophets whom Paul proceeds to cite in order to apply their truths to his own day. The

(e) See also, e.g., Rom 1:18; 3:1, 21; 4:1; 5:1; 6:1, 11; 10:4–5, 16–17; 13:7–8; 15:7

(f) Also in Rom 1:32; 4:16, 23–24; 5:3, 11; 8:23; 9:24; 13:5; 16:4

---

[166] Cranfield, *Romans*, 497–98; Matera, *Romans*, 228, asserts that 9:24 marks "the conclusion of 9:23."

[167] Pelagius, *Romans* (Bray, *Romans*, ACCS NT 6:266).

cumulative evidence of all of these Scripture quotations combines to refute any notion that "God's Word has failed [or] remains fallen" (9:6). "May it never come to be!" (μὴ γένοιτο, 9:14).

Finally, Dunn reminds us that most of the original recipients heard the letter orally; he then suggests that "the awkwardness of the phrasing is presumably deliberate and almost certainly meant that in being read aloud the words would have to be taken slowly and with emphasis, particularly on the awkward ἡμᾶς ['us,' 9:24]."[168] Indeed, the first person plural pronoun in 9:24 stands out as the verse's most striking feature. Thus far from being something that "is slipped in,"[169] *"us" (ἡμᾶς) makes the point emphatic*. In fact, it reaches all the way back to the thematic term in the letter's introduction, the three occurrences of the adjective "called" (κλητός) in 1:1, 6, 7. The declaration of 9:24 that "he called *us*" includes Paul and his addressees, both Jews and Gentiles who are among "all the ones in Rome who are loved by God, … those called, holy" (1:7). Indeed, it still reaches out to encompass all of "us" who hear the call of God's Word of mercy today.[170]

---

[168] Dunn, *Romans*, 570; cf. 1 Cor 12:28.

[169] As Cranfield, *Romans*, 498, maintains.

[170] See also "The Connection of Romans 9:24 with the Catena of Romans 9:25–29" in the commentary on 9:24–29.

God's Word Stands—for Both Jews and Gentiles

Translation

9 … ²⁴**whom he also called, [namely,] us, not only from Jews but also from Gentiles?** ²⁵**Even as he says in Hosea: "I will call the 'not my people' 'my people' and the 'not having been loved' 'having been loved and still beloved.'"** ²⁶**"And it will be in the place where it was said to them, 'You [are] not my people,' there they will be called 'sons of the living God.'"**

²⁷**But Isaiah cries out in behalf of Israel: "If the number of the sons of Israel might be as the sand of the sea[shore], the remnant will be saved.** ²⁸**For while completing and cutting short, the Lord will accomplish [his] Word on the earth."**

²⁹**And even as Isaiah spoke previously and still holds forth: "If the Lord of armies had not left seed to us, we would have become as Sodom and we would have been the same as Gomorrah."**

Textual Notes

9:24 This hinge verse is included in both 9:14–24 and this section. See the textual notes on it in that previous section and the commentary on it there, as well as "The Connection of Romans 9:24 with the Catena of Romans 9:25–29" in the commentary below.

9:25 ὡς καί—While ὡς, meaning "*as*," can "introduce an example" (BDAG, 2 d α), Paul clearly intends it to function as much more than that here. The καί also carries an intensive force, "*even*" (BDAG, 2 b). These two words, "even as," indicate that what follows serves to validate 9:24 but also advances the argument.

ἐν τῷ Ὡσηέ λέγει—The quote is from Hos 2:23 (MT/LXX 2:25). The Greek name Ὡσηέ is the transliteration of the name of the minor prophet Hosea, הוֹשֵׁעַ. The reading τῷ Ὡσηὲ λέγει in 𝔓⁴⁶ and B lacks the preposition ἐν and reflects God speaking "*to* Hosea." But the more difficult reading and, therefore, more likely the original one retains ἐν. The phrase then "functions metonymically of his book" (BDAG, s.v. Ὡσηέ): "even as he says *in* Hosea," that is, as God says in the prophet's writing.

καλέσω—The future indicative active of καλέω, "call," maintains the presence of that thematic verb in Romans 9 (see the commentary on 9:12; also 4:17; 8:30; 9:7, 24, 26). In this passage καλέω appears in 9:24, 25, 26, which are the last instances in the book of Romans. MT Hos 2:25 (ET 2:23) has the perfect with *waw* consecutive וְאָמַרְתִּי, "and I will *say*," which is rendered literally by LXX Hos 2:25 (ET 2:23) with καὶ ἐρῶ, using the future indicative of λέγω, "say." Therefore the presence of καλέω, "call," here likely reflects Paul's own alteration of the Hosea text to indicate and reinforce his emphasis. Here καλέω takes a double accusative; the first accusative object is τὸν οὐ λαόν μου, "the 'not my people'" (see the next textual note), and the second is λαόν μου, "my people." Sanday and Headlam insist that καλέσω with the double accusative

913

"can only mean 'I will name,'" but allow that the use of καλέω with the meaning "to call" in 9:24 may have influenced its use here.[1]

τὸν οὐ λαόν μου—The noun λαός represents the "people" of God. See "God's People" in the introduction to Romans 9–11. This negated phrase, literally, "the not people of mine," then refers to those who are "not" regarded as such. In MT Hos 2:25 (ET 2:23) God speaks לְלֹא־עַמִּי, which could mean "to [a people who is] not my people," or it could mean "to Lo Ammi," since in Hos 1:9 God assigns this phrase to be the Hebrew name of Hosea's son: לֹא עַמִּי, Lo Ammi. LXX Hos 1:9 renders the son's name as Οὐ-λαός-μου, "not my people," and this name seems to be intended in LXX Hos 2:25 (ET 2:23): καὶ ἐρῶ τῷ Οὐ-λαῷ-μου, "and I will say to the 'not my people.'" See the commentary.

τὴν οὐκ ἠγαπημένην ἠγαπημένην—For the verb ἀγαπάω, "to love," in reference to God's love, see the commentary on 5:5. In the wording here the first perfect passive participle of ἀγαπάω is negated to speak of a past act of rejection, literally, "the (female) 'not having been loved,'" but the immediate repetition of the same form, ἠγαπημένην, indicates the remedy and an ongoing situation, "having been loved and still beloved." By using ἀγαπάω, "love," Paul has altered the emphasis on "mercy" in the wording of MT/LXX Hos 1:6; 2:25 (ET 2:23). In Hos 1:6 God prescribes the name of Hosea's daughter to be לֹא רֻחָמָה, Lo Ruḥamah, meaning "she who has not been shown mercy" (רֻחָמָה is a Pual perfect third feminine singular in pause; its meaning is the passive of the corresponding active meaning of the Piel רִחַמְתִּי, "I will have mercy," in MT Hos 2:25 [ET 2:23]). LXX Hos 1:6 translates the MT with a perfect passive participle, Οὐκ-ἠλεημένη, "she who has not been shown mercy," and LXX Hos 2:25 (ET 2:23) has the accusative form, Οὐκ-ἠλεημένην. For ἐλεέω, "show mercy," see the first textual note on Rom 9:15. See further the commentary.

9:26 καὶ ἔσται ἐν τῷ τόπῳ οὗ—Paul now quotes from Hos 1:10 (MT/LXX 2:1). The word οὗ, in form the genitive singular of the relative pronoun ὅς, serves as a "marker of a position in space" (BDAG, s.v. οὗ, 1), "in the place where."

ἐρρέθη αὐτοῖς—The verb is the aorist passive of λέγω. The first person singular pronoun in the following clause ("my people"; see the next textual note) indicates that the verb should be understood as "a divine passive (or theological passive)."[2] "It was said" to and about Israel by God through his prophet.

οὐ λαός μου ὑμεῖς—See the similar wording in the fourth textual note on 9:25, where οὐ λαόν μου is a name. Here the addition of the plural pronoun ὑμεῖς forms a statement in a quote of what was formerly said to the people: "you [plural] [are] not my people."

κληθήσονται—The thematic verb καλέω, "call," appears again in a future indicative form (see the future active καλέσω in the third textual note on 9:25), but now in the passive voice. As in the second textual note on this verse, the implied speaker once again

---

[1] Sanday and Headlam, *Romans*, 264. According to BDAG the verb with the double accusative may mean either "call, address as, designate as" (s.v. καλέω, 1 b, citing Rom 9:25) or "name" (s.v. καλέω, 1 c).

[2] Wallace, *Greek Grammar*, 437–38.

is God, though this does not preclude a wider recognition of the statement by others (cf. Is 61:9). For the applicability of καλέω in the sense of naming, see the commentary.

θεοῦ ζῶντος—The participle ζῶντος, "living," functions adjectivally to modify θεοῦ, "God."[3] The verb ζάω, "to live," can depict "beings that in reality ... are not subject to death" (BDAG, 1 a ε). This definition certainly stands applicable to God. See θεός ζῶν also in 2 Cor 6:16; 1 Thess 1:9.

9:27 Ἡσαΐας—To introduce his citation of Is 10:22–23 (he also draws initially upon Hos 1:10 [MT/LXX 2:1]) in Rom 9:27–28, Paul uses this Greek form of the name of the OT prophet "Isaiah," which is יְשַׁעְיָהוּ in Hebrew. It reveals how significantly names can be altered in transliteration. The double dots over the Greek iota, -ϊ-, are a diaeresis,[4] indicating that the two vowels αι, which normally form a diphthong, are separate sounds and syllables; a diaeresis is used here because the Greek vowel -ι- represents the Hebrew consonant י.

ὑπὲρ τοῦ Ἰσραήλ—When followed by the genitive (here τοῦ Ἰσραήλ, "of Israel"), ὑπέρ most often functions as "a marker indicating that an activity or event is in some entity's interest, *for, in behalf of, for the sake of someone/someth[ing]*" (BDAG, A 1). See also ὑπέρ in the third textual note on 5:6 regarding its disputed sense in 5:6–8. Note the significance of ὑπέρ in 8:31–34 as well. Another suggestion is that the preposition here might instead serve as a "marker of general content ... *about, concerning*" (BDAG, A 3, as in, e.g., 2 Cor 1:8; 8:23).[5] See further the commentary.

ἐὰν ᾖ—The conjunction ἐάν (εἰ + ἄν) followed by the subjunctive ᾖ (from εἰμί) introduces a third class or future more vivid conditional, "if it might be." This kind of conditional generally expresses "the condition as *uncertain of fulfillment, but still likely*. There are, however, many exceptions to this."[6] In this quotation from Isaiah (eighth century BC), the protasis had already been fulfilled; at the time of Solomon (ninth century BC), the Israelites were already as many as "the sand on the seashore" (1 Ki 4:20). The fulfillment of the apodosis ("the remnant will be saved") was certain in Isaiah's time, and it remains so in Paul's time and in ours.

ὁ ἀριθμός—The English noun "arithmetic" derives from this Greek noun, which here means "number."

ἡ ἄμμος τῆς θαλάσσης—Literally, this expression means "the sand of the sea[shore]." But it is used figuratively to describe "things that cannot be counted" (BDAG, s.v. ἄμμος; see also Heb 11:12; Rev 20:8). As reflected in this passage, the phrase refers most significantly to the number of descendants promised to Abraham using the corresponding Hebrew terms (Gen 22:17), a promise reiterated to Jacob (Gen 32:12 [MT 32:13]).

ὑπόλειμμα—This noun depicts "a relatively small surviving group, *remnant*" (BDAG). In the NT it occurs only here, but the synonym λεῖμμα appears in 11:5. Both

---

[3] See Wallace, *Greek Grammar*, 617–19.

[4] See Mounce, *Basics of Biblical Greek*, 11.

[5] For a full discussion, see Wallace, *Greek Grammar*, 383–89.

[6] Wallace, *Greek Grammar*, 696; see 696–99.

nouns derive from the verb λείπω, "to leave"; see ἐγκατέλιπεν in the fifth textual note on 9:29. These Greek nouns represent the Hebrew theological terminology, common and significant, for the "remnant." See שְׁאָר in, e.g., Is 10:19–22; 11:11, 16; and the synonym שְׁאֵרִית in, e.g., Gen 45:7; Is 46:3; Jer 23:3; 24:8; Ezek 11:13; Amos 5:15; Micah 2:12; 4:7; 5:7 (ET 5:8). The OT can also use other terminology for the remnant, such as שָׂרִיד (Is 1:9), mentioned in the sixth textual note on Rom 9:29.

σωθήσεται—For the verb σῴζω, "to save," see the fourth textual note and the commentary on 5:9, as well as the cognate noun σωτηρία, "salvation," in 1:16. The verb occurs eight times in Romans (also 5:9, 10; 8:24; 10:9, 13; 11:14, 26). This form is a future passive with God as the implied actor.[7]

9:28 συντελῶν καὶ συντέμνων—Both of these participles are nominative singular masculine, agreeing with κύριος. They are used adverbially to modify what "the Lord [κύριος] will accomplish [ποιήσει] ... on the earth," but their precise meaning remains unclear. BDAG places συντελέω in this passage under its second definition, "to carry out or bring into being someth[ing] that has been promised or expected, *carry out, fulfill, accomplish.*" But BDAG's first definition seems more appropriate, "to complete someth[ing] that has been in process, *bring to an end, complete, finish, close.*" The verb συντέμνω means "to put a limit to someth[ing], freq[uently] w[ith an] implication of abruptness, *cut short, shorten, limit*" (BDAG). For the contextual meaning of both participles, see the commentary.

ποιήσει—In this verse, ποιέω means "to undertake or do someth[ing] that brings about an event, state, or condition, *do, cause, bring about, accomplish, prepare*" (BDAG, 2). The future indicative active depicts what the Lord "will do" or "will accomplish."

9:29 προείρηκεν—This form of the compound verb προλέγω is a perfect indicative active. The perfect tense of the indicative "describes an event that, completed in the past ... has results existing in the present time (i.e., in relation to the time of the speaker)."[8] Therefore προείρηκεν depicts what Isaiah "spoke previously," and since his inspired words still stand, the verb asserts that Isaiah "still holds forth."

Ἠσαΐας—For "Isaiah," see the first textual note on 9:27. This quote is from Is 1:9.

εἰ μὴ ... ἐγκατέλιπεν ... ἂν ἐγενήθημεν ... ἂν ὡμοιώθημεν—This sentence contains a conditional sentence with a protasis in the negative ("if the Lord ... had *not* left") and then a double apodosis, that is, two "then" clauses, each rendered with "we would have." Its form expresses a contrary to fact or second class condition, which "indicates *the assumption of an untruth (for the sake of argument),*"[9] and the untruth would be that "the Lord *did not* leave seed."[10] The aorist tense verbs in both the protasis and the two apodoses indicate a past contrary to fact: "*if X had been ... then Y would have*

---

[7] See Wallace, *Greek Grammar,* 437–38.

[8] Wallace, *Greek Grammar,* 573; see 572–82.

[9] Wallace, *Greek Grammar,* 694.

[10] In the words of Kuske, *Romans 9–16,* 71, "the horrible event of no Jews being left did not happen."

been."[11] This Greek conditional precisely renders the Hebrew conditional sentence in Is 1:9, which begins with the conjunction לוּלֵי (also spelled לוּלֵא), "if not," and continues with perfect verbs, referring to what would have happened in the past. For further discussion about the verbs, see the following textual notes.

κύριος σαβαώθ—This translates the Hebrew יְהוָה צְבָאוֹת, "Yahweh of Sabaoth/hosts/armies" (Is 1:9; cf. also, e.g., Is 6:3, 5; 47:4; 54:5).

ἐγκατέλιπεν—The doubly compound verb ἐγκαταλείπω (ἐν + κατά + λείπω) means "to cause someth[ing] to remain or to exist after a point in time, *leave* of posterity" (BDAG, 1). The form here is a second aorist indicative active, "he left." Cf. the related meaning of the nouns translated as "remnant," ὑπόλειμμα in 9:27 and λεῖμμα in 11:5, as well as the compound verbs with λείπω, the same root, ὑπολείπω in 11:3 and καταλείπω in 11:4.

σπέρμα—For "seed," see the third textual note on 1:3; note also 4:13 and 9:7. Usually this is the Greek translation of the Hebrew noun זֶרַע, which appears in the promises to Abraham and his "seed" regarding his "seed" (e.g., Gen 12:7; 15:5; 22:17–18; 26:3–4; cf. also Gen 3:15), and thus Paul uses σπέρμα regarding Abraham's seed in Rom 4:13, 16, 18; 9:7, 8; 11:1. Here, however, it renders the Hebrew שָׂרִיד (Is 1:9), literally, "an escapee, survivor."

ὡς Σόδομα ... ὡς Γόμορρα—A comparison to "Sodom" (and "Gomorrah") appears elsewhere in the NT in warnings of divine judgment. See the words of Jesus in Mt 10:15; 11:23–24 (∥ Lk 10:12); Lk 17:29; and in the epistles, see 2 Pet 2:6; Jude 7. Cf. Rev 11:8.

ἂν ἐγενήθημεν—The verb is an aorist indicative passive of γίνομαι, "to become." Since the conditional sentence (see the third textual note on 9:29) expresses what is unreal or contrary to fact,[12] the translation inserts "would," which produces "we would have become."

ἂν ὡμοιώθημεν—The verb ὁμοιόω means to "*make someone like a person* or *thing*," according to BDAG, 1, which then offers a translation for the aorist passive here, "*we would have resembled Gomorrah.*" However, "resembled" weakens the reality of the assertion (which would, in fact, be true if the Lord had not left seed). "We would have been *the same as* Gomorrah"[13] stresses the more appropriate notion of equivalency.

Commentary

The Connection of Romans 9:24 with the Catena of Romans 9:25–29

The previous section in this commentary concluded with a discussion of the role and meaning of 9:24.[14] It demonstrates that the verse ought to be treated as the triumphant conclusion of 9:14–23. Rom 9:24 concludes the extended, and incomplete, question of 9:22–23 as follows:

---

[11] Wallace, *Greek Grammar*, 695.

[12] See Wallace, *Greek Grammar*, 694.

[13] Dunn, *Romans*, 574; emphasis added.

[14] See "God Called Us: A Conclusive Hinge (9:24)" in the commentary on 9:14–24.

²²And [who are you to talk back] if God, willing to demonstrate [his] wrath and to make known his [saving] power, bore with much patience vessels of wrath which have been fitted for and are headed toward destruction, ²³and in order to make known the abundance of his glory upon vessels of mercy which he prepared beforehand for glory, ²⁴whom he also called, [namely,] us, not only from Jews but also from Gentiles?

At the same time, the swinging door of 9:24 also serves effectively as a hinge into a "catena of confirmatory OT quotations"[15] which provide prophetic documentation for the truths just enunciated. While references from Hosea and Isaiah corroborate Paul's assertion in 9:24, Paul also utilizes them to advance his argument. Most predominantly, however, they wrap up the opening assertion of 9:6, which has dominated the discussion ever since. Paul continues to maintain that what he writes is fully in concert with God's prophetic Word, which has not failed and is not fallen (see 1:2 and 9:6).

The most relevant facet of 9:24 for what follows is the presence of another "not only ... but also" expression.[16] Paul's most emphatic and remarkable point in 9:24 is his assertion that God actually reached out in mercy and "called us" (ἐκάλεσεν ἡμᾶς). Then he adds "not only from *Jews* but also from *Gentiles*" (9:24). In chiastic fashion, Paul then *turns* to *Gentiles* first and applies two citations from Hosea to them (9:25–26). He then *returns* to the *Jews* with two Isaiah quotations which refer to Israel (9:27–29). Paul effectively uses these passages to verify what he has just said about God's call in 9:24.

"He Called Us ... Also from Gentiles" (9:24–26)

Paul's application of two quotations from Hosea to Gentiles seems, at least initially, considerably different from how the prophetic text was originally meant to be heard in Hosea's day. Before proceeding, a pertinent portion from the general introduction to Romans in volume 1 of this commentary is reproduced below:[17]

> It is not necessary, however, to insist that the meaning of quotations that Paul cites from the OT is always simply equivalent with the intended meaning of the original author. When Paul quotes or alludes to an OT text, he is, at times, revealing more, "extending its meaning in new directions," in order to apply the inspired Word to his own context and time.[18] In so doing, he does *not* deny what the original author meant. Instead, in and through Christ, and by inspiration of the Spirit, Paul sees new or additional meaning in the ancient words. When this happens, the OT quote then *also* means what Paul intends it to mean as he uses it in the context of Romans.[19]

---

[15] Cranfield, *Romans*, 498.

[16] See "Our 'Not Only ... But Also' God" in the commentary on 9:14–24.

[17] Middendorf, *Romans 1–8*, 37.

[18] Hays, *Echoes of Scripture in the Letters of Paul*, 5; see his application of this principle on 34–83, especially 35, 41, 61, 69, 82–83.

[19] See, for example, Hab 2:4 in Rom 1:17; Is 52:5 in Rom 2:24; Deut 30:12–14 in Rom 10:6–8; Is 65:1–2 in Rom 10:20–21. For a more complete discussion, see the excursus "Paul's Use of the Old Testament in Romans" following the commentary on 15:7–13.

But Paul is no innovator here.

> Already these Scriptures were awash in what scholars call "intertextuality," fragments of earlier stories echoing in the later chambers of sacred words and promises. Later ... texts and stories ... are told with allusions to earlier stories. ... Paul continues the interpretive practices of his ancestors in faith, extending Scripture beyond their day to his own, finding its fullness in the Lord Jesus Christ.[20]

Furthermore, as discussed in the introduction to Romans 9–11, the OT passages Paul cites in this section are not employed specifically to prove the Messiahship of Jesus. Instead, Paul applies God's infallible Word (9:6) to the present situation of *the NT people of God*. In Romans 9–11 Paul focuses on how the Christ-event is playing itself out in the ongoing life of God's people on earth, now comprised of both believing Israelites and Gentiles (see "God's Word" and "God's People" in the introduction to Romans 9–11). Notice, for example, how Paul uses the present tense of λέγει, "*says*," in both 9:17 ("the Scripture says") and 9:25 ("he [God] says"). God spoke the words cited in 9:17 to Moses and then also through Moses to the Pharaoh (Ex 9:16). He similarly spoke prophetically to his people in Hosea's day and, with the very same words, still speaks of "us" Jews and Gentiles whom he has also called to be vessels of his mercy (9:23–24). All of this comes with Paul's present tense introduction in 9:25, "even as he *says* in Hosea."

Now My Beloved People (Hos 2:23 in Rom 9:25)

This brings us to Paul's citations from Hosea in Rom 9:25–26. The first obvious change is chronological. Not only does Paul quote two verses from Hosea out of the order in which they occur in the prophet's writings, but he also reverses the order of the two clauses *within* the first quote from Hos 2:23 (MT/LXX 2:25). Below is the initial Hosea text as it appears in Romans, followed by the LXX and, finally, the original Hebrew.

> καλέσω τὸν οὐ λαόν μου λαόν μου καὶ τὴν οὐκ ἠγαπημένην ἠγαπημένην.

> I will call the "not my people" "my people" and the "not having been loved" "having been loved and still beloved." (Rom 9:25)

> ἐλεήσω τὴν Οὐκ-ἠλεημένην καὶ ἐρῶ τῷ Οὐ-λαῷ-μου λαός μου εἶ σύ.

> I will mercy the "not having been mercied," and I will say to the "not my people," "My people you are." (LXX Hos 2:25 [ET 2:23])

> וְרִחַמְתִּי אֶת־לֹא רֻחָמָה וְאָמַרְתִּי לְלֹא־עַמִּי עַמִּי־אַתָּה

> And I will have mercy on "not mercied," and I will say to "not my people," "You are my people." (MT Hos 2:25 [ET 2:23])

While Rom 9:25 conveys the same thought as Hos 2:23 (MT/LXX 2:25), both the words and their order are considerably different than the LXX. At the same time, the LXX translates the MT very accurately. This indicates that the alterations

---

[20] Capes, Reeves, and Richards, *Rediscovering Paul*, 262.

most probably come from the hand of Paul himself. They are, therefore, both substantial and revelatory.[21]

Paul's use of Hos 2:23 (MT/LXX 2:25) in Rom 9:25 prior to his citation from Hos 1:10 (MT/LXX 2:1) in Rom 9:26 allows him to position the thematic verb "to call" (καλέω) strategically at the beginning of the catena of quotes in 9:25–29. In order to do so, Paul also reverses the order of the two clauses in Hos 2:23 (MT/LXX 2:25). He then *inserts* the future form of the verb "to call" (καλέσω) in place of the future of "to say" (ἐρῶ, which opens the second clause of the verse in the LXX and which more literally conveys the Hebrew; see the third textual note on Rom 9:25). The impact of "call" (καλέω), therefore, continues to reverberate throughout Romans and within chapter 9 in particular (see 9:12; also 4:17; 8:30; 9:7, 24, 26; cf. also the cognate adjective κλητός, "called," in 1:1, 6, 7).

Paul also omits the emphatic second person singular statement which concludes that promise in LXX Hos 2:25 (ET 2:23), "my people *you are*" (λαός μου εἶ σύ, which, in turn, accurately translates the second singular masculine Hebrew pronoun אַתָּה in MT Hos 2:25 [ET 2:23]). Hosea's son was originally given the name *Lo Ammi*, meaning "not my people" (Hos 1:9). While the singular Greek verb and pronoun "you are" in LXX Hos 2:25 (ET 2:23) are, therefore, fitting in the original reference to that son, Paul's omission of it may be explained by his emphasis on the collective sense of "people" (λαός), already present in Hosea (see below). It also allows him to maintain the plural force of the pronoun "us" (ἡμᾶς) from Rom 9:24 (see also the plural pronoun ὑμεῖς, "you," in 9:26).

Perhaps most surprisingly, Paul uses "to love" (ἀγαπάω) twice in the second clause of the quote in Rom 9:25 instead of the verb "to show mercy" (ἐλεέω), which appears twice in LXX Hos 2:25 (ET 2:23; reflecting the two instances of the Hebrew verb רָחַם). This seems particularly odd in view of the significance of "show mercy" (ἐλεέω or ἐλεάω) in Romans 9 (9:15 [twice], 16, 18; also the cognate noun in 9:23; see also 11:30–32). An adequate explanation is not readily apparent.

"Sons of the Living God" (Hos 1:10 in Rom 9:26)

The textual situation in Rom 9:26 is just the opposite. Paul's citation of Hos 1:10 (MT/LXX 2:1) is identical to the text of the LXX.

Rom 9:26 and LXX Hos 2:1 (ET 1:10):

καὶ ἔσται ἐν τῷ τόπῳ οὗ ἐρρέθη αὐτοῖς· οὐ λαός μου ὑμεῖς, ἐκεῖ κληθήσονται υἱοὶ θεοῦ ζῶντος.

And it will be in the place where it was said to them, "You [plural] [are] not my people," there they will be called "sons of [the] living God."

---

[21] Cf. Paul's apparent alteration of Hab 2:4 in Rom 1:17; see Middendorf, *Romans 1–8*, 99–106.

The LXX and Paul render MT Hos 2:1 (ET 1:10) accurately:

וְהָיָה בִּמְקוֹם אֲשֶׁר־יֵאָמֵר לָהֶם לֹא־עַמִּי אַתֶּם יֵאָמֵר לָהֶם בְּנֵי אֵל־חָי׃

And it will be in the place where it was said to them, "You [plural] [are] not my people," it will be said to them, "Sons of [the] living God."

Paul certainly appreciates that the Hebrew יֵאָמֵר לָהֶם, "it will be said to them," was translated by the LXX with κληθήσονται, "they will be called."[22] While an idiom for "to name" is properly drawn from the Hebrew construction קָרָא שֵׁם, "to call (someone) a name," in Hos 1:6, 9, or קָרָא לְ, literally, "to call to (someone)," as in MT Hos 2:18 (ET 2:16), the expression in MT Hos 2:1 (ET 1:10) is different. For Rom 9:26, as well as LXX Hos 2:1 (ET 1:10), the English translation "they will be called" makes better sense than "they will be named." To be sure, God himself named Israel and, thereby, his descendants, but that event took place long ago (Gen 32:28 [MT 32:29]). Hosea emphasizes God's call going out to Israel even in the places where the people will be exiled in order to reclaim them as his "sons." Such general consensus does not name God's people; only God does. Furthermore, the consistent translation with "call" for καλέω in Rom 9:26, as in Rom 9:24, 25, establishes a connection with Paul's repeated use of it thematically in reference to God's call (see 9:12; also 4:17; 8:30; 9:7).

Extended to Gentiles

In Paul's chiastic structure[23] he refers these two texts from Hosea[24] most directly to the "us" whom God called in 9:24 *from among Gentiles*. A striking change of referent has occurred thereby. But Paul is not the first to understand the Hosea passage in terms of more than one referent.[25] The initial application within Hosea's life was to his children with the harlot Gomer. After their first son, given the symbolic name Jezreel (Hos 1:4–5), they have a daughter, to whom God gives the name *Lo Ruhamah*, "not pitied" (Hos 1:6), and then a second son, *Lo Ammi*, "not my people" (Hos 1:9). God's explanation to Hosea extends the referent from the prophet's children to the children of Israel, that is, the Northern Kingdom of Israel and the Southern Kingdom of Judah (Hos 1:6–2:1 [MT/LXX 1:6–2:3]). "Hosea's prophecy promises the restoration of

---

[22] In the OT the Hebrew idiom with the Niphal (passive) of אָמַר, "say," and the preposition לְ, "to," can refer to calling someone by a term (Is 4:3; 32:5; 61:6), naming someone (Is 62:4), or naming something (Is 19:18; cf. Jer 7:32).

[23] The chiastic structure is "Jews … Gentiles" in 9:24 and then Gentiles followed by Jews in 9:25–29. See "The Connection of Romans 9:24 with the Catena of Romans 9:25–29" above.

[24] The two texts are Hos 2:23 (MT/LXX 2:25) in Rom 9:25 and Hos 1:10 (MT/LXX 2:1) in Rom 9:26.

[25] The conversion of Gentiles and their inclusion in God's people was envisioned by many OT prophets; see, for example, Is 2:1–4; 11:1–16; 19:18–25; 56:6–8; 60:1–11; 66:18–23; Ezek 16:53–63; Amos 9:11–12; Micah 4:1–3; Zeph 3:9–10; Zech 2:11 (MT 2:15); 14:16. The inclusion of believing Gentiles began already in the OT, as is witnessed, for example, by the "mixed multitude" that participated in the exodus (Ex 12:38); Ruth the Moabitess (the book of Ruth); and Uriah the Hittite (2 Samuel 11).

a sinful and wayward Israel … to covenant relationship with God."[26] While the Northern Kingdom of Israel was soon to be destroyed and exiled by the Assyrians in 722 BC (prophesied in Hos 1:4–5; fulfilled in 2 Kings 17), Hosea's children and his prophecy stand as a promise. They foretell Israel's return to the promised land, as well as a reunification of the brother and the sister, namely, those from both Judah and Israel (Hos 1:10–2:1 [MT/LXX 2:1–3]).

Paul does not dismiss the original application of the names of Hosea's children to the Israelites.[27] Neither does Paul skip over OT Israel to assert that OT prophecies of a renewed Israel find their fulfillment only in the church.[28] But it is also an unfair characterization to contend that Paul "deconstructs the oracle and dismantles Israel's privilege; with casual audacity he rereads the text."[29] The prophecy was, indeed, applicable to and at least partially fulfilled by Judah's return from exile.

Paul's citations do (as discussed above) serve to *extend the referent* of God's prophetic and enduring Word even further to those Gentiles whom God called in the apostle's own day (Rom 9:24), including most explicitly those "called" in Rome (1:6–7). While the phrase "not my people" in Hos 1:9–10 (MT/LXX 1:9–2:1; perhaps also in Hos 2:23 [MT/LXX 2:25]) originally described apostate Israel soon to be exiled, Paul here applies the term to formerly excluded Gentiles who are now among God's beloved people in Christ. Peter does much the same thing while echoing Hos 2:23 (MT/LXX 2:25) very loudly in 1 Pet 2:10: "formerly [you were] not a people, but now [you are the] people of God; [you are] the ones who had not been shown mercy, but have now been shown mercy" (οἵ ποτε οὐ λαὸς νῦν δὲ λαὸς θεοῦ, οἱ οὐκ ἠλεημένοι νῦν δὲ ἐλεηθέντες). Paul himself develops the theme most completely in Eph 2:11–22. The Gentiles referenced by the emphatic "but also" of Rom 9:24 are the ones to whom the words "even as he [the Lord] says in Hosea" now apply (Rom 9:25). One must emphasize, however, that Paul extends the meaning of the prophecy to yet another referent *only in and through Christ*. See the excursus "Beyond Typology" following the commentary on 12:1–8.

At the same time, the inclusion of Gentiles marks a striking reversal of some intertestamental texts. *Jubilees* 2:19–20, for example, records God as saying, "Behold I shall separate for myself a people from among all the nations. … And I have chosen the seed of Jacob from among all that I have seen."[30] *4 Ezra* 6:55–58 places these words about Israel into Ezra's mouth:

---

[26] Hays, *Echoes of Scripture in the Letters of Paul*, 66.

[27] Early church fathers debated whether the original referent of Hos 2:23 (MT/LXX 2:25) was to Israelites or to Gentiles. Chrysostom, *Homilies on Romans*, 16, contended: "Hosea obviously was speaking about the Gentiles here" (Bray, *Romans*, ACCS NT 6:266). But Theodoret of Cyrus, *Romans*, maintained: "This passage originally applied to Jews, not to Gentiles" (Bray, *Romans*, ACCS NT 6:266).

[28] Cf. Moo, *Romans*, 613.

[29] Hays, *Echoes of Scripture in the Letters of Paul*, 67.

[30] O. S. Wintermute, "Jubilees," *OTP* 2:57.

All this I have spoken before you, O Lord, because you have said that it was for us that you created this world. As for the other nations which have descended from Adam, you have said that they are nothing, and that they are like spittle, and you have compared their abundance to a drop from a bucket. And now, O Lord, behold, these nations, which are reputed as nothing, domineer over us and devour us. But we your people, whom you have called your first-born, only begotten, zealous for you, and most dear, have been given into their hands.[31]

Käsemann notes the "sharp antithesis" between such passages and Paul's assertions here, as well as the "great audacity" with which Paul "takes the promises to Israel and relates them to the Gentile-Christians."[32]

In What Place?

In regard to the context of Paul's day, the location(s) he intends by the expressions "in the place" (ἐν τῷ τόπῳ) and "there" (ἐκεῖ) in Rom 9:26 remain perplexing. On the basis of other prophecies (e.g., Is 2:2–4; 60:1–22; Micah 4:1–3; Zech 8:20–23), Munck proposes that Paul imminently expects the following:

He is referring to the gathering of the Gentile peoples in Jerusalem and the foundation there of the Messianic kingdom. …

In Palestine the Gentiles will be acknowledged as children of God, it may be hoped, now, even at the conclusion of Paul's third journey.[33]

Cranfield overreacts in the opposite direction by charging that "it remains exceedingly hazardous to assume that Paul was thinking of any particular place."[34] Cranfield proposes that the Hebrew prepositional phrase (בִּמְקוֹם, MT Hos 2:1 [ET 1:10]) Paul translates as "in the place" (ἐν τῷ τόπῳ) should be understood as "instead of" rather than as a reference to a place.[35] But the LXX wording (ἐν τῷ τόπῳ) quoted by Paul supports the notion of "in the place." Matera more properly suggests: " 'This place' no longer refers to Jerusalem but to any place where God speaks to people and calls them to belong to this new people, be they Gentiles or Jews."[36] At the same time, Matera's reference to a "new" people should not be misunderstood; Paul portrays those in Christ as a continuation of the OT people of God (see 11:17–24). The "place" envisioned by Hosea likely would have been "in the land of exile, the dispersion"; there God would "call out a people

---

[31] B. M. Metzger, "The Fourth Book of Ezra," *OTP* 1:536.

[32] Käsemann, *Romans*, 274.

[33] Munck, *Christ and Israel*, 72–73.

[34] Cranfield, *Romans*, 501.

[35] Cranfield, *Romans*, 501, including n. 1, citing BDB, s.v. מָקוֹם, 7 b, for that possible meaning for בִּמְקוֹם in MT Hos 2:1 (ET 1:10).

[36] Matera, *Romans*, 229.

for himself."[37] But Paul would not limit the spread of the Gospel only to areas of Jewish dispersion; he refers to the entire world.[38]

"He Called Us … from Jews" (9:24, 27–29)

While recognizing the striking application being made to Gentiles in 9:25–26, one must also keep in mind the first part of the "not only … but also" of 9:24. Paul initially affirms that God called "from Jews" (ἐξ Ἰουδαίων, 9:24). The promise to the patriarchs is fulfilled in the Good News coming "to [the] Jew first" (1:16; see also 2:9–10; 3:9, 29; 10:12; 15:8). In 9:27–29 Paul turns to Isaiah (Is 10:22–23 in Rom 9:27–28 and Is 1:9 in Rom 9:29) and focuses upon the impact of Isaiah's words on Israel. His introductory clause makes the shift clear: "but Isaiah cries out in behalf of Israel" (9:27).

The presence of the verb "cry out" (κράζω) recalls the NT prophetic proclamation of John the Baptist (e.g., Jn 1:15) and Jesus himself (e.g., Jn 7:28, 37; 12:44). However, the meaning of the preposition in the phrase "in behalf of Israel" (ὑπὲρ τοῦ Ἰσραήλ, Rom 9:27) is disputed. When followed by the genitive, ὑπέρ most commonly means *"on behalf of, for the sake of,"* but it can also express "respect: *concerning, with reference to* (= περί)."[39] While the latter is a typical translation (ESV, RSV), Hays counters that "on behalf of" ought to be adopted so that "Isaiah's cry might be heard not as a threat, but as a voice of hope."[40] It is difficult to see how either choice alters the clear meaning of the citations to follow.

In keeping with much of Paul's "both/and" argument thus far, *both* Isaiah quotations (Is 10:22–23 and then Is 1:9) express *two truths*. They stand comparable to the situation which exists between the vessels of wrath headed for destruction and those of mercy, which are headed toward the abundant glory God has prepared for them in advance (Rom 9:22–23; see the commentary there). Thus, as with the paradoxical impact of God's righteousness in Rom 1:18–4:25, Isaiah's words have a condemnatory effect at the same time as they serve as an expression of hope.

The Remnant of Israel and the Lord's Word (Hosea and Isaiah in Rom 9:27–28)

Hosea and Isaiah

In 9:27–28, the linguistic complexities increase in intensity as Paul conflates two texts, an additional one from Hosea with another from Isaiah. Paul's

---

[37] Moo, *Romans*, 614.

[38] See Paul's inclusion of "the earth" from Is 10:23 in Rom 9:28. Cf. Paul's statements "bring salvation to the ends of the earth" in Acts 13:47, quoting Is 49:6, and "in every place" in 1 Cor 1:2; 1 Tim 2:8. The OT already envisioned believing worshipers in every nation; see Is 52:10; 62:11; Mal 1:11. See also Jesus' discussion of the location of true worship in Jn 4:20–24.

[39] The quotes are from Wallace, *Greek Grammar*, 383, §§ A 1 a and A 1 b, respectively. See the second textual note on 9:27.

[40] Hays, *Echoes of Scripture in the Letters of Paul*, 68.

quotation remains "a passage not only of uncertain interpretation, but fraught w[ith] textual difficulties as well" (BDAG, s.v. συντέμνω). Rom 9:27–28 reads:

²⁷ἐὰν ᾖ ὁ ἀριθμὸς τῶν υἱῶν Ἰσραὴλ ὡς ἡ ἄμμος τῆς θαλάσσης, τὸ ὑπόλειμμα σωθήσεται· ²⁸λόγον γὰρ συντελῶν καὶ συντέμνων ποιήσει κύριος ἐπὶ τῆς γῆς.

²⁷If the number of the sons of Israel might be as the sand of the sea[shore], the remnant will be saved. ²⁸For while completing and cutting short, the Lord will accomplish [his] Word on the earth.

Aside from the initial and critically significant "if" and the following verb (ἐὰν ᾖ), the remainder of the first clause in Rom 9:27 replicates LXX Hos 2:1 (ET 1:10). Hos 2:1 reads as follows in the LXX and MT:

καὶ ἦν ὁ ἀριθμὸς τῶν υἱῶν Ισραηλ ὡς ἡ ἄμμος τῆς θαλάσσης.

And the number of the sons of Israel *was* as the sand of the sea[shore]. (LXX Hos 2:1 [ET 1:10])

וְהָיָה מִסְפַּר בְּנֵי־יִשְׂרָאֵל כְּחוֹל הַיָּם

And the number of the sons of Israel *will be* as the sand of the sea. (MT Hos 2:1 [ET 1:10])

Paul skillfully uses the Hosea verse as a bridge into Is 10:22–23, which begins with similar wording. The complete text of Is 10:22–23 in the LXX and the MT is as follows:

²²καὶ ἐὰν γένηται ὁ λαὸς Ισραηλ ὡς ἡ ἄμμος τῆς θαλάσσης, τὸ κατάλειμμα αὐτῶν σωθήσεται· λόγον γὰρ συντελῶν καὶ συντέμνων ἐν δικαιοσύνῃ, ²³ὅτι λόγον συντετμημένον ποιήσει ὁ θεὸς ἐν τῇ οἰκουμένῃ ὅλῃ.

²²And if the people of Israel might become as the sand of the sea, the remnant of them will be saved. For [he is] completing and cutting short a word in righteousness ²³because God will accomplish a word being cutting short in the whole inhabited world. (LXX Is 10:22–23)

²²כִּי אִם־יִהְיֶה עַמְּךָ יִשְׂרָאֵל כְּחוֹל הַיָּם שְׁאָר יָשׁוּב בּוֹ כִּלָּיוֹן חָרוּץ שׁוֹטֵף צְדָקָה:
²³כִּי כָלָה וְנֶחֱרָצָה אֲדֹנָי יְהוִה צְבָאוֹת עֹשֶׂה בְּקֶרֶב כָּל־הָאָרֶץ:

²²For if your people, Israel, *will be* as the sand of the sea, a remnant in him will return. Complete destruction is decided, overflowing with righteousness. ²³For a complete end, decided, is the Lord Yahweh of hosts making in the midst of all the earth. (MT Is 10:22–23)

Instead of the Greek imperfect indicative verb ἦν, "it was," which opens the passage in LXX Hos 2:1 (ET 1:10),⁴¹ Rom 9:27 opens with a conditional present subjunctive, "if it might be" (ἐὰν ᾖ). This stands comparable to the opening subjunctive clause in LXX Is 10:22, "and if it might become" (καὶ ἐὰν γένηται). The phrase "the number of the *sons* of Israel" in Rom 9:27 (ὁ ἀριθμὸς τῶν υἱῶν

---

⁴¹ MT Hos 2:1 (ET 1:10) has a Hebrew perfect with *waw* consecutive, וְהָיָה, "and (it) *will be*." The LXX translated as if the *waw* were simply conjunctive and the Hebrew perfect referred to past action, hence καὶ ἦν, "and (it) was."

Ἰσραήλ), however, matches LXX Hos 2:1 (accurately translating MT Hos 2:1 [ET 1:10]). Is 10:22 speaks, rather, of "the people, Israel" (ὁ λαὸς Ισραηλ). Both Hosea and Isaiah then contain the phrase, "as the sand of the sea[shore]." The opening conflated clause of Rom 9:27, therefore, provides a nice segue from the Hosea quotes in Rom 9:25–26 to Is 10:22–23.

The rest of Rom 9:27 compares favorably with the remainder of Is 10:22. Romans lacks the LXX's plural pronoun αὐτῶν, "the remnant *of them* will be saved." The omission may serve to make the statement more broadly applicable beyond any specific group of Israelites (cf. the omission of the third singular pronoun from Hab 2:4 in Rom 1:17). The underlying Hebrew of Is 10:22 contains a preposition with a masculine singular pronominal suffix, שְׁאָר יָשׁוּב בּוֹ, literally, "a remnant will return in/with/by *him*." Since the previous verse speaks of a remnant returning "to the mighty God" (Is 10:21), the Hebrew pronoun might refer back to God; if so, the prepositional phrase emphasizes that God is the one who enables the remnant to return. However, the Hebrew implies that the masculine preposition refers back to "your people, Israel" (עַמְּךָ יִשְׂרָאֵל), earlier in the verse (in harmony with the LXX understanding). Therefore the verse conveys the promise that "a remnant *in him* [in Israel] will return."[42]

In his quotation Paul omits these words from the middle of LXX Is 10:22–23: "in righteousness because a word being cutting short" (ἐν δικαιοσύνῃ, ὅτι λόγον συντετμημένον). Cranfield resorts to calling Paul's quotation "an abbreviation."[43] But the omission is not problematic in regard to the overall sense of the passage. However, the absence of "in righteousness" (ἐν δικαιοσύνῃ) seems odd in light of the significance of righteousness throughout Romans. Why would Paul delete it? It is possible the phrase was not present in the text of the LXX Paul had, though the MT supports it with צְדָקָה. Finally, at the end of the quotation, Rom 9:28 has "on the earth" (ἐπὶ τῆς γῆς) instead of the LXX's comparable expression, "in the whole inhabited world" (ἐν τῇ οἰκουμένῃ ὅλῃ).

Paul's Application in Romans 9:27

The bigger question surrounding Rom 9:27 concerns the meaning of the Isaiah text as Paul quotes it. The insertion of "*only* a remnant will be saved" in many English translations makes it sound rather negative (e.g., ESV, RSV, NRSV). Cranfield even contends that "the LXX must be translated 'only a remnant,' "[44] but Hays counters: "The rendering '*only* a remnant will be saved,' found in many English versions, is an interpretive paraphrase with no textual

---

[42] This view is also supported by the parallelism between Is 10:21 and Is 10:22. Is 10:21 promises that שְׁאָר יָשׁוּב שְׁאָר יַעֲקֹב, "a remnant will return, *a remnant of Jacob*," and the wording in Is 10:22, שְׁאָר יָשׁוּב בּוֹ, "a remnant will return *in him*," is parallel. "A remnant of Jacob" in Is 10:21 has been replaced by "in him" in Is 10:22, implying that "him" refers to "Jacob," that is, the people of Israel.

[43] Cranfield, *Romans*, 501.

[44] Cranfield, *Romans*, 502.

basis in any Greek manuscript."[45] As in the following quotation from Isaiah (Is 1:9 in Rom 9:29), Paul expresses both a negative and a positive message. The term "remnant" (see the sixth textual note on 9:27) means only a portion, not everybody. Therefore, while one should certainly avoid inserting the word "only" into the text, the very term "remnant" presupposes a judgment that will exclude many. However, the Hebrew phrase "a remnant *in him* will return" (MT Is 10:22) provides great assurance, an element heightened even further by the LXX verb "will be saved" (σωθήσεται).

What then is Paul's intended application of Is 10:22 in Rom 9:27? In one sense Chrysostom is correct: "This prophecy was actually fulfilled in the captivity, when most of the people were taken away and perished, with only a few being saved."[46] But it surely also points forward as Paul again hears the prophetic words in an extended sense in his own day wherein the same dual emphasis remains. The positive aspect stands completely consistent with 9:24. God called some of "us" from among Jews to believe and be saved in Christ. The phrase "from Jews" (ἐξ Ἰουδαίων) in 9:24 affirms that in Paul's day a remnant from Israel exists, some people of Israel who are both called and saved (9:24, 27), something 11:1–6 and 11:26 make even more explicit. This proves that God continues to call "vessels of mercy" (9:23) *from among Jews*. But the partitive sense of ἐκ[47] in "from Jews" (ἐξ Ἰουδαίων, 9:24), *some* from, also implies a portion or segment (as does "remnant," 9:27). As in Isaiah's day, the remnant does not include everyone, but only "some." Thus the twofold application of Is 10:22 exhibited by Rom 9:27 stands fully consistent with what is "characteristic especially of the prophets, [where] the remnant doctrine contains both a word of judgment and a word of hope."[48]

The Meaning of Romans 9:28

Rom 9:28 reads: "For while completing and cutting short, the Lord will accomplish [his] Word on the earth" (λόγον γὰρ συντελῶν καὶ συντέμνων ποιήσει κύριος ἐπὶ τῆς γῆς). Aside from the significant omission in the middle (see "Hosea and Isaiah" above), the verse is roughly equivalent to LXX Is 10:22b–23. Most problematic is the second of the two linked adverbial participles, συντελῶν καὶ συντέμνων, "completing and cutting short."[49] Interestingly, these two compound verbs with the prefixed preposition σύν, "with," are also

---

[45] Hays, *Echoes of Scripture in the Letters of Paul*, 68.

[46] Chrysostom, *Homilies on Romans*, 16 (Bray, *Romans*, ACCS NT 6:268).

[47] See Wallace, *Greek Grammar*, 84–86.

[48] Moo, *Romans*, 615, referencing Gerhard F. Hasel, *The Remnant: The History and Theology of the Remnant Idea from Genesis to Isaiah* (Berrien Springs, Mich.: Andrews University Press, 1972).

[49] See also συντετμημένον, "being cutting short," in LXX Is 10:23, which was omitted from Paul's quotation, and συντετελεσμένα καὶ συντετμημένα, "finished and cut short" (*NETS*), in LXX Is 28:22.

combined in the warning of swift judgment in LXX Dan 5:26.[50] The first, συντελῶν, denotes completion (see the first textual note on 9:28). God will carry out his word fully or completely as promised. The second, συντέμνων, literally means "cut short, shorten, limit." But to what does it refer? BDAG (s.v. συντέμνω) summarizes two options:

> The shortening is thought of as referring either to God's promise to Israel, which will be fulfilled only to a limited degree … , or to the Israelite nation, which is to enter into salvation trimmed and cut down [i.e., the remnant of 9:27].

BDAG continues by noting that others take it temporally:

> *The Lord will act by closing the account and shortening (the time)*, i.e. God will not prolong indefinitely the period of divine patience.

Murray, for example, contends that Israel will be cut off, that is, reduced to a remnant: "So widespread will be the destruction that only a remnant will escape."[51] Morris, however, reads συντέμνων as a reference to *time* that will be cut short.[52] This is the preferred interpretation, which then conveys that the Lord's Word will be accomplished speedily. Jesus' use of the verb "to shorten" (κολοβόω) in Mt 24:22 ‖ Mk 13:20 corroborates this view since he similarly speaks of time being shortened for the sake of saving people.

In either case, the two participles combine to reinforce the "decisive execution" and fulfillment of the Word of the Lord.[53] Both Isaiah and Paul announce that God is "completing and abridging His sentence, i.e., accomplishing it completely and decisively (indicating the thoroughness and dispatch with which it is executed)."[54] In keeping with the dual emphasis of the previous part of the quotation, Is 10:22a in Rom 9:27, this message need not be viewed purely as a "word [of judgment]."[55] On the other extreme, neither is the message solely positive, asserting only that "in the salvation of the remnant God will accomplish his purposes."[56] Instead, both aspects are present. Although the expression is not used in this verse, the verse's dual message is similar to Paul's frequent

---

[50] LXX Dan 5:26 reads in part: συντέτμηται καὶ συντετέλεσται ἡ βασιλεία σου, "your kingdom has been cut short and has been ended." These words appear after the translation of MT Dan 5:26 and seem to combine parts of MT Dan 5:27–28. According to MT Dan 5:26–28, Daniel explains a portion of the text from the hand that wrote on the wall as follows:

> This is the interpretation of the writing: *mene'*, God has numbered [Aramaic: *menah*] [the days of] your kingdom and has ended it; *teqel*, you have been weighted [Aramaic: *teqiltah*] in the balances, and you have been found lacking; *peres*, your kingdom is divided [Aramaic: *perisat*] and given to the Medes and Persians.

[51] Murray, *Romans*, 2:41.

[52] Morris, *Romans*, 372; see also "quickly" in NASB and GNT and "without delay" in ESV.

[53] Moo, *Romans*, 615, n. 25.

[54] Cranfield, *Romans*, 502.

[55] As λόγον in Rom 9:28 is explained by Moo, *Romans*, 615.

[56] Schreiner, *Romans*, 529.

expression "not only ... but also."[57] Most importantly, the emphatic declaration that "the Lord will accomplish [his] Word on the earth" indicates that Rom 9:28 *functions structurally. It serves to frame the thematic assertion of Rom 9:6a, which was similarly rooted in Isaiah:* "but by no means is it that God's Word [ὁ λόγος τοῦ θεοῦ] has failed and remains fallen." Indeed, "the Lord will accomplish [his] Word [λόγον]" (Rom 9:28) so that "the Word of our God stands forever" (LXX Is 40:8, quoted in 1 Pet 1:25).

The Lord Leaves the Promised Seed (Is 1:9 in Rom 9:29)

The final quotation in this section is from the opening chapter of the same prophet. The perfect tense of the verb προείρηκεν (see the first textual note on 9:29) in Paul's introductory clause asserts that these words are still in force: "And even as Isaiah *spoke previously and still holds forth:* 'If the Lord of armies had not left seed to us, we would have become as Sodom and we would have been the same as Gomorrah' " (9:29). Here Paul's citation comes verbatim from LXX Is 1:9. The LXX also translates the Hebrew literally except for one alteration that Paul certainly appreciated. For the Hebrew noun "a survivor, escapee" (שָׂרִיד), the LXX chose σπέρμα, "seed." In both Rom 9:29 and LXX Is 1:9, the passage reads as follows, with the Hebrew below:

καὶ εἰ μὴ κύριος σαβαωθ ἐγκατέλιπεν ἡμῖν σπέρμα, ὡς Σοδομα ἂν ἐγενήθημεν καὶ ὡς Γομορρα ἂν ὡμοιώθημεν.

And if the Lord of armies had not left to us seed, as Sodom we would have become and as Gomorrah we would have been the same.

לוּלֵי יְהוָה צְבָאוֹת הוֹתִיר לָנוּ שָׂרִיד כִּמְעָט
כִּסְדֹם הָיִינוּ לַעֲמֹרָה דָּמִינוּ׃

If Yahweh of hosts had not made remain for us a survivor as a few,
as Sodom we would be; to Gomorrah we would be like.

The form of the Greek conditional beautifully captures the dual impact of judgment and mercy here as well. The "if" clause is contrary to fact; it assumes, for the sake of argument, that something is true when in fact it has not happened.[58] Therefore, if Yahweh of hosts had not caused offspring to remain for us, then what follows would indeed be true—but he did, and so it is not true. In the second half of the quote, Isaiah boldly declares what Israel actually deserves. They are vessels of God's wrath (9:22) who justly ought to suffer the same fate as did the Gentiles in Sodom and Gomorrah. The sins of those cities certainly included homosexual activity.[59] But, as Ezekiel points out in his condemnation of Jerusalem's harlotries, those cities were involved in other iniquities as well:

---

[57] See "not only ... but also" in 1:32; 4:12, 16, 23–24; 5:3, 11; 8:23; 9:24; 13:5; 16:4.

[58] See the third textual note on 9:29.

[59] See Gen 19:1–13. See also the comments on Romans 1, particularly "The Unrighteous Exchange, Part 3 (1:26b–31)" and the excursus "Homosexual Conduct Is Contrary to Nature (Romans 1:26–27)" in Middendorf, *Romans 1–8*, 134–41 and 145–50, respectively.

Behold, this was the iniquity of Sodom, your sister: pride, satiation with food, and leisurely prosperity were hers and her daughters', and she did not strengthen the hand of the afflicted and needy. They were arrogant, and they did abomination before me. So I removed them when I saw. (Ezek 16:49–50)[60]

Thankfully, the assumption is false: Yahweh *did* leave "a few survivors" (Is 1:9). The LXX's use of σπέρμα, "seed, offspring," enhances the sense of God fulfilling his promise to Abraham (e.g., Gen 13:16; 15:5, 13; 16:10; 21:12; see Rom 4:13, 16, 18; 9:7, 8; cf. 1:3). Although Abraham witnessed the conflagration of Sodom and Gomorrah (Gen 19:27–28), God "remembered Abraham" and spared a remnant, Lot and his family (Gen 19:29; see also Gen 19:15–17). Isaiah declares that although Israel rightly deserves to suffer the fate of Sodom and Gomorrah, Yahweh will preserve his promised seed. Because of God's mercy, then, as now, the conclusion of the "then" clause does not happen; the facts remain to the contrary. At the same time, the verb "left" (ἐγκατέλιπεν) maintains the notion of a remnant, as it is cognate to the noun "remnant" (ὑπόλειμμα) in 9:27.[61]

The message of Isaiah in the eighth century BC applied initially to the exile of northern Israel in 722 BC, and then it would also apply to that of Judah in 586 BC. In each case, destruction came, but a few survivors were left; out of the many apostates, a few believers remained. This resonates in Paul's day as well. In spite of widespread unfaith in Israel (see 3:3–4; cf. 11:14, 20), a remnant of believers in Christ is left, including the "us" among Paul's addressees whom God *called from Jews* (9:24; see 11:1–6). The fact that in Paul's day God had also left a remnant looks forward in a manner which holds out "hope for the future of Israel."[62] "The remnant will be saved" (9:27).

Conclusion in Christ

The catena of quotations in 9:25–29 illustrates how Paul extends the meaning of God's OT Word. "After all, Paul reread and reinterpreted Israel's scriptures in light of Christ's resurrection"[63] (see 1:2–4). In so doing, Paul hears what God "says in Hosea" anew and afresh (9:25). As the Lord "still holds forth" from Isaiah (9:29), Paul hears the words fulfilled again in his own day when God "also called us, not only from Jews but also from Gentiles" (9:24). Ambrosiaster succinctly establishes the legitimacy of Paul's reading: "This has been done in Christ."[64] Paul details how God's Word accomplishes this task

---

[60] In Hebrew terminology the "daughters" of a city can refer to nearby smaller cities, and such communities were destroyed in the conflagration of Sodom and Gomorrah (Deut 29:23 [MT 29:22]; cf. Gen 14:2, 8). The verbs and the pronoun translated as "they …" and "them" are feminine plural, referring to all the cities involved.

[61] See the sixth textual note on 9:27. Note also the presence of ὑπολείπω, "leave behind/alone"; καταλείπω, "leave remaining"; and λεῖμμα, "remnant," in 11:3–5.

[62] Moo, *Romans*, 616.

[63] Matera, *Romans*, 234.

[64] Ambrosiaster, *Romans* (Bray, *Romans*, ACCS NT 6:267).

in 10:6–15. For a template to express and apply the "in Christ" application of God's OT Word more broadly, see the excursus "Beyond Typology" following the commentary on 12:1–8.

Paul has, thereby, established the veracity of his assertion regarding God's Word in Rom 9:6. "His immediate purpose in Rom. 9 is to show that despite the failure of most of his contemporaries to believe in the Messiah, God's word has not failed."[65] Why then does only a remnant believe and only this seed is saved from destruction? Why not all? (Note the implications here for 11:26.) Beginning in 9:30 and running all the way through chapter 10, Paul explains. Albeit briefly, Paul's focus moves away from God's actions to explain how and diagnose why some in Israel have responded improperly to God's Word and his call of mercy (9:30–10:5, 16–21). Then, beginning already in 10:19 and extending into Romans 11, we see how God reacts to Israel's response.

---

[65] Matera, *Romans*, 234.

Introduction to Romans 9:30–10:15: Returning to God's Righteousness

Rom 9:30 begins with "what then will we say?" (τί οὖν ἐροῦμεν;). As in 4:1; 6:1; 7:7; 8:31; and 9:14, this question introduces a new segment of Paul's argument. In 3:5; 6:1; 7:7; and 9:14, the rhetorical question "what (then) will we say?" is followed by another question which draws an *improper* conclusion that Paul proceeds to rebut. Here Paul employs the rhetorical question to introduce what he *affirms*, as signaled by the following ὅτι clause, "that Gentiles …" As a result, the chapter division at 10:1 is poorly placed. It would have been better to insert the chapter break between 9:29 and 9:30. What we call "Romans 10" for the most part applies the content of what Paul asserts in 9:30–33.

Righteousness Returns

What is Paul's new topic? Matera proposes that "Paul now focuses his attention on Israel's response to God's word (9:30–10:21)."[1] But Israel's response, at least to the Gospel message of God's merciful call, which serves as the theme of 9:6–29, is *not* the major point of discussion until 10:16. In 9:30–10:5, Paul, instead, diagnoses the problematic attempt to attain God's righteousness via the Law. Thus he is more concerned with Israel's *attempted approach to* God, rather than their response to the Good News of Jesus Christ.

Moo titles 9:30–10:21 "Understanding Israel's Plight: Christ as the Climax of Salvation History."[2] While the Christocentricity is appreciated, Christ is mentioned only once (10:4) in 9:30–10:5. He also is the unspecified referent of one pronoun (αὐτῷ), "on *him*," in 9:33. In both cases, however, Christ stands primarily as a contrast to the Law's approach. More problematic, Moo improperly views "Israel's plight" as the result of what is irrevocably rooted in "the sovereign determination of God," which Moo finds expressed in 9:6–29 in terms of unconditional double predestination.[3] He also wrongly contends that "Paul's criticism of the Jews with respect to the law is mainly salvation-historical: they have failed to see that its era has come to an end."[4] This assertion creates a nonexistent era where the Law supposedly had a divinely intended role in establishing Israel's righteousness *coram Deo*. This is contrary, for example, to

---

[1]   Matera, *Romans*, 235.

[2]   Moo, *Romans*, 616.

[3]   Moo, *Romans*, 616–17; see also, e.g., 571, 578, 598; cf. also Käsemann, *Romans*, 265; Schreiner, *Romans*, 501, 522. In the present volume, for the Lutheran understanding of the biblical teaching of election (versus Calvinistic double predestination), see "God" in the introduction to Romans 9–11; "Not 'Hated,' but 'Spurned' " and "What Paul Does *Not* Say" in the commentary on 9:6–13; and especially "Is This Fair to the Pharaoh? (9:17–18)" and "Thou Art the Potter; We All Are like Clay (9:19–21)" in the commentary on 9:14–24.

[4]   Moo, *Romans*, 619, n. 12.

Deut 9:1–6. To assert that the Law actually established Israel's righteousness is to disregard both Romans 4 and, even more glaringly, what Paul has just stated in Romans 9 regarding what was and was not the basis of the OT people's relationship with God. For example:

> [2]Indeed, if Abraham was declared righteous from works, he has a boast, but not toward God. [3]For what is the Scripture saying? "And Abraham believed God, and it was credited to him for righteousness." [4]Now to the one who works, the payment is not credited as a favor, but according to what is owed. [5]But to the one who is not working, but believing on the One who declares the ungodly righteous, his faith is being credited for righteousness. (4:2–5)

> Indeed, not through the Law was the promise to Abraham and to his seed, that he [would] be the heir of the world, but through [the] righteousness of faith. (4:13)

> [11]… in order that the purpose of God in accordance with [his] choice might endure, [12]not from works, but from the One who calls. (9:11b–12a)

> Consequently then, [God's mercy is] not of the one willing nor of the one striving, but of the God who shows mercy. (9:16)

As has been true throughout the letter, Paul's primary focus is not anthropocentric, but theocentric.[5] The title above, "Returning to God's Righteousness," calls to mind the letter's thematic statement in 1:16–17:

> [16]For I am not ashamed of the Good News, because it is [the] power of God into salvation for everyone who believes, to Jew first and also to Greek. [17]For [the] righteousness of God is being revealed in it from faith[fulness] into faith, just as it stands written: "But the righteous person will live from faith."

The vocabulary of 1:16–17 resurfaces particularly and repeatedly in 9:30–10:17. For example:

- Of the main "right-eous-ness" (δικη-) words,[6] only the noun "righteousness" (δικαιοσύνη) occurs in Romans 9–11 (as in 1:17). Yet all ten (or eleven) of its appearances are in 9:30–10:10 (9:30 [three times], 31; 10:3 [two or three times], 4, 5, 6, 10).

- In Romans 9–11 all of Paul's uses of "faith/believe" words,[7] aside from one (πίστις, "faith," in 11:20), are in 9:30–10:17 (the noun πίστις, "faith," in 9:30, 32; 10:6, 8, 17, as in 1:17 [three times], and the cognate verb πιστεύω, "believe," in 9:33; 10:4, 9, 10, 11, 14 [twice], 16, as in 1:16).

- Other terminology from 1:16–17 also reappears: "Gospel" (the noun εὐαγγέλιον, 10:16, as in 1:16; see also the cognate verb εὐαγγελίζω, "bring the Good News," in

---

[5]   See Middendorf, *Romans 1–8*, 21–22, 27, 29–30, 51; in this volume, see "Romans 1–4: The Righteousness of God" in the introduction to Romans 9–16, as well as "God" in the introduction to Romans 9–11.

[6]   For a summary, see "The Background and Meaning of 'Righteousness' Words" in the commentary on 1:17 (Middendorf, *Romans 1–8*, 92–96; see also 106–7).

[7]   For a summary, see "The Background and Meaning of 'Faith' Words" in the commentary on 1:16 (Middendorf, *Romans 1–8*, 88–90); " 'From Faith[fulness] into Faith' (1:17)" on 96–98; and also 106–7.

10:15); "save/salvation" (the verb σῴζω in 10:9, 13, and the cognate noun σωτηρία in 10:1, 10, as in 1:16); "every, all" (the adjective πᾶς, 10:4, 11, 12 [twice], 13, 16, as in 1:16), "Jew" and "Greek" (Ἰουδαῖος and Ἕλλην, 10:12 [cf. 9:30–31], as in 1:16); and "to live" (ζάω, 10:5, as in 1:17).

Righteousness Defined

The prominence of "righteousness" (δικαιοσύνη) in particular reveals that the courtroom language which dominated Romans 1–4 reemerges in this section. Recent studies have affirmed the forensic or legal nature of Paul's earlier argument, as expressed repeatedly in volume 1 of this commentary and with further implications here.[8] Wright asserts this about what he calls "the running metaphor of the *law-court*" in Paul:

> This is not arbitrary, as though it was simply one metaphor among others for how God forgives people their sins, brings them into a relationship with himself and assures them of their future hope. It is the utterly appropriate metaphor through which Paul can express and develop the biblical understanding that God, the Creator, must "judge" the world in the sense of putting it right at the last—and that God has brought this judgment into the middle of history, precisely in the covenant-fulfilling work of Jesus Christ. … According to this judgment, this "verdict" which is accomplished and publicly announced through the death and resurrection of Jesus, all those who are "in him" are "reckoned" to have died and been raised with him, so that from God's point of view their sins are no longer accounted against them and they stand on resurrection ground, free at last to live as genuine human beings. And the sign of this Spirit-given membership in the family of God's renewed covenant is neither more nor less than faith—specifically, the faith that Jesus is Lord and that God raised him from the dead. This faith, by being equally open to all, Jew and Gentile alike, indicates in its reach as well as its content that here we are witnessing the beginning of that cosmic renewal.[9]

Surburg's study then supports the translations generally adopted by this commentary:

> "Righteous" and "righteousness" serve as very suitable renderings of δίκαιος and δικαιοσύνη. With Westerholm, we can agree that "declare righteous" is an accurate translation of δικαιόω. Since this is what Lutherans mean by "to justify," they are completely accurate and true to Paul when they use this word to translate δικαιόω within the framework of forensic eschatological judgment.[10]

---

[8] See Middendorf, *Romans 1–8*, 92, 108, 176, 179, 182, 259–60, 262, 341, 389, 402, 434, 449, 467, 701. In addition to the authors cited there, see also Grieb, "The Righteousness of God in Romans"; Westerholm, *Righteousness Reconsidered*; and Das, *Galatians*, 243–45.

[9] Wright, *Justification*, 251.

[10] Surburg, "Rectify or Justify?" 77, including n. 141, citing Stephen Westerholm, *Perspectives Old and New on Paul: The "Lutheran" Paul and His Critics* (Grand Rapids: Eerdmans, 2004), 286.

The Structure of Romans 9:30–10:15

In this commentary's outline, 9:30–10:15, then, comes under the heading "Righteousness Reaffirmed." Determining an obvious division within this section remains difficult due to the skillful manner in which Paul utilizes hinge verses as he develops the progression of his thought (see 8:1–4).[a] Rom 10:4 provides a clear example. The first half of 10:4 makes an assertion about the "Law" (νόμος) prior to Paul's concluding statement about it in 10:5. From there on, the "Law" disappears until 13:8, 10, and the Gospel holds sway entirely in 10:6–15. Although the phrase "the end of the Law" in 10:4 serves mainly to signal the end of the "Law" section, it also introduces the message of Christ, who provides "righteousness for everyone who believes" (10:4b). "The righteousness from faith" (10:6) is then the theme developed fully in 10:6–15. This commentary's outline and section titles reflect that division: the "righteousness of God" (1:17; also 10:3) is "not from works of the Law" (9:30–10:5), but received through "Christ proclaimed—the word of the faith for all" (10:6–15).[11]

(a) See also, e.g., Rom 1:18; 3:1, 21; 4:1; 5:1; 6:1, 11; 9:24; 13:7–8; 14:13; 15:7

The separation of this section into 9:30–10:5 and 10:6–15 vividly illustrates the distinction between Law and Gospel in Paul's thought.[12] This dichotomy further buttresses the notion that Paul now revisits the twofold argument he expounded thoroughly and with universal implications earlier. He demonstrated unequivocally the righteous wrath of God on all under the Law in 1:18–3:20, followed by the Good News of God's saving righteousness for all in 3:21–4:25. In this light, it is intriguing that while Paul uses "Law" (νόμος) seventy-four times in Romans, it appears only four times in Romans 9–11. All four occurrences are in this section as well (9:31 [twice]; 10:4, 5). Afterward, "Law" (νόμος) appears only twice in the rest of the letter (13:8, 10). Therefore, rather than focusing specifically on Israel, or Gentiles for that matter, Paul instead hones in to diagnose two opposite avenues for attaining righteousness before God and then states their divergent outcomes. Note the following:[13]

9:30	δικαιοσύνην ... τὴν ἐκ πίστεως	
9:31–32	νόμον δικαιοσύνης ...	οὐκ ἐκ πίστεως ἀλλ᾽ ὡς ἐξ ἔργων
10:3	τὴν τοῦ θεοῦ δικαιοσύνην	τὴν ἰδίαν [δικαιοσύνην]
10:5–6	τὴν δικαιοσύνην τὴν ἐκ [τοῦ] νόμου	ἡ ... ἐκ πίστεως δικαιοσύνη

9:30	the righteousness which is from faith	
9:31–32	a Law of righteousness ...	not from faith but as if from works
10:3	the righteousness of God	their own [righteousness]
10:5–6	the righteousness which is from the Law	the righteousness from faith

A final introductory observation recognizes how Paul continues to employ numerous quotations from the OT to advance or buttress his argument at

---

[11] See Middendorf, *Romans 1–8*, 31, or the table of contents in this volume.

[12] Moo, *Romans*, 644, observes how Paul's "theological 'law'/'gospel' antithesis is at the heart [of 10:5–13]."

[13] Cf. Dunn, *Romans*, 577.

virtually every step. Romans 9–11 contains "35 direct quotations from the OT (39% of the verses)."[14] Eleven of these were in 9:6–29. Now in 9:30–10:21, Paul cites the OT ten times in twenty-five verses.[15] He even emphasizes a key point by using the quotation of Is 28:16 in Rom 9:33 and again in 10:11.[16] Paul thereby demonstrates that his proclamation of the Good News about God's righteousness and how it is received stands in full continuity with what God himself states in the Scriptures, which have not failed and are not fallen (9:6).

---

[14] Hultgren, *Romans*, 348, including n. 2, who is counting the verses identified as OT quotations in NA[27].

[15] See the excursus "Paul's Use of the Old Testament in Romans" following the commentary on 15:7–13.

[16] Notice how 1 Pet 2:6–10 similarly unites Hos 2:23 (MT/LXX 2:25), cited by Paul in Rom 9:25, with Is 28:16 and Is 8:14. Paul quotes both of those Isaiah passages together in Rom 9:33 and then repeats Is 28:16 in Rom 10:11.

Righteousness Reaffirmed, Part 1: Not from Works of the Law

Translation

9 ³⁰What then will we say? [We say] that Gentiles, those who were not pursuing righteousness, got righteousness, that is, the righteousness which is from faith, ³¹but Israel, while pursuing a Law of righteousness, did not attain to the Law. ³²On what account? Since [they were attempting to attain a Law of righteousness] not from faith but as [if it could be attained] from works, they stumbled on the stone of stumbling, ³³just as it stands written:

> "Look! I am placing in Zion a stone of stumbling and a rock of offense,
>> and the one who believes on him will not be put to shame."

10 ¹Brothers, as for me, the favorable desire of my heart and my plea to God in their behalf [are] for salvation. ²Indeed, I bear witness for them that they have zeal for God, but not in accordance with proper recognition. ³For while ignoring the righteousness of God and seeking to establish their own [righteousness], they were not submissive to the righteousness of God. ⁴You see, Christ is the end of the Law into righteousness for everyone who believes. ⁵For Moses writes [concerning] the righteousness which is from the Law that "the person who does them will live in them."

Textual Notes

9:30 τί οὖν ἐροῦμεν;—See the third textual note on 3:5 and the initial paragraph of the introduction to 9:30–10:15.

ὅτι—Here the conjunction ὅτι serves as a "marker of narrative or discourse content, direct or indirect, *that*" (BDAG, 1). After a verb of saying (ἐροῦμεν), ὅτι introduces a statement that answers the question just posed (BDAG, 1 a). Thus here after "what then will we say?" the sense is "[we say] that …" The question which opens 9:32, διὰ τί; "on what account?" also supports this sense.

ἔθνη τὰ μὴ διώκοντα δικαιοσύνην—The nominative plural ἔθνη is of the neuter noun ἔθνος. The absence of the article before ἔθνη means Paul is *not* speaking collectively of "*the* Gentiles" (KJV), as if *all* Gentiles "got righteousness." Therefore, as was true with the similarly anarthrous noun in the prepositional phrase ἐξ ἐθνῶν, "(some) from Gentiles," in 9:24, what follows does not apply to " 'the Gentiles' as a class, but (some) Gentiles,"[1] as the following clause shows. The article τά, "those who … ,"

---

[1] Dunn, *Romans*, 580. The same is true with Paul's reference to "Israel" in 9:31, as is evident by his statements about "Israel" in 9:6, 27. See "God's People" in the introduction to Romans 9–11.

goes with the negated participle διώκοντα and indicates that the participle performs an adjectival function[2] as Paul *begins* to modify specifically which Gentiles are under consideration. For the implications, see the commentary. The article τά confirms that the form of the active participle διώκοντα is neuter plural, and it must be nominative, matching ἔθνη (in form the participle could also be accusative neuter plural or accusative masculine singular). The verb διώκω often means "to pursue" with hostile intent, "to prosecute" or "persecute."[3] But Paul employs it figuratively, meaning to "*strive for, seek after, aspire to* someth[ing]" (BDAG, 4 b). Cranfield adds that here it denotes "an energetic, zealous quest" (see Rom 12:13; 14:19; 1 Cor 14:1).[4]

For the noun δικαιοσύνη, see "Righteousness Returns" and "Righteousness Defined" in the introduction to 9:30–10:15. The noun appears a total of eight or nine times in this pericope: three times in 9:30; once in 9:31; two or three times in 10:3; and once each in 10:4 and 10:5.

κατέλαβεν δικαιοσύνην—The basic meanings of καταλαμβάνω are "to seize, lay hold of" (BDAG). For this passage, BDAG then offers "to make someth[ing] one's own, *win, attain*" (BDAG, 1). Käsemann gives "ultimately get hold of."[5] On the one hand, Phil 3:12 reveals the verb can have a dynamic force; there Paul describes how "I was taken hold of [κατελήμφθην] by Christ Jesus." On the other hand, a more passive sense is appropriate here and elsewhere. See the commentary.

δικαιοσύνην δὲ τὴν ἐκ πίστεως—The conjunction δέ serves here as "a marker linking narrative segments, *now, then, and, so, that is*" (BDAG, 2). The article τήν functions like a relative pronoun,[6] which serves to define the "righteousness" under consideration as "the righteousness which is *from faith*." For ἐκ πίστεως, see 1:17; cf. also 10:6. Paul explicitly states the key contrast to this phrase in 10:5 with the full phrase τὴν δικαιοσύνην τὴν ἐκ [τοῦ] νόμου, "the righteousness which is *from the Law*."

9:31 νόμον δικαιοσύνης—For "a Law of righteousness," see the commentary.

εἰς νόμον—Here the preposition εἰς serves here as a marker "involving a goal" (BDAG, 1), "extension toward, in the direction of, a specific place to be reached" (BDAG, 1 a α). The translation "attain *to* the Law" is somewhat awkward. The full thought focuses upon failing to attain the goal of the Law, which is the righteousness of God in Christ (10:4). The sense of νόμος is clarified by the preceding phrase, "a Law of righteousness," and by Paul's fuller explanation in 10:5.

οὐκ ἔφθασεν—The verb φθάνω means "to come to or arrive at a particular state, *attain*" (BDAG, 3). Moo summarizes:

> While φθάνω does mean "come first," "precede," once in Paul (1 Thess. 4:15), in all other NT occurrences, it means "attain," "arrive at" (Matt. 12:28;

---

[2] See Wallace, *Greek Grammar*, 617–19.

[3] See LSJM; cf. Mounce, *Basics of Biblical Greek*, 420. Paul uses the verb διώκω to describe his own former persecution of the church in, e.g., Acts 22:4; 1 Cor 15:9; Gal 1:13; cf. Acts 9:4–5.

[4] Cranfield, *Romans*, 507, n. 2.

[5] Käsemann, *Romans*, 277.

[6] See Wallace, *Greek Grammar*, 213–15.

Luke 11:20; 2 Cor. 10:14; Phil. 3:16 [also 1 Thess 2:16]). The situation is the same in the LXX.[7]

The meaning here parallels that of κατέλαβεν in 9:30 (see the fourth textual note on that verse). Dunn translates εἰς νόμον οὐκ ἔφθασεν as "has not reached the law,"[8] which aligns with the race imagery that may run throughout this section. See the commentary.

9:32 διὰ τί;—This phrase "in direct questions" can be rendered as "*why?*" (BDAG, s.v. διά, B 2 b; see Acts 5:3; 1 Cor 11:11). But a more literal and revealing translation asks "on what account?"

ὅτι—In contrast to its use in 9:30 (see the second textual note on that verse), here ὅτι serves as a marker of causality, "*because, since*" (BDAG, 4 a).

ὡς ἐξ ἔργων—The particular nuance of ὡς here is that it has a "focus on what is objectively false or erroneous," namely, seeking righteousness "*not through faith but through deeds* (the latter way being objectively wrong)" (BDAG, 3 c). The phrase here, then, means "*as* [if righteousness *could* be attained] from works," with the implication that the assumption is *false*: righteousness *cannot* be attained from works. For ἐξ ἔργων, see the second textual note and the commentary on 3:20 and the excursus "The Background of 'Works of the Law'" following the commentary on 3:9–20.

προσέκοψαν—The verb προσκόπτω has two literal senses: Transitively it means "to cause to strike against someth[ing], *strike against*" (BDAG, 1; see LXX Ps 90:12 [MT/ET 91:12], cited in Mt 4:6; Lk 4:11). In a less direct action, it is defined as "to make contact w[ith] someth[ing] in a bruising or violent manner, *beat against, stumble*" (BDAG, 2; see Mt 7:27; Jn 11:9). This then becomes figurative for "to experience or cause offense" (BDAG, 3): "*take offense at, feel repugnance for, reject*" (BDAG, 3 a).

τῷ λίθῳ τοῦ προσκόμματος—The definite article τῷ with λίθῳ, "*the* stone," supports identifying this as "a special kind" of stone (BDAG, s.v. λίθος, 2).[a] The noun πρόσκομμα is a cognate of the verb προσκόπτω (see the preceding textual note) and refers to the "act of stumbling" (BDAG, s.v. πρόσκομμα, 1). In Koine Greek nouns that end in -μα usually "specify the *result* of the action,"[9] *not* the *cause* of the action. Therefore it is overly interpretive to translate this phrase as "*a stone that causes people to stumble*" (BDAG, s.v. πρόσκομμα, 1 a); that implies that the stone is somehow active(!) and designed by God to make people stumble. The phrase is better understood as denoting a stone established by God for a constructive purpose, to serve as a foundation and cornerstone (as stated in Is 28:16, which Paul quotes next in Rom 9:33), but those who reject the stone stumble over it and therefore "make a misstep" or "take offense" at it (BDAG, s.v. πρόσκομμα, 2). The meaning of the phrase here stands parallel with πέτραν σκανδάλου, "a rock of offense," in the quote of Is 28:16 in Rom 9:33 (see the third textual note on that verse).

(a) See also Mt 21:42; Mk 12:10; Lk 20:17; cf. Acts 4:11; Eph 2:20; 1 Pet 2:4, 6

9:33 καθὼς γέγραπται—For "just as it stands written," see the fourth textual note on 1:17.

---

[7] Moo, *Romans*, 622, n. 28.

[8] Dunn, *Romans*, 581.

[9] BDF, § 109.2 (emphasis added), citing πρόσκομμα among other words.

λίθον προσκόμματος—See the fifth textual note on 9:32.

πέτραν σκανδάλου—In some passages σκάνδαλον (*skandalon*, whence the English "scandal") can denote "a device used to catch someth[ing] alive, *trap*" (BDAG, 1, citing, e.g., LXX Josh 23:13; Ps 140:9 [MT/ET 141:9]; and Rom 11:9, quoting LXX Ps 68:23 [MT 69:23; ET 69:22]). However, here and in 1 Pet 2:8 it refers to "an action or circumstance that leads one to act contrary to a proper course of action or set of beliefs" (BDAG, 2). Thus some react to this rock in a way contrary to God's salvific intent. Isaiah speaks of "a rock of offense," that is, a rock by which one may be offended.

ὁ πιστεύων ἐπ᾽ αὐτῷ—With the article, ὁ πιστεύων is a nominative singular participle used substantively,[10] "the one who believes."[11] Paul uses πιστεύω with the preposition ἐπί, "believe (up)on," for faith in the God who justifies the ungodly (4:5) and who raised Jesus from the dead (4:24); see also 10:11. The preposition ἐπί with the dative (here αὐτῷ) serves as a "marker of basis for a state of being, action, or result, *on*" (BDAG, 6). Grammatically αὐτῷ refers back to the masculine antecedent, λίθον, "stone" (not the feminine πέτραν, "rock"), and so it could be translated as "on *it*," but Paul most likely intends it to be heard as a double entendre, which now and primarily serves as a personal reference to the Messiah/Christ, "on *him.*" See the commentary.

οὐ καταισχυνθήσεται—For the verb καταισχύνω, see the first textual note on 5:5, where the negated active means that Christian hope "will not put [us] to shame." The eschatological sense of the future tense identified there[12] is also present in this future passive. While the believer "will not be put to shame" (9:33) by circumstances or enemies (as in Isaiah's context), the emphasis here resides in one's relationship with God himself (*coram Deo*). It is less likely that the future should be read in a gnomic or logical manner[13] as "*is* not being put to shame," as with the future ζήσομεν, "will we still live (now)," in 6:2.

10:1 ἀδελφοί—For 'brothers," see the second textual note on 1:13; but cf. the fourth textual note and the commentary on 9:3. The vocative here does not signal a new section or chapter. In fact, ἀδελφοί generally does not do so; instead, it typically shows up in the midst of a discussion, providing an engaging point of contact (e.g., Rom 1:13; 7:4; 8:12; 1 Cor 1:11; 7:24, 29).

ἡ μὲν εὐδοκία—The particle μέν has no corresponding δέ later in the verse. According to BDF, § 447.4, this use of μέν alone reflects a classical use, "so far as it depends on." The translation of μέν here, "as for me,"[14] abbreviates the sense. The noun εὐδοκία can refer to the state or condition of goodwill, pleasure, or favor (see BDAG, 1 and 2; e.g., Lk 2:14; Eph 1:5; Phil 1:15; 2:13; 2 Thess 1:11). Here, however,

---

[10] See Wallace, *Greek Grammar*, 619–21.

[11] See the fifth textual note on 1:16; "The Background and Meaning of 'Faith' Words" in the commentary on 1:16 (Middendorf, *Romans 1–8*, 88–90); " 'From Faith[fulness] into Faith' (1:17)" on 96–98; and also 106–7.

[12] See "Hope Assured and Love Outpoured (5:5)" in the commentary on 5:1–11 (Middendorf, *Romans 1–8*, 395–97).

[13] See Wallace, *Greek Grammar*, 571.

[14] Cranfield, *Romans*, 504.

εὐδοκία is parallel in meaning with δέησις, "plea" (see the next textual note), and conveys a "desire, usually directed toward someth[ing] that causes satisfaction or favor, *wish, desire*" (BDAG, s.v. εὐδοκία, 3). Particularly in Sirach, where εὐδοκία occurs fourteen times and the cognate verb εὐδοκέω appears six times, "the range of meaning includes the more active sense of a will which asserts itself."[15] The positive emphasis of the prefixed εὐ- is conveyed here by modifying the noun as "the *favorable* desire."

ἡ δέησις πρὸς τὸν θεὸν ὑπὲρ αὐτῶν—The noun δέησις is used for an "urgent request to meet a need, exclusively addressed to God, *prayer*" (BDAG). Paul employs the prepositional phrase πρὸς τὸν θεόν for his prayers "to God" also in Rom 15:30. Paul often identifies a δέησις, "plea," as offered "in behalf of" people with the preposition ὑπέρ (as in 2 Cor 1:11; 9:14; Phil 1:4; 1 Tim 2:1–2; cf. Eph 6:18). In Rom 10:1 he pleads ὑπὲρ αὐτῶν, "in behalf of them," that is, of Israel. The collective singular Ἰσραήλ, "Israel," in 9:31 is then the subject of the plural verb προσέκοψαν in 9:32 and is the antecedent of the plural pronoun αὐτῶν here. It is also the antecedent of αὐτοῖς in 10:2 (see the first textual note there).

εἰς σωτηρίαν—The preposition εἰς, "*for* salvation," here expresses the goal or outcome (BDAG, s.v. εἰς, 4). In regard to Paul's specific plea, the preposition defines "the vocation, use, or end indicated *for, as*" (BDAG, 4 d). The identical phrase occurs in 1:16, although in a different sense, "*into* salvation" (BDAG, 4 e).

10:2 μαρτυρῶ γὰρ αὐτοῖς ὅτι—The conjunction γάρ functions as a "marker of clarification, *for, you see*" (BDAG, 2). Under this heading, BDAG adds: "Indeed, in many instances γάρ appears to be used adverbially like our 'now' (in which the temporal sense gives way to signal an important point or transition), 'well, then,' 'you see.' " Other suggested translations are "moreover" and "indeed." The verb μαρτυρέω provides the connotation of legal testimony, attested here by Paul's personal statement in the first person, "I bear witness." The dative to follow, αὐτοῖς, "for them" (i.e., for Israel; see the discussion of αὐτῶν in the third textual note on 10:1), indicates those about whom testimony is given, while ὅτι introduces its content (see BDAG, s.v. μαρτυρέω, 1). Together with the resurgence of δικη-, "right(eous)," terminology (see the third textual note on 9:30), this phrase reinforces the forensic nature of this section (cf. 1:18–3:31).

ζῆλον θεοῦ—Dunn summarizes the noun ζῆλος, "zeal; jealousy":

In itself [ζῆλος] is neither good nor bad, and in the NT usage is almost equally divided between the two [see BDAG]; in Paul, positive—2 Cor 7:7, 11; 9:2; 11:2 (cf. 1 Cor 12:31; 14:1, 39; Titus 2:14); negative—Rom 13:13; 1 Cor 3:3; 2 Cor 12:20; Gal 5:20 (cf. 1 Cor 13:4). But the usage here [in Rom 10:2 with θεοῦ] is one not found in secular Greek and is characteristic of Jewish piety, passionate consuming zeal focused on God.[16]

Käsemann affirms the Jewish background, noting that the phrase ζῆλον θεοῦ became "a technical term to characterize the piety which is oriented to the model of Phinehas and

---

[15] Dunn, *Romans*, 585.

[16] Dunn, *Romans*, 586; for the last comment, see also A. Stumpff, "ζῆλος," *TDNT* 2:877–80.

Elijah among the Maccabees and Zealots, at Qumran, and in many rabbinic circles."[17] The noun ζῆλος and its cognates ζηλωτής, "zealous person, zealot," and ζηλόω, "be zealous," do at times refer to God's own zeal.[b] But here the genitive θεοῦ is objective,[18] depicting human zeal *for* God," that is, directed toward him. Stumpff comments that this zeal "may be very good, but it may also be misplaced or perverted."[19] Paul illustrates the latter with his own "zeal" as a Pharisee (ζῆλος, Phil 3:6) and as a "zealot" (ζηλωτής, Acts 22:3; Gal 1:14). Cf. the compound verb παραζηλόω, "provoke to envy," in Rom 10:19; 11:11, 14.

(b) E.g.,
LXX Ex
20:5; 34:14;
Deut 4:24;
5:9; 6:15;
Josh 24:19;
Nah 1:2;
Zeph 1:18;
3:8; Zech
1:14; Zech
8:2

κατ᾽ ἐπίγνωσιν—For the noun ἐπίγνωσις, see 1:28 and 3:20. Here the prepositional phrase conveys *"in accordance w[ith] (real) knowledge"* (BDAG, s.v. ἐπίγνωσις) or, more appropriately, "in accordance with proper recognition."

10:3 ἀγνοοῦντες ... ζητοῦντες—Paul connects the action of these two participles, "while ignoring ... seeking." Both are present active nominative plural in form and used adverbially in relation to the negated main verb, ὑπετάγησαν, "they were not submissive" (see the fifth textual note on 10:3). The first participle is of the verb ἀγνοέω, which occurs six times in Romans. Some uses simply reflect the passive notion, "to be uninformed about, *not to know, be ignorant (of)*" (BDAG, 1; e.g., Rom 1:13; 6:3; 11:25), which Paul typically proceeds to remedy (see the first textual note on 6:3). But other uses go beyond a mere lack of knowledge. Here the active voice of the participle extends the sense. BDAG lists this passage under the definition "to pay little or no attention to, *not to recognize, disregard, ignore*" (BDAG, 2; see also Rom 2:4; 7:1). ζητοῦντες then reflects the opposite action. While "ignoring" one thing, they are "seeking" after another. BDAG elaborates upon the meaning of ζητέω in terms of *"strive for, aim (at), try to obtain, desire, wish (for)"* (BDAG, 3).

τὴν τοῦ θεοῦ δικαιοσύνην—This is equivalent to the phrase δικαιοσύνη ... θεοῦ, "[the] righteousness of God," in 1:17; see the commentary there.[20]

τὴν ἰδίαν [δικαιοσύνην]—The repetition of δικαιοσύνην may be original (e.g., 𝔓⁴⁶ א). If not (e.g., A B D), the context clearly assumes it.[21] The key contrast comes from the adjective that modifies "righteousness," ἴδιος, which means "belonging or being related to oneself, *one's own*" (BDAG, 1).

στῆσαι—This first aorist infinitive of ἵστημι completes the action of ζητοῦντες:[22] they are "seeking" to "set up or put into force, *establish*" (BDAG, 3) their own righteousness.

---

[17] Käsemann, *Romans*, 280.

[18] For the objective genitive, see Wallace, *Greek Grammar*, 116–19.

[19] A. Stumpff, "ζῆλος," *TDNT* 2:881.

[20] Middendorf, *Romans 1–8*, 91–96.

[21] Moo, *Romans*, 630, n. 2, concludes that "it is more likely that scribes added" δικαιοσύνην "to clarify τὴν ἰδίαν"; similarly, Käsemann, *Romans*, 281, who says that the addition "leads to a superfluous interpretation." Metzger, *A Textual Commentary on the Greek New Testament*, 524, affirms the lack of significance by not discussing the variant.

[22] For the complementary (supplementary) use of the infinitive, see Wallace, *Greek Grammar*, 598–99.

οὐχ ὑπετάγησαν—Paul here negates the aorist indicative passive of ὑποτάσσω, "submit." For the meaning of the verb, see the fourth textual note and the commentary on 8:7. Moo suggests that "the confusion of middle and passive in Hellenistic Greek, and especially with this verb, makes it possible to understand the passive ὑπετάγησαν as a reflexive middle,"[23] which would mean that "they did not subject themselves." In a sense, this is correct due to the nature of this verb's meaning which can have something like a stative sense in the passive. BDAG describes its passive as denoting "submission in the sense of voluntary yielding" (s.v. ὑποτάσσω, 1 b β). God's righteousness actively came to unbelieving Israel (see 10:6–8), but, as a result of their active "ignoring" and "seeking" (see first textual note on 10:3), their response (or reflex) entails a failure to yield; thus "they were not submissive" to what God provided.

10:4 τέλος γὰρ νόμου—For the translation of the conjunction γάρ as "you see," see the first textual note on 10:2. The major options for understanding τέλος in relation to νόμου here are the Law's "end," "goal," "result," "termination," or some combination thereof.[24] The commentary fully discusses the complex matter.

εἰς δικαιοσύνην—With "righteousness" the preposition εἰς serves as a marker of a goal (BDAG, 4), more specifically indicating "the result of an action or condition indicated *into, to, so that*" (BDAG, 4 e), the actual receiving of "righteousness." The preposition εἰς has the same sense in the phrase εἰς σωτηρίαν in 1:16. Cf. εἰς the second textual note on 9:31 and in the fourth textual note on 10:1.

παντὶ τῷ πιστεύοντι—See 1:16 for the identical phrase with the same meaning: "for everyone who believes."

10:5 Μωϋσῆς γὰρ γράφει—Moo observes that "this is the only place where Paul uses the present tense of γράφω ['write'] to introduce an OT quotation; the emphasis is on the current applicability of the quotation."[25] This matches the comparable use of present tense verbs to introduce Scripture citations in 9:25 (λέγει, "says") and 9:27 (κράζει, "cries out"). While the present impact is highlighted here, it is also conveyed by Paul's use of the perfect tense γέγραπται, "it has been and now stands written," sixteen times in Romans (e.g., 9:33; see 1:17).

τὴν δικαιοσύνην τὴν ἐκ [τοῦ] νόμου—In contrast to the similar formula δικαιοσύνην ... τὴν ἐκ πίστεως, "the righteousness which is from faith," in 9:30, Paul here refers to "the righteousness which is from the Law." As in 9:30, the second appearance of the definite article τήν functions as a relative pronoun, "which."[26] Depending on the textual placement of ὅτι (see next textual note), this accusative phrase could be the object within the quotation of what "Moses writes." But it more likely should be read as an accusative of respect or a (general) reference employed "to qualify a statement that would otherwise typically not be true."[27] In such a use, translations "can usually

---

[23] Moo, *Romans*, 633, n. 18.

[24] For an exhaustive overview, see Cranfield, *Romans*, 515–19.

[25] Moo, *Romans*, 645, n. 5.

[26] See the fifth textual note on 9:30 and Wallace, *Greek Grammar*, 213–15.

[27] Wallace, *Greek Grammar*, 203; he cites 10:5 as an example (204).

supply the words *with reference to*, or *concerning*."[28] The translation above includes "concerning." See the commentary.

ὅτι—The location of the conjunction ὅτι varies in the textual tradition. In ℵ and A, ὅτι occurs between γράφει and τὴν δικαιοσύνη. NASB adopts this reading: "for Moses writes *that* the man who practices the righteousness which is based on law shall live by that righteousness" (emphasis added; cf. RSV).[29] However, 𝔓⁴⁶ B and D² have ὅτι after νόμου at the conclusion of the phrase discussed in the previous textual note. Metzger properly supports this placement for the following reasons:

> (1) because of early and diversified external support; (2) because copyists would have been more likely to move the ὅτι to a position immediately after γράφει than conversely; and (3) because the expression ποιεῖν τὴν ἐκ νόμου δικαιοσύνην is non-Pauline.[30]

The translation above, "the Law *that* … ," reflects that reading, in which ὅτι introduces the Scripture quotation (see the next textual note).

ὁ ποιήσας αὐτὰ ἄνθρωπος—For ποιέω, "do," see the second textual note on 7:15. This citation of Lev 18:5 from the LXX illustrates the adjectival use of a Greek participle.[31] The definite article ὁ indicates that the participle ποιήσας modifies ἄνθρωπος, literally, "the doing man," meaning "the man who does." The participle also has its own object, αὐτά, "them," referring to the Lord's commandments/statues and judgments (see Lev 18:5). As an aorist participle, ποιήσας "denotes *antecedent* time to that of the controlling verb."[32] Thus the future tense of the main verb, ζήσεται, "will live," places the action of ποιήσας in the present: "the person who *does* them."

ζήσεται—The same future form of ζάω, "to live," occurs in the thematic Hab 2:4 quotation in Rom 1:17. See the commentary there.[33]

ἐν αὐτοῖς—The translation of this prepositional phrase expresses the basic sense, "in them," in keeping with the underlying Hebrew in Lev 18:5, בָּהֶם. For a discussion of whether ἐν should be taken as indicating sphere (locative)[34] or as a dative of means/instrument,[35] see the commentary.

Commentary

Overview

Paul's Law/Gospel antithesis is at the center of 9:30–10:15.[36] The initial section, 9:30–10:5, contains Paul's last reference to the "Law" (νόμος) until 13:8. Grammatically, a string of four sequential verses beginning with γάρ ("indeed,

---

28 Wallace, *Greek Grammar*, 203.

29 Also Cranfield, *Romans*, 520–21.

30 Metzger, *A Textual Commentary on the Greek New Testament*, 524–25.

31 See Wallace, *Greek Grammar*, 617–19.

32 Wallace, *Greek Grammar*, 614.

33 Middendorf, *Romans 1–8*, 98–109.

34 See Wallace, *Greek Grammar*, 153–55.

35 See Wallace, *Greek Grammar*, 162–63.

36 Cf. Moo, *Romans*, 644.

for, you see"),[37] 10:2–5, is also disrupted by the disjunctive δέ, "but," at the start of 10:6, further signaling a shift. Thematically, the "Gospel" side of the antithesis then dominates 10:6–15, where Paul writes exclusively about the Good News of salvation through faith in Christ.

In 9:30–10:5 Paul evaluates the role of the Law in relation to the righteousness of God. While the topic was dealt with previously, particularly in 2:17–3:20, Paul revisits it here specifically in relation to Israel. As Moo points out, in 9:30–10:4 Paul seems "especially interested in explaining the plight of unbelieving Jews. The Gentiles' involvement was mentioned only briefly (9:30) or allusively (10:4b: 'for all who believe')."[38] Similarly, references to Christ (the "stone" and "rock" in 9:33; "Christ" in 10:4) and faith/believing (9:30, 32, 33; 10:4) occur here primarily as foils to the Law. Theologically, 9:30–10:5 centers on diagnosing why those characterized as "Israel" fail to receive the righteousness of God in faith. Paul contends that their attempt to secure "their own" righteousness (10:3) "as [if it could be attained] from works" of the Law explains their stumbling (9:32). Yet Paul also includes his own fervent "plea" for a change (10:1).

Got Righteousness? (9:30–32a)

Gentiles and the Righteousness from Faith (9:30)

Paul begins this section with a question[39] to which he himself then affirmatively responds: "What then will we say? [We say] that Gentiles, those who were not pursuing righteousness, got righteousness, that is, the righteousness which is from faith" (9:30). As in 9:25–26, Paul again turns to speak regarding Gentiles first, but they then drop from view as Paul interacts primarily with "Israel" through 10:3. However, his references are applicable generally to "Israel," yet not universally to all descendants, but to "some" (3:3; see the commentary there and "God's People" in the introduction to Romans 9–11). The lack of the definite article with "Gentiles" (ἔθνη, 9:30) similarly indicates that Paul does not refer to all Gentiles, but speaks only of some, namely, those who believe.[40]

The use of the verbs διώκω and καταλαμβάνω "is a familiar sequence denoting pursuit and catching up or overtaking ... ,[41] but the imagery of the race may be closer to Paul's mind (as in Phil 3:12; cf. 1 Cor 9:24)."[42] Paul depicts the Gentiles as "not pursuing righteousness" at all (Rom 9:30). This is not to

---

[37] Paul uses γάρ 144 times in Romans. Similar sequences occur in 1:16, 17, 18, 19, 20; 2:11, 12, 13, 14; 6:19, 20, 21, 23; 8:13, 14, 15.

[38] Moo, *Romans*, 644.

[39] For the introductory interrogative, see the initial paragraph of the introduction to 9:30–10:15.

[40] Observed also by Cranfield, *Romans*, 506; Barrett, *Romans*, 192–93.

[41] See LXX Gen 31:23; Ex 15:9; Deut 19:6; 2 Ki 25:5; Sirach 11:10; see also καταδιώκω and καταλαμβάνω in LXX Deut 28:45; Josh 2:5; 1 Sam 30:8; Ps 7:6 (ET 7:5); Lam 1:3.

[42] Dunn, *Romans*, 580.

be understood only in terms of failing to follow a moral lifestyle, as intimated by Barrett with the translation "who do not make righteousness their aim."[43] Paul speaks about righteousness in terms of a relationship with God (see 1:17). This is affirmed by the quotation from Is 65:1 in Rom 10:20, where God himself declares, "*I was found among the ones not seeking me.*"

Such Gentiles as have now believed, Paul asserts, actually "got righteousness" (κατέλαβεν δικαιοσύνην). This compound verb, καταλαμβάνω, can have an active sense (see the fourth textual note on 9:30). But the simple verb λαμβάνω also can convey more passive meanings, "to be a receiver, *receive, get, obtain*" (BDAG, 10). Delling properly proposes " 'to attain definitively,' in R[om]. 9:30 in respect of the righteousness of faith, and paradoxically, without any effort."[44] This significant ambiguity carries over into the English verb "get," which works well as a general translation for λαμβάνω. Depending on the context, "get" can be active, e.g., "get that book!" or passive, e.g., "did you get a letter?"[45] In the latter, passive sense, the Gentiles under consideration were not actively pursuing righteousness in order to "take" it. Yet they "got" it anyway, even in spite of themselves and, paradoxically, "without effort." This coincides with and reinforces the passive nature of "faith" (πίστις) later in the verse, as well as for Paul in general.[46] Delling adds that in the compound verb καταλαμβάνω, whose aorist here in 9:30 is translated as "got," the prefixed preposition κατά adds "the character either of intensity ... or of suddenness."[47] The latter applies here, as 10:17 corroborates.

What those Gentiles "got" is "righteousness, that is, the righteousness which is from faith [ἐκ πίστεως]" (9:30). The fact that "righteousness" is the topic most prominently on Paul's mind, and not Israel or the Law, stands out clearly in 9:30. Three out of four consecutive Greek words are "righteousness" (δικαιοσύνην κατέλαβεν δικαιοσύνην, δικαιοσύνην). The linking of "righteousness" (δικαιοσύνη) with "faith" (πίστις) recalls the central role of both words in 1:16–17, establishing themes which have reverberated throughout the letter ever since.[48] There righteousness is shown to be an essentially relational term *coram Deo* with forensic connotations. As Abraham found to be the case, God "declares the ungodly righteous" (4:5). Properly understood, the action comes solely from God to humanity and is received "from faith" (ἐκ πίστεως). This critical prepositional phrase at the end of 9:30 occurs twice in the thematic

---

[43] Barrett, *Romans*, 192.

[44] G. Delling, "καταλαμβάνω," *TDNT* 4:10.

[45] Both the active and passive senses of λαμβάνω are illustrated in the Words of Institution. In Mt 26:26 ‖ Mk 14:22, Jesus actively "took" (λαβών) bread, but then gave it to his disciples and invited them to passively "receive" (λάβετε) it from his hand.

[46] See "The Background and Meaning of 'Faith' Words" in the commentary on 1:16 (Middendorf, *Romans 1–8*, 88–90); " 'From Faith[fulness] into Faith' (1:17)" on 96–98; and also 106–7.

[47] G. Delling, "καταλαμβάνω," *TDNT* 4:10.

[48] For a more thorough discussion of both "righteousness" (δικαιοσύνη) and "faith" (πίστις), see the treatment of 1:16–17 in Middendorf, *Romans 1–8*, 83–109.

statement of 1:17 and serves to identify faith as the sole source (ἐκ) of receiving God's righteousness in Christ. In his comments on 1:17, Lenski states:

> As regards salvation, as regards true righteousness, as regards life spiritual and everlasting, and that means as regards the gospel, all else is excluded, race, nationality, culture (Jew, Greek, barbarian), law, works, human prerogatives, claims, and everything else, and only the believer, only faith—faith—faith (Paul has the word three times) is included.[49]

Israel and a Law of Righteousness (9:31)

The blessed situation of those Gentiles who are righteous "from faith" in 9:30 serves as a contrast to what Paul states in 9:31: "but Israel, while pursuing a Law of righteousness, did not attain to the Law." In contrast to Gentiles, Israel is actively "pursuing" (διώκων). Just as Paul is not speaking of all Gentiles in 9:30, so he does not speak of all Israel in 9:31. Instead, he employs an adverbial participle to express attendant circumstance, "Israel, while pursuing," a picture comparable to his use of "the one striving" in 9:16. In other words, he refers to the segment of the people who are actually doing what follows.

The object of Israel's pursuit is "a Law of righteousness" (νόμον δικαιοσύνης). One might expect Paul to say they are pursing "the righteousness which is from the Law," as stated in 10:5, so here Paul writes surprisingly. Dunn perhaps overstates the importance by asserting: "Everything hangs on how νόμος δικαιοσύνης is understood,"[50] but the "phrase has become a storm center of debate."[51] The easiest solution may be to follow the RSV, which reverses the order of the Greek terms in order to translate the verse as equivalent to 10:5, "the righteousness which is based on law." However, Cranfield responds: "In such a situation it is important that we should try to resist both the temptation to rewrite Paul's sentence for him and also the temptation to treat Greek grammar as though it were a waxen nose that can be pulled into any shape one pleases."[52]

If one reads the text as is, the primary contested point, once again, is the referent of νόμος ("Law"). As in previous passages (e.g., 3:27; 7:21, 23; 8:2), Sanday and Headlam resort to a metaphorical interpretation and render the phrase as "a rule of life which would produce righteousness."[53] Murray similarly suggests that νόμος refers to a "principle or rule or order. Israel is represented as pursuing that order or institution which was concerned with justification."[54] This view largely comes from rejecting the notion that Paul could be depicting the revealed Law of God or some aspect thereof. Previously, for example,

---

[49] Lenski, *Romans*, 82.

[50] Dunn, *Romans*, 581.

[51] Moo, *Romans*, 622.

[52] Cranfield, *Romans*, 507.

[53] Sanday and Headlam, *Romans*, 279 (see also 95, 182–83, 190). Cf. ESV: "a law that would lead to righteousness."

[54] Murray, *Romans*, 2:43.

what Paul says of νόμος in 7:21–23 is deemed too negative to be a reference to the Law of God; what he attributes to νόμος in 3:27 and 8:2a is regarded as too positive.[55] But dismissing the Mosaic Law from this context removes one of the main factors under consideration![56]

Dunn properly responds that the referent of νόμος "is certainly the (Jewish) law, as usual (not 'norm' or 'rule,' …)."[57] Westerholm more specifically points to "the Mosaic law code which demands righteousness."[58] Thus νόμος reflects its most common Pauline understanding, as a reference to the commands of God's Law.[59] The phrase then communicates that "the law 'promises' righteousness when its demands are met" (as in 7:10; see also 10:5).[60] Schreiner explains the genitive that follows (δικαιοσύνης) as an objective genitive, which portrays Israel as "seeking the law 'for righteousness,' for a right relationship with God."[61] As Ambrosiaster states: "They claimed the righteousness which is commanded in the law, i.e., the sabbath, circumcision, etc. … They did not fulfill the law, and those who do not fulfill the law are guilty of it."[62] If one pursues that commanded righteousness via the Law, then, as Käsemann counters, the Law has unfortunately been "misunderstood and made a summons to achievement."[63]

Käsemann, however, reads νόμος in 9:31 as an expression of God's promise: "The law is thus viewed as the witness of righteousness, as in 3:21."[64] Cranfield similarly contends: "It was intended and designed to show the people of Israel how they could be righteous before God, to show them that the way to this righteousness is—faith."[65] While such positive understandings of νόμος are appropriate in other contexts (e.g., 3:21b, 27; 8:2), here Paul focuses upon the inability of the Law's command to enable people to attain righteousness (see 8:3). At the same time, these interpretations allude to an important point: *whether from God or his Law, righteousness is righteousness.* However, due to

---

[55] See the commentary on those passages; see also the excursus "Paul and the Law" following the commentary on 13:8–14.

[56] This commentary consistently understands νόμος, "Law," throughout the epistle to refer to the Torah of Moses. See, e.g., Middendorf, *Romans 1–8*, 278–80 (on 3:21), 294–95 (on 3:27), 301–3 (on 3:31), 573–74 (on 7:21–23), and 604–9 (on 8:2). See also "Positive Conclusions" in the commentary on 10:4.

[57] Dunn, *Romans*, 582; he later adds that the phrase should be understood as "lived in terms of its (God's) demands."

[58] Westerholm, *Israel's Law and the Church's Faith*, 127.

[59] See the textual notes on 2:12 and the excursus "Paul and the Law" following the commentary on 13:8–14.

[60] Moo, *Romans*, 625, including n. 39.

[61] Schreiner, *Romans*, 537; Moo, *Romans*, 626, similarly speaks of the "pursuit of this 'law for righteousness.' " For the objective genitive, see Wallace, *Greek Grammar*, 116–19.

[62] Ambrosiaster, *Romans* (Bray, *Romans*, ACCS NT 6:269).

[63] Käsemann, *Romans*, 277.

[64] Käsemann, *Romans*, 277.

[65] Cranfield, *Romans*, 508.

humanity's fall into sin and the resulting incapacity of any person to keep the Law, one cannot choose between pursing righteousness from the Law (10:5) or another righteousness "from faith" (9:30). The only avenue available receives the righteousness God freely grants to those who believe (e.g. 1:17; 3:22–24; 4:3–5; 10:4). The problem Paul identifies is that Israel's "pursuit of the law with respect to the righteousness that it promised should have been carried out on the basis of faith."[66]

The yearning for righteousness in relationship with God is appropriate (see 10:2). A desire to follow the Law is also good (e.g., 7:12, 18, 22). But 9:31 reflects "the typical Jewish understanding of the law, as a goal to be pursued (διώκω), as a standard which defines what God requires of his covenant people."[67] Wisdom 2:11 reflects this attitude by urging: "And let our strength be [the] Law of righteousness" (ἔστω δὲ ἡμῶν ἡ ἰσχὺς νόμος τῆς δικαιοσύνης).

From Faith or Works? (9:32a)

In light of the controversy over "Law" (νόμος) in 9:31, discussed above, it is fair to conclude that "Paul's meaning in v 31 would not have been wholly clear (and deliberately so) without v 32a."[68] Fortunately, Paul continues by explaining why Israel did not attain righteousness by pursing it: "On what account? Since [they were attempting to attain a Law of righteousness][69] not from faith but as [if it could be attained] from works, they stumbled on the stone of stumbling" (9:32). *Paul has now established his "righteousness" antithesis, not in terms of Law and promise/Gospel, but in terms of faith versus works* (οὐκ ἐκ πίστεως ἀλλ᾽ ὡς ἐξ ἔργων, 9:32).[70] Rom 9:30–32 then stands consistent with foundational passages from earlier in Romans:[71]

> Consequently, from works of the Law, every fleshly person will not be declared righteous before him, because through the Law [is] a recognition of sin. (3:20)

> For we conclude that a person is being declared righteous by faith apart from works of the Law. (3:28)

---

[66] Moo, *Romans*, 626, n. 44; he later adds that Israel "was pursing the law *in terms of its promise of righteousness*" (627).

[67] Dunn, *Romans*, 581.

[68] Dunn, *Romans*, 582.

[69] The implied verb here in 9:32 is φθάνω, "attain," which was the last Greek word of 9:31 (ἔφθασεν). Cranfield, *Romans*, 509, and Dunn, *Romans*, 582, contend that the assumed verb here must be διώκω, "pursue," as in 9:30–31, but to imply that Israel ought to have been pursuing from faith negates the point of 9:30 and 10:22 and contradicts the passive receptivity of faith in receiving righteousness. The implied object is the difficult phrase from the previous verse (9:31), "a Law of righteousness." The commentary on 9:31 discusses it extensively (see above); see also 10:4, which succinctly and definitively identifies how and through whom the Law's goal is attained with its resulting righteousness.

[70] Westerholm, *Israel's Law and the Church's Faith*, 129, states: "For, paradoxically, the *goal of the law* can only be attained *apart from the law*, by faith." But the antithesis is not with regard to the Law as a whole, but with pursuing righteousness "from works" (ἐξ ἔργων).

[71] See also the excursus "The Background of 'Works of the Law' " following the commentary on 3:9–20.

²Indeed, if Abraham was declared righteous from works, he has a boast, but not toward God. ³For what is the Scripture saying? "And Abraham believed in God, and it was credited to him for righteousness." ⁴Now to the one who works, the payment is not credited as a favor, but according to what is owed. ⁵But to the one who is not working, but believing on the One who declares the ungodly righteous, his faith is being credited for righteousness. (4:2–5)

¹¹… in order that the purpose of God in accordance with [his] choice might endure, ¹²not from works, but from the One who calls. (9:11b–12)

The problem with Israel's pursuit is not really self-deception "as to the goal"; instead, "on the pathway on which they set out they come to a fall."[72] Righteousness is indeed a goal of the Law (9:31); Paul himself will soon speak of "the righteousness which is from the Law" (10:5). But pursing that goal via the pathway of works renders the goal unattainable. It is not that "Israel's mistake was to understand righteousness as something peculiarly theirs" in nationalistic terms.[73] Equally inadequate is Sanders' assertion that "Israel's failure is not that they do not obey the law in the correct way, but that they do not have faith in Christ."[74] On the contrary, Paul's faith/works antithesis is *not* presented in both/and terms, but as an *either/or* proposition. Righteousness remains unattainable via works of the Law precisely because the corrupted flesh of sinful, fallen humanity renders all people wholly unable to meet the Law's righteousness requirements (e.g., 1:32; 3:9–20; 5:12; 7:18, 23; 8:3). Theodore of Mopsuestia aptly summarizes Paul's assessment of the human condition:

> It is impossible to be justified by the works of the law because it would be necessary to keep the whole law, which is not possible. But anyone who sins (which is inevitable) lies under the judgment of the law.[75]

This is why Paul adds the critical qualification ὡς ἐξ ἔργων, "*as if* [righteousness could be attained] from works" (9:32).[76] Attempting to live in relationship with God based upon works of the Law simply will not work because every person's works fall short (3:23). This explains why Israel, while actively "pursuing a Law of righteousness," nevertheless "did not attain to the Law" (εἰς νόμον

---

[72] Käsemann, *Romans*, 278, asserts both. In regard to the first quotation, the deception is not about the goal, righteousness. Instead, in keeping with Käsemann's second quotation, Dunn, *Romans*, 582, similarly identifies the problem as "the way that pursuit was envisaged and practiced."

[73] As Dunn, *Romans*, 583, contends.

[74] Sanders, *Paul, the Law, and the Jewish People*, 37.

[75] Theodore of Mopsuestia, *Romans* (Bray, *Romans*, ACCS NT 6:269).

[76] Note how the older son in Luke 15 similarly based his relationship with his father on his own works in obedience to the father's commands: "Look for how many years I am serving [as a slave, δουλεύω] for you, and I never passed by/transgressed your commandment" (ἐντολήν σου, Lk 15:29). This parable is used illustratively in the commentary on Rom 10:19 and 11:11–12.

οὐκ ἔφθασεν, 9:31; see 10:4). As Origen clarifies: "It was because they relied on works, not on faith."[77]

Paul states that one gets or receives righteousness (κατέλαβεν δικαιοσύνην, 9:30) not by pursuit of it (see also 9:12, 16) but by God's declaration in Christ, which is received "from faith" (1:17; 9:30; see also 3:28; 10:6–15; 11:20). Thus Paul's discussion is *not* simply about different paths to choose in regard to one's relationship with God. Instead, the entire matter revolves around which way the traffic is going. *In regard to attaining righteousness, Paul insists there is only a one-way street, from God toward us in Jesus Christ.*

Responding to the Rock: A Stone of Stumbling or Believing? (9:32b–33)

When Israel attempted to attain righteousness "as [if it could be attained] from works, they stumbled on the stone of stumbling" (9:32). In order to explain, Paul returns to Isaiah (whom he cited in Rom 9:27–29) and borrows a metaphor from the prophet. Dunn claims that Rom 9:33 combines Is 28:16 and Is 8:14 in a manner "such as we do not find in Jewish exegesis."[78] But that assertion is unwarranted since *Paul himself is a Jewish exegete* (cf. 11:8, 26–27). So is Peter, who utilizes the same Isaiah texts in a comparable manner in 1 Pet 2:6–8 (along with Ps 118:22; see also the quotation of Ps 118:22 in, e.g., Mk 12:10–11; Acts 4:11). It also overlooks the comparable reworking of other OT Scriptures in light of the coming of the Jewish Messiah by fellow Jews including Matthew, John, and James (e.g., Mt 2:15, 17–18, 23; Jn 7:38; James 4:5).

In regard to the "stone" imagery in non-Christian Jewish literature, Jeremias demonstrates that it is interpreted messianically in the Targum and more broadly in rabbinic literature based upon Is 28:16 and other OT texts (e.g., Gen 28:18; Ex 17:6; Num 20:7–11; Dan 2:34–35, 44–45). "The fact that Rock is often a name for Yahweh in the OT prepared the ground and made the way smoother for the Messianic understanding of many OT stone passages."[79]

Isaiah's Stone Texts (Is 28:16 and Is 8:14 in Rom 9:33)

At the same time, Paul's conflation of the two Isaiah texts seems quite remarkable. Paul's words are given below, followed by the LXX and MT of Is 28:16 and Is 8:14:

> καθὼς γέγραπται· ἰδοὺ τίθημι ἐν Σιὼν λίθον προσκόμματος καὶ πέτραν σκανδάλου, καὶ ὁ πιστεύων ἐπ᾽ αὐτῷ οὐ καταισχυνθήσεται.

> Just as it stands written: "Look! I am placing in Zion a stone of stumbling and a rock of offense, and the one who believes on him will not be put to shame." (Rom 9:33a)

---

[77] Origen, *Romans* (Bray, *Romans*, ACCS NT 6:269).

[78] Dunn, *Romans*, 583.

[79] J. Jeremias, "λίθος," *TDNT* 4:272–73.

διὰ τοῦτο οὕτως λέγει κύριος ἰδοὺ ἐγὼ ἐμβαλῶ εἰς τὰ θεμέλια Σιων λίθον πολυτελῆ ἐκλεκτὸν ἀκρογωνιαῖον ἔντιμον εἰς τὰ θεμέλια αὐτῆς, καὶ ὁ πιστεύων ἐπ᾽ αὐτῷ οὐ μὴ καταισχυνθῇ.

On account of this, thus the Lord says, "Look! I myself will put into the foundations of Zion a stone, precious [and] chosen, an honored cornerstone into her foundations, and the one who believes on him will certainly not be ashamed." (LXX Is 28:16)

לָכֵן כֹּה אָמַר אֲדֹנָי יְהוִה הִנְנִי יִסַּד בְּצִיּוֹן אָבֶן
אֶבֶן בֹּחַן פִּנַּת יִקְרַת מוּסָד מוּסָד הַמַּאֲמִין לֹא יָחִישׁ׃

Therefore thus says the Lord Yahweh, "Look, I founded in Zion a stone, a stone of testing, a precious corner foundation being founded; the one who believes will not be dislodged." (MT Is 28:16)[80]

Romans has the present verb τίθημι, "I am placing," instead of the comparable future verb in the LXX, ἐμβαλῶ (future of ἐμβάλλω), "I will cast, lay, put in(to)."[81] The MT has the more specific verb "to found, establish" (יִסַּד, Piel perfect of יָסַד).[82] More striking is that the stone's impact, as described in the LXX, is completely positive; it is "precious [and] chosen, an honored cornerstone [which God has placed] into her foundations." However, the original MT indicates that the stone can evoke either a positive or a negative response: "*a stone of testing*, a precious corner foundation being founded." The two nouns in the construct phrase אֶבֶן בֹּחַן, "a stone of testing," could have a verbally passive meaning, "a stone that has been tested," but the phrase may also have a verbally active meaning, "a stone that tests people." The latter meaning would explain Paul's adaptation in Romans, which speaks negatively of "a stone of stumbling and a rock of offense" (λίθον προσκόμματος καὶ πέτραν σκανδάλου, Rom 9:33).

The end of the Romans quotation aligns closely with LXX Is 28:16. Rom 9:33 concludes with "and the one who believes on him will not be put to shame" (καὶ ὁ πιστεύων ἐπ᾽ αὐτῷ οὐ καταισχυνθήσεται). The LXX is identical except it has the more emphatic οὐ μή, "certainly not," instead of simply οὐ, "not," and

---

[80] Most of the Hebrew vocabulary is readily understandable, but the syntax is difficult. First, the verb יִסַּד is third person (masculine singular Piel perfect), so a literal translation of הִנְנִי יִסַּד would be "look, I, *he* founded." The implied subject of the third person verb might be "the Lord Yahweh." In any case, the meaning is clear: God is the one who establishes the foundation stone. Second, the middle of the verse features an unusual three-word construct chain, פִּנַּת יִקְרַת מוּסָד, literally, "corner of a precious of a foundation." Note the alliteration of the noun "foundation" and the Hophal participle of יָסַד, "to found": מוּסָד מוּסָד, "a foundation being founded." Third, at the end of the verse, the Hiphil of חוּשׁ, the imperfect יָחִישׁ, would ordinarily mean "to hasten" (intransitive or transitive), but the contextual meaning here must be something like "*hasten away* (flee)" (BDB, s.v. חוּשׁ I, Hiphil, 1) or "give way, be dislodged" (*DCH*, s.v. חוּשׁ I, Hiphil, 3). In the context of constructing a building, "not be dislodged" is appropriate for other stones placed upon the foundation established with the precious cornerstone.

[81] For these meanings, see LEH, s.v. ἐμβάλλω.

[82] Regarding the syntax, see the footnote above on the Hebrew of Is 28:16.

the negated aorist subjunctive καταισχυνθῇ, "will certainly not be ashamed," rather than the negated future indicative καταισχυνθήσεται, "will not be put to shame." The Hebrew literally promises that "he who believes will not make haste." The expression communicates confident reliance which implies there is no need to rush or hurry. The negated verb might also mean "will not (need to) flee." Or, if the believer is envisioned as a stone in the building constructed upon the foundation established by the cornerstone, it may mean that the believer "will not be dislodged" from the foundation.[83] The Greek clause ὁ πιστεύων in LXX Is 28:16 and Rom 9:33, "the one who believes," literally translates the Hebrew Hiphil participle in Is 28:16, הַמַּאֲמִין, whose meaning is well established.[84] Next in LXX Is 28:16 and Rom 9:33, the Greek prepositional phrase with the third person pronoun, ἐπ᾽ αὐτῷ, "on him," has no counterpart in the underlying MT. Hebrew can use "to believe" in an absolute sense, without any object or subordinate clause (e.g., Is 7:9; 28:16; Job 29:24), and this absolute usage is fairly common in the Greek NT,[85] but the addition of the prepositional phrase clarifies the object of faith; for its Christological significance, see the fourth textual note on 9:33.

Comparing Romans to Isaiah 28, Moo's analysis postulates:

> Paul's wording is, then, mainly LXX, but similarities with the wording in 1 Pet. 2:6 (cf. esp. τίθημι ["I am placing"], which never in the LXX translates the Hebrew word used here) suggest that Paul may be relying on a Greek version of the text circulating among the early Christians.[86]

Where, then, does Paul get the notion of "a stone of *stumbling* and a rock of *offense*" (λίθον προσκόμματος καὶ πέτραν σκανδάλου, 9:33)? Once again, it comes from Isaiah, but now Is 8:14. The LXX and then the MT of Is 8:14 follow:

> καὶ ἐὰν ἐπ᾽ αὐτῷ πεποιθὼς ᾖς, ἔσται σοι εἰς ἁγίασμα, καὶ οὐχ ὡς λίθου προσκόμματι συναντήσεσθε αὐτῷ οὐδὲ ὡς πέτρας πτώματι· ὁ δὲ οἶκος Ιακωβ ἐν παγίδι, καὶ ἐν κοιλάσματι ἐγκαθήμενοι ἐν Ιερουσαλημ.

> If you trust in him, he will become your holy precinct, and you will not encounter him as a stumbling caused by a stone nor as a fall caused by a rock, but the house of Jacob is in a trap, and those who sit in Ierousalem [Jerusalem] are in a pit. (LXX Is 8:14 *NETS*)

---

[83] For these two possible meanings of the Hebrew, see the third point in the footnote above on the Hebrew of Is 28:16.

[84] The Hiphil of אָמַן commonly means "to believe" in God or his Word. See, e.g., Gen 15:6; Ex 4:31; 2 Chr 20:20; famously Is 7:9 and Is 53:1; Jonah 3:5.

[85] See BDAG, s.v. πιστεύω, 1 d. See also "The Background and Meaning of 'Faith' Words" in the commentary on 1:16 (Middendorf, *Romans 1–8*, 88–90); " 'From Faith[fulness] into Faith' (1:17)" on 96–98; and also 106–7.

[86] Moo, *Romans*, 629, n. 54.

וְהָיָה לְמִקְדָּשׁ וּלְאֶבֶן נֶגֶף וּלְצוּר מִכְשׁוֹל לִשְׁנֵי בָתֵּי יִשְׂרָאֵל
לְפַח וּלְמוֹקֵשׁ לְיוֹשֵׁב יְרוּשָׁלָ͏ִם׃

And he will become a sanctuary and a stone of striking and a boulder[87] of stumbling to the two houses of Israel, a trap and a snare to the inhabitants of Jerusalem. (MT Is 8:14)[88]

The LXX and MT diverge on a number of counts, though Paul's phrasing borrows from both texts and conveys the same basic sense of both. Most importantly, the opening words of the LXX express the notion of trusting or, more accurately, "if you might be (having been and now) persuaded upon him" (ἐὰν ἐπ᾽ αὐτῷ πεποιθὼς ᾖς) in a manner comparable to "the one who believes on him" in LXX Is 28:16 and Rom 9:33 (ὁ πιστεύων ἐπ᾽ αὐτῷ) and "the one who believes" in MT Is 28:16.

Specifically relevant to the phrase "a stone of *stumbling* and a rock of *offense*" (λίθον προσκόμματος καὶ πέτραν σκανδάλου) in Rom 9:33, the LXX has "as a stumbling caused by a stone … as a fall caused by a rock" (*NETS*; ὡς λίθου προσκόμματι … ὡς πέτρας πτώματι). Dunn observes: "The use of Isa 8:14, while more problematic [than the use of Is 28:16], seems to indicate a Greek rendering closer to the MT than the LXX, but reflected also in Aquila and Theodotion."[89] In the MT, Is 8:13 makes clear that it is "Yahweh of hosts" who himself will be "a stone of striking and a boulder of stumbling" (Is 8:14). While the difficulties are not all readily explainable, Moo again points out how "Paul's wording of the phrase from [Is] 8:14 agrees neither with the LXX nor the MT, but is identical (except for a change of case) with 1 Pet. 2:8. … Again, this suggests Paul is drawing his reference from an early Christian tradition."[90] Jesus' use of the imagery of the rejected stone from Ps 118:22 is worth noting, particularly in Lk 20:17–18, where he may also allude to Is 8:14 (see also Mt 21:42; Mk 12:10–11).

Negative Implications

The compilation of both Isaiah passages allows Paul to speak of *the same stone* being *both* the object of stumbling/offense *and* the object of believing/

---

[87] The Hebrew noun צוּר often refers to a "rock cliff" or, figuratively, to God as a "rock mountain" of refuge, but here the meaning *"block of stone, boulder"* (BDB, s.v. צוּר I [under the root צור V], 1 c) is most appropriate.

[88] The first Hebrew construct phrase (two nouns), literally translated as "a stone of striking," may have a verbally passive meaning, "a stone against which a person's foot strikes," or a verbally active meaning, referring to "a stone that strikes people" (cf. Dan 2:34–35). But in Jesus' sayings in Mt 21:44 and Lk 20:18, a person *first* stumbles and falls over the rock, and only afterward does Jesus speak of the rock falling on a person. The second Hebrew construct phrase, "a boulder of stumbling," likely has a passive meaning, referring to a stationary "boulder" or "rock cliff" over which people "stumble" and fall; this means that the first construct phrase likely has a passive meaning too.

[89] Dunn, *Romans*, 584, quoting Aquila: εἰς λίθον προσκόμματος καὶ εἰς στερεὸν σκανδάλου, and Theodotion: εἰς λίθον προσκόμματος καὶ εἰς πέτραν πτώματος.

[90] Moo, *Romans*, 629, n. 55.

faith. What determines which will happen? The fact that the Lord himself places the stone in Zion does not mean that "Israel's fall was intended by God."[91] Instead, the Lord God intends the stone to serve as the solid foundation (Is 28:16). The "stumbling" in Rom 9:32–33, as indicated by the use of the same Greek noun (πρόσκομμα) later in 14:13, 20, depicts *human reaction, not divine causation* (see the fifth textual note on 9:32).[92] More importantly, Paul clearly explains within this very context the manner in which the Isaiah citation in 9:33 should be understood. *The negative human response is caused not by God but by people's own actions* in "seeking to establish their own [righteousness]" (10:3); by attempting to attain righteousness "*from works*, they stumbled on the stone of stumbling" (9:32). As Gundry observes:

> Paul is not criticizing the Jews' unbelief in Christ *instead of* their attempt to perform the law, but ... he is criticizing their unbelief *as caused by* an attempt to perform the law. That attempt leads to self-righteousness, but not because of any fault in the law itself or in obedience as such.[93]

According to 9:32, if one attempts to attain righteousness from works, then one will stumble over the stone. (Pseudo-)Constantius observes how people, "thinking that they could be justified by the works of the law, were unable to come to the law of righteousness, that is to say, to faith in Christ."[94]

The imagery of stumbling reinforces the notion that the picture of an athletic race underlies Paul's thought throughout this section (see also 9:16, 31).[95] Those who pursue righteousness "as [if it could be attained] from works" (ὡς ἐξ ἔργων, 9:32) are the ones who "stumbled" (προσέκοψαν; see the fourth textual note on 9:32) and even took "offense" at the rock (σκάνδαλον, 9:33). As Paul moves ahead, he explains further why running after righteousness leads to stumbling. Seeking to establish one's own righteousness results in not submitting to the righteousness of God, which, through faith in Christ, comes to everyone who believes (see 10:3–4).

Positive Implications in Christ

But for those "not pursuing righteousness" via their works (9:30), the Lord himself does the action. He places "in Zion a stone ... and the one who believes in him will not be put to shame" (9:33). Here is the positive Gospel side, which Paul returns to briefly in 10:4 and expounds upon most fully in 10:6–15. Paul clearly establishes that *Christ is the referent of the stone* when he repeats his citation of the end of Is 28:16 in Rom 10:11 with an introductory πᾶς: "*everyone* who believes on him will not be put to shame." There again, God takes the

---

[91] As Dunn, *Romans*, 584, maintains.

[92] See also the discussion of 1 Pet 2:8 in the commentary on Rom 9:22.

[93] Gundry, "Grace, Works, and Staying Saved in Paul," 19.

[94] (Pseudo-)Constantius, *Romans* (Bray, *Romans*, ACCS NT 6:269).

[95] Observed by Dunn, *Romans*, 580, 589, 593; Matera, *Romans*, 240, 242; Stowers, *A Rereading of Romans*, 312–15; see also the commentary on 11:11.

initiative and sends the message of Christ out to those who are not even seeking it (see 10:14–15, 17, 20). The critical role of "faith" (ἐκ πίστεως, "from faith," in 9:32; see also 9:30; 10:6, 8, 17; 11:20) is reinforced by the verb "believe" (πιστεύω) in 9:33. Although this verb occurs only four times in the LXX of Isaiah[96] and has not appeared in Romans since 6:8, its presence in Is 28:16 allows Paul to reintroduce it here. He then utilizes "believe" (πιστεύω) thematically seven more times in the verses that follow (10:4, 9, 10, 11, 14 [twice], 16).

Thus this very same stone, Jesus the Messiah/Christ, provides righteousness for the getting from faith (9:30) but is a cause of stumbling and offense for those who pursue it "from works" (9:32). If one believes on the rock placed by the Lord as the solid foundation, he gets righteousness through faith and will not be put to shame (9:30, 33). If, on the other hand, one actively pursues righteousness from works, he stumbles over the Rock and is offended by him (9:32–33). Of whom does Paul speak in each case? In this context he depicts "Gentiles, those who were not pursuing righteousness" (9:30), as representing the former; "Israel, while pursuing a Law of righteousness" (9:31), characterizes the latter. As Paul continues into what we now call chapter 10, he maintains his primary focus upon diagnosing the latter situation.

The introduction to Romans 9–11 discusses how Paul's descriptions in this section are general characterizations, not uniformly applicable to all people in either group (Jews or Gentiles). Nevertheless, what Paul says to both is universally relevant for all people since (1) sinful human nature is naturally inclined to pursue righteousness through works and (2) the Gospel call to believe and not be ashamed is for all people. Before we continue, Chrysostom reminds us of the universal and ongoing implications of 9:30–33:

> This is said not of the Jews only but of the entire human race. ... The wonder is that the prophet [Isaiah] speaks not only of those who will believe but also of those who will not believe. For to stumble is to disbelieve.[97]

Matera draws this equally valid, but positive, conclusion which anticipates 10:4 and 10:6–15:

> For if righteousness is a relational concept that involves a right relationship with God rather than an ethical notion of personal achievement, and if all have sinned (3:9), then only God can bring about this right relationship. And if only God can effect this relationship, the proper response to what God has accomplished is trusting faith.[98]

---

[96] In Isaiah the verb πιστεύω, "believe," appears only in LXX Is 7:9; 28:16; 43:10; 53:1.

[97] Chrysostom, *Homilies on Romans*, 16 (Bray, *Romans*, ACCS NT 6:270).

[98] Matera, *Romans*, 242.

Paul's Plea to Restore the Righteousness
Unbelieving Israel Ignored (10:1–3)

Paul's Heartfelt Desire and Plea to God (10:1)

"Brothers, as for me, the favorable desire of my heart and my plea to God in their behalf [are] for salvation" (10:1). The insertion of the vocative ἀδελφοί, "brothers," heightens the connection Paul seeks to make with his hearers. In contrast with 9:3, the referent here is the audience of all believers in Rome (1:6–7) who receive this letter (as ἀδελφοί, "brothers," is used also in 1:13; 7:1, 4; 8:12). The source of the "great sorrow and unceasing anguish" Paul expressed in 9:2 "in behalf of my brothers, my kinsmen according to [the] flesh; such ones are Israelites" (9:3–4) returns to the fore here. This indicates that those in Israel depicted in 9:31 are the ones in whose behalf Paul also prays here. The expression "the favorable desire of my heart" (ἡ … εὐδοκία τῆς ἐμῆς καρδίας, 10:1) expresses more than an emotional appeal. The sentiment permeates Paul's entire being. He then puts that yearning into action with his ongoing petitions to God. "In praying for his own people's salvation, Paul would be conscious that he stood in a noble tradition."[99] At the same time, Paul's prayerful pleading "for salvation" (εἰς σωτηρίαν, 10:1) clearly implies the somber conclusion that those for whom he intercedes are not currently in a state of salvation (see 10:9, 10; 11:26). It also conveys his fervent desire that the current situation be remedied, which again dispels any notion of predeterminism or double predestination.[100]

Zeal: Good or Bad? (10:2)

Paul proceeds to explain the reason for his favorable desire, as well as the cause of the problem, in 10:2: "Indeed, I bear witness for them that they have zeal for God, but not in accordance with proper recognition." The presence of the verb "bear witness" (μαρτυρέω) reflects the forensic language which dominated 1:18–3:31 (e.g., 3:21; see also συμμαρτυρέω, "testify," in 2:15). This adds credence to the notion that Paul also develops a courtroom picture here. At the very least, the resurgence of legal terminology in 9:30–10:15 presumes an awareness of the case Paul argued persuasively in those earlier chapters.

Paul offers positive testimony in Israel's behalf regarding their zeal for God. While "zeal" sounds good, its use in the NT can have either salutary, positive or dire, negative connotations, depending upon the basis for one's zeal and the end to which it is directed. The OT often characterizes God himself as "zealous" (see the second textual note on 10:2). In the intertestamental era,

---

[99] Dunn, *Romans*, 586, citing as examples of that tradition Ex 32:11–14; Num 21:6–9; 1 Sam 7:8–9; Ps 99:6; Jer 42:2–4, 19–22; Ezek 11:13; *Testament of Moses* 11:17.

[100] Despite the expected protests of Murray, *Romans*, 2:47; Moo, *Romans*, 632, including n. 9. Regarding the Lutheran understanding of the biblical teaching of election versus Calvinistic double predestination, see "God" in the introduction to Romans 9–11; "Not 'Hated,' but 'Spurned' " and "What Paul Does *Not* Say" in the commentary on 9:6–13; "Is This Fair to the Pharaoh? (9:17–18)" and "Thou Art the Potter; We All Are like Clay (9:19–21)" in the commentary on 9:14–24; and the introduction to 9:30–10:15.

Mattathias exhibits zeal most famously as he issues this summons which instigates the Maccabean revolt:

> And Mattathias cried out in the city with a great voice, saying: "Let everyone who is zealous for the Law [πᾶς ὁ ζηλῶν τῷ νόμῳ] and who upholds [the] covenant come out after me!" And he and his sons fled to the mountains and left as much as they had in the city. (1 Macc 2:27–28)

The negative aspect of the zeal initially commended by Paul in Rom 10:2 comes across with his added assertion that it is "not in accordance with proper recognition" (ἀλλ᾽ οὐ κατ᾽ ἐπίγνωσιν, 10:2). Here again, previous uses of the term ἐπίγνωσις, "recognition, knowledge," are instructive. In 1:28, Paul speaks of those who "did not approve to have God in [proper] recognition" (ἐν ἐπιγνώσει). As discussed in the commentary there, Paul's description is not exclusively applicable to Gentiles, but encompasses at least some Jews as well. Rom 3:20 identifies one divinely intended outcome of a proper "recognition" (ἐπίγνωσις) which clearly seeks to encompass *all* people. Paul concludes: "Consequently, from works of the Law, every fleshly person will not be declared righteous before him, because through the Law [is] a *recognition of sin*" (ἐπίγνωσις ἁμαρτίας). Therefore, as exhibited by those Jews who fit the descriptions characterized by Paul in this context, "zeal" (10:2) clearly has negative connotations (cf. 2:17–20 and the commentary there).

"Seeking to Establish Their Own" Righteousness (10:3)

In the context of 9:30–10:5, the phrase "not in accordance with proper recognition" (10:2) defines unbelieving Israel's zeal as "misdirected—that is, not based on a recognition of how God's righteousness is bestowed."[101] As Pelagius observes: "The Jews are zealous in pursing the law, but they do not understand that Christ came according to the law and that they cannot be justified by the law."[102] This conclusion is evident from 9:31–33 and defined even more specifically in 10:3: "for while ignoring the righteousness of God and seeking to establish their own [righteousness], they were not submissive to the righteousness of God."

Paul again connects a number of simultaneous actions. In 9:31, "Israel, while pursuing a Law of righteousness, did not attain to [the goal of] the Law." Now "ignoring" one thing and seeking to establish another leads to not submitting to the righteousness of God. Understanding the verb ἀγνοέω ("to ignore") as a passive lack of knowledge can hardly be applicable to those in Israel who "were entrusted with the sayings of God" (3:2; see also 9:4–5). Instead, the *active* participle ἀγνοοῦντες implies an active "ignoring." Its grammatical direct object restates the dominant theme of Romans 1–4, "the righteousness of God" (τὴν τοῦ θεοῦ δικαιοσύνην, 10:3; see also 1:17). In 1:17, Paul declares how the "righteousness of God is being revealed" from God to us in Christ. In 10:3,

---

[101] Dunn, *Romans*, 587.

[102] Pelagius, *Romans* (Bray, *Romans*, ACCS NT 6:272).

unbelieving Israel's active "ignoring" is accompanied by an active "seeking." While "ignoring" the divine disclosure in Christ, those Paul describes continue "seeking" (present participle, ζητοῦντες) to establish something else.

The action of "seeking" (ζητοῦντες) in 10:3 stands synonymous with that of "pursuing" (διώκων) in 9:31. The object being pursued in 9:31 is "a Law of righteousness." In 10:3, Paul states another critical flaw in the arena of righteousness: *it resides not merely in the direction of the action but also its purported goal, "to establish their own" righteousness*. Paul underscores the determinative significance of the direction of the action with the complementary infinitive "to establish" (στῆσαι, from ἵστημι) which follows "seeking" (ζητοῦντες). Dunn notes that "στῆσαι ['to establish'] reflects the Hebrew הֵקִים (hiphil of קוּם) and in particular the characteristic use of the verb in connection with the covenant—usually of God's 'establishing' his covenant."[103] Thus, when *God* is establishing his covenant to give his righteousness *to Israel*, things are on the right track and going in the proper direction. Note, however, the quotation of 1 Macc 2:27 cited above. There Mattathias depicts every person being zealous for the Law as one "who upholds [the] covenant" (ἱστῶν διαθήκην). The verb ἱστάω (equivalent to ἵστημι), "uphold," literally means "cause to stand."[104] When ἵστημι is used transitively, as in Rom 10:3 (as is ἱστάω in 1 Macc 2:27), the verb carries connotations of "set up or put into force, *establish*" and "cause to be steadfast" (BDAG, s.v. ἵστημι, A 3 and 5). In regard to a covenant relationship with God, humans inappropriately and ineffectually presume to undertake any such action.

Similarly, the sense of establishing "their own" (τὴν ἰδίαν) righteousness in Rom 10:3 should not be diminished to "the sense of 'mine' as belonging to me in contrast to what someone else can claim as belonging to him, 'mine' as 'peculiar to me.' "[105] There is no element of comparison among humans here (and Paul is speaking with plural participles about groups in general, not individuals). It is not a matter of my righteousness versus their lack of righteousness (see Lk 18:9–12). Instead, the alternative to "their own" in Rom 10:3 is the very "righteousness *of God*," which they are "ignoring." In other words, it is not the righteousness of one community versus that of another; it is "their own" versus "God's." Augustine captures the point even more specifically: "For they were ignorant of the righteousness of God, not that righteousness whereby God is righteous but the one which comes to man from God"[106] (e.g., 1:17; 3:21–22).

---

[103] Dunn, *Romans*, 588, citing ἵστημι, "to establish," in LXX Gen 6:18; 9:11; 17:7, 19, 21; 26:3; Ex 6:4; Lev 26:9; Deut 8:18; 9:5; 29:12 (ET 29:13); Jer 11:5; Sirach 17:12; 45:7, 24.

[104] See LSJM, s.vv. ἱστάω and ἵστημι I; Mounce, *Basics of Biblical Greek*, 426.

[105] As maintained by Dunn, *Romans*, 587.

[106] Augustine, *Grace and Free Will*, 12.24 (Bray, *Romans*, ACCS NT 6:272).

Corroboration and Consequences

What is sought, then, can be described as "a righteous status of their own earning."[107] It is "the righteousness which man exerts himself to achieve by fulfilling the 'works of the Law' [e.g., 3:20]."[108] No one exemplifies this more than Paul himself did. In Philippians 3 Paul employs much of the same terminology and provides an insightful parallel to Rom 9:30–10:5. He speaks of his zeal for God which previously exhibited itself in persecuting the church (κατὰ ζῆλος διώκων τὴν ἐκκλησίαν, Phil 3:6). "According to righteousness which is in the Law" (κατὰ δικαιοσύνην τὴν ἐν νόμῳ), Paul the Pharisee considered himself "blameless" (ἄμεμπτος, Phil 3:6). The fallacy lies in the fact that all the action was *from Paul toward God*. Now, as a believer, Paul's righteousness is rooted elsewhere. In regard to his earlier zeal and his supposed righteousness in the Law, he writes:

> καὶ ἡγοῦμαι σκύβαλα, ἵνα Χριστὸν κερδήσω ⁹καὶ εὑρεθῶ ἐν αὐτῷ, μὴ ἔχων ἐμὴν δικαιοσύνην τὴν ἐκ νόμου ἀλλὰ τὴν διὰ πίστεως Χριστοῦ, τὴν ἐκ θεοῦ δικαιοσύνην ἐπὶ τῇ πίστει.

> And I regard [them as] dung in order that I might gain Christ ⁹and be found in him, *not* having *my own righteousness*, which is from the Law, but that [righteousness] which is through faith of/in Christ,[109] the *righteousness* which is *from God* upon faith. (Phil 3:8b–9)

"While seeking to establish their own" righteousness, Jews like Paul before his conversion "were not submissive to the righteousness of God" (Rom 10:3). As with the stumbling discussed in 9:32–33, the refusal to be under the righteousness given by God occurs in connection with other actions. Here it is ignored because righteousness is sought elsewhere. The negated verb "they were not submissive" certainly includes the outright rejection of Jesus as the Messiah.[c] But, as the history of the OT illustrates, that rejection of the Messiah in the flesh (Rom 9:5) is the culmination of Israel's all-too-common propensity not to submit to God's righteousness as he proffered it already in the OT means of grace (Rom 9:4–6). As in 9:32, the alternatives "from faith" or "from works" already pertained to OT Israel. Abraham showed the propriety and exclusive nature of the righteousness received from God through faith (see Gen 15:6 and Rom 4:1–5). *But when people strive to drive their own righteousness toward God, they ignore and even impede the one-way traffic flow of the righteousness of God toward them.*

> Paul acknowledges ... the reality of Israel's zeal for God [10:2], but refers to the disastrous failure of comprehension which distorts and perverts their zeal, their blindness to the righteousness which is God's gift and obstinate determination to establish their own righteousness on the basis of their works,

(c) Cf., e.g., Lk 23:21, 23; Jn 1:11; Acts 2:23, 36; 3:14–15; 17:3–5; 18:5–6

---

[107] Cranfield, *Romans*, 515.

[108] Bultmann, *Theology of the New Testament*, 1:285.

[109] For the ambiguous translation "through faith of/in Christ," see the excursus "πίστις Ἰησοῦ Χριστοῦ, 'Faith of/[in] Jesus Christ' " following the commentary on 3:21–31.

which result in a refusal to accept God's proffered gift humbly as the undeserved gift of His mercy.[110]

What then of "a Law of righteousness" (9:31)? As Paul will soon state in 10:4 and explain fully in 10:6–15, "since righteousness is always something received from God (God's accepting and sustaining power), only the faith which receives that righteousness sustains the law."[111] This section, then, aligns completely with Paul's conclusion in Romans 3: "Then do we make the Law ineffective through the faith? May it never come to be! But we confirm the validity of the Law" (3:31; see also 9:31).

"Christ Is the End of the Law"—Righteousness for All (10:4)

"You see, Christ is the end of the Law into righteousness for everyone who believes" (10:4; cf. 1:16). This verse contains "one of the most famous of all of Paul's theological 'slogans.' "[112] "Believe" (πιστεύω) was already introduced in the citation of Is 28:16 in Rom 9:33, and Paul's emphasis will be upon believing and the righteousness of faith in 10:6–15. Yet what predominantly occupies Paul's mind here remains his diagnosis of the problematic and unattainable approach of seeking one's own righteousness from works of the Law (see 9:31–32; 10:3). On the purely human side of things, that pursuit will not attain righteousness due to human failure, as 10:5 will soon imply. Such seeking not only ignores and, therefore, will not submit to the righteousness of God (10:3), but it also fails to recognize that Jesus the Messiah/Christ is the Rock on whom one is to believe (9:33) and that, in fact, he is "the end of the Law" (τέλος … νόμου, 10:4).

The Multivalent τέλος, "End" (10:4a)

But what is the sense of "the end of the Law" (10:4)? In this context, νόμος must refer to the Mosaic Law and not to some generic principle.[113] But does Paul speak of the Law's commands (e.g., the Law one must do; see 7:12, 15–22; 10:5) or of the entire Torah, which testifies to the righteousness of God (3:21b, 31; illustrated throughout Romans 4)? The answer probably depends upon one's definition of the multifaceted and disputed term τέλος, "end." Moo summarizes the main categories as follows:

> Does "end" mean (1) "termination," as in the sentence "The end of the class finally came!" or (2) "goal" as in the sentence "The end of government is the welfare of the people"; or (3) "result," as in the sentence "She did not foresee

---

[110] Cranfield, *Romans*, 505; his use of "blindness" calls to mind Paul's comparable discussion utilizing the metaphor of a veil in 2 Cor 3:14–16. As "Christ is the end of the Law" (Rom 10:4), so also in Christ the veil is set aside or removed (ἐν Χριστῷ καταργεῖται, 2 Cor 3:14).

[111] Dunn, *Romans*, 588.

[112] Moo, *Romans*, 636.

[113] That νόμος refers to a "principle" is suggested even here by Sanday and Headlam, *Romans*, 284.

the end of her actions." Each of these meanings is possible for the Greek word *telos*, and each is attested by Paul.[114]

To illustrate each sense in Paul's writings, Moo then cites these passages:

(1) "Termination": "Then shall come τὸ τέλος, when he shall hand over the kingdom to God the Father …" (1 Cor. 15:24); (2) "Goal": "The τέλος of the commandment is love from a pure heart …" (1 Tim. 1:5); (3) "Result": "The τέλος of these things [sinful actions] is death" (Rom. 6:21).[115]

Not the Law's Termination

The suggestion that "end" here means "termination" might seem attractive. BDAG initially places Rom 10:4 under "*end, termination, cessation*" (s.v. τέλος, 1). But this definition contradicts the words of Paul in Romans and those of Jesus himself. The Law continues to have a role in the life of believers.[116] Paul dramatically illustrates this in 7:14–25 (especially 7:16, 22, 25) and asserts it clearly in 13:8–10. There Paul speaks of the ongoing love of believers for one another as the fullness of the Law (πλήρωμα οὖν νόμου ἡ ἀγάπη, 13:10). More importantly, Jesus himself rejects this understanding of the Law's "end" in the Sermon on the Mount:

[17]μὴ νομίσητε ὅτι ἦλθον καταλῦσαι τὸν νόμον ἢ τοὺς προφήτας· οὐκ ἦλθον καταλῦσαι ἀλλὰ πληρῶσαι. [18]ἀμὴν γὰρ λέγω ὑμῖν· ἕως ἂν παρέλθῃ ὁ οὐρανὸς καὶ ἡ γῆ, ἰῶτα ἓν ἢ μία κεραία οὐ μὴ παρέλθῃ ἀπὸ τοῦ νόμου, ἕως ἂν πάντα γένηται.

[17]Do not think that I came to do away with the Law or the Prophets; I did not come to do away with [them], rather, to fulfill [them]. [18]For truly I say to you, until the heaven and earth pass away, one letter or one stroke will certainly not pass away from the Law until all things take place. (Mt 5:17–18)[117]

Gibbs properly observes:

[Mt] 5:17 is a programmatic statement about Jesus' relationship to the entire OT, and "fulfill" in such a statement must have the sense "that he enacts or manifests God's purposes" in a broad sense.

… If the forward-looking nature of the OT and Christ's enactment of its promises are in view in the verb "fulfill," then the antonym of such meaning would entail "ending, abolishing, doing away with."[118]

Dunn attempts to maintain the sense of termination by interpreting τέλος in Rom 10:4 as "the end of the law as so understood—ὡς ἐξ ἔργων ['as if from

---

[114] Moo, *Romans*, 638.

[115] Moo, *Romans*, 638, n. 37.

[116] For a complete discussion of the matter, see the excursus "Paul and the Law" following the commentary on 13:8–14. A summary of the Lutheran view of the ongoing role of the Law in the Christian life is given in FC Ep VI and FC SD VI. See also the treatments of the Ten Commandments in Luther's Small and Large Catechisms.

[117] This is the translation of Gibbs, *Matthew 1:1–11:1*, 263.

[118] Gibbs, *Matthew 1:1–11:1*, 263, including n. 3, quoting Warren Carter, "Jesus' 'I Have Come' Statements in Matthew's Gospel," *CBQ* 60 (1998): 52–53.

works,' 9:32]."[119] If one is speaking of failed attempts to establish one's righteousness via works of the Law, Paul endeavors to show how the work of Christ ought to end any such striving. Indeed, Paul has already demonstrated why that pursuit (9:30–31) has *always* been misdirected, futile, and fatal (2:17–29; 3:9–20). While the picture of a race is appropriate in this context (see 9:31–32; see also 11:11–12), it should not be used to argue that those seeking righteousness from the Law have now reached "the goal (= finishing line)" and "the race has ended."[120] In reality, works done to attain righteousness are not simply misguided, but they are also running in the *opposite* direction, away from the righteousness of God. "Such a righteousness, as Paul has already shown (9:31–32a; 10:3), is a phantom righteousness,"[121] which leads to the ultimate dead end (7:10).

Not a Salvation-Historical Distinction

Despite the assertions of a number of commentators, this cannot become a salvation-historical argument. Käsemann, for example, contends that the Law "comes to an end with Christ because man now renounces his own right in order to grant God his right."[122] Hultgren similarly proposes that righteousness is no longer a matter of Law observance because Christ "has replaced" it.[123] Moo likewise speaks of "the salvation-historical disjunction between the era of the law and the era of Christ," concluding that "Christ has brought an end to the law and the era of which it was the center."[124] So also Morris suggests that "the saving work of Christ has brought to a close any attempt to attain righteousness by way of law."[125]

Murray properly counters that only "an erroneous interpretation" puts forth the notion "that the Mosaic law had propounded law as the means of procuring righteousness," which has finally now ended with the coming of Christ.[126] The assertion that the Law was *ever* a means to righteousness before God stands contrary to numerous statements Paul has already made (and to the Law of Moses itself, e.g., Deuteronomy 9). For example, he contends that "the Law brings about wrath" (Rom 4:15) and "the Law came in alongside that the trespass might

---

[119] Dunn, *Romans*, 590.

[120] As suggested by Dunn, *Romans*, 589.

[121] Moo, *Romans*, 645.

[122] Käsemann, *Romans*, 283.

[123] Hultgren, *Romans*, 383.

[124] Moo, *Romans*, 640, who also says: "Christ consummates one era of salvation history" (641), and Paul "is picturing the Mosaic law as the center of an epoch in God's dealings with human beings that has now come to an end. The believer's relationship to God is mediated in and through Christ, and the Mosaic law is no longer basic to that relationship" (642).

[125] Morris, *Romans*, 381.

[126] Murray, *Romans*, 2:50.

multiply" (5:20).[127] Indeed, any approach to righteousness via our works has *always* been unbiblical; thus Paul repeatedly denounces it as an eternal dead end.

Positive Conclusions

More consistent, then, is the view that, properly understood, Christ is the *culmination* of the Law: "it was to faith in Christ that the law was all along leading."[128] BDAG also lists τέλος in 10:4 under definition 3: "the goal toward which a movement is being directed, *end, goal, outcome.*" Along these lines, Christ as the *fulfillment* of the Law is certainly a biblically appropriate understanding (e.g., Mt 5:17; Lk 24:44), but that idea does *not* seem to be within the semantic domain of τέλος. It is best to leave τέλος as "end" and allow *the multifaceted lack of specificity*, present in both Greek and English, to remain (see the points cited from Moo above).[129]

Returning to νόμος, "Law," if Paul here means the entire Torah, as in 3:21b (probably also 3:27, 31; 8:2), one can readily understand how Christ is the goal of the Torah since it testifies to the "righteousness of God through faith of/[in] Jesus Christ" (3:22).[130] Thus Luther:

> The entire Scripture deals only with Christ everywhere, if it is looked at inwardly, even though on the face of it it may sound differently by the use of shadows and figures. Hence [Paul] also says that *Christ is the end of the Law* (v. 4), as if to say that all Scripture finds its meaning in Christ. That this is absolutely true he proves by the fact that this word which is most alien to Christ yet signifies Christ.[131]

Hays similarly summarizes the essence of Rom 10:4:

> The sum and substance of the Torah, according to the whole argument of this letter, is righteousness through faith. This is what Israel failed to grasp, and that is what God's act in Christ now makes evident—to Paul—beyond all possible doubt.[132]

The assertion that Christ is the goal of the entire Torah in terms of its end and purpose certainly then *includes* the aspect that Christ himself fulfills the Law's commands. In this context, which speaks of "works" (9:32) and "seeking to establish their own [righteousness]" (10:3), the referent of νόμος, "Law," includes and *most likely emphasizes* the demands of its commands. The next verse, in particular, emphasizes that the Law requires doing (10:5). Therefore

---

[127] See also Rom 3:19–21; 4:13; 7:5; Gal 3:10–11, 17–22; 4:21–31. For a thorough interpretation of the Galatians passages, see Das, *Galatians*, 310–22, 352–71, and 477–511, respectively.

[128] Cranfield, *Romans*, 505.

[129] For example, this multivalence allows Morris, *Romans*, 381, to conclude: "It is true that Christ is the fulfilment of the law. It is true that Christ is the goal of the law. But here Paul is saying that Christ is the end of the law."

[130] Morris, *Romans*, 380, parenthetically states: "Of course Paul also thinks that the law of Moses pointed people to Christ and this function is not altered."

[131] Luther, *Lectures on Romans*, AE 25:405.

[132] Hays, *Echoes of Scripture in the Letters of Paul*, 76.

τέλος includes the fact that Christ brings an end to being under the Law and its lordship (6:14; 7:1), which means the termination of *the condemnation* which results when the Law's demands are not observed.[133]

Rom 8:1–4 explains why Paul himself, after admitting his ongoing and frustrating failures to do the Law (7:14–24), can nevertheless express his "thanks to God through Jesus Christ our Lord!" (7:25a):

> [1]Consequently now, nothing [is] condemnation for the ones in Christ Jesus. [2]For the Law of the Spirit of life in Christ Jesus freed you from the Law of sin and death. [3]For the inability of the Law, in that it was weakened through the flesh, God, after sending his own Son in [the] likeness of [the] flesh of sin and as a sin offering, condemned sin in the flesh, [4]so that the righteous requirement of the Law might be fulfilled in us, the ones who are not walking in accord with the flesh, but in accord with the Spirit. (Rom 8:1–4)

Jesus "completes, fulfills the law. … In Christ and by the Spirit God has at last done what Torah wanted to do but could not do, that is, to give life (7:10; 8:11)."[134] Thus, the Law is *not* terminated, but the requirement of works, to "do the Law or else" (see 2:25, 27; 3:19–20; cf. Gal 3:10; 5:3), has been satisfied fully. This is because Jesus Christ actively observed all of the Law's commands and also was the sin offering which covers the punishment our disobedience deserves (3:25; 8:3–4).

In this context, then, "Israel has not 'attained Torah' [9:31], because the mode of 'works' [9:32] is not the way whereby one can attain it."[135] It is, instead, "from faith" (ἐκ πίστεως, 9:32). Origen summarizes the point and also points forward to the remainder of 10:4 by stating: "Christ is the end of the law, but only for those who believe. Those who do not believe and who do not have Christ do not have the end of the law."[136]

The Thematic "for Everyone Who Believes" (10:4b)

Before ending his section on the Law in 10:5, the remainder of 10:4 points ahead to Paul's exposition of the Good News in 10:6–15. The language and thought of 10:4b also loudly echoes thematic statements from 1:16–17. The final three Greek words in 10:4, παντὶ τῷ πιστεύοντι, "for everyone who believes," are reproduced exactly from 1:16. As the Good News "is [the] power of God into salvation for everyone who believes" (1:16), so "Christ is the end of the Law into righteousness for everyone who believes" (10:4). Rather than simply speaking of "the Law" as being "into righteousness" (εἰς δικαιοσύνην), that

---

[133] In this sense, Voelz, *Mark 1:1–8:26*, 223, correctly asserts: "Our Lord is himself the τέλος ('end') of the Law (Rom 10:4), both as its goal and as its termination"; see also 471.

[134] Wright, "Romans," 657–58.

[135] Wright, "Romans," 657. He then interprets 3:27 in a manner comparable to this commentary's view: "In 3:27 the critical question as to how boasting is excluded is amplified: 'By what sort of Torah? A Torah of works?' and the answer comes back, 'No; by a Torah of faith' (3:27)" (658).

[136] Origen, *Romans* (Bray, *Romans*, ACCS NT 6:273).

prepositional phrase explains the goal of the entire first half of 10:4.[137] Thus "into righteousness" in 10:4 not only grabs on to the thematic noun "righteousness" in 1:17 but also clearly articulates how and in whom "the righteousness of God" (10:3) is received. Therefore, rather than being a statement about divergences in salvation history, 10:4 focuses on Christ as the all-encompassing factor. It is he who brings "everyone who believes" (10:4) into righteousness and salvation, even as he did throughout the OT era. In and through Christ, the prepositional phrase "into righteousness" in 10:4 stands synonymous with "into salvation" (εἰς σωτηρίαν) in 1:16, a point soon to be verified in 10:10. Paul's Christocentric emphasis also becomes unmistakable as he moves forward into 10:6–15 (see χριστός, "Christ," in 10:6, 7, 17; see also Ἰησοῦς, "Jesus," in 10:9 and κύριος, "Lord," in 10:9, 12, 13).[138]

A Final Word on the Law (10:5)

Paul wraps up this section in which he proves that righteousness does not come from works but from Christ in faith with a final explanation of why this is so: "For Moses writes [concerning] the righteousness which is from the Law that 'the person who does them [the Lord's commandments/statues and judgments] will live in them' " (10:5). In light of the reappearance of other terminology from 1:16–17 in 10:4, it is intriguing that the same form of ζάω, "to live," which occurs in the Habakkuk quotation (Hab 2:4) in Rom 1:17 recurs here, the future indicative ζήσεται, "he will live." Yet the emphasis of Paul's quotation of Lev 18:5 in Rom 10:5 falls upon "the person who does them" (ὁ ποιήσας αὐτὰ ἄνθρωπος). Critical to the sense of Lev 18:5 in all versions and as quoted in Rom 10:5 is the force of the phrase translated as "in them," which in the Greek is the preposition and pronoun ἐν αὐτοῖς, representing the Hebrew preposition and pronoun בָּהֶם.

Leviticus 18:5 in Romans 10:5

The Greek in Romans and the entirety of Lev 18:5 from the LXX and MT appear below:

... ὅτι ὁ ποιήσας αὐτὰ ἄνθρωπος ζήσεται ἐν αὐτοῖς.

... that "the person who does them will live in them." (Rom 10:5b)

καὶ φυλάξεσθε πάντα τὰ προστάγματά μου καὶ πάντα τὰ κρίματά μου καὶ ποιήσετε αὐτά, ἃ ποιήσας ἄνθρωπος ζήσεται ἐν αὐτοῖς· ἐγὼ κύριος ὁ θεὸς ὑμῶν.

---

[137] Dunn, *Romans*, 590, initially expresses the former, more limited option, suggesting that Paul "probably intended εἰς δικαιοσύνην ['into righteousness'] to go with νόμος ['Law']," before properly agreeing that "strictly speaking, it would make better grammatical sense to take εἰς δικαιοσύνην with the whole of the preceding phrase ['Christ is the end of the Law']."

[138] See also the brief analysis of the function of 10:4 as a hinge verse in "Introduction to the Hinges of Romans 10:4 and 10:16–17: Their Rhetorical, Theological, and Contextual Functions" at the start of the commentary on 10:6–15, 16–17.

> And you will guard all my commandments and all my judgments, and you will do them which, while doing, a person will live in them; I [am the] Lord, your God. (LXX Lev 18:5)

> וּשְׁמַרְתֶּם אֶת־חֻקֹּתַי וְאֶת־מִשְׁפָּטַי אֲשֶׁר יַעֲשֶׂה אֹתָם הָאָדָם וָחַי בָּהֶם אֲנִי יְהוָה׃

> And you will keep my statutes and my judgments, which a person will do them and live in them; I [am] Yahweh. (MT Lev 18:5)

The textual matters seem minor. One difference between Romans and the LXX is the placement of αὐτά, "them," but it can be explained simply by the observation that Paul has altered the relative clause of the LXX into a full statement by placing αὐτά after ὁ ποιήσας and deleting the relative pronoun ἅ. The Hebrew also has a relative clause that begins with אֲשֶׁר, "which," and this leads to the conclusion that the LXX likely added ποιήσετε αὐτά prior to the relative clause for clarification. In any case, the LXX's clause ποιήσετε αὐτά, "you will do them," conveys almost the same meaning as Paul's clause ὁ ποιήσας αὐτὰ ἄνθρωπος, "the person who does them." Yet, while Paul omits the second person plural indicative verb ποιήσετε, "*you* will do," he inserts the article ὁ, thereby making the participle substantival.[139] Now the person is defined more problematically as "the one who does."

Living in the Commandments: The Old Testament Context

The essence of the Law's command according to this passage is that it requires doing. But one might ask, "*Why* is the person doing?" This question points to the significance of the phrase "in them." Murray correctly observes that "in the original setting [Lev 18:5] does not appear to have any reference to legal righteousness as opposed to that of grace."[140] The Israelites at Sinai had already been redeemed by Yahweh from the death of slavery into the freedom of life under and with their God (e.g., Ex 20:2). Yahweh provided the tabernacle as the dwelling place for his name (Lev 20:3; 21:6; 22:2, 32; Deut 12:5, 11, 21), along with the priesthood and sacrificial system (see the entire book of Leviticus), to bestow the forgiveness of sins[141] on his people annually (Leviticus 16), regularly (Leviticus 1–7), and even twice daily (Ex 29:38–42) and continually (e.g., Lev 6:12–13 [MT 6:5–6]; 24:1–8).[142] But how would they respond?

"The context of Lev. 18 shows that obedience to the law results in life and blessing for Israel, but those who violate its precepts will 'be cut off from the people' (Lev. 18:29)."[143] Thus the commandments/statutes and judgments are

---

[139] See Wallace, *Greek Grammar*, 619–21.

[140] Murray, *Romans*, 2:51.

[141] The forgiveness of sins is a recurring refrain throughout Leviticus; see, e.g., the passive verb "be forgiven" in Lev 4:20, 26, 31, 35; 5:10, 13, 16, 18; 6:7 (MT 5:26); 19:22. The forgiveness of sins is also implicit in the book's language of "atone(ment)," as in the Day of Atonement for all of the iniquities of Israel (Leviticus 16).

[142] See Kleinig, *Leviticus*, 1–13, 24–30, as well as his commentary on the Leviticus verses cited.

[143] Matera, *Romans*, 236.

not depicted in Leviticus as the means by which one attained righteousness or membership within God's covenant people. They were *not* the source of life, but described "the pattern of religion and life which marked out the righteous, the people of the covenant."[144] *When Israelites lived "in them" (Lev 18:5), further blessings were promised to follow* (see, e.g., Deuteronomy 26–30; Psalms 1 and 119).[145] Thus "Lev 18:5 can be regarded as a typical expression of what Israel saw as its obligation and promise under the covenant."[146] But the covenant itself and the means through which God bestowed his forgiving grace on his people had already been established by God himself.

Paul's Use of the Passage: Works Are Not a Means to Life

In the context of Rom 9:30–10:5, Paul does *not* cite Lev 18:5 to demonstrate that, according to Moses, life is obtained through doing the Law's works. The problematic notions of "pursuing a Law of righteousness … from works" (9:31, 32) and "seeking to establish their own" righteousness by such doing (10:3) identify the critical factor at hand. Paul's use of the OT passage conveys that any person who is "seeking to establish a relationship with God through the law … must be content in seeking that relationship through 'doing.' "[147] In other words, he implies that the one who does them *seeks to live before God by means of doing them*, that is, "from works" of the Law (9:32). The normally very literal NASB grasps this with an unusually interpretive but contextually appropriate rendering of 10:5: "for Moses writes that the man who practices the righteousness which is based on law shall live by that righteousness."

The vital question then becomes quantitative: "Doing how many and how well?" The Law again is inappropriately and ineffectively used if one attempts to employ it to keep score in the arena of righteousness *coram Deo*. Moo proposes

---

[144] Dunn, *Romans*, 601.

[145] Origen, *Romans* (Bray, *Romans*, ACCS NT 6:273), observes that "Moses did not say that the man who practices the righteousness of the law will live forever but only that he will live by it in this life." It is true that in Leviticus the vocable "forever" is associated with, for example, the terms "covenant" (Lev 24:8), "statute" (e.g., Lev 3:17), and "decree" (e.g., Lev 6:18 [MT 6:11]), and not explicitly with "life/live," but the eschatological dimension of the "life" given by God should not be ignored (cf. Ex 20:12; Deut 5:16, 33; 6:2; 11:9). As Luther maintained, where there is the forgiveness of sins, and where God's name is, there also is (eschatological) life and salvation (SC VI,"The Sacrament of the Altar," 6; LC IV, "Baptism," 27).

Jerome, *Sermons*, 76 (Bray, *Romans*, ACCS NT 6:274), comments: "Scripture says not that he will find life through the law, in the sense that through it he will live in heaven but that he will find life through it to the extent that he will reap what he deserves in this world." However, the Torah of Moses emphasizes that God's gifts of life and blessing are gifts of grace and are not earned or deserved by works, but are received by his faithful people (e.g., Deut 26:1–19; 28:1–14). On the other hand, it is true that by evil works of disobedience (unfaithfulness) to the Torah the people deserve the curses (Deut 27:14–26; 28:15–68). For the proper understanding of good works, evil works, and merit in relation to justification through faith alone, see AC VI and Ap IV.

[146] Dunn, *Romans*, 601, citing as examples Deut 4:1; 5:32–33; 8:1; 16:20; 22:7; 30:15–20; Neh 9:29; Ezek 18:9, 17, 19, 21; 20:11, 13, 21; 33:15–16, 19.

[147] Moo, *Romans*, 649.

that "Paul does think that the law embodies, in its very nature, the principle that perfect obedience to it would confer eternal life (see 2:13 and 7:10),"[148] and Jesus might seem to affirm the point when he says this of the Law's command: "Do this [continually], and you will live" (τοῦτο ποίει καὶ ζήσῃ, Lk 10:28; cf. Mt 5:48). However, perfect obedience is the very problem, since it is impossible for sinners to attain—and in this present life all Christians still remain sinners.[149] Paul has pointed to the futility of attempting "righteousness by doing" earlier in Romans. To fail to do the Law *as required* (perfectly! e.g., Deut 18:13) equates to sinning (cf. James 4:17). Jews and Greeks alike are all under sin, which is to say, all have sinned (e.g., Rom 3:9, 19–20, 23). The Law pronounces judgment and condemnation upon all who rely on works because no one does the works required "under [the] Law" (6:14). Gal 3:12 utilizes Lev 18:5 to make the same point as Rom 10:5 about the Law's requirement for "doing."[150] In Galatians 3 Paul uses another OT text in order to answer the quantitative question for all who seek righteousness from the Law. Gal 3:10–11 cites Deut 27:26 and then the thematic passage for all of Romans, Hab 2:4b, in order to establish this decisive contrast:

> [10]ὅσοι γὰρ ἐξ ἔργων νόμου εἰσίν, ὑπὸ κατάραν εἰσίν· γέγραπται γὰρ ὅτι ἐπικατάρατος πᾶς ὃς οὐκ ἐμμένει πᾶσιν τοῖς γεγραμμένοις ἐν τῷ βιβλίῳ τοῦ νόμου τοῦ ποιῆσαι αὐτά. [11]ὅτι δὲ ἐν νόμῳ οὐδεὶς δικαιοῦται παρὰ τῷ θεῷ δῆλον, ὅτι ὁ δίκαιος ἐκ πίστεως ζήσεται.

> [10]Indeed, for as many [people] as are from works of the Law, they are under a curse. For it stands written: "Cursed is everyone who is not remaining in *all* the things having been written in the scroll of the Law *to do them*." [11]But since no one is being declared righteous before God in [the] Law, [it is] evident that "the righteous person will live from faith."[151]

Conclusion

If one depends upon "the righteousness which is from the Law" (Rom 10:5), all are hemmed in by the Law and doomed (3:19–20; 4:15; 5:20). As cited earlier, Theodore of Mopsuestia accurately and ominously summarizes Paul's assessment of the human condition:

> It is impossible to be justified by the works of the law because it would be necessary to keep the whole law, which is not possible. But anyone who sins (which is inevitable) lies under the judgment of the law.[152]

---

[148] Moo, *Romans*, 648.

[149] See the excursus "Who is the 'I' in Romans 7:14–25? Christian or Non-Christian?" following the commentary on 7:14–25.

[150] See Das, *Galatians*, 322–24.

[151] For a thorough interpretation, see Das, *Galatians*, 310–22. For Paul's thematic use of Hab 2:4 in Rom 1:17, see Middendorf, *Romans 1–8*, 98–108.

[152] Theodore of Mopsuestia, *Romans* (Bray, *Romans*, ACCS NT 6:269).

This is why those in Israel who were "pursuing a Law of righteousness … did not attain to the Law" (9:31). Furthermore, they then stumbled over the Rock (9:32–33), who "is the end of the Law into righteousness for everyone who believes" (10:4). But Paul has already hinted at the true route "into righteousness." It comes not from "the person who does them [the works of the Law]" (10:5). Instead, "Gentiles, those who were not pursuing righteousness, got righteousness, that is, the righteousness which is from faith" (9:30).

Rom 9:30–10:5 dissects an improper approach to righteousness, as does 2:17–3:20. But this serves only as Paul's penultimate goal. It is not the "end" (cf. τέλος, 10:4) of his argument earlier or here; *Christ is* (10:4, 6–15; 3:21–26). The Formula of Concord captures the "proper recognition" (10:2) which Paul seeks to convey toward all those who presume righteousness could be attained via humanity's works toward God:

> The proclamation of the law and its threats will terrify the hearts of the unrepentant and bring them to a knowledge of their sin and to repentance, but not in such a way that they become despondent and despair therein. Rather, since "the law was our custodian until Christ came, that we might be justified by faith" (Gal. 3:24), and hence points and leads not away from but toward the Christ who is the end of the law (Rom. 10:4), the proclamation of the Gospel of our Lord Christ will once more comfort and strengthen them with the assurance that if they believe the Gospel God forgives them all their sins through Christ, accepts them for his sake as God's children, and out of pure grace, without any merit of their own, justifies and saves them. (FC SD V 24–25)

As in 3:21–31, Paul now turns to elaborate upon the divinely provided route by which the "righteousness of God" (1:17; 10:3) comes to us. It is through Christ proclaimed—the Word of the faith for all (10:6–15).

Righteousness Reaffirmed, Part 2: Christ Proclaimed—the Word of the Faith for All

Translation

10 ⁶But the righteousness from faith says thus: "Do not begin to say in your heart, 'Who will go up into the heaven?' (this is, to lead Christ down) ⁷or, 'Who will go down into the abyss?' (this is, to lead Christ up from [the] dead)." ⁸But what is it saying? "The Word is near you, in your mouth and in your heart," this is, the Word of the faith which we are proclaiming, ⁹that if you acknowledge with your mouth, "Jesus [is] Lord," and believe in your heart that God raised him from [the] dead, you will be saved. ¹⁰For with the heart it is being believed into righteousness, and with [the] mouth it is being acknowledged into salvation. ¹¹For the Scripture says: "Everyone who believes on him will not be put to shame." ¹²For there is not a difference [between] a Jew and a Greek, for the same Lord [is] of all, being rich to all the ones who are calling on him. ¹³For "everyone who ever might call on the name of [the] Lord will be saved."

¹⁴How, then, might they call [on him] on whom they did not believe? And how might they believe [on him] of whom they did not hear? And how might they hear without one proclaiming? ¹⁵And how might they proclaim if they are not sent? Just as it stands written: "How timely [are] the feet of the ones bringing the Good News [of] the good things."

¹⁶But they did not all listen responsively to the Good News. For Isaiah says: "Lord, who believed our message?" ¹⁷Consequently, faith [comes] from hearing, and the hearing through [the] Word of Christ/[the] Messiah.

Textual Notes

10:6 ἡ δὲ ἐκ πίστεως δικαιοσύνη οὕτως λέγει—The adversative δέ serves as a "marker of contrast, *but, on the other hand*" (BDAG, 4). The change in content indicates that it signals a new section. "The personification of the righteousness of faith is a rhetorical device"[1] indicating that just as the present tense verb λέγει, "says/speaks," is used for "Moses" (9:15; 10:19), "the Scripture" (4:3; 9:17; 10:11; 11:2), and "the Law" (3:19), so also "the righteousness from faith" here "speaks" (λέγει). For the feminine noun δικαιοσύνη, "righteousness," see the commentary on 1:17.[2] Likewise, for

---

[1] Cranfield, *Romans*, 522.

[2] See "The Background and Meaning of 'Righteousness' Words" in the commentary on 1:17 (Middendorf, *Romans 1–8*, 92–96; see also 106–7). In this volume, see "Righteousness Returns" and "Righteousness Defined" in the introduction to 9:30–10:15.

ἐκ πίστεως, "from faith," see the commentary on 1:16, as well as the commentary on 1:17, where this prepositional phrase appears twice.[3]

μὴ εἴπῃς ἐν τῇ καρδίᾳ σου—This prohibition warns "do not *begin* to say in your heart."[4] The negative μή with the subjunctive mood εἴπῃς conveys a potential action. This clause is reproduced from LXX Deut 8:17; 9:4.

τίς ἀναβήσεται—When accented (rather than enclitic) τίς serves as an interrogative, and it is masculine singular, "who?" The verbal form of ἀναβήσεται is the future middle (deponent in meaning) of the compound verb ἀναβαίνω (ἀνά + βαίνω), which refers to "any upward movement *ascend, go up*" (BDAG, 1 a β); cf. ἄνω, "above," in Phil 3:14; Col 3:1. The clause represents a portion of LXX Deut 30:12; see the commentary.

τοῦτ' ἔστιν—Paul employs this clause three times in 10:6–8 to introduce his interpretation. A comparable Hebrew phrase occurs in the writings of Qumran, but τοῦτ' ἔστιν is used more broadly in biblical and secular Greek as well.[5]

καταγαγεῖν—The compound verb κατάγω (κατά + ἄγω) means to "*lead/bring down*" (BDAG). The former translation, "to lead down," is used here to distinguish this verb from the more common verb for "to bring," φέρω. The form καταγαγεῖν is a second aorist active infinitive.

10:7 ἤ—This particle serves as a "marker of an alternative, *or*" (BDAG), in this case of complementary opposites (up or down).

τίς καταβήσεται—See τίς ἀναβήσεται in the third textual note on 10:6. The preposition κατά prefixed to βαίνω here expresses the opposite direction, "go *down*."

τὴν ἄβυσσον—The Greek noun ἄβυσσος, transliterated into English as *abyss*, is defined for this passage by BDAG, 2, as a "place associated with the dead and hostile powers, *netherworld, abyss*, esp[ecially] the abode of the dead." In the LXX ἄβυσσος occurs over forty times, usually translating תְּהוֹם, "the deep," which normally denotes the depths of waters; the Hebrew תְּהוֹם is translated as ἄβυσσος by the LXX in, e.g., Gen 1:2; 7:11; Deut 8:7; 33:13; Is 51:10; 63:13; Jonah 2:6 (ET 2:5). In Rom 10:7 Paul is quoting Deut 30:13, and *if* Deut 30:13 referred to "the deep," that might explain why Paul in Rom 10:7 can refer to "the abyss," but the terminology in Deut 30:13 is that of the "sea" (MT: יָם; LXX: θάλασσα), and the LXX never translates יָם, "sea," by ἄβυσσος, "abyss." Therefore a better explanation for Paul's ἄβυσσος, "abyss," is Cranfield's observation that the phrase ἐκ τῶν ἀβύσσων τῆς γῆς, "from the abysses of

---

[3] See "The Background and Meaning of 'Faith' Words" in the commentary on 1:16 (Middendorf, *Romans 1–8*, 88–90); " 'From Faith[fulness] into Faith' (1:17)" on 96–98; and also 106–7.

[4] See Wallace, *Greek Grammar*, 469; note also the extended discussion on 714–17 titled "Introduction: The Semantics of Commands and Prohibitions ('Do Not Start' vs. 'Stop Doing'?)," which concludes: "Thus if the conditions are right, the aorist prohibition may well have the force of 'Do not start' " (717).

[5] See Dunn, *Romans*, 603, quoted in the commentary below. For references to biblical and secular uses, see BDAG, εἰμί, 2 c α; note especially τοῦτ' ἔστιν in Philemon 12 and similar expressions in Eph 4:9; Heb 7:2.

the earth," in LXX Ps 70:20 (MT/ET 71:20) "is used of the depths of the earth as the place of the dead, i.e. Sheol, and it is clearly in this sense that Paul uses it here."[6]

τοῦτ᾽ ἔστιν—See the fourth textual note on 10:6.

10:8 ἀλλὰ τί λέγει;—"But what is it saying?" The third singular present tense verb personifies "the righteousness from faith" still "speaking," as in 10:6.[7]

ἐν τῷ στόματί σου καὶ ἐν τῇ καρδίᾳ σου—A multifaceted use of the preposition ἐν with the dative occurs when these words, quoted from LXX Deut 30:14, are repeated in Rom 10:9. The locative or spatial/sphere sense applies here in 10:8, "near you, *in* your mouth and *in* your heart." In 10:9, the first ἐν is instrumental, "acknowledge *with* your mouth," whereas the second use in 10:9 is again locative, "believe *in* your heart."[8]

τὸ ῥῆμα τῆς πίστεως—The noun ῥῆμα denotes "that which is said, *word, saying, expression, or statement of any kind*" (BDAG, 1). No firm distinction should be pressed between it and λόγος, "word," derived from λέγω, "say." Indeed, most of the principal parts of the verb λέγω utilize forms related to the stem of ῥῆμα, i.e., ἐρῶ, εἴρηκα, ἐρρέθην.[9] In regard to λόγος, Kittel, who treats all these terms together in one article, concludes:

> The main G[reek] terms for דָּבָר are λόγος and ῥῆμα.
>
> The LXX uses them as full synonyms, so that we may treat the two together. In the usage of the Pentateuch the proportion between λόγος and ῥῆμα is 56 to 147, so that ῥῆμα easily predominates.[10]

Not surprisingly then, Paul here draws ῥῆμα from LXX Deut 30:14. In the context of LXX Deuteronomy, Moses uses ῥῆμα to refer to the Torah, the now-written Word (see LXX Deut 30:10–11). In regard to the relationship with τῆς πίστεως, "of the faith," Dunn issues this reminder:

> As so often with such genitive constructions, we need not press for an either-or meaning, as though Paul could have in mind only the word "which calls for (the response of) faith" (Cranfield), or only the word which proclaims the faith that is believed (Käsemann …).[11]

κηρύσσομεν—κηρύσσω means "to make public declarations, *proclaim aloud*" (BDAG, 2). Paul uses the verb four times in Romans, three of which are in this immediate context (10:8, 14, 15; also 2:21). The verb occurs thirty-one times in the LXX, where it translates various Hebrew verbs. Friedrich concludes: "As the linguistic basis

---

[6] Cranfield, *Romans*, 525.

[7] Cranfield, *Romans*, 525.

[8] Moo, *Romans*, 657, including n. 55; cf. Dunn, *Romans*, 607. For both the locative (spatial/sphere) and the instrumental usages of ἐν with the dative, see Wallace, *Greek Grammar*, 372.

[9] Mounce, *Basics of Biblical Greek*, 429.

[10] G. Kittel, "The Word of God in the Old Testament," *TDNT* 4:92; for his entire article on λέγω and its related terms, see *TDNT* 4:69–143.

[11] Dunn, *Romans*, 606; Cranfield, *Romans*, 526, contends that the phrase "the Word of the faith" "denotes not the confession of faith but the gospel message itself"; similarly, Barrett, *Romans*, 200. Käsemann, *Romans*, 290, states: "The reference is to the faith which is believed (*fides quae creditur*)."

varies, so does the meaning. … Against all expectation κηρύσσειν is seldom used of the proclamation of the prophets."[12] Dunn adds:

> But the surprisingly infrequent usage for the preaching of the prophets is nevertheless significant and no doubt influenced the Christian usage, particularly the messianic and eschatological references (Isa 61:1; Joel 2:1; Zeph 3:14; Zech 9:9; so elsewhere in the NT—Mark 1:4, 7, 14, 38–39; etc.; note, e.g., Luke 4:18–19; Acts 20:25; and [Acts] 28:31), and not least in Paul's case those who envisaged a proclamation to the nations (Joel 3:9 [MT/LXX 4:9]; Jonah 1:2; 3:2–7; …).[13]

For κηρύσσω as evangelistic proclamation, see the excursus "The New Testament Connotations and Context of Words Commonly Translated as 'Preach,' 'Teach,' and 'Prophesy' " following this pericope.

10:9 ὅτι—The conjunction ὅτι commonly functions as a "marker of narrative or discourse content" and a "marker of explanatory clauses" (BDAG, 1 and 2). Moo argues for the latter at the beginning of 10:9 "because it would be awkward to have two 'content' clauses in a row (e.g., 'that is the word of faith …' [10:8b], 'that if you confess …' [10:9a])."[14] If Moo is correct, the initial ὅτι clause in 10:9 may explain how "the Word is near you" (10:8). But ὅτι may perform both functions. Dunn observes: "English translation is unable to reproduce the ambiguity present in … the ὅτι—'that' (Barrett) and 'because' (Cranfield). … Once again 'either-or exegesis' should be avoided."[15] Both appearances of ὅτι in 10:9 are translated as "that," although this English word fails to capture the possible dual intent of the initial use.

ἐὰν ὁμολογήσῃς—Paul uses ὁμολογέω, "acknowledge, confess," only four times in all his epistles (Rom 10:9, 10; 1 Tim 6:12; Titus 1:16) and the cognate noun ὁμολογία, "confession (of the faith)," only three times (2 Cor 9:13; 1 Tim 6:12, 13). The compound verb ἐξομολογέω, "to indicate acceptance of an offer or proposal, *promise, consent*" (BDAG, 1), occurs three times in Paul, all in OT quotations (Rom 14:11; 15:9; Phil 2:11). Paul's use of the word does not make verbal confession a required work necessary for salvation; instead, he gives a Gospel promise for those who do confess. While the term has developed formal usages, "lit[erally] ὁμολογεῖν means 'to say the same thing,' 'to agree in statement.' "[16] BDAG, s.v. ὁμολογέω, 4, similarly offers "to acknowledge someth[ing], ordinarily in public, *acknowledge, claim, profess*." After ἐάν, the form ὁμολογήσῃς is an aorist active in the subjunctive mood, forming a third class conditional, referring to a potential action in the future (and with the future indicative σωθήσῃ in the apodosis).[17] The word "may" or "might" typically renders the subjunctive mood in translation. However, here no uncertainty exists on God's part. Although the conditional "if" clause may not always be fulfilled on the part of humanity, God's

---

[12] G. Friedrich, "κηρύσσω," *TDNT* 3:700–701.

[13] Dunn, *Romans*, 621.

[14] Moo, *Romans*, 657.

[15] Dunn, *Romans*, 607; see Barrett, *Romans*, 200; Cranfield, *Romans*, 526.

[16] O. Michel, "ὁμολογέω," *TDNT* 5:200.

[17] See Wallace, *Greek Grammar*, 696–97.

gracious actions remain certain. Of course, believers in Christ are still promised "you will be saved" even if they do not confess the faith in these exact words.

ἐν τῷ στόματί σου—See the second textual note on 10:8.

κύριον Ἰησοῦν—The verb ὁμολογέω is followed by a double accusative here (κύριον and Ἰησοῦν), as also in Jn 9:22; 1 Jn 4:2; 2 Jn 7; cf. also 2 Cor 4:5.[18] Literally, the word order is "confess Lord Jesus," but the meaning is "confess Jesus (to be) Lord" (and not "confess [the] Lord Jesus," as if κύριον Ἰησοῦν were a single accusative phrase). For the grammatical construction and the content of the confession, see "Faith's Essential Content, Part 1 (10:9a)" in the commentary.

ἐν τῇ καρδίᾳ σου—See the second textual note on 10:8.

σωθήσῃ—The form of σῴζω, "to save," is a future indicative passive (second singular). The passive voice illustrates a divine or theological passive "when *God is the obvious agent*,"[19] that is, "God will save you." See the fourth textual note on 5:9 and the commentary on 5:9–11.

10:10 καρδίᾳ—Although the preposition ἐν is omitted here, the instrumental sense of the dative,[20] "*with* the heart," should be presumed, as for ἐν τῷ στόματί σου, "*with* your mouth," in 10:9 (and not the locative sense as for ἐν τῇ καρδίᾳ σου, "*in* your heart," in 10:8, 9). See the second textual note on 10:8.

πιστεύεται—The thematic verb πιστεύω, "believe," occurs twenty-one times in Romans, seven of them in chapter 10.[21] The form here is a present indicative passive, "it is being believed." The implied subject of the passive ("it") is τὸ ῥῆμα, "the Word," in 10:8.

εἰς δικαιοσύνην ... εἰς σωτηρίαν—In both prepositional phrases εἰς, "into," expresses "the result of an action or condition indicated *into, to, so that*" (BDAG, 4 e). Thus "acknowledge into salvation" means "*so as to receive salvation*" (BDAG, 4 e). See the commentary on 1:16–17 for a discussion of both of the nouns, "righteousness" and "salvation," which are the objects of the repeated preposition here. Note the same sense of εἰς σωτηρίαν in 1:16 (although different in 10:1) and also of εἰς δικαιοσύνην in 10:4.

10:11 ἡ γραφή—"The Scripture" quoted is Is 28:16.

ὁ πιστεύων ἐπ᾽ αὐτῷ οὐ καταισχυνθήσεται—The identical wording was quoted in Rom 9:33, reflecting LXX Is 28:16. See the fourth and fifth textual notes on Rom 9:33 and "Isaiah's Stone Texts (Is 28:16 and Is 8:14 in Rom 9:33)" in the commentary on 9:30–10:5. See also the discussion of the verb καταισχύνω, "put to shame," and its future tense in the first textual note and the commentary on 5:5.

10:12 οὐ γάρ ἐστιν διαστολή—This repeats "for there is not a difference" between Jew and Greek from 3:22; see the last two textual notes on that verse and "The Righteousness of God for All (3:22–24)" in the commentary on 3:21–31.

---

[18] See Wallace, *Greek Grammar*, 187–88, and BDF, § 157.2.

[19] Wallace, *Greek Grammar*, 437.

[20] See Wallace, *Greek Grammar*, 162–63.

[21] See "The Background and Meaning of 'Faith' Words" in the commentary on 1:16 (Middendorf, *Romans 1–8*, 88–90); " 'From Faith[fulness] into Faith' (1:17)" on 96–98; and also 106–7.

ὁ γὰρ αὐτὸς κύριος πάντων—This clause assumes a form of the verb "to be," here ἐστίν, "is," to link ὁ γὰρ αὐτὸς κύριος, "for the same Lord," with πάντων, "[is Lord] of all." Wallace notes: "When modifying an articular substantive in the *attributive* position, αὐτός is used as an identifying adjective. As such it is translated *same*."[22]

πλουτῶν—This is a present participle of πλουτέω, "to be plentifully supplied with someth[ing], *be rich*" (BDAG, 2). Paul uses πλουτέω only here in Romans and four times elsewhere (1 Cor 4:8; 2 Cor 8:9; 1 Tim 6:9, 18). After the parable of the Rich Fool, Jesus uses this stative verb to speak of the consequences for humans who are not "being rich" toward God (Lk 12:21). But here the Lord Jesus provides what God requires; he "gives of his wealth generously to all" (BDAG, 2). See further the commentary.

εἰς πάντας τοὺς ἐπικαλουμένους αὐτόν—This prepositional phrase serves as the indirect object of πλουτῶν (see the preceding textual note). The compound verb ἐπικαλέω, "call on," occurs in Romans only in the three consecutive verses 10:12, 13, 14. Here the form is a present middle participle which functions substantively,[23] "*people who are calling on.*" ἐπικαλέω carries the general notion of "to call upon deity for any purpose" (BDAG, 1) and can be used for pagans invoking their gods (e.g., worshipers of Baal in LXX 1 Ki 18:25). But the overwhelmingly predominant usage in the LXX is for Israelites who "call on" (the name of) the Lord their God.[24] Note the importance of the simple verb καλέω, "to call," with God as the (implied) subject in Romans 9 (see especially 9:12; also 9:7, 24, 25, 26; earlier in the book, see 4:17; 8:30).

10:13 ἐπικαλέσηται—This verse is quoted from Joel 2:32 (MT/LXX 3:5). Here the form of ἐπικαλέω, "call on," is an aorist subjunctive middle. The presence of ἐπικαλέω in LXX Joel 3:5 (ET 2:32) serves as the basis for Paul's general usage of ἐπικαλέω in the immediate context of Rom 10:12–14 versus his preference for the simple verb καλέω, "to call," in earlier chapters; see the previous textual note.

τὸ ὄνομα κυρίου—The Hebrew of MT Joel 3:5 (ET 2:32) has בְּשֵׁם יְהוָה, "on the name of Yahweh," referring to the personal name of the covenant God, whereas Paul quotes LXX Joel 3:5 (ET 2:32) with the title κύριος, "Lord." See the commentary on this verse for the implications here, as well in the confession of Rom 10:9.

σωθήσεται—This is another future indicative passive form of σῴζω, "to save." See the sixth textual note on 10:9.

10:14 πώς—When accented πώς and as an enclitic, the word functions as an adverb. However, with the circumflex, πῶς serves as an "interrog[ative] reference to manner or way, *in what way? how?*" (BDAG, 1). Its four occurrences in 10:14–15 introduce a sequence of "rhetorical questions, which call an assumption into question or reject it altogether, inviting the response 'It is impossible.'"[25] The translations of all four subjunctive verbs (ἐπικαλέσωνται ... πιστεύσωσιν ... ἀκούσωσιν ... κηρύξωσιν) which

---

[22] Wallace, *Greek Grammar*, 349.

[23] See Wallace, *Greek Grammar*, 619–21.

[24] See, e.g., LXX Gen 4:26; 21:33; Deut 4:7; 2 Sam 22:7; Pss 4:2 (ET 4:1); 17:7 (MT 18:4; ET 18:3); Is 55:6; Zech 13:9; cf. Dunn, *Romans*, 610.

[25] Dunn, *Romans*, 620, citing also 3:6; 6:2; 8:32.

follow the four interrogative uses of the particle πῶς include "might," since they are deliberative subjunctives.[26]

ἐπικαλέσωνται εἰς ὃν οὐκ ἐπίστευσαν—The prepositional phrase with relative pronoun εἰς ὅν can connect nicely with either of the two adjacent verbs, "call *on whom*" or "*on whom* they did not believe." If one accepts the latter, which seems more probable, this is one of only three times in Paul that the verb πιστεύω (see 10:10) takes the preposition εἰς to indicate the object in/on whom one believes (also Gal 2:16; Phil 1:29).[27] But the expression is characteristic of John's Gospel for literally "believing into" Jesus[a] (cf. "into" God in Jn 14:1). In Romans 10 the use of πιστεύω with εἰς moves beyond simple believability or an intellectual judgment about facts; it even means much more than personal trust and reliance on another person or thing. It stands equivalent to the "in Christ" incorporation language so common in Paul[28] (see the commentary on 6:11).

(a) E.g., Jn 6:29, 40; 7:38; 9:35; 11:26; 12:44; 14:12; 17:20

πιστεύσωσιν οὗ οὐκ ἤκουσαν—Since πιστεύω, "believe," normally does not take the genitive, the genitive singular form of the relative pronoun, οὗ, most likely attaches to the verb that follows, ἤκουσαν, and serves as its object, "*of whom* they did not hear." A direct object in the genitive typically follows sensory verbs like ἀκούω, "hear."[29] The genitive form οὗ may be masculine, "of whom," referring to a person, namely, the "Lord" in 10:13, or neuter, "of which," referring to the "Word" in 10:8. Dunn argues for the former since he contends that "in accordance with normal grammatical usage the οὗ must mean the speaker rather than the message."[30] Certainly the referent of the relative pronoun ὅν, "whom," in the parallel prior question (see the preceding textual note), is similarly the Lord "on whom" they might call and believe.

χωρὶς κηρύσσοντος—The adverb χωρίς is used as a preposition, "without," that takes the genitive. κηρύσσοντος is the present active participle genitive masculine singular of κηρύσσω, "proclaim," for which, see fourth textual note on 10:8.

10:15 ἐὰν μὴ ἀποσταλῶσιν—This is the sole instance in Romans of the verb ἀποστέλλω, "send." Its form is aorist subjunctive passive (liquid verbs [-λ-] regularly lose the θ of the regular passive suffix). The use of "might" in translation renders the subjunctive mood after ἐάν in a third class condition, referring to a potential future action.[31] Although the outcome of God's sending remains certain, whether those who are sent actually go cannot always be presumed (e.g., Jonah), and those sent may be insufficient for the mission (cf. Mt 9:37–38; Acts 13:13; 15:38). The verb ἀποστέλλω occurs 132 times in the NT, but only 12 times outside of the Gospels and Acts. Paul uses

---

[26] See Wallace, *Greek Grammar*, 465–68.

[27] See Dunn, *Romans*, 620; Moo, *Romans*, 663, n. 10; see also BDAG, s.v. πιστεύω, 2 a β.

[28] Morris, *John*, 335–37.

[29] Wallace, *Greek Grammar*, 131, identifies four types of verbs which take a genitive object, those of "*sensation, emotion/volition, sharing, ruling.*" For a complete discussion, see 131–34.

[30] Dunn, *Romans*, 620; also Sanday and Headlam, *Romans*, 296, who contend it "must be interpreted by assuming that the preaching of Christ's messengers is identical with the preaching of Christ Himself." However, this assumption has certainly not always been the case throughout church history nor is it now.

[31] See Wallace, *Greek Grammar*, 696–97; cf. the second textual note on 10:9.

it only three times elsewhere (1 Cor 1:17; 2 Cor 12:17; 2 Tim 4:12). Rengstorf treats ἀποστέλλω together with πέμπω as synonymous "sending" verbs but concludes: "We can say in general that when πέμπειν is used in the NT the emphasis is on the sending as such, whereas when ἀποστέλλειν is used it rests on the commission linked with it."[32] The technical NT use of the title ἀπόστολος, "apostle," which Paul employs to identify himself in Rom 1:1 (see the third textual note and the commentary there), then influences the understanding of the verb.[33] The connection between being sent and proclamation occurs also in Is 61:1; Mk 3:14; Lk 4:18, 43–44; 1 Tim 2:7; 2 Tim 1:11.

ὡς ὡραῖοι—For this use of ὡς, BDAG, 7, offers "a relatively high point on a scale involving exclamation, *how!*" Dunn gives the following as the basic meaning of the adjective ὡραῖος: " 'timely, produced at the right season,' with the idea of 'beautiful, graceful' a natural derivative."[34] The original Hebrew of the passage Paul quotes, Is 52:7, has a verb after the exclamation, מַה־נָּאווּ, "how beautiful are … ," and its reference to a lovely appearance is confirmed by the identical verb form in Song 1:10, "comely are your cheeks with bangles."[35] Dunn properly argues that although the sense of beauty is present for ὡραῖος elsewhere in the NT (Mt 23:37; Acts 3:2, 10), "timely" is most likely "intended here by Paul."[36]

οἱ πόδες—The nominative singular form of this noun is πούς, "foot." πόδες illustrates the regular nominative plural ending in the third declension, -ες.

τῶν εὐαγγελιζομένων [τὰ] ἀγαθά—To add the "good things" (ἀγαθά) seems redundant in English when the verb εὐαγγελίζομαι is already translated as "bring the Good News." One could more literally say "evangelizing the good things." The inclusion of the direct object points toward the content of the message, which Paul defines more explicitly with τῷ εὐαγγελίῳ, "the Gospel," in 10:16 and ῥήματος Χριστοῦ, "[the] Word of Christ," in 10:17.

10:16–17 Note that 10:16 clearly *begins* Paul's discussion of Israel's response (10:16–21), as indicated in the commentary outline shown in this volume's table of contents. However, Paul masterfully ties together the sections 10:6–15 and 10:16–21 by introducing the element of response in 10:16, but he wraps up the thought of 10:6–15 with the summative statement of 10:17, introduced by ἄρα, "consequently." Therefore 10:16–17 is included in the translation above and mentioned briefly in the commentary immediately below. However, the detailed textual notes and major treatment of those verses more properly belong in the section on 10:16–21.

---

[32] K. H. Rengstorf, "ἀποστέλλω," *TDNT* 1:404.

[33] K. H. Rengstorf, "ἀποστέλλω," *TDNT* 1:406.

[34] Dunn, *Romans*, 621; BDAG, 1 and 2, is comparable.

[35] The translation is from Mitchell, *The Song of Songs*, 624.

[36] Dunn, *Romans*, 622; that sense in 10:15 is advocated by BDAG, 1, and considered possible by Moo, *Romans*, 664. The NEB translates with "how welcome."

Commentary

Introduction to the Hinges of Romans 10:4 and 10:16–17:
Their Rhetorical, Theological, and Contextual Functions

Paul here continues his discussion of righteousness in relationship with God. There are two proposed avenues to righteousness which, Paul argues, are mutually exclusive. The one from us toward God has been proven to be a dead end (3:19–20; 9:31–10:5). Indeed all terms related to that approach (e.g., "Law," "works," "doing") disappear beginning at 10:6. Thus 10:4 appropriately declares how the Law, in fact, reaches its goal/end: "you see, Christ is the end of the Law into righteousness for everyone who believes" (τέλος γὰρ νόμου Χριστὸς εἰς δικαιοσύνην παντὶ τῷ πιστεύοντι, 10:4). After a brief concluding statement in 10:5 about the righteousness from the Law that is unattainable for us, Paul moves completely away from any talk of human-centered or works-based righteousness stemming from performance of the Law. Instead, Paul turns exclusively to describe the second route, wherein the motion drives solely from God to us. In so doing, he demonstrates how God gives us his own righteousness through the Messiah/Christ, who accomplishes salvation for us! Paul, in effect, *expounds upon the positive Gospel aspects of 10:4 throughout 10:6–15*. Thus that verse functions as another masterful hinge (as does 10:16–17).

This section (10:6–15) also draws repeatedly on the key terms of Paul's *thematic statement in 1:16–17:*

> [16] For I am not ashamed of the Good News, because it is [the] power of God into salvation for everyone who believes, to Jew first and also to Greek. [17] For [the] righteousness of God is being revealed in it from faith[fulness] into faith, just as it stands written: "But the righteous person will live from faith."

In 10:6–15 Paul describes how "the Good News" (τὸ εὐαγγέλιον) announced in 1:16 (see also 1:1) comes near to all people. Eventually, he uses the cognate verb in 10:15, "the ones bringing the Good News" (τῶν εὐαγγελιζομένων), as well as the noun "Good News" (εὐαγγέλιον), in 10:16. But Paul also draws on numerous other terms from his thematic verses. He equates "salvation" (σωτηρία, 1:16; 10:10) with the "righteousness" of God (δικαιοσύνη, 1:17; 10:6, 10), and this salvation-righteousness in Christ is for "everyone who believes" (παντὶ τῷ πιστεύοντι, 1:16; 10:4; also 10:11). Note especially "everyone who believes" (πᾶς ὁ πιστεύων) in 10:11, as well as the threefold use of πᾶς in 10:12–13: "all ... all" in 10:12 and "everyone" in 10:13. The verb "believe" (πιστεύω) appears in 10:9, 10, 11, 14, 16. Here then we get important details about how God's saving righteousness comes near to all people, as it did to ancient Israel and does to present-day Israel, through the Word of Christ (10:17) and of faith (10:8).

Citing Melanchthon, Witherington insightfully describes 3:21–31 as a recapitulation and expansion of the epistle's proposition or main thesis.[37] Yet 10:6–17 also contains an equally profound amplification of the Good News which resounds throughout the letter. In the midst of his discussion of the righteousness of God and Israel in Romans 9–11,[38] Paul provides an explanation of how Christianity "works," not at all by our works, but all by the work of God, whose Word draws near to work faith in those who hear the Word of Christ.

In regard to the boundaries of this passage, the conjunction "but" (δέ) which opens 10:6 is emphatically contrastive between "the righteousness which is from the Law" (10:5) and "the righteousness from faith" (10:6; see δέ in the same contrast in 4:15; 9:30–31; see also Gal 3:11–12). But where does this section *conclude*? Romans presents consistent difficulties in identifying hard breaks due to the smooth movement of thought throughout the letter. Here again, opinions vary. Moo breaks after 10:13 and titles 10:14–21 "Israel's Accountability."[39] Käsemann even more *in*appropriately calls 10:14–21 "Israel's Guilt."[40] But 10:14–15 continues the thought of 10:6–13 by explaining how God's initiative in bringing the message of salvation *near to all* of humanity actually takes place through sent proclaimers (πᾶς, "everyone, all," occurs in 10:11, 12 [twice], 13; also 10:4).

The notion of an improper *human response does not enter the picture until 10:16*. That Paul is at least focusing on Israel in 10:16 becomes explicit in 10:19 and 10:21. While Dunn agrees with Moo that "it is much more natural to link vv 14–15 with vv 16–17," he also notes that "other divisions of the text are possible ... , particularly the suggestion that vv 14–15 go with the preceding context,"[41] to which they are attached in this commentary.

Paul makes the decisive move *from* speaking about God's Word coming to us in 10:6–15 *to* human responses to the Good News beginning in 10:16,[42] and 10:16 introduces a thought which continues to the end of the chapter. In this commentary, then, 10:16–21 forms a separate section. This shift marks the clearest break, but, even then, Dunn refers to the "awkwardness of vv 16–17." This is because the "consequently" (ἄρα) of 10:17 indicates that that verse recaps the

---

[37] Witherington, *Romans*, 21, including n. 51, citing Melanchthon, *Romans*, 98. For a more complete discussion of the contribution of 3:21–31 to the message of the epistle, see "Structure and Outline" in the introduction of this commentary.

[38] See "Introduction to Romans 9–11" as well as "Structure and Outline" in the introduction of this commentary.

[39] Moo, *Romans*, 661.

[40] Käsemann, *Romans*, 292.

[41] Dunn, *Romans*, 620; he, however, calls 10:14–21 "Israel's Failure to Respond to the Gospel" (618). As stated above, the notion of any human response does not arise until 10:16. Denney, "St. Paul's Epistle to the Romans," 672–73, also advocates taking 10:14–15 with what precedes.

[42] Lenski, *Romans*, 664, appropriately begins a new section at 10:16 titled "Jewish Unbelief—Gentile Faith."

previous section by pronouncing a key summative statement which can properly be viewed as the conclusion to 10:6–15. In a manner comparable to 10:4, therefore, 10:16–17 provides further evidence of Paul's use of hinge statements to conclude one section while also serving as a bridge leading directly into what follows.[b] As a result, 10:16–17 is included in the translation in both commentary sections but expounded more fully in the section on 10:16–21.[43]

(b) See also, e.g., 1:18; 3:1, 21; 4:1; 5:1; 6:1, 11; 8:1–4; 9:24; 13:7–8; 14:13; 15:7

It is truly extraordinary how Paul carefully affirms each assertion with scriptural validation throughout the rest of Romans 10. OT citations are present in 10:6, 7, 8, 11, 13, 15, as well as in 10:16, 18, 19, 20, 21. These serve to buttress Paul's argument at each step. Rom 10:9–10 is attested by the OT quote in 10:11. Next, 10:12 is validated by the OT citation in 10:13. And 10:14–15a is supported by the OT excerpt in 10:15b. Paul begins this section in 10:6 with Deuteronomy and ends it with a quote from Isaiah in 10:15. Paul's supporting citations draw rather creatively on a diversity of OT texts to make his points. Nevertheless, their cumulative effect is to maintain the assertion of 9:6: "but by no means [is it] that God's Word has failed and remains fallen."

"The Righteousness from Faith" Comes to You in "the Word of the Faith" (10:6–8)

"But the righteousness from faith says thus" (10:6a). Notice that, like "the Scripture" and "the Law," the personified "righteousness from faith" also now "says" or "speaks" (λέγει, 10:6).[44] "Paul follows the biblical pattern of personifying activities and concepts that are closely related to God. The 'righteousness based on faith' [10:6] is active and powerful because it is also 'the righteousness of God' [10:3]."[45] The defining prepositional phrase "from faith" (ἐκ πίστεως) draws the hearer back to its two thematic uses in 1:17. It is surely wrong to define "faith" here merely "as the principle of righteousness,"[46] just as this commentary also deems "principle" as an inappropriate translation for νόμος, "Law," in other places (e.g., 3:27, 31; 7:21, 23; 8:2; 9:31). Here "from faith" establishes a marked contrast with "the righteousness which is *from the Law*" (τὴν δικαιοσύνην τὴν ἐκ [τοῦ] νόμου, 10:5). What follows in 10:6–15 is solely an exposition of the righteousness from faith, without further contrast.

---

[43] A similar rationale is given in the textual note on 10:16–17 above in this section.

[44] See the first textual note on 10:6. There is no intended contrast between what this "righteousness" "says" (in the present tense) and what Moses "writes" (in the present tense) about "the righteousness which is from the Law" in 10:5. Kruse, *Romans*, 407, n. 107, rightly observes that drawing such a contrast "is to build too much upon the distinction between *writing* and *saying* in respect to Paul's citations from Scripture. He often uses *legō* when speaking of what Scripture says in quite straightforward ways … cf. 4:3; 9:17; 10:11; 11:2; Gal 4:30; 1 Tim 5:18) even though he uses *graphō* far more often in this connection."

[45] Moo, *Romans*, 650, including n. 24; he cites as other examples of personification Wisdom in Proverbs 8–9; the Word in Is 55:10–11, and Righteousness itself in Ps 85:10–13 (MT 85:11–14); Is 45:8.

[46] Sanday and Headlam, *Romans*, 288.

Deuteronomy 30:12–14 in Romans 10:6b–8

The actual *content* which the righteousness from faith speaks occupies 10:6b–8. Therein Paul not only cites Deut 30:12–14 but also offers an exegetical and Christological exposition of those verses.[47] But he initially cites an introductory clause present identically in both LXX Deut 8:17 and Deut 9:4: "do not begin to say in your heart." Cranfield elaborates on the contextual meaning:

> It is significant that both these verses are warnings against a self-complacent, presumptuous boasting in one's own merit. In the former the Israelite is forbidden to say in his heart (i.e., to think to himself), "My power and the might of mine hand hath gotten me this (LXX adds: 'great') wealth"; in the latter to say, "For my righteousness (LXX: 'righteousnesses') the LORD hath brought me in to possess this (LXX adds 'good') land."[48]

Grammatically, this introductory clause also *introduces second person singular expressions* into Romans 10. The singular "you" subject of μὴ εἴπῃς then becomes the presumed (and presumptuous) speaker of the words Paul utilizes from Deuteronomy 30. He then carries that form of expression forward into 10:9, where he employs three second person singular verb forms of his own.

In the remainder of 10:6 through 10:8, Paul uses three clauses adapted from Deut 30:12–14. After the first two he makes Christological applications, and then he draws a summative explanation after the third. Paul's *use* of these words in this context may strike the modern reader as quite extraordinary, as it perhaps did his first-century audience as well, due to the subject matter at hand in Deuteronomy.[49] The Hebrew and LXX of Deut 30:10–14 are provided below with translations:

^{10}כִּי תִשְׁמַע בְּקוֹל יְהוָה אֱלֹהֶיךָ לִשְׁמֹר מִצְוֹתָיו וְחֻקֹּתָיו הַכְּתוּבָה
בְּסֵפֶר הַתּוֹרָה הַזֶּה כִּי תָשׁוּב אֶל־יְהוָה אֱלֹהֶיךָ בְּכָל־לְבָבְךָ
וּבְכָל־נַפְשֶׁךָ: ^{11}כִּי הַמִּצְוָה הַזֹּאת אֲשֶׁר אָנֹכִי מְצַוְּךָ הַיּוֹם
לֹא־נִפְלֵאת הִוא מִמְּךָ וְלֹא רְחֹקָה הִוא: ^{12}לֹא בַשָּׁמַיִם הִוא
לֵאמֹר מִי יַעֲלֶה־לָּנוּ הַשָּׁמַיְמָה וְיִקָּחֶהָ לָּנוּ וְיַשְׁמִעֵנוּ
אֹתָהּ וְנַעֲשֶׂנָּה: ^{13}וְלֹא־מֵעֵבֶר לַיָּם הִוא לֵאמֹר מִי יַעֲבָר־לָנוּ
אֶל־עֵבֶר הַיָּם וְיִקָּחֶהָ לָּנוּ וְיַשְׁמִעֵנוּ אֹתָהּ וְנַעֲשֶׂנָּה:
^{14}כִּי־קָרוֹב אֵלֶיךָ הַדָּבָר מְאֹד בְּפִיךָ וּבִלְבָבְךָ לַעֲשֹׂתוֹ:

^{10}For you will listen to the voice of Yahweh your God to keep his commandments and his statutes, that which is written in the scroll of this Torah, because you will turn to Yahweh your God with all your heart and with all your soul.

---

[47] Contrary to Sanday and Headlam, *Romans*, 289, who contend that here "the Apostle carefully and pointedly avoids appealing to Scripture" and that "the quotation is singularly inexact" and that "the words had certainly become proverbial."

[48] Cranfield, *Romans*, 523.

[49] See, for example, Hays, *Echoes of Scripture in the Letters of Paul*, 1–5, 79–83, who treats this example paradigmatically in regard to Paul's use of Scripture as a whole and who also presents diverse rabbinic uses of Deut 30:11–14.

¹¹For this commandment which I am commanding you this day is not too miraculous for you, and it is not far away. ¹²It is not in the heavens, as if to say, "Who will go up for us to the heavens and get it for us and make us hear it so we will do it?" ¹³And it is not from over the sea, as if to say, "Who will cross over for us to the other side of the sea and get it for us and make us hear it so we will do it?" ¹⁴For the Word is exceedingly near to you, in your mouth and in your heart to do it. (MT Deut 30:10–14)

¹⁰ἐὰν εἰσακούσῃς τῆς φωνῆς κυρίου τοῦ θεοῦ σου φυλάσσεσθαι καὶ ποιεῖν πάσας τὰς ἐντολὰς αὐτοῦ καὶ τὰ δικαιώματα αὐτοῦ καὶ τὰς κρίσεις αὐτοῦ τὰς γεγραμμένας ἐν τῷ βιβλίῳ τοῦ νόμου τούτου, ἐὰν ἐπιστραφῇς ἐπὶ κύριον τὸν θεόν σου ἐξ ὅλης τῆς καρδίας σου καὶ ἐξ ὅλης τῆς ψυχῆς σου ¹¹ὅτι ἡ ἐντολὴ αὕτη, ἣν ἐγὼ ἐντέλλομαί σοι σήμερον, οὐχ ὑπέρογκός ἐστιν οὐδὲ μακρὰν ἀπὸ σοῦ. ¹²οὐκ ἐν τῷ οὐρανῷ ἄνω ἐστὶν λέγων τίς ἀναβήσεται ἡμῖν εἰς τὸν οὐρανὸν καὶ λήμψεται αὐτὴν ἡμῖν καὶ ἀκούσαντες αὐτὴν ποιήσομεν; ¹³οὐδὲ πέραν τῆς θαλάσσης ἐστὶν λέγων τίς διαπεράσει ἡμῖν εἰς τὸ πέραν τῆς θαλάσσης καὶ λήμψεται ἡμῖν αὐτὴν καὶ ἀκουστὴν ἡμῖν ποιήσει αὐτήν, καὶ ποιήσομεν; ¹⁴ἔστιν σου ἐγγὺς τὸ ῥῆμα σφόδρα ἐν τῷ στόματί σου καὶ ἐν τῇ καρδίᾳ σου καὶ ἐν ταῖς χερσίν σου αὐτὸ ποιεῖν.

¹⁰If you might heed[50] the voice of [the] Lord your God to guard and to do all his commandments and his righteous pronouncements and his judgments which stand written in the scroll of this Law, if you might turn upon [the] Lord your God from your whole heart and your whole soul ¹¹because this commandment which I myself am commanding to you today is not difficult nor far off from you. ¹²For it is not in heaven above, saying, "Who will go up for us into the heaven and get it for us and after hearing we will do it?" ¹³Neither is it across the sea, saying, "Who will cross over for us to the other side of the sea and get it for us and make it heard for us and we will do [it]?" ¹⁴The Word is exceedingly near you, in your mouth and in your heart and in your hands to do it. (LXX Deut 30:10–14)

Before analyzing Paul's use of Deuteronomy 30, it is intriguing that Baruch 3:29–30 contains this comparable thought about seeking wisdom:[51]

²⁹τίς ἀνέβη εἰς τὸν οὐρανὸν καὶ ἔλαβεν αὐτὴν καὶ κατεβίβασεν αὐτὴν ἐκ τῶν νεφελῶν; ³⁰τίς διέβη πέραν τῆς θαλάσσης καὶ εὗρεν αὐτὴν καὶ οἴσει αὐτὴν χρυσίου ἐκλεκτοῦ;

²⁹Who went up into the heaven and got her and who took her down from the clouds? ³⁰Who went over across the sea and found her, and who will buy her [with] precious gold?

Baruch appears to make use of the same Deuteronomy passage and, thereby, illustrates its wider significance. But it is impossible to determine whether Baruch influenced Paul's thinking. Note, for example, that in contrast to the

---

[50] For εἰσακούω, BDAG, 2, gives "to listen, with implication of heeding and responding, *hear*."

[51] Recognized by Bruce, *Romans*, 192; Kruse, *Romans*, 413; and Sanday and Headlam, *Romans*, 289, who also point to *Jubilees* 24:31, but the thought there regarding the inability of the Philistines and/or the Kittim to escape judgment seems very different.

consistent future tenses in Romans, Baruch has all past tense verbs, aside from the final one, which is future (οἴσει is the future of φέρω).

Paul's Use of the Deuteronomy Text

Two general matters arise in regard to Paul's use of the Deuteronomy passage in Rom 10:6–8. The first is the apparent contrast between the topic at hand in Deuteronomy and in Romans. The second concerns the specific applications Paul draws from the clauses he utilizes.

The most striking of these is the first. In Deuteronomy Moses speaks explicitly of "this commandment" (הַמִּצְוָה הַזֹּאת, Deut 30:11; LXX: ἡ ἐντολὴ αὕτη). In the context of Deut 30:10, the use of the definite article with the singular form and a demonstrative adjective ("this commandment") encompasses the whole Torah (הַתּוֹרָה הַזֶּה, "this Torah") with all of "its commandments" (מִצְוֹתָיו, Deut 30:10; LXX: τὰς ἐντολὰς αὐτοῦ, as in Deut 11:22; 19:9). The emphasis on "doing" (Deut 30:14; cf. Deut 30:10) identifies the specific referent as the "dos" and "don'ts" contained in the scroll of Deuteronomy as it resides within the context of the entire Torah. The main point in Deuteronomy is that Yahweh himself brought "this commandment" down to Israel through Moses on Mount Sinai or, in the case of portions of Deuteronomy, revealed it to Israel through Moses before his death. Thus Israel did not have to go anywhere to seek out the commandments in order to know God's will. *Yahweh himself brought them to Israel.* "Moses' purpose is to prevent the Israelites from evading responsibility for doing the will of God by pleading that they do not know it."[52]

In the context of Romans (e.g., 2:17–22; 3:19–20), it is quite extraordinary to hear the full passage in Deuteronomy declare that "this commandment" is *"not difficult"* (οὐχ ὑπέρογκος, LXX Deut 30:11; the Hebrew could be translated as "too difficult," but it has the connotation of "too miraculous, wonderful, extraordinary"). When received and followed in the context within which Yahweh gave "this commandment" to Israel, it was not intended to be problematic. Israel had already been chosen by Yahweh, redeemed by him from slavery, and saved through the Red Sea to be his covenant people (Ex 20:1–2; Deut 5:1–6, 10, 15), quite apart from any righteousness of their own, as Moses himself had already made clear (Deut 7:6–11; 9:1–6; cf. Rom 10:3).[53] Only after the Lord manifested himself to Israel through the exodus redemption and through his sustaining of them in the wilderness as a "God whose prior grace is the presupposition of all He requires"[54] does God in his Law show his people what good things they are to do in grateful response. The commandments were not given by God, or to be followed by Israel, as the means to pursue salvation or holiness or to attain a right status before God. Rather, in following them,

---

[52] Moo, *Romans*, 651.

[53] See Middendorf, *Romans 1–8*, 43–44, and the excursus "Paul and the Law" following the commentary on 13:8–14.

[54] Cranfield, *Romans*, 523.

Israel, already saved and justified, would be further blessed by God upon entering the promised land, to whose border Yahweh had also now brought them (as Moses delivers Deuteronomy to them on the plains of Moab [Deut 1:5; 34:1]). Moses makes this point immediately afterward in Deut 30:15–20 (see also Lev 18:5 as discussed in the commentary on Rom 10:5).

But if one seeks to earn "the righteousness which is from the Law" by works (10:5; also 9:32), then Paul's words earlier in Romans and most recently in 9:30–10:5 stand to exclude any such possibility. As stated earlier, "Paul consistently opposes all those who *misuse the Law to gain merit with God or keep score with others*"; any such approach is "*universally futile and ultimately fatal*."[55]

Instead of using Deut 30:12–14 to expound further upon "this commandment" (Deut 30:11), however, Paul uses segments of that text to articulate what "the righteousness from faith says" (Rom 10:6).[56] This righteousness might appear to stand in explicit contrast with what the Law's commandment offered! Dunn assembles and then critiques those who improperly criticize Paul's apparent misuse as follows:

> To describe Paul's use of Deut 30:12–14 as "purely fanciful" (Dodd), "drastic and unwarrantable allegorizing" (Kirk), "especially crass" (Gaugler) or "most arbitrary" (Byrne, *Reckoning*, 196) is therefore inappropriate and betrays a twentieth-century perspective insufficiently tutored by first-century parallels and techniques.[57]

Neither does Paul "replace" the commandments with Christ in some dispensational sense which suggests a new era in which the Law is now obsolete.[58] The Law's command remains fully in force, as does its condemnatory impact apart from Christ (e.g., Mt 5:17–20; Rom 3:19–20, 31; 7:5, 10–11; see the commentary on Rom 10:4).

Instead, by employing these words in Romans 10, Paul characteristically *extends*[59] the meaning of the OT passage. He uses Moses' words in order to

---

[55] Middendorf, *Romans 1–8*, 44; see also the excursus "Paul and the Law" following the commentary on 13:8–14.

[56] Cranfield, *Romans*, 522, states: "What is specially noteworthy here is the fact that it is in the law itself, in Deuteronomy, that Paul hears the message of justification by faith." Similarly, Leenhardt, *Romans*, 268.

[57] Dunn, *Romans*, 605, quoting Dodd, *Romans*, 166; K. E. Kirk, *The Epistle to the Romans* (Oxford: Clarendon, 1937), 225; Ernst Gaugler, *Der Römerbrief* (2 vols. Zürich: Zwingli, 1945, 1952), 2:124; and Brendan Byrne, *Reckoning with Romans* (Wilmington, Del.: Michael Glazier, 1986), 196.

[58] Moo, *Romans*, 653; in commenting on 10:4, he speaks of "the Mosaic law as the center of an epoch in God's dealings with human beings that has now come to an end" (642) and "the preparatory period of which the law was the center" (643).

[59] The term comes from Hay, *Echoes of Scripture in the Letters of Paul*, 5; for Paul's interpretation of Deut 30:12–14, which Hays highlights, see 1–5, 74–83. For the understanding of the term as used in this commentary, see Middendorf, *Romans 1–8*, 37–38, and the excursus "Paul's Use of the Old Testament in Romans" following the commentary on 15:7–13.

assert that what was true of the divine command for Israel also stands true in regard to the righteousness from faith. In both instances, the fundamental point of both Moses and Paul remains that *God's action brings his Word near to humanity*, and his Word is both one of commandment (Law) and one of faith (Gospel). Moo says it well:

> As Paul therefore uses Lev. 18:5 to summarize the essence of "the law," so he quotes Deut. 30:12–14 to encapsulate "the gospel." Throughout salvation history, these two "words" from the Lord have operated side-by-side: God making his demand of his people on the one hand and providing in his grace their deliverance on the other. ... He is reminding the Jews of his day that righteousness before the Lord can never come from the law, involving as it does human effort, but from the gospel of God's grace.[60]

God's consistency in using the same method to reveal his Word to humanity reinforces one of the prominent themes in Romans 9–11: God's Word has not failed and is not fallen (9:6).[61] In terms of their divine origin, means of revelation, and ongoing relevance, Paul maintains that these words from Deuteronomy stand "completely in conformity with the doctrine of 'justification by faith.' "[62] And Paul will now connect these words to the righteousness from faith in Christ.

Don't Say This of Christ! (10:6b–7)

In the latter half of 10:6 and in 10:7, Paul incorporates portions of Deut 30:12–13, followed by his own interpretive application. These two complementary thoughts convey what "the righteousness from faith" (10:6a) excludes one from saying:

> Do not begin to say in your heart, "Who will go up into the heaven?" (this is, to lead Christ down) [7]or, "Who will go down into the abyss?" (this is, to lead Christ up from [the] dead).

Paul's Interpretive Method

What technique does Paul use to apply the words he cites from Deuteronomy to the death and resurrection of Christ?[63] In both 10:6 and 10:7, after a clause from Deuteronomy Paul introduces his Christological application with "this is" (τοῦτ' ἔστιν). This brings up the question of the background for Paul's use of the interpretive clause "this is." Dunn notes:

> Particularly in the light of the DSS [Dead Sea Scrolls] we can now recognize more clearly characteristic features of Jewish exposition of a scriptural text: specifically the partial citing of a passage followed by an explanation of it (as most clearly in 1QpHab 5.6–8; 6.2–8; 7.3–5; 10.2–4; 12.2–10); with the explanation introduced by an identifying formula—"it/he/this is ..." (as

---

[60] Moo, *Romans*, 654.

[61] See the "Introduction to Romans 9–11."

[62] Cranfield, *Romans*, 523.

[63] For an overview of interpretations, see "Paul's Use of the Old Testament in 10:6–8" in Kruse, *Romans*, 413–14; also Hays, *Echoes of Scripture in the Letters of Paul*, 1–5, 79–83.

in 1QS 8.14–15; 4QFlor 1.11; 4QpIsaᵇ 2.6–7), or "the interpretation is …" (repeatedly in the Qumran exegetical writings).[64]

Cranfield offers two specific examples: 1QS 8:14–15 quotes Is 40:3 and then identifies "the way" of the Lord and "the highway" of our God as follows: "This is the study of the law which He commanded through Moses."[65] 1QpHab 12:7–8 defines "the city" referenced in Hab 2:17 in this way: "That is Jerusalem, where the Wicked Priest …"[66]

These parallels are interesting, but the notion that Paul follows the specific methodology of the Qumran scrolls is conjectural at best. First of all, we do not know whether Paul was even aware of the sectarian Qumran writings. Second, even if he was, "the phrase 'that is' does not clearly signal the Qumran 'pesher' technique; nor is it evident that Paul views his explanations of Deuteronomy as an exegesis of the 'real' meaning of the text."[67] On the contrary, Paul does not in any way discount the original meaning of the words of Moses or seek to disclose some secret or allegorical understanding. Finally, the fact that Paul's introductory expression "this is" (τοῦτ' ἔστιν) "is widely used in the LXX, Philo, and the NT to introduce an explanation"[68] demonstrates the broader context of his own use of it. The NT itself provides important parallels (e.g., Eph 4:8–11; Heb 10:5–10).

Ascending to Bring Christ Down (10:6b)

Aside from deleting the pronoun ἡμῖν, "for us," Paul cites the question in Deut 30:12 from the LXX: "who will go up into the heaven?" (τίς ἀναβήσεται εἰς τὸν οὐρανόν; Rom 10:6). On our own, none of us can go up to heaven. This negative assumption is most relevant for Paul's argument. In fact, "in the OT, the language of 'ascending into heaven' becomes almost proverbial for a task impossible for human beings to perform."[69] Jesus' statement in the Gospel of John also comes to mind: "And no one has ascended into the heaven except he who came down from the heaven, the Son of Man" (καὶ οὐδεὶς ἀναβέβηκεν εἰς τὸν οὐρανὸν εἰ μὴ ὁ ἐκ τοῦ οὐρανοῦ καταβάς, ὁ υἱὸς τοῦ ἀνθρώπου, Jn 3:13; cf. Jn 6:62). We are not able nor expected by God to go up to him in order to obtain righteousness. If "the righteousness from faith" (Rom 10:6) involved this, it would, like the righteousness which is from the Law, also be dependent upon our "doing" toward God (10:5). *If no mere human can ascend to heaven, how much less can anyone lead Christ down from there (10:6b)!*

---

[64] Dunn, *Romans*, 603.

[65] Cited from Cranfield, *Romans*, 524.

[66] Cited from Cranfield, *Romans*, 524.

[67] Moo, *Romans*, 654.

[68] Moo, *Romans*, 654, n. 40.

[69] Moo, *Romans*, 654, including n. 37, citing as examples Is 14:13; Amos 9:2; Ps 139:8; Prov 30:4.

The glorious fact, of course, is that Christ himself has instead come down from heaven to us. Many scholars conclude that Paul's interpretative comment about leading Christ down (τοῦτ᾿ ἔστιν Χριστὸν καταγαγεῖν, 10:6) alludes to the incarnation.[70] The temporal sequence of the actions depicted in 10:6–7 stand in favor of this view. Dunn, however, rejects the reference to the incarnation and argues that 10:6 refers to bringing down the risen and exalted Christ: "Christ features here … as one whose coming (again) from heaven (where he now reigns as Lord) … would make 'the word' [10:8] easier to believe and confess."[71] However, Dunn bases his interpretation on the faulty premise of finding "no evidence that Christian thought had so far evolved the idea of incarnation, or that the language of preexistence when referred to Christ (1 Cor 8:6) would as yet be taken to imply his personal preexistence."[72] Passages such as 1 Cor 15:47; Gal 4:4; Phil 2:5–6; and Col 1:15–17 refute that assessment; therefore, "there is no reason to reject an allusion to Christ's incarnation."[73] Lenski even applies Rom 10:6b more broadly to encompass "Christ's coming from heaven on his mission of righteousness (his whole mission and not only the incarnation)."[74] The temporal sequence in 10:6–7 lends convincing support to this interpretation. Therefore it seems most likely that Paul refers to that momentous event when the eternal Word came down to live among us by becoming flesh himself (Jn 1:1–3, 14).

And Descending to Bring Christ Up (10:7)

The source of Paul's question in 10:7 remains a bit more nebulous. The question "who will go down into the abyss?" (τίς καταβήσεται εἰς τὴν ἄβυσσον;) does not occur in Deuteronomy 30. Yet the notion of "going down" may well creatively capture the general idea expressed by Deut 30:13, which asks: "Who will cross over for us to the other side of the sea and get it for us and make it heard for us and we will do [it]?" (LXX Deut 30:13). Moreover, the LXX often uses "abyss" as a translation of the Hebrew term for the watery "deep."[75] As Moo points out:

> In fact, the "sea" and the "abyss" were somewhat interchangeable concepts in the OT and in Judaism; and some Aramaic paraphrases of Deut. 30:13 used the language of the abyss. Therefore, Paul could very easily change the horizontal imagery of the crossing of the sea in Deut. 30:13 to the conceptually similar vertical imagery of descent into the underworld.[76]

---

[70] Cranfield, *Romans*, 525; similarly, Barrett, *Romans*, 199; Moo, *Romans*, 655; Murray, *Romans*, 2:53; Nygren, *Romans*, 381; Sanday and Headlam, *Romans*, 287; Franzmann, *Romans*, 188.

[71] Dunn, *Romans*, 605.

[72] Dunn, *Romans*, 615.

[73] Kruse, *Romans*, 409, referencing David B. Capes, "YHWH and His Messiah: Pauline Exegesis and the Divine Christ," *Horizons in Biblical Theology* 16 (1994): 130–31.

[74] Lenski, *Romans*, 652.

[75] See the third textual note on 10:7.

[76] Moo, *Romans*, 655–56.

Less likely is the suggestion of Dunn: "Paul may possibly echo, whether consciously or unconsciously," Ps 107:26 (LXX 106:26).[77] The psalmist depicts those who go out to the sea on ships as follows: "They are going up into the heavens, and they are going down into the abyss. Their life dissolves in evils" (ἀναβαίνουσιν ἕως τῶν οὐρανῶν καὶ καταβαίνουσιν ἕως τῶν ἀβύσσων, ἡ ψυχὴ αὐτῶν ἐν κακοῖς ἐτήκετο). While the language is comparable, the context of the passage seems very distant from both Deuteronomy and Romans.

Whether the wording is a substitution or an adaptation, the challenge "who will go down into the abyss?" (10:7) drives Paul toward his second Christological application: "this is, to lead Christ up from [the] dead" (10:7). It is similarly impossible for any fallen human to lift Christ from the dead, but mercifully it is also unnecessary because he has already been raised bodily by the Father on Easter. Paul more commonly uses the verb ἐγείρω, "to raise," often in the passive, "be raised," to depict Jesus' resurrection from the dead, as in 10:9 (also 4:24–25; 6:4, 9; 7:4; 8:11, 34). The use here of ἀνάγω, "lead up," is unusual. However, Heb 13:20 does use this verb in an explicit statement about "the God of peace, the one who *led up* from the dead [ὁ ἀναγαγὼν ἐκ νεκρῶν] ... our Lord Jesus." It may well be that both Paul and the author of Hebrews take the prophetic language of LXX Ps 70:20 (MT/ET Ps 71:20) as fulfilled in Christ:

> ὅσας ἔδειξάς μοι θλίψεις πολλὰς καὶ κακάς,
>   καὶ ἐπιστρέψας ἐζωοποίησάς με
> καὶ ἐκ τῶν ἀβύσσων τῆς γῆς
>   πάλιν ἀνήγαγές με.

> As much as you showed to me afflictions, many and evil,
>   you also, after returning, made me alive,
> and from the abysses of the earth
>   again *you led me up*.

In any case, the application to Jesus' resurrection, "to lead Christ up from [the] dead" (Χριστὸν ἐκ νεκρῶν ἀναγαγεῖν), most clearly *explains Paul's alteration from going "to the other side of the sea" (Deut 30:13) to "into the abyss" (Rom 10:7).*[78] Dunn then postulates that "this imagery, as distinct from that of resurrection—that is, of a descent into the realm of the dead and return—presumably is the basis of the creedal affirmation of Christ's descent into hell, already developed in 1 Pet 3:19 and 4:6."[79] The latter assertion may be appro-

---

[77] Dunn, *Romans*, 606. For a brief introduction to such echoes, see Middendorf, *Romans 1–8*, 108–9; the term "echo" is from Hays, *Echoes of Scripture in the Letters of Paul*; see especially 14–33.

[78] This is the only use of ἄβυσσος, "abyss," by Paul. Elsewhere in the NT it appears only in Lk 8:31 and Rev 9:1–2, 11; 11:7; 17:8; 20:1, 3, all in reference to the abode of the devil and evil spirits. See also the third textual note on Rom 10:7.

[79] Dunn, *Romans*, 606; similarly, Käsemann, *Romans*, 289.

priate, but there is no need to push it here.[80] Paul may simply equate "the abyss" with the realm of the "dead" as expressed in Rom 10:7, 9 and elsewhere with the phrase "from [the] dead" (ἐκ νεκρῶν, 1:4; 4:24; 6:4, 9; 7:4; 8:11; cf. 14:9).

In 10:6–7, Paul *excludes* elements from what "the righteousness from faith says" (10:6). But even here, while eliminating any notion of even the plausibility of our works toward God in the arena of righteousness, he skillfully manages to proclaim the Gospel in something of a backhanded way. *What was impossible for us is precisely what Jesus has done*! In so doing, Paul demonstrates a Christ-centered reading of the OT whose impact is aptly summarized by Diodore: "The Word of God leaves believers in no doubt either about the descent of the Lord from heaven for our sake or about the resurrection from the dead and the ascent into heaven."[81]

The Word of the Faith Comes Near to You (10:8)

After asserting negatively what "the righteousness from faith says" you should "*not* begin to say" (10:6), Paul now asserts the affirmative side in 10:8. He asks and then answers as follows: "But what is [the righteousness from faith] saying? 'The Word is near you, in your mouth and in your heart,' this is, the Word of the faith which we are proclaiming" (10:8). The Greek words Paul cites here (ἐγγύς σου τὸ ῥῆμά ἐστιν ἐν τῷ στόματί σου καὶ ἐν τῇ καρδίᾳ σου) are all present in the Septuagint text of Deut 30:14 (see "Deuteronomy 30:12–14 in Romans 10:6b–8" above). However, their order is different; Paul also omits the adverb "exceedingly" (σφόδρα) and the concluding clause, "and in your hands to do it" (καὶ ἐν ταῖς χερσίν σου αὐτὸ ποιεῖν). The reason for the omission of the clause containing the verb "to do" seems obvious in light of the contrast between the righteousness of faith and that of the Law as expressed in 10:5. The righteousness which is from the Law *demands doing*; the righteousness of faith *excludes* it. Similarly, "in your hands" further conveys the notion of something you do (e.g., "the work of your hands"), and so Paul has not cited it.

---

[80] In Eph 4:8–10 Paul employs the same two verbs to refer to Christ that are in Rom 10:6–7: ἀναβαίνω, "go up, ascend" (Rom 10:6; Eph 4:8–10), and καταβαίνω, "go down, descend" (Rom 10:7; Eph 4:9–10). For a discussion of Paul's language in Eph 4:8–10, Christ's descent into hell, and a critical evaluation of the early church's development of it into the harrowing of hell, see Winger, *Ephesians*, 439–48, 490–93. The Apostles' Creed employs three clauses to confess this of Christ: "He descended into hell. The third day He rose again from the dead. He ascended into heaven" (*LSB* 159).

[81] Diodore, *Romans* (Bray, *Romans*, ACCS NT 6:275). When Diodore speaks of "the descent of the Lord *from heaven*" (emphasis added), he refers to Christ's incarnation, and this reflects "to lead Christ down [from heaven]" in Rom 10:6. Paul's statements that Christ "descended" in Eph 4:9–10 may best be interpreted as references to his incarnation. Likewise, when Diodore refers to Christ's "ascent *into heaven*" (emphasis added; rather than his "ascent" from the abyss or from the dead), his thought is consistent with Paul's "ascend" statements in Eph 4:8–10, where he declares that Christ victoriously "ascended far above the heavens" (Eph 4:10). See Winger, *Ephesians*, 490–93.

"The Word" (τὸ ῥῆμα)

The main point in both Deuteronomy 30 and Romans 10 is that the Word has come close and, therefore, "is near you" (ἐγγύς σου τὸ ῥῆμά ἐστιν, 10:8). Paul's rare use of the Greek noun τὸ ῥῆμα for "the Word" here surely stems from its presence in LXX Deut 30:14. It is impossible to draw any firm distinction between this Greek noun and Paul's usual term, ὁ λόγος, e.g., the oral "Word" versus the written "Word."[82] Both synonymous nouns typically translate the Hebrew דָּבָר, "word," and τὸ ῥῆμα actually dominates in the Pentateuch in the LXX. In regard to the singular noun here (ῥῆμα), BDAG, 1, recognizes that "gener[ally] the sing[ular] brings together all the divine teachings as a unified whole."

Paul expounds upon what "the righteousness from faith says" (10:6) throughout 10:6–15. He will eventually use this same noun (ῥῆμα) to speak explicitly of "[the] *Word* of Christ" (10:17). Already here in 10:8, does the phrase "the Word of the faith" (τὸ ῥῆμα τῆς πίστεως) express something about what its *content* entails? Cranfield suggests that "the essentially gracious character of the law" inherent in the assertion of Deut 30:14 points to "the close relation between the law and Christ."[83] But that identifies both Christ and faith too closely with the commandment (Deut 30:11). While there is surely no contradiction between Deuteronomy's and Paul's understanding of "the Word," Paul in no way claims that "the Word" (Deut 30:14) of "this *commandment*" (Deut 30:11) and "the Word of the *faith*" (Rom 10:8) have the same *content*. Yet while these "Word" (ῥῆμα) expressions may not be synonymous in meaning, they are interrelated. Kruse speaks more appropriately of "a Christologically determined exegesis, one which identifies a correspondence between what Moses says about the law and the way the apostle understands the gospel."[84] The commonality resides in the *divine origin* of both and the fact that both have become "accessible and understandable" because "God has brought them 'near' [10:8]."[85] They have, in fact, even been internalized "in your mouth and in your heart" (Deut 30:14; Rom 10:8). Perhaps it is best at this point to let Paul himself expound upon what he means by "the Word of the faith" (10:8) in the verses which immediately follow (10:9–11).

"Near" (ἐγγύς)

For Israel, "this commandment" (Deut 30:11) was "near" (Deut 30:14) because God came down on Sinai and imparted through Moses the things which stand "written in the scroll of this Torah/Law" (Deut 30:10). Paul briefly references how "the Word is near you" (Rom 10:8). It is that "Word of the faith

---

82   See the third textual note on 10:8.

83   Cranfield, *Romans*, 526.

84   Kruse, *Romans*, 414, including n. 127, referencing Mark A. Seifrid, "Paul's Approach to the Old Testament in Rom 10:6–8," *Trinity Journal* 6 (1985): 27.

85   Moo, *Romans*, 656.

which we are proclaiming" (10:8; the first person plural of κηρύσσω, "we proclaim[ed]," also occurs in 1 Cor 1:23; 15:11; 2 Cor 4:5; 11:4; 1 Thess 2:19; see also 2 Cor 1:19). In other contexts, Paul explicitly states the object of the proclamation as the Good News (Gal 2:2; Col 1:23; 1 Thess 2:9) or Christ himself (1 Cor 1:23; 15:12; 2 Cor 1:19; 4:5; 11:4; Phil 1:15). Here he returns to fill out the role and content of the verb "proclaim" (κηρύσσω) in both Rom 10:14 and 10:15. Its overall NT use is discussed more fully in the excursus "The New Testament Connotations and Context of Words Commonly Translated as 'Preach,' 'Teach,' and 'Prophesy' " following this pericope.

Paul will soon give more details of the process whereby the Word arrived in your proximity (10:14–15). But first he powerfully and concisely encapsulates its *message* in 10:9–10. He then provides further scriptural validation, specifically regarding those to whom "the righteousness from faith" (10:6) is available and efficacious (10:11–13). Thus we have this exposition on "the Word of the faith" (10:8):

The Essential Content of the Word of the Faith … for You (10:9–10)
The Word of the Faith for Whom? For All! (10:11–13)
How the Word of the Faith Comes Near: The Process of Proclamation (10:14–15)

The Essential Content of the Word of the Faith … for You (10:9–10)

Linguistically the phrase "the Word of the faith" masterfully frames 10:6–8. Paul began with "the righteousness from faith" (10:6) and ends with "the Word of the faith" (10:8). Now Paul begins to define the specific content of "the Word of the faith which we are proclaiming" (10:8). Similarly, the reference to "mouth" and "heart" in 10:8 concludes the expressions utilized from Deuteronomy 30. But the conjunction "that" (ὅτι)[86] which opens 10:9 also draws both bodily organs forward into 10:9–10.

In order to demonstrate how "the Word is near you, in your mouth and in your heart" (10:8), Paul utilizes "mouth" and "heart" in a chiastic manner in 10:9–10: "mouth … heart … heart … mouth." The initial order "mouth … heart" stems from the order in Deut 30:14. But Paul's repetition of both body parts in reverse order in 10:10 makes his point evident. He is not interested in a specific sequence *at this point* (but see 10:14–15). The structure, rather, reinforces the "*both/and*" involvement of what Ambrose describes as the "twin trumpets of mouth and heart."[87] The chiasm also nicely emphasizes the ultimate purpose of "the Word of the faith" (10:8) as its centerpiece (10:9–10):[88]

---

[86] See the first textual note on 10:9.

[87] Ambrose, *On the Death of His Brother Satyrus*, 2.112 (Bray, *Romans*, ACCS NT 6:276).

[88] See Capes, Reeves, and Richard, *Rediscovering Paul*, 65. Matera, *Romans*, 248, similarly identifies this as "a ring pattern" with only four parts, placing references to "salvation" at the end of the second and fourth lines.

A   ... [9]that if you acknowledge with your *mouth*, "Jesus [is] Lord,"
    B   and believe in your *heart* that God raised him from [the] dead,
       C   you will be saved.
    B'   [10]For with the *heart* it is being believed into righteousness,
A'   and with [the] *mouth* it is being acknowledged into salvation.

"Acknowledging" the Word of the Lord (ὁμολογέω, 10:9)

The first notion to dispel in 10:9 is the requirement of an oral statement as a human work necessary for salvation. Such a requirement might come to mind when Cranfield asserts: "All that one has *to do*, in order to be saved, is to confess with one's mouth."[89] Moo's proper retort, however, improperly diminishes the significance of the thought: "Paul's rhetorical purpose at this point should make us cautious about finding great significance in the reference to confession here, as if Paul were making oral confession a second requirement for salvation."[90]

The proclaimed Word of the faith has drawn near by being proclaimed into your ears (see 10:14–15, 17). As a result, it is now in your mouth and in your heart (10:8). This Word of the faith, thus delivered, calls you to "acknowledge, confess" (ὁμολογέω) it "with your mouth" (10:9). The sense of how the verb's action should be heard bears repeating from the textual note: "Lit[erally] ὁμολογεῖν means 'to say the same thing,' 'to agree in statement.' "[91] BDAG, s.v. ὁμολογέω, 4, offers "to acknowledge someth[ing], ordinarily in public, *acknowledge, claim, profess*." The critical factor recognizes that one can only "acknowledge" or "say the same thing" back after it has been *spoken first by someone else*. This is why Paul began by affirming how "the Word of the faith" comes near you first (10:8). It contains and conveys God's promise in Christ.

Only then have you been brought to the point where, by divine initiative and empowerment, you can "say the same thing" back in agreement with God. A variety of English translations seem appropriate, e.g., "acknowledge," "confess," "reply," "affirm," and even "repeat," though none is fully adequate. An echo provides a good analogy. A canyon echoing back words previously spoken into it does no active work. Similarly, ὁμολογέω in 10:9 should not be construed as establishing a legalistic requirement for an action we must do toward God in order to be saved (e.g., "you have to confess, make confession, go to confession"). Instead, Paul gives us the Gospel assurance that all who confess Jesus as Lord are indeed saved. *Thus the verb means to hear something and then to acknowledge or affirm its validity in faith*, as corroborated by the verb "believe" in the second half of the verse.[92] Unfortunately, unlike an inanimate

---

[89]   Cranfield, *Romans*, 526 (emphasis added).

[90]   Moo, *Romans*, 657.

[91]   O. Michel, "ὁμολογέω," *TDNT* 5:200. The English verb "confess" derives from the Latin equivalent (*con + fateri*).

[92]   Consider, for example, a pastor who speaks the Gospel to a patient in a hospital. The patient who hears and believes the message receives saving faith or continues in it without having to do anything in return other than, perhaps, nod the head or close the eyes in prayer or mouth the

canyon, humans are able to actively refuse and even contradict what is heard, a problem Paul begins to dissect in 10:16–21. But first he continues with the positive intention of God.

Before proceeding, one should note how the same situation applies in regard to the confession of sin. It is most properly based on the Word, which first draws near to us. The familiar passage from 1 Jn 1:9, which contrasts the "righteous[ness]" of God with our own "unrighteousness," illustrates the point: "if we confess [ὁμολογῶμεν] our sins, he is faithful and righteous to forgive our sins and cleanse us from all unrighteousness."[93] If we claim that we have no sin (1 Jn 1:8), we contradict what God's own Word clearly declares to be true: "all sinned" (Rom 3:23; see Rom 3:9–20). This is why John says that whenever we deny this reality in regard to ourselves, "we act as if he were a liar and his Word is not in us" (1 Jn 1:10).[94] To confess sin, then, simply means *to acknowledge what God's Word already says about us.* The solid foundation for biblical confession, therefore, does not originate within oneself; neither does it rely on one's feelings (e.g., "I don't feel like a sinner") or stem from comparing oneself with others. Instead, the invitation of ὁμολογῶμεν (1 Jn 1:9) means heeding God's Word and accepting his assessment of our fallen state. Here again, reality involves seeing things from God's perspective rather than based on our own self-assessment.[95]

The basic sense of ὁμολογέω, "acknowledge, confess," in Romans 10 is the same as in 1 Jn 1:9. However, the content of what is confessed in Romans 10, of what God's Word comes near to proclaim, is the saving message of Christ (10:6, 7, 8). The Good News for those "in Christ Jesus" is God's other and dominant declaration "nothing [is] condemnation" (Rom 8:1; cf. James 2:13; 1 Jn 2:1–2). God then enables and summons those who hear "[the] Word of Christ" (10:17) to receive it as "the Word of the faith" (10:8) and to say the same thing back as has already been heard.

Faith's Essential Content, Part 1 (10:9a)

The first content which "the Word of the faith" (10:8) proclaims is a momentous, reality-altering assertion about the person of Jesus. "Jesus [is] Lord" (κύριον Ἰησοῦν, 10:9) utters one of the earliest and most concise NT statements of the Christian faith. Wallace answers a basic grammatical point as follows:

---

words "amen" or "thank you." Silent gestures like these acknowledge that the Word of Christ (10:17) has been heard and believed, and so, according to Paul, the person has the assurance of salvation.

[93] See Schuchard, *1–3 John*, 101–50, for a complete exposition of 1 Jn 1:5–2:2. He makes the interesting observation that "in no other NT passage is the verb [ὁμολογέω, 'confess'] used as here with reference to the confessing of sin, although the similar expression with the related compound verb ἐξομολογέω, 'confess,' is well attested" (114, n. 106).

[94] This is the translation of Schuchard, *1–3 John*, 101.

[95] See Middendorf, *Romans 1–8*, 46, 51, 473.

First, which is the object and which is the complement? Since the object-complement construction is an embedded subject-predicate nom[inative] clause the same rules apply here. Thus, since Ἰησοῦν is a proper name, it is the object (and κύριον is the complement).[96]

This brief statement "Jesus [is] Lord" therefore involves

attributing lordship to the particular historical individual, Jesus (as in 4:24; 1 Cor 11:23; 12:3; cf. Rom 14:14; 1 Cor 5:4; 9:1; 2 Cor 4:14; Eph 1:15; 1 Thess 2:15; 2 Thess 1:8), and perhaps reflects its early fixation as a formula (before "Jesus Christ" became the standard referent …).[97]

There is certainly no tension between calling Jesus "Lord" (κύριος) and "Christ" (χριστός). Both figure prominently in the angelic announcement of his birth (Lk 2:11) and in the earliest proclamation of the church (see Acts 2:36!). By the time Paul writes Romans, "Jesus is Lord" has become "a well-established creedal formula."[98] This may be explained by the suggestion that the confession "was used in connexion with baptism," something Cranfield deems "probable."[99] The formulaic use of comparable expressions in Paul's own writings signals that the essential content already had a liturgical function which became further established as a result of his repeated uses (e.g., 1 Cor 8:6; 12:3; 2 Cor 4:5; Phil 2:11; Col 2:6).

The Background and Meaning of "Jesus [Is] Lord" (10:9a)

Some understandings of "Jesus [is] Lord" (κύριον Ἰησοῦν, 10:9) are inadequate. For example, it should not be viewed primarily as an expression of anti-imperial sentiment.[100] In fact, as Dunn points out, later acclamations that κύριος Καῖσαρ ("Caesar is lord") are "not yet in evidence" when Romans is written.[101] Cranfield agrees:

It is not likely it [the confession "Jesus is Lord"] originated as a response to κύριος Καῖσαρ ["Caesar is lord"]. That Christians in the Greek-speaking world were well aware of the fact that κύριος ["lord"] and κυρία ["lordess, goddess"] were commonly used with reference to the various pagan deities,

---

[96] Wallace, *Greek Grammar*, 188.

[97] Dunn, *Romans*, 607.

[98] Dunn, *Romans*, 607.

[99] Cranfield, *Romans*, 527; see also 530. While the NT itself does not explicitly use the statement "Jesus is Lord" as a baptismal formula, some passages speak of being baptized "in the name of the Lord Jesus," and affirmations that Jesus is "Lord" (often "Christ" also) can appear in close association with Baptism. See, e.g., Acts 2:36–38; 8:16; 10:48; 11:16–17; 16:15; 19:5. See also Paul's creedal "one Lord, one faith, one Baptism" (Eph 4:5) and his baptismal allusion "washed … in the name of the Lord Jesus Christ" (1 Cor 6:11).

[100] Suggested by Jewett, *Romans*, 639–40; Elliot, *The Arrogance of Nations*, 44, asserts that Paul's "titles for Christ ('lord,' *kyrios*, and 'son of God,' *huios tou theou*), for example, were titles that the Caesars also claimed" (see also 14–15). For a general rebuttal of anti-imperial readings throughout the NT, see McKnight and Modica, *Jesus Is Lord, Caesar Is Not*.

[101] Dunn, *Romans*, 608.

especially of the oriental-Hellenistic religions, is, of course, unquestionable (Paul himself refers to these κύριοι πολλοί ["many lords"] in 1 Cor 8.5).[102]

While clearly establishing a contrast with other deities, the main impact of "Jesus [is] Lord," however, does not derive from extrabiblical uses of the title "lord" (κύριος). Neither can it simply be described as a "slogan of identification"[103] which expresses "a transfer of allegiance."[104] All of these fail to capture the primary theological gist of the assertion. Similarly, in our own day, the main theological freight is *not about the lordship or sovereignty of Jesus.* Instead, the very origin of the confession points us in another direction, which more profoundly conveys the Good News contained therein.

Cranfield begins to steer us in the right direction by referencing the transliteration of the Aramaic expression μαράνα θά, *marana tha,* "our Lord, come" in 1 Cor 16:22 as an indication "that we have to look to the primitive Aramaic-speaking church" for its origin.[105] Then he cites the most relevant evidence: "The use of κύριος ['Lord'] more than six thousand times in the LXX to represent the Tetragrammaton [Yahweh] must surely be regarded as of decisive importance here."[106] Dunn affirms that the title was "at least an acceptable translation of יהוה [Yahweh] in diaspora circles" and then adds:

κύριος ["Lord"] would almost certainly have been used when the text was *read.* The reference of several such passages to *Jesus* as Lord is a striking feature in Paul's letters ([Rom 10:]13; 1 Cor 2:16; Phil 2:[10–]11—using the powerfully monotheistic Isa 45:23; 1 Thess 5:2 and 2 Thess 2:2—"the day of the Lord").[107]

Contextually, Paul's use of a passage from the prophet Joel in Rom 10:13 (see below) proves conclusively that the meaning of the confession "Jesus [is] Lord" (κύριον Ἰησοῦν, 10:9) *predominantly refers to the person of Jesus and identifies him as Yahweh,* the personal name of the God of Israel (Ex 3:13–16). Jesus makes the claim repeatedly by applying the "I AM" of Ex 3:14 to himself (ἐγώ εἰμι, "I AM," in, e.g., Mk 6:50; 14:62; Jn 8:24, 28, 58; cf. Rev 1:17; 22:13).[108] The Greek text of the Gospels makes this more apparent than most

---

[102] Cranfield, *Romans,* 528.

[103] Dunn, *Romans,* 607.

[104] Dunn, *Romans,* 608.

[105] Cranfield, *Romans,* 528.

[106] Cranfield, *Romans,* 529.

[107] Dunn, *Romans,* 608.

[108] The Gospel of John has the richest presentation of Jesus' claim to be "I am." His absolute (no predicate) ἐγώ εἰμι, "I am," occurs in Jn 4:26; 6:20; 8:24, 28, 58; 13:19; 18:5, 6, 8. The seven "I am" statements with a predicate are "I am the bread of life" (Jn 6:35, 48; cf. Jn 6:41, 51); "I am the light of the world" (Jn 8:12; cf. Jn 9:5); "I am the gate" (Jn 10:7, 9); "I am the Good Shepherd" (Jn 10:11, 14); "I am the resurrection and the life" (Jn 11:25); "I am the way and the truth and the life" (Jn 14:6); and "I am the true vine" (Jn 15:1; cf. Jn 15:5). The foundational OT passage for "I am" is Ex 3:14. In the LXX, see ἐγώ εἰμι, "I am," in LXX Ex 3:14; Is 43:25; and also, e.g., LXX Gen 17:1; Ex 3:6; 7:5; Is 41:4; 43:10; 45:18. In the MT, see

English translations,[109] but the divine assertion was readily grasped by his original audience as proven by their reaction (e.g., Mk 14:62–64; Jn 8:58–59; cf. also Jn 10:30–31). The divine identification conveyed by Paul's assertion that "Jesus [is] Lord" (κύριον Ἰησοῦν, Rom 10:9) becomes unmistakable in 10:13. It will, in fact, eventually be acknowledged by each and every person at the parousia. Some will do so in dismay, but believers will utter the words "Jesus Christ [is] Lord" with inexpressible joy (Phil 2:11).

What source leads one to make this startling declaration? It was first heard in the proclaimed Word of the faith, which has come near you (10:8). How that Word arrives is unpackaged further in 10:14–15. But once it has arrived, the hearer is called to affirm its content, to "acknowledge with your mouth, 'Jesus [is] Lord' " (ὁμολογήσῃς ἐν τῷ στόματί σου κύριον Ἰησοῦν, 10:9).

Believing in Jesus' Resurrection Results in Righteousness and Salvation (10:9b–10)

Faith's Essential Content, Part 2 (10:9b)

As Paul continues, it becomes clear that such an acknowledgment of Jesus as Lord with the mouth exists together with belief in the heart. In the latter half of the verse, Paul adds: "If you … believe in your heart that God raised him from [the] dead, you will be saved" (10:9). In other words, the content of the confession involves more than a simple verbal assent. As Jesus declares, "Not everyone who says to me, 'Lord, Lord' will enter the kingdom of heaven" (Mt 7:21). Thus what Paul describes is "not merely a recitation of a creedal form" apart from faith,[110] but a confession of faith.

Does one, therefore, need to believe first? The order of "mouth" then "heart" in 10:9 might be "at first sight surprising," but Paul surely draws it from Deut 30:14.[111] As he continues, the chiastic structure illustrated above conveys that assent and belief in 10:9 are not to be understood sequentially. Instead, what the mouth speaks is joined with what the heart believes. Paul's repetition of both in 10:10, but in the order "heart" then "mouth," serves to make them a "both/and" which, at least according to God's intent, might be distinguished but cannot be divided. Fundamentally, rather than expressing two requirements for salvation, the proclamation of "the Word of the faith" (10:8) conveys a gracious, but also rejectable (10:16), message into your mouth and heart, which you are invited to both acknowledge and believe. The question of specific order is resolved in 10:14; then, the means by which faith comes into existence becomes clear in 10:17.

אֲנִי הוּא, "I am he," in Deut 32:39; Is 41:4; 43:10, 13; 46:4; 48:12; 52:6, and likewise אָנֹכִי הוּא, "I am he," in Is 43:25; 51:12.

[109] Middendorf, "The Bud Has Flowered: Trinitarian Theology in the New Testament," 298–303.

[110] Dunn, *Romans*, 609, though he goes beyond what Paul says in suggesting that it "indicates clearly enough that an affective and deeply motivating belief (καρδία ['heart'] …) is in view" (608–9).

[111] Cranfield, *Romans*, 527.

The "believing" in 10:9 flows from the use of "for everyone who believes" in 10:4 and also more distantly echoes that same clause in 1:16. Now "faith" becomes the dominant term that it was earlier in Romans.[112] Paul uses the verb πιστεύω, "believe," six times in 10:6–17. The cognate noun πίστις, "faith," also occurs thematically three times. This entire section explicates "the righteousness from faith" (ἐκ πίστεως, 10:6) and, even more specifically, describes "the Word of the faith which we are proclaiming" (τῆς πίστεως, 10:8). The noun πίστις, "faith," occurs again in 10:17, where the topic reaches its culmination.

As in Romans 4, this faith created by the Word involves *both* a receptive relationship *and* accepting specific content. In Romans 4 Abraham believes that God "declares the ungodly righteous" (4:5) and is "the one who makes the dead alive" (4:17) because God "is powerful also to do" what he promises (4:21).[113] By the end of that chapter the explicit point affirmed here is restated (4:23–25):

> [23]But "it was credited to him" was not written on [Abraham's] account only, [24]but also on our account, to whom it is about to be credited, to those who believe upon the one who raised Jesus our Lord from the dead, [25]who was handed over on account of our trespasses and was raised on account of our becoming righteous.

The *content* which "you believe in your heart" in 10:9 relates directly to the same Lord Jesus acknowledged earlier in the verse. "God raised him from [the] dead." While one might cite other texts regarding the primacy of the crucifixion, Paul does not identify that as the critical factor of faith here; "from [the] dead" assumes that his crucifixion and death had already occurred. To assert "Christ crucified" without his resurrection would leave us in sin and without hope (1 Cor 15:17–19). As in Rom 1:4 and referenced more recently in 10:7b, the essential content of belief articulated in 10:9 is the resurrection of Jesus. The significance of this for Christian proclamation and teaching is discussed in the excursus "Jesus' Resurrection in Romans" following this pericope. Similarly, note that we have died to sin by being baptized into Christ's death, that we may also be united with him in his resurrection (6:1–5).

"You Will Be Saved" (10:9c)

Acknowledging Jesus as Lord *and* believing that God raised him from the dead result in one of the most gracious affirmations in Scripture: "you will be saved" (σωθήσῃ, 10:9). Both the verb "save" and its cognate noun "salvation" have appeared prominently and been discussed previously (see σωτηρία, "salvation," in 1:16; also 10:1, 10; and the verb σῴζω, "save," in 5:9). The form here in 10:9, σωθήσῃ, is a future indicative passive. The divine passive conveys the certain truth that "*God* will save you." The future tense should primarily be heard in a temporal and eschatological sense, though there is, perhaps, also a logical

---

[112] See "The Background and Meaning of 'Faith' Words" in the commentary on 1:16 (Middendorf, *Romans 1–8*, 88–90); " 'From Faith[fulness] into Faith' (1:17)" on 96–98; and also 106–7.

[113] See Middendorf, *Romans 1–8*, 329–31, 359–65.

nuance which conveys the present blessing as well. As Barrett states: "Paul means that believers, already justified, will be saved at the last day; though, of course, he does not deny that preliminary effects of salvation are already apparent through the work of the Holy Spirit."[114]

The singular verb σωθήσῃ (10:9) refers to each individual "you" whom God will save. This singular "you" exhibits these two essential things: (1) acknowledgment of the Word with the *mouth*, (2) accompanied by believing in the *heart*. These are reaffirmed in reverse order in 10:10: "for with the *heart* it is being believed into righteousness, and with [the] *mouth* it is being acknowledged into salvation." While the *content* which "is being believed" and acknowledged is not restated, the referents of the two uses of "it" are clear from 10:9: the affirmation both of the divinity of Jesus with "Jesus [is] Lord" (κύριον Ἰησοῦν) and of the fact "that God raised him from [the] dead" (10:9).

Resulting Righteousness and Salvation (10:10)

Now Paul adds two complementary results contained within two prepositional phrases: "for with the heart it is being believed *into righteousness*, and with [the] mouth it is being acknowledged *into salvation*" (10:10). The objects of the repeated preposition "into" (εἰς) reproduce significant thematic nouns from 1:16–17: "righteousness" (δικαιοσύνη) and "salvation" (σωτηρία). First, Paul articulates "the righteousness from faith" (10:6) in another way: believing results in "righteousness." Similarly, the result of uttering the confession of 10:9 is "salvation." Paul connects the terms as he did when describing the Good News in 1:16–17. In fact, the OT itself had "already firmly established the connection between those two terms by regularly using them synonymously."[115]

> The parallel nature of these texts indicates that God's "righteousness" (*dikaiosynē*) is God's "salvation" (*sōtēria*). Righteousness, then, is not a static quality whereby God exercises justice but a dynamic quality whereby God effects salvation.[116]

Thus God's imputation of his righteousness to his people has already and repeatedly been equated with his salvation of them.

The intriguing element of 10:10, however, is the change in person and voice. Paul ceases to speak of "you" singular as the active subject of the verbs ("you acknowledge ... you believe," 10:9). Instead, both of the verbs become passive ("it is being believed ... it is being acknowledged," 10:10). To be sure, the passive voice enhances *both* the more passive sense of echoing in faith what was proclaimed (10:9) *and* the divine passive of "you will be saved" in 10:9.

---

[114] Barrett, *Romans*, 201–2.

[115] Middendorf, *Romans 1–8*, 94, including n. 47, citing as examples Pss 40:10 (MT 40:11; LXX 39:11); 51:14 (MT 51:16; LXX 50:16); 71:15 (LXX 70:15); 98:2 (LXX 97:2); Is 45:8; 46:13; 51:5, 6, 8; 56:1; 59:16–17; 61:10; 62:1; for a more detailed discussion of one reference, Ps 98:2 (LXX 97:2), see 109.

[116] Matera, *Romans*, 35–36.

It further underscores the passively receptive nature of faith in the theology of Paul.[117] Furthermore, after properly and personally taking to heart the second person singular forms in 10:8–9, these third singular passives prompt the addressee to move beyond self. Pragmatically, 10:10 drives one to ask, "Is being believed *by whom?*" and "Is being acknowledged *by whom?*"

Rather than having a summative effect,[118] the unspecified subject drives Paul forward to expand upon the reality of salvation for one "you" (10:9) by affirming that God intends it to be *for all.* In 10:11, Paul proceeds to speak not in terms of "one who believes," but of "*everyone* who believes" (πᾶς ὁ πιστεύων). The same clause appears identically in 1:16 and 10:4 (in the dative case: παντὶ τῷ πιστεύοντι). It encompasses the Good News of which Paul is not ashamed; it is the Word of the living Lord Jesus Christ who seeks to encompass every person and all people. And, as in 1:17, the OT Scriptures continue to validate Paul's all-inclusive assertions.

The Word of the Faith for Whom? For All! (10:11–13)

Paul introduces his affirmation in 10:11 with the first of four sequential uses of the conjunction "for" (γάρ, 10:11; 10:12 [twice], 13).[119] He then retrieves Is 28:16 from Rom 9:33 (see the commentary on that verse) and redeploys it here with a notable insertion at the beginning: "For the Scripture says: '*Everyone* who believes on him will not be put to shame' " (Rom 10:11). Neither LXX Is 28:16 nor Rom 9:33 contains "everyone, all" (πᾶς). The underlying Hebrew does not explicitly express the thought either.[120] Therefore Paul has clearly added "everyone" (πᾶς) here. While it does not contradict or fundamentally alter the Isaiah passage, *the insertion of "everyone" underscores Paul's emphasis.* The adjective was used in relation to believing in 10:4 ("*everyone* who believes") and then it recurs twice in 10:12 ("all") and again in 10:13 ("everyone"). Thus Paul's primary point in 10:11–13 is to widen the scope. What was stated in 10:6–9 in terms of direct address and in the singular, "you," and then depicted impersonally in 10:10 now expands and expressly stands applicable to all.[121] Thus the Formula of Concord cites Rom 10:12, along with a string of other passages, to buttress this assertion:

---

[117] See "The Background and Meaning of 'Faith' Words" in the commentary on 1:16 (Middendorf, *Romans 1–8*, 88–90); " 'From Faith[fulness] into Faith' (1:17)" on 96–98; and also 106–7.

[118] As suggested by Moo, *Romans*, 658, n. 62, who says: "It is better to think that Paul uses the passive to connote an impersonal nuance: 'one believes,' 'one confesses.' He thereby gives to the verse a summary and principal character."

[119] Similar sequences with γάρ, "for," occur in 1:16–20; 2:11–14; 6:19–23; 8:13–15; and, most recently, 10:2–5.

[120] The Hebrew participle translated as "the one who believes" (הַמַּאֲמִין) in Is 28:16 can readily be interpreted as a universal promise. However, Is 28:16 lacks the term כֹּל, "all, everyone," which is present in MT Joel 3:5 (ET 2:32), the verse Paul will quote in Rom 10:13.

[121] Moo, *Romans*, 659 states: "Paul unpacks the universality inherent in 'everyone.' "

Hence if we want to consider our eternal election to salvation profitably, we must by all means cling rigidly and firmly to the fact that as the proclamation of repentance extends over all men (Luke 24:47), so also does the promise of the Gospel. (FC SD XI 28)

The "everyone" (πᾶς) prefaced to Isaiah's words causes the "for everyone who believes" (παντὶ τῷ πιστεύοντι) of Paul's overall theme in Rom 1:16, recently repeated in 10:4, to reverberate once again. The negated verb "will not be put to shame" (οὐ καταισχυνθήσεται) cited here in Rom 10:11 from Is 28:16 (LXX: οὐ μὴ καταισχυνθῇ) establishes another link with Rom 1:16. Although the prefixed preposition differs, the same verbal root appears in the opening words of Paul's thematic statement: "I am not ashamed" (οὐ … ἐπαισχύνομαι, 1:16).

No Difference/No Partiality (10:12a)

As was the case earlier in Romans (e.g., 2:9–10; 3:29–31), and more recently in 9:30–10:5, the main challenge to "everyone" (πᾶς, 10:11) is the purported distinction between Jew and Greek/Gentile. Beginning already in 1:16, Paul primarily and positively endeavors to completely flatten out any such distinction in order to assert what stands true for all people, individually and universally.[122] He also just turned any notion of Jewish prerogative on its head in 9:30–10:5. Through faith Gentiles attain by "not pursuing" the righteousness Israel sought so earnestly by works and did not attain (9:30–32). Paul now employs "everyone, all" (πᾶς) twice to declare: "For there is not a difference [between] a Jew and a Greek, for the same Lord [is] of *all*, being rich to *all* the ones who are calling on him" (10:12).

Paul uses the noun διαστολή, "difference, distinction," only twice in Romans (3:22; 10:12) and three times altogether.[123] Yet the negated word nicely encapsulates his theology. In 3:22–23 Paul removed any "difference" (διαστολή), "for all sinned." Indeed, "both Jews and Greeks are *all* under sin" (πάντας, 3:9). Paul has proven that this is so for all people under the Law (1:18–3:20; note especially 2:12–16). If any such distinction currently existed in the mind of any of his hearers in regard to the Gospel, Romans 3 proceeded to describe how the fact that "there is not a difference" (3:22) also entails "being declared righteous undeservedly by his grace through the redemption, the one in Christ Jesus" (3:24). That the same God is Lord over all people *and* treats all of them the same in regard to "the righteousness from faith" (10:6) was affirmed via allusion to the *Shema* of Deut 6:4 in Rom 3:29–30:

---

[122] Moo, *Romans*, 662; Cranfield, *Romans*, 533; Morris, *Romans*, 389. See also "Conclusion: A Contextual Letter with Universal Application" in the introduction (Middendorf, *Romans 1–8*, 49–51).

[123] Paul's only use outside Romans is in reference to the difference in sound of musical instruments in 1 Cor 14:7. Note the use of διαστολή in LXX Ex 8:19 (ET 8:23), where God makes a "distinction" between the Israelites and the Egyptians by sending the plague of flies throughout the land of Egypt but sparing the Israelites in Goshen.

²⁹Or is God [the God] of Jews only? Is he not also [the God] of Gentiles? Yes, also of Gentiles, ³⁰since *God is one*, who will declare righteous the circumcised from faith and the uncircumcised through the same faith.

But the reason *why* God makes no distinction among people does *not* reside within humanity; rather, it is rooted firmly in *an essential attribute of God himself*. Romans as a whole, including chapters 9–11, is primarily about God.[124] As 2:11 concluded, "there is no partiality [προσωπολημψία] in the presence of God." Peter finally comprehended the Gospel side of this truth in Acts 10:36. Cyril of Alexandria applies the theological truth in this way:

> Israel ought not to suppose that salvation by faith is a blessing peculiar to it. For Scripture says that everyone who calls on the name of the Lord will be saved, whether Jew or Gentile, whether slave or free. The universal God saves everyone without distinction, because all things belong to him.[125]

The Same Lord Jesus Is Rich to All Who Call on Him (10:12b)

Indeed, "the same Lord [is] of all, being rich to all the ones who are calling on him" (10:12b). In light of "Jesus [is] Lord" (κύριον Ἰησοῦν) in 10:9, the referent of "the same Lord" (ὁ ... αὐτὸς κύριος) here must be Jesus himself (see also 10:13). On the Last Day even unbelievers will be forced to confess that "Jesus Christ [is] Lord" (Phil 2:11), but in the present era Jesus does not coerce people into faith, as if grace were irresistible (see Rom 10:16, 21). Rather, Paul states that Jesus richly showers his grace upon all who call on him in faith. Paul utilizes the stative verb "be rich" (πλουτέω) only here in Romans. However, in 2:4, the cognate noun πλοῦτος, "riches, abundance," expresses "the abundance of his kindness and forbearance and patience." In 9:23 the same noun speaks of "the abundance of his glory." The noun πλοῦτος then occurs twice in 11:12 ("richness"), as well as in the doxology of 11:33 ("riches").[126] Paul's usage of the noun elsewhere involves gifts from God in Christ such as "grace," "the forgiveness of sins," "glory," "inheritance," "kindness," supplying for "every need," and "assurance."[127] Without further description in Rom 10:12, however, the verb "be rich" (πλουτέω) conveys how the Lord Jesus responds "to all the ones who

---

[124] Middendorf, *Romans 1–8*, 21–22, 27, 49–51; in this volume, see "Romans 1–4: The Righteousness of God" in the introduction to Romans 9–16, as well as "God" in "The Three Foci of Romans 9–11" in the introduction to Romans 9–11. See also the commentary on 1:17, 32; 2:11, 16, 29; 3:1–8, 19–20, 29–30; 4:21; 9:5, 11b–12a, 16, 22–24, 29; 10:21; 11:1–2, 32–36; 12:19; 13:1–2; 14:10–12; 15:5, 8, 13; 16:25, 27.

[125] Cyril of Alexandria, *Romans* (Bray, *Romans*, ACCS NT 6:277). See Joel 2:32 (MT 3:5); Zech 13:9; Acts 2:21; Gal 3:28.

[126] See further the commentary on 11:12, 33.

[127] See Paul's use of πλοῦτος, referring to God's "riches" for us in Christ, in Eph 1:7, 18; 2:7; 3:8, 16; Phil 4:19; Col 1:27; 2:2. He employs the verb πλουτέω, "be rich," for the wealth Christians have gained by Christ's poverty in 2 Cor 8:9, and for Christians "being rich" in good works in 1 Tim 6:18.

are calling on him" (εἰς πάντας τοὺς ἐπικαλουμένους αὐτόν).[128] In the context of 10:10, the riches which the Lord delivers are primarily "righteousness" and "salvation," though innumerable other blessings accompany those two foundational gifts.[129]

The identification of "the same Lord" (ὁ ... αὐτὸς κύριος) in 10:12 with the one confessed in "Jesus [is] Lord" (κύριον Ἰησοῦν) in 10:9 lends greater significance to the presence of the verb "call on" (ἐπικαλέω, 10:12). In biblical contexts, this verb often means to "call on" God in prayer (e.g., LXX Ps 4:2 [ET Ps 4:1]; 1 Cor 1:2),[130] and so "calling on" the Lord Jesus (Rom 10:12) is an affirmation of his divinity (see also Rom 9:5).

> That the word has its technical sense of "invoke in prayer" here is confirmed by v. 13. The fact that Paul can think of prayer to the exalted Christ without the least repugnance is, in the light of the first and second commandments of the Decalogue, the decisive clarification of the significance which he attached to the title κύριος ["Lord"] as applied to Christ (e.g. in this verse [10:12] and in v. 9).[131]

Chrysostom also recognizes the intricate connection between other terms used in close proximity to one another here: "The words *Everyone who believes* [10:11] point out faith, but the words *Everyone who calls upon* [10:13] point out confession."[132] Thus he correctly points out that Paul's use of "call on" (ἐπικαλέω) in 10:13, as well as in 10:12 and 10:14, should be linked with the understanding of "acknowledge, confess" (ὁμολογέω) in 10:9, as discussed above.

Jesus, the LORD/Yahweh of All (Joel 2:32 in Rom 10:13)

As Paul moves forward, Moo suggests the "catchword 'call upon' [10:12, 13, 14] is clearly the link between the context and the quotation" from Joel.[133] But the use of "everyone, all" (πᾶς) in 10:11, twice in 10:12, and once in 10:13 exerts even more force. This view stems not only from the *insertion* of "everyone" into the Isaiah citation in 10:11[134] but also from the corroboration Paul draws regarding "everyone, all" (πᾶς) from another prophet. Paul validates the

---

[128] Moo, *Romans*, 660, calls the verb "be rich" in Rom 10:12 an absolute expression of "the unlimited resources of God," but that seems unnecessarily vague.

[129] For example, see the "blessing" from "righteousness" in Rom 4:6; "the undeserved gift of righteousness" leads to reigning in "eternal life" (Rom 5:17, 21; cf. 6:13); "righteousness" involves the indwelling "Spirit," who "is life," and the promise of the resurrection of the body (8:10–11); and "the kingdom of God" is "righteousness and peace and joy in [the] Holy Spirit" (14:17).

[130] See also the fourth textual note on 10:12. Dunn, *Romans*, 611, elaborates: "Such 'calling on' can be described as prayer, but it has less the character of entreaty (δέησις—10:1) and more the character of an appeal to the covenant partner to honor his (covenant) obligations."

[131] Cranfield, *Romans*, 532.

[132] Chrysostom, *Homilies on Romans*, 17 (Bray, *Romans*, ACCS NT 6:278).

[133] Moo, *Romans*, 660.

[134] See "The Word of the Faith for Whom? For All! (10:11–13)" in the commentary above.

assertion of 10:12 by citing Joel: "For 'everyone who ever might call on the name of [the] Lord will be saved'" (10:13). Aside from the introductory "for" (γάρ), Paul cites the clause exactly from LXX Joel 3:5 (ET 2:32). The Hebrew of Joel 3:5 (ET 2:32) is as follows:

וְהָיָה כֹּל אֲשֶׁר־יִקְרָא בְּשֵׁם יְהוָה יִמָּלֵט

And it will be that everyone who will call on the name of Yahweh will escape/ be delivered. (MT Joel 3:5 [ET 2:32])

Peter's use of Joel 2:28–32 (MT/LXX 3:1–5) as his Pentecost "text" (Acts 2:16–21) provides corroboration for the significance of the passage in the very earliest Christian proclamation. Note how Peter concludes: "God made this Jesus whom you crucified both Lord and Christ" (καὶ κύριον αὐτὸν καὶ χριστόν, Acts 2:36). In Romans 10, Paul has already identified "Jesus [is] Lord" (κύριον Ἰησοῦν) as the essential content of the Word of the faith that is to be echoed back to God (Rom 10:9). Thus it is significant that the name in the original of Joel is the Tetragrammaton, יהוה, Yahweh. "This implies a striking identification of Jesus Christ with Yahweh."[135] Unfortunately, the LXX here, and also customarily (more than six thousand times!), replaces God's personal name, "Yahweh," with the title κύριος, "Lord." Moo summarizes the chronology of the terminology involved as follows:

> The significance of NT quotations that use the title κύριος ["Lord"] of Christ are debated because it is apparently the case that pre-Christian MSS of the LXX did not use this Greek word to translate the tetragram (reproductions of the Hebrew script were used [for יהוה]). But there is good evidence that Greek-speaking Jews before the time of Christ were already at least orally substituting the Greek word κύριος ["Lord"] for the tetragram [יהוה]. The NT application of texts that identify Christ with "the Lord" therefore suggest that the early Christians viewed Christ as in some sense equivalent to Yahweh.[136]

Wallace asks and then answers the essential question specifically in regard to Rom 10:9 and then the verses to follow:

> What does Paul mean here by "Lord"? Since the complement κύριον *precedes* the object [Ἰησοῦν, 10:9], it is possible that it is definite though anarthrous. Thus, the confession would be that Jesus is *the* Lord, that is, *Yahweh*. This is substantiated by the context: Since Paul is alluding to and even directly quoting the OT here, his thought is colored by it. In vv 11 and 12, Christ is still clearly in view. And in v 13 he again mentions κύριος without indicating that a different Lord is in view. Thus to confess that Jesus is *the* Lord is to confess that he is the Lord mentioned in v 13. This verse is a quotation of Joel 3:5 (Hebrew; 2:32 in [English]), in which "Lord" is in reference to Yahweh. Such an allusion is hardly accidental, but part of the Pauline

---

[135] Kruse, *Romans*, 412.

[136] Moo, *Romans*, 660, n. 77.

soteriological confession. For Paul, to confess that Jesus is Lord is to confess that he is Yahweh.[137]

Wallace thus clearly enunciates the position of this commentary regarding "Jesus [is] Lord" (κύριον Ἰησοῦν, Rom 10:9). Jesus not only "shares the name and the nature, the holiness, the authority, power, majesty and eternity of the one and only true God,"[138] but he, in fact, is Yahweh himself in the flesh.[139]

On Pentecost, Peter effectively countered the notion that salvation was based or dependent upon our action in calling out to God. Instead, he concludes his call to repent and be baptized in the name of Jesus Christ (which Baptism confers "the forgiveness of sins" and "the gift of the Holy Spirit," Acts 2:38) by making clear who does the initial and decisive calling: "Indeed, the promise is for you [plural] and for your children and for all the ones in far off [places], as many as ever [the] Lord our *God might call to himself*" (ὑμῖν γὰρ ἐστιν ἡ ἐπαγγελία καὶ τοῖς τέκνοις ὑμῶν καὶ πᾶσιν τοῖς εἰς μακράν, ὅσους ἂν προσκαλέσηται κύριος ὁ θεὸς ἡμῶν, Acts 2:39). Paul will make the same point about divine, salvific action in the verses to follow (Rom 10:14–15). In so doing he may well be drawing upon the entire passage from Joel.[140] The full verse of LXX Joel 3:5 (ET 2:32) reads:

καὶ ἔσται πᾶς ὃς ἂν ἐπικαλέσηται τὸ ὄνομα κυρίου σωθήσεται· ὅτι ἐν τῷ ὄρει Σιων καὶ ἐν Ιερουσαλημ ἔσται ἀνασῳζόμενος, καθότι εἶπεν κύριος, καὶ εὐαγγελιζόμενοι οὓς κύριος προσκέκληται.

And it will be that everyone who ever might call on the name of [the] Lord will be saved, because in the mountain of Zion and in Jerusalem there will be [one] being saved, just as [the] Lord said, and [there will be] people proclaiming the Good News to those whom [the] Lord has called and continues to call to himself.

In Rom 10:14–15 Paul similarly details how "the same Lord" (10:12) now calls *all* people to himself by bringing the Gospel "near" (10:8) to them.

How the Word of the Faith Comes Near: The Process of Proclamation (10:14–15)

This section on "the righteousness from faith" (10:6) concludes by describing how God calls people to himself by bringing the Good News to them. Paul uses three parallel questions (cf. 5:3–5; 8:29–30) about events, and the order of his questions is the reverse of the chronological order in which the

---

[137] Wallace, *Greek Grammar*, 188. Wallace also notes that two other NT confessions of Jesus as Lord allude to the OT and specifically to Yahweh: Is 45:23 in Phil 2:11 and Is 8:13 in 1 Pet 3:15 (188, n. 43).

[138] Cranfield, *Romans*, 529.

[139] See Middendorf, "The Bud Has Flowered: Trinitarian Theology in the New Testament," 298–303.

[140] Dunn, *Romans*, 611; for a complete discussion of such OT echoes, see Hays, *Echoes of Scripture in the Letters of Paul*, 14–33; see also Middendorf, *Romans 1–8*, 108–9.

events actually occur (10:14). He also now switches to third person plural verbs, "they …" These should not be identified with the earlier third person plural references to Jews in 9:32 and 10:2–3.[141] Instead, the four forms of "everyone, all" (πᾶς) in 10:11–13, together with the explicit reference to "a Jew and a Greek" in 10:12, mean that *the third person plural verbs are all-encompassing* (cf. "all the world" in 10:18).[142] The only possible distinction is chronological, "to Jew first and also to Greek" (1:16), but ultimately "there is not a difference" (10:12). The Good News of salvation is "for *everyone* who believes" (1:16; 10:4; also 10:11).

In this divinely mandated process,[143] Paul draws attention away from human activity. Instead, he emphasizes the divine initiative by explaining how "the same Lord" (10:12) reaches out to all people via "the Word of the faith," which draws near to them (10:8). Humanity, left to its own, could never come to the saving message of righteousness in Christ (10:6–8) and is not even seeking it (9:30–32; 10:20–21). Instead, through God's sending, the Good News comes from outside of us (*extra nos*) to us so that we might believe it and then call on the Lord Jesus for salvation. Paul asks and then answers as follows (10:14–15):

> [14]How, then, might they call [on him] on whom they did not believe? And how might they believe [on him] of whom they did not hear? And how might they hear without one proclaiming? [15]And how might they proclaim if they are not sent? Just as it stands written: "How timely [are] the feet of the ones bringing the Good News [of] the good things."

Note how the chiastic alteration in 10:9–10 emphasizes the "both/and" nature of acknowledging and believing. In 10:14 *the sequential order is clarified*: they cannot call on the one in whom they do not *first* believe. Those who believe come to faith only because they have heard (ἤκουσαν, 10:14) "the Word of the faith which we are proclaiming" (κηρύσσομεν, 10:8; see also 10:17). Only what is first heard and then believed may be confessed unto salvation (see 10:9–10).

The Passive Hearing of Faith (10:14)

Paul uses the verb "to hear" (ἀκούω), common elsewhere in the NT, only five times in Romans. Two are in this verse and another is in 10:18. The other two occur in OT quotations in 11:8; 15:21. However, Paul uses a prefixed compound form of this verb (ὑπακούω) three times in Romans 6 (6:12, 16, 17), as well as once in 10:16, where it serves as a synonym of πιστεύω, "believe." All three uses of the cognate noun ἀκοή, "hearing; message heard," are congregated in 10:16–17, appearing once in 10:16 ("message") and twice in the summative

---

[141] As does Cranfield, *Romans*, 533. In light of the intervening verses (10:4–13), it is unlikely that any restriction is present here.

[142] Dunn, *Romans*, 620, says that "Paul leaves the subject ambiguous," but that fails to convey the universality of the Gospel mission and invitation.

[143] Moo, *Romans*, 664, refers to this as a "chain of requirements," but that sounds quite legalistic. This process here marks God's gracious provision of proclaimers, of the Good News to be heard and believed, and of the name of Jesus as the Lord to be invoked.

statement of 10:17 ("hearing"). In its discussion "The Background and Meaning of 'Faith' Words" in the commentary on 1:16, volume 1 of this commentary asserts the following about the relationship between hearing and believing:

> Hearing is passive. If you are in a place where something is being proclaimed (i.e., the kerygma), you do not have to do anything to hear it. In fact, you would have to take some action in order not to hear. The passive nature of faith/believing is also illustrated by how Paul often uses the term in the context of righteousness. There, for Paul, the opposite of "faith" is not so much "unbelief," as it is "works" and, specifically, "works of the Law" (ἔργων νόμου, Rom 3:20, 28; Gal 2:15–16; see also Rom 4:4–5; 10:5–11). This refers to humans doing something *toward God* in the arena of righteousness. Faith, therefore, in these contexts means to not do anything; it is simply to let oneself be given to in the sense of passively receiving the gift of salvation. The direction of the action is all *from God* to us.[144]

That description fits this context well. The thought will be reengaged in 10:17.

God's Sent Proclaimers (Is 52:7 in Rom 10:15)

The passive nature of hearing depends upon a prior action which produces sound waves.[145] In Romans 10, "the Word of the faith" (10:8) cannot be heard "without one proclaiming" (10:14). The indefinite present active participle here, κηρύσσοντος, emphasizes the action of "one *proclaiming*" more than the personal "*we* are proclaiming" expressed with κηρύσσομεν in 10:8. For the specific context and use of the verb "proclaim" (κηρύσσω) in the NT, see the excursus "The New Testament Connotations and Context of Words Commonly Translated as 'Preach,' 'Teach,' and 'Prophesy'" following this pericope. This proclaiming is not done directly by the divine voice booming out from the sky; neither does it come from within ourselves. Most importantly, it is *not* a message we need to go out and find (10:6–8). Instead, it *comes to us*, and it does so incarnationally by those whom God has sent.

"How might they proclaim if they are not sent?" (10:15). As 10:17 makes clear, the essential component resides in the message of Christ being proclaimed, not in the qualities or motivations of the proclaimer himself.[146] Yet

---

[144] Middendorf, *Romans 1–8*, 89–90.

[145] Paul envisions the hearing of oral proclamation as the typical way for the Gospel to be disseminated. His description, however, does not preclude other ways in which the Good News of Christ may be received and believed. For example, the written Word may be read by those who are unable to hear or who live in an area of the world where preaching is prohibited. Likewise, those who receive Christian Baptism are incorporated into the death and resurrection of Christ, even if they are children too young to understand verbal communication; see "Our Baptismal Death and Life with Christ (6:1–8)" in the commentary on 6:1–11 in Middendorf, *Romans 1–8*, 451–70. The baptized are given faith and salvation under the confession of Jesus as Lord; see the baptismal passages cited in a footnote in "Faith's Essential Content, Part 1 (10:9a)" above. Note also the inclusion of "your children" in Acts 2:39 and the Baptism of entire households in Acts 16:15, 33; 1 Cor 1:16.

[146] For example, Dodd, *The Apostolic Preaching and Its Developments*, 7, states: "The word here [1 Cor 1:21] translated 'preaching,' *kerygma*, signifies not the action of the preacher, but that

for the message to be heard, God uses flesh and blood proclaimers and sends them out to do it. First of all, Jesus himself was sent by the Father, and as he was sent, so he sends those who speak for him.[147] The divine passive "they are sent" (ἀποσταλῶσιν) *by God* calls to mind the technical use of the cognate noun "apostle" (ἀπόστολος), as in 1:1. To be sure, the apostles were called by Jesus himself and sent (ἀποστέλλω in, e.g., Mt 10:5, 16; Mk 6:7; Acts 26:17) as authoritative heralds of the Gospel.[148] Furthermore, the apostolic Scriptures of the NT serve as the normative basis for all subsequent proclamation. But to assert that the "sending" and "proclaiming" (Rom 10:15) refer *only* to the apostles in a restrictive sense would be inappropriately narrow here; the application is broader.[149] For example, the NT also speaks of the "sending" of the seventy-two (Lk 10:1) and of co-workers of the apostles (Acts 19:22; 2 Cor 12:17–18; 1 Thess 3:2; 2 Tim 4:12), and even of the "sending" of Ananias for the conversion of Paul himself (Acts 9:17).[150] As the excursus following this section demonstrates, prominent NT proclaimers include Jesus and his apostles, notably Paul, but others also "proclaim" (κηρύσσω), e.g., a healed leper in Mk 1:45; a healed demoniac in Mk 5:20; a crowd in Mk 7:36; Philip the deacon in Acts 8:5. The authoritative proclamation of Christ is now provided in the NT documents, written under inspiration by apostles and also others (Mark, Luke-Acts, James, Jude). And the proclaiming continues as God sends Christian pastors, missionaries, teachers, singers, radio and television broadcasters, family members, co-workers, friends, neighbors, and so on into their various vocations so that they might herald the Word of Christ into the ears of others.

The origin of the believing community in Rome provides a most relevant example. This commentary's introduction concludes that it stems from

---

which he preaches, his 'message.' " Note Phil 1:15–18, where Paul rejoices whenever Christ is being proclaimed, even by those with improper motives such as envy and rivalry.

[147] See, e.g., ἀποστέλλω for the Father's "sending" of Jesus in Lk 4:18; Jn 3:17; 5:36; 7:29; 8:42; 17:3. As Jesus was sent, so he sends his disciples (Jn 20:21).

[148] Cranfield, *Romans*, 535, draws upon the quotation of Is 52:7 cited later in the verse to point out: "If the apostolic preaching is truly the fulfilment of the prophecy, then it is attested as a true κηρύσσειν ['to proclaim']."

[149] Käsemann, *Romans*, 294, explains that both of the verbs in 10:15, "proclaim" (κηρύσσω, also in 10:8, 14) and "bring the Good News" (εὐαγγελίζω, also in 1:15; 15:20), "mean Christian preaching, which includes the element of proclamation. The authorization of sending presented by ἀποστέλλειν ['to send'] thus belongs to it. … The interpretation of the quotation [Is 52:7 in Rom 10:15] will show that the apostolic commission is specifically meant." Cranfield, *Romans*, 534, similarly elaborates: "The point of the fourth question [Rom 10:15a] is that true Christian preaching, through which Christ Himself speaks, is not something which men can accomplish on their own initiative: it can only take place where men are authorized and commissioned by God. It is illuminating to compare what is said concerning prophetic authority in Jer 14.14; 23.21; 27.15."

[150] See also, e.g., the statement that the men Cornelius sent to Peter were actually sent (ἀποστέλλω) by the Spirit (Acts 10:19–20) so that the entire household of the Gentile Cornelius might hear and believe the Good News (Acts 10–11).

the visitors from Rome who were present on Pentecost (Acts 2:10).[151] They heard firsthand the apostolic proclamation of Peter that momentous day and, in all likelihood, listened to the other apostles as well. Their faith came from hearing this Word of Christ (Rom 10:17). As they returned home in due course, their timely feet (10:15) carried the Good News back to Rome. Various house churches then emerged, apart from any local apostolic activity of which we are aware.[152] In keeping with 10:14–15, we should presume that God himself sent those Pentecost visitors back to Rome for his evangelistic purposes.

This divinely mandated process is nothing new. Rather, it remains "just as it stands written" (καθὼς γέγραπται) in Is 52:7, quoted in Rom 10:15. Paul does not closely cite the LXX nor offer a strict translation of the MT. Below are the MT and LXX with literal translations:

מַה־נָּאווּ עַל־הֶהָרִים רַגְלֵי מְבַשֵּׂר מַשְׁמִיעַ שָׁלוֹם מְבַשֵּׂר טוֹב
מַשְׁמִיעַ יְשׁוּעָה אֹמֵר לְצִיּוֹן מָלַךְ אֱלֹהָיִךְ:

How lovely they are upon the mountains—the feet of one bringing Good News, causing peace to be heard, bringing Good News of good, making salvation be heard, saying to Zion, "Your God reigns!" (MT Is 52:7)

ὡς ὥρα ἐπὶ τῶν ὀρέων, ὡς πόδες εὐαγγελιζομένου ἀκοὴν εἰρήνης, ὡς εὐαγγελιζόμενος ἀγαθά, ὅτι ἀκουστὴν ποιήσω τὴν σωτηρίαν σου λέγων Σιων βασιλεύσει σου ὁ θεός.

As a moment upon the mountains, as feet of one bringing as Good News a message of peace, as bringing Good News of good things, because I will make be heard your salvation, saying [to] Zion, "Your God will reign!" (LXX Is 52:7)

Five textual comments are in order. First, the presence of the noun ὥρα, "moment, hour," in the LXX points toward a more temporal, rather than adjectival, understanding of Paul's use of the adjective ὡραῖοι, which is translated here as "timely" (see the second textual note on 10:15). Second, after the LXX's participle εὐαγγελιζομένου, "of one bringing as Good News," which Paul makes plural, he omits the reference to "a message of peace." In fact, he passes over all of the LXX wording ἀκοὴν εἰρήνης, ὡς εὐαγγελιζόμενος, but retains ἀγαθά, "good things," which follows those words in the LXX and which, in Rom 10:15, is the object of εὐαγγελιζομένων, "ones bringing Good News [of]." In some manuscripts of Romans the noun εἰρήνην, "peace," was inserted, perhaps "in order to make the citation correspond more fully to the Septuagint."[153] The KJV and NKJV retain the textually disputed reference to "peace." Third, the presence of ἀκοή, "message, something heard," in LXX Is 52:7 likely prompts Paul's

---

[151] Middendorf, *Romans 1–8*, 10–11.

[152] See Middendorf, *Romans 1–8*, 17–18, as well as the concluding section of the commentary on 16:1–16, which identifies seven congregations in Rome at the time Paul sends the letter. Klein, "Paul's Purpose in Writing the Epistle to the Romans," contends that Paul wrote Romans and intended to visit Rome in order to lay the necessary apostolic foundation.

[153] Metzger, *A Textual Commentary on the Greek New Testament*, 525. The noun εἰρήνην is present in ℵc D G, but not in 𝔓46 ℵ* A B C.

use of the noun twice in Rom 10:17. Fourth, Paul does not proceed beyond the first half of the Isaiah passage to include any mention of "Zion."

Finally, and as a result of those previously cited textual differences, Dunn suggests that Rom 10:15 may also include "an echo of Nah 2:1 [ET 1:15]."[154] In the MT and the LXX, Nah 2:1a (ET 1:15a) reads:

הִנֵּה עַל־הֶהָרִים רַגְלֵי מְבַשֵּׂר מַשְׁמִיעַ שָׁלוֹם

Look upon the mountains! The feet of one bringing Good News, one making peace be heard. (MT Nah 2:1a [ET 1:15a])

ἰδοὺ ἐπὶ τὰ ὄρη οἱ πόδες εὐαγγελιζομένου καὶ ἀπαγγέλλοντος εἰρήνην.

Look upon the mountains! The feet of one bringing Good News and announcing peace. (LXX Nah 2:1a [ET 1:15a])

It seems more likely that the earlier (eighth century BC) Isaiah text influenced Nahum (seventh century BC) and that Paul may have a conflation of both. The passage from Isaiah has had an even broader impact.

> That the verse lent itself to a messianic or eschatological sense is self-evident from the original context (the prospective return from exile to the promised land). That such an interpretation was already current in Jewish circles at this time is now confirmed by 11QMelch 15–19, where Isa 52:7 is explicitly interpreted of "the anointed by the Spirit."[155]

In Rom 10:15 Paul connects three critical verbs, "proclaim" (κηρύσσω), "send" (ἀποστέλλω), and "bring the Good News" (εὐαγγελίζομαι). All three verbs appear together in Lk 4:18, in the quote of Is 61:1, which Jesus reads aloud in the Nazareth synagogue to inaugurate his public ministry. The first two verbs occur together when Jesus *sends* his twelve apostles *to proclaim* the kingdom of God and to heal (Lk 9:2; also Mk 3:14). Jesus applies the combination of "send" (ἀποστέλλω) and "to bring the Good News" (εὐαγγελίζομαι) to his own mission in Lk 4:43–44, while Paul designates his ministry as that of a "proclaimer and apostle" (κῆρυξ καὶ ἀπόστολος) in 1 Tim 2:7; 2 Tim 1:11. Dunn says that "at this point the κῆρυξ ['proclaimer'] and the ἀπόστολος ['apostle'] are largely overlapping concepts,"[156] and he contends that "bring the Good News" (εὐαγγελίζομαι) "is more or less synonymous with" the verb "proclaim" (κηρύσσω).[157] In the NT, both verbs typically convey the action of proclaiming the Good News to unbelievers (i.e., evangelizing), as will be demonstrated in the excursus "The New Testament Connotations and Context of Words Commonly Translated as 'Preach,' 'Teach,' and 'Prophesy'" following this pericope.

The focus of all these verbal actions emphasizes *God's initiative* and purpose in sending the Good News to be proclaimed, heard, believed, and confessed. Interestingly, Paul does *not* use the nouns for "proclaimer" (κῆρυξ), "apostle"

---

[154] Dunn, *Romans*, 621; see also Moo, *Romans*, 663, n. 12.

[155] Dunn, *Romans*, 622. For the OT basis for "the anointed by the Spirit," see Is 61:1; also Is 11:1.

[156] Dunn, *Romans*, 622.

[157] Dunn, *Romans*, 621; similarly, Käsemann, *Romans*, 294.

(ἀπόστολος), or "evangelist" (εὐαγγελιστής) at all in 10:14–15; in fact, his only noun simply depicts timely "feet" (οἱ πόδες, 10:15). Otherwise Paul uses verbal forms, including participles. Therefore, while God uses real flesh and blood proclaimers, in this passage Paul does not place his *emphasis* upon the human beings who bring the Good News.[158] Instead, the all-encompassing character of his argument (e.g., four forms of the adjective πᾶς, "everyone, all," in 10:11–13) assures us that whenever the action of these verbs is done, *the main actor is the Lord himself*, who bestows the riches of his righteousness and salvation on all who call on him (10:12–13). Thus far, the Gospel is entirely *God reaching toward all of us* through the Word about the Lord Jesus, whom he raised from the dead (10:8–9). This is how it is with "the righteousness from faith" (10:6).

The Divinely Intended Outcome (10:16–17)

The abrupt "but" (ἀλλά) which opens 10:16 (also 10:18, 19) introduces the matter of human response.[159] As a result, this verse introduces a new thought, but it is a hinge. Mirroring 10:4–5, Paul uses the thought of 10:16 to move ahead into a new section and then utilizes 10:17 as a summative statement for 10:6–15:[160]

> [16]But they all did not listen responsively to the Good News. For Isaiah says: "Lord, who believed our message?" [17]Consequently, faith [comes] from hearing, and the hearing through [the] Word of Christ/[the] Messiah.

To acknowledge Jesus as Lord and believe in his resurrection is to receive righteousness and salvation (10:9–10). Paul has just made clear that believing comes first, from hearing what is proclaimed (10:8, 14). This is "the Word of the faith" (τὸ ῥῆμα τῆς πίστεως, 10:8). Now 10:17 reiterates even more explicitly that "faith [comes] from hearing." This "faith" receives "the righteousness from faith" (10:6), which has been the topic at hand ever since 10:6, indeed, ever since 1:17!

Together with Paul's interpretive applications in 10:6 and 10:7, 10:17 proves that "the Word" (τὸ ῥῆμα) of 10:8 refers to the message of Christ. *We cannot and did not go and seek him. He comes near to us* (10:6–8). He does so in his Word, as "the Word" (τὸ ῥῆμα) is being proclaimed. Those who proclaim the Word have been sent by God to bring the Good News (10:14–15). The content of their message is the "Word of Christ" (ῥήματος Χριστοῦ, 10:17). He is the source of righteousness and salvation, and he *is* righteousness and salvation, for anyone and everyone who believes (10:10–11). For a full treatment of 10:16–17, see the commentary on 10:16–21.

---

[158] Against Kruse, *Romans*, 417, who suggests that 10:15b–16 serves "to underline the importance of the preachers."

[159] See "Introduction to the Hinges of Romans 10:4 and 10:16–17: Their Rhetorical, Theological, and Contextual Functions" in the commentary above, as well as the opening section of the commentary on 10:16–21.

[160] Other hinges appear in, for example, 3:1, 21; 4:1; 5:1; 6:1, 11; 8:1–4; 9:24; 10:4; 12:1; 13:8; 15:7.

Conclusion

Ambrosiaster concisely summarizes what leads up to 10:6–15 and affirms its universal application:[161]

> Paul says that in general everyone is lumped together because of unbelief or else exalted together because of their belief, because apart from Christ there is no salvation in God's presence, only punishment or death. For neither the privileges of their ancestors nor the law can do the Jews any good if they do not accept the merit and promise made to them. Neither do the Gentiles have anything to boast about in the flesh, if they do not believe in Christ.[162]

This section wonderfully conveys how God has acted to alter our dire situation. Through his sending of people to proclaim "the Word of the faith" (10:8), the message spreads so that all might hear, believe, and acknowledge it. Thus Paul's primary focus here is *evangelistic*.[163] In keeping with the specific aim of his apostolic ministry to bring the Good News where Christ was not yet named (εὐαγγελίζεσθαι οὐχ ὅπου ὠνομάσθη Χριστός, 15:20), he explains to his Roman hearers, and to all, *how faith comes to those who had not previously heard or believed it*. The Lutheran Confessions corroborate this by using the sequence leading up to 10:17 in discussing *conversion*:

> In order that we may come to Christ, the Holy Spirit creates true faith through the hearing of God's Word, as the apostle testifies, "Faith comes from the hearing of God's Word" (Rom. 10:17).[164]

"The righteousness from faith" (10:6) comes through "*the Word of the faith*" (10:8) proclaimed/preached/heralded (κηρύσσω) by those whom God has sent out to bring the Good News (10:14–15). The essential message declares *who Jesus is*, namely, the "Lord" (10:9), Yahweh, the God of Israel in human flesh (9:5), *and what he has accomplished* climactically in his death and resurrection (10:9). Those who believe and acknowledge what they have heard receive righteousness and will be saved (10:9–10). This saving message is *for all* who hear it in faith, so that they might call on the Lord Jesus, who has first called out to them (10:11–13).[165] In other words, and in keeping with the form of expression in 10:8–9, it is most certainly *for you*.

---

[161] See the conclusion to the introduction of this commentary subtitled "A Contextual Letter with Universal Application" (Middendorf, *Romans 1–8*, 49–51).

[162] Ambrosiaster, *Romans*, on 10:12 (Bray, *Romans*, ACCS NT 6:278).

[163] The evangelistic nature of Paul's terminology is developed more completely in the excursus "The New Testament Connotations and Context of Words Commonly Translated as 'Preach,' 'Teach,' and 'Prophesy' " following this pericope.

[164] FC SD XI 69; see also FC SD II 50–52, as well as FC Ep II 4–5, quoted in the excursus "The New Testament Connotations and Context of Words Commonly Translated as 'Preach,' 'Teach,' and 'Prophesy' " following this pericope and in the commentary on 10:16–21.

[165] The Formula of Concord confesses this comforting assurance, citing Rom 10:12 in support of its affirmation that "as the proclamation of repentance extends over all men (Luke 24:47), so also does the promise of the Gospel" (FC SD XI 28).

Excursus

Jesus' Resurrection in Romans

The Essential Fact

Paul defines the essence of the Gospel right at the outset of his letter to Rome (1:2–6). It is God's Good News "concerning his Son, the one who came from the seed of David according to flesh, the one designated Son of God in power according to [the] Spirit of holiness out of [his] resurrection from [the] dead, Jesus Christ our Lord" (1:3–4).[1] Later in 10:9, he concisely summarizes the content of the believer's saving faith: "If you acknowledge with your mouth, 'Jesus [is] Lord,' and believe in your heart that God raised him from [the] dead, you will be saved." This excursus simply recognizes how both of these critical passages *identify the Gospel with a single event, and that is the fact of Jesus' resurrection from the dead*. In regard to 10:9, Cranfield remarks: "For Paul the belief that God raised Jesus from the dead is the decisive and distinctive belief of Christians, the *articulus stantis et cadentis ecclesiae*."[2]

It is certainly true that you cannot have any kind of resurrection unless a death has first preceded it; "God raised him *from [the] dead*" (10:9). Thus early in his first letter to the Corinthians, Paul claims not "to know anything among you except for Jesus Christ and this one having been crucified" (τι εἰδέναι ἐν ὑμῖν εἰ μὴ Ἰησοῦν Χριστὸν καὶ τοῦτον ἐσταυρωμένον, 1 Cor 2:2). At the same time, Paul obviously believes that knowing Christ crucified involves a great deal of wisdom and Christian practice that he must impart to the Corinthians, as is evident from the length of his prior eighteen-month ministry in Corinth (Acts 18:11), as well as the sixteen chapters he writes (just in this first epistle) covering numerous topics along with this claim!

Furthermore, as Paul argues most emphatically in 1 Corinthians 15, if you disregard Jesus' resurrection, you have no saving faith; moreover, without the fact of his resurrection, the Christian faith would be false and you would

---

[1] Note how Gal 1:1 also emphasizes the resurrection. Das, *Galatians*, 78, observes: "Paul can barely introduce God without immediately adding that he raised Jesus Christ from the dead."

[2] Cranfield, *Romans*, 530, citing 1 Cor 15:14, 17. Lutherans have long identified "the article [of the faith] by which the church stands or falls" (*articulus stantis et cadentis ecclesiae*) as the doctrine of justification—by grace alone and through faith in Christ alone. Cranfield's application of the phrase to the resurrection is compatible with the way Paul connects the resurrection to justification: he "was raised for our justification" (ἠγέρθη διὰ τὴν δικαίωσιν ἡμῶν, Rom 4:25). For the history and meaning of the Latin phrase, see J. A. O. Preus III, "Justification by Faith: The *Articulus Stantis et Cadentis Ecclesiae*," in *And Every Tongue Confess: Essays in Honor of Norman Nagel on the Occasion of His Sixty-fifth Birthday* (ed. Gerald S. Krispin and Jon D. Vieker; Dearborn, Mich.: Nagel Festschrift Committee, 1990), 264–82. Preus (279, n. 5) attributes the first use the exact Latin phrase to the Lutheran theologian Balthasar Meisner (Ἀνθρωπολογίας sacrae, disputatio XXIV [Wittenberg: Johannes Gormannus, 1613], A 2 b).

perish in your sins (1 Cor 15:12–19). Thus you *cannot* simply know *only* that Jesus Christ was crucified. You also need to know and confess his resurrection, without which the faith would be "empty" (κενή, 1 Cor 15:14) and "useless" (ματαία, 1 Cor 15:17). To stop with Jesus' death ultimately leaves the Christian dead in his own tracks. Yet how often has the Christian faith been reduced to the message that "Jesus died for you" with the implication that his death stands as the essential "be all and end all" of our message?

In similar fashion, an emphasis upon the theology of the cross is totally and profoundly appropriate when properly explained.[3] Yet it should not be comprehended in a manner which neglects Paul's theology of resurrected glory. This future glory springs forth from Christ's vicarious satisfaction on the cross, his resurrection, ascension, and current reign, and surely extends to the fulfillment of his promise regarding our own bodily resurrection on the Last Day. Thus Jesus' death *points ever forward* to his resurrection and beyond. For by it he escapes from and overcomes death, thereby producing new, abundant life for us as well (Jn 10:10; 14:19; Rom 6:2–4; see below). Finally, when he returns "in his glory" (Mt 25:31), we will "also be glorified" with him (Rom 8:17; see also 8:18, 30).[4]

What about in a Lutheran context? It was disheartening for this professor at a Lutheran university to read this student's response to reading the Gospels in a NT course: "I enjoyed reading all four Gospels, but my favorite [part] was the coming back to life of Jesus. I grew up as a Lutheran but I never read this." This surely is an isolated example that, hopefully, involves some type of misunderstanding by the student during his Lutheran upbringing. Yet the experience of this author concurs with the assessment of Gibbs. He makes the following observations about the emphasis of Lutheran proclamation:

> My strong impression is, however, that we have majored in proclaiming the biblical truth of the *death* of Jesus, especially his death as atoning sacrifice for sins (see Rom 3:21–26). If this is at all an accurate observation—that Good Friday has been primary, with Easter as Good Friday's validation—then perhaps there is a place for us as Lutherans to bear witness more fully and joyfully not only to the *fact* of Jesus's bodily resurrection (on which we have not wavered), but also to the *significance* of Jesus' resurrection.[5]

Gibbs also notes:

---

[3] For a brief summary, see Mueller, *Called to Believe, Teach, and Confess*, 33–34; for monographs on the subject, see Loewenich, *Luther's Theology of the Cross*; McGrath, *Luther's Theology of the Cross*.

[4] This is encapsulated in the Nicene Creed: "He will come again with glory to judge both the living and the dead, whose kingdom will have no end. ... I acknowledge one Baptism for the remission of sins [the Baptism into Christ's death and resurrection, Rom 6:1–5], and I look for the resurrection of the dead and the life of the world to come" (*LSB* 158).

[5] Gibbs, "Filling in the Blanks on 'Witness': God Raised Jesus from the Dead," 114.

There is a need to reclaim the significance of Easter. There are promises here for our faith to claim, promises related to the lordship of Christ, the reign of God, the new creation, and the Holy Spirit.[6]

To be sure, Jesus' death and his resurrection should never be severed from or pitted against each other. Obviously, "for us men and for our salvation" (Nicene Creed) we always need both and get even more! In fact, "Good Friday and Easter (along with Ascension and Pentecost) go together, one event, in a sense."[7]

A Plea for Both Cross *and* Resurrection

This excursus simply pleads that we be cautious about consistently, or even occasionally, ending our proclamation of the Gospel with the event of Jesus' death only. On occasions like Good Friday this may be appropriate. Indeed, at strategic points in Romans, Paul speaks only of Jesus' sacrificial death (e.g., 3:25; 5:6, 7, 8; 8:3; 14:15). But our full proclamation should not leave Jesus hanging on the cross, and, thereby, our hearers' faith hanging as well. Similarly, we faithfully display crosses and regularly make the sign of the cross. Perhaps we should ponder ways in which our visible testimony to the resurrection can also be made prominent. As Gibbs reminds us, "the biblical testimony forces us to say that *only Easter makes it possible for the death of Jesus to be not bad news, but good news*."[8]

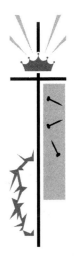

As indicated by the two significant Romans passages cited above which refer to Christ's resurrection from the dead (1:3–4; 10:9), *Paul's emphasis resides upon the victorious, life-giving proclamation of Jesus' resurrection.*[9] Yes, Paul speaks powerfully of both Jesus' death and his resurrection throughout Romans. Certainly this provides the best model for our efforts to faithfully pass on what the Spirit has entrusted to us through Paul's inspired writings. Rom 4:24–25 illustrates how the two events should be held together. Paul applies the account of Abraham's faith to those who now "believe upon the one who raised Jesus our Lord from the dead, who was handed over on account of our trespasses and was raised on account of our becoming righteous" (4:24b–25).

Paul's discussion of Baptism references both events, but repeatedly moves Christ and us from death to life. He thereby stresses the implications of Christ's resurrected life and our renewed life in him:

> [3]Or do you not know that as many of us as were baptized into Christ Jesus, [that] we were baptized into his death? [4]Consequently, we were buried with him through this Baptism into [his] death, so that just as Christ was raised from [the] dead through the glory of the Father, thus also we might walk in

---

[6] Gibbs, "Christ Is Risen, Indeed," 113.

[7] Gibbs, "Christ Is Risen, Indeed," 113.

[8] Gibbs, "Christ Is Risen, Indeed," 115. Thus the disciples themselves remained grief-stricken until they came to believe what happened on Easter (e.g., Lk 24:10–11, 37; Jn 20:11–15, 24–25).

[9] See Gaffin, *The Centrality of the Resurrection.*

life's renewal. [5]Indeed, since we have become united and grow together with the likeness of his death, we will certainly also be [united in the likeness] of his resurrection. ...

[9]Understanding that Christ, after being raised from [the] dead, no longer dies; death is no longer lord of him. [10]For what he died, he died to sin once for all, and what he lives, he lives to God. (6:3–5, 9–10)

Similarly, Romans 8 climactically summarizes the work of Christ for us, which extends beyond his empty tomb into the present and the future: "Christ Jesus [is] the one who died and, moreover, [who] was raised, who is even at the right hand of God, who is also pleading in our behalf. ... Neither present things nor the things about to come ... will be able to separate us from God's love which is in Christ Jesus our Lord!" (8:34, 38–39).

Thus the fact that Jesus lives, reigns, and intercedes for us not only enlivens, encourages, and edifies our present faith, but it also embodies, as he himself does, the essence of our future hope. "And since the Spirit of the one who raised Jesus from the dead is dwelling in you, the one who raised Christ from the dead will also make your mortal bodies alive through his Spirit, who indwells within you" (8:11). This is why 14:8–9 comforts believers with this assurance: "For not only if we live are we living to the Lord, but also if we die we die to the Lord. Therefore not only if we live, but also if we die, we are the Lord's. For to this [end] Christ died and lived [again] so that he might be Lord of both [the] dead and [the] living ones."

(a) Rom 1:32; 4:16, 23–24; 5:3, 11; 8:23; 9:10, 24; 13:5; 16:4

Paul uses the formula "not only ... but also" ten times in Romans (οὐ μόνον ... ἀλλὰ καί).[a] He might then similarly and repeatedly urge us to proclaim *not only the cross of Christ but also his resurrection.*

The New Testament Connotations and Context of Words Commonly Translated as "Preach," "Teach," and "Prophesy"

It is always a privilege and joy to return to the original languages of the Scriptures and to reexamine the meaning and connotations of its verbally inspired words. This excursus aims to make such a survey of the NT vocabulary typically translated into English with forms of "preach," "teach," and "prophesy." The goal is to make our understandings and explanations of those words adhere more closely to their biblical nuances, as well as to the contexts in which the authors of Scripture use them. Perhaps the reader will also evaluate his own practice of evangelistic proclamation and prophetic instruction on that basis.

Terms Commonly Translated as "Preach": κηρύσσω, "Proclaim," and εὐαγγελίζομαι, "Bring the Good News"

The Synoptic Gospels and Acts

κηρύσσω, "Proclaim"

One Greek verb commonly translated as "preach" in the NT is κηρύσσω, as in Rom 10:8, 14, 15.[1] The verb is cognate to the noun κῆρυξ, a term for a "*herald*" or "*proclaimer*" (BDAG, κῆρυξ, 2), whose role is "to make an official announcement" or "to make public declarations" (BDAG, κηρύσσω, 1 and 2). Yet our modern understanding of "preach" in English is often inconsistent with the *context* of the NT's use of the term.[2] In church circles "preaching" normally describes the authoritative proclamation and exposition of the Word of God by the pastor in the public gathering of God's people; that is to say, the "preacher" does it from the pulpit in the church during worship. What about κηρύσσω in the NT?

According to Friedrich:

---

[1] Translations which use forms of "preach" for κηρύσσω in Rom 10:8, 14, 15 include KJV, NASB, NKJV, and RSV. ESV has "preach" in Rom 10:14, 15, but "proclaim" in 10:8. NRSV consistently uses "proclaim." Among commentators, Matera, *Romans*, 250, uses "preach" or "preacher" three times in 10:14–15; similarly, Kruse, *Romans*, 417, uses "preach" and "preaching" in 10:14–15a before suggesting that 10:15b–16 serves "to underline the importance of the preachers." For renditions of κηρύσσω in other NT passages, see below.

[2] In secular society at large, "preach" often conveys a condescending tone of "talking down" to someone in an accusatory manner, e.g., "don't preach at me!"

Teaching is usually in the synagogue, whereas proclamation takes place anywhere in the open. Different hearers are present. διδασκαλία ["teaching"] is the exposition of Scripture in synagogue worship; it is for the righteous with a view to increasing their knowledge. κήρυγμα ["proclamation"] is the herald's cry ringing out in the streets and villages and in houses. The herald goes to all, publicans and sinners; he attracts the attention of those who are without (Lk. 18:13) and who do not attend the gatherings of the righteous.[3]

A strict separation in the meaning of different terms does not always seem warranted. For example, the two verbs διδάσκω, "teach," and κηρύσσω, "proclaim," appear synonymously in Mt 11:1 as descriptors of Jesus' own ministry. Furthermore Mk 1:39 and Lk 4:44 utilize the verb κηρύσσω for Jesus' proclamation in synagogues, which in any case would have included his evangelistic announcement of the kingdom's arrival. Nevertheless, the distinction asserted by Friedrich above generally holds. Note how Mt 4:23 and Mt 9:35 depict Jesus "teaching in their synagogues" (διδάσκων ἐν ταῖς συναγωγαῖς αὐτῶν), and in both passages the verb κηρύσσω, "proclaim," then follows, indicating that *the sphere of this activity typically takes place in numerous and widespread contexts.* Matthew uses κηρύσσω to depict the "proclaiming" of the kingdom by John the Baptist in the wilderness (Mt 3:1). Jesus does the action denoted by that verb at the outset of his ministry (Mt 4:17) and later "in their cities," that is, in the cities of Galilee (Mt 11:1).[4] He sends his disciples out to do the same (κηρύσσω, "proclaim," Mt 10:7, 27). These uses highlight the *evangelistic nature of the verb κηρύσσω, "proclaim."*

The Synoptics reveal how others engage in that activity as well. Those who "proclaim" (κηρύσσω) include a healed leper (Mk 1:45); the healed Gerasene demoniac (Mk 5:20 ‖ Lk 8:39), likely a Gentile heralding the Good News of the kingdom among Gentiles;[5] and an entire crowd after Jesus heals a deaf and mute man (Mk 7:36)! More general uses of the verb also appear (e.g., Mt 24:14 ‖ Mk 13:10; Mt 26:13).

---

[3]   G. Friedrich, "κηρύσσω," *TDNT* 3:713; for more on διδάσκω, "teach," see the discussion below regarding Paul's use of the word. Dodd, *The Apostolic Preaching and Its Developments*, 7–8, makes this similarly qualified proposal:

Teaching (*didaskein*) is in a large majority of cases ethical instruction. Occasionally it seems to include what we should call apologetic. … Sometimes, especially in the Johannine writings, it includes the exposition of theological doctrine. Preaching, on the other hand, is the public proclamation of Christianity to the non-Christian world. The verb *keryssein* properly means "to proclaim." …

It would not be too much to say that wherever "preaching" is spoken of, it always carries with it the implication of "good tidings" proclaimed.

[4]   Johnston, *Why Christians Sin*, 142, observes:

Christ met unbelievers where they were. … According to one count, the gospels record 132 contacts that Jesus had with people. Six were in the Temple, four in the synagogues and 122 were out with the people in the mainstream of life.

[5]   See Voelz, *Mark 1:1–8:26*, 340, 351, 356.

Finally, the dominant evangelistic element stands out climactically in Luke's equivalent to the Great Commission in Matthew (Mt 28:19–20). Jesus declares that repentance into forgiveness of sins is "to be proclaimed" (κηρυχθῆναι) in his name to all the nations, beginning from Jerusalem (Lk 24:47; cf. Mk 16:15).

An examination of Acts supports the same basic context for forms of κηρύσσω, "proclaim." After Jesus' death, resurrection, ascension, and Great Commission, it encompasses the announcement of Jesus as the Messiah among Jews who have not yet heard this Good News (e.g., Acts 9:20; 10:42), but it moves out beyond them. Philip heralds the message to unbelieving Samaritans (ἐκήρυσσεν, Acts 8:5). Paul proclaims it among the Gentile Ephesians (κηρύσσει, Acts 19:13). Indeed, κηρύσσω, "proclaim," characterizes the overall thrust of Paul's ministry and apostolic calling, his desire "to bring the Good News" (εὐαγγελίζεσθαι) where Christ was not yet named (Rom 15:20).[6]

εὐαγγελίζομαι, "Bring the Good News"

The passage just cited (Rom 15:20) uses the other Greek verb often translated as "preach," εὐαγγελίζομαι, euangelizomai, "bring the Good News." The context of εὐαγγελίζομαι throughout the NT is, in fact, quite accurately conveyed by our use of the transliterated noun "evangelism." However, we do not commonly transliterate the verb as "evangelize" in English. As a result, "preach (the Word/Good News)" has become a typical translation for εὐαγγελίζομαι, as in Rom 10:15.[7] Since its main NT thrust depicts the action of reaching out to *unbelievers* with the εὐαγγέλιον, "the Good News" (e.g., Rom 1:16; 10:16), the same contextual issue recurs with it as with κηρύσσω, "proclaim."

Some thematic examples in Acts confirm the point.[8] Disciples (other than the twelve apostles) who scattered from Jerusalem after Stephen's martyrdom "went about preaching the word" (εὐαγγελιζόμενοι, Acts 8:4 ESV; forms of "preach" are also in KJV, NKJV, NASB, RSV). Although Philip the deacon was appointed to distribute food to widows (Acts 6:3, 5), this Philip becomes "the evangelist" (τοῦ εὐαγγελιστοῦ, Acts 21:8) who *evangelizes* among the Samaritans, then *evangelizes* the Ethiopian eunuch, and, finally, *brings the Good News* all the way from Azotus to Caesarea (the preceding *italicized* words indicate forms of εὐαγγελίζομαι, "bring the Good News," in Acts 8:25, 35, 40).

Acts 14:21 states that in Derbe Paul and Barnabas "brought the Good News [εὐαγγελισάμενοι] to that city and discipled a considerable number." After Paul sees a vision calling him into Europe for the first time, Luke reports

---

[6] Paul uses κηρύσσω thematically to describe his ministry in Acts 20:25 as κηρύσσων τὴν βασιλείαν, "proclaiming the kingdom" (see also τὸ εὐαγγέλιον, "the Good News," in the preceding verse, Acts 20:24).

[7] Translations which use "preach" for εὐαγγελίζομαι in Rom 10:15 include ESV, KJV, and RSV. NRSV and NASB utilize the translation "bring good news" (cf. NKJV), and this commentary consistently employs "bring the Good News" for εὐαγγελίζομαι.

[8] See εὐαγγελίζομαι, "bring the Good News," also in Acts 8:12; 11:20; 13:32; 14:7, 15; 17:18, and τὸ εὐαγγέλιον, "the Good News, Gospel," in Acts 15:7; 20:24.

how "we sought to go on into Macedonia, concluding that God had called us to *preach the gospel* [εὐαγγελίσασθαι] to them" (Acts 16:10 ESV; similarly with "preach" again are KJV, NKJV, NASB, RSV). In all of these cases, the verb εὐαγγελίζομαι, "bring the Good News" (as well as the cognate noun τὸ εὐαγγέλιον, "the Good News," in Acts 15:7), occurs in the context of *outreach to Gentile unbelievers.*

Paul's Use of κηρύσσω, "Proclaim," and εὐαγγελίζομαι, "Bring the Good News"

In Paul's letters the evangelistic setting of the two Greek verbs often translated as "preach," as well as a contextual distinction with "prophecy" and "teaching" or "instruction," is supported even more clearly. Rom 10:14–17 profoundly describes how unbelievers receive the proclamation from someone who has been sent to "proclaim" the Good News of Jesus to them (κηρύσσω, 10:14, 15). The content of this public proclamation is the "Word of Christ/[the] Messiah" (10:17). This fulfills what Isaiah prophesied regarding those who "bring the Good News" or "evangelize" (εὐαγγελίζομαι in 10:15, citing Is 52:7). Here both words are used to describe how Christ's Word is *proclaimed to unbelievers.* It is the means by which they are brought to faith, which receives the Good News of salvation and confesses that Jesus is Lord (10:9–10, 17).

Later in 15:14–22 Paul uses the noun "Good News, Gospel" twice (εὐαγγέλιον, 15:16, 19) and the verb "bring the Good News" once (εὐαγγελίζομαι, 15:20) to characterize his own apostolic mission. It entails "striving eagerly to bring the Good News" where Christ was not yet named (15:20; cf. 11:13). In the Pastoral Epistles, Paul's use of cognate nouns reinforces the point. He twice describes his threefold role as follows: "I myself was appointed a proclaimer and apostle and teacher" (ἐτέθην ἐγὼ κῆρυξ καὶ ἀπόστολος καὶ διδάσκαλος, 2 Tim 1:11; also 1 Tim 2:7). The apostolic designation (ἀπόστολος) encompasses his entire ministry (see the commentary on Paul's call in Rom 1:1). As in the Synoptics, a strict separation between the other two "speaking" terms may not always be possible. However, the noun listed first, "proclaimer" (κῆρυξ), places primary emphasis upon his apostolic role of bringing the Gospel to unbelievers (cf. Rom 11:13; see also Acts 9:15; 22:17–18), whereas his role as a "teacher" (διδάσκαλος), listed third, focuses upon the significant responsibility he also bore for giving authoritative instruction to Christians (see next section). In further explaining his role as a "proclaimer" (κῆρυξ), he uses the cognate noun κήρυγμα for the for the Lord's purpose that "through me the *proclamation*" (δι' ἐμοῦ τὸ κήρυγμα) might be heard by "all the Gentiles" (2 Tim 4:17) and to affirm that God manifested the "proclamation" with which he had been entrusted (Titus 1:3). His usage of these cognate nouns lends further support to the evangelistic context of κηρύσσω, "proclaim," as does the use of that verb in 1 Tim 3:16: Christ "was proclaimed [ἐκηρύχθη] among the nations." The same general implications, then, come with Paul's evangelistic imperatives to Timothy: "Proclaim the Word" (κήρυξον τὸν λόγον, 2 Tim 4:2) and "Do the work of an evangelist" (ἔργον ποίησον εὐαγγελιστοῦ, 2 Tim 4:5).

The Contextual Use of "Prophesy" and "Teach" (προφητεύω and διδάσκω) in Paul

In Romans 12, Paul discusses gifts which are used *within* the body of Christ. There he uses *neither* κηρύσσω, "proclaim," *nor* εὐαγγελίζομαι, "bring the Good News." Instead, Paul speaks of "prophecy" (προφητεία, 12:6) and of "the one who teaches" (ὁ διδάσκων, 12:7). Both terms are dealt with below and explained more fully in the commentary on these verses.

In keeping with the discussion above, 1 and 2 Corinthians use κηρύσσω, "proclaim," to describe the evangelistic proclamation of Paul and others.[9] But Paul switches to διδάσκω in order to describe how "I *teach* in every church" (ἐν πάσῃ ἐκκλησίᾳ διδάσκω, 1 Cor 4:17). Elsewhere, he regularly uses διδάσκω, "teach," for instruction which takes place among believers.[a] The same applies with the cognate noun διδάσκαλος, "teacher," in 1 Cor 12:28–29; Eph 4:11; 1 Tim 2:7; 2 Tim 1:11; 4:3.

(a) Eph 4:21; Col 1:28; 2:7; 3:16; 2 Thess 2:15; 1 Tim 2:12; 4:11; 6:2; 2 Tim 2:2

Interestingly, when it comes time to speak of the various gifts exercised within the body of believers in 1 Corinthians 11–14, the "preach" words (κηρύσσω, "proclaim," and εὐαγγελίζομαι, "bring the Good News") once again *do not appear at all*. Instead, within the body of Christ other speaking gifts are received and shared mutually. 1 Cor 12:8–10 and 1 Cor 12:28 illustrate:

[8]ᾧ μὲν γὰρ διὰ τοῦ πνεύματος δίδοται λόγος σοφίας, ἄλλῳ δὲ λόγος γνώσεως κατὰ τὸ αὐτὸ πνεῦμα, [9]ἑτέρῳ πίστις ἐν τῷ αὐτῷ πνεύματι, ἄλλῳ δὲ χαρίσματα ἰαμάτων ἐν τῷ ἑνὶ πνεύματι, [10]ἄλλῳ δὲ ἐνεργήματα δυνάμεων, ἄλλῳ [δὲ] προφητεία, ἄλλῳ [δὲ] διακρίσεις πνευμάτων, ἑτέρῳ γένη γλωσσῶν, ἄλλῳ δὲ ἑρμηνεία γλωσσῶν. … [28]καὶ οὓς μὲν ἔθετο ὁ θεὸς ἐν τῇ ἐκκλησίᾳ πρῶτον ἀποστόλους, δεύτερον προφήτας, τρίτον διδασκάλους.

[8]For, on the one hand, through the Spirit to one is given a word of wisdom, but to another a word of knowledge according to the same Spirit, [9]to another faith [is given] in the same Spirit, but to another gracious gifts of healing in the one Spirit, [10]but to another [the] workings of powers and to another prophecy and to another [the] discerning of spirits, to another kinds of tongues, but to another [the] interpretation of tongues. … [28]And, on the one hand, God placed in the church first apostles, second prophets, third teachers.[10]

This progression through Paul's letters could continue further, but that is beyond the scope of this excursus. At this point, the repeated pattern of "speaking" terms *used and also not used based upon the context in which they are exercised implies a significant distinction among them*, at least in the

---

[9] See κηρύσσω, "proclaim," in 1 Cor 1:23; 9:27; 15:11, 12; 2 Cor 1:19; 4:5; 11:4, and τὸ κήρυγμα, "the proclamation," in 1 Cor 1:21; 2:4; 15:14.

[10] For a complete discussion of these terms in their context, see Lockwood, *1 Corinthians*, 421–25.

mind of Paul. This buttresses the assessment of the evangelistic connotations of κηρύσσω, "proclaim," and εὐαγγελίζομαι, "bring the Good News," in the Synoptics and Acts presented above.

What Paul Means by "Prophesy" (προφητεύω)

Unfortunately, another significant misunderstanding occurs in regard to the "Word" gift most valued by Paul within the body of Christ in Corinth, "prophesy" (the verb προφητεύω, "prophesy," and the nouns προφήτης, "prophet," and προφητεία, "prophecy," appear a total of twenty-two times in 1 Corinthians 11–14). In our culture and among many Christians, this verb predominantly entails predicting the future. However, such a definition proves to be inadequate even for the OT prophets. Fee and Stuart propose that only eight percent of the material in the writing prophets of the OT is directed toward the distant future.[11] The bulk of their prophetic words (ninety-two percent!) either remind Israel of God's work and words in the past or declare his will for Israel in the present or imminent future. Most commonly, the prophets applied the written Word of the Torah to their own day and setting.[12]

Although NT prophets did not typically produce inspired Scripture as did the writing prophets in the OT, the function of NT prophecy is essentially similar. NT prophets take God's written Word and the handed-down words of the Lord Jesus and seek to apply them in ways that are relevant for their specific context. In a manner comparable to statements by Luther, the Commission on Theology and Church Relations of The Lutheran Church—Missouri Synod observes how NT prophecy "includes also the God-given ability to interpret Scripture correctly and to apply its message of Law and Gospel to the needs of men. It is the gift of expressing what the will of God was in a given situation."[13] Therefore Lenski properly concludes:

> All true preachers and teachers of the gospel are prophets in the general or broader sense because they offer edification, admonition, and consolation to

---

[11] Fee and Stuart, *How to Read the Bible for All Its Worth*, 188.

[12] Fee and Stuart, *How to Read the Bible for All Its Worth*, 190–95.

[13] *The Charismatic Movement and Lutheran Theology*, 19. This coincides with the descriptions of prophecy made by Paul in 1 Cor 14:3–5, 19, 29–33. Luther uses the term thus to describe himself as the "prophet of the Germans" (AE 47:29); furthermore, in "To the Councilmen of All Cities in Germany That They Establish and Maintain Christians Schools," AE 45:363, he defines "prophets" as those equipped to "dig into Scripture, expound it, and carry on disputations." Similarly, *Spiritual Gifts*, a report of the Commission on Theology and Church Relations of The Lutheran Church—Missouri Synod, 34, states: "There is evidence to suggest that prophecy in the New Testament includes what we would today call preaching or expounding Scripture." For this understanding of NT prophecy, I credit Louis Brighton, long-time professor at Concordia Seminary, St. Louis. Brighton, *Revelation*, 6, contends that even in the last book of the NT, John's

> purpose is not primarily to reveal secrets to God's people, but rather to call them to repentance and faith, and to worship—to the blessedness of faithful service in the confidence of God's love and care.

See also the commentary on Rom 12:6, which includes "prophecy" (προφητεία).

their hearers. All true Christians who are able to impart the gospel truth privately in a similar manner exercise the gift of prophecy.[14]

This prophesying happens largely *within* the gathered body of Christ in order to build up the community of faith (e.g., 1 Cor 14:3–4). As Paul himself asserts: "But prophecy is not for the unbelieving, but for those who believe" (ἡ δὲ προφητεία οὐ τοῖς ἀπίστοις ἀλλὰ τοῖς πιστεύουσιν, 1 Cor 14:22). Therefore it is a gift to be sought and exercised by a wide variety of people in the church. "For you all, each one of you, is able to prophesy" (δύνασθε γὰρ καθ᾽ ἕνα πάντες προφητεύειν, 1 Cor 14:31; cf. also 1 Cor 14:1).[15] Yet Paul cautions the Corinthians since "it could easily happen that in their prophecy they let their own and erring thoughts enter. … Therefore, the apostle admonishes the Christians to judge and test the prophecy" (1 Cor 14:29).[16] Likewise in the OT, God gave Israel criteria by which to test prophecy, i.e., whether or not it comes true (Deut 18:21–22; 1 Ki 22:28), and even if it does come true, whether it was spoken in the name of the true God or of false gods (Deut 13:1–15 [MT 13:2–16]; 18:20). But the messages given by the true prophets were recognized to be divinely inspired, and so their writings were received as canonical and authoritative.

Implications to Ponder

What does all this mean for trying to distinguish preaching, teaching, and prophecy based upon the meaning and contextual usage of the underlying words in the NT? Those who know the original languages can strive to explain the verbally inspired words of Scripture as they are utilized in the Greek NT. Perhaps we can also then employ them similarly in appropriate ways in our contemporary languages and cultures. The remainder of this section provides some possible settings to consider.

In our day, many Christians have spoken loudly in the public square on moral and lifestyle issues. The NT certainly has much to say about proper and improper behavioral conduct which can be promulgated in the public square based upon natural law arguments, as well as the biblical witness (e.g., Rom 1:18–32). But in all cases, judgment should be left in God's hands.[17] Unfortunately, even if the message is firmly grounded in God's Word and sorely needed by society, the speaker is often perceived as self-righteous and holier than thou.[18] Perhaps this is why the NT directs most of its exhortations toward God-pleasing living to those within the Christian community (see the introduction to Romans 12–16). Such paraenesis fits within the categories of "prophecy"

---

[14] Lenski, *St. Paul's First and Second Epistles to the Corinthians*, 579.

[15] Lockwood, *1 Corinthians*, 430–31, n. 26, cites but then disagrees with applying this broader understanding of prophecy in 1 Corinthians.

[16] Stoeckhardt, *Romans*, 172–73.

[17] See Middendorf, *Romans 1–8*, 172–74.

[18] Kinnaman and Lyons, *Unchristian: What a New Generation Really Thinks about Christianity—and Why It Matters*; see also Kimball, *They Like Jesus but Not the Church*.

(προφητεία) and "teaching" (διδασκαλία) as outlined above.[19] Note the contexts in which Paul calls Christians to pronounce judgment and to refrain from judging in 1 Cor 5:9–13 (cf. Mt 7:1–2):

[9]I wrote to you in the letter not to associate with sexually immoral people. [10]By no means [was I referring] to the sexually immoral people of this world or to the greedy and rapacious or to idolaters—for otherwise you would have to go out of the world. [11]But now I wrote to you not to associate if anyone called a "brother" should be sexually immoral or covetous or idolatrous or abusive or a drunkard or a swindler—not even to eat with such a person. [12]For what business of mine is it to judge those outside? But isn't it for you to judge those on the inside? [13]Those on the outside God will judge. "Remove the wicked person from among yourselves!"[20]

The ongoing purification of the church envisioned by Paul takes place as believers gather to hear the proclamation of convicting Law followed by the absolving and consoling Gospel week after week. In so doing, we *are* indeed following the pattern of "preaching" evident in the NT and are delivering it primarily to those already within the body of Christ. The connotations of NT usage remind us that *unbelievers out in world even more desperately need to hear that proclamation* for the salvation of their souls. Unfortunately, they do not typically come to church to receive that Word, and we ought not expect them to do so without a winsome invitation. This is why God continues to send those with beautiful feet out into the world to bring them the Good News of Christ (see the commentary on 10:14–17). The Formula of Concord relies on the sequence of Romans 10 which culminates in 10:17 in order to describe how the Holy Spirit works through the proclamation of the Word:

God the Holy Spirit, however, does not effect conversion without means; he employs to this end the preaching and the hearing of God's Word, as it is written that the Gospel is a "power of God" for salvation [Rom 1:16]; likewise, that faith comes from the hearing of God's Word (Rom. 10:17). It is God's will that men should hear his Word and not stop their ears. The Holy Spirit is present with this Word and opens hearts. (FC Ep II 4–5; similarly, FC SD II 50–52)[21]

To be sure, believers repeatedly need to hear the accusations of the Law, pointing out how they, like Paul himself (Rom 7:14–25), give in to their sinful nature all too often. They should also be reminded regularly of where they would be in God's eyes apart from Christ (e.g., Rom 1:18–3:20; Eph 2:1–3). "But thanks [be] to God" (Rom 7:25) that they are now in Christ in whom "nothing

---

[19] Thus the early Christian catechetical document called the *Didache* ("teaching") contains a significant amount of moral instruction as it addresses how Christians are to live and conduct themselves amid the sinful world.

[20] For this translation and a complete exposition of this text, see Lockwood, *1 Corinthians*, 178–86.

[21] The Formula also recognizes how "the Father wills that all men should hear this proclamation and come to Christ," quoting Rom 10:17 for support (FC SD XI 68–69).

is condemnation" (8:1). Believers can never get too much of that Good News as pastors and teachers expound the Gospel to them in all of its biblical richness![22]

Yet the format of Paul's letters urges us not to stop here. We should not neglect offering the body the edifying meat of "prophecy" (προφητεία) and "teaching" (διδασκαλία) that comes later (Rom 12:6–7).[b] After Romans 1–11, the Gospel-motivated lifestyle instructions of chapters 12–16 follow, in keeping with a well-established pattern in Paul's letters (e.g., Galatians 5–6; Ephesians 4–6; Colossians 3–4; 1 Thessalonians 5).[23] In this way, we believers are called together to be mutually encouraged not only by our hope in the faithful one whom we confess (Rom 10:9–10) but also to "spur one another on to love and good deeds" (Heb 10:23–25).

(b) See also, e.g., 1 Cor 3:2; 14:3, 5, 12; Eph 4:21; Col 3:16; 1 Tim 4:11; 6:2; 2 Tim 2:2; Heb 5:12–14

Conclusion

The NT use of the vocabulary of κηρύσσω, "proclaim," and εὐαγγελίζομαι, "bring the Good News," almost exclusively conveys the notion of proclaiming the Word of Christ to *unbelievers* out in the world. In NT terms, those who have been brought to faith through the proclamation of that Good News then gather together to hear what can be called "prophecy" (προφητεία) and "teaching" or "instruction" (διδασκαλία), as well as the other "Word" gifts cited above (1 Cor 12:8–10), and to receive the Sacrament of Christ's body and blood (1 Cor 10:16–17; 11:23–32). We may well be stuck with conventional translations of the vocabulary of "preaching" terms. But we can be sensitive to the connotations that come with the verbally inspired Greek words of the NT and strive to *utilize them in contexts comparable to those in which Scripture uses them.*

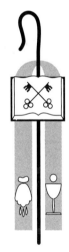

Finally, there is Good News in all of this. Wherever God's Word is present and whenever the Spirit has gifted God's people to preach, teach, and prophesy, as well as to speak, evangelize, proclaim, utter, herald, announce, or verbalize it, whether to believer or unbeliever, those who hear encounter the living and faith-giving Word of God through the heralds sent to them (Rom 10:14–17; Heb 4:12) and, therefore, the Word made flesh himself, Jesus Christ (Jn 1:14).

---

22 For an explanation of the various Gospel metaphors in Romans, see the excursus "Paul's Gospel Metaphors" following the commentary on 4:1–12; for a thorough exposition of the topic, see Preus, *Just Words.*

23 For a more thorough overview, see the introduction to Romans 12–16. Note, for example, how Walther, *The Proper Distinction between Law and Gospel,* 93, identifies three parts to the "true pattern of the correct sequence," which he locates in Romans:

> What do we find in the first three chapters? The sharpest preaching of the Law. This is followed, towards the end of the third chapter and in chapters 4 and 5, by the doctrine of justification—nothing but that. Beginning at chapter 6, the apostle treats of nothing else than sanctification. Here we have a true pattern of the correct sequence: first the Law, threatening men with the wrath of God; next the Gospel, announcing the comforting promises of God. This is followed by an instruction regarding the things we are to do after we have become new men.

Israel's Response
(and God's Reaction Introduced)

Translation

10 ¹⁶But they did not all listen responsively to the Good News. For Isaiah says: "Lord, who believed our message?" ¹⁷Consequently, faith [comes] from hearing, and the hearing through [the] Word of Christ/[the] Messiah.

¹⁸But I say, it is not that they did not hear, is it? On the contrary:

"Their voice went out into all the world
    and their words into the limits of the inhabited world."

¹⁹But I say, it is not that Israel did not know, is it? First, Moses says:

"I will provoke you to envy over [what is] not a nation;
    over a nation without understanding I will make you angry."

²⁰But Isaiah is bold and says:

"I was found among the ones not seeking me;
    I became visible to the ones not inquiring after me."

²¹But to Israel he says:

"The whole day I stretched out my hands
    to an unpersuaded and contradicting people."

Textual Notes

10:16–17 Note that 10:16 clearly *begins* Paul's discussion of Israel's response (10:16–21), as indicated in the commentary outline shown in this volume's table of contents. However, Paul masterfully ties 10:6–15 to this section by introducing the element of "response" in 10:16, but then he wraps up the thought of 10:6–15 with the summative statement of 10:17, introduced by ἄρα, "consequently." Therefore, while 10:16–17 was included briefly in the commentary on the previous section, the detailed textual notes and major treatment of these verses properly belong in this section.

10:16 οὐ πάντες—The same phrase appears in 9:6. The nominative plural of πᾶς negated with οὐ means "not 'all,' without specification of how many."[1] The implication, therefore, is that some or even many did listen. See the commentary.

ὑπήκουσαν—For the verb ὑπακούω, "listen responsively," see the third textual note on 6:12 and the commentary on 6:16. See also the third textual note and the commentary on the cognate noun ὑπακοή in 1:5.

τῷ εὐαγγελίῳ—For the noun εὐαγγέλιον, "Good News," see the fifth textual note on 1:1 and the commentary on 1:16. Note also the cognate verb εὐαγγελίζομαι in

---

[1] Dunn, *Romans*, 622.

10:15. The dative case of the noun here is influenced by the Hebrew expression שָׁמַע לְ, "to listen/hearken *to*."[2]

Ἠσαΐας—This is the Greek form of the Hebrew name "Isaiah." See the first textual note on 9:27.

κύριε—Paul follows the LXX, which adds this vocative singular form of κύριος, "Lord," to the beginning of Is 53:1. Note the LXX's regular use of κύριος, "Lord," to translate the divine name יהוה, as in the second half of Is 53:1. For the significance, see "The Background and Meaning of 'Jesus [Is] Lord' (10:9a)" and "Jesus, the LORD/Yahweh of All (Joel 2:32 in Rom 10:13)," both in the commentary on 10:6–15.

ἐπίστευσεν—This is the aorist indicative active of πιστεύω, "believe." Paul quotes this LXX translation of הֶאֱמִין in Is 53:1.[3]

τῇ ἀκοῇ ἡμῶν—Paul quotes this phrase from LXX Is 53:1, which literally translates the Hebrew phrase לִשְׁמֻעָתֵנוּ. The Hebrew noun שְׁמֻעָה is derived from the verb שָׁמַע, "to hear," and denotes the "message" heard. The noun ἀκοή occurs three times in Romans, here and twice in 10:17; Paul also employs it in, e.g., Gal 3:2, 5; 1 Thess 2:13. As the substantive of the verb ἀκούω, "to hear," ἀκοή can refer to the "*ear*" itself (BDAG, 3) or the "ability to hear" as one of the senses (see BDAG, 1). Later in 10:17 it depicts "the act of hearing, *listening*" (BDAG, 2). But in 10:16 it denotes "that which is heard" and means "*account, report, message*" (BDAG, 4 and 4 b). For the difficulty in providing a consistent English translation, see the commentary.

10:17 ἄρα—This particle occurs twelve times in Romans. See the second textual notes on 5:18 and 8:1. As in those passages, ἄρα should "be given its proper force as introducing a conclusion or summing up, 'so then, consequently.' "[4]

ἐξ ἀκοῆς—For the noun ἀκοή, see the seventh textual note on 10:16. For the force of the preposition ἐκ (ἐξ before a vowel), see the commentary.

διὰ ῥήματος—For the force of the preposition διά, see the commentary. For the noun ῥῆμα, "Word," see the third textual note and the commentary on 10:8.

Χριστοῦ—A textual variant here supports reading θεοῦ (Textus Receptus אᶜ A Dᶜ), forming the phrase ῥήματος θεοῦ, "Word of God" (ῥῆμα θεοῦ occurs also in Lk 3:2; Jn 3:34; Eph 6:17; Heb 6:5; 11:3). But Χριστοῦ, "of Christ," is well supported (𝔓⁴⁶vid א* B C D*) and the more unusual reading. In fact, the Greek phrase ῥῆμα Χριστοῦ, "Word of Christ," occurs only here in the NT.[5] The use of the genitive Χριστοῦ need not be pigeonholed into one category. It communicates possession, "Christ's Word," as well as source, "the Word from Christ," but most emphatically serves as an objective genitive, describing the content being proclaimed: "[the] Word about Christ/[the] Messiah."[6]

---

[2] Cf. Murray, *Romans*, 2:59, who translates: "But they did not all hearken to the glad tidings."

[3] See "The Background and Meaning of 'Faith' Words" in the commentary on 1:16 (Middendorf, *Romans 1–8*, 88–90); " 'From Faith[fulness] into Faith' (1:17)" on 96–98; and also 106–7.

[4] Dunn, *Romans*, 623; see also Cranfield, *Romans*, 536.

[5] See Metzger, *A Textual Commentary on the Greek New Testament*, 525; Moo, *Romans*, 661, n. 2.

[6] For the dominant objective sense, see Sanday and Headlam, *Romans*, 298; Fitzmyer, *Romans*, 598; Jewett, *Romans*, 641. For the many possible categories of such a genitive, see Wallace,

10:18 μὴ οὐκ … ;—"In questions with μή the verb itself can already be negated (class[ical] also), producing μή … οὐ with an affirmative answer implied" (BDF, § 427.2). Thus "it is *not* that they did *not* hear, is it?" means "they *did* hear."

μενοῦνγε—See second textual note on 9:20.

ὁ φθόγγος—Paul begins his quote of LXX Ps 18:5 (MT 19:5; ET 19:4). The noun φθόγγος describes "any clear or distinct sound" (BDAG). Paul's only other use of it refers to the tone of a musical instrument (1 Cor 14:7; BDAG, a). Here the parallelism to τὰ ῥήματα, "the words," in the second line Paul quotes from LXX Ps 18:5 (MT 19:5; ET 19:4) indicates that φθόγγος refers to words spoken by "the human *voice*" (BDAG, b).[7]

εἰς τὰ πέρατα τῆς οἰκουμένης—The neuter plural of the noun πέρας functions geographically, expressing the "farthest end of a space, *end, limit, boundary*" (BDAG, 1). In form οἰκουμένη would seem to be a passive participle, but it is used as a noun, meaning "*the inhabited earth, the world*" (BDAG, 1). It is the usual LXX translation of תֵּבֵל, a poetic synonym of אֶרֶץ, "earth" (the LXX normally translates אֶרֶץ with γῆ). In synonymous parallelism in Hebrew poetry, אֶרֶץ, "earth, the world," normally is used in the first line, and then תֵּבֵל, "inhabited world," appears as its parallel in the second line, as is the case in MT Ps 19:5 (ET 19:4).[8] Both Greek synonyms are in its translation in LXX Ps 18:5, with γῆ in the first line and οἰκουμένη in the second.

10:19 μὴ Ἰσραὴλ οὐκ ἔγνω;—The same interrogative with μή … οὐκ was used in 10:18; see the first textual note on that verse. For Paul's use of Ἰσραήλ, see God's People" in the introduction to Romans 9–11. Note that its eleven appearances in Romans are all congregated in chapters 9–11.

πρῶτος Μωϋσῆς λέγει—Paul uses "first" (πρῶτος) here without a second item, as in 3:2; see the second textual note and the commentary there. Thus it does not perform its typical function to introduce the "first" in a series or list (BDAG, 1 b). Sanday and Headlam propose that "first, Moses says" has a temporal understanding: "even as early in Israel's history as" when Moses spoke.[9] But it more likely conveys the Torah's "prominence, *first, foremost*" (BDAG, 2).

ἐγὼ παραζηλώσω ὑμᾶς—Paul quotes LXX Deut 32:21b, but omits the conjunction in κἀγώ, "*and* I," leaving just ἐγώ, "I," and twice changes the third person plural pronoun αὐτούς, "them," to the second person plural ὑμᾶς, "you." The future indicative form παραζηλώσω represents the first of three appearances in Romans of the verb παραζηλόω, "*provoke to jealousy, make jealous*" (BDAG; also Rom 11:11, 14; cf. the noun ζῆλος, "zeal," in 10:2). Moo summarizes the connotations of the verb:

Greek Grammar, 72. Käsemann, *Romans*, 295, argues that here "the genitive cannot be resolved in such a way" as to choose any one specific category to the exclusion of others. For the broader issue of grammatical categories, see Middendorf, *Romans 1–8*, 53–54.

[7] While the reading and meaning of the suffixed Hebrew noun קַוָּם in MT Ps 19:5 (ET 19:4) is debated, it likely means "their voice," as it is parallel to קוֹלָם, "their voice," in MT Ps 19:4 (ET 19:3). According to *DCH*, s.v. קַו I 2, the noun, which literally means "chord," has in MT Ps 19:5 (ET 19:4) the nuance "sound, music, melody."

[8] See also, e.g., 1 Sam 2:8; Is 14:21; 24:4; Jer 10:12; Pss 24:1; 33:8; 96:13. Occasionally the two Hebrew nouns occur in the reverse order, e.g., Is 18:3; Ps 97:4.

[9] Sanday and Headlam, *Romans*, 300.

Unlike its more common root verb ζηλόω, which can denote either a positive "zeal" for the Lord or a negative "jealousy" of others, παραζηλόω in the Bible always denotes "jealousy": either God's jealousy for his people (1 Cor. 10:22; 3 Kgdms. 14:22 [MT/ET 1 Ki 14:22]; Ps. 77:58 [MT/ET 78:58]) or a person's jealousy of others (Ps. 36:1, 7, 8 [MT/ET 37:1, 7, 8]; Sir. 30:3). Only in Deut. 32:21 and here [in Romans] does the word suggest that human jealousy might be a positive thing.[10]

The connection between "zealous" and "jealous" supports translating παραζηλόω as "make jealous." However, in a positive sense, God is properly "jealous" for his people, not wanting to share them with any other gods (Ex 20:5; 34:14). Thus their idolatry makes God jealous (παραζηλόω with God as its object in LXX Deut 32:21; 1 Ki 14:22; Ps 77:58 [MT/ET 78:58]). But for the relationship between Israel and the Gentiles, "stir ... up to envy"[11] or "provoke to envy" better communicates the idea here and in the other two occurrences in Romans (11:11, 14). Thus the blessings God gives to Gentiles in Christ hopefully will cause Israel to be envious and desire them as well.[12]

ἐπ' οὐκ ἔθνει—This negated prepositional phrase literally means "over not a nation" (cf. BDAG, s.v. ἐπί, 9 b). The phrase without the negative, ἐπ' ἔθνει, "over a nation," occurs in the next line here and in LXX Deut 32:21, which Paul is quoting. See the commentary.

ἀσυνέτῳ—For this adjective, ἀσύνετος, "without understanding," see the final textual note on 1:21; it also appears in 1:31.

παροργιῶ—This is the future indicative of the verb παροργίζω, "*make angry*" (BDAG). It parallels and lends a more negative sense to the future παραζηλώσω in the citation of Deut 32:21 (see the third textual note on Rom 10:19). Paul's only other use of παροργίζω tells fathers not to do this to their children (Eph 6:4).

10:20 Ἠσαΐας—For this Greek form of the name "Isaiah," see the first textual note on 9:27. Paul quotes the first half of Is 65:1 in Rom 10:20 and then the first half of Is 65:2 in Rom 10:21.

ἀποτολμᾷ—This compound stative verb, ἀποτολμάω (ἀπό + τολμάω), means "*be bold*" (BDAG) and occurs only here in biblical literature. But its sense is readily drawn from the simple verb τολμάω, "be brave" (see the final textual note on 5:7; also in 15:18). The verb with the prefixed preposition ἀπό may "underline the astonishing nature of what is said in Isa 65.1a."[13]

εὑρέθην—This aorist passive form of εὑρίσκω, "to find," is first singular. For the tolerative sense, "I *allowed* myself to be found," see the commentary.

---

[10] Moo, *Romans*, 688, n. 23, discussing παραζηλόω in 11:11.

[11] Barrett, *Romans*, 206; for the simple verb ζηλόω, BDAG, 2, gives "to have intense negative feelings over another's achievements or success, *be filled w[ith] jealousy, envy*."

[12] The identities of the subject and object often determine how a verb must be understood and translated. Cf. the verb λογίζομαι, which is best rendered as "credit" when God is the subject, while "count" serves better when humans do the action; see the first textual note on 4:3, the second textual note on 6:11, and the fourth textual note on 8:36.

[13] Cranfield, *Romans*, 540.

[ἐν] τοῖς ἐμὲ μὴ ζητοῦσιν—The presence of the preposition ἐν with this first participial clause, in contrast to its absence before the second one in 10:20 (τοῖς ἐμὲ μὴ ἐπερωτῶσιν; see the second textual note below), reflects the more difficult reading of 𝔓⁴⁶. It also explains alterations aimed at consistency by either including or omitting ἐν in both places. The sense of the preposition as "*among*" (BDAG, 1 d) is illuminated by the simple dative case of the substantival participial clause[14] without the preposition: τοῖς ἐμὲ μὴ ζητοῦσιν. The dative expresses place or sphere,[15] and so the clause is translated with "among": "among the ones (who are) not seeking me." Thus the translation is the same whether or not the preposition is included. Note the present tense of the participle ζητοῦσιν, as well as the contrast between "*not* seeking" and 10:3, τὴν ἰδίαν [δικαιοσύνην] ζητοῦντες στῆσαι, "seeking to establish their own [righteousness]."

ἐμφανὴς ἐγενόμην—For "I became visible," see the commentary.

τοῖς ἐμὲ μὴ ἐπερωτῶσιν—The verb ἐπερωτάω in the LXX carries the meaning "*inquire after God*" (BDAG, 1 c). The entire clause, "the ones not inquiring after me," is parallel in form, function, and meaning and denotes the same group as τοῖς ἐμὲ μὴ ζητοῦσιν, "the ones not seeking me" (see the second textual note above). Here, though, the dative functions more as an indirect object, "became visible *to*" them.

10:21 ὅλην τὴν ἡμέραν—The adjective ὅλος, "*whole, entire, complete*" (BDAG, 1), regularly occurs prior to a definite noun, as here with τὴν ἡμέραν, "the day." The phrase is an idiom for "continually"[16] and occurs also in Rom 8:36. Here, as in LXX Is 65:2, it translates the Hebrew phrase כָּל־הַיּוֹם in MT Is 65:2, which occurs also in, e.g., Deut 28:32; Is 65:5; Jer 20:7, 8.

ἐξεπέτασα τὰς χεῖράς μου—The aorist indicative first singular ἐξεπέτασα is from the compound verb ἐκπετάννυμι. Note the temporal augment (-ε-) between the preposition (ἐξ-) and the root (-πέτασα). Here, as in LXX Is 65:2, the entire expression is again drawn from the Hebrew being translated from MT Is 65:2: פֵּרַשְׂתִּי יָדֵי. The idiom means to "*spread/hold out* τὰς χεῖρας *the hands* in an imploring gesture" (BDAG, s.v. ἐκπετάννυμι).

πρὸς λαὸν ἀπειθοῦντα καὶ ἀντιλέγοντα—For the noun λαός, "people," see the fourth textual note and the commentary on 9:25. The two indefinite active participles (ἀπειθοῦντα ... ἀντιλέγοντα) function adjectively,[17] modifying the similarly indefinite form of "people." Both participles begin (ἀ-) with an *alpha* privative (BDF, § 117.1), which indicates their negative meaning. For the first participle, ἀπειθοῦντα (from ἀπειθέω), as "unpersuaded," see the first textual note on 2:8 (cf. ἀπειθής, "disobedient," in 1:30). It signifies that unbelief is the core problem. The less literal definition "*be disobedient*" (BDAG) might imply that the problem is not a lack of faith, but a need for (better) obedience; see " 'Obey' Is a Problematic Translation of ὑπακούω" in the commentary on 10:16a. The second participle, ἀντιλέγοντα, literally means "speaking

---

[14] See Wallace, *Greek Grammar*, 619–21.

[15] See Wallace, *Greek Grammar*, 153–55.

[16] Cranfield, *Romans*, 541.

[17] See Wallace, *Greek Grammar*, 617–19.

against." The concept is effectively translated as "contradicting,"[18] which serves as the antithesis of ὁμολογέω, "acknowledge, confess," in 10:9–10.

MT Is 65:2 has only one participle in this clause, סוֹרֵר, compared to the two participles in the LXX and Paul. There are several possible reasons for this difference. The two Greek participles may be intended to capture the full force of the single Hebrew participle. Another proposal is that a textual issue is involved. In place of סוֹרֵר 1QIsaᵃ reads מורה. The two Greek participles in LXX Is 65:2a might possibly reflect a Hebrew text that had two participles (see סוֹרֵר וּמוֹרֶה in Deut 21:18, 20; Jer 5:23; Ps 78:8), but no such Hebrew text of Is 65:2 is extant.

Commentary

Introduction: Romans 10:16–17—Another Hinge

The merciful call of God's enduring Word was summarized in 9:6–29. The opposing avenues of attempting to seek righteousness from human works versus receiving it from faith in the proclaimed Word of the Lord Jesus were laid out and diagnosed from 9:30 through 10:15. Beginning with an emphatic "but" (ἀλλά) in 10:16, Paul clearly shifts *from* the topic of how God sends his Word *to* people (10:14–15) to a discussion of *how people, and Israel in particular, respond* to the Good News both in the past and in the present.[19] Paul states the negative human reaction most directly at the bookends, 10:16 and 10:21, but also expresses it in 10:18 and 10:19.

At the same time, 10:17 provides a key summative statement for the previous section, 10:6–15. Moo, therefore, calls 10:17 "awkwardly placed" and then characterizes 10:16 as "premature, interrupting Paul's assertion of those points that have found fulfillment. What Paul says in v. 17 is therefore a necessary transition back into this topic."[20] A better appraisal discerns how 10:16–17 serve characteristically as yet another effective hinge.[21] This stands comparable to the role of 10:4. The first half of that verse states the definitive end of the Law, which was the topic engaged from 9:30–10:5. The second half of 10:4 then sets the stage for 10:6–15. Here, 10:17 draws together the thoughts of 10:6–15,

---

[18] Franzmann, *Romans*, 194; BDAG, s.v. ἀντιλέγω, 1, gives "*speak against, contradict*," but then unnecessarily resorts to "*obstinate*" for this passage (BDAG, 2). However, "obstinate" describes the people as (passively) unresponsive, whereas ἀντιλέγοντα depicts them as actively hostile toward God, "contradicting" his Word to them.

[19] Lenski, *Romans*, 664, begins a new section at 10:16 titled "Jewish Unbelief—Gentile Faith." The argument is *not* purely chronological as Matera, *Romans*, 253, suggests: "The story that Paul creates has three movements: Israel's past (9:1–29), Israel's present (9:30–10:21), and Israel's future (11:1–36)." Paul, instead, asserts that God, his Word, and Israel have acted consistently throughout history. Kruse, *Romans*, 417, recognizes: "If this happened in Isaiah's day, it is not surprising that it should recur in Paul's day." The same is true in our day.

[20] Moo, *Romans*, 665.

[21] Cranfield, *Romans*, 537, similarly notes that "hearing becomes the hinge, so that [10:17] leads naturally into v. 18." Prominent hinges also occur in 3:1, 21; 4:1; 5:1; 6:1, 11; 8:1–4; 9:24; 10:4; 12:1; 13:7–8; 14:13; 15:7.

while 10:16 points forward by bringing up the element of human response. Thus the critical nature of 10:16–17 cannot be overemphasized.[22]

As Paul continues in 10:18–21, he then also begins to incorporate elements of *God's reaction* to Israel's response, or lack thereof, already in 10:19 and 10:20. The subject of God's reaction then comes to dominate the discussion in Romans 11, introduced by the provocative question posed in 11:1. In this way all of 10:16–21 has a transitional function as well.

Hearing Responsively the Message of Christ … or Not! (10:16–17)

Responding to the Good News (10:16a)

"But they did not all listen responsively to the Good News" (10:16a). The Good News came near to Israel via the process depicted in 10:8, 14–15. Yet, after an emphatic "but" (ἀλλά, also 10:18, 19), 10:16 states that "they did not all listen responsively" (οὐ πάντες ὑπήκουσαν). In contrast with the four uses of "all, everyone" (πᾶς) in 10:11–13, the term here is negated, "*not* all." A number of commentators contend the "not all" (οὐ πάντες) in 10:16 represents a deliberate understatement which really means "only a few."[23] Jewett even categorizes it as "a gratuitous insult to the already large number of Roman converts, and it would weaken the rhetorical connection with 'all' in 10:4, 11, 12, and 13."[24] But that certainly reads more into the text than Paul says. The expression stands equivalent to the "some" in 3:3 and replicates "*not all* these from Israel are Israel" in 9:6, which produces a framing effect (see also 11:14, 17).[25] In other words, some believed, but "not all." Although Paul does not identify specifically those to whom he refers in this verse, the context makes it clear that he speaks of unbelieving Jews/Israel (e.g., 9:31–32; 10:19, 20, 21).[26] The citation from Is 53:1 in Rom 10:16b points in that direction; 10:19 and 10:21 make it explicit.

"Obey" Is a Problematic Translation of ὑπακούω

The verb ὑπακούω in 10:16 is translated as "listen responsively" and conveys "a positive response in faith to the gospel."[27] This verb and its cognate noun (ὑπακοή), "responsive hearing," have been discussed previously.[28] Heb

---

[22] See also "Introduction to the Hinges of Romans 10:4 and 10:16–17: Their Rhetorical, Theological, and Contextual Functions" at the beginning of the commentary on 10:6–15.

[23] Fitzmyer, *Romans*, 598, and Moo, *Romans*, 664, call this a litotes. Sanday and Headlam, *Romans*, 297, and Cranfield, *Romans*, 536, describe it comparably as a meiosis. Hultgren, *Romans*, 390, similarly interprets "not all" as "some have, such as Paul himself, but the overwhelming majority has not."

[24] Jewett, *Romans*, 641.

[25] Cranfield, *Romans*, 536: "We may compare his τινες ['some'] in 3.3."

[26] So Sanday and Headlam, *Romans*, 298: "It is of the Jews the Apostle is thinking."

[27] Jewett, *Romans*, 641, who translates it as "hearken." For other options, see below.

[28] See especially the third textual note and the commentary on 1:5 with "the responsive hearing of faith" (the noun ὑπακοή; also in 5:19, 6:16) and the second textual note and the commentary

5:9 provides yet another example of where the translation "obey" is not merely inadequate but also misleading. It declares that Christ "became the cause of eternal salvation for all the ones who ὑπακούουσιν him" (Heb 5:9). To translate "obey" in Heb 5:9 (ESV, KJV, RSV, NRSV) makes salvation contingent upon our obedience. But the intended sense in context is clearly that we "listen responsively" or "hear in faith" what Jesus says and, thereby, believe and receive what he has accomplished for us (Heb 5:7–9a).

Rom 10:16 illustrates how the verb simply cannot be translated as "obey" as is done here by ESV, KJV, NKJV, RSV, NRSV.[29] In English "obey" generally conveys the notion of something *we* must *do*. For example, the *OED* defines the transitive sense of the English verb as follows:

> a. To comply with, or perform, the bidding of; to do what one is commanded by (a person); to submit to the rule or authority of, to be obedient to. …

> b. To comply with, perform (a command, etc.). …

> c. To submit to, subject oneself to; to act in accordance with (a principle, authority, etc.).

Paul's Gospel is at the very least confused, if not totally obscured, by these translations and definitions of "obey."

This same thing happens when one stretches the meaning of the verb in 10:16 to include all of "becoming subject to the gospel, giving it one's consent, and conforming one's life to it."[30] The Good News becomes further obfuscated when the effects of the Gospel are made contingent upon human obedience[31] or the issue at hand is defined in terms of "moral accountability."[32] In all of these interpretations, we would, at least to some degree, be back in 10:5, where "Moses writes [concerning] the righteousness which is from the Law that 'the person who does them [the works of the Law] will live in them.'" However, any possibility of basing saving righteousness before God to any degree upon our works is something Paul repeatedly excludes from the way of the Gospel (e.g., 3:19–20, 28; 4:4–5; 9:31–32)! For him works have *no* role in salvation; in fact, in the arena of righteousness, our active obedience to the Law typically stands diametrically *opposed* to the Good News, which is received through the hearing of (the) faith (1:16; 10:6–8, 17).

Paul reveals his understanding of ὑπακούω as "listen responsively" most obviously in 10:16, where the parallel statement he cites from Isaiah equates

---

on 6:17 with "respond" (the verb ὑπακούω; also in 6:12, 16). For the noun ὑπακοή, see also 1 Pet 1:22.

[29] Dunn, *Romans*, 622, contends that Paul here "sees the opportunity to reinforce the note of obedience which he also sees as fundamental to the gospel." Moo, *Romans*, 665, similarly equates faith with obedience, as well as disobedience with unbelief.

[30] Hultgren, *Romans*, 390.

[31] Matera, *Romans*, 251, asserts: "If the gospel is to bear fruit, those who 'hear' must 'obey' (*hypakouō*) the word they have heard."

[32] Keener, *Romans*, 128.

it with πιστεύω, "believe" (see "Romans 10:16b and Isaiah 53" below).[33] His use demonstrates that the basic verbal root "to hear," ἀκούω, significantly influences the meaning of this related compound verb.[34] Thus ὑπακούω essentially means "to listen and respond appropriately."[35]

> In the LXX it [ὑπακούω] represents the broad Hebrew usage of שָׁמַע, "to hear, listen (to)," followed by a preposition.[36] The key to determining the meaning more specifically is contextual; it is discerned by identifying what follows the summons to hear. If the Word is a law, a command to perform an action or works, then "obedience" works well as an acceptable English translation. However, in many passages the emphasis of the verb ὑπακούω is on receiving, believing, and trusting the Word, including its Gospel promises (e.g., LXX Gen 22:18; 26:5; Ps 17:45 [MT 18:45; ET 18:44]; Prov 2:2).[37]

Paul's point with ὑπήκουσαν τῷ εὐαγγελίῳ (Rom 10:16) is that all did not "hearken to,"[38] "heed,"[39] or "listen responsively to"[40] the "Good News" God sent to them. Here Kruse at least recognizes the problematic nature of "obey" and offers the more passive "accept."[41] Lenski similarly defines it as " 'hearken' in the full sense of the word, namely with faith and acceptance."[42]

Romans 10:16b and Isaiah 53

All of this is in keeping with what "Isaiah says: 'Lord, who believed our message?' " (10:16). Paul's quotation presents identically the first half of Is 53:1 from the LXX. The LXX, in turn, aside from adding the introductory vocative, κύριε, "Lord," renders the Hebrew accurately. Here is the MT, followed by the LXX:

---

[33] While Cranfield, *Romans*, 536, regards the two verbs in 10:16, ὑπακούω and πιστεύω ("believe") as "equivalent," he confuses the works of the Law with faith in the Gospel rather hopelessly by asserting:

> The obedience which God requires is faith. To obey the gospel is to believe it and to believe in Him who is its content; and to believe the gospel and believe in Christ involves obeying it, obeying Him.

[34] Though largely lost in contemporary usage, the etymology of the English word "obey" reveals a similar origin rooted in the Latin verb "to hear" (*audio*). According to the *OED*, it is derived from the Latin *ob-* + *audīre*, "to hear."

[35] Middendorf, *Romans 1–8*, 67. In contrasting it with the middle/passive of ὑποτάσσω, "be subject to," in 13:1, Dunn, *Romans*, 761, later acknowledges that ὑπακούω "has more the sense of 'respond.' "

[36] This follows the approach of Hill, *Greek Words and Hebrew Meanings*. Note that *obaudire*, the Latin root of the English word "obey," also contains the verb *audire*, "to hear." Unfortunately, "obey" in English has come to convey "doing" in almost all contexts.

[37] Middendorf, *Romans 1–8*, 66–67; see also the third textual note on 1:5 and page 293.

[38] So Jewett, *Romans*, 641; Lenski, *Romans*, 664; Murray, *Romans*, 2:59.

[39] Fitzmyer, *Romans*, 598; Nygren, *Romans*, 386.

[40] See the discussion of 1:5 and 6:17 in Middendorf, *Romans 1–8*, 60, 66–67, 489, 500.

[41] Kruse, *Romans*, 416–17; while "accept" is not particularly literal, it is at least better than "obey."

[42] Lenski, *Romans*, 665.

מִי הֶאֱמִין לִשְׁמֻעָתֵנוּ וּזְרוֹעַ יְהוָה עַל־מִי נִגְלָתָה:

Who believed our message? And the arm of Yahweh, to whom was it revealed?
(MT Is 53:1)

κύριε, τίς ἐπίστευσεν τῇ ἀκοῇ ἡμῶν; καὶ ὁ βραχίων κυρίου τίνι ἀπεκαλύφθη;

Lord, who believed our message? And to whom was the arm of [the] Lord
revealed? (LXX Is 53:1)

Paul cites Is 53:1 as a prophetic affirmation that "not all" who heard Isaiah, that
is, "not all" in Israel, would accept their Messiah when he arrived. Thus the universal tone of the discussion, present ever since 10:11 ("everyone … a Jew and
a Greek," 10:11–12), begins to move in a more specific direction, namely, the
people Israel.

The *context* of the quotation in Isaiah deserves comment, especially since
Is 53:1 is just eight verses removed from Is 52:7, which Paul quoted in Rom
10:15, the previous verse of Romans (Paul also cites Is 52:5 in Rom 2:24 and Is
52:15 in Rom 15:21). As the chapter divisions in Romans (e.g., 3:1; 8:1; 10:1;
15:1) regularly deter us from recognizing the close interconnections within the
flow of Paul's thought, so it is with the chapter division in Isaiah at Is 53:1. "The
quotation is from Isaiah 53:1, part of a passage (Isa 52:13–53:12) depicting the
suffering and glory of the Servant of the Lord. Included [within it] is Isaiah's
lament that his message was not believed. Paul's experience was similar."[43]

Hays suggests these quotations from within, or very nearby, that famous
portion of Isaiah occur in Romans together with "several passages that seem
to echo the Suffering Servant motif of Isaiah 53 (e.g., Rom. 4:24–25, 5:15–19,
10:16, 15:21)."[44] Thus, in keeping with early Christian proclamation, the NT
repeatedly identifies Jesus as the fulfiller of this Servant role (e.g., Mt 8:17;
Lk 22:37; Acts 8:32–35; 1 Pet 2:24–25). The apostle John understood Is 53:1
as predictive of the unbelief among many of those who witnessed or heard the
report of Jesus' "miraculous signs" (σημεῖα, Jn 12:37–38). The fulfillment of
Isaiah's prophecy regarding "the ones bringing the Good News [of] the good
things" (Is 52:7, cited in Rom 10:15), therefore, is the Gospel message about
Jesus Christ, the Servant of Yahweh.[45]

---

[43] Kruse, *Romans*, 417. Despite the unfortunate chapter division at Is 53:1, commentators often
refer to the entire passage of Is 52:13–53:12 as "Isaiah 53," as does Hayes in the quote that
immediately follows above. For a brief structural analysis that affirms the unity and integrity
of Is 52:13–53:12 as a single poem, see Mitchell, *Our Suffering Savior*, 13–14.

[44] Hays, *Echoes of Scripture in the Letters of Paul*, 63. With some hyperbole, Hays adds that
Paul "hints and whispers all around Isaiah 53 but never mentions the prophetic typology that
would supremely integrate his interpretation of Christ and Israel." The NT is replete with
quotations and allusions to the Suffering Servant depicted in the four Isaian poems (42:1–9;
49:1–13; 50:4–11; 52:13–53:12), and these NT passages (including Paul's), considered individually and together, certainly exemplify prophetic Christology. See Mitchell, *Our Suffering
Savior*, 28–40.

[45] For an exposition of the text, see Lessing, *Isaiah 40–55*, 578–623; for an exegesis of the text
with examples for using it in Christian proclamation, see Mitchell, *Our Suffering Savior*,
41–147.

As the two verbs "listen responsively" and "believe" function synonymously in 10:16, so do the nouns that are the objects of those verbs, "the Good News" (τῷ εὐαγγελίῳ) and "the message" (τῇ ἀκοῇ), respectively. Paul lays out his own Christocentric understanding of the message promised in Is 53:1 already in the letter's introduction. There he specifically delineates the content of "the Good News of God" (1:1) as that

> [2]which [God] promised beforehand through his prophets in holy writings [3]concerning his Son, the one who came from the seed of David according to flesh, [4]the one designated Son of God in power according to [the] Spirit of holiness out of [his] resurrection from [the] dead, Jesus Christ our Lord. (1:2–4)

Faith from Hearing the Word of Christ (10:17)

Paul makes his Christological understanding of the fulfillment of Isaiah's message explicit in 10:17: "consequently, faith [comes] from hearing, and the hearing through [the] Word of Christ/[the] Messiah." This verse then draws together a number of themes and explicates the interrelationship between faith, hearing, and the Word of Christ. As in 10:14–15, the chronological sequence actually goes in reverse.

The order of the nouns in 10:17 is "faith," "hearing," and the "Word of Christ." But the *first* event in the sequence of conversion to the faith is that the "Word of Christ" (ῥήματος Χριστοῦ, 10:17) comes "near" (ἐγγύς, 10:8). The presence of "Word" (ῥῆμα) in 10:17 continues to stem from its use in LXX Deut 30:14, quoted in Rom 10:8 (translating דָּבָר in MT Deut 30:14; see the commentary on Rom 10:8). In this context it may be envisioned primarily as the Word proclaimed orally (see below on ἀκοή, "hearing"). But already in Deuteronomy "Word" refers to words written on a scroll (Deut 30:10). This "Word" is also conveyed through the now-written words of Isaiah and Joel just cited in Rom 10:11, 13, 15.

The genitive "of Christ" is primarily objective and refers to the content of the message being proclaimed (see the fourth textual note on 10:17). The "Word of Christ" (ῥήματος Χριστοῦ) in 10:17 specifically identifies the Word's content. It also stands equivalent to "the Word of the faith" (τὸ ῥῆμα τῆς πίστεως) spoken of earlier in 10:8. Paul's parenthetical interpretations in 10:6 and 10:7, as well as the content expressed in 10:9, make it clear that "the Word" in 10:8 is *about* Christ and that the Word *is* Christ, who has come "near" to us through his incarnation and resurrection (see the commentary on 10:6–7).

Second, what happens "through [the] Word of Christ" (διὰ ῥήματος Χριστοῦ) is "the hearing" (ἡ ... ἀκοή, 10:17). Unfortunately, English presents seemingly insurmountable difficulties in regard to consistently translating the noun ἀκοή.[46] The three occurrences in 10:16–17 illustrate this. At times, the context points toward a designation of content, "what is heard" (BDAG, 4), and so

---

[46] Note the even more significant English deficiencies with the "faith" and "righteousness" word groups discussed by Middendorf, *Romans 1–8*, 88 and 92.

it is translated as "message" in 10:16. At other times, however, the noun empha-sizes the reception of the Word, which is best rendered as "hearing" (10:17; see BDAG, 2). The cognate verb "to hear/listen" (ἀκούω) is discussed in the commentary on 10:14. Note also the relationship of that simple verb with the compound verb ὑπακούω, "listen responsively," just addressed in 10:16.[47] As a result, the ability to recognize the presence of all these related Greek terms has become problematic in English. Thank God for Greek!

In this context and in accordance with the prophecy of Isaiah, "the message" (ἡ ἀκοή) of "the Good News" (10:16) is the "Word of Christ" (10:17). Indeed, "hearing, the kind of hearing that can lead to faith, can only happen if there is a definite salvific word from God that is proclaimed."[48] Therefore, as laid out in 10:14–15, God sends proclaimers to speak it into the ears of those who do not yet believe, and the result is "hearing" (ἡ ἀκοή, 10:17 [twice]).

What is the *third* step? Moving backward to the beginning of the verse, Paul compactly states what God intends to happen as a result of such hearing: "Consequently, faith [comes] from hearing" (ἄρα ἡ πίστις ἐξ ἀκοῆς, 10:17). Throughout 10:6–15, Paul explicates various facets of "the righteousness from faith" (ἡ ... ἐκ πίστεως δικαιοσύνη, 10:6). In addition to the noun "faith" (πίστις) in 10:6 and 10:8, Paul also uses the cognate verb "believe" (πιστεύω) five times in 10:9–15, as well as in the previous verse (10:16) when quoting Is 53:1. All of these come together concisely in Rom 10:17, where the topic reaches its apex. Paul introduces his discussion in 10:6 with "the righteousness from faith says thus." He then announces: "The Word is near you, ... this is, the Word of the faith [τῆς πίστεως] which we are proclaiming" (10:8). Now he concludes it with "faith [comes] from hearing" (10:17).

The clause "faith [comes] from hearing" (ἡ πίστις ἐξ ἀκοῆς, 10:17), like "from faith" (ἐκ πίστεως) in 10:6, echoes one of the major themes of the let-ter.[49] In 1:17, where "from faith" (ἐκ πίστεως) occurs twice, the preposition "from" (ἐκ) expresses source.[50] The same basic sense applies to the preposi-tion here. The directional connotation then validates the bracketed insertion of the verb "comes" (rather than "is," which is more typically assumed in nomi-nal sentences). Rom 10:17 teaches that faith comes *from* (ἐκ) a source, "from hearing," and that hearing comes *through* (διά) a message, "through [the] Word of Christ." Righteousness, as expounded by Paul so thoroughly earlier in the letter, similarly comes "from" and "through" faith (3:21–31).[51] Rigid distinc-tions among the prepositions are not always appropriate (see 3:30). But Lenski

---

[47] See " 'Obey' Is a Problematic Translation of ὑπακούω" in the commentary on 10:16a.

[48] Moo, *Romans*, 666 (on 10:17).

[49] See "The Background and Meaning of 'Faith' Words" in the commentary on 1:16 (Middendorf, *Romans 1–8*, 88–90); " 'From Faith[fulness] into Faith' (1:17)" on 96–98; and also 66–67, 106–7.

[50] Middendorf, *Romans 1–8*, 104–5 (on 1:17).

[51] See Middendorf, *Romans 1–8*, 268–69, 280 (on 3:22), and 297–98 (on 3:28).

properly argues against simply equating "from" and "through" in 10:17 and proposes that they convey source and medium, respectively:

> Right "out of" [ἐκ, "from"] the thing one is made to hear comes this justifying faith; it never has another source. But what the gospel heralds make men to hear is not their own so that men might be justified if they were disbelieving; it is mediated by [διά, "through"] nothing less than "Christ's own utterance."[52]

As discussed earlier,[53] *10:14–17 focuses upon how people come to saving faith. It is evangelistic. Thus the Formula of Concord quotes 10:17 to affirm how "the Father wills that all men should hear this proclamation and come to Christ" (FC SD XI 68–69).* The Formula also relies on the sequence which culminates in 10:17 in order to describe how the Holy Spirit works through the proclamation of the Word:

> God the Holy Spirit, however, does not effect conversion without means; he employs to this end the preaching and the hearing of God's Word, as it is written that the Gospel is a "power of God" for salvation [Rom 1:16]; likewise, that faith comes from the hearing of God's Word (Rom. 10:17). It is God's will that men should hear his Word and not stop their ears. The Holy Spirit is present with this Word and opens hearts. (FC Ep II 4–5; similarly, FC SD II 50–52)

Conclusion to Romans 10:16–17: The Passive Meaning of Faith—Faith Meant for All

The passive nature of *both hearing and believing* was discussed previously.[54] Paul excludes any active role on the part of humanity in 10:6 and 10:7. Of course he has also done so repeatedly and effectively throughout the letter (e.g., 1:18–3:21; 9:30–10:5). The passive nature of faith becomes especially critical when Paul discusses righteousness.

> There, for Paul, the opposite of "faith" is not so much "unbelief," as it is "works" and, specifically, "works of the Law" (ἔργων νόμου, Rom 3:20, 28; Gal 2:15–16; see also Rom 4:4–5; 10:5–11). This refers to humans doing something *toward God* in the arena of righteousness. Faith, therefore, in these contexts means to not do anything; it is simply to let oneself be given to in the sense of passively receiving the gift of salvation. The direction of the action is all *from God* to us.[55]

---

[52] Lenski, *Romans*, 667–68.

[53] See the commentary on 10:14–15 and the excursus "The New Testament Connotations and Context of Words Commonly Translated as 'Preach,' 'Teach,' and 'Prophesy'" following the commentary on 10:6–15.

[54] See the commentary on 10:14; see also "The Background and Meaning of 'Faith' Words" in the commentary on 1:16 (Middendorf, *Romans 1–8*, 88–90); "'From Faith[fulness] into Faith' (1:17)" on 96–98; and also 106–7.

[55] Middendorf, *Romans 1–8*, 89–90; see also the excursus "The Background of 'Works of the Law'" following the commentary on 3:9–20.

Believing, then, is not something people strive after ("nor of the one striving," οὐδὲ τοῦ τρέχοντος, 9:16); it does not even involve our Law-abiding works of obedience (it is "apart from works of the Law," χωρὶς ἔργων νόμου, 3:28; cf. 9:32). In regard to its source, faith does not stem from intellectual assent or originate within our volitional human will ("not of the one willing," οὐ τοῦ θέλοντος, 9:16). As Käsemann states: "Faith and unbelief are not arbitrary human decisions."[56] Dunn retorts that "Käsemann exemplifies typical Lutheran nervousness on the point."[57] But to diminish the matter in that way overlooks *the significance of what, for Paul, is, in effect, the whole ball game, the issue of eternal salvation.*

Throughout the entire letter Paul insists that righteousness is *either* sought futilely and fatally from human works *or* it is the gift of God available by virtue of Christ's death and resurrection and passively received "from faith" (e.g., 1:17; 9:32; 10:6; cf. 10:17). The confusion in this context stems partially from the critical *misunderstanding* of ὑπακούω in 10:16 as "obey," as an expression of active and necessary human obedience,[58] rather than "listen responsively," that is, a passive human response of faith created by the active divine Word of Christ that is heard. If righteousness were to be attained by obedience, we would be back to salvation by faith *plus* works, a notion Paul vehemently rejects by repeatedly setting "faith" *versus* "works" as antitheses to each other (e.g., Rom 3:21–22, 28; 4:4–5; 9:32; 10:4–6; Gal 2:16; 3:6, 11).

Faith comes solely from hearing the Good News, whose specific content is the Word of the promised Messiah (10:16–17), the one of whom Isaiah prophesied and whom Paul proclaims as the risen Lord Jesus (10:9, 15). Those who heed what they hear and believe in their hearts are then also called to confess it with their mouths (10:9–10). With the four uses of "everyone, all" (πᾶς) in 10:11–13, Paul repeatedly insists that this is the way of the Gospel *for each person and for all people*, as it has always been, according to Isaiah and Joel: "[11]For the Scripture says, 'Everyone who believes on him will not be put to shame.' … [13]For 'everyone who ever might call on the name of [the] Lord will be saved'" (Rom 10:11, 13, citing Is 28:16 and Joel 2:32 [MT/LXX 3:5], respectively; see also the conclusion to this section).

Then wherein lies the problem addressed by Paul beginning in 9:1 and more immediately in 10:16? Keener contends one simply does not exist! "Far from Jewish unbelief posing a credibility problem for Paul's Jewish message, it simply fulfilled what the prophets had predicted."[59] But that hardly explains Paul's anguish, his fervent prayers, and a focus of his entire ministry (e.g., 9:1–3; 10:1–2; 11:14).

---

[56] Käsemann, *Romans*, 293.

[57] Dunn, *Romans*, 622.

[58] See "'Obey' Is a Problematic Translation of ὑπακούω" in the commentary on 10:16a.

[59] Keener, *Romans*, 128.

God's intends for all those who hear the "Word of Christ" (10:17) to passively receive, believe, and responsively hear its message. But 10:16 has brought up the only possible *active human role* in regard to the Good News of Christ and stated it in *negative* terms. Melanchthon articulates the problem simply: "They are not willing to believe the Gospel."[60] Humans can "stop their ears" (FC Ep II 5), that is, they can exert their will by refusing to listen responsively to the Good News or believe its messianic message (10:16). Paul's specific concern remains that, "as far as some of the Jews are concerned, the fourth and final condition (i.e. the one mentioned first in vv. 14–15a) has not been fulfilled. They have not believed in Christ."[61]

Why the Problem? (10:18–21)

The Psalm Says That All Heard (Ps 19:4 in Rom 10:18)

Through the remainder of this chapter, Paul seeks to explain the improper response of Israel,[62] a matter which causes "great sorrow and unceasing anguish in [his] heart" (9:2). But Paul proceeds by insisting that *the fault in no way resides with God, his Word, or his Messiah*. Indeed, the sending and proclaiming of the Word of Christ have gone according to God's plan and purpose (10:14–15). Paul demonstrates this in 10:18 by citing Ps 19:4 (MT 19:5; LXX 18:5):

> But I say, it is not that they did not hear, is it? On the contrary:
> "Their voice went out into all the world
>   and their words into the limits of the inhabited world." (Rom 10:18)

The quotation matches LXX Ps 18:5 (MT 19:5; ET 19:4) exactly:

> εἰς πᾶσαν τὴν γῆν ἐξῆλθεν ὁ φθόγγος αὐτῶν
>   καὶ εἰς τὰ πέρατα τῆς οἰκουμένης τὰ ῥήματα αὐτῶν.

Originally the psalmist David applies these words to God proclaiming his glory daily and to all people through his creation (Ps 19:2–3 [MT 19:3–4]), a sentiment Paul clearly affirms (see the commentary on Rom 1:20). This provides another excellent example of Paul extending the meaning of an OT Scripture passage (cf. also 9:25–26; 10:6–8). As Hays puts it: "Paul transmutes the psalmist's graceful depiction of the heavens' glory into a description of the universal scope of Christian preaching. ... He has simply appropriated [the] language to lend rhetorical force to his own discourse."[63] Paul cites the verse to refute any

---

[60] Melanchthon, *Romans*, 193, commenting on 9:30–32.

[61] Cranfield, *Romans*, 536.

[62] Thus this section (10:16–21) is titled "Israel's Response (and God's Reaction Introduced)."

[63] Hays, *Echoes of Scripture in the Letters of Paul*, 175. On the one hand, he contends: "This mode of intertextual reading is traditionally stigmatized as prooftexting, but that pejorative label misconstrues the rhetorical function of such intertextual strategies in Paul." At the same time, he seems to engage in what he critiques, by asserting:

notion that the message was not received or not heard.[64] On the contrary, the "voice" and "words" (10:18) went out to Israel and beyond to the Gentiles. In 10:18, the phrase "the words" (τὰ ῥήματα, from LXX Ps 18:5 [MT 19:5; ET 19:4]) functions in direct connection with the two singular forms of "word" (ῥῆμα) in 10:8, "the Word is near" and "the Word of the faith," and the singular "word" (ῥῆμα) in 10:17, the "Word of Christ." Paul thereby applies the psalmist's words about creation to the Good News as proclaimed by Isaiah, Paul, and numerous others (10:14–15). Through many and various ways, in written and oral form, *the message has resounded "into all the world"* (Ps 19:4 [MT 19:5; LXX 18:5], quoted in Rom 10:18). The parallel phrase "into the limits/corners of the inhabited world" (εἰς τὰ πέρατα τῆς οἰκουμένης) clarifies that "into all the world" (εἰς πᾶσαν τὴν γῆν) encompasses everywhere humanity lives. The Gospel is for everyone!

Yet one need not overpress the literal and temporal fulfillment of that aspect of the passage, as if Paul meant that at the time of his writing every person on earth had already heard the Gospel.[65] Indeed, Paul himself wants the assistance of the Roman believers as he strives to bring the Good News where Christ was not yet named (15:20; i.e., Spain; see 15:24). Thus it is not improper to recognize a note of hyperbole.[66] At the same time, Paul can describe his current situation as "no longer having a place in these regions" to do such new evangelistic work (15:23). From its beginnings in Jerusalem, the message had already spread remarkably far, even as far as Rome itself, well ahead of Paul and apparently apart from the personal presence of other apostles. Therefore, the scope should not be unnecessarily limited simply to Paul's ministry or "the gentile

---

There is no indication that Paul has wrestled seriously with the texts from which the citations are drawn. He has simply appropriated their language to lend rhetorical force to his own discourse, with minimal attention to the integrity of the semiotic universe of the precursor. ... The citation of Ps. 19:4 [MT 19:5] does not prove that Jews have had the opportunity to hear the gospel; rather, it gives Paul a "vocabulary of a second and higher power" with which to *assert* that they have heard it. (Quoting Thomas M. Greene, *The Light in Troy: Imitation and Discovery in Renaissance Poetry* [New Haven, Conn.: Yale University Press, 1982], 39)

For a brief evaluation of Hays' approach, see Middendorf, *Romans 1–8*, 37, and the excursus "Paul's Use of the Old Testament in Romans" following the commentary on 15:7–13.

[64] Thus Paul's use of Ps 19:4 (MT 19:5) is consistent with the verse's context, as the preceding verse literally declares that "there is no utterance and there are no words without their voice being heard" (Ps 19:3 [MT 19:4]).

[65] Similarly, Col 1:23 refers to "the Gospel ... , which has been proclaimed in all the creation under the heaven" (τοῦ κηρυχθέντος ἐν πάσῃ κτίσει τῇ ὑπὸ τὸν οὐρανόν), but Paul does not mean that at the time he wrote that epistle the church's evangelistic mission had already been completed. Rather, Paul refers to the universal scope of the mission. See, e.g., Mt 28:19–20; Acts 1:8. While the longer ending of Mark is likely secondary, it records Jesus giving this commission: "After going into all the world, proclaim the Good News in all the creation" (πορευθέντες εἰς τὸν κόσμον ἅπαντα κηρύξατε τὸ εὐαγγέλιον πάσῃ τῇ κτίσει, Mk 16:15).

[66] Kruse, *Romans*, 419; also Moo, *Romans*, 667, who cites Col 1:23 in note 39.

mission."[67] On the contrary, the "Word of Christ" (10:17) going out "to [the] Jew first" (1:16; cf. Mt 15:24) and among Diaspora Jews validates the direct application Paul makes in this specific context (10:19, 21). As Chrysostom observes: "If the ends of the world have heard, how can the Jews claim that they have not?"[68] The fact that "they did not all listen *responsively* to the Good News" was because they did not believe the message (10:16); "it is not that they did not hear, is it?" (10:18).

The Torah Affirms That They Knew (Deut 32:21 in Rom 10:19)

In 10:19, Paul focuses more intensively upon the primary issue which has been on his mind ever since 9:1:

> But I say, it is not that Israel did not know, is it? First, Moses says:
> "I will provoke you to envy over [what is] not a nation;
> over a nation without understanding I will make you angry." (10:19)

At first glance, the passage Paul cites here (Deut 32:21b) seems like an odd reply! *He expresses his main point in introducing the quote: Israel knew.* In so doing, he builds upon what he has already enunciated in 3:1; 9:4–5; and 10:18 by adding yet another privilege enjoyed by Israel over the Gentiles. Each of Israel's advantages excludes potential excuses for the reality that they all did not believe the Good News (10:16).

The half verse cited (Deut 32:21b), however, depicts *God's* action. The entire verse in the context of Deuteronomy makes it clear that Yahweh's future action in making Israel envious is not arbitrary, but a response to Israel's idolatrous apostasy.[69] Thus "Israel's present lack of 'faith' is the eschatological equivalent of Israel's unfaith in its most idolatrous periods."[70]

LXX Deut 32:21 reads:

> αὐτοὶ παρεζήλωσάν με ἐπ' οὐ θεῷ,
> παρώργισάν με ἐν τοῖς εἰδώλοις αὐτῶν·
> κἀγὼ παραζηλώσω αὐτοὺς ἐπ' οὐκ ἔθνει,
> ἐπ' ἔθνει ἀσυνέτῳ παροργιῶ αὐτούς.

> They provoked me to jealousy over [what is] not a god;
> they made me angry with their idols.
> And I will provoke them to envy over [what is] not a nation;
> over a nation without understanding I will make them angry.

---

[67] As does Dunn, *Romans*, 624; similarly, Cranfield, *Romans*, 537; Origen, *Romans* (Bray, *Romans*, ACCS NT 6:281), who states: "This passage, taken from Psalm 19[:4 (MT 19:5)], must refer to the Gentiles."

[68] Chrysostom, *Homilies on Romans*, 18 (Bray, *Romans*, ACCS NT 6:281).

[69] Ticciati, "The Nondivisive Difference of Election," 269, points out that Israel's jealousy "occurs in this verse [Deut 32:21] *in parallel with God's jealousy*" and argues that this notion "may be harnessed to illuminate Rom 9–11 in a most intriguing way." However, Paul never refers to *God's jealousy* over Israel, so it is difficult to perceive how this element can have significance for the hearers or readers of Romans.

[70] Dunn, *Romans*, 625.

Paul reproduces the latter half of the verse almost exactly, but in place of the third person plural objects "them" he substitutes the second person plural "you."[71] Certainly this alteration then encompasses those Jews who do not believe the Word of Christ, but it may also apply to those in Paul's audience who are wavering (cf. the weak in Rom 15:1 and the addressees of Hebrews). This provides yet another indication that at least some Jews in Rome are being addressed.[72] In any event, the refusal of some in Israel to listen responsively to the Gospel and believe its message (10:16; cf. 3:3; 9:6) leads to the reaction by God predicted in Deuteronomy and taking place in Paul's day.

Why Provoke to Envy/Jealousy?

The first verb in Deut 32:21b indicates that God's reaction to their rejection hopes to provoke a different, ultimately more positive response. LXX Deut 32:21 introduces παραζηλόω, either "provoke to *jealousy*" or "provoke to *envy*" (see the third textual note on Rom 10:19), a verb Paul employs here in 10:19 and twice in the following chapter (11:11, 14). The corresponding Hebrew verb in Deut 32:21 is אַקְנִיאֵם, "I will cause them to be jealous." Elsewhere, both the MT and the LXX use the respective cognate adjectives and nouns to depict a prominent self-characterization of Yahweh God as being "jealous" or having "jealousy."[73] Thus the vocabulary has the connotation of a positive attribute, as with a husband who is similarly "jealous" in regard to his wife, i.e., loving her and not wanting to share her with others. When used of Yahweh, then, his "jealousy" means that he is their only God, the only one who loves them, and he protectively enjoins them to be exclusively devoted to him; he will not share Israel with other gods, who are false and abusive.

The cognate noun ζῆλος also has generally positive connotations when transliterated with a "z," "zeal."[74] Paul offers this personal attestation in 10:2–3:

> [2]Indeed, I bear witness for them that they have *zeal* for God, but not in accordance with proper recognition. [3]For while ignoring the righteousness of God and seeking to establish their own [righteousness], they were not submissive to the righteousness of God.

---

[71] See the third through the sixth textual notes on 10:19.

[72] See Middendorf, *Romans 1–8*, 12–14 and 17–18, as well as "Who Are the 'Weak' and the 'Strong'? Addressees Again!" in the introduction to 14:1–15:13 and the final portion of the commentary on 16:1–16, titled "What Can We Conclude?"

[73] See the adjective קַנָּא, "jealous," in Ex 20:5; 34:14; Deut 4:24; 5:9; 6:15; the adjective קַנּוֹא, "jealous," in Josh 24:19; Nah 1:2; and the noun קִנְאָה, "jealousy," in Zeph 1:18; 3:8; Zech 1:14; 8:2. In the LXX, see ζηλωτής, "jealous"; ζῆλος, "jealousy"; or ζηλόω, "to be jealous," in those same verses.

[74] Dunn, *Romans*, 625, identifies the connection with "zeal" (ζῆλος) in 10:2, but further contends that "in a neat reversal [Paul] was using it to explain Israel's present role within God's overall purpose." However, the rejection of the "Word of Christ" (10:17) by some in Israel was not God's plan. See "Conclusions: Monergism (Romans 9) *and* Resistibility (Romans 10)" below.

Israel's proper "zeal for God" misdirected *some* of them to seek "their own" righteousness (10:3), which led to a rejection of the Word of faith, resulting in righteousness and salvation for the Gentiles (see 11:11–12). Thus, as discussed in the commentary on 10:2, "not in accordance with proper recognition" (οὐ κατ᾽ ἐπίγνωσιν) does not convey a lack of *knowledge*, that is, ignorance. On the contrary, 10:18 affirms that the unbelievers in Israel *know*; what they lack is *a proper recognition* in regard to that knowledge, a response in faith created by the Word of Christ.

Rom 3:2 points out the primary advantage of Israel in this regard: "they were entrusted with the sayings of God." Rom 9:4–5 spells out many more of Israel's privileges. The critical problem, therefore, does *not* reside with God, who graciously revealed his Word and poured out all these blessings on Israel so they would "know" (10:19). In spite of this knowledge, the problem is the response articulated in 10:16: "but they did not all listen responsively to the Good News." Now in 10:19 Paul describes how "they have been the recipients of God's special self-revelation, and yet they have been uncomprehending."[75] Moo describes this as Israel's

> willful refusal to recognize the fulfillment of these texts in the revelation of God's righteousness in Christ. Israel, Paul suggests, "sees, but does not perceive; hears, but does not comprehend" (Isa. 6:9; cf. Mark 4:12 and par[allels]; John 12:40; Acts 28:26–27).[76]

This correlates with what Paul asked earlier in response to the advantage of Israel cited in 3:2: "What, then, if some were unfaithful? Their faithlessness will not make the faithfulness of God ineffective, will it?" (3:3). He makes the same move in 10:19, stating the response of some in Israel followed by God's reaction to it.

By "Not a Nation" Gentiles

At the same time, the Deuteronomy text brings up those who are "not a nation" (οὐκ ἔθνει). While the form of the neuter noun ἔθνος, "nation," is singular, its presence in Deuteronomy conveys the typical biblical connotations of the plural, "those who do not belong to groups professing faith in the God of Israel, *the nations, gentiles, unbelievers*" (BDAG, 2 a). The referent is an unspecified nation, representing all the Gentiles, depicted in the second line of the quotation as "without understanding." What the Gentile "nation" lacks is what Israel knows.

The text says nothing positive about the generic "not a nation" (οὐκ ἔθνει) under consideration or how it would be used to provoke Israel's envy. Note, however, the underlying Hebrew of Deut 32:21, where both עַם, "people" (often used for Israel), and the generally more negative גּוֹי, "nation," are present as parallel terms:

---

[75] Cranfield, *Romans*, 538.

[76] Moo, *Romans*, 668, who refers to it as "ignorance."

אַקְנִיאֵם בְּלֹא־עָם בְּגְוֹי נָבָל אַכְעִיסֵם:

I will provoke them to envy by not-a-people;
  by a foolish nation I will cause them to be angry.

Earlier Paul had employed the phrase "not my people" in his quote of Hos 2:23 (MT/LXX 2:25) in Rom 9:25 and then of Hos 1:10 (MT/LXX 2:1) in Rom 9:26. While the LXX of Hosea uses λαός rather than ἔθνος to translate עַם, "people," in the phrase "not my people" (לֹא עַמִּי, Hos 1:9; 1:10 [MT/LXX 2:1]; 2:23 [MT/LXX 2:25]), Moo speculates:

> The phrase "no people" was probably the catch phrase that drew Paul's attention to this text, since he quotes the Hosea prophecy about those "not my people" becoming the people of God in [Rom] 9:25–26. Paul sees in the words a prophecy of the mission to the Gentiles.[77]

The explicit mention of Gentiles in 9:24 had already pointed toward them as the referent of *Paul's* "not my people" in Rom 9:25–26 (though Hosea was referring to Israel; see the commentary on Rom 9:25–26). The contrast Paul soon draws between 10:20 and 10:21 accomplishes that same purpose in this passage.

Thus the referent of "a nation" (ἔθνος) in 10:19 has been further defined for Paul as a result of the Word(s) of Christ going out into all the inhabited world (10:17, 18). The means by which God intends to provoke Israel to envy in order to fulfill Moses' words has already come to fruition, at least partially, through the mission in which Paul himself has participated mightily (see 11:13–14). In the blessed plan of God the "nation" in 10:19 now encompasses "*non-Israelite Christians, gentiles* of Christian congregations composed of more than one nationality and not limited to people of Israel" (BDAG, s.v. ἔθνος, 2 b). This resounds throughout the letter from 1:16 all the way to its conclusion (e.g., 16:4, 25–26; see also Eph 2:11–3:12).

The Father's Intended Outcome

How, then, will God (in response to Israel's unbelieving response), by reaching out to Gentiles, "provoke to envy" (παραζηλόω, 10:19) those in Israel who did not believe the Good News of their Messiah? Paul's only use of this verb outside of Romans warns the Corinthians against provoking the Lord to jealousy (παραζηλοῦμεν τὸν κύριον, 1 Cor 10:22). Such a negative connotation is heightened further by the parallel verb from LXX Deut 32:21 cited later in Rom 10:19, "I will make angry" (παροργιῶ). But the concept need not carry the "sinful" connotations often heard in English with the terms "jealous(y)/envy" or "anger."[78] *The notion of being understandably and even properly "envious" of the blessings someone else has* communicates the contextual meaning

---

[77] Moo, *Romans*, 668.

[78] For examples where this terminology has positive connotations, see God's depiction of himself as "jealous" in Ex 20:5 and Paul's imperative for Christians to "be angry and not sin" in Eph 4:26 (ὀργίζεσθε καὶ μὴ ἁμαρτάνετε; in form ὀργίζεσθε could be an indicative rather than an imperative).

well and anticipates a point developed in more detail when "provoke to envy" (παραζηλόω) occurs again in 11:11, 14.

Pelagius offers an analogy:

> It is just as if someone has a disobedient son and in order to reform him gives half his inheritance to his slave, so that when he finally repents he may be glad if he deserves to receive even that much.[79]

A better biblical comparison would be Jesus' parable of the Waiting Father,[80] or the Prodigal Son (Lk 15:11–32). As with the God-centered argument of Romans,[81] so that parable focuses our attention on the initial (Lk 15:11) and primary character, who represents our heavenly Father. At the end of the parable, the welcoming, joy-filled dad hosts a great celebration in his home with the newly returned prodigal (Lk 15:23, 25). This should entice the older son to come in and enjoy it! The father hopes that he will be provoked to envy over missing the party from which he has excluded himself; indeed, the older son "was angry" about the feast (ὠργίσθη, Lk 15:28).

God the Father similarly hopes that those in Israel who did not at first believe the Word of Christ will rejoin the family for the "necessary" (ἔδει, Lk 15:32) joyful celebration with the believing Gentiles. For these Gentiles, when they were unbelieving, used to form a nonexistent "nation" (Rom 10:19). Their previous spiritual state was far worse than the initial role of the younger son who grew up as an heir within a loving father's family (Lk 15:12). But the "prodigal," by breaking the filial relationship with his father, deliberately walked away (Lk 15:13–17) and became "dead … also having perished" (νεκρὸς … καὶ ἀπολωλώς, Lk 15:32), much like the former existence of Gentiles (e.g., Eph 2:11–12). But everyone among them who now believes "became alive … and was found," just like the son upon his return (ἔζησεν … καὶ εὑρέθη, Lk 15:32; e.g., Eph 2:13, 19; cf. Rom 10:12–13; 11:15). The open-ended scenario at the end of the parable matches the summation Paul draws in the final two verses of Romans 10 and in Romans 11 as well (see 11:11–12; also 11:14–15).

Applying the Prophets: Isaiah 65:1–2 in Romans 10:20–21

The Text

Paul concludes Romans 10 by engaging in another rather extraordinary use of yet another Scripture passage. Paul uses only the first half of each of the first two verses from Isaiah 65. In so doing, he completes his triumvirate of citations in Rom 10:18–21 by drawing from each section of the Hebrew Bible. He quotes from the Psalms (representing the Writings) in 10:18, the Torah in 10:19, and, finally, the Prophets in 10:20–21. In fact, for the fourth time in Romans 9–11,

---

[79] Pelagius, *Romans* (Bray, *Romans*, ACCS NT 6:282).

[80] This more appropriate title for the parable comes from a collection of sermons by Thielicke titled *The Waiting Father*.

[81] See "Romans 1–4: The Righteousness of God" in the introduction to Romans 9–16, as well as "God" in "The Three Foci of Romans 9–11" in the introduction to Romans 9–11.

Paul identifies his "favorite prophet" by name (10:20; also 9:27, 29; 10:16).[82]
Rom 10:20–21 reads:

> [20]But Isaiah is bold and says:
> > "I was found among the ones not seeking me;
> > > I became visible to the ones not inquiring after me."
> [21]But to Israel he says:
> > "The whole day I stretched out my hands
> > > to an unpersuaded and contradicting people."

The full text of LXX Is 61:1–2 follows:

> [1]ἐμφανὴς ἐγενόμην τοῖς ἐμὲ μὴ ζητοῦσιν,
> > εὑρέθην τοῖς ἐμὲ μὴ ἐπερωτῶσιν·
> εἶπα ἰδού εἰμι,
> > τῷ ἔθνει οἳ οὐκ ἐκάλεσάν μου τὸ ὄνομα.
> [2]ἐξεπέτασα τὰς χεῖράς μου ὅλην τὴν ἡμέραν
> > πρὸς λαὸν ἀπειθοῦντα καὶ ἀντιλέγοντα,
> οἳ οὐκ ἐπορεύθησαν ὁδῷ ἀληθινῇ,
> > ἀλλ᾽ ὀπίσω τῶν ἁμαρτιῶν αὐτῶν.

> [1]I became visible to the ones not seeking me;
> > I was found by the ones not inquiring after me.
> I said, "Look! [Here] I am!"
> > to the nation whose people did not call my name.
> [2]I stretched out my hands the whole day
> > to a people unpersuaded and contradicting,
> who did not go on the true way
> > but after their [own] sins.

Again, a number of observations are in order. First, as noted above, Paul quotes only the first half of each verse.

Second, while the words and forms he employs are all the same as in the LXX, the word order is changed. In MT Is 65:1 the order of the verbs that begin the first two clauses is נִדְרַ֫שְׁתִּי ... נִמְצֵ֫אתִי, "I was sought ... I was found," and LXX Is 65:1 has the verbs in that same order: "I became visible ... I was found" (ἐμφανὴς ἐγενόμην ... εὑρέθην). Paul reverses their order in Rom 10:20 to "I was found ... I became visible" (εὑρέθην ... ἐμφανὴς ἐγενόμην). Dunn suggests: "The inversion is what one would expect in a quotation from memory."[83] But rather than a careless citation from memory, it is more likely that Paul deliberately changed the word order to emphasize the verb which he placed first, "I

---

[82] Capes, Reeves, and Richards, *Rediscovering Paul*, 194, have a sidebar titled "Paul's Favorite Prophet." In it they contend:

> Paul's favorite prophet was probably Isaiah. The apostle quoted him more than any of the [other] Old Testament prophets. For him, Isaiah was the quintessential seer, the faithful witness, the one who—perhaps more than any—saw Israel's and the world's future with the coming of the Messiah. ... It was Isaiah who convinced Paul that Israel's unbelief and disobedience are not new; they have characterized the contrary members of God's covenant people all along (Rom 10:21, quoting Is 65:2).

[83] Dunn, *Romans*, 626.

was found." Similarly, when Paul utilizes Is 65:2 in Rom 10:21, he places "the whole day" (ὅλην τὴν ἡμέραν) at the front of the line. The notion that Paul cites haphazardly from memory is again put forward as a possible explanation, but it is more probable that Paul alters the order intentionally to add emphasis to the opening phrase.

Third, while the Hebrew is generally well represented by Paul and the LXX, two further points should be noted, one about Is 65:1a and another about Is 65:2a. MT Is 65:1a reads:

נִדְרַ֙שְׁתִּי֙ לְל֣וֹא שָׁאָ֔לוּ נִמְצֵ֖אתִי לְלֹ֣א בִקְשֻׁ֑נִי

The two Niphal verbs נִדְרַ֙שְׁתִּי֙ and נִמְצֵ֖אתִי are tolerative Niphals.[84] Thus נִדְרַ֙שְׁתִּי֙ means "I *allowed myself* to be (successfully) sought," that is, God led the people to inquire of him and responded when they did. Likewise, נִמְצֵ֖אתִי means "I *allowed myself* to be found," that is, God prompted the people to look for him and enabled them to find him. Therefore it is appropriate for BDAG to translate the Greek of Paul and the LXX that renders the first verb, ἐμφανὴς ἐγενόμην, reflexively as "*I have made myself known* (i.e. *revealed myself*)" (s.v. ἐμφανής, 2). Then MT Is 65:2a reads:

פֵּרַ֧שְׂתִּי יָדַ֛י כָּל־הַיּ֖וֹם אֶל־עַ֥ם סוֹרֵֽר

(a) See, e.g.,
Is 1:23; 30:1;
Jer 5:23;
6:28; Hos
4:16; 9:15;
Ps 78:8; Neh
9:29

The MT has the participle סוֹרֵֽר, from the verb סָרַר, which means "to revolt, rebel," continuing even after discipline and admonition to cease (Deut 21:18), and usually against Yahweh.[a] The Hebrew therefore supports the interpretation that Paul is not merely describing a (passive) stubbornness or obstinacy, but willful disbelief; the rejection of the Word of Christ is active rebellion against God. The MT has this single participle in this clause, whereas the Greek of the LXX and Paul has two participles, ἀπειθοῦντα καὶ ἀντιλέγοντα (see the third textual note on 10:21).

An Extended Application

Isaiah prophesied all these words *to Israel*. They were applicable to Israel at the many times in their history when they were not seeking Yahweh, but he nevertheless revealed himself so that he was found by them. These words certainly apply to God's calling of Abraham out from idolatry (Josh 24:2–3). He unexpectedly revealed himself to Moses in the burning bush and appointed him, despite his protestations, to lead Israel out from slavery in Egypt (Exodus 3). He visibly manifested himself to all Israel in the pillar of cloud and fire and later at Mount Sinai; he spoke his Word and established his sanctuary so that they could call upon him and be found by them.[85] Yahweh's self-revelation extends *all* the way back to Abraham and remained with Israel in *all* the ways noted in

---

[84] See Lessing, *Isaiah 56–66*, 391–92, 415–16; he includes discussion of Rom 10:20–21. See also Cranfield, *Romans*, 540, n. 5; similarly, Moo, *Romans*, 669, n. 49; Dunn, *Romans*, 626.

[85] Already at the consecration of the first temple Solomon prayed that not only Israelites (1 Ki 8:27–40) but Gentiles too (1 Ki 8:41–43) would find Yahweh there as the God who forgives sins and answers prayer.

Rom 3:1–2 and 9:4–5. They were then to listen responsively to the invitation Isaiah gives in Is 55:6: "Seek Yahweh while he allows himself to be found! Call on him while he is near!"[86]

Isaiah foresaw how Yahweh would be found and worshiped in faith by Gentile peoples.[87] Paul now extends the meaning of Is 65:1 in that direction. In Rom 9:30, he describes how "Gentiles, those who were not pursuing righteousness, got righteousness, that is, the righteousness which is from faith." In 10:20 he declares that what was once true of Israel *now applies to Gentiles*. They are "the ones who are not seeking me" and "the ones not inquiring after me." Yet God sends out those who proclaim the Good News "into the limits of the inhabited world" (10:18). Thus he was found by Gentiles because he revealed himself to them "through [the] Word of Christ" which they have heard (10:17).

But what generally characterized Israel in Isaiah's day according to the first half of Is 65:2 remains all too familiar: "But to Israel he says: 'The whole day I stretched out my hands to an unpersuaded and contradicting people' " (Rom 10:21, quoting Is 65:2a). As Paul cites Isaiah's words, he indicates the *continuing* problem of unbelief by using the two *participles* from the LXX (ἀπειθοῦντα, "unpersuaded," and ἀντιλέγοντα, "contradicting"). More important thematically, each of these two verbs expresses the direct opposite of a key verb for saving faith:[88]

- "Be unpersuaded" is an antonym of "believe" (πιστεύω in 10:4, 9, 10, 11, 14, 16; cf. also ὑπακούω in 10:16). The two verbs (ἀπειθέω and πιστεύω) stand as opposites in Jn 3:36: "the one who *believes* in the Son has eternal life; the one who *is unpersuaded* [disbelieves] in the Son will not see life, but the wrath of God remains on him."

- "Contradict" (ἀντιλέγω) is an antonym of "acknowledge, confess" (ὁμολογέω, 10:9, 10). Thus Christ himself is a sign that will be "contradicted/spoken against" (Lk 2:34), as is also the Christian church (Acts 28:22).

Instead of listen responsively or believing (10:16), Paul characterizes Israel as "unpersuaded" (ἀπειθοῦντα, 10:21; cf. the commentary on 2:8; 11:30–32; 15:31). They all heard and knew the Word of Christ (10:17, 18). "But they did not all listen responsively to the Good News. For Isaiah says: 'Lord, who believed our message?' " (10:16). The content of what all of them were intended to believe is the essential message of Jesus the Messiah's resurrection (10:9, 17).

---

[86] The translation is from Lessing, *Isaiah 40–55*, 649. In the immediately preceding verse (Is 55:5) Isaiah makes a statement comparable to Is 65:1. There, however, Yahweh utilizes Israel as his instrument to draw in the peoples. Lessing translates Is 55:5 as follows: "Behold, to a nation you do not know you will call out, and a nation that does not know you—to you they will run on account of Yahweh your God, and of the Holy One of Israel, because he glorified you."

[87] See, e.g., Is 19:19–25; 56:3–8; 66:19–21; and the universal scope of the salvation brought by the Servant in Is 42:1–6; 49:1–6.

[88] That these verbs are "the direct opposites" is recognized by Cranfield, *Romans*, 541.

God also called them to join with that belief a confession that this "Jesus [is] Lord" (10:9), namely, the Lord/Yahweh (see the commentary on 10:9 and 10:13). But instead of saying the same thing back in affirmation (ὁμολογήσῃς, 10:9; ὁμολογεῖται, 10:10), some in Israel did the opposite. The message they heard announcing the fulfillment of the prophecies they know (e.g., Is 52:7 and Is 53:1 in Rom 10:15–16) is one that they are, literally, "speaking against" (ἀντιλέγοντα, 10:21). Rather than confessing, they are "contradicting." Therefore what grieves Paul (9:1–2) is the result—they have not attained righteousness and salvation (9:31; 10:1, 10). None of this is new in regard to Israel. Isaiah already spoke of Israel in this way in his own day (Is 53:1; cf. Is 10:22–23 and Is 1:9, cited earlier in Rom 9:27–29). Jesus similarly lamented:

> Jerusalem, Jerusalem! The one killing the prophets and stoning the ones having been sent [τοὺς ἀπεσταλμένους; cf. Rom 10:15] to her. How many times I willed to gather together your children, in the manner in which a hen gathers her chicks under her wings, and you were not willing. (Mt 23:37)

While it remains true that "not all" listened responsively to the Good News (Rom 10:16), that very same expression certainly implies that others *did believe* the Word of Christ (see the first point of the conclusion below)!

How then will *God react* to those who respond to the Good News by refusing to be persuaded by it and instead contradict it? Isaiah tells us an extraordinary truth which Paul affirms: "the whole day I [God] stretched out my hands" to them (10:21). "The spreading out of the hands ... is here a gesture of appealing welcome and friendship."[89] Such is Yahweh's extraordinary goodness. "The passage stresses both God's constant offer of grace to his people and their stubborn resistance to that grace."[90] Nevertheless, he stretched out his hands (aorist tense) to them.[91] Are the hands of grace still stretched out? Paul delves into that topic in Romans 11.

Conclusions: Monergism (Romans 9) *and* Resistibility (Romans 10)

God's Acts

Paul's summation in 10:16 that "not all" listen responsively to the Good News obviously implies some did (cf. 3:3; 9:6)! In fact, Acts repeatedly makes it clear that *many Jewish people* within and outside the land of Israel *listened*

---

[89] Cranfield, *Romans*, 541.

[90] Moo, *Romans*, 669.

[91] In their commentaries on Romans, Ambrosiaster, Diodore, and Pelagius all interpret the verb to refer to Jesus' hands being spread out on the cross (Bray, *Romans*, ACCS NT 6:283). While a nice homiletical connection, the comparison is not precise exegetically. Here the hands are stretched out toward Israel rather than out to the sides as on the cross. The pastor seeking more precise exegetical connections to the crucifixion of Jesus might consider passages such as "behold, I have engraved you upon [my] hands" (Is 49:16, with the feminine singular "you" referring to Zion); "they have pierced my hands and my feet" (Ps 22:16 [MT Ps 22:17; LXX Ps 21:17]); and "they shall gaze upon me, whom they have pierced" (Zech 12:10).

responsively and believed the "Word of Christ/[the] Messiah" (10:17).[b] This aligns perfectly with the sense of "confess" (ὁμολογέω) in 10:9, as well as "listen responsively" (ὑπακούω) and "message; hearing" (ἀκοή) in 10:16–17. Through hearing the Word of Christ faith comes. As the message is believed in the heart, God's desire is that it be confessed and affirmed with the mouth so that all may call upon the Lord Jesus for salvation (10:9–10, 13–14). Therefore, as Paul will soon affirm, a faithful remnant continues to exist by God's grace (see 11:1–6). In this aspect, no distinction exists between Jew and Greek (10:12). Origen remarks: "Not all the Gentiles have believed the gospel nor have all the Jews, but many [of both] have."[92]

> (b) E.g., Acts 2:41; 4:4; 6:7; 13:43; 14:1; 17:4, 12; 18:8; 19:8, 10; 28:24

How then does one explain the "not" in "not all" (10:16)? On the one hand, *God* has done it all by sending out into the world those who proclaim the Word of Christ (10:15). Furthermore, *Jesus* himself came down to bring his Word near to Israel and to all (10:6, 8, 17). All in Israel both *knew* the prophetic promises of the Messiah (10:19) and *heard* the message (10:18). The problem, however, occurs between the hearing and the believing, between the human ear and the heart.

God does not *force* faith; the message which is passively heard can be actively rejected.[93] Neither does one have to confess the astonishing assertion of 10:9, "Jesus [is] Lord" (κύριον Ἰησοῦν), at least not until the Last Day when all people, believers and unbelievers alike, shall do so (Phil 2:11). The last Greek word of Romans 10, ἀντιλέγοντα, "contradicting" (10:21), makes it clear that humans can speak against that seemingly impossible declaration rather than confessing it. Similarly, God does not make people believe he raised Jesus from the dead (10:9, cf. Acts 17:32), again, at least not for now, for they shall see him, raised and exalted, when he returns on the Last Day. They can hear the Word of faith being proclaimed (10:8, 17) and refuse to be persuaded by it (ἀπειθέω, 10:21; the same verb as in 2:8; 11:30, 31; 15:31; also Acts 14:2; 19:9). As Paul has just stated: "But they did not all listen responsively to the Good News. For Isaiah says: 'Lord, who believed our message?' " (Rom 10:16, quoting Is 53:1).

Yet what is *God's* plan, purpose, will, and intent for *all* who hear? In the Lord Jesus Christ and through his Word (10:9, 17), "there is not a difference [between] a Jew and a Greek, for the same Lord [is] of all, being rich to all the ones who are calling on him. For 'everyone who ever might call on the name of [the] Lord will be saved' " (10:12–13). As Paul writes to Timothy, God "wills all people to be saved and to come to a proper recognition of [the] truth" (ὃς πάντας ἀνθρώπους θέλει σωθῆναι καὶ εἰς ἐπίγνωσιν ἀληθείας ἐλθεῖν, 1 Tim 2:4). Therefore he sends the Word (Rom 10:14–15, 18) of the Christ who has done it all "for us men and for our salvation" (Nicene Creed) out to *all*. He intends for the Good News to be heard by all and for all who hear to believe. After

---

92 Origen, *Romans* (Bray, *Romans*, ACCS NT 6:280).

93 See "Some Reject God's Gift of Salvation" in Mueller, *Called to Believe, Teach, and Confess*, 287.

citing Rom 10:17, the Formula of Concord captures this well: "It is God's will that men should hear his Word and not stop their ears" (FC Ep II 4–5). This is divine monergism,[94] which provides the only route which results in righteousness and salvation (10:10). These last two sections of Romans 10 (10:6–15 and 10:16–21) then resolve all the difficult passages in chapters 8 and 9 regarding God's plan, purpose, and desire (e.g., 8:29–30; 9:11–13, 18, 20, 22–23; see the commentary on those verses).

Human Response-ability

But along with divine monergism as the only way to salvation, humans retain the ability to *resist* and *refuse* salvation. People can hear the Word of Christ and, contrary to God's will, actively "stop their ears" (FC Ep II 5). We can refuse to believe or acknowledge its message. We can exercise our free will to be "unpersuaded and contradicting" (ἀπειθοῦντα καὶ ἀντιλέγοντα, 10:21). This has always been true among all who have heard the Word of Christ. It was true of those in Israel who heard the Word of Christ, which came to them in the form of the OT Word of promise. This ability to disbelieve is revealed *already in the original contexts* of the words of Isaiah cited here (Is 53:1; 65:1–2 in Rom 10:16, 20–21; see also, e.g., Deut 30:12–14 in Rom 10:6–8; Is 28:16 in Rom 10:11; Joel 2:32 [MT/LXX 3:5] in Rom 10:13).

> If this happened in Isaiah's day, it is not surprising that it should recur in Paul's day, the corollary being that there is nothing wrong with the gospel message or its messenger. The problem lies with the hearers.[95]

It was so in the first century among both Jews and Gentiles, as illustrated by Paul's experience in the many towns he visited on his missionary journeys.[96] It surely also *remains true today* among all those who hear the Word of Christ from those who have been sent to proclaim it (10:14–15), even though God's will is for the hearers to believe it.

God's Reacts

But how does God react to such rejection? While those individuals who die in unbelief do perish eternally, Paul will soon insist that God does *not* push away his people as a whole (11:1–2). Instead, he keeps sending out those who proclaim the "Word of Christ" (10:17). He still draws near to those not inquiring after or seeking him (10:8, 20). And, like the father in Jesus' parable about *two* lost sons (Lk 15:28; discussed in detail in the commentary on Rom 10:19;

---

[94] Divine monergism is the biblical teaching (-ism) that God (divine) alone (mono-) does all the work (-erg-) for our salvation. Neither human works nor human free will contribute to salvation in any way. For the topic, see further Article IV, "Justification," and Article XVIII, "Freedom of the Will," in both the Augsburg Confession and the Apology of the Augsburg Confession.

[95] Kruse, *Romans*, 417.

[96] See, e.g., Acts 19:9 (see also Acts 14:2), where people "were unpersuaded," that is, they disbelieved the Good News (ἀπειθέω, the same verb as in Rom 10:21).

see also the commentary on Rom 11:11–15), his hands remain stretched out to the unpersuaded and contradicting, inviting them to come in (Rom 10:21). Until the Day of Judgment, God the Father continues to urge those who have already heard the Good News, but not (yet) responsively, to believe the Word of Christ and confess the risen Lord Jesus and so to receive his righteousness and salvation through faith alone (10:9–10, 16, 18).

God's Response to Israel

Translation

11 ¹I say, then, God did not push his people away from himself, did he? May it never come to be! For I am also an Israelite, from the seed of Abraham, of the tribe of Benjamin. ²"God did not push his people away from himself" whom he knew relationally beforehand. Or do you not know in [the time of] Elijah what the Scripture says as he pleads to God against Israel? ³"Lord, they killed your prophets, they tore down your altars, and I myself was left alone, and they are seeking my life." ⁴But what does the divine oracle say to him? "I left for myself seven thousand men, such ones who did not bend a knee to Baal." ⁵Thus therefore also in the present momentous time a remnant has come to be and still exists according to [the] choice of grace. ⁶But if [his choice is] by grace, it is not from works since the grace would no longer be grace.

⁷What then? That which Israel seeks earnestly, this it did not obtain, but the chosen obtained, and the rest were hardened. ⁸Just as it stands written: "God gave to them a spirit of callousness, eyes to not see and ears to not hear, [and it has been that way] until this very day." ⁹And David says: "Let their table come to be for a trap and for a snare and for stumbling and for payback to them. ¹⁰Let their eyes become darkened to not see and bend their back continually."

¹¹I say, therefore, it is not that they tripped with the result that they might remain fallen, is it? May it never come to be! But by their stumble the salvation [comes] to the Gentiles in order to provoke them to envy. ¹²But if their stumble [is] richness of [the] world and their loss [is] richness of [the] Gentiles, how much more their fullness?

Textual Notes

11:1 λέγω οὖν—Aside from Eph 4:17, Paul uses this exact clause, "I say, then," only here and in 11:11. Thus it frames this section by highlighting Paul's opening and conclusion. Comparable statements with λέγω alone occur elsewhere in Romans (3:5; 6:19; 12:3; 15:8). Note λέγω, "I say," especially in 9:1 and congregated here (10:18, 19; 11:1, 11), emphasizing the personal nature of the subject for Paul.

μὴ ἀπώσατο … μὴ γένοιτο—In questions, μή indicates that a negative answer is expected,[1] one reinforced emphatically here by μὴ γένοιτο, "may it never come to be!" (see the first textual note on 3:4; see also 3:5–6; 9:14; 11:11). μὴ γένοιτο also serves as the sole negative response to neutral questions in 3:31; 6:2, 15; 7:7, 13. The literal sense of the compound verb ἀπωθέω is *push aside* (BDAG, 1) or "push away" based on the prefixed ἀπό. This physical meaning conveys the sense better than the metaphorical

---

[1] Voelz, *Fundamental Greek Grammar*, 261.

"*reject, repudiate*" (BDAG, 2). In the NT the verb ἀπωθέω occurs only in the middle voice; this voice of the aorist is translated in 11:1–2 as "he pushed away *from himself.*" The verb occurs elsewhere in Paul's writings only in 1 Tim 1:19, but note its use in Acts, as cited in the commentary. Paul's wording "God did not push his people away from himself" is drawn from 1 Sam 12:22 ‖ Ps 94:14 (LXX 93:14). Here in Rom 11:1 Paul alludes to those verses in his question. In 11:2 he quotes the verses as an affirmation.

τὸν λαὸν αὐτοῦ—The noun λαός, "people," occurs in Romans eight times, but seven are within direct quotations from the OT. This is the only exception, but it is anticipated from the quotation of 1 Sam 12:22 ‖ Ps 94:14 (LXX 93:14) in Rom 11:2. For Paul's use of λαός, see the commentary. 𝔓⁴⁶ has τὴν κληρονομίαν, "the inheritance," in place of τὸν λαόν, "the people," but this is drawn from the second clause of LXX Ps 93:14 (MT/ET 94:14). That verse reads ὅτι οὐκ ἀπώσεται κύριος τὸν λαὸν αὐτοῦ καὶ τὴν κληρονομίαν αὐτοῦ οὐκ ἐγκαταλείψει, "because [the] Lord will not push his people away from himself, and his inheritance he will not leave behind." τὸν λαόν, "the people," in the first clause, which Paul alludes to in 11:1 and quotes in 11:2, stands parallel to τὴν κληρονομίαν, "the inheritance," in the second clause. Thus the variant in 𝔓⁴⁶ is "a Western assimilation" to the psalm.[2]

Ἰσραηλίτης—The only other occurrence of "Israelite" in Romans is the plural in 9:4. See "God's People" in the introduction to Romans 9–11. Paul claims this and the next phrase as his own lineage also in 2 Cor 11:22: "They are Israelites; I am too. They are the seed of Abraham; I am too." Cf. Phil 3:5.

σπέρματος Ἀβραάμ—For σπέρμα, "seed," see the third textual note on 1:3, as well as 4:13. For the significance of "the seed of Abraham" as a consistent word of promise, see the commentary on 9:7.

φυλῆς Βενιαμίν—The noun φυλή designates "a subgroup of a nation characterized by a distinctive blood line, *tribe*" (BDAG, 1). It occurs only here in Romans. Paul uses the same phrase to describe himself as "of the tribe of Benjamin" in Phil 3:5. Cf. Rev 7:8.

11:2 οὐκ ἀπώσατο—Here οὐκ negates an indicative statement in answer to the question of 11:1, where this verb, ἀπώσατο, was already negated, first by μή and then again by μὴ γένοιτο. See the second textual note on 11:1.

προέγνω—This is the aorist indicative active third singular of προγινώσκω, "know beforehand." In Romans this verb appears here and in 8:29; see the second textual note and the commentary there.

ἐν Ἠλίᾳ—This is the dative form of Ἠλίας, which is the spelling the LXX sometimes uses for the rare short form of the Hebrew name אֵלִיָּה, "Elijah," which appropriately and prophetically means "my God [is] Yah[weh]."[3] The preposition ἐν

---

[2]   Metzger, *A Textual Commentary on the Greek New Testament*, 526.

[3]   In the canonical books of the OT, the LXX uses Ηλιας or Ηλια only in Mal 3:22 (MT 3:23; ET 4:5), which refers to God sending a (new) "Elijah," and in Ezra 10:26; 1 Chr 8:27 (cf. Ezra 10:21), which refer to other Elijahs. The LXX consistently uses the spelling Ηλιου for the prophet Elijah, regardless of whether he is designated in Hebrew by the usual long form of the name, אֵלִיָּהוּ, "Elijahu," or the rare short form, אֵלִיָּה, "Elijah."

along with the dative Ἠλίᾳ here could mean "in the section of Scripture which narrates the story of Elijah."[4] Sanday and Headlam support this by (1) noting how "the O. T. Scriptures were divided into paragraphs to which were given titles derived from their subject-matter" and (2) references from the Talmud and Hebrew commentaries.[5] Moo gives as the only NT parallels ἐπὶ τοῦ βάτου in Mk 12:26 and ἐπὶ τῆς βάτου in Lk 20:37, which he interprets as "[in the section of the Book of Moses] about the bush."[6] But Sanday and Headlam suggest that the use of the preposition ἐπί in those passages is "perhaps purely local" and that those verses thus are probably not comparable.[7] It seems simplest to read ἐν here in Rom 11:2 temporally as an expression of "time within which."[8] Cf. ἐν τῷ Ὡσηέ, "in Hosea," in Rom 9:25.

ἐντυγχάνει ... κατὰ τοῦ Ἰσραήλ—For the verb ἐντυγχάνω, "plead, intercede," see the fourth textual note on 8:27, where the Spirit "pleads" for the saints; it appears also in 8:34, where Christ "is pleading" for us. In both earlier cases a more positive sense of "pleading" is adopted. Here the preposition κατά followed by the genitive τοῦ Ἰσραήλ indicates opposition:[9] Elijah is not interceding on behalf of Israel but, rather, pleading "*against* Israel," as is evident from 1 Ki 19:10, 14, quoted in Rom 11:3. See the commentary.

11:3 κύριε—For the vocative "Lord," see the fifth textual note on 10:16.

τὰ θυσιαστήρια—The noun θυσιαστήριον denotes "a structure on which cultic observances are carried out, including esp[ecially] sacrifices, *altar*" (BDAG, 1). The plural reflects a general sense of multiple altars for pagan deities (plural θυσιαστήρια in, e.g., Judg 2:2; 2 Ki 11:18; 23:12, 20), indicative of the Divided Kingdom era, in contrast to *the* altar in Jerusalem (singular θυσιαστήριον in, e.g., 1 Ki 8:54, 64).

κατέσκαψαν—The simple verb σκάπτω means to "*dig*" or "*cultivate*" (BDAG, 1 and 2). The compound verb here, κατασκάπτω (κατά + σκάπτω), adds emphasis: "*tear down, raze to the ground*" (BDAG). The form is aorist active. It translates הָרַס in 1 Ki 19:10, 14, which also is the verb in God's command to tear down pagan shrines in Ex 23:24.

ὑπελείφθην—This is an aorist passive of ὑπολείπω, "*leave remaining*" (BDAG). The basic root λείπω means "leave behind" or "*lack*" (BDAG, 1 and 2). The compound verb ὑπολείπω (ὑπό + λείπω) occurs only here in the NT, but the more common compound καταλείπω is in 11:4. Note also the cognate noun λεῖμμα, "remnant," in 11:5.

τὴν ψυχήν μου—This translates נַפְשִׁי in 1 Ki 19:10, 14. Due to the influence of the Hebrew נֶפֶשׁ, the noun ψυχή in the NT often denotes the "whole self" or "life,"

---

[4] Sanday and Headlam, *Romans*, 310.

[5] Sanday and Headlam, *Romans*, 310, followed by Cranfield, *Romans*, 545; BDAG, s.v. ἐν, 1 a.

[6] Moo, *Romans*, 675, n. 22.

[7] Sanday and Headlam, *Romans*, 311.

[8] Wallace, *Greek Grammar*, 372, including n. 44, speaking of the temporal use of ἐν plus the dative in general; he adds this comment which explains the presence of the preposition: "This 'time within which' notion is almost never found with the simple dat[ive]."

[9] See Wallace, *Greek Grammar*, 376.

including the soul, whereas in secular Greek literature it typically refers to the "soul" as conceived in Greek thought. For further explanation, see the second textual note on 2:9; note especially ψυχή in 1 Pet 3:20.

11:4 ὁ χρηματισμός—This noun refers to "a *divine statement, answer*" (BDAG). The term occurs only here in the NT. But its meaning in 2 Macc 2:4 is comparable, and elsewhere in the NT the cognate verb χρηματίζω can refer to divine revelation (e.g., Lk 2:26; Acts 10:22; Heb 8:5). This supports the meaning of the noun here as "the divine oracle." See the commentary.

κατέλιπον—The compound verb καταλείπω, with prefixed κατά, means "to cause someth[ing] to remain in existence or be left over, *leave over*" (BDAG, 4). Paul employs it in other contexts in Eph 5:31; 1 Thess 3:1. It is another verb based upon λείπω in another OT quotation (here 1 Ki 19:18); see previously the fourth textual note on Rom 11:3 (quoting 1 Ki 19:10, 14), which has ὑπολείπω, a synonym (ὑπελείφθην, "I was left"). See also the cognate noun λεῖμμα, "remnant," in 11:5.

ἑπτακισχιλίους—The compound of ἑπτά, "seven," with χίλιοι, "thousands," forms the Greek number seven thousand.

ἔκαμψαν γόνυ—The verb κάμπτω means "to bend or incline some part of the body, *bend, bow*" (BDAG, 1). It is followed by the singular accusative noun γόνυ, "knee," as its direct object, conveying the idea "to bend a knee" in religious devotion or worship. LXX 1 Ki 19:18 has a similar idiom, ὤκλασαν γόνυ, but in the Hebrew original, "knees" are the subject: כָּל־הַבִּרְכַּיִם אֲשֶׁר לֹא־כָרְעוּ, "all the knees which did not bow." See the commentary.

τῇ Βάαλ—Since בַּעַל, "Baal," is a masculine Hebrew name, and LXX 1 Ki 19:18 has the masculine article τῷ before Βααλ, "Baal," Paul's use of the feminine article τῇ before the name is intriguing. Nineteen other LXX passages do use the feminine Greek article with his name.[10] The likely reason is that the feminine Greek noun αἰσχύνη, "shame," was implied as an equivalent or replacement for "Baal."[11] The LXX actually makes that substitution in a couple verses: whereas MT 1 Ki 18:19, 25 refer to "the prophets of Baal" (וּנְבִיאֵי הַבַּעַל), LXX 1 Ki 18:19, 25 refer to "the prophets of *the shame*" (τῆς αἰσχύνης). The LXX substitution, in turn, likely derives from Hebrew practice. Within the Hebrew canon of the MT, the name בַּעַל, "Baal," is in some cases replaced by the feminine Hebrew noun בֹּשֶׁת, "shame."[12]

11:5 ἐν τῷ νῦν καιρῷ—See the third textual note on 3:26.

---

[10] The same phrase as in Rom 11:4, τῇ Βααλ, appears in, e.g., LXX Judg 2:13; 2 Ki 1:2–3; 21:3; and often in Jeremiah, e.g., LXX Jer 2:8, 28; 7:9; 11:13, 17; 12:16.

[11] Similar explanations are in Cranfield, *Romans*, 547, and Munck, *Christ and Israel*, 109, including n. 157, citing C. F. A. Dillmann, "Über Baal mit dem weiblichen Artikel (ἡ βάαλ)," *Monatsbericht der Königlich Preussischen Akademie der Wissenschaften zu Berlin* 16 (1881): 601–20.

[12] The name of Saul's fourth son is given as אֶשְׁבַּעַל, "Eshbaal," meaning "man of Baal," in 1 Chr 8:33; 9:39. However, in 2 Samuel 2–4 he is named אִישׁ־בֹּשֶׁת, "Ish-bosheth," meaning "man of shame." Whereas MT 2 Sam 2:8 reads אִישׁ־בֹּשֶׁת, "Ish-bosheth," some manuscripts of LXX 2 Sam 2:8 read Εισβααλ, "Ish-baal." For this and other examples of such substitutions, see Tov, *Textual Criticism of the Hebrew Bible*, 267–69.

λεῖμμα—This noun occurs only here in the NT, but it is a theologically important term for the "remnant." See the commentary. See also the related vocabulary in the sixth textual note on 9:27 and the fifth textual note on 9:29.

κατ᾿ ἐκλογὴν χάριτος—For ἐκλογή, "choice," see the fifth textual note on 9:11; it also occurs in 11:7, 28. For χάρις, "grace," see the second textual note on 1:5 and the commentary on 1:7; note also 3:24. Although χάρις appears twenty-four times in Romans, only four occurrences are in Romans 9–11, here and three more in the next verse, 11:6. The entire phrase in 11:5 expresses "an election characterized by grace."[13] The genitive χάριτος may reflect a Hebrew construct state, which can have an adjectival meaning, hence "a gracious election."[14] Dunn further describes it as "God's free and unconditional choice."[15] Cf. κατὰ χάριν in 4:4, 16.

γέγονεν—The verb γίνομαι occurs thirty-five times in Romans. In the perfect tense, as here, the verb conveys both "to come into being" (BDAG, 1) and "to be present at a given time" (BDAG, 8). Cf. γεγόναμεν, "we have become," in 6:5. For the theological significance, see the commentary.

11:6 εἰ δὲ χάριτι—For χάρις, see 11:5. As in 3:24, the dative case expresses means:[16] "*by* grace."

οὐκέτι ἐξ ἔργων—For "from works," see 3:20 and the excursus "The Background of 'Works of the Law' " following the commentary on 3:9–20. The presence of οὐκέτι might at first seem problematic since it often conveys a temporal element, "*no longer*" (BDAG, 1), as it means in the next textual note. However, οὐκέτι can also serve as a "marker of inference in a logical process, *not*" (BDAG, 2, citing this instance in 11:6a), as also in, e.g., Rom 7:17, 20; 14:15; Gal 3:18 (see the first textual note on Rom 7:17). The context within a conditional sentence introduced by εἰ identifies its function here as logical: "*if* by grace, *then not* from works." The thought of 11:5b–6 can be expressed more fully in this way: since God's choice *is* by grace, therefore (logically) it *cannot* be from works, since *if* it *were* from works (which it is not), then the "grace" in "choice of grace" could not be or mean "grace."

ἐπεὶ ἡ χάρις οὐκέτι γίνεται χάρις—Here the conjunction ἐπεί, rather than having a temporal element (BDAG, 1), functions according to its most common use as a "marker of cause or reason, *because, since, for*" (BDAG, 2); cf. οὐκέτι in the preceding textual note. Here, however, οὐκέτι is translated temporally: if the divine choice were from works, then "the grace would *no longer* be grace."

At the end of the verse, the Textus Receptus and ℵᶜ add the sentence εἰ δὲ ἐξ ἔργων οὐκέτι ἐστὶ χάρις ἐπεὶ τὸ ἔργον οὐκέτι ἐστὶν ἔργον, "but if [it is] from works, it is no longer grace, since the work is not/no longer work." This is retained in translation

---

[13] Moo, *Romans*, 677, n. 35.

[14] Wallace, *Greek Grammar*, 86–88, including n. 44, discusses the attributive genitive (Hebrew genitive), citing BDF, § 165. Hebrew has a paucity of adjectives and commonly employs nouns in construct phrases to express attributive or adjectival meanings.

[15] Dunn, *Romans*, 639.

[16] See Wallace, *Greek Grammar*, 162–63.

by the KJV and NKJV. But the shorter reading is far better attested (e.g., $\mathfrak{P}^{46}$ א*A C D) and preferred.[17]

11:7 τί οὖν;—See the first textual note on 3:1.

ἐπέτυχεν—The verb ἐπιτυγχάνω occurs only twice in Romans, both times in this verse and in the identical form, the aorist indicative active third singular. The verb means "to be successful in achieving or gaining what one seeks, *obtain, attain to, reach* w[ith] gen[itive] of what is reached" (BDAG), but no genitive object follows here. In light of 9:30–31 and the parallel sense of φθάνω in 9:31, the thought can be similarly expanded here to "did not obtain *righteousness*," with all that God's righteousness entails.

ἡ δὲ ἐκλογή—Whereas this noun had an active meaning, referring to God's "choosing" or "choice" in 11:5 (also 9:11; 11:28), here it has the corresponding passive meaning, what God has "*chosen*" (BDAG, 2).

οἱ δὲ λοιποί—The adjective λοιπός (here in the nominative plural) "pert[ains] to being one not previously cited or included, *other, rest of*," and functions substantively here (BDAG, 2 and 2 b). For the specific referent, see the commentary.

ἐπωρώθησαν—This is the first aorist passive of πωρόω, which means "to cause someone to have difficulty in understanding or comprehending, *harden, petrify*, mostly of hearts" (BDAG; see πωρόω with καρδία, "to harden the heart," in Mk 6:52; 8:17; Jn 12:40). Cranfield notes how πωρόω "was used with reference to the formation of a stone in the bladder or of a callus by which the extremities of fractured bones are reunited, and so came to be used metaphorically of the hardening of men's hearts."[18] Note the cognate noun πώρωσις, "hardening," in 11:25. In light of ἔδωκεν ... ὁ θεός, "God gave," in the next verse (11:8), the passive here should be interpreted as "a *divine passive* (or *theological passive*)" wherein "*God is the obvious agent*,"[19] thus "they were hardened" by God. The verb πωρόω is a synonym of σκληρύνω, "harden," which Paul used in 9:18. See "Hardening" in "Is This Fair to the Pharaoh? (9:17–18)" in the commentary on 9:14–24.

11:8 καθὼς γέγραπται—This is Paul's usual formula for citing Scripture: "just as it stands written." See the fourth textual note on 1:17. Most of the quote is from Deut 29:4 (MT/LXX 29:3), but Paul includes a phrase from Is 29:10.

πνεῦμα κατανύξεως—The noun κατάνυξις, meaning "*stupefaction*" (BDAG), occurs only here in the NT, but the phrase πνεῦμα κατανύξεως, "a spirit of callousness," is drawn from Is 29:10, which has the Hebrew construct phrase רוּחַ תַּרְדֵּמָה, "a spirit of deep sleep." See the commentary.

ὀφθαλμοὺς τοῦ μὴ βλέπειν καὶ ὦτα τοῦ μὴ ἀκούειν—The two articular infinitives, τοῦ βλέπειν, "to see," and τοῦ ἀκούειν, "to hear," are each negated with μή and convey

---

[17] Metzger, *A Textual Commentary on the Greek New Testament*, 526; Moo, *Romans*, 670, n. 2, is even "certain that the shorter reading is original."

[18] Cranfield, *Romans*, 549.

[19] Wallace, *Greek Grammar*, 437–38.

the result of the stupefaction: the eyes do not see and the ears do not hear.[20] See the commentary for the differences between Paul's wording and LXX Deut 29:3 (ET 29:4).

ἕως τῆς σήμερον ἡμέρας—This seemingly redundant expression, literally, "until the today day," means "until today, this very day" (see BDAG, s.v. σήμερον). The entire phrase is drawn from the underlying Hebrew in Deut 29:3 (ET 29:4), עַד הַיּוֹם הַזֶּה, "until this day."

11:9–10 In these two verses Paul quotes from LXX Ps 68:23–24 (MT 69:23–24; ET 69:22–23). In Rom 11:9 only the initial part of his wording follows the LXX, but he reproduces it exactly in Rom 11:10.

11:9 γενηθήτω ... εἰς—In Paul's wording, the aorist imperative of γίνομαι is followed by four prepositional phrases, each beginning with εἰς, "let it be for ..." This reflects the construction of the Hebrew jussive יְהִי- followed by לְ, "let it become ... ," in MT Ps 69:23 (ET 69:22). While εἰς is translated with "for," all four of the Greek prepositional phrases function as predicate nominatives "due to a Semitic influence (Hebrew לְ)."[21]

ἡ τράπεζα—This noun refers to any "structure or surface on which food or other things can be placed, *table*" (BDAG, 1). While early LXX references are restricted to the table of showbread (as in Heb 9:2), its extension to other tables via *shared* sacrificial meals seems likely.[22] This informs the religious importance of the fellowship involved at any "*table* upon which a meal is spread out" (BDAG, 1 b). See τράπεζα in Lk 22:30; 1 Cor 10:21; cf. other vocabulary for table fellowship in Acts 2:42; 11:3; Rom 14:1–3. In the Greek Orthodox tradition the noun τράπεζα is used for the dining hall in a monastery, where monks and guests gather for food and discussion.

εἰς παγίδα—The noun παγίς denotes a "*trap, snare*" (BDAG, 1). Paul quotes παγίδα from LXX Ps 68:23 (MT 69:23; ET 69:22), where it renders the Hebrew noun פַּח. Elsewhere the LXX can use παγίς to translate the Hebrew noun רֶשֶׁת, "net," as in LXX Ps 9:16 (ET 9:15) and LXX Ps 56:7 (MT 57:7; ET 57:6), where unbelievers set a "net" to entrap David, but, ironically, the enemies themselves are the ones who become ensnared in it. Similar is the LXX use of παγίς to translate פַּח in Jer 18:22; see also παγίς translating פַּח in references to divine judgment in LXX Is 24:17–18; Jer 31:43–44 (MT/ET Jer 48:43–44). The change of a mealtime "table" into "that which causes one to be suddenly endangered or unexpectedly brought under control of a hostile force, *trap, snare*" (BDAG, 2) is both abrupt and ominous. Cf. Lk 22:21.

εἰς θήραν—In Classical Greek and in the LXX the noun θήρα usually refers to hunting or to the beasts hunted as prey, but it can also denote a "*net, trap*" (BDAG). It appears in that sense as a synonym in parallel with παγίς here and in LXX Ps 34:8 (MT/ET 35:8). This noun too is used in passages depicting God's judgment (e.g., LXX Is 31:4; Amos 3:4; Nah 2:13–14 [ET 2:12–13]; 3:1).

---

[20] Wallace, *Greek Grammar*, 592–94, discusses the infinitive of result, though this passage is included among disputed verses where purpose may also be involved (592, n. 8).

[21] Wallace, *Greek Grammar*, 40, 47–48 (quote 47); see also BDF, § 145.2; this construction also occurs in 4:3, 5.

[22] See the commentary and Schreiner, *Romans*, 589, n. 6, for various views.

εἰς σκάνδαλον—This noun usually refers to "stumbling"; see the third textual note on 9:33. Dunn notes that the prepositional phrase εἰς σκάνδαλον "may be translated 'as a lure or trap' and appears quite often in the LXX."[23] See the commentary for this other meaning as an explanation for Paul's reordering of the psalm verse.

εἰς ἀνταπόδομα—BDAG, s.v. ἀνταπόδομα, 2, defines this noun as "that which is given in return for behavior, *recompense.*—As punishment, as mostly in LXX (w[ith] σκάνδαλον)." BDAG then translates it in this verse as "retribution." This commentary renders it with the common term "payback" to convey the thought.

11:10 σκοτισθήτωσαν—As in 1:21, the passive of the verb σκοτίζω, "to darken," functions metaphorically for "*be/become inwardly darkened*" (BDAG, 2). The form here is an aorist passive imperative: "may they become darkened."

τοῦ μὴ βλέπειν—See the identical expression in the third textual note on 11:8.

τὸν νῶτον—The noun νῶτος, "*back*" (BDAG), occurs only here in the NT and comes in Paul's quotation of LXX Ps 68:24 (MT 69:24; ET 69:23).

διὰ παντός—This is an expression of time, literally, "through all." BDAG gives "*always, continually, constantly*" (s.v. διά, 2 a). Against "for ever" in RSV, Cranfield properly argues that "the recent tendency to translate διὰ παντός by 'for ever' ... is surely mistaken. The meaning is rather 'continually.' "[24] The underlying Hebrew adverb תָּמִיד (MT Ps 69:24 [ET 69:23]) validates Cranfield's view since it means "going on without interruption = *continuously*" (BDB, 1 a).

σύγκαμψον—The compound verb συγκάμπτω, "*(cause to) bend*" (BDAG), occurs elsewhere in the NT only as a variant reading in Lk 13:11, where it is used literally. Here the aorist active imperative is addressed to God, asking him bend someone's back in a metaphorical sense, for which, see the commentary.

11:11 λέγω οὖν—See the first textual note on 11:1.

μὴ ἔπταισαν—The μή indicates that a negative answer is anticipated,[25] and this is further reinforced by μὴ γένοιτο, "may it never come to be!" as in 11:1, where a question phrased with μή is then followed by μὴ γένοιτο (see the second textual note on 11:1). The verb πταίω means "to lose one's footing, *stumble, trip*" (BDAG, 1). In contrast with the passive voice ἐπωρώθησαν, "were hardened," in 11:7, the active voice here is significant.[26] Thus "they stumbled/tripped." *Paul does not say or imply they were tripped (by God).*

ἵνα πέσωσιν—Both elements here are important. The conjunction ἵνα expresses result, *not* divine purpose.[27] One should note that the subject of this active verb, as well as the one in the preceding textual note, is third person plural, referring to those in Israel

23 Dunn, *Romans*, 643, citing LXX Josh 23:13; Judg 2:3; 8:27 A; 1 Sam 18:21; Ps 105:36 (MT/ET 106:36); Wisdom 14:11; 1 Macc 5:4.

24 Cranfield, *Romans*, 552; also against Barrett, *Romans*, 210.

25 Voelz, *Fundamental Greek Grammar*, 261.

26 Cranfield, *Romans*, 554.

27 Wallace, *Greek Grammar*, 473, citing this passage as an example of a result ἵνα clause; so also Cranfield, *Romans*, 554; Sanday and Headlam, *Romans*, 321; contra Käsemann, *Romans*, 304; Murray, *Romans*, 2:76.

who "tripped." Thus *God is not doing or causing either action*. Therefore Sanday and Headlam's discussion properly concludes: "It is only a confusion of ideas that can see any [divine] purpose."[28] See the commentary. The aorist subjunctive of πίπτω "suggests lying after a fall rather than the fall itself,"[29] and so conveys a different sense than the form of πταίω which immediately precedes this clause (see the previous textual note). Thus this commentary translates πέσωσιν as "they might remain fallen"; one could also say "they might lie felled." When used figuratively, πίπτω has the extended sense of "to experience loss of status or condition, *fall, be destroyed*" (BDAG, 2). Cranfield contends: "This verb is here used to denote that falling which means irreversible ruin,"[30] but Paul's response to the query is in the negative; see the next textual note.

μὴ γένοιτο—For "may it never come to be!" see the first textual note on 3:4; see also the second textual note on 11:1.

τῷ αὐτῶν παραπτώματι—For the noun παράπτωμα, see the second textual note on 4:25; note also its repeated use for Adam's "trespass" and its consequences in 5:15, 16, 17, 18, 20. But the contextual sense here and in 11:12 is the more literal "stumble." It depicts "one making a false step so as to lose footing" (BDAG); see the commentary. In regard to the dative case, Moo argues that "the common instrumental meaning has moved over into a causal sense."[31] But a dative of means[32] seems most appropriate: "by their stumble."

εἰς τὸ παραζηλῶσαι αὐτούς—For the verb παραζηλόω, "provoke to envy," see the third textual note and the commentary on 10:19. The articular infinitive τὸ παραζηλῶσαι preceded by εἰς can express purpose and/or result.[33] Both make sense here as the active infinitive conveys that God provokes unbelieving Israelites in order to make them envious of what believing Gentiles now have in Christ, but it is also his *hoped for* result, ultimately leading to a far greater good for them.

11:12 παράπτωμα—See the fifth textual note on 11:11.

πλοῦτος κόσμου ... πλοῦτος ἐθνῶν—For the noun πλοῦτος, "richness," see 2:4; also 9:23; 11:33. Note the cognate verb πλουτέω in 10:12, where the Lord is "being rich" to all who call on him. The genitives that follow here are objective,[34] indicating that the κόσμου, "world," that is, ἐθνῶν, "Gentiles," stands as the recipient of God's "richness." Paul does not specify the explicit *content* of this abundance here. Yet it can be identified as ἡ σωτηρία τοῖς ἔθνεσιν, "the salvation to the Gentiles," in 11:11, together with all its accompanying "richness" (πλοῦτος in Eph 1:7, 18; 2:7; 3:8; Col 1:27; 2:2; cf. πλουτίζω in 1 Cor 1:5; 2 Cor 6:10). Moo emphasizes "the richness of

---

[28] Sanday and Headlam, *Romans*, 321.

[29] W. Michaelis, "πίπτω," *TDNT* 6:164.

[30] Cranfield, *Romans*, 555, including n. 1, citing LXX Is 24:20; Ps Sol 3:10; Heb 4:11.

[31] Moo, *Romans*, 687, n. 19.

[32] See Wallace, *Greek Grammar*, 162–63.

[33] See Wallace, *Greek Grammar*, 590–94, 611.

[34] See Wallace, *Greek Grammar*, 116–19.

spiritual blessing," noting that "Paul frequently uses the word to refer to the riches of God's grace and mercy."[35]

τὸ ἥττημα αὐτῶν—The noun ἥττημα occurs elsewhere in the Greek Bible only in LXX Is 31:8 and 1 Cor 6:7, where it expresses "defeat."[36] Here BDAG properly gives "*loss*." The noun is derived from the verb ἡττάομαι, "to be vanquished, *be defeated, succumb*" (BDAG, 1). In response to the KJV's use of "diminishing" here, Cranfield properly rejects "the habit of explaining ἥττημα as meaning here either 'diminution' or 'fewness,' in order to have a neat antithesis to πλήρωμα ['fullness']" later in the verse.[37] See further the commentary and the second textual note below.

πόσῳ μᾶλλον—This expression, "how much more" (also in 11:24), is comparable to πολλῷ … μᾶλλον discussed in the first textual note on 5:9 (also used in 5:10, 15, 17).

τὸ πλήρωμα αὐτῶν—Cranfield offers the following possible definitions for πλήρωμα here: "(i) complete conversion, complete restoration; (ii) fulfilment, consummation, perfection; (iii) obedience (fulfilment of God's will—cf. πλήρωμα … νόμου in 13.10); (iv) full and completed number."[38] Here πλήρωμα likely conveys the last option; it refers to "that which is brought to fullness or completion" (BDAG, 3). Thus the entire phrase describes "their *full number*" (see BDAG, 3 a). The genitive case of αὐτῶν, "their," is partitive, "of them; of the Israelites." It "denotes *the whole of which* the head noun is a part,"[39] i.e., "their" refers to all the Israelites, and "the fullness" refers to part of the Israelites. See the commentary.

Commentary

Introduction to Romans 11:1–12

A Connected Beginning

The initial "I say, then" (λέγω οὖν) in 11:1 indicates that Paul is clearly moving forward here, but, as usual, in reaction to what precedes. The connections between 10:16–21 and 11:1–12 are indicated both by form and content. In regard to form, note the interrogatives which begin 10:18, 19; 11:1, 11. Cranfield observes:

> Common to all these four questions are λέγω ["I say"] and μή ["not"], introducing a question expecting a negative answer, and the use of a verb in the aorist [past] tense. This similarity of form underlines the connexion between 11.1 and the preceding verses.[40]

This commentary contends that this section extends through 11:11–12,[41] which follows the same format.

---

[35] Moo, *Romans*, 688, n. 28.
[36] Cranfield, *Romans*, 557.
[37] Cranfield, *Romans*, 557.
[38] Cranfield, *Romans*, 558.
[39] Wallace, *Greek Grammar*, 84; see 84–86.
[40] Cranfield, *Romans*, 543.
[41] So also Hultgren, *Romans*, 396.

A second formal connection with the previous section stems from the manner in which the Word of God replies to Paul's questions. Dunn lays out the pattern as follows:[42]

Question	Scripture
10:18a	10:18b
10:19a	10:19b–21
11:1a	11:2a
11:2b	11:3
11:4a	11:4b
11:7a	11:8–10
11:11	

Thus the sequence of nearly continuous questions answered by passages Paul draws from the OT continues unabated from the end of Romans 10 and straight into chapter 11.

Paul again draws his sources from each of the major sections of the Hebrew Bible. As in 10:18–21, and later in 15:9–12, Paul chooses his OT texts broadly in order to represent the Torah, the Prophets,[43] and the Psalms (chief among the Writings):

Scripture Cited	Romans 11
1 Sam 12:22 ‖ Ps 94:14 (LXX 93:14)	11:2 (cf. 11:1)
1 Ki 19:10, 14	11:3
1 Ki 19:18	11:4
Deut 29:4 (MT/LXX 29:3)	11:8
Is 29:10	11:8
Ps 69:22–23 (MT 69:23–24; LXX 68:23–24)	11:9–10

While the chapter break at 11:1 is appropriate, the presence of "people" (λαός, 10:21; 11:1, 2) in three consecutive verses ties the thought of 10:21–11:2 together. In terms of subject matter, the final section of Romans 10 (10:16–21) depicts the inadequate response of some in Israel to God. Now how will God react? Will he "push away" (11:1, 2) those who did not listen responsively to or believe the Good News he sent to them (10:14–16), a message they both heard and knew (10:18–19)? How will he respond "to an unpersuaded and contradicting people" (10:21)? Specific reactions of God are stated in 11:2, 4, 7, 8, 11. The character of God remains central to Paul's discussion in Romans 9–11 and throughout the entire letter.[44] He perhaps hones in on it most directly beginning in 11:1.

---

[42] Dunn, *Romans*, 634.

[43] In the Hebrew canon of the OT, the books of Samuel and Kings are considered prophetic and are included among the Former Prophets.

[44] Middendorf, *Romans 1–8*, 21–22, 27, 49–51; in this volume, see "Romans 1–4: The Righteousness of God" in the introduction to Romans 9–16, as well as "God" in "The Three Foci of Romans 9–11" in the introduction to Romans 9–11. See also the commentary on 1:17, 32; 2:11, 16, 29; 3:1–8, 19–20, 29–30; 4:21; 9:5, 11b–12a, 16, 22–24, 29; 10:21; 11:1–2, 33–36; 12:19; 13:1–2; 14:10–12; 15:5, 8, 13; 16:25, 27.

A Contested Conclusion

But where does this section conclude? A sizable number of scholars contend it ends with 11:10.[45] But to insist that the "I say, therefore, it is not ..." (λέγω οὖν, μὴ ...) of 11:11 must mark a new section overlooks 10:18 and 10:19, where a very similar expression, "but I say, it is not ..." (ἀλλὰ λέγω, μὴ ...), occurs twice in sequential verses treating the same topic. Breaking after 11:10 is both structurally unwarranted and theologically misleading.

Instead, Paul *frames* his focus on God's response to Israel by using "I say, then/therefore" (λέγω οὖν) twice, at the beginning (11:1) and again to signal his concluding thought at the end (11:11). Both clauses introduce interrogatives which Paul proceeds to answer in 11:1–2 and 11:11–12 respectively. More importantly, God's response to those in Israel who did not listen responsively to the Good News does *not* end with "the rest were hardened" in 11:7. That action, while supported with Scripture in 11:8–10, is not yet explained and cannot be left unresolved. *What possible good can come of this hardening, and does it provide an indication that God has, in fact, pushed away his people, as 11:1 asks?* Käsemann properly recognizes that 11:11–12 deals with "the problem posed in v. 1a."[46] Paul rejects the notion that God's hardening action toward some in Israel is the final end for the whole people.[47] On the contrary, he intends for it to serve his ultimate, overarching goal of salvation for *both* Israel *and* Gentiles. This becomes clear only in 11:11–12.[48]

A further indication of the transition at 11:13 is the shift in addressees marked by the emphatic placement of the personal pronoun which begins 11:13: "But to *you Gentiles* I say" (ὑμῖν δὲ λέγω τοῖς ἔθνεσιν). Bruce and others properly mark 11:13 as the beginning of a new section wherein Paul speaks more narrowly to Gentile Christians.[49] Paul then focuses his attention on them throughout 11:13–24 (see the next commentary section). This narrowing of addressees at 11:13 adds further support to placing a break after 11:12.

---

[45] For example, Barth, *Romans*, 400; Cranfield, *Romans*, 542; Dunn, *Romans*, 634; Franzmann, *Romans*, 197; Kruse, *Romans*, 421; Moo, *Romans*, 670, Morris, *Romans*, 397; and Nygren, *Romans*, 361.

[46] Käsemann, *Romans*, 304, though he points out that the problem posed in 11:1a is also dealt with in 11:15 and 11:23–24.

[47] For those *individuals* (Jews and Gentiles alike) who die "unpersuaded" (10:21), without God's righteousness in Christ, their hardening is indeed final, and their stumbling (11:11–12) ends in eternal death.

[48] Keener, *Romans*, 133, n. 12, observes how "Paul reinforces the point rhetorically in 11:12 by key nouns ending in *-tōma, -tēma,* and *-ōma,* as well as four nouns beginning with *p* (*paraptōma, ploutos* [twice], and *plērōma*)." Greek nouns ending in *-ma* (-μα) "express the result of an action" (BDAG, s.v. δικαίωμα, 3), as they do so predominantly in 5:15–21. All of this underscores the culminating nature of 11:12, and it militates against viewing 11:11–12 as inaugurating a new line of thought.

[49] Bruce, *Romans*, 203, titles the section "Admonition to Gentile Christians (11:13–24)." That 11:13 begins a new section is recognized also by Matera, *Romans*, 260, who titles 11:13–24 "A warning to Gentile believers," and Hultgren, *Romans*, 405, who entitles the section "How Should Gentiles Think in the Present Situation? 11:13–24."

An Abhorrent Thought Rejected (11:1–4)
God Did Not Push His People Away (11:1–2a)
Paul's Shocking Proposal (11:1a)

The last verse of Romans 10 speaks directly about Israel—"to Israel he says" (πρὸς ... τὸν Ἰσραὴλ λέγει, 10:21)—and characterizes them as "an unpersuaded and contradicting people" (λαὸν ἀπειθοῦντα καὶ ἀντιλέγοντα, 10:21). How will God react to a people who respond to him in such a way? That is the focus of the discussion as Romans 11 opens. "I say, then, God did not push his people away from himself, did he? May it never come to be!" (11:1a). Rather than pushing them away, 10:21 has already stated just the opposite. There Paul cites Is 65:2, where the Lord himself declares: "The whole day I stretched out my hands" (ἐξεπέτασα τὰς χεῖράς μου, Rom 10:21) toward them.

Without further definition, "people" (λαός) in 11:1 refers to the chosen people collectively. As with the term "Israel," however, the primary emphasis is theological, not ethnic (see "God's People" in the introduction to Romans 9–11). In the approximately two thousand occurrences of "people" (λαός) in the LXX, most are singular and translate the Hebrew עַם.[50] This term (λαός), therefore, denotes "a specific people, namely, Israel, and it serves to emphasize the special and privileged religious position of this people as the people of God."[51] This positive connotation in the OT is exemplified by passages like 1 Chr 17:21. LXX 1 Chr 17:21 reads: "And there is not a nation yet upon the earth like your *people* Israel, as God led him [Israel] to redeem for himself a *people*" (καὶ οὐκ ἔστιν ὡς ὁ λαός σου Ισραηλ ἔθνος ἔτι ἐπὶ τῆς γῆς, ὡς ὡδήγησεν αὐτὸν ὁ θεὸς τοῦ λυτρώσασθαι ἑαυτῷ λαόν; the MT begins וּמִי כְעַמְּךָ יִשְׂרָאֵל). It is intriguing, therefore, that except in Titus 2:14, Paul uses this term for "people" (λαός) only in OT allusions or quotations.[a]

The radical suggestion that God might push away his own people is by no means novel. Dunn notes: "Paul clearly has in mind the regular OT usage, where the thought of God rejecting his people was entertained as a prospect, or question or conclusion."[52] Dunn continues: "The assurance that God has *not* rejected or will not reject his people was voiced much less frequently, at least in the same terms."[53] Cranfield contends that Rom 11:1 is "clearly reminiscent of OT passages which declare categorically that God will not cast off His people."[54] Paul negates the shocking proposal here within the form of the

(a) Rom 9:25–26; 10:21; 11:1–2; 15:10–11; 1 Cor 10:7; 14:21; 2 Cor 6:16

[50] The noun λαός, "people," occurs 1,966 times in the LXX. Of these 144 instances are plural. According to H. Strathmann, "λαός," *TDNT* 4:32, the underlying Hebrew is עַם in all but about 40 of the occurrences.

[51] H. Strathmann, "λαός," *TDNT* 4:32.

[52] Dunn, *Romans*, 634, citing Judg 6:13; 2 Ki 23:27; Pss 44:9, 23 (MT 44:10, 24); 60:1, 10 (MT 60:3, 12); 74:1; 78:60, 67; 108:11 (MT 108:12); Jer 7:29; 31:37 (but LXX Jer 38:35 inserts οὐκ, "not"); Lam 2:7; 5:22; Ezek 5:11; 11:16; Hos 9:17.

[53] Dunn, *Romans*, 634, citing 1 Sam 12:22; Ps 94:14; Lam 3:31.

[54] Cranfield, *Romans*, 542, citing 1 Sam 12:22 and Ps 94:14, the verses quoted in Rom 11:2.

question by introducing it with μή, "God did not … , did he?" Then he emphatically reinforces that answer with "may it never come to be!" (μὴ γένοιτο). The remainder of 11:1 and the verses to follow (11:2–4) provide three pieces of evidence against it: (1) Paul's Jewish remnant perspective in 11:1b; (2) his Scripture citation in 11:2a; and (3) his recounting of Elijah in 11:2b–4.[55]

Paul's Jewish Remnant Perspective (11:1b)

Paul's initial retort is this: "For I am also an Israelite, from the seed of Abraham, of the tribe of Benjamin" (11:1b). While his point may well include much more, the "for" (γάρ) serves "to introduce a *reason* for Paul's denial. … Paul himself, as a Jewish Christian, is living evidence that God has not abandoned his people Israel."[56] But the whole truth is probably more profound. The matter of perspective, discussed in the commentary introduction,[57] comes to the fore here. As Dunn notes:

> That Paul puts himself forward in a representative capacity (God has not rejected his people because he has not rejected me!) both misses and cheapens the point. … As in 2 Cor 11:22 and Phil 3:5–6 what is at stake is Paul's claim to express an authentically Jewish viewpoint and understanding of God's workings, to be speaking *as* a Jew.[58]

Luther builds upon Paul's past persecution of the church to assert: "For if God had rejected His own people, He surely would have rejected the apostle Paul, who with all his strength had contended against God."[59] *Thus if God had not permanently rejected even a blasphemous persecutor of his own Son, he surely has not cast off Israel as a whole.* In words reminiscent of Rom 5:20–21, Paul recounts this truth when writing to Timothy: "But the grace of our Lord overflowed above and beyond [to me]" (ὑπερεπλεόνασεν δὲ ἡ χάρις τοῦ κυρίου ἡμῶν, 1 Tim 1:14) in a manner which serves as an example (ὑποτύπωσις) for others (1 Tim 1:16). Cranfield extends the emphasis forward in Paul's life to the paradox that this Jew "is God's chosen apostle to the Gentiles."[60] But the emphasis on Gentiles at this point seems premature (see 11:13).

Both of the descriptors "Israelite" (11:1; cf. 9:4) and "the seed of Abraham" (11:1; cf. 4:13–18; 9:7–9, 29) place Paul within the line of promises given to

---

[55] Paul's evidence is selective, and much more could be cited. For example, one can also observe that even in some of the most scathing prophetic books and oracles of judgment against Israel, a Gospel promise of restoration is appended. See, for example, Ezek 16:53–63 in the context of Ezekiel 16 and, for the book as a whole, the final chapters of restoration, Ezekiel 40–48. See also Amos 9:11–15 at the conclusion of that prophetic book, and Obad 19–21 at the end of Obadiah's prophecy.

[56] Moo, *Romans*, 673; Cranfield, *Romans*, 544, agrees: "Paul's existence as a Jew who is also a Christian proves that the Jewish people as a whole cannot have been rejected"; similarly, Barrett, *Romans*, 207; Käsemann, *Romans*, 299.

[57] Middendorf, *Romans 1–8*, 40–49.

[58] Dunn, *Romans*, 635.

[59] Luther, *Lectures on Romans*, AE 25:421.

[60] Cranfield, *Romans*, 544.

Abraham and his offspring already discussed in detail in 4:13–18; 9:7–8. Paul's mention of his tribe, "Benjamin," in 11:1, as in Phil 3:5, gives further specificity to his identification. As Cranfield notes, it seems unlikely that Paul intends his hearers to correlate this reference with the knowledge that Benjamin "had once been nearly exterminated (Judg 20–21) or that it was the tribe of another Saul, the king whom God had rejected, or that (according to Rabbinic tradition) it had been the first tribe to enter the Red Sea."[61] These may, however, be homiletically informative.

Scriptural Affirmation: 1 Samuel 12:22 // Psalm 94:14 in Romans 11:2a

Paul's second piece of evidence which refutes the notion that God pushed Israel away comes in 11:2a. He answers the rhetorical question of 11:1a by repeating it as a statement, cited from a passage in 1 Samuel (12:22a), whose first clause recurs almost identically in a psalm which the LXX attributes to David (MT Ps 94:14a differs only by the omission of אֶת; the clause is identical in LXX 1 Sam 12:22 and Ps 93:14). When Israel admits their sin in making the evil request for a king (1 Sam 12:19), Samuel assures them with the words of 1 Sam 12:22a:

כִּי לֹא־יִטֹּשׁ יְהוָה אֶת־עַמּוֹ בַּעֲבוּר שְׁמוֹ הַגָּדוֹל

For Yahweh will not forsake his people on account of his great name. (MT 1 Sam 12:22)

ὅτι οὐκ ἀπώσεται κύριος τὸν λαὸν αὐτοῦ διὰ τὸ ὄνομα αὐτοῦ τὸ μέγα.

Because the Lord will not push his people away from himself on account of his great name. (LXX 1 Sam 12:22)

οὐκ ἀπώσατο ὁ θεὸς τὸν λαὸν αὐτοῦ.

God did not push his people away from himself. (Rom 11:2)

Paul uses only the first part of the OT verse. He omits the initial "for/because" (ὅτι in LXX 1 Sam 12:22; Ps 93:14, translating כִּי in MT 1 Sam 12:22; Ps 94:14). The psalm, like Romans, omits the explanatory "on account of his great name" in 1 Sam 12:22. Instead, Ps 94:14 continues with a parallel thought, "and he will not leave behind his inheritance" (LXX Ps 93:14: καὶ τὴν κληρονομίαν αὐτοῦ οὐκ ἐγκαταλείψει), which is reflected in the textual tradition of Romans (see the third textual note on Rom 11:1). The variant reading in Rom 11:1 associates Paul's quotation more closely with the Psalter, though one need not choose one OT source over the other.

In both OT texts, the personal name of God in the MT, "Yahweh," has been replaced, as usual, in the LXX by κύριος, "Lord."[62] Paul, however, does not

---

[61] Cranfield, *Romans*, 545. The rabbinic tradition is also cited by Käsemann, *Romans*, 299; see *Mekilta* 14:22; Str-B 3:286–88. Note that King Saul had first repeatedly rejected the Word of Yahweh before he was rejected by God (see 1 Sam 15:26). Likewise, the portion of Israel under consideration here repeatedly rejected God's Word before they became hardened.

[62] See the commentary on 10:9 and 10:12–13 for a complete discussion.

use κύριος, "Lord," but instead has θεός, "God," perhaps due to his preference of reserving κύριος, "Lord," for Jesus (see 10:9, but cf. 11:3).[63] He further changes the verb from a Greek future tense (ἀπώσεται in the LXX, translating יִטֹּשׁ, the Hebrew imperfect of נָטַשׁ) to an aorist, indicating that a once-future promise uttered by Samuel and David has already come to fulfillment. Most interesting is that instead of using the remainder of the passage in either Samuel ("on account of his great name") or the psalm ("and he will not leave behind his inheritance"), Paul provides another explanation (ὃν προέγνω). Thus Rom 11:2 begins " 'God did not push his people away from himself' whom he knew relationally beforehand."

Moo suggests that Paul "uses the verb 'foreknow' to indicate God's election."[64] But Moo then contrasts this with his interpretation of the same verb in 8:29 since "the context demands that Paul here be speaking of God's election of the people as a whole."[65] It would be wrong to say that Israel *as a whole* was *elected to salvation*, since many individual Israelites rejected God's Word and died as apostates, as the OT amply illustrates. Paul does use a different term for God's "choosing" or perhaps "election" later, namely, the noun ἐκλογή, translated as "choice" in 11:5 and, passively, as "chosen" in 11:7. But what of the verb "know relationally" (προγινώσκω) here? The relational nature of the term is discussed fully in the commentary on 8:29. At this juncture, one should reaffirm that God's eternal foreknowledge transcends all time and that he chose Israel apart from any quality in Israel or works performed by the people.[b]

More to the point, God *established a relationship with his people in history* beginning with his promise to Abraham and his offspring (Gen 12:1–3; 18:18; 22:17–18; 26:3–4; 28:13–14). This relationship was manifested most vividly through the exodus, when Israel as a whole was redeemed from Egypt, and at Mount Sinai, when God established his covenant with all Israel (e.g., Ex 3:6, 13–15; 20:1–2). Moo cites Amos 3:2 to support his discussion of "election" in Rom 11:2;[66] there Yahweh reminds Israel: "Only you did I know from all the tribes of the earth" (Amos 3:2). This statement comes immediately after describing them as the people "I brought up from the land of Egypt" (Amos 3:1). While Moo's terminology of "election" cannot be applied to Israel as a whole if an election to salvation is intended (as not all individual Israelites were saved eternally), the words in Rom 11:2, "his people … whom he knew relationally beforehand" (τὸν λαὸν αὐτοῦ ὃν προέγνω), like those in Amos 3:1–2,

(b) E.g., Gen 12:1–3; Deut 4:32–39; 7:6–8; 10:15–22; Josh 24:1–13; Rom 9:10–12

---

[63] W. Foerster, "κύριος," *TDNT* 3:1087, observes that apart from quotations from the OT, "κύριος ['Lord'] was not a very common term for God" in the NT. Middendorf, "The Bud Has Flowered: Trinitarian Theology in the New Testament," 303, concludes: "κύριος normally refers to the 'Lord' Jesus who is distinguished from God the 'Abba' Father (e.g., 1 Cor. 1:3; 2 Cor. 1:2; Gal. 1:3; Eph. 1:2; etc.)."

[64] Moo, *Romans*, 674.

[65] Moo, *Romans*, 674.

[66] Moo, *Romans*, 674.

carry with them the relationship God has steadfastly established and exhibited throughout Israel's history. These texts rest upon the revealed, saving grace of God, rather than on any notion of "His secret election."[67]

That God has foreknown Israel as "his people" (Rom 11:2) certainly conveys a *collective sense*, that is, God's choosing of the people as a whole (see "God's People" in the introduction to Romans 9–11). Some interpreters equate God's foreknowledge and historical choosing with "election." For example, Cranfield, commenting on "whom he foreknew" in Rom 11:2, speaks of "the general election of the people as a whole."[68] Dunn cites the Jewish interpretation that God's choice bestows eternal life on all the people of Israel, and he too then speaks of "election":

> This was to reach classic expression in *m. [Mishnah] Sanh[edrin]* 10.1: "All Israelites have a share in the world to come." Paul differs from this not in the matter of the assurance which derives from the belief in election, but in the self-definition of the elect.[69]

However, both that Jewish assumption and these commentators' use of "election" for the whole people are misguided.[70] Moreover, the phrase "self-definition" does not express the decisive factor involved, which is God's grace in Jesus Christ (see further the commentary on 11:5).

The entire OT recognizes that individual Israelites and entire groups within Israel could and did remove themselves from the gracious relationship God had established. *God never did push away his people, but they could most certainly push God away!* They were allowed to reject his choice of them as his own people, particularly by turning aside to other gods (e.g., the golden calf, Korah's rebellion, Achan, Israel in general at the behest of rulers such as Jeroboam

---

[67] Calvin, *Romans*, 239. For the Lutheran understanding of the biblical teaching of election versus Calvinistic double predestination, see "God" in the introduction to Romans 9–11; "Not 'Hated,' but 'Spurned'" and "What Paul Does *Not* Say" in the commentary on 9:6–13; "Is This Fair to the Pharaoh? (9:17–18)" and "Thou Art the Potter; We All Are like Clay (9:19–21)" in the commentary on 9:14–24; and the introduction to 9:30–10:15. See further the exposition of the biblical doctrine of election in FC SD XI and FC Ep XI. FC SD XI 9–13 says:

> We are not to view this eternal election or divine ordering to eternal life only in the secret and inscrutable counsel of God. ...

> Such a view, however, leads many to draw and formulate strange, dangerous, and pernicious opinions and causes and fortifies in people's minds either false security and impenitence or anxiety and despair. ...

> Scripture presents this doctrine in no other way than to direct us thereby to the Word. ... We should consider the counsel, purpose, and ordinance of God in Christ Jesus, who is the genuine and true "book of life" [Phil 4:3; Rev 3:5; 20:15] as it is revealed to us through the Word.

[68] Cranfield, *Romans*, 545. So also Moo, *Romans*, 674: "The context demands that Paul here be speaking of God's election of the people as a whole."

[69] Dunn, *Romans*, 636.

[70] The biblical distinctions between God's foreknowledge, causation, and his election by grace and the proper way in which election is to provide the comfort of the Gospel are discussed at length in "Eternal Foreknowledge and Divine Election" in FC SD XI and FC Ep XI.

the son of Nebat, Ahab and Jezebel [see below on Rom 11:3–4]), Manasseh, and so forth). This is *not* in any way to suggest that God *foreknew* just part of Israel; but again, foreknowledge is not the same as determination nor election.[71] Instead, this position recognizes the very topics Paul engages, namely, God's saving Word(s) going out to all (10:11–15, 18) *and* the reality of human ability to respond negatively to it with unbelief and contradiction (10:16–21), followed by God's reaction to that rejection (10:19, 21; 11:1–12; see the conclusion to the commentary on 10:16–17 in the commentary on 10:16–21).

As in Elijah's Time (1 Kings 19 in Rom 11:2b–4)

Paul draws his third and final piece of evidence to demonstrate that "God did not push his people away" (11:1) from Israel's own history. It comes "in [the time of] Elijah" or "in [the section of Scripture about] Elijah" (see the third textual note on 11:2) from the book of Kings, among the Former Prophets in the Hebrew canon. Paul's introduction presumes his hearers know the passage and its context, perhaps much better than many contemporary believers. In Elijah's day, the prophet stands seemingly alone as zealous for Yahweh against Ahab, Jezebel, and all the prophets of Baal. Shortly after his brutal, but resounding, triumph on Mount Carmel (1 Kings 18), Elijah flees to Mount Horeb, i.e., Mount Sinai (1 Kings 19). In Rom 11:2b–4, Paul reminds his hearers of the encounter between Elijah and Yahweh which took place on that mountain:

> [2]… Or do you not know in [the time of] Elijah what the Scripture says as he pleads to God against Israel? [3]"Lord, they killed your prophets, they tore down your altars, and I myself was left alone, and they are seeking my life." [4]But what does the divine oracle say to him? "I left for myself seven thousand men, such ones who did not bend a knee to Baal."

In the OT, Elijah's complaint comes in 1 Ki 19:10 and is repeated in 1 Ki 19:14, with the substitution of only one word with a synonym (καθεῖλαν for κατέσκαψαν). The portion of 1 Ki 19:10 referenced by Paul reads as follows in the LXX and then in Rom 11:3:

---

[71] FC SD XI 4–8 explains:

> At the very outset we must carefully note the difference between God's eternal foreknowledge and the eternal election of his children to eternal salvation. …

> The eternal election of God or God's predestination to salvation does not extend over both the godly and the ungodly, but only over the children of God, who have been elected and predestined to eternal life [Eph 1:4, 5]. …

> The source and cause of evil is not God's foreknowledge … but rather the wicked and perverse will of the devil and of men, as it is written [in Hos 13:9 in Luther's translation; Ps 5:4 (MT 5:5)].

> God's eternal election, however, not only foresees and foreknows the salvation of the elect, but by God's gracious will and pleasure in Christ Jesus it is also a cause which creates, effects, helps, and furthers our salvation and whatever pertains to it [Mt 16:18; Jn 10:28; Acts 13:48].

τὰ θυσιαστήριά σου κατέσκαψαν καὶ τοὺς προφήτας σου ἀπέκτειναν ἐν ῥομφαίᾳ, καὶ ὑπολέλειμμαι ἐγὼ μονώτατος, καὶ ζητοῦσι τὴν ψυχήν μου λαβεῖν αὐτήν.

They tore down your altars, and they killed your prophets with the sword. And I myself have been left all alone, and they are seeking my life to take it. (LXX 1 Ki 19:10)

κύριε, τοὺς προφήτας σου ἀπέκτειναν, τὰ θυσιαστήριά σου κατέσκαψαν, κἀγὼ ὑπελείφθην μόνος καὶ ζητοῦσιν τὴν ψυχήν μου.

Lord, they killed your prophets, they tore down your altars, and I myself was left alone, and they are seeking my life. (Rom 11:3)

Paul adds the introductory vocative κύριε, "Lord," which represents the Hebrew name Yahweh, for whom Elijah just asserted that he has been "intensely zealous" (1 Ki 19:10, 14).[72] Although Paul omits Elijah's charge that the Israelites have forsaken the Lord's covenant (1 Ki 19:10, 14), he does essentially replicate Elijah's four complaints. However, Paul switches the order of the first two and omits "with the sword" (ἐν ῥομφαίᾳ) as the instrument by which the prophets were killed. The vocabulary of the third is the same, but the forms are different: the LXX has the verb in the perfect tense, ὑπολέλειμμαι, "I *have been* left," and the superlative form of the adjective, μονώτατος, "most alone, all alone," whereas Romans has the verb in the aorist tense, ὑπελείφθην, "I *was* left," and the positive form of the adjective, μόνος, "alone." Paul then omits "to take it" (λαβεῖν αὐτήν) from the end of the final clause. Nevertheless, the overall thought remains the same.

Paul introduces God's response in Rom 11:4 with "but what does the divine oracle say to him?" (ἀλλὰ τί λέγει αὐτῷ ὁ χρηματισμός;). The noun "divine oracle" (χρηματισμός) occurs only here in the NT. However 2 Macc 2:4 uses it in association with God sending Jeremiah to Mount Sinai, depicting "the prophet after a divine oracle came to him" (ὁ προφήτης χρηματισμοῦ γενηθέντος αὐτῷ). The cognate verb χρηματίζω, "impart a divine revelation," reinforces the meaning by similarly describing God's warnings to the wise men and Joseph in dreams (Mt 2:12, 22), the revelation of the Holy Spirit to Simeon (Lk 2:26), and the angel's revelation to Cornelius in Acts 10:22. Thus the notion of "an authoritative divine answer"[73] seems appropriate.

The MT and LXX of 1 Ki 19:18, followed by the text in Romans, are presented below:

וְהִשְׁאַרְתִּי בְיִשְׂרָאֵל שִׁבְעַת אֲלָפִים
כָּל־הַבִּרְכַּיִם אֲשֶׁר לֹא־כָרְעוּ לַבַּעַל
וְכָל־הַפֶּה אֲשֶׁר לֹא־נָשַׁק לוֹ:

---

[72] In the MT, 1 Ki 19:10 begins וַיֹּאמֶר קַנֹּא קִנֵּאתִי לַיהוָה ׀ אֱלֹהֵי צְבָאוֹת, "and he said, 'I have been zealously zealous for Yahweh, the God of hosts,'" which the LXX translates as ζηλῶν ἐζήλωκα τῷ κυρίῳ παντοκράτορι, "being zealous, I have been and remain zealous for the Lord Almighty."

[73] Cranfield, *Romans*, 546.

And I will leave in Israel seven thousand,
> all the knees which have not bowed to Baal
> and every mouth which has not kissed him. (MT 1 Ki 19:18)

καὶ καταλείψεις ἐν Ισραηλ ἑπτὰ χιλιάδας ἀνδρῶν,
> πάντα γόνατα ἃ οὐκ ὤκλασαν γόνυ τῷ Βααλ
> καὶ πᾶν στόμα ὃ οὐ προσεκύνησεν αὐτῷ.

And you will leave in Israel seven thousand of men,
> all knees which did not bow a knee to Baal
> and every mouth which did not worship him. (LXX 1 Ki 19:18)

κατέλιπον ἐμαυτῷ ἑπτακισχιλίους ἄνδρας,
> οἵτινες οὐκ ἔκαμψαν γόνυ τῇ Βάαλ.

I left for myself seven thousand men,
> such ones who did not bend a knee to Baal. (Rom 11:4)

While the thought is certainly the same, the vocables in Paul's Greek text diverge quite markedly from the LXX and the underlying Hebrew as well. For example, in contrast to the second person singular expression "*you* will leave" of the LXX, Paul, in keeping with the MT, renders Yahweh's words in the first person, "I," which he further emphasizes by the addition of the reflexive pronoun ἐμαυτῷ, "for myself." As in 11:2, Paul also alters the tense from the future καταλείψεις, "you *will* leave," in the LXX (which corresponds to the future sense of the Hebrew perfect with *waw* consecutive[74]) to the second aorist κατέλιπον, "I *left*."

The number of males being "seven thousand" in all three texts (cf. πεντακισχίλιοι ἄνδρες, "five thousand men," in Mk 6:44) prompts Cranfield to read the number as "a symbol of completeness, perfection," not "a mere reflection of a traditional estimate of the actual number of those who remained faithful in this time of national apostasy."[75] Moo, perhaps, overreacts: "It is doubtful, however, that Paul intends any symbolic allusions: he takes the number from his text and makes nothing of it."[76] But completely separating an accurate, literal count of people from a symbolic significance presents a false alternative. Surely we are to hear "7,000 as an open, not closed, number indicating the open-endedness of God's covenant promise."[77]

In drawing on this passage from Kings and applying it in his own day, "Paul as an Israelite (11:1) echoes Elijah's complaint against Israel. To that extent Paul

---

[74] The accent on the Hebrew verb וְהִשְׁאַרְתִּי (1 Ki 19:18) is on the final syllable, indicating that the form is *waw* consecutive, referring to the future. If the *waw* were merely conjunctive, the accent would be on the penultimate syllable, וְהִשְׁאַרְתִּי.

[75] Cranfield, *Romans*, 547; K. H. Rengstorf, "ἑπτά," *TDNT* 2:629, seems skeptical of the literal sense of the number since he opines: "We cannot be sure from the context whether Paul connected with the OT number the thought of the totality of the true Israel which is certainly present in 1 K. 19:18."

[76] Moo, *Romans*, 676, n. 24.

[77] Dunn, *Romans*, 638.

sees himself ... as a latter-day Elijah."[78] The degree of comparison is debatable. Munck summarizes plausible connections between Elijah's circumstances and the immediate journey ahead of Paul as he writes Romans:

> Elijah on his way to Mount Carmel[79] and Paul heading for Jerusalem are much alike. Both are risking their lives by going to Palestine, and both aim in God's name to change the destiny of their people by making them believe in God and persuading them to turn away from the error that has made them his enemy.[80]

The key matter at hand, however, resides neither with Elijah nor Paul,[81] but in the vocabulary related to the Greek noun "remnant" (λεῖμμα, Rom 11:5) in the texts that Paul cites. He draws on cognates of that Greek noun, the Greek verbs "I was left" (ὑπελείφθην, 11:3) and "I left" (κατέλιπον, 11:4),[82] in order to make a foundational proposition about the "remnant" (the noun λεῖμμα) in the very next verse (11:5; cf. also the cognate noun ὑπόλειμμα, "remnant," in 9:27). In so doing, Paul explains *how God relates to his people*, even when they are wayward.[83]

A Remnant by God's Gracious Choice (11:5)

Paul now returns to the present and draws his conclusion. He signals his emphasis by beginning with "thus therefore also" (οὕτως οὖν καί). This "tripling of connectives is found only here in Paul"[84] and underscores the importance of what follows. So also does the present, eschatological force of a phrase replicated from 3:26, "in the present momentous time" (ἐν τῷ νῦν καιρῷ; see the commentary on 3:26; cf. also 8:18). The verse, then, reads "thus therefore also in the present momentous time a remnant has come to be and still exists according to [the] choice of grace" (11:5).

---

[78] Dunn, *Romans*, 636.

[79] After Elijah declared to King Ahab that the Lord was going to send a drought in Israel, Elijah was told by God to hide by the Cherith Brook, east of the Jordan River, and then to stay in Zarephath, north of Israel (1 Kings 17). In the third year, God sent Elijah back to Israel to show himself to Ahab (1 Ki 18:1). Elijah then confronted Ahab and the prophets of Baal on Mount Carmel (1 Kings 18).

[80] Munck, *Christ and Israel*, 109; for further arguments supporting the interrelationship between Romans and Paul's impending journey to Jerusalem, see Jervell, "The Letter to Jerusalem," and Bornkamm, "The Letter to the Romans as Paul's Last Will and Testament"; for a brief evaluation, see Middendorf, *Romans 1–8*, 16–17, 19–20.

[81] For the God-centered focus of the entire letter, see Middendorf, *Romans 1–8*, 21–22, 27, 49–51. In this volume, see "Romans 1–4: The Righteousness of God" in the introduction to Romans 9–16, as well as "God" in "The Three Foci of Romans 9–11" in the introduction to Romans 9–11.

[82] As described above in the textual analysis of the quotes, the verbs Paul uses, but in different tenses, are from the LXX version of the texts he quotes: ὑπολείπω (1 Ki 19:10, 14, quoted in Rom 11:3) and καταλείπω (1 Ki 19:18, quoted in Rom 11:4). Both mean "to leave."

[83] Käsemann, *Romans*, 300, states: "The [remnant] motif is set in the context of Paul's doctrine of justification."

[84] Dunn, *Romans*, 638.

God did not push his people away (11:1–2). On the contrary, his hands remain stretched out toward them (10:21). Therefore, as in Elijah's day, a "remnant" (λεῖμμα, 11:5) remains. Surprisingly, this particular Greek noun occurs only here in the NT and only twice in the LXX (2 Sam 21:2; 2 Ki 19:4). But the theological concept of the remnant has a critical function throughout the OT. It can be expressed by a variety of vocabulary, often by the Hebrew noun שְׁאֵרִית (sixty-six instances in the OT), which the prophets in particular use as a technical term to depict the "faithful *remnant* of Israel or Judah" (BDB, 1; see further the sixth textual note on Rom 9:27). As Dunn notes: "It came particularly into prominence at the great Assyrian and Babylonian crisis points of Israel's ([and] Judah's) history."[85]

The remainder of 11:5 contains a number of profound theological expressions about the "remnant." It is "according to [the] choice of grace" (κατ᾽ ἐκλογὴν χάριτος). Moo suggests that the preposition κατά is causal, "because of,"[86] but "according to" is more to the point. The two nouns which follow, "choice" (ἐκλογή) and "grace" (χάρις), have been used in Romans previously and profoundly. See especially the discussion of "choice" (ἐκλογή) in 9:11 and of "grace" (χάρις) in 1:5 and 3:24. Paul's major point asserts that God's "choice" was purely a matter "of grace."[87]

It must also be affirmed that God in grace chose Israel as his treasured people. *He chose the whole people to be his own—all of Israel, not just some of them* (e.g., Deut 4:37; 7:6–8; 10:15). To be sure, Paul discusses the present reality in terms of "two groups: a 'remnant,' enjoying the blessings of salvation and existing by virtue of God's gracious election ([11:]5–6; cf. 9:6b–13, 15–16, 18a, 22–23, 27–29), and 'the rest' [11:7]."[88] But as just noted,[89] the presence of a saved remnant amid widespread apostasy is by no means new to the NT era. More importantly, the latter group of unbelievers, "the rest" (οἱ … λοιποί, 11:7), did *not* come into existence as the result of God's purposeful action, i.e., because God did not choose them or did not call them to believe or much less because he willed them to perish and so deliberately hardened them in spiritual obduracy.[90] Instead, they have become hardened by their own actions, by rejecting the Word God sent near to them (Romans 10). The Good News is most certainly "for everyone who believes" (παντὶ τῷ πιστεύοντι, 1:16; 10:4; cf. 10:11), but "they did not all listen responsively to the Good News" (10:16a). Although they heard

---

[85] Dunn, *Romans*, 638, citing 2 Ki 19:4, 31 ‖ Is 37:4, 32; its frequent use in Jeremiah, including Jer 6:9; 15:9; 23:3; 24:8; Ezek 9:8; 11:13; Ezra 9:8.

[86] Moo, *Romans*, 677, n. 35.

[87] On this point, Sanders, *Paul and Palestinian Judaism*, 421, is correct: "Election and ultimately salvation are considered to be by God's mercy rather than human achievement." But see the concluding paragraph of "Faith Receives Grace—Works Are Antithetical (11:6)" below.

[88] Moo, *Romans*, 671–72.

[89] See the second paragraph of "A Remnant by God's Gracious Choice (11:5)" above.

[90] Contrary to Moo, *Romans*, 672.

and knew (10:18, 19), they are, nevertheless, "unpersuaded and contradicting" (10:21). Paul thus deals with the problematic and tragic response of unbelief. He raises the matter in regard to Israel and the Jewish people repeatedly, already in Romans 3 ("some were unfaithful," "their faithlessness," 3:3), then reinforces it with a citation from Isaiah (53:1) in Romans 10 ("who believed?" Rom 10:16), and makes it explicit again in 11:22–23 ("unbelief," 11:23).

The Word of Christ enables a response of faith (10:14–17), allowing one and all (10:11–13) to receive the "message" (ἀκοή, 10:16) through "hearing" (ἀκοή, 10:17, twice). The Good News, the hearing, and the believing are all "according to [God's] choice of grace" (11:5). The "Word of Christ" (10:17) announces and delivers

> [22]... a righteousness of God through faith of/[in] Jesus Christ into all those who believe [εἰς πάντας τοὺς πιστεύοντας]. You see, there is not a difference, [23]for all sinned and are lacking the glory of God, [24]while being declared righteous undeservedly by his grace through the redemption, the one in Christ Jesus. (3:22–24)

The Word of God, that is, Jesus, has always been the specific means of grace for all[91] and remains so now "in the present momentous time" (ἐν τῷ νῦν καιρῷ) referred to both in 3:26 and here in 11:5. Therefore, the "remnant" (λεῖμμα) now includes "the company of Jews who have believed in Christ."[92] "Its existence was a pledge of God's continuing interest in, and care for, the nation, a sign of God's faithfulness to His election of Israel."[93] According to 11:5, this remnant exists *by virtue of God's doing*, his "gracious choosing."

Faith Receives Grace—Works Are Antithetical (11:6)

What, then, was *not* involved in God's choosing? This leads to the key diagnosis Paul makes in this section: "but if [his choice is] by grace, it is *not* from works since the grace would no longer be grace" (11:6). If the remnant exists "by grace" (χάριτι), those in Israel attempting to obtain God's favor "from works" (ἐξ ἔργων) *exclude themselves* from it (see 9:32; also 11:7).

If the first occurrence in 11:6 of the adverb οὐκέτι had the temporal meaning "no *longer*," the verse might have been susceptible to being conscripted into support for a dispensational scheme: it *was/used to be* from works, but now *no longer*! But in this Greek conditional sentence οὐκέτι has a logical force (see the second textual note on 11:6). Therefore the verse expresses the same contrast set up already repeatedly in Romans. For example:

> For we conclude that a person is being declared righteous by *faith apart from works* of the Law. (3:28)

---

[91] In 10:6–8 Paul affirmed that this was so already at the time of Moses.

[92] Cranfield, *Romans*, 548.

[93] Cranfield, *Romans*, 548.

[4]Now to the one who *works*, the payment is *not* credited as a *favor*, but according to what is owed. [5]But to the one who is *not working*, *but believing* on the One who declares the godless righteous, his faith *is* being credited for righteousness. (4:4–5)

[30]What then will we say? [We say] that Gentiles, those who were *not pursuing* righteousness, *got righteousness*, that is, the righteousness which is *from faith*, [31]but Israel, while *pursuing* a Law of *righteousness*, *did not attain* to the Law. [32]On what account? Since [they were attempting to attain a Law of righteousness] *not from faith but as if [it could be attained] from works*, they stumbled on the stone of stumbling. (9:30–32)

In 9:32 and 11:6 "from works" (ἐξ ἔργων) is short for "from works of the Law" (ἐξ ἔργων νόμου, as in 3:20).[94] The specific point "from works," considered in 11:6 and then excluded by "not," would be to allow a role for "Israel's intrinsic merit" or for "her achievement in obeying the law."[95]

The Romans passages cited above convey Paul's insistence that righteousness in relationship with God *always has been and remains* an *either/or* proposition. As 9:30–10:5 further demonstrates, the avenue to righteousness is one-way only, from God to humanity, and the directions God-to-people and people-to-God "are mutually exclusive."[96] Rom 11:6 concisely encapsulates the two diametrically opposed options by (1) *affirming* that it is *from* God *to* people ("by grace," χάριτι) and (2) *denying* that it is *from* people *toward* God ("not from works," οὐκέτι ἐξ ἔργων).[97] Whenever and wherever a faithful remnant exists, it is *only and wholly* because of God's gracious action. And, as Paul's repeated use of forms of "everyone, all" (πᾶς) makes abundantly clear (e.g., 3:23–25; 10:11–13), *God intends for his grace to encompass not only Israel but all people. Conversely, the route of works is excluded for all.* Therefore, "Paul's polemic, while focused on Israel because of his particular situation, is applicable to all human beings and finds its ultimate basis in the human condition."[98]

The Remnant: An Enduring Reality (11:5–6)

It is also critical to recognize both aspects of the perfect tense of the Greek verb γέγονεν, which is the last word in 11:5: the remnant "has come to be and still exists." First, it would be wrong to suggest that Paul means that this remnant "has come into being" only recently, in Paul's day.[99] On the contrary, after

---

[94] Dunn, *Romans*, 639; see the excursus "The Background of 'Works of the Law'" following the commentary on 3:9–20.

[95] Moo, *Romans*, 677.

[96] Cranfield, *Romans*, 548.

[97] Paul encountered the misguided attempt to mix the two when he was in Galatia earlier; see Das, *Galatians*, 15–18.

[98] Moo, *Romans*, 678.

[99] Paul used another perfect of the same verb (but in the first person plural), γεγόναμεν, in 6:5 to say that "we have become" united with Christ in his death and resurrection in Baptism. At the time Paul wrote that, the Sacrament of Baptism had been instituted relatively recently, by

the fall into sin, a remnant by faith has existed ever since the promise was sent forth (Gen 3:15). Paul cited the Elijah narrative (Rom 11:2b–4) to confirm the existence of the remnant in the ninth century BC. Second, Paul emphasizes that the remnant still exists "in the present momentous time" (11:5). The scope of the verb's perfect tense encompasses *both* the remnant's coming into being long ago *and* its continued existence in the present. On the one hand, Paul's prepositional phrase "according to [the] choice of grace" could modify the preceding noun ("a remnant," λεῖμμα). If so, it characterizes the remnant as chosen in accord with God's grace, a foundational biblical truth. However, on the other hand, the lack of a definite article preceding the phrase means it could also modify the verbal action. Contextually, *the basis of God's choice* seems to be the primary emphasis, so the translation connects the prepositional phrase to the verb ("has come to be and still exists," γέγονεν). It asserts that the remnant not only *originated* by grace but also *continues* to exist in the present by grace as well. The exclusion of works discussed above applies to both aspects of the verb, past and present. Dunn states:

> The remnant is not constituted as a group within Israel by their faithfulness to the law ([as was believed to be constitutive for] 'the righteous' of the Psalms of Solomon, or the covenanters at Qumran; …), but as a group sustained by God's grace; *that* is how election is to be understood and how it is sustained.[100]

The perfect tense of γέγονεν in 11:5 supports both of the main verbs Dunn uses, "constituted" and "sustained."

This is noteworthy in light of the influential characterization of Judaism by Sanders. He proposed that any religion can be analyzed in terms of "how getting in and staying in are understood."[101] Based upon his review of Jewish literature, Sanders concludes that first century AD Judaism was not legalistic. Instead, he categorizes it as *covenantal nomism*, which understood that "getting in" the covenant was a sheer act of God's mercy. According to Sanders, obedience to the Law (i.e., "works") was not about earning grace, reward, or merit. It was simply the divinely offered means of "staying in."[102] Sanders's appraisal has been effectively challenged.[103] But even if he were correct about *Judaism*,[104]

Christ himself, and Paul and his Roman audience had been baptized even more recently. In that passage, then, the verb does refer to a new reality that came into being only recently, in the NT era.

[100] Dunn, *Romans*, 639.

[101] Sanders, *Paul and Palestinian Judaism*, 17 (emphasis removed); note the recent reevaluation by Sprinkle, *Paul and Judaism Revisited*.

[102] Sanders, *Paul and Palestinian Judaism*, 75, 141, 146–47, 420.

[103] For example, Westerholm, *Israel's Law and the Church's Faith*; Schreiner, *The Law and Its Fulfillment*; Das, *Paul, the Law, and the Covenant*; Kim, *Paul and the New Perspective*.

[104] Judaism emerged with its distinctive teachings in the intertestamental period, after the close of the OT era. The texts on which Sanders bases his argument are from ca. 200 BC to AD 200 (Sanders, *Paul and Palestinian Judaism*, 1). In other words, his argument is *not* based on the canonical texts of the OT.

Paul's treatment of the Law—that is, the Torah of Moses[105]—in Romans 7 and his concise statement here in 11:5 with γέγονεν counter any notion regarding the use of human works as necessary *either* for entering *or* for remaining in God's good graces. That was not the case according to God's Word in the OT, nor is it the case in the apostolic writings of the NT.[106] Paul maintains that both *entrance into* and *remaining in* the people of God have always been and remain now by grace alone.

Analysis and Scriptural Support (11:7–10)

The Three Parts of Romans 11:7

"What then?" (11:7). Rather than drawing "a comprehensive conclusion"[107] or stating "the implication of his teaching about the remnant,"[108] in 11:7 Paul gives a concise three-part overview of what has happened to Israel. First, "that which Israel seeks earnestly, this it did not obtain" (11:7a). The comparable thought and language of 9:30–10:5 are extremely close. Thus that section helps to fill in the blanks of Paul's thought here. As there, Paul does not speak of Israel as a whole in 11:7a,[109] otherwise there would be no one who did, in fact, obtain (see "obtain" in the very next clause: "the chosen obtained," 11:7b; "the chosen" [11:7b] are the "remnant" by God's "choice of grace" in 11:5). Instead, he modifies those to whom he refers as the portion of Israelites who *seek earnestly*. These are the same ones described in 9:31–32 as "pursing [διώκων] a Law of righteousness" "as if [it could be attained] from works [ὡς ἐξ ἔργων]." Although properly zealous for God (10:2), they similarly did not attain righteousness (οὐκ ἔφθασεν, 9:31).

Why and how did this happen? Those "seeking [righteousness] earnestly" (11:7a) based upon their works toward God *did* hear the "message," the "Word of Christ" (10:16–17), which drew near to them (10:8). But "they were not submissive to the righteousness of God" (τῇ δικαιοσύνῃ τοῦ θεοῦ οὐχ ὑπετάγησαν, 10:3) because they were *working* in the opposite direction; righteousness is *from* God *to* all who believe. Paul depicts them as "seeking to establish their own [righteousness]" (τὴν ἰδίαν [δικαιοσύνην] ζητοῦντες στῆσαι, 10:3) by the doing of the Law (10:5). As a result, they did not listen responsively to the Good News they heard (10:16), and, rather than believing on the Rock, they stumbled over him (9:32–33). This is why they "did not obtain" (οὐκ ἐπέτυχεν, 11:7) the righteousness they earnestly sought. Further explanation comes in

---

[105] This commentary consistently understands νόμος, "Law," throughout Romans to refer to the Torah of Moses. See, e.g., Middendorf, *Romans 1–8*, 604–9. See also "Positive Conclusions" in the commentary on 10:4.

[106] See especially 11:22. See further Middendorf, *Romans 1–8*, 596–97; see also Middendorf, *The "I" in the Storm*, 257–64.

[107] As maintained by Cranfield, *Romans*, 548.

[108] As asserted by Moo, *Romans*, 679.

[109] Against Moo, *Romans*, 679, who says that this is Israel "as a corporate entity."

11:11. Philippians 3 also reveals how this approach to God was exemplified most zealously (Gal 1:14) by an Israelite from the seed of Abraham and the tribe of Benjamin named Saul/Paul (Phil 3:4–6; cf. Rom 11:1). But Paul now realizes that since God's "choice" is "of grace" (ἐκλογὴν χάριτος, 11:5), it is "by grace" (χάριτι, 11:6) and "not from works" (οὐκέτι ἐξ ἔργων, 11:6).

In the *second part* of 11:7, Paul adds: "But the chosen obtained" (ἡ δὲ ἐκλογὴ ἐπέτυχεν, 11:7b). "The chosen" (ἡ ... ἐκλογή) refers to the remnant by faith which Paul has just been discussing (11:1, 4, 5)[110] and which he himself exemplifies (11:1). They obtained, not by works, but by God's "choice of grace" (ἐκλογὴν χάριτος, 11:5). They are, after all, *the chosen people!*[111] They, like Abraham, believe and passively receive what was promised (Gen 15:6). Thus God's gracious and active choosing of Israel is nothing new; the promises to Abraham and God's saving power at work in the exodus (see 9:22) and in Israel's preservation and eventual return from exile all demonstrate this fact, as does the divinely sent proclamation of the "Word of Christ" (10:17) "in the present momentous time" (11:5; also 10:14–15, 17). All those in Israel who receive and listen responsively to God's Good News "from faith" (ἐκ πίστεως, 1:17; 9:30; 10:6) obtain righteousness and salvation (10:10). In this context, then, "obtain" (ἐπιτυγχάνω, 11:7b) stands synonymously with the passive sense of "get, receive" (καταλαμβάνω) in 9:30 (as well as the negated φθάνω, "attain," of 9:31).

In contrast, the *third part* of 11:7 reveals God's reluctant reaction to the obdurate response of others in Israel who were depicted earlier in 11:7a as "seeking earnestly": "the rest were hardened" (οἱ δὲ λοιποὶ ἐπωρώθησαν, 11:7c). Both 9:18 and the verse to follow here, 11:8, indicate "that God is also the implied agent of the passive verb in this verse: 'the rest have been hardened (by God).' "[112] But this is *not* because they "were rejected by God before the foundation of the world" due to something he "freely determined before the fall."[113] Neither is human sinfulness the essential cause of God's hardening. Certainly, God's hardening acts on those who are sinners, but if it were enacted purely on that basis, all would be hardened, for all are sinners![114] Furthermore, Paul cannot be thinking about the hardening of all Israel as an entire national

---

[110] See Moo, *Romans*, 680; surely it is not an exclusive reference to Gentile believers, since they do not reenter the picture until 11:12.

[111] Paul employs the same Greek word, ἐκλογή, for both the "*choice* of grace" (11:5) and the "chosen" (11:7).

[112] Moo, *Romans*, 680. While Paul uses a different verb for "harden" in 9:18 (σκληρύνω), the divine reaction to Pharaoh there seems synonymous.

[113] As maintained by Calvin, *Romans*, 244. The biblical teaching of election does not allow Calvinistic double predestination; see "God" in the introduction to Romans 9–11; "Not 'Hated,' but 'Spurned' " and "What Paul Does *Not* Say" in the commentary on 9:6–13; "Is This Fair to the Pharaoh? (9:17–18)" and "Thou Art the Potter; We All Are like Clay (9:19–21)" in the commentary on 9:14–24; the introduction to 9:30–10:15; and the commentary on 11:5.

[114] Sanday and Headlam, *Romans*, 313, suggest that those who have been hardened "have been hardened because they have failed" to attain righteousness through their works, and "sin is

group because he vehemently denounced the idea of God rejecting his entire people in 11:1–2, and here he carefully says that only "the rest" (οἱ … λοιποί) were hardened. "The rest" are the "not all" (οὐ πάντες) of 9:6 and 10:16 who did not listen responsively to or believe the Good News. Franzmann explains: "*God petrified them in their stony resistance to the truth.* God hardened them, but He hardened them because of their unbelief. He did not harden them from everlasting, to prevent them from believing."[115] Finally, the progression of Paul's argument shows that he does not keep "God's hardening of people and their own refusal to believe in tension."[116] *Instead, he seeks to resolve it* (see 11:11–12; see also 11:14–15, 23–24).

Application of Romans 11:7

God chooses and calls by grace and not from works (11:5–6; cf. 9:11b–12a). Those who are "the rest" (11:7) are so not because *God* did not graciously choose them. He chose *all* Israel as his people. But grace is not irresistible; neither does it coerce, force, or demand acceptance.[117] This means grace may be rejected by those who refuse to receive and believe the Word. Therefore, Paul insists they have *not* become "the rest" because God pushed them away (11:1–2) or forsook them. Just the opposite! They, in effect, pushed God away by scorning the righteousness from him (10:3) now revealed in the Gospel of Jesus Christ (1:16–17), the righteousness which those of the present remnant receive now, as those of the remnant in the past always have, from faith.

As discussed above, Paul has diagnosed *why* previously in 9:30–10:5. In short he said: "On what account? Since [they were attempting to attain a Law of righteousness] not from faith but as if [it could be attained] from works" (διὰ τί; ὅτι οὐκ ἐκ πίστεως ἀλλ᾽ ὡς ἐξ ἔργων, 9:32). Thus "not from faith" is the key. "The rest" in 10:7, then, are comprised of people such as the "some" who did not believe in 3:3, the "not all" who failed to listen responsively to and believe the Good News in 10:16 just as Isaiah prophesied, and those who remain "unpersuaded" and "contradicting" in 10:21 (see also 9:6; 11:23). The response of "not from faith" (9:32) by many in Israel entails their rejection of God's grace, his message, and his Messiah.

---

represented as God's punishment inflicted on man for their rebellion." However, all humanity has failed to attain righteousness through works, and all have sinned (3:9–20, 23).

[115] Franzmann, *Romans*, 197 (emphasis added).

[116] As claimed by Moo, *Romans*, 681, n. 55. Barrett, *Romans*, 210, similarly asserts: "It is impossible here to distinguish between 'hardened because disobedient' and 'disobedient because hardened'; the two processes are concurrent." But the example of the Pharaoh, whom Paul cited in 9:17–18, shows that hardening is the result of a stubborn unbelief that continues to reject the Word of God. See "Hardening" in "Is This Fair to the Pharaoh? (9:17–18)" in the commentary on 9:14–24.

[117] Moo, *Romans*, 678, says that "grace demands that God be perfectly free to bestow his favor on whomever he chooses." See the concluding sections of the commentary on 9:6–13 and 9:14–18.

Paul also explains the reason why they fail to respond properly. It is because they seek to obtain righteousness "as if from works" (9:32). Those who seek earnestly *by working toward* the righteousness of God do not obtain it (11:7) because their earnest seeking goes in the wrong direction. If people seek him by works, then they spurn his grace; if God's "choice of grace" (11:5) could be obtained by works, then "the grace would no longer be grace" (11:6). Therefore, those who try to obtain righteousness by their works drive the wrong way down the one-way road. The ensuing collision results in *their refusal to be graciously given righteousness* through believing the Word of Christ, which God brings near to them (10:8, 15; see the conclusion to the commentary on 10:16–17 in the commentary on 10:16–21). They are the ones who, unless they repent, will become hardened. Thus the passive voice of "they were hardened" in 11:7 (ἐπωρώθησαν) should be understood as expressing *God's reaction to something which has already occurred: the negative response of unbelief on the part of some in his chosen Israel.*

Verification of God's Hardening from the Old Testament (11:8–10)

Deuteronomy 29:4 and Isaiah 29:10 in Romans 11:8

Paul contends that the three-part sequence in 11:7 reveals nothing new. For example, at the Red Sea, the Israelites "believed in Yahweh and in Moses his servant" (וַיַּאֲמִ֙ינוּ֙ בַּֽיהוָ֔ה וּבְמֹשֶׁ֖ה עַבְדּֽוֹ, Ex 14:31). But this was followed by the years of testing in the wilderness. During that time, some remained steadfast in faith (e.g., Deut 1:1–25). Others, however, were unfaithful and no longer desired to be Yahweh's chosen people (e.g., Numbers 16; Deut 1:26–46; Amos 5:25–27). When some in Israel reject their God, Paul asserts that God's reaction to such a response remains the same as it was then. It is "just as it stands written" (Rom 11:8) regarding those in the wilderness in MT Deut 29:3 (ET 29:4):

וְלֹֽא־נָתַן֩ יְהוָ֨ה לָכֶ֥ם לֵב֙ לָדַ֔עַת וְעֵינַ֥יִם לִרְא֖וֹת וְאָזְנַ֥יִם לִשְׁמֹ֑עַ עַ֖ד הַיּ֥וֹם הַזֶּֽה׃

Yahweh did not give to you a heart to know and eyes to see and ears to hear, [and it has been that way] until this day. (MT Deut 29:3 [ET 29:4])

καὶ οὐκ ἔδωκεν κύριος ὁ θεὸς ὑμῖν καρδίαν εἰδέναι καὶ ὀφθαλμοὺς βλέπειν καὶ ὦτα ἀκούειν ἕως τῆς ἡμέρας ταύτης.

The Lord God did not give to you a heart to know and eyes to see and ears to hear, [and it has been that way] until this day. (LXX Deut 29:3 [ET 29:4])

ἔδωκεν αὐτοῖς ὁ θεὸς πνεῦμα κατανύξεως, ὀφθαλμοὺς τοῦ μὴ βλέπειν καὶ ὦτα τοῦ μὴ ἀκούειν, ἕως τῆς σήμερον ἡμέρας.

God gave to them a spirit of callousness, eyes to not see and ears to not hear, [and it has been that way] until this very day. (Rom 11:8)

The MT and LXX line up fairly well here. In Romans, however, significant differences exist, though not so many as to regard the reference as "Paul's own creation."[118]

First, Paul turns what Yahweh "did not give" or withheld into what God actively "gave" (ἔδωκεν).

Second, the infinitives become articular and are negated. As a result, instead of expressing how God did *not* give what was needed "to know … to see … to hear," Paul contends that God actively gave the negative, "eyes to not see and ears to not hear" (ὀφθαλμοὺς τοῦ μὴ βλέπειν καὶ ὦτα τοῦ μὴ ἀκούειν). The explanation may simply be Paul's desire for consistency in order to avoid causing confusion among those hearing the letter read orally. His alteration makes the infinitive clauses in 11:8 match a comparable negated articular infinitive in LXX Ps 68:24 (MT 69:24; ET 69:23), which he is about to cite in Rom 11:10 (οἱ ὀφθαλμοὶ αὐτῶν τοῦ μὴ βλέπειν). As a result, however, "Paul has considerably strengthened the statement of Deuteronomy, so as to bring out more clearly the thought of divine hardening."[119] That aspect is discussed further below (see in "Psalm 69:24 in Romans 11:10").

Third, in place of "a heart to know" in the Deuteronomy text, Paul substitutes "a spirit of callousness" as the first element God gave. This phrase likely comes from LXX Is 29:10, where God poured out on false prophets and rulers a "spirit of callousness" (πνεύματι κατανύξεως). The original Hebrew depicts Yahweh pouring out "a spirit of deep sleep" (רוּחַ תַּרְדֵּמָה, Is 29:10). Sanday and Headlam suggest that Paul intends something comparable; they acknowledge that the noun κατάνυξις ("callousness") is derived from the verb κατανύσσομαι, "to strike, stun," but propose that the meaning of the noun has been influenced by some confusion with the verb νυστάζω, "to nod in sleep."[120] However, the verb κατανύσσομαι, from which the noun is derived, means "in the passive, 'be sorely pricked,' hence 'be bewildered, stunned' (e.g. Isa 6:5; 47.5; Th[eodotion] Dan 10.15). … πνεῦμα κατανύξεως here in Romans, as in Isa 29.10, must denote a state of spiritual insensibility."[121] Thus the translation "callousness"[122] aims to combine both the physical picture and the spiritual connotations. As with the Pharaoh (see Rom 9:17–18), so also with Israel; *this hardening is God's reaction to those in Israel who did not listen responsively to or believe the Gospel (10:16), who were unpersuaded and contradicting (10:21), who earnestly seek righteousness by works (11:6–7).* Paul cites these words from Deuteronomy and Isaiah in order to explain what the verb "they

---

[118] Moo, *Romans*, 681, n. 57.

[119] Cranfield, *Romans*, 549.

[120] Sanday and Headlam, *Romans*, 314–15.

[121] Cranfield, *Romans*, 550.

[122] Matera, *Romans*, 263–64, translates ἐπωρώθησαν at the end of 11:7 as "were made calloused." He then equates this divine action with the "spirit of stupefaction" in 11:8. See the fifth textual note on 11:7 and the second textual note on 11:8.

were hardened" (ἐπωρώθησαν) means at the end of 11:7. God reacts to their unbelief by acting on the spirit, making it calloused.

The other two elements in 11:8 express more clearly how God takes away or negatively changes a sensory function that previously existed. He has just demonstrated that Israel heard and knew (10:18, 19). But when they heard the message of the Good News and contradicted it (10:16, 21), God responded by replacing ears that were divinely intended to hear so as to believe (10:16–17) with those "not to hear" (11:8). Israel knew (10:19), but their refusal to be persuaded and their contradicting (10:21) led God to remove that insight and give them, instead, "eyes to not see" (11:8). Such a state exists, literally, "until the today day" (ἕως τῆς σήμερον ἡμέρας, 11:8), that is, "until this day" or "until the present," when Paul is writing.

A number of scholars connect Paul's use of Deuteronomy 29 and Isaiah 29 with Is 6:9–10, a passage in Isaiah's call to be a prophet (Is 6:1–13). Moo concludes that it is quite probable that Is 6:9–10 undergirds Paul's use of the other OT passages:

> [Is 6:9–10] became the standard early Christian "proof-text" to explain the spiritual obduracy of the Jews (Mark 4:12 and par[allels]; John 12:40; Acts 28:26) and has important verbal ("eyes that do not see," "ears that do not hear") and conceptual ("hardening"; the verb in LXX Isa. [6:10] is παχύνομαι, a synonym of πωρόω [used in Rom 11:7]) parallels with Paul's quotation (note also the link between Deut. 29:4 [MT 29:3] and Isa. 6:10 in their reference to the heart).[123]

While the comparable vocabulary and thought are interesting, it seems unwise to import that *text* (whether directly from Isaiah or from citations of Is 6:9–10 elsewhere in the NT) into the context here or to presume too much from perceived connections.[124]

Psalm 69:22 in Romans 11:9

Having cited from the Former Prophets in 11:2–4 and then from the Torah with a phrase from the latter prophet Isaiah in 11:8, Paul now draws on what "David says" (11:9) in Ps 69:22–23 (MT 69:23–24; LXX 68:23–24) (cf. Rom 4:6). LXX Ps 68:23 (MT 69:23; ET 69:22) and Rom 11:9 read:

γενηθήτω ἡ τράπεζα αὐτῶν ἐνώπιον αὐτῶν εἰς παγίδα
καὶ εἰς ἀνταπόδοσιν καὶ εἰς σκάνδαλον.

---

[123] Moo, *Romans*, 682, n. 59; see also Dunn, *Romans*, 641, who properly notes: "There is no specific allusion to Isa 6:9–10 as such here, but the theme is so close ... it would be surprising if Isa 6:9–10 was not in Paul's mind at this point."

[124] At the same time, one should recognize that Isaiah 6 contains the same kind of message as Romans 9–11, namely, unbelief by most of Israel. But the passage concludes with the promise of a remnant. Is 6:13 uses the simile of a tree that is chopped down, but a stump remains, and "the holy seed" is the stump that can then sprout again (as in Job 14:7–9, 14; cf. Paul's development of his olive-tree analogy in Rom 11:16–24).

Let their table come to be before them for a trap
>   and for recompense and for stumbling.
>   (LXX Ps 68:23 [MT 69:23; ET 69:22])

γενηθήτω ἡ τράπεζα αὐτῶν εἰς παγίδα
>   καὶ εἰς θήραν καὶ εἰς σκάνδαλον καὶ εἰς ἀνταπόδομα αὐτοῖς.

Let their table come to be for a trap
>   and for a snare and for stumbling and for payback to them.
>   (Rom 11:9)

Note the following:

- First, Paul deletes "before them" (ἐνώπιον αὐτῶν), though this element is picked up by the third person pronoun added at the end of Rom 11:9, "to them" (αὐτοῖς).

- Second, he inserts "and for a snare" (καὶ εἰς θήραν), which is parallel in meaning with "for a trap" (εἰς παγίδα). Dunn suggests that Paul may have added "and for a snare" either "deliberately or subconsciously from the very similar maledictory passage" in Ps 35:8 (LXX 34:8).[125]

- Third, the phrase "for stumbling" (εἰς σκάνδαλον) is the third prepositional phrase with "for" in both verses. However, it is the final phrase with "for" in the psalm, but the penultimate one in Rom 11:9, where Paul has a total of four phrases with "for."

- Finally, whereas "for recompense" (εἰς ἀνταπόδοσιν) is the second phrase with "for" in the psalm, Paul has an equivalent as his fourth phrase with "for": "for payback" (εἰς ἀνταπόδομα).[126] Dunn explains that "the thought of 'recompense, repayment,' is more clearly in ἀνταπόδομα" (Paul's term, which we have translated as "payback"), since in the LXX this term usually refers "to punishment."[127]

Cranfield correctly observes: "The general sense of this is no doubt a wish that even the good things which these enemies enjoy may prove to be a cause of disaster to them."[128] Various elucidations of the picture in the Psalter and in Paul have been suggested. The detail of the "table" can be explored further.[129]

---

[125] Dunn, *Romans*, 642; LXX Ps 34:8 reads ἐλθέτω αὐτοῖς παγὶς ἣν οὐ γινώσκουσιν, καὶ ἡ θήρα ἣν ἔκρυψαν, συλλαβέτω αὐτούς, καὶ ἐν τῇ παγίδι πεσοῦνται ἐν αὐτῇ.

[126] The MT has וְלִשְׁלוֹמִים, which might mean "and for their peaces [the plural of 'peace']," since שָׁלוֹם usually denotes "peace, completeness, wholeness." However, in this context the noun may refer to punishment or retribution that is "complete" or "entire" for them. The LXX reading, along with other ancient versions (see the *BHS* apparatus) translating the unpointed text, may have vocalized the consonants as וּלְשִׁלּוּמִים, "and for their recompenses/retribution," as the uncommon cognate noun שִׁלֻּם denotes "recompense, retribution," or "payback" (in the MT it appears only in Deut 32:35).

[127] Dunn, *Romans*, 643, citing as examples LXX Gen 50:15; Ps 27:4 (MT/ET 28:4); Lam 3:64; Joel 4:7 (ET 3:7); Judith 7:15; Sirach 14:6.

[128] Cranfield, *Romans*, 551.

[129] Schreiner, *Romans*, 589, wrongly says that "we transgress the boundaries of the text, then, in attempting to explain it precisely." Moo, *Romans*, 683, similarly contends that "it is fruitless to inquire about what the 'table' might stand for, or what 'bending the backs' might connote."

First, Käsemann contends that "a cultic sense ... alone seems to make good sense here."[130] Dunn offers support for this interpretation by asserting that "prior to the destruction of the temple τράπεζα seems to have been used only for the table of showbread."[131] A reference to Israel's worship sanctuary with all it entailed would then align with the advantages laid out in 9:4–5. Käsemann concludes: "Precisely the cultus which represents Jewish piety causes the blindness and fall of Israel."[132] If so, the extended connotations of "table" apply to those who continue to adhere to the necessity of the temple for atonement and fellowship with God, even though the "once for all" sacrifice of Christ (6:10) has now made the temple and its sacrifices obsolete (see also Heb 8:13). The overall argument of Hebrews provides a more extensive rebuttal to those who insist on adherence to the old covenant.[133] However, in this context, it seems difficult to perceive why one would pray for the blessings of the temple service (Rom 9:4) to become "a trap," "a snare," "stumbling," and "payback" (see the textual notes on these terms in 11:9).

Second, Barrett suggests that Paul envisions the issue of table fellowship, which he describes as "highly valued in Judaism."[134] It was also a cause for stumbling or offense among Jews and Gentiles within the early church (e.g., Acts 11:2–3; Gal 2:11–14).[135] Indeed, Paul discusses it later in Rom 14:1–3 and 14:13–15, where he again uses the term "stumbling" (σκάνδαλον, 14:13; also 9:33; 16:17).

Third, Sanday and Headlam interpret the reference to a table metaphorically. They define it as "that Law and those Scriptures wherein they [the unbelieving Jews] trusted," which "are to become the very cause of their fall and the snare or hunting-net in which they are caught."[136] If so, the thought of 9:32–33 applies here as both passages employ "stumbling" (σκάνδαλον). The "stumbling," then, is in regard to righteousness from works, a point reiterated in 11:6 and implied in 11:7. This interpretation is plausible; one needs to affirm that using works of the Law to seek righteousness remains a *misapplication* of the Law contrary to God's intent.[137]

The last interpretation seems most relevant. Yet Paul does not explicitly define his intended sense in regard to "table." This may reveal some deliberate

---

[130] Käsemann, *Romans*, 302; he cites 1 Cor 10:21 as a comparable cultic use of the noun in Paul.

[131] Dunn, *Romans*, 643, citing particularly Ex 39:36 (LXX 39:17); 1 Chr 28:16; 2 Chr 29:18; 1 Macc 1:22; he adds that after AD 70 "the function of atonement [transferred] from altar to table," but that thought would be anachronistic here.

[132] Käsemann, *Romans*, 302; considered also by Dunn, *Romans*, 643, who speaks of Paul's "fellow Jews' dependence on atonement through the sacrificial system."

[133] See Middendorf and Schuler, *Called by the Gospel*, 282–87, 289.

[134] Barrett, *Romans*, 211.

[135] For an interpretation of the Galatians text, see Das, *Galatians*, 204–32, which includes an excursus titled "The Issue at Antioch."

[136] Sanday and Headlam, *Romans*, 315; also considered by Morris, *Romans*, 404.

[137] See Rom 3:19–21, 28; 9:10–10:5; also Jn 1:45; 5:45–47; 2 Cor 3:14–16; Gal 2:15–21.

ambiguity on his part.[138] In any case, the ambiguity allows for a broader application of the "table" which can encompass a number of the views espoused
above without being restricted to a single identification.

Psalm 69:23 in Romans 11:10

The citation of Ps 69:23 (MT 69:24) in Rom 11:10 replicates LXX Ps
68:24 exactly. In light of the discrepancies in Rom 11:9 with LXX Ps 68:23
(MT 69:23; ET 69:22) noted above, this might seem almost surprising. It does,
however, reveal Paul's awareness and general reliance upon the Greek translation. LXX Ps 68:24 (MT 69:24; ET 69:23) reads:

σκοτισθήτωσαν οἱ ὀφθαλμοὶ αὐτῶν τοῦ μὴ βλέπειν
καὶ τὸν νῶτον αὐτῶν διὰ παντὸς σύγκαμψον.

Let their eyes become darkened to not see
and bend their back continually.

As suggested in regard to 11:8, Paul may have modified the negation in the text of
Deut 29:4 (MT/LXX 29:3) in order to match the comparable use of the negated
infinitive here, "to not see" (τοῦ μὴ βλέπειν). It is intriguing that the initial verb
is an aorist passive imperative, "let them become darkened" (σκοτισθήτωσαν).
Paul may intend for the passive verb to convey an active but intransitive sense.[139]
But understanding it as a divine passive fits with 11:7c, the action of God in
11:8, and the tone of the imprecatory psalm. If so, the plea is, in effect, "may
God darken them." This also makes the sense comparable to the aorist active
imperative, "bend [σύγκαμψον] their back." Cranfield offers various connotations for this image:

> The thought could be of, for example, being bowed down under oppressive
> slavery, being bent under a heavy burden, cowering with fear, being bowed
> down by grief, being too weak to stand upright, or stooping to grope on the
> ground because one's sight is bad or one is blind. Of these the third or fourth
> could be held to correspond best to the Hebrew, while the last would fit the
> first half of the verse very neatly.[140]

The psalmist requests for the enemies darkened eyes "to not see" (as in Rom
11:8) and for bent backs to become a present reality in a spiritual sense.

But this should *not* be understood as conveying that God's predetermined
will is to blind people so that they will stumble into eternal judgment. His will
is to save "everyone" (10:13), and for this reason he sends his Word near, to be
heard and believed (10:6–15). For those in Israel who sought by works to attain
righteousness, who did not believe in the Good News or obtain its proffered

---

[138] The terminology comes from the title of an article by Raabe, "Deliberate Ambiguity in the
Psalter." Note this commentary's application of the phrase "deliberate ambiguity" to Paul's
quotation from Hab 2:4 in Rom 1:17; see Middendorf, *Romans 1–8*, 106.

[139] See Voelz, *Fundamental Greek Grammar*, 144–46; for a good example, see the third textual
note on 1:21.

[140] Cranfield, *Romans*, 552.

righteousness, and consequently "were hardened" (11:7) as a result of their persistent rejection of the prophetic "message" (10:16), God's will is that the judgment pronounced in Ps 69:22–23 (MT 69:23–24; LXX 68:23–24) and Rom 11:9–10 may yet move them to repentance. Only if they perish in unbelief will this judgment become eternal. Therefore Barrett and the RSV mistranslate when they render διὰ παντός at the end of 11:10 as "for ever."[141] Neither the psalmist nor Paul prays for that! In fact, it would contradict 11:11 and 11:14–15. While the phrase διὰ παντός in 11:10 literally means "through all," it conveys the underlying Hebrew, which expresses continuity (see the fourth textual note in 11:10). In other words, "so long as it does go on, it is to be not intermittent but continuous and sustained."[142] God desires this state of hardening to be reversed, which happens when obstinate unbelievers cease resisting his Word and, instead, listen responsively to the Good News of Christ (10:16–17). They then recognize that God's patience sought all along to lead them to repentance (2:4). But if they remain in a "spirit of callousness" (11:8), deaf to the Word to the end of life, they will be consigned to everlasting darkness.

Concluding Implications

Both the setting of these words within the entirety of Psalm 69 and its NT applications are important. Moo notes that "quotations and probable allusions to this psalm occur in Mark 3:21; 15:23 and par[allels]; Luke 13:35; John 2:17; 15:25; Acts 1:20; Rom. 15:3; Phil. 4:3; Rev. 3:5; 16:1."[143] He then concludes:

> This interpretive tradition, according to which David's own sentiments in the psalm are applied to Jesus, makes it natural for Paul to apply to the enemies of Jesus Christ what David says about his own enemies. … What David prayed would happen to his persecutors, Paul suggests, God has brought upon those Jews who have resisted the gospel.[144]

The prayer of David, therefore, expresses a comparable reality to the words from Deut 29:4 (MT/LXX 29:3) cited in Rom 11:8, which Moses originally applied to the Israelites in the wilderness. Centuries later, Paul contends that this is true in his day as well, though he will soon insist that God's hardening of those who resist his will *need not* be permanent (11:11, 15, 23–24).

As with the hardening of Pharaoh (see 9:17–18), so it is now for those in Israel who heard and knew but refused to believe the Good News (10:16–21). Paul cites the psalmist's prayer calling upon God to act in a comparable manner. But, as in the exodus and in spite of divine hardening, the result remains that God's "[saving] power" (τὴν δύναμίν, 9:17) and his name are proclaimed in Egypt, in Israel, and to the ends of the earth (9:17; 10:18).

---

[141] Barrett, *Romans*, 210.

[142] Cranfield, *Romans*, 552.

[143] Moo, *Romans*, 682, n. 61.

[144] Moo, *Romans*, 682–83.

Though the psalmist's words may sound ominous and harsh, they are no more so than the searing indictment Paul files against all people, including every Jew and Gentile, earlier in the letter. Käsemann points out that by the end of 11:10 "there is confirmed in Israel what 1:18–3:20 established about the whole world. Just for that reason the turning can come to Israel which is announced in 3:21," namely, the turning away from works righteousness to the righteousness of God through faith in Christ which brings salvation to all,[145] Jew and Gentile alike, as just reiterated in 10:11–13.

What Happens Next? (11:11–12)

Those Who Tripped ... (11:11a)

Before turning to address Gentiles directly beginning in 11:13, Paul wraps up the consequences of 11:1–10 in 11:11–12 (see "Introduction to Romans 11:1–12" above). Since both 11:11 and 11:12 mention "the Gentiles," they provide an effective segue into the following section. Paul also nicely frames this section by returning to the format of 11:1. He opens both 11:1 and 11:11 with the same introduction, "I say, then/therefore" (λέγω οὖν), followed, in both places, by a negated question, and further rebuke of it.

"I say, therefore, it is not that they tripped with the result that they might remain fallen, is it? May it never come to be!" (11:11a). Who are the "they" under consideration? Paul returns to *the beginning* of 11:7 in order to elaborate further: "What then? That which *Israel* seeks earnestly, this it did not obtain" (11:7a). Thus the subject of "tripped" (ἔπταισαν) is "those Jews who have rejected the gospel."[146] Significantly, the voice of the verb "they tripped" is *active* (see the second textual note on 11:11). Thus this does *not* represent a divine passive; neither does it refer to any action on God's part. In other words, God did *not* knock them down or trip them up. They *actively* tripped, and why is clear from 9:30–10:5.

This tripping (ἔπταισαν, 11:11) stands equivalent to the "stumbling" (προσέκοψαν) discussed and explained in 9:32. It occurs on the same "stone of stumbling" and "rock of offense" of which/whom Isaiah prophesied (λίθον προσκόμματος καὶ πέτραν σκανδάλου, 9:33, citing Is 8:14; 28:16). Those in Israel who pursue righteousness "as if [it could be attained] from works" (9:32) are running in the wrong direction and, thereby, fail to recognize God's actions toward them. They rely on their own willing and striving (9:16; cf. 9:31) and, in looking to establish "their own" righteousness (10:3; 11:7), trip over the stone in whom they were to believe (9:32–33). That is, they refuse to listen responsively to the "Word of Christ" (10:16–17) or to be persuaded by the message; instead, they contradict it (10:21). *Therefore, this "trip up" occurs from earnestly seeking righteousness "not from faith but as if [it could be attained] from*

---

[145] Käsemann, *Romans*, 303.

[146] Cranfield, *Romans*, 554; he adds that they are equivalent to "the rest" (οἱ ... λοιποί) in 11:7. But the description applies more properly to those "seeking earnestly" earlier in 11:7.

works" (ἐξ ἔργων, 9:32).[147] Furthermore, it results in a fall from grace, for "if [his choice] is by grace, it is not from works" (ἐξ ἔργων, 11:6).

… Need Not Remain Fallen (11:11a)

The ἵνα clause in 11:11, "with the result that they might remain fallen," does *not* introduce an expression of (divine) purpose.[148] Rather it conveys the resulting state of those who tripped. The verb for "fall" here, πίπτω, conveys a result "consequent upon and more serious than πταίειν ['to trip' earlier in the verse]."[149] Michaelis notes that "in most instances" this verb (πίπτω) is used literally in the NT, where it "denotes an unintentional fall."[150] "But the notion of spiritual ruin is present in three of Paul's other uses of the term (Rom. 11:22; 14:4; 1 Cor. 10:12) and in Heb. 4:11."[151] It should be reinforced that, as with "they tripped" earlier in Rom 11:11, God is neither the source of the action nor the cause of its result.

The reason for the current fallen state of *some* in Israel is not sin in a general or moral sense or its consequent guilt.[152] Instead, when Paul uses πίπτω again in 11:22, in "the ones who fell" (τοὺς πεσόντας), the context specifies that it involves falling from faith, that is, into "unbelief" (τῇ ἀπιστίᾳ, 11:23). Rom 11:20 also clarifies that "due to unbelief" fallen branches "were broken off" (τῇ ἀπιστίᾳ ἐξεκλάσθησαν). The fall under consideration in 11:11, then, results from refusing to believe the Good News they heard, just as Isaiah foretold (Is 53:1, quoted in Rom 10:16; see also 10:18).

The question now concerns whether those who now lie fallen must *remain* so (see the third textual note on 11:11). Is recovery now impossible? Sanday and Headlam construe the verb πίπτω as denoting "a complete and irrevocable fall."[153] Moo defines it as "irretrievable spiritual ruin."[154] From a purely *human* perspective, this may be true; the verb depicts a fall from which one cannot recover *on one's own*. But this does not mean that the result of their tripping is

---

[147] Dunn, *Romans*, 653, recognizes that this is how "Israel's endeavor has been misdirected (9:31–32; 10:3; 11:7): this maintains the coherence of the imagery Paul has been using—in 'pursuing' ἐξ ἔργων ['from works'] they have erred and in thus 'slipping up' have failed to obtain their goal."

[148] As maintained by Käsemann, *Romans*, 304; Murray, *Romans*, 2:76; see the third textual note on 11:11.

[149] Dunn, *Romans*, 653.

[150] W. Michaelis, "πίπτω," *TDNT* 6:162.

[151] Moo, *Romans*, 687, n. 14.

[152] Sanday and Headlam, *Romans*, 320 conclude: "They have stumbled and sinned." They take "trip" (πταίω) in an ethical sense, as it is used elsewhere (they cite Deut 7:25; James 2:10; 3:2; 2 Pet 1:10). W. Michaelis, "πίπτω," *TDNT* 6:164, improperly imports the notion of guilt into Paul's discussion here.

[153] Sanday and Headlam, *Romans*, 320–21.

[154] Moo, *Romans*, 687.

unalterable from a *divine* perspective, as 11:12 makes clear.[155] The image of a race[156] may or may not be in Paul's mind, but a number of expressions readily cause the image to emerge. In this case, one envisions a runner stumbling or tripping over a stone (9:32–33; 11:11). After falling he might be able to right himself, regain his balance, and resume the race. At other times, however, when a runner trips and falls over a rock, he is unable to recover and cannot continue *on his own*. But what if help comes from the outside?

Paul vehemently rejects the notion that they must remain fallen: "May it never come to be!" (μὴ γένοιτο, 11:11). It is just as preposterous as the suggestion that God pushed away his own people, which Paul renounced just as emphatically (11:1). "Israel's fall, then, is not the end of the race."[157]

As in 11:1, Paul's personal experience illustrates that this fall need not be permanent. He was once a blasphemous and violent persecutor, acting in ignorance and "in unbelief" (ἐν ἀπιστίᾳ, 1 Tim 1:13; see Rom 11:23). His pursuit of his own righteousness via works (Phil 3:6, 9) caused him to stumble or trip over the rock of his salvation. After being confronted by the risen Christ, he was knocked off of his "high horse" and literally "fell" to the ground (πεσών, Acts 9:4, is a form of the same verb, πίπτω, as used here, πέσωσιν, Rom 11:11). For three days he was also given "eyes to not see" (ὀφθαλμοὺς τοῦ μὴ βλέπειν, Rom 11:8, 10): "although his eyes were opened, he was seeing nothing" (ἀνεῳγμένων δὲ τῶν ὀφθαλμῶν αὐτοῦ οὐδὲν ἔβλεπεν, Acts 9:8; cf. his companions who were "seeing no one," μηδένα δὲ θεωροῦντες, Acts 9:7). Yet God intervened to show him grace and mercy "in Christ Jesus our Lord" (1 Tim 1:12; see also 1 Tim 1:14, 16).[158]

---

[155] Middendorf and Schuler, *Called by the Gospel*, 285, make the same divine/human distinction in regard to Heb 6:4–6:

> The "falling away" here [παραπεσόντας, Heb 6:6] is not simply a falling into sin due to fear or the weakness of our human nature. Instead, it describes outright apostasy and a complete renunciation of the faith by one who once believed. It is the repeated hardening of one's own heart against God and his will. It is, therefore, obstinate unbelief, the "unforgivable sin" against the Holy Spirit spoken of by Jesus (Mark 3:28–29). Is someone in this situation gone for good?

> The Greek word translated "impossible" in 6:4 more accurately asserts that such a person is "unable" or "powerless" to return to God. According to Jesus, people are "unable" or "powerless" in terms of their own ability to be among the saved in the first place (Luke 18:24–27). Indeed, apart from God's intervention, it is impossible for any of us to repent and be saved. And so, the book of Acts speaks of repentance as God's gracious action in our lives (Acts 5:31; 11:18). This passage in Hebrews reinforces the point that such turning or, in this case, returning to God is something we are powerless to do; it happens only and always by the work of God's Spirit.

[156] Matera, *Romans*, 265. Dunn, *Romans*, 653, compares Israel's tripping and falling to "the sprawling on one's face which puts a runner out of the race."

[157] Matera, *Romans*, 265.

[158] Note the use of phrases comparable to "Jesus Christ our Lord" throughout Romans 5–8; see Middendorf, *Romans 1–8*, 377–79.

Israel's Stumbling Leads to Gentile Salvation (11:11b)

In the meantime, God has already worked a benevolent result out of the unfortunate fact that they tripped. "But by their stumble the salvation [comes] to the Gentiles" (11:11b). "By their stumble" (τῷ αὐτῶν παραπτώματι) needs explanation. The noun here rendered as "stumble" (παράπτωμα) is used six times in 5:15–20 to describe Adam's "trespass" and its consequences. Cranfield explains:

> The substantive παράπτωμα is frequently used by Paul to denote "trespass," "sin" (in the sense of a particular sinful deed), and it is clear that what is referred to here is the sin committed by the λοιποί [the "rest" in 11:7] in rejecting the gospel.[159]

While essentially correct, two points of clarification should be noted. *First, one cannot blame God for this sinful παράπτωμα.* Schreiner does so by asserting: "Romans 9:30–11:10 has clarified sufficiently that Israel's rejection of the gospel is sinful, even if it had been planned by God."[160] Paul in no way regards anyone's refusal to believe the Gospel as involving God's intent, action, or plan. On the contrary, God's Good News is for all to hear, believe, and confess, so everyone may call on the Lord Jesus and be saved (10:6–13; also 1:16).

Second, the specific "stumble" (παράπτωμα) under consideration in 11:11–12 is not simply a moral "trespass" consisting of acting contrary to God's commandments (cf. Paul's sinning in 7:14–25). Instead, the contextual language of tripping and falling in 11:11, as well as the ongoing connotations of a foot race (9:30–33; 11:7, 11),[161] indicates that this noun should "be given its more obvious etymological sense,"[162] namely, "making a false step so as to lose footing" (BDAG; see the fifth textual note on 11:11). This sinful "false step"[163] or "stumble"[164] (cf. 9:32–33) stands equivalent to "Israel's unbelief"

---

[159] Cranfield, *Romans*, 555.

[160] Schreiner, *Romans*, 594.

[161] The image of running a race is suggested by, for example, "pursuing" (9:30, 31); "stumbling" (9:32, 33); "seeking earnestly" (11:7); "obtaining" (11:7); "tripping" and "falling" (11:11); cf. also 1 Cor 9:24–26; Phil 3:12–14; 2 Tim 4:7–8. Matera, *Romans*, 265, states: "As he did in 9:30–32, Paul makes use of the metaphor of a race"; similarly, Stowers, *A Rereading of Romans*, 312–15; Dunn, *Romans*, 580, 589, 593, refers to the metaphor repeatedly and then contends that in Rom 11:11 "the imagery of 9:33 ['a stone of stumbling and a rock of offense'] is obviously still in mind" and that "Paul is drawing out a connected train of thought from a familiar sequence of interrelated imagery" (652). He then suggests that "παράπτωμα ['stumble'] can mean 'false step, or slip,' so Paul may consciously or unconsciously be continuing with the same circle of imagery" (653).

[162] Barrett, *Romans*, 213. The basic root πτῶμα in the noun παράπτωμα is technically a cognate noun of the verb "to fall" (πίπτω) used earlier in the verse (πέσωσιν), rather than of πταίω, "to trip"; see Morris, *Romans*, 407, n. 51, and Cranfield, *Romans*, 555. (In the NT this root noun, πτῶμα, denotes a fallen "body" or "corpse," e.g., Mt 14:12; 24:28; Rev 11:8–9.) Nevertheless, Munck, *Christ and Israel*, 118, maintains the connection: "παράπτωμα ['stumbling'], therefore, must refer back to ἔπταισαν ['tripped']."

[163] Sanday and Headlam, *Romans*, 321.

[164] Barrett, *Romans*, 213.

(BDAG, s.v. παράπτωμα, 2 b β; Rom 3:3; 10:16; 11:20, 23). Chrysostom puts it succinctly: "To stumble is to disbelieve,"[165] which is, in fact, the ultimate condemning sin. As Pieper clarifies:

> Of course, all sins, original sin and actual sins, are indeed damnable in themselves ... , and this truth must be urged against all who minimize sin; but in fact (*actu*) only unbelief results in damnation. This truth must be brought home to all who minimize the work of Christ, the complete reconciliation He brought about through His vicarious satisfaction. ... But where unbelief reigns, all other sins again assume their condemnatory character [citing Mk 16:16; Jn 3:18, 36].[166]

Israel's unbelieving rejection of grace stems from striving for righteousness based upon works instead of receiving it from faith (9:30–32; 10:3; 11:6–7). But by means of this sinful stumble, Paul contends that "the salvation" (ἡ σωτηρία, 11:11; see 1:16) God promised and brought to Israel has also now gone out to the Gentiles as well (note 10:10–12).

A Pattern Established from Paul's Ministry in Acts

Repeated events from Paul's own ministry experience are particularly illustrative. He goes "to [the] Jew first" (see 1:16) and has some success. But when he encounters rejection and hostility, most often from Jewish leaders, he turns to the Gentiles. An example from his first missionary journey establishes a pattern. After speaking at the synagogue in Pisidian Antioch, "many of the Jews" (πολλοὶ τῶν Ἰουδαίων) and devout proselytes "were persuaded [ἔπειθον] to remain in the grace of God" (Acts 13:43; i.e., in the olive tree of Rom 11:17–24; cf. 11:5–6; contrast "unpersuaded" in 10:21). The following Sabbath a great crowd gathered, but some other Jews were filled with "jealousy" or "envy" (ζῆλος, the same word used in Rom 10:2; cf. παραζηλόω, "provoke to envy," in Rom 10:19; 11:11, 14) and "spoke against" (ἀντιλέγω, the same verb used to describe Israel as "contradicting" in Rom 10:21) the apostolic message (Acts 13:44–45). But Paul and Barnabas were emboldened to answer:

> ⁴⁶It was necessary that the Word of God be spoken to you *first* [πρῶτος; see Rom 1:16]. Because you push it away from yourselves [ἀπωθεῖσθε, from ἀπωθέω, the same verb used in Rom 11:1–2] and you judge yourselves not worthy of eternal life, look, we are turning *to the Gentiles* [εἰς τὰ ἔθνη]. ⁴⁷Indeed, so the Lord himself has commanded and still directs us, "I have placed you, and so you now are a light of the Gentiles so that you might be *for salvation* [εἰς σωτηρίαν, the same phrase used in Rom 1:16; 10:1, 10; see also the noun in Rom 11:11] until the last [part] of the earth. (Acts 13:46–47)

This sequential pattern, repeated numerous times with slight variations throughout Acts (e.g., Acts 14:1–3; 18:4–7; 19:8–10; 28:23–29), is similar to and perhaps even helped to form the content outlined in Romans 10–11. God

---

[165] Chrysostom, *Homilies on Romans*, 16 (Bray, *Romans*, ACCS NT 6:270).

[166] Pieper, *Christian Dogmatics*, 3:548.

sends out messengers to proclaim the Word of Christ "to [the] Jew first" (1:16), where it *engenders faith in ma*ny (10:14–17; see also Acts 13:43). But *both* groups referenced in 11:7a ("Israel … did not obtain") and 11:7b ("the chosen obtained") are represented. "Not all" listen responsively to or believe the Good News of salvation (οὐ πάντες, 10:16). Those who are unpersuaded speak against it (10:21). They push God's Word away from themselves (ἀπωθεῖσθε, Acts 13:46). Does God then react by pushing away (ἀπώσατο, Rom 11:1–2) those who stumble over the Christ in whom they are being called to believe? By no means! (11:1). He stretched out his hands to them (10:21), but, at a certain point, as with the Pharaoh of Romans 9, "they were hardened" (11:7c).[167] Paul's experience in Pisidian Antioch and in the other places mentioned in the Acts passages cited above *serves as an illustrative example of this section in Romans*. More accurately in a chronological sense, these events in Acts form the backdrop which may well have produced the sequence Paul pulls together here.

By salvation going to the Gentiles, God hopes to accomplish what Moses first prophesied in Deut 32:21, as cited by Paul already in Rom 10:19 (see the textual notes and the commentary there). He hopes that this will result in making those in Israel who initially rejected the Good News envious (εἰς τὸ παραζηλῶσαι αὐτούς, 11:11).[168] However, this entire scenario, since it includes the unbelief of most in Israel, should not be viewed as consisting of God's prior will or gracious intention.[169] Instead, we see in the hardening here (11:7–10) the divine *reaction* to those who refused the message of Christ. God endeavors to reclaim those who disbelieved and consequently tripped over the Stone (9:32–33; 11:11) by sending salvation out to the Gentiles too. The ultimate end, God and Paul hope, is the salvation of Israel as well (see 11:14; see also 10:1; 11:22–23). Clearly then, this very hope means God has *not* pushed away his people (11:2) and that the current fallen state of the people as a whole, depicted in 11:11, *need not* be permanent. The next verse makes this even more apparent as Paul clarifies precisely what he means with a provocative question.

Great Riches and a Greater Goal (11:12)

Richness for Gentiles (11:12a)

"But if their stumble [is] richness of [the] world and their loss [is] richness of [the] Gentiles, how much more their fullness?" (11:12). Israel's "stumble" (παράπτωμα), as discussed in the comments on the previous verse (11:11), resulted in the Gospel of salvation going out to the Gentiles. The Gospel of

---

[167] See also "Hardening" in "Is This Fair to the Pharaoh? (9:17–18)" in the commentary on 9:14–24.

[168] Ticciati, "The Nondivisive Difference of Election," 269, argues that Israel's jealousy "occurs in this verse [Deut 32:21] *in parallel with God's jealousy*" and that this notion "may be harnessed to illuminate Rom 9–11 in a most intriguing way." But Paul never refers to *God's* jealousy over Israel, so it is difficult to perceive how this element can have significance for the hearers or readers of Romans. See also 10:19.

[169] Cranfield, *Romans*, 556, calls it "the divine intention."

Christ is the "richness" (πλοῦτος) referred to here. Along with this salvation come innumerable other riches (see the second textual note on 11:12). Barth locates Israel's stumble and the richness of the Gentiles at the cross: "The *fall* and *loss* of Israel, as they are manifested in the crucifixion of Christ, are the *riches of the world* and the *riches of the Gentiles.* But only in the light of the Cross of Christ is this wealth revealed to the world."[170] However, this would seem to discount the fact that Jesus' death actually won salvation for Jew and Gentile alike. A more applicable pattern of Israel's stumble becoming richness for the Gentiles takes place repeatedly within Paul's own ministry as the Gospel spread out into the Gentile world (e.g., Acts 13:46–47; see "A Pattern Established from Paul's Ministry in Acts" in the commentary on Rom 11:11b). On that basis one might simply then equate the "richness of [the] world" with that "of the Gentiles" (11:12). But Paul does not view this "richness of [the] *world*" in any restrictive sense, as if these riches are only for Gentiles and not for Israel as well. His thematic expression of "to [the] Jew first and also to [the] Greek" emphasizes this (1:16). More immediately pertinent for the noun "richness" (πλοῦτος) is the cognate verb, "be rich" (πλουτέω), which Paul employs to make the inclusivity explicit in regard to the Lord Jesus in 10:12: "For there is not a difference [between] a Jew and a Greek, for the same Lord [is] of all, being rich [πλουτῶν] to all the ones who are calling on him."

The "stumble" of the unbelieving Jews is then equated with their "loss" (ἥττημα, 11:12). The KJV translates ἥττημα as "diminishing" (i.e., a fewer number of people), which serves as a contrast with Paul's use of "fullness" at the end of the verse. But Moo discounts that understanding, properly arguing that Paul more likely uses ἥττημα in order to depict their "defeat" or "loss."[171] The term then denotes a current state of being which stands equivalent with "remain fallen" (πέσωσιν) in 11:11. Paul utilizes it in order to describe how the reaction of those in Israel who did not believe the Gospel (10:16) and, therefore, are now lost has led some Gentiles to hear, believe, and receive the riches of salvation. The latter result is surely a good thing!

God's "How Much More" Hope (11:12b)

How much better, then, Paul queries, would be "their fullness" (τὸ πλήρωμα αὐτῶν, 11:12)? Cranfield argues that the pronoun "their" (αὐτῶν) must refer *only* to unbelieving Jews; he concludes that the phrase describes

> the unbelieving majority's being brought up to its full numerical strength (i.e., the full strength of Israel as a whole …) by being reunited with the believing minority through its own (i.e., the majority's) conversion.[172]

However, Paul employs the pronoun "their" (αὐτῶν) in the same general manner as when he speaks of the entirety of ethnic "Israel" in 9:31; 10:19, 21 (see

---

[170] Barth, *Romans*, 403.

[171] Moo, *Romans*, 688; for ἥττημα, see the third textual note on 11:12.

[172] Cranfield, *Romans*, 558; similarly, Barrett, *Romans*, 213.

"God's People" in the introduction to Romans 9–11). The referent of "their" in "their fullness" refers to Israel as a whole and so encompasses unbelieving Jews, but it need not imply that all of them will be part of "the fullness" (11:12).

What then of "the fullness" (τὸ πλήρωμα, 11:12)? Numerous possibilities exist for understanding the precise meaning of the noun here (see the fifth textual note on 11:12). Examples of this noun "with a straightforward numerical sense are rare" in extrabiblical literature and are "entirely absent" elsewhere in the NT and in the LXX.[173] Nevertheless, Moo properly recognizes that the influence of the comparable phrase in 11:25 "strongly favors a numerical sense" here, which he identifies as "the full number."[174] It seems almost certain, then, that the phrase "their fullness" (τὸ πλήρωμα αὐτῶν, 11:12) conveys a meaning comparable to the parallel expression "the fullness of the Gentiles" (τὸ πλήρωμα τῶν ἐθνῶν) in 11:25. There Paul certainly does *not* envision the conversion or salvation of *every* Gentile. Instead, "the fullness of the Gentiles" indicates the full number "*of*" or "*from among*" the Gentiles who will be saved. In *both* 11:12 *and* 11:25, then, the genitive case after the same noun, "the fullness" (τὸ πλήρωμα), communicates the same partitive sense, "*which is a part of.*"[175] This is corroborated by the phrase "some from them" in 11:14 (τινὰς ἐξ αὐτῶν; see the commentary on 11:14). It also maintains the truth Isaiah announced and Paul affirms: "If the number of the sons of Israel might be as the sand of the sea[shore], the remnant will be saved" (Is 10:22, cited in Rom 9:27).

"Their fullness" (11:12), then, refers to the full number of those comprising the remnant, which is a part of Israel.[176] Again, as Paul will soon make clear, "their fullness" consists of all those who do "not remain in unbelief" (11:23). Thus Paul hopes "that when the [unbelieving] Jews saw that the Gentiles were being allowed into the kingdom of God, they might perhaps repent more easily"[177] and imitate the faith of those Gentiles who "were so unexpectedly accepted by God"[178] (11:14; cf. Heb 13:7).

An Open-Ended Conclusion: How Will the Older Brother Respond?

The references cited already from what Paul will soon articulate in the remainder of Romans 11 illustrate the necessity of moving forward. But before proceeding, one could return to the open-ended conclusion of the parable of the

---

[173] Moo, *Romans*, 689–90, including n. 35.

[174] Moo, *Romans*, 689; he adds that πλήρωμα has "a qualitative denotation" that "is attained through a numerical process" (690).

[175] Wallace, *Greek Grammar*, 84, discussing the partitive genitive in general.

[176] Keener, *Romans*, 133, refers to "the turning of the requisite portion of Israel to Jesus (versus the current smaller remnant)," but that is inadvisable since it implies that a certain number is required for "Israel's restoration," which he supposes will "bring about even the promised time of the resurrection of the righteous."

[177] Pelagius, *Romans* (Bray, *Romans*, ACCS NT 6:291).

[178] Cyril of Alexandria, *Romans* (Bray, *Romans*, ACCS NT 6:291).

Waiting Father[179] (Prodigal Son) utilized earlier in Rom 10:16–21 (see "The Father's Intended Outcome" in the commentary on 10:19). The younger son, like the lost tax collectors and "sinners" (Lk 15:1; cf. the Gentiles), has heard and believed his father's good news. He has been welcomed home by his father, the main character in the story (cf. the God-centered focus of Romans), with the "richness" (Rom 11:12) of an elaborate celebration (Lk 15:22–24). The older son protests (cf. Rom 10:21) against the father's lavish grace (cf. Rom 11:6) and, instead, relies slavishly on his own works as the basis of his claim to a righteous relationship with his father (Lk 15:29; cf. the Pharisees and scribes in Lk 15:2). This trips him up, and he stumbles by refusing to come in to the feast (Lk 15:28; Rom 11:11). In fact, the father's lavishness in killing the fatted calf to graciously provide a most undeserved celebration for his younger brother makes the older brother angry and provokes him to envy (cf. Rom 11:11). "You never gave a goat to me!" (Lk 15:29).

This unpersuaded and contradictory response (Rom 10:21) to the father's welcome of the outcast is met how? Does the father react by pushing his older son away? "By no means!" (Rom 11:1–2). He takes the initiative to go out (Lk 15:28) and reassure him of the good news—"all my things are yours" (Lk 15:31). The older son has removed and excluded himself from his own home, but he need not remain outside (Rom 11:11). The Father stretches out his hands (Rom 10:21) and invites him to join together with his brother and to reenter his father's house, which belongs to the older brother too.

How do these events resolve themselves for the characters in the parable? Will the older brother remain in self-exclusion or rejoin his own family? Jesus does not tell us. But the situation in Romans 11 is comparable. How will those analogous to the older son, namely, Jews who do not currently believe in their Messiah, respond? Must they "remain fallen … ? May it never come to be!" (11:11). The father rejoiced at the return of the younger son, who once was dead, but is now alive (Lk 15:32). "How much more" (Rom 11:12) would he rejoice if the older son heard, believed, and listened responsively to his invitation, which is the prophetic "message" (10:16). It would also be "life from [the] dead" (11:15).

Paul continues by directing his words more narrowly: "But to you Gentiles I say …" (11:13). He offers counsel to the newly welcomed Gentiles about their elder brothers in Israel (11:13–16). Then he describes how the Father's entire household operates by employing the analogy of an olive tree (11:17–24). Finally, Romans 9–11 culminates with resolution and doxology (11:25–36).

---

[179] The more appropriate title for the parable comes from a collection of sermons by Thielicke titled *The Waiting Father*.

How Gentiles Should Respond to Israel and to God: An Olive-Tree Analogy

Translation

11 **¹³**But to you Gentiles I say (as for me, then, insofar as I myself am an apostle of Gentiles), I glorify my ministry **¹⁴**[so that] if, somehow, I might provoke my flesh to envy, I will also save some from them. **¹⁵**Indeed, if the loss of them is reconciliation of [the] world, what is the acceptance [of them] if not life from [the] dead? **¹⁶**And if the firstfruits are holy, the lump [of dough] is also, and if the root is holy, so also are the branches.

¹⁷And if some of the branches were broken off, but you, while being a wild olive [branch], you were grafted in among them and you became a fellow sharer with the root of the oily sap of the olive tree, **¹⁸**then do not boast against the branches. But if you are boasting against [them, know that] you are not bearing the root, but the root [bears] you. **¹⁹**You will then say, "Branches were broken off so that I might be grafted in." **²⁰**Well [said]! Due to unbelief they were broken off, but you have stood and remain standing by faith. Do not set your mind on proud [thoughts], but reverently fear! **²¹**Indeed, if God did not spare the branches [which were] in accord with nature, neither will he spare you.

²²See then [the] kindness and severity of God. On the one hand, upon the ones who fell, severity, but, on the other hand, upon you, God's kindness, if you remain in his kindness; otherwise you also will be cut off. **²³**And those also, if they do not remain in unbelief, they will be grafted in; for God is powerful to graft them in again. **²⁴**For if you, in accord with nature from the wild olive tree, you were cut off and, contrary to nature, you were grafted into a cultivated olive tree, how much more will these, the ones in accord with nature, be grafted into their own olive tree?

Textual Notes

11:13 ἐφ᾽ ὅσον μὲν οὖν εἰμι ἐγὼ ἐθνῶν ἀπόστολος—This is a parenthetical aside: "(as for me, then, insofar as I myself am an apostle of Gentiles)." Under the thirteenth of eighteen (!) listed categories for the preposition ἐπί, BDAG identifies its use as a "marker of number or measure" and translates ἐφ᾽ ὅσον as *to the degree that, in so far as* (as also in Mt 25:40, 45). The latter is best; see the commentary.

As in 10:1, μέν has no corresponding δέ; see the second textual note on 10:1. It is hard to give μέν the force of "contrary to what you might expect,"[1] as that is more typically the force of the absent δέ clause.

Paul referred to himself by his office as ἀπόστολος, "apostle," at the start of the letter (see the third textual note on 1:1 and "Paul's Call [1:1]" in the commentary there;

---

[1]   Moo, *Romans*, 691.

the only other instance of ἀπόστολος in Romans is the plural in 16:7). Here, however, he modifies his vocation by the genitive ἐθνῶν, "of Gentiles." This likely is an example of the rare genitive of destination/direction or purpose ("destined for, toward"),[2] meaning "an apostle (purposely sent to) Gentiles." Paul uses the same kind of genitive in Gal 2:7 when he declares, πεπίστευμαι τὸ εὐαγγέλιον τῆς ἀκροβυστίας, "I have been entrusted with the Good News *of uncircumcision*," meaning he has been entrusted with the mission of bringing the Gospel *to* the uncircumcised, i.e., to the Gentiles. See further " 'An Apostle of Gentiles' (11:13b–c)" in the commentary.

τὴν διακονίαν μου—This is the first of the three occurrences of διακονία, "ministry," in Romans. In 12:7 it depicts Christian service more generally. But here and in 15:31 Paul speaks specifically of his own (μου, "my") apostolic ministry, whereby he is "functioning in the interest of a larger public" (BDAG, 3), a ministry which explicitly aims at reaching out to Gentiles.

δοξάζω—Usually the verb "glorify" has God as its direct object and signifies worship (e.g., Lk 2:20; 7:16). Here, with the direct object τὴν διακονίαν μου, "my ministry," Paul seeks "to influence one's opinion about" it "so as to enhance" its "reputation," and so the verb can be translated as "*praise, honor, extol*" (BDAG, 1). Paul is speaking to Gentiles and extolling his own ministry to them. However, for consistency with the translation of this verb elsewhere in Romans (8:30; 15:6, 9; negated in 1:21), "glorify" is used here. Cf. 8:17–18.

11:14 εἴ πως παραζηλώσω—Beginning in 11:14, four consecutive verses are each introduced by the particle εἰ, "if," which appears a total of eight times in 11:12–18 (11:12, 14, 15 [twice], 16 [twice], 17, 18). Here and in 1:10 εἰ is strengthened by πώς (see also Acts 27:12; Phil 3:11). While not a literal translation, the suggestion that εἴ πως here conveys the expectation of fulfillment and should then be understood as "in the hope that" or "in order to" or "so that" makes contextual sense.[3]

For discussion of the verb παραζηλόω, "provoke to envy," see the third textual note on 10:19. The form here, παραζηλώσω, is ambiguous. It could be an aorist subjunctive; however, the form of this conditional sentence means that, in all likelihood, it should be read as a future indicative. Here εἴ πως introduces a first class conditional, which indicates "*the assumption of truth for the sake of argument*."[4] But this does not imply that the "if" clause is false, as in a second class conditional.[5] Although noncommittal, "the point of the argument is based on the assumption of reality."[6]

μου τὴν σάρκα—"My flesh" does not refer to Paul's own body (as it does in Col 1:24; cf. Gal 2:20; Phil 1:22, 24). Paul's use of σάρξ here for his fellow Israelites is

---

[2] See Wallace, *Greek Grammar*, 100–101, who cites Rom 8:36 and Gal 2:7 as clear examples.

[3] Cranfield, *Romans*, 560, including n. 6, citing BDF, § 375; see also Dunn, *Romans*, 656; Moo, *Romans*, 692, n. 46.

[4] Wallace, *Greek Grammar*, 690; he later explicitly identifies this verse as a first class conditional in which the future indicative illustrates that "the time criterion is not an ontological criterion" (707).

[5] See Wallace, *Greek Grammar*, 694.

[6] Wallace, *Greek Grammar*, 692.

similar to his use of the phrase "my kinsmen according to [the] flesh [σάρξ]" in Rom 9:3; see the sixth textual note and the commentary on that verse.

σώσω—For σῴζω, "to save," see the fourth textual note and the commentary on 5:9. This form, like παραζηλώσω earlier in the verse, could be either an aorist subjunctive or a future indicative. The formula of a first class conditional (see the first textual note on this verse) allows either in the apodosis.[7] The sense of the passage, however, points to another future indicative. The "some" Jews who come to believe as a result of Paul's ministry to the Gentiles *will certainly be saved* (cf. the future indicative σωθήσῃ in 10:9).

τινάς—For "some" (plural) as a reference to a portion of the Israelites, see the first textual note and the commentary on 3:3.

11:15 εἰ—See the first textual note on 11:14.

ἡ ἀποβολὴ αὐτῶν—BDAG notes that the noun ἀποβολή corresponds to the various meanings of the verb from which it is derived, ἀποβάλλω, "to remove, throw away" or "to lose." BDAG, s.v. ἀποβολή, 1, then gives "rejection" for this verse, though its only other citation for this meaning[8] is qualified as "not of people as such, but repeated loss of their cities and temple through divine providence." The noun appears only one other time in the NT and that reference, Acts 27:22, refers to the potential loss of people when a ship sinks (ἀποβολὴ ... ψυχῆς). The genitive here serves as a comparable expression of apposition and defines "*who is*" among those lost: "the loss of them."[9] It should *not* be heard as an objective genitive, implying that someone (e.g., God) caused their loss (see the commentary).

καταλλαγή—This noun, "reconciliation," occurs in the NT only here and in Rom 5:11; 2 Cor 5:18–19. The cognate verb καταλλάσσω appears twice in Rom 5:10 (see the third textual note on that verse). For an explanation of these words in Paul, see the commentary on 5:10–11 and "Friendship" in the excursus "Paul's Gospel Metaphors" following the commentary on 4:1–12.

ἡ πρόσλημψις—In the Greek canon this noun occurs only here and means "acceptance into a relationship, *acceptance* (by God)" (BDAG). This theological connotation is supported by the strategic use of the cognate verb προσλαμβάνω, "receive (someone to oneself)," in 14:3 and 15:7. πρόσλημψις, "acceptance," remedies the previous state of estrangement expressed by ἀποβολή, "loss," earlier in the verse. The genitive αὐτῶν is implied here from the preceding parallel phrase ἡ ἀποβολὴ αὐτῶν, and the genitive is objective here: "the acceptance of them." See the commentary.

11:16 εἰ—See the first textual note on 11:14.

ἡ ἀπαρχὴ ἁγία—The singular noun ἀπαρχή is translated as "the firstfruits"; see the third textual note on 8:23; it recurs in 16:5. These "firstfruits" are deemed ἁγία, "holy." The LXX often associates these two technical terms (ἀπαρχή and ἅγιος) in

---

[7] See Wallace, *Greek Grammar*, 689.

[8] Josephus, *Antiquities*, 4.314.

[9] Wallace, *Greek Grammar*, 95; see 95–100 for a full discussion; he also titles this category "Epexegetical Genitive, Genitive of Definition" (95).

liturgical settings, e.g., "the firstfruits for the holy" refers to contributions for building the tabernacle in LXX Ex 36:6 (similarly, LXX Ex 39:1 [MT/ET 38:24]; 2 Chr 31:14). "The firstfruits of the holy things" in LXX Lev 22:12 refers to the portions of sacrifices that were given to the priests to eat (similarly, LXX Num 18:32). "The holy firstfruits" refers to a sacred portion of the land at the conclusion of Ezekiel's eschatological vision (LXX Ezek 48:10, 12, 18, 20, 21).

τὸ φύραμα—This neuter noun denotes "that which is mixed/kneaded, *mixture/batch of dough*" (BDAG, 1). As ἀπαρχὴν φυράματος in LXX Num 15:20–21 refers to "the firstfruits of the dough," the application here refers to bread dough, as does φύραμα in 1 Cor 5:6–7; Gal 5:9; but note τὸ φύραμα for the mixture of clay used by a potter in Rom 9:21.

ἡ ῥίζα—The noun ῥίζα (11:16, 17, 18) denotes "the underground part of a plant, *root*" (BDAG, 1). But the definition BDAG gives for this passage in Paul's figure of the olive tree, "its root *and branches*" (BDAG, 1 b; emphasis added), is odd. Paul explicitly contrasts the "branches" (κλάδοι, see the next textual note) with *this* part of the olive tree, which remains below ground; thus it is "the root" alone. ῥίζα also functions "in imagery" (BDAG, 1 b), as in Jesus' parable of the Sower (e.g., Lk 8:13); here "the root" represents the patriarchs of Israel (literally, "the fathers" in Rom 11:28), who currently are unseen, yet are a living (Mk 12:26–27) part of the tree. See further "Background and Introduction" in "Elaboration on the Olive Tree—Faith or Unbelief? (11:17–24)" in the commentary.

οἱ κλάδοι—The noun κλάδος means "a branch." As with "the root" (see the previous textual note), a parable of Jesus employs this term metaphorically (the parable of the Mustard Seed, e.g., Lk 13:19), as does Sirach 23:25, where branches represent children.

11:17 εἰ … τινες τῶν κλάδων—For εἰ, "if," and τινες, "some," see the first and fourth textual notes on 11:14, respectively. After τινες, the genitive case of τῶν κλάδων provides a clear example of a partitive genitive:[10] "some *of* the branches."

ἐξεκλάσθησαν—The verb ἐκκλάω means "to separate someth[ing] from someth[ing] with force, *break off*" (BDAG). As with ἐπωρώθησαν, "they were hardened," in 11:7, the aorist passive form here implies God as the actor:[11] "they were broken off" by God. The identical third plural aorist indicative passive form recurs with the same meaning in Rom 11:19, 20.

ἀγριέλαιος ὤν—The compound feminine noun ἀγριέλαιος (ἀγρός, "wild," + ἐλαία, "olive tree") denotes a "*wild olive tree*" (BDAG, s.v. ἀγριέλαιος, ου, ἡ), as in 11:24. But the same spelling forms an adjective here. Together with the singular participle of εἰμί it describes "(growing) *from a wild olive tree*" (BDAG, s.v. ἀγριέλαιος, ον; see also BDF, § 120.3) or, more contextually in this verse, "being a wild olive [branch]."

ἐνεκεντρίσθης—The compound verb ἐγκεντρίζω, formed with the preposition ἐν and the verb κεντέω, "prick, pierce," means "to cause (a shoot or bud: scion) to unite

---

[10] Wallace, *Greek Grammar*, 84–86.

[11] See Wallace, *Greek Grammar*, 437–38.

with the stock of a growing plant, *graft* of trees" (BDAG). Again, the form is aorist passive and the implied actor is God:[12] "you [singular] were grafted in" by God.

συγκοινωνός—In secular Greek the compound noun συγκοινωνός can apply to business partners (BDAG). But the image here conveys a grafted-in branch being a "fellow sharer" with the "root" (see the next textual note). Yet the theological connotations of the term, which are prominent in its other NT occurrences (1 Cor 9:23; Phil 1:7; Rev 1:9), should be recognized here as well. Dunn observes that "nearly 70 percent of the κοινων- words in the NT come in the Pauline corpus."[13] See the commentary.

τῆς ῥίζης τῆς πιότητος τῆς ἐλαίας—This string of three genitives (literally, "of the root of the sap of the olive tree") requires some interpretive explanation. The apparent difficulty has spawned a number of textual emendations, but this reading of ℵ* B and C "appears to explain best the origin of the other readings."[14] The best interpretation, which Wallace hints at in regard to this passage, is to connect the first noun, τῆς ῥίζης, with the previous συν- compound, συγκοινωνός (see the previous textual note), identify the genitive as one of association, "*with*,"[15] and render the phrase as "a fellow sharer with the root." In commenting on συναπαγόμενοι in Rom 12:16, Moo notes how a comparable "συν- prefix … will have an 'associative' flavor."[16] While a literal "root" is not personal, it is a metaphor here, clearly referring to people ("the fathers, patriarchs," 11:28). Note comparable συν- compounds together with a genitive in Rom 8:17; 11:34; Eph 2:19; 5:7; Phil 3:17.

The second noun in the string, πιότης, occurs only here in the NT and describes a "state of oiliness, *fatness*" (BDAG). In this context, it refers to the life-giving nourishment provided by the sap. The translation "oily sap" conveys the idea, even though the olive oil is not in the sap itself; the sap enables the tree to thrive and produce the olives, which are then compressed to extract the precious olive oil. The genitive case of τῆς πιότητος could modify the "root" qualitatively as "the rich root."[17] It may also restate "the root" in terms of what it supplies: the water and minerals absorbed by "the root" make it the source of "the sap" of the olive tree.[18] But the understanding of "the root" as a metaphor for the patriarchs[19] renders those complexities unnecessary. The third

---

[12] See Wallace, *Greek Grammar*, 437–38.

[13] Dunn, *Romans*, 661.

[14] Metzger, *A Textual Commentary on the Greek New Testament*, 526. Murray, *Romans*, 2:86, including n. 34, supports the same reading as Metzger, but then interprets the passage according to the variant which inserts καί, meaning "partaker of the root *and* the fatness of the olive tree" (emphasis added).

[15] Wallace, *Greek Grammar*, 130; for the genitive of association, see 128–30.

[16] Moo, *Romans*, 784, n. 73.

[17] Moo, *Romans*, 702, n. 28; Barrett, *Romans*, 217.

[18] Cranfield, *Romans*, 567, says that τῆς πιότητος is likely a genitive of apposition; Moo, *Romans*, 702, n. 28, says that it may be an epexegetical genitive.

[19] See the preceding paragraph in the text and the fourth textual note on 11:16; see further "Background and Introduction" in "Elaboration on the Olive Tree—Faith or Unbelief? (11:17–24)" in the commentary.

genitive, τῆς ἐλαίας, expresses source or possession,[20] the entity that has both "the oily sap" and "the root." (The feminine noun ἐλαία recurs at the end of 11:24.) The phrase then reads as "a fellow sharer with the root of the oily sap of the olive tree."

11:18 μὴ κατακαυχῶ—The simple verb καυχάομαι, "to boast," figures prominently earlier in Romans; see the fourth textual note on 2:17 (also 2:23; 5:2, 3, 11). The prefixed κατά of the compound verb κατακαυχάομαι here (twice in this verse) adds the force "against" (BDAG, s.v. κατά, A 2 b). Thus the compound means to "boast at the expense of another, *boast against, exult over*" (BDAG, 1), as in its only other NT occurrences, James 2:13; 3:14. Here the present imperative second singular with μή forms a prohibition. A present imperative with μή may imply the cessation of activity that is in progress,[21] but this is not always the case, since it "can also have the force of a *general precept*. This kind of prohibition really makes no comment about whether the action is going on or not."[22] The sequence of 11:20 implies that 11:18 expresses a general precept. See also the fourth textual note on 11:20.

τῶν κλάδων—See the fifth textual note on 11:16.

εἰ δὲ κατακαυχᾶσαι—This "if" clause is the protasis of a first class conditional indicative construction (see the first textual note on 11:14).[23] For εἰ, see the first textual note on 11:14; for κατακαυχάομαι, "to boast," see the first textual note on 11:18. The form κατακαυχᾶσαι is a present indicative middle of this deponent verb.

οὐ σὺ τὴν ῥίζαν βαστάζεις ἀλλὰ ἡ ῥίζα σέ—This is the apodosis or "then" clause in case of boasting. The verb βαστάζω means "to sustain a burden, *carry, bear*" (BDAG, 2). βαστάζεις is a negated second singular indicative form and is preceded by the emphatic singular pronoun σύ, "you," therefore "you, you are not bearing." In context, Paul stresses that the root bears the weight of the tree and supports the branches, not vice versa.

11:19 ἐρεῖς οὖν—For "you will then say," see the first textual note 9:19.

ἐξεκλάσθησαν κλάδοι—For these two terms, see the second textual note on 11:17 and the fifth textual note on 11:16, respectively.

ἵνα ἐγὼ ἐγκεντρισθῶ—The personal pronoun ἐγώ, "I," emphasizes the first person singular subject of the aorist subjunctive passive ἐγκεντρισθῶ. For the verb ἐγκεντρίζω, see the fourth textual note on 11:17. Here the force of ἵνα plus the subjunctive in the *assertion* suggests purpose, but the reality is actually one of result.[24] See the commentary.

11:20 καλῶς—The adverb of καλός is used as an exclamation, "*Quite right! That is true! Well said!*" (BDAG, s.v. καλῶς, 4 c).

τῇ ἀπιστίᾳ ἐξεκλάσθησαν—For the noun ἀπιστία, "unbelief," see the second textual note on 3:3 and the first textual note on 4:20. For the overall concept of faith versus

---

[20] Moo, *Romans*, 702, n. 28; see Wallace, *Greek Grammar*, 109–10.

[21] See Wallace, *Greek Grammar*, 724.

[22] Wallace, *Greek Grammar*, 724.

[23] See Wallace, *Greek Grammar*, 450–51, 690–94.

[24] For the purpose-result ἵνα clause, see Wallace, *Greek Grammar*, 473–74.

unbelief, see "The Background and Meaning of 'Faith' Words" in the commentary on 1:16.[25] As in 3:3, the reference is not to a lack of faithfulness, but to unbelief (see also 10:16). The dative case of τῇ ἀπιστίᾳ expresses cause; it "indicates the *why*" and "the *basis*"[26] for the verb "they were broken off." The sense is "due to" or "because of" their unbelief. Note the phrase's emphatic position prior to the verb; for ἐκκλάω, see the second textual note on 11:17.

τῇ πίστει ἕστηκας—While the dative case of the noun ("by faith") matches that of τῇ ἀπιστίᾳ in the preceding textual note, the nuance of the dative here is more an expression of means which "indicates the *how*" and "the *method*"[27] for the verb "stand." For πίστις, see "The Background and Meaning of 'Faith' Words" in the commentary on 1:16.[28] The verb ἕστηκας is the perfect active of ἵστημι used intransitively to express "stand firm in belief" (see BDAG, B 4). See the second textual note on 5:2, which has ἑστήκαμεν, another perfect active form of the same verb. Both the past and the present aspects of the perfect tense are significant here: "you *have* stood and *remain* standing." See the commentary.

μὴ ὑψηλὰ φρόνει ἀλλὰ φοβοῦ—The adjective ὑψηλός "pert[ains] to being arrogant, *exalted, proud, haughty*" (BDAG, 2). For φρονέω, "set your mind," see the third textual note and the commentary on 8:5. Note also the combination of this adjective and verb to form a compound verb with the same force, also negated with μή, in 1 Tim 6:17: μὴ ὑψηλοφρονεῖν, "not to be haughty." Here in place of ὑψηλὰ φρόνει that compound verb's imperative, ὑψηλοφρόνει, is the reading in C and D (and some other manuscripts). For the force of μή with a present imperative (φρόνει or ὑψηλοφρόνει), see the first textual note on 11:18. Wallace offers this further advice:

> In many of the NT letters the force of a particular present prohibition will not always be focused on the cessation of an activity in progress. It is *not*, then, safe to say that when an author uses the present prohibition the audience is being indicted for not heeding this command. Other factors—especially the overall context and *Sitz im Leben* of the book—must be taken into account.[29]

The second mandate, ἀλλὰ φοβοῦ, "but fear," is applicable to all believers, whether or not they have been boasting proudly. Therefore, instead of an awkward temporal sequence addressed only to boasters, "first, stop being proud, but then, second, fear," it makes better sense to understand the meaning of both imperatives as *general precepts*[30] addressed to all Christians. (The same is true for μὴ κατακαυχῶ; see the first textual note on 11:18.) Therefore these mandates are translated as "do not set your mind on proud [thoughts], but reverently fear!"

---

[25] Middendorf, *Romans 1–8*, 88–90.

[26] Wallace, *Greek Grammar*, 167; see 167–68.

[27] Wallace, *Greek Grammar*, 167; see 162–63.

[28] See also "'From Faith[fulness] into Faith' (1:17)" in Middendorf, *Romans 1–8*, 96–98; and 106–7.

[29] Wallace, *Greek Grammar*, 725.

[30] See Wallace, *Greek Grammar*, 724.

The second imperative, φοβοῦ, is Paul's first use of the verb φοβέομαι, "to fear," in Romans (later it is in 13:3, 4). For a discussion of its meaning in relation to the cognate noun φόβος, "fear," see the first textual note on 3:18 and the commentary here. The form of this deponent verb here is a present imperative.

11:21 τῶν κατὰ φύσιν κλάδων οὐκ ἐφείσατο—For οἱ κλάδοι, "the branches," see the fifth textual note on 11:16. Here the phrase is genitive because the verb φείδομαι takes the genitive. The preposition κατά with the accusative φύσιν, "nature,"[31] serves as a "marker of norm of similarity or homogeneity, *according to, in accordance with, in conformity with, according to*" (BDAG, s.v. κατά, 5; later, s.v. κατά, 7 a, suggesting an adjectival translation here, "*the natural branches*"). More literally, we have "the branches [which were] in accord with nature," i.e., where they grew originally. Paul expresses the complete contrast below in 11:24, where the opposite of κατὰ φύσιν is παρὰ φύσιν, "contrary to nature," the same phrase as in 1:26; see the discussion of παρὰ φύσιν in the excursus "Homosexual Conduct Is Contrary to Nature (Romans 1:26–27)" following the commentary on 1:18–32.

For the verb φείδομαι, "to spare," see the third textual note on 8:32. ἐφείσατο is the same form as in 8:32, an aorist indicative middle (deponent). The third and final use of this verb in Romans occurs later in this verse.

[μή πως]—The inclusion of these bracketed words, "that perhaps" (BDAG, s.v. πώς, 2 b), is supported by 𝔓[46] and D, but omitted in ℵ B and C. "The effect of this addition would be to add a nuance of uncertainty"[32] which seems to detract from Paul's point. Thus the general principle that the shorter reading should be preferred applies here. Metzger supports including the bracketed phrase because it represents "a typically Pauline expression" and, curiously, due to "its apparent unrelatedness … and its grammatical inappropriateness."[33]

φείσεται—This form of φείδομαι, "to spare," is a future indicative middle (deponent). Cf. ἐφείσατο in the first textual note on 11:21, and see the third textual note on 8:32.

11:22 χρηστότητα—See the third textual note on 2:4, where χρηστότης similarly expresses the divine "quality of being helpful or beneficial, *goodness, kindness, generosity*" (BDAG, 2).

ἀποτομίαν—The noun ἀποτομία, "*severity*" (BDAG), occurs only here in the NT (twice in this verse). In this context Paul's use of the noun may play off the meaning of the cognate verb ἀποτέμνω, "to cut off,"[34] as a synonym of ἐκκλάω, "break off," in Rom 11:17, 19, 20. See the commentary.

---

[31] In Romans Paul employs the noun φύσις, "nature," in 1:26; 2:14, 27; 11:21, 24 (three times).

[32] Moo, *Romans*, 697, n. 2.

[33] Metzger, *A Textual Commentary on the Greek New Testament*, 526–27.

[34] The compound verb ἀποτέμνω is absent from the NT but found in the LXX and extrabiblical Greek. Another compound verb from the same root, περιτέμνω, "to circumcise," is of course common in the LXX and NT.

ἐπὶ μὲν τοὺς πεσόντας ... ἐπὶ δὲ σέ—For πίπτω, "to fall," see the third textual note and the commentary on 11:11. The aorist participle here is used substantively.[35] For the μέν ... δέ construction, "on the one hand ... on the other hand," see the first textual note on 2:7.

ἐὰν ἐπιμένῃς—In the analogy of immobile tree branches, the subjunctive of ἐπιμένω (ἐπί, "on," + μένω, "remain; dwell") conveys the more passive sense "to remain at or in" (BDAG, 1), rather than the active connotations *"persist (in), persevere"* suggested for this verse by BDAG, 2. See the discussion of the related noun ὑπομονή (ὑπό + μένω) in the commentary on 5:3.

τῇ χρηστότητι—For the noun χρηστότης, see the first textual note on this verse. The definite article functions as a personal pronoun,[36] *"his* kindness."

ἐκκοπήσῃ—The compound verb ἐκκόπτω means "cut so as to sever, *cut off/down*" (BDAG, 1). In this context, it is essentially synonymous with ἐκκλάω in 11:17, 19, 20. ἐκκοπήσῃ is a future indicative passive with a divine passive sense: "otherwise you also will be cut off" by God.

11:23 κἀκεῖνοι—This is a combination or "crasis"[37] of καί with the masculine plural form of the demonstrative pronoun ἐκεῖνος, "those ones also."

ἐὰν μὴ ἐπιμένωσιν—Paul used ἐὰν ἐπιμένῃς in 11:22 (see the fourth textual note), but here he negates the subjunctive form of ἐπιμένω with μή and changes it from second singular to third plural: "if they do not remain." This begins a third class conditional sentence: the protasis has ἐάν plus the subjunctive, while the apodosis (see the second textual note below) can have a verb in any mood and tense.[38]

τῇ ἀπιστίᾳ—See the second textual note on 11:20.

ἐγκεντρισθήσονται—For ἐγκεντρίζω in the passive voice, see the fourth textual note on 11:17. Here, too, the passive has God as the implied actor, the cultivator. This future indicative passive is the apodosis of the third class conditional, which can have a wide range of semantic potentialities; the fulfillment can be unlikely, possible but uncertain, or, as is often the case and applicable here, likely.[39]

δυνατὸς ... ἐστιν ὁ θεός—See the discussion of δυνατός, "powerful," as an attribute of God in the commentary on 4:21.

ἐγκεντρίσαι—This is the aorist active infinitive of ἐγκεντρίζω, "to graft in"; see the fourth textual note on 11:17.

11:24 εἰ—See the first textual note on 11:14.

σὺ ἐκ τῆς κατὰ φύσιν ἐξεκόπης ἀγριελαίου—All of these terms have occurred already in this section. For ἀγριέλαιος, "wild olive tree," see the third textual note on

---

[35] See Wallace, *Greek Grammar*, 619–21.

[36] See Wallace, *Greek Grammar*, 211–12.

[37] Mounce, *Basics of Biblical Greek*, 69, 111.

[38] See the chart of conditionals in Wallace, *Greek Grammar*, 689.

[39] See Wallace, *Greek Grammar*, 696–99; he notes: "In classical Greek the third class condition was usually restricted to the first usage (known as *more probable future*)," which indicated "what is *likely to occur* in the *future*," but by NT times the range of options had expanded (696).

11:17. For the verb ἐκκόπτω, "cut off," see the sixth textual note on 11:22. Here it is an aorist indicative passive form with a divine passive force: "you were cut off" by God.[40] The preposition ἐκ, "from," as well as the prefixed ἐκ on ἐξεκόπης, "cut off from," expresses source:[41] *"from the wild olive tree."* The prepositional phrase κατὰ φύσιν, "in accord with nature" (see the first textual note on 11:21), likely modifies the second singular verb's subject, "you," which is emphasized by the pronoun σύ. Since 11:17 the second singular forms have continued to refer to a singular Gentile "you."[42] The prepositional phrase ἐκ τῆς … ἀγριελαίου, "from the wild olive tree," performs a double function related to both κατὰ φύσιν and the verbal action of ἐξεκόπης. The full thought is this: "for if you, who are in accord with nature from the wild olive tree, you were cut off from the wild olive tree."

παρὰ φύσιν ἐνεκεντρίσθης—For ἐνεκεντρίσθης, "you were grafted in," see the fourth textual note on 11:17. The prepositional phrase παρὰ φύσιν, "contrary to nature," stands here as the opposite of κατὰ φύσιν, "in accord with nature," in 11:21, 24 (twice). παρὰ φύσιν has the same meaning in 1:26. The prepositional phrase is discussed at length in the excursus following 1:18–32: "Homosexual Conduct Is Contrary to Nature (Romans 1:26–27)." This verse, then, reinforces the interpretation of 1:26 in the commentary on it.

καλλιέλαιον—This is Paul's only use of the compound noun καλλιέλαιος (καλός, literally, "beautiful," + ἔλαιος, "olive tree" [ἔλαιος is a masculine synonym of the feminine ἐλαία in 11:17, 24]) for a *"cultivated olive tree"* (BDAG), but this tree has been under consideration since 11:16.

πόσῳ μᾶλλον—This expression occurs also in 11:12. For the comparable expression πολλῷ … μᾶλλον (5:9, 10, 15, 17), see the first textual note on 5:9. Both expressions are translated as "how much more."

ἐγκεντρισθήσονται—For the meaning of the verb ἐγκεντρίζω, see the fourth textual note on 11:17; for its future indicative passive form, see the fourth textual note on 11:23.

Commentary

Introduction: Addressing "You Gentiles" (11:13a)

"But to you Gentiles I say" (11:13). As the Christians in Rome heard the letter read aloud, these words would certainly have caught their attention. In fact, "this is first time in the letter that Paul explicitly addresses the Gentile members of the Roman community."[43] The emphatic placement of "to you" (ὑμῖν)

---

[40] It is not a participle as Moo, *Romans*, 708, n. 63, suggests; note the temporal augment (-ε-) between the prefixed preposition and the basic root (ἐξ-ε-κόπης), which indicates a past tense indicative form.

[41] See Wallace, *Greek Grammar*, 371.

[42] The second person plural pronoun ὑμῖν, "to you," in 11:13 addresses the plural τοῖς ἔθνεσιν, "the Gentiles."

[43] Matera, *Romans*, 266; Cranfield, *Romans*, 559, describes the addressees as "the Gentile element in the church." Dunn, *Romans*, 655, adds that this "does not necessarily mean that the Roman congregations were exclusively Gentile, since Paul could intend by this phrase to

as the first Greek word of the verse heightens the shift. A change or modification of the addressees usually provides a solid indication of a transition to a new section. This is generally recognized in Romans 2, for example, at 2:1 and 2:17. However, as discussed above in the introduction to 11:1–12, most scholars break the first section of the chapter after 11:10 and begin a new section at 11:11.[44] But the harder break, signaled by the narrower target audience for Paul's words, comes at 11:13.[45]

The second person form of direct address ("you"), begun with the Greek second person plural pronoun (ὑμῖν) emphatically placed at the beginning of 11:13, continues throughout this section. Paul, however, switches to Greek second person *singular* forms (English unfortunately requires the same translation, "you") to speak even more directly in the following verses: 11:17 (three times), 18 (five times), 19, 20 (four times), 21, 22 (five times), 24 (three times).[46] Earlier he used the second person singular to speak a warning (2:1–5) to every one of "you … who judges" (2:1). He also directly addressed a word of caution to a singular "you [who] are calling yourself a Jew" (2:17) in 2:17–29.[47]

Now Paul turns specifically to "you Gentiles" in the church (11:13). "Making use of this rhetorical technique and the allegory of the olive tree, he will argue against Gentile boasting just as he has argued against Jewish boasting

---

catch the attention specifically of the Gentile members of the Christian groups to whom his letter would be read." Moo, *Romans*, 691, n. 39, contends that "this address suggests that the majority of the Christians at Rome were Gentiles, since Paul does not say 'I am speaking to those of you who are Gentiles.'" That the Gentiles outnumbered the Jews seems possible, but this evidence by itself is not convincing. See Middendorf, *Romans 1–8*, 10–14, 17–22, and, especially, "Who Are the 'Weak' and the 'Strong'? Addressees Again!" in the introduction to 14:1–15:13.

[44] As do Dunn, *Romans*, 634; Kruse, *Romans*, 421; Moo, *Romans*, 670; and Cranfield, *Romans*, 542, who says that 11:13 "is not the beginning of a new paragraph" (558), although his reasoning sounds odd: "For the thought of vv. 11–12 is continued in vv. 15ff." (558–59). See "Introduction to Romans 11:1–12" in the commentary on 11:1–12.

[45] Recognized by Bruce, *Romans*, 203; Matera, *Romans*, 260; Hultgren, *Romans*, 405. Dunn, *Romans*, 655, breaks after 11:10, but then asserts that the μὲν οὖν ("as for me, then") in 11:13 "probably has the force of summarizing what has been said in moving to a new subject (BDF, §451.1)."

[46] These statistics indicate the number of times each verse uses a Greek second person singular pronoun or verb. Moo, *Romans*, 698, says that "you" in the singular makes Paul's "address all the more pointed." For the possibility of and cautions regarding the diatribe, see Middendorf, *Romans 1–8*, 24–27, 151.

[47] While Paul surely intends for his apostolic words to be heard by any and all who will listen, the original recipients of the letter are believers in Rome (1:7). Therefore sections like 2:17–29 originally were intended to be heard by those who, by the grace of God, no longer relied upon the Law as a cause for boasting before him (2:17, 23; also 6:14). Yet Paul's words there and, indeed, throughout 1:18–3:20, continually remind those in Christ of where they were, and would be, apart from grace. Those earlier chapters, like 11:17–21, also serve to warn believers against adopting any kind of presumptuous, self-centered, or boastful attitude. For an analysis of Paul's pragmatic purposes when referring to himself throughout his writings, see Middendorf, *The "I" in the Storm*, 226–37.

(2:17–29)."[48] In this section, Israel, by way of contrast, continues to be referenced by third person plural forms, as well as indefinite and demonstrative plural pronouns and a plural participle, in 11:14 (twice), 15, 17 (three times), 19, 20, 22, 23 (four times), 24 (twice),[49] which focus most specifically on those in Israel who do not now believe. It may be tempting to view Paul's "development of the analogy" in 11:17–24 as a "detour."[50] But, as Jesus often enlightens his difficult teachings with parables, so Paul's metaphor provides key interpretive insights into the contested propositional statements which precede and follow the olive-trce analogy (especially 11:26a).

Instead of speaking generally about what is happening to Israel, Paul now turns to tell Gentile Christians how they ought to respond to God's reaction to the improper response of those in Israel who refused to hear the Good News. Indeed, "Gentiles might think that a long discussion of the remnant of Israel had little to do with them."[51] Perhaps their attention has waned in the midst of it. Based upon 11:18, 25 and 14:3, Moo proposes:

> Paul knew that Gentile Christians in Rome were engaging in such inappropriate bragging [boasting of their superiority over Jews and even Jewish Christians]; and the need to curb this sinful pride was one of his main motivations in writing chaps. 9–11 and, indeed, the letter as a whole.[52]

While plausible, the verbal constructions do not insist that such boasting is currently taking place in Rome.[53] More importantly, the overall content of Romans should dissuade interpreters from asserting that Paul directs the letter *exclusively* to a Gentile audience; neither should these verses be put forth as revealing that his primary purpose in writing is to silence Gentile boasting against Jews.[54] On the other hand, that such boasting has occurred in Rome seems an all-too-real possibility; it may even be *improperly* fueled by some of what Paul himself writes (e.g., 2:25–27; 3:9; 4:10; 9:6, 31; 10:2, 21). Therefore, whether the conduct is past, present, or future, this section rebukes Gentile hearers for any and all sinful pride against Jews; it also seeks to prohibit Gentiles from adopting such an unwarranted, arrogant attitude.

---

[48] Matera, *Romans*, 268; similarly, Staples, "What Do the Gentiles Have to Do with 'All Israel'? A Fresh Look at Romans 11:25–27," 385.

[49] These statistics indicate the number of times each verse uses a Greek third person plural pronoun ("them," "their") or verb (whose subject is "they" or a plural noun or pronoun), an indefinite pronoun ("some"), a demonstrative pronoun ("those," "these"), or a plural participle ("ones").

[50] As characterized by Ticciati, "The Nondivisive Difference of Election," 264.

[51] Barrett, *Romans*, 214; this is more correct than presuming with Cranfield, *Romans*, 559, "that what [Paul] is about to say is contrary to what the Gentile Christians will probably be inclined to think."

[52] Moo, *Romans*, 685.

[53] See the first textual note on 11:18 and the fourth textual note on 11:20.

[54] See "Who Are the 'Weak' and the 'Strong'? Addressees Again!" in the introduction to 14:1–15:13. For a discussion of the letter's purpose, see Middendorf, *Romans 1–8*, 14–22.

In any case, Paul reminds Gentiles, then and now, that something of *a chain reaction has occurred in God's plan of salvation as evident also in the development of Paul's argument*. God acts first through the Word of Christ proclaimed for all (10:6–15) in order to bestow the righteousness from faith. Paul then focuses upon the unbelieving response of some in Israel (10:16–21), followed by a description of God's reaction to impenitent Israel's hardened response (11:1–12). Now he depicts how believing Gentiles in his audience ought to respond to all of this (11:13–24). Hultgren and Matera treat 11:13–24 as a unit, which Hultgren aptly entitles "How Should Gentiles Think in the Present Situation?"[55]

It is generally acknowledged that 11:25 marks the beginning of the concluding section of Romans 9–11, which this commentary subtitles "Resolution and Doxology" (11:25–36). There Paul returns to the second person plural "you," but with "brothers" in apposition. Thus he directs his words, once again, to all the believers in Rome (as in 1:13; 7:1, 4; 8:12; 10:1; 12:1; 15:14, 30; 16:17).[56]

At the same time, it is important to remember that all of these section, chapter, and verse divisions were not in Paul's original but have been imposed later and, therefore, are somewhat arbitrary. Furthermore, Paul's intricate and skillful interweaving of his argument makes the attempt to divide his text even more tendentious. Moo, for example, recognizes that throughout the remainder of the chapter Paul's argument "oscillates between Israel and the Gentiles."[57]

Paul's Perspective (11:13b–15)

"An Apostle of Gentiles" (11:13b–c)

After turning to speak to "you Gentiles," Paul emphatically validates the vantage point from which he addresses them. In somewhat of a parenthesis, he identifies it and himself: "as for me, then, insofar as I myself am an apostle of Gentiles" (11:13b). The grammar may be incomplete (see the first textual note on 11:13), but the thought is clear. His role as an apostle was asserted right at the outset of the letter (1:1). Now he defines its missional direction to the Gentiles to whom he directly speaks. Dunn points out that "the absence of the definite article should be observed"[58] in ἐθνῶν ἀπόστολος, "*an* apostle of Gentiles," for Paul was not the *only* apostle to Gentiles (see Peter in Acts 10–11). However, the indefinite phrase rather indicates how his apostleship reached "to [the] Jew first and also to [the] Greek" (1:16; see the commentary there). The conduct of Paul's ministry in Acts clearly illustrates his mission to Jews,[a] but also regularly includes Gentiles,[b] as does Paul in his epistles.[c]

(a) E.g., Acts 13:5, 14; 14:1; 17:1–3; 18:4; 19:8; cf. Acts 13:46; 17:17

(b) E.g., Acts 9:15; 13:46–47; 14:27; 18:6; 21:19–20; 22:21; 26:17

(c) E.g., Rom 1:5; 15:16; Gal 1:16; 2:7, 9; 1 Tim 2:7

---

[55] Hultgren, *Romans*, 405; Matera, *Romans*, 260, titles 11:13–24 "A warning to Gentile believers"; similarly, Bruce *Romans*, 203: "Admonition to Gentile Christians (11:13–24)."

[56] See "Introduction to Romans 11:25–36" in the commentary on 11:25–36.

[57] Moo, *Romans*, 684.

[58] Dunn, *Romans*, 656.

The propriety of the verse division is uncertain, but 11:14 seems to explain *why* Paul extols his apostolic service.[59] The last clause of 11:13 then points forward: "I glorify my ministry [14][so that] if, somehow, I might provoke my flesh to envy, I will also save some from them" (11:13c–14). Paul refers to his "ministry" with the noun διακονία here and in 15:31, contexts in which it has a "theological-technical use,"[60] as does the related noun διάκονος in 15:8, where Paul states that Christ became "a *servant* of [the] circumcision," whereas διακονία has a more general connotation of Christian "service" in 12:7. This technical sense stems from Paul's role as an apostle (1:1), rather than from the noun διακονία itself as an "office."[61] Far from robbing God of his glory, Paul's glorification of his ministry (δοξάζω) reveals "a praise which is expressive of commitment of life. … [Paul] was by no means unwilling to speak out and make much of his ministry (as here and Gal 2:1–10), though not for any vainglorious end."[62] Paul's glorifying means that *he honors the ministry given to him by Christ and dedicates himself to fulfill it to the best of his ability* (see 15:15–19).

In Order to Save Some Jews (11:14)

Paul then adds this additional aim in 11:14: "[so that] if, somehow, I might provoke my flesh to envy, I will also save some from them." Paul here shows one way in which the "provoking to envy" which God spoke of originally in Deut 32:21 takes place. Paul cited that passage in 10:19 and referenced the action again in 11:11. These passages establish that the recipient of God's provocative action is Israel, those whom Paul here describes as "my flesh." As in 1:3; 4:1; 9:3, 5, "flesh" (σάρξ) has no negative connotations. Instead, it reflects "the use of *bāśār* in Hebrew in the sense of 'kindred' and the corresponding use of σάρξ ['flesh'] in the LXX (e.g. Gen 37.27; Lev 18.6; 25.49; Judg 9.2; 2 Sam 5.1)."[63] "[My] own flesh and blood"[64] conveys the sense well. Here one desired outcome of Paul's ministry comes full circle. Although some Jews have not believed the Gospel (10:16; cf. 3:3), Paul insists that his living relatives in the flesh are not

> beyond hope. God loved them so much that the Gentiles were called for their salvation, so that when the Jews saw that the Gentiles were being allowed into the kingdom of God, they might perhaps repent more easily.[65]

In so doing, "they would imitate those who were so unexpectedly accepted by God,"[66] namely, "you Gentiles" (11:13).

---

[59] See the first textual note on 11:14.

[60] Cranfield, *Romans*, 560.

[61] As properly noted by Käsemann, *Romans*, 306; see the commentary on 12:7.

[62] Dunn, *Romans*, 656; for an interpretation of the Galatians text, see Das, *Galatians*, 156–95.

[63] Cranfield, *Romans*, 561.

[64] Moo, *Romans*, 692.

[65] Pelagius, *Romans* (Bray, *Romans*, ACCS NT 6:291).

[66] Cyril of Alexandria, *Romans* (Bray, *Romans*, ACCS NT 6:291).

Paul's goal that "I will also save *some* from them" (σώσω τινὰς ἐξ αὐτῶν, 11:14) has been viewed in a minimal sense as a deliberate avoidance of "excessive claims for the success of his ministry."[67] But that seems to contradict his words elsewhere.[d] On the other extreme, Käsemann contends that this section reveals

(d) E.g.,
Rom
15:14–22;
2 Cor
10:1–12:21;
Gal 1:1,
11–12;
2:6–10; Eph
3:1–13

> the apocalyptic dream of a man who tried to do in a decade what two thousand years have not managed to do. … For Paul the conversion of Israel is an integral part of the end of history. He himself, however, as directly the apostle to the Gentiles and indirectly, precisely in virtue of the Gentile mission, a minister in the eschatological conversion of Judaism, is nothing other than a precursor of the parousia. … The apostle regards himself as one who brings about the divinely willed conclusion of salvation history.[68]

A review of Paul's ministry in Acts and his letters provides a far less apocalyptic assessment. "Paul's view of his role in the process was much more modest. Like the rest of the NT, Paul leaves the timing of these events in the hands of God."[69]

In the meantime, 1 Cor 9:22 speaks in language comparable to Rom 11:14 and provides a more balanced assessment of Paul's view of the purpose of his apostolic ministry:

> I have come to be and still am all things to all [people] in order that by all means *I might save some*. And I am doing all things on account of the Good News, so that I might become a fellow sharer of it. (1 Cor 9:22b–23)[70]

Paul becomes "all things to all" people, including both Jews and Gentiles (1 Cor 9:20–21), in order that he might save *some* from among both Jews and Gentiles. Paul's assertion that "*I* will/might save" in Rom 11:14 and 1 Cor 9:22 is comparable to him speaking of "*my* Gospel" (Rom 2:16). Of course we are to understand that "faith [comes] from hearing … [the] Word of Christ" (10:17). Paul's apostolic ministry sends him to proclaim Christ crucified and risen (Rom 10:14–15; 1 Cor 2:2; 15:1–4). All those who hear, listen responsively to, believe, and acknowledge the Gospel will be saved, *not* by Paul, of course, but by the risen Christ in whom they believe (10:9). This is the eschatological reality, received and experienced already now, that Paul articulates throughout Romans (see the introduction to Romans 5–8). Therefore one need not resort to limiting the verb "save" (σῴζω) by saying that here it means "convert."[71]

---

[67] Murray, *Romans*, 2:80.

[68] Käsemann, *Romans*, 307; Dunn, *Romans*, 658, speaks similarly of Paul seeing "his own work as triggering off that final sequence." For a response regarding the overall influence of apocalyptic thinking on Paul, see Middendorf, *Romans 1–8*, 653–55.

[69] Moo, *Romans*, 696.

[70] The Greek of 1 Cor 9:22b–23 reads τοῖς πᾶσιν γέγονα πάντα, ἵνα πάντως τινὰς σώσω. πάντα δὲ ποιῶ διὰ τὸ εὐαγγέλιον, ἵνα συγκοινωνὸς αὐτοῦ γένωμαι.

[71] As does Cranfield, *Romans*, 561.

Paul's Anticipated Outcome (11:14)

What kind of results did Paul experience and does he envision? Paul uses "some" (τινάς) both here and in 1 Cor 9:22 to acknowledge that some will believe his message; others will not. The "some from them" (Rom 11:14) who believe will be saved, as stated already in Rom 1:16. *The company of those saved is the fullness of Israel (11:12) and of Gentiles (11:25).* As with "some" (τινές) in 3:3 and 11:17, "some from them" (τινὰς ἐξ αὐτῶν) in 11:14 does not express a "surprisingly limited" number.[72] Neither is there an implied contrast between "a few of them" and a "lot of them."[73] Instead, τινὰς ἐξ αὐτῶν means "some from/of them" in contrast to "none of them" (as rejected in 11:1–2), as well as to "all of them" (see the commentary on 11:26). In other words, it stands roughly opposite to the "not all" (οὐ πάντες) in 9:6 and 10:16.

As Paul continues, the determining factor seems clear. Just as in 3:3 and 10:16, it is a matter of faith or unbelief (see 11:20–23). One might argue that this reads into this verse an element Paul has not yet expressed in this context. However, many other interpreters seem to be reading much of this chapter in light of what Paul says of Israel in 11:26 as well. Up to this point, Paul insists that God has not pushed his people away from himself (11:1), nor must they remain fallen (11:11). Instead,

> Paul is showing the Gentiles here how much he loves the Jews. For he magnifies his ministry, by which he is the apostle of the Gentiles, if by loving his own people he wins them to the faith as well. For he is more honored still if he wins to eternal life those to whom he has not been sent. For he who finds his lost brothers will have the greatest honor with his parents.[74]

Lost and Welcome(d) Back (11:15)

"The Loss of Them" (11:15)

Paul continues: "Indeed, if the loss of them is reconciliation of [the] world, what is the acceptance of them, if not life from [the] dead?" (11:15). Cranfield contends that "the loss of them" (ἡ ἀποβολὴ αὐτῶν) "must mean their temporary casting away by God."[75] Dunn also interprets it as a "divine action," which he similarly depicts as "throwing away, jettison, rejection."[76] Those who support this view contend that "loss" (ἀποβολή) has an active sense and that the genitive

---

[72] As Barrett, *Romans*, 215, contends.

[73] Murray, *Romans*, 2:81, insists that "in terms of the whole passage, as noted repeatedly, this must refer to Israel as a whole." For example, Murray speaks of "a mass restoration of Israel" (2:80) and "the conversion of the mass of Israel" (2:84). But Paul does not use such language.

[74] Ambrosiaster, *Romans* (Bray, *Romans*, ACCS NT 6:292); however, his clause "to whom he has not been sent" unnecessarily limits Paul's clear understanding that he was sent "to [the] Jew first" (1:17) as evident from Acts 13:5, 14; 14:1; 17:1–3; 18:4; 19:8.

[75] Cranfield, *Romans*, 562.

[76] Dunn, *Romans*, 657.

"of them" is objective and that taken together they provide the necessary contrast with "the acceptance" or "reception" (ἡ πρόσλημψις) later in the verse.[77]

However, Matera astutely recognizes that such an understanding stands contrary to 11:1–2, where Paul insists that "God has not 'repudiated' ... his people. How, then, can Paul claim that 'their repudiation' ... has led to the reconciliation of [the] world?"[78] Instead of reading both of the genitives as objective (referring to Israel as the *object* of the actions: God rejecting and accepting "them") Matera concludes:

> I am persuaded by those (such as Fitzmyer [*Romans*,] 1993, 612) who construe "their repudiation" as a subjective genitive; that is, *Israel's repudiation* of the Messiah has paradoxically resulted in the reconciliation of the world. If this interpretation is correct, the phrase "their acceptance" (*hē proslēmpsis*) should be taken in the same way: *their acceptance* of the Messiah."[79]

This view is certainly preferable to the previous suggestion. However, Moo points us to Rom 14:3 and 15:7, where the cognate verb προσλαμβάνω, "accept, receive," refers "to God's and Christ's 'accepting' of believers. This strongly suggests that 'acceptance' [11:15] refers to 'God's acceptance of the Jews.' "[80] If the second genitive is objective, God's "acceptance [of them]," what then does Paul mean by the first genitive phrase?

A consistent interpretation defines the "loss" (ἀποβολή) here the same way as in its only other appearance in Biblical Greek. Acts 27:22 uses the noun to describe those who suffer "loss" of life in the sinking of a ship (BDAG, 2). This aligns perfectly with ἥττημα in 11:12, also translated as "loss," and should be the meaning here as well. Dunn points out the congregating of various cognates referring to reconciliation and life in both 5:10 and 11:15, as well as the presence of "salvation" terms in both contexts (5:9–10; 11:11, 14).[81] In Romans 5, the previous relationship with God was that of being "enemies" (ἐχθροί, 5:10; also 11:28). This was in no way due to God's action, but to humanity's own turning against God. The same remains true in regard to "the loss of them" in 11:15.

The response of some in Israel who are unpersuaded by and contradicting toward the Good News (10:16, 21) has been depicted actively with "they tripped" and "their "stumble" (11:11–12), followed by a resulting fall (11:11), and now "the loss of them" (11:15). All of these expressions apply to the "not all" who did not believe or listen responsively to the Good News (10:16; cf. 3:3; 9:6). Therefore the third person pronouns in 11:11, 12, 14, 15 do *not* apply to

---

[77] Dunn, *Romans*, 657; Moo, *Romans*, 693; Murray, *Romans*, 2:81, n. 26, contends that "the meaning is fixed by the contrast with πρόσλημψις ['acceptance']." At the same time, however, Murray draws the meaning of "the reconciling ... of the world" from parallel phrases in 11:11–12. Why does he not allow the same thing for the meaning of ἀποβολή, "loss"?

[78] Matera, *Romans*, 267.

[79] Matera, *Romans*, 267; similarly, Hultgren, *Romans*, 408.

[80] Moo, *Romans*, 693; see the first and third textual notes on 11:15.

[81] Dunn, *Romans*, 657.

"all Israel" or "Israel as a whole."[82] Instead, they refer only to those "seeking earnestly" righteousness from works, who, therefore, did not obtain it (11:7a; also 9:32). Only they in Israel were hardened (11:7c); only they tripped and stumbled (11:11); only they are lost and need to be received back (11:12, 15). *These unbelievers are the "some" whom Paul seeks to save (11:14).* The only possible exception to these references to *part* of the people thus far is the disputed reference to "the fullness of them" in 11:12 (see the commentary there). The proleptic tendency to read one's understanding of Paul's sole use of the phrase "*all* Israel" in 11:26 into his entire discussion bedevils much of the interpretation of the earlier verses of this chapter.

The fact that some tripped and stumbled and lost life, moreover, is not "God's responsibility";[83] nor did it happen by his initiative. While God *reacts* to an unbelieving rejection of the Gospel on the part of some in Israel, he most emphatically does not actively push his people away from himself (11:1–2). Instead, he holds out his hands toward them (10:21) and seeks their reconciliation. Once again, these are the "some" (τινάς) whom Paul endeavors to save (11:14); indeed, the chosen who obtained righteousness through faith already are saved (11:7b).

Reconciliation and Acceptance (11:15)

Paul describes a positive consequence resulting from "the loss of them," namely, the "reconciliation of [the] world" (11:15; see 5:10–11). In keeping with 11:11–12, the "world" (κόσμος, 11:15) denotes specifically the Gentiles (as in 11:12),[84] but not in any restrictive sense, as the latter half of the verse makes evident.

Then Paul speaks of the "acceptance" (πρόσλημψις) of those who had previously been lost. This Greek noun occurs only here in the NT, but Paul employs the cognate verb "to accept" (προσλαμβάνω) thematically in 14:1, 3 and, especially, 15:7. There the middle voice of the verb supports the notion that "'acceptance' may be too passive a translation."[85] Instead, the verbal action behind the noun implies that *God actively receives* these people back to himself. Here it refers specifically to God's "acceptance of what is now unbelieving Israel, His admittance of them to the community of believers."[86] One should add a qualifier, as Paul soon will: "if they do not remain in unbelief" (11:23).

"Life from [the] Dead" (11:15)

Paul speaks even more positively of their reception back as "life from [the] dead" (ζωὴ ἐκ νεκρῶν, 11:15). This depicts the spiritual life granted already

---

[82] In regard to the latter, Murray, *Romans*, 2:81, insists that "in terms of the whole passage, as noted repeatedly, this must refer to Israel as a whole." Similarly, Moo, *Romans*, 698.

[83] As Moo, *Romans*, 693, contends.

[84] Dunn, *Romans*, 657; Moo, *Romans*, 694.

[85] Dunn, *Romans*, 657.

[86] Cranfield, *Romans*, 562; he defines this as "final acceptance."

now to those who believe in Christ.[87] "ζωή ['life'] as divine gift usually has an eschatological character (even when αἰώνιος ['eternal'] is not added)—the life of the new age already experienced in this age and continuing into the new age (as in 5:17, 8:2, 6, 10 …)."[88] Murray thoroughly and persuasively argues that Paul intends the sense of "*spiritual* life and death" in 11:15 based upon the larger context of the NT:

> "Life" frequently denotes the new life in Christ (*cf.* Acts 11:18; Rom. 5:18; 6:4; 8:6; II Cor. 2:16; Eph. 4:18; Phil. 2:16; I John 3:14; 5:11–13). The corresponding verb ['to live'] also is used in this religious sense (*cf.* Rom. 6:10, 11, 13; 8:12, 13; 10:5; II Cor. 5:15; I John 4:9). The word "dead" has also this same figurative [sense but opposite] meaning on many occasions (*cf.* Luke 15:24, 32; Rom. 6:11, 13; Eph. 2:1, 5; Col. 2:13; Heb. 6:1; 9:14; James 2:17; Rev. 3:1). It is significant that so many of these instances occur in Paul's epistles and not a few in the epistle to the Romans.[89]

While weighing the possibility that a spiritual sense is correct, Cranfield categorically insists that

> since ζωὴ ἐκ νεκρῶν ["life from (the) dead"] must clearly denote something surpassing everything signified by σωτηρία ["salvation"] in v. 11, by πλοῦτος κόσμου ["richness of (the) world"] and πλοῦτος ἐθνῶν ["richness of (the) Gentiles"] in v. 12, and by καταλλαγὴ κόσμου ["reconciliation of (the) world"] in the present verse, it cannot denote the spiritual blessings already being enjoyed by the believing Gentiles. If it is to be interpreted figuratively, it must mean—so it would seem—a spiritual vivification which Paul expects to come upon the whole world as a result of the conversion of the mass of Israel.[90]

One wonders, however, why the repeated "must" and "cannot" must be so. Cranfield then asserts that the interpretation he summarizes "seems inconsistent" with 11:25–26 and concludes that the phrase "should be taken to mean the final resurrection itself … the final consummation of all things."[91] Dunn similarly insists that by "life from [the] dead" Paul "must mean … the final resurrection at the end of the age/history," especially since "from the dead" (ἐκ νεκρῶν) "elsewhere always denotes resurrection."[92]

Murray responds:

---

[87] Note the comparable move from baptismal death to life in 6:1–4; for the spiritual life granted to believers already now, see Middendorf, *Romans 1–8*, 459–60 (on 6:4); and for the dominance of the "life" theme throughout Romans 5–8, see 378.

[88] Dunn, *Romans*, 658; see also BDAG, 2 b β.

[89] Murray, *Romans*, 2:83 (emphasis added).

[90] Cranfield, *Romans*, 562; similarly, Moo, *Romans*, 695: "These descriptions suggest that 'life from death' must be an event distinct from Israel's restoration, involving the whole world, and occurring at the very end of history."

[91] Cranfield, *Romans*, 563.

[92] Dunn, *Romans*, 658.

If Paul meant the resurrection, one wonders why he did not use the term [ἀνάστασις] occurring so frequently in his epistles and elsewhere in the New Testament to designate this event … (Rom. 1:4; 6:5; I Cor. 15:12, 13, 21, 42; Phil. 3:10; *cf.* Acts 4:2; 17:32; 23:6; 24:15, 21; 26:23; Heb. 6:2; I Pet. 1:3). … Nowhere else does "life from the dead" refer to the resurrection and its closest parallel, "alive from the dead" (6:13), refers to spiritual life.[93]

Thus Paul himself challenges the overly emphatic categorical assertions of Cranfield and Dunn on this point, as well as their conclusion.

As Paul continues he speaks of unbelievers in Israel as branches cut off from the tree (i.e., "dead," 11:15) due to unbelief (11:17, 20). He then reminds Gentiles that those same branches are able to be reattached and become alive again (11:23–24). Thus "dead" (νεκρός) at the end of 11:15 equates to "the loss" earlier in the verse (ἡ ἀποβολή; also τὸ ἥττημα in 11:12); "life" (ζωή) similarly expresses their "acceptance" (πρόσλημψις) back into the community of faith (11:15). As referenced by Murray,[94] one again hears the words of Jesus to the older brother at the conclusion of the parable of the Waiting Father: "it was necessary to celebrate and to rejoice because your brother was dead and he lives [νεκρὸς ἦν καὶ ἔζησεν], even perishing, and he was found" (Lk 15:32).

Enlightenment from Analogies (11:16–24)
Of Firstfruits and Roots (11:16)

Paul introduces two analogies in 11:16. He quickly drops the first, on "firstfruits," but then develops the second, regarding an olive tree, throughout 11:17–24. Thus, while 11:16 can be viewed as somewhat "transitional," its assertion that " 'the part' of something can convey holiness to the 'whole' "[95] moves mainly forward. Indeed, aside from the disputed reference to "their fullness" (11:12; see the commentary there), Paul has not yet spoken directly of the whole of Israel in this context (he will in 11:26). Just the opposite; he explicitly refers to "some" (11:14; as in 3:3; cf. "not all" in 9:6; 10:16). He also speaks collectively of both "Israel" and "Gentiles" in a manner which clearly does not apply to the whole of either, that is, every person in either case (see 11:14; see also "God's People" in the introduction to Romans 9–11).

"And if the firstfruits are holy, the lump [of dough] is also" (11:16). The first "proverb-like statement … clearly alludes to the offering of a cake from the first of the dough enjoined in Num 15.17–21."[96] LXX Num 15:20–21 contains the phrase "firstfruits of the lump" (ἀπαρχὴν φυράματος), and the offering of the firstfruits of the promised land consecrates the rest of the land's produce for

---

93 Murray, *Romans*, 2:83.

94 Murray, *Romans*, 2:83.

95 Moo, *Romans*, 697; he concedes: "The connection [of 11:16] with vv. 11–15 is not as obvious" as its connection with what follows (698).

96 Cranfield, *Romans*, 563; Moo, *Romans*, 699, n. 7, notes that the offering of firstfruits was prescribed also for grain (Lev 2:12); the harvest (Lev 23:10); and grain, wine, and fleece (Deut 18:4, which also mentions oil).

use by the people. The idea is that the consecration of this lump extends holiness to the rest of the dough or harvest, although that is not stated explicitly in the OT passage.[97] Cranfield seeks to root the idea in a discussion of trees whose fruit was deemed to be uncircumcised until an offering is made for them (Lev 19:23–25).[98] Käsemann looks to Philo.[99] Dunn suggests that the manner in which the holiness of the temple sanctified the rest of the city of Jerusalem provides a comparable theological truth.[100] Whatever relevant OT applications there were, if any, the principle Paul states is clear.

He reinforces it with this second, parallel statement: "and if the root is holy, so also are the branches" (11:16). While the OT background may not be as specific, the uses of the metaphor are certainly more widespread.[101]

> For the dependence of branches on root cf. Job 18:16; Jer 17:8; Ezek 31:7; Hos 9:16; Sir 1:20 and 40:15. Paul is certainly drawing here on a long-established imagery of Israel as God's planting (Ps 92:13 [MT 92:14]; Jer 11:17; *Pss. Sol.* 14.3–4; *1 Enoch* 84.6). ... [Closely related are] the eschatological overtones of the messianic hope of a branch from the root of Jesse (Isa 11:1, 10; Jer 23:5; 33:15; Zech 3:8; 6:12).[102]

Considering that most of Paul's hearers listened to the letter read orally, there would need to be some signal in the text or overwhelming evidence to counter the seemingly obvious observation that *the second half of 11:16 provides a restatement of the same point with a different illustrative example.*[103] As Paul continues in 11:17–18 and makes quite explicit in 11:28, the patriarchs are to be identified as the "root." Therefore, "*first fruits* and *root* both refer here to the patriarchs. ... *Lump* and *branches* refer to the whole of the Jewish people";[104]

---

[97] Cf. Dunn, *Romans*, 658.

[98] Cranfield, *Romans*, 563–64.

[99] Käsemann, *Romans*, 307, asserts: "Being consecrated to God, it is sanctified and it also sanctifies the whole lump according to Philo *De specialibus legibus* [*On the Special Laws*] i.131–144."

[100] Dunn, *Romans*, 658, citing Neh 11:1, 18; Is 11:9; 48:2; 66:20; Jer 31:23, 40; Ezek 20:40.

[101] Isaiah 6 seems especially relevant, especially since Paul seems to allude to Is 6:9–10 in Rom 11:8. God's judgment on Israel is likened to the felling of a tree, and even though only a fraction of its stump remains, it contains "the holy seed" (Is 6:13). The image in Isaiah is of a remnant of Israel saved by grace, which then holds the promise that a holy tree will grow from the stump.

[102] Dunn, *Romans*, 659; see the commentary on Rom 15:12 for a discussion of Paul's quotation of Is 11:10 in that verse.

[103] Barrett, *Romans*, 216: "The meaning is the same"; Murray, *Romans*, 2:85, describes the imagery in the two halves as "parallel"; Sanday and Headlam, *Romans*, 526, state this about the second half of the verse in comparison with the first half: "The same idea expressed under a different image." However, Cranfield, *Romans*, 564, contends: "There seems to be no sufficient reason for assuming that ἡ ἀπαρχή ['the firstfruits'] and ἡ ῥίζα ['the root'] must have the same application"; similarly, Dunn, *Romans*, 659: "There is no reason why the two halves of v 16 should be synonymous rather than complementary."

[104] Diodore, *Romans* (Bray, *Romans*, ACCS NT 6:293); to the patriarchs he adds "the lawgiver [i.e., Moses] and the prophets." While not objectionable, they are not specifically mentioned by Paul later (11:28).

see "Background and Introduction" in "Elaboration on the Olive Tree—Faith or Unbelief? (11:17–24)" below.

Other suggestions include identifying "firstfruits" (ἀπαρχή, 11:16) as Jewish Christians based upon Paul's use of the term in Rom 16:5; 1 Cor 16:15; and 2 Thess 2:13 for the first converts in a region. Cranfield appears to accept that interpretation of the first analogy, concluding that "the existence of Jewish Christians serves to sanctify the unbelieving majority of Israel, as the faith of one partner in a marriage sanctifies both the other partner and the children (1 Cor 7.14)."[105] But this lacks consistency with the second metaphor and is not the proper understanding of the Corinthians text.[106] Along the same lines, Moo cites "the lack of solid support in the OT or in Jewish theology for the idea that the remnant would have a 'sanctifying' effect on the people of Israel as a whole."[107] Paul describes Christ himself as the firstfruits elsewhere (1 Cor 15:20, 23). But maintaining consistency with the second metaphor seems to exclude that application here as well.

Elaboration on the Olive Tree—Faith or Unbelief? (11:17–24)

Background and Introduction

The last half of 11:16 then puts in place an "image which the Apostle develops somewhat elaborately" on the basis of the following:

> Israel the Divine nation is looked upon as a tree; its roots are the Patriarchs; individual Israelites are the branches. As then the Patriarchs are holy, so are the Israelites who belong to the stock of the tree, and are nourished by the sap which flows up to them from those roots.[108]

The only qualification needed for that concise summary is that "the patriarchs are a holy root, not because of any innate worth or merit of their own, but by virtue of God's election of grace."[109] Paul's earlier discussion of Abraham and his faith in God's credited righteousness provides excellent corroboration for this clarification (see the commentary on 4:1–5).[110] Abraham and the rest of the patriarchs grant spiritual benefits to their descendants insofar as they receive God's ancient promises in faith, for those promises are bequeathed to their descendants in the faith (Rom 8:14, 16; 9:8; Gal 3:26–29). The blessings given to the patriarchs already included the promise of the ingrafting of Gentiles, and all believers are supported and nourished by the fulfillment of those patriarchal promises in Christ, the "Seed."[111] God's purpose from the very beginning was "that *the bless-*

---

[105] Cranfield, *Romans*, 564.

[106] See Lockwood, *1 Corinthians*, 242–43.

[107] Moo, *Romans*, 700.

[108] Sanday and Headlam, *Romans*, 526.

[109] Cranfield, *Romans*, 565.

[110] Middendorf, *Romans 1–8*, 322–27.

[111] God promised Abraham that all the peoples of the earth would be blessed through him and his descendants, notably his Seed; see Gen 12:1–3; 18:18; 22:17–18; 26:3–4; 28:13–14. See also Gal 3:6–14.

ing of Abraham would come to the Gentiles in Christ Jesus, so that we might receive the promise of the Spirit *through faith*" (Gal 3:14). Thus Paul declares that "the promise is certain to every seed" of Abraham, that is, everyone who has "the faith of Abraham, who is the father of all of us" (Rom 4:16).

Paul's extended analogy in 11:17–24 deals specifically with an olive tree, a metaphor for Israel twice in the OT. One is rather ominous. In Jer 11:16 Yahweh declares this of Judah and Jerusalem: "Yahweh called your name 'a verdant olive tree, beautiful with desirable fruit.' But with the sound of a great tempest he will set it on fire, and its branches will be consumed." On the Gospel side, Hosea concludes with a word of promise for Israel: "his shoots shall go out; may his splendor be like the olive" (Hos 14:6 [MT 14:7]).

Paul's description of grafting practices "has often been criticized on the ground that in actual arboricultural practice one grafts slips from cultivated into wild trees, not slips from wild into cultivated trees."[112] For example, Pelagius observes: "It is against nature to graft a wild olive tree into a cultivated olive tree, because the branch usually alters the effectiveness of the root."[113] Ambrosiaster also notes the contrary application: "The Gentiles, who were from a bad root, were grafted into a good tree, which is the opposite of what happens in agriculture."[114] Dodd supposes that Paul was unfamiliar with agricultural practice,[115] but "the olive tree was the most widely cultivated fruit tree in the Mediterranean area."[116] Thus, as with Jesus' parables, his picture was readily relatable. Paul's use of the metaphor serves a ministerial purpose. Moo offers this witty principle: "It is not the logic of nature" which drives Paul's discussion "but the *theo*logic" of God.[117]

Establishing the Components of the Analogy (11:17)

As initiated in 11:13, Paul again speaks directly to the Gentiles in Rome, but now with the second person singular "you" (see the introduction to 11:13–24 above):

> And if some of the branches were broken off, but you, while being a wild olive [branch], you were grafted in among them and you became a fellow sharer with the root of the oily sap of the olive tree, [18]then do not boast against the branches. But if you are boasting against [them, know that] you are not bearing the root, but the root [bears] you. (11:17–18)

---

[112] Cranfield, *Romans*, 565.

[113] Pelagius, *Romans* (Bray, *Romans*, ACCS NT 6:296).

[114] Ambrosiaster, *Romans* (Bray, *Romans*, ACCS NT 6:294).

[115] Dodd, *Romans*, 180.

[116] Dunn, *Romans*, 660–61.

[117] Moo, *Romans*, 707; Cranfield, *Romans*, 566, similarly states that the imagery serves "simply as a medium for the expression of his meaning. … The verisimilitude of the metaphorical details is not important; the important thing is that the author's meaning should be quite clear."

The "some" (τινες) in 11:17 is hardly "surprising"[118] (see 11:14; also 3:3). Ever since at least 11:7, Paul has been focusing primarily upon those in Israel who "did not obtain" righteousness (11:7a), who tripped, stumbled, and fell (11:11; see also 9:32–33). He has already diagnosed why (9:30–32; 10:2–3, 16) and will make his point clear again in 11:20. These "some" (11:17) are "the rest" who were hardened (11:7c).

Thus Moo misstates when he says that "the essential tragedy that sparks Rom. 9–11: Jews, the recipients of God's blessing through their ancestry, have been severed from those blessings—through both God's hardening (cf. vv. 7b–10) and their own unbelief (cf. v. 20)."[119] First, the Jews as a whole have *not* been severed, but, as Paul says, only "some" have been (τινες, 11:17; also 3:3; cf. 9:6; 10:16). Second, *their unbelief came first* (10:16), before their hardening, as result of earnestly seeking to establish their own righteousness by works, rather than receiving it from faith (9:31–32; 10:3; 11:7a). This is what led to their stumbling and failure to attain/obtain (9:31; 11:7a, 11). Their hardening, that is, the hardening of "the rest" (οἱ ... λοιποί, 11:7c, = "some" in 11:17), by God then *followed* as a reactive response to their unbelief (10:16, 18–21; 11:7c–10).

Yet Paul's declaration that "not all listened responsively to the Good News" (10:16) simultaneously implies that others did. *These believing Jews simply remain where they already were and, in fact, always belonged by God's choice of grace (11:5, 7b).* Now, extraordinarily, Gentiles are included "among them" (ἐν αὐτοῖς, 11:17), namely, among believing Israel, those Jews who longed for and now receive their Messiah in faith (10:17). Finally, God's inclusion of (some) Gentiles hopes to provoke envy among at least some of those who fell in Israel (10:21; 11:11) so that they might not remain fallen (11:11) but, rather, be saved (11:14).

But what of Gentiles? *None* of them were originally part of the tree; instead, they were from a "wild olive (tree)" (ἀγριέλαιος, 11:17, 24), which conveys a lack of fruitfulness.[120] Nevertheless, God graciously grafted in *some* Gentiles.[121] They are now supported by Israel's patriarchal "root" (11:18b, 28) and also share in the nourishing, life-giving sap the olive tree provides, that is, the blessings Israel receives from God (see 3:1–2; 9:4–5). "Fellow sharer" (συγκοινωνός, 11:17) implies that both the root and the branches benefit from the rich sap of the tree. It also brings up the significance of the concept of *koinonia* (κοινωνία):

> Fundamental to Paul's soteriology is this emphasis on "sharing with"—sharing with Christ (6:4; 1 Cor 1:9; 10:16; Phil 3:10), sharing in the Holy Spirit

---

[118] As suggested by Dunn, *Romans*, 660.

[119] Moo, *Romans*, 701.

[120] Dunn, *Romans*, 661, says that "the wild olive was notoriously *un*productive."

[121] Eph 2:11–22 more fully develops the change from *before* to *after* for those Gentiles now in Christ.

(2 Cor 13:13 [ET 13:14]; Phil 2:1), sharing with fellow Christians (e.g., 12:13; 15:26; 2 Cor 1:7; Phil 1:7), and here not least Gentile sharing with Jews (see also 15:27).[122]

Irenaeus then observes: "If the wild olive takes kindly to the graft ... it becomes a fruit bearing olive. ... So likewise men ... receive the Spirit of God and bring forth the fruit."[123]

A Warning to Wild Gentiles (11:18)

The "then" clause of 11:18 completes the thought: "then do not boast [μὴ κατακαυχῶ] against the branches." The Gentile reaction to being so blessed certainly should not provoke boasting against Jewish people, *whether fellow Christians or not.*[124] In fact, the latter seems most prominent, particularly in light of 11:20–21.[125] Thus, while 14:1–15:7 affirms that Jew-Gentile tensions are present *within* the believing community in Rome, it seems overly conjectural to assert, as does Moo, that Paul knew that "these Gentile believers [in Rome] were apparently convinced that they belonged to a new people of God that had simply replaced Israel"[126] (see the discussion of the force of the prohibition in the first textual note on 11:18). Neither does the boasting against the Jews imply a general anti-Semitic sentiment among the Romans. On the contrary, as evident from Paul's nearly continuous use of the OT throughout this letter, many of the early Gentile Christians there had likely been a part of Jewish synagogues and, thus, previously and positively rooted in the OT and among its people.[127]

A more appropriate comparison exists with the boasting Paul dealt with earlier in Romans 2 (καυχάομαι, "to boast," 2:17, 23, which is a cognate to κατακαυχάομαι, "to boast against," 11:18 [twice]). There, predominantly Jewish boasting against Gentiles was excluded (3:27). Here, then, Paul similarly warns Gentiles against a presumptuous attitude over and against Jews. In both cases, such behavior stems from failing to acknowledge one's *complete dependence upon the God who graces us with his saving righteousness totally apart from any of our works.* Gentiles have been incorporated into the tree of Israel and are nourished in and through the blessings promised to Israel's patriarchs.[128] "No amount of boasting on the part of the branches which have been grafted in can reverse their relation to the root."[129]

---

[122] Dunn, *Romans*, 661.

[123] Irenaeus, *Against Heresies*, 5.10.1 (Bray, *Romans*, ACCS NT 6:293–94).

[124] Dunn, *Romans*, 661.

[125] So Barrett, *Romans*, 217, speaks of "boasting over the unbelieving Jew"; similarly, Murray, *Romans*, 2:87: "look with disdain upon the fallen."

[126] Moo, *Romans*, 704.

[127] See Middendorf, *Romans 1–8*, 10–12.

[128] See "Background and Introduction" in "Elaboration on the Olive Tree—Faith or Unbelief? (11:17–24)" in the commentary above.

[129] Cranfield, *Romans*, 568.

A Presumptive Reply (11:19)

As often in Romans, Paul presumes and enunciates a plausible response (e.g., 6:1, 15; 7:7; 9:19, 30): "You will then say, 'Branches were broken off so that I might be grafted in'" (11:19). While one need not assert that a Gentile is actually saying these words, they seem closer to reality for some of Paul's audience than his discussion of a judgmental person and/or a boasting Jew in 2:1–5, 17–27 (note the qualifiers there). Here the sense of reality seems closest to 9:19 both in form and as a representative reply. If the ἵνα clause ("so that") uttered by a presumptuous Gentile in 11:19 conveys result, it can be properly understood, i.e., "one result of branches being broken off is that I was then grafted in." But it more likely anticipates an egotistical (note the emphatic ἐγώ, "I") assertion of purpose. If so, it does not represent a true statement of God's purpose.[130] The actual reason why (ἵνα, purpose) some "were broken off" was *not* to make room for "me"; neither does it reside within the plan, desire, or act of God. Ambrosiaster identifies the actual explanation and the proper response for Gentiles:

> The Jews were not condemned by God in order to let the Gentiles in. They condemned themselves by rejecting God's gift, and by doing that they gave the Gentiles an opportunity to be saved. Paul wants to stop this boasting, so that we might rejoice in our salvation rather than insult the weak.[131]

The Only Human Distinction That Matters: Faith or Unbelief (11:20a)

Paul affirms Ambrosiaster's assessment with his own response in the first half of 11:20: "Well [said]! Due to unbelief they were broken off, but you have stood and remain standing by faith." With "well" (καλῶς) Paul partially affirms the previous assertion, properly understood. But he qualifies his agreement with references to "unbelief" (τῇ ἀπιστίᾳ), placed emphatically at the beginning of the clause, and "faith" (τῇ πίστει). Both nouns are in the dative case. Cranfield suggests treating them both the same, as causal, conveying "on the ground of."[132] While consistency is commendable,[133] the ground or basis for remaining standing in the tree is not human faith, but God's grace (11:5–6) and kindness (three times in 11:22). Therefore some distinction should be observed. Dunn proposes that "the first dative is causal (BDF, §196), but the second is more instrumental; the neatness of the contrast in Greek therefore cannot be easily reproduced in translation."[134] The inadequacies of English are even more pronounced in handling the relevant and related nouns in 11:20: "faith" (τῇ πίστει) versus "unbelief" (τῇ ἀπιστίᾳ).[135]

---

[130] Cf. Cranfield, *Romans*, 568–69.

[131] Ambrosiaster, *Romans* (Bray, *Romans*, ACCS NT 6:294–95).

[132] Cranfield, *Romans*, 569.

[133] See Middendorf, *Romans 1–8*, 52–54.

[134] Dunn, *Romans*, 663; similarly, Moo, *Romans*, 705, nn. 44 and 45.

[135] See Middendorf, *Romans 1–8*, 88.

Here, then, we have the fundamental explanation for what has happened to "some" in Israel (11:17). As already stated in 10:16, *everything hangs on faith* (also 3:3; 9:32). Ever since the emphatic statements about faith in 1:16–17, Paul has thematically emphasized faith/believing. This is particularly true in 3:21–31, where "faith" (πίστις) occurs eight times and Paul similarly excludes all boasting (cf. also 2:17–24). For example:

> [27]Then where is the boasting [ἡ καύχησις]? It was shut out. Through what kind of Law? Of works? No, but through the Law of faith [πίστεως]. [28]For we conclude that a person is being declared righteous by faith [πίστει] apart from works of the Law. (3:27–28)

This is also the faith of Abraham as Romans 4 demonstrated with its ten uses of the noun "faith" (πίστις) and six of the cognate verb "believe" (πιστεύω).[136] Even more recently, the critical nature of faith has been underscored further with the noun "faith" (πίστις) in 10:6, 8, 17 and the verb "believe" (πιστεύω) in 10:4, 9, 10, 11, 14, 16. Thus the distinguishing factor for one and for all resides in *either* receptive faith, which comes from hearing the Word, *or* the human ability to respond with unbelief (10:16).

> [11]For the Scripture says: "Everyone who believes [πᾶς ὁ πιστεύων] on him will not be put to shame." [12]For there is not a difference [between] a Jew and a Greek, for the same Lord [is] of all, being rich to all the ones who are calling on him. [13]For "everyone who ever might call on the name of [the] Lord will be saved."
>
> [14]How, then, might they call [on him] on whom they did not believe [οὐκ ἐπίστευσαν]? (10:11–14; cf. 3:22–23)

The reason for the response of "unbelief" (ἀπιστία, 11:20) by some in Israel has also been diagnosed repeatedly by Paul. It stems from seeking to attain righteousness "as if [it could be attained] from works" (9:32; cf. 9:31; 11:7a). However, attempting to "establish" (στῆσαι, aorist infinitive of ἵστημι, "to stand," 10:3) one's own righteousness by works results, ironically, in stumbling over the one in whom Israel (and everyone) is to believe (9:32–33; 11:11), through faith in whom one is credited with righteousness (Rom 4:3, citing Gen 15:6). The approach of works, then, is what prompts the "not all" to not listen responsively to or believe the Good News (10:16–17), to their tripping (11:11), not attaining/obtaining (9:31; 11:7a), and the resulting fallen state (11:11, 22). God then *reacts* to *unbelief* with breaking off (11:20) and hardening (11:7c). But, as in 3:3–4 and 11:1–2, this does not nullify his promises to everyone in Israel (and to all people). A remnant of those chosen by God remains in the tree by his grace (11:5, 7). Furthermore, those who fell into unbelief need not remain there (see 11:11–12, 23–24).

In contrast to being "broken off" (ἐξεκλάσθησαν, 11:20), Paul again utilizes a form of the verb "to stand" (ἵστημι, 11:20, as in 10:3) to make a critical

---

[136] See Middendorf, *Romans 1–8*, 313–14.

point. The dual force of its perfect tense[137] here (ἕστηκας) conveys that a past action brought about "by faith" (τῇ πίστει; see 3:28) also remains in effect through the very same faith in Christ. Therefore ἕστηκας means *"you have stood and remain standing* by faith" (11:20).[138] The Formula of Concord recognizes this by stating: "In other words, [Paul] attributes to faith alone the beginning, the middle, and the end of everything" (FC SD IV 34, followed by a citation of Rom 11:20). This verb "perfect[ly]" removes the wedge Sanders tries to drive between "getting in" and "staying in" the people of God.[139] "It is faith, and faith alone—characterized by ... receptivity—that is the only way to establish or to maintain a relationship with God (3:27–4:5)."[140]

Further Warning Shots to Gentiles (11:20b–21)

Paul now explicitly warns Gentiles. Since their relationship among God's people depends solely upon their receptive faith in Christ, any sense of self-assurance is unwarranted and all notions of superiority ought to be excluded (cf. 3:27), just as they were for the Jewish person characterized in 2:17–27. So Paul continues with this advice: "Do not set your mind on proud [thoughts], but reverently fear!" (11:20b). If everything depends on God's grace and kindness (11:5–6, 22) received from faith, then any haughty attitude toward others and all lofty thoughts about oneself are properly excluded (as again in 12:16; cf. 1 Tim 1:16). The Formula of Concord captures Paul's positive purpose:

> This will lead us to live in the fear of God and to recognize and glorify God's goodness to us without and contrary to our deserving, to whom he gives and preserves his Word and whom he does not harden and reject. (FC SD XI 59, following references to Rom 9:14ff.; 11:22ff. in FC SD XI 58)

While the imperative "fear!" (φοβοῦ, 11:20) does not admonish Gentiles to be scared or terrified of God (and so seek to avoid him), the warning goes beyond godly "awe" and "reverential respect."[141] It is an admonition to remain in faith, lest they, too, stumble and fall from grace. Such an admonition is often conveyed by calls to fear the Lord, e.g., "serve Yahweh in fear, and rejoice with trembling;

---

[137] According to Wallace, *Greek Grammar*, 573, the perfect tense "describes an event that, completed in the past (we are speaking of the perfect indicative here), has results existing to the present time (i.e., in relation to the time of the speaker)"; for a complete discussion, see 572–82.

[138] This may also be the sense of "from faith to faith" (ἐκ πίστεως εἰς πίστιν) in 1:17; see Middendorf, *Romans 1–8*, 96–98.

[139] Sanders, *Paul and Palestinian Judaism*, 17, proposes that any religion can be analyzed in terms of "how getting in and staying in are understood" (emphasis removed). See the commentary on 11:5; see also Middendorf, *Romans 1–8*, 596–97, and Middendorf, *The "I" in the Storm*, 257–64.

[140] Moo, *Romans*, 705.

[141] Moo, *Romans*, 705, speaks of "reverential respect for the God of majesty"; similarly, Dunn, *Romans*, 663.

kiss[142] the Son, lest he become angry" (Ps 2:11–12; see also Pss 34:9 [MT 34:10]; 111:10; 112:1; Prov 1:7; 3:7; cf. Mk 4:51).

Rom 11:21 proceeds to offer this ominous warning: "indeed, if God did not spare the branches [which were] in accord with nature, neither will he spare you." The form of the verb "spare" (ἐφείσατο, from φείδομαι) is exactly the same as in 8:32, which says that God "did not spare his own Son," but the "no sparing" in 11:21 hardly presents a comparable picture of Israel suffering punishment vicariously for the world.[143] After all, why did God not spare the branches of Israel? It was due to their unbelief (11:20). As Isaiah prophesied, they did not believe the message (Is 53:1, quoted in Rom 10:16) *specifically about a gracious God who "did not spare [ἐφείσατο] his own Son, but handed him over" (8:32) as the Suffering Servant of Is 52:13–53:12.* However, if God did not spare the unbelieving natural branches of Israel, neither will he spare you Gentiles if you, similarly, do not continue to stand in faith.

Paul, of course, readily reckons with the possibility that Gentiles, like some Jews, could forfeit or fall from faith and (re)turn to unbelief (e.g., Rom 8:13; Col 1:23; cf. Heb 3:6, 14).[144] As Dunn notes when commenting on Rom 11:21: "The possibility of believers 'falling away' … is one which Paul certainly did not exclude. On the contrary, he reckoned with it in all seriousness."[145] And as Dunn states with regard to 11:20: "The warning example continues to be Israel whose presumption transformed πίστις ['faith'] into ἀπιστία ['unbelief']."[146] Therefore any suggestion that the unbelieving Jews who were "broken off" from the tree (11:17) "had never been part of the tree at all" is beyond unnecessary.[147]

God's Kindness and Severity (11:22)

"See then!" (ἴδε οὖν, 11:22). With this interjection Paul grabs his hearers' attention in order to state the conclusion to be drawn from his discussion. As was often true in the opening chapters of the letter, his main lesson focuses upon neither Jews nor Gentiles, neither human faith nor unbelief. *Instead, he makes*

---

[142] The Hebrew verb "kiss" in this context denotes an act of worship in faith, and the "Son" who is worshiped is God's "Son" and "King" (Ps 2:6–7). Cf. 1 Ki 19:18, where the same Hebrew verb, "kiss," refers to worship of the false god Baal; Paul cites from 1 Ki 19:18 in Rom 11:4.

[143] As suggested by Hays, *Echoes of Scripture in the Letters of Paul*, 61.

[144] The entire argument of Hebrews also grapples with the all too real possibility; see Middendorf and Schuler, *Called by the Gospel*, 284–85.

[145] Dunn, *Romans*, 664.

[146] Dunn, *Romans*, 663.

[147] Moo, *Romans*, 707, n. 57, asks whether "a genuine Christian can lose his faith and thus be eternally condemned" and admits that "certainly it is possible to infer this from Paul's warning." That is indeed the reason for Paul's warning, as he elaborates in 11:21–22! However, Moo follows Calvin in wrongly suggesting that those who do not remain in faith (whether Israelites or Christians) "may never have been part of that tree at all," i.e., instead of losing faith, they never had faith.

an important assertion about God.[148] Earlier, Paul demonstrated how and why God's righteousness impacts humanity either in terms of his wrath (1:18–3:20) or as his most gracious Good News (1:1–4; 3:21–31). Now Paul similarly draws this theological truth from his olive-tree analogy: "See then [the] kindness and severity of God. On the one hand, upon the ones who fell, severity, but, on the other hand, upon you, God's kindness, if you remain in his kindness; otherwise you also will be cut out" (11:22). Paul reveals the dominant note here by referring to God's "kindness" (χρηστότης) three times. While "kindness" (χρηστότης) all too often is sorely lacking among humanity (3:12), it is abundant with God (2:4). Thus the basis upon which *anyone exists in the olive tree,* whether a branch "in accord with nature" (11:21, 24) or by being grafted into the tree (11:17), as well as *remains* there, *is always God's gracious "kindness"* (χρηστότης), received and sustained in faith (11:20).

Apart from the life-giving and nourishing sap (11:17) God provides in Christ, there is only "severity" (ἀποτομία, 11:22). This Greek term occurs only here in the LXX and the NT. "Hellenistic usage referred it to the law with the sense 'judicial strictness' or even 'pitiless severity.' "[149] When the cognate adjective "severe, relentless" (ἀπότομος) and the cognate adverb "severely, relentlessly" (ἀποτόμως) occur repeatedly in Wisdom (5:20, 22; 6:5; 11:10; 12:9; 18:15), a sense of "the 'unrelenting severity' of the diving judgment" prevails.[150] Whether or not Paul relies on this source as his background, the forensic connotations of "severity" (ἀποτομία) resonate well with his legal argument about the wrath of God in 1:18–3:20. All people have turned away from God (3:12) and, therefore, apart from divine intervention, are rightly and righteously condemned under divine judgment (1:32; 3:9–20; 5:12, 16, 18).

God's choosing of Israel, however, brought them under his kindness and grace. Those who tripped and stumbled over the Stone, in whom they were intended to believe, fell (9:32–33; 11:11), that is, they fell into unbelief (10:16; 11:20). Without faith in God's kindness, only his severity applies to all. If you are a Gentile believer, Paul reminds you that you have now been grafted in by God and, as a result, enjoy his kindness. God's promise (4:16) of continued "kindness" is also certain so long as "you *remain* in his kindness" (11:22).

In nature, branches do not actively *"persist"* (BDAG, s.v. ἐπιμένω, 2) in order to stay in place in a tree. Therefore the passive sense of the compound verb ἐπιμένω in 11:22 as *"remain"* (BDAG, 1) fits the metaphor.[151] Jesus similarly

---

[148] See Middendorf, *Romans 1–8*, 21–22, 27, 49–51; in this volume, see "Romans 1–4: The Righteousness of God" in the introduction to Romans 9–16, as well as "God" in "The Three Foci of Romans 9–11" in the introduction to Romans 9–11. See also the commentary on 1:17, 32; 2:11, 16, 29; 3:1–8, 19–20, 29–30; 4:21; 9:5, 11b–12a, 16, 22–24, 29; 10:21; 11:1–2, 33–36; 12:19; 13:1–2; 14:10–12; 15:5, 8, 13; 16:25, 27.

[149] Dunn, *Romans*, 664.

[150] H. Köster, "ἀποτομία κτλ.," *TDNT* 8:108; see 8:107–8.

[151] The related noun ὑπομονή in Rom 5:3, translated as "patient endurance," carries a somewhat more active sense, as it clearly does also in Heb 12:1; see the fourth textual note on Rom 11:22 and the commentary on 5:3.

employs the related simple verb μένω to describe a branch passively "remaining" in a nourishing vine (ten times in Jn 15:4–10).[152] As long as you stay where God has placed you, that is, remain in faith, you reside within God's kindness along with the patriarchs (11:17, 28) and those in Israel chosen by grace who did obtain righteousness (11:5–7). God's express will is that you remain in faith and that the Word of Christ (10:17) preserves you in faith, and thus Christ secures your place in the tree.[153] But on the human side of things, you can get yourself removed from the tree. If you do not continue to stand in faith, God will not spare you (11:20–21); you will be cut off and again face his severity (11:22).

God's Persistent Power to Save (11:23)

Yet God's kindness exerts itself so persistently that those who have fallen due to unbelief are *not* beyond recovery in this life. Paul speaks of those in Israel who did not believe in the Good News in 11:23: "And those also, if they do not remain in unbelief, they will be grafted in; for God is powerful to graft them in again." Paul again reinforces the significance of faith and unbelief. The "Word of Christ" (10:17) has been sent out, proclaimed, and heard (10:14–15, 18). Faith comes from hearing, but not all who heard believed the Good News (10:16–17). Yet God has not rejected his people (11:1–2), even those who have been unpersuaded and contradicting (10:21). His hands are stretched out (10:21). If his people do not persist in unbelief, but are brought (back) to faith by the Word (10:17), Paul affirms with an indicative verb that "they will be grafted in" (ἐγκεντρισθήσονται, 11:23a) and accepted back by God (11:15). He then affirms why: "For God is powerful [δυνατὸς γάρ ἐστιν ὁ θεός] to graft them in again" (11:23b).

The language of 11:23b recalls Abraham's steadfast relationship with the same God. Rom 4:20–21 depicts his faith and its object with striking similarity:

> [20]But he [Abraham] did not waver into unfaith [ἀπιστία, the same word translated as "unbelief" in 11:20, 23] in the promise of God, but he was *empowered in the faith* [ἐνεδυναμώθη τῇ πίστει], after giving glory to God. [21]And, after being fully convinced that what was promised [by God] and still in effect, *he [God] is powerful* [δυνατός ἐστιν] also to do.

---

[152] For the Johannine theme of "remaining" (μένω) in Christ, see " 'Where Are You Remaining?' (Jn 1:38–39)" in the commentary on Jn 1:35–51 in Weinrich, *John 1:1–7:1*, 279–81.

[153] The biblical teaching of preservation in faith and the means by which God preserves us are well expressed by Luther in his explanation of the Second Article of the Apostles' Creed:

I believe that by my own reason or strength I cannot believe in Jesus Christ, my Lord, or come to him. But the Holy Spirit has called me through the Gospel, enlightened me with his gifts, and sanctified and *preserved me in true faith*, just as he calls, gathers, enlightens, and sanctifies the whole Christian church on earth and preserves it in union with Jesus Christ in the one true faith. In this Christian church he daily and abundantly forgives all my sins, and the sins of all believers, and on the last day he will raise me and all the dead and will grant eternal life to me and to all who believe in Christ. This is most certainly true. (SC II 6; emphasis added; the first two sentences of Luther are also quoted in FC SD II 40)

The desire of God to move all people out from under his severity to a place in Christ where they receive his kindness also reinforces the interpretation of 9:22–23. There Paul speaks similarly of God being both "willing to demonstrate [his] wrath and to make known his [saving] power" (δυνατὸν αὐτοῦ, 9:22). *While his severity rests on all unbelievers, he desires to give to all people his mercy, kindness, and salvation—the gifts graciously given to all who believe* (1:16; 10:4, 11; 11:30–32). Therefore all these uses of the adjective "powerful" (δυνατός, 4:21; 9:22; 11:23) plus the cognate verb "empower" (ἐνδυναμόω, 4:20) stem from the cognate noun's presence in Paul's thematic description of the Good News as the "*power* [δύναμις] of God into salvation for everyone who believes, to Jew first and also to Greek" (1:16; cf. "my [God's] power," τὴν δύναμίν μου, in 9:17). Although resistible, God's saving power strives to work faith in all those who do not believe (10:17) and to keep those who do believe in faith.

A "How Much More" Natural Return (11:24)

Paul concludes the metaphor with an extensive interrogative thought for a representative Gentile to ponder: "For if you [singular], in accord with nature from the wild olive tree, you were cut out and, contrary to nature, you were grafted into a cultivated olive tree, how much more will these, the ones in accord with nature, be grafted into their own olive tree?" (11:24). In the first part of the verse, Paul asserts a positive promise. Every Gentile was once separated from God's people and under the severity of his wrath (see Eph 2:3, 11–12). But now, contrary to nature and all expectation, "you" were cut out and grafted into God's cultivated tree (Rom 11:24). By faith (11:20) you actually now receive the same nourishing sap of God's extraordinary kindness, which he bestowed upon the patriarchs and grants to believing Israelites through that "root" ever since (11:17, 22, 28). Remaining in faith, you Gentiles are "fellow citizens with the holy ones and members of the household of God" (Eph 2:19), with all its attendant blessings.

A further positive would seemingly be easier and "how much more" appropriate (πόσῳ μᾶλλον; see the fifth textual note on 11:24). Paul again refers to the branches which were born and grew up as part of the cultivated olive tree "in accord with nature" (κατὰ φύσιν, 11:24), but have now been broken off by God (11:17, 19) due to their unbelief (11:20). Yes, they are currently fallen from the tree (cf. 11:11). But as Ambrosiaster affirms: "These people have not fallen into unbelief in such a way as to make their ultimate conversion impossible."[154] *God is certainly willing and powerfully able to return them to what is, in fact, "their own olive tree" (τῇ ἰδίᾳ ἐλαίᾳ, 11:24); "if they do not remain in unbelief, they will be grafted in" (11:23).*[155] As Paul exclaimed previously: "But if

---

[154] Ambrosiaster, *Romans* (Bray, *Romans*, ACCS NT 6:290).

[155] Schreiner, *Romans*, 627, contends that God "has pledged … to graft them again onto the olive tree." While Paul asserts that this is surely God's intent and hope, as well as within his ability, he does not go so far as to *promise* that it will happen; see the textual notes and the commentary on 11:31.

their stumble [is] richness of [the] world and their loss [is] richness of [the] Gentiles, how much more their fullness?" (11:12).

Conclusions: God's One Tree—God's One People

One Tree

The severity of God's judgment and wrath applies justly to all people. "Every person, Jew or Gentile, stands under sin's power (3:9) and can be saved only by a special act of God's grace."[156] This means that "there is only one root and only one tree; branches, whether Jewish or Gentile, that do not remain attached to that tree are doomed to wither and die."[157]

Similarly, God's kindness is for all through faith. The faith of the patriarchal "root" (11:17, 28)[158] in God's promise has now come to fulfillment in Jesus Christ. Thus at the end of Romans 4, Paul identifies Abraham's faith in this way:

> [23]But, "it was credited to him" was not written on his account only, [24]but also on our account, to whom it is about to be credited, to those who believe upon the one who raised Jesus our Lord from the dead. (4:23–24)

While Paul does not explicitly put Christ in the picture of his olive tree in 11:16–24, Romans 10 certainly validates such an understanding (e.g., 10:4, 9, 17). Most specifically, Jesus' incarnation and his once-for-all salvific work for people of all times and places belong right at the center as the sturdy trunk of the tree (see 6:10 and figures 6–7). At the same time, his eternal existence and ongoing work can also be identified in other ways as well. For example, Pelagius contends: *"The richness of the olive tree* is the root of their fathers, the richness of Christ."[159] Cyril of Jerusalem asserts that Gentiles "became partakers of the good olive tree, Jesus Christ."[160] Homiletically, one might proclaim Christ in various other ways as well: Christ as the source of the (baptismal) living waters upon which the tree depends (cf. Ps 1:3); Christ as the Light of the world who enables the branches' leaves to photosynthesize; his shed, life-giving blood as the "oily sap" (11:17) that flows into the branches; or the "tree" as the cross (cf. Acts 5:30; 1 Pet 2:24) or even the "tree of life" (Gen 2:9; Rev 22:2, 14).[161]

The bow-tie diagram below (figure 6) is used by this author to summarize the story of salvation chronologically. The excursus "Beyond Typology" following the commentary on 12:1–8 explains it more thoroughly.[162]

---

[156] Moo, *Romans*, 708.

[157] Moo, *Romans*, 704.

[158] See "Background and Introduction" in "Elaboration on the Olive Tree—Faith or Unbelief? (11:17–24)" in the commentary above.

[159] Pelagius, *Romans* (Bray, *Romans*, ACCS NT 6:294).

[160] Cyril of Jerusalem, *The Mystagogical Lectures*, 2.3 (Bray, *Romans*, ACCS NT 6:294).

[161] A longstanding tradition of Christian interpretation has perceived the "apple tree" in Song 2:3 to represent Christ; see Mitchell, *The Song of Songs*, 693–95; also 671–72.

[162] See also Middendorf and Schuler, *Called by the Gospel*, 4; for a detailed explanation, see *Called by the Gospel*, 1–7, as well as this video: https://www.youtube.com/watch?v=-RJIQD_wV3k.

Figure 6

The Whole Story: The Bow-Tie Diagram

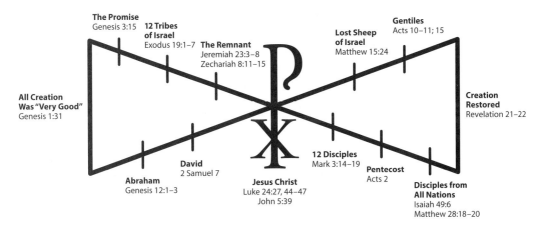

Here the OT (left side) all looks toward, narrows down to, and is fulfilled at the center point which represents the birth, life, ministry, death, and resurrection of Jesus the Christ/Messiah. Then, on the right side, everything flows out from him initially to the Twelve and the people of Israel and then into all of the world. If one merely flips the diagram up onto its left edge, it correlates fairly well with the olive-tree image Paul utilizes here with Christ as the trunk. See figure 7.

Figure 7

God's One Olive Tree

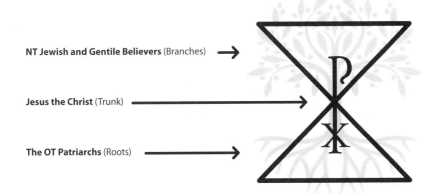

One People

As noted in "God's Word" in the introduction to Romans 9–11, these chapters of Romans primarily move past or, better, *through* the identification of Jesus as the promised Christ/Messiah (9:5; 10:17) and *concentrate on depicting the NT people of God in him.* In this way, Paul focuses on the right side of the bowtie diagram, which correlates with the broadened out branches of the olive tree in the olive-tree analogy. Moo nicely summarizes what this section means and thus what these diagrams convey in a manner which transitions into the next and final segment of Romans 9–11 (11:25–36):

> Basic to the whole metaphor is the unity of God's people, a unity that crosses both historical and ethnic boundaries. The basic point of the metaphor is that there is only one olive tree, whose roots are firmly planted in OT soil, and whose branches include both Jews and Gentiles. This olive tree represents the true people of God. The turn of the ages at the coming of Christ brought an important development in the people of God: the object of one's faith became clearer and more specific and the ethnic makeup of the people changed radically, as God extended his grace in vastly increased measure to Gentiles. … And "messianic Jews," following in the footsteps of their believing ancestors, belong to this same community.

> The picture Paul sketches reveals the danger of the simple and popular notion that the church has "replaced" Israel. For this formula misses the stress Paul places on historical continuity in the people of God. … Perhaps a better word to describe the movement from OT Israel to NT church is the same word the NT so often uses to denotes such relationships: "fulfillment." We thereby capture the necessary note of continuity—the church is the continuation of Israel into the new age—and discontinuity—the church, not Israel, is now the locus of God's work in the world.[163]

As a result, the use of the phrase "the new Israel" to convey the idea of replacement is similarly *misleading and inappropriate* (see "God's People" in the introduction to Romans 9–11).

In keeping with Paul's warnings in 11:20–23, Moo then issues this additional caution:

> The Gentiles' rejoicing at being *included* with Jews in God's people would all too easily lead to boasting that they had *replaced* the Jews as the people of God. Sorry to say, such an assumption is still rampant in the Christian church: witness the typical contrast "Jew"/"Christian."[164]

On this point, Moo is also correct. Assertions that "the Jews killed Jesus" are simply not true literally. The Jewish leaders turned him over, but a Roman execution squad crucified him on the orders of a Roman governor (Mt 27:26–31; Mk

---

[163] Moo, *Romans*, 709; in light of his correct conclusion at the end of this quotation, it is paradoxical for him to maintain that now Israel "as a national entity … continues to exist as the object of God's care and attention."

[164] Moo, *Romans*, 685.

15:15–20; Lk 23:25; Jn 19:16–18, 23; thus in the Nicene Creed we confess that Jesus "was crucified also for us under Pontius Pilate"). Moreover, since Christ died for the sins of the whole world, all of us are equally culpable; but "now, nothing [is] condemnation for the ones in Christ Jesus" (Rom 8:1).

Along the same lines, Murray's repeated statements that the kingdom of God has been "taken from" Israel, citing Mt 21:43,[165] are textually incorrect. The plural "you" from whom the kingdom is taken does *not* refer to the (singular) vineyard, which represents Israel (Is 5:1–7; Ps 80:8–16 [MT 80:9–17]). Instead, as Mt 21:45–46 makes clear, the former tenants correspond to the Jewish religious leaders whose role of tending God's vineyard ends.[166] The vineyard that is Israel, however, remains the same.

In keeping with the metaphor of Rom 11:17–24, God has *not* chopped down or replaced his olive tree with a new or different one. Any assertions that he has done so should be soundly dismissed. After all, Paul, a Jewish Christian himself, emphatically rejects the notion that God has pushed his people away from himself (11:1–2). On the contrary, he stretched out his hands toward them, even the unpersuaded and contradicting ones (10:21). So should Christians today with the same hope as Paul, that through our ministry God might save some of those who currently do not believe (11:13–14); whether they be Jew or Gentile makes no difference (3:22–23; 10:12).

One final question should be addressed before proceeding into 11:25–36. If Paul was asked to name the *one* olive tree in 11:17–24, what would he call it? As with the vineyard illustration discussed above (Mt 21:33–41), it seems that he would identify the tree in this way: God's one people, his "Israel."

---

[165] Murray, *Romans*, 2:78, 81.

[166] Middendorf, *Romans 1–8*, 225–26.

Conclusion to Romans 9–11: Resolution and Doxology

Translation

11 ²⁵Indeed, I do not want you to be without knowledge, brothers, [concerning] this mystery, so that you might not be wise within yourselves, that a hardening in part has come to be and still exists for Israel until which [time] the fullness of the Gentiles comes in, ²⁶and thus all Israel will be saved, just as it stands written:

"The Rescuer will come from Zion.

He will turn away godlessness from Jacob.

²⁷And this is the covenant from me for them,

when I take away their sins."

²⁸On the one hand, with respect to the Good News [they are] enemies for your sake, but, on the other hand, with respect to the choosing [of God, they are] loved on account of the patriarchs. ²⁹For the gracious gifts and the calling of God [are] without regret. ³⁰For just as you were formerly unpersuaded to God but now you were shown mercy by the unpersuadedness of these ones, ³¹thus also now these were unpersuaded for your mercy in order that they might also now be shown mercy. ³²Indeed, God locked up all people into unpersuadedness in order that he might show mercy to all.

³³O [the] depth of [the] riches and wisdom and knowledge of God!

How unfathomable his judgments and incomprehensible his ways!

³⁴"Indeed, who knew [the] mind of [the] Lord?

Or who has become his counselor?"

³⁵"And who has given previously to him

so that it should be repaid to him?"

³⁶Because all things [are] from him and through him and to him.

To him [is] the glory into the ages. Amen!

Textual Notes

11:25 οὐ γὰρ θέλω ὑμᾶς ἀγνοεῖν, ἀδελφοί—This clause virtually replicates a portion of 1:13; see the first two textual notes and the commentary there. Paul uses it similarly in 1 Cor 10:1; 12:1; 2 Cor 1:8; 1 Thess 4:13.

τὸ μυστήριον τοῦτο—The noun μυστήριον, *mysterion*, occurs in Romans only here and in 16:25, but twenty (or twenty-one) times total in Paul's writing. While it may be defined as "the unmanifested or private counsel of God, *(God's) secret*" (BDAG, 1), Paul asserts that the content of the "mystery" is, in fact, now revealed. See the commentary.

ἵνα μὴ ἦτε—The conjunction ἵνα with the subjunctive (ἦτε) expresses purpose.[1] As negated by μή, what follows is a negative purpose clause, "so that you might not be … ," which explains *why* Paul wants to correct any lack of knowledge.

[παρ'] ἑαυτοῖς φρόνιμοι—The elided preposition παρά is present in ℵ C and D, but 𝔓[46] omits it. The shorter reading is typically preferable, and the preposition was likely inserted to match the same expression in 12:16. For the influence of an idiom from Prov 3:7, "in your own eyes," see the commentary. Whether παρά is included or omitted, "the meaning is very little affected."[2] If omitted, the bare dative could express reference/respect, "*with reference to*," or sphere, "*in the sphere of* or *in the realm of*."[3] If present, παρά would similarly express sphere, "*in the sight of, before*" (as in 2:11, 13).[4] φρόνιμος "pert[ains] to understanding associated w[ith] insight and wisdom, *sensible, thoughtful, prudent, wise*" (BDAG). Properly grounded, it "is a very positive attribute."[5] But here the translation, "wise within yourselves," carries the full thought of being "*wise in your own estimation = relying on your own wisdom*" (BDAG).

ὅτι πώρωσις—The conjunction ὅτι is explanatory (BDAG, 2). BDAG defines the noun πώρωσις as the "state or condition of complete lack of understanding, *dullness, insensibility, obstinacy*" and for this verse suggests "*insensibility (=a closed mind)*." Note the cognate verb πωρέω, "to harden," in 11:7 (see the fifth textual note on that verse), which certainly influences the meaning here; for consistency, "hardening" is utilized for this noun.

ἀπὸ μέρους—The basic meaning of μέρος is "*part, in contrast to the whole*" (BDAG, 1). It is used as the object of various prepositions and appears with ἀπό three times in Romans. In 15:15 it has a partitive sense, "*in part*" (BDAG, s.v. μέρος, 1 c). But in 15:24 the same expression functions temporally, "*for a while*" (BDAG, s.v. μέρος, 1 c). Though its sense here is disputed, the translation "in part" recognizes the partitive meaning; for the contextual implications, see the commentary.

γέγονεν—In this context, as in 11:5, this perfect tense form of γίνομαι expresses both past and present aspects (see the fourth textual note on 11:5 and the commentary on 11:5–6). "It speaks of completed action (aorist) with existing results (present)."[6] The hardening "has come to be and still exists" up to the present. By no means does this imply that the hardening is permanent (see the commentary on 11:11, 24). Wallace refutes the "misleading" notion, "frequently found in commentaries, that the perfect tense denotes *permanent* or *eternal* results. Such a statement is akin to saying the aorist tense means 'once-for-all.' "[7]

---

[1]   See Wallace, *Greek Grammar*, 472.

[2]   Moo, *Romans*, 711, n. 1.

[3]   Wallace, *Greek Grammar*, 144–46, 153–55.

[4]   Wallace, *Greek Grammar*, 378.

[5]   Dunn, *Romans*, 679.

[6]   Wallace, *Greek Grammar*, 574.

[7]   Wallace, *Greek Grammar*, 574.

ἄχρι οὗ—Moo discusses the forty-eight uses of ἄχρι, "until; as far as," in the NT.[8] He summarizes that eleven convey a spatial sense. Of the other thirty-seven, twenty-five "rather clearly denote a period of time that will come to an end."[9] BDAG defines ἄχρι as a "marker of continuous extent of time up to a point, *until*" (BDAG, 1) and for this expression identifies the function as a conjunction (BDAG, 1 b) to be translated as "*until the time when*" (BDAG, 1 b α). The slightly more literal "until which [time]" is adopted here. When a verb follows the phrase, it regularly appears in the subjunctive mood (εἰσέλθη in 11:25; see also Lk 21:24; 1 Cor 11:26; 15:25; Gal 3:19). In these cases, the subjunctive does *not* express uncertainty regarding whether the event may or may not take place, but rather indicates an indefinite period of time until the occurrence. Thus the subjunctive that follows in 11:25 is translated as "comes in."

τὸ πλήρωμα—For "the fullness," see the fifth textual note and the commentary on 11:12.

11:26 καὶ οὕτως—Interpreters have understood this phrase in a number of ways. Its complexity and influence on one's interpretation of what follows warrants the placement of the discussion in the commentary below.

πᾶς Ἰσραήλ—Although the phrase "all Israel" occurs 136 times in the LXX,[10] the NT uses it or a similar phrase *only twice*, here and in Acts 2:36; see the commentary.

σωθήσεται—For the verb σῴζω, "to save," see the fourth textual note on 5:9. The future passive form (both here and there) is a divine or theological passive, wherein "*God is the obvious agent*":[11] "will be saved" by God.

καθὼς γέγραπται—For this frequent Pauline introduction to Scripture quotations, see the fourth textual note on 1:17.

ἥξει—This is the only occurrence of the verb ἥκω in Romans, drawn from LXX Is 59:20. ἥκω means "*be present*" or "*come*" (BDAG, 1 and 2); it is essentially synonymous with the more familiar ἔρχομαι. The form here is future indicative.

ὁ ῥυόμενος—For ῥύομαι, "to rescue, deliver," see the second textual note on 7:24 (it also occurs in 15:31). This form of the deponent verb ῥύομαι is a present participle used substantively for "the One who rescues" or "the Rescuer."[12]

ἀσεβείας—See the third textual note on 1:18, which has the only other occurrence of the abstract noun "godlessness, ungodliness" in Romans. Paul uses the cognate adjective ἀσεβής as a substantive, "godless/ungodly person," in 4:5; 5:6.

11:27 ἡ παρ᾽ ἐμοῦ διαθήκη—For διαθήκη, "covenant," see the fourth textual note on 9:4, where the plural form is the only other use of διαθήκη in Romans. Paul could have written simply ἡ διαθήκη μου, "my covenant."[13] Instead, he quotes the words from

---

[8] Moo, *Romans*, 717, n. 30.

[9] Moo, *Romans*, 717, n. 30; he adds: "and be followed by a change of those circumstances denoted," though that is disputed in this verse.

[10] Moo, *Romans*, 722, n. 55. See, e.g., LXX Josh 7:25; 1 Sam 7:5; 25:1; 2 Sam 16:22; 1 Ki 12:1; 22:17; 2 Chr 12:1; 24:5; 29:24; Dan 9:11; Mal 3:24 (MT 3:22; ET 4:4).

[11] Wallace, *Greek Grammar*, 437.

[12] For the substantival use of the participle, see Wallace, *Greek Grammar*, 619–21.

[13] The phrase in Rom 11:27 is translated as "my covenant" by ESV; Dunn, *Romans*, 683.

LXX Is 59:21 with the prepositional phrase παρ᾽ ἐμοῦ, which emphasizes divine origin, literally, "the from-me covenant," that is, "the covenant from me."

ὅταν ἀφέλωμαι τὰς ἁμαρτίας αὐτῶν—For the temporal particle ὅταν, "when, whenever," see the first textual note on 2:14. It regularly takes a verb in the subjunctive mood. ἀφέλωμαι is an aorist middle subjunctive first person singular of ἀφαιρέω. This compound verb (ἀπό + αἱρέω) means *"take away, do away with, remove"* (BDAG, 2). It occurs only here in Romans. In this context, the subjunctive does *not* express any uncertainty regarding whether the event may or may not take place (i.e., the taking away of sins). Rather, it indicates an indefinite period of time, in this instance, from Isaiah's day until the arrival of this promised covenant (cf. the eighth textual note on 11:25). Paul quotes ὅταν ἀφέλωμαι from LXX Is 27:9 but changes the singular words of the direct object in the LXX, αὐτοῦ τὴν ἁμαρτίαν, "his sin," to the plural τὰς ἁμαρτίας αὐτῶν, "their sins." See further the commentary.

11:28 κατὰ μὲν τὸ εὐαγγέλιον ἐχθροί—This is the first part of a complete μὲν ... δέ construction (see the first textual note on 2:7), "on the one hand ... on the other hand" (the δέ part is in the third textual note on this verse). The preposition κατά here conveys relationship, *"with respect to, in relation to"* (BDAG, B 6): "on the one hand, with respect to the Good News [they are] enemies." For the adjective ἐχθρός, used substantivally, see the second textual note on 5:10. The referent of "enemies" here must be those who "did not listen responsively to the Good News" (10:16); they are hostile to God because they refuse to believe (i.e., they reject) and contradict the Gospel he sent (see 10:14–16, 21; 11:20, 31). Thus Paul intends its active sense of bellicosity, as he does elsewhere.[14] But this cannot avert the resulting consequences: facing the severity (11:22) of enmity from God.

δι᾽ ὑμᾶς ... διὰ τοὺς πατέρας—The construction in both prepositional phrases is διά plus the accusative, but the preposition has a different nuance in each: "for your sake ... on account of the patriarchs." See " 'Enemies ... Loved' (11:28)" in the commentary.

κατὰ δὲ τὴν ἐκλογήν—Here κατὰ δέ completes the construction begun with κατὰ μέν (see the first textual note on this verse). The noun ἐκλογή refers to God's "choosing, choice," as in 9:11; 11:5 (but to people "chosen" in 11:7); see the fifth textual note on 9:11.

11:29 ἀμεταμέλητα—The doubly compound adjective ἀμεταμέλητος (ἀ- [*alpha* privative; see BDF, § 117.1] + μετά + μελητος, from μέλω) occurs only here and in 2 Cor 7:10 in the NT and is absent from the LXX. However, the cognate compound verb without *alpha* privative, μεταμέλω or μεταμέλομαι (μετά + μέλω), is well attested in both the NT and LXX; it can refer to God "regretting" (e.g., LXX 1 Sam 15:35) or "relenting" (e.g., LXX 1 Chr 21:15; Ps 105:45 [MT/ET 106:45]) or to a person "changing his mind" or "regretting" (e.g., LXX Ex 13:17; Mt 21:29, 32; 27:3; 2 Cor 7:8). Perhaps most relevant are passages where God swears an oath or issues a declaration

---

14   So also Dunn, *Romans*, 685. See Rom 5:10; 12:20; 1 Cor 15:25–26; Gal 4:16; Phil 3:18; Col 1:21; 2 Thess 3:15; cf. Rom 8:7; Gal 5:20.

and states that he "shall not change his mind" (οὐ μεταμεληθήσεται, LXX Ps 109:4 [MT/ET 110:4], quoted in, e.g., Heb 7:21; see his judgments with οὐ μετανοέω in LXX Jer 4:28; Zech 8:14). Thus God's promise about Christ ("a priest forever according to the order of Melchizedek," LXX Ps 109:4 [MT/ET 110:4]); see also Heb 5:6; 7:17) is immutable and eternal; cf. similar statements about God in Num 23:19; Mal 3:6. BDAG defines the adjective ἀμεταμέλητος as "*not to be regretted, without regret.* ... Hence also *irrevocable*, of someth[ing] one does not take back" (BDAG, 1). From God's perspective this is true, but ἀμεταμέλητα does not preclude the reality that what God offers can be revoked or rejected by humans, as is made clear by ἐχθροί, "enemies," in 11:28 (see rejection also in 10:16; 11:20, 31).

τὰ χαρίσματα—For a discussion of the noun χάρισμα, see the third textual note and the commentary on 1:11 ("spiritual gift"). The singular occurs also in 5:15, 16 and 6:23 ("gracious gift"). The plural is used here and in 12:6 to describe God's "gracious gifts."

ἡ κλῆσις—This is the only appearance of this noun for a "*call, calling*" (BDAG, 1) in Romans, but Paul uses it elsewhere.[15] The cognate verb καλέω, "to call," was used thematically five times in Romans 9 (see the fourth textual note on 9:7; also 9:12, 24, 25, 26, as well as 4:17; 8:30 [twice]). The adjective κλητός, "called," serves thematically in the letter's introduction, appearing three times (see the second textual note on 1:1; also 1:6, 7).

11:30 ὥσπερ γὰρ ὑμεῖς ποτε ἠπειθήσατε—For ὥσπερ, "just as," see the second textual note on 5:12. For ποτέ, "formerly," see the first textual note on 7:9; cf. 1:10. For ἀπειθέω, "be unpersuaded; disbelieve," see the first textual note on 2:8 and the third textual note on 10:21; see also the cognate noun ἀπείθεια in the second textual note below. The *alpha* privative (BDF, § 117.1) negates the verb for "persuade" (πείθω). Note that the aorist forms of this verb here, ἠπειθήσατε in 11:30 and ἠπείθησαν in 11:31, are *active*. When -θη- is added it typically signals an aorist or future *passive*,[16] but here the θ is part of the root and the η is lengthened from the vowel ε before a verbal ending. The key is that "you were unpersuaded," i.e., you refused to be persuaded by the Gospel. See further the commentary.

νῦν δὲ ἠλεήθητε—This is the first of two or three instances of the temporal adverb νῦν, "now," in 11:30–31 (see the third textual note on 11:31). For the passive of ἐλεέω, meaning "to be shown mercy," see the first textual note on 9:15; see also the third textual note on 9:16. There is no distinction in meaning between ἐλεέω (9:15 [twice], 18; 11:30, 31, 32; 12:8) and ἐλεάω (9:16). See also the cognate noun ἔλεος, referring to God's "mercy," in 11:31 (also 9:23; 15:9).

τῇ τούτων ἀπειθείᾳ—In Romans the noun ἀπείθεια occurs only here and in 11:32; elsewhere Paul uses it in Eph 2:2; 5:6; Col 3:6. BDAG defines it as "*disobedience, in our lit[erature] always of disob[edience] toward God* ... ; somet[imes] w[ith] the

---

[15] See κλῆσις referring to God's "call" to Christians or their "calling" in 1 Cor 1:26; 7:20; Eph 1:18; 4:1, 4; Phil 3:14; 2 Thess 1:11; 2 Tim 1:9.

[16] Mounce, *Basics of Biblical Greek*, 214, comments: "Almost every time you see the θη you can assume the verb is an aorist passive" or, if -θησ-, a future passive.

connotation of *disbelief* in the Christian gospel (see ἀπειθέω)." Disbelief is certainly the emphasis in this verse. Dunn helpfully points to "the synonym παρακοή (5:19; cf. 2:8) and the preferred antonym ὑπακοή" (5:19; also, e.g., 1:5; 6:16; 15:18).[17] The dative (τῇ … ἀπειθείᾳ) conveys an instrumental sense and expresses cause, "*because of* or *on the basis of*"[18] or "by." The demonstrative pronoun in the genitive (τούτων) identifies the specific group within Israel that Paul is discussing. The phrase is translated literally: "by the unpersuadedness of these ones."

11:31 οὗτοι νῦν ἠπείθησαν—For the verb, see the first textual note on 11:30.

τῷ ὑμετέρῳ ἐλέει—The adjective ὑμέτερος, "your," is addressed "to persons … as possessors or recipients" (BDAG). Here the emphasis is on *reception* of ἔλεος, God's "mercy," and so the sense is objective, "*the mercy shown to you*" (BDAG, s.v. ὑμέτερος, b), not subjective, "the mercy shown by you." The objective sense is required by the *passive* cognate verb ἠλεήθητε, "you were shown mercy" (11:30). Cranfield argues extensively that the phrase here goes with what follows, translating it with the last part of the verse: "in order that they too may now receive mercy by the mercy shown to you."[19] However, Dunn, Moo, and Schreiner all consider but properly reject that suggestion based upon the parallel and chiastic structure of 11:30–31.[20] Moo translates the phrase with the first part of the verse: "They disobeyed for the sake of mercy for you."[21] The translation above is "these also are now unpersuaded for your mercy." The dative case of the phrase τῷ ὑμετέρῳ ἐλέει then expresses interest or advantage, which "has a *to* or *for* idea" wherein the reader can "supply *for the benefit of.*"[22]

ἵνα καὶ αὐτοὶ [νῦν] ἐλεηθῶσιν—The construction ἵνα plus the subjunctive (ἐλεηθῶσιν; see the second textual note on 11:30) expresses purpose.[23] Thus "the focus is on the *intention* of the action of the main verb," regardless of whether the intention is accomplished or not, and "this subordinate clause answers the question *Why?*"[24]

The temporal adverb νῦν, "now," undisputed in the first clause of the verse, is textually disputed here. Regarding this variant Metzger contends that the

> external evidence and internal considerations are rather evenly balanced. A preponderance of early and diverse witnesses favors the shorter reading [e.g., 𝔓⁴⁶ and A]. On the other hand, the difficulty in meaning that the second occurrence of νῦν [in, e.g., ℵ and B] seems to introduce may have prompted … its deletion.[25]

---

[17] Dunn, *Romans*, 687.

[18] Wallace, *Greek Grammar*, 167.

[19] Cranfield, *Romans*, 583; see 583–85; see also Murray, *Romans*, 2:102, n. 59.

[20] Dunn, *Romans*, 688; Moo, *Romans*, 734–35; Schreiner, *Romans*, 627–28.

[21] Moo, *Romans*, 735.

[22] Wallace, *Greek Grammar*, 142.

[23] See Wallace, *Greek Grammar*, 472.

[24] Wallace, *Greek Grammar*, 472.

[25] Metzger, *A Textual Commentary on the Greek New Testament*, 527.

His last sentence seems slightly more persuasive. In other words, the (second) νῦν here was more likely in the autograph, but was later omitted in some copies by scribes; see the commentary. Even if not original, the two other uses of νῦν in 11:30–31 make much the same point.

Kaden conducts a thorough study of this variant and concludes that the νῦν was more likely deliberately added by a later scribe.[26] His methodology, however, relies on the influence of "increasing social tension between Jews and Christians in the first and second centuries CE."[27] By using that methodology, he follows a troubling "general trend in early Christian textual criticism toward examining the social context of variants in the first and second century CE *prior* to the time when our first manuscripts appear, and away from any notion of an 'original' text.' "[28]

11:32 συνέκλεισεν γὰρ ὁ θεὸς τοὺς πάντας εἰς ἀπείθειαν—The verb συνέκλεισεν is the aorist indicative of συγκλείω, "to confine to specific limits, *confine, imprison*" (BDAG, 2). BDAG translates and explains the clause as follows: "*He has imprisoned them all in disobedience*, i.e. put them under compulsion to be disobedient or given them over to disobedience." However, to suggest that God compelled people to disobey him is problematic. See also συγκλείω in Gal 3:22–23, where the Law "imprisoned" humanity "under sin"; God did not give his Law to cause sin, but rather, sinful humanity's imprisonment was the consequence of its inability to obey the Law (cf. the responsive actions of God depicted by παρέδωκεν in 1:24, 26, 28). See further the commentary below.

ἀπείθειαν—For this noun, rendered as "unpersuadedness," see the third textual note on 11:30; cf. also the cognate verb in the first textual note on 11:30.

ἵνα τοὺς πάντας ἐλεήσῃ—Again, ἵνα plus the subjunctive forms a purpose clause; see the third textual note on 11:31, where the subjunctive verb was passive voice, ἐλεηθῶσιν, "they might be shown mercy." Here the subjunctive ἐλεήσῃ is active voice, "he might show mercy."

11:33 ὦ βάθος—This is the only NT exclamation introduced by ὦ, "O," although examples are found in Hellenistic Greek.[29] Here ὦ functions as "an exclamatory utterance" (BDAG, 2); cf. 2:1, 3; 9:20, where it introduces a vocative address (ὦ ἄνθρωπε, "O you human being"). For the noun βάθος, "depth," in a spatial sense, see 8:39 (the only other occurrence in the letter) and, e.g., Mt 13:5; Lk 5:4. For the spiritual sense of βάθος, see "the depths of God" in 1 Cor 2:10 and, similarly, "depth" in Eph 3:18.[30]

πλούτου—For this noun, see the second textual note on 2:4 ("abundance"); see it also in 9:23 ("abundance") and 11:12 ("richness").

---

[26] Kaden, "The Methodological Dilemma of Evaluating the Variation Unit in Romans 11:31," 179.

[27] Kaden, "The Methodological Dilemma of Evaluating the Variation Unit in Romans 11:31," 167.

[28] Kaden, "The Methodological Dilemma of Evaluating the Variation Unit in Romans 11:31," 167.

[29] Cranfield, *Romans*, 589.

[30] Contrast the adjectival synonym in τὰ βαθέα τοῦ σατανᾶ, "the deep things of Satan" (Rev 2:24).

ὡς—For ὡς as "how," see the second textual note on 10:15 (an OT quotation). For ὡς "as a feature of hymnic style," see LXX Pss 8:2, 10 (MT 8:2, 10; ET 8:1, 9); 65:3 (MT/ET 66:3); 83:2 (MT 84:2; ET 84:1); 103:24 (MT/ET 104:24); Sirach 17:29.[31]

ἀνεξεραύνητα—The doubly compound adjective ἀνεξεραύνητος means "*unfath-omable*, lit[erally] 'unsearchable'" (BDAG). It occurs only here in Biblical Greek. Its root (-εραύνητος) is derived from the verb ἐραυνάω, "to search," with the prefixed preposition ἐκ (-εξ-, "search *out*") and an *alpha* privative (ἀν-), which negates its meaning, hence, "not able to be searched out" by people. But in 1 Cor 2:10 Paul employs the verb ἐραυνάω to declare that the Holy Spirit has this ability: he "searches out all things, even the depths of God" (πάντα ἐραυνᾷ, καὶ τὰ βάθη τοῦ θεοῦ); see Paul's similar use of ἐραυνάω in Rom 8:27. The form of the adjective here is analogous to the adjective in the next textual note; see also the first textual note on 11:29.

ἀνεξιχνίαστοι—The doubly compound adjective ἀνεξιχνίαστος, "lit[erally] 'not to be tracked out,'" means "*inscrutable, incomprehensible*" (BDAG). Here the reference is to God's ways; it is used of Christ in Eph 3:8. ἀνεξιχνίαστος also appears in Job 5:9; 9:10; 34:24. Like the adjective in the preceding textual note, its root is derived from a verb, ἰχνεύω, "track out, hunt after, seek out," with the prefixed preposition ἐκ and an *alpha* privative.

11:34 τίς γὰρ ἔγνω—Twice in this verse and once in 11:35 the interrogative pronoun τίς is used as a substantive ("who?") "in questions to which the answer 'nobody' is expected" (BDAG, 1 a α ℵ, citing also, e.g., Rom 8:24, 33–35; 1 Cor 9:7; 2 Cor 11:29).[32]

νοῦν κυρίου—The noun νοῦς refers to the "result of thinking, *mind, thought, opinion, decree*" (BDAG, 3). It is used of divine thought in 1 Cor 2:16, as here with the genitive of possession, κυρίου, "of the Lord," but of human thought in Rom 1:28; 7:23, 25.

ἤ—This is *not* the feminine definite article, ἡ. The particle ἤ, with the accent and smooth breathing, serves as a "marker of an alternative, *or*" (BDAG, 1; see 2:4). It recurs at the beginning of 11:35.

τίς σύμβουλος αὐτοῦ—The noun σύμβουλος means "*adviser, counsellor*" (BDAG). It appears in the NT only here, but is common in the LXX (usually translating יוֹעֵץ), and Paul draws it from LXX Is 40:13 (MT: אִישׁ עֲצָתוֹ, "a man of his counsel").

11:35 ἢ τίς προέδωκεν αὐτῷ—This verse appears to be Paul's adaptation of the Hebrew of Job 41:3 (ET 41:11), where God asks: מִי הִקְדִּימַנִי וַאֲשַׁלֵּם, "who came before me [with a gift] so that I should have to repay [him for his gift]?"

The Hiphil of קָדַם probably has the same nuance as the Piel can have, "to come before someone (bearing a gift for him)," as in Deut 23:5 (ET 23:4); Neh 13:2; Is 21:14; Ps 21:4 (ET 21:3). Micah 6:6 speaks of coming before Yahweh with sacrifices; cf. also Ps 95:2. Paul conveys "before" in a temporal sense, rather than the spatial sense of the

---

[31] Dunn, *Romans*, 699.

[32] Although BDAG also cites Rom 7:24 under this heading, it is clearly not applicable in light of 7:25; see the commentary on those verses.

Hebrew, by rendering it with the compound verb προδίδωμι, "to be beforehand in giving, *give in advance*" (BDAG, 1) or "give previously."

καὶ ἀνταποδοθήσεται αὐτῷ—The conjunction καί probably translates the Hebrew *waw* on וֵאֲשַׁלֵּם (Job 41:3 (ET 41:11; see the previous textual note), which can introduce a circumstantial clause (BDB, s.v. וְ, 1 k). *If* someone had previously presented a gift to God, *then*, under those circumstances, God would owe him, and "so that it should be repaid to him." The doubly compound verb ἀνταποδίδωμι (ἀντί + ἀπό + δίδωμι) expresses "to practice reciprocity with respect to an obligation, *repay, pay back*" (BDAG, 1). It can have a positive sense, as here, or a negative nuance when used of God's judgment in 12:19 (also 2 Thess 1:6).

11:36 αὐτῷ ἡ δόξα—The verb normally assumed when none is present is supplied here, ἐστίν, "is," the third person indicative form of εἰμί. Many translations utilize the imperative "be." However, the indicative captures the theological truth. All glory *is* his, whether we give him that acclaim or not. "To him [is] the glory" (see also 16:27; cf. "the Lord *is* with you" in accord with his Word of promise in Lk 1:28; similarly, in Mt 1:23; 28:20).

ἀμήν—For "amen," see the third textual note on 9:5.

Commentary

Introduction to Romans 11:25–36

Addressees and Romans 11:25a

As has been the case throughout Romans, Paul skillfully weaves together the flow of his thought. Paul begins by replicating a clause he used in 1:13, "I do not want you to be without knowledge, brothers" (11:25a).[33] The conjunction "indeed" (γάρ) "ultimately connects vv. 25–32 with the whole preceding argument."[34] It indicates that Paul now draws together the argument of Romans 9–11 and drives toward the conclusion he wants all the Christians in Rome to hear.[35] Thus "brothers" (ἀδελφοί) matches its nearly universal use in the NT to encompass all believers (see the second textual note on 1:13). Paul's use of the term in 9:3, however, referred exclusively to his fellow Jews, where he spoke of them in the third person (see the fourth textual note on 9:3). Jewish believers are surely part of the audience and thus represented among the "brothers" referenced here.[36]

A much more remarkable aspect is that "brothers" (ἀδελφοί) now also includes Gentiles who have been grafted into the olive tree of Israel (11:17, 19–20, 24), that is, incorporated into God's one family of faith. As stated repeatedly in this commentary, the letter seems directed toward a group of house

---

[33] The only difference is that Paul swaps the postpositive δέ in 1:13 for γάρ, "indeed," in 11:25.

[34] Moo, *Romans*, 714.

[35] Schreiner, *Romans*, 611–12, is a rare commentator who does not begin a section at 11:25. He divides midway through the olive-tree analogy and treats 11:23–27 as a unit.

[36] See Middendorf, *Romans 1–8*, 12–14, 17–18; see also "Who Are the 'Weak' and the 'Strong'? Addressees Again!" in the introduction to 14:1–15:13.

churches with a majority of Gentiles.[37] Paul speaks directly to "you Gentiles" for the first time in 11:13 and then uses second person forms ("you") to admonish any haughty attitude from any Gentile over and against the Jewish people in 11:17–24.[38] These Gentile believers are *primarily* the "you" plural warned here in 11:25, though Dunn suggests "a reference to Jewish confidence attacked in 2:17–24 is likely too."[39]

After a brief respite in 11:26–27, second plural forms return in 11:28, 30 (three of them in the Greek), 31. These "you(r)" forms again direct Paul's address toward *all of his believing brothers and sisters, both Gentiles as well as Jews.* This is so because the "they/these" in those verses are *not* Jews as a whole, but the unbelieving (10:16; 11:7a, 20) and, consequently, hardened portion of Israel (11:7c, 25). Only "they" are currently enemies according to the Good News (11:28) because they have not listened responsively to the Gospel message, namely, the Word of Christ (10:16–17). They actively refuse to be persuaded and remain unbelieving (10:21; 11:23, 31).

As a fitting conclusion to Romans 9–11, then, 11:32–36 exhibits the all-encompassing and universal scope of the argument characteristic of so much of the letter.[40] More importantly, Paul once again concludes a section with a resounding declaration that turns the spotlight away from all of humanity and places it squarely where it belongs, upon God himself.[41] Rom 11:32 summarizes "with breathtaking brevity"[42] how there is no difference among people, including particularly Jew and Gentile. God deals with all people in the same ways, both by locking them all up under his Law's judgment due to their sin and also in his desire to show mercy to all, mercy received by all who call on the name of the Lord Jesus (10:13; cf. 2:11; 3:22–23; 9:22–24; 10:11–12). What then is left other than to marvel at the unfathomable graciousness of such a God and to revel in attributing all glory to him (11:33–36; see also 16:25–27; cf. the framing doxology of 9:5)?

The Structure of Romans 11:25–26a

As noted above, the opening line of 11:25 replicates words from the opening chapter: "indeed, I do not want you to be without knowledge, brothers" (1:13;

---

[37] See Middendorf, *Romans 1–8*, 12–14, 17–18; "God's People" in the introduction to chapters 9–11; "Who Are the 'Weak' and the 'Strong'? Addressees Again!" in the introduction to 14:1–15:13; and the concluding section of the commentary on 16:1–16.

[38] See "Introduction: Addressing 'You Gentiles' (11:13a)" in the commentary on 11:13–24.

[39] Dunn, *Romans*, 679.

[40] See "Conclusion: A Contextual Letter with Universal Application" in Middendorf, *Romans 1–8*, 49–51.

[41] Romans is theocentric. See Middendorf, *Romans 1–8*, 21–22, 27, 49–51; in this volume, see "Romans 1–4: The Righteousness of God" in the introduction to Romans 9–16, as well as "God" in "The Three Foci of Romans 9–11" in the introduction to Romans 9–11. See also the commentary on 1:17, 32; 2:11, 16, 29; 3:1–8, 19–20, 26, 29–30; 4:21; 9:5, 11b–12a, 16, 22–24, 29; 10:21; 11:1–2, 33–36; 12:19; 13:1–2; 14:10–12; 15:5, 8, 13; 16:25, 27.

[42] Dunn, *Romans*, 677.

11:25). After both verses Paul then proceeds to fill in what is missing and/or to reinforce what is already known, but not properly recognized, by his fellow believers (as with the same verb, ἀγνοέω, "be without knowledge," in 6:3; 7:1). In 11:25 the knowledge concerns "this mystery" (τὸ μυστήριον τοῦτο); see "The 'Mystery' (μυστήριον) Made Known in Christ (11:25a)" below. Structurally, the opening line points forward as indicated by the explanatory ὅτι, "*that* a hardening … ," later in 11:25. Thereafter, Paul defines the mystery in three clauses, two in the rest of 11:25 and the third, climactically, in the beginning of 11:26 (unfortunately, the verse division between 11:25 and 11:26 is particularly disruptive). Paul reveals it as follows: "that a hardening in part has come to be and still exists for Israel until which [time] the fullness of the Gentiles comes in, [26]and thus all Israel will be saved" (11:25b–26a).

The intervening ἵνα purpose clause, "so that you might not be wise within yourselves" (11:25), is parenthetical. It explains why Paul does not want his "brothers" to be without cognizance of the mystery. The grammar of the phrase seems awkward in Greek ([παρ'] ἑαυτοῖς φρόνιμοι), with or without the variant παρά (see the fourth textual note on 11:25). But it repeats the sentiment of 11:20 and likely echoes the Hebrew expression in Prov 3:7: "do not be wise in your own eyes [בְּעֵינֶיךָ], but reverently fear Yahweh." Although Paul renders with a Greek plural "you" rather than the singular of the MT and LXX, his expression is comparable to the LXX: "do not be wise within yourself, but fear God" (μὴ ἴσθι φρόνιμος παρὰ σεαυτῷ φοβοῦ δὲ τὸν θεόν, Prov 3:7). The full meaning then warns against being "*wise in your own estimation = relying on your own wisdom*" (BDAG, s.v. φρόνιμος); cf. Prov 1:7; 2:5–10; 3:5.

The "Mystery" (μυστήριον) Made Known in Christ (11:25a)

Background

The term "mystery" has a significant background in both Jewish and Gentile contexts:

> The most common meaning for μυστήριον in the Greco-Roman world would be in reference to the mystery cults ("the mysteries"—usually in the plural), their secret teachings and rituals, known only to initiates, and kept secret so effectively that we today know little about them. … But, unlike Alexandrian Judaism, Paul's usage shows no knowledge whatsoever of or interest in the vocabulary of the mysteries. The background which informs his language is exclusively Jewish, and specifically Jewish apocalyptic. For in Jewish apocalyptic language, "mystery" has the sense not of undisclosed secrets, but rather of divine secrets now revealed by divine agency.[43]

---

[43] Dunn, *Romans*, 677–78; he suggests that this meaning occurs "typically … in the classic apocalyptic writings," citing, for example, *1 Enoch* 41:1; 46:2; 103:2; 104:10, 12; 106:19; *2 Enoch* 24:3; *4 Ezra* 10:38; 12:36–38; 14:5.

Dunn's "Jewish apocalyptic" needs qualification because in addition to intertestamental Jewish texts, he refers to the OT book of Daniel.[44] The Aramaic passages Dan 2:18–19, 27–30, 47; 4:6 (ET 4:9) use the noun רָז, "mystery," and speak of "revealing" it (the verb גְּלָא); the prophet Daniel interprets enigmatic dreams as revelations of God's plan of salvation. While this "mystery" terminology first appears in Daniel, the idea of divine revelation—revealing what previously was known only by God—is, of course, apparent throughout the OT and commonly expressed with other terminology (e.g., God "speaks" his "word," inspires "prophecy," shows a "vision"). Moreover, the ingathering of Gentiles into the kingdom of God—what Paul deems the "mystery" (Rom 11:25)—was spoken of by the prophets in various ways.[45] As for the technical terminology of the "mystery," Moo summarizes its use in apocalyptic literature as follows:

> In these writings "mystery" usually refers to an event of the end times that has already been determined by God—and so, in that sense, exists already in heaven—but which is first revealed to the apocalyptic seer for the comfort and encouragement of the people of Israel.[46]

These observations are helpful for understanding the general milieu in which Paul writes. Schreiner agrees that the term "'mystery' hails from an apocalyptic background," but then adds:

> Μυστήριον in Paul does not signify a riddle or a puzzle that surpasses human comprehension. In the OT and second temple literature it refers to a secret element of God's plan that has been hidden from human beings but has now been revealed. According to Paul the mystery of God has been disclosed particularly in the gospel of Jesus Christ (Rom. 16:25; 1 Cor. 2:1, 7; 15:51; Eph. 1:9; 3:3, 4, 9; 5:32; 6:19; Col. 1:26–27; 2:2; 4:3; 1 Tim. 3:9, 16).[47]

Therefore apocalyptic influence should be acknowledged, but not overstated.[48] For example, Paul does not engage in visions and dreams that require special interpretation. Instead, the mystery, "though once hidden, is now revealed in Christ and is to be proclaimed so that all who have ears to hear may hear it."[49]

Other Pauline Uses

Moo agrees that in Pauline usage "usually the mystery involves an event or insight associated with Christ's coming and the preaching of the gospel."[50] But

---

[44] Historical-critical scholars commonly date the book of Daniel very late (even into the intertestamental period) to fit their theories about the development of apocalyptic, rather than acknowledge the book's historical setting and authorship in the sixth century BC. See Steinmann, *Daniel*, 1–19.

[45] See the OT verses cited below in "Paul's Source(s)."

[46] Moo, *Romans*, 714.

[47] Schreiner, *Romans*, 613.

[48] See Middendorf, *Romans 1–8*, 653–55.

[49] Cranfield, *Romans*, 573.

[50] Moo, *Romans*, 714, including n. 13, citing for Paul's usual use of "mystery" (μυστήριον) Rom 16:25; 1 Cor 2:1, 7; 4:1; 15:51; Eph 1:9; 3:3, 4, 9; 6:19; Col 1:26, 27; 2:2; 4:3; 1 Tim 3:9, 16.

he then advocates for two exceptions: "Here and in 1 Cor. 15:51 it refers to an event at the end of history."[51] However, Moo makes an unwarranted distinction. Before dealing with Rom 11:25 in detail, a couple points should be stated:

The only other use of "mystery" (μυστήριον) in Romans must be taken into consideration. In the culminating verses of the letter, it carries its typical meaning for Paul. There he asserts that "my Gospel, namely, the proclamation of Jesus Christ" (τὸ εὐαγγέλιόν μου καὶ τὸ κήρυγμα Ἰησοῦ Χριστοῦ, 16:25) is "in accord with the revelation of the mystery … now revealed" (κατὰ ἀποκάλυψιν μυστηρίου … φανερωθέντος … νῦν, 16:25–26; cf. "is being revealed," ἀποκαλύπτεται, 1:17; "but now … has been revealed," νυνὶ δὲ … πεφανέρωται, 3:21). The combination of these phrases together in 16:25 suggests that the mystery revealed in Romans consists of (1) a *present knowledge* and, more importantly, (2) a *Christocentric focus* (as also in 1 Cor 2:1, 7; 4:1; 15:51; Eph 1:9; 3:3, 4, 9; 5:32; 6:19; Col 1:26–27; 2:2; 4:3; 1 Tim 3:9, 16). Schreiner recognizes a third key component of the mystery for Paul: "Many scholars have failed to see that the mystery also relates to the Gentiles."[52] Not only has this mystery been made known "into all the nations/Gentiles" (εἰς πάντα τὰ ἔθνη, Rom 16:26), but Paul also explicitly connects the mystery with (3) *the inclusion of Gentiles* (e.g., Eph 3:6; Col 1:27; 1 Tim 3:16).

All three components are evident in Eph 3:1–13, where Paul explains his understanding of the "mystery" in detail. He uses the noun three times (μυστήριον, Eph 3:3, 4, 9) and defines the now-revealed (Eph 3:3, 5) mystery as follows: "the Gentiles [are] fellow heirs and of the same body and fellow sharers of the promise in Christ Jesus through the Good News" (τὰ ἔθνη συγκληρονόμα καὶ σύσσωμα καὶ συμμέτοχα τῆς ἐπαγγελίας ἐν Χριστῷ Ἰησοῦ διὰ τοῦ εὐαγγελίου, Eph 3:6; cf. Eph 3:8). As clearly inferred in Ephesians 2, the Gentiles in Christ now share in "the citizenship of Israel" (τῆς πολιτείας τοῦ Ἰσραήλ, Eph 2:12). They do not take over or replace Israel but, as in the olive-tree analogy, are incorporated into the one people of God (see "Conclusions: God's One Tree—God's One People" in the commentary on 11:13–24).

Although Moo's other exception, 1 Cor 15:51, does not speak specifically of Gentiles, it fits more generally within the category of the "mystery" (μυστήριον) as Paul speaks of it elsewhere. While the mystery in that passage is "something that can only be known by divine revelation," Paul proceeds to "tell them" precisely what it is:[53] "See, I am telling you a mystery: we will not all sleep, but we will all be changed" (1 Cor 15:51).[54] On the Last Day, when Christ returns, those who have died in Christ will be raised bodily in glory, and those still physically alive in Christ will be glorified; thus all in Christ will be "changed" by entering the fullness of eternal life in their incorruptible bodies (1 Cor 15:41–53).

---

[51] Moo, *Romans*, 714.

[52] Schreiner, *Romans*, 614.

[53] Lockwood, *1 Corinthians*, 600.

[54] This is the translation of Lockwood, *1 Corinthians*, 596.

Therefore, even if "mystery" refers to an event that has not yet happened, the mystery itself stands revealed *already now by virtue of Christ's resurrection* (see 1 Cor 15:20–24, 45–49). 1 Cor 15:51, then, stands squarely within Paul's "now/not yet" understanding of the Gospel.[55] What will happen is already "now" known and certain to take place; humanity has just "not yet" experienced it.

Paul's Source(s)

How did Paul come to know the mystery of which he speaks in Rom 11:25? Cranfield suggests that it was "discerned in the OT seen in light of the gospel events" and cites Luther,[56] who finds its roots in the OT and its development in words from Jesus himself.[57] Paul's understanding could have begun as early as on the Damascus road, when the revelation of Christ required him to reevaluate the message of the OT which he knew so well,[58] and he unveils the revelation repeatedly in his letters (see above). While what follows may serve as something of "an answer to the anguish he expressed in 9:1–3 and 10:1,"[59] the "mystery" surely is not a fresh insight that came to Paul only midway through his writing of the letter or in a manner that contradicted what he had written up to this point. As Wright contends: "The 'mystery' is not a new revelation, standing over against the previous argument. It is the unveiled righteousness of God."[60] (Note the present tense of ἀποκαλύπτεται in 1:17: in the Gospel "[the] righteousness of God *is being revealed*.")

The Mystery Solved (11:25b–26a)

Exhibit 1: "Hardening in Part" (11:25b)

As Paul begins to explain the mystery at hand, he returns to the thought at the end of 11:7: "the rest were hardened" (ἐπωρώθησαν). The noun here in 11:25, "hardening" (πώρωσις), replicates the content of that cognate verb in 11:7. Now Paul reaffirms that "a hardening in part has come to be and still exists for Israel" (11:25). In regard to the much-contested sense of "in part" (ἀπὸ μέρους) Moo summarizes:

> There has been considerable debate over whether this phrase is adjectival, modifying Ἰσραήλ—"hardening has come on part of Israel" (Barrett; Käsemann), or adverbial, modifying either the verbal concept present in πώρωσις—"a partial hardening has come on Israel" (Dunn)—or γέγονεν—"a

---

[55] See Middendorf, *Romans 1–8*, 441–42.

[56] Cranfield, *Romans*, 574, including n. 1.

[57] Luther, *Lectures on Romans*, AE 25:429–30, citing, in this order, Lk 21:23–24; Deut 4:30–31; Hos 3:4–5; 5:12, 15; Mt 23:38–39; Gen 37:28.

[58] See OT promises for the inclusion of Gentiles in, e.g., Is 2:1–4; 11:1–16; 19:18–25; 56:6–8; 60:1–11; 66:18–23; Ezek 16:53–63; Amos 9:11–12; Micah 4:1–3; Zeph 3:9–10; Zech 2:11 (MT 2:15); 14:16; Ps 22:27 (MT 22:28).

[59] Dunn, *Romans*, 679.

[60] Wright, "Romans," 690; for those who advocate for a new revelation coming midway through the letter, see Moo, *Romans*, 715, n. 14.

hardening has come partially on Israel" (Godet; Michel; Schlier). The last of the alternatives is most likely syntactically (ἀπὸ μέρους is adverbial in its four other Pauline occurrences [Rom. 15:15, 24; 2 Cor. 1:14; 2:5]), but the difference in meaning is not great.[61]

Paul's repeated references to "some" (plural forms of τίς in 3:3; 11:14, 17) and "not all" (οὐ πάντες, 9:6; 10:16) in ethnic Israel points toward adopting an *adjectival sense*: "on a part of Israel."[62] This is how the phrase ἀπὸ μέρους also functions in 15:15. The segment of Israel under consideration is comprised of those who do not believe God's Good News proclaimed in the Word of Christ (10:16–17).

Moo again misreads the flow of Paul's rehearsal of events by suggesting that "Israel's present hostility toward God, manifested in her general refusal of the gospel (cf. 9:30–10:21), is itself part of God's plan, for it is the result of God's act of hardening."[63] Paul clearly maintains that the Gospel is for *all* who hear (10:4, 8, 11–13). It is only *after* a human refusal to respond properly to God's Word (10:16–21; 11:7a) that he reacts with hardening (10:7c).[64]

The perfect tense of the verb γίνομαι asserts that this hardening "has come" upon part of Israel *and* that it "exists" up to the present.[65] But, again, as Paul has repeatedly stated, the hardening is not final or unalterable for those who still remain alive (11:11, 12, 14, 15, 23, 24). By no means does the verb[66] mean that the hardening of Israel *must* "continue to the end."[67] On the contrary, Paul's apostolic ministry endeavors to "save some from them" (11:14); he has also just asserted that the currently unbelieving branches which are now cut off "will be grafted in" again "if they do not remain in unbelief" (11:23). Indeed, *Paul here gives it an explicit terminus*: "until which [time] the fullness of the Gentiles comes in" (11:25). The "until" phrase (ἄχρι οὗ) should be understood in a temporal sense, as is most often the case (see the eighth textual note on 11:25). However, to add "and then it will be removed"[68] inserts an element into the text which the grammar does not convey and Paul does not imply.

---

[61] Moo, *Romans*, 717, n. 28.

[62] Jewett, *Romans*, 699, adding that this is "consistent with" 9:27; 11:7, 14, 17 (699–700).

[63] Moo, *Romans*, 713.

[64] See "Hardening" in "Is This Fair to the Pharaoh? (9:17–18)" in the commentary on 9:14–24 and also "The Three Parts of Romans 11:7" in the commentary on 11:1–12.

[65] Morris, *Romans*, 420, n. 111: "The perfect tense denotes a continuing state." Cf. the dual impact of the same form in 11:5; see "The Remnant: An Enduring Reality (11:5–6)" in the commentary on 11:1–12.

[66] See the seventh textual note on 11:25.

[67] Lenski, *Romans*, 722, rightly condemns the millennial view that Scripture promises an end-time mass conversion of all Jews (he includes the extreme view that "all the petrified Jews who have died will be raised up and also be converted"). However, Lenski overreacts by saying Paul teaches that the petrifaction of a portion of Jews "will continue to the end." Paul's earnest prayer is that all would believe (9:2–3), and he does not give up on any.

[68] Moo, *Romans*, 717.

Exhibit 2: "The Fullness of the Gentiles" Enter (11:25c)

Paul speaks of the hardening continuing "until which [time] *the fullness of the Gentiles*" enters (τὸ πλήρωμα τῶν ἐθνῶν). The use of the same noun, "fullness" (πλήρωμα), in regard to Israel was discussed extensively in 11:12 ("the fullness of them," τὸ πλήρωμα αὐτῶν; see the commentary there). Here "fullness" certainly does *not* refer to *all* Gentiles. The genitive "of the Gentiles" is partitive,[69] and the phrase denotes the full number of non-Jews who believe.[70] This strongly suggests the same is true regarding the genitive referring to Israel, "the fullness of them" (τὸ πλήρωμα αὐτῶν), in 11:12.

The Gentiles coming in has been interpreted as representing the "Jewish expectation of an eschatological conversion and pilgrimage of the nations to Zion."[71] Passages that express this expectation include, for example, Is 2:1–4; 11:1–16; 19:18–25; 56:6–8; 60:1–11; 66:18–23; Ezek 16:53–63; Amos 9:11–12; Micah 4:1–3; Zeph 3:9–10; Zech 2:11 (MT 2:15); 14:16; Ps 22:27 (MT 22:28); Tobit 13:11 (LXX 13:13); 14:6–7; Ps Sol 17:26–46. See, for example, the description of the Messiah's work from Ps Sol 17:26–46:

> He will gather a holy people whom he will lead in righteousness. … He will have Gentile nations serving him under his yoke, and he will glorify the Lord in (a place) prominent (above) the whole earth. And he will purge Jerusalem (and make it) holy as it was even from the beginning, (for) nations to come from the ends of the earth to see his glory, to bring as gifts her children who had been driven out, and to see the glory of the Lord with which God has glorified her. (Ps Sol 17:26, 30–31)[72]

Moo then notes how "Paul … reverses the order of events and 'spiritualizes' the process: instead of Gentiles coming to worship Yahweh in Jerusalem as a result of Israel's restoration, Israel is saved in response to the extension of salvation to the Gentiles."[73]

---

[69] See Wallace, *Greek Grammar*, 84–86.

[70] Staples, "What Do the Gentiles Have to Do with 'All Israel'?" 385, posits this theory regarding " 'the fullness of the Gentiles.' Despite the terseness of Paul's language, the passage becomes quite clear once the phrase … is recognized as an allusion to Gen 48:19, where Jacob blesses Joseph's sons" and explains that Ephraim will be greater than his brother because Ephraim's " '*seed will become the fullness of the nations*' [מְלֹא־הַגּוֹיִם, Gen 48:19]." However, Ephraim's offspring are, in fact, ethnic Israelites, rather than Gentiles. It is also difficult to perceive how Paul intends for his hearers to grasp this connection to Gen 48:19 without some signal in the text. Finally, as Staples acknowledges (386, including nn. 72–73), while "Paul's use of πλήρωμα ["fullness" in Rom 11:25] accords with the usual LXX translation for מלא elsewhere" (citing LXX 1 Chr 16:32; Pss 23:1 [MT/ET 24:1]; 49:12 [MT/ET 50:12]; 88:12 [MT 89:12; ET 89:11]; 95:11 [MT/ET 96:11]; 97:7 [MT/ET 98:7]; Eccl 4:6; Jer 8:16; 29:2 [MT/ET 47:2]; Ezek 12:19; 19:7; 30:12), the LXX uniquely renders it with πλῆθος, "multitude," in Gen 48:19.

[71] Dunn, *Romans*, 680; Käsemann, *Romans*, 312, speaks similarly of "the apocalyptic expectation of the restitution of Israel and the associated pilgrimage of the nations to Zion."

[72] R. B. Wright, "Psalms of Solomon," *OTP* 2:667; cf. Moo, *Romans*, 684, n. 2.

[73] Moo, *Romans*, 684, n. 2.

These changes indicate why one should not read into Paul's theological statement ("comes in," Rom 11:25) a literal pilgrimage of Gentiles walking into present-day Jerusalem. It is also difficult to argue that Paul views his impending trip to Jerusalem with the offering from the Gentiles (Acts 20:2–5) as a (or *the*) fulfillment of it (see also Rom 15:27).[74] Paul does not cite any of the OT texts referenced above as predicting such geographical travel.[75] Furthermore, Paul alters the reference of Is 59:20. The MT has the Redeemer coming "*to* Zion," but Paul says he "will come *from* Zion" (Rom 11:26b; see below). Finally, while Paul is aware of the severity of threats against him in Judea (15:31), he also clearly envisions his missionary work extending beyond his trip to Jerusalem (1:1–12; 15:23–26).[76]

It seems more plausible to see the language and ministry of Jesus, as well as the mission activity of Paul, as depicting the manner in which Gentiles come in (εἰσέλθῃ, 11:25). First, Dunn observes "the frequency of the verb εἰσέρχομαι ['come in'] in the Jesus tradition in talk of entering into the 'kingdom' or into 'life.'"[77] Dunn believes that these references coupled with the verb's "infrequency in Paul (only three times elsewhere) make it likely that Paul is drawing here on pre-Pauline tradition which stems from Jesus."[78] The image of Gentile branches being grafted into an olive tree in Rom 11:17 and 11:19 also provides a link with the previous section (11:13–24). Note that the image there does not imply Gentiles entering Israel geographically or ethnically, but in terms of becoming part of the community of God's people by faith (11:20). Therefore the final clause of 11:25, "until which [time] the fullness of the Gentiles comes in," refers to their entrance into the kingdom of God during the present era of salvation.[79] Second, Jesus' expectation of Gentiles entering into the kingdom is often coupled with a comment that others, namely, Jews who reject his invitation, will be cast out from it (e.g., Lk 13:23–29; 14:15–24).

---

[74] As argued by Jervell, "The Letter to Jerusalem"; see Middendorf, *Romans 1–8*, 5–6, 16–17.

[75] The list above, compiled by this commentary, is of course simply representative, and not exhaustive. Donaldson, "'Riches for the Gentiles' (Rom 11:12)," 92, claims that Paul does not quote any of the standard OT texts that promise the salvation of the Gentiles, but his point is rejected as unwarranted skepticism by Moo, *Romans*, 684, n. 2, who notes that "Paul's quotation of Isa. 59:20–21 comes from the immediate context of one of the most important of the texts (Isa. 60:1–7)." Dunn, *Romans*, 680, states that in his own shorter list of OT passages, the LXX version never uses the verb Paul uses in Rom 11:25, εἰσέρχομαι, "come in." However, in the fuller list of OT passages given above, that verb is used in LXX Is 19:23. Moreover, since the OT promise is expressed with a wide variety of vocabulary, it is unreasonable to require the presence of that particular verb.

[76] Against Bornkamm, "The Letter to the Romans as Paul's Last Will and Testament," who, as the title of his article indicates, views Romans as Paul's last will and testament; this is based upon passages such as Acts 20:38; 21:10–13, 30–31; 23:12.

[77] Dunn, *Romans*, 680. See, e.g., Mt 5:20; 7:13–14, 21; 18:3; 19:17; Mk 9:43, 45, 47; 10:15, 23, 24, 25; Jn 3:5; see also Lk 13:24; 14:23.

[78] Dunn, *Romans*, 680.

[79] Moo, *Romans*, 718, says it "probably" does so.

Paul's Summation, Part 1: "And Thus …" (11:26a)

Meaning

The first half of 11:26 stands as "the storm center" in the interpretation of Romans 9–11.[80] The opening "and thus" (καὶ οὕτως) is critical for understanding the connection between 11:25 and 11:26. What does it mean? Several options have been proposed:

First, Barrett, Käsemann, and Witherington opt for a temporal sense, translating καὶ οὕτως as "when this is done," "so, then," and "then," respectively.[81] But Fitzmyer counters that "a temporal meaning of *houtōs* is not otherwise found in Greek,"[82] though that does not make it impossible here. More decisive is the contextual observation that "in every other occurrence in Romans *houtōs* obviously means 'in this way,' and never comes close to meaning 'then' or 'after that' (1:15; 4:18; 5:12, 15, 18–19, 21; 6:4, 11, 19; 9:20; 10:6; 11:5, 31; 12:5; 15:20)."[83] Thus there seems to be no solid evidence to support the temporal reading adopted by many, whether literally by those cited above or *de facto* by those who argue that "and thus" points toward a future mass conversion of Jews or salvation for "all" Jews at the end.[84] The adverb οὕτως simply does not mean or imply "then" or "in/at the end" or "at last."

Second, Dodd and Morris translate καὶ οὕτως as "this done" and "and so," respectively, giving οὕτως a logical sense which indicates a consequence or conclusion regarding what precedes.[85] Similarly, Moo suggests the translation "and in consequence of this process," but then dismisses it since only four of seventy-four uses of οὕτως by Paul are said to fit this category.[86] However, the fact that these instances include 1:15 and 6:11 means that it should not be summarily dismissed here. BDAG defines οὕτως in 1:15 and 6:11 as "drawing an inference fr[om] what precedes *so, hence*" (s.v. οὕτω/οὕτως, 1 b). In fact, the opening phrase of 11:25 points in this direction. Aside from γάρ in place of δέ,

---

[80] Moo, *Romans*, 719.

[81] Barrett, *Romans*, 223; Käsemann, *Romans*, 311; Witherington, *Romans*, 275 ("then" is his translation of οὕτως).

[82] Fitzmyer, *Romans*, 622; see 622–23.

[83] Wright, "Romans," 691.

[84] Commentators who fall in that *de facto* category (who rightly reject a temporal meaning for οὕτως but who then, in effect, interpret the passage as a temporal sequence) include Moo, *Romans*, 719–20, including n. 39: "Neither LSJ nor BAGD indicate a temporal meaning for the word [οὕτως]; and the two NT examples of a temporal meaning often cited (Acts 17:33; 20:11) are better explained in other ways." Cranfield, *Romans*, 576, rejects the temporal view, advocating the logical sense, as in 5:12. Dunn, *Romans*, 681, supports the nuance of manner, but hedges, saying that "some temporal weight cannot be excluded." Yet all of these then interpret 11:25–26 as a temporal sequence (see the discussion of their positions in "Most All of Ethnic Israel Alive at the Parousia" in "Alternative Interpretations of 'All Israel Will Be Saved' (11:26a)" below). Wright, "Romans," 691, n. 459, offers a proper critique of such commentators on this point, asserting that a temporal sense is smuggled back into the meaning.

[85] Dodd, *Romans*, 173, 182; Morris, *Romans*, 418, 420.

[86] Moo, *Romans*, 720, including n. 41.

the first clause of 11:25 replicates 1:13, which is followed by this same use of οὕτως in 1:15. The clause in 1:13 is also replicated almost identically in 1 Thess 4:13: "we do not want you to be without knowledge, brothers" (οὐ θέλομεν δὲ ὑμᾶς ἀγνοεῖν). It is again followed by a logical use of οὕτως in 1 Thess 4:17. Thus *the pattern seems formulaic for Paul*, which indicates that he is, in fact, using οὕτως here *to draw a conclusion* based upon what precedes.

Third, BDAG asserts that the use of οὕτως in 11:26 "pert[ains]" to what follows in discourse material, *in this way, as follows*," adding that it functions "correlatively" with καθώς, "just as," later in the verse (BDAG, s.v. οὕτω/οὕτως, 2). Like the first option, however, this third one would also be unprecedented; "Paul never elsewhere pairs *houtōs* and 'just as it is written.' "[87] Furthermore, οὕτως draws from what precedes in 11:25, rather than pointing ahead to what follows in 11:26b–27.

Fourth, Moo concludes that taking οὕτως "to indicate manner and linking it with what comes before … is to be preferred."[88] Dunn similarly says that the basic sense of the word here is "thus, in this manner."[89]

The translation "thus" here seeks to convey *both the second and fourth options. Paul is drawing a conclusion. What follows in 11:26 also happens "in the manner" he has already described*. But what exactly does "thus" refer back to, and how does what precedes serve as the basis for the conclusion which follows?

Contextual Implications and Insights from the Olive Tree

It is possible that Paul intends for us to read the entire sequence outlined earlier in the chapter into the shorthand phrase "and thus" (11:26a). Moo, for example, proposes that "the 'manner' of Israel's salvation is the process that Paul has outlined in vv. 11–24 and summarized in v. 25b."[90] If so, Paul speaks of the conversion of those Jews who had previously sought righteousness from works, had not believed the Gospel, and, consequently, had been hardened. Furthermore, Paul presumes we understand that "and thus/in this manner" (καὶ οὕτως) includes the sequence whereby the "conversion of the Gentiles will be the means of provoking Israel to jealousy and converting them."[91] Thus we should retrieve and insert the thought of 10:18; 11:7, 11–12, 14 in order to fill in the blanks in 11:25 and between 11:25 and 11:26 as well. *But there are two problems with this*. First, it is difficult to perceive how 11:25 is meant to rehearse or imply that whole process. Second, Paul repeatedly holds out the hope that *some* unbelieving Jews might be saved "if they do not remain in unbelief"

---

87 Moo, *Romans*, 720.

88 Moo, *Romans*, 720.

89 Dunn, *Romans*, 681.

90 Moo, *Romans*, 720.

91 Dunn, *Romans*, 681.

(11:14, 23). But he has not previously stated that he envisions that reality happening to the degree of completeness that these interpreters contend (see below).

It seems more realistic to assume that Paul intends for his hearers to base what follows in 11:26a upon what he has, in fact, just stated in 11:25, as well as from the immediately preceding illustration of the olive tree. It may be tempting to view Paul's "development of the analogy" of an olive tree as something of a "detour."[92] But Jesus often enlightens his difficult teachings with parables so that his hearers might come "to know the mysteries ... of the kingdom of God" (γνῶναι τὰ μυστήρια τῆς βασιλείας τοῦ θεοῦ, Lk 8:10; cf. Mt 13:11; with the singular τὸ μυστήριον in Mk 4:11). In a comparable manner, Paul's metaphor of the olive tree provides key interpretive insights into the contested propositional statements he makes in 11:25–26, so that we might not be without knowledge "[concerning] this mystery" (11:25).

The OT believing patriarchs (11:16, 28) and believing Jews, "in accord with" the "nature" of Israel as the people called and chosen to believe in God (11:24), reside in the cultivated olive tree. Due to the unbelief (11:23) of "part" (μέρος, 11:25) of Israel, that is, "some" (τινες, 11:17) in Israel, those branches (only the unbelieving ones) were broken off by God (11:17, 19, 20) and consequently hardened (11:7c, 25). Then by a divine "mystery" (11:25), that is, "contrary to nature" (11:24), (many but not all) Gentiles believed and were grafted into God's one tree (11:17, 20); this is how the fullness of the Gentiles enters in (τὸ πλήρωμα τῶν ἐθνῶν εἰσέλθῃ, 11:25). *In this way (οὕτως, 11:26) the fullness of believing ethnic Israelites (11:12), who remain where they belong by God's gracious choosing (11:5, 7b, 28), and the fullness of the Gentiles, who mysteriously now enter (11:25), will be saved together as the one "Israel of God" (Gal 6:16; the second "Israel" in Rom 9:6b).*[93] This is what 11:25 does state.

Paul's Summation, Part 2: "... All Israel ..." (11:26a)

"And thus" or "in this manner," Paul concludes, "all Israel will be saved" (πᾶς Ἰσραὴλ σωθήσεται, 11:26). The referent of "all Israel" remains the critical matter of dispute. Kruse organizes the numerous interpretations into these six categories, the first five of which pertain to ethnic Israel:

> (i) all Israelites from every age; (ii) all the elect of Israel of all time; (iii) all Israelites alive at the end of the age; (iv) Israel as a whole alive at the end of the age, but not including every individual Israelite; (v) a large number of Israelites at the end of the age; (vi) Israel redefined to include all Jews and Gentiles who believe in Jesus Christ.[94]

---

[92] As characterized by Ticciati, "The Nondivisive Difference of Election," 264.

[93] Paul's *alteration* of the citation from Is 27:9 later in Rom 11:26 adds further support to this view; see below. For Gal 6:16, see Das, *Galatians*, 646–52.

[94] Kruse, *Romans*, 448; Cranfield, *Romans* 576, gives only four options:
> (i) all the elect, both Jews and Gentiles;
> (ii) all the elect of the nation Israel;

The advantage of Kruse's categories is that he separates the temporal application, which is a significant factor among interpreters. But he fails to make clear the basis of salvation for "all Israel" in options 1–5, though perhaps one can read it into the categories. Wright helpfully includes this aspect by expanding the matter into three separate questions: "who is 'all Israel,' when will its 'salvation' occur, and how will it be accomplished?"[95] The latter is the most critical matter at hand and will be addressed, together with other views on this passage, in the concluding section below titled "Alternative Interpretations of 'All Israel Will Be Saved' (11:26a)."

Cranfield begins by asserting that Kruse's final option "must surely be rejected; for it is not feasible to understand Ἰσραήλ in v. 26 in a different sense from that which it has in v. 25."[96] However, at the very outset of his argument in Romans 9–11, Paul opens the door for such a possibility.

> In particular, 9:6 gives the lie to the constantly repeated assertion that one cannot make "Israel" in 11:26 mean something different from what it means in 11:25. … Paul opened his great argument with a clear signal that he was redefining "Israel," and here the argument comes full circle.[97]

"For not all these from Israel [Ἰσραήλ] are Israel [Ἰσραήλ]" (9:6).[98] Here the first "Israel" denotes Israelites ethnically, while the second "Israel" refers only to the believing segment, that is, the community of faith *within* Israel, a group God has now graciously *expanded beyond* those ethnic bounds.[99] This undermines Moo's pronouncement that "Paul has used the term 'Israel' ten times so far in Rom. 9–11, and each refers to ethnic Israel."[100] Rom 9:6 proves that Paul can and does change the referent of the name, even within the same sentence. Furthermore, Rom 11:26 "is the only place in all the letters of Paul where the

---

(iii) the whole nation Israel, including every individual member;

(iv) the nation Israel as a whole, but not necessarily including every individual member.

Cranfield, however, fails to include a distinction regarding temporal considerations, i.e., Israel exactly when. Moo, *Romans*, 723–24, discusses these in terms of ethnic Israel in a "diachronic" sense throughout time (options i–ii of Kruse, listed above) or a "synchronic" reference to Israel at a specific point in time, normally at the end of the age (options iii–v of Kruse, listed above).

[95] Wright, "Romans," 689.

[96] Cranfield, *Romans*, 576; this is his first view as cited two notes above.

[97] Wright, "Romans," 690; similarly, Franzmann, *Romans*, 212.

[98] See the commentary on 9:6. The two different, though partially overlapping, referents are acknowledged by Moo, *Romans*, 721–22; they are cited also by Lenski, *Romans*, 726, though he mistakenly refers to the relevant verse as 9:7 and somewhat contradictorily asserts: "In that same brief sentence 'Israel' is used in different senses. In fact, this is not an analogous example, it is the same truth that is now stated in v. 25, 26, but is now positively stated with regard to the entire future."

[99] The expansion of "Israel" (in the sense of the second "Israel" in Rom 9:6) to include believing Gentiles began already in the OT, as is witnessed, for example, by the "mixed multitude" that participated in the exodus (Ex 12:38); Ruth the Moabitess (the book of Ruth); and Uriah the Hittite (2 Samuel 11).

[100] Moo, *Romans*, 721.

expression '*all* Israel' occurs."[101] This also at least allows for the possibility of a different or fuller understanding of "Israel" in 11:26. The phrase with "all" may even push "Israel" in that direction.

All Israel Equals the Olive Tree of Romans 11:16–24

A general hermeneutical principle is to interpret analogies and parables in light of direct statements. The specific referent of "all Israel" in 11:26, however, remains so contested as to validate the opposite approach, which is also, if not equally, valid. Luke's Gospel, in particular, illustrates: direct statements repeatedly determine rather definitively how a parable, either preceding *or* following, should be understood and applied. At the same time, the parable provides an explication of the statement used to introduce or conclude it. Thus, properly understood, the parable also explains the assertion. Note, for example, Lk 7:47 for Lk 7:41–46; Lk 10:37 for Lk 10:30–35; Lk 12:15 *and* Lk 12:21 for Lk 12:16–20; Lk 16:8b–13 for Lk 16:1–8a; Lk 18:1 for Lk 18:2–5; Lk 20:17–18 for Lk 20:9–16.

As illustrated above, many interpreters read more into Rom 11:25–26a from earlier in the chapter (see 11:7, 11–12, 15) than what Paul actually states. At the same time, they overlook the olive-tree analogy (11:17–24), which does, in fact, immediately precede this section (11:25–36). It seems wise to presume that *the extended analogy of the olive tree provides the corresponding points which clarify how the elements of the "mystery" (11:25) detailed in the verses to follow should be understood.* This can be summarized by six points of correspondence:

1. Roots (11:16, 17)   Believing patriarchs (11:28)
2. Branches "in accord with nature" (11:18, 24)   Ethnic Israelites/Jews
3. Some broken-off branches (11:17, 19, 20)   Unbelieving part of Israel (11:20, 23, 25b)
4. Remaining ("them," 11:17) and regrafted (11:23) natural branches   Fullness of Israel/believing Jews (11:12)
5. Contrary to nature, grafted-in branches (11:17, 19, 24)   Fullness of believing Gentiles come in (11:11–12, 25)
6. Olive tree (11:17–24)   "All Israel," meaning all believers (11:26)

Since there is, in fact, only one tree, that tree would, it seems, be God's "Israel." In it are the patriarchs and other believing Israelites, who always belonged in it according to God's gracious choosing (11:5–6, 7b). Now, mysteriously, believing Gentiles have been ingrafted and have come into Israel by the merciful act of God in Christ (11:25).

Identifying "all Israel" (11:26a) as the entire olive tree of 11:17–24, that is, the whole people of God, does not entail any fundamental change in the nature

---

[101] Franzmann, *Romans*, 211; the only other NT use of "all Israel" or a phrase similar to it is "all the house of Israel" in Acts 2:36.

of Israel.[102] The true Israel has always been the Israel of faith. Yet this identification acknowledges an add-on, namely, the *now-revealed mystery of how God has brought Gentiles into Israel (11:25)*. Paul's only other use of "mystery" (μυστήριον) in Romans (16:25) and the dominant sense of the term throughout his writings support this as his characteristic understanding of the term; see "The Mystery [μυστήριον] Made Known in Christ (11:25a)" above. *The parallels with the olive-tree analogy provide persuasive clues for how the mystery spoken of in 11:25 should be understood.* "It is a secret [previously] unknown to mankind why the Gentiles were saved,"[103] but Paul has just described how they come in (11:25), that is, into Israel, by being grafted into the olive tree by faith in Christ (11:20, 24).

Paul's Summation, Part 3: "… Will Be Saved" (11:26a)

Rom 11:26, then, asserts that "thus" or "in this manner" (οὕτως) the entire tree and all who belong to it, that is, all of God's Israel, which consists of all believers in Christ, "will be saved" (σωθήσεται, future passive indicative). Seven of eight occurrences of the verb "to save" (σῴζω) in Romans are future indicatives (5:9, 10; 9:27; 10:9, 13; 11:14, 26).[104] The lone exception among all these futures is the aorist indicative in 8:24. Otherwise, "as usual in Paul the concept of 'salvation' is future-oriented."[105] But the future tense of "will be saved" (σωθήσεται, 11:26) should *not be restricted* to an exceptional end-times event. On the contrary, the verb in the active voice essentially means "*bring* Messianic *salvation, bring to salvation*" (BDAG, s.v. σῴζω, 2). The divine passive conveys the same sense here; people "will be saved" *by God* as the message of his fulfilled promise reaches out to all (see the third textual note on 11:26; cf. 10:14–15; 11:26b–27). This matches the thematic force of the cognate noun "salvation" (σωτηρία) in 1:16. Thus "*sōzein* is a missionary term associated with the goal of Paul's ministry of the gospel … , which knows of no distinction between Jew and Greek."[106] Paul can declare, "Look! Now [is the] acceptable time. Look! Now [is the] day of salvation" (ἡμέρα σωτηρίας, 2 Cor 6:2).[107] "All Israel will be saved" (11:26), then, encompasses *the rescue*

---

[102] Moo, *Romans*, 721, incorrectly speaks of "a shift from this ethnic denotation to a purely religious one." Believing ethnic Jews remain where they always were as members of God's Israel. Fitzmyer, *Romans*, 624, improperly reduces the meaning to the Platonic-sounding "spiritual Israel." God's faithful people, Jew and Gentile, are not merely spiritual but also remain a visible, corporeal entity in the world.

[103] Pelagius, *Romans* (Bray, *Romans*, ACCS NT 6:298).

[104] Re the verb in 11:14, see the third textual note on that verse.

[105] Dunn, *Romans*, 258; see Middendorf, *Romans 1–8*, 400–402, commenting on the future passive indicatives in 5:9–10. The same future connotation is present with the noun "salvation" (σωτηρία) in at least four of its five uses in Romans (10:1, 10; 11:11; 13:11; debatable in 1:16).

[106] Fitzmyer, *Romans*, 623.

[107] Note the two uses of "now" (νῦν) in 2 Cor 6:2; cf. the two (or three) uses in Rom 11:30–31.

and deliverance of God's people throughout their salvation history, as well as at its culmination.[108]

Rom 11:26 should also be heard in concert with other uses of "save" (σῴζω) in Romans 9–11. One of these seems to be improperly overlooked in this entire discussion. Isaiah foresees the exile (Is 10:5, 20–21) and announces: "And if the people of Israel might become as the sand of the sea, the remnant of them will be saved" (σωθήσεται, LXX Is 10:22). Paul cites the passage in Rom 9:27 to affirm the same truth in his own day. Second, and more recently, 10:9–13 explains how and on what basis God's Israel, which includes both Jewish and Gentile believers, will be saved:

> [9]If you acknowledge with your mouth, "Jesus [is] Lord," and believe in your heart that God raised him from [the] dead, you will be saved [σωθήσῃ]. [10]For with the heart it is being believed into righteousness, and with [the] mouth it is being acknowledged into salvation [σωτηρίαν]. [11]For the Scripture says: "Everyone who believes on him will not be put to shame." [12]For there is not a difference [between] a Jew and a Greek, for the same Lord [is] of all, being rich to all the ones who are calling on him. [13]For "everyone who ever might call on the name of [the] Lord will be saved" [σωθήσεται].

Corroboration for This Interpretation

The interpretation of 11:26 advocated here has, at least in general terms, been present throughout church history. For example, note the following:[109]

> [Theodoret of Cyrus:] *All Israel* means all those who believe, whether they are Jews, who have a natural relationship to Israel, or Gentiles, who are related to Israel by faith.[110]

> [Augustine:] Not all the Jews were blind; some of them recognized Christ. But the fullness of the Gentiles comes in among those who have been called according to the plan, and there arises a truer Israel of God ... the elect from both the Jews and the Gentiles.[111]

> [Calvin:] I extend the word *Israel* to include all the people of God. ... The salvation of the whole Israel of God, which must be drawn from both [Jews and Gentiles], will thus be completed, and yet in such a way that the Jews, as the first born in the family of God, may obtain the first place. I have thought that this interpretation is the more suitable, because Paul here wanted to point to the consummation of the kingdom of Christ, which is by no means confined to the Jews, but includes the whole world. In the same way, in Gal. 6.16,

---

[108] Thus Jesus uses the *perfect* tense of "save" (σῴζω) as an action already accomplished when he declares, "Your faith *has saved* you" (e.g., Lk 7:50; 8:48; 17:19; 18:42), as does Paul, "by grace you *have been* saved" (Eph 2:5, 8; in Eph 2:8 he adds "through faith").

[109] Kruse, *Romans*, 450–51, helpfully identifies much of this evidence, though he ends up advocating a different position, his option ii; see "Paul's Summation, Part 2: '... All Israel ...'" (11:26a) above.

[110] Theodoret of Cyrus, *Romans* (Bray, *Romans*, ACCS NT 6:299).

[111] Augustine, *Letters*, 149 (Bray, *Romans*, ACCS NT 6:298); for the unwise use of "truer," see the paragraph to follow above.

he calls the Church, which was composed equally of Jews and Gentiles, the Israel of God.[112]

[Franzmann:] "All Israel" signifies the whole redeemed people of God from among Jews and Gentiles. ... "All Israel" corresponds to the "all" of Gal. 3:26–29; in this "all" there is neither Jew nor Greek ... , for all are now one in Christ Jesus, all are Christ's, all are Abraham's offspring and heirs according to the promise.[113]

[Wright:] I remain convinced that ... God will save "all Israel"—that is, the whole family of Abraham, Jew and Gentile alike; this will take place during the course of present history; it will happen through their coming to Christian faith.[114]

Moo acknowledges:

Paul's view of the continuity of salvation history certainly allows him to transfer the OT title of the people of God to the NT people of God, as Gal. 6:16 probably indicates (cf. also Phil. 3:3). And this same theology surfaces in Romans itself, as Paul argues that Abraham's "seed" consists of faithful Jews *and Gentiles* (4:13–18).[115]

To be sure, this line of interpretation has certainly not always been articulated properly.[116] For example, by no means should it in any way imply Gentiles have replaced Israel. Believers who happen to be Gentiles are *not* now exclusively the true (or "truer," as Augustine says above) Israel or a new Israel which exists apart from old believing Israel itself. Gentile believers have not superseded Israel; instead of supplanting Israel, they are transplants into Israel (cf. 11:17). Neither has "Israel" become "spiritual" in some Platonic sense of the term.[117]

On the contrary and as the olive-tree analogy makes abundantly clear, believing Gentiles now *belong to or within Israel*. Thus Israel does not undergo "a polemical redefinition," as Wright suggests,[118] but has rather been *expanded*.[119] God still has his one and only tree, which stems from the patriarchs, as it always has.

Paul has spent half his writing life telling his readers that Abraham's family, Israel, the Jews, the circumcision, are neither reaffirmed as they stand,

---

[112] Calvin, *Romans*, 255.

[113] Franzmann, *Romans*, 211.

[114] Wright, "Romans," 689, citing Rom 2:29; 4:1–25; 9:6–9; Galatians 3; 6:16; Phil 3:3 (690).

[115] Moo, *Romans*, 721.

[116] The parable of the Talents (Mt 21:33–46) has often been similarly mishandled; see Middendorf, *Romans 1–8*, 225–26.

[117] As portrayed by Fitzmyer, *Romans*, 624.

[118] Wright, "Romans," 690; Kruse, *Romans*, 448, also mentions Israel being "redefined," but properly discounts that view (450–51).

[119] As noted above, the expansion of Israel to include believing Gentiles began already in the OT; see, e.g., the "mixed multitude" that participated in the exodus (Ex 12:38); Ruth the Moabitess (the book of Ruth); and Uriah the Hittite (2 Samuel 11).

nor "superseded" by a superior group, nor "replaced" with someone else—
that is what he is arguing against in 11:23–24—but transformed, through the
death and resurrection of Israel's own Messiah and the Spirit of Israel's own
God, so that Israel is now, as was always promised, both less and more than
the physical family of Abraham: less, as in 9:6–13; more, as in 4:13–25.[120]

The effect of this *interpretation*, then, would hardly "be to fuel the fire
of the Gentiles' arrogance by giving them grounds to brag that '*we* are the
true Israel.'"[121] They may be tempted to do so based upon the *mis*understandings cited above. If so, Paul counters, they are not merely without the
knowledge (11:25) he here provides but also presumptuously and falsely wise
within themselves (11:25; cf. 11:19–20). The fact that God took them out from
under the severity of his wrath, where they rightly belonged as a godless people (1:18–2:11; 11:22), and incorporated them where they in no way deserve
to be (11:17, 24, 25) ought to drive them not to think "proud [thoughts]" but
instead to "reverently fear" (11:20), as well as to affirm with Paul the awe for
God which he will soon express (11:33–36).

Alternative Interpretations of "All Israel Will Be Saved" (11:26a)
The Elect of Ethnic Israel/All Israelites of All Time Who Believe

In regard to the other five views categorized above by Kruse,[122] Lenski
argues forcefully for the second, "all the elect of Israel of all time": "'All Israel'
here means one thing, and only one, namely *totus coetus electorum ex Israele*
['the complete assembly of the elect/chosen from Israel'] (ἡ ἐκλογή ['the chosen'] in [Rom 11:]7 furnishing this designation). ... The 'all' who will be saved
[are] the spiritual Israel, which alone God regards as Israel."[123] Kruse similarly, but more cautiously, concludes that the referent encompasses "all faithful
Israelites of all time."[124] In favor of this view is its linguistic consistency, defining saved "Israel" *within* the ethnic community of Israel and, theologically,
basing their salvation in a manner coherent with Paul's argument elsewhere in
Romans (see below).

Yet Schreiner responds: "The difficulty with this interpretation is that the
mystery revealed is stunningly anticlimactic."[125] While that may overstate the
case, the second view does overlook three key elements: (1) Paul's ingrafting of
Gentiles into the one olive tree (11:17, 24), which is equivalent to (2) the "mystery" of Gentiles entering in (11:25), and (3) how Paul repeatedly lays out the
Gentile element of the mystery more conclusively and inclusively elsewhere

---

[120] Wright, "Romans," 690, citing also Rom 2:29; 4:16; Gal 3:28–29; Phil 3:3–4.

[121] As Moo, *Romans*, 721, claims.

[122] Kruse, *Romans*, 448; see "Paul's Summation, Part 2: '... All Israel ...' (11:26a)" above.

[123] Lenski, *Romans*, 726–27.

[124] Kruse, *Romans*, 451.

[125] Schreiner, *Romans*, 617; similarly, Cranfield, *Romans*, 577.

(e.g., Rom 16:25–27; Eph 3:6; Col 1:27; 1 Tim 3:16); see "The 'Mystery' (μυστήριον) Made Known in Christ (11:25a)" above.

Most All of Ethnic Israel Alive at the Parousia

The difference between Kruse's fourth and fifth options[126] appears to be merely one of degree, "most" versus "a large number." He offers: "(iv) Israel as a whole alive at the end of the age, but not including every individual Israelite; (v) a large number of Israelites at the end of the age."[127] The slenderness of this distinction makes it difficult to separate interpreters clearly into either the fourth or the fifth category. Thus these two interpretations will be treated together. Cranfield opts for the wording in the fourth view by suggesting that the referent is "the nation Israel as a whole, but not necessarily including every individual member."[128] Dunn, whom Kruse places in the fifth category,[129] categorically states:

> πᾶς Ἰσραήλ ["all Israel"] must mean Israel as a whole, as a people whose corporate identity and wholeness would not be lost even if in the event there were some (or indeed many) individual exceptions. ... The idiom is well enough known and should not cause confusion (cf. 1 Sam 25:1; 1 Kgs 12:1; 2 Chron 12:1; Dan 9:11; ...).[130]

Morris concurs: "Clearly *all Israel* indicates the people as a whole, but it leaves open the possibility that there may be exceptions. So much is clear."[131] For support he cites the following:

> Particularly instructive is a passage in the Mishnah which assures the reader that "All Israelites have a share in the world to come" (*Sanh[edrin]* 10:1) and then goes on to give a considerable list of Israelites who "have no share in the world to come," sometimes mentioning classes such as those who deny the resurrection of the dead and sometimes individuals such as Jeroboam.[132]

However, the invocation of the Mishnah, which generally assumes an ethnic commonality among Israelites, muddles *the basis of salvation* for "all Israel" in or at the end. Is the identity of the "all Israel" to be saved based on ethnicity or faith or some combination thereof? On the one hand, Fitzmyer contends that it happens "though faith in the gospel."[133] But an ethnic dimension appears

---

[126] See "Paul's Summation, Part 2: '... All Israel ...' (11:26a)" above.

[127] Kruse, *Romans*, 448.

[128] Cranfield, *Romans*, 576–77; Kruse, *Romans*, 448, defines this as "Israel as a whole alive at the end of the age, but not including every individual Israelite."

[129] Kruse, *Romans*, 450, including n. 248.

[130] Dunn, *Romans*, 681.

[131] Morris, *Romans*, 421; similarly, Munck, *Christ and Israel*, 136; Sanday and Headlam, *Romans*, 335.

[132] Morris, *Romans*, 420–21; also referenced by Cranfield, *Romans*, 577; Moo, *Romans*, 722, n. 55.

[133] Fitzmyer, *Romans*, 623; Jewett, *Romans*, 702, speaks similarly of "evangelical conversion."

when Moo says that "all Israel" refers to "the nation generally"[134] and defines this synchronically in terms of "a large-scale conversion of Jewish people at the end of this age."[135] Witherington similarly envisions "a mass conversion of non-Christian Jews at the end of salvation history."[136] Schreiner speaks of a time when "a great number of Jews will turn back to Christ in faith."[137] He explains: "The focal point of the mystery is the timing and manner of Israel's salvation: Israel will be saved *after* the inclusion of the Gentiles."[138]

But this view relies on interpreting "and thus" (καὶ οὕτως, 11:26a) as indicating some type of temporal sequence, a sense which Fitzmyer argues "is not otherwise found in Greek."[139] These commentators typically adopt a temporal scheme even though many of them at the same time reject a temporal meaning of "and thus."[140] It is revealing how Cranfield asserts that this end-times temporal sequence "indicates an inversion of the order in which salvation is actually offered to men according to 1.16,"[141] that is, "to Jew first and also to Greek" (1:16). Herein lies one major problem with this interpretation of "all Israel will be saved" within the context of Romans.

To be sure, Paul's ongoing prayer is that those in Israel currently seeking a righteousness of "their own" from works might repent, trust in Christ, and thus be saved (10:1–3; see also 9:1–3, 31–32; 11:7a). Indeed, he himself extols his ministry to the end that it might "save some from them" (11:14). Following Paul's lead, our own prayers and ministries ought to be directed toward *both* the conversion of unbelieving Jewish people (and *now*, without waiting for the end of this age) *and*, with equal fervor, the conversion of unbelieving Gentiles as well. But to insist that Paul teaches that a mass conversion of Jews will or must

---

[134] Moo, *Romans*, 722.

[135] Moo, *Romans*, 724; similarly, Keener, *Romans*, 136–37.

[136] Witherington, *Romans*, 275. Morris, *Romans*, 418, even titles 11:25–32 "The Conversion of Israel."

[137] Schreiner, *Romans*, 617.

[138] Schreiner, *Romans*, 614.

[139] Fitzmyer, *Romans*, 622.

[140] Wright, "Romans," 691, n. 459, points out how Moo, *Romans*, 720, "appears to agree [that a temporal meaning is unprecedented], but then smuggles back a temporal sequence that the text does not suggest." Moo, *Romans*, 716, states: "What stands out in vv. 25b–26a ... is the sequence by which 'all Israel' will be saved: Israel hardened *until* the Gentiles come in and *in this way* all Israel being saved." Later, Moo adds: "But this means that *houtōs* ['thus'], while not having a temporal *meaning*, has a temporal *reference*: for the manner in which all Israel is saved involves a process that unfolds in definite stages" (720). Similarly, Schreiner, *Romans*, 618, n. 16, argues that "the temporal element of the text is present regardless of the meaning of καὶ οὕτως ['and thus']. Indeed, I will argue that καὶ οὕτως is not temporal"; he later attempts to explain: "Thus Paul denotes the manner or way in which Israel would be saved, and in this context what is distinctive about the manner is the time frame" (620–21); see also 614, quoted above. Cranfield, *Romans*, 576, rejects the temporal view, advocating the logical sense of the phrase, as in 5:12. Dunn, *Romans*, 681, supports manner, but hedges, saying that "some temporal weight cannot be excluded."

[141] Cranfield, *Romans*, 576.

occur prior to Christ's return places an unbiblical requirement on the imminence of the second coming (cf., e.g., 1 Cor 15:51; 1 Thess 5:1–3). Nor does Paul define "this mystery" (Rom 11:25) in such a manner anywhere else.[142] In other words, he does not assert or imply that all or most of the broken-off branches will or must be grafted back into the tree. He insists that *it is possible*, but *only* if they do not remain in unbelief (11:23–24), and he does not foresee or reveal the degree to which it will happen. *The fullness of Israel (11:12) thus is to be interpreted in the same manner as the fullness of the Gentiles (11:25), that is, as all who believe (1:16; 3:22–23; 10:4, 11–13).*

As a result, for Moo to suggest that the end times must include "the salvation of the nation [Israel] as a whole" and that "this salvation of Israel in the last days will vindicate God's impartiality (v. 32)"[143] would seem to vindicate just the opposite. *It would, in fact, demonstrate an ethnic partiality by God,* whereas Paul explicitly rejects any "partiality in the presence of God" (2:11). On the contrary, Paul insists that God treats both Jew and Gentile/Greek alike in regard to both his judgment (2:9–11) and the salvation he offers to all who believe (1:16; 10:4, 9, 11–13).

Up to this point, one might properly acknowledge a certain level of uncertainty regarding which interpretation is correct. At the same time and with a certain degree of humility, one ought to advocate for the one which is the best. Specifically in regard to the previous interpretation (Kruse's fourth and fifth combined), Lenski offers the following wise advice:

> Good, orthodox men have believed in a final conversion of the Jewish nation. Yes, they had other misconceptions also. They are a warning and not a shield and not a cause for hesitation. When we note the best straying on any point, let us watch and pray the more lest we be found straying or far off on more than one.[144]

The Critical Matter: The Basis of Salvation for Israel

The more critical matter, unclear within all six of Kruse's categories,[145] is the basis of salvation for "all Israel" (11:26). If he intends for the basis of salvation to be subsumed under "(i) all Israelites from every age" and/or "(iii) all Israelites alive at the end of the age,"[146] *these categories appear to presume that Israelites are (and Jews will be) saved by virtue of their ethnicity/physical ancestry.* Kruse notes that "few have supported the first interpretation" (but see Matera, Jewett, and Hultgren in the second paragraph below), and he vaguely asserts that there is "some support" for the third view; in regard to the third, he

---

[142] See "The 'Mystery' (μυστήριον) Made Known in Christ (11:25a)" above.

[143] Moo, *Romans*, 713.

[144] Lenski, *Romans*, 727.

[145] See "Paul's Summation, Part 2: '… All Israel …' (11:26a)" above.

[146] Kruse, *Romans*, 448.

cites Witherington, who seems closer to the fourth (discussed above in combination with the fifth).[147]

A Separate Way of Salvation?

The basis of Israel's salvation has been brought to the forefront by those who support a position characterized by the German term *Sonderweg*. In contrast to those who envision a mass conversion of Jews to Christ, *Sonderweg* conveys that there is a "special way" to salvation for Jews apart from faith in Jesus the Messiah.[148] Stendahl, an early advocate, contends that, along with the Gentile church, Paul simultaneously "sees that God has mysterious and special plans for the salvation of Israel. This, the mystery of Israel's separate existence, Paul proclaims to the Gentiles."[149] Gaston similarly stresses "the right of Israel to remain Israel … as equal but elder recipients of the grace of God."[150] Various permutations of this view reflect a two-covenant theory which generally asserts that Jews are saved by God's choice according to their race (and/or works), while Christ opens the door to grace for Gentiles.[151]

Specifically in regard to Rom 11:26, Matera adopts Kruse's first option by asserting: "Paul is speaking of ethnic Israel, which includes not only the remnant that has believed but also the vast majority that has not. Historical Israel (past, present, and future) will be the beneficiary of God's salvation."[152] Jewett agrees that Paul means to "include all members of the house of Israel, who, without exception, would be saved."[153] Hultgren similarly concludes that the "expression 'all Israel' has to be taken for what it is, and that is that it refers to the people of Israel, the Jewish people, who have not accepted the gospel."[154]

A Separate Way Is Rejected in Romans

First of all, this two-covenant interpretation contradicts the words of Is 10:22, reaffirmed by Paul himself in Rom 9:27: "If the number of the sons of Israel might be as the sand of the sea[shore], the *remnant* will be saved." This remnant exists by grace and through faith.[155] Second, the contention that all (*or*

---

[147] Kruse, *Romans*, 448–49, including n. 239, citing Witherington, *Romans*, 275.

[148] See "Additional Note: A Special Way of Salvation for Israel (11:1–32)?" in Kruse, *Romans*, 453–56, and Moo, *Romans*, 725, n. 61, for more extensive lists of those who espouse some form of this view.

[149] Stendahl, "Paul among Jews and Gentiles," 4.

[150] Gaston, "Paul and the Torah," 66.

[151] Moo, *Romans*, 725, characterizes it this way: "Gentiles are saved in *their* ('new') covenant by faith in Christ while Jews are saved in *their* (Mosaic) covenant by their adherence to torah." See Stendahl, "Paul among Jews and Gentiles," 28.

[152] Matera, *Romans*, 273.

[153] Jewett, *Romans*, 702.

[154] Hultgren, *Romans*, 420.

[155] The immediate context of 9:27 defines the remnant as what the Lord accomplishes by his Word (9:28–29), that is, by the "Word of Christ" (10:17). See also 11:2–6, where the remnant exists solely by God's "choice of grace" and "*not* from works" (nor ethnicity), since then "grace would no longer be grace."

any!) Israelites are saved by their ethnicity and apart from faith *attacks the very heart of Romans*. As Moo concisely responds: "Paul knows nothing of it."[156] Wright reacts more fully:

> If v. 26*a* does indeed teach a special kind of salvation for all or most Jews, with or without Christian faith, awaiting them at the end of time, then it is exegetically out of step with the passage before it (11:1–24) and, as we shall see, with the one that follows (11:28–32); it is theologically incompatible with the entire argument of 9:6–10:21; and it undermines what Paul has emphasized again and again in Romans 1–8. If Paul has indeed, while writing the letter, received as some suggested a fresh revelation to the effect that the whole Jewish race will at the last be saved by some special means, he did the wrong thing by adding it to what he had already written. He would have been better to put the previous eleven chapters on the fire.[157]

Indeed, the assertion of a "special way" to salvation for ethnic Israel (or for anyone else[158]) runs counter to the argument of the bulk of the letter. Paul's main theme is that "the righteous person will live from faith" (Rom 1:17b, citing Hab 2:4), that is, faith in Jesus Christ (3:22–26), to the exclusion of anything and everything else.[159] Paul "insists that salvation has never been *based* on ethnic descent (see 2:1–29; 4:1–16)."[160] Neither is salvation attainable by virtue of any person's supposed adherence to the Torah understood in terms of works. Paul's entire argument denies any such possibility under the Law (e.g., 2:17–24; 3:19–20, 28; 9:31–32; 10:5). Apart from faith in Christ, *all* deserve God's righteous wrath (1:18, 32; 3:9, 19–20). *Paul insists that the hard truths of 1:18–3:20 stand applicable to all, including both Jews and Gentiles. In fact, he insists that this has always been true and remains so.* Thus Kruse's first and third options[161] are properly rejected for all and for any.

In regard to salvation, "Paul's ministry of the gospel (see 10:9–10, 12; 11:14; 1 Cor 7:16; esp. [1 Cor] 9:20–22; 10:33) … knows of no distinction between Jew and Greek."[162] In regard to one's relationship with God, the righteousness from faith (Rom 1:17; 9:32; 10:5) *transcends* all ethnic distinctions.

---

[156] Moo, *Romans*, 725.

[157] Wright, "Romans," 689.

[158] In this modern age of religious pluralism, it is a common belief that there are multiple ways to salvation. Many presume that, in addition to Christianity, other religions also offer valid paths to God for their adherents (contra Jn 14:6; Acts 4:12).

[159] See Middendorf, *Romans 1–8*, 104–6, and, particularly, the quotation from Lenski, *Romans*, 82.

[160] Moo, *Romans*, 573. Preceding that quote Moo states: "Paul does not deny that ethnic Israel remains God's people, in some sense (cf. 9:4–5; 11:1–2, 28)." Possibly that statement could be understood properly, if interpreted in light of all Paul says in Romans 9–11. But such a proper understanding would exclude other assertions by Moo such as his reference to "the 'holiness' of even the broken-off branches in [11:]16" (718). Paul in 11:16 refers to branches that are "holy" because they are connected to the olive tree's holy root, not to branches that have been broken off.

[161] See "Paul's Summation, Part 2: '… All Israel …' (11:26a)" above.

[162] Fitzmyer, *Romans*, 623.

This is the main point of the mystery as Paul describes it in Ephesians 2–3; for μυστήριον, "mystery," in Eph 3:3, 4, 9, see "The 'Mystery' (μυστήριον) Made Known in Christ (11:25a)" above. In Romans itself, "the 'all' of 11:26 looks back to the 'all' of 10:11–13, and behind that of 4:16 ('all the seed. ... Abraham as the father of all of us')."[163] Romans 4 forcefully argues that uncircumcised Abraham was declared righteous by God through faith in the promise (Gen 15:6; see, e.g., Rom 4:3–5, 9–12); the promise to Abraham and his offspring, who come from "many nations" (4:18), now stands fulfilled by God's grace given in Jesus Christ (4:23–25).

Romans 9–11 further demonstrates that salvation depends upon God's choosing (9:11; 11:5, 5, 28), call (9:12, 24–26), mercy (9:16, 23), and grace (11:5–6; cf. 3:24; 6:23) and is for all who listen responsively to and believe the Word of Christ (10:8, 16–17). Therein lies salvation for any and for all. As Isaiah, Joel, and Paul have together written:

> [11]For the Scripture says: "Everyone who believes on him will not be put to shame." [12]For there is not a difference [between] a Jew and a Greek, for the same Lord [is] of all, being rich to all the ones who are calling on him. [13]For "everyone who ever might call on the name of [the] Lord will be saved." (Rom 10:11–13, quoting Is 28:16; Joel 2:32 [MT 3:5]; cf. Rom 3:22–23)

The Lord to whom Paul refers in 10:13 is Jesus; 10:9 makes this identification irrefutable (see the commentary there). The Good News of salvation for Jew first and also for Greek (1:16) is from faith in him (1:1–4, 17; 10:4). Moo, therefore, gives this effective rebuttal to any notion that some kind of "special way" exists:

> Nor can the absence of the name of Christ in Rom. 11 justify the conclusion that this faith need not be faith in Christ. Paul has defined the faith he is talking about here quite adequately in the first ten chapters of the letter: it is faith in Jesus Christ (see esp. 3:22, 26; 10:4–13). As Paul has made clear in the immediately preceding chapter, faith is inextricably tied to Jesus and his resurrection victory (10:9), and it is this faith that brings salvation to Gentile and Jew alike (10:10–13). Jews, like Gentiles, can be saved only by responding to the gospel and being grafted into the one people of God. Paul has certainly not forgotten his great summary of the theme of his letter [Rom 1:16] as he writes chap. 11."[164]

Yes, unbelieving Israel may most certainly be grafted back into the tree (11:24; cf. 11:12, 14), but only, Paul says, "if they do not remain in unbelief" (11:23), that is, if they believe in Jesus. He offers no hint that it will be any different for Jew as for Gentile "in [the] day when God judges the hidden things of people, according to my Gospel, through Jesus Christ" (2:16).

---

[163] Wright, "Romans," 690.

[164] Moo, *Romans*, 725–26.

Old Testament Attestation of the Mystery Made Known (11:26b–27)
Isaiah 59:20–21a and 27:9 in Romans 11:26b–27

As Paul does fourteen times in Romans, he employs "just as it stands written" (καθὼς γέγραπται) in the middle of 11:26 to introduce the scriptural support which follows in the rest of 11:26 and in 11:27:

> 26"The Rescuer will come from Zion.
>> He will turn away godlessness from Jacob.
> 27And this is the covenant from me for them,
>> when I take away their sins."

The first three lines here replicate LXX Is 59:20–21a exactly, except for one insignificant omission (the καὶ before ἀποστρέψει) and one very significant change, the preposition before "Zion."

The LXX and then the MT of Is 59:20–21a read as follows:

> 20καὶ ἥξει ἕνεκεν Σιων ὁ ῥυόμενος
>> καὶ ἀποστρέψει ἀσεβείας ἀπὸ Ιακωβ.
> 21καὶ αὕτη αὐτοῖς ἡ παρ᾽ ἐμοῦ διαθήκη.

> 20And the Rescuer will come on account of Zion,
>> and he will turn away godlessness from Jacob.
> 21And this is the covenant from me for them. (LXX Is 59:20–21a)

> 20וּבָא לְצִיּוֹן גּוֹאֵל
>> וּלְשָׁבֵי פֶשַׁע בְּיַעֲקֹב נְאֻם יְהוָה:
> 21וַאֲנִי זֹאת בְּרִיתִי אוֹתָם אָמַר יְהוָֹה

> 20"And a Redeemer will come to Zion,
>> and to those turning away [from] transgression in Jacob," oracle
>> of Yahweh.
> 21"And I—this is my covenant with them," says Yahweh. (MT Is 59:20–21a)

Whereas the LXX has "the Rescuer" coming "on account of Zion" or "for the sake of Zion" (ἕνεκεν Σιων), Paul has him coming "*from* Zion" (ἐκ Σιών). Even more striking is the difference between Paul and the underlying Hebrew, which depicts the Redeemer, Yahweh himself, coming "*to* Zion" (לְצִיּוֹן).[165] Another noteworthy difference is that in the MT, those who do the action of "turning away" (intransitively; from "transgression") are the repentant people, who are parallel to "Zion"; the Redeemer comes "to Zion" by coming to the penitent, suggesting that in the MT "Zion" consists of those who repent of their transgression. In the LXX and Paul, however, it is the Rescuer who "will turn away" (transitively) the "godlessness from Jacob," that is, the Rescuer removes godlessness from the people.

---

[165] In the context of the Hebrew verb of motion בּוֹא, "to come," with the place name צִיּוֹן, "Zion," the ordinary sense of the Hebrew preposition לְ is to travel "toward" or "to" the place in a spatial sense. See BDB, s.v. לְ, 1 g (a). Most commentators recognize this sense, e.g., Moo, *Romans*, 727, n. 66.

The final line of 11:27 in Romans then defines the covenant differently than what follows in Is 59:21. In the rest of Is 59:21 Yahweh addresses his Suffering Servant and promises that "my Spirit" (the Spirit of Yahweh), who rests upon the Servant (as in Is 11:2; 42:1; 48:16; 61:1), and the Word of Yahweh ("my words"), which he has placed in the Servant's mouth (as in Is 50:4), shall not depart from the Servant nor from the Servant's "seed" or "offspring" (זֶרַע, as in Is 53:10). The "covenant" is that the children of God engendered by the Servant shall continue to have the "Spirit" and "words" of God "forever."[166]

Paul may have associated this covenant promise in Is 59:21 with the "new covenant" promise of Jeremiah, where God declares, "I will forgive their iniquity" (Jer 31:34) and "I will cleanse them. … I will forgive all their iniquities which they sinned against me" (Jer 33:8). But for the forgiveness of sins, instead of quoting the phraseology from Jeremiah, Paul instead draws the language from Is 27:9 for the last clause of Rom 11:27. LXX Is 27:9, which differs significantly from the MT, promises that in the midst of "the lawlessness of Jacob" (ἡ ἀνομία Ιακωβ) will be this blessing: "when I take away his sin" (ὅταν ἀφέλωμαι αὐτοῦ τὴν ἁμαρτίαν). Paul's clause is identical to the LXX, aside from his use of the plural "their sins" (τὰς ἁμαρτίας αὐτῶν), in all likelihood to match the plural pronoun from Is 59:21 earlier in Rom 11:27, "for them" (αὐτοῖς).

First, what should one make of Paul's linking of the thought of these two verses from Isaiah (Is 59:21 and Is 27:9)?

> There is a certain grammatical awkwardness in the composite quotation as it stands; … but the general sense is of course clear enough—the substance of the new covenant which God will establish with Israel consists in His gracious forgiveness of their sins.[167]

Paul is no innovator here. A plethora of OT passages speak of a covenant renewal with the forgiveness of sins.[168] This idea was also "well established in Jewish expectation" (e.g., *Jubilees* 22:14–15; Ps Sol 18:5).[169] Paul declares that the new covenant with its longed-for assurance of the forgiveness of sins has now arrived in Jesus Christ.[170]

Second, what about the significant change in preposition regarding the relationship between "the Rescuer" and "Zion"? "Not only does Paul's reading differ from the LXX, it differs also from the Hebrew text and from every known pre-Pauline text and version."[171] Rather than ascribing it to "the influence"

---

[166] See Lessing, *Isaiah 56–66*, 183–85, 202–6.

[167] Cranfield, *Romans*, 578–79.

[168] See, e.g., Is 1:18; 4:4; 40:2; 43:25; 44:22; 53:6; Jer 31:31–34; 33:6–8; 36:3; Micah 7:18–19; Zech 3:4, 9; 13:1.

[169] Dunn, *Romans*, 684; see J. Behm, "μετανοέω, μετάνοια," *TDNT* 4:991–92, 998–99.

[170] See the second textual note on 11:27 and the discussion of Mt 26:28 in "The Rescuer and Zion: 'To,' 'For the Sake of,' and 'From'" below. Cf. also Rom 3:21, 26; 16:25–26.

[171] Moo, *Romans*, 727.

of other texts,[172] the most plausible explanation, particularly in this context, assesses it as "a deliberate alteration by Paul."[173] A comparable example is provided by the varying pronouns, or lack thereof, in the text of Hab 2:4 as present in the MT and LXX and as quoted in Heb 10:38 and Rom 1:17. In a remarkable correspondence with Rom 11:27, a seemingly slight change in the pronouns in Hab 2:4; Rom 1:17; and Heb 10:38 makes a significant difference in meaning, but all three texts convey profound theological truths.[174]

The Rescuer and Zion: "To," "For the Sake of," and "From"

As for the Rescuer coming "*to* Zion" in the original Hebrew of Is 59:20, Paul does not discount at all the fact that Isaiah's prediction was fulfilled in Jesus' first advent. An applicable literal fulfillment is Palm Sunday. Matthew and John explicitly identify Jesus' coming to Zion on that day as the fulfillment of Zech 9:9: "Say to the daughter of Zion, 'Look! Your king *is coming to you*'" (εἴπατε τῇ θυγατρὶ Σιών· ἰδοὺ ὁ βασιλεύς σου ἔρχεταί σοι, Mt 21:5; similarly, Jn 12:15). Jesus himself describes the events of that coming to Zion as the fulfillment of the covenant which grants forgiveness of sins when, later that week, during the Last Supper, he gives his disciples the cup from which they all are to drink, saying, "For this is my blood [τὸ αἷμά μου] of the *covenant* [τῆς διαθήκης], the [τό] [blood] being poured out in behalf of many *for the forgiveness of sins*" (εἰς ἄφεσιν ἁμαρτιῶν, Mt 26:28). Jesus procures the forgiveness of sins for all humanity by the giving of his body into death and the shedding of his blood on the cross. He bestows this forgiveness together with his body and blood in the Lord's Supper. This inaugurates the "covenant" promised by Is 59:21 (also Jer 31:34; 33:8; cf. Is 27:9) and cited in Rom 11:27. The fulfillment by Jesus aligns with Is 59:20 according to both the MT and the LXX: Jesus comes both "*to* Zion" (לְצִיּוֹן, MT Is 59:20) and "*for the sake of* Zion" (ἕνεκεν Σιων, LXX Is 59:20).

Why, then, does Rom 11:26 have Isaiah predicting that the Rescuer "will come *from* Zion" (ἐκ Σιών)? Moo identifies this as a reference to the incarnation, but that depends on Paul presuming that his hearers will identify "Zion" as the heavenly Jerusalem or the "Jerusalem above" (Gal 4:26; cf. Heb 12:22).[175] Without any textual indication, that seems implausible and forced.

More common is the suggestion that the quotations from Isaiah refer to the second advent of Christ, the parousia.[176] If so, they align with the eschatological

---

[172] As does Cranfield, *Romans*, 577, who cites as possibilities Pss 14:7 (LXX 13:7); 53:6 (MT 53:7; LXX 52:7); 110:2 (LXX 109:2).

[173] Dunn, *Romans*, 682, though he guardedly calls it "quite conceivable"; similarly, Moo, *Romans*, 727, considers that Paul "may have deliberately changed the wording to make a point."

[174] See Middendorf, *Romans 1–8*, 99–106. For a more general overview of Paul's use of the OT, see 37–38 and the excursus "Paul's Use of the Old Testament in Romans" following the commentary on 15:7–13.

[175] Moo, *Romans*, 728.

[176] Schreiner, *Romans*, 619; similarly, Käsemann, *Romans*, 313–14; Cranfield, *Romans*, 578.

force of a comparable text like 1 Thess 1:10. There Paul calls us to wait expectantly for Jesus' second coming when he will be "the Rescuer of us from the coming wrath" (τὸν ῥυόμενον ἡμᾶς ἐκ τῆς ὀργῆς τῆς ἐρχομένης), that is, the wrath of God against sin. Wright comments that this reading of Rom 11:26b–27 "has undoubtedly been popular. But it is demonstrably mistaken."[177]

Wright then cites Deut 33:2, in which Moses remembers how "Yahweh came from Sinai" (יְהוָ֞ה מִסִּינַ֣י בָּ֗א; LXX: κύριος ἐκ Σινα ἥκει). He sees Rom 11:26 as a parallel.

> So far from pulling the text toward the parousia, he [Paul] seems rather to be emphasizing the opposite: the redeemer, by whom he must mean Jesus the Messiah, "comes" from Zion into all the world like YHWH "coming" from Sinai to establish the covenant and give Israel its inheritance. As the Messiah does so, he will banish ungodliness from Jacob. Once again texts that were unambiguously about YHWH in the Scriptures are taken by Paul to refer to Jesus.[178]

The OT prophetic expectation of the Gentiles streaming *to* Zion was discussed above.[179] Here Dunn properly recognizes that if Paul has those prophecies in mind, "he is in process of *transforming*—not merely taking up—the expectation of an eschatological pilgrimage of Gentiles to Zion."[180] Indeed, instead of Gentiles coming to Zion, *the Rescuer comes to them*. In this context, Paul sees this as the mysterious action by which "the fullness of the Gentiles comes in" (Rom 11:25). They do so *not by their coming to Zion*, but by the Word of Christ, the Rescuer, *going out to them* (10:14–15, 17), that is, "to Jew first and also to Greek" (1:16).

This began to be fulfilled in Jesus' own ministry (Mt 15:22–28). It was then expanded out exponentially according to his commission and in his name after Pentecost (e.g., Mt 28:19–20; Lk 24:45–49; Acts 1:8), with Paul himself playing no small part (Acts 13–20). As predicted by Isaiah, the Good News of the Messiah is sent out, proclaimed, heard, and believed (Is 52:7, quoted in Rom 10:15; Is 53:1, quoted in Rom 10:16) in "all the world" (Ps 19:4 [MT 19:5], quoted in Rom 10:18). It has been accepted by many, Jew and Gentile alike. God has, indeed, turned them from godlessness and taken away their sins;[181] this fulfills his covenant promise through Isaiah (Rom 11:26b–27). This is then

---

[177] Wright, "Romans," 691.

[178] Wright, "Romans," 692. For other texts, see the discussion of 10:9, 12–13 in this commentary.

[179] See "Exhibit 2: 'The Fullness of the Gentiles' Enter (11:25c)" above.

[180] Dunn, *Romans*, 682.

[181] As used in the context above, "take away their sins" (11:27) refers to subjective justification. Objective justification is the biblical truth that the universal atonement of Jesus Christ on the cross for the sins of all people has (objectively) taken away the sins of the whole world (e.g., Jn 1:29). However, the righteousness of God in Christ is credited or imputed to individuals through faith alone (Gen 15:6; Rom 4:3), and so only those who believe in Christ are justified subjectively, that is, only they stand before God as individuals whose sin has been taken away. Those who refuse to believe in Jesus thereby reject his atonement for their sins and therefore remain in them and under the wrath of God (Jn 3:16–18, 36).

"the same process of God's dealing with Israel's (and the world's) sins that he has already described in 9:24–26 and especially 10:6–13, with 2:25–29 and 8:1–11 in the immediate background."[182]

"But they did not all listen responsively to the Good News" (10:16a). As Isaiah also predicted, there would be those who do not believe the message (Is 53:1, quoted in Rom 10:16b). What of them? This explains Paul's transition into 11:28.

A Summary of the Theology of Romans 9–11 (11:28–32)

"Enemies … Loved" (11:28)

Moo suggests that "the immediate purpose of this paragraph is to ground and elaborate [on] Paul's prediction of Israel's final salvation."[183] But the two or three uses of "now" (νῦν) in 11:30–31[184] attest convincingly to the *present* reality being discussed. This aligns with the overall argument of the letter from beginning to end as Paul articulates the mystery of the Gospel which has *now been revealed* and made known as "[the] power of God into salvation for everyone who believes" (1:16; see also 1:17; 3:21; 11:25; 16:25–26).

In 11:28, Paul speaks of "enemies." But he is *not* referring to Israel as a whole or all Jewish people. Instead, he refers only to "some," namely, the "part" of Israel that did not believe the Gospel (3:3; 9:6; 11:25; cf. also 10:16; 11:7, 11, 14, 17), and he maintains that these "enemies" nevertheless are still "loved": "on the one hand, with respect to the Good News [they are] enemies for your sake, but, on the other hand, with respect to the choosing [of God, they are] loved on account of the patriarchs" (11:28). The structure of this verse carefully alternates a pair of prepositions, κατά, "with respect to," and διά, "for the sake of, on account of." Both prepositions are used twice, and all four times the objects are in the accusative case. Thus we have these parallels:

κατά	τὸ εὐαγγέλιον	ἐχθροὶ	δι᾽ ὑμᾶς
κατά	τὴν ἐκλογὴν	ἀγαπητοὶ	διὰ τοὺς πατέρας

with respect to	the Good News	enemies	for your sake
with respect to	the choosing	loved	on account of the patriarchs

The preposition κατά expresses reference both times. While διά conveys cause, it is translated two different ways in this verse: "for the sake of" and then "on account of."[185]

Cranfield incredulously contends that "the Good News/Gospel" (τὸ εὐαγγέλιον) must *not* mean "the gospel message" or "the content of the gospel,"

---

[182] Wright, "Romans," 691.

[183] Moo, *Romans*, 729.

[184] See the third textual note on 11:31.

[185] Dunn, *Romans*, 684, cautions that "the prepositions are chosen not because they necessarily mean the same thing each time, but, on the contrary, because their range or diversity or indeed ambiguity of meaning can be expressed in the same preposition + accusative form."

but instead "the progress of the gospel in the world."[186] But Paul clearly refers to those Jews who did not listen responsively to or believe "the Good News," as τὸ εὐαγγέλιον means in 10:16 (see also 1:1, 16). They are "unpersuaded and contradicting" (10:21) toward the "Word of Christ" (10:17). They are the "some" branches which were broken off due to unbelief (11:17, 20). Therefore, " 'enemies according to the gospel' succinctly summarizes the point that Paul has made in 9:30–10:21: [namely,] … their failure to respond to the revelation of God's righteousness in Christ, the heart of the gospel."[187]

As a result, they are currently at enmity with those who do believe, as well as with God himself (see 5:10). This is the division Jesus himself spoke about which separates those who do not believe in him from those who do and even from the patriarchs themselves (see Lk 12:49–53; 13:22–30). Apart from faith, unbelieving Israelites, *just like all other people*, are "under the wrath of God" and subject to the severity of "divine hostility"[188] (see, e.g., Rom 2:8–11; 3:9, 22; 11:22). Paul has previously discussed how this refusal on the part of some Jews to be persuaded by the Gospel has worked for the benefit of those Gentiles who now believe (10:19; 11:11, 17, 25). This sequence plays itself out repeatedly in the narrative of Acts (e.g., Acts 13:44–47; 14:1–3; 18:4–7; 19:8–10; 28:23–29).

But Beloved Nevertheless (11:28)

Nevertheless, the Jews who do not believe in Christ remain natural branches that were originally attached to the patriarchal roots "in accord with nature" (κατὰ φύσιν, 11:21, 24), that is, by virtue of God's prior "choosing" (κατὰ … τὴν ἐκλογήν, 11:28). "Choosing" (ἐκλογή) in 11:28 recalls the thematic use of this noun for God's "choice" of Jacob over Esau in 9:11,[189] as also does "loved" (11:28), for "Jacob I loved, but Esau I spurned" (Rom 9:13, quoting Mal 1:2–3). As a result, even though they are unbelieving branches broken off due to unbelief (11:20), they are still loved by God "on account of the patriarchs" (διὰ τοὺς πατέρας, 11:28), that is, because they are the physical descendants of Abraham, Isaac, and Jacob. The basis for this love is *not* the works of the patriarchs.[190] Paul had declared in Rom 9:11 that God's "choice" of Jacob took place before either he or Esau were born or had done anything good or evil. "We can rule out the idea that they [the natural branches now severed] were beloved because of the fathers' merits since verse 29 [of Romans 11] grounds God's love for the fathers in his gifts and gracious call,"[191] which they received through faith. As

---

[186] Cranfield, *Romans*, 579.

[187] Moo, *Romans*, 730; though he wrongly applies this to "Israel as a whole" instead of the "some" in Israel who disbelieve in Christ.

[188] Cranfield, *Romans*, 580.

[189] The noun ἐκλογή, "choosing; chosen," also appears thematically in 11:5, 7, but in those verses it refers to the remnant of believers in Christ.

[190] See Sanday and Headlam, *Romans*, 330–32; also Middendorf, *Romans 1–8*, 322–25.

[191] Schreiner, *Romans*, 626.

Romans 4 demonstrates, Abraham exemplifies such faith in the promises God gave to him and then reiterated to the other patriarchs.[192]

As discussed in "God's People" in the introduction to Romans 9–11 and in the concluding section of the commentary on 10:16–21, God chose "the people as a whole"[193] to be his own. "Loved" (ἀγαπητοί) here conveys "God's faithfulness to his chosen, despite their hostility to his fuller purpose of grace."[194] While those who do not believe are currently "enemies" (11:28), they are most certainly able to be reconciled through faith and be reattached to their patriarchal roots "if they do not remain in unbelief" (11:23). Indeed, Paul not only repeatedly and emphatically insists that this remains a possibility (11:1–2, 11, 15, 24), but he also fervently prays for and serves tirelessly toward that end (e.g., 10:1; 11:13–14).[195]

God's Choosing, Gracious Gifts, and Calling—No Regrets! (11:29)

Paul's explanation (γάρ, "for") of *why* this is possible comes in 11:29: "for the gracious gifts and the calling of God [are] without regret." The dual subjects here coincide with terms used significantly earlier in Romans. The word "gracious gifts" (χαρίσματα), here in the plural, denotes all "which is freely and graciously given" (BDAG, s.v. χάρισμα) by God (note the word's use also in 5:15, 16; 6:23). His grace bestows righteousness, forgiveness, redemption, life, and salvation to all who believe. In this context, the term certainly also includes the particular advantages bestowed upon Israel as listed by Paul in 3:1–2 and 9:4–5.

While 11:29 contains the lone appearance in Romans of the noun (κλῆσις) for God's "calling," it recalls Paul's thematic use of the cognate verb "to call" (καλέω), particularly in Romans 9. In 9:12 he even defines God as "the One who calls" (τοῦ καλοῦντος). And he climactically affirms that God "also called ... us, not only from Jews but also from Gentiles" (9:24). Moo contends that "the 'call' of God clearly refers to the election according to which the Jews are beloved,"[196] but that confuses the eternal *election* of God with his *calling* in time through the Word of Christ (10:17).[197] While God's election may transcend

---

[192] See, e.g., Gen 12:1–3; 15:1–6; 18:18; 22:15–18; 26:1–5; 28:13–15; Rom 4:3, 5, 9, 13, 14, 16, 20.

[193] Cranfield, *Romans*, 580.

[194] Dunn, *Romans*, 685.

[195] Note the objective reconciliation (objective justification) of all "enemies" of God by the death of his Son in 5:10. See Middendorf, *Romans 1–8*, 403, 432; Pieper, *Christian Dogmatics*, 2:347.

[196] Moo, *Romans*, 732.

[197] Similar to Moo is Jewett, *Romans*, 700, who speaks of "the predestined number of the elect according to an apocalyptic scheme" and "the completion of a fore-ordained number of converts." But Paul does not use any such language. For the Lutheran understanding of the biblical teaching of God's eternal election and historical calling through his Word (versus Calvinistic double predestination), see "God" in the introduction to Romans 9–11; "Not 'Hated,' but 'Spurned' " and "What Paul Does *Not* Say" in the commentary on 9:6–13; "Is This Fair to

earthly time, *all* of Paul's uses of the verb "to call" (καλέω) in Romans refer to actions of God that take place *within* salvation history in the world.[198] The same is true with the cognate adjective "called" (κλητός, 1:1, 6, 7; 8:28) for those who have been called to faith through the Gospel. In other words, *God's call comes in this time and to all who hear his invitation in Christ*. He also delivers his gracious gifts to his people here in this world.

Paul insists that God's gracious gifts and his call to Israel remain "without regret" (ἀμεταμέλητα, 11:29). This term conveys God's continuing actions toward Israel in a manner which reiterates the thought of 10:21–11:2:

> But to Israel he says: "The whole day I stretched out my hands to an unpersuaded and contradicting people."
>
> I say, then, God did not push his people away from himself, did he? May it never come to be! For I am also an Israelite, from the seed of Abraham, of the tribe of Benjamin. "God did not push his people away from himself" whom he knew relationally beforehand.

"Without regret" (ἀμεταμέλητα, 11:29) means that God has not pulled back his hands, even to those who are unpersuaded by the Word of Christ. God has not rejected Israel, as evidenced by the ongoing existence of the believing remnant "according to [the] choice of grace" (11:5; see 11:1–7). The translation of ἀμεταμέλητα as "immutable" or "irrevocable" is appropriate, therefore, in regard to *God's perspective toward Israel* and, specifically, those Jews who do not believe. He continues to call them (and all people) to faith by the evangelical process portrayed in 10:6–17. This serves to reinforce the assertion of 9:6: "by no means [is it] that God's Word has failed and remains fallen."

However, this does *not* mean that his gracious gifts and call are irresistible on the human side. The Gospel message of his grace, proclaimed through the Word of Christ, can be resisted, stumbled over, and rejected by humans (see 3:3; 9:32–33; 10:16, 21; 11:11, 20). The passion of the Christ graphically illustrates the human ability to reject him and to be unpersuaded by his message. On this point, there is no difference between Jews and Gentiles. Yes, God mercifully calls to faith all who hear (9:24; 10:16–17), but he does not forcibly impose some kind of irresistible grace upon people; neither does he *make them* accept his call. This is the area where God's permissive will includes allowing people to "exercise their freedom."[199] After the fall into sin, humanity retains "free will"

---

the Pharaoh? (9:17–18)" and "Thou Art the Potter; We All Are like Clay (9:19–21)" in the commentary on 9:14–24; the introduction to 9:30–10:15; and the commentary on 11:5. See especially FC SD XI and FC Ep XI. For a broad discussion, see Pieper, *Christian Dogmatics*, 1:489–94.

[198] Rom 4:17; 8:30 (twice); 9:7, 12, 24, 25, 26. See the discussion of 8:29–30 in Middendorf, *Romans 1–8*, 690–96.

[199] Cranfield, *Romans*, 587.

understood as the ability to choose to disbelieve God and his Word, although not the ability to choose to believe or to contribute to salvation in any way.[200]

In regard to the "not all" of 9:6 and 10:16, the "some" in 3:3, and the "part" of 11:25, their unbelief results in their being broken off from the tree by God (11:17, 20) and becoming his "enemies" (ἐχθροί, 11:28); these are *the dire straits of all humanity apart from Christ* (see 5:6–10). Nevertheless, they, like the older brother in the parable, will be readily welcomed back with joy (Lk 15:28; Rom 11:15) "if they do not remain in unbelief" (11:23). In other words, God's gracious gifts and his inviting call are now still there for them, as they are for all!

Human Unpersuadedness Met by God's Mercy (11:30–31)

As illustrated repeatedly already, Paul is drawing together the argument of Romans 9–11. Dunn contends, with some hyperbole, that 11:30–31 "is the most contrived or carefully constructed formulation which Paul ever produced in such a tight epigrammatic form, with so many balancing elements."[201] This may be illustrated in Greek as follows:

[30]ὥσπερ γὰρ   ὑμεῖς ποτε ἠπειθήσατε τῷ θεῷ,   νῦν δὲ ἠλεήθητε   τῇ τούτων ἀπειθείᾳ,
[31]οὕτως καὶ   οὗτοι νῦν ἠπείθησαν   τῷ ὑμετέρῳ ἐλέει,   ἵνα καὶ αὐτοὶ [νῦν] ἐλεηθῶσιν.

It is difficult to reproduce the parallels precisely in English, but 11:30–31 is rendered here as follows, with slashes dividing the four parts of each verse; each part is paralleled in the other verse:

[30]For just as / you were formerly unpersuaded to God / but now you were shown mercy / by the unpersuadedness of these ones,

[31]thus also / now these were unpersuaded / for your mercy / in order that they might also now be shown mercy.

Unpersuaded?

The *dominant note sounded three times in 11:30–31 is one of mercy* (also 11:32). This echoes the thematic use of "mercy" words in Romans 9 (9:15, 16, 18, 23). However, some explanation is required for the admittedly awkward use of the translations "be unpersuaded" and "unpersuadedness" (instead of "disbelieved" and "unbelief" [cf. KJV]; many versions use "be disobedient" and "disobedience"). The noun ἀπείθεια refers to *not* being persuaded in regard to something received or heard, and so in some contexts it denotes "*disbelief* in the Christian gospel (see ἀπειθέω)" (BDAG). That definition applies in regard to those in Israel referred to throughout 11:28–31. Dunn helpfully points to the synonym παρακοή, translated as "disobedience" (5:19), and its antonym

---

[200] See the commentary on 10:16–17, 21. God alone does all the work for our salvation, including the gift of faith, which is wrought by the Holy Spirit through the power of the Word. Neither human works nor free will contribute anything. See further Article IV, "Justification," and Article XVIII, "Freedom of the Will," in both the Augsburg Confession and the Apology of the Augsburg Confession.

[201] Dunn, *Romans*, 687.

ὑπακοή, "obedience" (5:19; also, e.g., 1:5; 6:16; 15:18).[202] "Be unpersuaded" also fits the active sense of the verb ἀπειθέω in 11:30–31 (see below).

BDF, § 187.6, groups the following related verbs together, noting that they typically take the dative case, as does ἀπειθέω in 11:30: "Πείθεσθαι, ὑπακούειν, ἀπιστεῖν, ἀπειθεῖν with dat[ive] as usual. Πιστεύειν often with dat[ive]." It is also interesting to observe that *passive* forms of πείθω function almost equivalently with "believe" in Acts 17:4 and Acts 28:24 (KJV translates both as "believed"). Therefore a point made in regard to ὑπακοή, usually rendered as "obedience" but translated as "responsive hearing" in 1:5, is generally applicable to this entire group of verbs.

> The key to determining the meaning more specifically is contextual; it is discerned by identifying what follows the summons to hear [or believe, be persuaded about, etc.]. If the Word is a law, a command to perform an action or works, then "obedience" works well as an acceptable translation. However, in many passages the emphasis of the verb ὑπακούω is on receiving, believing, and trusting the Word, including its Gospel promises.[203]

When the Gospel is involved (as discussed extensively in the commentary on 10:16), rendering forms of ὑπακούω/ὑπακοή with "obey"/"obedience" misleads the English reader since those translations imply an active doing, i.e., works instead of faith. In regard to righteousness and salvation, such a translation contradicts Paul's teaching: "for we conclude that a person is being declared righteous by faith apart from works of the Law" (3:28).

Formerly Unpersuaded Gentiles Receive Mercy (11:30)

What then do the four words in 11:30–32 that are forms of ἀπειθέω (11:30, 31) and ἀπείθεια (11:30, 32) mean? Again, it depends on the object. At the outset, it is important to note that both of the forms of the verb ἀπειθέω are *active* voice (11:30, 31; see the textual notes). In the overall context of Romans, the clause "you were formerly unpersuaded [ἠπειθήσατε] to God" (11:31) encapsulates how formerly the Gentiles in general not only lacked faith in Christ but were not even convinced that the eternal power and divine majesty of God displayed in his creation were a sufficient summons to all of humanity to glorify and thank him (1:20–21). Instead, they actively "exchanged" (ἀλλάσσω, 1:23; μεταλλάσσω, 1:25, 26) all that providential evidence for utter and increasing depravity, to which God, then, reluctantly "gave them over" (παρέδωκεν, 1:24, 26, 28).[204] They were also generally unpersuaded by "the work of the Law" written by God on their heart and conscience (2:15) and are accountable for not heeding it (2:12, 16). Paul then charges the boastful Jewish person addressed in 2:17–29 with failing to be persuaded to act according to the revealed Law: "through the transgression of the Law you are dishonoring God" (2:23). In 2:8,

---

[202] Dunn, *Romans*, 687.

[203] Middendorf, *Romans 1–8*, 66.

[204] See "The Content and Structure of Romans 1:18–32" in Middendorf, *Romans 1–8*, 113–14.

Paul depicts both Jews and Gentiles as "those who, out of self-centeredness, are unpersuaded [ἀπειθοῦσι] by the truth, but are persuaded [πειθομένοις] by the unrighteousness" (see also 2:9). This reveals "one reason why God's wrath falls on both Jew and Gentile alike" (e.g., 1:18; 3:9, 19–20; see also 11:32).[205]

The "but now" in the middle of 11:30 announces that those Gentiles who believe in Christ are "now … shown mercy" (νῦν δὲ ἠλεήθητε). This marks a dramatic shift

> from the era when Gentiles were "alienated from the commonwealth of Israel, and strangers to the covenants of promise, having no hope and without God in the world" (Eph. 2:12b) to the present era in which God's righteousness has been manifested "for all who believe," whether Jew or Gentile ([Rom] 1:16; 3:22; 10:11–13).[206]

Unpersuaded in Israel (11:30b)

The final phrase of 11:30 says that this occurred "by the unpersuadedness [ἀπειθείᾳ] of these ones." It should continually be pointed out that many Jews did believe the Gospel.[a] But "these ones" (τούτων) in 11:30 refers specifically to those Jews who refused to be persuaded in regard to the Good News of Christ. This is the sense of the noun ἀπείθεια in 11:30, as well as the *active* form of the verb ἀπειθέω in 11:31.[207] Note that the forms of ἀπειθέω in 10:21 (ἀπειθοῦντα), as well as in Acts 14:2 and Acts 19:9, are all in the *active* voice. Thus they convey an *active rejection* of the message. Faith comes from passive hearing, but humans can choose to refuse to believe what they hear. Thus "they did not all listen responsively to" or believe the Word of Christ which they heard (οὐ πάντες ὑπήκουσαν, 10:16; cf. 10:17; 11:20, 23; "not all" is equivalent to the "some" in 3:3; 11:17).

Translating with "the disobedience of these ones" and "they were disobedient" in 11:30–31 can create the mistaken impression that the critical problem stems specifically from a failure to obey, that is, to do the works of the Law (cf. 10:5). Various church fathers who perceived that to be the issue then misdiagnosed the reason why some in Israel are enemies of God (11:28), attributing it to "their wickedness"[208] and "their sins,"[209] as if they were greater transgressors of God's commandments than others were. But if moral wickedness separated one from God's mercy, all would stand apart from it forever (1:18; 3:9, 23). Furthermore, the avenue of righteousness pursued via obedient works does not simply lead into a misleading and futile dead end (3:20, 28; 9:32), but it also

[205] Moo, *Romans*, 733.

[206] Moo, *Romans*, 733.

[207] Although the forms of ἀπειθέω in 11:30 (ἠπειθήσατε) and 11:31 (ἠπείθησαν) may at first appear passive, the θ is part of the root; see the first textual note on 11:30.

[208] Cyril of Alexandria, *Romans*; Ambrosiaster, *Romans* (Bray, *Romans*, ACCS NT 6:291, 295).

[209] Chrysostom, *Homilies on Romans*, 19 (Bray, *Romans*, ACCS NT 6:292).

(a) E.g., Acts 2:41; 4:4; 6:7; 13:43; 14:1; 17:4, 12; 18:4, 8; 19:8, 10; 28:17–24

results in tripping or stumbling over the true source of God's mercy (9:32–33; 10:3–4; 11:7a, 11).

Unpersuaded Equals Unbelieving

Paul repeatedly stresses that the critical issue remains *a specific sin, that of unbelief* (3:3; 10:16; 11:11, 20, 23).[210] Instead of hearing the Good News and listening responsively to it, believing it, acknowledging it, and being persuaded by it (10:9, 16–17), Paul depicts some Jews as being actively "unpersuaded and contradicting" (ἀπειθοῦντα καὶ ἀντιλέγοντα, 10:21; see also 11:31). But, once again, that unpersuadedness in response to the Gospel has resulted in the message of mercy going out to the Gentiles who have now received mercy as a result of the Word of Christ being sent out and proclaimed to them (10:14–17). This chronological sequence occurs repeatedly during Paul's missionary journeys in Acts (e.g., Acts 13:44–47; 14:1–3; 18:4–7; 19:8–10; 28:23–29) and is encapsulated in Rom 1:16, "to Jew first and also to Greek." Rom 11:30, therefore, reiterates what Paul reveals about the mystery in 11:25. *Due to the rejection and hardening of some unbelieving Jews, Gentiles are shown mercy and, thereby, "come in" (11:25).*

Ambrosiaster and Pelagius both affirm this understanding of ἀπείθεια and ἀπειθέω in 11:30–31:

> Paul recalls the unbelief of the Gentiles so that being ashamed of it they may not insult the Jews who have not believed but rejoice when they accept the promise of God.[211]

> To consign everything to disobedience means that this decree comes as a gift from God at a time when everyone was laboring in unbelief, so that grace might appear to be the freest of all rewards.[212]

> God has not imprisoned them by force, but for a good reason he has confined all those whom he found in unbelief, i.e., all Jews and Gentiles. He confined the Jews because previously they were only sinners, not faithless as well. But since they have not believed Christ they are equal to the Gentiles and receive mercy in the same way.[213]

---

[210] See the commentary on 11:11b. Pieper, *Christian Dogmatics*, 3:548, clarifies the point in this manner:

> Of course, all sins, original sin and actual sins, are indeed damnable in themselves … , and this truth must be urged against all who minimize sin; but in fact (*actu*) only unbelief results in damnation. This truth must be brought home to all who minimize the work of Christ, the complete reconciliation He brought about through His vicarious satisfaction. … But where unbelief reigns, all other sins again assume their condemnatory character [citing Mk 16:16; Jn 3:18, 36].

[211] Ambrosiaster, *Romans* (Bray, *Romans*, ACCS NT 6:300).

[212] Ambrosiaster, *Romans* (Bray, *Romans*, ACCS NT 6:301).

[213] Pelagius, *Romans* (Bray, *Romans*, ACCS NT 6:301).

God's Present Merciful Response (11:31)

Rom 11:31 summarizes how God reacts to the response of unbelief by some in Israel (as in 10:19–11:12). Initially, it benefitted Gentile believers ("for your mercy," τῷ ὑμετέρῳ ἐλέει, 11:31a),[214] a great good in and of itself (10:20; 11:11–12, 15). Yet God intends that bestowing his mercy on Gentiles will further serve his "how much more" (11:12, 24) purpose, "in order that they might also now be shown mercy" (11:31b). Paul perceives that his own ministry to the Gentiles promotes this: "[so that] if, somehow, I might provoke my flesh to envy, I will also save some from them" (11:14; cf. 10:19; 11:11; 1 Cor 9:20, 22). Paul's fervent hope aligns with God's intended result, that mercy might be received by "the fullness of them" as well (Rom 11:12, 15, 24).

While the "now" (νῦν) in the second half of 11:31 (the third "now" in 11:30–31) is textually disputed, its inclusion seem likely.[215] *The repeated presence of "now" seriously challenges those who contend that Paul expects a uniquely spectacular end-time reversal* which includes "a great future conversion of Jews."[216] On the contrary, these Gospel uses of "now" describe the entire NT era, "the time which begins with the gospel events and extends to the Parousia"[217] (as with νῦν in 3:26; 5:9, 11; 8:1; 11:5; 16:26). As Paul says in 2 Cor 6:2: "Look! *Now* [νῦν] [is the] acceptable time. Look! *Now* [νῦν] [is the] day of salvation."

Furthermore, the ἵνα clause at the end of Rom 11:31 conveys divine *intent*: "in order that they might also now be shown mercy." However, the possibility expressed with the subjunctive verb, "they *might* be shown mercy" (ἐλεηθῶσιν; see the third textual note on 11:31), does not mean that God "has *pledged* ... to graft them again onto the olive tree."[218] Paul insists that God is certainly "powerful" to do so (δυνατός, 11:23) and "how much more" than willing to do so (πόσῳ μᾶλλον, 11:12; 24), but Paul modifies the statement "they *will* be grafted in" by the condition "*if* they do not remain in unbelief" (11:23).

Paul's Conclusion: God's Action toward All (11:32)

As Paul draws near to the end of the extraordinary discourse we call Romans 9–11, he utters this climactic and all-inclusive assertion:[219] "Indeed, God locked up all people into unpersuadedness in order that he might show mercy to all"

---

[214] See the second textual note on 11:31 for a discussion of where to attach this phrase, as well as the significance of its dative case.

[215] See the third textual note on 11:31. According to Schreiner, *Romans*, 628, the second "now" (νῦν) in 11:31 "is surely original"; similarly, though less emphatically, Dunn, *Romans*, 687; Käsemann, *Romans*, 316; Moo, *Romans*, 711, n. 2.

[216] As Moo, *Romans*, 735, maintains, though he later admits "that Paul's teaching about a final ingathering of Jewish people has no parallel elsewhere in his writings" (739).

[217] Cranfield, *Romans*, 586.

[218] As Schreiner, *Romans*, 627, contends (emphasis added).

[219] Cranfield, *Romans*, 586; Dunn, *Romans*, 689; Moo, *Romans*, 712; Schreiner, *Romans*, 629; see also the introduction to Romans 9–11.

(11:32). This verse also concisely encapsulates earlier themes. "As the ἀπείθεια ['unpersuadedness,' 11:32; also 11:30] sums up the first part of Paul's exposition (1:18–3:20), so the ἐλεέω ['show mercy,' 11:32; also 11:30–31] sums up the second (3:21–5:11)."[220] The repeated use of "all, everyone" (πᾶς) further heightens the universal applicability.[221]

> The "all" includes both parties in the preceding verses (you Gentiles, and Israel); Israel has been included in the blanket condemnation of humankind in order that humankind as a whole, including Israel, might be recipients of his mercy in its character as unconditional grace.[222]

However, this commentary has repeatedly emphasized that *the primary focus of Romans is not on humanity, but, rather, directs our attention toward God.*[223] This "final explanatory statement, as is appropriate, is about God" as well[224] and most immediately prompts the doxological assertions about him soon to follow in 11:33–36.

All Locked Up (11:32a)

"God locked up [συνέκλεισεν] all people" (11:32). This was a divine *reaction* to sinful humanity's inadequate response to the revelations of God in creation (1:18–32) and in his Word (2:1–3:20). Here the broader sense of "into unpersuadedness" (εἰς ἀπείθειαν) encompasses a disbelieving response to God's creative power (1:18–21), his work of the Law on heart and conscience (2:12–16), his revealed Law (2:17–29), and, at times, his Gospel promise as well (see the commentary on 11:30–31). Note, for example, in 1:18–32 that humanity first "exchanged" the glory of God (1:23) *before* God "gave them over" (1:24).[225] Note also that God did not *begin* by hardening Israel (or Pharaoh), but *only* did so to Pharaoh and to *some* in Israel after they refused to listen responsively to his good Word and saving will (see the commentary on 9:17–18; 10:16–17, 19; 11:7). *Thus "God locked up" is, in its broadest sense, a reaction to all of humanity's failures to hearken to him, to listen and respond appropriately in faith, to "obey" his Law, and to listen responsively to the call of his mercy.* God thus confirms and confines all "people in the state that they have chosen for

---

[220] Dunn, *Romans*, 689; similarly, Käsemann, *Romans*, 317.

[221] As also in 1:5, 16, 18; 2:9–10; 3:9, 19–20, 22–23; 4:11, 16; 5:12, 18; 10:4, 11–13. See Middendorf, *Romans 1–8*, 49–51.

[222] Dunn, *Romans*, 689.

[223] See Middendorf, *Romans 1–8*, 21–22, 27, 49–51; in this volume, see "Romans 1–4: The Righteousness of God" in the introduction to Romans 9–16, as well as "God" in "The Three Foci of Romans 9–11" in the introduction to Romans 9–11. See also the commentary on 1:17, 32; 2:11, 16, 29; 3:1–8, 19–20, 26, 29–30; 4:21; 9:5, 11b–12a, 16, 22–24, 29; 10:21; 11:1–2, 33–36; 12:19; 13:1–2; 14:10–12; 15:5, 8, 13; 16:25, 27.

[224] Wright, "Romans," 694; similarly, Kruse, *Romans*, 448; Schreiner, *Romans*, 629.

[225] Dunn, *Romans*, 689, misses this by referring only to the three uses of παραδίδωμι, "give over," in 1:24, 26, 28; he ignores that this divine action was always *preceded by* an inappropriate human action of "exchanging" (ἀλλάσσω, 1:23; μεταλλάσσω, 1:25, 26); see Middendorf, *Romans 1–8*, 113–14.

themselves"[226] and announces the resulting and impending consequences (e.g., 1:18, 32; 2:8–10; 3:19–20). All are locked up. And "all" means "all." Will "all" or any then receive mercy?

The parallel use of "lock up" (συγκλείω) in Gal 3:22–23 is similarly all-encompassing and helpful in filling out Paul's thought here:[227]

[22]ἀλλὰ συνέκλεισεν ἡ γραφὴ τὰ πάντα ὑπὸ ἁμαρτίαν, ἵνα ἡ ἐπαγγελία ἐκ πίστεως Ἰησοῦ Χριστοῦ δοθῇ τοῖς πιστεύουσιν.

[23]πρὸ τοῦ δὲ ἐλθεῖν τὴν πίστιν ὑπὸ νόμον ἐφρουρούμεθα συγκλειόμενοι εἰς τὴν μέλλουσαν πίστιν ἀποκαλυφθῆναι.

[22]But the Scripture locked up all things under sin, in order that the promise from [the] faith of/in Jesus Christ might be given to those who believe.

[23]But before the faith came, we were being guarded by the Law, while locked up toward the about-to-be-revealed faith.

Two aspects are worthy of comment. First, Galatians specifically delineates the role of the Law since it has become more problematic in the context of that region's churches (e.g., Gal 3:10–11; 5:2–4). But comparable effects of the Law have been repeatedly articulated in Romans. The work of the Law on heart and conscience (Rom 2:15) and the revealed Law (2:17) both have a role in explaining how God "locked up all people" here.[b] But Galatians, *like Romans,* emphasizes that, "although man had no ground for hope through the law,"[228] the actual imprisonment exists as bondage "under sin" (ὑπὸ ἁμαρτίαν, Gal 3:22; see also Rom 3:9; 5:20–21). Second, Galatians makes clear that the merciful resolution of this locked up condition does not require an eschatological event that will take place only later in the end times, but, rather, consists in a present *Christological* event, the revelation of faith.

(b) E.g., Rom 3:19–20; 4:15; 5:20; 7:7–11; 9:31–32; 10:3–5

Mercy in Christ for All (11:32b)

This Christological focus, affirmed also repeatedly in Romans (e.g., 3:21–22, 26; 10:4, 9, 17),[229] offers the proper response to the assertion that "in order that he might show mercy to all" in 11:32 teaches universalism.[230] "Such a

---

[226] Moo, *Romans,* 736. Cf. the responsive actions of God depicted by παρέδωκεν, "he gave over," in 1:24, 26, 28; see Middendorf, *Romans 1–8,* 113–14.

[227] See a complete exposition in Das, *Galatians,* 367–74.

[228] Ambrosiaster, *Romans* (Bray, *Romans,* ACCS NT 6:301). He adds: "The law was given so that the human race would be held back by the fear engendered by the revealed law. But because they did not restrain themselves and were counted guilty under the law, mercy was proclaimed" (6:302).

[229] Moo, *Romans,* 726; see the block quote of Moo, *Romans,* 725–26, in "A Separate Way Is Rejected in Romans" in the commentary on 11:26a.

[230] Dunn, *Romans,* 689, contends that "it certainly does not exclude universalism"; similarly, Cranfield, *Romans,* 588. Dodd, *Romans,* 187, sees all "humanity redeemed"; Christ certainly has "redeemed" all humanity in an objective sense, but only believers are "redeemed" in a subjective sense, that is, justified through faith. See the distinction between objective and subjective justification in the footnote on that topic in "The Rescuer and Zion: 'To,' 'For the Sake of,' and 'From'" above. See also Middendorf, *Romans 1–8,* 403, 432.

conclusion is obviously contradictory to Paul's teaching elsewhere."[231] Murray explains:

> In verse 32 the emphasis falls upon that which is common to all without distinction, that they are shut up to unbelief and fit objects for that reason of *mercy.* ... Thus "mercy upon all" means all without distinction who are the partakers of this mercy.[232]

This echoes 9:22–23, which maintains *both* God's wrath *and* mercy but also emphasizes his patient desire to have mercy on all those still under his wrath:

> [22]And [who are you to talk back] if God, willing to demonstrate [his] wrath and to make known his [saving] power, bore with much patience vessels of wrath which have been fitted for and are headed toward destruction, [23]and in order to make known the abundance of his glory upon vessels of mercy which he prepared beforehand for glory ... ?

As Paul reaffirms in 11:22, God's kindness does not eliminate his severity. Since he does not force his mercy on people, those who reject it face the reality and severity of his wrath. But God's desire to show mercy to all provides great assurance to all those who both need and receive it through faith in Christ. "You see, there is not a difference, for all sinned and are lacking the glory of God, while being declared righteous undeservedly by his grace through the redemption, the one in Christ Jesus" (3:22b–24).

Implications of Romans 11:32 in the Letter

First, 11:32 resolves Paul's earlier open-ended statement that "[to] whom he wills he shows mercy and whom he wills he hardens" (9:18). *The question of "whom" has now been decisively answered: God desires to show mercy to "all"* (πάντας, 11:32), "for there is no partiality in the presence of God" (προσωπολημψία, 2:11). Romans 9–11 has shown that God responds with hardening only toward those who repeatedly reject his merciful call (see the commentary on 9:17–18; 11:7, 25).

The repeated "all" (πάντας) in 11:32 has a *second,* salutary effect. It negates any problematic doubts regarding election which purport to restrict God's mercy to a "requisite portion."[233] As characteristic throughout Romans, *God remains the primary subject and actor.*[234] *In 11:32 he does both of the active verbs and includes "all" people as the object of both verbs.* The Formula of Concord concludes:

---

[231] Moo, *Romans*, 736. See, e.g., Rom 1:32; 2:8–9, 12, 16; 3:6; 5:9; 1 Thess 5:3; 2 Thess 2:7–10.

[232] Murray, *Romans*, 2:103.

[233] Keener, *Romans*, 133, uses the phrase.

[234] See Middendorf, *Romans 1–8*, 21–22, 27, 49–51; in this volume, see "Romans 1–4: The Righteousness of God" in the introduction to Romans 9–16, as well as "God" in "The Three Foci of Romans 9–11" in the introduction to Romans 9–11. See also the commentary on 1:17, 32; 2:11, 16, 29; 3:1–8, 19–20, 26, 29–30; 4:21; 9:5, 11b–12a, 16, 22–24, 29; 10:21; 11:1–2, 33–36; 12:19; 13:1–2; 14:10–12; 15:5, 8, 13; 16:25, 27.

Hence if we want to consider our eternal election to salvation profitably, we must by all means cling rigidly and firmly to the fact that as the proclamation of repentance extends over all men (Luke 24:47), so also does the promise of Gospel. (FC SD XI 28, citing in this order Jn 3:16; 1:29; 6:51; 1 Jn 1:7; 2:2; Mt 11:28; Rom 11:32; 2 Pet 3:9; Rom 10:12; 3:22; Jn 6:40; Lk 24:47 again; Mk 16:15)[235]

Finally, looking ahead in the letter, Paul's theological assertions about God's mercy for all are soon to be applied in Rom 14:1–15:7 to the current divisions among Jews and Gentiles in Rome (see the introduction to Romans 9–16 and the introduction to 14:1–15:13). There Paul will demonstrate how then, as now, "a Christianity which takes the 'all' seriously cannot operate with any kind of ethnic, national, cultural, or racial particularism or exclusiveness."[236]

This provides a critical criterion for evaluating the interpretations of 11:25–26 discussed above. It also *excludes* statements like this which contradict Paul's assertion of God's impartiality in 2:11:

> Yet in chap. 11 Paul seems to smuggle back into salvation history the principle of ethnic privilege that he excludes in chap. 9 and elsewhere: Jews, just because they are Jews, can look forward to a time when a great number of them are saved.[237]

It is also confusing, if not contradictory, to argue that a sequential or chronological "oscillation between the salvation of the Jews, then the Gentiles, and then the Jews again hammers home the point that no ethnic group deserves salvation and that God's saving work is a result of his merciful grace."[238] On the contrary, "there are no exceptions—Jews and Gentiles are both in the same prison"; yet at the same time God's mercy in Christ is for "all alike."[239] As a result, Paul repeatedly insists that before God no difference exists between Jew and Gentile (e.g., 3:22–24; 10:11–13; cf. also 1:16; 2:11; 3:9, 28–30; Gal 3:26–29; Ephesians 2–3). He will soon exhort the Roman Christians, and believers ever since, to manifest a similar impartiality toward one another in their life together in Christ.

Wrapping Up Romans 9–11

As discussed in the introduction to Romans 9–11, these chapters are not a stand-alone piece, nor are they in any way out of step with the rest of the letter. Instead, *these chapters skillfully draw out the implications of what the letter's*

---

[235] For the Lutheran understanding of the biblical teaching of election versus Calvinistic double predestination, see "God" in the introduction to Romans 9–11; "Not 'Hated,' but 'Spurned'" and "What Paul Does *Not* Say" in the commentary on 9:6–13; "Is This Fair to the Pharaoh? (9:17–18)" and "Thou Art the Potter; We All Are like Clay (9:19–21)" in the commentary on 9:14–24; the introduction to 9:30–10:15; and the commentary on 11:5. See also the entirety of FC SD XI and FC Ep XI.

[236] Dunn, *Romans*, 689.

[237] Moo, *Romans*, 737.

[238] As Schreiner, *Romans*, 629, maintains.

[239] Kruse, *Romans*, 448, who adds: "What Paul is saying in this verse [11:32] is no different in essence from what he said back in 3:22–24."

opening chapters teach about the place of Jews and Gentiles among the NT people of God. Paul directly applies these words to those to whom he writes in Rome (1:6) and, as 11:32 concisely demonstrates, to "all."

The culminating and all-encompassing nature of this section becomes particularly clear as it reaches its conclusion. Paul draws together Romans 9–11, while adroitly recapturing and, thereby, reasserting the bulk of his argument from earlier in the letter. Dunn, for example, illustrates the culminating character of 11:28–32 as follows:

> The use of ἐκλογή ["choice/chosen"], κλῆσις ["calling"], and ἐλεέω/ ἔλεος ["show mercy"/"mercy"] gather together the key elements and main thrust of chaps. 9–11 (ἐκλογή ["choice/chosen"]—9:11; 11:5, 7; καλέω/κλῆσις ["call"/"calling"]—9:7, 12, 24–26; ἐλεέω/ἔλεος ["show mercy"/"mercy"]—9:15–16, 18, 23). The repeated contrasts between ἀπειθέω/ ἀπείθεια ["be unpersuaded"/"unpersuadedness"] and ἐλεέω/ἔλεος ["show mercy"/"mercy"] (4 times in vv. 30–32) rehearses in summary form the indictment of 1:18–3:20 ("shut up in disobedience") and the resolution of 3:21–5:11 ("have mercy"). And v. 32 repeats with breathtaking brevity the conclusion of 5:12–21.[240]

Paul teaches us about humanity and preeminently about God himself throughout the letter. God locked up all; God desires to show mercy to all and does so in Christ. Thus in 11:32 "that for which Paul has contended throughout the epistle receives its crowning and seal."[241] All who hear this message are driven to marvel at the astounding ways of God and to respond with worshipful adoration which most fittingly attributes all glory to him.

Doxology (11:33–36)

Content and Structure

It may be best at this point to simply let Paul's resounding conclusion speak for itself. However, some comments may help those who hear these remarkable verses to appreciate their profound meaning even further.

The most distinguishing structural component comes from the *three triads*. First, 11:33 rejoices in the "riches and wisdom and knowledge" of God. Second, 11:34–35 contains three rhetorical questions, each of whose implied answer is "no one." Third, 11:36 contains three prepositions, "from … through … to," each with the third person pronoun "him," referring to God. All three of these triads led church fathers such as Origen, Ambrosiaster, and Augustine to interpret the passage in Trinitarian terms.[242] While a plausible application, these readings go beyond the literal sense of the text.

---

[240] Dunn, *Romans*, 677; similarly, Käsemann, *Romans*, 317.

[241] Nygren, *Romans*, 408.

[242] Origen, *Romans*; Ambrosiaster, *Romans*; Augustine, *Faith and the Creed*, 16 (Bray, *Romans*, ACCS NT 6:303–4).

What Paul does say about God here, however, should *not* lead one to dwell on his "freedom,"[243] his "unknowability,"[244] or some apocalyptic and obscure transcendence.[245] Instead, the immediately preceding verses, where words for "mercy" occur four times (11:30–32; cf. 12:1), indicate that this doxological section primarily engages in, to borrow a phrase from Pelagius, "magnifying God's mercy."[246] In this way, "the *theo*logical breadth of the assurance expressed at the end of chaps. 9–11 appropriately matches the *Christo*logical focus of the assurance expressed at the end of chaps. 6–8" (e.g., 6:23; 7:25; 8:39; note also 4:24; 5:1, 11, 21).[247] Of course the benediction uttered in 9:5, most likely to Christ as "the One being over all, blessed God into the ages. Amen!" forms a *more obvious frame* with 11:33–36 for chapters 9–11.

Together these observations diminish the persuasiveness of Stendahl's claim:

> It is stunning to note that Paul writes this whole section of Romans (10:17–11:36) without using the name of Jesus Christ. This includes the final doxology (11:33–36), the only such doxology in his writings without any christological element.[248]

Furthermore, one should readily recall the numerous references to the Lord Jesus Christ in Romans 9–11 (e.g., 9:5; 10:4, 6, 7, 9, 13, 17; cf. also 9:33; 10:11). Moo also counters Stendahl's assertion by reminding us that

> Paul has defined the faith he is talking about here quite adequately in the first ten chapters of the letter. ... Faith is inextricably tied to Jesus and his resurrection victory (10:9), and it is this faith that brings salvation to Gentile and Jew alike.[249]

Sources(?)

While commenting on the style of 11:33–36, Cranfield also prompts us to consider possible sources for the doxology:

> Their [the verses'] poetic character is apparent. That this hymn was composed by Paul as a conclusion to this division of his epistle is far more probable than that he was taking over an already existing hymn; but in composing it he has freely borrowed from several sources, from the OT, perhaps also

---

[243] Cranfield, *Romans*, 589; Moo, *Romans*, 738.

[244] Dunn, *Romans*, 700.

[245] Dunn, *Romans*, 700, refers to apocalyptic parallels which deal with times in Israel's history "when the ruling purpose of God must have appeared especially obscure."

[246] Pelagius, *Romans* (Bray, *Romans*, ACCS NT 6:303).

[247] Dunn, *Romans*, 698; see Middendorf, *Romans 1–8*, 377–80, for the thematic significance of phrases about Jesus Christ our Lord throughout Romans 5–8.

[248] Stendahl, "Paul among Jews and Gentiles," 4.

[249] Moo, *Romans*, 726, citing also 1:16; 3:22, 26; 10:4–13. See the block quote of Moo, *Romans*, 725–26, in "A Separate Way Is Rejected in Romans" in the commentary on 11:26a.

from extra-biblical apocalyptic, from Hellenistic Judaism, from Stoicism as mediated through Hellenistic Judaism, and from the language of worship.[250]

Dunn concurs on the Pauline composition of the doxology and also insightfully links it with Paul's letters to Corinth, the place from which he writes Romans.[251] This is especially evident in the opening two lines of 11:33. Paul uses "depth" (βάθος, 11:33) in a manner comparable to its plural in 1 Cor 2:10, where "the Spirit searches out everything, including the deep things of God" (τὰ βάθη τοῦ θεοῦ, 1 Cor 2:10).[252] Paul then uses "wisdom" (σοφία) for the only time in Romans, a word he employs seventeen times in 1 Corinthians.[253] The noun for "knowledge" (γνῶσις) in Rom 11:33 occurs two other times in Romans (2:20; 15:14), but a total of sixteen times in 1 and 2 Corinthians. Finally, Paul's concluding verse closely parallels 1 Cor 8:6 (see below).

God's Unfathomable Magnitude (11:33a)

Paul begins: "O [the] depth of [the] *riches* and *wisdom* and *knowledge* of God" (11:33a). The three italicized genitives identify the profundity of God's attributes. "The combination of the two metaphors (depth and riches) jars at first, but increases the force of the imagery (a treasury which has no bottom)."[254]

In light of the noun for "riches" (πλοῦτος) also in 2:4; 9:23; and especially 11:12, it "connotes especially God's kindness as it is expressed in the blessing he brings on undeserving sinners—both Jew and Gentile alike."[255] It is followed by Paul's only reference to "wisdom" (σοφία) in Romans. But the term has an extensive background. "The wisdom of God in creation, revelation, and redemption is a focal topic," particularly in "wisdom literature."[256] See, for example, Job 12; 28; 38:2, 36–37; Psalm 19; Pss 90:12; 104:24; 111:10; the books of Proverbs and Ecclesiastes; Daniel 2. Along with God's "wisdom," Paul refers to the depth of his "knowledge" (γνῶσις); he pairs these nouns also in Col 2:3. The term goes beyond intellectual knowledge. As emphasized in regard to the related verb "know relationally beforehand" (προγινώσκω) in Rom 8:29 and 11:2 (see the commentary on those verses), "knowledge" conveys God's relational knowing of his people, a concept firmly rooted in Hebrew terminology, including the verb "know" (יָדַע, e.g., Gen 18:19; Ex 2:25; 3:7; Is 43:10; Jer 1:5) and the noun "knowledge" (דַּעַת, e.g., Ex 31:3; Is 11:2; 53:11; Hos 4:6; 6:6; Prov 1:7; 2:6).

---

[250] Cranfield, *Romans*, 589.

[251] Dunn, *Romans*, 698–99; for Paul's location in Corinth, see Middendorf, *Romans 1–8*, 5–7.

[252] Lockwood, *1 Corinthians*, 97; see also 100, 104.

[253] Moo, *Romans*, 741, n. 9, summarizes that Paul discusses "true Christian 'wisdom'" in 1 Cor. 1:17–2:16, a wisdom whose focus is the fulfillment of God's plan in the crucified Christ"; for a more thorough presentation, see Lockwood, *1 Corinthians*, 89–93.

[254] Dunn, *Romans*, 699, referencing Eph 2:7; 3:8.

[255] Moo, *Romans*, 741; see also Rev 5:12.

[256] Dunn, *Romans*, 699. For the wisdom theme in Jewish literature he cites Wisdom 7:15, 25–26; 9:2, 4, 6, 9, 17–18; 10:1; Sirach 1:1–10; 15:18; 42:21; *2 Enoch* 30:8; 33:3.

His Judgments and Ways (11:33b)

Paul continues with two synonymously parallel statements: "How unfathomable his judgments and incomprehensible his ways!" (11:33b). Here two obscure adjectives ("unfathomable" and "incomprehensible"; see the textual notes and below) describe two more common nouns, God's "judgments" and his "ways." In regard to the nouns, Paul first uses the plural form "judgments" (κρίματα), something he does only here and in 1 Cor 6:7 (note also LXX Pss 18:10 [MT 19:10; ET 19:9]; 35:7 [MT 36:7; ET 36:6]; 118:75 [MT/ET 119:75]).[257] Thus it likely serves a broader function than the singular form used elsewhere in Romans for divine "judgment" (2:2, 3; 3:8; 5:16; 13:2). The LXX reinforces this, since it regularly uses the Greek nouns κρίσις and κρίμα, "judgment; justice," to translate the Hebrew noun מִשְׁפָּט, "judgment; justice; justification,"[258] and thereby these Greek terms convey the broader covenantal connotations of that Hebrew word in the OT.[259] The forensic connotations of "judgments" (κρίματα) also recall the predominant use of courtroom language throughout Romans 1–4, as well as in 9:30–10:5.[260] The parallel reference to "his ways" (αἱ ὁδοὶ αὐτοῦ, 11:33) expresses a comparable OT concept as well, as in phrases such as "the way of the Lord."[261]

There is certainly much here which surpasses all human understanding (cf. Phil 4:7). Yet in light of all that Paul has written thus far in Romans, the two rare adjectives which modify these nouns do not simply leave us clueless about God's judgments and ways.[262] Instead, the first, "unfathomable" (ἀνεξεραύνητα), means that we cannot "fathom" the "depth" (βάθος) of his judgments. They involve *more than* judicial activity; God's decisions *also* put his riches, wisdom, and knowledge on public display and impart them to us in Christ (11:33a). Relevant here is "this mystery" (11:25), which now has been revealed as the inclusion of Gentiles on equal footing with Jews in the "all

---

[257] Moo, *Romans*, 742, n. 15; however, his use of "'executive' decisions" (742) sounds a bit too corporate.

[258] See, e.g., MT and LXX Ex 23:6; 28:15; Lev 19:15, 35; 25:18; Num 27:5; Deut 1:17; 4:5; Is 5:7; Amos 5:7, 15, 24; 6:12; see Middendorf, *Romans 1–8*, 92–93.

[259] BDB, 2, defines מִשְׁפָּט as an "attribute of the שֶׁפֶט, *justice, right, rectitude*." This captures the sense here in regard to God (cf. Rom 3:26). For a clear example of מִשְׁפָּט meaning "justification" in Christ, that is, the "justice" that is brought by the Suffering Servant and that is the basis for the salvation and faith even of Gentiles, see Is 42:1, 3, 4, where the LXX translates it with κρίσις, commonly, but sometimes infelicitously, rendered in English as "judgment."

[260] For a brief overview, see Middendorf, *Romans 1–8*, 341.

[261] See, e.g., Gen 18:19; Ex 33:13; Deut 26:17–18; Pss 5:8 (MT 5:9); 18:21 (MT 18:22); 25:4, 8, 10, 12; 27:11; 128:1; 145:17; Prov 10:29; Is 2:3; 26:8; 40:3; Jer 6:16; Micah 4:2. Cf. Dunn, *Romans*, 699.

[262] The Formula of Concord echoes this sentiment in regard to the topic of election:

> After a lengthy discussion of this article on the basis of the revealed Word of God, as soon as he comes to the point where he shows how much of this mystery God has reserved for his own hidden wisdom, Paul immediately commands silence and cuts off further discussion with the following words: [Rom 11:33–34 is then cited]. (FC SD XI 64)

Israel" that "will be saved" (11:26) through the "covenant" of the forgiveness of sins (11:27).

The second adjective, "incomprehensible" (ἀνεξιχνίαστοι), portrays God's "ways" as beyond comprehension *from our human perspective* in a manner which leaves us astounded and amazed. The last line of 11:33 serves to extol God's mercy—his way of providing salvation in Christ—as something beyond human understanding, yet also something we receive through faith.

While not quoted, the thought of Is 55:6–9 expresses the same progression that Paul articulates in a *remarkably similar manner*. Isaiah declares:

> ⁶Seek Yahweh while he allows himself to be found!
> Call on him while he is near!
> ⁷Let the unbeliever abandon his way,
> and [let] a man of wickedness [abandon] his thoughts,
>> and let him turn to Yahweh, and he will show him mercy,
>> and [let him turn] to our God, because he will abundantly forgive.
> ⁸"Because my plans are not your plans,
> and your ways are not my ways,"
>> utters Yahweh.
> ⁹"Because as the heavens are higher than the earth,
>> so my ways are higher than your ways
>> and my plans [are higher] than your plans."²⁶³

Consider these commonalities:

- Paul describes how the Word of faith and of Christ draws near to us (10:8, 17); Isaiah 55:6 similarly announces that Yahweh "allows himself to be found" and that "he is near" (see also Is 65:1, quoted in Rom 10:20).
- Rom 11:32 summarizes how God rightly locked up all people due to their "unpersuadedness" toward God; Isaiah speaks similarly of human unbelief in Yahweh's promises and of wickedness which violates his Law (Is 55:7).
- Paul then announces that God's mercy is nevertheless secured by Christ for all (Rom 11:32); Isaiah similarly assures those who turn to Yahweh that they will receive abundant mercy and forgiveness (Is 55:7).

Together these thoughts combine to demonstrate how God's "plans" and "ways are higher" than ours (Is 55:9; cf. Ps 103:1–12). *Above all, his forgiveness remains "unfathomable" and his mercy "incomprehensible" (Rom 11:33), yet they are ours through faith in Christ.*

Who? No One! (Is 40:13 and 41:11 in Rom 11:34–35)

Paul then asks three rhetorical questions, all of which assume the answer "no one." The *first two* comprise Rom 11:34: "Indeed, who knew [the] mind of [the] Lord? Or who has become his counselor?" Dunn observes that "similar thoughts are expressed in Job 15:8; Isa 55:8–9; and Jer 23:18" and that such rhetorical questions are found not only in the OT (e.g., Ps 106:2; Jer 10:7) but

---

²⁶³ The translation is from Lessing, *Isaiah 40–55*, 649; for his exposition, see 654–55 and 665–66.

also in later Jewish literature (Sirach 16:20; Wisdom 9:16–17; 11:21; Pss Sol 5:3, 12; 15:2; *1 Enoch* 93:11–14; *2 Baruch* 14:8–9).[264] More specific to Rom 11:34 is that, aside from adding "indeed" (γάρ), changing "and" (καί) to "or" (ἤ), and transposing two words, this verse replicates LXX Is 40:13. Although the context is different, Paul also cites Is 40:13 in 1 Cor 2:16 in order to pose the same question. There he provides a powerful answer: "But we have the mind of Christ" (1 Cor 2:16). Moo inserts that thought into Rom 11:34 as well:

> Since Paul sees Christ as the embodiment of wisdom, we are probably justified in adding to our expected answer "no one" a qualification: "no one, except Jesus Christ, who has revealed to us in his own person the plan of God for salvation history."[265]

Since, however, the questions remain unanswered in Rom 11:34, they express the totality of the *divine origin of all God has done for us and for our salvation* (Nicene Creed). The Lord's saving mercy proceeds solely from his mind and is based upon his own counsel alone without any influence, coercion, persuasion, or dependence upon human involvement. Both 11:35 and 11:36 reinforce the point further.

Paul asks a *third and final* rhetorical question in 11:35: "And who has given previously to him so that it should be repaid to him?" Here Paul appears to be quoting Job 41:11 (MT/LXX 41:3), but his Greek differs considerably from that of the LXX. LXX Job 41:3 (ET 41:11) is followed by the text in Rom 11:35:

ἢ τίς ἀντιστήσεταί μοι καὶ ὑπομενεῖ;

Or who will oppose me and will endure? (LXX Job 41:3 [MT 41:3; ET 41:11])

ἢ τίς προέδωκεν αὐτῷ, καὶ ἀνταποδοθήσεται αὐτῷ; (Rom 11:35)

Paul may be relying on a different text or translating directly from the Hebrew of Job 41:3 (ET 41:11): מִי הִקְדִּימַנִי וַאֲשַׁלֵּם, "who came before me [with a gift] so that I should have to repay [him for his gift]?" In that verse God goes on to say, "Everything under heaven is mine," which further supports Paul's use of the citation in the context of Romans 11, as also does the larger context in Job.[266]

---

[264] Dunn, *Romans*, 700.

[265] Moo, *Romans*, 743; see also 1 Cor 1:24, 30.

[266] Dunn, *Romans*, 701, considers the text "not-altogether-clear Hebrew"; see also Moo, *Romans*, 742, n. 19. However, the Hebrew text is lucid and readily understandable in its context; see the first textual note on 11:35. In the larger context Job and his friends have argued about the wisdom and justice of God and why Job is enduring such protracted suffering at the hands of God. Finally in Job 38–41 Yahweh himself speaks to Job of his own unfathomable wisdom and actions. Yet these are not random; they are part of his overarching purpose of redemption. To illustrate, Yahweh depicts the sea monster Leviathan (Job 41:1–34 [MT 40:25–41:26]), first introduced in Job 3:8; this dragon is supremely terrifying and dangerous ("on earth is not his equal," Job 41:33 [MT 41:25]). Only God is able to subdue him to save people from him. See the similar depictions of Leviathan in Is 27:1; Ps 74:14. Thus, when Yahweh queries Job in Job 41:11 (MT/LXX 41:3), he is highlighting Job's inability to contribute to his salvation; it is all God's doing, in harmony with Paul's theme in Romans.

Cranfield accurately perceives that "the purpose of the quotation is to underline the impossibility of a man's putting God in his debt."[267] We can lay no claim on God to benefit us in any way. Instead, *in our relationship with God, everything comes from God to us and in no way depends upon our initiative or works* (cf. 9:11b–12a, 16; 9:30–10:5). The financial expression[268] of 11:35 recalls what Paul draws out from Abraham's relationship with God, something foundational for all who follow in "the footsteps of the faith of our father Abraham" (4:12):

> [4]Now to the one who works, the payment is not credited as a favor, but according to what is owed. [5]But to the one who is not working, but believing on the One who declares the ungodly righteous, his faith is being credited for righteousness.[269] (4:4–5)

A Resounding and All-Inclusive Declaration of Praise (11:36)

Paul, therefore, appropriately concludes Romans 9–11 by speaking of God as the source of all things (ἐκ, "from"), the one "through" (διά) whom all things come to us, and the one toward whom all things are headed (εἰς, "to"), including also the remaining chapters of this great letter (see 16:27). Rom 11:36 pronounces:

> Because all things [are] from him and through him and to him.
> To him [is] the glory into the ages. Amen!

This final verse of Romans 11 has numerous intriguing parallels. Dunn lists eight of them, demonstrating that "the use of prepositions like 'from,' 'through,' and 'to' when speaking of God and the cosmos ('all things') was widespread in the ancient world and typically Stoic."[270] The second-century AD Stoic Marcus Aurelius provides an example subsequent to Paul: "From you are all things, in you are all things, for you are all things" (ἐκ σοῦ πάντα, ἐν σοὶ πάντα, εἰς σὲ πάντα).[271] Moo postulates that "Hellenistic Jews picked up this [Stoic] language and applied it to Yahweh; and it is probably, therefore, from the synagogue that Paul borrows this formula."[272] Even if that is true about the phraseology, however, Stoic thought is far removed from Paul's.[273]

The most helpful parallels come from Paul himself. In 1 Cor 8:6 he speaks distinctly of God the Father and the Lord Jesus in this manner:

---

[267] Cranfield, *Romans*, 591.

[268] Banking/finance is one of Paul's Gospel metaphors. See "Banking/Finance" in the excursus "Paul's Gospel Metaphors" following the commentary on 4:1–12 (Middendorf, *Romans 1–8*, 344).

[269] See Middendorf, *Romans 1–8*, 327–29.

[270] Dunn, *Romans*, 701.

[271] Marcus Aurelius, *Meditations*, 4.23, quoted from Moo, *Romans*, 743, n. 28; see also Dunn, *Romans*, 701.

[272] Moo, *Romans*, 743.

[273] For more on the similarities and fundamental contrasts between Paul and Stoicism, see Kruse, *Romans*, 486–89; see also "Introduction to Romans 12:9–21" in this commentary.

ἀλλ᾽ ἡμῖν εἷς θεὸς ὁ πατὴρ ἐξ οὗ τὰ πάντα καὶ ἡμεῖς εἰς αὐτόν, καὶ εἷς κύριος Ἰησοῦς Χριστὸς δι᾽ οὗ τὰ πάντα καὶ ἡμεῖς δι᾽ αὐτοῦ.

But for us [there is] one God, the Father, from whom [are] all things and we are for him, and one Lord Jesus Christ, through whom [are] all things and we [are] through him.

Col 1:16–17 then attributes all of this to Jesus Christ himself:

[16]ὅτι ἐν αὐτῷ ἐκτίσθη τὰ πάντα … · τὰ πάντα δι᾽ αὐτοῦ καὶ εἰς αὐτὸν ἔκτισται· [17]καὶ αὐτός ἐστιν πρὸ πάντων καὶ τὰ πάντα ἐν αὐτῷ συνέστηκεν.

[16]Because in him all things were created … ; all things have been created and exist through and to him; [17]and he himself is before all things, and all things stand together in him.

As the Nicene Creed aptly demonstrates, one need not drive any wedge between the Father and the Son here.[274] Paul effectively demonstrates that what he states of each can appropriately be attributed to both.

Conclusion

Romans 9–11 contains some of the deepest thoughts and some of the most contested passages in all of the NT. This commentary has endeavored to interpret these chapters within the context of the letter as faithfully as possible, while always humbly acknowledging human uncertainty and a limited perspective. As a result, the interpretations offered here, together with all those which have gone before, probably have not articulated all the answers convincingly or resolved the numerous matters of dispute to everyone's satisfaction.

Yet Paul himself demonstrates the most adequate response. As one considers the all-encompassing salvific work of God in Christ throughout history, Paul concludes by leading us in reverent and joyful praise (11:33–36). *Soli Deo gloria!* Then, "if we have followed him through these chapters with serious and open-minded attentiveness, we may well feel that he has given us enough to enable us to repeat the 'Amen' of his doxology."[275]

---

[274] See Middendorf, "The Bud Has Flowered: Trinitarian Theology in the New Testament," 298–300; Toon, *Our Triune God*, 113–30, discusses this more fully in a chapter titled "Mutation in Monotheism."

[275] Cranfield, *Romans*, 592.

Romans 12:1–16:27

From the Life God Gives (Romans 5–8) to the Life a Believer Lives (Romans 12–16)

Introduction to Romans 12–16: From the Life God Gives (Romans 5–8) to the Life a Believer Lives (Romans 12–16)

Faith and Life

Paul introduces the theme of this lengthy letter in 1:16–17:

> [16]For I am not ashamed of the Good News, because it is [the] power of God into salvation for everyone who believes, to Jew first and also to Greek. [17]For [the] righteousness of God is being revealed in it from faith[fullness?][1] into faith, just as it stands written: "But the righteous person will live from faith."

The key terms in Romans come from the quotation of Hab 2:4b: "righteous" (δίκαιος), "live" (ζάω), and "faith" (πίστις).[2] This commentary demonstrates how the interplay between these three words (and their cognates) dominates the development of thought in the letter. Note again the word counts first presented in the commentary on 1:17:[3]

Romans	1–4	5–8	9–11	12–16	Total
"Righteous(ness)" word group*	27	17	11	1	56
All "right-" terms	39	22	12	4	77
"Faith"/"believe" word group	37	3	16	10	66
"Live"/"life" word group	3	27	3	8	41

*A word group includes cognate nouns, adjectives, and verbs. The wider group of "right-" terms also counts compound words such as δικαιοκρισία, "righteous judgment" (2:5), negated terms such as ἀδικία, "unrighteousness" (e.g., 1:18), and other related forms. For the complete list with references, see Middendorf, *Romans 1–8*, 106.

Perhaps that interplay seems less obvious in Romans 12–16. The theme of "righteousness" appears to recede almost completely from Romans 12–16, much as "faith" terms did from chapters 5–8. In fact, the entire "righteousness" word

---

[1] For the possibility that "faithfulness" on God's part is an appropriate translation and understanding of Paul's intent, see "The Background and Meaning of 'Faith' Words" in the commentary on 1:16 (Middendorf, *Romans 1–8*, 88–90); "'From Faith[fulness] into Faith' (1:17)" on 96–98; and also the commentary on 3:3 (with "the faithfulness of God," ἡν πίστιν τοῦ θεοῦ) on 227–29.

[2] See Middendorf, *Romans 1–8*, 27–31. Note the difficulties English presents here since it lacks verbal cognates for the words "righteous" and "faith." Translations typically use forms of "justify" and "believe," respectively; for further details, see Middendorf, *Romans 1–8*, 88, 92.

[3] See Middendorf, *Romans 1–8*, 106–7.

group makes only one appearance (δικαιοσύνη, "righteousness," 14:17). In Romans 12–16, the other two terms are more influential. "Faith" words occur ten times and "life" ones a total of eight. Paul, therefore, discusses the interplay between faith and life.

"Life" terminology, however, occurs much more predominantly in Romans 5–8, appearing twenty-seven times. Beyond the simple matter of word counts, an even more critical distinction between Romans 5–8 and Romans 12–16 exists. The focus of the earlier chapters explains *the life God gives* in and through our Lord Jesus Christ.[4] Now Paul turns to elaborate upon *the life a believer lives*.[5] The dominant use of "life" words in Romans 5–8 expresses "the spiritual renewal or fullness of life in relationship with God through the life of our resurrected Lord Jesus (5:10, 17, 18, 21; 6:4, 10 [twice], 11, 13, 22, 23; 8:2, 6, 10, 13 [second occurrence])."[6] A few key examples are worth citing here:

> But where sin multiplied, grace overflowed above and beyond with the result that just as sin reigned in death, thus also grace might reign through righteousness to eternal life through Jesus Christ our Lord. (5:20b–21)

> Consequently, we were buried with him through this Baptism into [his] death, so that just as Christ was raised from [the] dead through the glory of the Father, thus also we might walk in life's renewal. (6:4)

> For the payment of sin is death, but the gracious gift of God is eternal life in Christ Jesus our Lord. (6:23)

> But since Christ is in you, on the one hand, the body is dead because of sin, and, on the other hand, the Spirit is life because of righteousness. (8:10)

This Gospel "now" already stands as a present reality. It began with Christ's own resurrection and then when his renewed life was given to us through Baptism into Christ (6:4), and it continues to be visible in our lives of service on earth. God's purpose, Paul says, is that through our baptismal life of suffering under the cross "the life of Jesus [ἡ ζωὴ τοῦ Ἰησοῦ] might be made visible in our bodies" (2 Cor 4:10; see also 2 Cor 4:8–9).

However, the "not yet" Paul articulates so powerfully in Romans 6–8 means that challenges still confront those who have been given a renewed life in Christ.[7] Nowhere does Paul demonstrate this so powerfully and personally as in 7:14–25. There we see Paul the believer striving to live according to God's will as revealed in his Law, but repeatedly and frustratingly falling short.[8] However,

---

[4] For an overview, see Middendorf, *Romans 1–8*, 377–80.

[5] Furnish nicely captures the interplay between the two sections with an article titled "Living to God, Walking in Love" (for the latter phrase, see the introductory section of the commentary on 12:9–21).

[6] Middendorf, *Romans 1–8*, 378.

[7] Middendorf, *Romans 1–8*, 440–42.

[8] Cranfield, *Romans*, 593, agrees that Romans 7 "underlines … this truth":

> For, while it indicates that rebellion against sin's tyranny is no easy matter but something with which the Christian is never done, so long as he is in the flesh, and reveals

even in the midst of that ongoing struggle, Paul gives thanks to God through Jesus Christ our Lord (7:25) and then announces triumphantly: "Nothing [is] condemnation for the ones in Christ Jesus" (8:1). Rom 8:2–4a explains why; 8:4b then calls believers to walk according to the Spirit in response (see also 8:5–13).

Here also in Romans 12–16, the Good News of Jesus Christ provides the basis for everything. Paul begins his appeal to all of his brothers in Christ "through the mercies of God" (διὰ τῶν οἰκτιρμῶν τοῦ θεοῦ, 12:1). He has recently used other Greek words for "mercy" (ἔλεος) and "show mercy" (ἐλεέω) four times in 11:30–32, climactically asserting that God desires to "show mercy to all" (τοὺς πάντας ἐλεήσῃ, 11:32). With the preposition διά, "through," Paul explains that just as righteousness comes "through faith" (διὰ πίστεως, e.g., Rom 3:22, 25, 30, 31; Gal 2:16), so also Christian living flows "through the mercies of God" (12:1).

The Habakkuk quote in Rom 1:17 sets the thematic basis for the entire letter within the context of the Lord's written Word ("just as it stands written," 1:17; note also "through his prophets in holy writings" in 1:2). Paul similarly roots his exhortations in Romans 12–16 in the words of the Word himself made flesh (Jn 1:14). In particular,

> the echoes of Jesus' teaching (particularly at 12:14, 18; 13:7, 8–10; and 14:10, 13, 14, 17, 18; 15:1, 2) indicate not only a greater dependence of Christian parenesis on the Jesus tradition than is usually recognized … , but also the greater coherence of the section (12:1–15:13) as a whole.[9]

Pauline Imperatives

On the firm foundation of God's gracious gifts of mercy, righteousness, and life, Paul urges his hearers to walk in life's renewal (6:4; cf. 12:2) as they actively present their bodies to God as living sacrifices (12:1). The moment one loses sight of God's mercy for all in Christ (e.g., 11:32), all of what Paul calls forth in Romans 12–15 will be misunderstood and misapplied, as well as impossible to achieve. For Paul

> will not turn Jesus into either a schoolmaster to give lessons or a policeman to make sure they are obeyed. The foundation of his ethic is what Jesus *accomplished*: the whole new world, the "age to come" of Jewish expectation, into which the baptized enter and in which they must live by the Spirit. This is where we see how important it is that in chapter 6 the Christian is precisely no longer an "old human being," but instead stands on resurrection ground.[10]

> with relentless frankness the tension, with all its real anguish, in which he is involved and from which he cannot in this life escape, it also makes it clear that there can be no question of his laying down his arms and settling for peace [with sin]. Standing as it does between chapters 6 and 8, 7.25 … is totally misunderstood, if it is taken to imply that the Christian may accept his continued sinning with complacence.

[9] Dunn, *Romans*, 706.

[10] Wright, "Romans," 706; see "Revisiting Romans 6" below.

Other Letters

At the same time, one should also not lose sight of the fact that God's abundant mercies in Christ do call forth a certain lifestyle in response. Paul is not shy about articulating and even commanding it. An analysis of his use of verbs in the imperative mood illustrates this. *The distinction between their minimal presence early in his letters provides a marked contrast with their more prominent appearances later.* For example, in Ephesians, *only one* imperative occurs in chapters 1–3, and it is a "command" to "remember" (μνημονεύετε, Eph 2:11). In Ephesians 4–6, however, Paul uses *forty* imperative forms as he calls his hearers to live a life worthy of the calling they have received (Eph 4:1).[11] The same pattern holds in a number of his other letters as evidenced by these statistics:

	Imperatives		*Imperatives*
Colossians 1–2	4 (all in 2:6–18)	Colossians 3–4	26
Philippians 1–2	9	Philippians 3–4	16
Galatians 1–4	9 (4 in OT quotes)	Galatians 5–6	12
1 Thess 1:1–4:17	0	1 Thess 4:18–5:28	20

Romans

Romans exhibits a similar shift. Romans 1–11 contains a total of thirteen imperatives; Romans 12–16 has forty-nine. A closer look heightens the contrast. Aside from 6:11–19, which contains five imperatives, *only one imperative* occurs throughout all of Romans 1–10! And that lone form has God as its subject, "but let God be true" (γινέσθω δὲ ὁ θεὸς ἀληθής, 3:4). Romans 11 then contains seven imperatives. Yet three of these occur in the citation from Psalm 69 in Rom 11:9–10. The other four are addressed primarily to Gentile believers, stating how they ought and ought not to regard their own ingrafting into the people of God vis-à-vis Jewish believers and unbelievers (11:18, 20 [two imperatives], 22). After introducing those admonitions in 11:18–22, Paul returns to take up a related matter in more detail when he addresses the "weak" and the "strong" in 14:1–15:13 (see the separate introduction to that section).

Romans 6 contains a similar preliminary section which serves to introduce a topic taken in greater detail later in the letter. In 6:11–19, Paul uses five imperatives to exhort the baptized to resist sin and, instead, to offer themselves in willing service to God (see below). He then returns to flesh that out in much greater detail beginning in 12:1.[12]

---

[11] For more on Ephesians, see Middendorf, "The New Obedience," 209–11.

[12] Note, for example, that forms of the verb παρίστημι, "to present," occur in 6:13 (twice), 16, 19 (twice), and then in 12:1 (also 14:10; 16:2; see the commentary on 12:1).

In Romans 12–16, Paul uses imperatives forty-nine times, distributed as follows:

Chapter	Imperatives	
12	11	
13	7	
14	9	
15	5	
16	17	(all but one are a request to "greet" [ἀσπάσασθε] various members of the Roman house churches)

It should also be noted that Greek lacks first person imperatives. Therefore, first person subjunctives typically perform the function of exhortation, though discerning the intended sense as a hortatory "let us" instead of "we might" remains an interpretive venture.[13] In all of Romans 1–11, one finds only two hortatory subjunctives, both in questions ("Let us persist in sin so that grace might multiply?" 6:1; "Should we sin because we are not under Law, but under grace?" 6:15), and Paul vehemently rejects both by responding, "May it never come to be!" (6:2, 15). However, in chapters 12–16, Paul uses three or four hortatory subjunctives positively to call forth proper conduct in response to God's mercies (13:12, 13; 14:13; probably also 14:19).

Conclusion

Such statistics are not decisive in and of themselves. But, as one considers the general flow of Paul's letters, a clear pattern emerges. Luther identifies it in Romans as he astutely discerns the predominance of the "righteousness" theme:

> The whole purpose and intention of the apostle in this epistle is to break down all righteousness and wisdom of our own, … and thus to show that for breaking them down Christ and His righteousness are needed for us. This he does up to chapter 12. From there to the end he teaches in what kind of works we should be involved, once that righteousness of Christ has been received. For in the presence of God this is not the way, that a person becomes righteous by doing works of righteousness … , but he who has been made righteous does works of righteousness.[14]

Thus Paul's writings contain *both* indicative and imperative.[15] But, as Paul moves from chapters 1–11 and into chapters 12–16, a more accurate overall appraisal would be indicative, *then* imperative. Moreover, the imperative is based on the indicative; it is only because of the (indicative) reality of what God has accomplished for us in Christ that we can then, by grace and the Spirit's aid, begin to live in the way he enjoins (imperative). This typical Pauline sequence, evident also in the other letters discussed above, establishes a biblical model for Christian proclamation and instruction.[16]

---

[13] See Wallace, *Greek Grammar*, 464–65.

[14] Luther, *Lectures on Romans*, AE 25:3.

[15] Middendorf, *Romans 1–8*, 484–85; see also 441–42.

[16] See Middendorf, "The New Obedience," 211–13.

Revisiting Romans 6

As noted above, aside from 6:11–19, the first ten chapters of the letter contain only one imperative (3:4). The five imperatives in 6:11–19 therefore establish a significant connection between that section and Romans 12–16 with its forty-nine imperatives.[17] Walther summarizes the flow of the chapters leading up to Romans 6 and captures the role of that chapter well:

> Let us pass on to the apostolic epistles, especially to that addressed to the Romans, which contains the Christian doctrine in its entirety. What do we find in the first three chapters? The sharpest preaching of the Law. This is followed, towards the end of the third chapter and in chapters 4 and 5, by the doctrine of justification—nothing but that. Beginning at chapter 6, the apostle treats nothing else than sanctification. *Here we have a true pattern of the correct sequence: first the Law, threatening men with the wrath of God; next the Gospel, announcing the comforting promises of God. This is followed by an instruction regarding the things we are to do after we have become new men.*[18]

Throughout Romans 6 Paul exhorts believers to resist sin and, instead, to walk in the renewal of life made possible by Baptism into Christ (6:4). This commentary divides and outlines the chapter as follows:[19]

Romans 6:1–11: Persist in Sin? No! We Were Baptized into Christ Jesus
    Our Baptismal Death and Life with Christ (6:1–8)
    Christ's "Once for All" Death and Life (6:9–10)
    Application (6:11)

Romans 6:12–23: Resisting Sin "in Christ Jesus Our Lord"
    Let the Struggle Begin! (6:12–14)
    The Analogy and Reality of Slavery (6:15–22)
    God's Gracious Gift (6:23)

The five imperatives occur in these four verses:

> Thus you also *count* [λογίζεσθε] yourselves to be dead to sin on the one hand, but, on the other hand, living to God in Christ Jesus. (6:11)

> Therefore continually *resist the reign* [the negated βασιλευέτω] of sin in your mortal body which results in being responsive to its desires. (6:12)

> And *do not continue to present* [the negated παριστάνετε] your bodily members to sin [as] instruments of unrighteousness; instead, *present* [παραστήσατε] yourselves to God as living from [the] dead and your bodily members to God [as] instruments of righteousness. (6:13)

---

[17] For example, Theodoret of Cyrus, *Romans*, 18 (Bray, *Romans*, ACCS NT 6:307), properly recognizes the connection with Romans 6 (see the full quotation of him in the commentary on 12:1); similarly, the Apology of the Augsburg Confession cites 6:19 and 12:1 consecutively to affirm that "after penitence (that is, conversion or regeneration) must come good fruits and good works in every phase of life" (Ap XII 131–32).

[18] Walther, *The Proper Distinction between Law and Gospel*, 93 (emphasis added); for a discussion of the old and new man, see the commentary on 6:6.

[19] Middendorf, *Romans 1–8*, 443–511.

> For just as you presented your bodily members [as] slavish to impurity and to a lawless mindset leading to lawless behavior, thus now *present* [παραστήσατε] your bodily members [as] slavish to righteousness leading to sanctification. (6:19)

These imperatives must all be heard in their context, which features numerous indicative verbs, and as a response to what Paul has just stated in 6:1–10. A portion of the concluding section of the commentary on Romans 6 is reproduced below:

> The introduction to 6:12–23 is titled "Indicative *and* Imperative." The eighteen indicative statements which permeate 6:12–23 counter the tendency to view it predominantly as imperative commands, only four of which occur. But it would also obscure Paul's purpose to exclude the exhortations to continually resist sin and, instead, to present one's entire self to God in righteousness, which has fruit for sanctified living. To highlight *either* the indicatives alone *or* the imperatives alone is a false alternative.

> The key, of course, is to consider both fully, with proper balance, and in the right order. The indicatives of God come first in 6:1–11, and they also lead throughout 6:12–23. The free gifts of God are passively received through Baptism and in faith. But Paul also calls for, indeed, even commands, a response which entails active resistance against sin, as well as the offering of one's bodily members in righteous service and for fruitful holy living to God. ...

> Paul's exhortations make no sense to an unbeliever; they make no sense to those who are still slaves to sin, even if that slavery is cleverly masquerading itself as slavery to some supposedly autonomous self. The ongoing struggle expressed in 6:12–23 also betrays the notion that holiness of living is somehow temporally attainable, rather than a continual battle this side of eternity. Yet they also do not make sense if our struggle against sin and our efforts to live for God are a matter of complete futility and, therefore, not to be energetically pursued. Such resignation to sin is an improper appropriation of Luther's "sin boldly"[20] and a simplistic misapplication of *simul justus et peccator*. Both Paul's indicatives *and* his imperatives are also not properly comprehended if one adopts a "God-does-it-all-so-I-can-be-lazy" attitude toward sanctified living. Yes, God does it all in our justification (e.g., 3:21–26, 28). We do well to reject all moralism and legalism. At the same time, we ought to confess that an indolent apathy is not what Paul teaches about sanctification. As the Formula of Concord states:

>> From this it follows that as soon as the Holy Spirit has initiated his work of regeneration and renewal in us through the Word and the holy sacraments, it is certain that we can and must cooperate by the power of the Holy Spirit, even though we still do so in great weakness. (FC SD II 65)

---

[20] In a letter to Melanchthon, Luther said: "Be a sinner and sin boldly, but believe and rejoice in Christ even more boldly, for he is victorious over sin, death, and the world" (AE 48:282). Luther, of course, was not advocating sin. Rather, since Melanchthon's keen awareness of his own sinfulness held him back from taking any action (out of fear that any action would be sinful), Luther encouraged Melanchthon to act in confident faith.

… Christian living is our responsibility, yet, thankfully, not ours alone. It is possible only "in Christ Jesus our Lord" (6:23), empowered by the Spirit, who was poured out on us richly (Titus 3:5) when we were baptized in the triune name, "so that just as Christ was raised from [the] dead through the glory of the Father, thus also we might walk in life's renewal" (Rom 6:4).[21]

The Exhortations of Romans 12–16

The title of this introduction to Romans 12–16 distinguishes between Paul's more theological expressions of *the life God gives* and his practical guidelines for *the life a believer lives*. The former was emphasized in chapters 5–8. Before we move to the latter, as articulated primarily in Romans 12–16, Raabe and Voelz make five helpful points about how this section should be heard:[22]

The first point that needs to be stressed is that Paul's exhortations are addressed to Christians, to those in Christ who want to and are able to live for God. …

Second, it is clear that, although the addressees are Christians, they cannot live for God by their own power and abilities. The power comes from the Spirit working through the Gospel. Therefore, Paul's exhortations are based on Gospel indicative statements.[23] …

Third, Paul exhorts his hearers to live out their lives practically and experientially in a way that conforms with what they are already by virtue of Baptism. He calls for their new status to be actualized in their daily life. …

Fourth, Pauline paraenesis exhibits a twofold character of negative warning and positive encouraging. This is necessary because it is still possible for Christians to return to their former life under sin that leads to death. Sin remains an ever-present threat. …

Fifth, it should be noted that Paul's intent in paraenesis is not to accuse the Romans as sinners. He does that in chapters 1–3, where the tone is notably different. Paraenesis uses the language of urging, appealing, and beseeching rather than that of harsh demanding and condemning.

Raabe and Voelz then articulate this "very basic and practical [Pauline] anthropology," which forms an effective segue into the text of Romans 12 itself:

The hearers are assumed to be ordinary, concrete human beings who actively participate in their everyday living. They seem to be in a position to make decisions, to be led astray, to be reminded, to be encouraged, and to be persuaded,

---

[21] Middendorf, *Romans 1–8*, 509–11; see also FC Ep II 18, quoted in "Everything Flows from and through God's Mercies (12:1a)" in the commentary on 12:1–8.

[22] Raabe and Voelz, "Why Exhort a Good Tree?" 158–60. They develop their analogy

by comparing two different approaches to physics, that of Newton and that of Einstein. There is an everyday sort of experiential and phenomenological understanding of the universe (= Newton), and there is a deeper, more theoretical, and ontological understanding (= Einstein). (161)

The "Einstein" perspective basically corresponds with Romans 5–8, while the Newtonian model aligns with Romans 12–16.

[23] Similarly, Dunn, *Romans*, 707, affirms this as "the balance necessary between personal commitment and divine enabling."

just as we all are. Paul addresses them as if they are a third party standing before two powers, sin and the Spirit, and he exhorts them to pay attention to the impulses of the Spirit and to resist those of sin. He urges them, for example, to be transformed by the renewing of their mind, to present their hands and feet, their intentions and actions, as weapons for God's service, and to offer their bodies as living sacrifices to God.[24]

Outline and Structure

Outline of Romans 12–16[25]

III.   EXHORTATION/APPLICATION: living in response to the mercies of God (12:1–15:13)[26]
   A.   Living sacrifices serve Christ's body (12:1–8)
   B.   Authentic love (12:9–21)
   C.   Submitting to earthly authorities (13:1–7)
   D.   Fulfilling the Law of love until the dawning day (13:8–14)
   E.   The weak and the strong in Christ: acceptance instead of judgment (14:1–15:7)
   F.   Conclusion: Christ for Jews and Gentiles as promised (15:8–13)
IV.   CLOSING (15:14–16:27)
   A.   Paul's ministry (15:14–21)
   B.   Paul's travel plans and intention to seek support (15:22–33)
   C.   Greetings to those in Rome (16:1–16)
   D.   A word of warning and greetings from Corinth (16:17–24)
   E.   Conclusion: final restatement of the theme and doxology (16:25–27)

The Structure of Romans 12–13

In addition to the sequential outline above, a chiastic structure provides another helpful way to portray the flow of thought in 12:1–13:14. Wright's layout and his encapsulation of Paul's thought are both informative:

> Rom 12:1–2 set out the Christian's obligation within the dawning "age to come," which joins up with 13:11–14. The appeal for unity and love (12:3–8, 9–13) is matched in turn by 13:8–10. This leaves 12:14–13:7 at the center of the section, dealing from two different angles with the problems of living

---

[24] Raabe and Voelz, "Why Exhort a Good Tree?" 160.

[25] See Middendorf, *Romans 1–8*, 29–31, for a complete outline of the letter. That outline is fleshed out more fully in this commentary's table of contents, which covers both volumes.

[26] "The mercies of God" comes from the phrase διὰ τῶν οἰκτιρμῶν τοῦ θεοῦ, "through the mercies of God," in 12:1, which strategically sets the stage for all that follows in chapters 12–16. Textually, 12:1 flows out of the climactic assertions of 11:30–32, where the verb, ἐλεέω, "show mercy," occurs three times (also in 9:15, 18; see also ἐλεάω, "show mercy," in 9:16; 12:8; note further the synonymous verb οἰκτίρω, "have compassion," in 9:15; the noun ἔλεος, "mercy," appears in 9:23; 11:31; 15:9). The important point is that the lifestyle Paul urges believers to adopt in chapters 12–16 only and always comes forth in response to God's mercy in Christ (see 15:9).

as citizens of God's kingdom (see Phil 3:20) while also continuing to live in the "present world" with its various challenges.[27]

Wright, however, identifies the first break in chapter 12 at 12:3 (between 12:1–2 and 12:3–13). Due to the titular nature of 12:9, that introductory verse provides a better first break (between 12:1–8 and 12:9–21); see the introduction to 12:9–21. Rom 12:9 also provides a more effective frame with 13:8–10, as both deal explicitly with the topic of Christian love in action toward others. Furthermore, rather than taking 12:14–21 as a unit, the content of 12:17–21 more closely parallels 13:1–7. Indeed, it leads directly into the latter discussion and almost makes it a necessity; see the introduction to 13:1–7, subtitled "An Alien Body? Not at All!" This commentary, then, prefers the following modified structure:

```
A    12:1–8
    B    12:9–16
        C    12:17–21
        C'   13:1–7
    B'   13:8–10
A'   13:11–14
```

---

[27] Wright, "Romans," 703. His layout of the structure is as follows:

```
A    12:1–2
    B    12:3–13
        C    12:14–21
        C'   13:1–7
    B'   13:8–10
A'   13:11–14
```

Living Sacrifices Serve Christ's Body

Translation

12 ¹I therefore urge you, brothers, through the mercies of God to present your bodies [as] a sacrifice, living, holy, [and] well-pleasing to God, [which is] your reasonable worship. ²And do not be conformed to this age, but be transformed by the renewing of the mind so that you may test and discern what [is] the good, well-pleasing, and perfect will of God.

³For through the grace which was given to me, I say to everyone who is among you not to elevate your mind high, beyond what is fitting to set your mind on, but to set your mind toward what is a proper mindset, as God apportioned to each one a measure of faith. ⁴For just as in one body we have many members, but all members do not have the same function, ⁵thus we, the many, are one body in Christ, and, [as] the [body], each one members of one another, ⁶and having different gifts in accordance with the grace which was given to us, whether prophecy, according to the analogy of faith, ⁷whether serving in the service, whether the one who teaches in the teaching, ⁸whether the one who encourages in the encouragement, the one who shares with simplicity, the one who stands before with eagerness, the one who shows mercy with cheerfulness.

Textual Notes

12:1 παρακαλῶ οὖν—The conjunction οὖν could be a "marker of continuation of a narrative, *so, now, then,*" wherein it serves to indicate "a transition to someth[ing] new" (BDAG, 2 and 2 b). But the emphasis here is "inferential, denoting that what it introduces is the result of or an inference fr[om] what precedes, *so, therefore, consequently, accordingly, then*" (BDAG, 1). Here οὖν flows most directly out of 11:30–36. The verb παρακαλέω (contracted form: παρακαλῶ) occurs fifty-four times in Paul and encompasses "three categories: (1) 'comfort' (14 occurrences; cf., e.g., 2 Cor. 1:4); (2) 'beseech' (a personal request; nine occurrences; cf., e.g., 2 Cor. 12:8); and (3) 'exhort.' "[1] The nuance here fits the last definition and is translated as "urge." The combination παρακαλῶ οὖν also occurs in 1 Cor 4:16; Eph 4:1; 1 Tim 2:1.

ὑμᾶς, ἀδελφοί—These two masculine plural words have the same referents. The first form is accusative, "you." The second form could be either nominative or vocative, but functions as the latter here, and "brothers" denotes fellow Christians (see 1:13; note the lone exception to that meaning in 9:3).

---

[1] Moo, *Romans*, 748, n. 18; see also O. Schmitz, παρακαλέω, παράκλησις," *TDNT* 5:793–99, who categorizes NT uses in four comparable ways as "asking for help," "exhortation," "consoling help," and "comforting by men and as God's act."

διὰ τῶν οἰκτιρμῶν—For διά, "through," see the second textual note on 3:22. The noun οἰκτιρμός expresses a "display of concern over another's misfortune, *pity, mercy, compassion*"; BDAG goes on to explain that it is "almost always pl[ural], partly to express the concrete forms of expression taken by the abstract concept" (referencing BDF, § 142). However, the plural more likely reflects the common OT use of the plural Hebrew noun רַחֲמִים,[2] "mercy, compassion," which is particularly frequent in Psalms.[3] Two of Paul's three other uses of οἰκτιρμός are also plural (2 Cor 1:3; Phil 2:1; cf. the singular in Col 3:12).

παραστῆσαι—Here the verb παρίστημι serves "as a t[echnical] t[erm] in the language of sacrifice *offer, bring, present*" (BDAG, 1 d). Though the verb is not used in this manner elsewhere in the LXX or the NT, its sacrificial connotation here reflects "a usage already well established in Greek literature and inscriptions."[4] The form is an aorist active infinitive, used to express indirect discourse. A verb of perception or communication (here παρακαλέω) "introduces the indirect discourse, of which the infinitive is the main verb."[5] The infinitive, as Wallace notes, "may represent an *imperative*."[6] The verb παρίστημι occurs also in 6:13 (twice, both imperatives), 16, 19 (twice, one an imperative); 14:10; 16:2. The aorist here "allows the speaker to focus—from his own point of view—upon *what* someone did, does, is to do, and so on"[7] and does not convey a simple one-time event.

τὰ σώματα—The noun σῶμα, "body," emphasizes the physical, corporeal aspect of a person in, e.g., 1:24; 4:19; 8:23, but here it encompasses the whole person. See the fifth textual note on 6:6.

θυσίαν—The noun θυσία can refer to the "act of offering" or to "that which is offered," as here (BDAG, 1 and 2), hence "a sacrifice." Note how the English word "offering" can have the same two meanings. Since the verb παρίστημι takes a double accusative, the translation inserts "as" ("[as] a sacrifice") to distinguish between the first accusative, σώματα, "bodies," and the second accusative, θυσίαν, "sacrifice."

εὐάρεστον—The adjective εὐάρεστος means "*pleasing, acceptable*" (BDAG). The prefixed εὐ- adds "well" to the translation: "well-pleasing."

τὴν λογικὴν λατρείαν—In the LXX and elsewhere in the NT the noun λατρεία usually refers to the formal, sacrificial worship at Israel's sanctuary (LXX Josh 22:27;

---

2   So Dunn, *Romans*, 709; also *The Lutheran Study Bible* (St. Louis: Concordia, 2009), 1934, though perhaps overstating the case.

3   The plural noun רַחֲמִים occurs thirty-nine times in the OT and is often associated with God. For example, David pleads, "According to the abundance of your mercies [רַחֲמֶיךָ], blot out my transgressions" (Ps 51:3 [ET 51:1]). In Psalms the word appears also in Pss 25:6; 40:12 (ET 40:11); 69:17 (ET 69:16); 77:10 (ET 77:9); 79:8; 103:4; 106:46; 119:77, 156; 145:9. Other OT instances where the "mercies" are by or from God include Gen 43:14; Deut 13:18 (ET 13:17); 2 Sam 24:14; 1 Ki 8:50; 1 Chr 21:13; Neh 9:19, 27, 28, 31; Is 54:7; 63:7; Jer 42:12; Lam 3:22; Dan 9:9, 18; Hos 2:21 (ET 2:19); Zech 1:16.

4   Dunn, *Romans*, 709.

5   Wallace, *Greek Grammar*, 603.

6   Wallace, *Greek Grammar*, 603.

7   Voelz, *Fundamental Greek Grammar*, 57, speaking of the aorist in general; similarly, Wallace, *Greek Grammar*, 501; Moo, *Romans*, 750.

1 Chr 28:13; Rom 9:4; Heb 9:1, 6; cf. its use for the Passover in Israelite homes in Ex 12:25–26; 13:5; cf. Jn 16:2). Thus the use here is exceptional; see the commentary. The modifying adjective λογικός, absent from the LXX, occurs only twice in the NT, here and 1 Pet 2:2. Generally it "pert[ains] to being carefully thought through, *thoughtful*" (BDAG), and so for λογικὴ λατρεία BDAG (s.v. λογικός) gives "*a thoughtful service (in a dedicated spiritual sense)*." But see the commentary for the wide range of meanings possible here.

12:2 μὴ συσχηματίζεσθε … ἀλλὰ μεταμορφοῦσθε—The first verb, συσχηματίζω, means "to form according to a pattern or mold, *form/model after someth[ing]*" (BDAG). A present imperative negated by μή (as here: μὴ συσχηματίζεσθε) may command the cessation of an activity in progress,[8] but here, as in 11:18 and 11:20, this construction more likely conveys a general precept.[9] The difference is whether Paul implies that the activity (i.e., conforming) is in progress or not. In either case, the negated present imperative issues an *ongoing command to resist conforming*. The second verb, μεταμορφόω, means "to change inwardly in fundamental character or condition, *be changed, be transformed*" (BDAG, 2). The imperative μεταμορφοῦσθε illustrates how the present tense "is used for the most part for general precepts—i.e., for habits that should characterize one's attitudes and behavior."[10] For this passage, BDAG (s.v. μεταμορφόω, 2) then suggests: "*Do not model yourselves after this age, but let yourselves be transformed by the renewing of your minds.*" An "outward versus inward" distinction between the terms is disputed and should not be regarded as exclusive in either case; see the commentary.

τῇ ἀνακαινώσει τοῦ νοός—The noun ἀνακαίνωσις occurs first in Paul and expresses a "*renewal*; of a person's spiritual rebirth" (BDAG). Cognates are connected to Baptism in Rom 6:4 and Titus 3:5. For νοῦς as "mind," see the commentary on Rom 7:23 (see also 1:28; 7:25).

εἰς τὸ δοκιμάζειν ὑμᾶς—The verb δοκιμάζω means "to draw a conclusion about worth on the basis of testing, *prove, approve*," and "here the focus is on the result of a procedure or examination" (BDAG, 2). See the first textual note on 1:28; cf. also the cognate noun δοκιμή, "tested character," in the textual note on 5:4. Thus the preposition εἰς with the articular infinitive τὸ δοκιμάζειν most strongly expresses result (as does the same construction in 3:26; 4:11, 18).[11] Yet the sense of purpose cannot be completely excluded from the thought as the two often merge.[12] To capture the force adequately the translation employs two verbs, "so that you may *test and discern.*"

---

[8] See Wallace, *Greek Grammar*, 724.

[9] See Wallace, *Greek Grammar*, 724–25. See the textual notes on the negated present imperatives in 11:18 and 11:20.

[10] Wallace, *Greek Grammar*, 721.

[11] Lenski, *Romans*, 751–52. See Wallace, *Greek Grammar*, 593, including n. 10, who says: "This [sense for εἰς τό plus the infinitive] is disputed by older works, but it is an established idiom in both the NT and extra-biblical literature."

[12] For the use of this construction to denote purpose, see Wallace, *Greek Grammar*, 591. Cranfield, *Romans*, 609, and Moo, *Romans*, 757, stress purpose. For a discussion of the merging of purpose and result, see Wallace, *Greek Grammar*, 473–74.

τί τὸ θέλημα—Three neuter singular forms appear together. The first, τί, is an interrogative pronoun, "what?" though Paul here provides the answer. The second is the definite article, τό, which goes with the following neuter noun θέλημα, "will." A form of εἰμί is assumed and inserted, "what [is] the will."

τέλειον—According to BDAG τέλειος refers "to meeting the highest standard … of things, *perfect*" (BDAG, 1 and 1 a). It also "pert[ains] to being fully developed in a moral sense" (BDAG, 4), as in Mt 5:48, "be perfect [τέλειοι] as your heavenly Father is perfect [τέλειος]." Both senses seem applicable here (cf. 1 Cor 2:6; 13:10; 14:20; Eph 4:13; Phil 3:15).

12:3 διὰ τῆς χάριτος τῆς δοθείσης μοι—For διά as "through," see the second textual note on 3:22; note the comparable use in 12:1. Paul redundantly defines "grace" with a passive participle used adjectivally,[13] "through the grace which *was given* to me." "Grace" must be freely "given" by God, not earned by human works; otherwise, "the grace would no longer be grace" (11:6). Cf. the comparable expression regarding the Holy Spirit in 5:5: διὰ πνεύματος ἁγίου τοῦ δοθέντος ἡμῖν, "through the Holy Spirit, who *was given* to us."

μὴ ὑπερφρονεῖν—After λέγω, "say," at the beginning of the verse, the infinitive conveys indirect discourse and has an imperatival force; for this construction, see the fourth textual note on 12:1. The compound verb ὑπερφρονέω means "*think too highly of oneself, be haughty*" (BDAG). Here in 12:3 the simple verb φρονέω, "set one's mind," appears twice (both times the infinitive φρονεῖν) along with two compound verb forms, each with a different prefixed preposition: ὑπερφρονέω, discussed in this textual note, and σωφρονέω, discussed in the second textual note below. For the basic sense of φρονέω as involving one's mindset, reflected in the translation of all four of these related verbs, see the third textual note and the commentary on 8:5.

παρ᾽ ὃ δεῖ φρονεῖν—The preposition παρά expresses "comparative advantage, *in comparison to, more than, beyond*" (BDAG, C 3) one's proper mindset (φρονέω). Rather than the more common "it is necessary" (BDAG, 1), the impersonal verb δεῖ here depicts what "should happen because of being fitting" or proper (BDAG, 2), thus "beyond what is fitting to set your mind on."

φρονεῖν εἰς τὸ σωφρονεῖν—For the verbs, see the second textual note on 12:3. The first infinitive is used in indirect discourse; for the construction, see the fourth textual note on 12:1. The preposition εἰς with the articular infinitive τὸ σωφρονεῖν expresses a goal, "*toward*" (BDAG, s.v. εἰς, 1). The compound verb σωφρονέω (σῶς, "safe, sound, whole," + φρονέω) means "to be prudent, with focus on self-control, *be reasonable, sensible, serious, keep one's head*" (BDAG, 2) and is translated as "a proper mindset." Moo notes that its "word group denoted a cardinal virtue among the Greeks, from whom it found its way into Hellenistic Jewish literature."[14]

---

[13] See Wallace, *Greek Grammar*, 617–19.

[14] Moo, *Romans*, 760, n. 12; for numerous examples, see U. Luck, "σώφρων κτλ.," *TDNT* 7:1097–1102.

ἐμέρισεν μέτρον πίστεως—The verb is an aorist form of μερίζω, which means to "*deal out, assign, apportion*" (BDAG, 2 b; cf. 1 Cor 7:17). The neuter noun μέτρον can refer to an instrument for measuring (BDAG, 1), but here applies to the resulting measurement (BDAG, 2). For various interpretations of the "measure of faith," see the commentary.

12:4 καθάπερ—This conjunction introduces a comparison: "just as."

ἐν ἑνὶ σώματι πολλὰ μέλη ἔχομεν—Whereas the plural σώματα in 12:1 referred to the "bodies" of individual Christians, here the singular number of σῶμα, reinforced by the cardinal number εἷς, refers to the "one body" of Christ, as also in the next verse: ἓν σῶμα (12:5). The neuter plural noun μέλη refers to the "members" of a body; see the second textual note on 6:13.

τὴν αὐτὴν ... πρᾶξιν—The form αὐτήν is the feminine accusative singular of αὐτός. Although αὐτός regularly is used as a third person pronoun, when it is preceded by the article (τὴν) it functions as "an identifying adjective. As such, it is translated *same.*"[15] The noun πρᾶξις denotes a "sustained activity, *acting, activity, function*" (BDAG, 1); cf. 8:13, its only other occurrence in Romans.

12:5 οὕτως—This adverb introduces the other side of the comparison begun in 12:4.

τὸ δὲ καθ' εἷς ἀλλήλων μέλη—The neuter singular article τό stands before the entire phrase and, thereby, renders it all as definite.[16] The article likely reflects an anaphoric use,[17] drawing its neuter gender and singular number from ἓν σῶμα earlier in the verse (thus the bracketed insertion of "body" in translation; cf. also ἑνὶ σώματι in 12:4). καθ' is the form of the preposition κατά before a vowel with a rough breathing mark and functions distributively as a "marker of division of a greater whole into individual parts" (BDAG, B 3; see also B 3 a). However, this meaning of κατά should be followed by the accusative (BDAG, B) instead of the nominative form εἷς. BDF, § 305, describes Paul's use of the nominative as a "vulgarism," but, while καθ' εἷς maybe be an "unusual construction,"[18] it functions appropriately as an idiom for "each one."[19] Kuske paraphrases τὸ καθ' εἷς as "we, each and every one of us taken one by one."[20] Furthermore, Paul's distributive use of the nominative εἷς[21] leans more strongly forward and serves to emphasize ἀλλήλων; literally the two words refer to "one of each other(s)/one another." For μέλη, "members," see the second textual note on 12:4. The

---

[15] Wallace, *Greek Grammar*, 349; for the various uses of αὐτός, see Mounce, *Basics of Biblical Greek*, 101–3.

[16] See BDAG, s.v. ὁ, 2 h α (cf. 13:8–9), and Wallace, *Greek Grammar*, 237–38.

[17] See Wallace, *Greek Grammar*, 217–20.

[18] Kuske, *Romans 9–16*, 190.

[19] Moo, *Romans*, 762, n. 25; BDAG, s.v. εἷς, 5 e, translates τὸ καθ' εἷς adverbially, "individually."

[20] Kuske, *Romans 9–16*, 190.

[21] In the LXX, forms of εἷς exhibit a similar distributive force (τοὺς υἱοὺς Ισραηλ κατὰ ἕνα ἕνα, LXX Is 27:12; τὸ καθ' ἓν πραχθέν, 1 Esdras 1:31; and ἐγὼ καθ' ἑνὸς ἑκάστου ὑμῶν θαυμάζω, 4 Macc 8:5).

entire phrase then depicts "the" body of Christ as one in which "each member is one with every other member."[22]

12:6 χαρίσματα κατὰ τὴν χάριν τὴν δοθεῖσαν—The plural χαρίσματα refers to various spiritual "gifts." See the commentary on 1:11, which has the singular χάρισμα. In 5:15, 16; 6:23 the singular has the broader meaning of the "gracious gift" of righteousness and salvation in Jesus Christ offered to all. The plural in 11:29 referred to the gifts of grace bestowed on OT Israel. The preposition κατά followed by the accusative τὴν χάριν means "*according to, in accordance with, in conformity with, according to*" (BDAG, s.v. κατά, B 5) "the grace" given to Christians. Similar is διὰ τῆς χάριτος τῆς δοθείσης μοι in the first textual note on 12:3.

διάφορα—The adjective διάφορος "pert[ains] to being different, w[ith] focus on distinctiveness, *different*" (BDAG, 1; cf. ἀδιάφορα, *adiaphora*, with *alpha* privative, "indifferent things"). The neuter plural modifies χαρίσματα, "different gifts."

τὴν ἀναλογίαν—The noun ἀναλογία, *analogia* (hence the English *analogue, analogy*, etc.), is "drawn from the world of mathematics and logic, where it denotes the correct proportion or right relationship."[23] It is absent from the LXX and appears only here in the NT. Many translations render it as "proportion" (ESV, KJV, NASB, RSV, NRSV; so BDAG), but they seem unduly influenced by μέτρον, "measure," in 12:3.[24] τὴν ἀναλογίαν is better transliterated as "the analogy." For the specific meaning of the phrase in relation to the following genitive τῆς πίστεως, "of faith," and the comparable expression μέτρον πίστεως, "measure of faith," in 12:3, see the commentary.

εἴτε—The four uses of this conjunction in Romans all occur in 12:6–8, meaning "whether." Curiously, Paul uses it with the first four gifts (12:6b–8a), but not the final three (12:8b–d).

12:7 διακονίαν ἐν τῇ διακονίᾳ—"Serving in the service" is the first of three gifts Paul defines with the preposition ἐν, "in," followed by a dative cognate noun of the listed gift. (The last four gifts also use ἐν, but in the sense of "with" and not with a cognate noun; see the first textual note on 12:8.) Here and in the following two gifts, "teaching" and "encouragement," the preposition ἐν with the dative conveys the sphere in which the gifts are used.[25]

ὁ διδάσκων ἐν τῇ διδασκαλίᾳ—This gift and the remaining four begin with the article and a substantival participle,[26] here "the one who teaches in the teaching." The definite participle ὁ διδάσκων could also be rendered as "the teacher."

12:8 ὁ μεταδιδοὺς ἐν ἁπλότητι—Paul used the verb μεταδίδωμι, "to impart, share," in 1:11 when he expressed his yearning to "give over" a spiritual gift to the Roman Christians. It refers to "sharing" with someone in need in Lk 3:11; Eph 4:28; 1 Thess 2:8. The feminine noun ἁπλότης can mean "*simplicity, sincerity, uprightness, frankness*," as

---

22 Kuske, *Romans 9–16*, 191.

23 Moo, *Romans*, 765; he adds (n. 36) that Josephus, *Antiquities*, 15.396, uses it to describe the proportionality of the porticos in the Jerusalem temple "to the temple as a whole" (cf. Philo, *On the Virtues*, 95).

24 Bolling, *Interpretation of Scripture*, 6, 13, 25–29.

25 See Wallace, *Greek Grammar*, 372.

26 Wallace, *Greek Grammar*, 619–21.

well as "*generosity, liberality*" (BDAG, 1 and 2). Both categories would be appropriate as a characteristic of "the one who shares"; see the commentary. The same ambiguity of meaning applies similarly in 2 Cor 8:2; 9:11, 13. Here and with the three remaining gifts, the sense of ἐν shifts to "denoting kind and manner" (BDAG, 11) and is translated as "*with*."[27]

ὁ προϊστάμενος ἐν σπουδῇ—The contextual meaning of the verb προΐστημι here also remains disputed. It can mean "to exercise a position of leadership, *rule, direct, be at the head (of)*" or "to have an interest in, *show concern for, care for, give aid*" (BDAG, 1 and 2), though the former is most likely here; see the commentary. The translation of the substantival participle as "the one who stands *before*" communicates the spatial sense of the prefixed preposition πρό, "*before, in front of*,"[28] in this compound verb. The preposition ἐν, denoting manner, takes the dative of the noun σπουδή, which originally meant "*haste, speed*" (BDAG, 1) but developed the sense of "earnest commitment in discharge of an obligation or experience of a relationship, *eagerness, earnestness, diligence, willingness, zeal*" (BDAG, 2). The clause means "the one who stands before with eagerness."

ὁ ἐλεῶν ἐν ἱλαρότητι—The substantival participle of ἐλεέω describes one who is "greatly concerned about someone in need" (BDAG, 1). The verb can mean "*have compassion/mercy/pity*" (BDAG, 1). But here, as when God is the subject, the verbal meaning is more active, "*show* mercy/compassion" (see 9:15, 18; 11:30, 31, 32; see also ἐλεάω in 9:16). The prepositional phrase with the noun ἱλαρότης defines this as being done with "*cheerfulness, gladness, wholeheartedness, graciousness*" (BDAG).

Commentary

Introduction: What the "Therefore" (οὖν) Is There for in Romans 12:1

Moo calls 12:1–2 "one of the best-known passages in the NT."[29] That might overstate the reality, but as Paul lays out the groundwork for all that follows,[30] these two verses seem "as dense as any passage" in his letters.[31] The force of "therefore" (οὖν) also indicates how they build upon the foundation of what Paul has already stated. The reference to "the mercies of God" (τῶν οἰκτιρμῶν τοῦ θεοῦ) later in 12:1 connects the "therefore" most immediately with four uses of the more common Greek words for "(showing) mercy" in 11:30–32 (ἐλεέω and

---

[27] Wallace, *Greek Grammar*, 372.

[28] Wallace, *Greek Grammar*, 379.

[29] Moo, *Romans*, 748.

[30] Cranfield, *Romans*, 595: "These two verses serve as an introduction to the rest of the main division 12.1–15.13"; Moo, *Romans*, 748, nicely titles 12:1–2 "The Heart of the Matter," though his subtitle, "Total Transformation," can ignore the ongoing struggle which makes Paul's exhortation necessary. During this life a believer continues to struggle against sin, as did Paul even while he was an apostle; see 7:7–25 and the commentary and excursuses on it in Middendorf, *Romans 1–8*, 527–97.

[31] Wright, "Romans," 703.

ἔλεος). Even though οὖν is a small Greek word, "therefore" properly focuses our attention where Paul has directed it throughout the letter: on God himself.[32]

> The οὖν makes clear right from the start the theocentric nature of all truly Christian moral effort; for it indicates that the source from which such effort springs is neither a humanistic desire for the enhancement of the self by the attainment of moral superiority, nor the legalist's illusory hope of putting God under an obligation, but the saving deed of God itself.[33]

The fact that "therefore" (οὖν) springs forth directly from the rousing doxology of 11:33–36 reinforces this further.

But the background inferred from "therefore" stands more deeply rooted *in all of the letter* up to this point.[34] For example, significant foundations in Romans 6 were discussed above in the introduction to Romans 12–16. Further verbal similarities will be pointed out as this section progresses. Perhaps the most intriguing parallels which permeate 12:1–2 mark a stark contrast to what Paul stated long ago in 1:24–28 and 2:18. Dunn identifies the following (translations added):[35]

1:24 ἀτιμάζεσθαι σώματα to the dishonoring of bodies	12:1 παραστῆσαι σώματα to present bodies
1:25 ἐλάτρευσαν τῇ κτίσει they worshiped the created thing	12:1 τὴν λογικὴν λατρείαν the reasonable worship
1:28 ἀδόκιμον νοῦν an undiscerning mind	12:2 [τῇ] ἀνακαινώσει [τοῦ] νοός by the renewing of the mind
2:18 γινώσκεις τὸ θέλημα καὶ δοκιμάζει you know the will [of God] and you are discerning	12:2 εἰς τὸ δοκιμάζειν τί τὸ θέλημα so that you may test and discern what [is] the will [of God]

Gratefully and graciously, the "downward spiral" of those early chapters "now finds its reversal."[36]

---

[32] Middendorf, *Romans 1–8*, 21–22, 27, 49–51; in this volume, see "Romans 1–4: The Righteousness of God" in the introduction to Romans 9–16, as well as "God" in "The Three Foci of Romans 9–11" in the introduction to Romans 9–11. See also the commentary on 1:17, 32; 2:11, 16, 29; 3:1–8, 19–20, 29–30; 4:21; 9:5, 11b–12a, 16, 22–24, 29; 10:21; 11:1–2, 33–36; 12:19; 13:1–2; 14:10–12; 15:5, 8, 13; 16:25, 27.

Note how the descent into "unrighteousness" (1:18) begins with the opposite, a failure to properly focus upon God by glorifying and giving him thanks (1:20–21); see Middendorf, *Romans 1–8*, 113–14.

[33] Cranfield, *Romans*, 595.

[34] Cranfield, *Romans*, 596; Moo, *Romans*, 748.

[35] Dunn, *Romans*, 708.

[36] Moo, *Romans*, 748.

Everything Flows from and through God's Mercies (12:1a)

The opening verb (παρακαλῶ) has a wide range of meanings from "comfort/console" to "beseech/ask for help" to "exhort" (see the first textual note on 12:1).[37] Cranfield insists that " 'exhort' is surely required here,"[38] but the more common English term "urge" stands comparable in meaning. In any case Cranfield properly identifies παρακαλέω "as a technical term for Christian exhortation, the earnest appeal, based on the gospel, to those who are already believers to live consistently with the gospel they have received"[39] (see the introduction to Romans 12–16). It is not necessary to import an added nuance of apostolic authority into the verb itself here, for that authority surely permeates the entire letter beginning already in 1:1 ("Paul … a called apostle"). Furthermore, the basis for Paul's exhortations comes across in other contexts with παρακαλέω when he, for example, invokes "our Lord Jesus Christ and … the love of the Spirit" (Rom 15:30; cf. 2 Cor 13:11) or "the name of our Lord Jesus Christ" (1 Cor 1:10; cf. 1 Thess 3:2; 4:1; 2 Thess 3:12) or uses the verb for God himself acting through the apostle on behalf of Christ (2 Cor 5:20; cf. 2 Cor 7:6). Here, then, Paul begins: "I therefore urge you, brothers, through the mercies of God" (Rom 12:1).

As discussed above, Paul's appeal "through the mercies of God" (διά τῶν οἰκτιρμῶν τοῦ θεοῦ) is rooted in his earlier expositions of God's "mercy" (expressed by other, more common terminology in 9:15–23; 11:30–32; see also 15:9; cf. 12:8). The preposition διά, translated as "through," expresses "the basis, or even the source, of the exhortation."[40] What Paul calls for and calls forth in the verses and chapters to follow all flows through God's mercies. He thus reminds his hearers that "they possessed nothing greater than the mercy of God because they had been set free by it."[41] Rom 11:32 climactically asserted God's desire to "show mercy to *all*" (τοὺς πάντας ἐλεήσῃ). The synonym here, the plural noun "mercies" (οἰκτιρμοί), regularly occurs in the LXX, particularly in Psalms. The predominant appearance of plural forms in the LXX and the NT, including three of Paul's four uses of the word (also 2 Cor 1:3; Phil 2:1), reflects the underlying Hebrew (see the third textual note on Rom 12:1). In this instance, the plural noun nicely encapsulates *all* the aspects of God's mercy-driven Good

---

[37] Wright, "Romans," 703, states that the verb παρακαλέω "is a many-sided word for Paul, ranging from 'comfort' to 'exhort,' and the present instance is clearly closer to the latter"; similarly, Moo, *Romans*, 748–49; cf. ὁ παρακαλῶν ἐν τῇ παρακλήσει in 12:8.

[38] Cranfield, *Romans*, 597.

[39] Cranfield, *Romans*, 597, including n. 2, citing Acts 2:40; 1 Cor 1:10; 4:16; 16:15; 2 Cor 10:1; Eph 4:1; Phil 4:2; 1 Thess 4:1; 1 Pet 2:11; 5:1.

[40] Moo, *Romans*, 749. He adds (n. 21) that when Paul uses the preposition διά, "through," following the verb παρακαλῶ, "urge," elsewhere (Rom 15:30; 1 Cor 1:10; 2 Cor 10:1), "the object of διά ['through'] is that which is ultimately making the appeal that is expressed." Those other uses contain more personal references to Christ and the Holy Spirit, so an instrumental sense might be best here, as suggested by Dunn, *Romans*, 709. Käsemann, *Romans*, 326, proposes less literal nuances: "with appeal to" or "in the name of."

[41] Pelagius, *Romans* (Bray, *Romans*, ACCS NT 6:307).

News (e.g., righteousness, life, hope), which Paul has fully and effectively presented thus far in the letter. *Together all these "mercies" serve as the foundation for what follows.* Along with "therefore" (οὖν), the phrase "through the mercies of God" emphasizes that, as Paul moves ahead, one must not lose sight of all that has gone before. Note the bracketing use of the more common terminology for "(showing) mercy" as the section (12:1–15:13) draws to a conclusion in 15:9 (God's "mercies," the plural of the noun ἔλεος),[42] as well as its more immediate use in 12:8 ("show mercy," the verb ἐλεέω).

If one ever loses sight of these mercies, Paul's exhortations run the danger of becoming legalistic or moralistic. So also Paul addresses believers who have received those mercies though faith in Christ and who thereby have been freed from the Law's condemnation and are credited with righteousness (e.g., 8:1–4). Therefore what follows is not meant, nor should it be taught or proclaimed, for the purpose of condemning believers by placing them back under the Law, contrary to 6:14.[43] Speaking of the paraenetic portions of Paul's epistles (and in keeping with the sense of παρακαλῶ, "urge," in 12:1) Raabe and Voelz point out:

> Paul's intent in paraenesis is not to accuse the Romans as sinners. He does that in chapters 1–3, where the tone is notably different. Paraenesis uses the language of urging, appealing, and beseeching rather than that of harsh demanding and condemning.[44]

At the same time, the reality "that God's mercy does not automatically produce the obedience God expects is clear from the imperatives in this passage."[45] Appeals based upon mercies, much like grace itself, are resistible and not coercive. The active imperatives Paul addresses to Christians throughout his letters make it clear that willing human involvement is necessary (see "Pauline Imperatives" in the introduction to Romans 12–16). Thus the notion that sanctified living is *totally* the work of God or done *solely* by the Holy Spirit should be rejected. The Formula of Concord observes:

> After the Holy Spirit has performed and accomplished this [conversion] and the will of man has been changed and renewed *solely by God's power and activity*, man's new will becomes an instrument and means of God the Holy Spirit, so that man not only lays hold on grace but also cooperates with the Holy Spirit in the works that follow. (FC Ep II 18; cf. FC SD II 65)[46]

But this does not warrant speaking about "the obedience that the gospel demands";[47] the Law demands obedience, but the Gospel is the gift of righteous-

---

[42] Dunn, *Romans*, 706.

[43] See Middendorf, "The New Obedience," 205–12.

[44] Raabe and Voelz, "Why Exhort a Good Tree?" 160.

[45] Moo, *Romans*, 749–50.

[46] See further the conclusion of the commentary on 12:2 below. See also Middendorf, *Romans 1–8*, 510–11.

[47] Moo, *Romans*, 750.

ness through faith (e.g., 1:17; 3:22; 4:13; 9:30; 10:6). Paul's language certainly serves us better. He urges us to respond actively and freely on the basis of mercies graciously given and already received.

The Worshipful Oxymoron of Living Sacrifices (12:1b–c)

Presenting Bodies to God (12:1b)

The content of Paul's exhortation is "to present your bodies [as] a sacrifice, living, holy, [and] well-pleasing to God" (12:1). Comparable uses of the verb "to present" (παρίστημι) occur five times in Roman 6 (6:13 [twice], 16, 19 [twice]), and three of these are imperatives (see the introduction to Romans 12–16). Here the infinitive "to present" (παραστῆσαι) following "urge" (παρακαλῶ) carries an *imperatival force*; its aorist tense focuses attention on the act itself and should not be viewed as a simple one-time event (see the first and fourth textual notes on 12:1).

Interestingly, this depiction of "presenting" a sacrificial offering to God *using this verb* (παρίστημι) stands unique in the Greek Bible, but appears in extrabiblical Greek.[48] Another observation "worth noting is the fact that σῶμα [the noun for 'body'] does not occur in connection with sacrifice" throughout the LXX.[49] Similarly, "the almost technical use of σῶμα for 'corpse' " is totally absent in Pauline usage.[50] Thus it seems best to allow Paul to fill out the meaning of his terms in the rest of the verse and within the broader context of the entire letter.

In Romans 6 Paul uses forms of the verb "present" (παρίστημι) five times to depict people presenting their "members" (μέλη, 6:13, 19) or "themselves" (ἑαυτούς, 6:13, 16) in service *either* to sin *or* to God. Here the object is "your bodies" (τὰ σώματα ὑμῶν, 12:1). While Romans 6 does not have the same sacrificial connotations present in 12:1, all six of these expressions with "present" (παρίστημι, 6:13 [twice], 16, 19 [twice]; 12:1) certainly convey comparable actions.[51] Romans 6 speaks of Baptism (6:3–4), a corporeal Sacrament in which the water is applied to the body along with the Word.[52] Moreover, the baptized are incorporated into the bodily death and resurrection of Christ (6:3–5), who thereby offered the perfect, all-availing sacrifice for sin; our own baptismal

---

[48] For references, see Cranfield, *Romans*, 598, n. 4.

[49] E. Schweizer, "σῶμα κτλ.," *TDNT* 7:1048.

[50] E. Schweizer, "σῶμα κτλ.," *TDNT* 7:1060.

[51] Theodoret of Cyrus, *Romans*, 18 (Bray, *Romans*, ACCS NT 6:307), properly recognizes the relationship with Romans 6:

> Paul has already exhorted us to make our members instruments of righteousness and to present ourselves before God as if we had risen from the dead [Rom 6:2, 11, 13]. But here he exhorts us to make our members a sacrifice, and one which he describes as *living*.

[52] Cf. Heb 10:22: "let us draw near [to God] with a true heart in the full assurance of faith, with our hearts sprinkled [with Christ's blood] from an evil conscience and with our bodies washed in clean water."

death to sin is the basis for Paul's exhortation that we no longer live in sin (6:2) but live to God, a new life that includes our bodily conduct (6:11–19). The best conclusion to draw is that all of the terms Paul uses as objects of "present" (παρίστημι) function synonymously for the *whole* person,[53] including the body, soul, and spirit. Thus while "body" (σῶμα, 12:1) may place an emphasis on physicality here, it primarily denotes wholeness (as in 6:6, 12; 7:4, 24; 8:10, 11, 13, 23).

Three Adjectives Modify the Sacrifice (12:1b)

Paul calls for the "bodies" of the baptized to become a "sacrifice" (θυσία). The manner in which he depicts sacrifice in 12:1–2 may be metaphorical[54] in that it does not require the shedding of the Christians' own blood.[55] But this does not render the sacrifice any less real. On the contrary, it calls for an ongoing commitment "to God" (τῷ θεῷ, 12:1, as in 6:11, 13) throughout one's daily baptismal life (Romans 6). Three adjectives modify the kind of sacrifice under consideration: "living, holy, [and] well-pleasing" (ζῶσαν ἁγίαν εὐάρεστον, 12:1b).

In regard to the *first*, Paul uses cognates of "life"/"living" in both the more common physical sense, as well as with the pregnant theological meaning of life in relationship with God through Christ, with the latter being prominent in chapters 5–8.[56] In 12:1, Cranfield argues for "a deep, theological sense—living in that 'newness of life' (καινότης ζωῆς, 6.4)."[57] Moo counters that ζῶσαν "modifies 'sacrifice.' This being the case, it is more likely to refer to the nature of the sacrifice itself: one that does not die as it is offered but goes on living."[58] If so, the oxymoronic nature of a "living" sacrifice is striking. It is possible only because of the unique nature of Christ's sacrifice; "he died … once for all" (ἀπέθανεν ἐφάπαξ, 6:10), and now "Christ, after being raised from [the] dead, no longer dies" (6:9). The distinction between the two interpretations of "living" here presents something of a false alternative. Both aspects of life stand as relevant and applicable to those in Christ being exhorted. And in both cases, the source is the freeing, resurrection-life-giving Spirit (1:4; 8:2, 10–11, 23), who is "the Lord and giver of life" (Nicene Creed). "They are living sacrifices, because the Spirit has given them life."[59]

The next two adjectives clearly have an OT background in the formal worship God prescribed for his sanctuary. The *second* adjective, "holy" (ἅγιος),

[53] Cranfield, *Romans*, 598; Dunn, *Romans*, 709; Moo, *Romans*, 751.

[54] See the excursus "Paul's Gospel Metaphors" following the commentary on 4:1–12.

[55] Cf. Heb 12:4: "in your struggle against sin you have not yet resisted to the point of [shedding your] blood." But see also Acts 22:20.

[56] See "eternal life" in Rom 5:21; 6:22–23. See further "The Background and Meaning of 'Life' Words" in Middendorf, *Romans 1–8*, 98–99.

[57] Cranfield, *Romans*, 600.

[58] Moo, *Romans*, 751.

[59] Luculentius, *Romans* (Bray, *Romans*, ACCS NT 6:307).

carries the OT notion of "set apart," the essence of the Hebrew קָדוֹשׁ. Thus it entails "being dedicated or consecrated to the service of God" (BDAG, 1). But as a modifier for "sacrifice" (θυσία), Paul surely intends a "shading over into the sense *holy = pure, perfect*" (BDAG, 1 b). The portion of the OT sacrifices given to the priests and also some other offerings were literally called "the holies" or "the holy things" (הַקֳּדָשִׁים, e.g., Ex 28:38; Lev 21:22; 22:1–7; Deut 12:26; 2 Ki 12:5 [ET 12:4]; Neh 10:34 [ET 10:33]) or even "a holy of holies" (קֹדֶשׁ קָדָשִׁים, e.g., Lev 2:3, 10; 6:18 [ET 6:25]; 7:1, 6) or, in the plural, "the holies of holies," "the most holy things" (קָדְשֵׁי הַקֳּדָשִׁים, Lev 21:22).[60] Thus "holy" describes a sacrifice that has been sanctified, purified, and cleansed. Already in Rom 1:7, Paul asserts that God calls the Roman Christians "holy" (κλητοῖς ἁγίοις).

Third, the sacrifice is "well-pleasing to God" (εὐάρεστον τῷ θεῷ, 12:1). One translation option would be to attach "to God" (the dative τῷ θεῷ) to the "sacrifice" (θυσία) in a manner which then encompasses all three adjectives: "a sacrifice to God that is living, holy, and well-pleasing." However, in almost every other NT instance of "well-pleasing" vocabulary (εὐαρεστέω, εὐάρεστος, εὐαρέστως), with Titus 2:9 as the exception, the sense is that of being well-pleasing to God or to Christ.[61] The grammatical attachment of the phrase to the final adjective, "well-pleasing to God," therefore, seems most appropriate. "To be well-pleasing to/before God" (with the cognate verb εὐαρεστέω) is LXX phraseology for people who live and walk by faith.[62] Comparable Hebrew expressions describe sacrifices upon which God looks with "favor"[63] and which are "pleasing" to God.[64] These expressions are the positive alternative to prophetic passages that speak of sacrifices not offered in faith that are unacceptable to God.[65] The latter Hebrew expression for "a pleasing/fragrant aroma" (רֵיחַ נִיחוֹחַ) underlies Paul's terminology for Christ's own sacrifice as "a pleasing/fragrant aroma" (ὀσμὴ εὐωδίας, Eph 5:2). In Phil 4:18 he applies that phrase to gifts sent by the Philippians to Paul, which he goes on to depict

---

[60] For an overview of the practice and theology of the OT sacrificial system, see Kleinig, *Leviticus*, 1–39, and specifically its degrees of holiness on page 9. For explanations of the Levitical terminology in the verses cited above, see Kleinig, *Leviticus*, 77, 165–72, 459, and for their fulfillment in Christ, see pages 80–82, 172–74.

[61] Cranfield, *Romans*, 610.

[62] E.g., LXX Gen 5:22, 24; 6:9; 17:1; 24:40; 48:15; Pss 25:3 (MT/ET 26:3); 55:14 (MT 56:14; ET 56:13); 114:9 (MT/ET 116:9). Sirach 44:16 refers to Enoch (reflecting Gen 5:22, 24); see also Wisdom 4:10; 9:10.

[63] See רָצוֹן, God's "grace, favor, acceptance," in sacrificial contexts in, e.g., Ex 28:38; Lev 1:3; 19:5; Prov 15:8; such a sacrifice must be perfect and without blemish (Lev 22:21); even Gentile converts will offer such sacrifices (Is 56:7).

[64] The phrase רֵיחַ נִיחוֹחַ, "a pleasing/fragrant aroma," applied to a sacrifice prescribed by God and pleasing when offered to him in faith, occurs forty-two times in the OT, mostly in Leviticus and Numbers; see, e.g., Ex 29:18, 25, 41; Lev 1:9, 13, 17; 2:2, 9, 12; Num 15:3, 7, 10, 13, 14, 24.

[65] E.g., Is 1:11; 43:23–24; 66:3; Jer 6:20; Hos 8:13; Amos 4:4; 5:22; Mal 1:8, 10, 13; 2:13. Similarly, Dunn, *Romans*, 711.

with the same adjective as in Rom 12:1: "a fragrant aroma, an acceptable sacrifice, *well-pleasing* to God" (ὀσμὴν εὐωδίας, θυσίαν δεκτήν, *εὐάρεστον τῷ θεῷ*, Phil 4:18).

"Reasonable Worship" (12:1c)

This entire presenting Paul now calls "your reasonable worship" (τὴν λογικὴν λατρείαν ὑμῶν, 12:1). Both terms here are significant: the sense of the adjective translated as "reasonable" (λογικός) is widely disputed, and the noun "worship" (λατρεία) exhibits another exceptional use. First, the noun: elsewhere in Scripture "worship" (λατρεία) usually refers to the liturgical worship God prescribed for his people (see the eighth textual note on 12:1). In its five appearances in the canonical books of the LXX, it always translates the Hebrew noun "service" (עֲבֹדָה Ex 12:25, 26; 1 Chr 28:13), sometimes when the word is used together with the cognate verb "to serve" (עֲבֹדָה with עָבַד, Ex 13:5; Josh 22:27).[66] But here, as is typical in the NT, the OT language of worship is transformed; it is not restricted to corporate, liturgical worship in specific locations on designated occasions, but characterizes the entire lives of individual believers on a daily basis in all of their vocations.[67]

Paul modifies this everyday worship with the adjective "reasonable" (λογικός). It is absent from the LXX and occurs in the NT only here and in 1 Pet 2:2. But it has a significant background elsewhere. Greek Stoic philosophers employed it to contrast their

> "rational" worship with what they considered to be the superstitions that were so typical of Greek religion. Hellenistic Jews took over this use of the term, applying it sometimes to the mental and spiritual attitude that was necessary for a sacrifice to have any merit before God.[68]

Moo then offers four possibilities for understanding λογικός in Rom 12:1, which may be summarized briefly as follows:[69]

1. "Spiritual" as "inner"
2. "Spiritual" or "rational" in the sense of appropriate for humans to offer to God, in contrast to the depraved worship in 1:23–25
3. "Rational" as "acceptable" to human reason, in contrast to "irrational"[70]
4. "Reasonable" or "logical" in terms of "fitting the circumstances" for those in Christ

---

[66] In Ex 13:5 עָבַד is translated with ποιέω, "to do," but in Josh 22:27 it is translated with λατρεύω, "to serve, worship," the cognate verb of λατρεία, "worship."

[67] Dunn, *Romans*, 708, speaks of "the sudden use of cultic language (sacrifice, worship), but transformed … : the service God looks for transcends the bounds of cult—it is the commitment of every day." Käsemann, *Romans*, 329, similarly states: "It is the offering of bodily existence in the otherwise profane sphere. As something constantly demanded this takes place in daily life."

[68] Moo, *Romans*, 752; for a discussion entitled "The Relationship between Pauline Ethics and Stoic Teaching," see Kruse, *Romans*, 486–89.

[69] Moo, *Romans*, 752–53.

[70] The contrast could also be with *nonrational* creatures. Gennadius of Constantinople, *Romans* (Bray, *Romans*, ACCS NT 6:307), puts it this way: "The offering of rational creatures is much more valuable than that of dumb ones."

"Reasonable" (as in KJV, NKJV) is chosen here as a translation in order to convey "the sense of being consistent with a proper understanding of the truth of God revealed in Jesus Christ."[71] As Franzmann puts it: "The new worship is inspired, not imposed *on* man but created *in* man by the God who gives life to the dead."[72] "Through the mercies of God" (12:1), such worship is, in fact, the only "reasonable," appropriate, and proper response.

Moo opts for the translation "true."[73] While an appropriate descriptor of worship in the Spirit, it is not a literal translation, for "true" would be expressed with a term such as ἀληθινός; see, for example, the "true worshipers" (ἀληθινοὶ προσκυνηταί) who will "worship" the Father "in Spirit and [in] truth [ἀλήθεια]" (Jn 4:23–24). Thus "spiritual" (Rom 12:1 ESV; NASB; RSV; NRSV) can also aptly describe Christian worship, but Paul does not use the normal adjective for "spiritual" here (πνευματικός). Furthermore, his call "to present your *bodies*" (Rom 12:1) makes that translation less desirable as it tends toward an overly "inner" interpretation. Barrett, for example, asserts: "Paul means, a worship consisting not in outward rites but in the movement of man's inward being."[74] Wright properly counters such platonic notions by the contextual observation "that the offering of the *body* is precisely the thing that *thinking* creatures ought to recognize as appropriate."[75] Franzmann then eloquently articulates the all-encompassing implications of Paul's thought in Rom 12:1b–c:

> Since all men have bodies, all can sacrifice, all have become priests. Since men are never without their bodies, worship is constant. Since bodies are visible, all worship becomes a witness and a proclamation, a lived doxology to God.[76]

Two Additional Thoughts on Romans 12:1

Two comments seem appropriate prior to moving on to 12:2. The first is general and has an overarching significance. Paul's consistent, but remarkable and *innovative*, use of OT worship terminology in 12:1 demonstrates an important aspect of the overall biblical theology he develops in this verse. The NT roots these OT realities in Christ and then, through him, induces them into the lives of his followers. The use of "sacrifice" exemplifies this. On the one hand, Christians no longer offer animal sacrifices nor the drink, grain, and firstfruits offerings specified for OT Israel, "for Christ has fulfilled and thus brought to an end the OT sacrificial system."[77] But it is incorrect to presume that Christ ends all sacrifice. Yes, his once-for-all bloody sacrifice accomplished the purpose

---

[71] Cranfield, *Romans*, 604–5; Murray, *Romans*, 2:112, translates the word as "spiritual" but adds: "Reasonable or rational is a more literal rendering."

[72] Franzmann, *Romans*, 216.

[73] Moo, *Romans*, 753.

[74] Barrett, *Romans*, 231.

[75] Wright, "Romans," 705.

[76] Franzmann, *Romans*, 217.

[77] Moo, *Romans*, 750.

anticipated by all the OT sacrifices as the all-availing sacrifice of atonement for sin (see 3:24–25; 6:10). He is *the* sin-offering of 8:3 (περὶ ἁμαρτίας; see the commentary there).

At the same time, the NT repeatedly calls for believers to sacrifice themselves to God and others in response to the Gospel. Phil 2:17 refers similarly to "the sacrifice and service of your faith" (τῇ θυσίᾳ καὶ λειτουργίᾳ τῆς πίστεως ὑμῶν). The NT describes these as "spiritual sacrifices" (πνευματικὰς θυσίας, 1 Pet 2:5) and "a sacrifice of praise" (θυσίαν αἰνέσεως, Heb 13:15), of good deeds, and of sharing with those in need; "indeed, God is well-pleased with such sacrifices" (τοιαύταις γὰρ θυσίαις εὐαρεστεῖται ὁ θεός, Heb 13:16). These examples illustrate some of what it means "to present your bodies [as] a sacrifice, living, holy, [and] well-pleasing to God" (Rom 12:1).[78]

A similar application of other significant OT theological themes (e.g., tabernacle/temple, priesthood, Abraham's seed/offspring) to NT believers occurs elsewhere in the NT and is discussed in the excursus "Beyond Typology" following this pericope. A potential weakness in the use of typology would come from utilizing it to speak *only* of an OT type and an antitype in Christ himself, leaving out the ongoing and present application to those in Christ. In the NT, each of these OT realities points toward and stands fulfilled in Jesus, but they do not end there. To use a word this commentary regularly applies to Paul's use of the OT,[79] the NT "extends" them on into the lives of the NT people of God. It should be emphasized, however, that they are all transformed as such *only in and through Christ*. Moo notes:

> For Christians, there is no more "cult" or "sacrifice" in any literal sense. … But Paul does not "spiritualize" the cult; rather, he extends the sphere of the cultic into every dimension of life. Thus the Christian is called to a worship that is not confined to one place or to one time, but which involves all places and all times.[80]

A second comment urges a fuller understanding of how to view our living sacrifice as "well-pleasing to God" (εὐάρεστον τῷ θεῷ). Wright states:

> Paul, unusually, repeats the word "well-pleasing" in the next verse [12:2], making it clear that for him at least what a Christian does, in Christ and by the Spirit, gives actual pleasure to God. This is counterintuitive for many Christians, schooled to insist that nothing we do can commend ourselves to God. But Paul insists in several passages that Christian worship and obedience,

[78] Gregory of Nyssa, *On Virginity*, 23 (Bray, *Romans*, ACCS NT 6:306), expands these even further. After noting that Paul commands "you to present your body as a sacrifice," he asks: "How can you be a priest for God, having been anointed for this very purpose of offering a gift to God?" Cf. also 1 Pet 2:5 as cited in the excursus "Beyond Typology" following this pericope.

[79] See, e.g., Middendorf, *Romans 1–8*, 37; the concluding section of the commentary on 9:24–29; the excursus "Beyond Typology" following this pericope; and the excursus "Paul's Use of the Old Testament in Romans" following the commentary on 15:7–13.

[80] Moo, *Romans*, 753–54.

holiness and unity do indeed please God, and if we have articulated his other doctrines (e.g., justification) in such a way as to exclude this notion, we have clearly misrepresented him. (See 14:18; 2 Cor 5:9; Eph 5:10; Phil 4:18; Col 3:20—all the same word as here; ... and, most strikingly, Rom 8:8, where "those in the flesh" cannot please God but, it is strongly implied, "those in the Spirit" can and do.)[81]

Transformed and Renewed (12:2)

"And do not be conformed to this age, but be transformed by the renewing of the mind so that you may test and discern what [is] the good, well-pleasing, and perfect will of God" (12:2). Rom 12:2 adds further content to Paul's appeal. While it might be tempting theologically to take the conjunction "and" (καί) which opens 12:2 as indicating means,[82] that certainly goes beyond its range of meaning. Similarly unwise is Fitzmyer's separation between the two verses, viewing 12:1 as expressing "somatic" (bodily; outward) and 12:2 as "noetic" (inward) commitment (see below).[83] While one may properly distinguish between body, mind, and spirit (cf. 1 Thess 5:23), these are not disconnected entities to be exhorted separately. Instead, in keeping with Hebraic and biblical anthropology, Paul speaks to the entire person in both verses (see the commentary on 12:1b and the second textual note on 2:9).

Conformation versus Transformation (12:2a)

The two imperatives translated as "be conformed" (συσχηματίζεσθε) and "be transformed" (μεταμορφοῦσθε) have different verbal roots, but they "are more or less synonymous in Koine Greek,"[84] and the wordplay in English is effective. The following distinction between the two in Greek has often been asserted: the first, συσχηματίζεσθε, indicates an outward conforming in contrast to the inward transformation of the second, μεταμορφοῦσθε (see, e.g., BDAG, cited in the first textual note on 12:2). Cranfield effectively argues that "there are serious difficulties in the way of accepting this claim."[85] Thus it seems wise not to push it very far. Indeed, a separation of the inner from the outer is unwise in regard to both. Resisting conformity is *not* simply outward since even Paul openly admits that sin still "is dwelling in me ... this is, in my flesh" (7:17–18; see also 13:14). Furthermore, the transformation *of bodies* (12:1) into a living sacrifice surely exhibits itself in outward manifestations. Note also how the second verb, "transform" (μεταμορφόω), describes the *outward* appearance

---

[81] Wright, "Romans," 704.

[82] Moo, *Romans*, 754, argues that 12:2 is probably subordinate to 12:1: Rom 12:2 gives "the means by which we can carry out the sweeping exhortation" of 12:1. "We can present our bodies to the Lord as genuinely holy and acceptable sacrifices only if we 'do not conform to this world.'"

[83] Fitzmyer, *Romans*, 638–41, who contends: "The metamorphosis [in 12:2] is not external but inward" (641).

[84] Dunn, *Romans*, 712.

[85] Cranfield, *Romans*, 605; see 605–7; also Moo, *Romans*, 756, n. 67.

of the divine majesty of the incarnate Jesus revealed at his transfiguration (Mt 17:2; Mk 9:2). Furthermore, God continues to use the tangible, outward means of water, bread, and wine to transform us in Baptism (Rom 6:1–13) and the Lord's Supper (1 Cor 10:16–21; 11:23–34).

The tense and voice of these two imperatives are also significant. The *voice* of the form of both imperatives could be either middle or passive. Since the second imperative is probably passive, "be transformed" (see below), the first, συσχηματίζεσθε, is also most likely passive and means to resist *being conformed* by outward pressures. The passive could feasibly have an active but intransitive sense, "do not conform."[86] If taken as a middle voice, the sense would similarly be more active, "do not conform yourselves." In any case, Origen describes those who conform as follows: "If there are those who love this present life and the things which are in the world, they are taken up with the form of the present age and pay no attention to what is not seen."[87]

Both imperatives are also *present tense*. The first present imperative, which is negated (μὴ συσχηματίζεσθε), could imply "stop being conformed" (see the first textual note on 12:2). Moo discounts this due to "Paul's generally positive attitude toward the Romans' spirituality."[88] However, the present tense of both imperatives is best understood as expressing general precepts which convey an ongoing activity, rather than something fulfilled in a single event (see the textual note). Thus Paul's commands reflect *an ongoing reality which calls for continual and necessary vigilance on the part of believers* (see, e.g., 13:12–14).

On the one hand, "not conforming" entails an ongoing resistance to "this age" (ὁ αἰὼν οὗτος, 12:2; also 1 Cor 1:20; 2:6, 8; 3:18; 2 Cor 4:4; Eph 1:21). "This age" refers to "the sin-dominated, death-producing realm in which all people, included in Adam's fall, naturally belong."[89] To be sure, the Gospel "now" of present Christian existence affirms that Christ has rescued us "from the present evil age" (Gal 1:4), but the "not yet" means that believers still live in it and continue to struggle against sin as long as they are in it (e.g., 6:12–21; 7:14–25).[90] Yet neither Jesus nor Paul calls for our withdrawal from this world (e.g., Jn 17:11, 15, 18). Instead, the fact of Christ's rescue means that we have now been enabled to resist and battle against its evil forces (see, e.g., the commentary on 6:12–14, 19).

The second imperative, "be transformed" (μεταμορφοῦσθε, 12:2), has a rich background. Dunn proposes that Paul's language draws on Jewish apocalyptic, in which the idea of metamorphosis is found "initially with regard to the resurrection" and "also as something consequential upon one being taken up to

---

[86] For the concept, see Voelz, *Fundamental Greek Grammar*, 144–46; in regard to this passage, so Moo, *Romans*, 755.

[87] Origen, *Romans* (Bray, *Romans*, ACCS NT 6:308).

[88] Moo, *Romans*, 755.

[89] Moo, *Romans*, 755.

[90] For a brief overview, see Middendorf, *Romans 1–8*, 441–42.

heaven while still alive."[91] The significant and typically Pauline move brings aspects of the age to come into our present reality (1 Cor 10:11). Thus already now we are being transformed into glory (2 Cor 3:18; see also Rom 8:29). The voice of the form here is more certainly passive. This divine or theological passive implies that *God effects the change* so that believers "receive from the Lord their reformation."[92] At the same time, the mood is imperative. Cranfield encapsulates the force of *both* mood *and* voice nicely: "While this transformation is not the Christians' own doing but the work of the Holy Spirit, they nevertheless have a real responsibility in the matter—to let themselves be transformed, to respond to the leading and pressure of God's Spirit."[93]

Paul calls believers to "be transformed by the renewing of the mind" (μεταμορφοῦσθε τῇ ἀνακαινώσει τοῦ νοός, 12:2). The noun rendered as "renewing" (ἀνακαίνωσις, Rom 12:2; Titus 3:5) "is first found in Paul's writings," as is also the verb "to renew" (ἀνακαινόω, 2 Cor 4:16; Col 3:10).[94] In light of his use of "newness, renewal" (καινότης) in the baptismal context of Rom 6:4, Paul surely intends us to hear a connection with Baptism and to view a renewed mind as one of its results.[95] Paul asserts that our baptismal union with Christ results in a stunning change of reality. First, being joined to Christ's death and burial through Baptism accomplishes our death and burial to sin (6:2–4a). Then, as a result of his resurrection, our Baptism means that "thus also we might walk in life's renewal" (οὕτως καὶ ἡμεῖς ἐν καινότητι ζωῆς περιπατήσωμεν, 6:4b). Paul's use of the same noun as in 12:2, "renewing" (ἀνακαίνωσις), in Titus 3:5 in direct relation to the Spirit's work in Baptism corroborates the connection to baptismal renewal (see the excursus "Baptism in Paul" following the commentary on 6:1–11).[96]

A Renewed Mind Discerns God's Will (12:2b)

Paul then says that "the renewing of the mind" (τῇ ἀνακαινώσει τοῦ νοός) both serves to and results in the ability to "discern what [is] the good,

91 Dunn, *Romans*, 713. In regard to the resurrection, he cites *1 Enoch* 104:6; *4 Ezra* 7:97; *2 Baruch* 51:5, as well as Dan 12:3; Mk 12:25; 1 Cor 15:51–53; Phil 3:21. For assumption into heaven, he refers to *1 Enoch* 71:11; *2 Enoch* 22:8; *Ascension of Isaiah* 9:9.

92 Augustine, *The Trinity*, 14.22 (Bray, *Romans*, ACCS NT 6:309); for this use of the passive voice, see Wallace, *Greek Grammar*, 437–38.

93 Cranfield, *Romans*, 607; for the attribution of both aspects to the work of the Holy Spirit, see also FC SD VI 11–12, where the Spirit "through the preaching of the Gospel ... renews the heart" and then also "employs the law to instruct the regenerate ... what the acceptable will of God is (Rom. 12:2)." See the fuller quote of FC SD VI 11–12 at the end of "Three Concluding Thoughts on Romans 12:2" below.

94 Cranfield, *Romans*, 609; see also Dunn, *Romans*, 713; J. Behm, "ἀνακαινίζω," *TDNT* 3:452–53.

95 Käsemann, *Romans*, 329–30, repeatedly and properly speaks of 12:1–2 as "baptismal exhortation."

96 The reticence of Dunn, *Romans*, 714, is unwarranted: "Here again the too quick referral of the thought to baptism can obscure the point." Quite the opposite! See " 'What? Water Baptism?' " (Middendorf, *Romans 1–8*, 467–70).

well-pleasing, and perfect will of God" (12:2b; see the textual note). The presence of a renewed "mind" (νοῦς) which discerns (δοκιμάζειν) God's will contrasts sharply with the unbeliever's "undiscerning mind" (ἀδόκιμον νοῦν) in 1:28. Yet it *coincides quite well with the way the "mind" (νοῦς) is portrayed in 7:23, 25*. In fact, throughout 7:14–25 the mind, as well as the will and inner man of the "I" (i.e., Paul the Christian), is fully aligned with carrying out God's Law. Whatever the "I" laments doing or not doing is attributed to "the sin which is dwelling in me" (7:17). But, as in 12:2, his mind properly discerns the will of God in the Law and consistently desires to carry it out (see the commentary on 7:15–20). The agreement with and even delighting in the excellent Law of God in 7:16 and 7:22 stems from the renewed mind of a believer, whose will is now aligned with the will of God.[97] This vocabulary affirms that Paul surely depicts his experience as a believer in 7:14–25. While first person singular forms dominate that section, the consistent second person plural forms here show that Paul now is thinking of Christians in the church as a corporate reality (as is made clear in 12:3–8).[98]

Three Adjectives Define God's Will (12:2b)

As with the "sacrifice" in 12:1, Paul proceeds with three adjectives that define the "will of God" (12:2). The lone article, "the" (τό), before all three adjectives indicates that together they modify God's will as "good, well-pleasing, and perfect."[99] The *first*, "good" (ἀγαθός), explicitly connects God's will with the commands of his Law. In 7:13, Paul describes the Law as "(the) good" (τὸ … ἀγαθόν). A verse earlier, he defines the Law as "holy" (ἅγιος, 7:12; cf. 12:1) and the commandment as "holy and righteous and good [ἀγαθός]." These descriptors from Romans 7 firmly connect the Law with the will of God in 12:2, which Christians are to "discern" (δοκιμάζειν, 12:2). Rom 2:18 further buttresses the point. A Jewish person who relies on the Law is depicted there as follows: "you know the will [τὸ θέλημα] [of God] and you are discerning [δοκιμάζεις] the differing things by being instructed from the Law" (ἐκ τοῦ νόμου, 2:18).

Paul describes the "holy" sacrifice called for (and forth) in 12:1 as "well-pleasing to God" (εὐάρεστον τῷ θεῷ). The *second* adjective in 12:2 indicates that God's will, articulated in his Law, expresses that which is "well-pleasing" (εὐάρεστος) to him. The *third* adjective is "perfect" (τέλειος). In the Sermon on the Mount, Jesus describes our heavenly Father as "perfect" (τέλειος, Mt 5:48), or perhaps "complete" (cf. BDAG, 1 b). Thus the "perfect" will of God provides a reflection of who he is so that those whom he transforms and renews may discern and then follow it. Apollinaris describes the believer's "spiritually

---

[97] See the commentary on 7:21–23, as well as the excursus "Who is the 'I' in Romans 7:14–25? Christian or Non-Christian?" following the commentary on 7:14–25.

[98] Cf. Dunn, *Romans*, 715.

[99] Against Dunn, *Romans*, 715, who argues that εὐάρεστον "is probably substantive here … not an adjective describing God's will."

minded heart" this way: "Filled with the goodness of the good Father it will want to do his will and will try to encourage everyone to do good."[100]

Three Concluding Thoughts on Romans 12:2

First, if pursued purely by human means, what Paul calls forth here "is not something manageable and achievable."[101] But such anthropocentric striving overlooks the essential ground of the appeal. It comes all and only "through the mercies of God" (12:1), which entail all that God has already done in Christ to grant mercy to all (11:32). This all-important phrase from 12:1 must continually be kept in the forefront as one deals with all of 12:1–15:13.

Second, the Spirit certainly guides the believer in how to carry out 12:1–2 in daily living (see 8:4–9, 12–13). However, the Spirit *does not force* the Christian to do good works; neither do they happen automatically apart from the believer's will. As occurs typically in Paul's letters, he spends the latter portion of this correspondence (Romans 12–16) urging and even commanding renewed believers to actively engage in striving to live according to God's will (see the commentary on 6:12–23 and "Pauline Imperatives" in the introduction to Romans 12–16; see also FC Ep II 18, quoted above, and FC SD II 65). Paul vividly illustrates the active and ongoing struggle this entails for his own renewed will in 7:14–25.[102]

Third, it is also misleading to assert that Christian "minds are so thoroughly renewed that we know from within, almost instinctively, what we are to do to please God in any given situation."[103] If that were so, Paul could simply stop writing here! Instead, he spends most of the remainder of the letter *spelling out the will of God for us at length and with specific details.* Furthermore, as demonstrated above, "the good, well-pleasing, and perfect will of God" (12:2) continues to be revealed in his unchanging Law (7:12; see especially 13:8–10). To be sure, the Law's lordship and condemnation have been brought to an end for those in Christ, who fulfilled its righteous requirements (7:1, 4–6; 8:1, 4; 10:4). But "the renewed mind of the believer" has not simply been "put in [the Law's] place."[104] A more balanced appraisal recognizes that "motivation has to come from constant inward renewal, without, however, denying the law its role as moral yardstick and norm."[105] The Formula of Concord expresses this well:

> The law indeed tells us that it is God's will and command that we should walk in the new life, but it does not give the power and ability to begin it or to do it. It is the Holy Spirit, who is not given and received through the law but through the preaching of the Gospel (Gal. 3:2, 14), who renews the heart.

---

[100] Apollinaris of Laodicea, *Romans* (Bray, *Romans*, ACCS NT 6:308).

[101] Cranfield, *Romans*, 610–11, citing in support Deut 6:5; Lev 19:18; Mt 22:37, 39; Mk 10:20; 12:30–31.

[102] Note, for example, the seven uses of θέλω, "to will," in 7:15–21; see Middendorf, *Romans 1–8*, 564–65; 591–92.

[103] As does Moo, *Romans*, 758.

[104] As Moo, *Romans*, 757, maintains.

[105] Dunn, *Romans*, 715.

Then he employs the law to instruct the regenerate out of it and to show and indicate to them in the Ten Commandments what the acceptable will of God is (Rom. 12:2) and in what good works, which God has prepared beforehand, they should walk (Eph. 2:10). (FC SD VI 11–12)

Grace, Faith, and One Body in Christ ... So No Attitude! (12:3–5)

Paul continues by stressing two things in 12:3–5. *The first is negative, an admonition against haughty thinking.* "The emphatic warning against inflated thinking (v 3) recalls the similar warning against Gentile presumption in 11:7–24 (particularly 11:20), but also the similar theme of the earlier diatribes against Jewish presumption (chaps. 2–4)."[106] Since everything comes to us as a gift of grace "through the mercies of God" (12:1), which are received in faith, any boastful attitude is excluded (3:27). Presumptuous self-boast also seems most inappropriate in light of the *second topic* Paul addresses, namely, the *relational interdependence* among all the members who have been baptized into Christ and by his Spirit into one body (12:4–5; cf. 6:3; 1 Cor 12:13). Paul then proceeds to detail how God gave members various gifts "so that we should enjoy harmony and friendship and the common salvation of all"[107] (see 12:6–8).

A Grace-Based Admonition (12:3a)

In Greek, Paul opens 12:3, as he did 12:1, with a first person singular appeal. Here he begins with "I say" (λέγω). While an element of apostolic authority has been present ever since 1:1, one can hardly characterize what follows as a "solemn command."[108] On the contrary, Paul emphasizes the very nature of grace as an *undeserved* gift. As with "through [διά] the mercies of God" in 12:1,[109] a comparable phrase with "through" (διά) in 12:3 stresses God's grace, which Paul then describes somewhat redundantly: "through the *grace* which was *given* to me" (διὰ τῆς χάριτος τῆς δοθείσης μοι). Paul makes explicit the divine or theological force of the passive verb "given" when he essentially repeats the phrase in 15:15 with an added "by God" (ὑπὸ τοῦ θεοῦ). Paul's own life vividly illustrates the personal, life-altering reality of grace, but not in any exclusive manner. Instead, he speaks of God's grace "to me" in order to provide a powerful example for all (see 1 Tim 1:12–17). He makes this abundantly clear in Rom 12:6, where he uses virtually identical language to describe "the grace which was given to *us*" (τὴν χάριν τὴν δοθεῖσαν ἡμῖν).

As is typical throughout Romans, Paul then addresses his hearers all-inclusively:[110] "I say to *everyone* who is among you [παντὶ τῷ ὄντι ἐν ὑμῖν]

---

[106] Dunn, *Romans*, 720.

[107] Gennadius of Constantinople, *Romans* (Bray, *Romans*, ACCS NT 6:310).

[108] As does Cranfield, *Romans*, 612.

[109] See the discussion of διὰ τῶν οἰκτιρμῶν in the third textual note and the commentary on 12:1. Cranfield, *Romans*, 612, including n. 2, suggests "by virtue of" here for διά, citing BDF, § 223.4, but maintaining a consistent translation with 12:1 is preferable.

[110] For an overview, see Middendorf, *Romans 1–8*, 50.

not to elevate your mind high, beyond what is fitting to set your mind on, but to set your mind toward what is a proper mindset' " (12:3a). While he does not appear to single out any specific group or gift(s) as in Corinth, his later repeated denunciations against judging in 14:3, 4, 10, as well as earlier in 2:1–3, may be in view. More immediately, his admonitions to Gentile believers in 11:18–21, 25 come to mind as Paul *now more broadly rebukes any haughty attitude*.

Four Greek verbs containing the basic root φρονέω, "set one's mind," occur in 12:3. The verb was introduced in 8:5, along with the cognate noun φρόνημα, "mindset," in 8:6, 7, 27. More recently, Paul admonishes Gentiles with the verb in 11:20 and the cognate adjective φρόνιμος, "wise," in 11:25. As discussed in the commentary on those passages, the translation "thinking" makes this application too narrow. This vocabulary encompasses one's active mindset or even worldview.[111] In Romans 8 the contrast was between the mindset of the flesh and that of the Spirit. Here Paul addresses those in Christ, who have the Holy Spirit. But, as in 8:10–13, instead of portraying a simplistic either/or contrast, he reveals that believers currently exist in a both/and situation.[112] Thus, while they have a renewed mind (12:2) and mindset, they must continually guard against lapsing into the negative attitude expressed in 12:3 with two prepositions. They are not to set their mind "high, above" (ὑπέρ in the compound verb ὑπερφρονεῖν) nor "beyond" (παρά) what is appropriate.

The "Measure of Faith" (12:3b)

Paul identifies a proper mindset in this way: "as God apportioned to each one a measure of faith" (12:3b). Cranfield argues extensively that Paul speaks of each person equally "measuring himself by the standard which God has given him in his faith."[113] Dunn counters that after the verb "apportion" (μερίζω) "the phrase is more naturally taken as an apportioning of *different* measures—as is the case in 1 Cor 7:17 and 2 Cor 10:13."[114] The metaphor of "rich diversity" in the body, coming soon in Rom 12:4–5, supports "recognizing that each is graced in some measure and each expression is indispensable to the community of faith."[115] But based upon what Paul has written thus far, it seems unwise to speak of "the quantity of faith" and "different levels of faith."[116] Paul has spoken only of grace and faith. Thus 12:3 affirms "the one common grace from

---

[111] Moo, *Romans*, 760, properly says that the verb φρονέω "connotes not so much the act of thinking in itself (the intellectual process) but the direction of one's thinking, the way in which a person views something." Cranfield, *Romans*, 613, describes it too narrowly as "a man's estimation of himself," but it certainly includes that aspect as well.

[112] See the commentary on 8:5–13, which is titled "Flesh *or* Spirit; Dead *and* Alive"; see also "The 'Now' and the 'Not Yet' " in Middendorf, *Romans 1–8*, 441–42.

[113] Cranfield, *Romans*, 615; see 613–16; similarly, Fitzmyer, *Romans*, 646; Barrett, *Romans*, 235: "faith [here] is a power given by God to do certain things"; Murray, *Romans*, 2:119.

[114] Dunn, *Romans*, 721; similarly, Jewett, *Romans*, 742, considers it "strongly suggested."

[115] Dunn, *Romans*, 722.

[116] As does Schreiner, *Romans*, 653.

which [the many different gifts] stem (v. 6). It is that faith which believers have in common ... that Paul here highlights as the standard against which each of us is to estimate himself."[117]

One Body—Many Members (12:4–5)

Analogy (12:4)

On the basis of God's *unifying grace received equally by all through faith in Christ*, Paul proceeds to speak of *diversity* with a favorite comparison: "for just as in one body we have many members, but all members do not have the same function, thus we, the many, are one body in Christ, and, [as] the [body], each one members of one another" (12:4–5). Various sources for the image of the body have been suggested. Dunn presents eight possibilities![118] Since Paul currently resides in Corinth as he writes Romans, the monument wall at the temple of Asclepius in Corinth with its dismembered terra-cotta body parts might have provided background for the image.[119] In any case, Paul develops the human body as a metaphor for the Christian community most fully in 1 Cor 12:12–27 (see also Eph 4:4, 12–16).[120] Then he proceeds to apply its ramifications in order to remedy the fractured state of the Corinthian community throughout 1 Corinthians 12–14. Their divisions resulted from an overemphasis on the more ostentatious spiritual gifts.[121]

Dunn repeatedly emphasizes the charismatic nature of the early churches.[122] However, as Paul quickly moves on to list seven gifts in Rom 12:6–8, he does not include any of the more "spectacular" gifts often associated with the charismatic movement. For example, he makes no mention of miraculous powers, healings, various kinds of tongues, or the ability to interpret them (see 1 Cor 12:28). Instead, he dwells on the *seemingly more mundane gifts* of speaking and serving.[123] Surprisingly, he does not even mention the Holy Spirit! Paul also uses the body image so briefly in Romans 12 that it seems safe to conclude that the divisive view of gifts which afflicted the Corinthians is not present in

---

[117] Moo, *Romans*, 761.

[118] Dunn, *Romans*, 722–24; Lockwood, *1 Corinthians*, 444, locates it in "Greco-Roman authors concerned for the unity of the body politic."

[119] In the second century AD, Pausanius wrote *Description of Greece*, in which he mentions the temple of Asclepius, the Greek god of healing, in Corinth (*Description of Greece*, 2.4.5). Archaeologists have found numerous terra-cotta figures of individual body parts presented as votive offerings to the god in thanks for the healing of such members; see Lang, *Cure and Cult in Ancient Corinth*, 14–29.

[120] See Lockwood, *1 Corinthians*, 441–54.

[121] See Lockwood, *1 Corinthians*, 411–515.

[122] See Dunn, *Romans*, 720 and 726, where he unjustifiably concludes: "It is a striking fact, worth noting once again, that Paul can so confidently take it for granted that congregations he had neither founded nor visited would be charismatic. ... This must imply that the pattern was widespread at least in the diaspora churches."

[123] See Lockwood's discussion entitled "Spiritual Gifts in 1 Corinthians" (*1 Corinthians*, 426–40).

Rome. Yet the analogy or "simile"[124] of the body proffered in 12:4 is then utilized in 12:5 to make the same general points addressed to Corinth, though with brevity.

Application (12:5)

The description of one human body with various members having different purposes compares to another reality. Paul, therefore, moves from the "just as" (καθάπερ) of 12:4 to the "thus" (οὕτως) in 12:5. But there is *more than metaphor* here. Paul starts with unity: "thus we, the many, are one body in Christ, and, [as] the [body], each one members of one another." The one body does not merely provide an analogy; it is actually what "we are in Christ" (ἐσμεν ἐν Χριστῷ, 12:5; for "in Christ," see the commentary on 6:11). The one body includes all those who "were baptized into Christ Jesus" (ἐβαπτίσθημεν εἰς Χριστὸν Ἰησοῦν, 6:3). 1 Cor 12:13 explicitly states that this corporate belonging results from and resides in the incorporating action of God's Spirit in Baptism.

While all Christians surely belong together as members of the body of Christ (e.g., Eph 4:4–6), *Paul utilizes the image primarily to describe the cohesion and interaction among a local group of believers*, rather than to paint a picture of the universal church.[125] In other words, the Christians in Rome or Corinth do not merely represent a segment of the body (e.g., a leg). Instead, the whole body exists in that place (e.g., Rom 12:5; 1 Cor 12:27). Romans 16 "makes clear that the Christians in Rome, all of whom Paul addresses in the letter (cf. 1:7), met in several 'house churches.' "[126] Together these various "congregations" are the body of Christ which encompasses "all the ones in Rome" in Christ (πᾶσιν τοῖς οὖσιν ἐν Ῥώμῃ, 1:7). Although meeting in various locations, the unity of all the believers in Rome provides a key insight into the direction in which the argument progresses in the remainder of the letter (see especially 14:1–15:13). It also militates against a narrow view of the body of Christ as congregational only, without consideration of what we might call a synod, district, or denomination. Paul views all the believers *in a given area* like Rome as members of the body, even though they might not all gather together regularly under one roof. Thus, for Paul's image here, a geographical view of the body of Christ may be more appropriate than an isolated congregational one.[127]

In this one body in Christ, Paul speaks of plural "members" (μέλη): "and, [as] the [body], each one members of one another" (12:5b). Even here, Paul's

---

[124] Cranfield, *Romans*, 617.

[125] Hultgren, *Romans*, 695, argues that for Paul "the body of Christ is not first of all the local congregation but the whole church; in the final analysis, the members of the body of Christ are not individual congregations but individual believers." He properly recognizes that individual body parts do not align with individual congregations. But Paul does envision that the whole body, with all its necessary parts, is present in Corinth, as well as in Rome.

[126] Moo, *Romans*, 763; Lampe, "The Roman Christians of Romans 16," 230, postulates "at least seven separate groups." For an overview of Christianity in Rome, see Middendorf, *Romans 1–8*, 10–14.

[127] For example, Dunn, *Romans*, 725, refers to "the Christian congregation."

initial point, though awkward grammatically (τὸ … καθ᾽ εἷς; see the second textual note on 12:5), stresses the *belonging of each one*. He further reinforces this unity by adding "members of one another" (ἀλλήλων μέλη). Therefore, "each and every member of the body is joined to each and every other member of the body."[128] Yet, as with the human body, a plurality of "members" (μέλη 12:4, 5) also points ahead to various functions (12:6–8). The foundation, however, has been laid. "Paul says not that one person received more and another less of God's gifts but only that they are different. We all have different functions, but the body is one and the same."[129]

Finally, the use of "one body" (ἓν σῶμα) in 12:5 connects nicely with the plural "bodies" (σώματα) in 12:1. When members present their *bodies* as a sacrifice, living, holy and well-pleasing to God (12:1), the one *body* functions as divinely intended (12:5). "By using the example of the body, Paul teaches that it is impossible for any one of us to do everything on our own, for we are members of each other and need one another."[130]

Seven Gracious Gifts (12:6–8)

Romans 12:6a—Not a New Sentence

The grammatical transition into 12:6, if Paul even intends one, is incomplete. The verse simply begins with an indefinite adverbial participle, "and having" (ἔχοντες δέ), with the same verb "have" (ἔχω) that he used twice in 12:4. Thereafter, the only verbal forms throughout the rest of 12:6–8 are definite participles. Therefore the connection with what precedes is stronger than most translations convey (as in Eph 5:21, which begins with a participle). For example, many presume that a new sentence begins at 12:6, which then requires inserting some type of main verb(s) into 12:6–8.[131] But should the verbal sense be that of a command or a statement?

The ESV and RSV put in "let us use them."[132] Some claim that the insertion of one or more *imperatives*, or at least the assumption of their presence, fits the context of 12:1–3. "Paul is then not just listing gifts; he is exhorting each member of the community to use his or her own gift diligently and faithfully."[133] The repeated uses in 12:7–8 of the preposition ἐν, "in," followed by a dative noun (e.g., "in the service") buttress this position, since these prepositional phrases depict *how or in what manner* the gifts are to be used. However, only two imperatives actually appear in 12:1–5, both in 12:2. The NRSV tries to break up the long sentence by translating the opening participle of 12:6 as an *indicative*

---

[128] Kuske, *Romans 9–16*, 191.

[129] Chrysostom, *Homilies on Romans*, 21 (Bray, *Romans*, ACCS NT 6:311).

[130] Ambrosiaster, *Romans* (Bray, *Romans*, ACCS NT 6:310).

[131] Schreiner, *Romans*, 654; Barrett, *Romans*, 237; Käsemann, *Romans*, 331.

[132] Similarly, KJV; NASB; Sanday and Headlam, *Romans*, 356; Schreiner, *Romans*, 654.

[133] Moo, *Romans*, 764.

verb: "we have gifts that differ."[134] It does seem *better* to hear what follows as primarily descriptive of various gifts functioning properly. But this happens *best* without inserting words into the text or breaking up the flow of the long sentence begun in 12:4. In this way, *Paul's more immediate emphasis remains upon the one who gives the gifts*: the God who apportions them to those who are one body in Christ (12:5).

We then have a typically Pauline extended thought resulting in a lengthy sentence. By continuing with an adverbial participle ("having") at the start of 12:6, Paul maintains strong continuity with the thought of 12:3–5. Dunn sees what follows as "a description of the Christian congregation functioning as 'one body in Christ'" (12:5).[135] The many members of the one body are depicted as "having different gifts in accordance with the grace which was given to us" (12:6a). Thus another continued theme comes from Paul's repeated reference to "the grace which was given" (12:3 and 12:6). The redundancy inherent in defining "grace" as "given" and the repetition of the phrase in both 12:3 and 12:6 *emphasizes that all gifts are given by God's grace*. And as God's grace is freely given to us in Christ (5:15, 16; 6:23; 11:29), so our Lord calls his people to freely give in response (Mt 10:8; cf. Acts 20:35). Thus "χάρισμα ['gift'] is the reality of χάρις ['grace'] coming to visible expression in the actual being and doing of members of the body."[136] This should counter the temptation to develop the attitude remonstrated in 12:3, which goes above and beyond what is proper. For example, Origen reminds us that "there is an enormous difference between speaking by grace and speaking by human cleverness."[137]

While Paul develops the "varieties of gifts" (1 Cor 12:4) and their uses more elaborately in 1 Corinthians 12–14, he targets that discussion at particular problems which had surfaced in the specific context of Corinth. By way of contrast, *Rom 12:6–8 provides us with a more general discussion*, comparable to that of Eph 4:11–16. Note, for example, that all of the more "supernatural" gifts that were being overemphasized in Corinth (e.g., miraculous powers, healings, various kinds of tongues; see 1 Cor 12:28) are omitted from Paul's discussion both here and in Ephesians 4.[138]

Romans 12:6b–8: Form and Content

Paul lists seven gifts of grace. The list is intriguing both in form and content. In terms of form, note the following:

---

[134] Similarly, Käsemann, *Romans*, 331; Cranfield, *Romans*, 618.

[135] Dunn, *Romans*, 725.

[136] Dunn, *Romans*, 726.

[137] Origen, *Romans* (Bray, *Romans*, ACCS NT 6:309).

[138] See Lockwood's discussion entitled "Spiritual Gifts in 1 Corinthians" (*1 Corinthians*, 426–40).

- Each gift besides the first ("prophecy") is defined by a prepositional phrase with "in" (ἐν) expressing the manner in which the gift is to be used.
- In the second, third, and fourth gifts, the object of "in" is a cognate noun which essentially restates the activity under consideration ("serving in the service," "teaches in the teaching," "encourages in the encouragement").
- The first two gifts ("prophecy" and "serving") are presented as nouns (προφητείαν ... διακονίαν) that denote the activity. Both Greek nouns appear in the accusative case and, along with the plural noun "gifts" (χαρίσματα), function as direct objects of the participle "having" (ἔχοντες).
- The last five identify the gift with a nominative participle which functions substantively, "the one who ..."[139]

A convincing explanation for these commonalities and alterations in format does not seem evident. One final feature does appear readily explainable. Paul does not use *any* denominative titles, e.g., "prophet," "teacher," or the others in Eph 4:11. For the first two he uses the noun for the gift itself, "prophecy" and "service," and for the last five he uses an active participle to stress the activity carried out, e.g., "the one who teaches." This aligns well with 10:14–15; there, as here, Paul emphasizes the function and the action, rather than the actor or the title.

In terms of content, Paul's other letters readily reveal that the list in 12:6–8 is not exhaustive. *The general nature* of these gifts stands out as the most overriding characteristic of the seven. Along with the absence of the more supernatural gifts noted above, another prominent omission here is any reference to apostleship, the *very first* gift mentioned in both 1 Cor 12:28 and Eph 4:11. However, one need not read between the lines to presume that its absence here reflects some deficiency in Rome, namely, the lack of an apostolic foundation which Paul endeavors to correct by his upcoming visit.[140] Indeed, if this were so, "apostle" would more likely appear prominently on the list![141]

The Greek words typically translated as "preach" (κηρύσσω) and "evangelize" (εὐαγγελίζομαι) also do not appear here among those exercised *within* the body of Christ. This is because those verbs, as well as their cognates, typically function as *evangelistic* terms in the NT.[142] Thus they function critically in answering Paul's earlier questions "And how might they believe [on him] of whom they did not hear? And how might they hear without one proclaiming?" (κηρύσσοντος, 10:14). People come to faith when they hear the Word of Christ spoken by those sent out to bring the Good News (εὐαγγελιζομένων, 10:15; cf. 10:17).

When Paul changes contexts from evangelism to speaking gifts that take place *within the body of Christ*, those word groups tend to disappear, and he,

---

[139] See Wallace, *Greek Grammar*, 619–21.

[140] As suggested by Klein, "Paul's Purpose in Writing the Epistle to the Romans."

[141] Paul does refer to himself as an "apostle" in 1:1; 11:13 and speaks of "the apostles" in 16:7.

[142] For an overview, see the excursus "The New Testament Connotations and Context of Words Commonly Translated as 'Preach,' 'Teach,' and 'Prophesy'" following the commentary on 10:6–15.

instead, uses the terminology of the two speaking gifts mentioned here, "prophecy" and "teaching" (12:6, 7).[143] These two stand prominently in Paul's other lists. "Prophets" or "prophecy" are the second gift listed in 1 Cor 12:10 and 1 Cor 12:28, as well as Eph 4:11; prophecies are also highlighted in 1 Thess 5:19–20. "Teachers" appear in 1 Cor 12:28 and Eph 4:11 (cf. "teaching" in, e.g., 1 Tim 4:13; 5:17; 6:3; 2 Tim 3:16; Titus 2:7).

The final four here, listed in Rom 12:8, do not appear as spiritual gifts elsewhere, at least not with the same terminology. Therefore attempting to establish the definitions of a number of these latter terms presents intriguing alternatives which will be discussed below.

Prophecy (12:6b)

Definition and Function

"And having different gifts … whether prophecy, according to the analogy of faith" (εἴτε προφητείαν κατὰ τὴν ἀναλογίαν τῆς πίστεως, 12:6). The common definition of "prophecy" entails predicting the future.[144] However, rather than simply being future-focused, the OT prophets readily drew upon God's words and deeds from Israel's past (e.g., the Torah, the exodus) and then generally spoke directly to the present-day situation of their hearers. As a result, their specific words of Law and Gospel were applicable to and vitally relevant within their contemporary setting. These OT spokesmen for God, then, were heard (and should be studied), at least initially, within their original context, even as they ultimately bore witness to the Word made flesh (Jn 1:14; cf. Lk 24:27, 44–47; Jn 5:39).[145] Diodore offers a better definition: "*Prophecy* means primarily the explanation of things which are unclear, whether future or past, whether present or hidden."[146] Therefore,

> NT prophecy could include predictions of the future (cf. Acts 11:28; 21:10–12), but this was not its essence. More broadly, rather, NT prophecy involved proclaiming to the community information that God had revealed to the prophet for the church's edification (see esp. 1 Cor. 14:3, 24–25, 30). The truth revealed by the prophet did not come with the authority of the truth taught by the apostles, for prophetic speech was to be scrutinized by other prophets (1 Cor. 14:29–32).[147]

---

[143] For further details, see the excursus "The New Testament Connotations and Context of Words Commonly Translated as 'Preach,' 'Teach,' and 'Prophesy'" following the commentary on 10:6–15.

[144] According to Fee and Stuart, *How to Read the Bible for All Its Worth*, 188, "many Christians refer to the [OT] Prophetic Books *only* for predictions about the coming of Jesus and/or certain features of the new-covenant age—as though prediction of events far distant from their own day was the main concern of the prophets."

[145] The title of Hummel's OT survey ingeniously covers both aspects: *The Word Becoming Flesh*.

[146] Diodore, *Romans* (Bray, *Romans*, ACCS NT 6:311).

[147] Moo, *Romans*, 765, referencing (in n. 35) Wayne A. Grudem, *The Gift of Prophecy in the New Testament and in the World Today* (Westchester, Ill.: Crossway, 1988).

The latter part of this definition leads one to question how restrictively one should view prophecy. If prophecy is "information God had revealed to the prophet," why would it be necessary for it "to be scrutinized"? That would involve selectively standing in judgment on God's message like some higher critical form critic. (To be sure, identifying whether a *person* is a true or false prophet based upon the message would, of course, be a different matter; see Deut 18:18–22.)

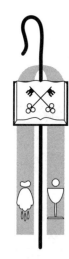

In this light, prophecy may more mundanely entail *applying God's inspired Word to his people in a specific context.*[148] Although none of the writers of the NT Scriptures is categorized as a "prophet,"[149] as were many in the OT, the function of NT prophecy remains similar. Prophets utilize the inspired words given in the Scripture (e.g., the Torah), as well as those now delivered through the evangelists and apostles, and apply them to a specific community for learning, upbuilding, exhortation, and encouragement (1 Cor 14:3, 31). Fitzmyer, who calls prophecy "inspired Christian preaching," adds: "It denotes not one who predicts the future, but one who speaks in God's name and probes the secrets of hearts (1 Cor 14:24–25)."[150] (In a few cases, however, a NT "prophet" does predict the future; see Acts 11:28; 21:11.) On the one hand, "prophecy fulfilled a truly pastoral function."[151] Lenski then properly broadens the scope:

> Thus all true preachers and teachers of the gospel are prophets in the general or broader sense because they offer edification, admonition, and consolation to their hearers. All true Christians who are able to impart the gospel truth privately in a similar manner exercise the gift of prophecy.[152]

---

[148] This better fits the descriptions of prophecy made by Paul in 1 Cor 14:3–5, 19, 29–33. Luther defines "prophets" as those equipped to "dig into Scripture, expound it, and carry on disputations" (AE 45:363). Similarly, *Spiritual Gifts*, a report of the Commission on Theology and Church Relations of The Lutheran Church—Missouri Synod, 34, states: "There is evidence to suggest that prophecy in the New Testament includes what we would today call preaching or expounding Scripture"; also *The Charismatic Movement and Lutheran Theology*, a report of the Commission on Theology and Church Relations of The Lutheran Church—Missouri Synod, 19, concludes that NT prophecy

> does not refer primarily to the gift of declaring coming events in advance, although this did occur in the apostolic church (Acts 11:27[–28]: Agabus). It includes also the God-given ability to interpret Scripture correctly and to apply its message of Law and Gospel to the needs of men. It is the gift of expressing what the will of God was in a given situation.

For more details, see the excursus "The New Testament Connotations and Context of Words Commonly Translated as 'Preach,' 'Teach,' and 'Prophesy' " following the commentary on 10:6–15.

[149] The NT contains a few messages from contemporary NT "prophets" (e.g., Acts 11:27–28; 13:1–2; 21:10–11), and the book of Revelation is characterized as a "prophecy" (προφητεία) in Rev 1:3; 22:7, 10, 18–19; cf. Rev 19:10. When the angel, speaking to John, refers to "your brothers the prophets" (τῶν ἀδελφῶν σου τῶν προφητῶν), he may be implying that John too is a prophet. Cf. also Rev 22:6.

[150] Fitzmyer, *Romans*, 647, citing also 1 Cor 12:10, 28; 13:2; 14:1, 3–6, 24, 39; 1 Tim 4:14.

[151] Cranfield, *Romans*, 620.

[152] Lenski, *St. Paul's First and Second Epistles to the Corinthians*, 579.

The prophecy under consideration in Rom 12:6, then, happens largely *within* the gathered body of Christ in order to build up the community of faith (e.g., 1 Cor 14:3–4). As Paul himself asserts: "But prophecy is not for the unbelieving, but for those who believe" (ἡ δὲ προφητεία οὐ τοῖς ἀπίστοις ἀλλὰ τοῖς πιστεύουσιν, 1 Cor 14:22). Therefore it is a gift to be sought by all, exercised in proper ways by all those who have received it, and esteemed in the church more highly than others (e.g., 1 Cor 14:1, 3–5, 24–25, 31).

"According to the Analogy of Faith" (12:6b)

Paul defines prophecy uniquely in this list as "according to the analogy of faith" (12:6). This is the lone use of the noun "analogy" (ἀναλογία) in all Biblical Greek. Uncertainty regarding its meaning also calls into question the sense of "faith," which follows in the genitive (τῆς πίστεως). In the fields of Greek mathematics and logic, "analogy" (ἀναλογία) expresses "a state of right relationship involving proportion" (BDAG). Numerous translations utilize "proportion" (see the third textual note on 12:6). That understanding of "analogy" (ἀναλογία) then leads commentators to define "faith" (πίστις) here in terms of the *content* of the Christian faith.[153] Fitzmyer, for example, suggests it is best understood "as *fides quae creditur* ['the faith which is believed'], the body of Christian belief, the believed-in object, as in 12:3; Gal 1:23; 3:23."[154] Paul does use πίστις for the content of the "faith," particularly in the Pastorals (e.g., 1 Tim 3:9; 4:1, 6; 6:21), but he does not seem to do so elsewhere in Romans (it may be a component of the meaning in 10:8; see the third textual note on that verse).

---

[153] Melanchthon, *Romans*, 215, defines ἀναλογία as "in agreement with the faith. It should not depart from the articles of faith"; similarly, Käsemann, *Romans*, 341–42.

Bolling, *Interpretation of Scripture*, 42–43, contends that τῆς πίστεως, "of faith," here "refers to the Bible" and that προφητεία, "prophecy," stands equivalent to "the Word/will of God." He properly advocates for transliterating ἀναλογία as "analogy." However, he then contends that 12:6b should be paraphrased as follows:

"If" (your gift is) "to speak God's Word" (that is, if your message is to convey the will of God to other people), "do it" (communicate the words or the teachings) "according to" (which are equal to or are in agreement with) "an analogy" (an analogy made up or consisting of two parts—one of which is clear [i.e. an intelligible, unquestionable propositional statement] and another part which is similar in meaning to the first part) "of the faith" (the teachings of the apostles and prophets, that is the objective words of the Bible).

This understanding of ἀναλογία in its lone appearance in Biblical Greek seems overly complex for the Roman hearers to grasp without some further explanation from Paul. Furthermore, Bolling's definitions of "faith" and "prophecy" both seem implausible in this context and within Romans. See "The Background and Meaning of 'Faith' Words" in the commentary on 1:16; see also the discussion of "prophecy" in 12:6 and the discussion of "prophesy" in the excursus "The New Testament Connotations and Context of Words Commonly Translated as 'Preach,' 'Teach,' and 'Prophesy'" following the commentary on 10:6–15.

[154] Fitzmyer, *Romans*, 647, who adds:

From this Pauline phrase comes the later theological expression about the ecclesiastical norm or the rule of faith, "according to the analogy of faith." It was often used by patristic and medieval writers to relate the teaching of the OT to the NT as promise and fulfillment and as an integrating principle in the development of dogma. (647–48)

If Paul is speaking of faith's content here, he insists "that prophets assess what they are saying against the standard of Christian truth."[155] This would align with Paul's counsel to the Corinthians that others should discern what is prophesied (οἱ ἄλλοι διακρινέτωσαν, 1 Cor 14:29), but it is something which would be superfluous if the prophetic content came straight from God.

However, the meaning of a comparable expression in 12:3 influences the understanding of this phrase.[156] Note the similarities between portions of 12:3 and 12:6:

διὰ τῆς χάριτος τῆς δοθείσης μοι … ἑκάστῳ ὡς ὁ θεὸς ἐμέρισεν μέτρον πίστεως

through the grace which was given to me … as God apportioned to each one a measure of faith

κατὰ τὴν χάριν τὴν δοθεῖσαν ἡμῖν διάφορα … κατὰ τὴν ἀναλογίαν τῆς πίστεως

in accordance with the grace which was given to us … according to the analogy of faith

These commonalities and the attachment of the phrase "according to the analogy of faith" to the first gift in the list, "prophecy," indicate that one's mindset about prophecy should "be extended by analogy to all the gifts."[157] The varieties of gifts bestowed on those in Christ's body (12:4–5) *are all grounded in the same grace and spring forth from what is passively received and given equally to all through faith in Jesus Christ* (i.e., *fides qua creditur*, "the faith by which one believes," as "faith" means in 12:3).[158] Thus grace and faith provide the sole standards for consideration. In keeping with the meaning of both terms throughout Romans, they serve also here as powerful Gospel reminders; in so doing, they reinforce the opening emphasis of 12:1, "through the mercies of God."

Paul makes much the same point at the beginning of his more lengthy discussion in 1 Corinthians 12: "Now there are varieties of gifts of grace, but the same Spirit. And there are varieties of services, and the same Lord. And there are varieties of workings, but the same God is the one who works all things in all" (1 Cor 12:4–6; cf. Rom 11:36).[159] The triune God bestows the gifts by vir-

---

[155] Moo, *Romans*, 765.

[156] Schreiner, *Romans*, 656, properly observes: "One's decision is significantly influenced by the understanding of 'measure of faith' in verse 3."

[157] Gennadius of Constantinople, *Romans* (Bray, *Romans*, ACCS NT 6:312).

[158] So Moo, *Romans*, 766; Dunn, *Romans*, 728; Cranfield, *Romans*, 621. Schreiner, *Romans*, 656, individualizes the notion: "Prophecy should be exercised in proportion to one's personal faith."

[159] The translation is from Lockwood, *1 Corinthians*, 417; see also his exposition (418–20), where he concludes that 1 Cor 12:4–6 serves in the following way (420):

> With his theological foundation in place—that the Holy Spirit's role is to glorify the Lord Jesus, and that all spiritual gifts ultimately come from the same triune God—Paul moves from these general principles to an extended discussion of specific gifts and their role within the body of Christ.

tue of his grace; faith receives them as such. When utilized with this proper perspective, prophecy and all the other gifts never become self-serving works that puff up those who exercise them (cf. 1 Cor 8:1), but are, rather, put into service to build up others.

Service (12:7a)

The second of the gracious gifts is "serving in the service" (διακονίαν ἐν τῇ διακονίᾳ, 12:7; both "serving" and "service" translate the same Greek noun). In fact, Paul uses the plural of "service" (διακονία) synonymously with the word "gifts" (χαρίσματα) itself in 1 Cor 12:4–5. "Service" (διακονία) also characterizes Paul's own ministry in Rom 11:13 (τὴν διακονίαν μου, "my service/ministry"; cf. 2 Cor 5:18; 6:3; Col 4:17; 2 Tim 4:5) and, even more specifically, the offering for Jerusalem in Rom 15:31. Cranfield argues for a different, but also narrow, sense here: "a range of activities similar to that which came to be the province of the deacon,"[160] specifically caring for the poor and needy.[161] But Paul covers those aspects later in the list.

The reference to "service" (διακονία) in 12:7 "is comprehensive"[162] and should be understood broadly as "a standard way [of] describing the work that Christians do on behalf of others."[163] As always, Jesus himself sets the standard. He "did not come to be served but to serve" (οὐκ ἦλθεν διακονηθῆναι ἀλλὰ διακονῆσαι, Mt 20:28; cf. Phil 2:5–11). By his service, giving his life as a ransom, we have life. Jesus then also provides us with a model for being a "servant" (διάκονος, Mt 20:26; 23:11), serving one another in our own lives as well. Phoebe, being a "servant" (διάκονος), exemplifies this exceptionally well (Rom 16:1–2).

Teaching (12:7b)

Next Paul depicts the one body in Christ as "having ... the one who teaches in the teaching" (ἔχοντες ... ὁ διδάσκων ἐν τῇ διδασκαλίᾳ, 12:6, 7). He thereby includes another speaking gift exercised by passing on sound instruction in keeping with the words of the Lord; indeed, Jesus reminds us, "Your teacher [καθηγητής] is one, the Christ" (Mt 23:10). Although separated in the list by "service" (see above), it seems that "the line between teaching and prophecy becomes very thin."[164] See the discussion of prophecy above under 12:6b and the treatment of both "teach" and "prophesy" in the excursus "The New Testament

---

Thus 1 Cor 12:4–6 functions in much the same way as Paul's repeated references to grace and faith in Rom 12:3 and 12:6.

[160] Cranfield, *Romans*, 622; Murray, *Romans*, 2:124, goes farther and concludes: "This reference is to the diaconate"; see 2:123–25 for his argument, which seems anachronistic.

[161] Sanday and Headlam, *Romans*, 357; Barrett, *Romans*, 238; Schreiner, *Romans*, 657.

[162] Chrysostom, *Homilies on Romans*, 21 (Bray, *Romans*, ACCS NT 6:312–13).

[163] Moo, *Romans*, 766; see Collins, *Diakonia*.

[164] Dunn, *Romans*, 729.

Connotations and Context of Words Commonly Translated as 'Preach,' 'Teach,' and 'Prophesy' " following the commentary on 10:6–15.

Encouragement (12:8a)

The first gift of 12:8 is "the one who encourages in the encouragement" (ὁ παρακαλῶν ἐν τῇ παρακλήσει). Paul began 12:1 by exercising the gift himself with the same verb (παρακαλέω), though translated as "urge" there. The notion of "pastoral application" certainly remains appropriate here as well.[165] But this encouraging should not be viewed in any restrictive sense. As discussed under 12:1, the verb has a wide range of meanings, e.g., "exhort," "urge," "comfort," "encourage" (see the first textual note and the commentary on 12:1; note the noun also in 15:4, 5), and the broad nature of its various components seems to be the point. The multifaceted encouragement, whenever exercised and by whomever, remains *a marvelous gift to give and an even more wonderful one to receive*!

As with prophecy and teaching, a significant overlap also presents itself here. According to 1 Corinthians 14, one purpose of prophecy is to provide encouragement (the noun παράκλησις in 1 Cor 14:3 and the verb παρακαλέω in 1 Cor 14:31). Furthermore, Cranfield concludes: "It is clear that in ancient, as in modern times, the activities denoted by these two verbs [παρακαλέω, 'to encourage,' and διδάσκω, 'to teach'] must have overlapped."[166] Thus all of these speaking gifts are intertwined and cannot be sharply separated one from the other.

Sharing (12:8b)

Establishing specific definitions for Paul's terminology becomes especially problematic with the final three participles. Each expresses a gift, followed by a noun which modifies how it ought to be used (see the textual notes on 12:8). Together, all three give concrete ways in which members of the body of Christ (12:5) love and care for others in his name.

Fifth, Paul refers to "the one who shares with simplicity" (ὁ μεταδιδοὺς ἐν ἁπλότητι, 12:8). The compound form here of the basic verb "to give" (δίδωμι) implies sharing a portion of something with someone else. Scholars debate whether this involves one's own wealth and property (e.g., Prov 11:26; Lk 3:11; Eph 4:28; cf. Job 31:17)[167] *or* describes one who distributes collective resources coming from and in behalf of the whole congregation (Acts 4:32–5:2; cf. Acts 2:44–45).[168] Whether or not the latter, more formal role was yet widespread or present in Rome remains unclear. Furthermore, the addition of "with simplicity" or, maybe, "with generosity" (ἐν ἁπλότητι, see the textual note), would appear to indicate the former understanding, *sharing of one's own possessions.*

---

[165] Cranfield, *Romans*, 624; as with prophecy as discussed under 12:6.

[166] Cranfield, *Romans*, 623.

[167] Sanday and Headlam, *Romans*, 357; Murray, *Romans*, 2:125–26.

[168] Calvin, *Romans*, 270; Käsemann, *Romans*, 342.

Here it is helpful to remember that all of our possessions come as gifts from God. This particular gift, then, involves sharing a portion of them with others and doing so without ulterior motives (cf. 2 Cor 8:2; 9:11, 13).[169]

Presiding (12:8c)

Next Paul speaks of "the one who stands before with eagerness" (ὁ προϊστάμενος ἐν σπουδῇ, 12:8). Whether this gift refers to the leadership of one who presides as the head *or* whether the verb (προΐστημι) has the alternate meaning "*care for*" or "*give aid*" (BDAG, 2; see the textual note) presents another matter of dispute. Murray cites Paul's use of the word for church leaders in 1 Thess 5:12 and 1 Tim 5:17 to assert: "There can be no question but those here referred to are those who exercise government and oversight in the church."[170] If so, Barrett points out that this need not be heard in a singular sense: "It ... refers to a function which may have been exercised by several persons, perhaps jointly or in turn."[171] This coincides with the regular portrayal of a plurality of elders in the NT.[a] A broader exercise of leadership is also supported by the fact that Paul uses this verb's participle (προϊστάμενος) for the "leader" of a household in 1 Tim 3:4, 12.[172]

Dunn argues for the other definition of προΐστημι, the giving of aid (so RSV), for two reasons: (1) a reference to the one who leads would more likely be in the perfect tense and (2) the location within the list; he contends leaders would have been nearer the top, rather than "set between two forms of aid giving."[173] Furthermore, Paul employs the following noun translated as "eagerness" (σπουδή, Rom 12:8) in the context of financial giving in 2 Cor 8:7–8, 16.

It is difficult to choose between the two. Cranfield, therefore, attempts something of a hybrid: "ὁ προϊστάμενος is the administrator in charge of the charitable work of the congregation."[174] But such a titled office may come as a later development. Overall, Dunn's points might initially seem slightly more persuasive. But Paul's use of the term elsewhere and his pattern here indicate that *he depicts "the one who leads"* (so ESV; comparably, KJV, NASB, NRSV). Paul strategically places "service" (12:7) second in his list, right between two speaking gifts, prophecy and teaching. Then, comparably, "the one who stands before/leads" shows up sixth, in between the gifts of sharing and showing mercy. Thus he *skillfully integrates gifts of speaking with those of serving*. In either case, those who carry out this function should do so "with eagerness" (ἐν σπουδῇ, see 12:11; see also 2 Cor 7:11–12).

(a) E.g., Acts 15:2, 4, 6, 22, 23; 16:4; 20:17; 21:28; Titus 1:5; cf. Heb 13:7, 17

---

[169] Dunn, *Romans*, 730; Moo, *Romans*, 786.

[170] Murray, *Romans*, 2:126.

[171] Barrett, *Romans*, 239.

[172] Cf. Schreiner, *Romans*, 660.

[173] Dunn, *Romans*, 731.

[174] Cranfield, *Romans*, 626.

Showing Mercy (12:8d)

Finally, Paul wonderfully frames 12:1–8 with another reference to "mercy." In 12:1, he began by running everything "through the mercies of God" (διὰ τῶν οἰκτιρμῶν τοῦ θεοῦ). Now, he mentions a final gracious gift, "the one who shows mercy with cheerfulness" (ὁ ἐλεῶν ἐν ἱλαρότητι, 12:8). Remarkably, "this is the only occasion in the Pauline literature in which ἐλεέω ['show mercy'] is used of human rather than divine mercy."[175] The cognate noun ἐλεημοσύνη is used in Mt 6:2–4 to describe Jewish "almsgiving," leading Dunn to suggest "that Paul might be thinking specifically of this ministry here. But the connection … is not widespread enough to justify this restriction of the reference."[176]

Here again, the more general understanding seems persuasive and consistent with the entire list. It surely encompasses all those who "tend the sick, relieve the poor, or care for the aged and disabled."[177] The prepositional phrase "with cheerfulness" (ἐν ἱλαρότητι) means that the one who engages in such merciful acts "will do it with a cheerful heart and not as if somebody was twisting his arm to do it"[178] (cf. the cognate adjective ἱλαρός, "cheerful," in 2 Cor 9:7).

Conclusion to Romans 12:1–8

Paul has adeptly moved us "through the mercies of God" received (διὰ τῶν οἰκτιρμῶν τοῦ θεοῦ, 12:1) to "the one who shows mercy with cheerfulness" (ὁ ἐλεῶν ἐν ἱλαρότητι, 12:8). Ambrosiaster provides a good summary. He addresses *the life God's mercy gives and how it impacts the life a believer lives* (see the introduction to Romans 12–16):

> Paul pleads with them through the mercy of God, by which the human race is saved. … This is a warning that they should remember that they have received God's mercy and that they should take care to worship the one who gave it to them.

> God's will is our sanctification [1 Thess 4:3], for bodies subject to sin are considered not to be alive but dead, since they have no hope of obtaining the promise of eternal life. It is for this purpose that we are cleansed from our sins by God's gift, that henceforth we should lead a pure life and stir up the love of God in us, not making his work of grace of no effect.[179]

God's grace gathers people together in faith and into the one body of Christ (12:3–6a). Paul then lists some of the most basic, general, and essential gifts exercised by its various members. As noted above under "Presiding (12:8c)," *his order integrates gifts which highlight speaking* (gifts 1, 3, 4, and 6) *with those that focus on acts of serving* (gifts 2, 5, 7). This does not mean that the

---

[175] Dunn, *Romans*, 731, citing Rom 9:15–16, 18; 11:30–32; 1 Cor 7:25; 2 Cor 4:1; Phil 2:27; 1 Tim 1:13, 16.

[176] Moo, *Romans*, 769, citing Dunn, *Romans*, 731–32.

[177] Cranfield, *Romans*, 627.

[178] Ambrosiaster, *Romans* (Bray, *Romans*, ACCS NT 6:313).

[179] Ambrosiaster, *Romans* (Bray, *Romans*, ACCS NT 6:306).

sequence lacks "any discernible order or structure."[180] Rather, Paul's point may well be that while words of faith and acts of love can be properly distinguished, they cannot be separated from one another. Otherwise, the many parts of the one body cease to function properly (12:5). For example, Chrysostom observes: "It is not just with money that Paul wants us to help those in need but with words, deeds, in person and in every other way."[181] Indeed, faith in Christ Jesus evidences itself by "working through love" (Gal 5:6; cf. James 2:8–26).

Yet Paul's *overall progression* is revelatory. He begins with grace received abundantly and equally through the apportioned faith God has given to all who "are one body in Christ" (12:3–6a). His body gathers before those who preside (gift 6) to hear nourishing words of prophecy, instruction, and encouragement from all those having been graced with such gifts of speaking (gifts 1, 3, 4). Then the members spring into action with deeds of serving, sharing, and caring for others (gifts 2, 5, 7). Thus they have been moved by the transforming and renewing mercies of God to offer themselves as a sacrifice of ongoing worshipful service, which remains living, holy, and well-pleasing to God (12:1–2).

---

[180] As Schreiner, *Romans*, 660, maintains.

[181] Chrysostom, *Homilies on Romans*, 21 (Bray, *Romans*, ACCS NT 6:313).

Beyond Typology

Introduction to Typology and Beyond

Jesus says that the OT Scriptures are "bearing witness concerning me" (μαρτυροῦσαι περὶ ἐμοῦ, Jn 5:39). The laudable goal of discerning the multifaceted ways in which the OT testifies to Christ remains a valuable, yet daunting, challenge. Too often such attempts are limited to direct, predictive messianic prophecies (e.g., Gen 3:15; Pss 16:10; 22:16 [MT 22:17]; 110:1–7; Is 52:13–53:12; Micah 5:2 [MT 5:1]; Zech 12:10). Another fruitful effort for locating Christ throughout the OT is typology, varieties of which have been practiced in the early church, in the medieval and Reformation eras (including Luther), in the era of Lutheran Orthodoxy (perhaps best represented by Johann Gerhard), and to the present day.[1] The *Handbook of Biblical Criticism* defines typology as "a method of Biblical exegesis or interpretation in which persons, events, or things of the OT are interpreted as being foreshadowings or prototypes of persons, events, or things in the NT."[2] Hill and Walton explain: "Usually the Old Testament correspondent is identified as the 'type'; the New Testament correspondent expressing the Old Testament truth in a greater way is regarded as the 'antitype.'"[3] For example, Jesus is the antitype of the OT priesthood and tabernacle, as well as of Moses, Joshua, David, and Solomon. Hummel properly contends "that all valid typology is both eschatological and Christological."[4] *The great strengths of typology are that it rightly recognizes the Christological character of the OT, finds Jesus prominently there, and illustrates how the entirety of Scripture is united as one in him.*[5]

A debate has transpired over the extent to which typology should be utilized. One side contends that only those things which the NT explicitly identifies as typological should be utilized as such. Another position observes *how* the

---

[1] Davidson, *Typology in Scripture*, 18–33, traces typological interpretations, evident already in second-century AD church fathers, through the medieval and Reformation eras and the era of Lutheran Orthodoxy before turning to the modern era.

[2] Soulen, *Handbook of Biblical Criticism*, 206.

[3] Hill and Walton, *A Survey of the Old Testament*, 225.

[4] Hummel, *The Word Becoming Flesh*, 16. According to the NT, the eschaton arrived with the first coming of Christ (e.g., 1 Cor 10:11; Heb 1:2), however a "now"/"not yet" tension remains; see Middendorf, *Romans 1–8*, 441–42.

[5] For detailed studies of typology, see the classic work of Goppelt, *Typos: The Typological Interpretation of the Old Testament in the New* (1982 translation of the 1939 German original), as well as Davidson, *Typology in Scripture: A Study of Hermeneutical τύπος Structures* (1981). For works that include typology as well as broader hermeneutical considerations, see, e.g., Baker, *Two Testaments: One Bible* (1st ed. 1976; 3d ed. 2010); Holwerda, *Jesus and Israel: One Covenant or Two?* (1995); and books by Sidney Greidanus such as *Preaching Christ from the Old Testament: A Contemporary Hermeneutical Method* (1999).

NT employs typology and then, so to speak, applies these words of Jesus from another context "go and do likewise" (Lk 10:37). The latter approach is preferable, though identifications which go beyond those given in the NT ought not be regarded as authoritative as those that do not go beyond them. However, to avoid the controversy, all of the types utilized in this excursus are explicitly applied to Jesus in the NT.[6]

In explicating how the NT extends these types through Jesus and then beyond to the NT people of God, *two errors* should be avoided. One would be to apply them to NT Christians apart from considering how they have been fulfilled and transformed in Christ. A second shortcoming stops at Christ; in so doing, it fails to recognize what the NT does with these types and neglects their ongoing relevance for Christ's people. But when the two (how types are fulfilled in Christ and then are extended to his people) are considered together, a complete biblical theology emerges.[7] From the Scriptures we can speak generally of OT types, of Christ as the antitype, and then of a third category, what might be called a "post-antitype" applicable to the church. Thus we need to recognize this third category in Scripture which extends beyond typology.[8]

Overview of Scripture

The bow-tie diagram on the next page illustrates the overarching metanarrative of the Scriptures.[9] It begins on the left edge with a creation that was "very good" (Gen 1:31). After the fall, God immediately promised to restore his

---

[6] Davidson, *Typology in Scripture*, 33–44, summarizes this debate among biblical theologians in the seventeenth through nineteenth centuries. The Cocceian school tended to maximize the use of typology, while the Marshian school minimized it, and Patrick Fairbairn advocated a mediating position.

[7] See Middendorf and Schuler, *Called by the Gospel*, 5–7. For a comprehensive resource, see the *New Dictionary of Biblical Theology* (*NDBT*).

[8] For an example of the first two categories, Paul designates Adam in the OT as a "type" (τύπος, Rom 5:14) of Christ, who then is implied to be the "antitype" (Rom 5:12–19; see Middendorf, *Romans 1–8*, 425–26). Yet the Greek terminology can be used in other ways. For the tabernacle, both of the words "type" and "antitype" pertained to the OT: the vision of the heavenly tabernacle shown to Moses on Sinai was the "type" (τύπος, LXX Ex 25:40; Acts 7:44; Heb 8:5), and so the earthly tabernacle completed under Moses was the "antitype" (ἀντίτυπος, Heb 9:24). Sometimes the movement is directly from the OT to the church, attesting what this excursus calls the "post-antitype," but even if Christ is not explicitly mentioned, he is always the basis for the link between the OT and the church. For example, Christian "Baptism," which "now saves," is the "antitype" (ἀντίτυπος) of the Noahic flood, and Christ is the connector for the typology, for Baptism saves "through the resurrection of Jesus Christ" (1 Pet 3:21). Likewise, in 1 Cor 10:1–11 the OT events are "types of us" (τύποι ἡμῶν, 1 Cor 10:6), that is, applicable to Christians in the church, and they happened "typologically" (τυπικῶς), that is, "for our instruction" (1 Cor 10:11). In still other passages both the "type" and the (implied) "antitype" are contemporary realities in the church. Paul and his associates serve as the "type" (τύπος) for other Christians to emulate (Phil 3:17; 2 Thess 3:9; ὑποτύπωσις in 1 Tim 1:16; 2 Tim 1:13). Similarly, Timothy, (1 Tim 4:12), Titus (Titus 2:7), the Thessalonian Christians (1 Thess 1:7), and pastors (1 Pet 5:3) are all designated as a "type" (τύπος) for other believers to imitate.

[9] See also the explanation of the bow-tie diagram given in this video: https://www.youtube.com/watch?v=-RJIQD_wV3k.

fallen creation through the offspring of a woman. That promise was applied to Abraham and progressively *narrowed down* on the left side through his descendants—Isaac, Jacob/Israel, and Judah—then on through the exodus, the royal family of King David, the exile to Babylon, the return of the remnant, and so on all the way to Jesus (from Abraham down to Christ in Mt 1:1–17; from Christ back to Adam in Lk 3:23–38).

Figure 6
_____

The Whole Story: The Bow-Tie Diagram

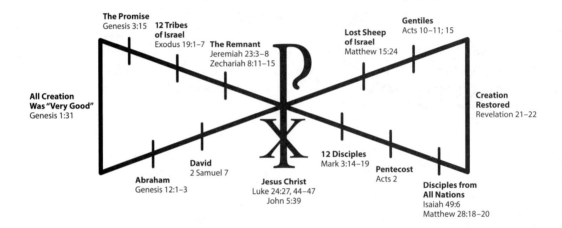

According to the NT and to Jesus himself, the whole point of the OT was narrowing down to the center point, Jesus the Christ (Lk 24:27, 44–47; Jn 5:39).[10] It all led to the coming of the Messiah, in whom God's promises now stand fulfilled. From Jesus the NT *broadens out* on the right side to include, sequentially, his twelve Jewish disciples, the lost sheep of Israel, and Jews scattered throughout the Mediterranean world. The Good News also reaches out to Gentiles as it strives to encompass all peoples and nations. God's NT people anticipate the end of the story on the far right edge. The Messiah will come again and restore God's creation as described in the closing chapters of Revelation, and those in Christ will reign with him forever (Rev 22:5).

Typology is one important way to apply the Christocentricity illustrated by this diagram. OT types fit on the *left side* of the diagram and all lead up to Christ, the antitype, at its *focal point*. But the NT doesn't stop there. It goes *beyond typology* as illustrated by the *right side*. In the NT, many significant

_____

[10] See also, e.g., Lk 4:16–21; Jn 1:14–18, 45; 3:14; 5:46; 8:39; Acts 3:12–26. And see the excursus "Paul's Use of the Old Testament in Romans" following the commentary on Rom 15:7–13. The symbol in the center of the diagram is a Chi-Rho, formed from the first two letters of the Greek word for "Christ" (Χριστός). It translates the Hebrew word מָשִׁיחַ, "Messiah." Both nouns serve as titles for the "Anointed One."

theological themes commonly identified as typological continue through Christ and are applied to God's people in a transformed way on the right side. They then also reach beyond the present and extend into the restored new creation. After laying out some examples, a few implications of going beyond typology will be offered.

Examples of All Three: An Old Testament Type, Christ the Antitype, and the New Testament Post-Antitype

1. A biblical theology of *sacrifice* is discussed under the treatment of 12:1 in the commentary.

2. In the OT, the descendants of Aaron, Moses' brother, served as *priests* to God. They were types of Christ, whom the NT identifies as our "great High Priest" (ἀρχιερέα μέγαν, Heb 4:14). Yet Peter tells the believers to whom he writes: "You are a chosen race, a royal priesthood" (βασίλειον ἱεράτευμα, 1 Pet 2:9). Revelation similarly states that by his death Jesus has "made us to be a kingdom, priests [ἱερεῖς] to his God and Father" (Rev 1:6; see also Rev 5:10; 20:6).

3. Those OT priests served at the *tabernacle* and, then, the Jerusalem *temple*, where God dwelled in the midst of his people. The opening chapter of John's Gospel identifies Jesus as the one who ultimately came and "tabernacled" or "dwelled" among us (ἐσκήνωσεν, Jn 1:14). When Jesus predicts, "Destroy this temple [τὸν ναόν], and in three days I will raise it" (Jn 2:19), Jn 2:21 concludes: "He was speaking about the temple of his body" (τοῦ ναοῦ τοῦ σώματος αὐτοῦ). The tabernacle and temple sanctuaries were types of Christ. Yet Paul reminds the Corinthian Christians: "Or do you not know that your body is a temple of the Holy Spirit, [who is] in you?" (τὸ σῶμα ὑμῶν ναός, 1 Cor 6:19). Note Paul's consistent use of plural forms of "you," as well as his comparable sanctuary expressions in 1 Cor 3:16; 2 Cor 6:16; Eph 2:21–22.

4. Peter expounds further by utilizing the image of the actual stones which were part of the OT temple. These very rocks cry out and point to Jesus, "the living Stone [λίθον ζῶντα], having been tested and rejected by men, but before God chosen [and] precious" (1 Pet 2:4; cf. Rom 9:32–33). *Peter then immediately and remarkably extends all four applications presented thus far to believers in one fell swoop*: "You yourselves also as living stones are being built [as] a spiritual house for a holy priesthood to offer up spiritual sacrifices acceptable to God through Jesus Christ" (καὶ αὐτοὶ ὡς λίθοι ζῶντες οἰκοδομεῖσθε οἶκος πνευματικὸς εἰς ἱεράτευμα ἅγιον ἀνενέγκαι πνευματικὰς θυσίας εὐπροσδέκτους [τῷ] θεῷ διὰ Ἰησοῦ Χριστοῦ, 1 Pet 2:5).

5. God's repeated promises to bless *Abraham and his offspring/seed* (MT: זֶרַע, as also in the first promise, Gen 3:15; LXX and NT: σπέρμα) stand as one of the foundational elements in the OT (e.g., Gen 12:1–3, 7; 13:15–16; 15:5; 17:8; 22:17–18; 24:7; 26:3–4; 28:13–14), as Paul affirms in Rom 4:13–17; 9:7–8. In identifying the recipient(s) of these promises, Paul points out that the Scripture "is not saying 'and to seeds,' as upon many [people], but as upon one,

'and to your seed,' who is Christ" (Gal 3:16; cf. Rom 1:3).[11] Yet later in the same chapter of Galatians, Paul declares: "But since you are of Christ, consequently you are Abraham's seed, heirs according to [the] promise" (Gal 3:29; cf. Rom 4:13, 16; Gal 3:7). Notice that "seed" is still singular, but the pronoun (ὑμεῖς) and verb (ἐστέ) are second person plural, "you."

6. Kings like David and Solomon pointed ahead toward Jesus (Ps 2:1–2 with Acts 4:25–27; Ps 16:8–11 with Acts 2:25–31; Lk 1:32; 20:41–44; Rom 1:3; and, for Solomon, Mt 12:42), who is the King of kings (Rev 19:16; cf. Jn 19:37). The NT then promises that believers "will reign (as kings) with him" (βασιλεύσουσιν μετ᾽ αὐτοῦ, Rev 20:6), starting already now during the present church age (the "thousand years" of Rev 20:6) and extending throughout eternity (Rev 22:5).

7. Even created light itself (Gen 1:3) serves as a type of Jesus, who asserts, "I am the light of the world" (ἐγώ εἰμι τὸ φῶς τοῦ κόσμου, Jn 8:12). In the Sermon on the Mount he then tells his disciples, "You yourselves are the light of the world" (ὑμεῖς ἐστε τὸ φῶς τοῦ κόσμου, Mt 5:14).

Applications

The examples could continue, but the point has been made sufficiently.[12] Typology says what needs to be said about Christ, but all too often interpreters stop short of saying all of what ought to be said. What are some applications of drawing these OT types to Jesus and then going beyond him as the antitype, extending the type through Jesus to his NT people?

First, in order to appreciate the NT's manifold ways of expressing the saving work of Christ and its effect in our lives, a fairly substantial understanding of the OT is often needed. The level of OT knowledge assumed by the NT is considerable.[13] Devoting more attention to that much larger portion of Scripture enables one to more fully appreciate the completeness of God's work in Christ.[14]

Second, emphasizing how these types flow through Christ to NT believers opens up a wide variety of biblical ways in which the Gospel can be expressed both objectively and subjectively.[15] Through Scripture's broad use of typology, *the objective work of Christ for the salvation of all is powerfully displayed.* Then, as these types extend through Christ as the antitype and on to those who

[11] For a thorough interpretation of Gal 3:16, see Das, *Galatians*, 337–38, 349–52.

[12] For further examples, see articles in the *NDBT* and also Preus, *Just Words*.

[13] As an illustration, see the introductory discussion of Hebrews in Middendorf and Schuler, *Called by the Gospel*, 279–81.

[14] A weakness of most lectionary systems comes into play here. Rarely are OT books or even sections within them given consistent, chronological, or sustained attention. Instead, the OT pericopes typically jump around throughout the OT to match the theme set by the Gospel or Epistle reading of the day.

[15] For the distinction between objective and subjective justification, see Middendorf, *Romans 1–8*, 403, 432; see also the footnote on that topic in "The Rescuer and Zion: 'To,' 'For the Sake of,' and 'From'" in the commentary on 11:26b–27.

believe in him, the subjective application of the Good News effectively hits home. For example, in and through our faith in Christ, God declares us to be Abraham's offspring, he bestows a royal priesthood upon us, and our bodies have already become the dwelling place of the Holy Spirit. Furthermore, all these manifestations of the Gospel extend into eternity, as abundant blessings to be enjoyed forever in the restored new creation.

Third and in the meantime, extending types through Jesus and on to us opens up a number of *biblical ways to speak of sanctified living* in a manner which quite literally flows through Christ to us and then through us to those around us.[16] For example, these "post-antitypes" provide a number of solidly Gospel-based and Christ-centered ways to speak of how and why we live as priests mediating the Gospel to the world as we offer ourselves in daily worship as "a sacrifice, living, holy, [and] well-pleasing to God" (Rom 12:1; see also 1 Pet 2:5, 9). They describe why and how those who actually are God's holy temple respond appropriately by honoring God with our bodies (Rom 12:1; 1 Cor 3:16; 6:19–20). They explain how we, who were once darkness but now bask in the light of the Lord, should live as children of light (Eph 5:8), shining as stars in this dark world (Phil 2:15), so that others might see our good works and join us in giving glory to our Father in heaven (Mt 5:16).

---

[16] This includes NT passages where the "type" (τύπος or ὑποτύπωσις) is an exemplary Christian for others to imitate. See these passages, discussed further in a footnote in "Introduction to Typology and Beyond" above: Phil 3:17; 1 Thess 1:7; 2 Thess 3:9; 1 Tim 1:16; 4:12; 2 Tim 1:13; Titus 2:7; 1 Pet 5:3.

Introduction to Romans 12:9–21

Paul's Title—"Love [Is] Without Hypocrisy" (12:9a)

In contrast with much of Romans, the problems with this section do not so much concern understanding exactly what Paul means. The greater degree of difficulty comes in striving to put what he says into practice.[1] The heading of the commentary section below on 12:9–21, "Authentic Love," attempts to convey the titular nature of the opening phrase of 12:9 (ἡ ἀγάπη ἀνυπόκριτος). It has no verb, and translations typically supply an imperative: "let love be …" This may be appropriate if Paul's primary "purpose is to exhort, not simply to describe"[2] (cf. 12:1). Yet an indicative is typically inserted when a verb is lacking. Furthermore, Dunn properly observes that "an imperative (implied) slightly obscures this 'thesis character' of v 9a."[3] The definite article also expresses a "par excellence" sense, which could be conveyed by "this love" or "*the* love."[4] Nygren reflects the titular nature well: "This is what love is like."[5]

Paul begins to expound upon authentic love in 12:9–21 and then returns to use the verb "to love" (ἀγαπάω) three times and the noun "love" (ἀγάπη) once in 13:8–10. Thus it seems most proper to view all of 12:9–13:10 as Paul's explication of authentic love. Love, then, not only includes the items detailed in 12:9–21 but also involves submitting to the authorities (see 13:1–7). When Paul wraps up his teaching on "love" in 13:8–10 he will even assert that *agape* (ἀγάπη) is the "fulfillment of the Law" (13:10). This stands in concert with Jesus himself, who similarly encapsulates the Law in terms of love (Mk 12:28–34; cf. Gal 6:2).

The "love defining" section of 12:9–21, and really all the way through 13:10, vividly demonstrates how Paul's God-given understanding of love stands in sharp contrast with what much of our world perceives love to be. All too often, our love degenerates into something like "I'll scratch your back if you scratch mine." In other words, love becomes a response to favorable treatment from someone else or at least depends upon such a response in return. Otherwise, love is withheld. Such "tit for tat" love, offered only selectively and conditioned upon what one can get back in return, is, Paul suggests, hypocritical. Thus he encourages us to love "without hypocrisy" (ἀνυπόκριτος, 12:9), that is, regardless of

---

[1] See the comparable discussion of Fee and Stuart, *How to Read the Bible for All Its Worth*, 21; they use Phil 2:14 as an example for asserting that "with such a text … the problem is not understanding it but obeying it—putting it into practice."

[2] As Moo, *Romans*, 775, maintains.

[3] Dunn, *Romans*, 739.

[4] See Wallace, *Greek Grammar*, 222.

[5] Nygren, *Romans*, 426.

what comes back in return, whether good, evil, or nothing. This same adjective also occurs in relation to love in 2 Cor 6:6; 1 Tim 1:5; 1 Pet 1:22.

Our culture also asserts that love consists primarily of subjective emotional feelings and/or sexual activity. Paul engages the matter of proper and improper sexual behavior at significant length in other letters (1 Cor 6:12–7:40; Eph 5:21–33; Col 3:18–19; 1 Thess 4:3–8). It is striking, therefore, that Romans contains only brief denunciations of improper sexual conduct (1:24, 26–27 and 13:13) and never addresses the positive aspects of sexuality at all within, for example, a table of duties.[6]

Instead, Paul follows a pattern established toward the end of 1 Corinthians. There a lengthy section on spiritual gifts within the body of Christ in chapter 12 flows into his most famous explication of love in 1 Corinthians 13.[7] The same pattern occurs more briefly in Romans: spiritual gifts in 12:3–8, followed by a description of love in action in 12:9–21. Paul's words here may lack the poetic beauty of 1 Corinthians 13, but he effectively illustrates the same thing: authentic love.

Forms and Function

After the brief, tone-setting title of 12:9a, "Paul fires off a volley of short, sharp injunctions with little elaboration."[8] These illustrate that "exhortation is therefore necessary—an exhortation which does not stop at the abstract and general, but is concrete and particular."[9] Paul uses imperatives in 12:9–21, but only nine. *Seventeen participles actually dominate the discussion.*[10] These are accompanied by two infinitives (12:15) and two additional phrases (12:10a, 11a) which, like the title, contain no verb at all. Thus one ought to be cautious of translations like the NRSV, which contains thirty-one imperatives in 12:9–21!

The sense of these dominant participles is disputed. For the most part, they have no article, but, nevertheless, do not seem to be dependent on other verbs as is the typical role of adverbial participles.[11] Based upon his work in 1 Peter, Daube proposes that NT imperatival participles reflect the use of participles in Tannaitic Hebrew to express admonitions, citing the seventeen dominant

---

[6] This is a factor which weighs against the assessment that Romans is a general summary of Christian teaching; see Middendorf, *Romans 1–8*, 15–16.

[7] This is recognized by Dunn, *Romans*, 737; Nygren, *Romans*, 425–26.

[8] Moo, *Romans*, 771; similarly, Kuske, *Romans 9–16*, 198.

[9] Cranfield, *Romans*, 594.

[10] These seventeen participles occur in the following verses: 12:9 (twice), 10 (once), 11 (twice), 12 (three times), 13 (twice), 16 (three times), 17 (twice), 18 (once), and 19 (once). In addition the section contains four participles that function in more usual ways (12:14, 15 [twice], 20).

[11] Wallace, *Greek Grammar*, 650–51, categorizes these dominant participles in 12:9–21 as independent verbal participles.

participles in 12:9–19 as examples.[12] However, Moo responds that "the late date of the clearest evidence" for this use makes its NT application "questionable."[13] Wallace suggests that "the participle may function just like an imperative," citing Rom 12:9 as a clear example, but then concludes "that *most* of the NT instances of this phenomenon will be found in Rom 12 or 1 Peter."[14] He also inserts a marker indicating that this is an "abused" category.[15]

One *may* speak of "hortative participles"[16] or "imperatival participles,"[17] but these participles do *not*, thereby, become "the equivalent of hortative subjunctives or imperatives."[18] Similarly, Paul employs two infinitives in 12:15. These have also been characterized as "hortative infinitives"[19] or "imperative infinitives."[20] Here again, hortatory subjunctives and imperatives were readily available to Paul if he wished to use them, and he does use imperatives nine times in 12:9–21. But he chooses participles seventeen times and infinitives twice.

One should, therefore, strive to maintain the appropriate verbal mood in translation, as is done here. Furthermore, Paul's choice of verbal moods throughout 12:9–21, as well as his statements which lack any verb, reinforce the point that his depiction of love here, as in 1 Corinthians 13, should be regarded as *more descriptive than prescriptive*. In other words, in response to God's love and mercies to us (e.g., 5:5, 8; 8:39; 12:1), Paul intends to elicit love from us primarily by portraying what it looks like in action, rather than by issuing injunctions which order us to produce it.

Structure

Moo characterizes the structure of 12:9–21 as an "apparently haphazard arrangement."[21] However, readily identifiable patterns exist within this section.[22] See, for example, the following:

---

[12] Daube, "Appended Note: Participle and Imperative in I Peter," 480–81; in regard to the mixed use of participles, infinitives, and imperatives in Rom 12:9–19, he contends that these "different imperative expressions follow one another with no corresponding difference in meaning."

[13] Moo, *Romans*, 776, n. 27.

[14] Wallace, *Greek Grammar*, 650–51.

[15] Wallace, *Greek Grammar*, xxxii, 650.

[16] Kuske, *Romans 9–16*, 204.

[17] Dunn, *Romans*, 738.

[18] As Kuske, *Romans 9–16*, 198, maintains.

[19] Kuske, *Romans 9–16*, 204.

[20] Lenski, *Romans*, 774; see also BDF, § 389; see "Forms and Function" above.

[21] Moo, *Romans*, 771.

[22] See the diagramming of Kuske, *Romans 9–16*, 197.

- After the title, the next two clauses in 12:9 begin with participles ("abhorring," "clinging"), the latter followed by a phrase in the dative case, "to the good" (τῷ ἀγαθῷ).

- This dative leads into nine consecutive phrases (12:10–13a) that begin with a dative Greek article (translated with "the" only in 12:11b, 13a), all but the last of which are singular. Thus the plural ταῖς in 12:13 ("*the* needs") signals the end of this sequence.

- Rom 12:13 then contains another pair of participles, first "sharing" and then concluding with "pursuing" (διώκοντες). A substantival participle of the same Greek verb then serves as the object of the first imperative in 12:14, "the ones who persecute" (τοὺς διώκοντας).

- Rom 12:15 has two clauses, each beginning with an infinitive ("to rejoice," "to weep"), and nicely utilizes assonance.

- Rom 12:16 utilizes three forms of the φρονε- word group ("having a mindset," "setting your mind," "wise").

- Rom 12:17–21 is a unit framed by four instances of the adjective "evil" (κακός). It appears as the second and fourth Greek word in 12:17 and as the fifth and the last word of 12:21. This subsection coheres around the topic of how believers are to respond in love toward those who do evil. This then leads into a discussion of how God is at work even now to punish evildoers through earthly authorities (13:1–7).

This demonstrates that in order to describe genuine love Paul stitches together various well-integrated segments, which are also fairly well-connected grammatically.

In regard to topical division, the clearest distinction is between Paul's instruction regarding authentic love among Christians (12:9b–13) and the manner in which they are to relate to unbelievers (12:17–21). Cranfield recognizes a comparable twofold division in 12:9–21, but his qualifying "mainly"[23] illustrates that the division is not exclusive and should not, therefore, be pressed too far.[24] For example, while 12:14 introduces relationships with non-Christians, "one another" in 12:16 clearly focuses upon inter-Christian behavior (12:15 encompasses both). Nevertheless, the general movement of thought demonstrates how genuine love operates within the community of believers and then flows outward toward nonbelievers. It even expresses itself by submitting to those in positions of governmental authority, behavior which "constitutes not the least part of love" (13:1–7).[25] Paul then wraps up his exposition of genuine love in action in 13:8–10, using the verb "love" three times and the noun once. Thus the beginning of 12:9 and the end of 13:10 provide this identical and skillful frame: "(the) love" (ἡ ἀγάπη).

---

[23] Cranfield, *Romans*, 629.

[24] As does Wright, "Romans," 703.

[25] Calvin, *Romans*, 285.

Sources

Rom 12:9–21 utilizes a recognized style categorized by the technical term "paraenesis."[26] Moo describes how the section "strings together admonitions of a general ethical content."[27] The introduction to Romans 12–16 above discusses how these "admonitions" should be properly presented and heard in the context of 12:1–2, which flows out of all of Romans 1–11.

From whence does Paul derive the specific content of 12:9–21?

- First, as will become apparent, repeated references to the profound and transformative teachings of Jesus himself regarding the lifestyle of his disciples stand out most prominently (e.g., compare Rom 12:14 with Mt 5:44; Lk 6:27–28; Rom 12:17, 21 with Lk 6:27–36).[28] The means by which Paul came to know these teachings remains obscure to us, whether from direct revelation, through the other apostles, or via written sources. But the source is less important than the fact that *Paul does know them and that his words have been shaped by the words of his Lord.*

- Second, similarities with other NT passages point to some stream of common catechetical-like instructions on living love (e.g., 1 Thess 5:12–21; 1 Pet 3:8–12). Paul both utilizes and assists in the formation of such material.

- Third, Paul draws on the OT Scriptures. He echoes their thought (compare Rom 12:16 with Prov 3:7 and Is 5:21; Rom 12:17 with Prov 3:4; Rom 12:18 with Ps 34:14 [MT 34:15]; Rom 12:19 with Lev 19:18) and makes explicit quotations (Deut 32:35 in Rom 12:19; Prov 25:21–22 in Rom 12:20).[29]

- Fourth, the presence of verbally comparable instructions in extrabiblical sources should not be surprising. For example, Kruse discusses "the relationship between Pauline ethics and Stoic teaching" at some length.[30] Such outward commonalities with extrabiblical sources exist elsewhere, notably in OT Wisdom literature,[31] and provide evidence of the work of the Law written on the heart and conscience of those without the revealed Word (see the commentary on 2:15). Yet in all these cases, the vastly different religious content of the biblical passages is also noteworthy. As Kruse concludes:

> There are certainly aspects of Paul's ethical teaching that would resonate with those acquainted with Stoic moral philosophy, but equally there are significant differences between them, the most obvious being the impact of Christian tradition and the experience of the Spirit reflected in Paul's ethical teaching.[32]

---

[26] See "The Exhortations of Romans 12–16" in the introduction to Romans 12–16.

[27] Moo, *Romans*, 772.

[28] Cf. Dunn, *Romans*, 738; see further details and examples in the commentary on 12:9–21; for a study of the overall topic, see Schoberg, *Perspectives of Jesus in the Writings of Paul.*

[29] Cf. Dunn, *Romans*, 738.

[30] Kruse, *Romans*, 486–89.

[31] See, for example, Hummel, *The Word Becoming Flesh*, 451–52, who discusses "the phenomenal parallelism" of much of Prov 22:17–24:22 with the "Teaching of Amenemope"; Amenemope was "an Egyptian sage who lived sometime in the latter half of the second millennium B.C., thus well before Solomon."

[32] Kruse, *Romans*, 488–89.

Finally, does 12:9–21 contain ethical content explicitly aimed at the situation of Paul's addressees in Rome? Unlike the content of most of his letters (e.g., Galatians, 1 and 2 Corinthians, 1 and 2 Thessalonians), this section does not seem to directly address troublesome issues specific to the context of the believers in Rome. But this does not mean that Paul is oblivious to tensions within and among the Roman congregations. Indeed, such matters clearly become Paul's focus beginning in 14:1. Therefore,

> Paul's selection of material suggests that he may have at least one eye on the situation of the Roman church. But there are no direct allusions; nor does he use the vocabulary characteristic of his discussion of the weak and the strong in 14:1–15:13. Moreover, the parallels between the sequence of exhortations here and in other Pauline texts also suggest that Paul may be rehearsing familiar early Christian teaching.[33]

---

[33] Moo, *Romans*, 772–73.

Authentic Love

Translation

12 [9]Love [is] without hypocrisy:

abhorring the evil, clinging to the good,

[10]in brotherly love [showing] familial affection for one another,

in honor leading the way for one another,

[11]in zeal not [being] lazy,

in the Spirit blazing,

serving as slaves to the Lord,

[12]rejoicing in hope,

enduring amid pressure,

holding fast to prayer,

[13]sharing for the needs of the holy ones,

pursuing the love of strangers.

[14]Bless the ones who persecute [you]; bless and do not curse!

[15]To rejoice with rejoicing ones, to weep with weeping ones,

[16]having the same mindset toward one another,

not setting your mind on the haughty things,

but associating with the lowly ones.

Do not become wise beyond yourselves;

[17]giving back to no one evil in place of evil,

but being preoccupied with excellent things before all people,

[18]if possible [in] that which is from you, being at peace with all people.

[19]While not avenging yourselves, loved ones, rather, give a place for the wrath [of God]; indeed, it stands written: " 'Vengeance [is] for me; I myself will pay [it] back,' says the Lord." [20]But "if ever your enemy is hungry, feed him. If he is ever thirsty, give him a drink. For, while doing this, you will heap burning coals of fire upon his head."

[21]Do not be conquered by the evil, but conquer the evil [thing] with the good.

Textual Notes

12:9 ἡ ἀγάπη—The article with abstract nouns is often difficult to translate.[1] The use here reflects a category called "par excellence," in which the article points out "a substantive that is, in a sense, 'in a class by itself.' It is the only one deserving of the name."[2] To say "this love" or "*the* love" would be appropriate. For ἀγάπη, see the com-

---

[1] See Wallace, *Greek Grammar*, 226.

[2] Wallace, *Greek Grammar*, 222.

mentary on 5:5. Note that Paul's letters contain 75 of the 116 uses of ἀγάπη in the NT. Moo's observations regarding the background of the word and its cognates are helpful:

> The noun ἀγάπη is rare in nonbiblical Greek before the 2d–3d centuries A.D. It occurs 20 times in the LXX, 11 times with reference to love between humans. … The verb ἀγαπάω, on the other hand, was much more common in NT times (over 250 occurrences in the LXX), denoting all kinds of relationships. … The early Christians chose the word [ἀγάπη] (perhaps because of unwanted nuances in other words for "love" in Greek) to convey their particular understanding of the nature of love.[3]

ἀνυπόκριτος—This adjective with ἀν-, an *alpha* privative (BDF, § 117.1), is translated literally, "without hypocrisy." Its background provides the picture of "not playing the part of an actor on the stage."[4]

ἀποστυγοῦντες—The verb ἀποστυγέω is attested in Classical Greek (Herodotus, Sophocles), meaning *"hate violently, abhor"* (LSJM), but it is absent from the LXX and appears in the NT only here. Its form here is a present active participle. See the commentary for more on the word.

τὸ πονηρόν … τῷ ἀγαθῷ—In both "the evil" and "the good," the definite article gives the adjective an "independent or substantival use" in which it takes on "the lexical nuance of a noun."[5]

κολλώμενοι—The verb κολλάω expresses the idea of being "closely associated, *cling to, attach to*" (BDAG, 2). The passive most frequently has an active but intransitive sense,[6] as here. In Paul's two other uses of this verb he refers to a sexual union (1 Cor 6:16) and to the believer's spiritual union with the Lord (1 Cor 6:17; in Mt 19:5 Jesus refers to the marital union with this word).

12:10 τῇ φιλαδελφίᾳ—The noun φιλαδελφία literally encompasses the *"love* [φιλ-] *of brother/sister* [ἀδελφός or ἀδελφή]" (BDAG), but "could also denote a wider fraternal concern, for which love for brother was the pattern (as in 2 Macc 15:14; and note its frequent uses as a title for kings, particularly the Ptolemies—see LSJ)."[7] For other NT uses in regard to fellow believers, see 1 Thess 4:9; Heb 13:1; 1 Pet 1:22; 2 Pet 1:7.

φιλόστοργοι—The adjective φιλόστοργος occurs only here in the NT and appears in the LXX only in 4 Macc 15:13. It denotes *"loving dearly"* (BDAG), "typically, love of parent for child … , but also of other family ties."[8] Here again, "the type of family affection can be understood as capable of being extended fittingly to such as country or king or a pet animal."[9] How much more fitting, then, is it for all those within God's

---

[3] Moo, *Romans*, 775, n. 24.

[4] Moo, *Romans*, 775, n. 26.

[5] Wallace, *Greek Grammar*, 294, referencing this passage on 295; see also Mounce, *Basics of Biblical Greek*, 65–66.

[6] See Voelz, *Fundamental Greek Grammar*, 144–46.

[7] Dunn, *Romans*, 741.

[8] Dunn, *Romans*, 740.

[9] Dunn, *Romans*, 741.

family! The bracketed insertion of "showing" in the translation aligns with the sequence of nine consecutive participles in 12:9b–13.

προηγούμενοι—The basic meaning of the compound verb προηγέομαι, which occurs only here in the NT, is "to go first and lead the way, *go before and show the way*" (BDAG, 1). Some early translations of this verse understood it to mean "*try to outdo one another in showing respect*" (BDAG, 3). The simple verb ἡγέομαι (without the prefix) is thought by some to point in the direction of "*consider better, esteem more highly*" (BDAG, s.v. προηγέομαι, 3) for the meaning of the compound verb here.[10] While the latter seems pertinent to the meaning of the simple verb in Phil 2:3 and 1 Thess 5:13, it seems best in this verse to stick with the meaning attested elsewhere for the compound verb, "leading the way."

12:11 τῇ σπουδῇ—See the second textual note on 12:8.

μὴ ὀκνηροί—The cognate verb ὀκνέω refers to holding "back from doing someth[ing], *hesitate, delay*" (BDAG). The adjective here, ὀκνηρός, then characterizes one negatively as "*idle, lazy, indolent*" (BDAG, 1). Its negation with μή is an example of this negative "in abrupt expressions without a verb" (BDAG, s.v. μή, 1 c ζ).

ζέοντες—The verb ζέω literally means to "boil or seethe" with the implications of resulting heat and came to be used figuratively in regard to being "stirred up emotionally, *be enthusiastic/excited/on fire*" (BDAG). The participle form should be rendered in a verbal sense as "boiling" or "blazing."

τῷ κυρίῳ δουλεύοντες—For (ὁ) κύριος, "(the) Lord," as a reference to Jesus, see the commentary on 10:9 and 10:12. For δουλεύω, "to serve," see the discussion of δοῦλος, "servant," in the first textual note on 1:1 and "Freed for Slavery to God (6:19)" in the commentary 6:12–23. An interesting textual variant to κυρίῳ is καιρῷ in D F G, in which case the clause refers to "serving the time" (cf. "redeeming the time" in Eph 4:16; Col 4:5). But the textual attestation for καιρῷ is weak, and the idea seems out of place here.[11]

12:12 τῇ ἐλπίδι χαίροντες—For ἐλπίς, "hope," see the commentary on 4:18. This is the first of three uses of the verb χαίρω in Romans, depicting "a state of happiness and well-being, *rejoice, be glad*" (BDAG, 1; also 12:15; 16:19).

τῇ θλίψει ὑπομένοντες—See the second and third textual notes and the commentary on 5:3, both for θλίψις, "affliction, pressure," and its relation to the verb ὑπομένω, "to endure," via its cognate noun ὑπομονή in 5:3.

τῇ προσευχῇ προσκαρτεροῦντες—The verb προσκαρτερέω means "to persist in someth[ing]" or "*hold fast to*" (BDAG, 2 and 2 b). Its only other occurrence in Romans applies to the governing authorities' diligence in their duties (13:6). But here the verb characterizes persistence in "prayer" (προσευχή), as also in Acts 1:14; 2:42; 6:4; Col 4:2.[12]

---

[10] Similarly, Cranfield, *Romans*, 632–33; Käsemann, *Romans*, 346; Sanday and Headlam, *Romans*, 361.

[11] See Metzger, *A Textual Commentary on the Greek New Testament*, 528; Moo, *Romans*, 769–70, n. 1.

[12] Dunn, *Romans*, 743.

12:13 ταῖς χρείαις τῶν ἁγίων—The noun χρεία denotes "that which is lacking and needed, *need, lack, want, difficulty*" (BDAG, 2). In the NT, the plural always involves material needs (see the commentary). The dative case functions as a dative of advantage, which indicates "*for the benefit of* or *in the interest of.*"[13] The plural of the adjective ἅγιος, "holy," with the article is used substantively for "the saints/holy ones" (cf. 1:7).

κοινωνοῦντες—The basic meaning of κοινωνέω is to "*share, have a share*" (BDAG, 1). The verb here conveys "giving a share" to those in need (as also in Gal 6:6; Phil 4:15). But note the use in regard to "sharing" in spiritual things in Rom 15:27. The cognate noun κοινωνία more often expresses theological notions of "fellowship" with God and others in the Gospel (e.g., 1 Cor 1:9; 2 Cor 13:13 [ET 13:14]; Phil 1:5; 2:1; cf. κοινωνέω in 1 Pet 4:13).

τὴν φιλοξενίαν—The noun φιλοξενία literally means "love [φιλο-] of a stranger [ξένος]," but it can be translated as "*hospitality*" (BDAG). Its only other NT use occurs in Heb 13:2.

διώκοντες—The basic notion of διώκω is "to move rapidly and decisively toward an objective" (BDAG, 1). This extends in divergent directions, to the notion of harassing/persecuting (BDAG, 2), as in the next verse, 12:14, as well as to that of "pursuing" a positive goal, as here (also Rom 14:19; 1 Cor 14:1; 1 Tim 6:11; 2 Tim 2:22).

12:14 εὐλογεῖτε—"Bless" is the *first actual imperative verb in the section*. The present tense conveys a durative sense[14] which implies the continued blessing of a persecutor and/or repeated blessing toward various persecutors. For the meaning, see the commentary.

τοὺς διώκοντας—See the last textual note on 12:13.

[ὑμᾶς]—Regarding "you" Metzger comments: "It is difficult to decide whether ὑμᾶς was deleted in order to extend the range of the exhortation, or whether copyists, recollecting the parallel sayings in Mt 5.44 and Lk 6.28, added the pronoun."[15] The latter seems more likely, especially due to the absence of ὑμᾶς in 𝔓⁴⁶ and B, "but it makes little difference to the meaning since some such object must in any case be assumed."[16]

μὴ καταρᾶσθε—This form too is a present imperative, as is εὐλογεῖτε (see the first textual note on 12:14). The deponent verb καταράομαι, then, expresses the opposite of εὐλογέω and means "to curse."

12:15 χαίρειν μετὰ χαιρόντων, κλαίειν μετὰ κλαιόντων—The entire verse is alliterative. For χαίρω, "to rejoice," see the first textual note on 12:12. The verb κλαίω means "to weep." Their infinitives here are *the first time Paul uses infinitives* in this section. As with the participles above, it is again tempting to translate them as if they were imperatives, particularly in light of the three actual imperatives in 12:14 (see "Introduction to Romans 12:9–21" before this pericope). But Wallace cautions: "*Very* rarely an infinitive may function like an imperative," and the two instances in Rom 12:15 plus the one in

---

[13] Wallace, *Greek Grammar*, 142; see also 144.

[14] Wallace, *Greek Grammar*, 485: "With the *present*, the force generally is to *command the action as an ongoing process.*"

[15] Metzger, *A Textual Commentary on the Greek New Testament*, 528.

[16] Moo, *Romans*, 770, n. 2.

Phil 3:16 "are apparently the *only* examples of this in the NT."[17] Moreover, he notes that στοιχεῖν in Phil 3:16 "more resembles a hortatory subjunctive than an imperative."[18] It again seems best to acknowledge that Paul could readily have used imperative forms if that was his intention, but instead, he asserts that "love without hypocrisy" (12:9) means "to rejoice … to weep" (12:15).

12:16 φρονοῦντες, μὴ τὰ ὑψηλὰ φρονοῦντες—For the verb φρονέω, see the third textual note on 8:5; see also the commentary on 8:5 and 12:3. Its participle is repeated identically here in 12:16, but translated somewhat differently each time, "have a mind-set" and then "set one's mind." For ὑψηλά, the neuter plural of the adjective ὑψηλός used substantively,[19] see the fourth textual note on 11:20, where too it is the object of φρονέω. The translation "haughty things" communicates its negative connotations.

τοῖς ταπεινοῖς συναπαγόμενοι—The doubly compound verb συναπάγω (σύν + ἀπό + ἄγω) in the passive voice with the dative can mean "to be led astray, carried away" by or to something (cf. BDAG, 1). Here, however, the passive means "to join the company of others, *associate with*" them (BDAG, 3), and the object is dative (τοῖς ταπεινοῖς) because of the συν- prefix of the verb, which has an "'associative' flavor."[20] That object is the plural of the substantival adjective ταπεινός, which "pert[ains] to being of low social status or to relative inability to cope, *lowly, undistinguished, of no account*" (BDAG, 1). BDAG takes the adjective as neuter in gender and suggests that this clause means "accommodate yourself to humble ways" (BDAG, s.v. συναπάγω, 2). But the dative form can also be masculine, and the consistent reference to people in this context makes a personal reference with the masculine gender more likely, "associating with the lowly ones."

μὴ γίνεσθε—This present imperative negated with μή forms a prohibition that conveys "a *general precept*":[21] "do not become." For the same construction, see the first textual notes on 11:18; 12:2, 21; and the fourth textual note on 11:20.

φρόνιμοι παρ᾿ ἑαυτοῖς—The same expression appears in 11:25; see the fourth textual note there.

12:17 ἀντὶ κακοῦ—The preposition ἀντί appears only here in Romans. It indicates "that one thing is equiv[alent] to another, *for, as, in place of*" (BDAG, 2) and takes its object in the genitive, here κακοῦ.

προνοούμενοι καλά—The verb προνοέω means "to give careful thought to, *take thought for, take into consideration, have regard for*" (BDAG, 1). Both here and in 2 Cor 8:21 it takes as its object the neuter plural καλά, "excellent things," and involves making up one's mind beforehand or "being preoccupied with." For the adjective καλός, "*excellent*" (BDAG, 2 c), see the third textual note on 7:16.

---

[17] Wallace, *Greek Grammar*, 608.

[18] Wallace, *Greek Grammar*, 608.

[19] See Wallace, *Greek Grammar*, 294–95.

[20] Moo, *Romans*, 784, n. 73.

[21] Wallace, *Greek Grammar*, 724–25.

12:18 εἰ δυνατόν—In contrast to Paul's confident description of divine ability with δυνατός in 4:21 and 11:23, God is "powerful," Paul now uses the neuter form of the adjective to speak of what is "possible" (BDAG, 2) for sinful humans in a fallen world. The verb assumed is ἐστίν: "if [it *is*] possible." But note the noncommittal conditional force of εἰ, "if." It introduces a first class conditional, which "indicates the assumption of truth for the sake of argument."[22] For the implications of this phrase with the next (τὸ ἐξ ὑμῶν) in this verse, see the commentary.

τὸ ἐξ ὑμῶν—In this abbreviated phrase, "that which is from you," the neuter article τό refers back to the neuter adjective δυνατόν, denoting that which is humanly "possible." The preposition ἐκ introduces "the reason which is a presupposition" for that possibility, "*as far as it depends on you*" (BDAG, 3 e). This expression also allows for the real possibility that in many human circumstances, believers, due to circumstances beyond their control, may not be able to be at peace with others, as when others are intent on hostility.

εἰρηνεύοντες—The verb εἰρηνεύω is cognate to the noun εἰρήνη, "peace." It has a more stative meaning, "*live in peace, be at peace*," or perhaps even "*keep the peace*" (BDAG, 2 a and b). Jesus extends the notion with the cognate substantival adjective εἰρηνοποιός, encouraging his disciples to be active "peacemakers" (Mt 5:9).

12:19 μὴ ἑαυτοὺς ἐκδικοῦντες—The verb ἐκδικέω can have a positive force, "procure justice for someone, *grant justice*" (BDAG, 1). Note, for example, this verb in Jesus' parable of the unjust judge who, nevertheless, is persuaded to "grant justice" (Lk 18:3, 5). The cognate noun ἐκδίκησις, "justice," appears later there (Lk 18:7, 8) and here (but in a different sense; see the third textual note on Rom 12:19). But here the object of the participle ἐκδικοῦντες is the accusative reflexive pronoun ἑαυτούς, "avenging *yourselves*," which signals the idea of "taking justice into one's own hands … *take one's revenge*" (BDAG, s.v. ἐκδικέω, 1). The negative force here is confirmed by the preceding μή, advising believers "not" to do so.

δότε τόπον τῇ ὀργῇ—The verb δότε is the aorist active imperative of δίδωμι, "give." The sense is permissive; do not take revenge into your own hands, but patiently "give," that is, allow a "place" (τόπον) "for the wrath [of God]," that is, allow room for God to execute his own wrath in your behalf. For ὀργή, "wrath," see the second textual note and the commentary on 1:18.

ἐμοὶ ἐκδίκησις—Both here (and in the next clause) the pronoun is fronted in emphatic position, literally, "*mine* [ἐμοί] [is] vengeance." The dative case of ἐμοί expresses possession, "*belonging to*" me.[23] The noun ἐκδίκησις carries the same judicial connotations as the cognate verb ἐκδικέω (see first textual note on this verse). But when God enacts his "retaliation for harm done" (BDAG, s.v. ἐκδίκησις, 2), it entails a "righteous" (note the δίκη root) or just "penalty inflicted on wrongdoers, abs[tract] *punishment*" (BDAG, 3), which then procures justice for his people.

---

[22] Wallace, *Greek Grammar*, 690.

[23] Wallace, *Greek Grammar*, 149; see 149–51.

ἐγὼ ἀνταποδώσω—Again, note the emphatic fronted pronoun, "*I myself* [ἐγώ] will give back in return." For the doubly compound verb ἀνταποδίδωμι, see the second textual note on 11:35. A notion of "reciprocity" exists which, in this future form, means that God will "exact retribution, *repay, pay back*" those who do evil (BDAG, 1 and 2).

12:20 ἀλλὰ ἐὰν πεινᾷ ὁ ἐχθρός σου—The verb πεινᾷ is the subjunctive of the contract verb πεινάω, "to hunger," in the protasis of a future more vivid (third class) conditional sentence. The general sense considers a situation "as *uncertain of fulfillment, but still likely*."[24] Thus with ἐάν (εἰ + ἄν), it conveys the sense of "if ever." This implies "not just once, but every time your enemy is 'hungry' (πεινᾷ)."[25] The picture described, drawn from Prov 25:21, could be realized in a literal way or a metaphorical one in terms of any need (see the fourth textual note on 12:20 regarding πότιζε).

ψώμιζε αὐτόν—This is the apodosis of the third class conditional (see the protasis in the previous textual note), whose "apodosis can have any tense and any mood."[26] The verb is the present imperative of ψωμίζω, "to feed."

ἐὰν διψᾷ—This is the protasis of another future more vivid (third class) conditional sentence (see the preceding two textual notes). The picture is synonymous, but with drink instead of food. The verb is the present subjunctive of διψάω, "to thirst."

πότιζε αὐτόν—This apodosis has the present imperative of ποτίζω, "to give (someone something) to drink." This verb can be used in either a literal or a metaphorical sense. A literal sense is intended in, e.g., Mt 27:48; Lk 13:15. The verb is clearly metaphorical in the giving of "milk" for the church to drink (1 Cor 3:2) and the "watering" of the church, pictured as a plant (1 Cor 3:6–8). While the Sacrament of Baptism uses physical water, the verb seems to be metaphorical when Paul speaks of Christians being given "the one Spirit" "to drink" in Baptism (1 Cor 12:13). The passages that use ποτίζω to speak of receiving or serving Jesus by giving a drink to his little ones or brothers (Mt 10:40–42; 25:35–40) may be either literal or metaphorical, or perhaps both. Contrast the negative use of ποτίζω in Mt 25:42–45; Rev 14:8.

ἄνθρακας πυρὸς σωρεύσεις—This is cited from LXX Prov 25:22. The verb σωρεύω means "to amass by setting one thing atop another, *heap/pile up*" (BDAG, 1). The object, ἄνθρακας πυρός, literally, "coals of fire," refers to burning coals. For the interpretation, see "The Image of Coals of Fire (12:20)" in the commentary.

12:21 μὴ νικῶ ... νίκα—The contract verb νικάω means "*conquer, overcome*" (BDAG, 1). The first form, νικῶ, is a present passive imperative, "be conquered." It is negated with μή to form a prohibition which has "the force of a *general precept*."[27] For other instances of a present imperative negated by μή forming a general prohibition, see the first textual notes on 11:18; 12:2; the fourth textual note on 11:20; and the third textual note on 12:16. The second form, νίκα, later in the verse is a present active

---

[24] Wallace, *Greek Grammar*, 696.

[25] Kuske, *Romans 9–16*, 210.

[26] Wallace, *Greek Grammar*, 696; so also Mounce, *Basics of Biblical Greek*, 341. Kuske, *Romans 9–16*, 210, incorrectly suggests that this is a present general conditional, which he himself asserts takes a "present indicative" in the apodosis.

[27] Wallace, *Greek Grammar*, 724.

imperative and has the same durative force. For both the passive and the active imperative, "the present tense indicates a call for dedicated persistence."[28]

ὑπὸ τοῦ κακοῦ … τὸ κακόν—The preposition ὑπό serves as a "marker of agency or cause, *by*" (BDAG, A). Its genitive object, τοῦ κακοῦ, is a definite substantival adjective,[29] whose form could either be neuter, "(the) evil," or masculine and personal, "the evil *one*"; cf. ἀπὸ τοῦ πονηροῦ, "from the evil one," in the final petition of the Lord's Prayer (Mt 6:13). The same adjective (κακός) at the end of the verse, also definite and substantival, is the direct object of νίκα, "conquer," and so it is accusative, τὸ κακόν. Its article (τό) is neuter, indicating that it denotes "the evil [thing]" or, less literally, "that which is evil."[30] This may signal that Paul intends the first to be read as neuter as well. On the other hand, if the first is masculine ("the evil one"), Paul may switch to the neuter at the end of the sentence to avoid telling Christians themselves to "conquer the evil one," since Christ alone can and has defeated the devil. For that reason we petition the Father in the Lord's Prayer to "deliver us from the evil one" (Mt 6:13), rather than asking the Father to enable us to deliver ourselves from him.

Commentary

The Source of Authentic Love and a General Expression (12:9)

"Love [is] without hypocrisy" (12:9a). The titular nature of 12:9a is discussed in "Introduction to Romans 12:9–21" before this pericope. A response to that statement in Rome and in our own day might well be "What does this mean?" or, more precisely, "What does such love look like?" What follows in 12:9b–21 answers those questions by explaining what *authentic love in action does*.[31] Matera captures this by listing "twelve maxims" from 12:9–21.[32] Paul also describes "love" (ἀγάπη) by using other "love" terminology as well (φιλαδελφία, "brotherly love," and φιλόστοργος, "familial affection," in 12:10; also φιλοξενία, "love of strangers," in 12:13). These various terms for "love" in Greek illustrate the richness of the language.[33]

Richer by far is the observation that *all* uses of the noun "love" (ἀγάπη) thus far in Romans communicate the love of the triune God—the Father (5:5, 8; 8:39), Christ (8:35), and through the Spirit (5:5; note also 15:30)—*for us*.

---

[28] Dunn, *Romans*, 751; Wallace, *Greek Grammar*, 485: "With the *present* [imperative], the force generally is to *command the action as an ongoing process*."

[29] See Wallace, *Greek Grammar*, 294–95; Mounce, *Basics of Biblical Greek*, 65–66.

[30] According to Wallace, *Greek Grammar*, 213, translations such as the latter regard "the article [as] equivalent to a relative pronoun in *force*"; see 213–15.

[31] Dunn, *Romans*, 736, captures this fairly well with the title "Love as the Norm for Social Relationships." However, Sanday and Headlam, *Romans*, 360, lose the "love" connection with the title "Maxims to Guide the Christian Life," as does Moo, *Romans*, 774, who concludes that the section serves "as a further elaboration of that 'good' which the person who is being transformed by the renewing of the mind approves of (v. 2)." Cranfield, *Romans*, 628, titles this section "A Series of Loosely Connected Items of Exhortation (12.9–21)."

[32] Matera, *Romans*, 291; unfortunately, he includes "let love be sincere" as the first in his list, rather than its heading.

[33] See the classic work of C. S. Lewis, *The Four Loves*.

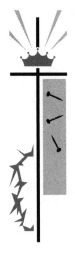

The same is true of the cognate verb "to love" (ἀγαπάω, 8:37; 9:13, 25), aside from 8:28 ("the ones loving God"). Only here does Paul begin to use ἀγάπη of the Christians' "love"; he does so again in 13:10 and 14:15. The verb "love" functions similarly in 13:8 (twice) and 13:9. *Love from God in Christ through the Spirit to us then serves as the foundation and motivation for all responsive Christlike behavior.*[34] This order corroborates what 1 Jn 4:19 says: "we love because he first loved us."[35] Origen summarizes the theological basis for what follows using Paul's language:

> It happens that we hate things we ought not to, just as we love things we ought not to. We are ordered to love our brothers, not to hate them. If you think someone is ungodly, remember that *Christ died for the ungodly*. And if you think that because your brother is a sinner you do not have to love him, remember that *Christ Jesus came into the world to save sinners*.[36]

Paul begins his lengthy depiction of authentic love by asserting that it entails "abhorring the evil, clinging to the good" (ἀποστυγοῦντες τὸ πονηρόν, κολλώμενοι τῷ ἀγαθῷ, 12:9b). The first verb, "abhorring" (the compound ἀποστυγέω), is related to the compound cognate adjective "hating God" (θεοστυγής), which Paul employed for fallen humanity in 1:30. The cognate verb (στυγνάζω) appears in the LXX when people are "appalled" at the divine punishment of heathen (Tyre and its king in Ezek 27:35; 28:19; Pharaoh in Ezek 32:10). The prefixed preposition on the verb here (ἀπό, "away from") enhances the sense of revulsion, as in Classical Greek.[37] Paul follows this forceful participle with his only use in Romans of πονηρός, another strong word meaning " 'wicked' in the active sense, … not merely κακόν, morally inferior."[38] The positive antithesis, "clinging to the good," conveys an emphatic and even intimate sense (see the last textual note on 12:9). This serves as one place to demonstrate the *general content* of Paul's material in Romans 12. Note the commonalities with 1 Thess 5:21b–22:

τὸ καλὸν κατέχετε, ἀπὸ παντὸς εἴδους πονηροῦ ἀπέχεσθε.

Hold fast to the good; hold yourself away from every appearance of evil.

Authentic Love within the Spirit-Filled Family of Faith (12:10–13)
Familial Ties (12:10a)

Paul adds comments about Christians relating to one another in genuine love by using two other "love" terms in 12:10a: "In brotherly love [showing] familial affection for one another" (τῇ φιλαδελφίᾳ εἰς ἀλλήλους φιλόστοργοι, 12:10a). The first (φιλαδελφία) normally applies to brothers and sisters; the

---

[34] For numerous biblical references outside of Romans, see Nygren, *Romans*, 423–25.

[35] See Schuchard, *1–3 John*, 491.

[36] Origen, *Romans* (Bray, *Romans*, ACCS NT 6:315), quoting in italics Rom 5:6 and 1 Tim 1:15.

[37] See the third textual note on 12:9.

[38] Lenski, *Romans*, 766–67.

second (φιλόστοργος) has the connotations of parental love (see the first two textual notes on 12:10). Paul here describes how "the brother love of Christians should be like that of the members of one family. … In brother love all are alike, stand on the same level."[39] His choice of terminology, then, effectively conveys "a sense of family belongingness which transcended immediate family ties and did not depend on natural or ethnic bonds."[40] This expands upon his earlier assertion that "we, the many, are one body in Christ" (12:5). And just as these bodily members "do not have the same function" (12:4), so "in a family, there is also a difference. There are children, parents, grandparents."[41] This leads into the next sequence, which details the ways in which believers honor and serve one another.

Love in Action (12:10b–11)

The next string of statements, in 12:10b–13, depicts actual expressions of authentic love within the Christian family, concluding with yet another "love" term, "love of strangers" (φιλοξενία, 12:13):

> [10b]In honor, leading the way for one another,
> [11]in zeal not [being] lazy,
> in the Spirit blazing,
> serving as slaves to the Lord,
> [12]rejoicing in hope,
> enduring amid pressure,
> holding fast to prayer,
> [13]sharing for the needs of the holy ones,
> pursuing the love of strangers.

Paul's Greek consistently places dative phrases at the beginning of all but the final statement. This Greek word order at times seems awkward in English, so the translation here only partially preserves it.

The meaning of the final participle in 12:10 is disputed, but the understanding of "going before" others in showing honor seems most appropriate (see the third textual note on 12:10). Thus do not wait to be honored, and do not seek honor for yourself (cf. Lk 14:7–11; 20:45–47). Instead, take the initiative in honoring others.

Prior to introducing a negative characteristic, Paul begins 12:11 by providing a positive attribute, "in zeal" (τῇ σπουδῇ). This phrase utilizes the same noun Paul employs to commend the "zeal/eagerness" of those in leadership roles in 12:8. Now "zeal also comes out of loving and gives it warmth."[42] Paul then counters the generally positive activities thus far with an opposing negative expression, "not [being] lazy." The adjective ὀκνηρός depicts a fault "often

---

[39] Lenski, *Romans*, 767–68.

[40] Dunn, *Romans*, 741.

[41] Lenski, *Romans*, 768.

[42] Chrysostom, *Homilies on Romans*, 21 (Bray, *Romans*, ACCS NT 6:315).

warned against in wisdom literature."[43] The antithesis of active zeal with passive laziness recalls the thematic exhortation to offer your bodies as a *living sacrifice* in 12:1, that is, the oxymoron of actively living (in Christ to God) even after dying (with Christ to sin); cf. 6:1–4.

Next Paul speaks of "bubbling," "boiling," and/or "blazing in the Spirit" (τῷ πνεύματι ζέοντες, 12:11). This verb (ζέω) conveys a number of vibrant pictures. In the Greek translation of Ezekiel, it refers to boiling water (LXX Ezek 24:5), and in that of Job, to fermentation (LXX Job 32:19), while Josephus uses it for glowing iron.[44] The only other use of the verb in the NT depicts Apollos in this same manner as "blazing in the Spirit" (ζέων τῷ πνεύματι, Acts 18:25). Thus it seems best to take the dative case as indicating basis or cause:[45] our "blazing" is the result of the Spirit's work in us. Moo then explains the phrase as "to allow the Holy Spirit to 'set us on fire,' "[46] but an active verbal translation should be preferred for the active Greek participle. While "boiling" is perhaps most literal, "blazing" also captures the essence well since both Testaments regularly connect fire with the Spirit of the Lord, most notably on Pentecost (Acts 2:2–4).[47] Thus the dative noun πνεύματι refers *primarily* to the Holy Spirit,[48] rather than to our own human spirit,[49] though one should again be cautious about completely separating a believer's spirit from the Holy Spirit (see the first textual note and the commentary on 8:16). Dunn holds both together, observing that "such emotive imagery [Paul] regularly uses of the Spirit (e.g., 5:5; 1 Cor 12:13c; 1 Thess 1:6)—he seems indeed concerned to keep the human emotional/spiritual dimension correlated to the Spirit (8:15–16, 26; 1 Cor 14:14–16; Gal 5:22–23)."[50]

[43] Dunn, *Romans*, 741, citing LXX Prov 6:6, 9; 20:4, 21:25, 22:13; 26:13–16; 31:27; Sirach 22:1–2; 37:11.

[44] Dunn, *Romans*, 742, citing for Josephus, *War*, 5.479.

[45] See Wallace, *Greek Grammar*, 167–68.

[46] Moo, *Romans*, 778, including n. 46.

[47] See also "Spirit of burning" in Is 4:4; in Is 30:27–28 Yahweh comes "burning in his anger," and "his tongue is like a consuming fire," while "his Spirit is like a flooding river." Jesus "will baptize you in the Holy Spirit and fire" (Mt 3:11; Lk 3:16). In 1 Thess 5:19 Paul counsels: "Do not extinguish the Spirit." Rev 4:5 refers to "seven burning torches of fire … , which are the seven spirits of God." Cf. the fiery theophany in Ezekiel 1–2 with the "Spirit" in Ezek 1:12, 20–21; 2:2. Cf. also Deut 33:2, as well as Heb 1:7, where God "makes his angels spirits and his ministers a flame of fire." The collocation of "love," "zeal," and "blazing" in Rom 12:10–11 might be compared to Song 8:6, which speaks of "love" and "zeal/jealousy" as "flashes of fire … the flame of Yah(weh)."

[48] Barrett, *Romans*, 240, makes the point too exclusively an "either/or" by asserting that "the parallel with 'the Lord' shows that here 'Spirit' means not the human spirit but the Holy Spirit."

[49] Against Murray, *Romans*, 2:130–31, who concludes: "It is not necessary to refer it to the Holy Spirit."

[50] Dunn, *Romans*, 742; Sanday and Headlam, *Romans*, 361, though weighted to the human side, similarly keep both together by describing the referent as "the human spirit instinct with and inspired by the Divine Spirit."

Moo buttresses this notion by connecting the description with the clause which follows, "serving as slaves to the Lord" (τῷ κυρίῳ δουλεύοντες, 12:11c). Together they remind us that "being set on fire by the Spirit must lead to, and be directed by, our service of the Lord."[51] Thus the Spirit need not quench ecstatic fervor or drive us away from emotional experience. Instead, the Spirit drives those passions into action, toward a self-sacrificial and willing enslavement to our Lord (12:11c), who desires that we act in ways that reflect him and benefit others. The clause recalls the language and exhortation of 6:12–23 (see the introduction to Romans 12–16) and most directly 6:19, which states: "thus now present your bodily members [as] slavish [δοῦλα] to righteousness leading to sanctification."

Hope and Its Companions (12:12)

Paul offers three brief characterizations of love in action in 12:12: *love* involves "rejoicing in hope, enduring amid pressure, holding fast to prayer." The first two expressions have *firm roots earlier in Romans*. In 4:18 Paul discussed Abraham's "hope" (ἐλπίς), built on faith: "he believed" (ἐπίστευσεν, as also in 4:3, 17; see the commentary on 4:18). Here also in 12:12 "hope" (ἐλπίς) conveys confident expectation, a notion rooted in faith in God's Word, for God is trustworthy to fulfill all his promises,[52] even if that fulfillment will take place only after this earthly life.[53] This stands in contrast with the secular Greek understanding of ἐλπίς ("hope") as an unknown fate. Shortly after his analysis of Abraham in Romans 4, Paul fills out what "hope" instills in 5:2b–5:

> [2b]And we boast upon hope [ἐλπίς] of the glory of God. [3]And not only [this], but we are also boasting within pressures [the plural of θλῖψις], knowing that pressure [θλῖψις] is accomplishing patient endurance [ὑπομονή], [4]and patient endurance [ὑπομονή] [is accomplishing] tested character, and tested character [is accomplishing] hope [ἐλπίς]. [5]And hope [ἐλπίς] will not put [us] to shame because the love [ἡ ἀγάπη] of God has been poured out and remains within our hearts through the Holy Spirit [πνεῦμα ἅγιον], who was given to us.

Romans 12 contains a similar sequence which also integrates love (ἡ ἀγάπη, 12:9), the Spirit (πνεῦμα, 12:11), hope (ἐλπίς, 12:12), pressure (θλῖψις, 12:12), and endurance (ὑπομένω, 12:12) with one another.

While 12:12 uses a different verb (χαίρω) for "rejoicing in hope" (τῇ ἐλπίδι χαίροντες), the clause stands comparable to the positive "we boast upon hope" (καυχώμεθα ἐπ᾽ ἐλπίδι) amid "pressures" (ἐν ταῖς θλίψεσιν) in 5:2–3. Now

---

[51] Moo, *Romans*, 778–79; noted also by Dunn, *Romans*, 742.

[52] While the LXX version of the Abraham narrative does not employ the Greek vocabulary of ἐλπίς, "hope," or ἐλπίζω, "to hope," Abraham's confident hope stems from his trust that God will indeed accomplish all of his promises, no matter how improbable they may seem; see especially Gen 15:6.

[53] Of the many promises given to Abraham in Genesis 12–24, only some were realized in his lifetime, yet he continued to trust God to complete his promises in the future (e.g., Gen 15:5; 22:17; 26:4). See the exposition of Abraham's faith in Heb 11:8–19, which included the belief that God is able to raise the dead.

"enduring amid pressure" (12:12) also connects with what God seeks to accomplish when various sufferings take place in the lives of those who have been declared righteous from faith (5:1, 3–4; cf. 8:18–25, 35–36). Above all, 5:5 makes it clear that the authentic love depicted throughout this section flows out from the love God has first poured into our hearts through the Holy Spirit. All our blazing in the Spirit (12:11) stems from his gift as well. And Paul has already reminded us that any and all "pressure" which might come our way cannot separate us from Christ's "love" (θλῖψις and ἀγάπη, 8:35). Here, then, we have "both the sense of eschatological excitement ('rejoicing') and the note of eschatological reserve ('in hope')."[54]

Therefore, in the meantime and in the midst of whatever might be encountered along the way (see 8:35–36, 38–39; cf. 12:14, 17), our *responsive love* exhibits itself in confidently "holding fast to prayer" (τῇ προσευχῇ προσκαρτεροῦντες, 12:12). Ambrosiaster points out that "prayer is essential if we are to survive tribulation!"[55] Surprisingly, this is the first occurrence of the common noun for "prayer" (προσευχή) since Paul spoke of his own "prayers" in 1:10. Later in 15:30 he uses the noun for a third and final time in asking the Roman believers to join him in their "prayers."[56] Rom 8:24–26 moves us similarly from "hope" (ἐλπίς) to "endurance" (ὑπομονή) and then connects endurance with "praying" (προσεύχομαι) guided by "the Spirit" (τὸ πνεῦμα):[57]

> [24]For we were saved in hope [τῇ … ἐλπίδι]. But while hope [ἐλπίς] is being seen, it is not hope [ἐλπίς]; indeed, who is hoping [ἐλπίζει] for what he sees? [25]But if we are hoping [ἐλπίζομεν] [for] what we are not seeing, we are eagerly awaiting [it] through patient endurance [δι' ὑπομονῆς]. [26]And likewise, the Spirit [τὸ πνεῦμα] is also alongside assisting [us] in our weakness. For we do not know what we should pray for [προσευξώμεθα] as it is appropriate, but the Spirit [τὸ πνεῦμα] himself pleads in our behalf with unspeakable groans.

Thus Paul understands and clearly communicates that the Spirit (12:11) enables, empowers, and encourages all the actions which Paul calls for and forth in 12:12.

Sharing and Serving Strangers (12:13)

Before turning his attention toward love for those outside the Christian community, Paul gives wider application to the serving and sharing gifts of 12:7–8. In 12:13 believers in general display *love* in action when "sharing for the needs of the holy ones" and "pursuing the love of strangers." The former clause uses the verb "to share, participate, have fellowship" (κοινωνέω), a member of the theologically important "fellowship" word group (see the second textual note on 12:13). However, the accompanying noun "need" (χρεία), particularly when

---

[54] Dunn, *Romans*, 742.

[55] Ambrosiaster, *Romans* (Bray, *Romans*, ACCS NT 6:316).

[56] For a summary of Paul's statements regarding prayer, see Kruse, *Romans*, 477–78.

[57] Moo, *Romans*, 779; Cranfield, *Romans*, 637, also notes "the special frequency with which the verb προσκαρτερεῖν ['to hold fast'] is used in the NT in connexion with prayer" (citing Acts 1:14; 2:42; Col 4:2; cf. Lk 18:1; Eph 6:18; 1 Thess 5:17).

it appears in the plural as here (ταῖς χρείαις), generally refers to supplying the physical necessities of others within the community of believers (Acts 6:3; 20:34; 28:10; Titus 3:14; cf. Acts 2:42–45). While not discounting the significance of the spiritual fellowship often conveyed by this verb and its cognates (see 15:26–27), the connection with "need" (χρεία) indicates a focus on material privations here. Paul also uses this verb "in the more specific sense of 'sharing by contributing (monetarily)' " in Gal 6:6 and Phil 4:15.[58] In fact, later in Romans, both the verb (κοινωνέω) and its cognate noun (κοινωνία) refer to the collection Paul is gathering for the "holy ones" (τῶν ἁγίων) in Jerusalem (15:26–27). The comparable wording there might lead his hearers to recall the phrasing here.

At this point, however, it seems best to view the expression in 12:13 as a general *and ongoing* expression of love, rather than limiting it to any particular offering. Thus Paul, like Jesus (e.g., Mt 10:42; 25:34–40), urges us "to have fellowship with, to participate in, the 'needs' of the saints. These 'needs' are material ones: food, clothing, and shelter."[59] It is surely always good to "provide for those who need the services of others for a while," especially those who "neglect their own affairs for the sake of Christ."[60]

The term in 12:13 translated as "love of strangers" (φιλοξενία) is another compound "love" term (see other such compounds in 12:10; cf. 12:9). Even though "love of strangers" (φιλοξενία) appears only once elsewhere in the NT (Heb 13:2), "the obligation to provide hospitality to the stranger was deeply rooted and highly regarded in ancient society."[61] Scripture regularly reinforces the importance of this behavior and commends its practice.[a] Although the translation "hospitality" captures the sense fairly well, it also seems weak for graciously granting *a stranger* welcome into one's home, along with providing food, shelter, and other essentials. The scope here seems specifically directed toward *traveling believers* whose "outsider's status is changed from stranger to guest."[62] For example, the ministry of Jesus and the ones he sent, including Paul, regularly relied on those who opened their homes and offered them gracious provision.[b] The epistles of John consider the reception of itinerant ministers of the Gospel to be a hallmark of the church. Christians are not to admit into their homes those who bring a false Gospel; but to refuse lodging for faithful ministers (as did Diotrephes) is a mark of apostasy (2 Jn 10–11; 3 Jn 5–10).[63] To receive or reject an emissary of Christ is to receive or reject Christ himself (Mt 10:40–42; Lk 10:9–12, 16).

(a) E.g., Gen 18:1–7; Lev 19:34; Deut 10:19; Mk 2:15–17; Lk 7:34; 14:1–24; 1 Tim 3:2; Titus 1:8; Heb 13:2

(b) E.g., Mk 1:29–31; 14:3; Lk 10:1–9, 38–42; Acts 16:15; 18:3

---

[58] Fitzmyer, *Romans*, 654.

[59] Moo, *Romans*, 779.

[60] Pelagius, *Romans* (Bray, *Romans*, ACCS NT 6:316).

[61] Dunn, *Romans*, 743; for additional details, see Kruse *Romans*, 478–79.

[62] Kruse *Romans*, 478; see 478–79 for a brief excursus on hospitality.

[63] See Schuchard, *1–3 John*, 631–33, 654–56, 675–85.

At the same time, the participle "pursuing" (διώκοντες, Rom 12:13) communicates more than simple openness to hosting other Christians. It means that authentic love actually *seeks out* opportunities to demonstrate such love for *strangers*. The verb also provides a link into the next section as Paul uses διώκω again in 12:14, but in a starkly different sense ("persecute").

Authentic Love Extends beyond the Christian Community (12:14–21)

Blessing Persecutors (12:14)

Aside from 12:16 (and perhaps 12:15), 12:14–21 moves beyond the bounds of the believing community. Paul thereby demonstrates that authentic love extends to all. He begins by asserting that it even encompasses those "who persecute" (διώκοντας, 12:14) Jesus' followers. Here Paul most clearly shows his awareness of Jesus' words from the Sermon on the Mount/Plain:

ἀγαπᾶτε τοὺς ἐχθροὺς ὑμῶν καὶ προσεύχεσθε ὑπὲρ τῶν διωκόντων ὑμᾶς.

Love your enemies and pray in behalf of the ones who are persecuting you. (Mt 5:44)

ἀγαπᾶτε τοὺς ἐχθροὺς ὑμῶν. ... εὐλογεῖτε τοὺς καταρωμένους ὑμᾶς.

Love your enemies. ... Bless the ones who are cursing you. (Lk 6:27–28)

εὐλογεῖτε τοὺς διώκοντας [ὑμᾶς], εὐλογεῖτε καὶ μὴ καταρᾶσθε.

Bless the ones who persecute [you]; bless and do not curse! (Rom 12:14)

Paul "saw persecution as par for the course for believers."[64] Jesus and Peter similarly portray persecution in some form as something to be expected and almost inevitable.[c] "Persecution in various forms—from social ostracism to legal action—was almost unavoidable in the early church"[65] and is resurgent in our own day. Without more information regarding particular forms of oppression the Roman Christians may have been enduring at the time Paul wrote to them, it may be best to conclude that Paul is "issuing a general command" that was "a staple item in the list of early Christian exhortation (see 1 Cor. 4:12; 1 Pet. 3:9)."[66]

These comparable commands from Jesus and Paul *were and remain countercultural*, both in terms of verbal meaning and overall content. Paul uses the verb "to bless" (εὐλογέω) with the meaning of the comparable Hebrew terminology of the OT, and not of Greek culture, in which it would simply mean that a person "speaks well of" or "praises" another.[67] The epitome of "blessing" in the OT is the Aaronic Benediction, with the trifold invocation of Yahweh to

(c) E.g., Mt 5:10–12, 44; 10:23; 23:34; Lk 11:49; 21:12; 1 Pet 3:13–17; 4:12–19

---

[64] Kruse, *Romans*, 482. See, e.g., 1 Cor 4:9; 2 Cor 6:4–5; 11:24–25; Gal 4:29; 5:11; 6:12; Phil 1:29; 1 Thess 2:14.

[65] Moo, *Romans*, 780.

[66] Moo, *Romans*, 780–81.

[67] Cf. Dunn, *Romans*, 744.

bestow his grace, favor, and peace (Num 6:24–26).[68] For Christians to "bless" their antagonists is to ask that they too might, through repentance and faith, receive the fullness of God's gracious blessings in Christ, in fulfillment of the Abrahamic promise of blessing for all through his Seed.[69] Conversely, to "curse" would be to request that they be cut off from God's grace in Christ, which would be contrary to his salvific will (Romans 10), but is the final state of those who persist in unbelief.[70]

Moo observes: "For Jesus' command that his followers respond to persecution and hatred with love and blessing was unprecedented in both the Greek and Jewish worlds."[71] One example of the uniqueness of the shared thought is that "since the contrast between blessing and cursing appears in this form only in Luke 6:28 and Rom 12:14 (Paul nowhere else uses καταράομαι ['to curse']), the obvious corollary is that the one who provided this decisive moral impetus was Jesus himself."[72]

At the same time, Paul does not quote Jesus directly, and it seems likely that he wrote Romans prior to the compilation of the completed Gospels. But this need not mean that a fixed form of Jesus' words on this subject had yet to be established. Paul's alteration of various OT texts throughout the letter demonstrates his flexibility even with written texts. Paul likely abbreviates the longer statements of Jesus into a single brief summary. He expresses the teaching even more concisely with only two Greek words in 1 Cor 4:12: "while being reviled, we are blessing" (λοιδορούμενοι εὐλογοῦμεν).

Empathy toward All (12:15)

The dominant verbal forms in 12:15 are infinitives. One should, therefore, be cautious about treating them too quickly as "hortative infinitives"[73] or "imperative infinitives."[74] Moo observes that such use of infinitives "is found as early as Homer and is very common in the papyri, though rare in the NT."[75] Therefore the words *function more descriptively as definitions*. Genuine love means "*to rejoice* with rejoicing ones, *to weep* with weeping ones" (12:15).

---

[68] Cf. Mitchell, *The Meaning of* BRK *"To Bless" in the Old Testament*, 96–98.

[69] See Gen 3:15; 12:1–3; 15:1–6; 18:18; 22:15–18; 26:1–5; 28:13–15; and the corresponding appropriations by Paul in Rom 4:3, 5, 9, 13, 14, 16, 20.

[70] God proffers blessing to all through faith, but those who continue to reject Abraham and his Seed and the Word's promise of covenant blessings in him will finally be cursed (Gen 12:3; Deut 11:26–29; 27:15–26; 28:15–68; 30:1, 19; cf. Job 2:9; Pss 37:22; 109:17, 28; Prov 3:33; Jer 11:3; 17:5).

[71] Moo, *Romans*, 781, citing Michael Thompson, *Clothed with Christ: The Example and Teaching of Jesus in Romans 12.1–15.13* (Sheffield: JSOT, 1991), 97–98.

[72] Dunn, *Romans*, 745.

[73] Kuske, *Romans 9–16*, 204.

[74] Lenski, *Romans*, 774; see also BDF, § 389; see "Forms and Function" in "Introduction to Romans 12:9–21" before this pericope.

[75] Moo, *Romans*, 782, n. 62, citing only Phil 3:16. See further the textual note on Rom 12:15.

In terms of content, Paul may appear to revert back to the context of how *believers* interact with one another, as is certainly the case in 12:16. The second half of 12:15, for example, might show how to respond in love by weeping together with persecuted believers. Similarly, "love that is genuine will not respond to a fellow believer's joy with envy or bitterness, but will enter whole-heartedly into that same joy."[76] Paul clearly directs the comparable words of 1 Cor 12:26 toward those *within* the body of Christ (cf. Mt 5:4, 11–12). But, in light of Rom 12:14, a broader general scope should also be envisioned. Indeed, such engagement with those *outside* the believing community would seem especially appropriate and effective. It would shine the light out into the midst of a dark world. Unfortunately, Pelagius' characterization remains all too relevant, even within the Christian community: "We do the opposite—we weep over those who rejoice and rejoice over those who weep. For if someone has been praised, we are unhappy. If someone has fallen, we leap for joy."[77]

A Glance Back Within: A Proper Mindset toward *Fellow Believers* (12:16)

While 12:15 *may* provide a segue primarily back to relations among believers, Paul clearly indicates this by the phrase "toward one another" (εἰς ἀλλήλους) near the beginning of 12:16 (see also 12:5, 10). Love *among believers* consists in these four connected clauses:

> Having the same mindset toward one another,
> not setting your mind on the haughty things,
> but associating with the lowly ones.
> Do not become wise beyond yourselves. (12:16)

Although translated differently, Paul employs the same form (φρονοῦντες) of the verb φρονέω, "have a mindset; set one's mind," twice in 12:16, as well as the cognate adjective φρόνιμος, "wise." This recalls the use of the verb and two of its compounds four times in 12:3. In contrast to the attitude negated in the second and fourth lines of 12:16, the first line calls again for "a common mind-set"[78] (see the commentary on 12:3; also 8:5). As in other comparable expressions (see also Rom 15:5; 2 Cor 13:11; Phil 2:2; 4:2), "having the same mindset toward one another" (Rom 12:16a) "does not mean that [Christians] must think the same thoughts, which is only seldom realized and not even desirable. It is rather a matter of orientation to the single goal of the community united in grace."[79]

The second and fourth lines of 12:16 replicate the thought of 11:20 (directed primarily against Gentiles) and 11:25, respectively. The problem with a high and haughty attitude again stems from its improper basis. Society often lauds "the

---

[76] Moo, *Romans*, 782.

[77] Pelagius, *Romans* (Bray, *Romans*, ACCS NT 6:318).

[78] Moo, *Romans*, 783.

[79] Käsemann, *Romans*, 347.

man who is self-sufficient in his confidence in his own wisdom."[80] But, as in chapter 11, Paul reiterates the warning of Prov 3:7 against relying on one's self-estimation. However, rather than simply serving as a generic warning against selfish ambition (Phil 2:3),[81] "it is still the tensions within the congregations that Paul has in view—probably still the temptation on the part of Jewish and Gentile Christians to claim a more favored status before God (2:17–20; 11:18–20)."[82] *The only reliable source of our self-worth comes from God's merciful perspective on us in Jesus Christ our Lord.*[83] Paul has reminded the Romans: "For there is not a difference [between] a Jew and a Greek, for the same Lord [is] of all, being rich to all the ones who are calling on him" (10:12).

A proper mindset rests its identity on what God credits to us (see 4:2–5; 6:11) and then exhibits itself in the behavior of the third line of 12:16, "associating with the lowly ones."[84] The form of the substantival adjective "lowly" (ταπεινοῖς) could be neuter; if so, the directive means to engage in lowly tasks.[85] However, the form could also be masculine, and a focus on people seems more appropriate, hence "lowly ones." Dunn observes how countercultural this behavior was, and we might add that it remains so:

> With ταπεινός ["lowly"] we meet once again a Jewish rather than Greek attitude. For the typical Greek mind with its idealization of the free man, ταπεινός denotes someone or something servile, menial, petty, and base. ... But in Jewish thought God is characterized precisely as one who chooses and favors the ταπεινός. ... Here again Paul takes it for granted that Christians should live in accordance with this insight, as also commended and exemplified by Jesus (in particular Matt 5:3–5; 11:29; 18:4; cf. Mark 10:42–45).[86]

Jesus, the "friend of tax collectors and sinners" (τελωνῶν φίλος καὶ ἁμαρτωλῶν, Mt 11:19; cf. Lk 15:1), thus demonstrates what God the Father is like in choosing that which appears foolish and weak in the eyes of the world (1 Cor 1:27).[87]

Love for All, Even in Response to Evil (12:17)

Equally radical is the thought of 12:17, which depicts love in action, now in clear view for all to see: "giving back to no one evil in place of evil, but being preoccupied with excellent things before all people." The two instances of "evil" (κακός) in 12:17 signal a new thought which extends to the two framing uses of

---

[80] Cranfield, *Romans*, 645.

[81] Noted, as often, but rejected here by Cranfield, *Romans*, 645.

[82] Dunn, *Romans*, 746.

[83] See Middendorf, *Romans 1–8*, 49, 51, 377–80; see also the commentary on 6:11.

[84] See the second textual note on 12:16.

[85] So Murray, *Romans*, 2:136; Sanday and Headlam, *Romans*, 364.

[86] Dunn, *Romans*, 746–47, citing for the use of ταπεινός, "lowly," for those favored by God LXX Judg 6:15; Job 5:11; Pss 9:39 (MT/ET 10:18); 17:28 (MT 18:28; ET 18:27); 33:19 (MT 34:19; ET 34:18); 81:3 (MT/ET 82:3); 101:18 (MT 102:18; ET 102:17); 137:6 (MT/ET 138:6); Prov 3:34; Is 14:32; 25:4; 49:13; 54:11; 66:2; Zeph 2:3; 3:12.

[87] Luther, *Lectures on Romans*, AE 25:463, points to 1 Cor 1:25, 27.

the same adjective in 12:21. In spite of common references to the *lex talionis*,[88] Schreiner observes the consistency of this biblical theme:

> The exhortation not to repay evil for evil is a mark of early Christian parenesis (cf. 1 Thess. 5:15; 1 Pet. 3:9), and it is likely that Paul's words here reflect his knowledge of the Jesus tradition (Matt. 5:38–39, 44–45; Luke 6:29, 35). We should not conclude that such a theme is lacking in the OT, for retaliation against enemies is censured there also (Exod. 23:4–5; Prov. 17:13; 20:22; …).[89]

Instead of striking back against evil with further evil, Paul describes genuine love as "being preoccupied with excellent things before all people" (Rom 12:17b). The participle translated as "being preoccupied with" (προνοούμενοι) describes what believers "take into consideration" or "take thought for."[90] The prefixed προ-, "before," also conveys that "doing good to all is something to be planned and not just willed."[91] A renewed mindset (12:2), therefore, involves thinking beforehand (temporally) about doing what is "in any respect *unobjectionable, blameless, excellent*" (BDAG, s.v. καλός, 2 c) before (in the sight of) everyone.

But who determines what things are "excellent" (καλός)? Cranfield thinks Paul does not refer to "a moral *communis sensus* of mankind."[92] But here and in 2 Cor 8:21, Paul draws on Prov 3:4, which points toward doing things approved by the Lord, first and foremost, and which people in general should also recognize as good:[93]

> καὶ προνοοῦ καλὰ ἐνώπιον κυρίου καὶ ἀνθρώπων.

> And be preoccupied with excellent things before [the] Lord and people. (LXX Prov 3:4)

---

[88] Hummel, *The Word Becoming Flesh*, 75, explains and clarifies in a manner which coincides well with Paul's upcoming discussion in 12:19 and then 13:1–7:

> Special comment seems mandatory only in the case of the so-called "*lex talionis*," the "eye for an eye" law governing retaliation in [Ex] 21:24. Times without number, it is irresponsibly cited as representative of the Old Testament's low morality and spirit of vengeance, in alleged contrast to the New Testament's law of love. The context makes plain, however, that the law enjoins *restraint*, not cold-blooded retribution. We here see ancient Israel in its "left-hand" aspect as a state rather than a church, and that the law's intent is to safeguard as much "love" as is possible in that realm. When in the world of power, retributive justice must operate, the law insists that the punishment must not be excessive, but must correspond to the severity of the infraction.

[89] Schreiner, *Romans*, 672; see also Kruse, *Romans*, 481–82; Gibbs, *Matthew 1:1–11:1*, 301–8; Just, *Luke 1:1–9:50*, 291–95.

[90] Dunn, *Romans*, 747.

[91] Käsemann, *Romans*, 348.

[92] Cranfield, *Romans*, 646.

[93] See Moo, *Romans*, 785; Dunn, *Romans*, 748; Pelagius, *Romans* (Bray, *Romans*, ACCS NT 6:319), also affirms this understanding: "But if you have such great patience and humility, you will be found praiseworthy not only in the Lord's eyes but also in the eyes of all people."

προνοοῦμεν γὰρ καλὰ οὐ μόνον ἐνώπιον κυρίου ἀλλὰ καὶ ἐνώπιον ἀνθρώπων.

For we are preoccupied with excellent things not only before [the] Lord but also before people. (2 Cor 8:21)

Thus, in accord with BDAG's definition cited above, Rom 12:17 envisions a both/and sense of excellence which extends out, and ought to be acknowledged as such, in the public square. Earlier in the letter, Paul confirms the existence of this God-given sense of right and wrong in all people (2:14–15),[94] though he also laments how it has been corrupted by sin and is regularly suppressed and even rejected (1:18–32).

Peace—Without and Within (12:18)

Paul then adds another directive for how to live among people in general, but introduces it with a *double qualification*: "If possible [in] that which is from you, being at peace with all people" (12:18). Paul's introduction admits two things. The first implies that it might not always be possible. The second expresses the notion "insofar as it depends on you." Origen explains:

> The apostle here gives a very balanced command because he knows perfectly well that peace depends on both parties, and the other party may well be hostile and block peace. What he asks is that our mind should always be ready for peace and that the blame for any discord should lie with the other side and not with us.[95]

Jesus extends the notion by blessing "the ones making peace" (οἱ εἰρηνοποιοί, Mt 5:9). But Paul's verb is more stative, "being at peace" (εἰρηνεύοντες, Rom 12:18), something Jesus also commands in Mk 9:50 when he says: "Be at peace with one another" (εἰρηνεύετε ἐν ἀλλήλοις).

It is perhaps too easy to limit the application of Rom 12:18 to the unbelieving world, which is certainly included. In that sphere, believers should, insofar as it remains possible without acting contrary to the will of God, live "at peace with all people" (12:18; cf. 1 Thess 5:15). Paul will soon expand upon that thought in Rom 13:1–7 by discussing how governments should serve to enhance the likelihood of this happening.

At the same time and in keeping with Jesus' plea cited above (Mk 9:50), *how much more should "with all people" include all those within the believing community*, where peace is so often threatened or even sorely lacking (see 14:1–15:13). If God's people live by the Gospel in peace with one another, this will display what is truly "excellent" (καλός, 12:17) to the unbelieving world. As Jesus says: "If you abide in my Word, you are truly my disciples" (Jn 8:31) and "In this all people will know that you are my disciples, if you have love for

---

[94] See Middendorf, *Romans 1–8*, 185–88.

[95] Origen, *Romans* (Bray, *Romans*, ACCS NT 6:319–20).

one another" (ἐν τούτῳ γνώσονται πάντες ὅτι ἐμοὶ μαθηταί ἐστε, ἐὰν ἀγάπην ἔχητε ἐν ἀλλήλοις, Jn 13:35).

God's Vengeance (Deut 32:35 in Rom 12:19)

When those who believe Paul's Gospel are wronged or even persecuted for it (12:14), living in peace might no longer be possible. In such cases, the fallen human nature in believers naturally reacts by striking back with equal or greater force. *But authentic love does not respond in that way.* Instead, "while not avenging yourselves, loved ones, rather, give a place for the wrath [of God]; indeed, it stands written: ' "Vengeance [is] for me, I myself will pay [it] back," says the Lord' " (12:19). Paul has already called for believers not to respond toward evil in kind (12:17a). While he now concedes that bad things will happen, he reminds his hearers they are "loved" by God (ἀγαπητοί, 12:19) and then insists that they not become vengeful vigilantes. Vengeance is left in the Lord's hands because he reserves it for himself to carry out. Kruse supports the bracketed insertion "wrath *[of God]*" in translation "because it is clearly God's wrath (not human wrath) that the apostle has in mind, as the quotation that follows immediately makes clear."[96]

Paul makes this explicit by citing God's promise in Deut 32:35. While "says the Lord" is not in that text, its addition following the quote in Romans is surely appropriate in light of numerous comparable utterances by Yahweh through Moses and the other prophets. However, the rest of the citation does *not* literally match the language of the MT or the LXX. Below is the text of the quotation in Rom 12:19, followed by the LXX and MT of Deut 32:35:

ἐμοὶ ἐκδίκησις, ἐγὼ ἀνταποδώσω.

For/to me [is] vengeance; I myself will pay [it] back. (Rom 12:19)

ἐν ἡμέρᾳ ἐκδικήσεως ἀνταποδώσω.

In [the] day of vengeance I will pay [it] back. (LXX Deut 32:35)

לִי נָקָם וְשִׁלֵּם

For/to me [is] vengeance and payback/retribution. (MT Deut 32:35)

The Hebrew has two nearly synonymous nouns. The LXX and Paul render the first Hebrew noun, נָקָם, "vengeance," with the corresponding Greek noun ἐκδίκησις. Cognate to that noun is the Greek verb ἐκδικέω, which occurs often in the LXX; "outside the prophets it is used as much of human vengeance as of divine. ... In the prophets, however, the thought is almost always of divine punishment."[97]

Both the LXX and Paul then translate the second Hebrew noun, שִׁלֵּם, "payback, retribution," with a future first person singular form of the Greek verb Paul just used in 11:35, ἀνταποδίδωμι, "repay, pay back" (cf. also the cognate

---

[96] Kruse, *Romans*, 483.

[97] Dunn, *Romans*, 749, citing as examples of the word's use in the Prophets LXX Jer 5:9; 23:2; Hos 4:9; Joel 4:21 (MT 4:21; ET 3:21); Amos 3:2, 14; Nah 1:2.

noun ἀνταπόδομα, "payback," in 11:9). The LXX may have assumed that in its unpointed text שלם (MT: שִׁלֵּם) was a Piel infinitive, or it may have been influenced by nearby verses such as Deut 32:43 and particularly Deut 32:41, where "vengeance" (נָקָם, the first Hebrew noun in Deut 32:35) is followed by the verb from which the second Hebrew noun in Deut 32:35 is derived:[98]

אָשִׁיב נָקָם לְצָרָי
וְלִמְשַׂנְאַי אֲשַׁלֵּם:

I will return vengeance to my adversaries;
    I will pay back to those who hate me. (MT Deut 32:41)

καὶ ἀνταποδώσω δίκην τοῖς ἐχθροῖς
    καὶ τοῖς μισοῦσίν με ἀνταποδώσω.

And I will pay back vengeance to the enemies,
    and to those who hate me I will pay back. (LXX Deut 32:41)

Paul's use of the verb ἀνταποδώσω, "I will pay back," in Rom 12:19 agrees with LXX Deut 32:35. But rather than using the temporal reference at the beginning of the LXX version, "in [the] day of vengeance," Paul used a more literal translation of the Hebrew of the beginning of Deut 32:35, "for/to me [is] vengeance." In MT Deut 32:35, temporal references follow the previously quoted words: "for/to me [is] vengeance and payback/retribution *for the time when their foot totters; for near is the day of their doom*." The temporal references indicate a specific time and day and, in particular, Judgment Day (see below). Paul's text, with its use of a literal translation of the Hebrew rather than the temporal phrase from the LXX, agrees exactly with Heb 10:30.[99] Paul's thought in this context provides a convincing explanation for his omission of any reference to a specific day. Elsewhere, he clearly affirms that God's revenge will be vented in all its fullness on Judgment Day (e.g., 2:5, 8–9, 16; note with ἀνταποδίδωμι, "pay back," in 2 Thess 1:6). None of those who have done evil to God's people will finally or ultimately get away with it. God's wrath will be poured out upon them fully "in [the] day of vengeance" (LXX Deut 32:35; cf. "a day of wrath," Zeph 1:15; Rom 2:5; and "great day of wrath," Rev 6:17; also Rev 11:18; 19:15), and "he will without doubt punish them far more severely than we ever could."[100]

---

[98] In addition to Deut 32:41, the first person singular of the Piel of שִׁלֵּם appears in other texts where God declares "I will pay back" (2 Ki 9:26; twice in Is 65:6; Jer 16:18). Another possible source of influence on Rom 12:19 is Prov 20:22, which has a similar (cohortative) form of the same verb, and where the believer is told "Do not say, 'I will pay back evil' " (אַל־תֹּאמַר אֲשַׁלְּמָה־רָע).

[99] The identical rendering of Deut 32:35 by two NT authors, in Rom 12:19 and Heb 10:30, leads Dunn, *Romans*, 749, to speculate: "Since the text of Paul and Heb[rews] agrees in part with the MT and in part with the LXX and is closest to the Targums, we should assume that a different text from the LXX was current among the diaspora churches." However, the influence of Deut 32:41 and the rest of the context may have been a factor in the translation of Deut 32:35, and the Targumim are notoriously unreliable for textual criticism.

[100] Origen, *Romans* (Bray, *Romans*, ACCS NT 6:320).

The reason Paul omits any temporal reference to a specific day seems clear, though an awkward chapter division obscures it.[101] At the beginning of Romans 13, Paul takes up the manner in which God's vengeance and wrath, as introduced in 12:19, *are currently active in the world*. This becomes unmistakable by 13:4, where a term related to "vengeance" and the same noun for "wrath" as in 12:19 appear: "an avenger for wrath" (ἔκδικος εἰς ὀργήν, 13:4). That his wrath is currently at work was stated in 1:18 with a present tense verb: already the "wrath of God is being revealed [ἀποκαλύπτεται] from heaven upon every ungodliness and unrighteousness of people." And one manner in which God carries out his wrath in the present is through the earthly rulers and authorities who serve as his servants (διάκονος, 13:4 [twice]). The Apology of the Augsburg Confession properly recognizes the connection:

> Thus private revenge is forbidden not [only] as an evangelical counsel but as a command (Matt. 5:39; Rom 12:19). Public redress through a judge is not forbidden but expressly commanded, and it is a work of God according to Paul (Rom. 13:1ff). (Ap XVI 7)

Responding to Enemies and Overcoming Evil with Good (12:20–21)

With confidence that God currently acts through earthly authorities, God's beloved can respond to evil in another way. Paul has also already expressed how genuine love does not simply remain passive in the face of evil, but goes the extra step by responding with active excellence and blessing (12:14, 17). Paul elaborates further in 12:20–21. What he calls for matches up well with the radical sentiments expressed by Jesus in the Sermon on the Mount (Mt 5:38–44). In responding to evil with active good works, his disciples act *as he did*, even on the cross (Lk 23:34), and *as their merciful heavenly Father does* in the way of the Gospel (Mt 5:44–45, 48; Rom 11:30–32). Paul also calls those who have received God's love ("loved ones," ἀγαπητοί, 12:19) to exhibit or, better, reflect that genuine love even the midst of the evils of this world.

"But 'if ever your enemy is hungry, feed him. If he is ever thirsty, give him a drink. For, while doing this, you will heap burning coals of fire upon his head'" (12:20). This gripping metaphorical language comes from Prov 25:21–22a. The LXX represents the Hebrew literally, and the text in Romans replicates the LXX, aside from introducing the reference with the strong adversative "but" (ἀλλά) and Paul's synonymous imperative "feed" (ψώμιζε) instead of τρέφε.[102]

---

[101] Unfortunately, this is one of a number of unfortunate chapter divisions throughout the letter which artificially disrupt Paul's thought (also 3:1; 8:1; 10:1; 15:1).

[102] Moo, *Romans*, 787, n. 96, evaluates a minor textual matter as follows:

> Paul's wording agrees exactly with that of LXX MS B, but B differs from the two other most important MSS, A and S, at one point, translating ψώμιζε in place of the roughly synonymous τρέφε. The reading of B has probably been assimilated to Paul's wording. The LXX and the Hebrew of the MT are similar.

The Image of Coals of Fire (12:20)

The more intriguing matter here concerns the *intended impact* of the language, both in Proverbs and as cited by Paul. Moo observes: "When used metaphorically in the OT, the words 'coals' and 'fire' usually refer to God's awesome presence, and especially to his judgment."[103] Psalm 140, for example, uses the image of burning coals being heaped upon the wicked in an imprecatory sense (Ps 140:10 [MT 140:11]). Chrysostom goes even further, adding: "There is nothing so sweet as to see an enemy chastised."[104] But, especially in this context of Romans (12:14, 17–18, 21), it is *very difficult* to conceive of this being Paul's intention. He can hardly define genuine love in terms of returning evil with good so that, intentionally or not, it would ultimately serve to increase guilt and, thereby, punishment from the hand of God. Furthermore, God can and does work toward one's ultimate good, even while punishing.[105] The history of Israel bears this out. Throughout the period of the judges God repeatedly allowed enemies to oppress his people when they became unfaithful and then promptly sent them saviors when they repented and cried to him for deliverance (e.g., Judg 2:11–19; 3:7–10). Even the destruction and exile of the Northern Kingdom of Israel and of Judah were designed to lead his people to repentance and purify a remnant by faith (cf. Rom 9:27; 11:5). Moreover, God intended to gather Gentiles into his people by the same process he used on Israel (compare Is 19:19–20 to the period of the judges). Cranfield points to Is 19:22 as an example:[106] "And Yahweh will strike Egypt, to strike and to heal, and they will turn to Yahweh."

What, then, does Paul mean? Just after citing the Lord's promise in Deut 32:35 to carry out vengeance himself, Paul moves the force of *our actions* in a different direction. His *insertion* of the strong adversative "but" (ἀλλά) prior to the words from Proverbs provides a sharp turn signal. *While giving a place for God to enact his judicial vengeance, we are to show genuine love (12:9), even for an enemy.* After all, God demonstrates this kind of love to his enemies (5:10), and Jesus calls us to put it into action in responding to our own foes (e.g., Mt 5:44). This seems to be the force of the expression in Proverbs as well, since it is followed by a promise of reward from Yahweh (Prov 25:22b; see also Prov 25:20). Moo suggests:

---

[103] Moo, *Romans*, 788, including n. 97, citing 2 Sam 14:7; 22:9, 13; Pss 18:8, 12 (MT 18:9, 13); 140:10 (MT 140:11); Is 5:24; cf. Job 41:19, 20 (MT 41:11, 12); Ps 120:4.

[104] Chrysostom, *Homilies on Romans*, 22 (Bray, *Romans*, ACCS NT 6:321).

[105] The Formula of Concord states: "Thus, even in the New Testament, [the Spirit of Christ] must perform what the prophet calls 'a strange deed' [God's 'alien' work; see Is 28:21] (that is, to rebuke) until he comes to his own work [God's 'proper' work] (that is, to comfort and to preach about grace)" (FC SD V 11); see also Mueller, *Called to Believe, Teach, and Confess*, 67–69; and Pieper, *Christian Dogmatics*, 2:412. Pieper states: "The wrath of God over the sin of men can and should be taught also from the suffering and death of Christ. ... In the Epitome [of the Formula of Concord] terrifying with Christ's suffering and death is called 'a foreign work [*alienum opus*] of Christ, by which He arrives at His proper office [*proprium suum officium*], that is, to preach grace'" (3:235, quoting FC Ep V 10).

[106] Cranfield, *Romans*, 648.

Paul views "coals of fire" as a metaphor for "the burning pangs of shame." Acting kindly toward our enemies is a means of leading them to be ashamed of their conduct toward us and, perhaps, to repent and turn to the Lord whose love we embody.[107]

BDAG (s.v. ἄνθραξ) similarly asserts that the idiom probably means to "cause the pers[on] to blush w[ith] shame and remorse."

Corroboration and Clarification regarding Coals of Fire (12:20)

A number of church fathers support the view espoused above and counter the notion that the purpose of our loving response is to increase the divine punishment of our adversaries. For example, Augustine winsomely argues:

> For how can it be love to feed and nourish someone just in order to heap coals of fire on his head, assuming that "coals of fire" mean some serious punishment? Therefore we must understand that this means that we should provoke whoever does us harm to repentance by doing him a good turn. For the coals of fire serve to burn, i.e., to bring anguish to his spirit, which is like the head of the soul, in which all malice is burnt out when one is changed for the better through repentance. These coals of fire are mentioned in the Psalms.[108]

Luculentius similarly observes:

> Some people give their enemies food and drink in order to inflict coals of fire, that is, punishments, on them. But whoever does that does not love his enemy as himself. It is not for that reason that we are supposed to give our enemy food and drink but rather to convert him to us. For as he detested us before, he will now start to love us. The person who loves his enemy in this way will heap coals of fire on his head, that is, the love which comes from charity.[109]

Pelagius also points in a positive direction: "When he realizes that coals have been heaped upon him through your undeserved mercy, he may shake them off, that is, repent, and may love you whom at one time he hated."[110] Jerome speaks similarly of an enemy being "softened by the fire of charity."[111]

Three relatively obscure points add further support to this line of interpretation. First, a number of scholars refer to an Egyptian practice of carrying a dish with burning coals in it as a sign of repentance.[112] Egyptian parallels to other texts in Proverbs have been fairly well-established,[113] so this practice may

---

[107] Moo, *Romans*, 788–89.

[108] Augustine, *Commentary on Statements in Romans*, 71 (Bray, *Romans*, ACCS NT 6:322); he then quotes Ps 120:3–4.

[109] Luculentius, *Romans* (Bray, *Romans*, ACCS NT 6:322).

[110] Pelagius, *Romans* (Bray, *Romans*, ACCS NT 6:322).

[111] Jerome, *Against the Pelagians*, 1.30 (Bray, *Romans*, ACCS NT 6:322).

[112] For example, Käsemann, *Romans*, 349; Moo, *Romans*, 789, n. 100; Dunn, *Romans*, 751; Cranfield, *Romans*, 650, including n. 1, who all cite a version of the following article: Siegfried Morenz, "Feurige Kohlen auf dem Haupt," in *Religion und Geschichte des alten Ägypten: Gesammelte Aufsätze* (Cologne: Böhlause, 1975), 433–44.

[113] See Hummel, *The Word Becoming Flesh*, 393–95, 453–54.

well inform the language of Proverbs and, thereby, of Paul as well. Second, a Targum on Proverbs translates the end of Prov 25:22 with consonants that can be vocalized as נַשְׁלְמֵיהּ לָךְ, which can be translated as either "[and God] will hand him over to you" or "will make him your friend."[114] Third, the last line of MT Prov 25:22 probably means "and Yahweh will pay back to you" (repay or reward you for the food and water you gave your enemy), and Dunn concludes that "Paul's omission of the final line … suggests that Paul is seeking to avoid any sense of self-seeking in the action advocated."[115]

A number of other earlier commentators try to incorporate *both* interpretations, depending on the reaction of the enemy: the coals of fire serve as a sign *either* of added judgment *or* prompting repentance. For example, (Pseudo-) Constantius suggests:

> In this passage Paul teaches that we ought to imitate God, who causes his sun to rise on the good and the evil [Mt 5:45], for by feeding our enemy and giving him something to drink we provoke him to peace or even to reconciliation. But if he persists in his wickedness, he will bring down fire on his head.[116]

Similarly, Origen:

> For insofar as we do good to our enemies and do not repay evil for evil, we store up wrath for them on the day of judgment. … Perhaps here also these coals of fire which are heaped on the head of an enemy are heaped for his benefit.[117]

Ambrosiaster also says:

> If by their ungodliness they continue in their evil ways, our service to them will lead to punishment for them. … Thus the Lord not only forbids us to repay our enemies in kind but also exhorts us to seek friendship by acts of kindness, both because that serves to mature us and because it is a means of winning others to eternal life.[118]

These interpretations properly rely on the imagery of coals and fire as depicting judgment elsewhere in Scripture (e.g., Pss 18:8, 12 [MT 18:9, 13]; 140:10 [MT 140:11]). Rom 12:19, along with 1:18–3:20 (e.g., 2:5, 8; 3:5), provides ample support for acknowledging that God will fully carry out his vengeance by heaping coals of wrath *on all those who do not repent.*

At the same time, God also yearns for something better. His patient kindness is intended to lead to repentance (2:4). Similarly, the overall content of Romans 12 indicates that providing food and drink for an enemy (12:20a) serves as a concrete demonstration of "love without hypocrisy" (12:9). Paul also calls

---

[114] See Dunn, *Romans*, 751, and Str-B 3:302; see also F. Lang, "σωρεύω κτλ.," *TDNT* 7:1095, n. 5.

[115] Dunn, *Romans*, 751.

[116] (Pseudo-)Constantius, *Romans* (Bray, *Romans*, ACCS NT 6:322).

[117] Origen, *Romans* (Bray, *Romans*, ACCS NT 6:321).

[118] Ambrosiaster, *Romans* (Bray, *Romans*, ACCS NT 6:321).

on believers to refuse to retaliate against those who do evil (12:17a, 19), but, instead, to "bless the ones who persecute [you]" (12:14) and to strive for peace with all (12:18). He now concludes by asserting that responding with good points forward to the ultimate hope of actually overcoming evil with the good (12:21). Thus Paul's words in 12:20b should primarily be understood as *desiring a positive final outcome*, even and especially for an enemy.

Conquering Evil with Good (Rom 12:21)

Paul continues and concludes: "Do not be conquered by the evil [thing], but conquer the evil [thing] with the good" (12:21). The first occurrence of "the evil" (τοῦ κακοῦ) could be masculine and personal. If so, Paul speaks initially of "the evil one/person." However, the form of the definite article before the second appearance of the same adjective indicates that the latter must be neuter, "the evil [thing]" (τὸ κακόν; see the second textual note on 12:21). It is possible that Paul uses the two forms *sequentially* to describe the evil person who does that which is evil or even to depict Satan himself, *the* evil one, who is the original cause of every evil thing that is done. However, it seems more likely that both uses of the word should be taken consistently as impersonal descriptions of "the evil [thing]" done to a believer. In either case, instead of being overcome by the evil one who and/or the evil thing which comes our way, Paul commands us to overcome evil with good. This would happen most blessedly if those doing evil actually turn to the Lord in repentance and faith (see the commentary on 12:20) and then respond "through the mercies of God" (12:1) by striving to cease and desist from further evil.

The present tense of the Greek verbs in 12:21 translated as "do not be conquered ... conquer" (μὴ νικῶ ... νίκα; see the first textual note on 12:21) communicate that this remains *an ongoing process and endeavor*, something applicable to the actions already described in 12:14–15, 17–18, 20. In fact, the forms here are both imperatives, parallel in force to the three present tense Greek imperatives in 12:14, "bless ... bless ... do not curse" (εὐλογεῖτε ... εὐλογεῖτε ... μὴ καταρᾶσθε). These five imperatives, along with the framing use of "evil" (κακός) twice in 12:14 and twice in 12:21, summarize the principal message of 12:14–21.[119] This effectively wraps up Paul's emphasis on how genuine love *extends toward those outside* the believing community (cf. 1 Pet 2:11–25; 3:13–17; 4:12–19; but see Rom 13:8–10).

Conclusion: Always Remember Why

The proper motivation for demonstrating "love without hypocrisy" (12:9), the reason why we continually strive to "conquer the evil [thing] with the good" (12:21), comes from the blessed assurance Paul previously gives to all those loved by God in Christ ("loved ones," ἀγαπητοί, 12:19; see also 8:35, 39). "Within all these things we are overwhelmingly victorious [ὑπερνικῶμεν]

---

[119] Cf. Dunn, *Romans*, 751.

through the One who loved [ἀγαπήσαντος] us" (8:37).[120] Thus the command to "conquer" (νίκα) in 12:21 *stands firmly grounded in the victory already accomplished by Christ himself, even if the final vanquishing of all enemies is yet to come.*

> It is the victory of the man who has been justified by faith, who is borne up by the grace of God in Christ, who is indeed confident, but confident in the knowledge of the victorious power of the gospel, and not in any sense of his own moral superiority.[121]

Similarities in terminology with Romans 5, cited above in the commentary on 12:12, also provide confidence. In response to being "declared righteous from faith" (5:1), along with all its accompanying effects (5:2–5), Paul explains how the believer can survive and even thrive in the midst of whatever evils may come before Christ returns. Finally, one should not lose sight of the opening words of this chapter. Paul begins 12:1 compactly with *both* a pregnant "therefore" (οὖν) *and* the foundational phrase for all of Romans 12–16, "through the mercies of God" (διὰ τῶν οἰκτιρμῶν τοῦ θεοῦ; see the commentary on 12:1). For "God's mercy does not abandon you in these circumstances, but you are constantly and everywhere helped by him in all things."[122]

Looking Ahead to Romans 13

Paul has left unstated the means by which the Lord currently exacts his vengeance against evildoers. But he reengages the thought of 12:19 immediately after 12:21 in what we call 13:1–7. Wright catches the connection by "taking 12:14–21 and 13:1–7 as two halves of a statement of Christian responsibility vis-à-vis outsiders. … Paul intends these two passages to be mutually interpretive."[123] Paul then returns to and wraps up the topic of love in 13:8–10 using the noun "love" (ἀγάπη) twice and the verb "to love" (ἀγαπάω) three times. What does authentic love look like or, better, act like? Paul has described *love* in detail in 12:9–21. In 13:8–10, where he makes his final references to the "Law" (νόμος) in this letter, he asserts that *love* in action looks remarkably like doing the Law's commandments (13:9). He even concludes: "Therefore love [is the] fulfillment of the Law" (πλήρωμα οὖν νόμου ἡ ἀγάπη, 13:10).

---

[120] The stative translation "overwhelmingly victorious" is to be preferred over the common "more than conquerors" (ESV, KJV, NKJV, RSV, NRSV) since the latter implies that we did the conquering. For an explanation of this stative translation, as well as other options, see Middendorf, *Romans 1–8*, 723–24.

[121] Cranfield, *Romans*, 651.

[122] Gennadius of Constantinople, *Romans* (Bray, *Romans*, ACCS NT 6:316).

[123] Wright, "Romans," 712.

Introduction to Romans 13:1–7:
An Alien Body? Not at All!

The Place of Romans 13:1–7 in the Letter

One extreme view excises this passage from its context. Käsemann contends: "Our section is an independent block. In view of its singular scope it can be pointedly called an alien body in Paul's exhortation."[1] He further asserts: "We do not find in it any sign of any specifically eschatological or christological motivation."[2] Nevertheless, he properly maintains that "there is no reason to dispute the authenticity of the text."[3] What then of its place here?

Romans 13:1–7 Flows from and Follows after Romans 12:14–21

The reason why Paul now writes 13:1–7 here may not seem obvious at first since his thought is once again disrupted artificially by an unfortunate chapter division at Rom 13:1 (as in 3:1; 8:1; 10:1; also 15:1). Rom 13:1 also begins abruptly grammatically without any of Paul's now familiar connecting terms. But after writing 12:14–21, Paul takes up the topic almost out of necessity.[4] If Christians do not take action against those who harm them (and others), but instead bless them and seek peace (12:14, 17–18), will chaos run rampant? Moo aptly identifies 12:19 as "the specific contextual trigger for Paul's teaching about government and its role in this world."[5] Paul just wrote:

> While not avenging yourselves, loved ones, rather, give a place for the wrath [of God]; indeed, it stands written: " 'Vengeance [is] for me; I myself will pay [it] back,' says the Lord." (μὴ ἑαυτοὺς ἐκδικοῦντες, ἀγαπητοί, ἀλλὰ

---

[1] Käsemann, *Romans*, 352; Moo, *Romans*, 790–91, agrees in part: "This argument comes on the scene quite abruptly, with no explicit syntactical connection with what has come before it—and not much evidence of any connection in subject matter either."

[2] Käsemann, *Romans*, 351. But Cranfield, *Romans*, 653–55, argues at length that the passage is Christological: "If we are to enter fully into Paul's communication here, we must understand these verses in the light of the central affirmation of Paul's, and the early Church's, faith, the affirmation κύριος Ἰησοῦς ['Jesus is Lord'] (cf. especially [Rom] 10.9)" (654). Cranfield also perceives an eschatological dimension (655):

> Though it is true that the governments of this world were, even before the death, resurrection, and ascension of Christ, subject to divine control, and that they are now no more submissive than they were before, yet the fact that God's claim over them, as over all other things visible and invisible, has been decisively and finally asserted, means that they fulfil their functions now under the judgment, mercy and promise of God in a way that was not so before.

[3] Käsemann, *Romans*, 351; as does, for example, Kallas "Romans xiii. 1–7: An Interpolation."

[4] Lenski, *Romans*, 783, assesses the situation well: "As chapter 12 is a unit, so is chapter 13, the latter naturally following the former. This is sometimes not clearly seen although it is rather obvious."

[5] Moo, *Romans*, 792.

δότε τόπον τῇ ὀργῇ, γέγραπται γάρ· ἐμοὶ ἐκδίκησις, ἐγὼ ἀνταποδώσω, λέγει κύριος, 12:19)

When Paul commands us to give a "place" for the eschatological wrath of God to be at work (τόπον τῇ ὀργῇ, 12:19), where is that place? Wright responds:

> The point he stresses throughout 12:14–21 dovetails exactly into what he says in 13:1–7. One must not call down curses on persecutors, nor repay evil with evil, nor seek private retribution; punishment is God's business. Now we see how Paul supposed, in part at least, that God went about that business. Of course, Paul believed in a final judgment (1:32; 2:1–16; 14:10) when all wrongs would be put to rights. But he now articulates, as a central point in 13:1–7, a standard Jewish and then Christian belief: that ruling authorities are what they are because God wants order in the present world.[6]

In 13:1–7, therefore, Paul engages in describing *the primary manner in which God's vengeance and wrath are currently at work against those who do evil.* This becomes unmistakable by 13:4, where the terminology of "wrath" and "vengeance" from 12:19 reappear: a human authority is "an avenger for wrath" (ἔκδικος εἰς ὀργήν, 13:4; see also "the wrath," τὴν ὀργήν, in 13:5). A present tense verb in 1:18 already asserted that the "wrath of God is being revealed [ἀποκαλύπτεται] from heaven upon every ungodliness and unrighteousness of people." Now Paul specifies one way in which this occurs. God enacts his vengeance through earthly "authorities" (13:1) and "rulers" (13:3), whom he describes twice as "God's servant" (θεοῦ … διάκονος, 13:4 [twice]) and as "God's ministers" (λειτουργοὶ … θεοῦ, 13:6). The Apology of the Augsburg Confession properly recognizes the connection:

> Thus private revenge is forbidden not [only] as an evangelical counsel but as a command (Matt. 5:39; Rom 12:19). Public redress through a judge is not forbidden but expressly commanded, and it is a work of God according to Paul (Rom. 13:1ff). (Ap XVI 7)

Schreiner then points away from an improper conclusion one could draw from Romans 12, and toward Paul's view:

> Even though believers are not to avenge themselves, it does not follow from this that the government abstains from punishing those who violate the law. … The ruling authorities have a responsibility to correct those who practice evil, so that society is peaceful and spared from anarchy.[7]

With confidence that God exacts his vengeance through these earthly authorities as promised (Deut 32:35, quoted in Rom 12:19), God's beloved can respond to evildoers as described in 12:20–21. Thus "the theme of quietist response and legitimate authority links 12:14–21" with 13:1–7[8] (cf. 1 Tim 2:1–3).

---

[6] Wright, "Romans," 718.

[7] Schreiner, *Romans*, 678, citing in the ellipses S. E. Porter, "Romans 13:1–7 as Pauline Political Rhetoric," *Filologia Neotestamentaria* 3 (1990): 118–19.

[8] Dunn, *Romans*, 759.

Romans 13:1–7 in the Context of Romans 12:1–15:13

The *universal language* which characterizes so much of Romans[9] unites 13:1–7 with what precedes and merges it into what follows even more profoundly. Paul spoke of how genuine love exhibits itself in the presence of and in interaction with "*all* people" (πάντων ἀνθρώπων) in both 12:17 and 12:18. Paul begins 13:1 with a reference to "*every* person" (πᾶσα ψυχή). Later he speaks about giving back "to *all* people the things that are owed" (πᾶσιν τὰς ὀφειλάς, 13:7). Paul then masterfully moves on to address another debt we owe in response to the Gospel by declaring: "Owe nothing to anyone [μηδενὶ μηδὲν ὀφείλετε] except *the* [obligation] to love one another" (13:8). Moo suggests that 12:9–21 and 13:8–10 both "focus on love and its outworkings."[10] Yet the reference to what is owed in both 13:7 and 13:8 establishes an even more obvious linguistic connection between 13:1–7 and the verses which immediately follow. Thus, in keeping with the theme established by 12:9, Calvin reminds us that submitting to God's governing authorities "constitutes not the least part of love."[11]

In the midst of the emphasis on human response to the Gospel throughout 12:1–15:13, one needs to always keep in the forefront an awareness that Paul's entire appeal flows "through the mercies of God" (12:1; see the commentary on that verse). Thus *God's gracious initiative in Christ* toward humanity impacts all of what Paul writes in these chapters. The *God-centered nature of the argument*, so prevalent throughout Romans,[12] rises to the forefront in 13:1–7, though in a *divergent* way.

Paul uses the noun "God" (θεός) six times in 13:1–7 to emphasize God's work in and through governing authorities. But he does so in a manner reminiscent of 1:18–2:16 and, in particular, 2:5–11.[13] There Paul argues that God's *future* eschatological judgment of all people will be on the basis of their works (2:5–6); he then elaborates as follows (2:7–10):

> [7]On the one hand, to the ones who, according to the endurance of good work, seek glory and honor and incorruptibility, [he will give] eternal life. [8]On the other hand, to those who, out of self-centeredness, are unpersuaded by the truth, but are persuaded by the unrighteousness, [there will be] wrath and fury, [9]tribulation and distress upon every person of man who works that which is

---

[9] Middendorf, *Romans 1–8*, 49–51.

[10] Moo, *Romans*, 791.

[11] Calvin, *Romans*, 285.

[12] Middendorf, *Romans 1–8*, 21–22, 27, 49–51; in this volume, see "Romans 1–4: The Righteousness of God" in the introduction to Romans 9–16, as well as "God" in "The Three Foci of Romans 9–11" in the introduction to Romans 9–11. See also the commentary on 1:17, 32; 2:11, 16, 29; 3:1–8, 19–20, 29–30; 4:21; 9:5, 11b–12a, 16, 22–24, 29; 10:21; 11:1–2, 33–36; 12:19; 13:1–2; 14:10–12; 15:5, 8, 13; 16:25, 27.

[13] Dunn, *Romans*, 758, recognizes "common themes shared by 2:7–11 and 13:3–4," e.g., good work/the good in 2:7, 10; 13:3–4; honor/praise in 2:7, 10; 13:3; the evil in 2:9; 13:3–4; and wrath in 2:5, 8; 13:4.

evil, of a Jew first and also of a Greek, [10]but glory and honor and peace to every person who works that which is good, to a Jew first and also to a Greek.

We see in 13:1–7 a *present, though partial and imperfect*, manifestation of "the righteous judgment of God" (δικαιοκρισίας τοῦ θεοῦ, 2:5) for "every person" (13:1; cf. also 1:18; 2:12–16). As a necessary explanation of 12:19, Paul emphasizes how God's "wrath" (ὀργή, e.g., 1:18; 2:5, 8; 12:19; 13:4) currently acts against and thereby also restrains "evil" (κακός, e.g., 1:30; 2:9; 12:17, 21; 13:3, 4, 10).

On a more positive note and in line with the discussion *which begins in 12:1–2*, Paul affirms that " 'not being conformed to this world' does not require Christians to renounce every institution now in place in society. For some of them—such as government and marriage—reflect God's providential ordering of the world for our good and his glory."[14] It also seems wise to consider whether "his exhortation is more closely related to the larger argument of Romans itself than has usually been appreciated."[15] If so, it seems reasonable to consider the presence of some tensions *between Jews and Gentiles* in general, as well as within "the political self-identity of the Christian groups" in Rome[16] (see the next section). Thus, as Paul works 13:1–7 into his flow of thought, far from appearing as "an alien body,"[17] it stands very well placed in regard to what comes immediately before and after. It also serves as an integral part of the letter as a whole.

Suggested Backgrounds for Romans 13:1–7

Two other preliminary questions should be addressed. First, what moves Paul to deal with the topic of earthly authorities at unprecedented length when writing to Rome? Second, how does what he says fit within the rest of what Scripture says on the topic of earthly rulers?

Historical Context

Moo reminds us that Paul writes from *Corinth*, where he encountered "the kind of extremism that would pervert his emphasis on the coming of a new era and on the 'new creation' [2 Cor 5:17; Gal 6:15] into a rejection of every human and societal convention—including the government."[18] On that basis, Käsemann suggests that Paul's "Corinthian experiences and the introduction in [Rom] 12:3" mean that he now engages in "calling enthusiasts back within the limits of earthly order."[19] But evidence of similar behavior among the believers in Rome does not exist within or outside of Paul's letter.

---

[14] Moo, *Romans*, 803.

[15] Dunn, *Romans*, 768.

[16] Dunn, *Romans*, 768.

[17] Käsemann, *Romans*, 352, quoted above.

[18] Moo, *Romans*, 791.

[19] Käsemann, *Romans*, 350.

1283

A more pertinent observation recognizes "the fact that he is addressing the church in the capital city of the empire."[20] Therefore, "it is not astonishing that this subject arises; Rome was the capital of the empire, and the relationship of believers to governing authorities was a natural subject of discussion."[21] But does Murray correctly postulate that "there was some urgent need for pressing home upon the believers at Rome the teaching which is given here?"[22] In other words, *was there a specific and identifiable political situation in Rome of which Paul was aware that led him to write this section?*[23]

A number of proposals rest upon the (incorrect) assumption that the believers in Rome had a predominantly Jewish character.[24] One hypothesis is that a violent anti-Roman Jewish Zealot movement was afoot and feared in Rome.[25] Schreiner responds: "It is unconvincing to posit that the text was written because of Zealot activity, for this was scarcely relevant to Romans believers and did not burst into full flame until A.D. 66."[26] Another explanation posits that the expulsion of Jews from Rome in AD 49 or 50 under Claudius may have been caused by "the belief that Jews were inimical to the imperial interests."[27] If so, when Paul writes Romans in AD 55 or 56,[28] he is responding about five years later with a call for his hearers to be subject to the authorities (13:1, 5) so that they might avoid pulling "the roof of Nero's wrath down on their heads as they had under Claudius."[29] But the Edict of Claudius was issued at least five years before Paul wrote Romans, and it had been revoked at Nero's ascendency in AD 54.[30] Perhaps Jewish privileges in regard to taxation caused a general antagonism toward Jews which Paul aims to counter in 13:6–7.[31] Yet taxation was

---

[20] Käsemann, *Romans*, 350.

[21] Schreiner, *Romans*, 678; see also Fitzmyer, *Romans*, 662; see Keesmaat, "Reading Romans in the Capital of the Empire," for an intriguing dialogical walk through the letter which traces the potential impact of the fact that Rome was the capital of the empire.

[22] Murray, *Romans*, 2:146.

[23] For a good overview, see Kruse, *Romans*, 490–92.

[24] This commentary argues for mixed Jewish and Gentile congregations with the Gentiles being in the majority; see Middendorf, *Romans 1–8*, 10–14, 17–19. Others, like Das, "The Gentile-Encoded Audience of Romans," argue for an exclusively Gentile composition of the churches. See "Who Are the 'Weak' and the 'Strong'? Addressees Again!" in the introduction to 14:1–15:13.

[25] Dodd, *Romans*, 201: "Many Jewish Christians brought over with them a traditional resentment of the Roman rule. Jewish national feeling was running high at this time, when things were brewing up to the crisis of A.D. 66." Similarly, Edwards, *Romans*, 303; Murray, *Romans*, 2:146; for a list of other advocates, see Moo, *Romans*, 792, n. 8.

[26] Schreiner, *Romans*, 678.

[27] Murray, *Romans*, 2:146.

[28] See Middendorf, *Romans 1–8*, 5–7.

[29] Edwards, *Romans*, 302–3, adopting the view of Willi Marxsen, *Introduction to the New Testament* (trans. G. Buswell; Philadelphia: Fortress, 1968), 100.

[30] See Middendorf, *Romans 1–8*, 10, 12.

[31] See Middendorf, *Romans 1–8*, 9; Nanos, *The Mystery of Romans*, 43–45; Dunn, *Romans*, 766, suggests that the "antagonism" of Cicero (*Pro Flacco*, 28.67) and Tacitus (*Histories*, 5.5.1) toward Jews was a response to such "special privileges, above all in the matter of taxation."

hardly the only source for such sentiments against the Jews, and they were not the only ones seeking tax relief.[32]

A more general theory suggests that a "mounting unrest regarding the *taxation system*" as a whole was currently underway.[33] Jewett documents evidence for "unrest in the period before 58 C.E. when a formal tax protest was brought to Nero, as reported by Tacitus *Ann[als]* 13:50–51."[34] If so, Paul writes in order "to be certain that the Christian community in Rome was not responsible for any unrest."[35] Moo responds:

> Evidence for a tax rebellion in Rome as early as 56–57 (the date of Romans) is sparse; and if Paul was concerned about the Roman Christians not paying taxes, it is peculiar that he would commend them for doing just that [paying taxes in 13:6].[36]

Therefore the contention that Paul rebukes such anti-taxation sentiments remains speculative.[37] In fact, the dominant political mood seems to have been just the opposite. "There was great and widespread hope, and not only in Rome, that Nero would keep the peace and govern wisely, fairly, and justly."[38] Along these general lines, and as corroborated by Acts, "Paul's own experiences with sensible Roman magistrates"[39] may have had a positive influence on his thoughts (see, e.g., events prior to the writing of Romans in Acts 13:6–8; 18:14–16; 19:35–40; but cf. Acts 16:37; 17:8; 18:17).

On the other hand, as benevolent as it may have been at the moment, the Roman Empire of the NT era came into existence and maintained its domain largely as a militaristic and expansionist dictatorship. Thus the manner in which Paul addresses believers in Rome may seem almost shocking to our twenty-first-century Western sensibilities. And surely *this section downplays any anti-imperial sentiment; indeed, it directly and repeatedly countermands it.* Therefore, those who attempt to identify a politically revolutionary undertone in

---

[32] Barclay, *The Mind of St Paul*, 9–10, summarizes:

> No nation was ever more bitterly hated than the Jews. Cicero called the Jewish religion "a barbarous superstition" (Cicero, *Pro Flacco* 28); Tacitus called the Jewish nation "the vilest of people" (Tacitus, *Histories* 5:8). …
>
> Tacitus believed that if a Gentile became a proselyte to Judaism, the first thing he was taught was to despise the gods, to repudiate his nationality, and to hold worthless his parents, children and friends (Tacitus, *Histories* 5:5).

[33] Dunn, *Romans*, 768 (emphasis added); he speculates: "Paul must have been aware that the subject was a particularly sensitive matter in Rome itself" (766).

[34] Jewett, *Romans*, 798, where the full text of Tacitus is quoted. Dunn, *Romans*, 766, summarizes: "We know from Tacitus (*Ann[als]* 13) that the year A.D. 58 saw persistent complaints against the companies farming indirect taxes and the acquisitiveness of tax collectors … so that some reform became essential."

[35] Schreiner, *Romans*, 679.

[36] Moo, *Romans*, 793.

[37] Cf. Käsemann, *Romans*, 350.

[38] Witherington, *Romans*, 306.

[39] Kruse, *Romans*, 491.

Romans[40] encounter their most serious problems here.[41] Indeed, it is difficult to believe that Paul intends his hearers to grasp that he is engaged in subtle counter-government subterfuge in the face of his *direct and repeated statements* which call for them to be subject to rulers and fear their authority (13:1, 3, 5, 6, 7).[42] While serious problems surrounding emperor worship lay ahead in the not-too-distant future,[43] "it is unlikely … that the Caesar cult was as yet provoking any clash of loyalties."[44] The same can be said regarding any direct persecution of Christians by the hand of Rome. However, the events of AD 64 would dramatically alter that situation, at least temporarily. In that year "Nero was suspected of starting the great fire in Rome in order to build a bigger palace. He blamed the fire on Christians and began executing them (Tacitus *Ann[als]* 15.44)."[45]

Kruse properly concludes: "It is impossible to be dogmatic about the exact *Sitz im Leben* of Paul's exhortations in 13:1–7."[46] Paul may well be concerned about one or more of the factors presented above as he writes to those who reside in the seat of imperial power. But *a general statement determined primarily by the flow of letter itself* seems the most plausible explanation for its content. The previous section of this introduction demonstrates the function of 13:1–7 in relation to its immediate context.[47]

Canonical Context

More important than chasing down a specific historical context is the recognition of how 13:1–7 fits squarely within the overall teaching of the Scriptures. In a broader canonical context, 13:1–7 parallels numerous OT statements regarding non-Israelite governments. They too are deemed to be established by God and, therefore, dependent upon and accountable to him. Through the

---

[40] For example, Elliott, *The Arrogance of Nations*, which is subtitled *Reading Romans in the Shadow of Empire*, 62–65; Wright, "Paul's Gospel and Caesar's Empire"; Wright, "Paul and Caesar: A New Reading of Romans"; cf. Wright, *Paul*, 71.

[41] See Middendorf, *Romans 1–8*, 69–70, 92–93; see also Kruse, *Romans*, 491–93, who notes that an anti-imperial undertone is unlikely due to Jesus' words in Mk 12:17 and what Paul says in Titus 3:1. For a general rebuttal of anti-imperial readings throughout the NT, see McKnight and Modica, *Jesus Is Lord, Caesar Is Not*.

[42] Carter, "The Irony of Romans 13," 226, attempts to evade the clear sense of the text by suggesting Paul employs "the rhetorical use of verbal irony, where the tension between the words and the reality they denote can be enough to reverse the plain meaning of the text"; if so, Paul actually engages in "blaming through apparent praise" and intends for his addressees to recognize that his rationale for submitting to authorities ought to be regarded as "spurious." But the pragmatic difficulties involved for Paul's hearers make this covert assumption difficult to accept.

[43] Brighton, *Revelation*, 355: "It was not until the latter part of the first century A.D. that such [emperor] worship was widespread."

[44] Dunn, *Romans*, 761.

[45] M. Reasoner, "Political Systems," *DPL*, 722; he adds: "It is probable that Paul was executed c. A.D. 64–65 after trial in Nero's court."

[46] Kruse, *Romans*, 491.

[47] See "Romans 13:1–7 in the Context of Romans 12:1–15:13" above.

prophets, the God of Israel frequently addresses the nations of the world in a manner which shows that they are under his authority and are to rule in justice on his behalf.[48] The OT Wisdom literature likewise declares that the order of the entire creation has been established by the wisdom of God. For example, "the book of Proverbs teaches us that kings do not come to rule apart from the dispensation and will of God,"[49] for Yahweh's personified Wisdom declares (Prov 8:15–16):

> By me kings reign and rulers prescribe righteousness;
>> by me princes exercise princedom, also nobles, all judges of
>>> righteousness.[50]

Fitzmyer illustrates further:

> What Paul teaches in this passage has to be understood against the background of the OT itself, in which Israel was instructed, especially in the time of the exile, to respect governing authorities, even to pray for them: Jer 29:7 ("Seek the welfare of the city to which I have exiled you and pray to the Lord on behalf of it, for in its welfare will be your welfare").[51]

Paul's words also serve as an appropriate expansion upon words of *Jesus himself*.[52] Jn 19:11 provides dominical support for Paul's opening assertion in 13:1. The command to pay taxes in Rom 13:6–7 aligns with Mt 17:24–27, where Jesus provided for the payment of a tax that he was considered to owe. Jesus also speaks comparably when asked a duplicitous question regarding how to respond to the Roman government's demand for taxes. The wording in Luke provides the closest verbal parallels to Romans (e.g., φόρος, "tax," in Lk 20:22 and ἀποδίδωμι, "pay/give back," in Lk 20:25 are both used comparably Rom 13:6–7). Here is the question asked of Jesus, followed by his reply:

---

[48] See, e.g., the prophetic oracles to the nations in Isaiah 13–23; Ezekiel 25–32; Amos 1:3–2:3; Jonah's mission to Nineveh; as well as Prov 21:1; Is 10:5–6; 41:2–4; 45:1–7; Jer 21:7, 10; 27:5–7; Dan 2:21, 37–38; 4:17, 25, 32 (MT 4:14, 22, 29); 5:21; Amos 9:7. Cf. also Wisdom 6:3; Sirach 10:4.

[49] Diodore, *Romans* (Bray, *Romans*, ACCS NT 6:324); he proceeds to quote Prov 8:15.

[50] Steinmann, *Proverbs*, 204, points out that the attributes of divine wisdom in Prov 8:1–21 match the wisdom attributes of the Spirit of Yahweh, who rests upon the Davidic Messiah in Is 11:2. He comments (203):

> Is 11:3–5 … goes on to describe how Christ will reign in righteousness and execute justice. This is parallel to Prov 8:15–16. Those in authority need the Spirit and divine Wisdom as well as strength and sound judgment if they are to rule in righteousness and bring about justice. … Since in this passage Wisdom/Understanding states that rulers only govern "by me" (Prov 8:15–16), it also implies that Wisdom is divine since only God establishes rulers (e.g., Dan 2:37–38; Neh 9:37; Jn 19:10–11; Rom 13:1–4).

[51] Fitzmyer, *Romans*, 665.

[52] Against Käsemann, *Romans*, 352, and Fitzmyer, *Romans*, 664, who downplay any direct influence.

²²ἔξεστιν ἡμᾶς Καίσαρι φόρον δοῦναι ἢ οὔ; ²³κατανοήσας δὲ αὐτῶν τὴν πανουργίαν εἶπεν πρὸς αὐτούς· ²⁴δείξατέ μοι δηνάριον· τίνος ἔχει εἰκόνα καὶ ἐπιγραφήν; οἱ δὲ εἶπαν· Καίσαρος. ²⁵ὁ δὲ εἶπεν πρὸς αὐτούς· τοίνυν ἀπόδοτε τὰ Καίσαρος Καίσαρι καὶ τὰ τοῦ θεοῦ τῷ θεῷ.

²²"Is it permissible for us to give tax to Caesar or not?" ²³After considering their trickery he said to them, ²⁴"Show me a denarius. Of whom does it have an image and inscription?" And they said, "Of Caesar." ²⁵And he said to them, "Well then, give back the things of Caesar to Caesar, and the things of God to God." (Lk 20:22–25)[53]

Jesus profoundly expands the topic far beyond mere taxation. He speaks of a proper stewardship of giving in regard not only to what the government claims as its own but also to *all the gifts of God* in a manner which coincides well with Paul's directives throughout 12:1–13:14. Augustine recognizes that "the balance which the Lord himself prescribed is to be maintained."[54]

Finally, a section of this length devoted entirely to the topic of governing authorities may be unique in Paul's letters (cf. the shorter passages 1 Tim 2:1–2; Titus 3:1). Yet the numerous commonalities that Rom 13:1–7 shares with 1 Pet 2:13–17 demonstrate that it stands right in line with early apostolic teaching. 1 Pet 2:13–14 and 1 Pet 2:17 are most comparable (1 Pet 2:15–16 also aligns well with Rom 12:14–20):

¹³ὑποτάγητε πάσῃ ἀνθρωπίνῃ κτίσει διὰ τὸν κύριον, εἴτε βασιλεῖ ὡς ὑπερέχοντι, ¹⁴εἴτε ἡγεμόσιν ὡς δι᾽ αὐτοῦ πεμπομένοις εἰς ἐκδίκησιν κακοποιῶν ἔπαινον δὲ ἀγαθοποιῶν. ... ¹⁷πάντας τιμήσατε, τὴν ἀδελφότητα ἀγαπᾶτε, τὸν θεὸν φοβεῖσθε, τὸν βασιλέα τιμᾶτε.

¹³Be subject, on account of the Lord, to every created order among men, whether to a king as holding a high place, ¹⁴whether to governors as having been sent through him for vengeance on ones doing evil and for praise of ones doing good. ... ¹⁷Honor all people, love the brotherhood [of believers], fear God, honor the king. (1 Pet 2:13–14, 17)

The phrase πάσῃ ἀνθρωπίνῃ κτίσει in 1 Pet 2:13 is difficult to translate in English. "To every human institution" is typical (e.g., ESV; similar is NRSV), but this obscures the meaning of κτίσις, literally, "creation, created thing." Its presence asserts that *these human institutions are, in fact, divinely created in order to benefit all humanity*. Paul repeatedly and explicitly makes the same assertion as he refers to God six times in Rom 13:1–7[55] and speaks specifically of governing authority as "the ordinance of God" (τῇ τοῦ θεοῦ διαταγῇ, 13:2). Moo further observes:[56]

---

[53] For a complete, contextual explication, see Just, *Luke 9:51–24:53*, 771–74.

[54] Augustine, *Commentary on Statements in Romans*, 72 (Bray, *Romans*, ACCS NT 6:325); he then quotes Mt 22:21.

[55] See θεός, "God," in 13:1 (twice), 2, 4 (twice), 6.

[56] Moo, *Romans*, 793, n. 11.

The 1 Peter text has a number of key words and concepts in common with Rom. 13:1–7: ὑποτάσσω ("order under, submit") as the basic command;[57] ὑπερέχω ("supreme"), used to denote governing powers;[58] the purpose of government as being ἐκδίκησιν κακοποιῶν ("taking vengeance on evildoers")[59] and ἔπαινον ἀγαθοποιῶν ("giving praise to doers of good");[60] the exhortation to give "honor" (τιμάω)[61] and "fear" (φοβέομαι).[62]

---

[57] 1 Pet 2:13; translated in this commentary as "be subject" in Rom 13:1, 5.

[58] 1 Pet 2:13; translated in this commentary as "be in a high position" in Rom 13:1.

[59] 1 Pet 2:14; compare "an avenger [ἔκδικος] for wrath to the one who practices evil [τὸ κακὸν πράσσοντι]" in Rom 13:4.

[60] 1 Pet 2:14; compare "do that which is good [τὸ ἀγαθὸν ποίει], and you will have praise [ἔπαινον] from it" in Rom 13:3.

[61] 1 Pet 2:17; compare "give back ... honor [τιμή] to the one [owed] honor [τιμή]" in Rom 13:7.

[62] 1 Pet 2:17; Rom 13:4 (cf. 13:3).

Submitting to Earthly Authorities

Translation

13 ¹**Let every person be subject to authorities who are in high positions. For there is not an authority except by God, and the ones which exist have been ordered and remain in place by God. ²So then the one who opposes the authority has stood against the ordinance of God, and the ones who stand against [God] will receive judgment for themselves. ³For the rulers are not a [cause of] fear for [one doing] the good work, but for [one doing] the evil. Do you then wish not to fear the authority? Do that which is good, and you will have praise from it. ⁴Indeed, he is God's servant to you for the good. But if you do evil, fear! For he does not bear the sword for no purpose. For he is God's servant, an avenger for wrath to the one who practices evil.**

⁵**Therefore [it is] a necessity to be subject, not only on account of the wrath but also on account of the conscience. ⁶Indeed, on account of this you are also paying taxes. For they are God's ministers, holding fast to this very thing. ⁷Give back to all people the things that are owed: the tax to the one [owed] the tax, revenue to the one [owed] revenue, fear to the one [owed] fear, honor to the one [owed] honor.**

Textual Notes

13:1 πᾶσα ψυχή—"Every person" encompasses all people, believers and unbelievers alike. Paul's use of ψυχή reflects a Hebraism for the entire "person." See the second textual note on 2:9.

ἐξουσίαις—The feminine noun ἐξουσία, "authority," appears 66 times in the LXX and 102 times in the NT. In the majority of verses its meaning is abstract, as when it described a potter's "authority" over the clay in Rom 9:21, the only other Romans passage with it besides 13:1–3. More concretely, ἐξουσία can refer to the actual realm or sphere under one's authority (Lk 7:8; 19:17; 20:20; 23:7), or it can designate a person who is a "bearer of ruling authority" (BDAG, 5). This last, personal meaning fits this context, as confirmed by Paul's parallel use of "the rulers" (οἱ … ἄρχοντες) in 13:3. Thus Paul speaks of "authorities, government officials"[1] in the anarthrous plural here. He also does so with the anarthrous singular of ἐξουσία later in the verse (see the fifth textual note on 13:1) and similarly with definite singular forms in 13:2 (τῇ ἐξουσίᾳ) and 13:3 (τὴν ἐξουσίαν).

ὑπερεχούσαις—The compound verb ὑπερέχω literally means "be at a point higher than another" (BDAG, 1). Figuratively, it then means "be in a controlling position, *have power over, be in authority (over), be highly placed*" (BDAG, 2). While "be highly placed" is passive, it nicely hints at Paul's emphasis upon the One who placed them

---

[1] Dunn, *Romans*, 760.

there. The form here is an active participle (dative feminine plural, to match ἐξουσίαις), translated as "who are in high positions" (see BDAG, 2), which readily applies to governing authorities. 1 Pet 2:13 uses ὑπερέχω similarly to describe a king (βασιλεῖ ὡς ὑπερέχοντι).

ὑποτασσέσθω—For the compound verb ὑποτάσσω, see the fourth textual note and the commentary on 8:7; for the simple verb τάσσω, see the last textual note on 13:1. This is a third person singular imperative in the present tense with a durative force.[2] The form could be middle, "let him subject himself,"[3] but more likely it should be understood as passive,[4] "let him be subject." This translation fits the context well (i.e., a ruler and his subjects), though "let him be under order" would better maintain the connection with the three other forms derived from τάσσω in 13:1–2 (τεταγμέναι, "ordered"; ἀντιτασσόμενος, "who opposes"; and διαταγῇ, "ordinance"; see the textual notes below). The specific parameters of meaning for ὑποτασσέσθω are critical for understanding the section as a whole. See "Applications" in the commentary.

οὐ γὰρ ἔστιν ἐξουσία εἰ μὴ ὑπὸ θεοῦ—An abstract meaning for the anarthrous ἐξουσία, "authority," is possible here, but a consistent personal meaning (referring to the people who wield governmental authority) is appropriate throughout 13:1–3; see the second textual note on 13:1. For εἰ μή, "except," see the fourth textual note on 7:7. The prepositional phrase ὑπὸ θεοῦ ("by God") makes explicit the often-implied notion of a divine or theological passive.[5]

αἱ δὲ οὖσαι ὑπὸ θεοῦ τεταγμέναι εἰσίν—The definite feminine plural participle of εἰμί (αἱ … οὖσαι) functions as a substantive in this clause,[6] "the ones which are/exist." The feminine plural form indicates that the participle refers back to the plural ἐξουσίαις, "authorities," in the first clause of the verse (see the second textual note on 13:1). The verb τάσσω means "to bring about an order of things by arranging, *arrange, put in place*" (BDAG, 1). Its perfect passive participle with the form of εἰμί (εἰσίν) forms a periphrastic construction which is equivalent to the force of a perfect indicative.[7] The perfect conveys both the ordering by which the authorities came to power *and* their continuing existence in those roles.[8] For ὑπὸ θεοῦ ("by God"), see the previous textual note. Thus "they have been ordered and remain in place by God."

13:2 ὥστε—The conjunction ὥστε regularly introduces a dependent result clause which contains an infinitive (BDAG, 2 and 2 a β). Here, however, it introduces an independent clause which has an indicative verb (ἀνθέστηκεν; see the fourth textual note on

---

[2] Wallace, *Greek Grammar*, 485: "With the *present*, the force generally is to *command the action as an ongoing process*."

[3] Murray, *Romans*, 2:148, argues that the form is middle and its meaning is reflexive, which "stresses active participation."

[4] Cranfield, *Romans*, 660, n. 4. (Moo, *Romans*, 797, n. 24, points out that aorist forms of this verb are always passive and never middle, but the form here is present.)

[5] See Wallace, *Greek Grammar*, 437–38; Mounce, *Basics of Biblical Greek*, 272–73.

[6] See Wallace, *Greek Grammar*, 619–21.

[7] See Wallace, *Greek Grammar*, 647–49; Mounce, *Basics of Biblical Greek*, 283–84.

[8] See Wallace, *Greek Grammar*, 572–74.

13:2) and serves to state a conclusion. BDAG gives "*for this reason, therefore*" (BDAG, 1). The comparable "so then" is used here. See the first textual note on 7:4, where ὥστε is translated as "for this reason."

ὁ ἀντιτασσόμενος τῇ ἐξουσίᾳ—The verb ἀντιτάσσομαι, "to oppose, resist," occurs only in the middle voice. The accompanying dative case τῇ ἐξουσίᾳ, "(to) the authority," indicates the person or thing opposed. The definite present middle participle ὁ ἀντιτασσόμενος functions substantively,[9] "the one who opposes." The translation "resist" is adequate but could be understood more passively in English, and passive resistance to an evil authority is permissible (i.e., the Christian need not actively volunteer to participate in an evil authority's endeavor). Therefore the translation uses "oppose" to convey the active meaning of the middle-form verb.

τῇ τοῦ θεοῦ διαταγῇ—The noun διαταγή is cognate to the verb διατάσσω, "to order, command, arrange." The verb is absent from Romans but employed by Paul elsewhere for his authoritative apostolic directives to the churches (1 Cor 7:17; 11:34; 16:1; Titus 1:5) or for the Lord's own command (1 Cor 9:14; cf. Gal 3:19). The noun refers to "that which has been ordered or commanded, *ordinance*" (BDAG), and the genitive τοῦ θεοῦ, "of God," specifies its source or origin.[10] Note that this noun is the fourth use of τάσσω or one of its cognates or compounds in 13:1–2 (see also ὑποτασσέσθω in the fourth textual note on 13:1; τεταγμέναι in the sixth textual note on 13:1; and ἀντιτασσόμενος in the second textual note on 13:2).

ἀνθέστηκεν—The verb ἀνθίστημι, literally, "stand against," means "be in opposition to, *set oneself against, oppose*" (BDAG, 1). Two perfect-tense forms of the verb occur sequentially in this verse; for the second one, see the next textual note. The translation of this first instance indicates the past aspect of the action, "he has stood against."

οἱ δὲ ἀνθεστηκότες—For the meaning of ἀνθίστημι, see the previous textual note. This definite perfect active plural participle functions substantively,[11] "the ones who ..." The translation of this second, participial, form expresses the abiding present result of the perfect tense:[12] "who (now continue to) stand against."

ἑαυτοῖς κρίμα—The dative case of the reflexive pronoun ἑαυτοῖς with the noun κρίμα, "judgment," functions as a "dative of disadvantage," which "has an *against* idea":[13] "judgment against themselves." But to avoid confusion with other uses of "against" in the immediate context, the more basic sense of "for" is retained in translation. "Judgment" (κρίμα) effectively indicates the negative force of "for themselves."

λήμψονται—This is the future middle indicative of λαμβάνω, to "*receive, get, obtain*" (BDAG, 10). Note the clearly passive nuance of the verb's meaning here, "they will receive." See the discussion of the similarly passive contextual nuance of καταλαμβάνω, "get," in the commentary on 9:30.

---

[9] See Wallace, *Greek Grammar*, 619–21.

[10] See Wallace, *Greek Grammar*, 109–10.

[11] See Wallace, *Greek Grammar*, 619–21.

[12] See Wallace, *Greek Grammar*, 572–74.

[13] Wallace, *Greek Grammar*, 142.

13:3 οἱ γὰρ ἄρχοντες—This form is actually an active participle of ἄρχω functioning substantively,[14] "the ones who rule/are ruling." But ἄρχων regularly serves as a noun, meaning "one who has administrative authority" (BDAG, 2), thus "the rulers."

οὐκ εἰσὶν φόβος—BDAG's first definition of the noun explains φόβος in an active, causative sense as an "intimidating entity" (BDAG, 1), and when used concretely, it describes someone/something that is *terrible/awe-inspiring, a terror*" (BDAG, 1 b). A desire for consistency[15] here leads to the translation "a [cause of] fear."

τῷ ἀγαθῷ ἔργῳ—Literally, "to the good work" (cf. 2:7), this phrase carries both a collective[16] and a personified[17] sense, "the person doing the good work." Paul makes this explicit later in the verse with the imperatival clause τὸ ἀγαθὸν ποίει, "do that which is good."

θέλεις δέ—The break in thought with the introduction of second person discourse in a question, "do you then wish … ?" means that a verse division would be well placed here; see the commentary. The particle δέ serves as "a marker linking narrative segments, *now, then, and, so, that is*" (BDAG, 2).

μὴ φοβεῖσθαι—The verb is the present infinitive of the deponent contract verb φοβέομαι. It means "be in an apprehensive state, *be afraid*" (BDAG, s.v. φοβέω, 1) as the result of and in response to a "source of fear,"[18] which is the meaning of the earlier noun φόβος (see the second textual note on 13:3). The verb recurs as the imperative φοβοῦ in 13:4.

τὸ ἀγαθὸν ποίει—The direct object, τὸ ἀγαθόν, is placed before the verb for emphasis: "the good [is what you are to] do." The verb is an active imperative of the contract verb ποιέω. Its present tense has an "iterative" force, which envisions a *repeated action*. That is, 'do it again and again.' "[19]

ἕξεις ἔπαινον ἐξ αὐτῆς—The form of the verb ἔχω here is a second person singular future indicative, "you will have." The direct object is the accusative of ἔπαινος, "praise"; see the third textual note on 2:29. Here the "praise" is explicitly ἐξ αὐτῆς, "from her/it," that is, from the (feminine gender) ἐξουσία, "authority," meaning the one in authority.

13:4 θεοῦ γὰρ διάκονός ἐστιν σοί—The placement of the genitive θεοῦ before the nominative noun διάκονος is emphatic, "*God's* servant," and the same emphatic word order recurs later in this verse (θεοῦ γὰρ διάκονός ἐστιν). The dative case of the second person singular pronoun σοί, "to you," expresses interest or advantage, to benefit you.[20]

εἰς τὸ ἀγαθόν—The preposition εἰς here expresses a goal "w[ith] the result of an action or condition indicated" (BDAG, 4 and 4 e). For consistency both uses of the

---

[14] See Wallace, *Greek Grammar*, 619–21.

[15] See Middendorf, *Romans 1–8*, 51–52.

[16] Sanday and Headlam, *Romans*, 367.

[17] Murray, *Romans*, 2:151.

[18] Moo, *Romans*, 800, n. 47.

[19] Wallace, *Greek Grammar*, 722.

[20] See Wallace, *Greek Grammar*, 142.

preposition in this verse are translated as "for" (see the fifth textual note on 13:4), here "for the good."

φοβοῦ—This form of the deponent verb φοβέομαι is a present imperative. For the meaning, see the fifth textual note on 13:3, with φοβεῖσθαι.

οὐ γὰρ εἰκῇ τὴν μάχαιραν φορεῖ—The adverb εἰκῇ occurs only here in Romans, where it "pert[ains] to being without purpose, *to no purpose*" (BDAG, 3). When used literally the noun μάχαιρα denotes a "*sword, dagger*" (BDAG, 1), but it can also be used metaphorically in a number of ways. Here it represents "the power of authorities to punish evildoers" (BDAG, 2 d). For a discussion of the applicability to capital punishment, see the commentary. The verb φορέω means "to carry or bear habitually or for a considerable length of time, *bear* ... constantly/regularly" (BDAG, 1). In contrast, φέρω, "carry, bring," can refer to bearing something only temporarily. Thus the choice of the verb φορέω here expresses an ongoing responsibility.

ἔκδικος εἰς ὀργήν—"An avenger for wrath" recalls the language of 12:19. That verse has ἐκδίκησις, "vengeance," which is a cognate of ἔκδικος, "avenger," here. See the third textual note there. The noun ὀργή refers to God's "wrath," as in 12:19; see the second textual note and the commentary on 1:18.

τῷ τὸ κακὸν πράσσοντι—This substantival participial clause[21] refers to "the one who practices evil." For the verb πράσσω, see the second textual note on 7:15. Though it may emphasize "practicing" something in an ongoing way, it essentially functions synonymously with ποιέω, "do," as in 13:3 and 13:4a.

13:5 διὸ ἀνάγκη ὑποτάσσεσθαι—The inferential conjunction διό draws a conclusion, "therefore." It occurs six times in Romans (also 1:24; 2:1; 4:22; 15:7, 22). The noun ἀνάγκη conveys a "necessity or constraint as inherent in the nature of things, *necessity*" (BDAG, 1) and regularly takes an explanatory infinitive, as here (also Mt 18:7; Heb 9:16, 23). An impersonal verb is supplied here, "[it is] a necessity." The form of the explanatory infinitive ὑποτάσσεσθαι could be either middle or passive, as was true of ὑποτασσέσθω in 13:1 (see the fourth textual note there). The present tense again here suggests an ongoing activity of being subject(ed).[22]

οὐ μόνον ... ἀλλὰ καί—Paul regularly uses a "not only ... but also" comparison to describe God's gracious interaction with humanity (see the first textual note and the commentary on 4:12; also 4:16, 23–24; 5:3, 11; 9:10, 24; cf. 3:29). But he also uses the expression to describe humanity's conduct in 1:32 and here. Normally the latter half conveys an aspect that is unexpected and/or broader. Here, the broader aspect is the universal human "conscience"; see the next textual note.

τὴν συνείδησιν—The noun συνείδησις here, as in 2:15, refers to "the inward faculty of distinguishing right and wrong, *moral consciousness, conscience*" (BDAG, 2), something possessed by all people (πᾶσα ψυχή, "every person," 13:1). (See the fifth textual note and the commentary on 2:15; the only other use of συνείδησις in Romans

---

[21] See Wallace, *Greek Grammar*, 619–21.

[22] This use of the present tense is either iterative or customary. See Wallace, *Greek Grammar*, 520–22.

conveys a different sense, Paul's personal conviction in 9:1.) See further "Reasons for Submitting (13:5)" in the commentary.

13:6 διὰ τοῦτο—The prepositional phrase "on account of this" refers to what precedes here and in 1:26; elsewhere its referent lies ahead (e.g., 4:16; 5:12).[23]

καὶ φόρους τελεῖτε—The noun φόρος is derived from the verb φέρω, "carry, bring," and refers to "that which is brought in as payment to a state … *tribute, tax*" (BDAG), indicating that the taxpayer is subservient. The verb τελέω generally means to "*finish, complete*" (BDAG, 1) or "*carry out, … fulfill*" (BDAG, 2; see 2:27; cf. the cognate noun τέλος in 10:4), but with the object φόρους here, the meaning is "to pay what is due" (BDAG, 3). The present-tense form τελεῖτε could be an imperative, but the preceding γάρ indicates an indicative assertion: "indeed, … you are paying taxes." This general statement becomes distinguished more specifically in 13:7; see the commentary.

λειτουργοὶ γὰρ θεοῦ εἰσιν—In contrast to other biblical uses (see the commentary), here λειτουργός stands as "more or less equivalent to 'public servant.' "[24] While the selected translation, "minister," typically has a dominant religious sense in English, the title can also, as here, apply to those in governmental positions, as in titles such as "prime minister" and "minister of defense."[25]

εἰς αὐτὸ τοῦτο—Here the pronoun αὐτό has an intensive force,[26] "to this very thing" (NASB, RSV, ESV). The antecedent of both neuter singular pronouns is the same, but also unclear. They could connect with λειτουργοί ("ministers") earlier in the verse and mean "their service itself."[27] Barrett identifies the referent as the actions "of promoting good, and of restraining evil" described in 13:3–4.[28] Cranfield and Dunn point to the specific action of collecting taxes in 13:6.[29] The initial suggestion seems best, particularly in combination with the participle; see the next textual note.

προσκαρτεροῦντες—This same participle of προσκαρτερέω described "holding fast" to prayer in 12:12. Here the persistent action is comparable, "*be busily engaged in, be devoted to*" (BDAG, 2 a). But the participle's relation to the rest of the sentence is ambiguous. Although a form of εἰμί is present (εἰσιν; see the third textual note on 13:6), it functions independently; therefore, this participle is not part of a periphrastic construction (as in 13:1).[30] Instead, "the present attributive (adjectival) participle προσκαρτεροῦντες states an ongoing important characteristic of good rulers."[31] The

[23] Cranfield, *Romans*, 668.

[24] Dunn, *Romans*, 767; for examples from secular Greek, see H. Strathmann, "λειτουργέω" and "λειτουργός," *TDNT* 4:216–22 and 4:229–30, respectively.

[25] In English, both the governmental and the religious usage of "minister" are attested from the fourteenth century AD onward. See the *OED*.

[26] See Mounce, *Basics of Biblical Greek*, 102–3.

[27] Moo, *Romans*, 805.

[28] Barrett, *Romans*, 247, whose translation of the end of 13:6 is in bold: "**attending upon the purpose I have described** (that is, of promoting good, and of restraining evil)."

[29] Cranfield, *Romans*, 669; Dunn, *Romans*, 767.

[30] See Moo, *Romans*, 805, n. 75.

[31] Kuske, *Romans 9–16*, 228.

verb προσκαρτερέω normally takes its object in the dative case, as in 12:12, but BDAG, s.v. προσκαρτερέω, 2, suggests that the preceding prepositional phrase εἰς αὐτὸ τοῦτο serves as the object here.[32] Although rejected as a grammatical possibility by Dunn,[33] this "rare (if not unprecedented)"[34] option makes good sense in resolving ambiguities regarding both the preceding prepositional phrase and this participle: "holding fast to this very thing."

13:7 ἀπόδοτε—This is the aorist active imperative of ἀποδίδωμι. Previously this verb referred to divine retribution in 2:6 and to Christians not repaying evil with evil in 12:17. In some contexts it can have a financial nuance, "to meet a contractual or other obligation, *pay, pay out, fulfill*" (BDAG, 2). While a financial nuance would apply to the first two items in Paul's list ("tax" and "revenue"), it is inappropriate for the third and fourth items ("fear" and "honor"). The basic idea of "*give back, return*" (BADG, 3) is equally applicable to all four. The prefixed preposition ἀπό on ἀποδίδωμι implies that you are "giving back *from*" (ἀπό) what you have received and, therefore, are returning a portion to the authorities in response.

τὰς ὀφειλάς—The noun ὀφειλή occurs "often in the papyri with references to financial debts."[35] Its singular has that meaning in Mt 18:32. Here, however, only the first two items in Paul's list of four are financial. Given the general nature of "fear" and "honor," the plural noun with the article is better translated as "the things that are owed." The only other NT instance of the noun ὀφειλή is in 1 Cor 7:3, where it refers to the conjugal obligation of husband and wife to each other. The cognate verb ὀφείλω in Rom 13:8 is also used in the context of general obligations (to love and not violate the commandments).

τῷ τὸν φόρον τὸν φόρον—Paul uses the same syntactical format in four consecutive phrases in order to lay "four specific examples (cf. the article with each noun) of the obligations owed to those in positions of authority."[36] All four phrases are controlled by the imperative ἀπόδοτε, "give back." In each case, the Greek word order is to give "to the one" (τῷ) who is owed "the [obligation]" "the [obligation]." The first definite noun (here, the first τὸν φόρον, "the tax") goes with the indirect object (τῷ, the one to whom it is owed), and the second, repeated definite noun (here, the second τὸν φόρον, "the tax") is the direct object of the imperative "give back." For the sake of English, the translation in effect reverses the Greek order of the two definite nouns by placing the direct object first and the (same definite) noun that is associated with the indirect object second: give back "the [obligation] to the one [owed] the [obligation]." For φόρος, see next textual note.

---

[32] So also Lenski, *Romans*, 796, who translates the phrase as rendered here "to this very thing."

[33] Dunn, *Romans*, 767: "εἰς αὐτὸ τοῦτο should not serve as object (προσκαρτερέω takes the dative)."

[34] Moo, *Romans*, 805, n. 76.

[35] Moo, *Romans*, 805, n. 81.

[36] Kuske, *Romans 9–16*, 229; see also 226 for his helpful diagramming.

τὸν φόρον … τὸ τέλος—These two singular terms seem to distinguish between direct and indirect taxes,[37] hence "tax" and "revenue." See the commentary for the details.

τὸν φόβον—This noun is the third item in the list of that which is owed. BDAG, 2 b β, defines this use of φόβος in terms of "*respect* that is due officials." Chrysostom agrees that "fear in this context means very great honor."[38] But here the noun "fear" also incorporates that which the same noun, "[cause of] fear," and its cognate verb φοβοῦ, "fear!" convey in 13:3–4; see the commentary.

τὴν τιμήν—This noun (τιμή) denotes "honor" (see also 2:7, 10; 9:21; 12:10). It too should not be separated from an appropriate godly fear. See, for example, the cognate verb in the pair of admonitions "fear God; *honor* the king" (τὸν θεὸν φοβεῖσθε, τὸν βασιλέα τιμᾶτε, 1 Pet 2:17).

Commentary

Earthly Authority—Divine Ordering (13:1–4)

Earthly Authorities (13:1a)

"It is only a slight exaggeration to say that the history of the interpretation of Rom. 13:1–7 is the history of attempts to avoid what seems to be its plain meaning."[39] But that does not provide an excuse for failing to seek and to heed the "plain meaning." In fact, by turning to the text itself, "we find in 13:1–7 a coherent and well-organized argument about a single topic."[40] Moo outlines the structure as follows:[41]

> General command (13:1a)
>   First reason (13:1b)
>   Consequences (13:2)
>   Second reason (13:3–4)
> Reiteration (13:5)
> Appeal to practice (13:6)
> Specific command (13:7)

Paul begins: "Let every person be subject to authorities who are in high positions" (13:1a). Dunn points to further "common themes shared by 2:7–11 and 13:3–4" (e.g., good work/the good in 2:7, 10; 13:3–4; honor/praise in 2:7, 10; 13:3; the evil in 2:9; 13:3–4; and wrath in 2:5, 8; 13:4).[42] In keeping with the universal applicability of those earlier verses, Paul explicitly indicates the equally "all-inclusive nature" of 13:1–3 by beginning with "every person"

---

[37] Moo, *Romans*, 805.

[38] Chrysostom, *Homilies on Romans*, 23 (Bray, *Romans*, ACCS NT 6:329).

[39] Moo, *Romans*, 806.

[40] Moo, *Romans*, 790.

[41] Summarized from Moo, *Romans*, 794.

[42] Dunn, *Romans*, 758.

(πᾶσα ψυχή).[43] While the phrase clearly includes all believers, it also extends beyond them to encompass all people. Thus the words which follow can be used properly by God's people in the public square to assert that those outside of the family of faith stand *equally accountable* for being subject "to authorities who are in high positions" (13:1a).

Cranfield summarizes the view advocated by Barth and Cullmann that Paul intends a double referent with "authorities" (ἐξουσίαι) to include also angelic ones.[44] The best evidence is that, aside from Titus 3:1, "in every other place in the Pauline epistles where ἐξουσία occurs in the plural or the plurally-used singular with πᾶσα ['every'] … it clearly signifies invisible angelic powers."[45] But that interpretation seems forced here in light of numerous other expressions in the context which must be taken as synonyms for earthly human powers. These clearly define the "authorities" (ἐξουσίαι) under consideration as "the rulers" (οἱ … ἄρχοντες, 13:3), "God's servant" (θεοῦ διάκονος, 13:4 [twice]) who bears the sword, and "God's ministers" (λειτουργοὶ … θεοῦ, 13:6) to whom taxes are due (13:6–7)! Furthermore, Paul provides no indication "to support the suggestion that ἐξουσίαι here mean also angelic powers behind and acting through the political authorities."[46] Some passages speak of evil angels who wield influence as "princes" or even "kings" over heathen nations,[47] but Paul certainly would not urge people (especially Christians) to submit to them. In Revelation 1–3 Christ exhorts the seven angels stationed over the seven churches, but does not command Christians to submit to these angels (cf. the prohibition against worshiping angels in Rev 19:10; 22:8–9).

Paul does speak of these earthly rulers in a broad sense as "authorities who are in high positions" (ἐξουσίαις ὑπερεχούσαις, 13:1a). Jewett observes:

> Since the participle οἱ ὑπερέχοντες ["who are in high positions"], as well as the noun ἐξουσίαι ["authorities"], can be used to refer to governmental officials, their somewhat redundant combination here has a cumulative sense that encompasses a range of officials placed in superior positions of political authority, duly appointed to their tasks and currently exercising their power.[48]

Paul views all people as subjects to them all and, therefore, commands his hearers to "be subject to" or, perhaps, "to submit themselves to" these authorities

---

[43] Kuske, *Romans 9–16*, 214.

[44] Cranfield, *Romans*, 656–60; argued at length in Barth, *Church and State*, 23–36; Cullmann, *The State in the New Testament*, 55–70.

[45] Cranfield, *Romans*, 657, citing 1 Cor 15:24; Eph 1:21; 3:10; 6:12; Col 1:16; 2:10; 15.

[46] Dunn, *Romans*, 760.

[47] See Dan 10:13–11:1 and the exposition of it in Steinmann, *Daniel*, 501–7; Steinmann (502–3) quotes Luther's "Preface to Daniel," AE 35:305–6. Cf. the "kings" in Dan 11:2–45, most of whom seem to refer to human earthly rulers, but the "king" in Dan 11:36–45 is the antichrist; see Steinmann, *Daniel*, 518–46. See also the evil powers that exert influence over human affairs in, e.g., Revelation 13 and 17, and those that harm churches in Rev 2:9–10, 13, 20–24. But Christians are to resist them, not submit to them.

[48] Jewett, *Romans*, 788.

without adding any qualification. However, the verb "be subject to" (the passive of ὑποτάσσω; see the fourth textual note on 13:1) is not one of the verbs typically translated as "obey." Therefore "be subject to" need not always include responding in complete conformity with what is heard (cf. ὑπακούω, "listen responsively to," in the commentary on 10:16). Neither does it demand total obedience in every instance (cf. πειθαρχέω in Acts 5:29, 32). Even if noncompliance or direct disobedience to a human authority becomes necessary for a believer (Acts 5:29), it is to be accompanied by the recognition that one still remains "subject to" the temporal power (*de jure humano*) of authorities whose response may well involve punishment. This becomes a key factor in the "Applications" section presented below.

While it is common to translate ὑπερεχούσαις in 13:1a with "governing" (ESV, NASB, RSV, NRSV), that might tend to limit those under Paul's purview to politicians in specific governmental positions (e.g., presidents, members of Congress, mayors). But Paul's wording in 13:1a speaks more broadly of "authorities who are in high positions," encompassing, therefore, all other civil servants such as judges, police officers, and teachers. BDAG offers the definition "*be highly placed*" (s.v. ὑπερέχω, 2). While less literal than "who are in high positions," BDAG's rendering effectively brings up an issue Paul proceeds to clarify, namely, who "placed" those in authority into such roles.

Divine Ordering (13:1b)

Paul answers immediately: "For there is not an authority except by God, and the ones which exist have been ordered and remain in place by God" (13:1b). Three implications follow: First, "government is not something that evolved simply because humans felt a need for it. Rather, it is God's doing."[49] This means, second, that all governing authorities have a *derived* authority, rather than one they can legitimately claim as inherently theirs. Third, Paul clearly acknowledges a higher authority from whom the ordering comes and by whom each and every one in authority has been put in place (τεταγμέναι, "ordered," 13:1b). Therefore those "who are in high positions" (13:1a) stand *dependent upon and responsible to God* for the exercise of their authority.

This does *not* mean that God predetermines how authorities use what he has entrusted to them. "For it is not the wickedness of individual rulers which comes from God but the establishment of the ruling power itself."[50] Regarding this distinction Origen provides a helpful analogy to the faculties endowed by our Creator:[51]

---

[49] Kuske, *Romans 9–16*, 214.

[50] Theodoret of Cyrus, *Romans* (Bray, *Romans*, ACCS NT 6:326).

[51] Luther's explanation of the First Article of the Apostles' Creed notes that the Creator has "given me my body and soul, eyes, ears, and all my members, my reason and all my senses" (SC II 2 [*LSB* 322]).

Nobody will deny that our senses—sight, sound and thought—are given to us by God. But although we get them from God, what we do with them is up to us. … God will judge us righteously for having abused what he gave us to use for good. Likewise, God's judgment against the authorities will be just, if they have used the powers they have received according to their own ungodliness and not according to the laws of God.[52]

His view, then, coincides with this "corollary, that those who abuse their God-given authority or call for greater submission than God has ordered will come under the judgment of God."[53]

As discussed in the introduction to 13:1–7, this appraisal fits squarely within the OT's worldview. Daniel, for example, tells Nebuchadnezzar: "The Most High rules the kingdom of men and gives it to whom he will" (Dan 4:25 [MT 4:22]; cf. Dan 4:17 [MT 4:14]). It also stands fully in concert with Jesus' words to Pontius Pilate: "You would not have authority against me at all unless it had been given to you from above" (οὐκ εἶχες ἐξουσίαν κατ' ἐμοῦ οὐδεμίαν εἰ μὴ ἦν δεδομένον σοι ἄνωθεν, Jn 19:11). His words to Pilate may be properly extended to include all earthly authorities, yet their power is derived from his, since the risen and ascended Lord Jesus now possesses "all authority in heaven and on earth" (πᾶσα ἐξουσία ἐν οὐρανῷ καὶ ἐπὶ [τῆς] γῆς, Mt 28:18).

Rebellion Has Consequences (13:2)

Paul then draws forth the results of failing to be subject to authorities by engaging in active and ongoing opposition against them: "So then the one who opposes the authority has stood against the ordinance of God, and the ones who stand against [God] will receive judgment for themselves" (13:2). When Paul speaks of the one "who opposes" (ἀντιτασσόμενος) and the "ordinance" (διαταγή) here, he uses his third and fourth τάσσω cognate or compound in 13:1–2 (see also ὑποτασσέσθω, "let him be subject," and τεταγμέναι, "ordered," in 13:1). Franzmann captures the emphasis in the original as follows:

> One could reproduce this feature of Paul's Greek in bad English somewhat as follows: "Be sub*ordin*ated … the authorities that exist have been *ordained* by God … (v. 1). He who refuses to sub*ordin*ate himself … is resisting God's *ordin*ance (v. 2). … Therefore one must sub*ordin*ate oneself" (v. 5).[54]

Thus Paul emphatically asserts that an order exists and, more importantly, a *divine* ordering. Note that "God" (the noun θεός) occurs three times in 13:1–2 and twice more in 13:4. In a broader sense, "Paul's point is that the structures of the world are God-given—there [1:18–32] the moral structures, here the social structures."[55] Paul spells out its details in the remainder of the section.

---

[52] Origen, *Romans* (Bray, *Romans*, ACCS NT 6:324).

[53] Dunn, *Romans*, 762, citing Dan 4:13–17, 23–25 (MT 4:10–14, 20–22); 5:20–21; Wisdom 6:4–5; *2 Baruch* 82:4–9.

[54] Franzmann, *Romans*, 232.

[55] Dunn, *Romans*, 765.

After "oppose" (ἀντιτάσσομαι, 13:2) Paul uses a synonym, the verb "to stand against" (ἀνθίστημι), twice in 13:2, both times in the perfect tense. The perfect, as usual, implies a past act, reflected by "he stood against," with present implications, "who stand [remain standing] against [God]." The following connotations, which are typical of its use in the LXX, may well come with the repeated use of this verb: "a resistance which is unavailing before superior strength"[56] or "a resistance to God which was inconceivable."[57]

Paul warns that those who thus stand against God "will receive judgment for themselves" (13:2b). The term for "judgment" (κρίμα) usually refers to God's eschatological judgment (e.g., 2:2, 3; 3:8; 5:16). In 11:33, however, the plural serves more broadly for God's acts within current salvation history (see the commentary there). The use of the word in 13:2 implies the certainty of eventual divine judgment, with the real possibility that it may be administered promptly through the earthly authority. Rom 13:4 expresses how "God's own judgment" may be "present in the punishment meted out by the ruler"[58] here and now; when this happens "through the state there takes place a partial, anticipatory, provisional manifestation of God's wrath against sin."[59] All too often, however, the evildoer evades temporal judgment entirely or does not receive the full extent of the punishment he deserves, and so justice does not take place as divinely intended. Yet even when that occurs, the future tense of the verb "will receive" (λήμψονται, 13:2) indicates that "divine judgment is clearly in view, and presumably eschatological, as the end result of such a deliberate policy" of resistance (see 2:2–3).[60] The ultimate retribution for such ongoing opposition remains certain.

The Dual Functions of Earthly Authorities (13:3–4a)

"For the rulers are not a [cause of] fear for [one doing] the good work, but for [one doing] the evil" (13:3a). Here, without doubt, Paul speaks of earthly "rulers" (ἄρχοντες). He also communicates a basic function "ordered" (13:1) by God.[61] It resides in God's providential ordering "that there should be rulers and ruled and that things should not just lapse into anarchy, with the people swaying

---

[56] Dunn, *Romans*, 762, citing LXX Lev 26:37; Deut 7:24; 9:2; 11:25; Josh 1:5; 7:13; 23:9; Judg 2:14; 2 Chr 13:7; Judith 6:4; 11:18.

[57] Dunn, *Romans*, 762, citing LXX Job 9:19; Ps 75:8 (MT 76:8; ET 76:7); Jer 30:13 (MT/ET 49:19); Judith 16:14; Wisdom 11:21; 12:12.

[58] Moo, *Romans*, 799.

[59] Cranfield, *Romans*, 666; on the basis of the phrase "to you for the good" (σοὶ εἰς τὸ ἀγαθόν) in Rom 13:4 and on the basis of 1 Tim 2:1–4, he adds that the authorities' "primary and pre-eminent" role is to benefit those whom they serve.

[60] Dunn, *Romans*, 762; his reference to a "deliberate policy" of rebellion against authority effectively conveys the double impact of the perfect tense verbs translated above as "has stood against" and "who stand against" (see the fourth and fifth textual notes on 13:2).

[61] See the four uses in 13:1–2 of τάσσω and its cognates as translated in the quote of Franzmann in "Rebellion Has Consequences (13:2)" above.

like waves."[62] For one who does "the good work," rulers should cause no fear. However, in keeping with the judgment envisioned in 13:2, rulers should bring the fear of judgment to anyone who does evil. This is one function God expects anyone whom he places in authority to carry out. On the basis of the correlations identified with 2:7–11,[63] Dunn suggests that with "good" and "evil" here "Paul is expressing himself in terms which would gain the widest approbation from men and women of good will (see on 2:10)."[64] This is further corroborated by Paul's use of "every person" at the inception of this discussion (πᾶσα ψυχή, 13:1).

As Paul did earlier in Romans 2, he utilizes the second person singular form of address to ask a direct question in the second half of 13:3: "Do you then wish not to fear the authority? Do that which is good, and you will have praise from it" (13:3b). Here again, those who do good should not (need to) be afraid of any ruler, whatever position they occupy; on the positive side, and in a manner equally applicable to every person in a position of authority, God expects those in authority to actively praise those who do good. In 2:29, the "praise" (ἔπαινος) that ultimately matters is "from God"; but here the same word for "praise" (ἔπαινος) is "from her/it" (ἐξ αὐτῆς, 3:3). The antecedent of the feminine pronoun ("her/it") is "the authority" earlier in the verse (τὴν ἐξουσίαν), which clearly applies to the one in authority.

One may properly identify this verse as another example of the diatribe style.[65] But, here again, *this does not mean the person being addressed is merely fictional.*[66] Instead, "when this [rhetorical] device is used in the course of such exhortation as we have here, it is natural to regard it as a singling out, for the purpose of effect, of the individual member of the group addressed."[67] Thus with the second person singular "do you wish?" Paul emphasizes that each person he addresses as "you" is responsible for his or her own conduct in this regard. The question in 13:3b *applies to any and "every person"* (πᾶσα ψυχή, 13:1), whether he does good or evil. This same reading of the second person singular should be applied throughout the letter. In other words, whatever persons fit the qualifying descriptions Paul indicates along with the "you" becomes the direct and intended referent being addressed.[68] Whether any or many are present in the audience during a given reading of the letter among the congregations in Rome (or today) does not diminish that reality. And in *no* case does Paul speak of *no one*.

---

[62] Chrysostom, *Homilies on Romans*, 23 (Bray, *Romans*, ACCS NT 6:325).

[63] See "Earthly Authorities (13:1a)" above.

[64] Dunn, *Romans*, 763.

[65] Dunn, *Romans*, 763.

[66] See Middendorf, *Romans 1–8*, 24, 151, 197–99.

[67] Cranfield, *Romans*, 666.

[68] See Middendorf, *Romans 1–8*, 197–202; see also "Who Are the 'Weak' and the 'Strong'? Addressees Again!" in the introduction to 14:1–15:13.

Paul continues the second person address in the first half of 13:4: "Indeed, he is God's servant to you for the good. But if you do evil, fear!" This repeats much the same thought. The authorities exist for the good of those who do good. They should, however, cause "you" to be afraid of them if you do evil. Paul now reiterates that God is the source of order and authority, as well as the one who puts individual rulers in place. Each is, in fact, "*God's* servant" (θεοῦ ... διάκονος; see the first textual note on 13:4).

Paul uses the noun for "service" (διακονία) three times in Romans. Twice it refers to his own ministry (11:13; 15:31); another time διακονία encompasses Christian service in its broadest sense (12:7). Now we meet a cognate noun, "servant" (διάκονος). Here also, the context defines the kind of servicing being envisioned. BDAG, 1, defines the noun here as "one who serves as an intermediary in a transaction, *agent, intermediary, courier.*" In 15:7–9, Paul exhorts the Jewish and Gentile Christians in Rome to receive one another because Christ received them; Christ became "a *servant* of [the] circumcision," that is, God's intermediary to save the Jews (15:8), also so that the Gentiles might glorify God for his mercies (15:9). In 16:1, "servant" (διάκονος) could possibly identify Phoebe as the courier of the letter (but see the commentary on that verse).

In 13:4, however, διάκονος refers to a servant in public, governmental office. This use is "well enough attested in inscriptional evidence in the sense '(civic) official or functionary' ... ; so in Esth 1:10; 2:2; and 6:3 for royal attendants, with no indication of a sacral or cultic reference."[69] Therefore "God's servant" (13:4) need *not* be a believer or even aware of the one true God whom he serves. The classic biblical example is Cyrus (Is 44:28–45:7).[70] But this does not mean that those in authority serve "unconsciously."[71] *They actively engage in their tasks, but in a specific sphere with two main obligations.* Those in authority are to be a source of praise for the doer of good; they are to be an ominous force against the doer of evil.

The Power of the Sword and Agents of Wrath (13:4b)

Paul himself then explains the extent and the power behind such a servant's authority to punish: "For he does not bear the sword for no purpose" (13:4b). The reference to the ongoing obligation of "bearing the sword" (μάχαιραν φορέω; see the fourth textual note on 13:4) has caused debate among commentators. Barrett suggests that it "recalls the technical term *ius gladii*, by which was meant the authority (possessed by all higher magistrates) of inflicting sentence of death."[72] But Cranfield responds: "In Paul's time (and, in fact, for the first two centuries of the Empire) the phrase *jus gladii* denoted the power given to provincial governors ... it was the right to condemn to death a Roman citizen

---

[69] Dunn, *Romans*, 764.

[70] See Lessing, *Isaiah 40–55*, 378–84.

[71] As Moo, *Romans*, 801, maintains.

[72] Barrett, *Romans*, 247, citing Tacitus, *Histories*, 3.68.

serving in the forces under one's own command."[73] He then posits other narrow interpretations, suggesting that Paul may be referring to military power or even the dagger worn by the emperor.

Murray responds with the evidence of other NT uses of "the sword"; these passages convey *a broader understanding which includes capital punishment* but does not require or always encompass it:

> It would not be necessary to suppose that the wielding of the sword contemplates the infliction of the death penalty exclusively. It can be wielded to instil the terror of that punishment which it can inflict. It can be wielded to execute punishment that falls short of death. But to exclude the right of the death penalty when the nature of the crime calls for such is totally contrary to that which the sword signifies and executes. We need appeal to no more than the New Testament usage to establish this reference. The sword is so frequently associated with death as the instrument of execution (*cf.* Matt. 26:52; Luke 21:24; Acts 12:2; 16:27; Heb. 11:34, 37; Rev. 13:10) that to exclude its use for this purpose in this instance would be so arbitrary as to bear upon its face prejudice contrary to the evidence.[74]

In Rom 13:4b, "he is God's servant, an avenger for wrath" (ἔκδικος εἰς ὀργήν) utilizes language reserved for the Lord in 12:19: "while not avenging yourselves, … give a place for the wrath [of God]" (τόπον τῇ ὀργῇ). Therefore the earthly "servant" in 13:4 serves as a "place" for "the wrath" of God to be carried out. Bruce properly makes the connection: "The state is thus charged with a function which has been explicitly forbidden to the Christian (12:17a, 19)."[75] This also fits squarely within an OT understanding, for the Scriptures often depict nations, even heathen ones, as God's agents for executing his wrath, particularly on his own rebellious people.[76]

Reasons for Submitting (13:5)

Next, Paul reiterates both the God-given *responsibility of rulers* to serve as instruments of his wrath and also the God-given *necessity for his hearers* to be subject to authorities; in so doing, he adds a most interesting component: "Therefore [it is] a necessity to be subject, not only on account of the wrath but also on account of the conscience" (13:5). In regard to "necessity" (ἀνάγκη), Dunn explains that Paul's audience would be familiar with its use in Greek philosophy "in reference to divine or immanent necessity—the way things are (laws of nature) and have to be (fate, destiny). … Paul appeals to this sense of the (divine) givenness of things"[77] in a manner which should be acknowledged by many outside the family of faith. He began by asserting that "every person"

---

[73] Cranfield, *Romans*, 667.

[74] Murray, *Romans*, 2:152–53.

[75] Bruce, *Romans*, 224.

[76] See, e.g., 2 Kings 17; 24–25; Jeremiah 20–27; Ezekiel 24; Obadiah; Hab 1:5–11. Dunn, *Romans*, 765, cites Is 5:26–29; 7:18–20; 8:7–8; 10:5–6, 25–26; 13:4–5.

[77] Dunn, *Romans*, 765.

should "be subject" (ὑποτασσέσθω, 13:1). How much more then should being subject (ὑποτάσσεσθαι, 13:5) characterize believers![78]

One reason to refrain from doing evil comes "on account of the wrath" (διὰ τὴν ὀργήν, 13:5) which should be duly and appropriately inflicted on God's behalf through rulers. This ought to provide a deterrent "to correct behavior and prevent bad things from happening."[79] But *another* is added via Paul's use of a favorite form of expression, "not only … but also" (see the second textual note on 13:5). In fact, fear of punishment "is only the minor reason for Christian submission, as Paul's 'not only … but also' sequence indicates. A more basic reason for Christian submission is 'because of conscience' [13:5]."[80] Moo speaks of conscience as applicable *only to Christians*.[81] Nygren defines it similarly, asserting: " 'for the sake of conscience,' that is, for the sake of God."[82] But does Paul limit the exercise of "conscience" (συνείδησις) in that manner?

Paul uses "conscience" (συνείδησις) two other times in Romans. Once it refers to the personal testimony of his own conscience (9:1). But the other use of the noun points, once again, to a broader sense which has general implications. Dunn properly recognizes:

> As in 2:15 Paul does not conceive the operation of conscience as something distinctively Christian. … Paul appeals to the moral sensibility of the ancient world. … And once again Paul does not separate moral or spiritual obligation from civic responsibility and political reality.[83]

The discussion of 2:12–16 in this commentary confirms Dunn's first point regarding the general application of the function of conscience. It responds on the basis of "the work of the Law written in" the hearts of all people (2:15). Cranfield equates "conscience" (συνείδησις) with knowledge,[84] but it is not merely a static awareness; conscience serves as a reactive guide as well (see the commentary on 2:15). Surely, a believer's conscience informed by the revealed Word has a prime advantage in this regard (cf. 3:1), and the active presence of the Spirit further enlightens one's conscience. Thus Augustine points out that "you [believers] should not submit simply to avoid the authority's anger, which can be done by pretense, but so that you might be assured in your conscience that you

---

[78] FC SD IV 14 cites Rom 13:5, 6, 9 as evidence that for Christians "good works are necessary" because "they necessarily follow faith and reconciliation" to God (see AC VI; XX; Ap IV 141, 189, 200, 214); Scripture uses words like "necessity," "necessary," "should," and "must" to indicate "what we are bound to do because of God's ordinance, commandment, and will." However, that article goes on to maintain that good works do not in any way contribute to our salvation nor our preservation in faith; see FC SD IV 15–36.

[79] Ambrosiaster, *Romans* (Bray, *Romans*, ACCS NT 6:326).

[80] Moo, *Romans*, 803; similarly, Käsemann, *Romans*, 358: "A Christian's political conduct should not be motivated by fear alone."

[81] Moo, *Romans*, 803, n. 62: "a guide to Christian conduct."

[82] Nygren, *Romans*, 431.

[83] Dunn, *Romans*, 765.

[84] Cranfield, *Romans*, 668.

are doing this out of love for him. For you submit at your Lord's command."[85] But in regard to the topics under discussion both in 2:12–16 and in 13:1–7, *the conscience is also present and expected to perform an active role in all those without the revealed Word* precisely because "the work of the Law" has been inscribed within their hearts (2:15). The conscience, therefore, reacts to the good or evil done with corresponding testimony, either "accusing or even defending" (2:15); here conscience (13:5) in "every person" (13:5) also prompts submission to authorities.

Paul's Summation (13:6–7)

"God's Ministers" (13:6)

Paul now draws his primary conclusion with an affirmation of what the Roman Christians *are doing*, something which continues to serve as an important reminder today: "Indeed, on account of this you are also paying taxes. For they are God's minsters, holding fast to this very thing" (13:6). The noun "taxes" here (the plural of φόρος) encompasses all forms of revenue, though Paul employs its singular in a narrower, technical sense in the next verse (τὸν φόρον; see the fourth textual note on 13:7). "This is evidently the climax of the discussion. … It was not simply that taxation is the point at which the power of the state most rudely impinges on daily life (as then, so now)."[86] Instead, Paul views it as a *response* to the activity of "God's minsters" (λειτουργοὶ … θεοῦ, 13:6). As they are devoted to carrying out their duties, those who receive the services outlined thus far respond appropriately (ἀπόδοτε, "give back," in 13:7) to the ruler and, more importantly, to the One in whose service the minister is employed, by paying taxes. This matches Jesus' instruction in Lk 20:22–25.[87]

Paul used the noun "worship" (λατρεία) in 12:1 in a unique manner, depicting the everyday lives of believers as living sacrifices offered in worship. Now a similar phenomenon occurs with the noun "minister" (λειτουργός). While its biblical usage normally designates one who conducts formal worship activities, Paul proceeds to utilize it in a less common, but not unheard of, setting.

> It is generally agreed that the context here is that of the secular technical usage in Hellenistic society, where λειτουργεῖν and λειτουργία refer to the rendering of public services to the body politic, traditionally the obligation which well-to-do citizens undertook for the benefit of the community.[88]

This application is not completely foreign to the biblical context. In the LXX, λειτουργός or a participle of the cognate verb λειτουργέω typically refers to

---

[85] Augustine, *Commentary on Statements in Romans*, 74 (Bray, *Romans*, ACCS NT 6:328).

[86] Dunn, *Romans*, 766.

[87] See the discussion of Lk 20:22–25 in "Canonical Context" in "Introduction to Romans 13:1–7" before this pericope.

[88] Dunn, *Romans*, 767.

a "minster" who serves at the temple;[89] λειτουργός can also describe a "servant" of a person or of the Lord in a more general sense.[90] The NT applies the term similarly to Epaphroditus (Phil 2:25), angels (Heb 1:7), and even Jesus (Heb 8:2).[91] Later in Rom 15:16 Paul also uses λειτουργός as a self-designation. However, significant for its use in Romans, λειτουργός *designates a court "official"* in LXX 2 Sam 13:18; 1 Ki 10:5; and 2 Chr 9:4. Context, therefore, determines how broadly or narrowly the ministry should be understood, as well as the sphere in which the "minister" operates. Even today the term has a dominant religious sense, but garners numerous governmental applications as well (e.g., prime minster, minister of defense).

Barrett contends that Paul's use here makes secular service sacred: "The Roman magistrates, little though they knew it, were public servants not of Rome but of God."[92] But that presents a false dichotomy. Instead, as they ministered in behalf of the people under their authority in service to Rome, they were, *at the same time*, in fact, also "God's minsters" (13:6). Paul's repeated use of references to God in regard to governing authorities, describing them twice as "God's servant" (θεοῦ … διάκονος, 13:4 [twice]) and also as "God's minsters" (λειτουργοὶ … θεοῦ, 13:6), remains both striking and significant. These expressions communicate a perspective of "secular" service as being *both divinely derived and directed*. Therefore they provide a framework from which a broader understanding of "vocation can clearly be developed"[93] (see "Applications" below).

Taxes (and More) Are Due! (13:7)

"Give back to all people the things that are owed: the tax to the one [owed] the tax [τὸν φόρον], revenue to the one [owed] revenue [τὸ τέλος], fear to the one [owed] fear, honor to the one [owed] honor" (13:7). Paul's final words in regard to governing authorities appear to draw a technical distinction between the first two terms as two kinds of taxation:

> The distinction between φόρος and τέλος (v 7) corresponds to the difference between *tributum* (direct taxes from which Roman citizens would have been exempt in Rome) and *vectigalia* (direct taxes comprised initially of revenue from rents on state property but in Paul's time also including customs duty, tax on slave sales and manumissions, death duties).[94]

---

[89] See, e.g., λειτουργός in LXX Ezra 7:24; Neh 10:40 (MT 10:40; ET 10:39); Is 61:6; and the participle of λειτουργέω in Num 4:37, 39, 41, 43; 1 Sam 2:11, 18; 3:1.

[90] See, e.g., LXX 2 Ki 4:43; 6:15; Pss 102:21 (MT/ET 103:21); 103:4 (MT/ET 104:4).

[91] Moo, *Romans*, 804, n. 71, adds this comparable observation: "The cognate λειτουργία (from which we get the word 'liturgy') denotes cultic service in Luke 1:23; Heb. 8:6; 9:21; and 'ministry' generally in 2 Cor. 9:12; Phil. 2:17 (with sacrificial allusions); Phil. 2:30."

[92] Barrett, *Romans*, 247.

[93] Dunn, *Romans*, 767.

[94] Dunn, *Romans*, 766; similarly, Moo, *Romans*, 805, including nn. 82–83; Sanday and Headlam, *Romans*, 368.

While a helpful insight into the original setting, "one ought not press the meaning of these two words too much. Paul's point is simply that citizens have an obligation to pay taxes of all kinds."[95] Origen offers this important reminder:

> The authorities demand taxes on our property and revenue from our business transactions. What can I say? Jesus Christ himself was obliged to pay taxes, not because he owed anything but so as not to cause scandal [Mt 17:24–27]. If he who owed nothing to Caesar and who had every right to refuse to pay taxes nevertheless agreed to pay them, who are we to refuse to do so?[96]

Paul then moves beyond the sometimes *easier matter of monetary payment* to that of attitude. Cranfield argues that "fear" (φόβος) here should be restricted to the reverent fear which believers properly owe to God alone. He bases this on the fact that, "apart from [Rom 13:]3 and possibly the verse which is under discussion, it is not used in connexion with rulers."[97] Peter directly makes the distinction "fear God; honor the king" (τὸν θεὸν φοβεῖσθε, τὸν βασιλέα τιμᾶτε, 1 Pet 2:17; cf. Lk 20:25). But, as Cranfield admits, in Rom 13:3 "fear" (φόβος) obviously refers to that shown to earthly "rulers,"[98] as does the cognate verb "to fear" (φοβέω) in 13:3, 4. Thus, without any explicit notice otherwise, all four elements in 13:7 ("tax," "revenue," "fear," and "honor") should be taken in reference to the ruling authorities.

Christians all across the spectrum have consistently failed in regard to giving appropriate "fear" and "honor." Although living under democratically elected, representative governments would seem to make it easier to submit to them, that appears to be less and the less the case.[99] Nevertheless, that which Paul commands believers in Rome to give to the Emperor Nero and his administrators remains in place due to the *divine offices* held by those persons who serve in government and all other positions of authority.[100] "Every person" (13:1) owes all of God's ministers taxes, revenue, fear, and honor (13:7).

Applications

O'Neill contends that "these seven verses [13:1–7] have caused more unhappiness and misery in the Christian East and West than any other seven verses in the New Testament."[101] What is the cause of such "misery?" Does Paul

---

[95] Kuske, *Romans 9–16*, 229.

[96] Origen, *Romans* (Bray, *Romans*, ACCS NT 6:329). Mt 17:24–27 affirms that Jesus himself provided for the payment of taxes that he was considered to owe. See also the discussion of Lk 20:22–25 in "Canonical Context" in "Introduction to Romans 13:1–7" before this pericope.

[97] Cranfield, *Romans*, 672.

[98] Cranfield, *Romans*, 672.

[99] Recognized by Edwards, *Romans*, 305.

[100] Chrysostom, *Homilies on Romans*, 23 (Bray, *Romans*, ACCS NT 6:325), errs here by arguing that Paul "does not speak about individual rulers but about the principle of authority itself." Without actual people in ruling positions, the "principle" would be void.

[101] J. C. O'Neill, *Paul's Letter to the Romans* (Harmondsworth, England: Penguin, 1975), 209, quoted in Morris, *Romans*, 457, n. 1.

really command every believer and, in fact, all people to be subject to governmental authority in any and all cases? Morris responds with a litany of situations in which, he implies, what Paul says here may not appropriately apply:

> Paul is writing in general terms to meet the need of the Romans and not legislating for every conceivable situation in which the Christian might find himself. He does not face, let alone resolve, the problem of when it is right to rebel against unjust tyranny (it has well been remarked that the first-century Romans had no experience of a successful revolt), or what to do when there are rival claimants to the crown or conflicts between civil and religious authorities. He does not distinguish between legitimate and usurped authority, nor go into the question of when a successful rebel may be held to have become the legitimate ruler. He does not speak of the situation in which the state asks the citizen to do something against the law of God. All the New Testament writers were clear that they must obey God rather than men (Acts 5:29), and Paul's whole manner of life shows that he accepted this wholeheartedly. He does not say what the Christian should do when the state fails in its duty. He is not trying to cover every situation. His concern is authority, however it has come to be possessed. He is writing out of a settled order where there is no doubt as to who the ruler is, and he is telling his readers something of the duty of a citizen in such a situation.[102]

But does this list from Morris provide a piling on of exceptions which seek to avoid the "plain meaning"[103] of what Paul writes?

It may seem troubling that 13:1–7 appears to "speak so absolutely about our need to 'be submissive to the authorities.' "[104] If it properly does so, *what of the many objections and exceptions such as those presented by Morris*? Moo gives seven possible answers,[105] the first five of which may be summarily dismissed as inadequate (see comments in brackets). However, the last two are worthy of further discussion. Moo's first five options are as follows:

> (1) Paul does not demand such submission at all. … [Yes, he does; see 13:1, 5.]

> (2) Paul is naive about the evil that governments might do or demand that we do. … [He is not; see 1:18–2:11.]

> (3) Paul was demanding submission to the government only for the short interval before the kingdom [of God] would be established in power. … [No, but see 13:11.]

> (4) Paul demands submission to "authorities," interpreted as both secular rulers and the spiritual powers that stand behind them, only as long as those authorities manifest their own submission to Christ. … [Nero, who was the Roman emperor when Paul wrote, certainly was not in submission to Christ.]

> (5) Paul is demanding submission to secular rulers only of the Roman Christians and only in the immediate situation they are facing. … [Nothing

---

in the text suggests this limitation, nor do the other corroborative biblical passages cited above.][106]

The sixth option Moo considers is that "Paul demands submission to government only as long as the government functions as Paul says it should function in vv. 3–4."[107] This application deserves a fuller explication. Achtemeier advocates for it as follows:

> In the first place, since governing authorities are in fact God's servants for the promotion of civil order, those governing authorities cannot claim for themselves divine prerogatives. A government that claims for itself the total and absolute devotion which a creature can give only to its Creator, ceases in the moment it makes that claim to be an agent of divine order, or a divine servant [referencing Rev 17:1–19:10].

> In the second place, Paul describes governments as agents of good, which are to promote civil good and punish evil and disorder. … But what happens when a government reverses those roles and begins to reward evil and punish people who do what is good? Again, clearly enough, that would no longer be the kind of government about which Paul here speaks. …

> If then a government claims for itself the kind of devotion proper only to God and demands of its subjects that they perform evil rather than good, and if it punishes those who disobey such demands to do evil, that government no longer functions as a servant of God and is therefore no longer to be obeyed as such.[108]

Achtemeier himself then brings up the major difficulty which bedevils this view:

> Yet the fundamental problem remains: How does one decide at what point a government has passed from the ranks of God's servants to the ranks of his opponents? On that matter this passage gives no specific advice. That decision will have to be reached on the basis of the larger content of this letter, and indeed of the whole of the Bible.[109]

While plausible, Achtemeier's application certainly allows for believers to come to divergent convictions of conscience and then conflicting conclusions about whether being subject to any given government is proper. Leenhardt illustrates the conundrum:

> It is significant that Paul has brought out in this connexion the positive character of obedience, because such a point of view at the same time implies the limits of obedience. If obedience is a matter of conscience, then it is no

---

[106] Moo, *Romans*, 807–8.

[107] Moo, *Romans*, 808.

[108] Achtemeier, *Romans*, 205; similarly, Kruse, *Romans*, 499, citing Stanley E. Porter, "Romans 13:1–7 as Pauline Political Rhetoric," *Filologia neotestamentaria* 3 (1990): 117–18, contends that "believers are to willingly submit to the authorities on the assumption that they are just" and that authorities "must rule in a way that is consistent with God's justice." Kruse cites with approval Porter's conclusion: "Unjust authorities are not due the obedience of which Paul speaks. … Rather than being a text which calls for submissive obedience, Rom 13:1–7 is a text which only demands obedience to what is right, never to what is wrong."

[109] Achtemeier, *Romans*, 205–6.

longer servile; when conscience is introduced as the motive of obedience, the latter can no longer be counted on![110]

This somewhat arbitrary position leans toward postmodern situational ethics and stands challenged by the more inclusive statements of Paul in this section.

A seventh and final option is preferable. Cranfield and Moo establish an important distinction between "being subject" (the passive of ὑποτάσσω, Rom 13:1, 5) and "obeying" (e.g., πειθαρχέω in Acts 5:29, 32; cf. ὑπακούω in Rom 10:16).[111] Cranfield concludes: "There are, of course, three perfectly good Greek verbs meaning 'obey,' all of which occur in the NT, namely, πειθαρχειν, πείθεσθαι, and ὑπακούειν,"[112] but the middle/passive of ὑποτάσσω, translated as "be subject" in 13:1, 5, "does not mean 'obey.' "[113] Murray asserts that "the term for 'subjection' is more inclusive than that for obedience. It implies obedience when ordinances to be obeyed are in view, but there is more involved."[114] However, subjection may actually be more limited, that is, submission does not always require obedience; see below.

Morris explains the use of ὑποτάσσω here as "a due recognition of the subordinate place that is part of the Christian understanding of life" under any and all divinely established orders.[115] It is certainly true that "being subject" (13:1, 5) entails "recognizing that one is placed below the authority by God."[116] Yet Paul's argument expresses how God exercises his authority in the governmental sphere *indirectly* through rulers who, along with all other people, remain sinful and imperfect (3:9–18, 23). Therefore, they dare not wield their limited powers, which they have derived from the omnipotent One (13:1), in such a way as to give the impression that they or their powers are on the level of his indisputable, divine authority; neither should personal convictions of conscience (13:5) be equated with the will of God himself.

For those under authorities, then, the best application is to draw this distinction: *being subject remains imperative always, regardless of whether actual obedience presents a godly option in a given situation.* Moo explains in his seventh answer:

> Paul demands a "submission" to government: not strict and universal obedience. ... The Christian submits to government by acknowledging this divinely ordained status of government and its consequent right to demand

---

[110] Leenhardt, *Romans*, 335, quoted with approval by Edwards, *Romans*, 308.

[111] Cranfield, *Romans*, 660–62; Moo, *Romans*, 797.

[112] Cranfield, *Romans*, 660.

[113] Cranfield, *Romans*, 661, speaking specifically of the use of ὑποτάσσω in Eph 5:21.

[114] Murray, *Romans*, 2:148; apparently Dunn, *Romans*, 760–61, advocates a similar position when he defines the middle/passive of ὑποτάσσω as " 'subject oneself, be subjected, subordinate' (stronger than ὑπακούω, which has more the sense of 'respond')"; the latter verb is typically translated as "obey."

[115] Morris, *Romans*, 461.

[116] Cranfield, *Romans*, 662.

the believer's allegiance. … Christians may continue to "submit" to a particular government (acknowledging their subordination to it generally) even as they, in obedience to a "higher" authority, refuse to do, in a given instance, what that government requires.[117]

Thus submission to a governing authority can coexist "with disobedience to government in certain exceptional circumstances."[118] These circumstances are situations where the government commands one to do something that is clearly contrary to the Word of God or when rulers prohibit allegiance to Christ alone. Conscience may also come into play in light of 13:5. For in such situations "it becomes possible to object to authority on the grounds of conscience."[119]

In these cases, it should be emphasized that submission then entails *willingly accepting whatever punishment the earthly authorities dole out* in response to disobedience. In the earliest days of the church, the apostles Peter and John illustrate this kind of godly behavior on both counts, particularly in Acts 4–5 (e.g., Acts 4:13–20; 5:12–16, 21, 25, 27–29, 42). Jesus himself exemplifies it most profoundly by his passive obedience to God in his own passion; he allowed himself to be arrested, and when interrogated by the governing authorities, he refused to reply or perform miracles for them.[120]

Conclusions

With the coming of the Christ, the people of God are no longer identified with a specific national or ethnic group as was true of Israel in OT times. As Paul writes, this transformed community of faith exists in numerous places under the civil control of a wide variety of local authorities, all currently subordinate to the auspices of imperial Rome.

> Paul thus approached the relation of church and state not as a Sadducee who lived from the advantages of the state, nor as a Zealot who lived to overthrow the state, nor as a Pharisee who divorced religion from the state, nor as a Roman citizen for whom the state was an end in itself.[121]

Instead, Paul insists that a higher authority exists from whom all governments derive their power and to whom governing authorities remain accountable (13:1b, 2, 4, 5). And believers clearly owe their ultimate allegiance to God (Acts 4:19–20; 5:29). Yet Paul reinforces the divine role of authorities in their earthly

---

[117] Moo, *Romans*, 809.

[118] Moo, *Romans*, 797.

[119] Leenhardt, *Romans*, 335.

[120] E.g., Mt 26:50–56; 27:14; Mk 14:61; 15:5, 30–32; Lk 23:8–9. The Scriptures also provide examples of believers who accepted punishment by governing authorities because they engaged in civil disobedience in order to obey God, e.g., Joseph (Gen 39:7–20); Micaiah (1 Ki 22:8–27); and Shadrach, Meshach, and Abednego (Daniel 3). Besides Christ himself and the apostles in Acts 5:17–33, 40–42, Paul did so on many occasions (e.g., Acts 16:19–24; 2 Cor 11:23–27). See also, e.g., Mt 14:3–12; Heb 11:35–38; Rev 1:9.

[121] Edwards, *Romans*, 308.

sphere of influence (13:3–4). He calls believers to be *not only submissive* (13:1, 5) *but also supportive* (13:6–7).

Two Overlapping Ages and Kingdoms

A necessary theological construct for understanding Paul's view of the believer's life in this world is the recognition of both the "now" and the "not yet."[122] While that underlying theme permeates Romans 6–8, Nygren properly identifies its influence in 13:1–7 as well:

> Again and again, in the preceding parts of the letter, we have been reminded of the tension in the life of the Christian due to the fact that it must be lived *in this aeon*. This aeon has its orders, quite apart from those that obtain in the new aeon. …
>
> The two aeons do interpenetrate, but that does not mean that they may arbitrarily be confused.[123]

Integral to a proper understanding of this eschatology is the basic distinction between God's Law and his Gospel, which is foundational for Paul's thought in Romans (e.g., 1:1, 9, 16; 3:19–24). The state, or civil government, is an expression of God's Law, while the church is built on the Gospel. While believers in Christ have already "now" been accounted righteous by the Gospel and freed from the Law's condemnation (8:1), we are still subject to civil law as long as we live in the present aeon. Only in the age to come will the civil orders of this world have passed away completely (cf. 1 Cor 7:31).

The Lutheran vocabulary of "the twofold kingdom of God," or "the two kingdoms," provides another helpful framework for grasping the manner in which Paul operates here.[124] The right-hand kingdom of grace (the church, enlivened by the Gospel) currently coexists with the left-hand kingdom of earthly power (the state, which rules by the power of law). Thus Herod Antipas (Mk 6:23) and Jesus (e.g., Lk 22:30; Jn 18:36) can each speak of "my kingdom." *Both kingdoms are ultimately God's, and in both of them he provides his blessings mediated through his servants and minsters.* In the right-hand kingdom of the church, these blessings are spiritual and eternal; in the left-hand kingdom, he providentially brings the temporal benefits of "peace and the blessings of

---

[122] For a brief overview, see Middendorf, *Romans 1–8*, 441–42.

[123] Nygren, *Romans*, 426–27.

[124] It is impossible to go into detail here. For an overview, see, for example, *Render unto Caesar … and unto God: A Lutheran View of Church and State*, a report of the Commission on Theology and Church Relations of The Lutheran Church—Missouri Synod; Mueller, *Called to Believe, Teach, and Confess*, 427–30. See also AC XVI, "Civil Government" (quoted below); Ap XVI, "Political Order"; SC IX, "Table of Duties," 4–5; FC Ep XII 12–19; Luther, "Temporal Authority: To What Extent It Should Be Obeyed," AE 45:75–129; and Luther, "Whether Soldiers, Too, Can Be Saved," AE 46:87–137. Other resources include Bornkamm, *Luther's Doctrine of the Two Kingdoms*; MacKenzie, "The Challenge of History: Luther's Two Kingdoms Theology as a Test Case"; Niebuhr, *Christ and Culture*; Stephenson, "The Two Governments and the Two Kingdoms in Luther's Thought."

civil institutions."[125] For now, these two kingdoms may be distinguished, but not divided, separated, or merged.[126] Believers, therefore, remain part of both kingdoms. They reside in the kingdom of Christ *and* within the various kingdoms of this world as ordered by God. But after the second coming, there shall be only one kingdom, as the heavenly voices shall proclaim: "The kingdom of the cosmos has become our Lord's and his Christ's" (Rev 11:15).[127]

Romans 12 calls forth dedicated service from all believers (12:1) and then, more specifically, from those who serve and preside over God's people (12:7, 8). Romans 13:1–7 demonstrates how it is also appropriate to speak of God's servants and minsters in the various spheres of earthly authority. The Lutheran *theology of vocation* provides a most helpful category here as well.[128] It aptly applies *both* to earthly authorities as God's servants and minsters in the left-hand kingdom (13:4, 6) *and* to their subjects, especially when blessed with opportunities for active citizenship and community service in return. In both kingdoms, those on the receiving end are commanded to give back what is appropriately owed. Paul engages that topic for believers directly in 13:8–10. In 13:1–7 he spells out what is owed to earthly authorities—being subject (13:1, 5) and willingly rendering back to them taxes, revenue, fear, and honor (13:7).

Three Final Points

First, it may be helpful to look briefly beyond the situation under Nero in Rome at the time Paul writes. As Christianity grew and spread, Christians were increasingly given opportunities to serve as God's servants in many and various roles of earthly authority.[129] Article XVI of the Augsburg Confession summarizes the Christian's relationship to earthly governing authorities, but also draws further conclusions regarding *roles of service which a believer may be called by God to fulfill* within various spheres of civil government:

> It is taught among us that all government in the world and all established rule and laws were instituted and ordained by God for the sake of good order, and that Christians may without sin occupy civil offices or serve as princes and judges, render decisions and pass sentence according to imperial and other existing laws, punish evildoers with the sword, engage in just wars, serve as soldiers, buy and sell, take required oaths, possess property, be married, etc. …

---

[125] Chrysostom, *Homilies on Romans*, 23 (Bray, *Romans*, ACCS NT 6:328).

[126] Origen, *Romans* (Bray, *Romans*, ACCS NT 6:327), also recognizes that "God wants these crimes to be punished by human judges and not by representatives of the church."

[127] For this translation and an exposition, see Brighton, *Revelation*, 304–5, 308–9.

[128] For a brief overview, see Mueller, *Called to Believe, Teach, and Confess*, 431–35. For more thorough treatments, see Veith, *God at Work*; Wingren, *Luther on Vocation*.

[129] The NT suggests that a few of the earliest Christians already held positions of military authority or social influence; see, e.g., Mk 15:39; Lk 7:2–10; Acts 10–11. However, it seems unwarranted to conclude with Chrysostom, *Homilies on Romans*, 23 (Bray, *Romans*, ACCS NT 6:326), that one of Paul's aims in 13:1–7 is "to draw civil governors who were unbelievers to accept the Christian faith."

The Gospel does not overthrow civil authority, the state, and marriage but requires that all these be kept as true orders of God and that everyone, each according to his own calling, manifest Christian love and genuine good works in his station of life. Accordingly Christians are obliged to be subject to civil authority and obey its commands and laws in all that can be done without sin. But when commands of the civil authority cannot be obeyed without sin, we must obey God rather than men (Acts 5:29). (AC XVI 1–2, 5–7; see also Ap XVI 5)

Second, an added thought seems appropriate in regard to the functions those appointed by God are expected by him to perform. The divine essentials are detailed in 13:3–4: avenging evildoers and praising those who do what is good. Thus rulers stand accountable to God for maintaining basic law and order. *The NT, however, does not envision government being responsible for carrying out broader roles typically referred to as "social welfare."* To be sure, the NT does not prohibit governments from engaging in such functions at whatever level. But the NT does not hold governments accountable for caring for the poor and needy, not to mention providing education and a host of other community services increasingly under their purview. Furthermore, the NT does not instruct believers to look to the government for such provision; neither does it suggest that those responsibilities may simply be delegated to governments and, thereby, taken off of our hands.

Instead, Paul asserts quite strongly that, first and foremost, the *extended family* is obligated to provide for those among them who are in need (e.g., 1 Tim 5:8, 16). Then he instructs God's *family of faith* to do the same, especially for the needy within the community of believers, but then also to those outside of it as well.[130]

Third, Paul himself provides the final and best explanation for how God's people properly live out Rom 13:1–7. Years later he writes this to Timothy:

¹παρακαλῶ οὖν πρῶτον πάντων ποιεῖσθαι δεήσεις προσευχὰς ἐντεύξεις εὐχαριστίας ὑπὲρ πάντων ἀνθρώπων, ²ὑπὲρ βασιλέων καὶ πάντων τῶν ἐν ὑπεροχῇ ὄντων, ἵνα ἤρεμον καὶ ἡσύχιον βίον διάγωμεν ἐν πάσῃ εὐσεβείᾳ καὶ σεμνότητι. ³τοῦτο καλὸν καὶ ἀπόδεκτον ἐνώπιον τοῦ σωτῆρος ἡμῶν θεοῦ, ⁴ὃς πάντας ἀνθρώπους θέλει σωθῆναι καὶ εἰς ἐπίγνωσιν ἀληθείας ἐλθεῖν.

¹Therefore, first of all, I urge that pleas, prayers, petitions, and thanksgivings be made in behalf of all people, ²in behalf of kings and all the ones being in a high position, so that we might lead a quiet and tranquil life in all godliness and respectfulness. ³This [is] good and acceptable before our Savior God, ⁴who desires all people to be saved and to come to a recognition of [the] truth. (1 Tim 2:1–4)

---

[130] See, e.g., Rom 12:8, 13; 2 Cor 8:13–15; 9:6–15; Gal 2:10; 6:10; 1 Tim 5:3, 9; cf. also Mt 10:42; 25:31–46; Lk 12:33–34.

Fulfilling the Law of Love
until the Dawning Day

Translation

13 **8Owe nothing to anyone except** *the* **[obligation] to love one another. For the one who loves the other has brought [the] Law to fulfillment. 9Indeed, the [commandments] "you will not commit adultery," "you will not murder," "you will not steal," "you will not [improperly] desire," and if [there is] some other commandment, it is brought under a heading in this word: "you will love your neighbor as yourself." 10Love does not work evil to the neighbor; therefore love [is the] fulfillment of the Law.**

11And [do] this, knowing the momentous time, because already [it is the] hour for you to be raised from sleep. For now our salvation is nearer than when we believed. 12The night has advanced far and the day has drawn near and is at hand. Therefore, let us take off from ourselves the works of the darkness, and let us clothe ourselves with the instruments of the light. 13Let us walk decently as in [the] day, not in excessive eating and drunkenness, not in sexual promiscuity and self-indulgence, not in strife and envy, 14but clothe yourselves with the Lord Jesus Christ, and do not make for yourselves provision for the flesh, for [its] desires.

Textual Notes

13:8 μηδενὶ μηδέν—The first form of μηδείς is dative masculine singular; the second is accusative neuter singular, thus "*to no one* [owe] *nothing*." In Greek such double negatives are emphatic, but in English two negatives cancel each other out, so one must be altered, thus "[owe] nothing to anyone." The emphasis could be retained with "[owe] nothing at all to anyone," but that would potentially be misleading if taken as a prohibition against Christians taking out any kind of loan or borrowing on credit even with their timely repayment. See the commentary.

ὀφείλετε—The verb ὀφείλω, "to be under obligation to meet certain social or moral expectations, *owe*" (BDAG, 2; also 15:1, 27), is cognate to the noun ὀφειλή, "that which is owed," in 13:7. Its form could be an indicative, but the context points to an imperative. The present tense implies an ongoing obligation.[1]

εἰ μή—Barrett argues that the force of these two words is adversative and that a second instance of ὀφείλω is to be supplied, but in the indicative mood and with the meaning "ought": "Owe no man anything—but you ought to love ..."[2] Cranfield con-

---

[1] Wallace, *Greek Grammar*, 485: "With the *present* [imperative], the force generally is to *command the action as an ongoing process.*"

[2] Barrett, *Romans*, 250.

cedes that this is possible (citing the use of εἰ μή with an adversative sense in Mt 12:4; Rom 14:14; 1 Cor 7:17), but points out that "the combination of change of sense and change of mood, where the verb is not repeated, is surely so harsh as to be extremely improbable."[3] Thus the more common understanding is that εἰ μή means "except" and no repetition of the verb is needed.

τὸ ἀλλήλους ἀγαπᾶν—BDAG points out that the infinitive with a neuter article "is used in a number of ways," one of which is to stand "for a noun."[4] Wallace similarly asserts that the article can be used as a substantiver, one function of which is "to nominalize the infinitive."[5] But the category *Par Excellence* or "Well-Known"[6] for the use of the article here seems more appropriate. *Par excellence* would mean that the command "to love" is the premiere commandment, the one that best summarizes the heart of the entire Law, as Jesus affirmed (Mt 22:34–40; Mk 12:28–34). Dunn expresses the meaning in this context as "the (well-known command to),"[7] though "to" is supplied by the infinitive form which follows, ἀγαπᾶν, "to love," and the implied noun "command" (ἐντολή) is feminine, whereas the article τό is neuter. Due to the verb ὀφείλετε, "owe," earlier in the verse, it seems best to presume the influence of its cognate neuter noun ὀφείλημα, which is represented by the bracketed insertion of "obligation" (BDAG, 2). The verb ἀγαπάω, "to love," twice in 13:8 and once in 13:9, refers here to the love of believers for others. In 8:37; 9:13, 25, it referred to the love of God or Christ for his people and in 8:28 to love for God (see further the commentary on 12:9). The accusative plural object, ἀλλήλους, means "one another" and is, therefore, reciprocal by definition. The term is usually "limited to fellow-Christians,"[8] but see the commentary.

ὁ γὰρ ἀγαπῶν τὸν ἕτερον νόμον πεπλήρωκεν—For ἀγαπάω, see the preceding textual note. The adjective ἕτερος "pert[ains] to being distinct from some other item implied or mentioned, *other*" (BDAG, 1). Grammatically, it could modify the following noun, νόμον, as ἕτερον νόμον means "another Law" in 7:23. In that case Paul would be saying, "the one who loves has fulfilled the other Law," but that is not likely; see the commentary. Paul almost certainly uses τὸν ἕτερον as the object of the participle ἀγαπῶν: "who loves *the other*." The perfect active of πληρόω has the particular connotation "to bring to a designed end, *fulfill*" (BDAG, 4; Rom 13:8 is cited in BDAG, 4 b). The translation "brought to fulfillment" strives to convey both the past and present aspects of the perfect tense. This is the third of six uses of πληρόω in Romans; note especially its relation to the Law in 8:4 (see the third textual note and the commentary there); also 1:29; 15:13, 14, 19.

13:9 τὸ γὰρ οὐ μοιχεύσεις—For the use of the neuter article τό, see the fourth textual note on 13:8. Here it introduces four well-known commandments from the Decalogue,

---

3   Cranfield, *Romans*, 674. See also Sanday and Headlam, *Romans*, 373.

4   BDAG, s.v. ὁ, ἡ, τό, 2 d and 2 d α, citing BDF, § 398ff.; Robertson, *A Grammar of the Greek New Testament*, 1062–68.

5   Wallace, *Greek Grammar*, 231, 234.

6   Wallace, *Greek Grammar*, 222–23, 225.

7   Dunn, *Romans*, 776.

8   Cranfield, *Romans*, 675.

beginning with "you will not commit adultery." For the verb μοιχεύω, see the first textual note on 2:22. Regarding Paul's choice of these particular commandments and their order, see the commentary. In the original Hebrew each negated verb form is a singular imperfect ("you will not …"). Paul cites each of them from the LXX: οὐ μοιχεύσεις, "you will not commit adultery" (LXX Ex 20:13 [MT/ET 20:14]; Deut 5:17 [MT/ET 5:18]); οὐ φονεύσεις, "you will not murder" (LXX Ex 20:15 [MT/ET 20:13]; Deut 5:18 [MT/ET 5:17]); οὐ κλέψεις, "you will not steal" (Ex 20:14 [MT/ET 20:15]; Deut 5:19); οὐκ ἐπιθυμήσεις, "you will not covet/[improperly] desire" (twice in each verse: LXX Ex 20:17; Deut 5:21). Each of those verbs (as well as ἀγαπήσεις, "you will love;" see the sixth textual note on 13:9) is a singular future indicative whose

> force is quite emphatic, in keeping with the combined nature of the indicative mood and future tense. It tends to have a universal, timeless, or solemn force to it. … [But] "it is not a milder or gentler imperative."[9]

Therefore, one should not make them into imperatives in translation, but render the forms as in the Greek text (reflecting the original Hebrew).

οὐ φονεύσεις—The verb φονεύω means "*murder, kill*" (BDAG). The underlying Hebrew in Ex 20:13 and Deut 5:17 is לֹא תִרְצָח, "you will not murder." In the OT רָצַח (forty-seven instances) always refers to the killing of a person but is not used for capital punishment. It occurs in contexts that describe what would generally be considered under the laws of the United States to be murder (in the first, second, or third degree); it is premeditated (first degree) in 1 Ki 21:19 and could be either premeditated or not (second degree) in, e.g., Num 35:16–21; Deut 22:26; Job 24:14; but it refers to manslaughter (involuntary, third degree) in, e.g., Num 35:11; Deut 19:4–6. The Decalogue does not employ one of the common and more general Hebrew terms for any kind of killing (such as הָרַג, 167 times in the OT, or the Hiphil of מוּת, 138 times), which would conflict with bearing the sword in Rom 13:4.

ἐν τῷ λόγῳ τούτῳ—"In this *word*" contains the noun λόγος. Three times the OT calls the Decalogue עֲשֶׂרֶת הַדְּבָרִים, "the Ten *Words*" (Ex 34:28; Deut 4:13; 10:4), which the LXX accurately translates with the plural of the same noun as here in Rom 13:9, τοὺς δέκα λόγους (Ex 34:28; Deut 10:4), and with a close synonym, τὰ δέκα ῥήματα (Deut 4:13). The phrase "Ten *Commandments*" never actually occurs in Scripture even though many English versions use it to translate the phrase in Ex 34:28; Deut 4:13; 10:4 (e.g., KJV, RSV, ESV, NASB). Luther, however, rendered the biblical phrase literally as *die zehen wort/Wort*[10] (in modern German: *die Zehn Worte*). See further the commentary.

ἀνακεφαλαιοῦται—The verb ἀνακεφαλαιόω is "used of literary or rhetorical summation *sum up, recapitulate*" (BDAG, 1). The literal sense (cf. κεφαλή, "head") conveys the notion of bringing "everything to a head."[11] Schlier demonstrates that it

---

[9] Wallace, *Greek Grammar*, 718, quoting Basil L. Gildersleeve, *Syntax of Classical Greek from Homer to Demosthenes* (2 vols.; New York: American Book Company, 1900–1911), 1:116 (§ 269).

[10] WA DB 8.311, 571, 591.

[11] Dunn, *Romans*, 778.

refers to "summing up in reflection or speech, but also ... the gathering together of things."[12] The latter applies here and in the verb's only other NT use, the gathering of all things together in Christ (Eph 1:10).

[ἐν τῷ]—This introductory prepositional phrase is not in 𝔓[46] or B. It is redundant here and most likely assimilated from Gal 5:14.[13]

ἀγαπήσεις τὸν πλησίον σου ὡς σεαυτόν—Paul quotes LXX Lev 19:18 verbatim. The underlying Hebrew verb is a singular perfect with *waw* consecutive, which should be understood in the same way ("*you will* love") as the Hebrew imperfects from the Decalogue (see the first textual note on 13:9). For ἀγαπάω, "to love," see the fourth textual note on 13:8. In form πλησίον is the neuter nominative or accusative of the adjective πλησίος, "near, close," but this neuter form is used as an adverb, which is indeclinable (see the next textual note). The Greek article, however, can be used as a "substantiver" that turns another part of speech, in this case an adverb, into a substantive.[14] Here, then, τὸν πλησίον denotes "the one who is near or close by, *neighbor, fellow human being*" (BDAG, 2). See the commentary for a proper application of "neighbor."

13:10 ἡ ἀγάπη τῷ πλησίον κακὸν οὐκ ἐργάζεται—As in the previous textual note, the article (here τῷ) turns the adverb πλησίον into a substantive. Although the article is in the dative case, the adverb is indeclinable; it retains its form as a nominative or accusative neuter adjective, πλησίον. The dative article τῷ indicates that the phrase serves as the indirect object of the verb ἐργάζεται, "love does not work evil *to* the neighbor."

πλήρωμα οὖν νόμου ἡ ἀγάπη—The noun πλήρωμα generally means "*sum total, fullness*" (BDAG, 3 b), whereas the related noun πλήρωσις describes an action of "fulfilling up," "filling in," or "completing."[15] The noun here, πλήρωμα, appears significantly also in 11:12 and 11:25, where its meaning is likewise disputed (see the commentary on 11:12, 25). Some propose that the meaning of πλήρωμα (here and in 11:12, 25) should be equated with that of πλήρωσις. For example, BDAG suggests that in 13:10 πλήρωμα describes the "act of fulfilling specifications, *fulfilling, fulfillment* (=πλήρωσις ...)" (BDAG, 4). "Fulfillment" works well (see the next paragraph), but the notion of our active "fulfilling" is problematic; it leads to the dubious suggestion that in 11:12 τὸ πλήρωμα αὐτῶν refers to "*their* (the people of Israel) *fulfilling* (the divine demand)" (BDAG, s.v. πλήρωμα, 4). Delling similarly defines πλήρωμα in 13:10 as the "act of filling."[16] Although Dunn admits that that sense would be "unusual," he defends it by relying on Paul's "liking for -μα words" and, more importantly, the active sense of the perfect verb πεπλήρωκεν, "brought to fulfillment," in 13:8.[17] But this definition and explanation for πλήρωμα here seem overly strained.

[12] H. Schlier, "ἀνακεφαλαιόομαι," *TDNT* 3:682.

[13] Cranfield, *Romans*, 677, n. 3. Metzger, *A Textual Commentary on the Greek New Testament*, does not even discuss the variant.

[14] See Wallace, *Greek Grammar*, 231–32.

[15] The noun πλήρωσις is absent from the NT but appears in Classical Greek (see LSJM) and in the LXX (see Muraoka).

[16] G. Delling, "πλήρωμα," *TDNT* 6:305.

[17] Dunn, *Romans*, 780–81; similarly, Sanday and Headlam, *Romans*, 374; Moo, *Romans*, 817.

The definition of the cognate verb πληρόω that is appropriate for 13:8 is "to bring to a designed end, *fulfill*" (BDAG, 4; see the last textual note on 13:8). Noun forms with the suffix -μα denote the result of a verbal action, so the corresponding meaning of πλήρωμα is " 'fullness,' … when one has achieved the result, 'fulfillment' in this sense."[18] The context here indicates that the noun conveys a divinely intended result; see the commentary.

13:11 καὶ τοῦτο—This introductory phrase "is resumptive or recapitulative, gathering up what has already been said," as in 1 Cor 6:6, 8; Eph 2:8.[19] In order to make the connection with the exhortations to "love" in Rom 13:8–10,[20] a bracketed "do" is inserted (so NASB, NKJV).

τὸν καιρόν—While the noun καιρός in 5:6 referred to a specific time or "opportune moment," here it denotes the "momentous time" ushered in by Christ, that is, the present NT era (as also in 3:26; 8:18; 11:5). Paul then describes this "time" in the rest of 13:11 and into 13:12a, before the first hortatory subjunctive (see the second textual note on 13:12).

ὥρα ἤδη ὑμᾶς ἐξ ὕπνου ἐγερθῆναι—The combination of ὥρα, "hour," with an infinitive "is a familiar construction in Greek to indicate the right time to do something."[21] The construction appears in LXX Gen 29:7; Ruth 2:14; Neh 8:3. Here the infinitive is ἐγερθῆναι, "to be raised"; cf. the imperative ἔγειρε, "rise!" in a similar context in Eph 5:14. For a complete explanation, see the commentary.

νῦν γὰρ ἐγγύτερον—The adjective ἐγγύτερον is the comparative form of ἐγγύς, "near," either in space (Rom 10:8) or time (BDAG, 1 and 2). In light of νῦν, "now," and the surrounding temporal expressions in 13:11–12, the comparative "nearer" clearly has a temporal sense here. It is cognate to ἐγγίζω, "draw near" (see the second textual note on 13:12).

ἐπιστεύσαμεν—Of the twenty-one appearances of πιστεύω, "believe," in Romans,[22] this is the third to the last (later only in 14:2; 15:13). The form is aorist indicative. In this context, it appears that ἐπιστεύσαμεν implies an ingressive sense which stresses "the beginning of an action or the entrance into a state."[23] This would highlight the specific point in time at which people began to believe. While probable, such a translation is also interpretive. "We began to believe" would be expressed conclusively with a construction like ἠρξάμεθα πιστεῦσαι. Thus the translation here simply retains "we believed."[24]

---

[18] Lenski, *Romans*, 800, citing Robertson, *A Grammar of the Greek New Testament*, 151.

[19] Dunn, *Romans*, 785, citing BDF, § 442.9.

[20] Cf. Lenski, *Romans*, 801.

[21] Dunn, *Romans*, 785; similarly, BDAG, s.v. ὥρα, 3; Cranfield, *Romans*, 680–81.

[22] See "The Background and Meaning of 'Faith' Words" in the commentary on 1:16 (Middendorf, *Romans 1–8*, 88–90); and " 'From Faith[fulness] into Faith' (1:17)" (96–98); for the appearances of all cognates, see 107.

[23] Wallace, *Greek Grammar*, 558.

[24] See "A Brief Explanation of This Commentary's Translation Style" (Middendorf, *Romans 1–8*, 51–54).

13:12 ἡ νὺξ προέκοψεν—Paul uses προκόπτω to convey the idea of "progress" or "advance" in Gal 1:14; 2 Tim 2:16; 3:9, 13. But here there is an added "temporal nuance."[25] The verb means "to move forward to a final stage, of time *be advanced, be far gone*" (BDAG, 1). The aorist indicative is difficult to render in English. It refers to the time of "the night" (ἡ νύξ) which has passed up until the present, thus "has advanced far."

ἡ δὲ ἡμέρα ἤγγικεν—The verb ἐγγίζω means "*draw near, come near, approach*" (BDAG, 1). The perfect, as usual, conveys both a past event, "the day has drawn near," with present implications, "and is now at hand" (cf. ἤγγικεν in, e.g., Mk 1:15; Lk 10:9, 11; 21:8, 20).[26] It is cognate to the adjective ἐγγύτερον (see the fourth textual note on 13:11).

ἀποθώμεθα—This is the aorist subjunctive middle of ἀποτίθημι, which here has a hortatory force:[27] "let us take off from ourselves." There is a variant in 𝔓[46], along with other Western texts, which reads ἀποβαλώμεθα, "let us throw off from ourselves." While the latter is adopted by Cranfield,[28] Metzger rejects it since ἀποβάλλω occurs "nowhere else in the Pauline Epistles and its middle voice is entirely absent from the New Testament."[29]

ἐνδυσώμεθα—The verb ἐνδύω, when used in the middle, means "to put any kind of thing on oneself, *clothe oneself in, put on, wear*" (BDAG, 2), as also in 13:14. The aorist middle subjunctive here has a hortatory sense:[30] "*let us* clothe ourselves with." Active forms of ἐνδύω take a double accusative construction: "to put (clothing) on (someone)" (e.g., Mt 27:31). Middle forms, as here and in 13:14, can be considered a direct middle:[31] a first accusative object is unexpressed but is implied to be a reflexive pronoun ("clothe [oneself] with"), and the accusative object that is expressed in the text serves as the second accusative ("clothe [oneself] with something"). Wallace cites Acts 12:21 as a good example of a direct middle; there "Herod clothed himself with royal clothing" (ὁ Ἡρῴδης ἐνδυσάμενος ἐσθῆτα βασιλικήν). Wallace properly observes: "Since the aorist has distinct forms for the middle and passive, this can hardly mean 'Herod was clothed.' "[32] The expressed accusative object here is τὰ ὅπλα (see the next textual note); in 13:14 it is τὸν κύριον Ἰησοῦν Χριστόν. Oepke adds that middle forms of ἐνδύω can at times "have a passive sense," citing Lk 24:49; 1 Cor 15:53, 54[33] (see the commentary on Rom 13:14).

---

[25] Moo, *Romans*, 820, n. 19.

[26] See Wallace, *Greek Grammar*, 573–74; Middendorf, *Romans 1–8*, 52–52.

[27] See Wallace, *Greek Grammar*, 464–65; note the discussion in the commentary on 5:1 (Middendorf, *Romans 1–8*, 390).

[28] Cranfield, *Romans*, 685.

[29] Metzger, *A Textual Commentary on the Greek New Testament*, 529–30.

[30] See Wallace, *Greek Grammar*, 464–65.

[31] See Wallace, *Greek Grammar*, 416–18.

[32] Wallace, *Greek Grammar*, 417.

[33] A. Oepke, "ἐνδύω," *TDNT* 2:320.

τὰ ὅπλα τοῦ φωτός—For the plural noun τὰ ὅπλα, "the instruments," see the third textual note on 6:13. For its accusative case following the verb ἐνδύω, see the previous textual note. The genitive τοῦ φωτός is descriptive.[34]

13:13 εὐσχημόνως—This adverb, "pert[aining] to being proper in behavior, *decently*" (BDAG, 1), occurs elsewhere in Biblical Greek only in 1 Cor 14:40 and 1 Thess 4:12 (the latter also with περιπατέω). The cognate adjective εὐσχήμων is slightly more common (Mk 15:43; Acts 13:50; 17:12; 1 Cor 7:35; 12:24). The adjective and its cognate noun εὐσχημοσύνη also "occur quite frequently in classical Greek. Originally referring to elegance of bearing, outward gracefulness (εὐ + σκῆμα),"[35] they then develop the metaphorical application to "proper conduct" or what is "appropriate."[36]

περιπατήσωμεν—For περιπατέω, "walk," as a manner of living, see the seventh textual note on 6:4; note also 8:4. This is another hortatory subjunctive (like ἀποθώμεθα and ἐνδυσώμεθα in 13:12). The verb here governs *both* the previous part of 13:13 *and* the string of negated nouns to follow.

The following six nouns are given in three pairs. Each pair is negated by one initial μή. The nouns in each pair are joined with καί. The nouns in the first two pairs are dative plural, while those in the third pair are dative singular. The datives indicate manner and answer the question of "how" a person lives.[37]

μὴ κώμοις καὶ μέθαις—The first noun, κῶμος, "originally referred to a festal banquet, but took on a negative meaning, 'excessive feasting,' 'carousing.' "[38] The second noun, μέθη, means "*drunkenness*," and the first noun "may influence μέθαι in the direction of *drinking-bout*" (BDAG, s.v. μέθη). The phrase is translated as "not in excessive eating and drunkenness."

μὴ κοίταις καὶ ἀσελγείαις—For κοίτη as "sexual relations" or "intercourse," see the second textual note on 9:10. The second noun, ἀσέλγεια, conveys a "lack of self-constraint which involves one in conduct that violates all bounds of what is socially acceptable, *self-abandonment*"; it is used especially "of sexual excesses" (BDAG). The phrase is translated as "not in sexual promiscuity and self-indulgence."

μὴ ἔριδι καὶ ζήλῳ—As in 1:29, ἔρις depicts "engagement in rivalry, ... *strife, discord, contention*" (BDAG; see 1 Cor 1:11; 3:3; Gal 5:20; Titus 3:9). For ζῆλος, "zeal," in a positive sense, see the second textual note and the commentary on 10:2. But here it has the negative connotations of "jealousy" or "envy."[39]

13:14 ἐνδύσασθε τὸν κύριον Ἰησοῦν Χριστόν—For the verb ἐνδύω, "put on, clothe," and its construction, see the fourth textual note on 13:12. Here its form is an aorist

---

[34] Wallace, *Greek Grammar*, 79–80.

[35] Cranfield, *Romans*, 687.

[36] Moo, *Romans*, 824.

[37] For the dative of manner, see Wallace, *Greek Grammar*, 161–62.

[38] Moo, *Romans*, 825, n. 45., citing for the use of the negative meaning also Wisdom 14:23; 2 Macc 6:4; Gal 5:21; 1 Pet 4:3.

[39] See Moo, *Romans*, 825, n. 48.

middle imperative second person plural, and it takes "the Lord Jesus Christ" as its accusative object.

καὶ τῆς σαρκὸς πρόνοιαν μὴ ποιεῖσθε—The Greek word order is, literally, "and of the flesh, provision do not make for yourselves." The negated middle imperative μὴ ποιεῖσθε, "do not make for yourselves," takes as its object the accusative noun πρόνοιαν, "provision," which is modified by the genitive τῆς σαρκός, "of the flesh." With the verbally based noun preceding ("provision"), the genitive case has an objective function which conveys providing "for the flesh."[40] Outside of the NT, the noun πρόνοια is used for God's "foresight," "forethought," and "provision."[41] It occurs in the NT only here and in Acts 24:2, both times as a human quality. Its connotation is positive in Acts 24:2, but here the provision is "for the flesh." In this verse making provision "for the flesh" does not simply mean meeting necessary bodily needs, but σάρξ has the more negative sense common in Paul, "the whole of our human nature in its fallenness,"[42] as in Rom 7:5, 18, 25; 8:3–9; see the commentary on 1:3.

εἰς ἐπιθυμίας—For ἐπιθυμία as "a desire for someth[ing] forbidden or simply inordinate, *craving, lust*" (BDAG, 2), see also 1:24; 6:12; 7:7, 8. Here it is used negatively in conjunction with the "flesh" (σάρξ) as also in Gal 5:16, 24; Eph 2:3; 2 Pet 2:10, 18; 1 Jn 2:16. Note the cognate verb ἐπιθυμέω, "to improperly desire, covet," in 13:9 in Paul's citation from the Decalogue.

Commentary
Love and the Law (13:8–10)
Introduction

Paul has just spoken about paying back to everyone "the things that are owed" (τὰς ὀφειλάς, 13:7). He then "cleverly uses"[43] the cognate verb "to owe" (ὀφείλω) as a segue into his next thought: "Owe nothing to anyone except *the* [obligation] to love one another" (13:8). The topic of love engaged in 13:8–10 then forms a frame with the heading in 12:9, "love [is] without hypocrisy" (ἡ ἀγάπη ἀνυπόκριτος). The titular noun of 12:9, "love" (ἀγάπη), appears twice in 13:10 and twice later in the letter (14:15; 15:30). The cognate verb "to love" (ἀγαπάω) occurs twice in 13:8 and again in 13:9, but those are the last of its eight uses in Romans.[44] This indicates that Paul here concludes his description of authentic love, which has been his dominant theme ever since 12:9. While 13:1–7 has been deemed a tangent by some, Calvin cautions against such

---

[40] See Wallace, *Greek Grammar*, 116–18.

[41] For the LXX, see Muraoka; see also Moo, *Romans*, 826, n. 52; BDAG, a.

[42] Cranfield, *Romans*, 689.

[43] Moo, *Romans*, 810, characterizes Paul's use of the idea of "obligation" this way; Cranfield, *Romans*, 673, deems Paul's repetition "in negative form" in 13:8 "the positive injunction" of 13:7 "a neat transition."

[44] For the other instances of "to love" (ἀγαπάω) in Romans, see the fourth textual note on 13:8.

thinking by reminding us that being subject to earthly authorities "constitutes not the least part of love."[45]

Perhaps more noteworthy, 13:8–10 contains the final two appearances of the "Law" (νόμος) in Romans. After seventy-two previous uses, it occurs in 13:8 and 13:10, but never again. As elsewhere in Romans, "Law" (νόμος) does not denote an undefined "principle";[46] neither does it function broadly to encompass "anything properly deserving the name 'law.' "[47] Instead, throughout Romans it consistently refers specifically to the Mosaic Torah (see "Defining the Disputed Term νόμος" in the excursus "Paul and the Law" following this pericope). Typically, Paul here focuses on the demands contained within the Torah. He makes this evident by alternating between "Law" (νόμος) and the noun for "commandment" (ἐντολή), which similarly makes its last appearance in the letter in 13:9. All other uses of "commandment" (ἐντολή) in Romans occur in chapter 7, where Paul uses the noun in six consecutive verses (7:8–13). In both Romans 7 and Romans 13 "commandment" (ἐντολή) indicates that *the specific content of the Law* under consideration is its commands, asserting what one is to do or not do (see the commentary on 7:12, 15–21). *Thus the themes of love and the Law are here brought together.* At first glance, this may sound odd for Paul, but Jesus himself firmly establishes the connection (see below). While the "Law" then drops from view, what Paul says about "love," at least to some degree, also "lays groundwork" for the next section (14:1–15:13; note 14:15).[48]

Love One Another and the Other (13:8)

"Owe nothing to anyone except *the* [obligation] to love one another" (13:8a). The opening clause does not mean that one ought never to borrow anything (e.g., never take out a mortgage or never use a credit card), but that such debts should not be left outstanding (e.g., the monthly payments to repay the loan or credit card should be paid on time when they come due; none of the bills should be neglected to become past due). In other words, Christians should have no *unpaid* obligations, especially the various forms of taxes listed in 13:6–7. Paul just said: "Give back to all people the things that are owed" (τὰς ὀφειλάς, 13:7; again, note the hinge with "owe," ὀφείλετε, in 13:8).[49]

The lone exception (εἰ μή, "except") to this mandate is definite, literally, "the 'to love another' " (τὸ ἀλλήλους ἀγαπᾶν). Paul uses the definite article (τό) substantively to introduce something well-known that also represents *the* best in a given category, the highest command that summarizes the whole Law (see the fourth textual note on 13:8). The notion of debt or obligation stems

---

[45] Calvin, *Romans*, 285; see "Introduction to Romans 13:1–7" before the commentary on 13:1–7.

[46] As Sanday and Headlam, *Romans*, 373, maintain.

[47] As Lenski, *Romans*, 798, maintains.

[48] Moo, *Romans*, 811.

[49] For other effective hinges which serve to pivot Paul's argument, see, e.g., 8:1–4; 9:24; 10:4–5, 16–17; 13:7–8; 14:13; 15:7.

from the imperative verb "owe" (ὀφείλετε) in the first half of the verse. That Paul also regards "to love one another" as a command becomes clear in the very next verse. Jesus himself explicitly identifies it as such when he tells his disciples: "I am giving a renewed commandment [ἐντολή] to you, that you love one another [ἀγαπᾶτε ἀλλήλους] just as I loved you, so that you also love one another [ἀγαπᾶτε ἀλλήλους]" (Jn 13:34). Jesus provides the motivation for such love, "just as I loved you." Paul's ongoing appeal throughout Romans 12–16 similarly comes "through the mercies of God" (12:1). Thus "to love one another" (13:8) poses "not merely an obligation but a responsive obligation, an obligation which arises from what those addressed have received."[50] The present tense of the Greek imperative ὀφείλετε ("owe") and of the infinitive ἀγαπᾶν ("to love") implies an *ongoing and continual* responsibility.[51]

In the first eleven chapters of Romans, all but one (8:28) of the uses of the noun "love" and the verb "to love" express the love of God or Christ for us.[52] Earlier, Paul shows how God's love has been poured into us (5:5); in 13:8 he declares that this love ought then to flow through us to "one another." Murray insists that the "one another" (ἀλλήλους) who are the objects of love "cannot be restricted in this case to believers."[53] But, as in Jesus' statement to his disciples in Jn 13:34 (quoted above), "Paul has fellow believers particularly in view but not in any exclusive way."[54] He clarifies this subtly as he continues.

The "for" (γάρ) midway through 13:8 does *not* state the reason *why* one must love others (i.e., in order to attempt to fulfill the Law). Instead, it offers further explanation[55] that "the one who loves the other has brought [the] Law to fulfillment," that is, to its divinely intended result or outcome (see the fifth textual note on 13:8). At first glance it might appear as though Paul speaks of "the other Law" (τὸν ἕτερον νόμον, 13:8b) since all three Greek words have the same accusative masculine singular ending. Some interpreters suggest that Paul contrasts the Mosaic Law with "another Law" which could be the "new/ renewed commandment" (Jn 13:34) or the "Law of Christ" (Gal 6:2). Gutbrod proposes that "the other Law" acknowledges the twofold command to love God and neighbor (e.g., Mt 22:34–40).[56] Another option is that Paul now identifies the Mosaic Law as "another" in contrast to the civil law of Rome under

---

[50] Dunn, *Romans*, 776.

[51] Wallace, *Greek Grammar*, 520–21, speaks of the iterative present, "used to describe an event that *repeatedly* happens. … It is frequently found in the imperative mood, since an action is urged to be done."

[52] See the fourth textual note on 13:8 and the commentary on 12:9.

[53] Murray, *Romans*, 2:160; similarly, Dunn, *Romans*, 776, who then extends the meaning so that ἀλλήλους "embraces all with whom the Roman Christians would come in contact."

[54] Dunn, *Romans*, 776.

[55] Cranfield, *Romans*, 676.

[56] W. Gutbrod, "νόμος," *TDNT* 4:1071.

consideration earlier in 13:1–7.[57] Wright responds that such interpretations are "very awkward in view of the quotation from the Decalogue that follows immediately; and Paul rarely uses the verb 'love' absolutely, without an object."[58]

The flexibility of Greek word order allows for another, more likely reading in this context. The clause "to love one another" earlier in the verse more plausibly leads to taking "the other" person here as the object of "love": "the one who loves the other" (ὁ ... ἀγαπῶν τὸν ἕτερον). Rather than a simple restatement, Paul uses a term that makes a subtle contrast with the earlier "one another" (ἀλλήλους). The substantival adjective "the other" (τὸν ἕτερον) denotes a person who is different and so could be an unbeliever; the Christian is to love every "other," that is, all others. Thus, when combined with the reference to "anyone" at the beginning of the verse (μηδενί; see the first textual note on 13:8), *these two terms encompass those within (*ἀλλήλους, *"one another") and then also outside (*any "other") *the believing community as proper objects of love.*[59] This reinforces what Paul has stated already in regard to genuine love (12:9); it extends to one another (12:10, 13, 16) and then outward toward "the other" (13:8) as well (12:14, 17–18, 20).

The Law Fulfilled (13:8b)

Paul concludes 13:8 by asserting what may at first seem an impossibility. The one who loves the other has, in fact, "brought [the] Law to fulfillment" (νόμον πεπλήρωκεν). For Käsemann, "the real problem of the text is that there is no polemicizing against" the Law.[60] In fact, this passage refutes the notion that Paul has a purely negative appraisal of the Law. Instead, it shows how "love and law are not polarized but belong together."[61] In so doing, "Paul shows a very positive attitude to the law—the law as something he expects Christians to 'fulfill'; there are no seeds of antinomianism here."[62] This is the same sense in which Jesus himself summarizes the Law (Mt 22:34–40; Mk 12:28–34). Perhaps this language reveals that

> Paul is almost certainly following, consciously or unconsciously, language already established in the Jewish-Christian debate with the Pharisees (cf. Matt 5:17–20), and the use of the perfect (πεπλήρωκεν) probably reflects the same debate (cf. James 2:10–11; 1 John 2:5).[63]

And that debate remains an ongoing one.

---

[57] This is the view of Leenhardt, *Romans*, 337–38, according to Cranfield, *Romans*, 675, including n. 6.

[58] Wright, "Romans," 725.

[59] Similarly, Moo, *Romans*, 813.

[60] Käsemann, *Romans*, 361.

[61] Schreiner, *Romans*, 695.

[62] Dunn, *Romans*, 777.

[63] Dunn, *Romans*, 777.

But what of the perfect tense of the verb (πεπλήρωκεν) in "he has brought [the] Law to fulfillment"?[64] Passages like 6:12–13; 7:14–25; 8:10–13; and 13:12–14 make it virtually impossible to conclude that Paul means that any believer has, by his own actions, "entered into the state of having fulfilled the law"[65] or has accomplished a "complete and final doing"[66] of it. Indeed, there is always and eternally more loving to do (e.g., 1 Cor 13:13). Nygren proposes: "Not by fulfillment of law is the law fulfilled, but by life 'in Christ' and 'in love.' "[67] But that explanation seems to dismiss the Law from the scene entirely, which contradicts Paul's view (as in 13:9–10).

Barrett gets closer to defining the sense of the verb by suggesting: "Love is not the *completion* but the *performance* of the law."[68] Schreiner affirms that "the idea of doing cannot be shucked off the word."[69] But neither can one shuck off what Paul has said earlier about how the Law has been fulfilled. God sent his Son as a sin offering "so that the righteous requirement of the Law might be fulfilled in us" (8:3–4). In 10:4, Paul declares: "Christ is the end of the Law into righteousness for everyone who believes." But now that this salvific "end" has been received by the believer, what comes next in his or her life?

In Romans 5–8 Paul's describes *the life God gives*. In 12:1–15:13 he moves to the life *believers are to live* in response (see the introduction to Romans 12–16). As will be concluded below regarding the cognate noun "fullness, fulfillment" (πλήρωμα) in 13:10, Paul means that the one who actively loves, in fact, does the Law as God intends. The Law can never be properly fulfilled when done out of fear or guilt; also improper are "works of the Law" done to earn righteousness or other merits.[70] Instead, *God desires (as he always has) for his people to follow the Law as a response to his love, and then out of love for others.* Therefore the verb "here probably has the sense of 'properly perform,'

---

[64] In Galatians Paul uses a perfect passive form (πεπλήρωται) of the same verb, "to fulfill," to make a comparable statement in regard to the Law prior to citing Lev 19:18, which he also quotes at the end of Rom 13:9. Gal 5:14 states: "For all the Law *has been brought to fulfillment* in one word [ὁ γὰρ πᾶς νόμος ἐν ἑνὶ λόγῳ πεπλήρωται], in the 'you shall love your neighbor as yourself.' " See the commentary on Rom 13:9–10; for the Galatians passage, see Das, *Galatians*, 551–54.

[65] Moo, *Romans*, 814, n. 25; he attributes this to Sanday and Headlam, but responds (815) "that such complete and consistent loving of others remains an impossibility, even for the Spirit-filled believer." (See Sanday and Headlam, *Romans*, 373.)

[66] Moo, *Romans*, 814; he notes that this "is possible only in the new age of eschatological accomplishment." While this will, in fact, occur in the eternal age of heaven, it is "not yet" possible even for renewed believers due to sin and death, which also continue as present realities within the current age (see Middendorf, *Romans 1–8*, 441–42).

[67] Nygren, *Romans*, 435.

[68] Barrett, *Romans*, 251.

[69] Schreiner, *Romans*, 692.

[70] See 3:19–20; 9:30–10:5; and the excursus "The Background of 'Works of the Law' " following the commentary on 3:9–20.

do what the law really asks for,"[71] with love as the motivation. In fact, it is only "by loving [that] one puts the law into practice"[72] as God desires. This, then, is the "love without hypocrisy" Paul has been describing ever since 12:9; such genuine love does, in fact, fill up the Law's intent in action.

The Law, therefore, does *not* have an exclusively negative function; it is *wrong* to contend, as does Nygren, that "for Paul the law is essentially God's restraint on sin."[73] On the contrary, "when Paul admonishes those who have been born anew to do good works, he holds up before them precisely the Ten Commandments (Rom. 13:9)" (FC SD VI 21). At the same time and particularly in light of the Law's double function in 7:14–25, one must also concede that during this earthly life "such complete and consistent loving of others remains an impossibility, even for the Spirit-filled believer."[74] But this does not dismiss the positive and active call to love, which means, per God's intent, to walk in accord with the Law (see "walk," περιπατέω, in 6:4; 8:4; 13:13). Paul immediately makes this explicit (13:9–10).

Specific Commandments (13:9a)

Paul proceeds by offering these concrete examples: "Indeed, the [commandments] 'you will not commit adultery,' 'you will not murder,' 'you will not steal,' 'you will not [improperly] desire'" (13:9a). The definite article in the neuter singular (τό) is present by itself at the beginning of the verse and functions in the same way as in 13:8. Paul uses "the" (τό) to introduce specific OT commandments which were well-known in Paul's time, something affirmed both within and outside the NT.[75] The specific content Paul cites validates the bracketed insertion of "commandments." His explicit reference afterward to "some other commandment" (τις ἑτέρα ἐντολή, 13:9b) further demonstrates that the word "commandments" represents the assumed category under consideration.

The Order of the Commandments

Interestingly, *Paul cites specific commandments from the Decalogue in only two of his letters, Ephesians and Romans.* In Ephesians, he echoes the Seventh Commandment in Eph 4:28 and quotes the Fourth Commandment in Eph 6:2–3.[76] Rom 2:21–22 references the Sixth and Seventh Commandments in

---

[71] Dunn, *Romans*, 777.

[72] Schreiner, *Romans*, 693.

[73] Nygren, *Romans*, 434.

[74] Moo, *Romans*, 815.

[75] See also the NT citations in the commentary below. Other early Jewish sources which "demonstrate the centrality of the Decalogue in the NT period" include Philo, *On the Decalogue*, 18–19; Josephus, *Antiquities*, 3.89, 93; Mishnah, *Tamid* 5:1 (Moo, *Romans*, 815, n. 33, citing Stuhlmacher, *Romans*, 209).

[76] The Decalogue is given in Exodus 20 and Deuteronomy 5. In the Roman Catholic and Lutheran traditions, the commandments are numbered as follows: (1) no other gods (Ex 20:3; Deut 5:7); (2) misuse of God's name (Ex 20:7; Deut 5:11); (3) the Sabbath (Ex 20:8; Deut 5:12); (4) honoring father and mother (Ex 20:12; Deut 5:16); (5) murder (Ex 20:13; Deut 5:17); (6) adultery

reverse order. The order in Rom 13:9 differs from the Hebrew OT as well; Paul cites, in order, the Sixth, Fifth, Seventh, and Ninth–Tenth Commandments.[77] Interestingly, this order matches James 2:11, which similarly quotes the Sixth Commandment before the Fifth. In Lk 18:20 the order is also the Sixth, Fifth, and Seventh Commandments, followed by the Eighth Commandment and then the Fourth! While these different orderings do not directly affect their meaning, the variations are interesting and once again indicative of the association of the book of Romans most directly with Luke's Gospel.[78] By way of contrast, note that in Mk 10:19 (which is parallel to Lk 18:20 and to Mt 19:18–19, cited below), Jesus cites the Fifth through the Eighth Commandments in the order found in the Hebrew OT. He does the same in Mt 19:18–19, followed by the Fourth Commandment (which is also quoted at the end of Mk 10:19) and a concluding reference to Lev 19:18, a verse Paul uses later in Rom 13:9 as well. Moo offers this plausible explanation for the altered sequence found in Romans:

> This order is the same as that found in MS B of the LXX in Deut. 5:17–18; in the Nash Papyrus (a first- or second-century-B.C. scrap of text with the Ten Commandments); it is reflected in several other Jewish and early Christian sources. … It may be an order popular in Diaspora Judaism.[79]

The Grammatical Form of the Commandments

Paul's reference to the Seventh and Sixth Commandments in Rom 2:21–22 utilizes infinitive verbs in order to reflect indirect discourse. But in 13:9, all four verbs are future indicative second person singular (see the first, second, and sixth textual notes on 13:9). This matches the LXX and the underlying Hebrew verbs of these "commandments." Though imperative verbs are readily available in

---

(Ex 20:14; Deut 5:18); (7) stealing (Ex 20:15; Deut 5:19); (8) false witness (Ex 20:16; Deut 5:20); (9) coveting the neighbor's house (Ex 20:17a; the second clause of Deut 5:21); and (10) coveting the neighbor's wife, servants, and other possessions (Ex 20:17b; Deut 5:21). Thus the order of what we call the Ninth and Tenth Commandments follows their order in Ex 20:17 but differs from their order in Deut 5:21. In the Reformed tradition, the prohibition against images (Ex 20:4; Deut 5:8) is counted as the Second Commandment, and the Third through Tenth Commandments (all coveting is included in the Tenth Commandment) correspond to the Catholic/Lutheran Fourth through Ninth/Tenth Commandments. The Jewish tradition counts Ex 20:2; Deut 5:6 as the First Commandment; Ex 20:3; Deut 5:7 as the Second Commandment; and then the Third through Tenth Commandments are numbered as in the Reformed tradition. The Jewish tradition has much to commend it; see further "Biblically, 'The Ten Words' (13:9b–c)" below.

[77] As noted below, the Fifth and Sixth Commandments are also transposed in LXX Deut 5:17–18 in manuscript B.

[78] The passage nearest to Rom 13:9 that demonstrates the association between Romans and Luke is Rom 13:7, with the terminology of Lk 20:22–25. This seems logical since Paul and the author of Luke-Acts were personally acquainted. The first person plural forms in Acts 16:10–15 verify that they spent some time together in Troas and Macedonia well before the writing of Romans which takes place in the context of Acts 20:2–3. For more details, see E. E. Ellis, "Coworkers, Paul and His," *DPL*, 183, who includes Luke in a list entitled "Long-Term Coworkers."

[79] Moo, *Romans*, 815, n. 31, citing, where the ellipses appear above, Lk 18:20; James 2:11; Philo, *On the Decalogue*, 36; 51; 121–37; 167–71 (cf. Clement of Alexandria, *Stromata*, 6.16).

both Hebrew and Greek, the only commandments with them are the positively stated Third and Fourth Commandments,[80] neither of which is quoted by Paul in Romans.[81] The *general avoidance of imperatives* surely conveys something significant. One should not ignore the reality of the actual grammatical forms in the inspired text (in the Hebrew and as cited by Paul); doing so also becomes theologically problematic.[82] Hummel offers this sound explanation and advice:

> It is of utmost importance to underscore the fact that grammatically the Decalogue is in *indicative*, not imperative form. (The negative is *lo'*, not *'al*.) These are statements of what the believer who has experienced God's grace *will* voluntarily do, not commands of what he *must* do to deserve or earn God's love. They represent perimeters or boundaries of God's kingship, beyond which the believer will not stray, but *within* which he is essentially free to respond joyfully and voluntarily, as illustrated by the rest of the "laws" or "codes" of the Old Testament.[83]

The Content of the Commandments

Why does Paul cite these four? At first glance, it seems curious that Paul does not cite any of the commands which refer directly to God, a point which becomes even more noticeable later in the verse (see below).[84] Indeed, this commentary repeatedly emphasizes how "the whole of Romans is radically God-centered. The probable reason for this omission is that Paul concentrates here on social and horizontal relations within the Christian community"[85] and with people outside the family of faith as well. Ever since 12:1 Paul has been focusing on how believers live out the life they have been given "through the mercies of God." *Within the earthly sphere of human interaction, Paul's*

---

[80] The LXX uses these imperatives: μνήσθητι, "remember" (LXX Ex 20:8); φύλαξαι, "keep" (LXX Deut 5:12); and τίμα, "honor" (LXX Ex 20:12; Deut 5:16). The Hebrew has the imperative כַּבֵּד in Ex 20:12; Deut 5:16, but an infinitive absolute is used in both Ex 20:8 (זָכוֹר) and Deut 5:12 (שָׁמוֹר).

[81] In Romans Paul never refers to the Sabbath. He may allude to the Fourth Commandment with the phrase γονεῦσιν ἀπειθεῖς, "disobedient to parents," in 1:30.

[82] For example, in an "exegetical insight" provided in Mounce, *Basics of Biblical Greek*, 155, Craig Blomberg says this of these Greek future indicatives: "This is not a prediction but a demand!" He then asserts: "God does remain faithful when we commit to his *commands*. And some of them come 'disguised' in the future tense" (156). God's words are not "disguised"; the terms in the inspired original texts express what he means. The larger context of Paul's argument throughout Romans shows that his Gospel is not a call for us to "commit to his commands," but to believe the Good News of righteousness from faith alone.

[83] Hummel, *The Word Becoming Flesh*, 74. He continues by rightly affirming an ongoing "*second* use of the Law" for those who remain "sinner as well as saint" (74–75).

[84] Philo, *On the Decalogue*, 121, had already separated the commandments into two sections relating to divine and human relationships.

[85] Schreiner, *Romans*, 693. For the God-centered focus throughout the letter, see Middendorf, *Romans 1–8*, 21–22, 27, 49–51; in this volume, see "Romans 1–4: The Righteousness of God" in the introduction to Romans 9–16, as well as "God" in "The Three Foci of Romans 9–11" in the introduction to Romans 9–11; see also the commentary on 1:17, 32; 2:11, 16, 29; 3:1–8, 19–20, 29–30; 4:21; 9:5, 11b–12a, 16, 22–24, 29; 10:21; 11:1–2, 33–36; 12:19; 13:1–2; 14:10–12; 15:5, 8, 13; 16:25, 27.

selection of commandments becomes more expected than surprising.[86] His reference to "some other commandment" (τις ἑτέρα ἐντολή, 13:9), immediately following the four cited commandments, further indicates that these four are not regarded as exclusive or even primary. They are *representative* of God's commandments in a general sense which Paul brings together at the end of the verse. Ambrosiaster captures the main point: "Although there may be other laws which Paul has not mentioned, love is the fulfillment of them all"[87] (see 13:8, 10).

The first cited commandment, "you will not commit adultery," was discussed already in 2:22 (see the first textual note and the commentary there). The second, "you will not murder," does not seek to prohibit all killing. It specifically forbids "murder" and not capital punishment, as is evident from the original Hebrew (see the second textual note on 13:9). Indeed, a command against any and all killing would seem especially out of place in light of 13:4, which notes that an earthly authority *as God's servant* "does not bear the sword for no purpose." The translation "kill" would also cause problems within the larger biblical context wherein God would then seem to command humans to violate his own commands (e.g., Numbers 21; Deuteronomy 13; Josh 6:17–19; 7:10–15). The next commandment cited, "you will not steal," was also referenced earlier in Rom 2:21, prior to the commandment against adultery (see the second textual note and the commentary on 2:21).

Finally, Paul quotes: "You will not [improperly] desire" (13:9). The traditional English translation "covet," though not even given as a definition of ἐπιθυμέω by BDAG, serves equally well here. However, in all of the other passages in the letter where the verb or its cognate noun ἐπιθυμία, "desire," appears (1:24; 6:12; 7:7–8; 13:14), "covet" seems inappropriately narrow.[88] Therefore to maintain consistency in translation, the broader notion of "desire" is maintained here.[89] The bracketed "improperly" is inserted here in order to acknowledge that the word group does have positive connotations for Paul outside of Romans (e.g., ἐπιθυμία in Phil 1:23; 1 Thess 2:17; ἐπιθυμέω in 1 Tim 3:1).

The Greek in Rom 13:9, οὐκ ἐπιθυμήσεις, replicates how the LXX begins both Ex 20:17 and Deut 5:21; each of these verses contains both the Ninth and the Tenth Commandments as numbered in the Roman Catholic and Lutheran traditions.[90] The Hebrew uses the same negated verb twice in Ex 20:17, לֹא תַחְמֹד, and this verb also begins Deut 5:21. In Deut 5:21, however, instead of a second לֹא תַחְמֹד, the prohibition against desiring the neighbor's "house" (Ninth

---

[86] As Dunn, *Romans*, 778, says: "The actual choice made was hardly arbitrary."

[87] Ambrosiaster, *Romans* (Bray, *Romans*, ACCS NT 6:331).

[88] See Middendorf, *Romans 1–8*, 531–32.

[89] See "A Brief Explanation of This Commentary's Translation Style" (Middendorf, *Romans 1–8*, 51–54).

[90] See the footnote about how the commandments are numbered in "The Order of the Commandments" above.

Commandment) employs a different, though essentially synonymous, Hebrew verb, וְלֹא תִתְאַוֶּה (Deut 5:21). Earlier, in Romans 7, Paul had used the identical clause as in Rom 13:9, "you will not desire" (οὐκ ἐπιθυμήσεις, Rom 7:7), as an introductory clause to illustrate the general interaction between sin and the Law's command in his own life (Rom 7:7–8; see the textual notes and the commentary there). Together the force of this evidence leads to the conclusion that *the Hebrew OT, the LXX, and Paul all regard the prohibitions not to improperly desire or to covet as the subject of a single command.* Does this leave us with (only) the Nine Commandments?

Biblically, "The Ten Words" (13:9b–c)

Not at all! Paul immediately adds: "And if [there is] some other commandment" (13:9b), which implies that there are others. The remainder of the verse also helps resolve the matter. Paul makes the following collective statement applicable to *both* the specific commandments of the Decalogue he does cite *and* to all others: "It is brought under a heading in this word: 'you will love your neighbor as yourself'" (13:9c). The addition of the plural noun in brackets earlier in the verse, "indeed, the [commandments]" (13:9a), certainly seems appropriate in light of Paul's use of the term "commandment" here (ἐντολή, 13:9b) to describe the content of the Torah under consideration. This was also the case in 7:7–13, where "Law" (νόμος) and "commandment" (ἐντολή) interchanged with one another in the context of what one does or does not do. Now Paul asserts that these various commands can be summed up or brought together under a single heading (ἀνακεφαλαιοῦται, 13:9c). He introduces this summative heading specifically as "in this word" (ἐν τῷ λόγῳ τούτῳ), which is similar to his phrase prior to citing the commandment from Lev 19:18 in Gal 5:14: "For all the Law has been brought to fulfillment in one word [ἐν ἑνὶ λόγῳ]: 'you will love your neighbor as yourself'" (Gal 5:14).[91] In both Rom 13:9 and Gal 5:14 he utilizes "word," the most proper biblical term for the Decalogue, "the Ten Words," and he also resolves the quandary created by uniting both instances of "you will not covet" (traditionally numbered as the Ninth and Tenth Commandments) into a single commandment.

Some may be shocked to hear that the Scriptures themselves *never* use the phrase "the Ten Commandments." Instead, whenever "ten" appears in reference to them, it modifies another noun.[92] After the Decalogue was given in Exodus 20, Moses recalls the event by referring to the tablets inscribed with "the *words* of the covenant" (דִּבְרֵי הַבְּרִית), which he identifies appositionally as "the ten *words*" (עֲשֶׂרֶת הַדְּבָרִים, Ex 34:28). LXX Ex 34:28 renders the latter phrase literally as τοὺς δέκα λόγους, and the Greek *deca logous* is transliterated by the English term "Decalogue." Twice more Moses recalls the writing

---

[91] Das, *Galatians*, 544, affirms that in Gal 5:14 "'one word' refers to one command or, better, to one *statement*"; see also 551–53.

[92] See the third textual note on 13:9.

of "the Ten Words" (עֲשֶׂרֶת הַדְּבָרִים), in Deut 4:13 and then (after the reiteration of the Decalogue in Deuteronomy 5) a third time in Deut 10:4. This title also appears in Philo and Josephus.[93]

The reason Scripture never refers to them as "the Ten Commandments" stems from the fact that the first is not a command in any sense at all. Instead, the First Word given at Sinai reminds God's people of their identification and salvation: "I am Yahweh your God, who brought you out of Egypt, from the house of slaves" (Ex 20:2). Hummel affirms:

> Two later Jewish usages underscore the same general point: (1) continuing the Biblical usage of speaking of ten *words*," not "commandments"; and (2) counting [Ex 20:]2, which plainly is indicative, as "word" #1.[94]

Thus the *biblical name* is "the Ten Words." Jewish tradition maintains this and, more importantly, begins them, as Scripture itself does, with a concise summary of the salvific covenant relationship God established with Israel. *Therein the First Word is Gospel, reminding Israel that Yahweh, their God, has already rescued them.*[95] Within the chronology of salvation history recounted in Exodus and in Deuteronomy, the remaining nine "words" (or "commandments") indicate *a way to live in response to mercies already received*. The use of future indicative verb forms, as discussed above, corroborates the point. This aligns with the sense in which believers are to hear the commands cited in Rom 13:8–10 as well. They come after and "through the mercies of God" (12:1).

"You Will Love Your Neighbor as Yourself" (Lev 19:18 in Rom 13:9c)

Understood and received in this context, the commandments can then be "brought under a heading in this word: 'you will love your neighbor as yourself'" (13:9c). Paul's quotation matches LXX Lev 19:18 exactly. Intriguingly, Lev 19:18 is one of the Torah passages most frequently quoted in the NT.[96] Most significant, of course, are the quotations of it by *Jesus himself*. He cites Lev 19:18 in his discussion with the rich young ruler (Mt 22:37–40; Mk 12:29–33). Lev 19:18, together with Deut 6:4–5, stands as the greatest commandment (Mk 12:29–31), upon which all the Law and the Prophets hang (Mt 22:40). Jesus also cites Lev 19:18 partially in the Sermon on the Mount (Mt 5:43). The expert in the Law of Moses correctly utilizes it in his dialogue with Jesus in Lk 10:25–28 as well.

Elsewhere, James quotes Lev 19:18 in a discussion of how to "complete the royal Law" (νόμον τελεῖτε βασιλικόν, James 2:8). Paul himself uses it in a

---

[93] E.g., Philo, *On the Decalogue*, 32; Philo, *Who Is the Heir?* 168; Josephus, *Antiquities*, 3.138.

[94] Hummel, *The Word Becoming Flesh*, 75.

[95] See also Middendorf, *Romans 1–8*, 200.

[96] Dunn, *Romans*, 779, considers it to be "the passage in all the Pentateuch most frequently cited by NT writers." The "Loci Citati vel Allegati" in NA[27] lists quotations of Lev 19:18 in Mt 5:43; 19:19; 22:39; Mk 12:31, 33; Lk 10:27; Rom 13:9; Gal 5:14; James 2:8 (Rom 12:19 is listed as well in reference to "you will not take vengeance" at the beginning of Lev 19:18).

similarly comprehensive manner in Gal 5:14.[97] The latter two examples demonstrate the influence of Jesus' use of the Leviticus text. It was also used as a summary of the Torah in the Jewish tradition:

> According to b. Šabb. [Babylonian Talmud, Šabbath] 31a, Hillel summed up the law in the negative form of the golden rule: "That which you hate do not do to your fellows; this is the whole law; the rest is commentary; go and learn it." … More striking still, Rabbi Akiba spoke of the same passage (Lev 19:18) as "the greatest general principle in the Torah" (Sipra on Lev 19:18).[98]

Jesus (Mt 22:37–39; Mk 12:29–31) and the expert in the Law (Lk 10:27) use Lev 19:18 *only after* citing the primary command "you will love the Lord your God …" (Deut 6:5).[99] Jesus thereby validates the assessment of the Ten Words as containing "Two Tables," or sections.[100] Yet, as discussed above, Paul cites Lev 19:18 by itself in Rom 13:9 (as it is cited also in Mt 5:43; Gal 5:14; James 2:8) because he is dealing with a believer's relationship with other people. Yet he does speak elsewhere of their love for God (e.g., Rom 8:28).

Who is the intended referent of "your neighbor" (13:9)? "Certainly the original context of Lev 19:18 is thus circumscribed" as referring to a "fellow Israelite."[101] But, as with "one another" and "the other" in Rom 13:8, this *never* ought to be applied in an exclusive sense, i.e., *only* to fellow Israelites. In Luke 10 the expert in the Law, seeking to justify himself, makes this all-too-common assumption in posing the question "And who is my neighbor?" (καὶ τίς ἐστίν μου πλησίον; Lk 10:29). Jesus countermands it forcefully in his answer, the parable of the Good Samaritan (Lk 10:30–37). "According to the parable of the Lord, who bids us show mercy to everyone without distinction, we must think of every person as our neighbor."[102] The application Jesus himself makes from the parable then is "go and do likewise" (Lk 10:37). In other words, *be a neighbor* by doing mercy to any and all who are in need (Lk 10:36–37; cf. Rom 12:8). Cranfield beautifully draws together Jesus' understanding of "neighbor" in a manner which impacts the rest of the NT:

> Fulfilment of the law involves not just loving someone other than oneself, but loving *each* man whom God presents to one as one's neighbour by the

---

[97] "For all the Law has been brought to fulfillment in one word, in the 'you will love your neighbor as yourself'" (ὁ γὰρ πᾶς νόμος ἐν ἑνὶ λόγῳ πεπλήρωται, ἐν τῷ· ἀγαπήσεις τὸν πλησίον σου ὡς σεαυτόν, Gal 5:14); see Das, *Galatians*, 551–54.

[98] Dunn, *Romans*, 778.

[99] In Mk 12:29–31 Jesus quotes the *Shemaʿ* (Deut 6:4) first of all, before the two "love" commands.

[100] The OT speaks of the "two tablets" (e.g., Ex 31:18; 32:15; Deut 4:13; 9:10–17; 1 Ki 8:9) without specifying which commandments were on the first or the second of the tablets. The Lutheran tradition speaks of the "Two Tables" of the Law, with the first consisting of love for God (the First, Second, and Third Commandments) and the second pertaining to love for the neighbor (Fourth through Tenth Commandments); for the numbering, see the footnote on that topic in "The Order of the Commandments" above.

[101] Dunn, *Romans*, 779.

[102] Pelagius, *Romans* (Bray, *Romans*, ACCS NT 6:331).

circumstance of his being someone whom one *is in a position to* affect for good or ill. The "neighbour" in the NT sense is not someone arbitrarily chosen by us: he is given to us by God.[103]

It should also be noted that when Leviticus, Jesus, and Paul say, "Love your neighbor *as yourself* [ὡς σεαυτόν]," they do not mean *"instead of* yourself" in the sense that you should hate or abuse yourself.[104] To be sure, either love or disdain for self can degenerate into self-centered and destructive behaviors to the detriment of self and others. Indeed, "unrighteousness is born when we love ourselves more than others."[105] Paul prohibits this in Phil 2:3–4. "As yourself" should be understood in terms of what Paul says in Ephesians while making an application to the sacrificial love of husband for wife in marriage (Eph 5:25–28): "For no one ever hated his own flesh, but he feeds and nourishes it" (Eph 5:29).[106] A person of sound mind and body naturally cares for himself, even if only to be able to attend to the needs of others. How much more should a believer live in love for his neighbor, since he is to regard himself as God does in and through Christ (e.g., Rom 6:11; 1 Cor 6:19–20; for more examples, see the excursus "Beyond Typology" following the commentary on 12:1–8).

Love and the Law's Fulfillment (13:10)

Love Divinely Defined

Are all the commandments then simply reduced to love?[107] Does the command "you will love your neighbor as yourself" (13:9) somehow replace all of God's other commandments? This conclusion would present just as much of a false alternative as the one exhibited by the Pharisees. In legalistically obeying the commandments, they ended up omitting love, that is, as Jesus charges, the more important matters of justice, mercy, and faithfulness (Mt 23:23; cf. Lk 20:46–47). But *today the mistake more often occurs in the opposite direction, where "love," as defined by our self-absorbed permissive society, takes precedence over all else.* It is misguided to follow our own inclinations of what we deem "love" to be without relying on God's defining guidance on the subject

---

[103] Cranfield, *Romans*, 676.

[104] Luther, *Lectures on Romans*, AE 25:475, asks: "For who is so useless that he hates himself? But no one is such a nothing that he does not love himself and does not love others in the same way." Later he again discusses Lev 19:18 while commenting on Rom 15:2:

Therefore, I believe that with this commandment "as yourself" man is not commanded to love himself but rather is shown the sinful love with which he does in fact love himself, as if to say: "You are completely curved in upon yourself and pointed toward love of yourself, a condition from which you will not be delivered unless you altogether cease loving yourself and, forgetting yourself, love your neighbor." (AE 25:513)

[105] Pelagius, *Romans* (Bray, *Romans*, ACCS NT 6:331).

[106] The connection between Lev 19:18 and Eph 5:29 is made by Murray, *Romans*, 2:163, who also comments: "The love of God is supreme and incomparable. We are never asked to love God as we love ourselves or our neighbour as we love God."

[107] Sanday and Headlam, *Romans*, 373, use language such as "substituted for" and "takes the place of." Räisänen, *Paul and the Law*, 27, describes it as "a radical *reduction*" of the Law to the love command.

of what love actually entails.[108] Augustine's suggestion: "Love, and do as you please"[109] will all too readily lead fallen humanity astray. That is *precisely why Paul has been providing an extensive definition of authentic love ever since 12:9 and why he continues to do so here by citing specific biblical commandments.* God's own Law, therefore, informs the renewed will of the believer about what is "good, well-pleasing, and perfect" in his eyes (12:2; cf. also 7:16, 18, 25). Schreiner strikes a good balance:

> Paul sees love and law as compatible in a wider way. ... The specific commands cited help Christians discern how love expresses itself in specific situations, but the other moral norms of the law also help believers define love. ... There is the danger of separating love from moral norms. If love is cut free from any commandments, it easily dissolves into sentimentality, and virtually any course of action can be defended as "loving."[110]

Finally, *why* "love your neighbor as yourself," and, more to the point, *how* is this done? The Formula of Concord refers to Rom 13:9 and, thereby, Lev 19:18, as well as Rom 13:5–6, as evidence that "good works are necessary"; these passages indicate "what we are bound to do because of God's ordinance, commandment, and will" (FC SD IV 14). By holding up *both* the specific commandments *and* the ongoing obligation to love others, Paul teaches us to hold them together in a healthy tension. Cranfield applies this by utilizing the metaphor of seeing both the forest and the trees:

> While we most certainly need the summary to save us from missing the wood for the trees and from understanding the particular commandments in a rigid, literalistic, unimaginative, pedantic, or loveless way, we are equally in need of the particular commandments, into which the law breaks down the general obligation of love, to save us from resting content with vague, and often hypocritical, sentiments.[111]

Paul wraps up this brief section (13:8–10), as well as the larger discussion of genuine love which he began in 12:9, with these words: "Love does not work evil to the neighbor; therefore love [is the] fulfillment of the Law" (13:10). One should not view the first half of the verse as defining love in simply negative terms of what "not" to do. Certainly, as illustrated by the four commandments Paul cites in Rom 13:9 from the Ten Words, that negative aspect remains an important part of love. However, Paul expresses *the active obligation to love*

---

[108] The matter of homosexual conduct provides a good illustration. See the commentary on 1:26 and the excursus "Homosexual Conduct Is Contrary to Nature (Romans 1:26–27)" following the commentary on 1:18–32. Some in our society today argue that since this conduct is claimed to be "loving" or "an expression of love" and purported to not harm anyone else, it is appropriate and positive behavior, despite the specific proscriptions of Scripture. But our motivations, however well-intentioned, do not make what is contrary to God's design and will appropriate or somehow pleasing to him. Our own definitions and self-determined expressions of love do not override his Law or biblical explanations of what is truly loving.

[109] *Ama, et fac quod uis* (Augustine, *Homilies on 1 John*, 7.8, cited from Bruce, *Romans*, 133–34).

[110] Schreiner, *Romans*, 694.

[111] Cranfield, *Romans*, 679.

in 13:8 and again at the end of 13:9. Unfortunately, the verse division before 13:10 artificially disrupts his thought. Here we simply have the flip side of the Leviticus verse just cited. Therefore,

> a sharp contrast between the positive form of the rule (Matt 7:12) and the neg-ative should *not* be pressed, as though the former was distinctively Christian and the latter characteristically Jewish. ... This two-sided exposition of the love command arises immediately from Lev 19:18 anyway and is reflected elsewhere in Jewish thought.[112]

As implied by the presence of the verb "to work" (ἐργάζεται, 13:10), 13:9c–10a presents another "both/and." Love means *both* beneficial actions (i.e., "good works") directed toward all those whom God deems to be our neighbor *and* a refusal to engage in any conduct or "work" which might be harmful to them.[113]

The Law's Fulfillment

Paul's final statement has prompted much dispute: "Therefore love [is the] fulfillment of the Law" (13:10b). The citation of commandments from the Law, as well as the positive reference to "some other commandment" (13:9), surely proves that Paul does not mean that the commandments of the Law have been replaced, whether by "the Law of love" or "the Law of Christ" (Gal 6:2).[114] Neither does "fulfillment" mean that the command to love expresses "the full content, the sum total" of the Law.[115] Paul uses the same term for "fulfillment" (πλήρωμα) here as in 11:12 and 11:25. One should not too readily contend that he really means πλήρωσις, which would more clearly convey an active "fulfill-ing" (see the second textual note on 13:10). That dimension was expressed in 13:8 by the perfect active verb "has brought to fulfillment" (πεπλήρωκεν; see the fifth textual note and the commentary on 13:8), but that earlier use of the verb does not make it equivalent to the noun here.[116]

Murray suggests that "the apostle has enriched and added to the notion of fulfillment expressed in verse 8 by indicating through the use of the noun in verse 10 that love gives to the law the full measure of its demand."[117] To be sure,

---

[112] Dunn, *Romans*, 780; for example, Tobit 4:15 states: "And what you hate you may not do to anyone" (καὶ ὃ μισεῖς μηδενὶ ποιήσῃς); see also the quote of Hillel cited above in "'You Will Love Your Neighbor as Yourself' (Lev 19:18 in Rom 13:9c)."

[113] To fail in either regard is a sin, either of omission (e.g., James 4:17) or of commission, respec-tively. Pelagius, *Romans* (Bray, *Romans*, ACCS NT 6:332), characterizes sins of omission as follows:

> Even not to do good is wrong. For if one sees that one's neighbor is in danger of starva-tion, does one not kill him if, while one has an abundance, one does not give him food, though one has not used up one's own provisions?

[114] For an excellent interpretation of Gal 6:2, see Das, *Galatians*, 606–12.

[115] As Dodd, *Romans*, 207, maintains.

[116] Moo, *Romans*, 817, improperly suggests that πλήρωμα here expresses the Law's "culmina-tion, its eschatological fulfillment." This would seem to imply that the manner in which the Law is fulfilled has somehow been altered with the coming of Christ.

[117] Murray, *Romans*, 2:164.

this "demand" no longer results in condemnation for those who are no longer under the Law, but now in Christ (6:14; 8:1). Yet the Law continues to assert requirements and to spell out obligations for believers (8:4; 13:8), ones which all believers fall short of fully attaining in this life (7:14–25). Yet Murray's expression "full measure" properly communicates that the noun πλήρωμα in 13:10 means that "one has achieved the result, 'fulfillment' in this sense."[118] Therefore *God's intent in giving the Law's commands reaches its fullness when, and only when, enacted in love.* This statement then offers a most appropriate culmination to Paul's description of genuine love in 12:9–13:10.

Conclusions: Love and the Law

First and foremost, Paul certainly "does not say that man is justified by fulfilling the law through love."[119] That would be a clear contradiction to his statements earlier in Romans (e.g., 3:19–20, 28; cf. Gal 2:16, 21), as well as to the Gospel itself. On the other hand, it is also unwarranted to speak of "the negative quality which always characterizes the law."[120] The Law remains as Paul defines it earlier, "the embodiment of the knowledge and the truth" (2:20). He also characterizes the Law as "holy" and "Spiritual" (7:12, 14) and declares that "the commandment is holy and righteous and good" (7:12). Furthermore, no "negative quality" adheres to the Law in Paul's final statements about it here in 13:8–10 because those in Christ are no longer under the Law's lordship (7:1; also 6:14, 15; 7:4; 8:4).[121] The Formula of Concord affirms: "In this respect Christians are not under the law but under grace because their persons have been freed from the curse and condemnation of the law through faith in Christ" (FC SD VI 23; see also Rom 8:1–4). Therefore, Kruse properly observes that Paul's Gospel "is not antinomian, for it results in the fulfillment of the law. … What the law sought, but was unable to produce, is fulfilled in [Christians] (cf. 8:3–4)."[122] As 8:3 clarifies, however, it is objectively fulfilled *for them* by the sacrificial obedience of God's Son "so that the righteous requirement of the Law might be fulfilled in us" (8:4; cf. 3:24–25).

Kruse then, while partially helpful, introduces a more problematic thought: "It is not a matter of the apostle, having argued that believers have died to the law in 7:1–6, reinstating it again as a regulatory norm for them in 13:8–10."[123] This statement improperly suggests the Law was somehow "uninstated" (contrary to Mt 5:17–19) and that it ceases to exist as "a regulatory norm." Rom

---

[118] Lenski, *Romans*, 800.

[119] Barrett, *Romans*, 251.

[120] As does Nygren, *Romans*, 434. The Law's accusatory function is provoked by human sin, not by any fault in the Law itself.

[121] Moo, *Romans*, 816, defines this lordship as the Law's "binding authority."

[122] Kruse, *Romans*, 502. However, this does not mean a reinstatement of the Law's lordship. Rather, the effect of Paul's Gospel is that believers, by walking in the Spirit, are enabled to love one another so that the Law is actually fulfilled according to its divine intent.

[123] Kruse, *Romans*, 502.

13:8–10 proves that the Law still stands and that it functions precisely as a norm for loving Christian behavior. Therefore Paul is also no antinomian in the usual sense of the term. Moo points out how this short section "serves the larger purpose of the letter—the explanation and defense of the gospel—by guarding" against "the assumption that Paul's gospel leads to a 'do whatever you want' libertinism."[124] Paul has previously and emphatically rebuked any such notion (e.g., 3:8; 6:1–2, 15; 8:12). Yet the defensive tone so prominent in his earlier rebukes is completely absent in 13:8–10.

Instead, Paul's treatment of *the Law in 13:8–10 is a purely positive one.* By reminding us of Paul's extensive treatment of the Law in Romans 7, Kruse provides a vital connection to understanding the manner in which believers properly grasp the role of the Law "through the mercies of God" (12:1).[125] Paul made this key contrast in 7:6: "But now we were released from the Law, after dying [to that] by which we were being confined, so that we might serve as slaves in [the] renewal of the Spirit [ἐν καινότητι πνεύματος] and not in [the] oldness of [the] letter." Those who have died to the reign of sin and the Law in Baptism have also been raised with Christ so that they might "walk in life's renewal" (ἐν καινότητι ζωῆς, 6:4). They are thereby also "transformed by the renewing of the mind [τῇ ἀνακαινώσει τοῦ νοός] so that [they] may test and discern what [is] the good, well-pleasing, and perfect will of God" (12:2). *The knowledge and truth of God's will remain embodied in his Law* (2:20). In the "renewal of the Spirit" (ἐν καινότητι πνεύματος, 7:6) believers now serve as slaves to God (6:19, 22) by loving others in the manner described in God's Law. But they no longer do so in the "oldness of [the] letter" (7:6) which demands, "Do the Law perfectly or face God's wrath!" Neither is the point a matter of striving to fulfill the Law as an end or goal in itself; that results in the exasperation of 7:14–25. Fortunately, Christ is the end of the Law (10:4), and nothing is condemnation for those in him (8:1).

Instead, renewed believers lovingly serve in the Holy Spirit, who "employs the law to instruct the regenerate out of it and to show and indicate to them in the Ten Commandments what the acceptable will of God is (Rom. 12:2)" (FC SD VI 12; see also Rom 13:8, 10). In fact, *the renewed mind joyfully delights to enslave itself to the good which the Law reveals (7:22, 25). In this way, the Law reaches the loving "fullness/fulfillment" that God lovingly intends (13:10).* Now, as Wright states in commenting on 12:1–2:

> Paul's vision of living sacrifice, and mind renewed, generates a picture of Christian behavior in which rules matter but are not the driving force, in which thought and reflection matter but without reducing ethics to purely situational decisions.[126]

---

[124] Moo, *Romans*, 811.

[125] See the quotation of Kruse, *Romans*, 502, at the start of the preceding paragraph.

[126] Wright, "Romans," 705–6.

Schreiner's concluding words on 13:8–10 bring and hold together well the balance between love and the Law:

> It seems to me that many commentators flee from the natural meaning of these verses. Fitzmyer (1993c: 677) says that Paul does not envision keeping the law as an ideal in the Christian life. But the wording of the text suggests otherwise. Love and law are not polarized but belong together. … The moral norms of the law were part of the law of love for Paul. … Nor do we need to pit the Spirit (contra Fee 1994: 603) against keeping the law. … In Paul's theology the Spirit is the means by which the law is observed, and thus keeping the law is not a heavy burden but a joy (Ps. 119).[127]

Of course these positive appraisals of the Law and such joyful interaction with its commands are possible only "because the love of God has been poured out and remains within our hearts through the Holy Spirit, who was given to us" (Rom 5:5). Then one can embrace the divine connection between love and the commandments articulated in 13:8–10 and, more importantly, enacted by Jesus himself, who said: "And just as the Father loved me, I also loved you; remain in my love. If you keep my commandments, you remain in my love, just as I have kept my Father's commandments [τὰς ἐντολάς] and continue to do so and I remain in his love" (Jn 15:9–10). "Therefore, whatever you do, do it for the love of Christ, and let the intention or end of all your actions look to him. Do nothing for the sake of human praise but everything for the love of God,"[128] who *gave you his Law to show you how to love others in his name.*

Once one grasps this understanding of the statutes and commandments in God's Law, the inspired words of the psalmist are properly enjoined (Ps 119:33–35 [LXX 118:33–35]):

33הוֹרֵנִי יְהוָה דֶּרֶךְ חֻקֶּיךָ
וְאֶצְּרֶנָּה עֵקֶב:
34הֲבִינֵנִי וְאֶצְּרָה תוֹרָתֶךָ
וְאֶשְׁמְרֶנָּה בְכָל־לֵב:
35הַדְרִיכֵנִי בִּנְתִיב מִצְוֹתֶיךָ
כִּי־בוֹ חָפָצְתִּי:

33Teach me, O Yahweh, the way of your statutes,
  and I will keep it until the end of time.
34Give me understanding, and I will guard your Torah [LXX: τὸν νόμον σου],
  and I will keep it with all [my] heart.
35Lead me in the path of your commandments [LXX: τῶν ἐντολῶν σου]
  because I delight in it.

---

[127] Schreiner, *Romans*, 694–95; the references are to Fitzmyer, *Romans*, 677, and Gordon D. Fee, *God's Empowering Presence: The Holy Spirit in the Letters of Paul* (Peabody, Mass.: 1994), 603.

[128] Caesarius of Arles, *Sermons*, 137.1 (Bray, *Romans*, ACCS NT 6:332).

The Dawning Day (13:11–14)[129]

Structure and Format

Paul begins 13:11 by drawing his thoughts together: "And [do] this, knowing the momentous time." But what is the referent of the pronoun "this" (τοῦτο)? Paul certainly includes most immediately the obligation to love according to the Law as laid out in 13:8–10.[130] Believers are called to do the Law's commands in love because they understand the fleeting times in which they live. But 13:8–10 clearly frames the discussion of authentic love begun in 12:9. The "this" of 13:11, therefore, reaches all the way back to chapter 12 and includes everything Paul has presented for believers to live out "through the mercies of God" (12:1) ever since. *The parallel bookends, then, are 12:1–8, which opens the discussion, and 13:11–14, which wraps up Romans 12–13 as a whole.*[131]

As Paul concludes this section, "striking is the mixture of first and second person exhortation, the triple mixed metaphor of 12b, and the contrast of three double negatives (v 13) with the single call to 'put on Christ' (v 14)."[132] But amidst these complexities of style, another common Pauline theological pattern emerges. As illustrated most clearly in 6:12–23,[133] Paul begins with *indicative* assertions in 13:11–12a utilizing the universally relevant images of "time," along with "hour," "night," and "day." On that basis, he moves to *exhortation* in 13:12b–14 (see "Pauline Imperatives" in the introduction to Romans 12–16). There he employs the metaphors of darkness and light (13:12b), clothing (13:12b, 14), and walking (13:13) to make appropriate contrasts in regard to Christian living.[134]

Theme: "Not Yet" and "Now"

Dunn titles Rom 13:11–14 "The Imminence of the End as Spur."[135] That certainly applies as Paul here looks ahead to the return of Christ. He depicts the parousia as "the day" (13:12) when we will experience the fullness of "our salvation" (13:11). That impending future event commonly serves as the basis for exhortation throughout the NT.[136] Rom 13:11–14 aligns most closely with Paul's earlier exhortation to the Thessalonians in 1 Thess 5:1–10. Both share the metaphorical contrasts between "day" and "night," as well as "light" and "darkness." They both then use "the day" to speak of the eschatological "not

---

[129] Wright, "Romans," 727, titles the section comparably as "Living by the Rising Sun."

[130] Murray, *Romans*, 2:165.

[131] So Cranfield, *Romans*, 680; Barrett, *Romans*, 252; Moo, *Romans*, 820; contrary to Lenski, *Romans*, 801, who contends that "we need not go back to 12:1, etc., or to 13:1, etc., for 13:8, etc., is ample."

[132] Dunn, *Romans*, 785.

[133] See "Romans 6:12–23: Indicative *and* Imperative" in Middendorf, *Romans 1–8*, 484–85.

[134] Moo, *Romans*, 819.

[135] Dunn, *Romans*, 782.

[136] Cranfield, *Romans*, 680; Moo, *Romans*, 819. See, e.g., Mt 25:31–46; Mk 13:33–37; Phil 4:4–7; 1 Thess 5:1–11, 23; Heb 10:24–25; James 5:7–11; 1 Pet 4:7–11.

yet" return of Christ (Rom 13:12; 1 Thess 5:4; cf. 1 Thess 5:2). But the parousia does not provide the exclusive motivation for godly living in either text.

Paul also speaks repeatedly of the "hour," the "light," and the "day" as already now present (Rom 13:11, 12, 13; 1 Thess 5:5, 8). Thus *his major focus resides in "the present momentous time"* ushered in by the death and resurrection of Jesus (ἐν τῷ νῦν καιρῷ, 3:26).[137] Rather than relying primarily on a future impetus, Paul's exhortations are more strongly based upon the fact that we already now live in the era inaugurated by the light of Christ's first coming. By way of analogy, the initial framing words of 12:1–2, which launch this section of the letter (12:1–15:13), lack any future focus. Augustine properly explains that the time primarily under consideration in 13:11–14 "relates to 2 Corinthians [6:2]: *Behold, now is the acceptable time, now is the day of salvation.* Paul means by this the time of the gospel."[138] Thus the theological framework of the "now" and the "not yet" so prominent in chapters 6–8 permeates 13:11–14 as well.[139] In this way, Paul's entire exhortation to Christian living "flows from the work of Christ already accomplished. But it also looks ahead to the completion of the process."[140]

Knowing the Time—Three Temporal Indicatives (13:11–12a)

"And [do] this, knowing the momentous time" (13:11a). As discussed above, Paul begins by reminding his hearers of the "momentous time" (καιρός) ushered in by Christ: the present NT era (see καιρός also in 3:26; 8:18; 11:5). Before moving on to the first of three hortatory subjunctives (13:12b–13), Paul describes this καιρός. He does so with *three temporal statements* which occupy the rest of 13:11 and extend through 13:12a: "[11]... because already [it is the] hour for you to be raised from sleep. For now our salvation is nearer than when we believed. [12]The night has advanced far and the day has drawn near and is at hand."

The Hour to Be Raised from Sleep (13:11a)

In regard to the first temporal statement, "sleep" in the OT can denote death, even everlasting perdition.[141] Rom 13:11 is the only NT passage that uses the

---

[137] Cranfield, *Romans*, 683, affirms that the early "Church was convinced that the ministry of Jesus had ushered in the last days, the End-time," and indeed it has.

[138] Augustine, *Commentary on Statements in Romans*, 76 (Bray, *Romans*, ACCS NT 6:333).

[139] For a brief overview, see Middendorf, *Romans 1–8*, 441–42; for a complete study, see Pate, *The End of the Age Has Come*.

[140] Moo, *Romans*, 818.

[141] See the noun "sleep" (שֵׁנָה) in Job 14:12; Ps 76:5 (MT 76:6); Jer 51:39, 57; the verb "to sleep" (יָשֵׁן) in Ps 13:3 (MT 13:4); Jer 51:39, 57; and the substantival adjective "sleeping" (יְשֵׁנֵי) in Dan 12:2. A negative and metaphorical meaning of "sleep" is also found in Jewish literature (Dunn, *Romans*, 786, citing 4 Macc 5:11; *Testament of Reuben* 3:1, 7; Philo, *On Dreams*, 1.121; 2.162) and in the Greek philosophical tradition (see "Disparagement of Sleep" in H. Balz, "ὕπνος κτλ.," *TDNT* 8:547–48).

Greek noun ὕπνος, "sleep," in a metaphorical sense.[142] However, its metaphorical meaning may correspond to that of the Greek verb καθεύδω, "to sleep"; the NT does not use any nouns derived from that verb, so the noun ὕπνος, "sleep," may serve as a nominal equivalent.[143] Paul employs καθεύδω, "to sleep," for the spiritual stupor of unbelief, that is, a kind of spiritual darkness and death even while still alive (Eph 5:14; 1 Thess 5:6).[144] In those two other epistles the word's context is similar to that of Rom 13:11. Paul urges the Thessalonian Christians not to sleep as do those (unbelievers) in darkness who will be overtaken by sudden destruction (1 Thess 5:2–9).[145] In Eph 5:14 Paul combines it with ἐγείρω, "arise; (in the passive) be raised" (ἐγείρω occurs also in Rom 13:11), when he implores: "Awake, O sleeper; arise from the dead, and Christ will shine on you." As in Rom 6:1–11, believers have already now died to sin and have been raised to new life through Baptism into Christ. Therefore Christians are not to revert to a life of sin (6:1–2) or "sleep" (13:11), that is, spiritual apathy or moribundity. Unfortunately, however, it aptly characterizes much of twenty-first-century culture as a whole and far too many churches as well. "Enough!" Paul says. "Wake up! Rise up!" More accurately, he uses an idiom and the *passive voice* to assert that it is the right time to *be raised* (ἐγερθῆναι, 13:11) from spiritual slumber *by the God* "who raised Jesus our Lord from the dead" (τὸν ἐγείραντα, 4:24; see ἐγείρω also in 4:25; 6:4, 9; 7:4; 8:11, 34; 10:9).

The sense of "hour" (ὥρα) in 13:11 is disputed. It could simply refer to "ordinary" time[146] and denote "a short period of time."[147] Elsewhere in Scripture, however, this noun (ὥρα) expresses the notion of "God's appointed eschatological hour."[148] Thus we have the same "now" and "not yet" tension addressed above. It is "already [the] hour"[149] since "the momentous time" (τὸν καιρόν) has come in Christ (13:11; cf. 3:26). But that does not dismiss the realities of everyday life. Paul will go on to speak quite specifically of how to live in the hour-by-hour grind of ordinary time in 13:12b–14.

---

[142] The noun ὕπνος, "sleep," may hint at spiritual lethargy in Lk 9:32 and is at least tangentially associated with physical death in the contexts of Jn 11:13; Acts 20:9.

[143] So Moo, *Romans*, 820, n. 18.

[144] The Greek verb καθεύδω, "to sleep," may have other nuances elsewhere in the NT. It is associated with physical death in Mt 9:24 ‖ Mk 5:39 ‖ Lk 8:52, but refers to Christians who have physically died and await the resurrection in 1 Thess 5:10 (as does the verb κοιμάω frequently, e.g., 1 Cor 15:18, 20, 51; 1 Thess 4:13–15). καθεύδω refers to a spiritual torpor that may be equivalent to lapsing into unbelief in Mt 25:5; Mk 13:35–36. Cf. Mt 26:40, 43, 45; Mk 14:37, 40–41; Lk 22:46.

[145] See also the comments about 1 Thess 5:1–10 in "Theme: 'Not Yet' and 'Now' " above in the commentary on 13:11–14.

[146] Cranfield, *Romans*, 680.

[147] Moo, *Romans*, 821, n. 23; he adds: "This is the case in all the other occurrences of the word in Paul" (citing 1 Cor 4:11; 15:30; 2 Cor 7:8; Gal 2:5; 1 Thess 2:17; Philemon 15).

[148] Dunn, *Romans*, 785–86, citing LXX Dan 8:17, 19; 11:35, 40; Jn 4:23; 5:25; 1 Jn 2:18; Rev 3:3, 10.

[149] See Sanday and Headlam, *Romans*, 378.

Salvation Is Nearer (13:11b)

But before that, Paul provides a second description of this momentous time: "For now our salvation is nearer than when we believed" (13:11b). Taking the pronoun (ἡμῶν) in reference to the noun, "our salvation"[150] (ἡμῶν ἡ σωτηρία; so KJV, NKJV; cf. 2 Cor 1:6; Phil 2:12), seems more likely than attaching it to the preceding adverb, "nearer to us"[151] (ἐγγύτερον ἡμῶν; so ESV, NASB, NRSV, RSV). But if Paul intends "nearer to us," he "is not thinking of salvation in a pietistic way as something that happens to *us* in *our* experience, but as a universal eschatological event."[152] While both translations convey appropriate truths, linguistic evidence tips the balance toward the former.[153]

In any case, "Paul regularly uses 'salvation' and its cognates to denote the believer's final deliverance from sin and death" when Christ returns.[154] This is illustrated by 10:9, 10, 13; 11:26 (also 1 Thess 5:8–9). In keeping with all these passages, "our salvation" (or the "salvation" that is nearer to us) means "the general resurrection on the last day, for it is then that we shall enjoy true salvation."[155] This conveys the impending "not yet." Here an eschatological emphasis stands out, yet Paul's strategic placement of "now" (νῦν) at the beginning of the clause in 13:11b enables him to stress the present as well (see also 3:21; 5:9).[156]

The Dawning Day (13:12a)

Paul's third and final description of "the momentous time" (τὸν καιρόν) introduces language implied in being "raised from sleep" (13:11), namely, moving from night to day: "The night has advanced far and the day has drawn near and is at hand" (13:12a). The temporal referent describes the moments of dawn before the actual sunrise when it seems to be, for a brief time, *both* night *and* day. It may be surprising to note that the illustration does not appear widely in Scripture. Dunn cites Ps 139:12; Is 21:11–12; Jn 9:4; 11:10, but based on its infrequency he also suggests that "Paul's usage therefore may be distinctively his own (the closest parallel is again 1 Thess 5:5–8)."[157]

"Night" in Rom 13:12 refers to the present age of darkness, sin, and death, which Paul asserts "has advanced far" (προέκοψεν) and nears its end. At the same time, Paul's verb implies that the "night," while retreating, still remains

---

[150] Dunn, *Romans*, 786; Kruse, *Romans*, 503; Moo, *Romans*, 821, including n. 25.

[151] Cranfield, *Romans*, 681.

[152] Barrett, *Romans*, 253.

[153] According to Moo, *Romans*, 821, n. 25, "when ἐγγύς ['near'] occurs in eschatological statements in the NT, it is never followed by a genitive object." It is, however, followed by a genitive object in Rom 10:8.

[154] Moo, *Romans*, 822.

[155] Theodore of Mopsuestia, *Romans* (Bray, *Romans*, ACCS NT 6:333).

[156] Dunn, *Romans*, 786.

[157] Dunn, *Romans*, 787.

at present. This provides evidence for the "not yet" which paradoxically counters the "now" assertions in 13:11.

In the midst of the darkness, however, *the early light of morning shines forth* by virtue of Jesus' first coming, which announces and inaugurates his kingdom.[158] Theodoret of Cyrus therefore properly concludes that "*day* refers to the time after the Lord's coming."[159] It is, in fact, the promised "Day of the Lord" which Paul insists *has now arrived*.

> Paul uses several variations of this common early Christian reference: "the day of [our] Lord Jesus Christ" (1 Cor. 1:8); "the day of our Lord Jesus" (2 Cor. 1:14); "the day of Jesus Christ" (Phil 1:6); "the day of Christ" (Phil. 1:10; 2:16); "the day of the Lord" (1 Cor. 5:5; 1 Thess. 5:2; 2 Thess. 2:2); "the day of redemption" (Eph. 4:30); "the day of wrath" (Rom. 2:5); "the day when God judges" (Rom. 2:16); … "that day" (2 Thess. 1:10; 2 Tim. 1:12, 18; 4:8); "the day" (Rom. 13:12, 13; 1 Thess. 5:4). These phrases all go back to the OT "day of the Lord," the time of eschatological judgment and salvation (cf., e.g., Isa. 27; Jer. 30:8–9; Joel 2:31 [MT 3:4]; 3:18 [MT 4:18]; Obad. 15–17).[160]

Paul's description, therefore, clearly exhibits his conception of the overlapping of the ages. Within it, he emphasizes that the *age of night*, though far along, *remains a present reality*. Yet the age to come, is, in spatial terms, right at the doorstep and, in that sense, here. Temporally, like the light of the dawning day, it became visible in Jesus, the light of the world (Jn 8:12), and can be experienced already by faith, if not yet by sight (2 Cor 5:7; cf. Jn 1:5).

The End Is "Nearer," but How Near?

Did Paul then conceive that Christ's return was immediately at hand? Barrett asserts that these verses (13:11–12a) mean that "the Age to Come must very soon dawn."[161] Dunn characterizes Paul as evoking a sense of "heightened imminence."[162] Others, however, speculate that Paul used to believe so, but has now changed his mind. Dodd, for example, summarizes what he postulates as Paul's progression:

---

[158] A theme of "(still) night, yet also (dawning) day" may be present in other texts not cited by Dunn (above). The brilliant angelic announcement of Christ's birth was at "night" (Lk 2:8–14), and a star led the Magi to the Christ Child (Mt 2:1–11). The genitive absolute descriptions of the time of Christ's resurrection on Easter morning indicate that it was both "when darkness still is being" (σκοτίας ἔτι οὔσης, Jn 20:1) and "when the sun had risen" (ἀνατείλαντος τοῦ ἡλίου, Mk 16:2). Song 2:17 and Song 4:6 have been interpreted to refer to the manifestation of salvation—already in the OT, and now, after the first advent of Christ, with greater luminosity for the church—for Christ can be seen as the Daystar shining in the present darkness, or as the Light of the world, who is turning the night into day. See Mitchell, *The Song of Songs*, 719–20, 735–38.

[159] Theodoret of Cyrus, *Romans* (Bray, *Romans*, ACCS NT 6:334).

[160] Moo, *Romans*, 821, n. 20.

[161] Barrett, *Romans*, 253; for an overview, see Cranfield, *Romans*, 683–84, who uses the term *Naherwartung* for the view of those who are convinced that Paul embraced a "near expectation."

[162] Dunn, *Romans*, 786.

Paul's earliest extant epistles, those to the Thessalonians, suggest that at that time he thought that the Advent of the Lord might come within a few months: it would certainly come within the lifetime of most present members of the Church. The same thought is present in 1 Corinthians. ... It is all the more striking that in this epistle there is no mention of the imminence of the Advent, apart from these few verses. ... Clearly the urgent sense of the imminence of "the End" was fading in Paul's mind as the years passed. He dwelt more and more on the thought that Christians were already living in the New Age, and the date at which it should be consummated became a matter of indifference.[163]

But Dodd's scenario overlooks the overlapping of ages discussed above. It also reads more into Paul's earlier letters than he actually says (where does Paul say "within a few months"?). In reality, Paul firmly acknowledges and even warns his contemporary hearers that the parousia could happen at any time (thus Phil 4:5; 1 Thess 4:15), yet "nowhere does he predict a near return."[164] In fact, in an early letter, Paul warns the Thessalonians that it still remains somewhat far off (2 Thess 2:1–12).

Paul consistently stresses that *time moves ever forward in a relentless march toward its culmination*; therefore the parousia stands ever nearer. "Every day the end comes closer, and we are already on the threshold of the resurrection."[165] The application for the church today then remains the same as it was for the early church, which "reckoned absolutely seriously with the *possibility* that the Parousia might occur very soon."[166] Alford eloquently articulates this proper response: "On the *certainty of the event*, our faith is grounded: by the *uncertainty of the time*, our hope is stimulated, and our watchfulness aroused."[167]

What to Wear as We Wait *and* Walk—Exhortation (13:12b–13)

Clothing of Light, not Darkness (13:12b)

What are some practical ways that those who have been "raised from sleep" (13:11) can now stand in vigilant watchfulness? Paul provides them in 13:12b–14. First, he shifts subtly from the picture of night and day to darkness and light: "Therefore, let us take off from ourselves the works of the darkness, and let us clothe ourselves with the instruments of the light" (13:12b). Paul's move from night and day in 13:12a to "the works of darkness" and "the instruments of the light" in the latter half of the verse mirrors 1 Thess 5:4–5, where Paul establishes the same correlation. The basic contrast between darkness and light occurs commonly throughout the Scriptures,[168] and the image is readily extended in

---

[163] Dodd, *Romans*, 209.

[164] Moo, *Romans*, 822.

[165] Gennadius of Constantinople, *Romans* (Bray, *Romans*, ACCS NT 6:333).

[166] Cranfield, *Romans*, 684.

[167] Alford, *The Greek Testament*, 2:449, quoted by Moo, *Romans*, 822.

[168] See, e.g., Gen 1:1–8, 14–19; Ex 10:21–23; 14:19–20; 2 Sam 22:29; Is 5:20; 8:22–9:2 (MT 8:22–9:1); 42:6–7; 45:7; 50:10; 60:1–3; Jer 13:16; Joel 2:2; Jn 1:4–9; 3:19; 8:12; Acts 26:18; Rom 2:19; 1 Cor 4:5; 1 Jn 1:5–6.

an eschatological way, "with darkness characterizing the present evil age and light the new age of salvation."[169]

Second, Rom 13:12b introduces yet another image, that of clothing. A debate has ensued over how relevant the metaphor of changing garments was in Paul's day. Can we presume a daily routine in which people took off their night clothes and put on their day clothes?[170] Cranfield argues that "it does not seem to have been normal practice in the first century to have special garments for wearing at night."[171] Nevertheless, Paul uses the verbs for "taking off" and "putting on" together several times (also Eph 4:22–25; Col 3:8–12).[172]

> The contrasting imagery of taking off and putting on clothes is again obvious and would be familiar to Paul's readers in metaphorical usage: putting off vices (a more Greek than Hebrew metaphor—e.g., Demosthenes [*Orations*] 8.46; Plutarch, *Coriolanus* 19.4; *Ep. Arist.* [*Epistle of Aristeas*] 122; in the NT—Eph 4:22, 25; Col 3:8; James 1:21; 1 Pet 2:1); and putting on virtues (more characteristically Hebraic—e.g., Job 29:14; Pss 93:1; 132:9, 16; Prov 31:25; Isa 51:9; 61:10; Wisd Sol [Wisdom of Solomon] 5:18; … in the NT—Eph 6:14; Col 3:12; 1 Thess 5:8; and here particularly Eph 6:11; …).[173]

Therefore, whether or not it was the normal practice for most people to change clothes in the morning and evening, the picture communicates readily and effectively.

The common use of "putting on" and "taking off" "in passages of moral teaching in the NT" suggests to Cranfield that their use may have been "a feature of primitive catechetical material."[174] Barrett counters that idea by arguing that "the metaphor is a very simple one, which might easily have occurred independently to many different minds."[175] That, however, seems too much of stretch. More likely, this illustration provides but one example of numerous expressions which *Paul shares with James, Peter, and others.* It seems very likely then that such expressions, along with those articulated by Jesus of course, *set the standard for what came to be standard forms of Christian instruction.* For example, in the praxis of the early church, the baptismal right came to include the preparatory removal of one's old clothing and subsequent putting on of a new, clean garment.[176] Paul applies the image of donning new clothing to Baptism when he says: "As many of you as were baptized into Christ, you clothed yourselves with

---

[169] Moo, *Romans*, 823, including n. 35, citing Amos 5:18, 20; Is 60:19–20; Mt 4:16; 1 Pet 2:9; Rev 22:5. From extrabiblical literature he cites *1 Enoch* 10:4; 92:4–5; 108:11; *2 Baruch* 18:2; 48:50; and especially Qumran, "where 'the sons of light' were sharply distinguished from 'the sons of darkness' in an eschatological context (e.g., 1QS 1:9; 2:16; 3:13; 1QM 1:1, passim)."

[170] Cf. Moo, *Romans*, 823.

[171] Cranfield, *Romans*, 685.

[172] Moo, *Romans*, 823, n. 32.

[173] Dunn, *Romans*, 787.

[174] Cranfield, *Romans*, 685.

[175] Barrett, *Romans*, 253.

[176] See Winger, *Ephesians*, 514–15, including n. 44; 544–49.

Christ" (Gal 3:27).[177] Before changing into clean clothes one might naturally wash, which reflects another baptismal theme.[178] The imagery of being clothed with new life in Christ fits with Paul's baptismal resurrection motif elsewhere (e.g., Rom 6:1–4; Col 2:12–13) and with the clothing imagery of the bodily resurrection (1 Cor 15:53–54; 2 Cor 5:4; Rev 3:5).[179]

Paul elaborates on the clothing metaphor by identifying six specific "works of the darkness" (Rom 13:12) to be put off in 13:13. However, what does Paul mean by being clothed with the antithetical "instruments of the light" referenced at the end of 13:12? Elsewhere when Paul employs the image of putting on clothes, he sometimes lists explicit components which comprise *military armor* (Eph 6:11, 14–17; 1 Thess 5:8). Therefore, in all likelihood, these connotations reside in Paul's mind here as well. If so, he envisions "dressing for battle, being kitted out with the full panoply of war (weapons and armor; cf. Eph 6:11)."[180] But to insist that the term here (ὅπλα, "instruments") "must mean 'armour,' and will include both defensive and offensive armour"[181] goes beyond the meaning of the text.[182]

Earlier in the letter, after speaking of Baptism (6:1–11) Paul uses the noun "instruments" (ὅπλα) twice in 6:13 for the Christians' bodily members: they are not to be presented as "instruments of unrighteousness" but as "instruments of righteousness." There, as here, Paul does not indicate any specific military connotations. Thus while military armor provides one prominent metaphorical example of "instruments" with which a believer might adorn himself,[183] it seems unlikely that Paul's hearers would have perceived "instruments" as restricted to armaments. Indeed, many other deeds can be "worn" as "instruments of the light" as well. One need only return to 12:1 and read from there up to this point to see many examples. *Altogether, these assemble a sufficient wardrobe which allows Paul to speak generally about God-pleasing living.* In the next verse, he similarly defines it very simply as walking "decently" (13:13).

---

[177] See "Here's What's Imperative (13:14)" below and the excursus "Baptism in Paul" following the commentary on 6:1–11.

[178] For washing as a baptismal theme, see, e.g., Acts 22:16; 1 Cor 6:11; Eph 5:26; Titus 3:5; Heb 10:22; 1 Pet 3:21; Rev 22:14.

[179] Cf. also Jesus' promise of his disciples being "clothed" with Holy Spirit in Lk 24:49 and being "baptized" with the Holy Spirit in Acts 1:5 (cf. Acts 1:8) and the fulfillment of those promises on Pentecost (Acts 2:1–4, 16–18) and through Baptism, beginning on that day (Acts 2:37–41).

[180] Dunn, *Romans*, 788.

[181] Cranfield, *Romans*, 686, citing 2 Cor 6:7; 10:4; Eph 6:11ff.; 1 Thess 5:8.

[182] The equipment in Eph 6:10–17 is generally defensive, and it is Christ who is the victor in the battle; see Winger, *Ephesians*, 728–31.

[183] Chrysostom, *Homilies on Romans*, 24 (Bray, *Romans*, ACCS NT 6:334) states: "The day is calling us to get ready for the battle."

Day-ly Walk (13:13a)

Paul's next exhortation employs another term used significantly earlier in Romans, the verb "to walk" (περιπατέω): Baptism enables us to "walk in life's renewal" (6:4) and "in accord with the Spirit" (8:4). Now he exhorts: "Let us walk decently as in [the] day, not in excessive eating and drunkenness, not in sexual promiscuity and self-indulgence, not in strife and envy" (13:13). Here again, theological issues emerge regarding the phrase Paul places emphatically at the very beginning of the verse in the Greek, "as [ὡς] in the day." Cranfield gives four options for understanding its impact in this verse, which are summarized below:[184]

1. Walking in the literal hours of daytime/daylight
2. Living "as if" it were already the age to come
3. Living in the "day" (the same "day" referenced in 13:12) "as" in some sense being already here
4. Living in the "day" (distinct from the "day" in 13:12) that is the state of regeneration and enlightenment

Cranfield correctly adopts his third option, concluding that in so living, Christians "are to recognize this as the *truth* which the gospel reveals."[185] This coincides with living according to God's perspective, a sense Paul urges most directly in Romans 6. To those who have experienced the realities of death and burial with Christ accomplished by God in Baptism (6:2–8), he declares: "Thus you also count yourselves to be dead to sin on the one hand, but, on the other hand, living to God in Christ Jesus" (6:11).[186] With the expression "as in [the] day" at the beginning of 13:13, "Paul intends more than a metaphor. ... Christians eagerly wait for the coming of the day (in its final phase) even as they experience, by faith, the power and blessings of that day in its present phase."[187]

A strong sense of the "now" and the "not yet" emerges once again. The day of salvation has already now dawned, but it is not yet here in its fullness (13:12); we await Christ's return. Therefore, "let us walk ... *as* in [the] day" (13:13), in the Light.

> In fact the double use of ἡμέρα ["day"] in v 12 and v 13 reflects very much the same Already/Not-yet tension which is evident in ... Jesus' proclamation of the kingdom of God. Indeed, we could almost replace ἡμέρα ["day"] by the word βασιλεία ["kingdom"]: for the Not-yet, cf., e.g., Mark 1:15 (ἤγγικεν ἡ βασιλεία ["the kingdom has drawn near"]) and 1 Cor 6:9–10; Gal 5:21; for the Already, cf., e.g., Matt 12:28; Luke 17:21; Rom 14:17; and Col 4:11.

---

[184] Cranfield, *Romans*, 686.

[185] Cranfield, *Romans*, 687.

[186] See H. W. Heidland, "λογίζομαι," *TDNT* 4:289, who speaks of the verb "count yourselves" (λογίζομαι) as "the saving act of God." See Middendorf, *Romans 1–8*, 49–51, and the commentary on 6:11.

[187] Moo, *Romans*, 824.

The point in all cases is that those who look for the coming of the kingdom/day must live as citizens of that kingdom, in light of that (coming) day.[188]

"Let us walk decently as in [the] day" (13:13a). The first person plural aorist subjunctive περιπατήσωμεν, "let us walk" (see the second textual note on 13:13), again performs the function of exhortation (as did ἀποθώμεθα and ἐνδυσώμεθα in 13:12; see the third and fourth textual notes on that verse). It is "a constative (summarizing) hortative aorist subjunctive. It considers our whole conduct as one grand unit."[189] Thus the aorist, outside of the indicative, should be regarded as emphasizing the act itself, rather than conveying a singular, once-for-all event.[190] This overall depiction of the Christian life coincides with the two previous uses of the verb "to walk" in Romans (περιπατέω, 6:4; 8:4).

> Consequently, we were buried with him through this Baptism into [his] death, so that just as Christ was raised from [the] dead through the glory of the Father, thus also we might walk [περιπατήσωμεν] in life's renewal. (6:4)

> [3b]God, after sending his own Son in [the] likeness of [the] flesh of sin and as a sin offering, condemned sin in the flesh, [4]so that the righteous requirement of the Law might be fulfilled in us, the ones who are not walking [περιπατοῦσιν] in accord with the flesh, but in accord with the Spirit. (8:3b–4)

Public Decency (13:13a)

As noted above, 13:13 utilizes a single adverb to provide a positive depiction of how believers ought to walk: "decently" (εὐσχημόνως). But Paul has already given numerous details about daily Christlike living (12:1–13:10). Here he simply adds that the conduct of Christians should conform to

> what would generally be regarded as decent, proper, presentable in responsible society. … Paul has no hesitation in calling on his readers to observe the conventional respectability of his day; he does not press for a Christian ethic distinctive in every element.[191]

Ambrosiaster recognizes the connotations of public-square behavior as well: "It is true that people do not sin in public, so let us behave as if we were constantly in the public eye."[192] Similarly, Pelagius: "The light of day keeps everyone from doing what he would freely do at night."[193]

Unfortunately, their observations appear less and less applicable to the "progressive" or "advanced" civilization of today. When one looks at the open flaunting of all sorts of wickedness in plain view for all to see, and all too often to celebrate, the present-day culture has declined sharply toward the dismal description of 1:18–32. There Paul concludes: "Such ones who, even though

---

[188] Dunn, *Romans*, 789.

[189] Lenski, *Romans*, 806.

[190] See Wallace, *Greek Grammar*, 556–57; see also Voelz, *Fundamental Greek Grammar*, 56–58.

[191] Dunn, *Romans*, 789.

[192] Ambrosiaster, *Romans* (Bray, *Romans*, ACCS NT 6:335).

[193] Pelagius, *Romans* (Bray, *Romans*, ACCS NT 6:335).

they recognize the righteous decree of God that the ones who practice things like these are deserving of death, not only do them, but also think well of those who practice [them]" (1:32). Perhaps the new aspect today is that these abhorrent and indecent behaviors are practiced more and more openly even by those who claim the name of Christ. As a result, "the works of the darkness" (13:12), examples of which Paul proceeds to list, are all too often on display, in public and even in the church. Certainly, these were all too prominent in Paul's day as well, even if they were more often kept under the cover of darkness. But whenever done, they belong to the night, both literally (often) and spiritually to be sure (see Jn 3:19–20).

Stumbling Deeds of Darkness (13:13b)

The last part of 13:13 provides six specific negative examples of vices to avoid: "Let us walk decently as in [the] day, not in excessive eating and drunkenness, not in sexual promiscuity and self-indulgence, not in strife and envy" (13:13; for specific explanations of each term, see the textual notes). Essentially, *Paul's list consists of three sets of paired nouns* (cf. 8:38–39). While each pairing contains terms related to one another, they do not simply merge into "one composite idea."[194] For example, the first two fit together since festival banquets and parties often involve both gluttonous overeating and intoxication from alcohol. At the same time, those sinful behaviors regularly take place separately as well, with equally detrimental results. Noteworthy also is the fourth term, "self-indulgence" (ἀσέλγεια). It encompasses all sorts of unrestrained living and figures prominently as "an obvious member of any list of vices."[195] The translation "self-indulgence" hints at its typical sexual overtones. Those connotations become explicit when the word is joined with its paired term, "sexual promiscuity" (κοίτη), which is inherently impure and narcissistic.

There may be an *intended sequencing* in the three pairs of nouns. Origen observes how the first term, "excessive eating" (κῶμος), "refers to dishonorable and extravagant banqueting, which inevitably is prone to sexual immorality."[196] Thus the first pair often leads to the second pair. The behaviors in the second then tend to result in the condition of "strife and envy" expressed by the final pair. Chrysostom similarly argues that Paul "does not merely attack [deadly passions] but goes to their source as well. For nothing kindles lust or wrath so much as excessive drinking."[197] All too often, drunkenness then produces "strife and envy" as well.

Due to the dangers involved in these items, some Christians have resolved to avoid them entirely through an ascetic lifestyle and/or complete abstinence. But Chrysostom reminds us that "Paul does not forbid alcohol; he is opposed

---

[194] As Cranfield, *Romans*, 687, maintains.

[195] Dunn, *Romans*, 789, citing Mk 7:22; 2 Cor 12:21; Gal 5:19; 1 Pet 4:3.

[196] Origen, *Romans* (Bray, *Romans*, ACCS NT 6:334).

[197] Chrysostom, *Homilies on Romans*, 24 (Bray, *Romans*, ACCS NT 6:335).

only to its excessive use. Nor does he prohibit sexual intercourse; rather, he is against fornication"[198] (e.g., 1 Corinthians 6 *and* 7). Thus he *does not disallow the proper use of God's gifts* of food and drink and sexual intimacy in marriage. On the contrary, these are blessings to be received with thanksgiving (1 Tim 4:4–5; see also 1 Cor 10:25–26, 31). *Paul exhorts us to avoid the improper abuse of them.*

The final noun, "envy" (ζῆλος), illustrates the same understanding. In 10:2 Paul uses this term in a positive manner to describe Israel's "zeal" for God. But here it occurs in a list of behaviors to be shunned and is paired with "strife" (ἔρις), as also in 1 Cor 3:3; Gal 5:19–21. Stumpff clarifies the distinction: "ζῆλος here denotes the kind of zeal which does not try to help others but rather to harm them, the predominant concern being for personal advancement."[199] Together, this final pair combines to describe "rivalry, party attachment."[200] They may then point ahead to the divisions introduced and addressed almost immediately, only two verses later in Rom 14:1.

Here's What's Imperative (13:14)

Positively, Clothe Yourselves with Christ! (13:14a; cf. Gal 3:27 and Baptism)

Finally, Paul summarizes proper Christian living with a single positive and a single negative expression: "But clothe yourselves with the Lord Jesus Christ, and do not make for yourselves provision for the flesh, for [its] desires" (13:14). Since Paul uses the same verb "clothe oneself with" (the middle of ἐνδύω) as in 13:12, one can relate clothing oneself in "instruments of the light" as roughly equivalent to putting on Christ himself.[201] Origen, of course, says it more eloquently: "The Lord Jesus Christ himself … is said to be the clothing of the saints."[202]

As with 6:1–8,[203] one encounters various views in regard to whether Baptism underlies 13:14 (and 13:12).[204] Dunn contends that the exhortation "clothe yourselves with the Lord Jesus Christ" "is not a description of baptism or of what baptism as such does; Paul is hardly calling for a further baptism (this needs to be borne in mind in cross-referencing to Gal 3:27)."[205] However, what Paul states explicitly about Baptism in Gal 3:27 does utilize remarkably similar terminology: "For as many of you as were baptized into Christ, you clothed yourselves

[198] Chrysostom, *Homilies on Romans*, 24 (Bray, *Romans*, ACCS NT 6:335).

[199] A. Stumpff, "ζῆλος," *TDNT* 2:881–82.

[200] Dunn, *Romans*, 790.

[201] Cranfield, *Romans*, 688.

[202] Origen, *On First Principles*, 2.3.2 (Bray, *Romans*, ACCS NT 6:335).

[203] In regard to Romans 6, see " 'What? Water Baptism?' " (Middendorf, *Romans 1–8*, 467–70).

[204] For 13:12, see "Clothing of Light, not Darkness (13:12b)" above.

[205] Dunn, *Romans*, 791.

with Christ" (ὅσοι γὰρ εἰς Χριστὸν ἐβαπτίσθητε, Χριστὸν ἐνεδύσασθε).²⁰⁶ For example, Paul employs the same verb (ἐνδύω) in the same voice, person, and number in both passages (middle second person plural). On that basis, Käsemann properly refers to this section of Romans (13:8–14) as "typical baptismal exhortation" and "part of the fixed baptismal vocabulary."²⁰⁷ In regard to the latter, Hultgren points out that "the use of the metaphor of putting on clothing … is derived most immediately from baptism."²⁰⁸

Yet the distinction between the *indicative* form of the verb in Gal 3:27 (ἐνεδύσασθε) in direct reference to Baptism (ἐβαπτίσθητε)²⁰⁹ and the *imperative* here (ἐνδύσασθε) should be properly considered. In fact, it conveys the same "now" and "not yet" framework present in so much of Paul's theology and in this section as well (see the introductory discussion to 13:11–14 titled "Theme: 'Not Yet' and 'Now' "). Thus Gal 3:27 depicts a *past tense indicative event* accomplished already in Baptism: "you clothed yourselves with Christ" or, possibly, "you were clothed with Christ" (see the discussion of the voice of the verb ἐνδύω in the fourth textual note on Rom 13:12 and in the commentary below on 13:14). Rom 13:14 communicates the "not yet," the *imperative exhortation* to live out the baptismal life "as in [the] day" (13:13; cf. 6:4).²¹⁰ On the one hand, the imperative in 13:14 should *not* simply be *equated* with the indicative statement of Galatians. But the language is so similar that, in Paul's mind, they are certainly *connected*. In fact, Schreiner recognizes how this "alteration between the indicative (you have been clothed with Christ and laid aside the old person) [and] the imperative (put on Christ and lay aside the old person) is characteristic of Pauline thought."²¹¹

Romans 6 provides further parallels which corroborate the baptismal connection.²¹² Note Paul's use of the verb "to walk" (περιπατέω) in 6:4 and 13:13

---

²⁰⁶ For a discussion of Gal 3:27 in its context, see Das, *Galatians*, 379–83, who cites Rom 13:12–14 among the passages where Paul "uses a clothing metaphor as he stresses a new identity in Christ along with the attendant behavioral traits" (382, citing also 2 Cor 5:2–3; 1 Thess 5:8; Eph 6:11–17; Col 3:10, 12).

²⁰⁷ Käsemann, *Romans*, 362–63.

²⁰⁸ Hultgren, *Romans*, 493, citing Gal 3:27 for corroboration.

²⁰⁹ For a convincing explanation of the baptismal interpretation of Gal 3:27, see Das, *Galatians*, 379–83.

²¹⁰ Das, *Galatians*, 382, captures both elements well, referencing Rom 13:12–14 in his commentary on Gal 3:27 as follows:

> Paul often uses a clothing metaphor as he stresses a new identity in Christ along with the attendant behavioral traits (Rom 13:12–14; 2 Cor 5:2–3; 1 Thess 5:8; Eph 6:11–17; Col. 3:10, 12; cf. Zech 3:3–5). That emphasis on a new identity is the strongest in Gal 3:27 when the believer puts on Christ.

²¹¹ Schreiner, *Romans*, 701; see "Romans 6:12–23: Indicative *and* Imperative" in Middendorf, *Romans 1–8*, 484–85.

²¹² See " 'What? Water Baptism?' " (Middendorf, *Romans 1–8*, 467–70) and the excursus "Baptism in Paul" following the commentary on 6:1–11. For discussion of additional connections to Romans 6, see "Pauline Imperatives" and "Revisiting Romans 6" in the introduction to Romans 12–16.

(see above). The subjunctive form of that verb in 6:4, "we might walk," conveys what has "now" become possible by virtue of being joined to Christ's death and burial in Baptism, as enunciated in 6:2–3. Yet Paul consistently holds off our complete union with Christ's resurrection until our own (the "not yet"; see the commentary on 6:5; see also 6:8; cf. 5:9, 10, 17, 21). The baptismal indicatives in 6:2–10 then serve as the essential basis for the five imperatives in 6:11–19.[213] Similarly, what occurred in Baptism according to Gal 3:27 leads toward the imperative in Rom 13:14. In this verse, "Paul calls upon his readers to recall their baptisms and confirm once more what happened then and has ongoing importance for their lives."[214]

What of the *aorist tense* of the imperative ἐνδύσασθε, "clothe yourselves with"? Lenski argues that the aorist hortatory subjunctive form of the verb in 13:12, ἐνδυσώμεθα, "let us clothe ourselves with," and the imperative in 13:14 denote the same "once for all" action.[215] But that interpretation does not coincide with the nature of Paul's ongoing exhortation. It seems best to take these aorist forms in 13:12 and 13:14 as ones "in which the action is viewed as a whole."[216] The imperative in 13:14 also likely has a constative force wherein "the stress is on the *solemnity* and *urgency* of the action; thus 'I solemnly charge you to act—and do it now!' "[217]

Finally, what of Paul's use of the *middle voice* of ἐνδύω, "clothe *oneself* with," in Rom 13:12, 14 and Gal 3:27?[218] No forms of this verb that *must be* passive appear in Biblical or Classical Greek. However, a number of forms that are identical in the middle and passive can be read as passive.[219] Furthermore, in Lk 24:49 and 1 Cor 15:53–54 the aorist middle forms of ἐνδύω do express a passive meaning.[220] Therefore the aorist middle forms in Rom 13:12, 14 and Gal 3:27 could feasibly be understood as passive in order to match the conclusively passive forms of baptismal verbs in Rom 6:3–6: "we were baptized"

---

[213] Aside from these five, only one other imperative appears in Romans 1–10 (3:4, where God is the subject).

[214] Hultgren, *Romans*, 493.

[215] Lenski, *Romans*, 805, states that in 13:12 "the aorist of the hortative subjunctive means, 'Let us once for all clothe ourselves'; it asks for finality." He later adds: " 'Let us draw (put) on ourselves' in v. 12 and 'draw (put) on yourselves' in v. 14 denote the same action" (808).

[216] Wallace, *Greek Grammar*, 719; similarly, Voelz, *Fundamental Greek Grammar*, 56–58.

[217] Wallace, *Greek Grammar*, 720; this fits better than the suggestion of Cranfield, *Romans*, 688: "To put on the Lord Jesus Christ means here to embrace again and again … Him to whom we already belong."

[218] For an overview of the verb's usage, see A. Oepke, "ἐνδύω," *TDNT* 2:319–20. In regard to Gal 3:27, Das, *Galatians*, 337, 379, translates the aorist middle verb form ἐνεδύσασθε in an apparently active sense, "put on Christ." Later (382) he depicts the verbal action in a passive manner, "to be clothed in Christ," but does not explain further.

[219] Duplicate middle/passive forms occur in all Greek tenses except the future and aorist. In the NT all middle/passive forms of ἐνδύω occur in the perfect; see Mk 1:6; Rev 1:13; 15:6.

[220] A. Oepke, "ἐνδύω," *TDNT* 3:320; BDAG, 2 b, asserts: "The mid[dle] sense is not always clearly right; the pass[ive] is somet[imes] better" (citing Lk 24:49; 1 Cor 15:53–54); see also the fourth textual note on Rom 13:12.

(ἐβαπτίσθημεν, twice in 6:3); "we were buried" (συνετάφημεν, 6:4); and "it was crucified with" (συνεσταυρώθη, 6:6).[221]

But, as 13:12 just demonstrated, the verb ἐνδύω also has a middle use which conveys a reflexive meaning wherein the subject acts upon himself (i.e., "clothe yourselves," 13:14; see the fourth textual note on 13:12).[222] The hortatory nature of 13:12b–14 points toward this interpretation (see the introductory section on 13:11–14 titled "Structure and Format"). Note, for example, the active form of περιπατέω in 13:13 ("let us walk"), which occurs similarly in the baptismal context of 6:4 (cf. also 8:4). Furthermore, the negated parallel verb later in 13:14 (ποιεῖσθε) must have a middle sense ("do not make for yourselves," rather than a passive sense, "do not be made"). Thus it seems most plausible that the middle forms of the verb ἐνδύω in both 13:12b (see above) and here in 13:14 convey a *reflexive action comparable to that of putting clothes on oneself*, though this comes along with the recognition that the precious garment itself was received purely as a divine gift.[223] Moo draws this application:

> As a result of our baptism/conversion, we have been incorporated into Christ, sharing his death, burial, and (proleptically) his resurrection (Rom. 6:3–6). … But our relationship to Christ, the new man, while established at conversion, needs constantly to be reappropriated and lived out, as Eph. 4:24, with its call to "put on the new man," makes clear. Against this background, Paul's exhortation to "put on the Lord Jesus Christ" means that we are consciously to embrace Christ in such a way that his character is manifested in all that we do and say. This exhortation appears to match the exhortation at the beginning of this section, "be transformed by the renewing of the mind" [Rom 12:2], suggesting that it is into the image of Christ that we are being transformed (cf. 8:29).[224]

This is well said, but one needs to remember that the *indicative* of Gal 3:27 (as in Rom 6:2–3) *conveys the reality*—in Baptism "you clothed yourselves with Christ" or, possibly, "you were clothed with Christ" (see above). The *imperative* "clothe yourselves with the Lord Jesus Christ" (Rom 13:14) then *can only follow, and always flows from*, that which was bestowed in Baptism,[225] never the other way around. Theodore of Mopsuestia has the correct order; he reaches

---

[221] Astley, "Morning People," 12, asserts: "Note that the verb ἐνδύσασθε [in Rom 13:14] is in the middle voice and thus can be translated as a passive."

[222] A. Oepke, "ἐνδύω," *TDNT* 3:320, affirms that the verb's middle forms can "be used as an ethical imperative, however, with an active accent" (citing Rom 13:14; cf. also Col 3:12; 1 Thess 5:8).

[223] More multivalent occurrences of ἐνδύω similarly convey the notion of putting on oneself or wearing what God alone has provided (e.g., Eph 4:24; 6:11, 14).

In the wedding parable of Mt 22:1–14, a wedding garment was evidently given to each guest by the king, and that is why the guest without his garment could be reprimanded in Mt 22:11–13. Cf. the garments to be given at the wedding of Samson in Judg 14:12–13.

[224] Moo, *Romans*, 825–26.

[225] See " 'What? Water Baptism?' " (Middendorf, *Romans 1–8*, 467–70) and the excursus "Baptism in Paul" following the commentary on 6:1–11.

back to the picture of 12:4–5 and skillfully weaves that thought into the eschatological tone of 13:11–14:

> Paul wants to say that by the regeneration of baptism we have been conformed to Christ and become members of the one body of the church, of which he is the head, and so we must put him on in the understanding of what we are expecting, in that we hope to share in his resurrection.[226]

Therefore, one need not insist with Käsemann (cited above) that Paul's language reflects the baptismal liturgy already extant in his day. But Paul's language certainly and appropriately *produces* liturgical forms, as did the momentous acknowledgment uttered in 10:9: "Jesus [is] Lord" (see the commentary on 10:9). Yet Paul goes a step further in 13:14 and uses the full salvific name "the Lord Jesus Christ." Volume 1 of this commentary emphasizes how variations of this formula function strategically and climactically throughout Romans 5–8.[227] Its presence here echoes all of those powerful expressions of *the life God gives* in and through our Lord Jesus Christ and powerfully wraps up Paul's explanation of *the life believers live* in response throughout Romans 12–13 (see the introduction to Romans 12–16). In short, what does it look like to clothe yourself with Christ? It means to wear the specifics laid out for you in these two chapters.

Negatively, No Provisions for the Flesh! (13:14b)

Moo claims:

> Paul implies concern that his proclamation of freedom from the law (vv. 8–10) might lead to a licentious lifestyle. Thus he urges his readers, in place of the law, to embrace Christ—who, through the Spirit, provides completely for victory over the flesh.[228]

But that assessment overlooks two significant factors. First, no concept of "in place of the law" exists for Paul since the Law remains firmly in place (see the excursus "Paul and the Law" following this pericope). He makes that abundantly clear in 13:8–10, which explicitly commands believers to fulfill the Law's commandments in love. Second, to contend that the Spirit "provides completely for victory over the flesh" runs counter to the final statement of the chapter. Paul's concluding command is "and do not make for yourselves provision for the flesh, for [its] desires" (13:14).

In this context, the term "flesh" ($\sigma \acute{\alpha} \rho \xi$) does not simply refer to the physical body. Instead, it has the negative nuance that is more common in Paul.[229] Thus Paul "is not speaking of necessities but of excess."[230] Though in no way due to the Sprit's lack of provision, "complete victory" over the sinful flesh remains a

---

[226] Theodore of Mopsuestia, *Romans* (Bray, *Romans*, ACCS NT 6:336).

[227] See Middendorf, *Romans 1–8*, 377–80.

[228] Moo, *Romans*, 826.

[229] See "flesh" ($\sigma \acute{\alpha} \rho \xi$) in 7:5, 18, 25; 8:3–9; see also the commentary on 1:3.

[230] Chrysostom, *Homilies on Romans*, 24 (Bray, *Romans*, ACCS NT 6:336).

"not yet" part of the believer's experience in the present age. The flesh, rather, causes the ongoing struggle portrayed so vividly by Paul himself in 7:14–25.

The present middle imperative in the prohibition "do not make for yourselves" (μὴ ποιεῖσθε, 13:14) expresses *a general precept and reflects an ongoing reality*.[231] Gal 5:17 describes the believer's current situation in this manner: "For the flesh [σάρξ] desires against the Spirit, and the Spirit against the flesh; indeed, these are opposing one another so that you might not do [μὴ ... ποιῆτε] these things which you will."[232] Rom 8:5–13 establishes the same dichotomy (see the commentary on it). Believers still exist in the sinful flesh, which has desires contrary to the Spirit. "The 'flesh' is not something which Paul regards as having been left behind by the believer; the believer is still ἐν σαρκί ['in the flesh'] (7:5) and must continually refuse to walk κατὰ σάρκα ['in accord with the flesh'], an all-too-realistic possibility (8:12–13)."[233] The ongoing battle in 13:14 involves a refusal to provide provisions for the flesh.

Conclusion: The Dawning Day

The reality depicted in 13:11–14 remains the same as in Romans 6–8. The believer's life in Christ, as well as the life a believer lives in Romans 12–13, is not simply an either/or situation, but *an ongoing both/and situation*.[234] Therefore, as 13:14 illustrates, along with the exhortation "clothe yourselves with the Lord Jesus Christ" comes the ongoing necessity to make no provision for fleshly desires. This reinforces the continuing applicability of the struggle delineated in 7:14–25 to believers. While those verses provide Paul's personal perspective on his own battle against the flesh while a Christian, God's resolution resounds triumphantly in 7:25a and, especially, in 8:1–4. "Consequently now, nothing [is] condemnation for the ones in Christ Jesus" (8:1). This is because

> [3b]God, after sending his own Son in [the] likeness of [the] flesh of sin and as a sin offering, condemned sin in the flesh, [4]so that the righteous requirement of the Law might be fulfilled in us, the ones who are not walking in accord with the flesh, but in accord with the Spirit. (8:3b–4)

That's the "now" (νῦν, 8:1; 13:11).

Rom 13:11–14 affirms the "now" but emphasizes the "not yet" in two ways. First, it reminds us that we remain in the "in between" times. Yes, our salvation draws ever nearer but has not yet fully arrived (13:11). The day only now dawns, and the residue of night, with its "works of the darkness," still remains

---

[231] Wallace, *Greek Grammar*, 724, states: "The present prohibition can also have the force of a *general precept*. This kind of prohibition really makes no comment about whether the action is going on or not" (cf. 11:18, 20; 12:2).

[232] For a complete explication, see Das, *Galatians*, 563–66.

[233] Dunn, *Romans*, 791; however, instead of citing 7:5 (which refers to the believers' former life before their Baptism and faith in Christ), better references to Christians as still fleshly would be 7:14, 18, 25.

[234] See Middendorf, *Romans 1–8*, 441–42.

(13:12). Second, in the meantime, which is to say, in this present "momentous time" (13:11; also 3:26), Paul urges believers to live "as in [the] day" already now (13:13). He exhorts us to engage daily in taking off all fleshly deeds of darkness (13:12–13, 14b); he calls us instead to clothe ourselves with Christ, the light of the world (Jn 8:12), and to let "the instruments of light" (13:12) shine forth through the good works Paul lays out for us to wear throughout 12:1–13:14 (cf. Mt 5:16; Phil 2:14–16). As Pelagius puts it: "Christ alone should be seen in us, not the old self, for *one who says he abides in Christ should walk as he walked*."[235]

---

[235] Pelagius, *Romans* (Bray, *Romans*, ACCS NT 6:336), citing 1 Jn 2:6.

Excursus
Paul and the Law

Introduction

In the latter half of the twentieth century, a movement called the "New Perspective on Paul" ignited a reevaluation of first-century Jewish religious thought.[1] The most influential publication is a 1977 work by E. P. Sanders titled *Paul and Palestinian Judaism*.[2] He contends that first-century Judaism should be properly characterized by the phrase "covenantal nomism." He believes it held that *getting in* the covenant was a sheer act of God's mercy and that obedience to the Law was not about earning grace, reward, or merit, but rather was simply the divinely offered means of *staying in*.[3] Sanders followed up with a later monograph titled *Paul, the Law, and the Jewish People*. Since the character and function(s) of God's Law reside at the heart of the discussion, the "New Perspective" has spawned numerous attempts to reassess what Paul teaches about the Law.

For example, Sanders' assertion that there was no legalism among first-century Jews produced a great deal of skepticism about Paul. If "works of the Law" were not required or promoted by Judaism, why does the apostle spend much of Romans and Galatians countering them?[4] Just who and what is Paul opposing? In numerous monographs and articles, various "New Perspective" scholars suggest that Paul engages imaginary straw men, deliberately mischaracterizes his opponents, or merely attacks aspects of the Law which gave exclusive covenant membership badges to Jews.[5] Others conclude that Paul has views on the Law which are hopelessly contradictory, inconsistent, and even nonsensical.[6]

---

[1]   For an introductory overview, see Meeks, "The New Perspective on Paul"; see also Middendorf, *Romans 1–8*, 40–49, especially 42–44. Numerous examples of proponents are cited in the following footnotes.

[2]   Other earlier influential works include Stendahl, "The Apostle Paul and the Introspective Conscience of the West"; Davies, *Paul and Rabbinic Judaism*; Montefiore, *Judaism and St. Paul*.

[3]   Sanders, *Paul and Palestinian Judaism*, 75, 141, 146–47, 420; see the critique with respect to 7:14–25 discussed in Middendorf, *The "I" in the Storm*, 257–64, and summarized in Middendorf, *Romans 1–8*, 596–97.

[4]   For the phrase, see the excursus "The Background of 'Works of the Law'" following the commentary on 3:9–20.

[5]   See, e.g., Loader, "Paul and Judaism: Is He Fighting Strawmen?"; Räisänen, *Paul and the Law*; Gaston, *Paul and the Torah*; and Dunn, "The New Perspective on Paul."

[6]   For example, Räisänen, *Paul and the Law*, 11, charges that "contradictions and tensions have to be *accepted* as *constant* features of Paul's theology of the law." Later he suggests Paul's view of the Law is nonsensical or "*strangely ambiguous*" (201) and uses descriptions such as "oscillates" and "blurred" (199); also Sanders, *Paul, the Law, and the Jewish People*, 77–81; Hübner, *Law in Paul's Thought*, 60–65, 135–36, who argues that Paul's view of the Law is

These challenges have been effectively countered, or at least reevaluated, by Das, Gundry, Kim, Neusner, Pate, Rosner, Schreiner, Sprinkle, Westerholm, and others.[7]

A comprehensive assessment of Paul and the Law in his historical context may not even be possible, given the diversity of Judaism in that era and the paucity of evidence for its mainstream beliefs in primary sources dating to the first century. Such an endeavor certainly would be beyond the bounds of a commentary on Romans. Readers are referred to the resources referenced in the preceding paragraph and its footnotes for detailed studies of the overall topic. This excursus focuses primarily upon what Paul does say about the Law here in Romans, the purview of this work. This limitation of the discussion does not allow for a complete treatment of Paul's perspective, but Romans often stands at or very near the center of the entire debate. Rosner summarizes:

> Most scholars come at Paul and the law above all as interpreters of Romans and/or Galatians. This is understandable, given the fact that the vast majority of Paul's references to *nomos* ["Law"] occur in these two letters. To use a metaphor, if the "law is the main subplot of Romans," in Galatians the law is personified and appears as a main character in the drama.[8]

Contested Matters

In *Paul and the Law*, Rosner identifies seven exegetical problems connected to Romans and Galatians. They are adapted below, with brief responses by the present author given in brackets:

1. Is Christ the end of the Law or its goal or both? [Both, though it depends on how one defines the multifaceted term τέλος, "end"; see the commentary on 10:4.]

2. Since we are no longer under the Law's condemnation, are we also liberated from its jurisdiction? [Believers are no longer "under Law" in regard to its lordship and power to condemn us before God (6:14; see also 7:1–4; 8:1–4; cf. Gal 5:1, 13). Nevertheless, the Law expresses God's eternal will and remains in force as his means to move us to repentance, curb our sin, and guide our Christian living, so believers are obligated to follow it (Rom 2:20; 7:12, 16, 22; 13:8–10). Inevitably, it also exposes how all people still fall short of its commands (e.g., 3:23; 7:14–25).]

3. Do believers fulfill the Law, or does Christ do it for us? [Christ's fulfillment of the Law's requirement for us has given us a righteous relationship with God (see

---

consistent in Romans but that it has developed from and stands in contrast with the earlier view of Galatians.

[7] For example, Das, "Beyond Covenantal Nomism"; Das, *Paul, the Law, and the Covenant*; Gundry, "Grace, Works, and Staying Saved in Paul"; Kim, *Paul and the New Perspective*; Neusner, *Judaic Law from Jesus to the Mishnah: A Systematic Reply to Professor E. P. Sanders*; Pate, *The End of the Age Has Come*, 125–36; Rosner, *Paul and the Law*; Schreiner, *The Law and Its Fulfillment*; Sprinkle, *Paul and Judaism Revisited*; Westerholm, *Israel's Law and the Church's Faith*. For a general overview, see especially Meeks, "The New Perspective on Paul"; Wedderburn, "Paul and the Law"; Westerholm, *Israel's Law and the Church's Faith*, 1–101.

[8] Rosner, *Paul and the Law*, 22; the thought in quotation marks comes from Dunn, *The Theology of Paul the Apostle*, 131.

8:1–4; see also 5:12–21); those who have received God's declaration of righteousness through faith are called to love one another in accordance with the Law. As they do so, the Law reaches its divinely intended purpose or fulfillment in that sense; see the commentary on 13:8–10.]

4. Is "the Law of Christ" (1 Cor 9:21; Gal 6:2; cf. Rom 8:2) a reconfiguration of the Law of Moses or a new set of commandments or something else? [The content of the Law remains the same; see 13:8–10. For "the Law of Christ," see Das on Gal 6:2.[9]]

5. Must we keep God's commandments? [The Decalogue provides a summary of the entire Law (Rom 7:7–12; 13:8–10). Obedience to the Law never was the basis for salvation and righteousness before God (3:21–22, 28; 10:10), but the Law remains a normative obligation for Christian living; see the response to point 2 above.]

6. Are "works of the Law" identity markers given by God to separate Israel from the Gentile nations or works God demanded of Israel by the Law? [Paul critiques them as the latter. For that phrase, see 3:19–20, 28; 4:4–5; see also the excursus "The Background of 'Works of the Law' " following the commentary on 3:9–20.]

7. Is Paul's reservation about doing the Law due to his concern that the Law marks off Jews as different from Gentiles? [No; his primary concern is one's relationship with God; see especially the commentary on 3:19–20. Paul is not at all opposed to doing the Law (see 13:8–10). He only rejects the possibility of attaining righteousness *coram Deo* by doing works demanded by the Law; see 3:28; 9:30–10:5.][10]

These brief responses generally direct readers to specific texts regarding the Law already dealt with at length throughout this commentary. In them Paul himself gives us his own view of the Law. The most critical sections to consider are 2:17–29; 3:19–21, 27–31; 4:13–15; 7:1–8:4; 9:30–10:5; and 13:8–10. It is impossible to encapsulate everything in Romans or to synthesize here Paul's appraisal of the Law throughout his letters and Acts. However, a few summative comments and reflections drawn from Romans are enumerated below.

The Law in Romans

Why place this excursus here? The term "Law" (νόμος) appears seventy-four times in Romans, all between 2:12 and 13:10. After 13:10, however, Paul has no more to say about it in the rest of the letter, or at least he never uses "Law" (νόμος) or "command(ment)" (ἐντολή) again. He has already said much about the Law. His critique of "works of the Law" has shown that *attempting to utilize them in order to attain righteousness before God is both futile and fatal* (2:17–29; 3:9–20; 9:30–10:5). As an earlier excursus demonstrated, early evidence exists that some Jews (e.g., Pharisees) used the Law in attempting to attain righteousness through works.[11] Furthermore, any attempt to *maintain* a righteous status through obedience similarly stands contrary to Paul's teaching,

---

[9] Das, *Galatians*, 606–12.

[10] Adapted from Rosner, *Paul and the Law*, 22.

[11] See the excursus "The Background of 'Works of the Law' " following the commentary on 3:9–20.

most evidently in 7:14–8:4. Paul consistently opposes those who thus misuse the Law to keep score with God and others. But, as we have just seen, the Law properly guides believers in the divinely ordained ways of loving others (13:8–10).

Watson nicely encapsulates the Law's impact in the context to which the letter was originally addressed:

> Gentile Christians must learn to respect and revere the law, acknowledging its roles both in preparing for the gospel and in articulating and reinforcing Christian ethical values, resisting the temptation to distance the God of the gospel from the God of the Jews. Christians of Jewish origin or outlook must learn that the Torah's significance lies in its subsidiary status in relation to a gospel which places them on a level with Gentiles under the judgment and mercy of God.[12]

Defining the Disputed Term "Law" (νόμος)

What does Paul mean by νόμος?[13] While interpreters suggest significant alternatives in certain passages (e.g., 3:27; 7:23; 8:2; 13:8), this commentary agrees with Käsemann's assessment that "law for [Paul] was always related to the Torah of Moses."[14] Ironically, attempts at identifying other referents or definitions of νόμος veer off in different directions for opposite reasons.[15] At times, what Paul says of νόμος is deemed to be too negative to possibly be a characterization of God's Law (e.g., 7:23, 25). At other times, scholars view what he says of νόμος to be too positive to be a reference to the Law (3:27; 8:2). Then, in both cases, scholars typically define νόμος as a nebulous "principle"[16] or a

---

12 Watson, "The Law in Romans," 106.

13 In regard to the presence or absence of the definite article in ὁ νόμος, "*the* Law," Sanday and Headlam, *Romans*, 58, follow Origen, *Romans* (on 3:21), in setting up general categories where νόμος with the article conveys the Law of Moses or a law familiar to the readers and the anarthrous use specifies "law in general." Yet they admit many difficulties and that it is not possible to maintain such a distinction. BDAG, 2 b, defines νόμος "specifically: of the law that Moses received from God" and then adds "without the art[icle] in the same sense" (citing Rom 2:13a, 13b, 17, 23a, 25a; 3:31a, 31b; 5:13, 20; 7:1a; also Gal 2:19b; 5:23). W. Gutbrod, νόμος, *TDNT* 4:1070, states: "It is certainly not true that νόμος is 'a' law as distinct from ὁ νόμος, 'the' Law." So also Grafe, *Die paulinische Lehre vom Gesetz nach den vier Hauptbriefen*, 5–8; and Kümmel, *Römer 7*, 55, who concludes that νόμος with or without the article means the same thing, "namely the Mosaic Law."

14 Käsemann, *Romans*, 282.

15 See, for example, Cranfield, *Romans*, 376; Lenski, *Romans,* 484; Matera, *Romans*, 191; Moo, *Romans*, 475–76; Morris, *Romans*, 300; Murray, *Romans*, 1:267; Newman and Nida, *A Handbook on Paul's Letter to the Romans*, 140; Sanday and Headlam, *Romans*, 190; Theissen, *Psychological Aspects of Pauline Theology*, 233; see especially the commentary on 7:21–23 and 8:2.

16 For example, BDAG contends: "A special semantic problem for modern readers encountering the term ν[όμος] is the general tendency to confine the usage of the term 'law' to codified statutes. Such limitation has led to much fruitless debate in the history of NT interpretation." BDAG then gives this as the first definition: "a procedure or practice that has taken hold, *a custom, rule, principle, norm*" (BDAG, 1), and then places Rom 7:21, 23a, 23b, 23c, 25b; and 8:2b under the first ("gener[al]") subsection of that definition (BDAG, 1 a), with this added explanation on 7:21:

general "constitutional or statutory legal system, *law*" (BDAG, 2 and 2 a).[17] A brief survey of Romans illustrates the complexity of the matter, but also points toward a consistent understanding in reference to the Torah or Law of Moses.

The noun for "commandment" (ἐντολή) appears in six consecutive verses in Romans 7 (7:8–13) and a final time in 13:9. In both chapters, it interchanges freely with "Law" (νόμος). Therefore, in keeping with the basic translation "Law," νόμος *typically has connotations of what one is to do or not do according to God's commandments*. Paul clearly expresses this when he employs the phrase noted above, "works of the Law," in Rom 3:20, 28 (also Gal 2:16 [three times]; 3:2, 5, 10). He further indicates it by the use of various "to do" verbs in relation to the Law (e.g., 7:15–21). "Law" (see BDAG, 2 b) conveys the most common sense of νόμος in Paul, but it is not always optimal.

Paul also uses νόμος in a broader sense. The prior decision of the LXX translators to render the Hebrew תּוֹרָה, *torah,* with the Greek word for "law," νόμος, readily explains how νόμος came to be the Biblical Greek term for the entire Torah, that is, "the Pentateuch, the work of Moses" (BDAG, 3 a).[18] Yet Genesis through Deuteronomy contains much more than "laws," e.g., the account of the good creation, the first Gospel promise (Gen 3:15), the subsequent genealogies of life, the covenants with Noah and the patriarchs, the blessing promises, and the narrative of the exodus deliverance, with Israel's "baptism" and sustenance by spiritual food and drink (cf. 1 Cor 10:1–4). In light of those salvation themes, the translation "Law" may properly be regarded as "most lamentable."[19] However, Paul is more or less stuck with it, and at times he uses νόμος to refer to the entire Torah.

Examples of a Twofold Use of νόμος, "Law" (3:21, 27; 8:2)

Rom 3:21 provides the best illustration of both senses. There the righteousness of God to which the "Law" (νόμος) testifies (3:21b) is said to be revealed "apart from the Law" (χωρὶς νόμου, 3:21a). As indicated by "from works of the Law" (ἐξ ἔργων νόμου) in 3:20 (cf. 3:28; 9:31–32), the phrase "apart from the Law" (3:21a) speaks of *the Law's commands* which one does (via "works") in order to attain righteousness before God. Paul has unequivocally demonstrated

---

According to Bauer, Paul uses the expression νόμος (which dominates this context) in cases in which he prob[ably] would have preferred another word. But it is also prob[able] that Paul purposely engages in wordplay to heighten the predicament of those who do not rely on the gospel of liberation from legal constraint: the Apostle speaks of a *principle* that obligates one to observe a code of conduct that any sensible pers[on] would recognize as sound and valid.

[17] BDAG places these passages under definition 2 a: Rom 3:27; 4:15b; 5:13b; and 7:1–2.

[18] Occasionally, νόμος also then extends to designate "Holy Scripture" generally (BDAG, 3 b), for example, in Rom 3:19; 1 Cor 14:21; see the commentary on Rom 8:2.

[19] Hummel, *The Word Becoming Flesh*, 62; he adds: "If it were possible to turn back the clock and expunge fateful and misleading renditions from our Bibles, this would surely be the place to start."

that whenever the commands of God's νόμος are misused in that manner, they function as "the Law of sin and death" (8:2).[20]

How then can the very same νόμος in the very same verse also testify to the "righteousness of God" through faith (3:21b)? It is because "the term 'Law' is used in Holy Writ also in a wider, or general, sense to designate all the divine revelation."[21] Here it *refers to the Torah as a whole*, that is, the entire Pentateuch (comprised of *Law and Gospel*), and even beyond (see "the Prophets" in 3:21; cf. 1:2; 11:3; see further 8:2a).

A similar twofold use can be established with Paul's use of νόμος in 3:27.[22] There Paul declares: "Then where is the boasting? It was shut out. Through what kind of Law [νόμου]? Of works? No, but through the Law of faith [διὰ νόμου πίστεως]." In light of Paul's attack upon "boasting" before God on the basis of "works of the Law" (ἔργων νόμου, 2:17, 23; 3:20, 28), the Law "of works" in 3:27 surely refers to the commands in the Mosaic Law.[23] As chapter 7 further demonstrates, the Law understood essentially in terms of *works done to fulfill its commands* provides no ground for boasting but, rather, functions as a "Law of sin and death" (8:2; cf. 7:23, 25). What, then, is "through the Law of faith" (διὰ νόμου πίστεως) in 3:27? Paul elaborates four verses later. In 3:31 he concludes that "through the faith" (διὰ τῆς πίστεως) "we confirm the validity of the Law" (νόμον ἱστάνομεν).[24] No better example is available than the one to which Paul immediately turns, the testimony provided by the Torah itself to Abraham as recounted in all of Romans 4. His account exemplifies that when God's sure promise is received through faith, νόμος as the *entirety of the Torah* has been established.[25]

---

[20] See also 3:20; 4:15; 5:20; 7:9–11, 13, 23–24, 25b; 9:31–10:5. In light of 7:12, Dunn, *Romans*, 419, appropriately paraphrases "the Law of sin and death" (8:2) as "the law as manipulated by sin and death." This is especially so when the Law is viewed apart from faith and the Spirit; see 2:17–29; 9:30–10:5.

[21] Pieper, *Christian Dogmatics*, 3:222–23: "The term 'Law' is used in Holy Writ also in a wider, or general, sense to designate all the divine revelation and, moreover, the divine revelation κατ' ἐξοχήν, the Gospel, as in Is. 2:3: 'For out of Zion shall go forth the Law (תּוֹרָה [*Torah*]).'" Pieper adds: "There can be no doubt that תּוֹרָה here signifies the Gospel, for it is the designation of that Word of God by which the Gentiles are gathered into the Christian Church" (223, n. 3).

[22] Hübner, *Law in Paul's Thought*, 144, states: "According to our reflections on 3.27, the genitives occurring there, 'of works' and 'of faith,' define the Law in regard to the perspective of the moment from which it is regarded. From this alone one might suppose that the same is also true of 8.2"; see also Friedrich, "Das Gesetz des Glaubens Röm. 3, 27."

[23] Middendorf, *Romans 1–8*, 294–95; cf. Dunn, *Romans*, 186.

[24] Räisänen, *Paul and the Law*, 51, objects because this interpretation ascribes "a very active role" to νόμος in both 3:27 and 8:2. Dunn, *Romans*, 187, responds that the preposition διά in "through the Law of faith" (διὰ νόμου πίστεως, 3:27) "has the same force as in the nearly synonymous phrase διὰ πίστεως ['through faith'] in 3:22, 25, 31." In addition, note the similarly active role of νόμος as it testifies to the righteousness of God through faith in 3:21–22.

[25] See the treatment of Romans 4 in this commentary; for an overview, see "Romans 4: The Account of Abraham" (Middendorf, *Romans 1–8*, 313–15).

The promise to Abraham now stands fulfilled in Christ, whom Paul later calls the "end of the Law" in all the multivalent senses of the term τέλος (10:4; see the commentary there). Through Christ and by his Spirit, who is the Lord, the veil which obscures the books of Moses (2 Cor 3:14–18) by improperly suggesting that they consist of commandments one must do to attain righteousness (Rom 9:31–32; 10:3) is removed. Then the "Law" (νόμος) directs faith toward its own fulfillment in Christ as "the Law of the Spirit of life" (ὁ … νόμος τοῦ πνεύματος τῆς ζωῆς, 8:2a). Thus verses like 3:21a, 27, 31; and 8:2a illustrate how Paul "can even use the hallowed term 'law' of the new order of things inaugurated by Christ and revealed in the Gospel."[26]

Conclusion

What then is the "Law" (νόμος) for Paul? Rosner, with general agreement, cites the following:

> And Donald Hagner, confronted with the problem of negative and positive comments in Paul's letters about the law, recommends that we "take the negative statements as referring to *nomos* understood *as commandments*, and the positive statements as referring to the broader meaning of *nomos*, namely *as Scripture*."[27]

Rosner then seeks to "sharpen this point" by proposing that "we are more in tune with Paul when we consider 'the law as commandments,' as well as 'the law as prophecy' and 'the law as wisdom.' "[28] One can utilize these three categories to emphasize what aspect of the Torah is under consideration. In this way, the category, "the law as prophecy," readily serves as a "witness to the gospel"[29] since the Torah contains, encompasses, and conveys Gospel promises (e.g., Rom 1:1–2; 4:1–25; 16:25–26). However, Paul uses νόμος more broadly in Rom 3:21a, 27, 31; 8:2a; and 10:4, where it essentially refers to the *whole of the Torah*, not just parts of it. This is evident in Paul's affirmation that "the Law [the entire Torah] and the Prophets" bear witness to the "righteousness of God" (Rom 3:21; cf. also "through his prophets in holy writings" in 1:2).

When Paul uses νόμος by itself without further identification, it should be understood in terms of the Law's required works; it then stands roughly equivalent to "the law as commandments."[30] But Hagner's appraisal that only the *negative* statements about the Law pertain to it as consisting of commandments

---

[26] Franzmann, *Romans*, 163. Schreiner, *Romans*, 400, commenting on 8:2, concludes: "Although it is difficult to be certain, the idea that the Mosaic law is intended in both uses of the word νόμος in verse 2 is more probable."

[27] Rosner, *Paul and the Law*, 29, quoting Donald A. Hagner, "Paul as a Jewish Believer— According to His Letters," in *Jewish Believers in Jesus: The Early Centuries* (ed. Oskar Skarsaune and Reidar Hvalvik; Peabody, Mass.: Hendrickson, 2007), 108 (italics added by Rosner).

[28] Rosner, *Paul and the Law*, 30.

[29] Rosner, *Paul and the Law*, 135.

[30] Rosner, *Paul and the Law*, 30.

(see above) is problematic and simply does not hold. Rom 13:8–10 proves that Paul utilizes both "Law" (νόμος) and "commandment" (ἐντολή) in a positive sense as well (see also 2:20; 7:12); see further "The Nature of the Law" and "Function(s) of the Law" below. Rosner categorizes passages like 13:8–10 in Paul's "reappropriation of the law as wisdom."[31] This properly acknowledges that the Law "was written for us Christians to teach us how to live."[32] While the category may be helpful, it should not imply that being in Christ somehow results in a replacement of the Law which then must be reinstated later. The Law remains constant (e.g., 2:20; 7:12; cf. Mt 5:17–19). Furthermore, his use of "wisdom" terminology does not coincide well with the language of Romans.[33]

The Nature of the Law

Paul does not consider the Law, in and of itself, to be a negative or evil force; neither is its influence limited merely to the old age of sin and death (see 3:31). On the contrary, Paul defines νόμος as "the embodiment of the knowledge and the truth" (2:20). It is intended for life (7:10). Whatever negative effects the Law might have upon sinners (e.g., 5:20–21; 7:7–11, 23; 8:2b), the Law remains "holy" and "Spiritual" (7:12, 14); "the commandment is holy and righteous and good" (7:12). Indeed, the Law stands aligned with love itself and has an ongoing, positive purpose in the believer's life (13:8–10). Therefore Paul "will not permit any shadow to rest on the law."[34] The essence of the Law as a whole, including the Law as commandments, remains unequivocally good.

Function(s) of the Law

Rather than proposing that Paul's appraisal of the Law's commandments is entirely negative, one should understand that these divine commands have various *effects* upon people or *functions* (cf. 7:7–11, 14–25; 13:8–10).[35] Thus instead of seeking to find a uniform evaluation of the Law's impact, one should recognize that the decisive element involves *whether a person stands under Law or under grace in Christ* (6:14). Under the Law, all people stand condemned as Paul charges in 3:9–20. All have sinned and are under its penalty of wrath and death (3:23; 5:12; 6:23). Apart from grace in Christ, the Law only makes this dire situation worse (4:15; 5:20; 7:7–11). Thus any and all who attempt to

---

[31] Rosner, *Paul and the Law*, 159, 163–64. This is the subtitle of his sixth chapter.

[32] Rosner, *Paul and the Law*, 222.

[33] The term "wisdom" occurs only once in the letter and that in reference to God (σοφία, 11:33). Moreover, the passage utilized as Rosner's main title for chapter 6 (159–205), "Written for Our Instruction," comes from 15:4, which speaks more emphatically of God's Gospel promises (see the commentary there). Better support for a link between the Law and wisdom can be found in other texts, e.g., Deut 4:5–6; 1 Chr 22:12; Neh 10:28–29 (MT 10:29–30); Pss 19:7 (MT 19:8); 111:7–10; 119:34; Prov 28:7; Is 2:3.

[34] Nygren, *Romans*, 298, citing Heb 7:18–19; 10:1.

[35] Dunn, *Romans*, 392, speaks of the "two-sidedness" of the Law and of its "two-dimensional character." While that is insightful, see "A Summary and Critique of Dunn's Interpretation of νόμος," in Middendorf, *Romans 1–8*, 572–76.

pursue, attain, or obtain righteousness before God through doing the Law or, fully stated, through doing the "works of the Law" are doomed to fail (3:19–20, 28; 9:30–10:5; 11:7). As discussed in the commentary on 9:30–10:5, righteousness comes totally and completely *from* God *to* all who receive his righteous declaration through faith in Christ. To seek to establish one's relationship with God based on obedience to the Law, that is, on human works done *for* or *toward* God, is both presumptuously vain and pursued in vain.[36]

But Paul repeatedly makes an *either/or* contrast which applies equally to all people, Jew or Gentile, in both the OT and NT eras. *Either* one stands before God under sin, Law, and works (i.e., on the basis of human effort) *or* one stands under God's promise of righteousness, grace, and mercy through faith (e.g., 3:28; 4:4; 9:11b–12a, 16; 9:32; 10:4–5; 11:5–6). For one under grace in Christ Jesus, "nothing [is] condemnation" (8:1). In echoing 1:16–17, 10:4 provides the best shorthand statement: "You see, Christ is the end of the Law into righteousness for everyone who believes" (see the commentary on 10:4).

Yet the Law, as it did for Israel when freed from bondage in Egypt (see Ex 20:1–2; see the commentary on Rom 13:9), then gives divine instruction for those already saved to love God and others in accordance with the eternal divine will. *For those in Christ*, the Law no longer lords itself over people at the behest of sin (5:20–21; 7:1, 5). Instead, the Law serves as divinely intended for his redeemed people. The "holy" and "Spiritual" Law and its "holy and righteous and good" commandment (7:12, 14) reveal the truth and the knowledge of God's good and pleasing and perfect will to those who endeavor to serve him and others in love (2:20; 12:2; 13:8–10). In this way, the Law fulfills its divinely intended purpose (13:8, 10).

Three Uses or Functions of the Law

Disputes regarding Paul's view of the Law stem largely from the multiple functions which he himself asserts that the Law performs, functions which are not exclusive of one another. The Lutheran Confessions helpfully present three categories within which the Law as commandment functions in relationship with humanity:

> The law of God serves (1) not only to maintain external discipline and decency against dissolute and disobedient people, (2) and to bring people to a knowledge of their sin through the law, (3) but those who have been born anew through the Holy Spirit, who have been converted to the Lord and from whom the veil of Moses has been taken away, learn from the law to live and walk in the law. (FC SD VI 1)

---

[36] Paul contends that every person, even one who lacks the Law revealed in Scripture, comes under the purview of the Law, insofar as "the work of the Law" is written on the human heart and conscience; see the commentary on 2:12–16 (cf. 13:1).

Specific examples in Romans of each of these three functions of the Law can be illustrated by reading the commentary on these passages from Romans: (1) 1:18–32; 2:12–16; 13:1–7; (2) 2:17–27; 3:9–20; 7:7–11; and (3) 12:1–13:10.

As noted above, *the Law can perform more than one function at a time*. It may operate in all three of the Confessional categories, as, for example, in 13:1–7. There Paul instructs "every person" (13:1), believer and nonbeliever alike, how to act in relation to earthly authorities (see also 2:12–16). This instruction serves to promote, or at least maintain, general order in society (function 1), but would also convict those who fail to interact with proper respect, honor, and revenue (function 2). In context, however, 13:1–7 serves *primarily* as a guide for believers to act in genuine love in that sphere of life (function 3). Furthermore, the contested and paradoxical depiction in 7:14–25 stems from the Law's command fulfilling *both functions 2 and 3 simultaneously in Paul's Christian life*. It, therefore, has the double function or effect discussed in the commentary on those verses and the excursus which follows it.[37]

To be sure, these various—and at times simultaneous—functions do, at first glance, seem to portray a contradictory attitude toward the Law on Paul's part. Is it good or bad? Is it holy or aligned with sin? However, Paul is aware that improper conclusions could be drawn from some of his assertions about the Law's command, and he actively and carefully opposes them (e.g., 6:15; 7:7, 12, 13, 16). Yes, in an unbeliever, sin's usurpation even of the Law's spiritual command enables sin to enhance its own rule of deception and death (e.g., 5:20; 7:7–11; 8:2b). Even for those no longer under the Law's condemnation, sin can use the Law in a manner which results in ongoing negative and frustrating effects (7:14–25). But this does not change the good character and divine quality of the Law (2:20; 7:12).

The Double Effect in Romans 7:14–25

Paul exhibits the resulting complexities[38] of the Law's roles within the Christian life most transparently in 7:14–8:4. Yet these fit squarely within Paul's theology, specifically the eschatology of the "now" and the "not yet."[39] The believer "now" no longer lives under the dominion and condemnation of the Law, but belongs, instead, to the age to come through the mercies of God. Therein, the believer delightfully agrees with and rejoices in obeying the commands of God's Law (7:16, 22, 25a; cf. 13:8–10). Yet at the present time believers still retain their sinful nature and also live in the fallen "not yet" world into which sin entered and spread to all people (5:12). As a result Paul the believer continues to admit: "I am fleshly, having been sold and still under sin. … Sin … is dwelling in me," that is, "in my flesh" (7:14, 17, 18). The

---

[37] See the commentary on 7:14–25 and the excursus "Who Is the 'I' in Romans 7:14–25? Christian or Non-Christian?" following that pericope.

[38] See Rosner, *Paul and the Law*, 19.

[39] See Middendorf, *Romans 1–8*, 441–42, and the commentary on 7:14–25 and 8:1–4.

Formula of Concord identifies how both functions 2 and 3 enumerated and explained above remain in play:

> Thus, when Paul admonishes those who have been born anew to do good works, he holds up before them precisely the Ten Commandments (Rom. 13:9), and he himself learns from the law that his works are still imperfect and impure (Rom. 7:18, 19). (FC SD VI 21)

The frustration expressed by Paul in 7:14–25 results. As a believer, he uses the first person singular "I" to give *his own perspective* regarding himself, the Law, and sin in 7:14–25. That section precludes his (and our) ability to vanquish sin or fulfill the Law completely in this earthly existence and, instead, beckons us to turn to God and trust in his rescue from "this body of death," which will come "through Jesus Christ our Lord" (7:24–25).

After all, what really counts is *God's perspective*, and Paul gives us just that throughout Romans.[40] God's declaration regarding our present and future reality stands: "Nothing [is] condemnation for the ones in Christ Jesus" (8:1). This change in perspective explains why Paul moves away from his first person singular language in chapter 7 ("I," "me," "my") to the plurals in 8:1–4 ("the ones," "us") to speak authoritatively of God's view, rather than his own, and to describe the decisive change in relationship with God by virtue of God "sending his own Son" (8:3). Therefore, even in the midst of the ongoing now/ not yet reality, all who know how God regards them in Christ can join Paul in declaring *all* of 7:25: "But thanks [be] to God through Jesus Christ our Lord! Consequently then, on the one hand, I myself am a slave to the Law of God with my mind. But, on the other hand, with my flesh [I am a slave] to the Law of sin."

Thus, for fallen humanity, it is proper to assert that *the Law* always accuses (*lex semper accusat*, Ap IV 128, 295).[41] Indeed, to some degree, any standard that has been set up reveals if one measures up or not, and to what degree; when one falls short, as is the case for all people under God's Law (3:23), that Law properly exposes one's shortcomings (3:19–20; 7:7–11, 14–25). To be sure, the Law may still function to accuse those in Christ for continuing to do the "don'ts" and failing to do the "dos" (7:14–25), and it is properly used in that way for church discipline (13:9–13) and civil order (13:1–7). But it will not, on the Last Day, condemn those upon whom God has bestowed the gift of his own righteousness. Surely *God* does *not* use his Law even now to pronounce eternal condemnation upon the baptized who have already repented and trust in Christ's forgiveness. Indeed, that punishment has been meted out fully already, "once for all" on the cross (ἐφάπαξ, 6:10; cf. 8:3). As Jesus declared: "It has been finished and stands completed" (τετέλεσται, Jn 19:30). Furthermore,

---

[40] See Middendorf, *Romans 1–8*, 49, as well as the author's preface in this volume.

[41] See also Article VI in the Formula of Concord, "The Third Use of the Law."

"in Romans 8 Christ fulfils the law *for us*"[42] (8:1–4). How then does a believer receive the Law?

Living Out the Good Law in Love

Raabe and Voelz express Paul's intent in Romans 12–16 in a manner which applies directly to the Law in 13:8–10:

> It should be noted that Paul's intent in paraenesis is not to accuse the Romans as sinners. He does that in chapters 1–3, where the tone is notably different. Paraenesis uses the language of urging, appealing, and beseeching rather than that of harsh demanding and condemning.[43]

Here the Holy Spirit himself "employs the law to instruct the regenerate out of it and to show and indicate to them in the Ten Commandments what the acceptable will of God is (Rom. 12:2)" (FC SD VI 12). Paul himself does the same thing with the Law's commandments in 13:8–10 at the conclusion of his lengthy depiction of genuine love (12:9–13:10). *In response to God's love, our love for others is informed and formed by the specific commandments of his good Law* (see the introduction to 12:9–21), something Paul himself asserts in Romans 7 (e.g., 7:16, 22, 25). Large sections of other epistles such as Ephesians 4–6 and Colossians 3–4 are intended to function in a similar manner (see "Pauline Imperatives" in the introduction to Romans 12–16).

When performed in response to God's love for us in Christ, doing the Law in love is most certainly good. Dunn insightfully points out that even in 9:32, "Paul does not disparage the idea of 'pursuit' (or of 'doing' the law; see on 10:5)"; rather, the problem with Israel's quest for righteousness "was the way that pursuit was envisaged and practiced,' "[44] that is, "as if [it could be attained] from works" (9:32). As stated above, if the Law is being used to keep score with God to earn one's own righteousness (10:3) or even to be regarded more favorably *coram Deo* by way of comparison with others, the Law is being *misused* and *misapplied* contrary to God's intent. If anyone hearing Romans is attempting to make the Law function in that manner, Paul strives to convince them unequivocally that such an effort is ultimately futile and fatal. But *the divinely intended use of the Law's commands for those in Christ is given in 13:8–10.* As the culmination of everything Paul has called for since 12:9, these verses assert that the divine intent of the Law is fully in concert with genuine love, a point Jesus also affirms (e.g., Mt 22:37–40; Mk 12:29–31; Lk 10:25–28; Jn 13:34). "Therefore love [is the] fulfillment of the Law" (Rom 13:10).

---

[42] Rosner, *Paul and the Law*, 124. Unfortunately, he then adds: "In Romans 13 and Galatians 5 Christ fulfils the law *through us*," which would seem to imply a second or ongoing fulfilling of the Law *by Christ*, something he finished "once for all" on the cross (Rom 6:10; 8:3).

[43] Raabe and Voelz, "Why Exhort a Good Tree?" 160.

[44] Dunn, *Romans*, 582.

Contemporary Cultural Complexities

In response to current views of morality, it should be emphasized that Paul is no postmodernist; neither would he be at all amenable to situational ethics. God has determined the "dos" and "don'ts," and his (not those of our own choosing) are the best for us under his loving guidance. His Law then reveals those things which are pleasing to him and truly loving to others. His Law also prohibits those which he deems to be harmful. *God does not set these standards arbitrarily or temporarily, and they do not change*, regardless of humanity's ongoing attempts to reinvent them (note 1:18–32; 13:8–10). Paul counters attempts to rely on human definitions of love apart from God's revealed commands most effectively in 13:8–10 (see especially the commentary on 13:10). Even believers "require the teaching of the law in connection with their good works, because otherwise they can easily imagine that their works and life are perfectly pure and holy" (FC SD VI 21).

The divinely inspired Law, therefore, reveals *God's* "good, well-pleasing, and perfect will" for humans (12:2). His Law articulates those things which are good for people in their relationship with God (and with others) and forbids those actions which would hinder it. Paul's quotation from Lev 19:18 about loving neighbor as self in Rom 13:9 is followed immediately by the assertion that love works no evil to a neighbor (13:10). Thus the Law serves the believer positively and beneficially by showing him how to act in genuine love for God and others and how to abstain from what is unloving.[45] And "the one who loves the other has brought [the] Law to fulfillment" as God intends (13:8).

Sin has made one's relationship with the Law problematic. This remains so not merely in terms of sinful acts but also due to the inherited corruption of the *sinful nature*. For example, the Bible condemns selfishness. A seemingly plausible excuse may be "God made me this way. Therefore, it is perfectly fine

---

[45] One controversial example may illustrate. The excursus "Homosexual Conduct Is Contrary to Nature (Romans 1:26–27)" in volume 1 of this commentary (Middendorf, *Romans 1–8*, 145–50) may not deal sufficiently with the popular argument that sexual behavior between consenting adults does not harm anyone. Homosexual conduct, according to this argument, ought not be considered outside the boundaries set by the Law as defined in Rom 13:10; it serves, instead, as a form of love for neighbor (Lev 19:18; Rom 13:9). Some wrongly conclude that consensual homosexual conduct should not be considered sinful or harmful; on the contrary, it is alleged to be a positive expression of who the person is according to his or her nature in a loving relationship with another.

In addition to the points made in the excursus in volume 1 referenced above, two additional responses can be offered here: (1) Homosexual behavior, by definition, requires at least two people to engage in the activity depicted by Paul in 1:26–27. Thus another person is always involved. If the behavior is contrary to God's Law, then, you are, in fact, doing harm to your neighbor by involving them in such an activity. (2) You also do not have to be harming someone else for a behavior to be harmful to yourself. Sins such as drunkenness, envy, and covetousness may, in some cases, affect only the person who engages in them. But they remain contrary to God's will to love your neighbor *as yourself* (Lev 19:18; Rom 13:9) and, therefore, are still harmful to the person who does them. Any sin, even if done "alone" (e.g., viewing pornography), is harmful to oneself and one's relationship with God and therefore is unloving (13:8–10). There is no such thing as a "victimless sin."

for me to act selfishly." However, this overlooks that it is our sinful nature/flesh (σάρξ), corrupted since the fall, that makes us selfish, *not* God, the Creator of good. Luther describes this with the phrase *incurvatus in se*, "curved in on self."[46] God's Law reveals that it is unhealthy for us to be absorbed with self. Therefore it directs us away from inward self and outward toward the love of God and neighbor wherein healthy relationships can be formed and fulfilled (e.g., Mt 22:37–40; Mk 12:29–31; Lk 10:25–28; Rom 13:8–10).

According to situational ethics, one might argue, for example, that a mother who steals from a grocery store to feed her hungry children does not violate God's Law. In fact, she fulfills a "higher law," her responsibility as a mother, and failing to provide food for her children would be a sin of omission (James 4:17). Nevertheless, no matter the motivation, stealing is still stealing, something *always* contrary to God's command (Ex 20:15; Deut 5:19; Rom 2:21; 13:9). The biblical response in such a situation is Christian charity; believers are to give freely to their brothers and sisters in need.[47] One might also argue that the grocery store would not be harmed substantially by the theft of so little, but by stealing, a person does "work evil" (13:10) against the owner and employees of the store, at least to some degree, and the degree itself does not affect the sinfulness of the action before God.

In a fallen world God's people may, at times, end up in situations where the only apparent alternative becomes the lesser of two evils. But even so, both still remain evil. In such cases, one joins with the tax collector in the temple pleading, "God, be propitiated (by an atoning sacrifice) to me, the sinner" (ὁ θεός, ἱλάσθητί μοι τῷ ἁμαρτωλῷ, Lk 18:13). It is then encouraging to know that God desires to show mercy to all (Rom 11:32) in Jesus, "whom God set forth publicly [as] an atoning sacrifice" (ἱλαστήριον, 3:25). For those covered with his blood, "nothing [is] condemnation"; "the ones in Christ Jesus" (8:1) are always under the grace of God instead of the lordship of the Law (6:14; 7:1). Then, on the basis of the renewed life God continually gives in Christ Jesus our Lord (6:4, 23; 12:2), believers also continue in their endeavor to live "through the mercies of God" (12:1).

Conclusion: Children of the Heavenly Father

The Father-children portrayal of our relationship with God, established by the Gospel, figures prominently in Jesus' teaching[48] and stands evident in Paul's as well (e.g., Rom 8:14–17; see the commentary there; see also Gal

---

[46] Luther, *Lectures on Romans*, AE 25:291, states: "Our nature has been so deeply curved in upon itself because of the viciousness of original sin" (see also AE 25:245, 292, 313, 345–46, 351).

[47] See, e.g., Deut 16:10–14; 24:19–21; Ruth 2; Acts 2:44–45; 4:32–37; Eph 4:28; 1 Jn 3:17.

[48] For example, "Father" occurs seventeen times in the Sermon on the Mount (Matthew 5–7), fifteen times in the phrase "your Father"; see also Lk 6:36; 11:1–13; Jn 5:36–37; 17:1–5; 20:17; see also Middendorf and Schuler, *Called by the Gospel*, 369–70. God's perfect fathering also stands in contrast to the imperfect parenting of our earthly fathers (e.g., Lk 11:11–13).

4:6–7). Paul then calls us to "be imitators of God, as loved children" (Eph 5:1; cf. Mt 5:44–48). Earthly parents establish rules for the benefit of their children. Similarly, in the Law our heavenly Father gives commands and instructions for how we are to imitate him and administers his discipline when we fall short (Heb 12:5–11). Both of these functions of the Law serve for our ultimate good in order to build us up so that we mature as his children (e.g., Eph 4:12–16).[49] As we grow in our faith relationship with God, we join with Paul in willingly and joyfully striving to do God's holy, righteous, and good commands (Rom 7:12, 16, 21, 25a), while also being increasingly frustrated by our failures to live according to his Law (7:14–15, 18–20, 23–24, 25b).[50] Nevertheless, with the confident assurance that we remain his children by grace through our baptismal union with Christ (6:1–11), we persist in our efforts to live out his "good, well-pleasing, and perfect will" (12:2) for the benefit of our neighbor (13:8–10), for our own good, and all to the glory of our gracious God.

---

[49] Note these statements from Ephesians 4: "toward the building up of the body of Christ" (εἰς οἰκοδομὴν τοῦ σώματος τοῦ Χριστοῦ, Eph 4:12); "toward a mature man" (εἰς ἄνδρα τέλειον, Eph 4:13); "so that we might no longer be infants" (ἵνα μηκέτι ὦμεν νήπιοι, Eph 4:14); "let us grow up into him" (αὐξήσωμεν εἰς αὐτόν, Eph 4:15); "the growing up of the body ... toward the building up" (τὴν αὔξησιν τοῦ σώματος ... εἰς οἰκοδομήν, Eph 4:16).

[50] The exasperation expressed in 7:14–25 by Paul is not from when he was still an unbeliever, nor is it characteristic of a "weak" Christian (as commentators often assert), but it signals the maturity evident in the apostle himself. See the excursus "Who Is the 'I' in Romans 7:14–25? Christian or Non-Christian?" in Middendorf, *Romans 1–8*, 584–97, particularly 594–97.

Introduction to Romans 14:1–15:13: The "Weak" and the "Strong" in Christ: Acceptance instead of Judgment

The Themes and Parameters of Romans 14:1–15:13

Acceptance

The verb "receive" (προσλαμβάνω) marks the opening and closing of this section (14:1, 3; 15:7 [twice]). The form προσλαμβάνεσθε in 14:1 is read as a second person plural present middle imperative, "receive to yourselves." The verb recurs as an aorist middle indicative in 14:3: "God received to himself" (ὁ θεὸς ... προσελάβετο). Then Paul uses each of those same two verb forms in 15:7: "receive one another to yourselves, just as the Christ also received you to himself." *The verbal action and the consistent middle voice, "receive to one-self," beautifully frame the entire discussion*. The indicatives in 14:3 and 15:7 powerfully articulate the Gospel, reminding the readers that God/Christ received them to himself. That Good News provides the motivation and the model for the receiving Paul urges those in Rome to do toward one another. In a manner comparable to 8:31–39 and 11:33–36, Paul then adds a profound epilogue in 15:8–13 which wraps up this section and, in many ways, the theological exposition of the entire letter.

Judgments

The other dominant note in this section sounds far less lofty, for it always refers to a human action, one that is most often negative. *Eight* of the eighteen appearances of the verb "to judge" (κρίνω) in Romans occur in chapter 14 (14:3, 4, 5 [twice], 10, 13 [twice], 22). Paul accents this emphasis further with the noun "judgments" (the plural of διάκρισις) in 14:1 and the culminating compound verbs διακρίνω, "make a distinction," and κατακρίνω, "pronounce a sentence," in 14:23. Thus a total of *eleven terms for judging permeate the chapter*. Even worse, these judgments are being made by and against those *within the family of faith* based upon personal convictions ("judgments over convictions," 14:1) in matters where the NT grants Christians freedom. On the one hand, Paul respects *both* those who understand and live out the extent of the liberty Jesus himself bestows in regard to foods and holy days *and* those who continue adhering to OT practices; they are the "strong" (15:1) and the "weak" (14:1–2; 15:1), respectively (see "Who Are the 'Weak' and the 'Strong'? Addressees Again!" below). On the other hand, he emphatically denounces those who despise fellow believers or pronounce judgments against them in these matters (e.g., 14:3, 10), and he also admonishes them to avoid causing others to stumble (e.g., 14:13, 21).

The Good News

At the same time that Paul prohibits judgmental attitudes and contempt in areas of Christian freedom, *the Gospel predominates.*[1] Paul grounds the reasons why all such behaviors are inappropriate in the relationship baptized believers have with the God who accepted all of them to himself in Christ (14:3; 15:7) and in the resulting relationship they have with one another in the Christ who died, rose, and lives for them all (14:7–9). As a result, believers live together in the righteousness, peace, and joy of God's kingdom (14:17). The section culminates with the assertion that Christ gave himself up for us in order to accept us to himself (15:3, 7). This Gospel truth is followed by a scriptural demonstration that Christ came to serve both Jews and Gentiles, that is, all alike (15:8–13). Thus, in Christ, we remain inseparably united with one another. Whether living or dying (14:8), nothing "will be able to separate us from God's love which is in Christ Jesus our Lord!" (8:39).[2]

Outline

Moo offers the following excellent analysis of Paul's structure and thought in 14:1–15:13:

> Paul's call for mutual acceptance in the Roman community falls into four larger sections. Each combines exhortation with theological rationale.
>
> 14:1–12—Both "strong" and "weak" Christians need to stop condemning each other because it is the Lord, and he alone, who has the right to assess the believer's status and conduct.
>
> 14:13–23—The "strong" Christians must be careful not to cause the "weak" Christians to suffer spiritual harm by their insistence on exercising their liberty on disputed matters. For such insistence violates the essence of the kingdom, which is to manifest love and concern for one another.
>
> 15:1–6—The "strong" Christians should willingly tolerate the tender consciences of the "weak" Christians, seeking thereby to foster unified praise of God in the community. Christians should exhibit such concern for others because of the example set for them by their Lord.
>
> 15:7–13—Both "strong" and "weak" Christians should receive each other as full and respected members of the Christian community, for God himself has shown, in fulfillment of Scripture, that he accepts both Jews and Gentiles as his people.[3]

---

[1] Franzmann, *Romans*, 243, states: "The question raised by differences in faith had to be answered from the church's central resource, from the Gospel itself." Later he also recognizes how "all three of Paul's appeals [14:1–12; 14:13–15:6; and 15:7–13] to the weak and strong for unity have been grounded in the Christian hope (14:9–12; 15:4; 15:13)" (261).

[2] For the thematic significance of repeated references to "Jesus Christ our Lord" throughout Romans 5–8, see Middendorf, *Romans 1–8*, 378–80.

[3] Moo, *Romans*, 832–33.

Who Are the "Weak" and the "Strong"? Addressees Again!

Identifying the Controverted Issues

Before considering the makeup of the factions being addressed in Rome, the precise nature of the conflict needs to be determined. Cranfield discusses a number of possibilities regarding *the specific matters of dispute*.[4] One scenario is that the situation in Rome stands equivalent to that in Corinth. Paul devotes a lengthy discussion in 1 Corinthians 8–10 to the eating of meat that had been sacrificed to idols, which was common practice in pagan society, and most of the Corinthian Christians seem to have been Gentile converts from paganism.[5] A number of church fathers identify the problem in Rome as such too.[6] Certain points of Paul's counsel in Romans are remarkably similar to those he gave when he first wrote to the Corinthians just a matter of months earlier.[7] For example, he includes references to the "weak" and to "weakness" (ἀσθενέω, ἀσθενής, ἀσθένημα, Rom 14:1–2; 15:1; 1 Cor 8:7, 9–12; 9:22); he warns Christians to avoid "scandalizing" or becoming a "stumbling block" (σκανδαλίζω, πρόσκομμα, ἀπρόσκοπος, προσκόπτω, Rom 14:13, 20, 21; 1 Cor 8:9, 13; 10:32) and against "destroying" a weak brother's faith (ἀπόλλυμι, Rom 14:15; 1 Cor 8:11).[8] But this view does not take into consideration the concerns unique to Romans: different convictions in regard to holy days (Rom 14:5–6), the description of foods as being "unclean" (κοινός, 14:14 [three times]), and Paul's conviction that all foods are "clean, pure" (καθαρός, 14:20).[9]

That the contentious matters in Rome were rooted in the OT seems indisputable. Whereas the "weak" Christians in 1 Cor 8:7–12 were susceptible to the allure of the pagan idolatry in which they formerly lived, Cranfield properly concludes that the "weak" Christians in Rome felt obligated to adhere to the ceremonial stipulations of the Torah. Even if the "weak" Romans had no scruples about Gentile Christians disregarding those Mosaic stipulations, they

---

[4] Cranfield, *Romans*, 690–97.

[5] For the situation in Corinth, see Lockwood, *1 Corinthians*, 271–74.

[6] For example, in interpreting Romans 14, (Pseudo-)Constantius, *Romans*, points out "that meats which were being sold in the markets of that time had been sacrificed to idols"; Augustine, *Commentary on Statements in Romans*, 78, also refers to "eating food which had been sacrificed to idols" (Bray, *Romans*, ACCS NT 6:337, 339, respectively).

[7] This commentary's view is that Paul wrote Romans during a three-month stay in Corinth in AD 55 or 56 (Middendorf, *Romans 1–8*, 7). Lockwood, *1 Corinthians*, 15, argues that Paul wrote 1 Corinthians in early AD 55.

[8] Cranfield, *Romans*, 691–92; Moo, *Romans*, 827, speaks similarly of "the impressive number of verbal and conceptual parallels." The language of a "stumbling block" appears also in Rev 2:14; there and in Rev 2:20 the Lord Jesus uses OT figures ("Balaam," "Jezebel") to characterize those people in Christian churches who were eating food sacrificed to idols and practicing sexual immorality.

[9] Curiously, three of the other options given in Cranfield, *Romans*, 693–94, deal exclusively with the "twofold abstinence" from meat and wine, rather than unclean foods, and also do not take the matter of holy days into consideration at all.

felt that, as far as they themselves were concerned, they could not with a clear conscience give up the observance of such requirements of the law as the distinction between clean and unclean foods, the avoidance of blood, the keeping of the Sabbath and other special days.[10]

Rom 14:1–15:13, then, seems *most directly addressed toward a conflict over ongoing issues related to the OT Law*, namely, the distinctions between clean and unclean foods and holy days. Both Acts and Colossians provide ample evidence that such disputes extended beyond Rome (e.g., Acts 10:13–16; 11:3; 15:1–6). Paul draws a more concise, but comparable, conclusion in Col 2:16–17; Christians should not be judged on the basis of OT observances, since they simply were types of Christ, who has now fulfilled them:

> [16]Therefore do not let someone judge you in food or in drink or in [the] matter of a festival or of a new moon or of Sabbaths, [17]which are a shadow of the things about to come, but the substance [is] of the Christ.

> [16]μὴ οὖν τις ὑμᾶς κρινέτω ἐν βρώσει καὶ ἐν πόσει ἢ ἐν μέρει ἑορτῆς ἢ νεομηνίας ἢ σαββάτων· [17]ἅ ἐστιν σκιὰ τῶν μελλόντων, τὸ δὲ σῶμα τοῦ Χριστοῦ. (Col 2:16–17)[11]

Cranfield's final option equates the context in Rome with the one Paul encountered in Galatia years earlier.[12] But in contrast with the contentious situation in that region regarding the Law (e.g., Gal 1:6–9; 5:10–12), in Romans "we hear nothing of circumcision, for instance, and Paul's calm and winning manner here is quite different from his volcanic outbursts in the Letter to the Galatians."[13] Whereas the Judaizers in Galatia held that circumcision was a requirement for righteousness and salvation,[14] the "weak" Roman Christians apparently did *not*.[15] Instead, the OT observances mentioned in Rom 14:1–15:13 became impediments to full fellowship *within* the community of Jewish and Gentile believers and among the various house churches in Rome.

---

[10] Cranfield, *Romans*, 695.

[11] See Deterding, *Colossians*, 112–24.

[12] Cranfield, *Romans*, 694–95. This commentary's view is that Paul wrote Romans during a three-month stay in Corinth in AD 55 or 56 (Middendorf, *Romans 1–8*, 7). Das, *Galatians*, 43–47, argues that Paul had traveled through Galatia during his first missionary journey in AD 46–47 or 47–48 and wrote his epistle to the Galatians shortly thereafter, around AD 48.

[13] Franzmann, *Romans*, 243; see also Middendorf, *Romans 1–8*, 20–21; Wright, *The Climax of the Covenant*, 234, suggests the two situations are a "mirror-image" of one another.

[14] Gal 1:6–7; 3:1–5; 5:1–4; 6:12–14. This was also the issue in Acts 15:1, where the Judaizers argued that "unless you are circumcised according to the custom of Moses, you *cannot be saved*."

[15] Dunn, *Romans*, 798, cites Rom 4:19 and 1 Cor 8:7, 9–10; 9:22 in the context of his argument that to be "weak in the faith" (Rom 14:1) is "to fail to trust God completely and without qualification. ... The weakness is trust in God *plus* dietary and festival laws, trust in God *dependent* on observance of such practices." However, Moo, *Romans*, 830, properly recognizes that "the 'weak' ... were not propagating a view antithetical to the gospel"; similarly, Cranfield, *Romans*, 690–91. See "The Situation at Galatia" in Das, *Galatians*, 1–19; for a full discussion of issues regarding table fellowship between Jews and Gentile, see the excursus "The Issue at Antioch" in Das, *Galatians*, 216–32.

The Composition of the Addressees—Reiterating This Commentary's View

Paul writes this letter "to all the ones in Rome who are loved by God, to those called, holy" (πᾶσιν τοῖς οὖσιν ἐν Ῥώμη ἀγαπητοῖς θεοῦ, κλητοῖς ἁγίοις, 1:7). In the previous verse, Paul directly addresses his audience in the second person plural as "called by Jesus Christ" (1:6). Thus his intended audience encompasses *all the Christians in Rome*, and chapter 16 proves that they include both Jews and Gentiles (see "What Can We Conclude?" at the end of the commentary on 16:1–16). The history and makeup of the Christian community in Rome was discussed in detail in the introduction to this commentary.[16] It contends that *Paul speaks to a mixed group of Jewish and Gentile believers, the latter having majority status.*[17] Yet a significant Jewish-Christian presence most adequately explains why the disputes over foods and holy days exist and why Paul needs to address them at length in 14:1–15:13. This presence also best accounts for the theological argument for "Israel" engaged throughout Romans 9–11.

Where did the lines of demarcation in the conflict addressed in 14:1–15:13 most likely fall? In light of the ethnic composition of the congregations in Rome, we concur with Kruse:

> The most widely accepted view, and that adopted in this commentary, is that the "weak" are Jewish Christians (including possible proselytes) who practiced essentially Jewish customs, and the "strong" were mainly Gentile Christians (including some Jewish believers who were liberated like Paul himself) who felt no obligation to practice these customs.[18]

Note, however, that in Romans 14–15 Paul *nowhere* expresses the debate in terms of "Jew" versus "Gentile." Instead, he employs the categories of "the one who is weak" (ὁ ἀσθενῶν, 14:1, 2; cf. 15:1) and "the strong" (οἱ δυνατοί),

---

[16] Middendorf, *Romans 1–8*, 10–14, 17–21; see also the introduction to Romans 9–16.

[17] Similarly, Fitzmyer, *Romans*, 76, in agreement with Klein, "Paul's Purpose in Writing the Epistle to the Romans," states:

> Paul regards the Christians of Rome as predominantly of Gentile background (1:5–6, 13; 15:15–16); but they are also Gentile Christians related to and aware of a Jewish Christianity stemming from Jerusalem. And there were also Jewish Christians from Jerusalem among them.

The latter assertion is plausible, but there are surely also Jewish Christians in Rome who had previously been part of the synagogue communities there.

[18] Kruse, *Romans*, 510, including n. 6, citing as representatives of "the most widely accepted view" Dunn, *Romans*, 795 (see also 804–5); Wright, "Romans," 731–32; Moo, *Romans*, 831; Fitzmyer, *Romans*, 686–88. Similarly, Watson, "The Two Romans Congregations," 203, 206; also Jewett, *Romans*, 71, who concludes:

> It is likely that the majority of the strong were Gentile believers, with Jewish liberals such as Paul and his close allies included in this group. It is also likely that the weak included Jewish adherents to the law, but this group probably included some Gentiles who had been close to synagogues before becoming believers.

For an overview of various positions, see Kruse, *Romans*, 509–10; Cranfield, *Romans*, 690–97.

though the latter does not even appear until 15:1, and only there. Therefore Rosner reinforces Kruse's parenthetical qualifiers (see above) and appropriately cautions those who separate the factions simply along ethnic lines:

> The two groups probably did not divide neatly into Jewish Christians and Gentile Christians: "the weak" may have included some Gentile Christians and "the strong" may have included some of Paul's Jewish-Christian friends in Rome, such as Prisca and Aquila.[19]

"To the Churches within the Synagogues of Rome"?[20]

Are these "weak" Christians at least *predominantly* Jewish? This would likely be so if, as Nanos suggests, "in Rome Christianity and Judaism shared a common heritage, and were probably inseparable before 60 c.e."[21] Disputes over foods and holy days would surely have arisen if Jewish believers in Jesus continued to worship and participate actively *within* their synagogue communities. This may well have happened for a time, at least as long as their acceptance of and witness to the Messiah was tolerated. But the story of Acts demonstrates a more common pattern:

> Those who advocated or accepted the messianic identity of Jesus were often forcibly removed from the synagogue by the Jewish leaders (e.g., Acts 13:45; 17:5–7, 13; 18:6; 19:9; cf. Jn 9:22; 16:1–2). In other words, the hostility went in the opposite direction.[22]

The previous expulsion of Jews from Rome by Claudius due to "disturbances at the instigation of Chrestus"[23] (AD 49 or 50) may well provide evidence that this conflict and separation had already taken place in Rome by the time Paul wrote his letter in AD 55 or 56.

In any case, Nanos' assertion that "*non-Christian Jews* were those Paul refers to as the 'weak' or 'stumbling' of Israel"[24] is definitely *untenable* in light of 14:8–9 and 15:7, as well as Paul's repeated use of "brother" (ἀδελφός, 14:10 [twice], 13, 15, 21) to refer to fellow believers in Jesus. Furthermore, Romans indicates that the viewpoint of the "strong" occupies the dominant position among Paul's addressees. If so, it seems most implausible that they were practicing their faith within synagogue communities.

---

[19] Rosner, *Paul and the Law*, 32, n. 36. Moo, Romans, 831, n. 22, points out that "Roman writers note the popularity of both the Sabbath and Jewish food laws even among Gentiles" (citing Juvenal, *Satirae*, 14.9–10b; Horace, *Satirae*, 1.9.67–72; Ovid, *Remedia amoris*, 219–20; Ovid, *Ars amatoria*, 1.76, 415–16).

[20] "To the Churches within the Synagogues of Rome" is the title of an article by Nanos.

[21] Nanos, *The Mystery of Romans*, 68.

[22] Middendorf, *Romans 1–8*, 13; see also 11–13 for further details.

[23] Suetonius, *Vita Claudius*, 25.4; for the edict, see Middendorf, *Romans 1–8*, 10.

[24] Nanos, *The Mystery of Romans*, 38 (emphasis added); in response, see also the commentary on 9:3; Middendorf, *Romans 1–8*, 12–13; Moo, *Romans*, 827.

An Exclusive(ly) Gentile Audience?

Worthy of more attention is the opposite assessment argued by Das and others.[25] Based upon passages such as 1:5–6, 13; 11:13; 15:15–16, Das argues that the Roman Christians "are themselves Gentiles"[26] and that Paul addresses them exclusively as "the gentile-encoded audience."[27] But what of those sections that appear directed specifically toward Jews?

Das contends that 2:17–3:1 speaks only of a "fictive Jew" and does not describe Christ-believing Jews.[28] However, the Jew addressed with the second person singular "you" in that section is clearly identified by a number of important qualifiers (see the commentary on 2:17). First, although Paul writes from a Christian perspective, *he does depict actual and common attitudes among non-Christian Jews*, e.g., relying on the Law (2:17) and boasting in God and the Law (2:17, 23).[29] The Pharisees exemplify these most vividly (e.g., Lk 11:42–46, 52; 18:9–12), and Paul himself recalls all too well that he did this in his own Pharisaic past (Phil 3:3b–6; 1 Tim 1:12–16). Furthermore, passages in Romans 3 also seem directed toward a general Jewish audience, believer and unbeliever alike. For example, the first person plural "we" in 3:9 presumes this reaction from a Jewish perspective, inclusive of Paul: "What then? Are we any better off?" Additionally, the echo of the *Shema‘* (Deut 6:4) at the end of Romans 3 counters a Jewish assumption within his audience as well: "Or is God [the God] of Jews only? Is he not also [the God] of Gentiles? Yes, also of Gentiles, since God is one" (Rom 3:29–30).

(a) See, e.g., Rom 5:1; 6:2–3, 14–15, 17–18; 7:6; 8:1, 4

On a larger scale, *all of 1:18–3:20* does not directly apply to Christians any longer.[a] But the section does have a pragmatic purpose.[30] It effectively reminds believers, Jew or Gentile, of where they were and would be without Christ and also serves to warn them against adopting (again) the lifestyle and attitudes depicted therein.[31] Thus the second person singular "you" addressed in 2:1–5

---

[25] Also Elliot, *The Arrogance of Nations*, 19–20, 128–30; Johnson Hodge, "A Light to the Nations," 169–70; Stowers, *A Rereading of Romans*, 21–33.

[26] Das, "The Gentile-Encoded Audience of Romans," 33.

[27] Das titles his article "The Gentile-Encoded Audience of Romans" and suggests: "The best clue to the letter's situation and purpose is with the encoded audience, that is, the audience as reconstructed from the letter itself and as conceptually distinguished from the *actual* original hearers" (29). This methodology is comparable to the "mirror reading" advocated by Longenecker, *Introducing Romans*, 55, and adopted in this commentary's introduction (Middendorf, *Romans 1–8*, 7–14). But it seems confusing to drive a wedge between a "reconstructed" audience and "the *actual* original hearers." At least from the point of view of the author, they are surely one and the same.

[28] Das, "The Gentile-Encoded Audience of Romans," 34.

[29] See also the excursus "The Background of 'Works of the Law' " following the commentary on 3:9–20.

[30] For a brief introduction to pragmatics, see Middendorf, *Romans 1–8*, 596, n. 34; see also Middendorf, *The "I" in the Storm*, 133–34, 226–27.

[31] The theory of Das, " 'Praise the Lord, All You Gentiles,' " 105, that 2:17–29 "forms the first stage of a layered rhetorical trap for the gentile reader that is not fully sprung until 11.11–26" seems an unrealistic stretch for Paul's first-century hearers to grasp and provides

may not be directly targeted at a specific judgmental person in Rome. But those verses do, in fact, serve to admonish those in the Christian community who act judgmentally, a *real* problem in Rome, as evident from the eight appearances of "judge" (κρίνω) in Romans 14 (14:3, 4, 5 [twice], 10, 13 [twice], 22). The same applies to the ongoing temptation to rely upon the Law and to boast before God on that basis; Paul counters those notions in 2:17–3:1. While a Gentile may also adopt such a presumptuous attitude on the basis of Law-based obedience, it seems more typical of a Jewish standpoint, something Paul articulates in his argument against it. Thus he does not create an artificial scenario, nor does he speak to a "fictive" person. Instead, *he critiques those actual Jews who do fit his qualifications and, thereby, also warns his Jewish and Gentile (over)hearers against any boastful reliance on the Law.*

Das argues that Paul's description in 6:19 "would be appropriate only for Gentiles" and that his discussion of remarriage in 7:1–6 "offers yet another tell-tale sign that his audience is Gentile."[32] However, just before engaging in his most extensive discussion regarding the Law, Paul describes his hearers as "brothers, for I am speaking to ones knowing the Law" (7:1). This experiential knowledge of the Law, particularly at the level engaged in Romans, could, of course, include Gentile proselytes.[33] But the description seems *most applicable to Jewish believers*; in any case, it certainly would not *exclude* them.

Furthermore, the impact of *Paul's own* wrestling with the Law in 7:7–25 again seems most emblematic of Jewish experience (i.e., his own!) and is targeted pragmatically in that direction. Das' interpretation of the "I" in 7:7–25 becomes especially problematic at this point. He aligns himself with "a handful of interpreters [who] have recognized Rom. 7.7–25 as an instance of *prosopopoiia*" as Paul supposedly "speaks from the vantage point of the gentile seeking assistance from Moses' Law in the battle against the passions."[34] But an analysis of Paul's letters reveals that *he simply does not use the first person singular in such a manner elsewhere.*

> In the vast majority of the passages where Paul uses the first person singular, he himself is the referent. As a rule, if Paul does not intend himself as the referent of the "I," he explicitly indicates this to his readers and makes evident who the referent is. … No such signal is present in the text of Romans 7. Nothing suggests that the referent is anything or anyone other than Paul.[35]

---

an unconvincing assessment of Paul's more theological purpose in the letter; see Middendorf, *Romans 1–8*, 14–21, 49–51, and the previous critique of this approach (13, n. 69).

[32] Das, "The Gentile-Encoded Audience of Romans," 35.

[33] Das, " 'Praise the Lord, All You Gentiles,' " 106.

[34] Das, " 'Praise the Lord, All You Gentiles,' " 106, citing in agreement Stowers, *A Rereading of Romans*, 251–84; Tobin, *Paul's Rhetoric in Its Contexts*, 225–50; Das, *Solving the Romans Debate*, 204–35.

[35] Middendorf, *The "I" in the Storm*, 156; passages where Paul does indicate a different referent include Rom 3:7; 11:19; 1 Cor 1:12; 3:4; for the complete survey, see 148–57.

In light of the sustained nature of the argument and the consistent and extensive use of first person singular forms throughout 7:7–25, it seems difficult to believe how the hearers in Rome were intended to grasp that Paul's "I" portrays a Gentile *to the exclusion of the Jewish author himself*![36] Indeed, Paul's own interaction with the Law, *both* in his Pharisaic past (7:7–11) *and* his apostolic present (7:14–25), serves as the foundation for the whole argument.[37]

As discussed in the introduction to Romans 9–11, those three chapters provide much of the theological groundwork to support the practical applications Paul will make in 14:1–15:13. While the place of Jewish believers within the community of faith exists as one of continuity between the OT remnant of Israel and the church (9:27–29; 11:1–6), the extraordinary "mystery" concerns how Gentiles have been ingrafted (see the commentary on 11:25–26). On the one hand, Das correctly notes: "Christ-believing Gentiles in the capital of the empire may be meeting separately from the Jews for the worship of Jesus, but the worship of Jesus cannot be severed from the historical privileges and heritage of Israel."[38] To be sure, Paul does address "you Gentiles" directly in 11:13 and repeatedly within 11:17–24. Yet the fact that he does so supports the notion that *the entire letter has a broader audience which Paul specifically narrows in this section in order to make targeted comments*.[39] Furthermore, he occasionally engages Gentile believers in order to instruct them precisely about how they should regard Jewish people. This includes Jews who currently do not believe (e.g., 11:28), but *it refers especially to believing Israel*, those with whom Gentiles in Rome now share in the nourishing sap of God's olive tree by virtue of having been grafted in among them (11:17–21, 25). Thus the core message of the Gospel *to Paul's addressees uses the first person plural* to affirm that God called "*us*, not only from Jews but also from Gentiles" (9:24).

In this way, Paul's discussion of God's interaction with Israel in chapters 9–11 moves ahead purposefully toward addressing the divided groups of Jewish and Gentile believers within and among separate house churches in Rome.

> Paul's complex theologizing in chaps. 9–11 has a very practical purpose: to unite the squabbling Roman Christians behind his vision of the gospel and its implications for the relationship of Jew and Gentile. As so often in Romans, Paul's approach is balanced. He insists, against the presumption of many Gentiles in the community, that the gospel does not signal the abandonment of Israel (chap. 11, especially). But he also makes clear that Jews and Jewish Christians who think that they have an inalienable salvific birthright are in

---

[36] See Middendorf, *The "I" in the Storm*, 157; that real practicality is raised against various interpretations by Dunn, *Romans*, 372; Theissen, *Psychological Aspects of Pauline Theology*, 251.

[37] See the commentary on Rom 7:7–11 and 7:14–25; cf. Phil 3:4–11; 1 Tim 1:12–16.

[38] Das, "The Gentile-Encoded Audience of Romans," 45.

[39] See "Introduction: Addressing 'You Gentiles' (11:13a)" in the commentary on 11:13–24.

error (chaps. 9 and 10, especially). Paul therefore criticizes extremists from both sides, paving the way for his plea for reconciliation in chaps 14–15.[40]

Finally, in chapter 16 Paul sends greetings to twenty-six people by name, among whom *at least four are certainly Jewish*, and very possibly as many as eight.[41] Das contends that "ancient admonitions to greet someone that employ second-person pronouns request the letter's recipients to greet a *third* party. … The named people would be *outside* the Roman congregations or perhaps new-comers into their midst."[42] But that misreads the force of Paul's repeated use of the plural imperative "greet" (ἀσπάσασθε, sixteen times in 16:3–16; see the commentary on 16:3). Furthermore, Paul's familiarity with these named believ-ers, particularly Prisca and Aquila (16:3–5a), cannot place them *outside* the Roman congregations. They, along with any newcomers, are certainly included among the intended recipients of the letter addressed "to all the ones in Rome who are loved by God" (1:7).

Conclusions

Within the text of Romans, Paul at times addresses Gentiles directly to emphasize the special role of Israel in order to counter any unwarranted Gentile boasting (e.g., 11:13, 17–24). Just as vociferously, however, he also feels the need to affirm the mysterious and even more surprising *inclusion of Gentiles* within the people of God (e.g., 3:29–30; 4:9–11; 15:9–12; probably also 3:26; cf. 3:9). To whom would such an argument need to be directed? *Surely the most plausible answer is Jewish believers in his audience.* On the basis of 1:1–17 and 15:14–33, Watson even argues that "Romans was addressed primarily to Jewish Christians" in order to persuade them "to accept the legitimacy of" Gentile Christianity![43]

Peering behind the text through "mirror reading" it, the historical background discussed in the commentary introduction provides plausible infor-mation which helps us to understand what the letter itself says.[44] The historical sequence of events leads Das to conclude that "a decisive break took place as Christ-believers began to meet for worship apart from synagogue gatherings and as a distinctive Gentile Christ-believing identity began to emerge."[45] That point has some commonalities with the position advocated here. But the problem comes with insisting that a *distinctive* Gentile community became an *exclusive* one or that this is so in regard to the letter's actual addressees. Paul, instead, addresses a situation which is divided, but *not* an audience that has become

---

[40] Moo, *Romans*, 552–53.

[41] See "What Can We Conclude?" at the end of the commentary on 16:1–16; see also Middendorf, *Romans 1–8*, 14, 17–18.

[42] Das, "The Gentile-Encoded Audience of Romans," 37–38.

[43] Watson, "Two Romans Congregations," 212.

[44] For the concept of "mirror reading," see Longenecker, *Introducing Romans*, 55; it is utilized in the overview of the Roman context in Middendorf, *Romans 1–8*, 10–14, 17–21.

[45] Das, "The Gentile-Encoded Audience of Romans," 44.

ethnically exclusive. In fact, Paul addresses Rom 14:1–15:13 to all the believers in Rome in order to avoid just such an outcome. Thus this section fits squarely within the flow of the entire letter:

> It was written to assist the Gentile Christian majority, who are the primary addressees of the letter, to live together with the Jewish Christians in one congregation, thereby putting an end to their quarrels about status.[46]

Application to Romans 14:1–15:13

Paul addresses the divisions in 14:1–15:13 in regard to *the issues themselves*; he does not employ any ethnic terms. Nevertheless, the matters of foods and holy days do reflect tensions which existed in the first century, mainly between Jewish and Gentile Christians. The NT provides evidence for the existence of such conflicts elsewhere (e.g., Acts 10:13–16; 11:3; 15:1–6; Gal 2:11–14), and the same controversies appear to have afflicted the believing communities in Rome. The entirety of Paul's letter aims to obliterate any Jew/Gentile "distinction/difference" before God (διαστόλη in 3:22 and 10:12; see also 1:16; 2:9, 10; 3:9, 29; 9:24; 10:12; 15:8–9). Dunn agrees that Rom 14:1–15:13 addresses both Jews and Gentiles and seeks to overcome disputes between them for these three reasons:

> (1) The whole letter is oriented to the issue of Jew and Gentile, and how they stand in relation to the gospel and to each other. …
>
> (2) The terms of the discussion itself (14:1–15:6) are most clearly applicable to particularly Jewish concerns. The talk of "clean" (καθαρός—[14:]20) and especially "unclean" (κοινός—[14:]14) is characteristically and in the latter case distinctively Jewish. … And the concern about festivals is equally characteristic of Judaism. …
>
> (3) Too little appreciated in discussions of this passage is the considerable importance of dietary laws for Jews of this period. It was not simply that the laws of clean and unclean food were so clearly stated in the Torah (Lev 11:1–23; Deut 14:3–21). Also and even more important was that fact that the Maccabean crisis had made observance of these laws a test of Jewishness … (1 Macc 1:62–63; cf. 2 Macc 5:27; …).[47]

Das helpfully reminds us that Paul's description of the "weak" would "be appropriate for *non*-Jews observing such customs."[48] His assessment that many Gentile believers in Rome had been part of synagogue communities also seems likely.[49] But this need not exclude the far more likely reality that *many Jewish believers*, also from synagogue communities, continued to practice "such customs." To suggest that "the offense of Paul's apparent relativizing of

---

[46] Wiefel, "The Jewish Community in Ancient Rome and the Origins of Roman Christianity," 96; see Middendorf, *Romans 1–8*, 19.

[47] Dunn, *Romans*, 800.

[48] Das, "The Gentile-Encoded Audience of Romans," 37.

[49] Das, " 'Praise the Lord, All You Gentiles,' " 106; see Middendorf, *Romans 1–8*, 10–14.

Law-observant customs in Rom. 14.1–15.6 would be alleviated if directed to a gentile audience"[50] minimizes the far more significant matter at hand. Paul bases his argument on the relationship established by the Gospel itself in which Jesus fulfills, overcomes, and transcends the necessity of such "Law-observant customs" for both Jew and Gentile (e.g., 14:7–8, 17–18; 15:5–12).

Therefore 14:1–15:13, like the Gospel itself, seems generally directed "to Jew first and also to Greek" (1:16). Here Paul spells out very specific implications of the Gospel to his Roman audience. *Initially, he takes aim mainly at Jewish believers, as well as some Gentile proselytes*, who judge those who do not observe OT regulations about foods and festivals (14:1–13a). But *he then cautions Gentiles, together with Jewish Christians (like himself!)*, to live out their freedoms regarding diet and days in a manner which will build up the "weak," rather than tear down and destroy them (14:13b–22a; 15:1–4).

Rom 15:5–7 contains Paul's climactic call for unity among the Christians in Rome. The language of those verses supports Watson's summation that they ought "to set aside their differences and to worship together,"[51] but it surely encompasses much more. Wright appropriately titles the section more broadly as "Romans 14:1–15:13, God's Call to Unity of Life and Worship across Barriers of Custom and Ethnic Identity."[52] Paul's practical plea for full fellowship stands firmly rooted in the all-sufficiency of "our Lord Jesus Christ" (15:6, 8–9a). Those whom Christ has "received … to himself" (15:7), whether categorized by Paul as "weak" or "strong," ought to exhibit the same attitude of acceptance instead of judgment toward one another (14:1; 15:1–3).

Paul concludes similarly, first by affirming that Christ became a servant to the "circumcision" in order to confirm God's promises to the patriarchs (15:8; see the commentary there). He then turns to show how the OT itself repeatedly expresses God's intention to reach out to include Gentiles as well (15:9–12). In many ways, these verses serve as the theological culmination of Paul's entire argument, which he wraps up with a concluding word of blessing (15:13).

---

[50] Das, " 'Praise the Lord, All You Gentiles,' " 106.

[51] Watson, "Two Romans Congregations," 211; Wright, "Romans," is similarly too narrow at times, for example: "The underlying message Paul wants to convey is about the glorifying of God in the united worship of Jew and Gentile together in the Messiah" (744) and "Shared worship, indeed, is central to Paul's vision" (749).

[52] Wright, "Romans," 730.

Do Not Judge Those Who *Also* Belong to the Lord Based on Your Convictions

Translation

14 [1]As for the one who is weak in the faith, receive [him] to yourselves, not for judgments over convictions. [2]On the one hand, [there is one] who believes [he has the freedom] to eat all things, but, on the other hand, the one who is weak is eating vegetables. [3]The one who eats, let him not despise the one who does not eat; but the one who is not eating, let him not judge the one who is eating, for God received him to himself.

[4]You, who are you, the one judging the household servant of another? To his own master he stands or falls, and he will be established, for the Lord is able to establish him. [5]Indeed, on the one hand, [there is one] who judges a day in preference to a day, but, on the other hand, [there is another] who judges every day [alike]. Let each one be fully convinced in his own mind. [6]For the one who sets his mind on a day sets [it] to the Lord. And the one who eats is eating to the Lord, for he gives thanks to God; and the one who does not eat is not eating to the Lord, and he gives thanks to God.

[7]Indeed, no one of us lives to himself, and no one dies to himself. [8]For not only if we live are we living to the Lord, but also if we die we die to the Lord. Therefore not only if we live, but also if we die, we are the Lord's. [9]For to this [end] Christ died and lived [again] so that he might be Lord of both [the] dead and [the] living ones.

[10]But you, why are you judging your brother? Or you, why are you also despising your brother? For we will all present ourselves before the judgment seat of God. [11]Indeed, it stands written: "'[As] I live,' the Lord says, 'to me every knee will bow, and every tongue will acknowledge itself to God.'" [12]Consequently then, each one of us will give an account concerning himself to God. [13a]Therefore let us judge one another no longer.

Textual Notes

14:1 τὸν δὲ ἀσθενοῦντα τῇ πίστει—The conjunction δέ serves as "a marker connecting a series of closely related data or lines of narrative, *and, as for*" (BDAG, 1). For the verb ἀσθενέω, "be weak," see the first textual note on 4:19. There Abraham was "*not weakening in the faith*"; the word occurs also in 8:3; 14:2. In both 4:19 and 14:1, the dative τῇ πίστει is one of respect, "in respect to the faith."[1] The definite active participle

---

[1] See Wallace, *Greek Grammar*, 144–46.

here is used substantively,[2] "the one who is weak in the faith." The accusative participle is the object of the following imperative προσλαμβάνεσθε.

προσλαμβάνεσθε—The verb προσλαμβάνω, "to take, receive," functions thematically, as it is repeated in 14:3 and climactically in 15:7 (twice).[3] BDAG, 4, defines it as "to extend a welcome, *receive in(to) one's home or circle of acquaintances,* ... of one Christian receiving another" (cf. Acts 18:26; 28:2; Philemon 17). The translation "welcome" (RSV, ESV, NRSV) is too weak for the full sense of fellowship involved here. The present tense form προσλαμβάνεσθε could be either indicative or imperative mood, but the context clearly points to an imperative. The form could also be either middle or passive voice. The middle is indicated because it takes a direct object (τὸν ... ἀσθενοῦντα in the preceding textual note); likewise, the identical form in 15:7 must be middle since it also takes a direct object (cf. the aorist indicative middle προσελάβετο with a direct object in 14:3; 15:7). Thus the meaning is "receive to yourselves."

μὴ εἰς διακρίσεις διαλογισμῶν—The preposition εἰς, "for," expresses purpose. The compound noun διάκρισις can have a positive or neutral meaning, "the ability to distinguish and evaluate," as between sprits in 1 Cor 12:10 (BDAG, 1). BDAG also suggests a negative meaning, "engagement in verbal conflict because of differing viewpoints, *quarrel*" (BDAG, 2). But the sense here is even more deleterious. The noun κρίσις is cognate to the verb κρίνω, "to judge," which appears eight times in this chapter, along with two additional cognate verbs in 14:23.[4] Therefore the condemnatory sense of "judgments" is certainly prevalent and the most appropriate translation of this plural form. The noun διαλογισμός describes the "content of reasoning or conclusion reached through use of reason, *thought, opinion, reasoning, design*" (BDAG, 2). BDAG translates it along with the preceding prepositional phrase as "*not for the purpose of getting into quarrels about opinions*" (s.v. διάκρισις, 2). But both "quarrels" and "opinions" seem weak, as does Cranfield's use of "scruples" for διαλογισμῶν.[5] The translation "for judgments over convictions" better conveys the meaning.

14:2 ὃς μὲν ... ὁ δέ—The postpositive μέν introduces a comparison with the δέ that follows.[6] Paul uses a relative pronoun ὅς, "who,"[7] in the first part of the comparison and the definite article in the second part of the comparison, ὁ δέ. The construction functions in essentially the same way as does ὃς μὲν ... ὃς δέ in 14:5, for which BDAG offers the contrast "*the one ... the other*" (BDAG, s.v. ὅς, 2 b). The translation here uses

---

2 See Wallace, *Greek Grammar*, 619–21.

3 See "Acceptance" at the start of the introduction to 14:1–15:13.

4 See the eight instances of the verb κρίνω, "to judge," in 14:3, 4, 5 (twice), 10, 13 (twice), 22; and the compound verbs διακρίνω, "make a distinction," and κατακρίνω, "pronounce a sentence," in 14:23. See further "Judgments" in the introduction to 14:1–15:13.

5 Cranfield, *Romans*, 698, 701; for the other suggestions, see the commentary.

6 Wallace, *Greek Grammar*, 672, lists them under "Correlative Conjunctions (paired conjunctions)."

7 Wallace, *Greek Grammar*, 339–40, explains that a relative pronoun can have an embedded demonstrative pronoun. While he deals with this usage under the heading "Omission of Antecedent," he notes that in such cases the antecedent is clear from the context.

the more literal rendering "who" for the relative pronoun and presumes an initial "to be" verb: "on the one hand, [there is one] who … but, on the other hand, the one …"

πιστεύει φαγεῖν πάντα—The verb "believe" (πιστεύω) followed by an infinitive has "the sense 'believe that, feel confident that' something is, will be, or has been."[8] Here the conviction recognizes that believers have been freed "to eat everything." φαγεῖν is the second aorist infinitive of the common verb ἐσθίω, "to eat." Its object is the neuter plural πάντα, "all things." Given the preponderance of "faith"/"believe" language in Romans,[9] Paul's use of πιστεύω here may also hint that this belief is correct: with faith in Christ, one may eat anything.

ὁ … ἀσθενῶν—For the definite substantival participle of ἀσθενέω, "the one who is weak," see the first textual note on 14:1. The form here is nominative.

λάχανα—The neuter noun λάχανον refers to an "*edible garden herb, vegetable*" (BDAG), but the issue does not simply involve being a vegetarian; see the commentary.

14:3 ὁ ἐσθίων τὸν μὴ ἐσθίοντα … ὁ δὲ μὴ ἐσθίων τὸν ἐσθίοντα—Each of the four definite participles of ἐσθίω is substantival, "*the one who* eats/does not eat."[10]

μὴ ἐξουθενείτω … μὴ κρινέτω—The verb ἐξουθενέω means "to show by one's attitude or manner of treatment that an entity has no merit or worth, *disdain*" and "despise" (BDAG, 1). In the NT it is employed only by Luke (Lk 18:9; 23:11; Acts 4:11) and Paul (Rom 14:10; 1 Cor 1:28; 6:4; 16:11; 2 Cor 10:10; Gal 4:14; 1 Thess 5:20). The form is a negated third person singular present active imperative. Paul surely perceives that this action is now happening, so "stop despising" would be appropriate. But the broader general precept is also certainly applicable, and the third person imperative is translated more smoothly as "let him not despise."[11] The same is true of the second negated third person singular present active imperative, "let him not judge."

ὁ θεὸς γὰρ αὐτὸν προσελάβετο—For the verb προσλαμβάνω, "receive," see the second textual note on 14:1. Since the aorist has separate middle and passive forms, the aorist indicative προσελάβετο can only be middle, which signals the present tense προσλαμβάνεσθε in 14:1 and 15:7 should be read as middle as well.

14:4 σὺ τίς εἶ ὁ κρίνων—"You, who are you, the one judging … ?" is comparable to the challenge in 2:1 (see the third textual note and the commentary on 2:1).

ἀλλότριον οἰκέτην—The noun οἰκέτης is related to the noun οἶκος, "house," and originally denoted a "household slave." The adjective ἀλλότριος indicates that the slave belongs to "another" rather than to "one's own lord/master" (see next textual note).

τῷ ἰδίῳ κυρίῳ … ὁ κύριος—The force of the dative is discussed in the commentary. The referent of κύριος changes here. In the initial phrase it describes an earthly

---

[8] Dunn, *Romans*, 799, citing LSJM, πιστεύω, I 3.

[9] For πιστεύω, "believe," and πίστις, "faith," see "The Background and Meaning of 'Faith' Words" in the commentary on 1:16 (Middendorf, *Romans 1–8*, 88–90); " 'From Faith[fulness] into Faith' (1:17)" on 96–98; and also 106–7.

[10] See Wallace, *Greek Grammar*, 619–21.

[11] See the discussions of the same issue—whether a command calls for cessation of current activity or is a general precept—in the first textual note on 11:18, the fourth textual note on 11:20, and the first textual note on 12:2. See also Wallace, *Greek Grammar*, 714–17, 724–25.

"lord": "to his own master" (cf. Lk 16:8). But in the latter phrase κύριος denotes "the Lord" Jesus himself.

στήκει ἢ πίπτει—This is the only use of the verb στήκω, "to stand," in Romans, though it is largely synonymous with ἵστημι (see next textual note). For πίπτω, "to fall," see the third textual note on 11:11; it occurs also in 11:22. BDAG explains the preceding τῷ ἰδίῳ κυρίῳ as a dative of advantage/disadvantage, *"stand or fall to the advantage or disadvantage of his own master,"* meaning that the slave is *"his own master's concern whether he stands or falls"* (s.v. στήκω, 2).

σταθήσεται—Due to the influence of the common use of Hiphil forms of the Hebrew verb קום to mean "to cause to stand," BDAG appropriately defines ἵστημι here as "to cause to be steadfast, *make someone stand"* (BDAG, A 5). Here it is rendered as "he will be established." For the sense of this future indicative passive, see the commentary.

στῆσαι—This aorist infinitive active of ἵστημι has the causative meaning "to establish," corresponding to the passive in the preceding textual note. See the commentary.

14:5 ὃς μὲν … ὃς δέ—See the first textual note on 14:2.

ἡμέραν παρ᾽ ἡμέραν—The preposition παρά indicates a "comparative advantage, *in comparison to, more than, beyond"* (BDAG, C 3). Thus "one man lays greater weight on one day as compared with another, and thus esteems it more highly."[12] In other words, a person judges one day as greater than or "in preference to" another day.

ἐν τῷ ἰδίῳ νοΐ—This prepositional phrase means "in his own mind." For ἴδιος, "one's own," see the third textual note on 10:3; for νοῦς, see the commentary on 7:23 (see also its use in 1:28; 7:25; 11:34; 12:2).

πληροφορείσθω—For the verb πληροφορέω, see the first textual note on 4:21. This form is a present imperative, which could be either middle or passive in voice. The translation considers it passive: "let him be fully convinced."

14:6 ὁ φρονῶν τὴν ἡμέραν—The verb φρονέω expresses one's mindset or outlook; see the third textual note and the commentary on 8:5; see also 12:3. The definite participle here is substantival: "the one who sets his mind on the day."

14:7 ζῇ—This is a present indicative active of the contract verb ζάω, "to live." In this chapter, ζάω recurs in 14:8 (three times), 9 (twice), 11. The verb appears thematically in the Habakkuk quotation in Rom 1:17. See "The Background and Meaning of 'Life' Words" in the commentary on 1:17.

14:8 ἐάν τε γὰρ ζῶμεν, τῷ κυρίῳ ζῶμεν, ἐάν τε ἀποθνήσκωμεν, τῷ κυρίῳ ἀποθνήσκομεν—The protasis of each of these two conditional statements has ἐάν, "if," with a subjunctive verb (ζῶμεν, ἀποθνήσκωμεν). In the first statement, the identical verb form, ζῶμεν, is repeated in the apodosis (τῷ κυρίῳ ζῶμεν), and this form of the contract verb ζάω, "to live," could be either indicative or subjunctive. Since the apodosis of the second statement has the indicative ἀποθνήσκομεν, "we die," ζῶμεν in the apodosis of the first statement is also likely indicative. The "present indicative in the apodosis" or "then" clause of both statements means that both of these are probably fifth

---

[12] E. H. Riesenfeld, "παρά," *TDNT* 5:734–35.

class conditionals.[13] "The *fifth* class offers a condition the fulfillment of which is realized in the *present time*. This condition is known as the *present general condition*."[14]

ἐάν τε οὖν ζῶμεν ἐάν τε ἀποθνήσκωμεν—BDAG identifies τὲ ... τέ as a "connecter of sentences and parts of sentences that are closely related to each other *as ... so, not only ... but also*" (BDAG, 2 b). The latter suggestion highlights Paul's emphasis (see 14:9). Jesus' blessed lordship encompasses us "not only if we live, but also if we die."

14:9 εἰς τοῦτο—This phrase expresses purpose, "*for this reason* or *purpose*" (BDAG, s.v. εἰς, 4 f).

ἔζησεν—This is the aorist indicative active of ζάω, "to live." See the textual note on 14:7.

ἵνα ... κυριεύσῃ—This construction with ἵνα and an aorist subjunctive is best translated as "so that he might be Lord." BDAG, s.v. ἵνα, 3, notes that "in many cases purpose and result cannot be clearly differentiated, and hence ἵνα is used for the result that follows according to the purpose of the subj[ect] or of God. ... Here ἵνα means both 'in order that' and 'so that.'" Wallace adds: "In other words, the NT writers employ the language to reflect their theology: what God purposes is what happens and, consequently, ἵνα is used to express both the divine purpose and the result."[15] According to Moo "the aorist κυριεύσῃ is almost certainly ingressive."[16] But this should be qualified since Jesus did not "become" Lord only at his resurrection. The lordship of the Son of God extends from all eternity; see the commentary.

14:10 ἐξουθενεῖς—For "despise," see the second textual note on 14:3. This form is present indicative active second person singular.

παραστησόμεθα τῷ βήματι—"We will present ourselves before the judgment seat." The verb is the future indicative middle of παρίστημι, "we will present ourselves" (cf. 12:1). The prefixed παρά, together with the dative case of τῷ βήματι, explains the preposition "before" in the translation (so also ESV, KJV, NASB, RSV, NRSV). The noun βῆμα describes "a dais or platform that required steps to ascend, *tribunal*" (BDAG, 3), which gives the verb a judicial connotation; see the commentary.

14:11 γέγραπται—For the Scripture citation formula "it stands written," see the fourth textual note on 1:17.

ζῶ ἐγώ, λέγει κύριος—This translates the introductory Hebrew expression חַי־אָנִי נְאֻם־יְהוָה, literally, "[as] I live, utterance of Yahweh" (e.g., Is 49:18). It appears

---

[13] Wallace, *Greek Grammar*, 696; structurally, he views the fifth class condition as "virtually identical" to the broader third class. However, the fifth class "requires a present indicative in the apodosis, while the *third* class can take virtually any mood-tense combination, including the present indicative." He does maintain that "semantically, their meaning is a bit different" in regard to the fulfillment of the condition since the third class views it as "*future*" and "*hypothetical*," whereas the fifth class places it in the present (696–97; see the quote following above).

[14] Wallace, *Greek Grammar*, 697.

[15] Wallace, *Greek Grammar*, 473; see his complete discussion of the matter on 471–74, as well as the fourth textual note on 3:8 and the commentary on 4:16 and 5:20.

[16] Moo, *Romans*, 845, n. 89; so also Cranfield, *Romans*, 708, n. 3.

some twenty times in the LXX,[17] though not in Is 45:23, which is the OT passage Paul quotes here. See the commentary.

κάμψει πᾶν γόνυ—The singular "every knee will bow" reproduces the singular Hebrew clause in Is 45:23. Cf. the fourth textual note on Rom 11:4, which has the singular (γόνυ, "knee") although the Hebrew and the LXX have the plural ("knees," 1 Ki 19:18).

καὶ πᾶσα γλῶσσα ἐξομολογήσεται—Paul's statement in Phil 2:11 is almost identical but has the aorist subjunctive ἐξομολογήσηται in place of the future indicative ἐξομολογήσεται here. The doubly compound verb ἐξομολογέω (ἐκ + ὁμός + λέγω), "to declare openly in acknowledgment, *profess, acknowledge*" (BDAG, 3), can specifically refer to confessing sins (Mt 3:6; Mk 1:5; James 5:16; cf. Acts 19:18) or to the offering of praise to God (Rom 15:9; by Jesus himself in Mt 11:25; Lk 10:21). This form is a future indicative middle, "it will acknowledge itself." This double compound appears again in an OT citation in Rom 15:9. See also the discussion of the compound verb ὁμολογέω (ὁμός + λέγω) in the commentary on 10:9.

14:12 ἄρα [οὖν]—The variant οὖν is included for the translation "consequently then." As in 5:18; 7:3, 25; 8:12; 9:16, 18; 14:19, the phrase "introduces a logical summary of what Paul has been saying."[18]

λόγον δώσει—While literally, "he will give a word," in this idiom, λόγος describes a "*computation, reckoning*," and the clause here entails "a formal accounting, esp[ecially] of one's actions" (BDAG, s.v. λόγος, 2 and 2 a). λόγος in this sense occurs with various verbs. See other examples of the idiom in the commentary.

[τῷ θεῷ]—The manuscript evidence for including "to God" is strong (א A C D), which "makes it difficult to reject the reading."[19] Metzger suggests that copyists could have supplied these two words "in order to clarify the reference of the verb."[20] But that explanation for an addition posits something unnecessary in light of the end of 14:11. The phrase is deemed original and included in the translation.

14:13a μηκέτι οὖν ἀλλήλους κρίνωμεν—The adverb μηκέτι means "*no longer, not from now on*" (BDAG). It appears also in 6:6 and 15:23. The form κρίνωμεν is subjunctive and should be interpreted in a hortatory sense, which functions "to exhort or command oneself and one's associates":[21] "*let us* judge one another no longer."

Commentary

Place and Structure of Romans 14:1–13a

The connection between the opening segment of chapter 14 and what immediately precedes it should be neither overstated nor ignored. The simple conjunction δέ, "as for," in 14:1 does *not* suggest a totally new line of

---

[17] LXX Num 14:28; Is 49:18; Jer 22:24; 26:18 (MT/ET 46:18); Ezek 5:11; 14:16, 18, 20; 16:48; 17:16, 19; 18:3; 20:3, 31, 33; 33:11; 34:8; 35:6, 11; Zeph 2:9 (cf. Moo, *Romans*, 847, n. 108).

[18] Morris, *Romans*, 297, on its use in 7:25.

[19] Metzger, *A Textual Commentary on the Greek New Testament*, 531.

[20] Metzger, *A Textual Commentary on the Greek New Testament*, 532.

[21] Wallace, *Greek Grammar*, 464; see 464–65.

thought. But Dunn's attempt to establish direct continuity, particularly in linking " 'flesh' (13:14) and being 'weak in faith' (14:1 …),"[22] is unconvincing. Cranfield strikes a good balance: "The δέ marks the transition to a new section within the main division 12.1–15.13."[23] At the other end of this section, 14:13 operates as yet another hinge which "forms a bridge between the two halves of chap. 14."[24]

Within 14:1–13a, the main divisions are 14:1–3, 4–9, 10–13a. Paul marks these off by beginning 14:4 and 14:10 with rhetorical questions. Both of them bear a "striking and probably deliberate" resemblance to comparable challenges to "you, every person who judges," in 2:1–3.[25] Moo further observes how 14:1–3 and 14:10–13a restate the issues of dispute "in almost identical language," while the middle section (14:4–9) provides Paul's profound, Gospel-based theological foundation.[26]

Acceptance of One Another, not Judgment! (14:1–3)

Conflict over Convictions (14:1)

"As for the one who is weak in the faith, receive [him] to yourselves, not for judgments over convictions" (14:1). In this opening form of address, the clause "the one who is weak in the faith" is the object of the imperative verb "receive to yourselves." In comparison to the weaker believers whom they are to "receive," those who are to do the action must be, in some sense, stronger in the faith. *Paul thereby directs his opening salvo primarily toward those whom he will later categorize as "strong"* (15:1). In so doing, he likely "implies that the 'strong' were the dominant element in the Roman church."[27]

As indicated in the introduction to 14:1–15:13, the verb "receive to oneself" beautifully frames the discussion (προσλαμβάνω in the middle voice, 14:1, 3; 15:7 [twice]). The form here in 14:1 is taken as a present middle imperative (see the second textual note on 14:1). The same verb appears as an aorist indicative middle in 14:3. The action of προσλαμβάνεσθε (14:1) surely means more than simply "welcome" (RSV, NRSV, ESV).[28] It encompasses the active and complete integration of the weak into the worshiping community and *also* includes them fully in all other formal and informal aspects of fellowship.[29]

Paul defines those who are to be received in the singular, as "the one who is weak in the faith" (τὸν … ἀσθενοῦντα τῇ πίστει 14:1), that is, in respect to

---

[22] Dunn, *Romans*, 797.

[23] Cranfield, *Romans*, 699.

[24] Wright, "Romans," 740; for other hinge verses, see, e.g., 8:1–4; 9:24; 10:4–5, 16–17; 13:7–8; 15:7.

[25] Dunn, *Romans*, 797.

[26] Moo, *Romans*, 835.

[27] Moo, *Romans*, 835.

[28] As Barrett, *Romans*, 256, also maintains.

[29] Cranfield, *Romans*, 700.

the faith. This need *not* mean that the person is weak regarding faith in Christ, the faith which receives the righteousness of God (1:17; 3:22). Thus "weak" does not imply that the person is about to fall from faith.[30] In fact, the description of being "weak" calls to mind how Paul "elsewhere regards human or physical weakness as the very locus of divine power."[31] More pertinent is the antithetical foil provided earlier in Romans 4. Although Abraham was credited with righteousness through faith (Gen 15:6; Rom 4:3), he continued to entertain doubts about the time and manner of the fulfillment of the promises that he would have an heir, possess the land, and become the father of many nations (Gen 15:2, 8; 16:1–16; 17:17–18; cf. Gen 18:11–15). Despite his difficult circumstances—being a century old and the "deadness" of his wife's womb (Rom 4:19)—the power of God's Word prevailed, so he was "*not* weakening in the faith" (μὴ ἀσθενήσας τῇ πίστει, Rom 4:19), but rather "was empowered in the faith" (ἐνεδυναμώθη τῇ πίστει, Rom 4:20). In light of what follows in Romans 14, the "weak" here might be compared to Abraham after he had been called and justified through saving faith (cf. Rom 8:30). He still wrestled with reservations about the manner of fulfillment, yet nevertheless was sustained by the powerful Word. More specifically, the "weak" in Romans 14 lack a full understanding of "the implications of their faith in Christ."[32] They believe in Jesus Christ, the Seed of Abraham, who has fulfilled the OT promises, but they struggle with the manner in which that fulfillment can or should change the daily habits and customs they inherited from the OT.

Paul prohibits the strong from engaging in a behavior described with a prepositional phrase at the end of 14:1 which is difficult to translate accurately (μὴ εἰς διακρίσεις διαλογισμῶν). It may entail "passing judgment on [the weak Christian's] opinions" (NASB) or "scruples."[33] But, as Paul proceeds in 14:3–4, it becomes apparent that actual people are the victims of judgment. An alternative translation forbids the strong from entering into "*quarrels about opinions*" (BDAG, s.v. διάκρισις, 2). But referring to mere "quarrels"[34] or "disputes"[35] also seems too weak, and the use of "opinions" does not communicate well in a postmodern age (which has reduced facts, truths, and doctrines to mere "opinions"). Rather than merely a matter of self-introspection or personal preference,

---

[30] For "fall" in this spiritual sense, see 11:11, 22; 14:4. In none of these passages does Paul refer to a "weak" person who "falls." In fact, in 14:4 it is one of the "strong" (15:1) who potentially "stands or falls," but Paul quickly adds that this person "will be established, for the Lord is able to establish him."

[31] Dunn, *Romans*, 798, citing 2 Cor 4:7–11; 11:30; 12:5, 9–10; 13:4, 9. See also 1 Cor 1:25, 27.

[32] Moo, *Romans*, 836.

[33] Cranfield, *Romans*, 698, 701; Murray, *Romans*, 2:171.

[34] This is also the translation of διακρίσεις by Moo, *Romans*, 833, 836; cf. NRSV: "quarrelling."

[35] This is the translation of Dunn, *Romans*, 795, 798, for διαλογισμῶν; Barrett, *Romans*, 256, takes "disputes" as the literal meaning of διακρίσεις, which he then translates weakly as "discussions."

Paul deals with different *convictions* believers have arrived at regarding issues which have *significant biblical and theological precedents.*

That these involve "judgments" (διακρίσεις, 14:1) stands evident from the *eight appearances of the cognate verb* κρίνω, *"to judge," in this chapter* (14:3, 4, 5 [twice], 10, 13 [twice], 22), accented further by the two culminating compound verbs in 14:23, διακρίνω, "make a distinction," and κατακρίνω, "pronounce a sentence."[36] Thus the translation "judgments over convictions" fits best in 14:1. Dunn nicely captures what Paul seeks to prohibit and why:

> What is in view seems to be the possibility that the majority group in a congregation would see the reception of "the weak in faith" as an opportunity to engage in an argument which, as the majority (and "the strong"), they would be able to arbitrate in favor of the majority opinion. … The liberty of the Christian assembly should be able to embrace divergent views and practices without a feeling that they must be resolved or that a common mind must be achieved on every point of disagreement.[37]

Thus Paul begins by addressing *the strong*, who are remonstrated against *instigating* such arguments; as we will soon see, he also admonishes the weak not to judge (14:3).

Conflicting Convictions over Foods (14:2–3)

What's the Matter with Food? (14:2)

In 14:2 Paul explicitly engages one specific matter over which there are contrary convictions: "On the one hand, [there is one] who believes [he has the freedom] to eat all things, but, on the other hand, the one who is weak is eating vegetables." In the first set of brackets "there is one" assumes a form of the verb "to be" (ἐστίν) prior to the relative pronoun ὅς, "who." In the second set of brackets "he has the freedom" completes the thought of the sentence. Its structure reflects the presence of divergent understandings regarding the applicability of OT food regulations now that the Messiah has come.

The first position, that the believer can "eat all things," presumably is based on the belief that Christ's fulfillment of the OT has rendered all foods "clean." The evangelist interprets the words of Jesus himself during his earthly ministry as asserting this (καθαρίζων πάντα τὰ βρώματα, "cleansing all the foods," Mk 7:19).[38] Subsequently, the account of Acts 10–11 affirms it. There the abolition of OT dietary laws goes hand in hand with the full acceptance of Gentiles into the infant Jewish-Christian church.

The second position, wherein the "weak" Christian is only "eating vegetables," might seem to indicate that the matter at hand simply concerns differences over whether to eat meat or not. Interestingly, "the practice of vegetarianism for

---

[36] See Moo, *Romans*, 838, including n. 51.

[37] Dunn, *Romans*, 798–99.

[38] See Voelz, *Mark 1:1–8:26*, 464, 468.

religious or philosophic reasons was quite well known in the ancient world."[39] But the overall context—the example of holy days (14:5–6), and, most decisively, the use of the technical terms for food that is either "unclean" (κοινός, 14:14 [three times]) or "clean" (καθαρός, 14:20)—indicates that the matter at hand resides in *different convictions regarding the food laws of the OT*.[40]

Thus the one who eats vegetables "probably decided to avoid meat altogether out of a concern to maintain OT laws of purity in a pagan context," where ritually clean meat "was not easily obtained."[41] Such a practice is attested already in the sixth century BC when Judean exiles taken to Babylon refused the royal diet offered them by the pagan king and instead thrived on a diet of vegetables and water (Dan 1:3–16). Observance of the OT dietary laws entailed not only avoiding unclean animals (e.g., Leviticus 11; Deut 14:2–21) but also ensuring that blood was properly drained.[a] The Torah also includes other stipulations about the cooking and consumption of meat and the portions that could or could not be eaten (e.g., Gen 32:32 [MT 32:33]; Ex 12:9; 23:19; Lev 8:31; Deut 14:21). Paul's general language, therefore, encompasses "the whole complex of food laws together."[42] The issue at hand concerns whether Christian freedom allows those in the NT era to eat what was formerly forbidden.

(a) E.g., Lev 3:17; 7:26–27; 17:10, 14; Deut 12:16, 23–24; 15:23; cf. Acts 15:20, 29

Problematic Actions from Both Sides (14:3)

The believers in Rome have arrived at divergent convictions about the relevance of these OT matters. Some assert the propriety of eating all things; others contend that OT food regulations remain normative and prohibit one from doing so. In 14:1, Paul pleads that this issue not become the cause for judgments against the weak. In 14:3, however, the language addresses those on *both sides* of the issue: "The one who eats, let him not despise the one who does not eat; but the one who is not eating, let him not judge the one who is eating, for God received him to himself." Here the "strong" (15:1), the ones who eat everything, *should not look down with disdain* on those who do not, as if the "weak" (14:1–2; 15:1) Christians were in any way inferior or lesser or in need of reproof. Thus Paul prohibits anything akin to the all-too-common condescending modern attitude that "I'm a better/more mature Christian than you are."[43]

---

[39] Dunn, *Romans*, 799, who cites several examples. For additional examples, see J. Behm, "ἐσθίω," *TDNT* 2:690. See also Cranfield, *Romans*, 693–94, n. 5.

[40] See the textual notes and the commentary on 14:14, 20.

[41] Moo, *Romans*, 837. Instead of the biblical category of "clean," Moo uses the later Rabbinic Hebrew terminology of "kosher."

[42] Dunn, *Romans*, 801. Besides biblical texts, Dunn also cites Jewish and early Christian literature where the concern is to avoid eating foods associated with idolatry.

[43] The example of the Rechabites may be instructive (Jeremiah 35). This small group of Israelites went beyond the Law of Moses by creating additional restrictions for themselves. Their father Jonadab the son of Rechab commanded them and their succeeding generations never to drink wine nor plant vineyards or any crops; neither were they to build houses, but live in tents (Jer 35:6–10). Therefore the Rechabites might be compared to the "weak" in Rom 14:1–2. (However, there is no indication that they judged other Israelites who did not observe these

Paul then counters that the weak likewise should not "judge" those who do eat. While fault exists on both sides,[44] Dunn argues effectively that the two negated imperatives, "let him not despise" (μὴ ἐξουθενείτω) and "let him not judge" (μὴ κρινέτω), "should not ... be regarded as synonymous"[45] and that the second verb frequently carries "the stronger note ... of 'condemn.' "[46] Thus in 14:3b Paul countermands a situation in which *the weak condemn the strong for violating a stricture of God's OT Law*, a stricture that Jesus himself has now set aside (Mk 7:19; Acts 10–11). Chrysostom characterizes the circumstances as follows:

> The stronger ones should not look down on the weak or be contemptuous of them. Likewise, those who abstain are not to pass judgment on those who eat. For just as the strong mocked the weak, ... so the others thought that the strong ones were lawbreakers.[47]

Why are both contempt for and judgment against another believer unwarranted and also invalid? It is because "God received him to himself" (ὁ θεὸς γὰρ αὐτὸν προσελάβετο, 14:3). Paul specifies the object of the action with the accusative pronoun "him" (αὐτόν). Grammatically here it refers back to "the one who is eating" everything (τὸν ἐσθίοντα). But the final clause of 14:3 functions more broadly as an expression of "Paul's theological 'bottom line' in this whole issue, one that he elaborates in vv. 4–9 and states again at the climax of his argument (15:7)."[48] The clause personally and powerfully expresses the grace and mercy of *the God who* does not charge sin to our account (Rom 4:7–8, quoting Ps 32:1–2) or condemn those in Christ (Rom 8:1), but, instead, *receives "ungodly" people to himself in Christ* (τὸν ἀσεβῆ, 4:5).

More Improper Judging (14:4–6)

Of the Lord's Servant (14:4)

At the beginning of 14:4, Paul continues to focus his attention on the judgmental attitude of the "weak" (14:1–2; 15:1) toward those he will later call the "strong" (15:1): "You, who are you, the one judging the household servant of another?" (σὺ τίς εἶ ὁ κρίνων, 14:4a). This language sounds reminiscent

---

traditions and who simply kept the Law of Moses; neither does the text suggest that relatively "strong" Israelites who kept only the Law of Moses despised the Rechabites as being "weak." The historical situation was that the majority of the Israelites had become unfaithful and did not abide by the Torah.) God did not render any verdict on the Rechabites' practices, whether they were lawful or commendable or to be repudiated as overly legalistic. Instead, God commended the Rechabites themselves for their fidelity in keeping the traditions passed down by their father. Therefore they would be spared and continue to have descendants after God executed his righteous judgment on the apostate Israelites (Jer 35:17–19).

[44] Moo, *Romans*, 838.

[45] Dunn, *Romans*, 803.

[46] Dunn, *Romans*, 802, citing κρίνω, "to judge," in Rom 2:1, 3, 12, 27; 3:7; 14:4, 10, 22; 1 Cor 5:3, 12–13; 11:31; 2 Thess 2:12.

[47] Chrysostom, *Homilies on Romans*, 25 (Bray, *Romans*, ACCS NT 6:339).

[48] Moo, *Romans*, 838.

of 2:1–5, where Paul admonishes against judging by using the second person singular to address "you, every person who judges" (εἶ, ὦ ἄνθρωπε πᾶς ὁ κρίνων, 2:1). There, however, the apostle's argument was based on the Law itself, whereas here his reasoning resides within the Gospel reality just expressed at the end of 14:3.

While οἰκέτης originally referred to the member of a household, it came to denote a "house or domestic slave … answerable only to his own master."[49] The reason why judging is improper follows: "To his own master he stands or falls, and he will be established, for the Lord is able to establish him" (14:4b). The dative case of "to his own master" (τῷ ἰδίῳ κυρίῳ) docs not express advantage, benefit, or responsibility, which would be directed toward the master.[50] Instead, it expresses relationship,[51] which can be categorized as a dative of "reference."[52] The emphasis rests not simply on whether the slave stands or falls, but that he does so *solely in relationship to his master*, regardless of others who may critique him.

Paul then makes a nice segue by repeating the noun κύριος. The first use in 14:4 refers to a slave's relationship toward his "master" or "lord." So it is too, Paul says, for a servant of the "Lord." The strong believer being judged by the weak believer "will be established, for *the Lord* is able to establish him" (14:4b). Now κύριος clearly has its typical divine referent in Scripture. But does Paul speak of God the Father or of Jesus, his Son? This poses a question which recurs repeatedly in Romans 14:

> The referent of "lord" (κύριος) throughout this passage is not easy to determine. Paul uses the title nine times (and the verb "lord it over" [κυριεύω] once), significantly interchanging it with God (θεός) and Christ (χριστός). …
>
> The ease with which Paul interchanges the titles suggests (1) that he may not have been intending to distinguish clearly in each case his referent, and (2) the degree to which he thought of Christ, Lord, and God on equal terms.[53]

In any and both cases, *the key factor is one's relationship to the Lord, as well as the nature of the servanthood under consideration*. Diodore captures it well: "A servant of Christ is anyone whom Christ has accepted"[54] (see below on 14:9; see also 1:1; 6:19, 22).

---

[49] Dunn, *Romans*, 803.

[50] Cranfield, *Romans*, 703, argues for advantage; Sanday and Headlam, *Romans*, 386, suggest responsibility. For the general category of "dative of interest," see Wallace, *Greek Grammar*, 142–44.

[51] Dunn, *Romans*, 804; Moo, *Romans*, 840, n. 59.

[52] See Wallace, *Greek Grammar*, 144–46.

[53] Moo, *Romans*, 840, n. 61. The nine occurrences of κύριος as a divine title, "Lord," are in 14:4 (second occurrence), 6 (three times), 8 (three times), 11, 14. In the first occurrence in 14:4, the reference is to an earthly "lord, master." The verb κυριεύω, "lord it over/be Lord," appears in 14:9 (and earlier in 6:9, 14; 7:1).

[54] Diodore, *Romans* (Bray, *Romans*, ACCS NT 6:340). Luther elaborates: "The little word 'Lord' simply means the same as Redeemer, that is, he who has brought us back from the devil to

Paul switches between two verbs which basically mean "to stand." In the first part of 14:4 he employs στήκω, but then switches to use ἵστημι twice in the remainder of the verse (see the textual notes). Relevant for the first verb, "he stands" (στήκει, intransitive), is the Hebrew verb קום in the Qal in passages where God's saving grace enables a person to "stand" on Judgment Day (Ps 1:5), during calamities (Ps 20:8 [MT 20:9]), and in his holy presence (Ps 24:3). Since Paul employs the second verb, ἵστημι, in a transitive sense, "to make or enable someone stand; to establish," it can be compared to the Hiphil of קום in passages where God "establishes" his people, that is, he raises them up and preserves them steadfast to life everlasting.[b] The first form of ἵστημι, translated by the passive "will be established," is σταθήσεται, a future indicative passive which grammatically could be utilized in an active but intransitive sense.[55] Moo argues for an intransitive rendering, "he will stand," because "a passive rendering of the verb would tend to duplicate what Paul says in the next clause."[56] However, Jewett observes that the passive "seems more likely because the logic of the passage depends on the power and authority of the lord to determine the status of house slaves."[57] Therefore it is translated passively here (so also KJV, RSV, ESV, NRSV) and understood as a divine or theological passive, i.e., "he will be established" by God.[58] Consequently, it reinforces, and is reinforced by, the final clause of the verse, wherein "the Lord" is named as the one who performs this action. In the last clause, the second instance of ἵστημι clearly has a transitive meaning, "to establish someone," since it takes a direct object (αὐτόν, "him"). With all three "stand" verb forms in 14:4, Paul emphasizes the believer's *relationship with the Lord*. The two forms of ἵστημι magnify the Gospel promise that each believer, credited with the righteousness of faith in Christ already now (cf. 5:9), will indeed stand acquitted on Judgment Day (overruling any presumptuous human judgments).

(b) E.g., Deut 28:9; 29:13 (MT 29:12); Is 49:6; Hos 6:2; cf. 1 Sam 2:8, 35; Ps 113:7

Debating Days (14:5–6)

In 14:5, Paul addresses a different issue, but with much the same phraseology. In addition to disputes over foods, he indicates that there are those in Rome who have come to personal "convictions" on both sides of another issue and that they are engaged to some degree in making "judgments" about it (14:1): "Indeed, on the one hand, [there is one] who judges a day in preference to a day, but, on the other hand, [there is another] who judges every day [alike]" (14:5a). Cranfield notes that many ancient and some modern interpreters interpreted the observance of days in relation to the foods in 14:1–3; if so, certain

God, from death to life, from sin to righteousness, and now keeps us safe there" (LC II 31). See also Middendorf, *Romans 1–8*, 379–80.

[55] See Voelz, *Fundamental Greek Grammar*, 144–46.

[56] Moo, *Romans*, 841, n. 63; so also Dunn, *Romans*, 804.

[57] Jewett, *Romans*, 843.

[58] So also Käsemann, *Romans*, 370; see Wallace, *Greek Grammar*, 437–38.

days were designated for abstaining from meat.[59] But that view seems too narrow.[60] More likely, as Cranfield suggests,[61] the issue was the observance of days specified in the OT, that is, the Sabbath and festival days in the liturgical calendar of Israel, and possibly the early Christians' change of congregational worship from the Sabbath to the Lord's Day, the day of the resurrection, the first day of the week.[c]

The point here does not simply involve a matter of whether one eats and drinks on a certain day, but entails a *preference in regard to the day itself*. A Christian has been prompted to ponder whether a particular day is the same or different in comparison to every other day. Furthermore, "judges" (κρίνει, 14:5) indicates that this does not simply entail what various believers prefer.[62] As with foods, it involves making "a judgment regarding" various days,[63] terminology which permeates the entire section.[64]

Why is a distinction regarding days an issue? While Paul engages the matter of foods in more clarifying detail shortly (see 14:14–15, 17, 20–23), he "does not elaborate" further on what is involved in distinguishing days one from another.[65] Dunn draws this plausible conclusion:

> Paul can express it so concisely and imprecisely because his readers would know well what he was referring to. This clearly implies that the issue is related to the overall situation among the Christian congregations in Rome and no doubt also to the main theme of the letter. That is to say, it is a disagreement which sprang in large part at least from or was expressive of the tensions in Rome between the Gentile- and Jewish-Christian members.[66]

Thus the criteria for judging between both foods and days reside within the Scriptures. It involves *discerning the applicability of relevant OT Laws for NT believers now that the Christ has come.*

The most obvious distinction between days comes from the Third Commandment (or Fourth Word).[67] The *Sabbath* as a day of rest and remembrance stems from creation itself (Gen 2:2–3). It also resides prominently in the Decalogue, receiving extensive explanations: Ex 20:8–11 bases the Sabbath on the creation, while Deut 5:12–15 bases it on Israel's salvation. Observing

(c) See Jn 20:1, 19; Acts 20:7; 1 Cor 16:2; Rev 1:10

---

[59] Cranfield, *Romans*, 705.

[60] See "Identifying the Controverted Issues" in "Who Are the 'Weak' and the 'Strong'? Addressees Again!" in the introduction to 14:1–15:13.

[61] Cranfield, *Romans*, 705.

[62] Moo, *Romans*, 842, n. 68, advocates "prefer."

[63] Dunn, *Romans*, 804.

[64] See the plural of διάκρισις, "judgments," in 14:1; the eight instances of the verb κρίνω, "to judge," in 14:3, 4, 5 (twice), 10, 13 (twice), 22; and the compound verbs διακρίνω, "make a distinction," and κατακρίνω, "pronounce a sentence," in 14:23. See further "Judgments" in the introduction to 14:1–15:13.

[65] Moo, *Romans*, 842.

[66] Dunn, *Romans*, 804.

[67] See "Biblically, 'The Ten Words' (13:9b–c)" in the commentary on 13:8–14.

the Sabbath involves a command of the Law and, therefore, an aspect of obedience to God. The entire issue of the Sabbath became a matter of dispute between Jesus and the Pharisees within the borders of the promised land (see Mk 7:1–23).[68] But it was no less so among the scattered Jewish communities. "Within the diaspora the importance of the sabbath ... is underlined ... by the concern of Josephus and Philo to document the right of sabbath observance granted to Jewish communities in Asia (Josephus, *Ant[iquities]* 14.241–46, 258, 263–64) and Rome (Philo, *Legat.* [*On the Embassy to Gaius*] 155–58)."[69]

In addition to the Sabbath, the entire *annual festival calendar* in OT Scripture also established a difference in days. This means that the different convictions in Rome also involved the propriety of observing the other holy days such as Passover and Unleavened Bread, Firstfruits, Weeks, Trumpets, the Day of Atonement, and Tabernacles as laid out together in Leviticus 23. As with the Sabbath, therefore, the matter at hand for God's people involves obedience to the Law.

The issue of days (the Sabbath and festival observances) remains a factor throughout the rest of Paul's treatment of the weak and the strong up until 15:7. However, it is most interesting that *from here on Paul makes specific references only to foods* (14:14–15, 17, 20–23). He does not again mention anything specific in regard to days. This would seem to indicate that the convictions and the judgments being made in Rome are more fiercely contested over foods. As a result, a few concluding comments about these OT holy days are offered here.

A Theology of Days

Both diet and days deal with prominent scriptural mandates, albeit from the OT. The NT alters these elements (similarly, the sacrifices, priesthood, temple, etc.) *only in and through Christ.*[70] Elsewhere, the NT asserts that we are freed from the *requirement* to keep the Sabbath as prescribed in the OT only because Jesus, the Lord of the Sabbath, has fulfilled it (Mk 2:23–28; cf. Heb 4:1–11).[71] Similarly, we need not observe the OT Passover because "Christ, our Passover Lamb, has been sacrificed" (1 Cor 5:7). The same, then, extends to the other festivals. But the believer remains *equally free to continue observing* the Sabbath and other festivals as holy days to the Lord so long as they are not made into or regarded as requirements for righteousness. Indeed, Paul himself willingly

---

[68] See Voelz, *Mark 1:1–8:26*, 448–74.

[69] Dunn, *Romans*, 805.

[70] See the excursus "Beyond Typology" following the commentary on 12:1–8.

[71] See Voelz, *Mark 1:1–8:26*, 222–24; he describes how Jesus "*changes the entire orientation*" (222). He adds (223):

> Jesus brings the eschatological reign and rule of God to earth (Mk 1:15), and that in a way that is fundamentally transforming. As (will be) described in [Mk] 7:1–23 (and expressed explicitly in 7:19), and as developed extensively in the letters of St. Paul (see, e.g., Gal 2:17–21; 6:15; Phil 3:3; Col 2:16–17 [cf. Acts 10:11–15]), *specifically old covenant configurations of belief and practice no longer obtain within the new creation.*

does so in order to avoid having his conduct get in the way of proclaiming the Gospel or living out the fellowship it gives among those who continue to live according to the OT (see 1 Cor 9:19–23).

The importance of the matters being engaged here and their impact on overall biblical theology should not be diminished. Dunn, for example, downplays the Sabbath and festivals as matters merely involving "ethnic identity and devotion to ancestral custom."[72] But, first, the issue at hand concerns the ongoing relevance of liturgical rites mandated by the OT Scriptures. Second, Paul deals with the most basic question of whether one even observes holy days at all; he does not even broach the subject of *how* one might keep the Sabbath or other festivals.[73] Therefore, contemporary issues of dispute involving the manner of worship according to ethnic or national customs do not rise to the level of those addressed here. These could involve largely cultural matters (e.g., language or instrumentation in worship); they could also involve denominational traditions (e.g., adherence to a particular church-year calendar, specific liturgical orders, or a lectionary system, as well as the commemoration of saints' days). Such matters reside below the threshold of the biblical mandates dealt with in 14:1–15:7. How much less, then, should they become criteria for judging others. The Formula of Concord offers this reminder:

> We believe, teach, and confess that no church should condemn another because it has fewer or more external ceremonies not commanded by God, as long as there is mutual agreement in doctrine and in all its articles as well as in the right use of the holy sacraments, according to the familiar axiom, "Disagreement in fasting does not destroy agreement in faith."[74]

For further applications, see "Romans 14:1–15:7—Summary and Application" at the end of the commentary on 15:1–7.

Both Practices Can Be God Pleasing (14:5b–6)

Remarkably, Paul not only allows for but also *defends and even commends the practice of both positions* with this caveat: "Let each one be fully convinced [πληροφορείσθω] in his own mind" (14:5b; see also 14:22b–23). Paul here retrieves a verb he used in 4:21 to describe Abraham's exemplary faith: "And, after being fully convinced [πληροφορηθείς] that what was promised [by God] and still in effect, he [God] is powerful also to do." Thus one's own observance or nonobservance of OT regulations concerning foods and festivals should be *rooted in one's faith relationship with the Lord, rather than in judgmental comparisons with or criticisms of others.*

---

[72] Dunn, *Romans*, 805.

[73] Maschke, *Gathered Guests*, 72, more broadly observes: "During the time of the New Testament, Christians worshiped in various ways, though little is actually recorded in Scripture."

[74] FC Ep X 7, quoting Irenaeus, *Epistle to Victor*, quoted in Eusebius, *Ecclesiastical History*, 5.24.13.

Paul elaborates upon how fully convinced convictions on both sides can be properly practiced in 14:6: "For the one who sets his mind on a day, sets [it] to the Lord. And the one who eats is eating to the Lord, for he gives thanks to God; and the one who does not eat is not eating to the Lord, and he gives thanks to God" (14:6). If "the one who sets his mind on a day" (ὁ φρονῶν τὴν ἡμέραν) describes those who continue to observe the OT Sabbath and festivals, then Paul initially depicts the position of the "weak" (14:1–2; 15:1), proceeds to the strong ("the one who eats"), and returns back to the weak ("the one who does not eat"). But the opening clause of 14:6 may somewhat ambiguously convey either or both mindsets regarding days.[75] If so, Paul's initial statement encompasses both positions, either setting one's mind on each day as the same or continuing to distinguish between them.

Paul clearly covers both sides in regard to the eating of or abstinence from foods in the second half of 14:6. The key evidence of being firmly convinced regarding either conviction does *not*, after all, involve human observance toward God (now that Christ has declared all foods clean [Mk 7:19]), but resides in "thankful dependence on God."[76] The giving of.thanks (εὐχαριστέω) certainly includes "the blessing spoken at meals,"[77] as when this verb is used of Paul in Acts 27:35 (cf. 1 Cor 10:30).[78] Both the eating of previously forbidden foods and restricting one's diet to foods declared "clean" in the OT should certainly include receiving them with thanksgiving. But an attitude of gratitude ought not be restricted merely to a mealtime prayer; it encompasses every area of life (1 Tim 4:4–5). More importantly, an all-inclusive and ongoing relationship with God in Christ permeates all of the believer's life (Rom 12:1–2).

Paul expresses this in 14:6 by the repeated datives "to the Lord" and "to God" (κυρίῳ ... τῷ θεῷ). Moo contends that they "are almost universally—and correctly—taken as datives of 'advantage' "[79] However, Paul can hardly envision the believer's behavior on either side of these issues as being " 'in the interest of,' 'for the benefit of,' the Lord," as Moo suggests.[80] We can do nothing to benefit God or increase his advantage. On the contrary, and as Paul goes on to describe, *the issue is whether the believer is fully convinced about his behavior*

---

[75] Dunn, *Romans*, 806, allows for this possibility; Moo, *Romans*, 843, agrees if the verb φρονέω, "set one's mind," is given "a general or neutral meaning."

[76] Dunn, *Romans*, 807.

[77] Dunn, *Romans*, 807; see also H. W. Beyer, "εὐλογέω," *TDNT* 2:760–61; H. Conzelmann, "εὐχαριστέω κτλ.," *TDNT* 9:410.

[78] Cf. also the uses of εὐχαριστέω, for Jesus "giving thanks" before he fed the five thousand (Jn 6:11 [cf. Jn 6:23]) and the four thousand (Mt 15:36; Mk 8:6) and when he instituted the Lord's Supper (Mt 26:27; Mk 14:23; Lk 22:19 [cf. Lk 22:17]; 1 Cor 11:24).

[79] Moo, *Romans*, 843, n. 78; so also Cranfield, *Romans*, 706.

[80] Moo, *Romans*, 843.

in relationship to his God and Lord.[81] Therefore, as Moo himself asserts in regard to the earlier dative in 14:4 (τῷ ἰδίῳ κυρίῳ, "to his own master"): "The issue here is not the 'benefit' derived by the Lord from the Christian's service but the integrity of the relationship between 'lord' and servant. The dative is better seen, then, as a dative of reference."[82] It seems inexplicable that one should not acknowledge the same sense in 14:6 as in 14:4. This is particularly so within the broader context of a letter where Paul repeatedly excludes from righteousness the performance of human works toward God. How much less, then, could our thanksgiving somehow be "for the benefit of" the Lord? Even more persuasively, the immediate context goes on to assert that everything revolves from and around one's relationship with the Lord Jesus. It is based solely on what he has done *for our benefit* (14:9) and, then, expresses itself in our relationship to him and with one another in and through him (14:8).

The Heart of the Matter: We Are Never Alone in the Lord (14:7–9)

> [7]Indeed, no one of us lives to himself, and no one dies to himself. [8]For not only if we live are we living to the Lord, but also if we die we die to the Lord. Therefore not only if we live, but also if we die, we are the Lord's. (14:7–8)

Paul's whole point in the discussion of diet and days continues to be relational. Selfishly living for oneself certainly contradicts God's will. But the point is *not* really "living for someone (or something's) benefit."[83] In other words, the fundamental issue does not involve our own *doing*, even when directed nobly toward God or others.

On the contrary, a greater and gracious reality prevails. The matter of ultimate importance, regardless of which position we advocate regarding food or days, resides *first and foremost in who we are. We belong to the Lord* (14:4). This theological underpinning explains why we live and die "to the Lord" (τῷ κυρίῳ, 14:8), "because we belong to Him both in life and in death."[84] Thus the dative "to the Lord" (τῷ κυρίῳ) in 14:8 maintains the relational sense of reference as with the dative "to his own master" (τῷ ἰδίῳ κυρίῳ) in 14:4 and the datives in 14:6, "to the Lord" (κυρίῳ, three times) and "to God" (τῷ θεῷ, twice). See also "living to God in Christ Jesus" (ζῶντας δὲ τῷ θεῷ ἐν Χριστῷ Ἰησοῦ) in 6:11. "Neither life nor death shall ever From the Lord His children

---

[81] Lenski, *Romans*, 823, buttresses the point in 14:6 textually as follows:

> Note that the emphasis is on the three Κυρίῳ ["to the Lord"] (minus the article = *Yahweh*, God) and on the two τῷ Θεῷ ["to God"]. This, Paul would say, is the right attitude and the right way: each "in his own mind" concerned about *God*.

[82] Moo, *Romans*, 840, n. 59; see also Wallace, *Greek Grammar*, 144–46.

[83] As Dunn, *Romans*, 807, maintains; BDAG, s.v. ζάω, 3 b, describes this use as "*for the other's benefit.*"

[84] Cranfield, *Romans*, 707.

sever."[85] Even death itself is no big deal. Believers do not grieve as those without hope (1 Thess 4:13) because their belonging to the Lord transcends death itself (Rom 8:38–39).

Paul's *introduction of the first person plural "we"* in 14:8 bears a *second fundamental* truth. Whether in living or in dying, a believer is never an isolated "I"-land. *We* live in his love together. Thus being in Christ has an added and eternal benefit, our interrelationship with one another. After all, "we, the many, are one body in Christ, and, [as] the [body], each one members of one another" (12:5).

How did we come to belong to Jesus? Rom 14:9 explains with this double statement which expresses both purpose and result (see the third textual note on this verse): "For to this [end] Christ died and lived [again] so that he might be Lord of both [the] dead and [the] living ones." Here "for to this" (εἰς τοῦτο γάρ) points forward to what follows and "so that" (ἵνα) further emphasizes the impact. Paul's simple portrayal of Jesus' resurrection here is unique (cf. Rev 2:8): he uses the single Greek word ἔζησεν, "he lived" (from ζάω), rather than the more familiar verbs ἐγείρω, "raise" (e.g., Rom 4:24–25; 6:4; 7:4), or ἀνίστημι, "rise" (e.g., Lk 24:7, 46; 1 Thess 4:14), which some manuscripts have here.[86] But this formulation serves to match the five other uses of the verb ζάω, "live," in 14:7–9. Thus Paul beautifully *ties the death and resurrected life of Christ*, which he considers to be "essentially one complex event"[87] (see 4:23–25), *together with another event, our own death with him in Baptism and the renewed life which springs forth from it* (6:3–4; cf. 1 Pet 1:3).

While Jesus' lordship as the eternal Son of God extends from all eternity (e.g., Ps 110:1; Col 1:15–17), his death and return to life have resulted in his acclamation as "Lord" (see κύριος in Rom 10:9, 13). The verb (κυριεύω) in the clause "so that he might be Lord" (ἵνα ... κυριεύσῃ) might also be interpreted to signify that Jesus has now been designated Lord in power "out of [his] resurrection from [the] dead" (1:4).

The genitive phrase "of both [the] dead and [the] living ones" does not merely assert "the completeness of [his] lordship" or the fact that no one "escapes his rule."[88] Neither does Paul emphasize here that "all parts of believers' lives ... are to be carried out with a view to what pleases and glorifies the Lord."[89] Instead, Chrysostom points in the right direction: "For nothing escapes his lordship. ... Christ put down his own life for our salvation. Having gone

---

[85] Carolina Sandell Berg, "Children of the Heavenly Father" (*LSB* 725:3; © Augsburg Publishing House; used by permission).

[86] In place of ἔζησεν, a few manuscripts (F G 629) read ἀνέστη. Others manuscripts have both verbs. But Metzger, *A Textual Commentary on the Greek New Testament*, 531, concludes that "the oldest and best attested reading appears to be ἀπέθανεν καὶ ἔζησεν (א* A B C ...)."

[87] Cranfield, *Romans*, 708.

[88] As Dunn, *Romans*, 808, maintains.

[89] As Moo, *Romans*, 844, maintains.

to so much trouble and expense, he is not likely to consider us as being of no value."[90] Paul seeks to emphasize that "everyone who ever might call on the name of [the] Lord" (10:13) lives and also dies united "in Christ Jesus our Lord" (6:23; 8:39).[91] As Theodore of Mopsuestia puts it, we always belong together "under his custody,"[92] a most blessed corporate relationship in which we are never alone. In fact, his most gracious lordship encompasses all who belong to him, *both* all of those who have died in the faith[93] *and* all of those who still live in this age, *as well as* those yet to come who will be baptized and will believe.[94] *Paul thus reasserts our Gospel-rooted relationship with Jesus and with one another in him.* In this context, his Gospel reminder effectively serves "to relativize the disputes on food and days within the perspective of God's overarching purpose in Christ."[95]

Therefore, No Judging! (14:10–13a)

After providing the proper theological and relational basis for whose and who we are, Paul returns to rebuke behavior which would be inconsistent with our gracious, common identity: "But you, why are you judging your brother? Or you, why are you also despising your brother?" (14:10a). As throughout much of the letter, the lively diatribe style cannot be reduced to the notion that Paul addresses some fictive or imaginary person. On the contrary, he continues to utilize it in order to effectively engage actual people in the audience who exhibit the characteristics being portrayed.[96] Here he returns to the verbs of 14:3 and, in reverse order, now directs his challenge to the weak who "judge" and then the strong who "despise." In both cases, they do so against one who is "your brother" (τὸν ἀδελφόν σου, 14:10a; cf. Lk 15:32). This designation for a fellow Christian reappears for the first time since Rom 12:1. "Brother" then recurs in 14:13, 15, 21. It sets the context for the judging and despising *within* the very body of Christ. Moo even suggests that "Paul's direct and lively style creates the

---

[90] Chrysostom, *Homilies on Romans*, 25 (Bray, *Romans*, ACCS NT 6:344).

[91] For the significance of variations of this phrase, particularly throughout Romans 5–8, see Middendorf, *Romans 1–8*, 378–79. Luther expresses the point well in the Large Catechism:

> The little word "Lord" simply means the same as Redeemer, that is, he who has brought us back from the devil to God, from death to life, from sin to righteousness, and now keeps us safe there. (LC II 31)

[92] Theodore of Mopsuestia, *Romans* (Bray, *Romans*, ACCS NT 6:343).

[93] Jesus' counterargument for the resurrection asserts that believers who have died (specifically the patriarchs) nevertheless remain "living": God "is not the God of the dead, but of the living" (Mt 22:32; Mk 12:27; Lk 20:38).

[94] Paul's phrase "[the] dead and [the] living" (Rom 14:9) has the reverse order of the phrase "the living and the dead" in Acts 10:42; 2 Tim 4:1; 1 Pet 4:5 (also the Apostles' and Nicene Creeds). The most plausible explanation is that Paul here matches the order of his reference to Jesus' death and resurrection earlier in the verse; so Moo, *Romans*, 845–46.

[95] Dunn, *Romans*, 808.

[96] See the introduction to Romans 2; the commentary on 2:1–5 and 2:17; and the discussion of the addressees in the introduction to 14:1–15:13.

picture of the apostle shifting his gaze from the 'weak' to the 'strong' as he publicly chastises these representative Christians from the Roman community."[97]

Accountability before God (14:10b–12, Quoting Is 45:23)

All Will Give an Account (14:10b, 12)

Not only does their behavior stand contrary to the Good News of Jesus' death and resurrection "for us men and for our salvation" (Nicene Creed; 14:9), but it is also ominously inappropriate for believers in view of what lies ahead.

> [10b]For we will all present ourselves before the judgment seat of God. [11]Indeed, it stands written: " '[As] I live,' the Lord says, 'to me every knee will bow, and every tongue will acknowledge itself to God.' " [12]Consequently then, each one of us will give an account concerning himself to God. (14:10b–12)

Here 14:10b and 14:12 articulate the same truth. The verb and noun for "presenting oneself" before a "judgment seat" in 14:10b clearly have forensic connotations.[98] The verb παρίστημι "is well known in the papyri in the judicial technical sense of appearing in court before a judge" (as in Acts 27:24).[99] So also the noun βῆμα describes a raised platform used for delivering public speeches and pronouncements "and hence the tribunal of a magistrate or judge (again very common in the papyri)."[100] Although "Paul is the only NT author to appropriate the term for theological purposes,"[101] he clearly employs "judgment seat" (βῆμα) to depict God's throne on the Last Day. Origen notes: "The judgment seat of God is the same thing as the judgment seat of Christ, to which Paul refers when writing to the Corinthians" (τοῦ βήματος τοῦ Χριστοῦ, 2 Cor 5:10).[102] The very *public* place of judgment in Rom 14:10b carries an "implied contrast to the more insidious carping and snide comments made in the 'in-group' language of

---

[97] Moo, *Romans*, 846.

[98] Compare the forensic connotations of Paul's pervasive language of being "credited" (λογίζομαι) with "righteousness" (δικαιοσύνη). See especially 4:1–12; see also "The Background and Meaning of 'Righteousness' Words" in the commentary on 1:17 (Middendorf, *Romans 1–8*, 92–96; see also 106–7); and in this volume, see "Righteousness Returns" and "Righteousness Defined" in the introduction to 9:30–10:15. See also "Legal" in the excursus "Paul's Gospel Metaphors" following the commentary on 4:1–12 (Middendorf, *Romans 1–8*, 341).

[99] Dunn, *Romans*, 808–9.

[100] Dunn, *Romans*, 809, citing for its use in this sense in the NT Mt 27:19; Jn 19:13; Acts 12:21; 18:12, 16–17; 25:6, 10, 17 (cf. Acts 12:21; 2 Cor 5:10). Kruse, *Romans*, 518, further observes:

> It may be significant that [Paul] refers to it both in 2 Corinthians and here in Romans, a letter written from Corinth, for according to Acts 18:12 it was in Corinth in the time when Gallio was proconsul of Achaia that Paul was brought before his judgment seat.

[101] Moo, *Romans*, 846, n. 104.

[102] Origen, *Romans* (Bray, *Romans*, ACCS NT 6:344–45). Moo, *Romans*, 847, n. 105, points out that some manuscripts assimilate the last phrase of Rom 14:10 to 2 Cor 5:10 by replacing "the judgment seat of *God*" (τοῦ θεοῦ) with that "of *Christ*" (τοῦ Χριστοῦ). But Metzger, *A Textual Commentary on the Greek New Testament*, 531, properly concludes that "God" (θεοῦ) "is supported by the best witnesses (א* A B C* D …)."

one group about the other."[103] Paul's words continue to deliver the same admonition to *all* those who engage in any kind of judgmental or contemptuous talk against one another in the family of faith. Unfortunately, such behind-the-back sniping persists to this day.

The *universal expressions* which permeate Romans resurface prominently here.[104] "All" (πᾶς, 14:10; see also "every" twice in 14:11) will appear on that day before that seat of judgment where each and every one of us (ἕκαστος ἡμῶν) "will give an account [λόγον δώσει] concerning himself to God" (14:12). The idiom "give an account [λόγος]" is financial, "to give an account or make an accounting" (see the second textual note on 14:12). Jesus utilizes it in his parables (Mt 25:19; Lk 16:2) and also applies it specifically to our speech: "Every worthless word which they speak, people will give an account for it [ἀποδώσουσιν περὶ αὐτοῦ λόγον] in the Day of Judgment" (Mt 12:36).

Paul clearly teaches that believers have been declared righteous freely by God's grace apart from anything they do (e.g., Rom 3:23, 28; 4:4–5). Salvation remains a gift given for the sake of Christ (e.g., 3:24; 5:15, 16, 17; 6:23; Eph 2:8–9). But the notion that "anything goes" abuses his grace (see 6:1–4). *Baptized believers remain responsible to God for how they conduct themselves as his people in this world.* Especially inappropriate, Paul insists, is judging and despising others within the community of faith on matters from which Christ has freed us. Who would want to have to answer for that before the ultimate Judge of all (see 2:1–6)?

As "the Lord Says" (Is 45:23 in Rom 14:11)

Paul reinforces this reality in 14:11 by citing the Lord's own Word from Is 45:23. Aside from an alteration in word order (πᾶσα γλῶσσα and ἐξομολογήσεται are transposed), the main quote represents the LXX identically.[105] However the introductory statement is not present in the LXX text of Isaiah, where the verse begins with the oath formula "I swear according to myself" (κατ᾽ ἐμαυτοῦ ὀμνύω, LXX Is 45:23). Nevertheless, the formula quoted by Paul, " '[as] I live,' says the Lord," replicates "a formula which occurs quite frequently in the prophets."[106] Thus it is not necessary to resort to explaining its inclusion here as an inadvertent substitution by Paul, who supposedly was "quoting from memory," of one common OT formula (" '[as] I live,' says the Lord") for another ("I swear according to myself").[107] The statement serves appropriately here, adding yet another form of the verb "to live" (ζάω), which

---

[103] Dunn, *Romans*, 809.

[104] See Middendorf, *Romans 1–8*, 50.

[105] The Hebrew of this portion of Is 45:23 reads:

כִּי־לִי תִּכְרַע כָּל־בֶּרֶךְ תִּשָּׁבַע כָּל־לָשׁוֹן

Because to me every knee will bow; every tongue will swear.

[106] Dunn, *Romans*, 809. See the second textual note on 14:11.

[107] As Cranfield, *Romans*, 710, asserts.

occurred six times in 14:7–9. Paul might have selected this formula to hint that "the Lord" who says "I live" (14:11) is the same "Lord," that is, "Christ," who "died and lived" (14:9).[108]

The actual portion of Isaiah quoted is "to me every knee will bow, and every tongue will acknowledge itself to God." Just prior to making that assertion, Yahweh pronounces: "There is no god besides me, a righteous God and Savior. ... By myself I have sworn. From my mouth has gone forth a word of righteousness, and it will not return" (45:21b, 23a).[109] One need not insist that the specific referent of "Lord" (κύριος) earlier in Rom 14:11 is Jesus, although it could be. As noted above (see the commentary on 14:4), Paul freely interchanges references to God the Father and the Lord Jesus throughout this section, using "Lord" (κύριος) for both (and for the Spirit elsewhere, e.g., 2 Cor 3:17–18). Furthermore, no tension exists between maintaining both "the lordship of Christ and the ultimate authority of God."[110] Therefore, one need not be troubled by the appellation of the same Isaiah verse to Jesus himself in Phil 2:10–11. He is one with the Father, the Lord Yahweh, who spoke to and through Isaiah (see, e.g., Jn 8:58; 10:30; see the commentary on Rom 10:9, 13).[111]

In this context, the portion cited from Isaiah provides an all-inclusive buttress to Paul's warning. The compound verb translated as "acknowledge" in 14:11 (ἐξομολογέω) carries the same meaning as the simple verb (ὁμολογέω) does in 10:9 (see the commentary there).[112] The singular future middle form of the verb here now conveys the truth that every person will give an account *for himself or herself* before Yahweh's throne. The repeated use of "every" (πᾶς) reinforces the notion that no person's tongue will be exempt from acknowledging itself to God (14:11; cf. Phil 2:10–11).

Conclusion: No More Judging! (14:13a)

Since this is the case, 14:13a "sums up succinctly the exhortation of the preceding paragraph. It may also be seen as the conclusion to be drawn from what has been said in vv. 10c–12."[113] "Therefore let us judge one another no longer" (14:13a). The command to cease judging in matters where God no longer does (as in 14:3, 4, 10) now comes immediately following a reminder of the harsh consequences for doing so. All of this stands in full concert with an admonition from Jesus himself: "Do not judge, so that you might not be judged. For in

---

[108] Black, *Romans*, 167, claims that this was Paul's "clear intention." If it was Paul's intention, then, as Black concludes, "it is to the Risen and Living Lord that every knee shall bow" (cited with reservations in Cranfield, *Romans*, 710, including n. 2).

[109] This is the translation of Lessing, *Isaiah 40–55*, 357.

[110] Dunn, *Romans*, 810, argues that Paul in this chapter seems to want to maintain a balance between the two.

[111] Lenski, *Romans*, 830, explains: "All men shall acknowledge God as God; in more detail, 'that Jesus Christ is Lord, to the glory of God the Father,' Phil. 2:11."

[112] Lenski, *Romans*, 830, defines it well as "make out-and-out acknowledgment."

[113] Cranfield, *Romans*, 711.

whatever judgment you judge, you will be judged" (μὴ κρίνετε, ἵνα μὴ κριθῆτε· ἐν ᾧ γὰρ κρίματι κρίνετε κριθήσεσθε, Mt 7:1–2).

In closing, an important caveat about judging ought to be stated, particularly in a postmodern culture where any and all judging, particularly by followers of Jesus, is deemed to be contrary to statements by Jesus and Paul. The fundamental point pertains to *who* judges. Jesus makes it emphatically clear that we humans do not. However, God has expressed his own judgments regarding numerous things quite clearly in his Word. Thus, while it would be wrong for believers to make judgments based upon their own standards, *it is not wrong to pronounce God's revealed judgments when appropriate* (see "Contemporary Cultural Complexities" in the excursus "Paul and the Law" following the commentary on 13:8–14). Indeed, we *must* do so if we are to remain salt and light in this world.[114] Augustine expresses the distinction well:

> Paul says this [Rom 14:4] so that, when something might be done with either good or bad motives, we should leave the judgment to God and not presume to judge the heart of someone else, which we do not see. But when it comes to things which obviously could not have been done with good and innocent intentions, it is not wrong if we pass judgment. ... In the case of that abominable immorality where a man had taken his stepmother, Paul taught us to judge [1 Cor 5:1–5]. For that man could not possibly claim that he committed such a gross act of indecency with good intentions. So we must pass judgment on things which are obviously wrong.[115]

---

[114] See Mt 5:13–16; yet note also Jesus' admonition "have salt in yourselves, and *be at peace with one another*" (Mk 9:50).

[115] Augustine, *Commentary on Statements in Romans*, 79 (Bray, *Romans*, ACCS NT 6:340).

To the Strong in Christ:
Do Not Become a Stumbling Block;
Build Up in Christ Instead!

Translation

14 ¹³Therefore let us judge one another no longer. But, rather, judge this: not to place a [cause for] stumbling or offense to [your] brother. ¹⁴I know and I have been persuaded and remain convinced in the Lord Jesus that nothing is unclean through itself, except to the one who considers something to be unclean; to that person [it is] unclean. ¹⁵For if on account of food your brother is being grieved, you are no longer walking according to love. Do not by your food destroy that person in behalf of whom Christ died. ¹⁶Therefore do not let that which is for your good be slandered.

¹⁷Indeed, the kingdom of God is not eating and drinking, but righteousness and peace and joy in [the] Holy Spirit. ¹⁸For the one who serves [as a slave] to the Christ in this [is] well-pleasing to God and tested and approved by people.

¹⁹Consequently then, we are pursuing the things of peace and the things of the building up for one another. ²⁰Do not, for the sake of food, tear down the work of God. On the one hand, all things are [ritually] clean, but [they can be] a bad thing for the person who eats through stumbling. ²¹[It is] better not to eat meat nor to drink wine nor [to do anything] in which your brother stumbles. ²²[As for] you, [the] faith which you have in accord with yourself, have before God.

Blessed is the one who is not judging himself in what he approves. ²³But the one who makes a distinction, if he eats, he has pronounced a sentence upon himself and remains under judgment because [the eating is] not from faith. And everything which is not from faith is sin.

Textual Notes

14:13 μηκέτι οὖν ἀλλήλους κρίνωμεν—The adverb μηκέτι means *"no longer, not from now on"* (BDAG). It appears also in 6:6 and 15:23. The form κρίνωμεν is a hortatory subjunctive:[1] *"let us* judge one another no longer."

ἀλλὰ τοῦτο κρίνατε μᾶλλον—Paul repeats the verb κρίνω, "judge," but in the form of an aorist imperative. Its direct object, the neuter demonstrative pronoun τοῦτο, "this," is explicated in the next clause.

τὸ μὴ τιθέναι ... τῷ ἀδελφῷ—The articular infinitive with the neuter article (τό) is in apposition to the neuter τοῦτο, "this," and, therefore, makes explicit the direct object

---

[1] See Wallace, *Greek Grammar*, 464–65.

of the imperative κρίνατε, "judge." The present infinitive of τίθημι means "to put" or "place." "Those persons are added, in the dat[ive], to whose advantage or disadvantage the example is given" (BDAG, s.v. τίθημι, 1 b θ). Here the dative τῷ ἀδελφῷ is of disadvantage; "to the brother" is to his detriment (πρόσκομμα, "stumbling"). The article τῷ functions as a possessive pronoun:[2] "[your] brother." The pronoun σου, "your," is included in relation to "the brother" in 14:10, 15, 21.

πρόσκομμα—Previously Paul used this neuter noun in conjunction with λίθος, "rock of stumbling" (9:32, 33), but here the accusative noun stands alone as "a [cause for] stumbling," as also in 14:20. See the fifth textual note on 9:32. It is cognate to the verb προσκόπτω, "stumble," in 14:21.

ἢ σκάνδαλον—The neuter noun σκάνδαλον, "scandal, offense," is a synonym of the preceding noun πρόσκομμα; the two were used together also in 9:33. See the third textual note on 9:33. σκάνδαλον appears also in 11:9; 16:17.

14:14 πέπεισμαι—For the significance of this verb and its perfect passive form, see the first textual note and the commentary on 8:38.

κοινόν—The Greek adjective κοινός can refer to that which is held in "common" (Acts 2:44; 4:32; cf. *Koine* Greek), including the Christian faith (Titus 1:4) and salvation (Jude 3). But more often it represents the OT category "unclean," referring particularly to unclean foods (its three instances in this verse; also Acts 10:14, 28; 11:8).[3] Regulations for animals—and their meat as food—deemed "unclean" (Hebrew טָמֵא), which also rendered the person eating them "unclean," are the main concern of Leviticus 11, although additional legislation about "unclean" things and persons is given in Leviticus 12–15; Numbers 19; and other passages (e.g., Deut 14:7–10; cf. also Judg 13:4; Ezek 22:26; 44:23; Hos 9:3). Jewish tradition extrapolated from the OT categories to impose further rituals, e.g., the hand-washings in Mk 7:2–5, to avoid being what they considered "unclean" (κοινός, Mk 7:2, 5). Since the NT regularly uses the adjective καθαρός for the category of "clean" (see the third textual note on 14:20), one might have expected its negated form with *alpha* privative, ἀκάθαρτος, to be the preferred adjective for "unclean." It and the adjective used here in Rom 14:14 are employed as synonyms by Peter in regard to foods in Acts 10–11 (κοινὸν καὶ ἀκάθαρτον, Acts 10:14; κοινὸν ἢ ἀκάθαρτον, Acts 10:28; 11:8), with the implication that Gentiles have now been rendered "clean" through Christ. In the NT ἀκάθαρτος is frequently used to describe evil spirits as "unclean,"[4] but κοινός usually serves to describe people and foods that are "unclean."[5]

δι' ἑαυτοῦ—Literally, "through itself," this prepositional phrase contains a reflexive pronoun as its object. Wallace points out that in this "especially common" use of a

---

[2] See Wallace, *Greek Grammar*, 215–16.

[3] Its sense is stronger in Heb 10:29, where it means that an apostate treats Jesus' blood of the covenant as "profane, unholy," and in Rev 21:27, where it refers to unbelievers as unfit to enter the new Jerusalem.

[4] E.g., Mk 1:23, 26, 27; see Voelz, *Mark 1:1–8:26*, 159–63.

[5] See Voelz, *Mark 1:1–8:26*, 452–54.

reflexive pronoun, it "overlaps to some degree with the intensive pronoun."[6] Thus, in context, the phrase implies something like "in and of *itself*."

τῷ λογιζομένῳ—For λογίζομαι, which occurs nineteen times in the letter, see the first textual note on 2:3. When humans are the subject, a translation other than "credit" becomes necessary. In such cases, this commentary regularly uses "count" to maintain the financial connotations (e.g., 2:3; 6:11; 8:18, 36). However, in the context of personal convictions (14:1), "consider" makes better sense (cf. 3:28). The verb form here is an articular substantival participle[7] in the dative, translated as "to the one who considers."

τι κοινὸν εἶναι—This clause defines the object of τῷ λογιζομένῳ as "something [τι] to be [εἶναι] unclean [κοινόν]." εἶναι is the present infinitive of εἰμί. For κοινόν, see the second textual note on 14:14.

14:15 εἰ … λυπεῖται—The particle εἰ, "if," with an indicative verb forms the protasis of a first class conditional sentence, which is assumed, for argument's sake, to be true.[8] See the commentary for the contextual significance. For the verb λυπέω BDAG gives definitions such as "*be sad, be distressed*" and translates it in this verse as "feelings are hurt" (BDAG, 2 b). However, the verb's force is surely stronger, for spiritual peril is at stake! In light of the severity of the situation, BDAG also offers a better option, "*grieve*" (BDAG, 2 b), a term associated with mourning at a death. See the commentary for a fuller explanation, as well as Luther's astute observation regarding the verb's meaning and its passive form.

διὰ βρῶμα—The preposition διά with the accusative often denotes cause, "*because of*" (BDAG, B 2 a) or "on account of." The neuter noun βρῶμα (from the verb βιβρώσκω, "eat," as in Jn 6:13) is a general term for anything "which is eaten, *food*" (BDAG, 1). It recurs later in 14:15 and again in 14:20. Cf. βρῶσις in the second textual note on 14:17.

περιπατεῖς—The apodosis of a first class conditional can have a verb of any tense and mood; this form is present indicative. For περιπατέω, "walk," as daily conduct, see the seventh textual note on 6:4; see also 8:4; 13:13.

μὴ τῷ βρώματί σου ἐκεῖνον ἀπόλλυε—"Do not by your food destroy that person." The verb ἀπόλλυμι in the active voice means "*ruin, destroy*" (BDAG, 1 a). The present imperative in the prohibition does not simply mean "stop destroying," as if that were progressive or already happening. Instead, it functions as a general, ongoing precept, which seeks to prohibit such an outcome[9] (see the first textual note on 11:18 and the last textual note on 11:20). The dative τῷ βρώματι expresses means: "by food."[10]

ὑπὲρ οὗ Χριστὸς ἀπέθανεν—The prepositional phrase ὑπὲρ οὗ means "in behalf of whom." Χριστὸς ἀπέθανεν, "Christ died," is used with the preposition ὑπέρ also in 5:6, 8. See the third textual note on 5:6 and the commentary on 5:6–8.

---

[6] Wallace, *Greek Grammar*, 350.

[7] See Wallace, *Greek Grammar*, 619–21.

[8] See Wallace, *Greek Grammar*, 690–94.

[9] See Wallace, *Greek Grammar*, 724–25.

[10] See Wallace, *Greek Grammar*, 162–63.

14:16 μὴ βλασφημείσθω—The present imperative in a prohibition conveys a general precept, as in 14:15 (see the fourth textual note there). For the verb βλασφημέω, "blaspheme," see the textual note on 2:24 and the second textual note on 3:8. The third person imperative here could be either middle or passive voice; the passive is indicated by the syntax as it has a subject (ὑμῶν τὸ ἀγαθόν) but no object. The term βλασφημέω "is regularly used in the NT with respect to God, his name, the Spirit, and Christ."[11] "In relation to transcendent or associated entities," BDAG gives "*slander, revile, defame, speak irreverently/impiously/disrespectfully of or about*" (BDAG, b). That fits the verb's use in 2:24. Here, however, its use is closer to the present passive in 3:8 ("we are being slandered"; see the second textual note on 3:8) as the action is not directed toward God himself, but toward his people or, here, to "things that constitute the significant possessions of Christians" (BDAG, b η; as also in Titus 2:5; 2 Pet 2:2). They are being "slandered." For the subject of the derision, see the next textual note.

ὑμῶν τὸ ἀγαθόν—This phrase denotes "that which is for your good." The article τό functions as a relative pronoun.[12] The genitive ὑμῶν expresses possession, "your."[13] See the commentary.

14:17 ἡ βασιλεία τοῦ θεοῦ—Although "the kingdom of God/heaven" is prominent in the Synoptic Gospels, references to the "kingdom" (βασιλεία) of God and/or Christ occur only fourteen times in Paul.[14] Normally, the reference is to the coming kingdom.[15] But here, in 1 Cor 4:20; Col 1:13; and, probably, 1 Thess 2:12, the kingdom is regarded as already present (see the commentary).

βρῶσις καὶ πόσις—These two nouns are paired in the same order in Jn 6:55; Col 2:16. The noun βρῶσις may be a synonym of βρῶμα, "what is eaten, food" (see the second textual note on 14:15), but here it more likely refers to "the act of partaking of food, *eating*" (BDAG, 1). If so, then πόσις likewise refers to the "act of drinking" (BDAG, 1), although it may denote what is drunk, "drink."

14:18 ὁ ... δουλεύων τῷ Χριστῷ—BDAG defines the verb δουλεύω as "to act or conduct oneself as one in total service to another, *perform the duties of a slave, serve, obey*" (BDAG, 2). The one to whom the service is rendered is given in the dative, τῷ Χριστῷ, "to the Christ" (cf. other datives used with this verb in 6:6; 7:25; 9:12; 12:11; 16:18). See the discussion of δοῦλος Χριστοῦ Ἰησοῦ, "a slave of Christ Jesus," in the first textual note and the commentary on 1:1 and the section titled "Everybody's Serving Someone (6:15–16)" in the commentary on 6:12–23.

ἐν τούτῳ—The meaning of the prepositional phrase is clear: "in this." But to what does "this" refer? See the commentary for a discussion of various possibilities.

---

[11] Moo, *Romans*, 855, n. 31.

[12] See Wallace, *Greek Grammar*, 213–15.

[13] See Wallace, *Greek Grammar*, 81–83.

[14] Paul's other references to the "kingdom" of God occur in 1 Cor 4:20; 6:9, 10; 15:24, 50; Gal 5:21; Eph 5:5 ("the kingdom of Christ and God"); 4:11; 1 Thess 2:12; 2 Thess 1:5; Christ's "kingdom" is also in Col 1:13; 2 Tim 4:1, 18.

[15] Moo, *Romans*, 857, n. 40.

εὐάρεστος—For this adjective, "well-pleasing," see the seventh textual note on 12:1; the only other occurrence in Romans is in 12:2.

δόκιμος—BDAG defines this adjective as "being genuine on the basis of testing, *approved (by test), tried and true, genuine*" (BDAG, 1). To convey its full meaning the translation uses two English terms, "tested and approved." See the discussion of the cognate noun δοκιμή, "tested character," in the textual note and the commentary on 5:4. On the human level, the term then extends "to being considered worthy of high regard, *respected, esteemed … among people* (in contrast to God)" (BDAG, 2).

14:19 ἄρα οὖν—See the first textual note on 14:12 for this phrase, "consequently then."

τὰ τῆς εἰρήνης—The two sequential forms of the definite article (τὰ τῆς) here and later in the verse (see the fourth textual note on 14:19) might at first seem odd grammatically, but the combination occurs with some regularity; see τὰ τῆς also in 8:5 and τὰ τοῦ in 2:14; 8:5.[16] The first, τά, is accusative neuter plural, "the things." The second, τῆς, is genitive feminine singular and modifies the feminine noun in the genitive, εἰρήνης, "of peace."

διώκωμεν—This presents a difficult textual problem. Did Paul write the indicative διώκομεν with a short "o" connecting vowel or the subjunctive διώκωμεν with a long "o" connecting vowel? The textual variation, when combined with other factors, renders this situation comparable to the ἔχομεν/ἔχωμεν debate in 5:1 (see the fourth textual note and the commentary on that verse).[17] However, the matter here provides a mirror image. In this instance, the best manuscripts (א A B) support the indicative διώκομεν, "we are pursuing," which also presents the more difficult reading, since one expects a hortatory subjunctive,[18] "let us pursue." The subjunctive connects better moving forward toward the imperative κατάλυε in 14:20, though it is in the second person and singular (whereas the verb here is first person plural). The indicative mood, however, aligns with the previous statements in 14:17 and 14:18. Metzger also points out that "elsewhere in Romans the phrase ἄρα οὖν [see the first textual note on 14:19] is always followed by the indicative (5.18; 7.3, 25; 8.12; 9.16, 18; cf. 14.12)." Nevertheless, his committee "felt that, on the whole, the context here calls for the hortatory subjunctive (cf. the imperatives in ver. 13 and ver. 20)."[19] In this commentary, however, the usual text-critical rules are followed: the better attested and more difficult indicative reading, "we are pursuing," is adopted.

τὰ τῆς οἰκοδομῆς τῆς εἰς ἀλλήλους—For τὰ τῆς, see the second textual note on 14:19. The feminine noun οἰκοδομή literally describes the "process of building,

---

[16] For additional examples, see Wallace, *Greek Grammar*, 235–36. Wallace, 235, describes this sequence as "the neuter plural article with a genitive, where the neuter article implies 'things.'"

[17] Lenski, *Romans*, 844, who considers the subjunctive to be the original reading, comments: "Some good texts have the indicative instead of the hortative subjunctive: 'we pursue,' we make this our rule of life. This is the same kind of a variant as that found in 5:1. The scribe wrote short *o* for long *o*."

[18] On the hortatory subjunctive, see Wallace, *Greek Grammar*, 464–65.

[19] Metzger, *A Textual Commentary on the Greek New Testament*, 532.

building, construction" (BDAG, 1). But Paul commonly uses it figuratively for "spiritual strengthening ... *edifying, edification, building up*" (BDAG, 1 b), as also in Rom 15:2; five times in 1 Corinthians; and four times each in 2 Corinthians and Ephesians. The following phrase with the repeated feminine genitive singular definite article, τῆς εἰς ἀλλήλους, modifies the feminine noun, "the building up for one another."

14:20 μὴ ... κατάλυε—The verb καταλύω, "tear down," can have the literal meaning of razing a building (cf. Mt 24:2; Acts 6:14) or refer to the destruction of people, e.g., the overthrowing of Christians and their faith (Acts 5:39) or the destruction of the body at death (2 Cor 5:1). The construction with the negated present imperative forms another general precept prohibition; see the fourth textual note on 14:15. It would also apply to action in progress of course: "if you are destroying, stop it!" But the stronger meaning is to make it your ongoing aim never to destroy any of God's work.

ἕνεκεν βρώματος—For the preposition ἕνεκεν, see the second textual note on 8:36, its only other use in Romans. It indicates the "cause of or reason for someth[ing]" and means *"because of, on account of, for the sake of"* (BDAG, s.v. ἕνεκα, 1). For the noun βρῶμα, see the second textual note on 14:15.

πάντα μὲν καθαρά—In this context, the adjective καθαρός refers to the OT category of being "clean," and it is the antonym of κοινός, "unclean"; see the second textual note on 14:14 and the passages cited there. The translation includes "ritually" in brackets to indicate this is a theological category, not a matter of hygiene. Cognate to the adjective here is the verb καθαρίζω, "to cleanse" or "to render someone 'clean,' " used in the Gospels to describe Jesus healing lepers (e.g., Lk 5:12–13; 7:22; 17:14–17), since that disease rendered one "unclean" in the OT sense (see Leviticus 14). In Mk 7:19 the verb καθαρίζω indicates that Jesus "declared all foods to be 'clean.' "[20] See "Jesus Said So" in the commentary on Rom 14:14.

τῷ ἀνθρώπῳ τῷ διὰ προσκόμματος ἐσθίοντι—The main sense is clear, "to/for the person who eats," but the prepositional phrase διὰ προσκόμματος is difficult. For the noun πρόσκομμα, "(cause of) stumbling," see the fourth textual note on 14:13. BDAG identifies διά here as indicating "attendant or prevailing circumstance" and translates the clause as *"eat with offense* (to the scruples of another)" (BDAG, A 3 c; see 2:27; 4:11b). The statement then references the action of the "strong" (15:1), who eat foods that the "weak" (14:1–2; 15:1) still consider as "unclean" (14:14) and thereby cause the weak to stumble. For further explanation and the implications, see the commentary.

14:21 καλὸν τὸ μὴ φαγεῖν κρέα μηδὲ πιεῖν οἶνον—The adjective καλός means "beautiful" or "excellent"; see the third textual note on 7:16; see also 12:17. Here the adjective with the articular infinitives has a comparative sense, "better" (BDAG, 2 d γ). The negated articular infinitives function as the grammatical subjects in the Greek:[21] "not to eat meat nor to drink wine is better," although the translation is adjusted to accommodate English idiom ("[it is] better not to ..."). The neuter noun κρέας, used

---

[20] For an analysis of the Greek vocabulary for "clean" and "unclean" in the LXX and the NT, see Voelz, *Mark 1:1–8:26*, 452–54.

[21] See Wallace, *Greek Grammar*, 600–601.

in the NT only here and in 1 Cor 8:13, means "meat" (BDAG). The common masculine noun οἶνος denotes "wine."

μηδὲ ἐν ᾧ ὁ ἀδελφός σου προσκόπτει—This clause generically extends the sense of the previous two articular infinitive clauses beyond the consumption of "meat" and "wine": "nor [to do anything] in which your brother stumbles." For the verb προσκόπτω, "to stumble," see the fourth textual note on 9:32. It is cognate to the noun πρόσκομμα, "(cause of) stumbling," in 14:13, 20.

14:22 σὺ πίστιν [ἣν] ἔχεις—The singular pronoun σύ, "you," emphasizes the subject of the singular verb ἔχεις, "you have," both by its redundant presence and by its emphatic placement at the beginning of the sentence. The object of the verb is πίστιν, "faith," which clearly pertains to an aspect of Christian faith, although the clause does not specify its basis or nature. When πίστις lacks specification, it can refer to a "*firm commitment*" (BDAG, 2 d) or to "true piety, genuine devotion" (BDAG, 2 d α). Here Paul speaks of the conviction of one's own Christian faith regarding the disputed matters of food and drink.

Textual evidence strongly supports the inclusion of the relative pronoun ἥν (ℵ A B C): "you, [the] faith *which* you have." If absent, the clause reads more smoothly as a statement ("you, you have faith") or, perhaps, even a question ("you, do you have faith?").[22] But the weight of the textual evidence and the more awkward reading with the relative clause both point to the relative pronoun being original.[23]

κατὰ σεαυτόν—The preposition κατά here expresses "isolation or separateness, *by ... keep someth[ing] to oneself*" (BDAG, B 1 c), or, in this case, specifically to "yourself." This could be understood in terms of privacy, "keep to yourself" (cf. ESV). However, the literal translation "in accord with yourself" conveys the sentiment expressed by the NASB's interpretive rendition "have as your own conviction." In this case, the conviction of the strong regarding freedom to eat and drink all foods should be "in accord with," that is, in agreement with the faith relationship one has with God.

ἔχε ἐνώπιον τοῦ θεοῦ—The verb ἔχε here is an imperative: "*have* before God." For ἐνώπιον τοῦ θεοῦ as a *coram Deo* expression, see 3:20.

μακάριος—For the adjective "blessed," see the first textual note and the commentary on 4:7; the only other occurrence in Romans is in 4:8.

ἐν ᾧ δοκιμάζει—BDAG notes that the verb δοκιμάζω can mean "to draw a conclusion about worth on the basis of testing, *prove, approve*, here the focus is on the result of a procedure or examination" (BDAG, 2). More specifically, the sense here is "*accept as proved, approve*" (BDAG, 2 b).

14:23 ὁ δὲ διακρινόμενος—BDAG provides a wide spectrum of possible definitions for the verb διακρίνω, a compound of κρίνω, "to judge," which appears eight times in Romans 14.[24] For this verse, BDAG prefers "to be uncertain, *be at odds w[ith] oneself, doubt, waver* (this m[eaning] appears first in NT)" (BDAG, 6). Paul uses the verb in

---

[22] See Metzger, *A Textual Commentary on the Greek New Testament*, 533.

[23] So Cranfield, *Romans*, 726; Käsemann, *Romans*, 378; Moo, *Romans*, 849, including n. 3; Sanday and Headlam, *Romans*, 393.

[24] Rom 14:3, 4, 5 (twice), 10, 13 (twice), 22. See "Judgments" in the introduction to 14:1–15:13.

that sense to assert that Abraham "did not waver into unfaith" (οὐ διεκρίθη τῇ ἀπιστίᾳ, 4:20). But here other, more common definitions fit better, for example, "to evaluate by paying careful attention to, *evaluate, judge*" (BDAG, 3; see 1 Cor 11:31; 14:29) or, even better, "to conclude that there is a difference, *make a distinction, differentiate*" (BDAG, 2; see Acts 15:9; 1 Cor 4:7). The application here is to "the one who makes a judgmental distinction" between clean and unclean foods.

ἐὰν φάγῃ—The particle ἐάν with the subjunctive φάγῃ (irregular aorist of ἐσθίω) forms a conditional: "if (ever) he eats." The present impact of the perfect indicative κατακέκριται in the apodosis ("then" clause; see the next textual note) gives it the force of a fifth class condition, which, if realized, would be "realized in the *present time*."[25]

κατακέκριται—For the compound verb κατακρίνω, see the fifth textual note on 2:1; it occurs also in 8:3, 34. Note that, like διακρίνω (see the first textual note on 14:23), it is a compound of κρίνω, "to judge." Here the verb is intensified by the prefixed preposition κατά to mean "pronounce a sentence after determination of guilt, *pronounce a sentence on*" (BDAG, s.v. κατακρίνω). The form is perfect middle/passive. The sense of the middle applies well here ("upon *himself*"), and the perfect tense implies an ongoing result ("remains"). Therefore it is translated as "he has pronounced a sentence upon himself and remains under judgment."

ὅτι οὐκ ἐκ πίστεως—The prepositional phrase ἐκ πίστεως, "from faith," represents one of the thematic statements of the letter. It appears twice in 1:17 (see the commentary there) and also twice in this verse. Here the prepositional phrase is negated with οὐκ and the conjunction ὅτι is causal: "because not from faith." This four-word phrase also appeared in 9:32 but is found nowhere else in the NT (although οὐκ ἐκ πίστεως occurs in James 2:24).

Commentary
Romans 14:13–23—Structure

Rom 14:13 operates as yet another hinge; it "forms a bridge between the two halves of chap. 14, introducing the new theme, which is the positive side of Paul's exhortation" in the first half.[26] Dunn divides 14:13–21 into three parts (14:13–15, 16–18, 19–21); each begins with οὖν, "therefore/consequently," and "features bluntly expressed negative warnings ('Do not …')."[27] As in 14:1–13, Moo does a better job of keeping the Gospel at the center of Paul's argument. He summarizes Paul's thought as follows:

His basic exhortation is found at the beginning and at the end of the text—"don't cause a weaker Christian to stumble" (vv. 13b–16 and vv. 19–23)—while

---

[25] Wallace, *Greek Grammar*, 697, who subsumes this under the third class condition; for further details, see 696–97 and the first textual note on 14:8.

[26] Wright, "Romans," 740; for other hinge verses, see 8:1–4; 9:24; 10:4–5, 16–17; 13:7–8; 15:7.

[27] Dunn, *Romans*, 816.

a central section sets forth the basic theological rationale for his exhortation—the nature of the kingdom of God (vv. 17–18).[28]

The words of Christ also remain prominent as Paul continues to provide "consistent echoes of Jesus' teaching";[29] for example, compare Rom 14:13 with Mt 7:1–2; Rom 14:14 with Mt 17:27; Rom 14:15 with Mk 7:18–19; and Rom 14:17 with Mt 6:33.

To the Strong (14:13b–16)

Cause No Stumbling; Give No Offense (14:13b)

The concluding exhortation of 14:1–13a properly admonishes both factions in the Christian community: "Therefore let us judge one another no longer" (14:13a). The second portion of the verse has a narrower target. Instead of judging (κρίνωμεν, i.e., condemning), *Paul particularly calls the strong* (although Paul waits until 15:1 to call them οἱ δυνατοί, "the strong") in his audience to make a different judgment (κρίνατε, 14:13b)—*to resolve or determine not to trip up a "weak" fellow believer* (he had labeled such a believer "the one who is weak in the faith" in 14:1; similarly, 14:2): "But, rather, judge this: not to place a [cause for] stumbling or offense to [your] brother" (14:13b).

Paul retrieves two essentially synonymous nouns, "(cause for) stumbling" (πρόσκομμα) and "offense, scandal" (σκάνδαλον), utilized already in 9:32–33, which he derived from Is 8:14 (quoted in Rom 9:33). There Christ himself was "a stone of stumbling and a rock of offense" (9:33) to those in Israel pursuing "their own" righteousness (10:3) "as if [it could be attained] from works" (9:32; similarly, 1 Pet 2:8). In chapter 9 unbelievers found the Gospel scandalous.[30] While the word picture remains the same in chapter 14, all parties here are baptized believers in Christ. Now the *skandalon … is that which arises as a result of differences of conviction in the Pauline churches.*[31] The context here applies to the negative impact one believer might have upon another (see 14:15, 21). This interpersonal dimension coincides with Paul's use of the noun "stumbling" (πρόσκομμα) in 1 Cor 8:9 and the verb "cause offense, scandalize" (σκανδαλίζω) in 1 Cor 8:13, a verb Jesus employs comparably in Mt 18:6.

This common terminology provides further evidence for how Paul's argument continues to parallel what he wrote earlier to the Corinthians (see

---

[28] Moo, *Romans*, 850; he further recognizes this chiastic structure in "the two exhortation sections" (14:13b–16 and 14:19–23): A (14:13b) and A' (14:21) warn against becoming a stumbling block; B (14:14a) and B' (14:20b) acknowledge all foods as clean; and C (14:15b) and C' (14:20a) are commands against ruining the work of God in Christ. Dunn, *Romans*, 816, sees a similar chiastic structure in 14:13–23 and then (817) points out how "the closing verses of chap. 14 pick up the themes of the opening": compare 14:1 and 14:23; 14:2a and 14:22a; 14:3 and 14:22b.

[29] Dunn, *Romans*, 817.

[30] G. Stählin, "σκάνδαλον κτλ.," *TDNT* 7:352, refers to "the σκάνδαλον ['offense, scandal'] of the Gospel."

[31] G. Stählin, "σκάνδαλον κτλ.," *TDNT* 7:355.

"Identifying the Controverted Issues" in the introduction to 14:1–15:13). However, the divisive matters in Rome are different from the eating of meat offered to Gentile idols in Corinth.[32] In Rome Paul deals with the ongoing applicability of OT regulations within and among the house churches.[33] The issue would be most acute for Jewish Christ-believers, although some Gentiles too may have been inclined to adhere to OT strictures. The most prominent concern is the OT categorization of foods, though instructions governing the Sabbath and other holy days remain in play (see 14:5–6). Yet Paul's personal conviction and his assessment of the "weak" remain the same (compare Rom 14:1–2, 14–15 to 1 Cor 8:4–12).

Affirming Jesus' Declaration with Qualification: No Food Is Unclean (14:14)

"I know and I have been persuaded and remain convinced in the Lord Jesus that nothing is unclean through itself, except to the one who considers something to be unclean; to that person [it is] unclean" (14:14; cf. 1 Cor 8:4–7). Paul begins this statement with a unique and emphatic *quadruple* emphasis: (1) "I know" (οἶδα); (2) "I have been persuaded" (the past aspect of the perfect πέπεισμαι); (3) "I remain convinced" (the present aspect of the perfect πέπεισμαι); and (4) "in the Lord Jesus" (14:14a). Paul employs the perfect tense verb πέπεισμαι identically in 8:38 and 15:14. While Dunn overlooks the two distinct aspects of the perfect and counts 2 *and* 3 as a single element, "[I] am convinced," he helpfully points out that "the nearest parallels have only two out of the three elements used here—Gal 5:10; Phil 1:25; 2:24; and 2 Thess 3:4."[34]

Unclean No More!

Paul himself is definitely certain that, in and of themselves, no foods remain "unclean" (14:14). He uses the Greek adjective κοινός in a distinctly OT sense.[35] In Mk 7:2, 5, the same adjective describes what the Pharisees considered to be ritually "unclean."[36] Furthermore, all of the NT instances of the cognate verb κοινόω have the meaning "to render/declare (something or someone) [ritually]

---

[32] On the issue in Corinth, see Lockwood, *1 Corinthians*, 271–74.

[33] As discussed in the commentary on 14:1–13a.

[34] Dunn, *Romans*, 818.

[35] See the second textual note on 14:14.

[36] The Pharisaic hand-washing ritual described in Mk 7:2–5 is not in the Law of Moses nor any other OT passage. Rather, as Jesus indicates in Mk 7:6–9, it was of human origin, part of the tradition handed down by the Jewish elders. Later rabbinic Jewish sources, whose composition began some two centuries after Christ (the Mishnah, compiled ca. AD 200, and the later Gemara, together forming the Talmud, ca. AD 600), would claim that the Jewish traditions of the elders had been given in oral form to Moses on Sinai, and this "oral Torah," considered just as authoritative as the written Torah, supposedly was passed down by word of mouth until the compilation of the Talmud. The Pharisees believed that their hand-washing tradition was needed to preserve the same distinction between "clean" and "unclean" that is in the regulations actually in the (written) Torah. See Voelz, *Mark 1:1–8:26*, 455–56, 466; he includes quotations on this topic from Josephus and the Mishnah.

unclean."[37] These NT words reflect the categories of "clean" and "unclean" in the Law of Moses.[38] Even after the resurrection and ascension of Christ, Peter, likely representative of the early Jewish Christians, initially deemed it vital to maintain these categories; when God offered him "unclean" foods he protested: "I have never eaten anything unclean or unclean" (the synonyms κοινὸν καὶ ἀκάθαρτον, Acts 10:14). Paul, therefore, does not speak simply to matters of indifference, but to those with strong biblical precedence.[39] The ecclesiastical term "adiaphora" (ἀδιάφορα) technically refers to "ceremonies and church rites which are neither commanded nor forbidden in the Word of God" (FC SD X 1). Romans 14, however, reflects the transitional period of the early NT era, when the question is whether the dietary and calendrical observances commanded and forbidden in the OT still remain in force or whether they have been fulfilled and/or transformed in and through the coming of Christ (see the excursus "Beyond Typology" following the commentary on 12:1–8). If they have been fulfilled in Christ, *have some OT commandments now moved into the category of NT adiaphora?*[40]

In 14:14, Paul asserts that now "nothing" (οὐδέν) is "unclean" (κοινός). He soon reinforces the point positively by adding that all things are "clean" (καθαρά, 14:20), much as the evangelist interprets the words of Jesus (καθαρίζων, Mk 7:19).[41] Such passages cannot be cited in order to buttresses the postmodern attitude expressed already by Shakespeare: " 'There is nothing either good or bad' morally, 'but thinking makes it so.' "[42] That would take Paul's words completely out of their context. His repeated references to "food" (βρῶμα, 14:15, 20) and "eating" (βρῶσις, 14:17) evaluated by the Levitical categories of "clean" (14:20) and "unclean" (14:14) clearly indicate the specific contextual application. Together these terms provide "almost indisputable

---

[37] This is the precise meaning of κοινόω, even though English versions typically use the shorter translation "to defile." Moo, *Romans*, 852, n. 14, cites the NT verses that have the verb κοινόω: Mt 15:11, 18, 20; Mk 7:15, 18, 20, 23; Acts 10:15; 11:9; 21:28; Heb 9:13. He adds that the adjective κοινός, "unclean," is "not used in this way in the earlier parts of the LXX; but see, e.g., 1 Macc. 1:47, 62; and Josephus, *Ant[iquities,]* 12.112; 13.4." See the more detailed presentation in Voelz, *Mark 1:1–8:26*, 452–54.

[38] Cranfield, *Romans*, 713, affirms that here κοινός means "ritually unclean" and represents the Hebrew טָמֵא. Sanday and Headlam, *Romans*, 390, add that κοινός functions as "the technical term to express those customs and habits, which, although 'common' to the world, were forbidden to the pious Jew," citing 1 Macc 1:47, 62; Josephus, *Antiquities*, 13.4. See further the second textual note on 14:14.

[39] Käsemann, *Romans*, 374–75.

[40] Regarding adiaphora, see also "Broader Implications of the Discussion" in the commentary on 14:20–22a below and "Romans 14:1–15:7—Summary and Application" in the commentary on 15:1–7.

[41] Voelz, *Mark 1:1–8:26*, 468–74, not only explains Mk 7:19 but also furnishes profound theological reflections regarding the Law and the Christian life.

[42] Cranfield, *Romans*, 713; he notes (713, n. 4) that "the words quoted refer, as they are used by Hamlet to Rosencrantz in *Hamlet* 2.2.259, not, of course, to what is morally good or morally bad, but to what is pleasing or unpleasing."

proof that the discussion moves within the context of distinctively Jewish concerns."[43] *Therefore, questions regarding the specific nature of the conflict which divides the Roman community are decisively answered* (see the introduction to 14:1–15:13). *Paul deals explicitly with OT laws regarding foods and days*, and *not* with the Decalogue or OT Law as a whole, which he recently did in Rom 13:8–10.

Underlying the food laws in Leviticus is its whole conception of God's holiness and his sanctification of his people through the liturgical and sacramental rites he prescribed for the sanctuary in which he dwelt.[44] Not only did the distinctive dietary practices maintain "a clear line of demarcation ... between the holy community and those outside,"[45] but, more importantly, only people in the state of being "clean" were able to enter into the realm of the "holy" to commune with God; the "unclean" could not. Now, however, Jesus is the new temple (Jn 2:19–22), the locus of holiness, the Holy One of God (Jn 6:69; 1 Jn 2:20), the one who cleanses and sanctifies his people through his Word and Sacraments.[a] He does so in a more perfect way than the OT rites and ceremonies. Since they were given to testify to Christ and to be accomplished and surpassed by his person, work, and ongoing ministry, literal obedience to them is no longer necessary.[46] Indeed, *Jesus himself has fulfilled all the Law and the entirety of the OT.*[47]

(a) See, e.g., Mt 11:5; Lk 17:14–17; Jn 13:10; 15:3; 17:17; Acts 15:9; Eph 2:21; 5:26–27; Titus 3:5; Heb 2:11; 10:19, 22; 13:12

Jesus Said So

Upon what does Paul base his conclusion that no food remains unclean? His understanding resides "in the Lord Jesus" (ἐν κυρίῳ Ἰησοῦ, 14:14). Cranfield presents a number of options for grasping the force of this prepositional phrase:

* It is drawn from "his fellowship with the risen and exalted Christ."

* "It was consonant with God's self-revelation in Jesus Christ as a whole, that is, with the gospel."

* "Its truth rested on the authority of the risen and exalted Christ."

* "We certainly cannot rule out the possibility that he had in mind some specific teaching of the historic Jesus."[48]

---

[43] Dunn, *Romans*, 818, speaking specifically of κοινός, "unclean."

[44] For an exemplary explication of the Levitical theology of "unclean," "clean," and "holy," see Kleinig, *Leviticus*, 1–13.

[45] Dunn, *Romans*, 819.

[46] Cf. Cranfield, *Romans*, 713–14.

[47] See the commentary on 8:4 and 10:4; see also the excursus "Beyond Typology" following the commentary on 12:1–8. For a broad theological exposition of how Jesus has now rendered the "unclean" to be "clean," see Voelz, *Mark 1:1–8:26*, 448–74. In his final comments on Mk 7:1–23, Voelz (470–71) says this of the new covenant: "For such a covenant, the law code of regulations not only *can* be abrogated, but *it actually must be abrogated for the visions of the prophets to be fulfilled.*"

[48] Cranfield, *Romans*, 712.

Cranfield, Dunn, and Moo all reference Paul's use of the personal name "Jesus" as, perhaps, indicative of the last option.[49] Franzmann adopts and explicitly articulates this view: "He knows that Jesus Christ his Lord has 'declared all foods clean' (Mark 7:19), and so pork is a good gift of God to him."[50]

Indeed, one can point specifically to Mt 15:10–20 and Mk 7:14–23 since "the point Paul is making in the first half of this verse [Rom 14:14] is essentially the same as that made in Mk 7.15a"[51] (and Mt 15:11a). The words of Jesus in Mt 15:11a are slightly more concise: "the thing that enters into the mouth does not defile the person" (οὐ τὸ εἰσερχόμενον εἰς τὸ στόμα κοινοῖ τὸν ἄνθρωπον).[52] The wording of Mk 7:15a is somewhat fuller: "nothing outside of the person is going into him which is able to make him unclean" (οὐδέν ἐστιν ἔξωθεν τοῦ ἀνθρώπου εἰσπορευόμενον εἰς αὐτὸν ὃ δύναται κοινῶσαι αὐτόν). Mark then elaborates that Jesus' words have the effect of "cleansing all foods" or "declaring all foods clean" (καθαρίζων πάντα τὰ βρώματα, Mk 7:19).[53] Novatian concludes:

> It is evident that all these foods enjoy again the blessings they received at their creation, now that the law has ended. We must not return to the legal prohibition of foods commanded for certain reasons and which evangelical liberty, setting us free from its bondage, has now discontinued.[54]

Dunn labels as "surprising" the "unwillingness of the earliest community of Jesus' disciples in Jerusalem to follow what, according to Mark 7:15, was unequivocal teaching (cf. Acts 10:14; 11:2–3; Gal 2:12)."[55] But more than a millennium of biblical precedent and practice,[56] as well as a desire to not offend

---

[49] Cranfield, *Romans*, 712–13; Dunn, *Romans*, 818; Moo, *Romans*, 853.

[50] Franzmann, *Romans*, 245.

[51] Cranfield, *Romans*, 713.

[52] The translation is from Gibbs, *Matthew 11:2–20:34*, 767. Matthew's account lacks a parallel to Mark's comment that Jesus by his words was "cleansing all foods" (Mk 7:19). Instead, at the conclusion of the Matthew passage Jesus returns to the Pharisaic hand-washing tradition (a tradition not found in the OT) and expressly refutes it: "to eat with unwashed hands does not defile a person" (Mt 15:20b). Gibbs (778–79) interprets Jesus in Mt 15:10–20 as invalidating the human laws of the Pharisees, but not yet as teaching his disciples that the Mosaic food laws were abrogated; later, "in the post-Easter period, God would reveal to the apostles the implications of Christ's fulfillment of the Law of Moses" (778).

[53] "Purifying all the foods (that there are)" is the translation of Voelz, *Mark 1:1–8:26*, 450.

[54] Novatian, *Jewish Foods*, 5.6 (Bray, *Romans*, ACCS NT 6:346).

[55] Dunn, *Romans*, 819.

[56] The traditional date for the exodus and the giving of the Torah of Moses is 1446 BC. For the practice of the food laws therein, see "What's the Matter with Food? (14:2)" in the commentary on 14:1–13a, as well as the second textual note on 14:14 and "Unclean No More!" above. These laws were considered permanent and binding regardless of location and social environment. For example, Judeans continued to observe them even while exiled in Babylon in the sixth century BC (Dan 1:3–16).

those who continued to follow those laws, certainly explain the hesitancy.[57] As Voelz states:

> *Jesus now relativizes the very teachings (Leviticus 11) of the divine, written Law!* If his (and Mark's) assessment of the oral law is radical and unsettling, how much more so this assertion? Such a critique of the divine written Law would have been truly offensive to any pious Jew. Indeed, the Maccabean Revolt was fought over just such an issue.[58]

Application to Rome

It seems hardly surprising, then, that different convictions about the matter of clean and unclean foods existed among the Christians in Rome. They were torn between "observance of the Torah on the one side and the unity of the community on the other side."[59] But Paul argues in such a way that different convictions regarding clean and unclean foods serve "not as a boundary dividing one group from another and preventing communion, but as an issue affecting the expression of liberty *within* a community which embraces diverse viewpoints."[60]

Paul adds this qualification: "except to the one who considers something to be unclean; to that person [it is] unclean" (14:14b; cf. 1 Cor 8:4–7). The verb "count" (λογίζομαι) describes those who still regard such foods as unclean. Unlike Paul and the "strong" (Rom 15:1), they have not been convinced that, in God's sight and according to his will, all foods are now clean. As a result, they have different "convictions" about foods (14:1). The physical, and often public, eating or avoidance of such foods, as well as judgments swirling around both consumption and abstinence, means that the matter involves more than inner convictions.[61]

Cautionary Warnings about Negative Consequences (14:15–16)

Watch Out for the Weak (14:15a)

Rom 14:14 serves an explanatory purpose, affirming the position of the "strong" (15:1) and the reality for the "weak" (14:1–2; 15:1). But Origen issues this word of caution:

> Although Paul establishes the principle that nothing is unclean in itself, and he gives complete freedom to believers to eat whatever they like, nevertheless

---

[57] One might add that "cleansing all foods" in Mk 7:19 is the evangelist's conclusion about the implication of Jesus' words, rather than a direct statement by Jesus himself, and no explicit parallel to this conclusion occurs in the other Gospels. It seems likely that the apostles did not realize the full implication of Jesus' words during the time of his earthly ministry but were given this realization only later (see Acts 10–11; Gal 2:11–14; cf. Jn 2:22).

[58] Voelz, *Mark 1:1–8:26*, 467–68. For the "oral Law" or "oral Torah," see the footnote on the Pharisaic hand-washing ritual described in Mk 7:2–5 in "Unclean No More!" above.

[59] Käsemann, *Romans*, 374.

[60] Dunn, *Romans*, 820.

[61] Käsemann, *Romans*, 375, properly concludes: "Stress lies, then, not on the limit of the decision of conscience … but on the duty of following it."

he proceeds to restrict that freedom for the sake of building up the freedom of brotherly love.[62]

In 14:15a Paul returns to the thought of 14:13b, that of causing stumbling or offense, and enunciates this foreboding consequence: "For if on account of food your brother is being grieved, you are no longer walking according to love" (14:15a). Paul's conditional sentence assumes reality for the sake of argument.[63] It does not insist that the fulfillment exists as a present reality; neither does the form imply that the situation is contrary to the current condition.[64] The supposition, "for if on account of food" (εἰ γὰρ διὰ βρῶμα, 14:15), presumes the open exercise of freedom to eat formerly unclean food in the presence of the weak. This might be happening within a specific house church in Rome. It could also happen if, whether by open flaunting or not, the practice of some of the strong house churches has become known to those weak congregations which still maintain OT food laws.

In any of these cases, it may cause offense to "your brother" (ὁ ἀδελφός σου, 14:15). The pronoun "your" modifying a fellow Christian here is singular, as again in 14:21–22. Paul thus speaks, as elsewhere, directly and personally. While BDAG speaks of "feelings [being] hurt" (see the first textual note on 14:15; cf. NASB), Dunn argues that the word has "a stronger meaning,"[65] which he translates as "is deeply upset."[66] Käsemann affirms: "What is in mind is the state of the wounded conscience, not irritation that I break conventions and do not follow traditions."[67] Thus the RSV and NRSV employ "is being injured." The use of "is being grieved" here (similar are ESV, NKJV, KJV) pushes further by bringing in the connotations of mourning a death. Since the result may be to "destroy that person" (14:15), it jeopardizes his very faith and salvation; the person is at risk of going to hell.[68]

Luther comments insightfully both on Paul's choice of verb and the implication of its passive voice:

> He uses the word "injured," disturbed, wounded in his conscience, which is much more than if he were deprived of his money or material things or were even wounded. And this because of food! Also notice that he does not say "if you grieve him," but rather "if he is grieved." Here he very adroitly rejects their excuse if they should say: "It is not my fault, I am not doing anything to

---

[62] Origen, *Romans* (Bray, *Romans*, ACCS NT 6:346–47).

[63] See the textual note. Wallace, *Greek Grammar*, 692, says: "The force of the indicative mood [in the apodosis/'then' clause], when properly understood, lends itself to the notion of *presentation* of reality." In this verse the indicative verb in the apodosis is περιπατεῖς, which is negated with οὐκέτι: "you are no longer walking."

[64] The former case would not be a conditional sentence; the latter requires ἄν in the apodosis and is called a second class, or contrary to fact, condition; see Wallace, *Greek Grammar*, 694–96.

[65] Dunn, *Romans*, 820.

[66] Dunn, *Romans*, 815; Cranfield, *Romans*, 714, gives "is … seriously hurt."

[67] Käsemann, *Romans*, 376.

[68] See "Gospel Motivation (14:15b)" below.

him. I am not grieving him, I am only doing what I am permitted to do." …
But it is not enough that you live by your own law and do what you wish with
your own things, unless you also look out for your brother. … Therefore you
act according to an alien law, that is, you commit wrong, if you act in such
a way that through you your brother is grieved. For thus today nearly everyone pays attention only to what is his own and what is permitted him under
his own rights, but not what he owes another and what is expedient for both.
"All things are lawful for me," [Paul] says, "But not all things are helpful or
edifying" (1 Cor. 6:12).[69]

Instead of following the "alien law" (foreign to Christian compassion) to which
Luther refers, Paul has already positively stated the proper guide: "Owe nothing
to anyone except *the* [obligation] to love one another. For the one who loves the
other has brought [the] Law to fulfillment" (13:8). Here he adds another negative
component; if your conduct leads to another being grieved, "you are no longer
walking according to love" (κατὰ ἀγάπην, 14:15; cf. 13:9–10).

This is the sole instance of the noun "love" (ἀγάπη) in 14:1–15:13. While
Dunn claims that it expresses "the key motive which links together all [Paul's]
parenesis in these chapters,"[70] it must be defined as the remainder of the verse
enunciates it; see "Gospel Motivation (14:15b)" immediately below. The noun
ἀγάπη also sums up all Paul illustrated in describing *how genuine love does walk*
from 12:9 through 13:10. Furthermore, the use of "walk" (περιπατέω, 14:15a)
in connection with "love" identifies it with the renewal of life made possible
by Baptism into Christ and in accord with the Spirit's leading (6:4; 8:4). Paul
recently rejected other indecent ways of "walking" in 13:13.

Gospel Motivation (14:15b)

The "key motive"[71] for not wounding your brother derives from the heart
of the Gospel as expressed in the last half of the verse: "Do not by your food
destroy that person [a 'weak' person] in behalf of whom Christ died" (14:15b).
This echoes the glorious truth of 5:6–8 very loudly: "While we were still being
weak, … Christ died in behalf of the ungodly. … God demonstrates his own
love toward us in that while we were still being sinners, Christ died in behalf
of us" (Rom 5:6, 8). Therefore, *how dare a believer destroy another person for
whom Christ also died by doing something so trivial as exercising freedom to
eat previously unclean food?*

What does "destroy" (14:15) mean? Moo points out:

Every time Paul uses the verb ἀπόλλυμι with a personal object, it refers to
spiritual ruin (with three possible exceptions): Rom. 2:12; 1 Cor. 1:18; 8:11;

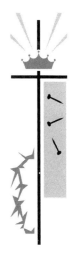

15:18; 2 Cor. 2:15; 4:3; 2 Thess. 2:10; the possible exceptions are 1 Cor. 10:9, 10; 2 Cor. 4:9.[72]

Thus "destroy" does not mean "annihilate,"[73] but the loss of faith, something Paul himself makes clear in 14:23. Since "to abandon entirely his faith in Christ" entails forfeiting the reception of righteousness and salvation, Dunn appropriately equates it with "final eschatological ruin."[74] All the dead shall be raised bodily; then unbelievers will be condemned to eternal derision and torments, while believers will enter eternal life (Is 66:23–24; Dan 12:2–3; Rom 2:5, 8–10; 6:5–8; 9:22–23; 1 Corinthians 15).

How might this destruction of a brother happen? One possibility would be a weak believer adopting practices contrary to his own convictions which might lead him to conclude that he has left the Christian faith (see 14:23).[75] More likely, the weak believer would be so appalled by the dietary conduct of the strong that he takes offense (14:13) and walks out of the believing community and away from the Christian faith as well. Particularly when the strong Christian is acting intentionally, Paul's words continue to remind us "of the terrible absurdity of the strong Christian's readiness to bring about his weak brother's spiritual ruin for the sake of such a triviality as the use of a particular food."[76] In our day, one could add numerous other trivialities which unnecessarily and grievously wound fellow Christians who end up suffering the same destructive consequences. In order to avoid this, Bengel simply advises: "Do not value your food [or anything else for that matter] more than Christ valued his life."[77]

God's Good Gifts Being Slandered (14:16)

Paul continues to speak *primarily to the strong* in concluding: "Therefore do not let that which is for your good be slandered" (14:16). Cranfield provides a thorough overview regarding various options for interpreting "the good" (τὸ ἀγαθόν). He agrees that Paul addresses the "strong" (as they will be called in 15:1) but then identifies "the good" as "the gospel itself"[78] (cf. 3:8). Dunn similarly contends that the phrase "sums up all God's covenanted blessings" and suggests that the plural "you" (ὑμῶν) encompasses "*all* the recipients of the

---

[72] Moo, *Romans*, 854–55, n. 28, unconvincingly attempts to interpret this text in a manner consistent with the Calvinistic doctrine that all believers are always preserved in faith, and, therefore, those who fall from the faith must not have truly been believers: "Rom. 14:15 does not refute the doctrine of the perseverance of the saints." Either, he suggests, the person ("brother"!) might not be "genuinely regenerate" or Paul only gives a hypothetical warning but "does not say that the destruction will actually take place."

[73] Cf. Middendorf, *Romans 1–8*, 672–73.

[74] Dunn, *Romans*, 821.

[75] Dunn, *Romans*, 821.

[76] Cranfield, *Romans*, 717.

[77] Bengel, *Gnomon Novi Testamenti*, 599, quoted in Dunn, *Romans*, 821.

[78] Cranfield, *Romans*, 717; for his complete discussion, see 715–17.

letter."[79] If so, the blasphemers or slanderers are deemed to be "those outside the church,"[80] that is, "gentile onlookers."[81]

But this seems contrary to the context of the dispute occurring *within the believing community* and/or among the various house churches. "The good" (14:16), instead, denotes those foods which may now be received in thanksgiving from the hand of God (14:6). In regard to such eating, Pelagius observes: "What is good is our freedom, which we have in the Lord, so that everything is clean to us."[82] Contrary to those who continue to advocate the necessity of, among other things, abstaining from certain foods (ἀπέχεσθαι βρωμάτων, 1 Tim 4:3), Paul reminds Timothy "that every created thing of God is good and nothing being received with thanksgiving [is to be] cast away" (ὅτι πᾶν κτίσμα θεοῦ καλὸν καὶ οὐδὲν ἀπόβλητον μετὰ εὐχαριστίας λαμβανόμενον, 1 Tim 4:4, cf. Rom 14:6). Indeed, "freedom from the dietary laws is a 'good' thing, a legitimate implication of the coming of Jesus the Messiah and the New Covenant."[83]

The slandering (βλασφημείσθω, 14:16), then, does not pertain to blasphemy by unbelievers against God or his people (as it did in 2:24; see the first textual note on 14:16). Instead, *it entails the reviling which comes along with the judging being done by the weak*.[84] The "weak in faith" (14:1) continue to regard the consumption of "unclean" foods (14:14) by the "strong" (15:1) to be a direct violation of God's Law; therefore, they are pronouncing judgments against the strong who consume this food (14:3, 10, 13a). One might picture the weak slanderously shouting that the strong are "Unclean! Unclean!" (cf. Lev 13:45). 1 Cor 10:29b–30 provides a key parallel in regard to eating meat offered to idols: "For why is my freedom being judged by another's conscience? If I am partaking in grace, why am I being slandered in behalf of [that for] which I am giving thanks?" (ἱνατί γὰρ ἡ ἐλευθερία μου κρίνεται ὑπὸ ἄλλης συνειδήσεως; εἰ ἐγὼ χάριτι μετέχω, τί βλασφημοῦμαι ὑπὲρ οὗ ἐγὼ εὐχαριστῶ; cf. Rom 3:8).[85] In both contexts, negative words of judgment and slander are being spoken within the community of believers, by the weak against the strong. Paul's mandate for the strong not to allow this to happen ("do not let ... ," 14:16) means that the strong are to avoid eating "unclean" (14:14) food—even though it is "good" (14:16)—in circumstances where the weak would notice and take offense at the action.

---

[79] Dunn, *Romans*, 821.

[80] Cranfield, *Romans*, 717.

[81] Dunn, *Romans*, 821–22.

[82] Pelagius, *Romans* (Bray, *Romans*, ACCS NT 6:348).

[83] Moo, *Romans*, 855.

[84] Sanday and Headlam, *Romans*, 391; see also Moo, *Romans*, 855.

[85] See Lockwood, *1 Corinthians*, 353–54.

God's Kingdom at the Center (14:17–18)

The Kingdom Defined (14:17)

In 14:1–13a, Paul quite literally centers his discussion of these sensitive and divisive matters in the Gospel truths of Christ's death and resurrection, as well as in the relationship all believers, whether living or dying, share together in him (14:7–9). The fact that God has received us to himself (14:3) in the One who is now our saving Lord ought to effectively remove even the possible hint that we might engage in judging and slandering one another. The added fact of our accountability before God for such detrimental conduct adds further force to Paul's point on the edges of his previous instructions (14:3–4, 10–13a).

Paul does the same here. At the heart of a discussion aimed primarily at the strong who, like him, properly consume all foods, *he reinforces what really matters*. In so doing, he moves away from imperatives and offers *these central indicative realities*: "Indeed, the kingdom of God is not eating and drinking, but righteousness and peace and joy in [the] Holy Spirit" (14:17). Such "theological underpinnings" provide much needed perspective.[86]

The phrase "the kingdom of God/heaven," occurs thematically around a hundred times in the Synoptic Gospels.[87] Paul uses phrases designating the "kingdom" of God and/or Christ relatively rarely, only here in Romans and thirteen other times (see the first textual note on 14:17).[88] Dunn offers a parenthetical explanation that this paucity in Paul is "perhaps for the simple reason that a preacher traveling through the Roman Empire speaking of another kingdom could leave himself open to charges of sedition; cf. Acts 17:6–7."[89] The vast majority of Paul's uses refer to the future eschatological kingdom (see the first textual note on 14:17). But here, as in 1 Cor 4:20; Col 1:13; and, probably, 1 Thess 2:12, Paul also speaks of *the kingdom as a present reality*.[90] Therefore, in agreement with Synoptic use, Paul affirms that "God's eschatological rule was already being manifested in the present."[91] Thus his expressions regarding God's kingdom fit squarely within his theological framework of the "now" and the "not yet."[92]

---

[86] Moo, *Romans*, 856.

[87] For the Synoptic perspective, see "The Reign of Heaven/God in Jesus" in Gibbs, *Matthew 1:1–11:1*, 47–51.

[88] Dunn, *Romans*, 822, points out "the inverse ratio" of references to the "kingdom" (βασιλεία) of God versus references to "righteousness" (δικαιοσύνη) and the "(Holy) Spirit" (πνεῦμα) in the Synoptics compared to Paul's epistles: "kingdom" references occur ca. 105 times in the Synoptics versus 14 times in Paul; references to "righteousness" (δικαιοσύνη) are 7 versus 57, and references to the "(Holy) Spirit" (πνεῦμα) are 13 versus more than 110.

[89] Dunn, *Romans*, 822.

[90] Both present and future aspects are noted by Cranfield, *Romans*, 717–18, n. 2; Dunn, *Romans*, 822; Käsemann, *Romans*, 377; Moo, *Romans*, 857, n. 40.

[91] Dunn, *Romans*, 822.

[92] For an overview, see "The 'Now' and the 'Not Yet' " in Middendorf, *Romans 1–8*, 441–42.

God's Kingdom Is Not

Paul begins by defining God's kingdom in negative terms. It does not consist in "eating and drinking" (βρῶσις καὶ πόσις, 14:17). For the first time "drinking" (or "drink") is added to "eating," and "drink wine" will appear in 14:21. "Eating" and "drinking" may appear here simply as something of a reflex resulting from the "natural combination" of the two elsewhere.[93] Moo supports this by noting yet another parallel with 1 Corinthians 8–10:

> The mention of "drinking" in 1 Cor. 10:31, toward the end of Paul's discussion of food sacrificed to idols and without any indication that this was a problem in Corinth, may especially suggest that in Rom. 14–15 also, Paul introduces "drinking" simply as a hypothetical matter.[94]

But "hypothetical" probably does not say enough. To be sure, drunkenness and its associate behaviors present an ongoing temptation (see 13:13). Murray also discusses how "wine" may have presented a case much like the meat offered to idols in Corinth, since it could be seen as contaminated by association with pagan religious practice.[95] Still, Paul's passing references to "drinking" in 14:17 and "wine" in 14:21 probably indicate that in Rome drink is not currently a prominent cause of divisive judgments based upon varying convictions (see "Identifying the Controverted Issues" in the introduction to 14:1–15:13).

God's Kingdom Is

Paul then defines God's "kingdom" positively with vocabulary he more regularly employs: "righteousness and peace and joy" (δικαιοσύνη καὶ εἰρήνη καὶ χαρά, 14:17). First, "righteousness" (δικαιοσύνη) appears here for the last time in Romans. This "key word of the whole letter … is unlikely to have a different sense from what has been a consistent but broad usage—God's gracious power reaching out"[96] toward all humanity with his declaration of "righteousness" received simply through faith in Christ (1:16–17; 3:22–25). Rom 5:1 connects the first two terms here: "therefore, after being declared *righteous* from faith, we have *peace* with God through our Lord Jesus Christ." "Peace" (εἰρήνη), therefore, also depicts a relationship enacted despite our enmity toward God, who has reconciled us to himself through the death and resurrection of Christ (5:10). Finally comes the first of three appearances of the noun for "joy" in Romans (χαρά; also 15:13, 32). The cognate verb "to rejoice" (χαίρω) also occurs only three times (12:12, 15; 16:19). But the related verb "to boast" (καυχάομαι), often translated as "rejoice" (e.g., ESV, RSV), appears prominently in the opening verses of Romans 5 as well (5:2, 3, 11).[97]

---

[93] Moo, *Romans*, 856, n. 38, citing as examples Mt 6:25; 11:18, 19; 1 Cor 9:4; 10:7; 10:31; 11:22.

[94] Moo, *Romans*, 856, n. 38.

[95] Cf. Murray, *Romans*, 2:260–61.

[96] Dunn, *Romans*, 823.

[97] Moo, *Romans*, 857, n. 46, makes the connection between joy and boasting/rejoicing.

"In the Holy Spirit" (ἐν πνεύματι ἁγίῳ, 15:17) may attach to all three nouns.[98] Note that "joy" and "peace" appear together also in 15:13 and that both are among the fruit of the Spirit in Gal 5:22. At the same time, Paul associates the Spirit particularly with "joy" (1 Thess 1:6). On that basis, Cranfield contends:

> By δικαιοσύνη ["righteousness"] Paul probably means the status of righteousness before God which is God's gift, by εἰρήνη ["peace"] the state of having been reconciled with God, by χαρά ["joy"] the joy which is the Spirit's work in the believer.[99]

In any case, all three are gifts of grace received from the Holy Spirit "through the mercies of God" (12:1).

The Kingdom Lived Out—Its Horizontal Dimensions (14:18)

Romans makes it clear that such gifts then have a horizontal dimension as well. They are to be *actively expressed within and by the believing community which has received them.*[100] Rom 6:19 implores believers to "present [their] bodily members [as] slavish to righteousness [τῇ δικαιοσύνῃ] leading to sanctification." The communal dimensions of peace and joy have been called forth more recently (12:18 and 12:12, 15 respectively). "εἰρήνη is the state of peace with one another which should characterize Christians; χαρά is the joy which comes from the indwelling Holy Ghost in the community."[101] To be sure, all of these come as a *response* to God's actions toward us in Christ. But that does not diminish the expectation that we will faithfully reflect them in our dealings with others.

The "strong" (15:1) who insist on consuming what is "unclean" (14:14), then, tend to major in the minors. They emphasize food and drink while ignoring the kingdom's real essentials.

> Theirs, paradoxically, is the same fault as that of the Pharisees, only in reverse: where the Pharisees insisted on strict adherence to the ritual law at the expense of "justice, mercy, and faith" (Matt. 23:23), the "strong" are insisting on exercising their freedom from the ritual law at the expense of "righteousness and peace and joy in the Holy Spirit" [Rom 14:17].[102]

---

[98] So Käsemann, *Romans*, 377; Moo, *Romans*, 857, n. 46; and Dunn, *Romans*, 824, who takes ἐν, "in," as expressing " 'in the power of' (embracing both a locative and instrumental sense)."

[99] Cranfield, *Romans*, 718.

[100] Similarly, note that aside from 8:28 all the references to love in the letter prior to 12:9 convey God's love to us in Christ. But in 12:9 Paul begins to define how divine love flows through us and then out to others via our authentic love for them. Ever since, he has been describing how we walk "according to love" in our dealings with others (14:15; note 13:8–10).

[101] Sanday and Headlam, *Romans*, 392.

[102] Moo, *Romans*, 856. Dunn, *Romans*, 822, similarly argues that Paul does not want to let the Gentile majority make "the same mistake as the devout Jew had fallen into in his boasting in the law (2:23–24)."

Slaves to the Christ (14:18a)

Paul then adds an explanation: "For the one who serves [as a slave] to the Christ in this [is] well-pleasing to God and tested and approved by people" (14:18). Whether slavery language (here the verb δουλεύω) is deemed derogatory or not *depends totally upon one's master or Lord*. It would seem oppressive if Paul intended to characterize "the believer as a servant who is required to satisfy the demands of his or her master (vv. 4, 7–8)."[103] But this legalistic and anthropocentric portrayal fundamentally misreads the relational aspect so prominent in this immediate context (see 14:4 and 14:8–9), as well as throughout the entire letter.

In the very first verse, Paul identifies himself as "a slave of Christ Jesus" (δοῦλος Χριστοῦ Ἰησοῦ, 1:1). This entails, first and foremost, belonging to Christ because he paid the redemption price (3:24; 14:9; 1 Cor 6:19–20). In chapter 6, Paul uses the language of slavery once again. It must be understood in the context of the biblical motif described by a section title in this commentary: "Everybody's Serving Someone (6:15–16)."[104] All who sin are slaves to sin (Jn 8:34; cf. Rom 3:9), a bondage that the Law makes increasingly negative (5:20–21; 7:7–11) and that results only in death and wrath (2:5, 8; 6:23). But being a slave of the Christ entails reigning in life now and eternally (5:17; 6:23). It then follows that *those who are slaves of Christ will live out that relationship responsibly* (6:18, 19, 22) with the full knowledge that they will give an account to their Lord and God himself (14:11–12).[105]

Conduct in the Kingdom (14:18b)

While this general truth applies to all of life, Paul speaks of it "in this" (ἐν τούτῳ, 14:18). The form of the demonstrative pronoun is singular, but most commentators take "this" as encompassing the three expressions of God's kingdom, "righteousness and peace and joy" (14:17), as a totality or whole.[106] In other words, things are done "in this" manner, in the way of the kingdom of God. Dunn argues for a more generic understanding, contending that the phrase "is best taken in a recapitulative sense but without a more specific reference = 'in this matter.' "[107] However, Moo observes that in all Pauline uses of this prepositional phrase (ἐν τούτῳ), "the antecedent of τούτῳ ['this'] is a 'matter' or

---

[103] Moo, *Romans*, 858.

[104] Middendorf, *Romans 1–8*, 497–99.

[105] While the phrase "their Lord and God himself" could speak of Jesus and the Father respectively, it could also refer in its entirety to Jesus. Paul stoutly asserts the divinity of the Lord Jesus by interchanging references to the Father and the Son using the terms "God" and "Lord"; see "Of the Lord's Servant (14:4)" and "As 'the Lord Says' (Is 45:23 in Rom 14:11)" in the commentary on 14:1–13a.

[106] E.g., Käsemann, *Romans*, 377; Murray, *Romans*, 2:194; Sanday and Headlam, *Romans*, 392; Cranfield, *Romans*, 720; see 719–20 for other options.

[107] Dunn, *Romans*, 824.

'circumstance' denoted in the previous context."[108] Therefore, "in this" *refers directly to the matter at hand*, namely, foods and, to a lesser extent, holy days (see 14:5–6).

In this circumstance and as slaves of Christ, Paul calls the Roman believers to conduct themselves in a way that is both "well-pleasing to God and tested and approved by people" (14:18). These descriptors recall the language of 12:1–2. The adjective "well-pleasing" (εὐάρεστος, 14:18) occurred in both 12:1 and 12:2. There Paul exhorts believers to offer their bodies as a sacrifice "well-pleasing to God" (εὐάρεστον τῷ θεῷ, 12:1); this means that they endeavor to "test and discern [δοκιμάζειν] what [is] the good, well-pleasing [εὐάρεστον], and perfect will of God" (12:2). The verb "discern" (δοκιμάζω) in 12:2 is cognate to the adjective translated as "tested and approved" (δόκιμος) in 14:18. Here the adjective refers to being verified *by people*. This contrasts sharply with the previously stated alternative, being "slandered" by people (14:16). Such "well-pleasing" (14:18) behavior toward God *combined with the discernment necessary for one's actions to be well regarded by others* is applied to the controverted situation addressed in Romans 14.

Primarily this would entail the "strong" (15:1) not offending the weak in what they eat. "Conduct which limited personal freedom in consideration for others is the opposite of the selfish insensitivity which was careless of the hurt caused" to others.[109] The strong, therefore, should walk according to love (14:15; cf. 6:4; 8:4; 13:13) and in a way that enhances "righteousness and peace and joy" within and among the community of congregations (14:17).

Yet one should *not* view Paul's instructions in simply moralistic terms as if one pursues these virtues for virtue's sake. Chrysostom reminds us: "Men will approve of such a person, not so much because of his perfect state but because of his devotion to peace and good relations."[110] Both Jesus and Paul provide *Gospel-motivated, positive role models for our willing, self-sacrificial living for one another* (e.g., Mt 20:28; Lk 22:27; Jn 15:12–15; 1 Cor 9:15–25; 11:1). Those who love one another in such a way also provide a positive witness that extends outward "before all people" (12:17; see the commentary on 13:8). Hopefully, unbelievers will then recognize such laudable behavior by Jesus' disciples and tend to regard Jesus and the Father favorably (Mt 5:16; Jn 13:35). Unfortunately, such Christian conduct toward those *within and among* various churches has, all too often, been sorely lacking throughout the history of the church. It has been replaced, instead, by slandering one another within the family of faith (14:16) and, then, as a result, by "the name of God … being blasphemed" by unbelievers (2:24). Paul points to a different way.

---

[108] Moo, *Romans*, 858, n. 55, citing 1 Cor 4:4; 7:24; 11:22; 2 Cor 5:2; 8:10; Phil 1:18.

[109] Dunn, *Romans*, 824.

[110] Chrysostom, *Homilies on Romans*, 26 (Bray, *Romans*, ACCS NT 6:349).

To the Strong: Implications and Applications (14:19–22a)

Pursuing Peace and Building Up (14:19)

"Consequently then" (ἄρα οὖν), which opens 14:19, takes the blessed theological truths of 14:17–18 and begins to apply them. Unfortunately, the verb in 14:19 presents a significant and difficult textual variation (διώκωμεν or διώκομεν; see the third textual note on 14:19). In point of fact, the typical guidance for textual criticism, which favors the reading that is best attested and most difficult, *points unmistakably to the indicative* διώκομεν, "we are pursuing." In a mirror of the case in 5:1,[111] commentators and translators seem to want Paul to have written the subjunctive διώκωμεν, "let us love,"[112] so much so that they overlook both of those basic text-critical principles. The indicative "has the weightier textual support (including ℵ and B), and alteration to the subjunctive to give an exhortation is more likely than the alternative change from the clear exhortation to the more surprising indicative."[113] Also, the imperative in 14:20 is a second person singular; this lessens support for reading the first person plural form as a hortatory subjunctive. The indicative, therefore, states Paul's own pursuit, one which serves as a model for "we, the strong" (15:1; cf. 1 Cor 11:1).

"Consequently then, we are pursuing the things of peace and the things of the building up for one another" (Rom 14:19). Those who have "peace" with God in his kingdom (5:1; 14:17) pursue the same with one another (as in Ps 34:14 [MT 34:15; LXX 33:15]; 2 Tim 2:22; Heb 12:14; 1 Pet 3:11). We also pursue things which build others up in their faith (τὰ τῆς οἰκοδομῆς, Rom 14:19). *The image of construction* appears prominently elsewhere in Scripture. Dunn observes how "Jeremiah in particular makes repeated use of it."[114] It also serves as a favorite picture for Paul. He uses it broadly to describe the purpose of his own ministry (Rom 15:20; 1 Cor 3:9–10; 2 Cor 10:8; 13:10), for the joining of Jews and Gentiles into one spiritual house (Eph 2:19–21; cf. 1 Pet 2:5), and for the building up of other believers within the community of the faith (Eph 4:12, 16, 29). The latter provides the emphasis here. This picture stands as the antithesis to the command which opens the following verse, "do not ... tear down" (μὴ ... κατάλυε, 14:20), as well as the earlier admonition "do not ... destroy" (μὴ ... ἀπόλλυε, 14:15).

The Individual and Communal Impact

Not only should the "strong" (15:1) avoid having a negative effect upon the "weak" (14:1–2; 15:1), but they should also reach out positively in active pursuit of "peace" and "building up" (14:19). Barrett argues that " 'edification'

---

[111] See Middendorf, *Romans 1–8*, 382, 390.

[112] Those who favor the subjunctive include Moo, *Romans*, 849, n. 1; Cranfield, *Romans*, 720–21; Metzger, *A Textual Commentary on the Greek New Testament*, 532.

[113] Dunn, *Romans*, 816; similarly, Käsemann, *Romans*, 378; Sanday and Headlam, *Romans*, 392.

[114] Dunn, *Romans*, 825, citing Jer 12:16; 31:4, 28 (LXX 38:4, 28); 33:7 (LXX 40:7); 42:10 (LXX 49:10); 45:4 (LXX 51:34).

is for Paul ... corporate. ... And 'building up' means the building up of the Church" rather than the individual.[115] But this surely posits a false alternative. The essence of Paul's argument toward the strong is not to grieve "your [singular] weak brother [singular]" (ὁ ἀδελφός σου) and not to "destroy that person [singular] in behalf of whom Christ died" (ἐκεῖνον, 14:15; see also 14:21). Therefore *Paul primarily envisions the impact upon individuals* with whom the strong interact. To be sure, this individual interaction will certainly affect an entire congregation. It will also have an influence on the entire believing community in Rome and, in many ways, determine the collective church's reputation. But this is a "both/and." "We, the many, are one body in Christ, and, [as] the [body], each one members of one another" (12:5). Therefore, one cannot dismiss *either* the effect on individual relationships *or* the corporate impact those relationships have, for better or worse, on a congregation, a denomination's reputation, and how the unbelieving world views all the followers of Jesus.

A Series of Assertions (14:20–22a)

In a manner out of character with the typically smooth flow of Paul's thought, he makes a series of seemingly disconnected (i.e., asyndetic) "authoritative pronouncement[s]"[116] in 14:20a, 20b, 21, 22a, 22b. He also uses second person singular forms in 14:20 and 14:21, followed by three more in 14:22a. Therefore, up until the blessing which begins midway through 14:22, one should interpret the statements in 14:20–22a as *directed primarily toward the "strong"* (15:1). Indeed, they have been the primary target of Paul's admonitions ever since 14:13b. Rom 14:22b–23 then switches to more general third person singular forms. Thus Paul concludes the chapter by offering all-encompassing instructions equally applicable to both sides. This parallels the more general language with which he began the discussion in 14:1–3 (see the commentary there).

Do Not Tear Down What God Has Built (14:20a)

Rom 14:20a essentially reiterates 14:15b and also makes a direct application regarding God's "kingdom," which was referenced in 14:17: "Do not, for the sake of food, tear down the work of God" (14:20a). The second person singular imperative "tear down" (κατάλυε) expresses the antithesis of "building up" (τῆς οἰκοδομῆς, 14:19). The specific cause under consideration is emphatically placed and remains "food" (βρῶμα). "Tearing down" would involve *the strong eating previously "unclean" food (14:14) in the presence or within the awareness of the "weak"* (14:1–2; 15:1) and thus injuring them. It could also include the strong urging the weak to join in consuming such foods contrary to their own convictions (14:1).

"The work of God" (14:20) stands equivalent to his "kingdom" work in Christ (14:17). As Jesus declares: "This is the work of God [τὸ ἔργον τοῦ

---

[115] Barrett, *Romans*, 265; Moo, *Romans*, 859, n. 61, also points "especially" in the collective direction.

[116] Cranfield, *Romans*, 724.

θεοῦ], that you believe in [the one] whom he sent" (Jn 6:29). Paul reminds his hearers that Jesus died in behalf of the brother and in behalf of all (Rom 5:6–8; 14:15) and then rose and lives (14:9) to bestow "righteousness and peace and joy in [the] Holy Spirit" (14:17) on all who receive him in faith. Chrysostom affirms that "here *the work of God* means the salvation of a brother."[117] Therefore Ambrosiaster recognizes: "Man is the work of God by creation, and again by his renewal in regeneration, and food is God's work as well."[118]

Commentators again engage in a false alternative regarding "the work of God" (14:20) which might potentially be destroyed. Some take it as a reference to "the Christian community rather than to the individual 'weak' believer."[119] Others argue that it pertains most specifically to "God's work in the weak brother."[120] But this either/or view separates what God has joined together. The collective view might tend to diminish the impact on an individual in service to the good of the church as a whole. But an exclusively corporate emphasis tilts the balance away from Paul's concern for the individual whom God has brought into his kingdom. At that same time, that kingdom and the body of Christ in each and every place exists as a collective entity which is impacted by the spiritual health and well-being of each of its members (e.g., Rom 12:3–8; 1 Cor 12:12–27).

All Foods Are Clean but Ought Not Cause Stumbling (14:20b–21)

In 14:20b, Paul restates the matter at hand in regard to food (and drink, 14:17, 21) and then gives a word of advice primarily to the "strong" (15:1): "On the one hand, all things are [ritually] clean, but [they can be] a bad thing for the person who eats through stumbling." In 14:14, Paul declares: "Nothing is unclean" (οὐδὲν κοινόν). Now he states the same thing positively: "All things are clean" (πάντα … καθαρά, 14:20b). For both "unclean" and "clean" the contextual referents specifically are foods, and these verses do not provide overarching moral statements (see 14:14). Cranfield identifies the statement in 14:20b as some kind of "slogan" chanted by the strong.[121] But it carries much more impact when identified with the teaching of Jesus in Mark 7, which had the effect of "declaring all foods clean" (καθαρίζων πάντα τὰ βρώματα, Mk 7:19).[122]

The specific idea in the last clause of Rom 14:20 remains uncertain. Who is "the person who eats" here, and what is the sense of the prepositional phrase "through stumbling" (διὰ προσκόμματος)? Dunn contends that Paul's statement

---

[117] Chrysostom, *Homilies on Romans*, 26 (Bray, *Romans*, ACCS NT 6:350).

[118] Ambrosiaster, *Romans* (Bray, *Romans*, ACCS NT 6:350).

[119] Moo, *Romans*, 860; similarly, Dunn, *Romans*, 825; Barrett, *Romans*, 265.

[120] Cranfield, *Romans*, 723; similarly, Murray, *Romans*, 2:195; Fitzmyer, *Romans*, 698.

[121] Cranfield, *Romans*, 723.

[122] See the discussion of Mk 7:19 in the third textual note on Rom 14:20 and in "Jesus Said So" in the commentary on 14:14.

ambiguously includes both the strong and the weak; the strong person is "caus-ing offense (to the weak)" by eating what the weak deems unclean, while the weak "eats with offense = with an offended, bad conscience" because of what he sees the strong doing.[123] While Paul makes that point directly in 14:23, it seems premature here. The noun πρόσκομμα, "a [cause for] stumbling," is used in 14:13 for the strong offending the weak by eating what the weak considers "unclean" (14:14); the cognate verb προσκόπτει in 14:21 similarly depicts the (weak) brother who "stumbles" because he sees the strong eating meat and drinking wine. The use of both those terms weighs heavily in favor of taking διά as expressing attendant circumstance (see the fourth textual note on 14:20) and understanding the noun in a causal sense. Therefore,

> context and grammar make it more likely that the "person who eats" here is the "strong believer." Paul is therefore warning the "strong" believer that it is wrong for him or her to eat "while causing offense" or "if it causes [another] to stumble"; cf. NRSV: "it is wrong for you to make others fall by what you eat."[124]

Paul insists that "all things are [ritually] clean" (14:20; see also 14:14). Therefore, previously "unclean" food can be received from the hand of God and eaten with thanksgiving (14:6) as "good" (ἀγαθός, 14:16). But the adjective at the beginning of 14:21 serves in a comparative construction (καλός, "better") in order to point out a more excellent way (cf. 1 Cor 12:31): "[it is] better not to eat meat nor to drink wine nor [to do anything] in which your brother stum-bles." This noun for "meat" (κρέας) occurs elsewhere in the NT only in 1 Cor 8:13, where Paul engages the matter of meat sacrificed to idols (1 Corinthians 8–10), but the primary background of Romans 14 is the OT, not idolatry as practiced by Gentiles in Corinth. The LXX uses this same term for the "meat" (κρέας) of animals considered unclean in the Law of Moses (e.g., Lev 11:8; Deut 14:8), as well as for "meat" (κρέας) that can be eaten (by both "clean" and "unclean" persons) if it has been drained of blood (Deut 12:15–16), as required by the Torah (Gen 9:4; Lev 17:10–14). In line with the interpretation of Rom 14:2 advocated by this commentary,[125] Dunn properly suggests that Paul's gen-eral language may well suggest "a policy of avoiding all meat in case any of the above taboos had been breached."[126]

Here again, *the eating likely involves the strong flaunting their freedom* in the presence or within the awareness of the weak who consider such food "unclean" (14:14). Due to this behavior by a strong believer, "your brother stum-bles" (ὁ ἀδελφός σου προσκόπτει, 14:21). This seems to reflect Paul's dominant

---

[123] Dunn, *Romans*, 826; Barrett, *Romans*, 266, similarly concludes: "The vagueness and obscu-rity of Paul's sentence is due to the fact that he is thinking of both possibilities."

[124] Moo, *Romans*, 860; Lenski, *Romans*, 848, similarly concludes that the clause refers to "the strong Christian who makes the weak stumble."

[125] See "What's the Matter with Food? (14:2)" in the commentary on 14:1–13a.

[126] Dunn, *Romans*, 827.

concern. Such stumbling could result from "the 'weak' in faith, under pressure from the arguments and example of the 'strong,' doing what they still think is wrong."[127] While plausible, one does not get a direct sense from *Paul's words* that the weak are "giving in to the pressure from the majority 'strong' " and joining with them to eat that which the OT forbids.[128] Instead, Paul speaks specifically to the strong about the effect of "*your* food" (τῷ βρώματί σου, 14:15), not the food of the weak.

"Drinking" (πόσις) was added to "eating" in 14:17 and discussed in the commentary on that verse. Here Paul uses the cognate verb "to drink" (πίνω, 14:21) and specifies the object, "wine" (οἶνος). He certainly does not issue any universal prohibition against the consumption of alcoholic beverages for all times and places; neither does the OT. "Drinking wine as such was also *not* forbidden (cf. Deut 7:13; 11:14, and the established Passover practice; not to mention Mark 14:23–25 … and John 2:1–11)."[129] Whether idolatrous concerns were at issue, as with the meat in Corinth (1 Corinthians 8–10), or drunken behavior (Rom 13:14), neither stand evident in this text. Thus, as with "drinking" in 14:17, the inclusion of "to drink wine" after "to eat meat" in 14:21 is best regarded as a reflex or as part of a "stereotyped phrase."[130]

Broader Implications of the Discussion

The additional words μηδὲ ἐν ᾧ in 14:21 seem to presume something like "nor [to do anything] in which." This should again be heard in the context of Romans 14: the Christian should not do anything that endangers the faith of a fellow believer. Certainly, this would apply to the behavior of the strong in no longer observing the Sabbath or other OT holy days, which Paul mentioned directly in 14:5–6, but has not recalled since. The OT mandates specific practices in regard to both diet and days. Since religious practices are in view, *the filling out of Paul's "nor [to do anything]" would most properly serve as the basis for developing a teaching on "adiaphora."* This technical term specifically applies to "ceremonies and church rites which are neither commanded nor forbidden in the Word of God" (FC SD X 1).[131]

On the basis of "everything" (πᾶς) in 14:23, Lenski broadens the discussion beyond ceremonies and church rites. He rejects the notion that Paul's guidance should be restricted "to the matter of the adiaphora alone" and applies it to

---

[127] Moo, *Romans*, 861; similarly, Chrysostom, *Homilies on Romans*, 26 (Bray, *Romans*, ACCS NT 6:351), concludes that Paul means "do not compel" the weak.

[128] As suggested by Dunn, *Romans*, 827.

[129] Dunn, *Romans*, 827.

[130] This is Cranfield's description of the phrase βρῶσις καὶ πόσις, "eating and drinking," in 14:17 (*Romans*, 725).

[131] Regarding adiaphora, see also "Unclean No More!" in the commentary on 14:14 above and "Romans 14:1–15:7—Summary and Application" in the commentary on 15:1–7.

"the Christian's whole life."[132] Is it appropriate to draw upon what Paul says in order to formulate guidelines in regard to *more general behaviors* (e.g., smoking, dancing, dress, the use of alcohol)? On the one hand, the use or nonuse of these created gifts may not fall specifically under Paul's purview here; neither do they reside at the heart of the matter addressed so comparably in 1 Corinthians 8–10, where idolatry is a serious concern (e.g., 1 Cor 10:14–22).[133]

On the other hand, Paul might well respond that *all* of a Christian's behavior is part of his or her "reasonable worship" (Rom 12:1), including physical, bodily activities ("present your bodies," 12:1; "glorify God in your body," 1 Cor 6:20), as well as thinking with the mind ("the renewing of the mind," Rom 12:2). Therefore, drawing forth guidance on how to responsibly handle such issues would be *an appropriate and valid extension of Paul's statements*.[134] Ambrosiaster summarizes Paul's instructions in a manner applicable to a wide variety of behaviors:

> Paul gives them peace of mind by telling them to make their own decision and putting an end to the disagreement through which the dispute had arisen. No one will dispute that either option is legitimate in itself. For the creation was given for voluntary use. There is no necessity imposed on anybody, one way or the other.[135]

The Influence of Faith (14:22a)

"[As for] you, [the] faith which you have in accord with yourself, have before God" (14:22a). The grammar of 14:22a appears to be idiomatic. The second person singular pronoun (σύ) which begins the verse provides emphasis: "[as for] you."[136] Another textual variant, whether or not to include the relative pronoun ἥν, "which," further complicates matters (see the first textual note on 14:22). If one accepts it as original, as reflected in the translation "[the] faith which you have," the only main verb in the first sentence of the verse is the imperative ἔχε: "have" that faith "before God."

Another question is how to connect the prepositional phrase "in accord with yourself" (κατὰ σεαυτόν) with the rest of the sentence. One could posit that the phrase attaches most closely to what precedes. If so, Paul asserts that the inner or private conviction of faith one has should then, in the latter part of the verse, be put on outward display publicly "before God" and all people. But that would

---

[132] Lenski, *Romans*, 854; he similarly reasserts that this section "applies to 'everything,' to all adiaphora, and also to all else."

[133] See Lockwood, *1 Corinthians*, 271–74, 337–46. Practical guidance in regard to such behaviors can be rooted more firmly in what Paul says in 1 Cor 6:12–14, 19–20; 7:17–24; see Lockwood, *1 Corinthians*, 210–22, 223–27, 247–50.

[134] So Middendorf and Schuler, *Called by the Gospel*, 156–59. Similarly, Moo, *Romans*, 881, states: "Paul here sets forth principles that are applicable to a range of issues that we may loosely classify as *adiaphora*"; see 881–84 for his discussion of these principles.

[135] Ambrosiaster, *Romans* (Bray, *Romans*, ACCS NT 6:351).

[136] Dunn, *Romans*, 827, claims that this is a "reversion to second person singular address," but Paul has already used that form of expression in both 14:20 and 14:21.

be just the opposite of the counsel he has been giving to the strong (14:20–21). Furthermore, that does not seem to be the meaning of the text. Instead, the prepositional phrase appears to be an idiom which attaches to the imperative that follows: it literally means "have/hold by yourself" or, perhaps, "have as your own conviction" (NASB; see the second textual note on 14:22). If this is correct, Paul's instruction applies directly to the strong. The relative clause refers to the faith that the strong have which recognizes their Christian freedom to eat all foods. This conviction should not only be in agreement or "in accord" with one's own faith but should also be consistent with one's standing before God.

In this context, Paul would certainly agree that a "person should keep his faith" (which allows him to eat all foods) "to himself and not try to impose it on others."[137] But since no note of coercion exists in the text, Paul more likely warns the "strong" (15:1) against their own eating of previously "unclean" (14:14) food in the presence or within the awareness of the "weak" (14:1–2; 15:1). *He urges them instead to keep their knowledge of that freedom, as well as their exercise of it, before God.* While the strong remain free to eat all foods (Mk 7:19), they ought not exhibit this publicly *before the weak.*[138] In other words, "the inward freedom does not have to be expressed outwardly in order to be enjoyed."[139] This aligns with "the tension Paul maintains between the liberty of personal conviction (vv 5, 14a, 22–23) and the exercise of liberty through love."[140] Indeed, a consistent theme throughout this chapter aims to strike the appropriate balance between living out one's freedom in Christ and the restraint which may be (self-)imposed upon it due to the higher calling of love. Paul properly illustrates both aspects in his own ministry. Particularly noteworthy is 1 Corinthians 9 since it occurs in the midst of the comparable discussion in 1 Corinthians 8–10 regarding eating meat offered to idols.

Of greater significance, Paul uses the thematic noun "faith" (πίστις) in 14:22 for only the second time since 12:6 (also 14:1). He then employs it twice more in 14:23 in the pregnant prepositional phrase utilized thematically twice in 1:17, "from faith" (ἐκ πίστεως). It appears to Cranfield that "faith" (πίστις) "is used in its special sense of confidence that one's faith allows one to do a particular thing."[141] Lenski agrees that " 'faith' is here the sure conviction that an act accords with God's will and his Word. A Christian must have that knowledge and that conviction."[142] The term "conviction" was used to translate διαλογισμός

---

[137] Origen, *Romans* (Bray, *Romans*, ACCS NT 6:351).

[138] Dunn, *Romans*, 826, contends that the aorist tense of the negated infinitive μὴ φαγεῖν, "not to eat," in 14:21, following immediately after the present tense participle ἐσθίοντι, "who eats," in 14:20, "suggests that Paul does not envisage the strong abstaining permanently."

[139] Cranfield, *Romans*, 726.

[140] Dunn, *Romans*, 820.

[141] Cranfield, *Romans*, 726.

[142] Lenski, *Romans*, 853; Moo, *Romans*, 861, similarly suggests that " 'faith' does not refer to general Christian faith but to convictions about the issues in dispute in Rome."

in 14:1, and Paul could have used that word again if that were his point. Instead, Paul utilizes the noun that he uses elsewhere for "faith" in Christ. Particularly in light of 14:23 (see below), Dunn is correct in asserting:

> As always in this letter πίστις denotes trust, reliance directly upon God. … The "stronger" the faith (that is, the more unconditional the trust), the less dependent is it on observance of particular traditions; the "weaker" the faith, the more dependent on such customs (hence the use of πιστεύειν ["believes"] only in the first half of [14:]2 …).[143]

Concluding Words to Weak and Strong (14:22b–23a)
A Blessing (14:22b)

The use of "blessed" (μακάριος) at the beginning of 14:22b indicates that *a general assessment ensues*. The switch from the consistent use of the second person singular in 14:20–22a to the exclusive use of third person singular expressions in 14:22b–23 buttresses this assessment. The verb "to judge" (κρίνω) has been absent since 14:13, but it returns in 14:22b and is joined in 14:23 by two additional verbs (διακρίνω, "make a distinction," and κατακρίνω, "pronounce a sentence") compounded from "to judge" (κρίνω). These terms signal that Paul now *incorporates the weak in his directives* since they were specifically admonished not to "judge" the strong earlier in the chapter (14:3–4).

"Blessed is the one who is not judging himself in what he approves" (14:22b). Paul begins by "commending believers who have no reservations about their own beliefs on these disputed matters and therefore have no cause to 'reproach' themselves for their conduct."[144] The verb "approve" (δοκιμάζω) entails that they have examined or tested these issues for themselves, reached a conclusion, and abide by it in their behavior (see this verb also in 12:2 and the cognate adjective δόκιμος, "tested and approved," in 14:18). This would include both the "strong" (15:1), who have the faith to eat all things and do so, as well as the "weak" (14:1–2; 15:1), who adhere faithfully to their conviction not to eat meat prohibited by the OT as "unclean" (14:14). In both cases, *the person is "not judging himself"* (μὴ κρίνων ἑαυτόν) based upon what he does or does not eat since he is acting in accord with the Word of God; the "weak" still abide by the OT, while the "strong" are mindful of Christ's pronouncement in Mk 7:19 (reiterated in Acts 10–11 and affirmed by Paul in Rom 14:20). Each kind of Christian is "free" to follow his practice. As Paul made clear earlier (14:3, 4, 10, 13), both ought to be "free" in regard to judging others as well, but that is not the point here. The contrast, instead, applies to eating which would result in judging *oneself*.

---

[143] Dunn, *Romans*, 827.

[144] Moo, *Romans*, 862.

A Dire Warning (14:23a)

"But the one who makes a distinction, if he eats, he has pronounced a sentence upon himself and remains under judgment because [the eating is] not from faith" (14:23a). The participle διακρινόμενος most likely refers to "making a distinction" between foods (see the first textual note on 14:23). The person who is "weak in the faith" (14:1) maintains the OT distinction between clean and unclean foods. The assumption of the protasis in the conditional, "if he eats," could become a reality for a number of reasons. The weak might eat what they still deem unclean at the insistence of the "strong" (15:1), though such external pressure is not evident in what Paul says. It seems *more likely that a weak person might succumb to a subtler peer pressure and eat in order to fit in or to appear strong*. The underlying issue is that the weak "do not have a strong enough faith to believe that they can ignore the ritual elements of the OT law."[145]

Moreover, the combination of the compound verb διακρίνω, "make a distinction," and the noun πίστις, "faith," points to the only other use of the compound verb διακρίνω in Romans, where πίστις also occurs in the near context. In 4:20 Paul states that Abraham "did not waver into unfaith [οὐ διεκρίθη τῇ ἀπιστίᾳ] in the promise of God, but he was empowered in the faith [πίστις]" (Rom 4:20). In other NT passages, the usage of the verb διακρίνω, "waver; make a distinction," is "precisely as a contrast to the unconditional trust in God which comes to expression in prayer."[146] If that sense is in view here, the matter does *not* simply include having doubts about the propriety of eating the food. Instead, "making a distinction" involves a far more serious matter, *wavering in one's faith in God*. The three appearances of the noun for "faith" (πίστις) in 14:22–23 means that it figures prominently in Paul's concluding statements.

The problem is that the Christian eats while still convinced in his own faith that the OT distinction between foods should be maintained. Therefore, such eating does not merely place one "outside the boundary marking off the people of God,"[147] as was true for Israelites who ate unclean food in the OT era. Such a Christian eats even though *he believes* his own action is contrary to the will and Word of God. This casts doubt on his own faith, and without faith in Christ a person stands under divine judgment. The result of such eating is indicated by another compound of the verb κρίνω, "to judge," namely, the perfect middle/passive indicative κατακέκριται. Its force involves *both* pronouncing a sentence upon oneself by acting contrary to one's assessment of God's will in the matter *and* then being under the resulting condemnation of God.

Paul explains the reason why in the compact phrase "because [the eating is] not from faith" (ὅτι οὐκ ἐκ πίστεως, 14:23). Cranfield (along with others) again argues that "πίστις here denotes one's confidence that one's *faith* (in the basic

---

[145] Moo, *Romans*, 863.

[146] Dunn, *Romans*, 828, citing Mt 21:21 ‖ Mk 11:23; James 1:6.

[147] As suggested by Dunn, *Romans*, 828.

NT sense of the word) allows one to do a particular thing."[148] Lenski defines it as "the *enlightened* Christian conscience with which faith operates."[149] But such human-centered understandings are too weak and even less plausible here than in 14:22b for two reasons. First, Paul retrieves not merely the noun "faith," but the prepositional phrase "from faith" (ἐκ πίστεως), which he employs so profoundly earlier in the letter. Instances include, most thematically, twice in 1:17 (as here!) and also in other extremely significant passages (3:26, 30; 4:16 [twice]; 5:1; 9:30, 32; 10:6). Second, Paul's concluding assertion, "and everything which is not from faith is sin" (14:23b), carries much broader contextual implications as well. As Franzmann recognizes:

> If it is true that our only righteousness is "the righteousness of God through faith in Jesus Christ" (3:22), then all that does not flow from this our faith in Him is sin. If an act ignores and overrides the redeeming death of Christ (v. 15), if it withdraws from the royal reign of God which gives men righteousness and peace and joy (v. 17), if it contradicts the lordship of the Christ, who died and rose for us that He might be our Lord in life and death (vv. 7–9), if it forgets that what we have received from God we have received in trust and that "each of us shall give account of himself to God" (vv. 10–12)—any act that forgets all that is sin.[150]

The climactic statement of 14:23b also retrieves the noun for "sin" (ἁμαρτία). It appears here for the last time in the letter and only the second time since 8:10. The other occurrence came in 11:27, where Paul cites God's promise in Is 27:9 to "take away their sins." Here it is possible that ἁμαρτία could describe "any act that does not match our sincerely held convictions about what our Christian faith allows us to do and prohibits us from doing."[151] If so, "the 'strong'… should not force the 'weak' to eat meat, or drink wine, or ignore the Sabbath, when the 'weak' are not yet convinced that their faith in Christ allows them to do so. For to do so would be to force them into sin."[152] Such coercion itself would surely also be "sin," but that reads "forcing" into the text. More likely, however, Ambrosiaster is accurate when he summarizes that the weak person "makes himself guilty when he does what he thinks he ought not to. If someone acts against his better judgment in a matter of conscience, then Paul says that it is a sin."[153] Fortunately, "whenever our heart condemns us, God is greater than our heart" (1 Jn 3:20). This explains Paul's emphasis upon "faith"

---

[148] Cranfield, *Romans*, 729; similarly, Murray, *Romans*, 2:196; Sanday and Headlam, *Romans*, 393; Fitzmyer, *Romans*, 700: " 'conviction,' … a confidence that proceeds from Christian faith."

[149] Lenski, *Romans*, 855; Moo, *Romans*, 863, speaks of it as " 'conviction' stemming from one's faith in Christ."

[150] Franzmann, *Romans*, 254.

[151] Moo, *Romans*, 863; he inserts the notion of conscience here based upon 1 Cor 10:25–30 (863, n. 90).

[152] Moo, *Romans*, 864.

[153] Ambrosiaster, *Romans* (Bray, *Romans*, ACCS NT 6:352).

(14:22–23). For if faith itself is destroyed (14:15, 20), a person's state before God reverts back to what it was apart from Christ and he "remains under judgment" (14:23), and sin regains its reign (e.g., 3:9; 5:20; 6:16–17, 20–21).

Conclusion: The Relational Focus of Faith (14:23b)

The primary grounding in this entire chapter rests upon theological and relational truths. This is evident from the following: the assertion that "God received him to himself" (14:3), which is equally applicable to both the strong and the weak person; the prominence of one's relationship to the Lord (14:6); the fact that, whether we live or die, together we belong to the Lord Jesus, who died for us and lives (14:7–9, 15); and God's kingdom defined in terms of "righteousness and peace and joy in [the] Holy Spirit" (14:17). All these, then, are obtained from God through Christ how? Paul clearly articulates that righteousness is received "from faith" (ἐκ πίστεως) and from nowhere else (see 1:17; 3:26, 30; 4:16 [twice]; 5:1; 9:30, 32; 10:6). Similarly, then, those declared righteous from faith have its resulting peace in relationship with God (5:1; see also 14:17). All of these kingdom gifts flow from God to us. They are to be received from faith and with thanksgiving (14:6). Rom 14:23b asserts that *to step outside of faith means to step out of that relationship and end up being back in sin, which results in condemnation*. This essential truth runs throughout Romans; it is encapsulated concisely and restated in 14:23b: "and everything which is not from faith is sin."

Those who advocate that "faith" (πίστις) in 14:22–23 deals merely with *our own* convictions reveal an anthropocentric tendency. But my convictions and whether or not I act in line with or contrary to them are *not* ultimately determinative in matters of sin or faith. But, for Paul, all that really matters consists in *what God says, does, and gives*.[154] As Dunn rightly notes, "faith" (πίστις) does not describe "a secondary conviction (confidence) deduced from [one's] faith."[155] Instead *it remains the channel through which God delivers all of his kingdom's gifts to us, and he does so in and through our Lord Jesus Christ* (e.g., 14:4, 8–9, 14, 15, 18).[156]

Sure, Paul knows and remains "persuaded in the Lord Jesus [πέπεισμαι ἐν κυρίῳ Ἰησοῦ] that nothing is unclean through itself" (14:14). But he has also already asserted: "I have been persuaded and remain convinced [πέπεισμαι]

---

[154] For the God-centered perspective and focus throughout the entire letter, see Middendorf, *Romans 1–8*, 21–22, 27, 49–51; in this volume, see "Romans 1–4: The Righteousness of God" in the introduction to Romans 9–16, as well as "God" in "The Three Foci of Romans 9–11" in the introduction to Romans 9–11. See also the commentary on 1:17, 32; 2:11, 16, 29; 3:1–8, 19–20, 29–30; 4:21; 9:5, 11b–12a, 16, 22–24, 29; 10:21; 11:1–2, 33–36; 12:19; 13:1–2; 14:10–12; 15:5, 8, 13; 16:25, 27.

[155] Dunn, *Romans*, 828.

[156] For more on the definition of "faith," see Middendorf, *Romans 1–8*, 88–90, 280–82, 295–98; for "life in and through Jesus Christ our Lord" as the dominant theme in Romans 5–8, see Middendorf, *Romans 1–8*, 377–80.

that neither death nor life, neither spiritual beings nor authorities, neither present things nor the things about to come, nor powers, neither height nor depth, nor any other created entity will be able to separate us from God's love which is in Christ Jesus our Lord!" (ἐν Χριστῷ Ἰησοῦ τῷ κυρίῳ ἡμῶν, 8:38–39). As Käsemann concludes: "Christ remains the only measure for all."[157]

---

[157] Käsemann, *Romans*, 379.

To the Strong and Then to All:
Bear With and Receive One Another
as Christ Received You to Himself

Translation

15 ¹And we, the strong, ought to bear the weaknesses of the ones without strength and not to please ourselves. ²Let each one of us please the neighbor for the good, toward building up. ³Indeed, even the Christ did not please himself, but just as it stands written: "The revilings of the ones who reviled you fell upon me." ⁴For as much as was written previously was written for our teaching so that through the patient endurance and through the encouragement of the Scriptures we might have hope.

⁵And may the God of patient endurance and of encouragement give to you the same mindset among one another in accord with Christ Jesus ⁶so that with the same purpose you might with one mouth glorify the God and Father of our Lord Jesus Christ. ⁷Therefore, receive one another to yourselves, just as the Christ also received you to himself to [the] glory of God.

Textual Notes

15:1 ὀφείλομεν—See the second textual note on 13:8, though the sense here is more accurately "to be constrained by circumstance, … *ought*" (BDAG, s.v. ὀφείλω, 3).

ἡμεῖς οἱ δυνατοί—The adjective δυνατός refers to "being capable or competent" (BDAG, 1). Here it is used in regard to a specific matter or with reference "to an area of competence or skill" (BDAG, 1 b). The form is plural and substantival and is used in apposition to the emphatic pronoun ἡμεῖς, which is the subject of the verb: "we, the strong."

τὰ ἀσθενήματα τῶν ἀδυνάτων—The noun ἀσθένημα occurs only here in Biblical Greek but is derived from the common verb ἀσθενέω, "be weak, sick," whose participle denoted the one "weak (in the faith)" in 14:1–2. This definite neuter noun is plural (τὰ ἀσθενήματα) and means "the weaknesses" (see BDAG). The definite genitive adjective that follows (τῶν ἀδυνάτων) is from ἀδύνατος and functions substantively: "the ones without strength" (cf. NASB).[1] With the negating *alpha* privative (BDF, § 117.1), ἀδύνατος expresses the opposite of the adjective used in the previous phrase οἱ δυνατοί, "the strong," and functions as a synonym of the participle ὁ ἀσθενῶν, "the one who is weak," in 14:1–2.

---

[1] See Wallace, *Greek Grammar*, 294–95.

βαστάζειν—This complementary infinitive,[2] used with the modal verb ὀφείλομεν, "we ought," means "to sustain a burden, *carry, bear*" (BDAG, s.v. βαστάζω, 2). For literal uses, see, e.g., Mk 14:13; Lk 7:14. Though figurative in meaning here, it does *not* have the negative connotations of "put up with" (BDAG, 2 b β) or, as Barrett suggests, "endure."[3] The only other occurrence of the verb in Romans is in the image of a root ungrudgingly bearing branches (11:18).

μὴ ἑαυτοῖς ἀρέσκειν—The infinitive is from ἀρέσκω, which means "*please, accommodate*" (BDAG, 2). It is negated (μή) and takes as its dative object the reflexive pronoun ἑαυτοῖς, "ourselves." Similarly, it is negated and takes a reflexive pronoun in 15:3 (οὐχ ἑαυτῷ ἤρεσεν). BDAG further observes: "Sacrifice of self-interest is a major component of the foregoing theme" (BDAG, 2 a). Three of the verb's four uses in Romans occur in three consecutive verses here (15:1–3); elsewhere in Romans it appears only in 8:8.

15:2 ἕκαστος ἡμῶν ... ἀρεσκέτω—For the verb ἀρέσκω, "to please," see the preceding textual note. ἀρεσκέτω is a third person singular present imperative: "let each one [ἕκαστος] of us [ἡμῶν] please ..." It takes the dative object discussed in the next textual note.

τῷ πλησίον—For this dative article and indeclinable adverb that forms a substantive, "the neighbor," see the first textual note on 13:10, as well as the sixth textual note on 13:9. Those two verses have the only other uses of πλησίον in Romans.

εἰς τὸ ἀγαθὸν πρὸς οἰκοδομήν—These two prepositional phrases, "for the good, toward building up," could both indicate purpose.[4] But there is also a sense of result or goal, particularly in the second phrase.[5]

15:3 οὐχ ἑαυτῷ ἤρεσεν—The form ἤρεσεν is an aorist active indicative. For ἀρέσκω, "to please," see the fifth textual note on 15:1, where too it was negated and took a dative reflexive pronoun as its object.

καθὼς γέγραπται—In Romans Paul is fond of the formula "just as it stands written," utilizing it fourteen times to introduce a Scripture citation. See the fourth textual note on 1:17 and the commentary on 1:17b. γέγραπται is the perfect passive indicative of γράφω, "to write." The next verse employs this verb, its compound προγράφω, and the cognate noun γραφή, all in reference to Scripture; see the first three textual notes on 15:4.

οἱ ὀνειδισμοὶ τῶν ὀνειδιζόντων—The noun ὀνειδισμός is followed by a genitive plural participle of its cognate verb, ὀνειδίζω, used substantively.[6] The verb means "to find fault in a way that demeans the other, *reproach, revile, mock, heap insults upon* as

---

2 See Wallace, *Greek Grammar*, 598–99.

3 Barrett, *Romans*, 269.

4 Dunn, *Romans*, 838, refers to the "double purpose phrases" and compares 1 Cor 10:33.

5 For the prepositions, see Wallace, *Greek Grammar*, 369 and 380; for the merging of purpose and result, see Wallace's discussion of purpose-result ἵνα clauses on 473–74.

6 See Wallace, *Greek Grammar*, 619–21.

a way of shaming" (BDAG, 1). The noun then refers to an "act of disparagement that results in disgrace, *reproach, reviling, disgrace, insult*" (BDAG).

ἐπέπεσαν—This aorist form is from the compound verb ἐπιπίπτω, "to fall upon" someone. Elsewhere its subject may be "fear" (Lk 1:12; Acts 19:17; Rev 11:11) or the Holy Spirit (Acts 8:16; 10:44; 11:15). Cf. the simple verb πίπτω, "to fall," in Rom 11:11, 22; 14:4.

15:4 ὅσα γὰρ προεγράφη—The compound verb προγράφω, "to write before," appears only here in Romans and elsewhere in the NT only in Gal 3:1; Eph 3:3; Jude 4. Here it refers to the OT Scriptures, while in Eph 3:3 Paul uses it for his own epistle to the Ephesians. Here the form is the third singular aorist indicative passive, whose neuter plural subject is the adjective ὅσος, which refers "to a comparative quantity or number of objects or events; *how much (many), as much (many) as*" (BDAG, 2): thus "for as much as was written previously."

εἰς τὴν ἡμετέραν διδασκαλίαν ἐγράφη—This clause has an aorist indicative passive of the simple verb γράφω, "to write," referring to the composition of the OT. The prepositional phrase with εἰς indicates "the vocation, use, or end ... *for*" (BDAG, s.v. εἰς, 4 d). ἡμετέραν is the accusative singular feminine form of the first person plural adjective ἡμέτερος, "our." For διδασκαλία, "teaching," see 12:7.

ἵνα διὰ τῆς ὑπομονῆς καὶ διὰ τῆς παρακλήσεως τῶν γραφῶν—For ὑπομονή, "patient endurance," see the third textual note and the commentary on 5:3; for παράκλησις, "encouragement," see the commentary on 12:8 and here below. Here ἵνα with the subjunctive (ἔχωμεν; see the last textual note on this verse) expresses purpose, answering the question Why?[7] But it also conveys the result of such instruction. BDAG, s.v. ἵνα, 3, notes that "in many cases purpose and result cannot be clearly differentiated, and hence ἵνα is used for the result that follows according to the purpose of the subj[ect] or of God. ... Here ἵνα means both 'in order that' and 'so that.' " Wallace adds: "In other words, the NT writers employ the language to reflect their theology: what God purposes is what happens and, consequently, ἵνα is used to express both the divine purpose and the result."[8] See also the first textual note on 15:6.

Dunn and Käsemann differentiate between the two uses of the preposition διά, suggesting that the first expresses attendant circumstance and that the second is causal.[9] But it seems more probable that the sense is the same and that διά is instrumental, "*via, through*" (BDAG, A 3). The definite plural of the noun γραφή, "a writing," denotes "the Scriptures" and is cognate to the preceding verbs γέγραπται, προεγράφη, and ἐγράφη (15:3–4).

τὴν ἐλπίδα—For ἐλπίς and the distinction between the Hebrew and Greek concepts of "hope," see the commentary on 4:18.[10]

---

[7] See Wallace, *Greek Grammar*, 472.

[8] Wallace, *Greek Grammar*, 473; see his complete discussion of the matter on 471–74, as well as the fourth textual note on 3:8 and the commentary on 4:16; 5:20; 14:9.

[9] Dunn, *Romans*, 839; Käsemann, *Romans*, 383; cf. Moo, *Romans*, 870, nn. 36–37, who says that the first is attendant circumstance and the second is instrumental.

[10] Middendorf, *Romans 1–8*, 361.

ἔχωμεν—This subjunctive of the verb ἔχω is the verb of the ἵνα clause (see the third textual note on this verse): "so that … we might have."

15:5 ὁ δὲ θεὸς … δῴη—The verb is the aorist active optative of δίδωμι. Wallace calls it a "voluntative optative," which occurs "in an independent clause to express an *obtainable wish* or a *prayer*";[11] thus "may (the) God … give."

τῆς ὑπομονῆς καὶ τῆς παρακλήσεως—For the two genitive definite nouns, see the third textual note on 15:4. Here the genitives are qualitative,[12] signifying divine attributes: the God "of patient endurance and of encouragement."

τὸ αὐτὸ φρονεῖν ἐν ἀλλήλοις—The pronoun αὐτός with the article (τὸ αὐτό) functions "as an identifying adjective," which is translated as "the *same*."[13] For φρονέω, "set one's mind on," see the third textual note and the commentary on 8:5. The articular infinitive of φρονέω functions as the direct object of the optative δῴη, "may he give" (see the first textual note on 15:5).[14] The entire clause means "may (the) God … give to you the same mindset among one another."

15:6 ἵνα … δοξάζητε—In this clause with ἵνα and a subjunctive verb, purpose and result merge as it "indicates *both the intention and its sure accomplishment*"[15] (see also the third textual note on 15:4). It expresses both the reason why God gives "the same mindset" (15:5) and what results from it: "so that you might glorify" God.

ὁμοθυμαδὸν ἐν ἑνὶ στόματι—The adverb ὁμοθυμαδόν (ὁμός, "the same, together" + θυμός, "desire, will," + the adverbial ending -δον) means "*with one mind/purpose/ impulse*" (BDAG). Here the translation "with the same purpose" conveys an underlying unity, which is then vocalized "with one mouth." See the commentary.

15:7 διό—This is an inferential conjunction used six times in Romans: "*therefore*" (BDAG).

προσλαμβάνεσθε … προσελάβετο—The verb προσλαμβάνω thematically marks the opening and closing of 14:1–15:7 (followed by an epilogue in 15:8–13).[16] In fact, these two forms are identical to the ones in 14:1 and 14:3, a present middle imperative second person plural and an aorist middle indicative third person singular (see the second textual note on 14:1 and the third textual note on 14:3). The commentary discusses the contextual significance of the middle voice, "receive *to oneself*."

---

[11] Wallace, *Greek Grammar*, 481–83.

[12] Wallace, *Greek Grammar*, 86–88, notes that the qualitative or "attributive" genitive in the NT corresponds to OT Hebrew usage. In the OT the Hebrew construct state is commonly used in place of an adjective.

[13] Wallace, *Greek Grammar*, 349–50; for the various uses of αὐτός, see Mounce, *Basics of Biblical Greek*, 101–3.

[14] See Wallace, *Greek Grammar*, 601–3.

[15] Wallace, *Greek Grammar*, 473; see 473–74.

[16] See "The Themes and Parameters of Romans 14:1–15:13" in the introduction to 14:1–15:13.

Commentary

An Unfortunate Chapter Break and an Overview (15:1–7)

While what we now call 15:1 marks a slight shift in Paul's argument, "the chapter break is poorly located in this instance."[17] Unfortunately, this is not the only example. At a number of points in Romans, chapter divisions become particularly disruptive and seem improperly inserted right in the midst of the development of Paul's argument (e.g., 3:1; 8:1; 10:1; 13:1). These artificial "chapters" tend to inhibit the understanding of those who do not grasp that they were added centuries later. In this case, people might imagine that 15:1 ushers in a new topic.[18]

However, *15:1–7 actually wraps up Paul's discussion, introduced in 14:1, of the ongoing relevance of OT regulations for festivals and, particularly, foods.* The issue of their (ir)relevance for the Christian life seems to have become particularly disruptive within and among the house churches in Rome.[19] Rom 14:1–13a hones in on the impropriety of the judging done mostly by the "weak" (14:1–2; 15:1) against those whom Paul now calls the "strong" (15:1). In 14:13b, Paul turns his attention more directly toward the strong, urging them not to cause the weak to stumble or take offense, even though the strong are right in understanding that all foods are now clean (Mk 7:19; Acts 10–11). Paul did offer a more general blessing and warning in 14:22b–23, which perhaps led to the insertion of a chapter break at 15:1. But 15:1–7 continues in the same vein as the previous section (14:13b–23) as it is also aimed most directly at the "strong" (15:1).[20]

Throughout Romans 14, Paul keeps Jesus Christ and the kingdom, which his death and resurrection graciously brings to us, at the heart of the discussion (14:3, 7–9, 15b, 17).[21] As Paul goes on to identify with and further describe those who concur with his "strong" position, he points out that their strength does not reside in themselves and certainly provides no warrant for pleasing themselves. It comes, instead, through a full recognition of what Christ accomplished in his suffering (15:3) and, thereby, how he received us to himself (15:7). As Paul stated in the opening of this lengthy letter, this "Good News of God" (εὐαγγέλιον θεοῦ, 1:1) is God's "power" to save (δύναμις, 1:16) and remains firmly rooted in the (OT) Scriptures themselves (ἐν γραφαῖς ἁγίαις, "in holy

---

[17] Dunn, *Romans*, 836.

[18] Note also the hypothesis that 14:23, followed by the doxology of 16:25–27, concludes the letter! For details, see the excursus "Textual Criticism and the End of Romans" following the commentary on 15:23–33.

[19] See the introduction to 14:1–15:13.

[20] Moo, *Romans*, 864, attempts "to steer a middle course" and contends: "The introduction of new vocabulary and new arguments suggests that 15:1 marks a new stage in the discussion" (865).

[21] Käsemann, *Romans*, 380, errs here suggesting that in 15:1–6 "we now have thematic reflection on the model of Christ."

writings," 1:2; γέγραπται, "it stands written," 15:3; προεγράφη, "was written previously," 15:4).

On the basis of a proper understanding of the Gospel, Paul *primarily calls out the strong* in 15:1–3. He reminds them of Christ who, rather than pleasing himself, suffered in order to receive them to himself (15:3, 7). Thus they should respond in the same way, receiving especially the weak with the same mindset as Christ, all to the glory of God (15:7). Of course, the weak, who were previously and repeatedly remonstrated against judging the strong (14:3, 4, 5, 10, 13), ought not revile the strong, but, instead, mutually receive them as well. Paul surely accepts and supports the notion that these two groups may well, at least for a time, maintain their different "convictions" on the disputed matters (14:1). He does not urge either side to change, but calls for mutual acceptance of one another in spite of their differences. This demonstrates that the unity Paul seeks (15:6) does not *require* a uniformity of practice. Instead, *it resides within God's acceptance of all believers in Christ (14:3; 15:7) and is, therefore, able to accommodate a variety of views on issues that fall into the category of adiaphora.*[22] In the midst of them, he implores God to grant us endurance and encouragement in Christ and through his Scriptures (15:4, 5)!

Paul then uses 15:7 as yet another effective hinge.[23] It nicely concludes the discussion of different convictions begun in 14:1 in a manner equally applicable to both weak and strong. At the same time, in a manner most comparable to 9:24, 15:7 also points ahead to a most profound conclusion, which marvelously culminates the overall theological content of the letter. To be sure, 15:7–13 functions as a great conclusion to 14:1–15:13, but its content truly reaches all the way back to 9:1 and, even more impressively, to 1:1. Most explicitly it returns to the thematic thought of 1:16, "to Jew first and also to Greek." Therefore, both commentary sections (15:1–7 and 15:7–13) include 15:7, and 15:7–13 is treated as a separate unit.

Paul's Plea: No Strong Self-Pleasers Please! (15:1–2)

"And we, the strong, ought to bear the weaknesses of the ones without strength and not to please ourselves" (15:1). Paul explicitly addresses those who now eat all foods and who no longer observe the Sabbath and other holy days (14:1–6). For the first time, he characterizes them as "the strong" (οἱ δυνατοί, 15:1). Dunn defines the term δυνατός, beginning with a reference to its

> regular usage in the historical books of the OT/LXX = "the mighty men" (1 Sam 2:10; 17:51; 2 Sam 1:25, 27; 10:7; 16:6; etc.; so also 1 Macc 4:3; Acts 25:5; 1 Cor 1:26). The implication is of a strength or power which gives prominence and the possibility of dominating others. Hence the thought of greater responsibility. ... For Paul, of course, the thought is not of physical

---

[22] Regarding adiaphora, see further "Romans 14:1–15:7—Summary and Application" below.

[23] For other hinges, see, e.g., 8:1–4; 9:24; 10:4–5, 16–17; 13:7–8; 14:13.

strength, but the strength of superior knowledge and understanding of how God's grace works (cf. 2 Cor 12:10; 13:9).[24]

Here the description applies to the relatively narrow matters under consideration. As discussed above, the strength of the strong resides not in themselves, but in the saving "power" of the Gospel (δύναμις, 1:16).

Theodore of Mopsuestia contends: "Paul is speaking to the Gentiles, who looked down on the Jews because they kept the law."[25] But such a simplistic ethnic categorization remains untenable. A more nuanced assessment recognizes how "Paul the Jew feels more at one with the gentile (and more liberated Jewish) believers than with the majority(?) of the Jewish Christians."[26] By emphatically beginning with "we, the strong" (ἡμεῖς οἱ δυνατοί, 15:1), Paul aligns himself with those who, he thereby implies, have come to the correct conclusion. This explains the *switch to the dominant use of first person plural forms here*, though they also appear sporadically in chapter 14 (14:7, 8, 10, 12, 13, 19). How the strong handle this recognition becomes a true mark of Christian maturity.

What the strong owe is "to bear the weaknesses of the ones without strength" (15:1). In regard to the weak, Paul speaks specifically of their conviction to continue adhering to OT regulations regarding foods and festivals even though the Christ has come. For the strong "to bear" (βαστάζειν, 15:1) their weaknesses does *not* simply mean passively putting up with, tolerating, or enduring the weak (see the fourth textual note on 15:1). As similarly in Gal 6:2,[27] Paul tells the strong *actively* "to bear" the weaknesses of the weak, that is, to take them upon themselves. Matthew uses the same verb when referencing Jesus' healing ministry in fulfillment of Is 53:11: "In order that what was spoken through the prophet Isaiah might be fulfilled, saying: 'He himself took our weaknesses [τὰς ἀσθενείας] and bore [ἐβάστασεν] our diseases" (Mt 8:17). In Romans 14–15, "bearing" weaknesses would entail not exercising one's freedom to indulge in such foods (see 14:22); it may also involve continued observance of the Sabbath and other OT festivals (e.g., gathering and worshiping on Saturday). In light of the verse to follow (15:2), it likely also means bearing up when being judged (improperly) by the weak without striking back. "The strong" (οἱ δυνατοί, 15:1) are able to do so because they are not seeking to please themselves.[28]

Instead, Paul urges the strong: "Let each one of us please the neighbor for the good, toward building up" (15:2). Paul's language moves from his general

---

[24] Dunn, *Romans*, 837.

[25] Theodore of Mopsuestia, *Romans* (Bray, *Romans*, ACCS NT 6:353).

[26] Dunn, *Romans*, 837. See "Who Are the 'Weak' and the 'Strong'? Addressees Again!" in the introduction to 14:1–15:13.

[27] See Das, *Galatians*, 606–7.

[28] The substantival adjective "the strong" (οἱ δυνατοί) is cognate to the verb δύναμαι, "be powerful, able"; see the discussion of the verb, including its use in Luke's Gospel, in Middendorf, *Romans 1–8*, 87; see also the discussion of the adjective δυνατός, "strong, able," but translated as "powerful" in 4:21 and substantivally as "power" in 9:22, in the commentary on 4:21 and 9:22.

form of address to the strong in the first person plural in 15:1, "we, the strong," toward an exhortation directed toward "each one" individually (ἕκαστος, 15:2).[29] The content of his plea coincides with the language of chapters 13 and 14. The reference to the singular "neighbor" (τῷ πλησίον, 15:2) likely stems from Lev 19:18 as cited in Rom 13:9: "you will love your neighbor [τὸν πλησίον] as yourself." Earlier Paul explained what this means in these negative terms: "love does not work evil to the neighbor" (13:10) and "for if on account of food your brother is being grieved, you are no longer walking according to love" (14:15). Now we get to *the positive, loving, and active behavior:* pleasing "the neighbor" (15:2). Moo makes this interesting observation:

> What is involved is not the "pleasing people" *rather than God* that Paul elsewhere condemns (Gal. 1:10; Col. 3:22; 1 Thess. 2:4; Eph. 6:6), but a "pleasing" fellow believers *rather than ourselves.*[30]

In Rom 15:2, Paul directs the pleasing toward specific ends. First, it is "for the good" (εἰς τὸ ἀγαθόν). While including an explanation of purpose, an expression of end or goal also applies (see the third textual note on 15:2). The ultimate "good" is eschatological salvation,[31] but this phrase also includes everything else which would be for a neighbor's good.

Paul adds to the thought of the first prepositional phrase by adding a second, "toward building up" (πρὸς οἰκοδομήν). It conveys an even stronger sense of goal. Paul recently used the noun οἰκοδομή in 14:19. There he asserted that we, the strong, "are pursuing the things of peace and the things of the building up for one another" (διώκωμεν καὶ τὰ τῆς οἰκοδομῆς τῆς εἰς ἀλλήλους). Indeed, the singular forms in 15:2 (ἕκαστος, "each one"; τῷ πλησίον, "the neighbor") counter any notion, already rebutted in the commentary on 14:19, that the goal of building up "does not have the individual as such in view."[32] Any attempt to distinguish "the growth to maturity of the whole congregation"[33] from that of the weaker brother surely presents a false alternative.

The Messiah Who Willingly Bore All Reviling (15:3)

But how is such selfless living possible? Origen identifies both the problem and its solution:

> We must not please ourselves but rather assume the example of Christ, who alone died to sin. ... We do not have this example of living in ourselves, but we get it from Christ. ...

---

[29] Moo, *Romans,* 867.

[30] Moo, *Romans,* 867.

[31] Cranfield, *Romans,* 732, suggests that the neighbor's salvation is most in view.

[32] As Dunn, *Romans,* 838, maintains.

[33] Dunn, *Romans,* 838.

> Christ did not please himself nor did he think it was robbery to be equal with God [Phil 2:6], but wanting to please men, that is, to save them, he suffered the reproaches of those who reproached God.[34]

Chrysostom goes so far as to claim that "Paul always points to Christ's self-sacrifice when he asks us to make sacrifices."[35] Yet Paul intends Christ to be more than an example for us to imitate; his self-sacrifice reconciled us to God and one another (5:10; 14:3; 15:7) and furnishes us with the "righteousness and peace and joy in [the] Holy Spirit" (14:17) that enables us to sacrifice ourselves to please our neighbor. Therefore 15:3 provides the basis for the imperative of 15:7 ("receive one another"), toward which Paul already aims. "Indeed, even the Christ did not please himself" (15:3a).[36]

Paul's use of the article indicates that "the Christ" (ὁ Χριστός, that is, "the Messiah," "the Anointed One"; cf. Jn 1:41; 4:25) functions as a title.[37] Contrary to the misconception of many modern readers who often regard "Christ" as equivalent to Jesus' last name (!), Cranfield correctly considers it "unlikely that Paul ever used the word (whether with or without the article) as a mere proper name without any consciousness of its titular character."[38]

His reference to "the Christ" (ὁ Χριστός) in 15:3 encompasses Jesus' self-denial which, much to the initial chagrin of his disciples (e.g., Mt 16:21–22; Mk 10:35–38; Lk 9:44–46; 18:31–34), accomplishes our ultimate good and continues to edify his followers (cf. Rom 15:2). In fact, Jesus' refusal to please himself comprises his entire messianic mission for our sake, beginning with his incarnation and extending through the cross (2 Corinthians 8; Galatians 4). But it surely reaches its culmination on Good Friday (e.g., 2 Cor 8:9; Phil 2:5–8). This becomes particularly evident when Paul proceeds to cite Ps 69:9 (MT 69:10; LXX 68:10): "But just as it stands written: 'The revilings of the ones who reviled you fell upon me' " (Rom 15:3b). Translating the noun ὀνειδισμός and its cognates consistently and effectively into English presents difficulties. The use of "insults" for the plural here seems too weak, the technical "reproaches" too unfamiliar. The use of "revilings" conjures up notions of vile spoken words and fits well (see Mt 27:39–44; Mk 15:29–32; Lk 23:35–39).

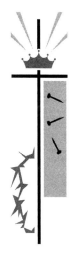

---

[34] Origen, *Romans* (Bray, *Romans*, ACCS NT 6:342, 354).

[35] Chrysostom, *Homilies on Romans*, 27 (Bray, *Romans*, ACCS NT 6:354).

[36] In 1 Cor 10:31–11:1, Paul uses the verb "to please" of himself as an example which then serves toward the imitation of Christ. Lockwood, *1 Corinthians*, 347, translates: "Just as I please [ἀρέσκω] all people in all things, not seeking my own advantage, but that of the many, that they may be saved. Be imitators of me, as also I am of Christ" (1 Cor 10:33–11:1); for his interpretation, see 354–55.

[37] See Käsemann, *Romans*, 382.

[38] Cranfield, *Romans*, 732, n. 5. Further discussion is provided by the excursus " 'Christ': Messianic Title or Proper Name? A Third Option?" in Das, *Galatians*, 90–94.

The Background and New Testament Use of Psalm 69:9

While Paul cites only the last clause of Ps 69:9 (MT 69:10), the entire verse, cited below from the MT and the LXX, is illuminating:

כִּי־קִנְאַת בֵּיתְךָ אֲכָלָתְנִי
וְחֶרְפּוֹת חוֹרְפֶיךָ נָפְלוּ עָלָי:

For the zeal of your house devoured me,
and the taunts of the ones taunting you fell upon me.

ὅτι ὁ ζῆλος τοῦ οἴκου σου κατέφαγέν με,
καὶ οἱ ὀνειδισμοὶ τῶν ὀνειδιζόντων σε ἐπέπεσαν ἐπ' ἐμέ.

For the zeal of your house consumed me,
and the revilings of the ones reviling you fell upon me.

In the original context of this Davidic psalm, the first half of the verse establishes that the second person singular pronoun ("*your* house") refers to God, who patiently endures the taunts of those opposing him.[39] The psalmist David, because of his own zeal for Yahweh's house, suffers the same vile words. Initially, then, Ps 69:9 (MT 69:10) expresses his own personal anguish in the midst of great distress. Note that he "laments his affliction at the hands not only of his enemies, but also, it would appear, of his own people and kinsfolk (69:8, 28 [MT 69:9, 29])."[40] David suffered such afflictions,[41] as did Christ all the more.

Psalm 69 then becomes quite prominent in the NT. Psalms 2, 22, 110, and 118 are quoted more often, but Psalm 69 may be next after them. "The most explicit allusions" to it are "usually with direct reference to Christ's passion and the events surrounding it."[42] *The NT extends the application of Psalm 69 to Jesus in a fuller way.* After the death and resurrection of Jesus, the razed and risen temple, Jn 2:17 recounts how the disciples remembered the words Jesus spoke when he cleansed the temple and connected those words to Ps 69:9 (MT

---

[39] One interpretation of "your [God's] house" in Ps 69:9 (MT 69:10) is that in David's day it referred to God's sanctuary or tabernacle. David had begun planning for the temple, which would house the ark he had brought to Jerusalem (2 Samuel 6), but the temple would not be built until later by his son Solomon (1 Kings 5–8). It is possible that "your house" might also refer to the Davidic dynasty, from whose lineage the Christ would be born. In God's promise to David in 2 Samuel 7, "house" (בַּיִת) refers in some verses to the sanctuary (tabernacle or temple) and in others to the line of Davidic kings, culminating in the Son (2 Sam 7:11–16; "he shall be to me a son," 2 Sam 7:14). Both interpretations support the NT presentation of Jesus Christ as the Son of David and the Son of God (e.g., Mt 1:1, 20; 22:42; Mk 1:1; Lk 1:35; 3:31, 38), whose own body is the temple which was destroyed and raised again on the third day (Jn 2:13–22).

[40] Dunn, *Romans*, 839.

[41] See, e.g., the persecution of David by Saul and his countrymen in 1 Samuel 18–27 and by his own son Absalom in 2 Samuel 13–18.

[42] Dunn, *Romans*, 839. In the accounts of Jesus' crucifixion, Ps 69:21 (MT 69:22) is alluded to in Mt 27:34, 48; Mk 15:23, 36; Lk 23:36; Jn 19:28–29. See also these quotations of the psalm: Ps 69:9 (MT 69:10) in Jn 2:17; Ps 69:4 (MT 69:5) in Jn 15:25; Ps 69:25 (MT 69:26) in Acts 1:20; and Ps 69:22–23 (MT 69:23–24) in Rom 11:9–10.

69:10).[43] They, like Paul, understood that Jesus himself was the ultimate first person singular referent of the "me" upon whom the "revilings" (ὀνειδισμοί) against God fell. At his crucifixion, the cognate verb ὀνειδίζω characterizes the taunts of the criminals: "and the ones being crucified with him kept reviling him" (ὠνείδιζον, Mk 15:32; also Mt 27:44).

Psalm 69:9 in Romans 15:3

As Paul uses the passage from Psalm 69 in Rom 15:3, *Christ himself is depicted as speaking the words*. Thus, as elsewhere in the NT, the referent of "me" has been extended beyond David, who originally composed the lyrics. Must the "you" then still be God, or may a change of refcrent be intended here as well? In agreement with Origen as cited above,[44] Cranfield asserts that "in this verse of Romans the σε ['you,' singular] must refer to God."[45] But that leads to a vague understanding of why Paul cites this verse, as well as the sense of the statement that follows in 15:4. Moo illustrates: "Why Paul uses this particular quotation is not clear since we have no reason to think that the 'strong' were enduring 'reproaches.' "[46] He then weakens the term for "reproaches" in order to suggest that Paul's pragmatic purpose for the strong serves "to put their own 'suffering' in perspective: occasionally abstaining from meat or wine or observing a special religious day should not seem like much of a burden in comparison with what Christ had to suffer for the sake of others."[47] While certainly true, the eight uses of the verb "to judge" (κρίνω) in Romans 14, along with three other cognates, lend credence to the notion that *the weak are, in fact, reviling the strong for violating OT scriptural injunctions* (see the introduction to 14:1–15:13). This appears most evident in 14:16: "therefore do not let that which is for your good be slandered" (μὴ βλασφημείσθω).

The excursus "Beyond Typology" following the commentary on 12:1–8 demonstrates how so many typological applications of the OT to Christ in the NT are also extended further beyond Jesus and applied to his disciples as well. The same phenomenon occurs with the verb ὀνειδίζω, "revile," which has Jesus as its object in Mt 27:44; Mk 15:32. Like Jesus, his disciples will endure "reviling" in their own lives as well (ὀνειδίζω, Mt 5:11; Lk 6:22; 1 Pet 4:14). Paul extends the meaning similarly, but in the opposite direction in Rom 11:9–10. There he takes words from this same psalm, Psalm 69 (LXX Psalm 68), which

---

[43] See Jn 2:17–22. In the quote of Ps 69:9 (MT 69:10) in Jn 2:17, the aorist verb of LXX Ps 68:10, κατέφαγεν, "devoured," is replaced by the future tense καταφάγεται, "shall devour" (Jn 2:17). Partly based upon this change, Weinrich, *John 1:1–7:1*, 346–48, interprets the verse to refer not so much to Jesus' zeal in cleansing the temple, but especially to Jesus' suffering and death on the cross as the event in which zeal for the Father's house "shall devour" him. "The Scripture" which the disciples then were able to "believe" after Easter (Jn 2:22) was Ps 69:9 (MT 69:10); see Weinrich, *John 1:1–7:1*, 354–55.

[44] Origen, *Romans* (Bray, *Romans*, ACCS NT 6:354), refers to "those who reproached God."

[45] Cranfield, *Romans*, 733; so also Murray, *Romans*, 2:198–99.

[46] Moo, *Romans*, 868.

[47] Moo, *Romans*, 869.

David implores regarding his enemies in Ps 69:22–23 (MT 69:23–24), and directs them toward those in Israel who earnestly sought to obtain righteousness on the basis of works rather than grace (Rom 11:6–7; see the commentary on 11:9–10).

This understanding makes contextual, ongoing, and Gospel-based applications of the psalm verse in Rom 15:3 relevant whenever "insults are cast, not only upon Christ but also upon the saints for God's sake."[48] When believers are reviled, whether by other believers or those outside the church, this verse describes what Paul goes on to say the Scriptures provide: "patient endurance and ... encouragement" (15:4). Those blessed results stem from the fact that *Christ himself took all of those vile words upon himself in his own passion*. As he himself bore our sin and all of its consequences (e.g., diseases) that have befallen us (Is 53:11 in Mt 8:17; see the discussion of βαστάζω, "to bear," in the commentary on Rom 15:1), so he also bore upon himself whatever vile things have been directed toward us. He died and rose to give us patient endurance and encouragement in the midst of them; even more remarkably, he did so in order that words of forgiveness might be spoken back toward those who revile him and us (Lk 23:34).

When viewed in this manner, Paul's next statement hardly swerves off into "a brief detour from his main argument."[49] Instead, Paul continues in the first person plural and offers added counsel particularly, though not exclusively, to the strong. Käsemann observes that Rom 15:4 shows "why the quotation" of the psalm verse in 15:3, "understood christologically, is being used in exhortation, and in a way similar to 4:24; 1 Cor 9:10; 10:11."[50] In fact, the passage just cited from Psalm 69 also provides an exemplar which demonstrates the overall purpose of all of the written Scriptures.

The Source of Patient Endurance, Encouragement, and Hope (15:4–5a)

The Purpose of the Scriptures (15:4)

"For as much as was written previously was written for our teaching so that through the patient endurance and through the encouragement of the Scriptures we might have hope" (15:4). Here, as with "in holy writings" (ἐν γραφαῖς ἁγίαις) in 1:2, Paul refers specifically to the contents of our OT. He now reasserts their Christocentricity, a point of heightened emphasis as Paul continues in 15:8–12.

The purpose of the written Scriptures is to deliver divine "teaching" (διδασκαλία, 15:4). Thus they are to be used according to one of the gracious gifts identified in 12:7, "the one who teaches in the teaching" (ἐν τῇ

---

[48] Pelagius, *Romans* (Bray, *Romans*, ACCS NT 6:354); similarly, Sanday and Headlam, *Romans*, 395.

[49] As Moo, *Romans*, 869, contends.

[50] Käsemann, *Romans*, 382.

διδασκαλίᾳ). While the noun διδασκαλία, "teaching," "becomes a key word in the Pastorals (15 out of 21 occurrences in the NT),"[51] one ought not press that point too far. Paul uses the cognate verb διδάσκω, "to teach," a total of sixteen times (in Romans, 2:21 [twice] and 12:7), only five of which are in the Pastorals. But the contexts in which the NT utilizes "teaching" words reinforce the point emphasized in the excursus "The New Testament Connotations and Context of Words Commonly Translated as 'Preach,' 'Teach,' and 'Prophesy' " following the commentary on 10:6–15. While the verbs κηρύσσω, "proclaim, preach," and εὐαγγελίζομαι, "evangelize, proclaim the Good News," and their cognates function almost exclusively as evangelistic terms in the NT, Paul uses προφητεύω, "prophesy," and διδάσκω, "teach," along with their cognates, for speaking gifts exercised *within* the body of Christ (e.g., 12:6–7). As a result, the emphasis on "teaching" in this verse and in the Pastorals is to be expected.

After Paul explains the purpose of the Scriptures, he lists two things which result from being taught them.[52] Written Scripture serves *both as the (intermediary) source of and the means through (διά) which one receives* "the patient endurance and … the encouragement" (15:4).[53] Paul uses the noun ὑπομονή, "patient endurance," significantly in 5:3–5 with the same sense as here (see the commentary there). When suffering slander, instruction from the Scriptures empowers one to patiently endure, literally, "remaining under" (ὑπομονή) God's declaration of righteousness with its resulting peace and access into grace (5:1–2).

Similarly, one receives "the encouragement" (τῆς παρακλήσεως, 15:4) from the Scriptures (τῶν γραφῶν, a genitive of source). This retrieves another one of the gifts listed in 12:6–8. Immediately after "teaching" in 12:7, Paul adds "the one who encourages in the encouragement" (ὁ παρακαλῶν ἐν τῇ παρακλήσει, 12:8; cf. 12:1). In the context of being reviled (15:3), the notion of "comfort" might better convey the meaning of the term, as illustrated particularly by the first chapter of 2 Corinthians (e.g., 2 Cor 1:4–7; also 2 Cor 7:4, 13). But "encouragement" maintains consistency with Romans 12 and encompasses both a sense of comfort[54] and exhortation.[55]

The purpose and outcome is "so that … we might have hope" (ἵνα … τὴν ἐλπίδα ἔχωμεν, 15:4).[56] Paul uses ἐλπίς, "hope," significantly throughout

---

[51] Dunn, *Romans*, 839. The noun διδασκαλία, "teaching," occurs eight times in 1 Timothy, three times in 2 Timothy, and four times in Titus.

[52] For ἵνα with the combined sense of purpose and result, see the third textual note on 15:4.

[53] Käsemann, *Romans*, 383, takes both prepositional phrases ("through the patient endurance and through the encouragement") as dependent upon τῶν γραφῶν, "of the Scriptures," stating: "Scripture gives comfort and leads to patience," though he concedes that it is "a debatable point." For other options, see Cranfield, *Romans*, 735; Moo, *Romans*, 870, n. 38.

[54] Cranfield, *Romans*, 737; Moo, *Romans*, 870; Murray, *Romans*, 2:199–200.

[55] Barrett, *Romans*, 270.

[56] This same combination of the verb "to have" (ἔχω) with the noun "hope" (ἐλπίς) as its object appears also in Acts 24:15; 2 Cor 3:12; 10:15; Eph 2:12; 1 Thess 4:13; 1 Jn 3:3. In all of these other verses the form of ἔχω is a present participle, "having hope."

Romans, beginning with the confident expectation which stemmed from Abraham's faith in God's promise (4:18). The noun then occurs prominently in both Romans 5 (5:2, 4, 5) and Romans 8 (8:20, 24), particularly in the context of present sufferings (also 12:12; 15:13). Paul clarifies the foundational basis for this certain "hope" in the next verse.

God, the True Source (15:5a)

"And may the God of patient endurance and of encouragement give to you the same mindset among one another in accord with Christ Jesus" (15:5). The main verb in 15:5 is the optative δῷη, "may he give." The optative mood expresses an *"obtainable wish* or a *prayer."*[57] "May he give" (δῷη) functions similarly in 2 Thess 3:16; 2 Tim 1:16, 18, as do other optatives in Rom 15:13 and, e.g., 1 Thess 5:23; 2 Thess 3:5; Philemon 20; Heb 13:21; 1 Pet 1:2; Jude 2. The form of the entire verse (Rom 15:5), then, "has a liturgical ring and suggests that Paul wrote with a view not only to winding up the section [begun in 14:1] … but also to the letter's being read within the context of a congregation gathered for worship."[58] Here Paul makes it clear that the Scriptures are the channel or instrument through which *God himself, the actual source of "patient endurance" and "encouragement,"* works in order to give us the "hope" referenced in 15:4.

Two other grammatical points are noteworthy. The postpositive conjunction δέ, "and," at the start of 15:5, "marks the fact that the prayer-wish brings the present paragraph to a conclusion,"[59] though that conclusion extends into 15:7. An observation of greater significance buttresses the point. The pronoun "to you" (ὑμῖν) is second person *plural*. Since the inception of this discussion in 14:1, Paul has used only three second person plural forms (imperatives in 14:1, 13; a pronoun in 14:16). In 15:1–4 he heavily utilizes the first person plural to address the strong, among whom he includes himself ("we," "our," "us," 15:1, 2, 4). But in 15:5 he *switches to the second person plural* and maintains that form of address in 15:6–7, as well as in 15:13. Paul thereby signals that "for the rest of the section [through 15:13] he addresses all the Christians of Rome alike and together."[60] It further indicates that Paul now wraps up his argument. But how does it end?

The Result: A Mindset of Unity (15:5b–6)

The prayer for God to "give to you the same mindset" (δῷη ὑμῖν τὸ αὐτὸ φρονεῖν) in 15:5 may sound like Paul wants the Roman Christians all to think the same thing. Specifically this would apply to the issues about which those in

---

[57] Wallace, *Greek Grammar*, 481; similarly, Cranfield, *Romans*, 736; Moo, *Romans*, 871.

[58] Dunn, *Romans*, 840.

[59] Cranfield, *Romans*, 736, who considers the present paragraph to be 15:1–6 (see 699).

[60] Cranfield, *Romans*, 737; Käsemann, *Romans*, 383, also recognizes that here "Paul is addressing the whole community."

Rome have different convictions (14:1), namely OT regulations about foods and days. These have led the weak to judge the strong and the strong to despise the weak (14:3, 5). If they would all have the same conviction, it seems the problems would dissolve. "But Paul's whole treatment of his subject throughout this section surely tells strongly against this view."[61]

A Unified Mindset Accepts Diversity in Adiaphora (15:5b)

This commentary consistently renders the φρονέω word group as expressing a "mindset." The verb fully means "to set one's mind or heart upon something, to employ one's faculty for thoughtful planning, w[ith] the emphasis upon the underlying disposition or attitude"[62] (see 8:5, 6; also 12:3, 16; 14:6). In 12:16 Paul defines authentic love as "having the same mindset toward one another" (τὸ αὐτὸ εἰς ἀλλήλους φρονοῦντες). The sense in 15:5 does *not* insist on everyone reaching the same conviction regarding foods and holy days, but, rather, urges them to have *the same attitude of Christian love toward or regarding one another*. Moo captures this by describing τὸ αὐτὸ φρονεῖν (15:5) as expressing "a common perspective and purpose."[63] Dunn's translation of τὸ αὐτὸ εἰς ἀλλήλους φρονοῦντες as "to live in harmony among yourselves"[64] seems overly interpretive, but the analogy to musical harmony with more than one pitch serves as a good illustration. Paul's teaching in 14:5–6 (with the verb φρονέω twice in 14:6) similarly encompasses the acceptance of both positions on days and diet. *Therefore, the same mindset in 15:5 means the acceptance of one another, whether "weak" (14:1–2; 15:1) or "strong" (15:1), rather than uniform agreement on the controverted issues of adiaphora.*[65]

Rom 15:7 will soon make abundantly clear that Jesus Christ freely and fully received us to himself without insisting that we achieve anything approaching a uniformity of practice with the holy Son of God. On the contrary, while we were still weak and sinful enemies of God and one another, "Christ died in behalf of us" (5:8; see 5:6–10). Paul then calls us to receive one another in the same manner (15:7; cf. 14:1).

Paul therefore pleads that the mindset of all those in Rome be "in accord with Christ Jesus" (κατὰ Χριστὸν Ἰησοῦν, 15:5b). One can hardly avoid thinking of Phil 2:5, "have this mindset among yourselves which is also in Christ Jesus" (τοῦτο φρονεῖτε ἐν ὑμῖν ὃ καὶ ἐν Χριστῷ Ἰησοῦ). That sentiment certainly incorporates setting one's mind in accord with the will of Christ Jesus.[66] But it more emphatically means a mindset which adheres to his example in the treatment of others, loving even those who disagree with and sin against us,

---

[61] Cranfield, *Romans*, 737.

[62] Rogers and Rogers, *The New Linguistic and Exegetical Key to the Greek New Testament*, 330.

[63] Moo, *Romans*, 871.

[64] Dunn, *Romans*, 840.

[65] Regarding adiaphora, see further "Romans 14:1–15:7—Summary and Application" below.

[66] Cranfield, *Romans*, 737; Käsemann, *Romans*, 383.

as he loved those who disagreed with and sinned against him. Indeed, as Paul continues in Philippians 2, Jesus humbled himself to become a man and to die for all humanity. That is the servant mindset Paul sets forward for imitation in Rom 15:2–3, 7 (cf. 12:7).

The Resulting Praise (15:6)

The reason for and the result of such a common mindset is "so that with the same purpose you might with one mouth glorify the God and Father of our Lord Jesus Christ" (15:6). BDAG defines ὁμοθυμαδόν as "*with one mind/purpose/ impulse*." Originally, the term occurs in political contexts, where it "confers particular weight on the decision of a corporate body" (cf. Acts 15:25).[67] The sense conveys unity and concord regarding an underlying purpose which transcends differences. Paul clearly allows for the divergent views in regard to foods and festivals in Rome to continue (e.g., 14:5–6); in fact, he insists that neither side pressure the other to conform to their position.

What accords "with Christ Jesus" (15:5b) in his multifaceted body is the variety Paul envisions and describes repeatedly, as in 12:4–6:

> [4]For just as in one body we have many members, but all members do not have the same function, [5]thus we, the many, are one body in Christ, and, [as] the [body], each one members of one another, [6]and having different gifts in accordance with the grace which was given to us, whether prophecy, according to the analogy of faith.[68]

Franzmann draws upon these earlier verses in order to describe Paul's intended outcome:

> Unanimity is essential to the worship of the new people of God. All must put on Christ and live their lives of faith and love and hope together; there is no room for self-centered individualism. It has already become apparent that this unanimity of the members of the church does not mean that all individuality is suppressed; no monotonous uniformity is imposed. … The unanimity and health of the church are maintained by the functioning of "gifts that differ according to the grace given" to each member of the church. (12:6)[69]

The marvel remains that within the body of Christ, even with a diversity of practices regarding adiaphora, *a unity permeates and prevails*, as with the human body. Thus the unifying prepositional phrase "with one mouth" (ἐν ἑνὶ στόματι, 15:6) resonates nicely alongside a mindset that allows for and embraces the strongly held divergent positions present in Rome. In fact, Paul here describes how such differences, including potentially divisive convictions (14:1), can be "continually transcended when the community addresses itself

---

[67] H. W. Heidland, ὁμοθυμαδόν, *TDNT* 5:185. The adverb occurs thirty-six times in the LXX and eleven times in the NT, but, aside from this instance, all are in Acts. Luke regularly uses it to describe the early church (e.g., Acts 1:14; 2:46; 4:24; 5:12; 15:25).

[68] See also 1 Cor 12:12–27; Eph 3:6; 4:11–16.

[69] Franzmann, *Romans*, 241.

to the magnifying of the one Lord."[70] The differing members of the various congregations in Rome can "with one mouth glorify the God and Father of our Lord Jesus Christ" (15:6). The verb "glorify" or "praise" (δοξάζω) connects this verse with what follows, as Paul uses the verb again in 15:9 and the cognate noun δόξα, "glory," in 15:7.[71]

While they glorify the one true God, the recipient of their praise here is designated in Trinitarian terms, "the God and Father of our Lord Jesus Christ" (15:6; the Holy Spirit is soon to be referenced as well [15:13]). Elsewhere, Paul uses similar phraseology to speak of God the Father and God the Son in 2 Cor 1:3; 11:31; Eph 1:3, 17 (cf. also 1 Pet 1:3). In Romans he speaks repeatedly about the relationship between the Father and the Son (e.g., 1:3–4; 5:10; 8:3, 15–17, 29, 32) and the Spirit's relationship both to Christ and God the Father.[72] The assertion that God is "the God and Father of our Lord Jesus" (15:6) does not in any way lessen the Godhead of the Son.[73] Instead, it serves to unite the eternal roles of God the Father and God the Son. Indeed, the risen Christ himself sends Mary Magdalene to tell his brothers: "I am ascending to my Father and your Father, and to my God and your God" (ἀναβαίνω πρὸς τὸν πατέρα μου καὶ πατέρα ὑμῶν καὶ θεόν μου καὶ θεὸν ὑμῶν, Jn 20:17).[74]

"Our Lord Jesus Christ" (15:6)

While Christ and then God's kingdom served as the centerpieces of previous segments of 14:1–15:7 (see 14:7–9 and 14:17–18), Jesus becomes increasingly prominent toward the conclusion. Paul speaks of "the Christ" in 15:3, "Christ Jesus" in 15:5, and "the Christ" again climactically in 15:7. Most noteworthy in the overall context of Romans is Paul's return in 15:6 to the full Christological title "our Lord Jesus Christ" (τοῦ κυρίου ἡμῶν Ἰησοῦ Χριστοῦ). Though absent since 8:39, this complete designation appears with slight variation throughout Romans 5–8, where it repeatedly functions thematically in culminating

---

[70] H. W. Heidland, ὁμοθυμαδόν, *TDNT* 5:186.

[71] Paul's reference to one "mouth" (στόμα) also brings to mind his three uses of "mouth" (στόμα) in 10:8–10, where he asserts that one who confesses with the "mouth" that Jesus is Lord and believes that God raised him from the dead will be saved. The common profession of this saving faith in Christ establishes the unity of every worshiping community that glorifies God "with one mouth" (15:6).

[72] See, e.g., "the Spirit of the one [God the Father] who raised Jesus from the dead" (8:11); the role of the Spirit in Christ's resurrection and session in power in 1:4; "the Law of the Spirit of life in Christ Jesus freed you" (8:2); the "Spirit (of God)," 8:9, 14; see also, e.g., 5:5; 14:17; 15:19, 30.

[73] In addition to " 'Our Lord Jesus Christ' (15:6)" immediately below, see also the exposition of "Jesus [is] Lord" in the commentary on 10:9 and the discussion of how Paul asserts the divinity of the Lord Jesus by interchanging references to the Father and the Son using the terms "God" and "Lord" in "Of the Lord's Servant (14:4)" and "As 'the Lord Says' (Is 45:23 in Rom 14:11)" in the commentary on 14:1–13a.

[74] All three persons of the Trinity are named shortly afterward when Jesus refers (in this order) to "the Father," "I," and "the Holy Spirit" (Jn 20:21–22).

statements (5:1, 11, 21; 6:23; 7:25; 8:39; cf. 4:24).[75] The combined references to Jesus in these verses heighten the fervor of the argument as well. Paul seeks to make his hearers more and more aware of their personal relationship with Jesus Christ so that this bond might extend through our common Lord toward one another. Rom 15:7 then serves as the climactic assertion and appeal of this entire section.

Romans 15:7—Another Effective and Evangelical Hinge
The Pivot of Romans 15:7

Some translations and commentators begin a new section at 15:7.[76] On the one hand, the assertion in 15:7 that "Christ ... received you to himself" does point forward. The following verse begins "for I say" (λέγω γάρ, 15:8), which introduces a catena of scriptural quotations that confirm the service of the Christ/ Messiah first to the Jews (15:8) and, then, also to the Gentiles (15:9–12). This reinforces themes which have dominated the entire letter (see the commentary on 15:7–13).

However, beginning a new section at 15:7 *obscures the very "therefore"* (διό, 15:7) *moment when Paul gets to his main point* regarding the issues under consideration ever since 14:1. The verse primarily functions as the culmination of 14:1–15:7. The most obvious textual indication of this is the return to the opening verb of 14:1, "receive to yourselves" (προσλαμβάνεσθε). Two verses later Paul adds that God "received to himself" (προσελάβετο, 14:3) the one whom the "weak" (14:1–2) person is judging and, by implication, rejecting. Now Paul uses the identical two forms of the same verb in the same order: προσλαμβάνεσθε, "receive to yourselves," and προσελάβετο, Christ "received to himself" (15:7). Clearly these four uses of προσλαμβάνω in the middle voice provide a frame for the discussion which ensued at 14:1 and wraps up at 15:7.[77] Where then does one properly place a break?

This commentary has demonstrated Paul's repeated and skillful use of hinge verses (e.g., 8:1–4; 9:24; 10:4–5, 16–17; 13:7–8; 14:13). Rom 15:7 provides one of the most prominent illustrations. Trying to separate the verse in either direction presents a false alternative. Instead, it needs to be considered in both directions.[78] The frequency of such hinge verses, at least in Romans, reminds us again of the artificial nature, and at times misleading insertion, of paragraph divisions, as well as demarcations between chapters and verses.[79] It might also caution against citing isolated proof-texts or reading separated sections (e.g., pericopes) without giving due consideration to the larger context and the overall

---

[75] Middendorf, *Romans 1–8*, 377–80.

[76] RSV, NRSV; also Dunn, *Romans*, 844; Franzmann, *Romans*, 258; Hultgren, *Romans*, 528; Käsemann, *Romans*, 384; Schreiner, *Romans*, 752.

[77] See also the discussion of these verbs in "Acceptance" in the introduction to 14:1–15:13.

[78] See Moo, *Romans*, 873–74, for a discussion of factors on both sides.

[79] See "An Unfortunate Chapter Break and an Overview (15:1–7)" above.

flow of the letter. Paul intends his recipients to hear all of Romans in the order in which he wrote it and to consider every verse within its narrower and broader contexts.

Responsive Receiving (15:7)

As the culmination of everything Paul has said since 14:1, he now provides this profound framing thought: "Therefore, receive one another to yourselves, just as the Christ also received you to himself to [the] glory of God" (15:7). The action Paul calls for, "receive to yourselves" (προσλαμβάνεσθε), is identical to the one he began with in 14:1. He directs this present middle imperative in the second person plural inclusively to all his hearers in Rome, as signaled by the switch to the second person plural pronoun already in 15:5 (ὑμῖν, "to you").[80] In spite of their different convictions on the matters at hand, Paul commands the Christians in Rome not merely to tolerate or give perfunctory recognition to one another, but actually to "receive one another" (ἀλλήλους, 15:7) to themselves in worship and with full fellowship, together with all that entails. Thus, while the language of 15:6 demonstrates that "shared worship, indeed, is central to Paul's vision,"[81] 14:1–15:13 more broadly issues "God's call to unity of life and worship across barriers of custom and ethnic identity."[82]

"Just as" (καθώς, 15:7) firmly plants the command to do so within the Good News. It establishes a comparison,[83] "just as the Christ also received you to himself" (καθὼς καὶ ὁ Χριστὸς προσελάβετο ὑμᾶς, 15:7; note the continuing second person plural pronoun). He receives any and all who come to him; you all should do the same for all fellow believers. The notion that "just as" (καθώς) also expresses cause[84] resides less in the meaning of the word than in the switch of mood and tense with the second form of the verb προσλαμβάνω, "receive." The second form in 15:7, as in 14:3, is an aorist middle indicative. *It conveys the basic and essential fact of the Gospel:* "Christ … received you to himself," just as "you" were, with no preconditions. True enough, "both Jews and Greeks are all under sin" (3:9). But even more marvelously certain is this fact: "Jesus sinners doth receive"[85] (see, e.g., Mt 9:11–13; Lk 5:30–32; 15:1–2).

Again, modern English fails to express the significance of the second person *plural*. He did not just receive "you" ["thee"] individualistically; he received "you (all)" ["ye"]. The same should follow as Christians accept to themselves all other baptized believers. This, of course, reflects the opposite of judging and despising (14:3, 5). More importantly, Paul does not follow the ways of the

---

[80] Chrysostom, *Homilies on Romans*, 27 (Bray, *Romans*, ACCS NT 6:356), observes: "It is no longer just the weak that he is encouraging, but everyone."

[81] Wright, "Romans," 749.

[82] Wright, "Romans," 730; this is Wright's title for Rom 14:1–15:13.

[83] Dunn, *Romans*, 846.

[84] Käsemann, *Romans*, 385, deems καθώς "an indication of reason"; it is taken similarly as an expression of cause by Cranfield, *Romans*, 739; Moo, *Romans*, 875.

[85] This is the title of a hymn by Erdmann Neumeister (*LSB* 609).

world in promising conditionally: "*If* you Romans accept one another, shape up, and act rightly toward one another, *then* Christ will accept you." Instead, Christ *has already* accepted you all. In *response* Paul implores those in Rome to do the same for one another, even in the midst of their ongoing differences in regard to foods and holy days.

Of course, his letter is now part of the written Scriptures which continue to teach us (15:4) the same: first, Christ received you (plural) to himself; do the same for one another in spite of and even in the midst of whatever adiaphora convictions might cause divisions. Paul reminds us that Jesus Christ freely and fully received us to himself (15:7; cf. 14:3) without insisting that we achieve anything approaching a uniformity of practice with the holy Son of God. On the contrary, while we were still weak and sinful enemies, "Christ died in behalf of us" (5:8; see 5:6–8). Paul then calls us to receive one another in the same manner (15:7; cf. 14:1). This does not, of course, envision the abuse of that acceptance by openly flaunting or willfully ignoring actions outside of God's will (e.g., 1 Corinthians 5–6).[86] But it *does* apply to accepting all other believers as brothers and sisters in Christ, whatever their diverse practices might be in those areas where God's Word has not spoken (see the concluding application section below).

To God Be the Glory! (15:7)

This, Paul says, resounds "to [the] glory of God" (εἰς δόξαν τοῦ θεοῦ, 15:7). Moo takes the phrase as expressing purpose, "in order that God might be glorified,"[87] but result also factors into the meaning.[88] Cranfield argues that this concluding prepositional phrase should be attached to the command to "receive one another" in the first part of the verse;[89] others attach it only or primarily to the action of Christ, who "received you."[90] But this surely presents another false and potentially misleading alternative. The two actions expressed by forms of προσλαμβάνω, "receive," in 15:7 can and should be properly distinguished and kept in their proper order, but the two should not be severed from one another, grammatically, theologically, or in practice.[91] To be sure, our receiving of one another to ourselves does not resound to the glory of God in any way apart from Christ's acceptance of us. His action always comes first in time (the aorist indicative προσελάβετο refers to a past event: Christ "received") and remains foremost in significance. But Paul's thought does not end there. Instead and on that basis, he uses the present tense imperative προσλαμβάνεσθε, "receive,"

---

[86] For a discussion of that passage, see Lockwood, *1 Corinthians*, 178–95.

[87] Moo, *Romans*, 875.

[88] For the merging of purpose and result, see the discussion of purpose-result ἵνα clauses in Wallace, *Greek Grammar*, 473–74.

[89] Cranfield, *Romans*, 739–40; similarly, Moo, *Romans*, 875.

[90] Murray, *Romans*, 2:204; Sanday and Headlam, *Romans*, 397.

[91] With Barrett, *Romans*, 270; Dunn, *Romans*, 846, properly asks: "Would Paul want to choose between these alternatives?"

to implore the Roman believers (and us) to do the same for one another. Surely this also resounds "to [the] glory of God."

Romans 14:1–15:7—Summary and Application

Summary

The "judgments over convictions" (14:1) which had become divisive among the Roman house churches centered on OT mandates regarding foods and festivals (see "Identifying the Controverted Issues" in the introduction to 14:1–15:13, as well as the commentary on 14:2–3 and 14:5–6). These five factors summarize Paul's response:

- First, now that Christ has come, these OT stipulations have been fulfilled and have come to an end *as requirements* and may not be imposed; Christians who do not observe them should not be judged (e.g., 14:1–4, 10, 13a).

- Second, within the arena of Christian freedom, these mandates in the Word of God still present a legitimate lifestyle option; Christians who observe them should not be despised (e.g., 14:5–6, 22).

- Third, a person's own conviction may mean he ought not engage in a behavior if he views it as being contrary to his own faith (e.g., 14:14, 22–23).

- Fourth, the strong recognize their freedom in regard to these particular OT regulations (14:14, 20), but ought to be more concerned that their exercise of it does not cause a weak brother in the faith to stumble (e.g., 14:13b, 15, 20–21; 15:1–2).

- Finally, the Gospel resides at the center throughout Paul's treatment of these disputed matters (14:3, 7–9, 17; 15:3, 7) and always ought to remain there whenever similarly contentious issues arise in the church.

Application of Paul's Instruction in the Lutheran Confessions

What Paul states specifically about the OT in 15:4 stands equally true of the ongoing relevance of his own writings: "For as much as was written previously was written for our teaching." The Lutheran Confessions provide an illustrative example of how Paul's words in 14:1–15:7 continue to provide the Gospel and normative guidance based on it. They reference verses from this section fifteen times, eight of which occur in the Formula of Concord.

Parameters of Applicability

Käsemann points out that, strictly speaking, "Paul is not formulating a doctrine of adiaphora,"[92] that is, a doctrine of things neither commanded nor forbidden by Scripture. Paul is addressing specific mandates that are in the OT Scriptures. The Law of Moses clearly requires the people of God to eat clean foods and abstain from those that are unclean (see the commentary on 14:14).[93]

---

[92] Käsemann, *Romans*, 375–76, referring to 14:13–23. For a review of the extension of "adiaphora" to encompass all of a Christian's life, including nonreligious activities, see "Broader Implications of the Discussion" in "A Series of Assertions (14:20–22a)" in the commentary on 14:13–23.

[93] In 1 Corinthians 8–10 the issues regarding meat offered to idols similarly should not be called "adiaphora" because idolatry is involved, which violates the First Commandment (Ex 20:3;

It repeatedly specifies when and how they are to observe the Sabbath and other holy days. As a result, it is more accurate to say that 14:1–15:7 deals primarily with *hermeneutical issues regarding whether or not OT commands regarding foods and holy days continue to apply now that the NT era has dawned.*

At the same time, Paul's apostolic words provide guidance for the church of all times and places in dealing with practices which God's Word neither commands nor forbids for his NT people. It must be maintained that such practices are not binding upon NT believers. Yet, as this section of Romans demonstrates, they all too easily become one of two things:

1. The basis for judgments against "strong" (15:1) believers who recognize and enjoy their freedom in Christ

or

2. A cause of stumbling in faith for the "weak" (14:1–2; 15:1) who view themselves as bound in regard to these issues

The Lutheran Confessions illustrate how 14:1–15:7 should be applied in response to both problematic situations. While the Formula of Concord defines the term "adiaphora" specifically as "ceremonies and church rites which are neither commanded nor forbidden in the Word of God" (FC SD X 1),[94] the Confessions as a whole apply Paul's treatment on a broader scale to encompass rules about "food, drink, clothing, and similar matters" (Ap XXVIII 7) which reside within the category of human tradition.[95]

Under the Gospel: To Follow Traditions or Not?

A disruption of fellowship among the house churches in Rome presents the immediate challenge to which Paul responds. His remedy comes to the fore in the bracketing exhortations for baptized believers to "receive to yourselves" (προσλαμβάνεσθε, 14:1; 15:7) other Christians, even in the midst of ongoing diverse practices regarding foods and holy days. The Gospel itself, a positive point to which Paul continually returns (14:3, 7–9, 17; 15:3, 7), serves as the proper foundation for united worship and fellowship (15:6). The Augsburg Confession aligns well with this part of Paul's instruction:

> For it is sufficient for the true unity of the Christian church that the Gospel be preached in conformity with a pure understanding of it and that the sacraments be administered in accordance with the divine Word. It is not necessary for the true unity of the Christian church that ceremonies, instituted by men,

---

Deut 5:7; e.g., 1 Cor 8:7, 10; 10:14, 21–22), and that commandment remains normative for Christians; see Lockwood, *1 Corinthians*, 337–46.

[94] Regarding adiaphora, see also "Unclean No More!" in "Affirming Jesus' Declaration with Qualification: No Food Is Unclean (14:14)" and "Broader Implications of the Discussion" in "A Series of Assertions (14:20–22a)" in the commentary on 14:13–23.

[95] For a thorough discussion of religious traditions, rites, and ceremonies, see Article X of the Formula of Concord, "The Ecclesiastical Rites That Are Called Adiaphora or Things Indifferent." For the wider application to human traditions in general, see also Ap VII/VIII 34 and Ap XV, "Human Traditions in the Church," 25–26.

should be observed uniformly in all places. (AC VII 2–3; see also Ap VII/VIII 30–31; FC Ep X 4)

On the one hand, then, the Apology of the Augsburg Confession cites 14:17 in order to remind us that Christian freedom from the necessity of conforming to human traditions must be maintained within God's kingdom of liberating grace:

> It is evident that human traditions do not quicken the heart, are not works of the Holy Spirit (like love of neighbor, chastity, etc.), and are not means by which God moves the heart to believe (like the divinely instituted Word and sacraments). Rather, they are customs that do not pertain to the heart and "perish as they are used." Therefore we must not believe that they are necessary for righteousness before God. He says the same in Rom. 14:17, "The kingdom of God does not mean food and drink but righteousness and peace and joy in the Holy Spirit." (Ap VII/VIII 36; see also FC Ep X 7; FC SD X 14, 30)

On the other hand, Paul also commands those who are "strong" in the faith, as he is ("we, the strong," 15:1), to give up the legitimate practice of their freedom in such matters if and when their practice grieves a brother (14:13–15, 20–21). When necessary and in deference to those whom he characterizes as "weak" (14:1–2; 15:1), the "strong" are to follow the human traditions. The Formula of Concord echoes Paul's plea:

> Paul instructs us how we can with a good conscience give in and yield to the weak in faith in such external matters of indifference (Rom. 14) and demonstrates it by his own example (Acts 16:3; 21:26; I Cor. 9:10). (FC SD X 9; see also AC XXIV 1–3)

The Formula's reference to Paul's example calls to mind the incredible flexibility the "strong" apostle demonstrates and models for us in service to the Good News of Christ. He himself characterizes it in this way:

> For while being free from all, I enslave myself to all in order that I might gain the more. Namely, to the Jews I became as a Jew in order that I might gain Jews. To those under the Law [I became] as under the Law, though not being under the Law myself, in order that I might gain those under the Law. To those outside the Law, [I became] as outside the Law, though not being outside the Law of God, but in the Law of Christ, in order that I might gain those without the Law. *To the weak I became weak* in order that I might gain the weak. I have become all things to all people so that by any means I might save some. And I do all things on account of the Gospel. (1 Cor 9:19–23a; cf. Rom 15:15–21)[96]

So when should a Christian yield freedom in regard to human traditions and follow them, and when should he refuse to do so? The Formula of Concord observes how Paul's conduct illustrates both responses:

---

[96] See Lockwood, *1 Corinthians*, 309–15. Paul is not willing to engage in sin, of course. But he is open to living according to OT and/or Jewish stipulations about food, worship, washings, and so forth, and he is also willing to live free from them, depending on how he cannot offend and reach people in different contexts.

> Thus Paul yielded and gave in to the weak as far as foods, times, and days were concerned (Rom 14:6). But he would not yield to false apostles who wanted to impose such things on consciences as necessary, even in matters that were in themselves indifferent. (FC SD X 13; see also Col 2:16–17)

The decision, then, depends upon *context*. At times, as the citation of 1 Cor 9:19–23 above demonstrates, Paul passionately exhibits remarkable adaptability in order to share the Good News of Christ more effectively. But whenever the Gospel itself was at stake, as in Galatia, where "false brothers" attempted to abolish "our freedom" (Gal 2:4) by requiring works of the Law (circumcision) in addition to Christ, the apostle vehemently opposed the additional requirements and rebuked those who complied with them (Gal 2:11–14).[97] Indeed, when any practice *not* mandated by the NT is put forth as necessary for salvation, righteousness, or unity in the faith, it becomes an impediment to the Gospel or even turns it into "a different gospel" (Gal 1:6), that is, a false one. Paul adamantly insists that "salvation" always and only comes through "the Good News" of "the righteousness of God" now revealed in Jesus Christ, which is received by "faith" and faith alone (1:16–17; 3:21–22; "by faith apart from works of the Law," 3:28).

Conclusion

The Lutheran Confessions utilize 14:1–15:7 in order to show us how to handle issues that are not (or are no longer) commanded or forbidden by God's Word. On the one hand, such practices cannot be put forth as a requirement for salvation, righteousness before God, or membership in Christ's body. The Apology of the Augsburg Confession relies on 14:17 in affirming that

> in the church we must keep this teaching, that we receive forgiveness of sins freely for Christ's sake by faith. We must also keep the teaching that human traditions are useless as acts of worship, and that therefore neither sin nor righteousness depends upon food, drink, clothing, and similar matters. Christ wanted to leave their use free when he said (Matt. 15:11), "What goes into the mouth does not defile a man." And Paul says (Rom. 14:17), "The kingdom of God is not food or drink." (Ap XXVIII 7)

On the other hand, 14:1–15:7 also teaches that human traditions should not be arbitrarily or carelessly discarded in a manner which harms the weak, that is, those who still view them as essential, even though they are not. Whatever the tradition under consideration might be, the Formula of Concord similarly advises that "in this matter all frivolity and offenses are to be avoided, and particularly the weak in faith are to be spared (1 Cor. 8:9–13; Rom. 14:13ff)" (FC Ep X 5; see also FC Ep X 3; FC SD X 9).

In order to steer us pastorally toward a middle course which avoids either extreme, the Apology of the Augsburg Confession relies on Paul as "our constant champion":

---

[97] For further details, see "The Situation at Galatia" in Das, *Galatians*, 1–19.

This subject of traditions involves many difficult and controversial questions, and we know from actual experience that traditions are real snares for consciences. When they are required as necessary, they bring exquisite torture to a conscience that has omitted some observance. On the other hand, their abrogation involves its own difficulties and problems. … Here Paul is our constant champion; everywhere he insists that these observances neither justify nor are necessary over and above the righteousness of faith. Nevertheless, liberty in these matters should be used moderately, lest the weak be offended and become more hostile to the true teaching of the Gospel because of an abuse of liberty. (Ap XV 49–51)

This often delicate balance should be maintained, always in service to that which resides at the heart and center of Paul's discussion throughout 14:1–15:7 (14:3, 7–9, 17; 15:3, 7), the Good News of what God has done for us all in "our Lord Jesus Christ" (15:6).[98]

---

[98] For the thematic significance of repeated references to "Jesus Christ our Lord" throughout Romans 5–8, see Middendorf, *Romans 1–8*, 377–80.

Conclusion to Romans 14:1–15:6 *and* to the Message of Romans: Christ—for Jews as Promised, for Gentiles as Prophesied

Translation

15 ⁷Therefore, receive one another to yourselves, just as the Christ also received you to himself to [the] glory of God. ⁸For I say that Christ came to be and remains a servant of [the] circumcision in behalf of [the] truth of God in order to confirm the promises of the fathers ⁹and [in order that] the Gentiles might glorify God for [his] mercies, just as it stands written: "On account of this, I will acknowledge you among the Gentiles and I will sing to your name."

¹⁰And again it says: "Rejoice, Gentiles, together with his people!"

¹¹And again: "Praise the Lord, all the nations, and let all the peoples praise him!"

¹²And again Isaiah says: "The root of Jesse will be, even he who arises to rule the Gentiles; on him [the] Gentiles will hope."

¹³Now may the God of hope fill you [with] all joy and peace while believing, so that you might have an abundance in hope by [the] power of [the] Holy Spirit.

Textual Notes

15:7 See the textual notes on this verse in the commentary on 15:1–7.

15:8 λέγω γὰρ Χριστὸν διάκονον γεγενῆσθαι περιτομῆς—After the verb λέγω, "I say," the infinitive γεγενῆσθαι indicates indirect discourse.[1] It is the perfect infinitive of the deponent verb γίνομαι, "become." The perfect tense conveys both a past action and ongoing effect:[2] "he came to be and remains" (see the commentary). For the background and uses of the noun διάκονος, "servant," see the commentary on 13:4. Here its accusative, διάκονον, is modified by the genitive noun περιτομῆς, "of circumcision." Here περιτομή denotes "*one who is circumcised*" (BDAG, 2) in contrast to the uncircumcised (e.g., Rom 3:30; 4:9, 12; Eph 2:11; Col 3:11; 4:11). It functions, then, as a synonym for the Jews or "Judeans" (BDAG, 2 a) in distinction from Gentiles; see the commentary.

εἰς τὸ βεβαιῶσαι τὰς ἐπαγγελίας τῶν πατέρων—The preposition εἰς followed by an articular infinitive expresses purpose, "in order to," though the concept of result

---

[1] See Wallace, *Greek Grammar*, 603–5.

[2] Wallace, *Greek Grammar*, 573–74.

(e.g., 1:20) or a combination of both seems plausible (see 15:13).[3] The verb βεβαιόω means "to put someth[ing] beyond doubt, *confirm, establish*" (BDAG, 1). The cognate adjective βέβαιος appears in 4:16, where it is translated as "certain." For "the promises of the fathers," see the commentary.

15:9 τὰ δὲ ἔθνη—The syntactical relationship of 15:9 to 15:8 is challenging. Dunn first proposes that the most natural reading would be to take δέ as "adversative to v 8"[4] (cf. BDAG, 4: "marker of contrast"), which would set up a contrast between the salvation of Jews ("circumcision") by Christ the "servant" in accord with "the promises of the fathers" (15:8) and the salvation of "the Gentiles" through God's "mercies" (15:9). Dunn then rightly concludes that such a contrast "seems antithetical to everything Paul has so far argued" (citing 4:16; 9:8).[5] Instead, δέ serves here and commonly as a connecting marker (BDAG, 1), perhaps also indicating an "additive relation" (BDAG, 3). ἔθνη is the plural form of ἔθνος, which regularly denotes the "Gentiles," that is, non-Israelite or non-Jewish foreign nations (see BDAG, 2 a; see also the fourth textual note on 1:5 and the commentary on 10:19). The noun occurs six times in 15:9–12, as well as in 15:16 and 15:18.

ὑπὲρ ἐλέους—BDAG places this use of ὑπέρ under a "marker of the moving cause or reason, *because of, for the sake of, for*" (BDAG, A 2). Earlier Paul used the noun ἔλεος to refer to the "mercy" of God by which Gentiles are saved (11:31); see also the cognate verb ἐλεέω, "have/show mercy," in 11:30–32.

δοξάσαι—This aorist infinitive of δοξάζω is also governed by the εἰς τό in 15:8 (see the second textual note on that verse), so the translation inserts "in order that." The verb is used for "glorifying" God also in 15:6; for the *failure* to glorify God, see 1:21.

καθὼς γέγραπται—Paul introduces a Scripture quotation with this formula fourteen times in the letter; see the fourth textual note on 1:17.

ἐξομολογήσομαί σοι—The doubly compound verb ἐξομολογέω (ἐκ + ὁμός + λέγω) means "to declare openly in acknowledgment, *profess, acknowledge*" (BDAG, 3). See the fourth textual note on 14:11, and note the comparable use of ὁμολογέω in 10:9 (see the second textual note and the commentary there). Here the thought extends toward "the more general sense *to praise*, in acknowledgment of divine beneficence and majesty" (BDAG, 4).

ἐν ἔθνεσιν—The dative expresses location or sphere:[6] "among the Gentiles." For ἔθνος, see the first textual note on 15:9.

τῷ ὀνόματί σου ψαλῶ—The verb is the future of the liquid ψάλλω, "*sing, sing praise*." It is the root from which we get the title "Psalms." The verb takes the dative "of the one for whom the praise is intended" (BDAG); τῷ ὀνόματί σου is, literally, "to the name of you."

---

[3] See Wallace, *Greek Grammar*, 590–92, 611; see 473–74 for his discussion of the merging of the two concepts; for other examples, see 4:16; 5:20; 14:9; 15:4.

[4] Dunn, *Romans*, 847.

[5] Dunn, *Romans*, 848.

[6] See Wallace, *Greek Grammar*, 153–55.

15:10 εὐφράνθητε—The verb εὐφραίνω means "to be glad or delighted, *be glad, enjoy oneself, rejoice, celebrate*" (BDAG, 2), and the passive is often used in an active sense. The form here is an aorist passive imperative, "rejoice!"

15:11 αἰνεῖτε—αἰνέω is another general verb meaning "*to praise*" (BDAG); the form is a present active imperative.

πάντα τὰ ἔθνη … πάντες οἱ λαοί—For ἔθνη, see the first textual note on 15:9. Here, however, instead of "Gentiles," it is translated as "nations" because the phrase functions all inclusively. "All the nations" is parallel to "all the peoples," which would encompass Israel as well. Paul uses λαός for Israel in 10:21; 11:1, 2; 15:10.

ἐπαινεσάτωσαν—The verb ἐπαινέω is a compound of αἰνέω (see the first textual note on 15:11) with a comparable meaning. The form is an aorist active imperative third person plural: "let them praise!"

15:12 Ἠσαΐας—For this Greek form of "Isaiah," see the first textual note on 9:27. The rest of 15:12 consists of three clauses quoted verbatim from LXX Is 11:10.

ἡ ῥίζα τοῦ Ἰεσσαί—The noun ῥίζα can denote "the underground part of a plant, *root*" (BDAG, 1), as in its use for the root of the olive tree in 11:16–18. Is 11:1 speaks of the royal Messiah who will sprout "*from* the root of Jesse" (LXX: ἐκ τῆς ῥίζης Ιεσσαι), and he, anointed with the Spirit (Is 11:2), is then called "the root of Jesse" in Is 11:10 (LXX: ἡ ῥίζα τοῦ Ιεσσαι; MT: יִשַׁי שֹׁרֶשׁ). In context, then, ῥίζα more clearly refers to "that which grows from a root, *shoot, scion*, in our lit[erature] in imagery *descendant*" (BDAG, 2). Ἰεσσαί is the Greek form of the name יִשַׁי, "Jesse," David's father (Ruth 4:17, 22; 1 Samuel 16).

ὁ ἀνιστάμενος ἄρχειν—This masculine participle of ἀνίστημι, "to arise," is adjectival.[7] It modifies the noun ῥίζα, "root," which is feminine, but since the phrase ἡ ῥίζα τοῦ Ἰεσσαί refers to a man (see the preceding textual note), the participle is masculine. The infinitive ἄρχειν expresses purpose:[8] "he who arises to rule."

ἐλπιοῦσιν—This is the future indicative of ἐλπίζω, "to hope" (also in 8:24, 25; 15:24). See the discussion of the cognate noun ἐλπίς, "hope," in the commentary on 4:18 and the commentary on 15:13; it appears twice in the next verse.

15:13 ὁ δὲ θεὸς τῆς ἐλπίδος—The conjunction δέ has the effect of "linking narrative segments, *now, then, and, so, that is*" (BDAG, 2). For "the God of hope" as a "plenary genitive," which functions as "*both* subjective and objective,"[9] see the commentary.

πληρώσαι ὑμᾶς πάσης χαρᾶς—This is the aorist optative of πληρόω, "to fill," used in a prayer-wish; see the discussion of the optative voice of δῴη in the first textual note on 15:5. πληρόω employs the accusative (ὑμᾶς, "you," plural) for the object that is filled and the genitive (πάσης χαρᾶς καὶ εἰρήνης, "all joy and peace") to indicate what the object is filled with (BDAG, s.v. πληρόω, 1 b). Thus "may he fill you [with] all joy and peace."

---

[7] For adjectival participles, see Wallace, *Greek Grammar*, 617–19.

[8] See Wallace, *Greek Grammar*, 609.

[9] Wallace, *Greek Grammar*, 119; see 119–21.

ἐν τῷ πιστεύειν—The preposition ἐν with the articular infinitive expresses con-temporaneous time:[10] "while believing."

εἰς τὸ περισσεύειν ὑμᾶς—For εἰς with the articular infinitive, see the second tex-tual note on 15:8. Here the sense of result seems stronger,[11] if not dominant: "so that." When περισσεύω is used intransitively with persons as the subject, it means "*have an abundance, abound, be rich*" in something (BDAG, 1 b). The thing possessed can be in the genitive case, but here it is given in the following prepositional phrase (see the next textual note).

ἐν τῇ ἐλπίδι ἐν δυνάμει—The initial preposition ἐν expresses sphere: "in (the) hope." The second instance of ἐν is instrumental: "by [the] power."[12] For ἐλπίς, which appears thirteen times in Romans and twice in this verse, see the commentary on 4:18; for δύναμις, with eight occurrences in the letter, see the commentary on 1:16.

Commentary

Romans 15:7–13—A Conclusion *and* a Summation

A Review of the Hinge in Romans 15:7

The previous section of this commentary provides an analysis of the pivot Paul performs at 15:7 and also offers a detailed exegesis of the verse.[13] While these will not be repeated here, it is important to reemphasize how Paul skill-fully utilizes the verse as yet another effective hinge.[14] In the verse "therefore, receive one another to yourselves, just as the Christ also received you to himself to [the] glory of God" (15:7), we may ask, Who are the "you" (plural) whom Christ received to himself to the glory of God? In light of the replicated verb "receive to yourselves" (προσλαμβάνεσθε) in both 14:1 and 15:7, the "you" are the "weak" (14:1–2; 15:1) and the "strong" (15:1) who have been addressed since 14:1. This verse *concludes the intervening discussion* of 14:1–15:6 with a call for mutual acceptance and properly roots its motivation in the accepting action of God in Christ ("God received him," 14:3; "Christ … received you," 15:7; cf. 14:4, 9, 17).[15]

As discussed above,[16] some of the "strong" were Jews ("we, the strong" in 15:1 notably includes Paul!), and some among the "weak" likely were Gentiles (e.g., former proselytes to Judaism). However, since these two groups were

---

[10] See Wallace, *Greek Grammar*, 611.

[11] For the infinitive of result, see Wallace, *Greek Grammar*, 592–94; he notes: That εἰς τό plus the infinitive can indicate result "is disputed in older works, but it is an established idiom in both the NT and extra-biblical literature" (593, n. 10).

[12] See Wallace, *Greek Grammar*, 372.

[13] See "An Unfortunate Chapter Break and an Overview (15:1–7)" and "Romans 15:7—Another Effective and Evangelical Hinge" in the commentary on 15:1–7.

[14] See other hinges in, e.g., 8:1–4; 9:24; 10:4–5, 16–17; 13:7–8; 14:13.

[15] Similarly, Dunn, *Romans*, 845; Cranfield, *Romans*, 740–41; Käsemann, *Romans*, 384; Moo, *Romans*, 873; Schreiner, *Romans*, 753–54.

[16] See "Who Are the 'Weak' and the 'Strong'? Addressees Again!" in the introduction to 14:1–15:13.

divided over the ongoing necessity of abiding by OT regulations regarding foods and holy days (14:2–6), it seems "inevitable that the two parties would split along basically ethnic lines."[17] Paul reinforces this line of interpretation in 15:8–12, where he speaks about two groups, the "circumcision" in 15:8 and "Gentiles" throughout 15:9–12. Therefore, it seems clear that *15:7 also leads forward into the content of 15:8–13.*[18] The three uses of the accusative second person *plural* pronoun ὑμᾶς, "you" (once in 15:7 and twice in 15:13), provide an effective literary frame and a unifying theological theme as well.

Romans 15:7–13 as Paul's Concluding Theological Statement

At the same time, Käsemann calls for "not seeing vv. 7–13 merely as the doxological conclusion of the special exhortation"[19] of 14:1–15:13. Instead, the language Paul uses in 15:7–13 brings together a number of important threads which reach back further than 14:1 to connect with his discussion of the people of Israel beginning in 9:1, his treatment of Abraham in Romans 4, and all the way back to the letter's opening chapter (see examples below). In fact, the referent of the second person plural "you" whom Christ received to himself in 15:7 is explicated in 15:8–12 in a manner which resonates strongly with a key phrase in the letter's thematic opening, "to Jew first and also to Greek" (1:16).[20]

Paul's concluding prayer in 15:13 utilizes both the verb "believe" (πιστεύω) and the noun for the Gospel's "power" (δύναμις) from 1:16 as well. Dunn provides a more detailed example of this extended reach backward by pointing out how

> the vocabulary of [15:]8–9 is particularly carefully chosen to tie together central themes in the whole discussion: ὑπὲρ ἀληθείας θεοῦ ["in behalf of (the) truth of God," 15:8]—the truth (= faithfulness) of God abused by both Gentile and Jew (1:18, 25; 2:8; 3:7) has thus been vindicated: "the promise to the fathers" [15:8]—2:25–29; 4:9–22; 9:4, 8, 9; God's mercy to Gentiles [15:9]—9:15–18, 23; 11:30–32; and thus the primal failure to glorify God (1:21) is reversed [by "glorify God" in 15:9].[21]

All of this lends considerable credibility to the notion that in 15:7–13 "Paul is in fact broadening out his perspective to take in the main thrust of the whole letter."[22] The strongest evidence that Paul here wraps up his theological exposition rests on what follows. The content of 15:14–33 details Paul's plans to visit Rome in a manner which returns the reader to comparable sentiments expressed

---

[17] Moo, *Romans*, 874.

[18] RSV and NRSV begin a new paragraph at 15:7; so also Dunn, *Romans*, 844; Franzmann, *Romans*, 258; Hultgren, *Romans*, 528; Käsemann, *Romans*, 384; Schreiner, *Romans*, 752–53.

[19] Käsemann, *Romans*, 380.

[20] Murray, *Romans*, 2:203, appropriately titles 15:7–13 "Jews and Gentiles One." Dunn, *Romans*, 844, similarly offers "Concluding Summary: God's Mercy and Faithfulness—Jew First, but Also Gentile (15:7–13)."

[21] Dunn, *Romans*, 845.

[22] Dunn, *Romans*, 845.

in 1:8–15.[23] Therefore Romans 15:7–13 serves as the *culminating theological statement of the letter's main body*, which extends from 1:18 through 15:13.[24] Pelagius grasps this well:

> Once more Paul urges both Jews and Gentiles to unity with each other. He agrees with the Jews that Christ was promised to them and came to them first and that the Gentiles were called later on, because of God's mercy. Nevertheless, both peoples have now been made into one.[25]

This section then effectively serves a *twofold purpose*. Schreiner properly observes how "15:7–13 both functions as the conclusion of 14:1–15:6 and also contains a summary of some of the major themes of the letter."[26] Moo encapsulates how Paul, in accomplishing both goals in a single section, masterfully

> sets the local conflict in Rome against the panorama of salvation history. … This exhortation to the two groups in the Roman church is not the main driving force of the letter; but it is one of the key converging motivations that led Paul to write about the gospel the way that he has in Romans.[27]

The Servant Christ (15:8–12)

To the Jew First (15:8; cf. 1:16)

"For I say that Christ came to be and remains a servant of [the] circumcision in behalf of [the] truth of God" (15:8a). Paul's introductory words "for I say" convey the sense of "a solemn doctrinal declaration."[28] Identifying Christ with the title "servant" (διάκονος) expresses Jesus' own self-understanding of his mission. He "came not to be served [διακονηθῆναι] but to serve [διακονῆσαι] and to give his life as a ransom in behalf of many" (Mt 20:28; cf. Mt 20:26; 23:11; Lk 22:27).[29]

The Circumcision (15:8)

Paul explicitly asserts that Christ is "a servant of [the] circumcision." As in 3:30 and 4:9 the noun περιτομή, "circumcision," by synecdoche "means 'the circumcised'—the Jewish people identified by one of their most distinctive features."[30] Contextually this seems obvious (1) in light of the reference to the "fathers," the circumcised patriarchs, later in the verse, (2) "his people" in the OT citation in 15:10, and (3) the sixfold use of the term ἔθνη for "Gentiles" or

---

23 See "Wrapping Up the Letter: Romans 15:14–16:27" before the commentary on 15:14–22.

24 See "Structure and Outline" (Middendorf, *Romans 1–8*, 22–31).

25 Pelagius, *Romans* (Bray, *Romans*, ACCS NT 6:357).

26 Schreiner, *Romans*, 753; Wright, "Romans," 404, similarly calls 15:1–13 "a final summing up of the subject," but it is difficult to see why 15:1–6 should be included in that description.

27 Moo, *Romans*, 874.

28 Cranfield, *Romans*, 740, quoted with approval by Dunn, *Romans*, 846.

29 Primary OT background for this servant Christology in the NT is the Suffering Servant in Isaiah (Is 42:1–9; 49:1–13; 50:4–11; 52:13–53:12; 61:1–11).

30 Dunn, *Romans*, 846–47; similarly, Moo, *Romans*, 877; Kruse, *Romans*, 532–33, who even translates the word here as "the Jews."

other "nations" in contrast to Israel in 15:9–12.[31] Sanday and Headlam argue that περιτομή refers only to the rite of "circumcision" here,[32] but that presents a false dichotomy. Origen incorporates both aspects when he points out that Christ "was himself circumcised and so identified himself with [those who were circumcised]"[33] (Lk 2:21; cf. Gal 4:4) in order to reach out to them.

Das, however, contends that Paul's use of " 'the circumcision,' a negative category earlier in the letter (2.25–3.30; 9.18), is hardly apt if he is also addressing Jewish Christians."[34] Das defines περιτομή in 15:8 as depicting Jews who exhibited an "absence of a response to Christ's work."[35] But the resulting exclusion of Jewish *believers* from the picture is unwarranted. Paul references the circumcised "fathers" later in this verse in language that points the hearer much more strongly to Romans 4. There Abraham "received [the] sign of circumcision" as divinely intended, "a seal of the righteousness of the faith" (4:11). Morris recognizes how "this way of putting it brings out the fact that Christ was the minister of the covenant of which circumcision was the seal (so Murray), that covenant with Abraham which Paul earlier argued was of such relevance to the Gentiles (ch. 4)."[36]

To be sure, 15:8–9 does not imply that all circumcised Jews or uncircumcised Gentiles(!) did or would heed God's call, but Christ's saving service (15:8) was accomplished for all (i.e., objective justification[37]) and remains available to all people, both the circumcised and the uncircumcised. Thus the connotations of "circumcision" (περιτομή) here are much more akin to how it functions in the all-inclusive formulations of 3:29–30 and 4:9–12. Instead of driving a wedge between Jew and Gentile, the sequencing of 15:8–9 maintains "a critical theological balance basic to Paul's argument in Romans: the equality of Jew and Gentile and the salvation-historical priority to the Jew (e.g., 1:16b …)."[38] In 15:8, then, as in 3:30; 4:9, 12, "*circumcision* is taken as a collective, equivalent to 'the Jews' "[39] (as also in Eph 2:11; Col 3:11; 4:11). Bruce reminds us

---

[31] Murray, *Romans*, 2:205, identifies the first and third as conclusive; Schreiner, *Romans*, 754, cites the third.

[32] Sanday and Headlam, *Romans*, 397–98.

[33] Origen, *Romans* (Bray, *Romans*, ACCS NT 6:356); Origen adds: "He fulfilled the promises of the law," the matter Paul discusses in the remainder of 15:8.

[34] Das, " 'Praise the Lord, All You Gentiles,' " 90; see also 105. Note, however, that Paul has not used the noun for circumcision (περιτομή) since 4:9–12, and those references do not fit into a "negative category" (note particularly 4:11).

[35] Das, " 'Praise the Lord, All You Gentiles,' " 97.

[36] Morris, *Romans*, 503; he references Murray, *Romans*, 2:204–5.

[37] For this term and the distinction between objective and subjective justification, see the footnote on that topic in "The Rescuer and Zion: 'To,' 'For the Sake of,' and 'From' " in the commentary on 11:26b–27. See further Mueller, *Called to Believe, Teach, and Confess*, 233–35.

[38] Moo, *Romans*, 876.

[39] Barrett, *Romans*, 271; so also Jewett, *Romans*, 890: "the Jewish people as a whole," citing 3:30 and 4:12. See "God's People" in "The Three Foci of Romans 9–11" in the introduction to Romans 9–11.

that "on his own testimony, during his earthly ministry, Jesus was 'sent only to the lost sheep of the house of Israel' (Mt. 15:24)."[40]

Jesus' Ongoing Ministry to the Jews (15:8)

The double aspect of the perfect tense of γεγενῆσθαι in 15:8, "came to be and remains," surely conveys a significant truth. It means that Jesus' service to the Jewish people encompasses *both* his past earthly ministry, death, and resurrection accomplished in their behalf (and in behalf of all) *and* his ongoing delivery of the benefits attained by that salvific work. His salvation is delivered through his Word and is received through faith whenever anyone hears the Good News and believes (10:6–15).[41] Contrary to any two-covenant way of thinking (see the commentary on 11:26a), Christ came to be and remains a servant to the Jewish people. Earlier Paul described how the Law/Torah is "the embodiment of the knowledge and the truth" (2:20). In 9:1 he also begins to speak the "truth" regarding Israel. Here Christ's ongoing role as a servant who receives all believers (Jews and Gentiles) to himself not only resounds to God's glory (15:7) but also serves as an affirmation "in behalf of [the] truth of God" (ὑπὲρ ἀληθείας θεοῦ, 15:8a). As in 3:4 and 3:7, the vocabulary of "truth" (ἀλήθεια) carries the Hebrew sense of faithfulness.[42] God's faithfulness is expressed by Christ's work "to confirm the promises" (15:8), which included all nations as the beneficiaries,[43] hence "the Gentiles" in 15:9.

The best analysis of the complex structure of 15:8b–9a takes "in order" (εἰς τό) in the middle of 15:8 as governing the rest of the verse, as well as the initial half of 15:9.[44] Both clauses have infinitive verb forms which are used with "in order" (εἰς τό) to express purpose: "to confirm" (βεβαιῶσαι, 15:8) and to "glorify" (δοξάσαι, 15:9). They explain "why."[45]

First, Christ became and remains such a servant "in order to confirm the promises of the fathers" (15:8b), God's pledges to the patriarchs.[46] This language loudly echoes Romans 4. There Paul uses the noun "promise" four times

---

[40] Bruce, *Romans*, 242.

[41] Christ's accomplishment of salvation for all people is what is meant by objective justification, and the reception of his salvation through faith refers to subjective justification. See the footnote on that topic in "The Rescuer and Zion: 'To,' 'For the Sake of,' and 'From' " in the commentary on 11:26b–27; see also Middendorf, *Romans 1–8*, 403.

[42] Cranfield, *Romans*, 741; Dunn, *Romans*, 847; Käsemann, *Romans*, 385; see Middendorf, *Romans 1–8*, 230.

[43] See the footnote below on patriarchal promises.

[44] Sanday and Headlam, *Romans*, 398; Barrett, *Romans*, 271; Murray, *Romans*, 2:205; against Dunn, *Romans*, 847–48. See the overall analysis by Cranfield, *Romans*, 742–43, and Das, " 'Praise the Lord, All You Gentiles,' " 91–96.

[45] See Wallace, *Greek Grammar*, 590–92, 611.

[46] The bulk of the patriarchal narratives (re Abraham, Isaac, Jacob, and Joseph in Genesis 12–50) concerns the giving, transmission, and anticipatory fulfillments of the promises to Abraham and his offspring, which included that all nations of the earth shall be blessed in him and his seed: Gen 12:1–3; 18:18; 22:17–18; 26:3–4; 28:13–14. In Romans "seed" (σπέρμα) appears in 1:3; 4:13, 16, 18; 9:7, 8, 29; 11:1. In Galatians Paul argues that the Seed is Christ (Gal

in reference to Abraham, the father of the fathers, who received and believed it (ἐπαγγελία, 4:13, 14, 16, 20). There Paul describes Abraham as the "father of [the] circumcision" (πατέρα περιτομῆς, 4:12). He assures his hearers that God's promise is from faith and on account of grace "so that the promise is certain to every seed" (εἰς τὸ εἶναι βεβαίαν τὴν ἐπαγγελίαν παντὶ τῷ σπέρματι, 4:16). In 15:8, together with the noun "promise," Paul employs the verb βεβαιόω, "to confirm," which is cognate to the adjective βέβαιος, "certain," in 4:16. Thus God's "truth" (ἀλήθεια, 15:8) now declares that what was "certain" for the patriarchs (4:16) has reached its confirmation in Christ (15:8). As "in 9:5 and 11:28, Paul applies the language of 'promise' and 'fathers' (i.e., the patriarchs) to the Jewish people specifically."[47]

According to OT expectations, this is precisely what the Christ/Messiah would come to accomplish. Jesus confirms, fulfills, and embodies "the Good News of God which he promised beforehand through his prophets in holy writings concerning his Son, the one who came from the seed of David according to the flesh" (1:1b–3). But those same holy writings promised even more. Already in Romans 4, Paul insists that Abraham is *also* the father of the uncircumcised faithful (4:11–12). Similarly, in 9:24, a hinge verse comparable to 15:7, Paul addresses *his hearers in the first person plural*, reminding them inclusively that God also called "us, not only from Jews but also from Gentiles." "The promises of the fathers" (15:8) also encompass "the Gentiles" (15:9).[48]

And Also to the Greek (15:9–12; cf. 1:16)

Christ's Service Adds Gentiles (15:9a)

In keeping with Paul's earlier expressions (e.g., 3:29–30; 4:12; 9:24), the δέ at the beginning of 15:9 surely expresses an added bonus (see the first textual note on that verse). Christ also became a servant in order that "the Gentiles might glorify God for [his] mercies" (15:9). While translated differently, the prepositional phrase "for [his] mercies" (ὑπὲρ ἐλέους) has the same Greek preposition as "in behalf of [the] truth of God" (ὑπὲρ ἀληθείας θεοῦ, 15:8). Moreover, in the LXX the Greek nouns ἔλεος, "mercy," and ἀλήθεια, "truth," are often paired as translations of the Hebrew words חֶסֶד and אֱמֶת in phrases like חֶסֶד וֶאֱמֶת, which ascribes these qualities to God in his salvific actions for the sake of his people.[49] The same Hebrew pair is likely intended by the description of Christ himself as "full of grace and truth" (πλήρης χάριτος καὶ ἀληθείας) in

---

3:5–16). Not to be overlooked is the first Gospel promise in Scripture, given for all humanity: the fall into sin will be overcome by Eve's "Seed" (Gen 3:15).

[47] Moo, *Romans*, 877–78.

[48] Again, the original patriarchal blessing promises extended to include all nations (Gen 12:1–3; 18:18; 22:17–18; 26:3–4; 28:13–14), as was latent already in God's first promise to humanity (Gen 3:15).

[49] This pairing occurs about thirty times in the OT. See, e.g., Gen 24:27; 32:10 (MT 32:11); Ex 34:6; Pss 25:10; 40:10–11 (MT 40:11–12); 115:1; 117:2. English versions translate the pair with vocabulary such as "lovingkindness" and "truth" (Ps 138:2 NKJV) or "steadfast love" and "faithfulness" (Ps 138:2 ESV).

Jn 1:14.[50] The theme of mercies for *all* was articulated most decisively in Rom 11:32: "in order that he show mercy to all" (ἵνα τοὺς πάντας ἐλεήσῃ). There Paul continues similarly with the doxology of 11:33–36, which also concludes with the most appropriate response, the ascription of "glory" to God (ἡ δόξα, 11:36; cf. δοξάσαι τὸν θεόν, 15:9).

Therefore Gentile Christians also stand among the "you" whom Christ received to himself "to [the] glory of God" (15:7). They are included in the "many" (πολλῶν, Mt 20:28) whom Christ came to serve by giving his own life as a ransom for them. The inclusion of Gentiles among the people of God coincides with the illustration of grafting wild Gentile branches into the olive tree of Israel in 11:17, 19, 24. The "mystery" of 11:25 similarly involves the fullness of Gentiles entering God's Israel. While *the manner in which this would happen* was once a mystery, that mystery has come to be and now stands revealed through the servanthood of Christ (15:8; 16:25–26; cf. 1:17; 3:21). Furthermore, Paul insists that the extension of mercies to Gentiles should *not* have been totally unanticipated. On the contrary, their inclusion is "just as it stands written" (καθὼς γέγραπται, 15:9b).

Paul selects his scriptural attestations strategically in 15:9–12. He cites passages sequentially in 15:9–12 first from the Psalms (though this psalm is virtually replicated in the Former Prophets), next from the Torah, then back to the Psalms, and, finally, from the Latter Prophets. Thus, as in 10:18–20 (note also the Former Prophets in 11:3–4), Paul draws evidence from each of the three main sections of the Hebrew Scriptures (Torah, Prophets, Writings) in order to show that God's "promise was written in every part of the Old Testament canon."[51] The textual issues here are minimal, but a number of points should be noted in regard to each.

Scriptural Affirmation 1: Psalm 18:49 in Romans 15:9b

The remainder of Rom 15:9 cites Ps 18:49 (MT 18:50; LXX 17:50), which appears with slight variation also in 2 Sam 22:50.[52] The only differences between those two texts in Hebrew are the form of the final verb and the location of the divine name "Yahweh," represented in Greek by the vocative "Lord" (κύριε). Paul's citation omits "Lord" (κύριε) entirely. Otherwise, Rom 15:9 matches LXX Ps 17:50 (MT 18:50; ET 18:49) exactly:

> διὰ τοῦτο ἐξομολογήσομαί σοι ἐν ἔθνεσιν, κύριε,
>> καὶ τῷ ὀνόματί σου ψαλῶ.
> On account of this I will acknowledge you among [the] Gentiles, O Lord,
>> and I will sing to your name. (LXX Ps 17:50)

---

[50] See the sixth textual note on Jn 1:14 and "The Word Dwelt among Us (Jn 1:14b)" in Weinrich, *John 1:1–7:1*, 111–13, 177–80.

[51] Franzmann, *Romans*, 260.

[52] Identifying this citation as coming from the Former Prophets would be attractive. However, LXX 2 Sam 22:50 differs from *both* LXX Ps 17:50 *and* Rom 15:9 by inserting the article τοῖς in front of ἔθνεσιν and the preposition ἐν before τῷ ὀνόματί σου. It reads διὰ τοῦτο ἐξομολογήσομαί σοι κύριε, ἐν τοῖς ἔθνεσιν καὶ ἐν τῷ ὀνόματί σου ψαλῶ.

עַל־כֵּן ׀ אוֹדְךָ בַגּוֹיִם ׀ יְהוָה
וּלְשִׁמְךָ אֲזַמֵּרָה:

For this reason I will praise you among the nations, Yahweh,
and to your name I will sing. (MT Ps 18:50 [ET 18:49])

The omission of "Lord" (κύριε) from Rom 15:9 likely indicates that, while David was the original human speaker ("I"), Paul also understands *Christ as the prophetic referent* of the first person singular. In Psalm 18 David rejoiced in the victory given to him by God and, therefore, directed his praise *to* the LORD/ Yahweh. Now the exalted Lord Jesus speaks these same words to his Father as he rejoices that his suffering, death, and victorious resurrection have opened the kingdom of God (cf. Rom 14:17) to Gentiles. And as his Gospel is being proclaimed among them, Christ is receiving them to himself to the glory of God (15:7; cf. 14:3). Therefore Christ is the one in whom the words ultimately come to fulfillment (as with Ps 69:9 [MT 69:10] in Rom 15:3).[53] *Paul, then, as proclaimer of the Gospel, also assumes the role of the speaker* ("I") in his ministry (e.g., 11:13; 15:16, 18) as he acknowledges Christ ("you," σοι) among the Gentiles.[54]

Scriptural Affirmation 2: Deuteronomy 32:43 in Romans 15:10

After an introductory "and again it says" (καὶ πάλιν λέγει), Paul's citation in Rom 15:10 matches the third clause of LXX Deut 32:43 exactly. The more compact underlying Hebrew clause is well represented:

εὐφράνθητε, ἔθνη, μετὰ τοῦ λαοῦ αὐτοῦ.
Rejoice, Gentiles, with his people. (LXX Deut 32:43c and Rom 15:10)

הַרְנִינוּ גוֹיִם עַמּוֹ
Shout for joy, nations, [with] his people. (MT Deut 32:43)

Here, however, the *context* of this clause in Hebrew stands markedly different from the LXX. In the Hebrew verse this is the first of four clauses or lines of poetry, whereas in the LXX it is the third of eight clauses or lines. LXX Deut 32:43 is roughly twice as long as MT Deut 32:43, "mainly by addition of lines calling for heavenly rejoicing as well; hence also the quotation in Heb 1:6."[55] Dunn further summarizes:

---

[53] Cranfield, *Romans*, 745, including n. 5; Moo, *Romans*, 878–79.

[54] Käsemann, *Romans*, 386.

[55] Dunn, *Romans*, 849. *NETS* renders LXX Deut 32:43 as follows:

Be glad, O skies, with him,
    and let all the divine sons do obeisance to him.
Be glad, O nations, with his people,
    and let all the angels of God prevail for him.
For he will avenge the blood of his sons
    and take revenge and repay the enemies with a sentence,
and he will repay those who hate,
    and the Lord shall cleanse the land of his people.

The verse's original Hebrew was clearly intended as a strong promise of God's covenant faithfulness to his people, with more than a hint of the "us/them, God's people/others" attitude ("he avenges the blood of his servants, and takes vengeance on his adversaries, and makes expiation for the land of his people" [RSV]). The expansion of the Greek allows not only a much more universal perspective, but the crucial reading μετὰ τοῦ λαοῦ αὐτοῦ ["*with his people*"] transforms a potentially very hostile meaning into one much more sympathetic to the Gentiles. This is only hinted at in the LXX. … But it enables Paul to lift out this single line and to use it as an expression of his own theology, that in accordance with God's original purpose and promise the covenant made to Israel is now open to all who believe.[56]

Scriptural Affirmation 3: Psalm 117:1 in Romans 15:11

In Rom 15:11, Paul introduces Ps 117:1 (LXX 116:1) simply with "and again" (καὶ πάλιν). The Hebrew is straightforward. The LXX begins with αλληλουια, "alleluia," which the LXX uses elsewhere (e.g., Ps 110:1 [MT/ET 111:1]) as a transliteration of הַלְלוּ יָהּ (absent from this Hebrew text). The initial αλληλουια is redundant because it essentially repeats the meaning of the first Hebrew clause, הַלְלוּ אֶת־יְהוָה, "praise Yahweh," which the LXX goes on to translate literally as αἰνεῖτε τὸν κύριον, "praise the Lord." In comparison to the LXX, Paul omits the opening "alleluia" (αλληλουια). He also reverses the word order of the subject, "all the nations," and the object, "the Lord," inserts "and" (καί) at the start of the second line, and uses a third person plural imperative instead of the LXX's second person plural imperative in the second line.

αἰνεῖτε, πάντα τὰ ἔθνη, τὸν κύριον
  καὶ ἐπαινεσάτωσαν αὐτὸν πάντες οἱ λαοί.
Praise the Lord, all the nations [τὰ ἔθνη],
  and let all the peoples praise him! (Rom 15:11)

αλληλουια. αἰνεῖτε τὸν κύριον, πάντα τὰ ἔθνη,
  ἐπαινέσατε αὐτόν πάντες οἱ λαοί.
Alleluia! Praise the Lord, all the nations;
  praise him, all the peoples! (LXX Ps 116:1)

הַלְלוּ אֶת־יְהוָה כָּל־גּוֹיִם
שַׁבְּחוּהוּ כָּל־הָאֻמִּים׃
Praise Yahweh, all the nations;
  laud him, all the peoples. (MT Ps 117:1)

The phrase πάντα τὰ ἔθνη could represent "all the Gentiles." However, it stands in synonymous parallelism with "all the peoples" (πάντες οἱ λαοί). The summons, therefore, is universal, *including Israel among "all the nations"* (see the second textual note on 15:11). This seems especially clear when one examines the reasons for this call to praise. The second and final verse of this short psalm provides them: "his mercy" (τὸ ἔλεος αὐτοῦ) and "the truth of the

---

[56] Dunn, *Romans*, 849.

Lord" (ἡ ἀλήθεια τοῦ κυρίου, LXX Ps 116:2 [MT/ET 117:2]). These are the same two divine attributes which serve as the object of the preposition ὑπέρ in Rom 15:8 ("in behalf of [the] truth of God") and 15:9 ("for [his] mercies"). Those phrases are in verses that speak to the Jews (15:8) and then to the Gentiles (15:9), underscoring the all-inclusive emphasis in 15:11.

Scriptural Affirmation 4: Isaiah 11:10 in Romans 15:12

Finally, 15:12 begins "and again Isaiah says." This is the only quotation in Rom 15:7–13 for which Paul identifies the source. Isaiah is "his favorite prophet—explicitly named more often than anyone else" (see also 9:27, 29; 10:16, 20).[57] Perhaps together with the dual references to ἔθνη, "Gentiles," this signals the end of the catena. The text in Romans omits "in that day" (ἐν τῇ ἡμέρᾳ), a phrase "Paul may have preferred to reserve for the final day of judgment."[58] The omission makes translating the initial verb somewhat awkward. Paul also does not include the final clause of the verse. Otherwise, however, Rom 15:12 largely matches LXX Is 11:10. While the Hebrew meaning is comparable, it depicts the root of Jesse standing "as an ensign" or battle standard for all nations and that they "will seek him."

> ἔσται ἡ ῥίζα τοῦ Ἰεσσαὶ καὶ ὁ ἀνιστάμενος ἄρχειν ἐθνῶν, ἐπ᾽ αὐτῷ ἔθνη ἐλπιοῦσιν. (Rom 15:12)

The root of Jesse will be, even he who arises to rule the Gentiles; on him [the] Gentiles will hope.

> καὶ ἔσται ἐν τῇ ἡμέρα ἐκείνῃ ἡ ῥίζα τοῦ Ιεσσαι καὶ ὁ ἀνιστάμενος ἄρχειν ἐθνῶν, ἐπ᾽ αὐτῷ ἔθνη ἐλπιοῦσιν, καὶ ἔσται ἡ ἀνάπαυσις αὐτοῦ τιμή.

And in that day, the root of Jesse will be, also the one who arises to rule the nations; on him the nations will hope, and his resting place will be honor. (LXX Is 11:10)

> וְהָיָה בַּיּוֹם הַהוּא שֹׁרֶשׁ יִשַׁי אֲשֶׁר עֹמֵד לְנֵס עַמִּים
> אֵלָיו גּוֹיִם יִדְרֹשׁוּ וְהָיְתָה מְנֻחָתוֹ כָּבוֹד׃

And in that day the root of Jesse [will be the one] who stands for an ensign of nations; nations will seek him, and his resting place will be glory. (MT Is 11:10)

Even though ῥίζα is translated as "root" (as it means in Is 11:1), in Is 11:10 it alludes to the Messiah as a "shoot" that grows from the royal line of David after the "family tree" of Israel would be chopped down in divine judgment and only the "stump" would remain with the "holy seed" (Is 6:13).[59] Northern Israel would be conquered by the Assyrians, and then the Southern Kingdom of Judah would fall to the Babylonians. "The root of Jesse" (ἡ ῥίζα τοῦ Ἰεσσαί, Rom 15:12)

---

57 Dunn, *Romans*, 850.
58 Dunn, *Romans*, 850, citing as examples Rom 2:5, 16; 13:12; 1 Cor 1:8; 3:13; 5:5.
59 See the second textual note on Rom 15:12.

"was already established as a title for the royal Messiah."[60] "Root" has the same meaning in the Fourth Suffering Servant Song (Is 53:2; MT: שֹׁרֶשׁ; LXX: ῥίζα). So too do Hebrew terms for the messianic "branch" in Is 4:2; 11:1; Jer 23:5; 33:15; Zech 3:8; Zech 6:12.

The verb ἀνίστημι, "arise" (Rom 15:12), may refer to Jesus' incarnation and epiphany, but it also connects with his resurrection as Paul himself utilizes it in Acts 17:3 and 1 Thess 4:14 (cf. also, e.g., Lk 24:7, 46; Acts 2:24, 32; 3:26). Jewett acutely observes:

> Here Paul returns to the same Jewish Christian creedal tradition with which the letter began, referring to Jesus as "born of the seed of David" (1:3). Even the expression ἐξ ἀναστάσεως νεκρῶν ("from the resurrection of the dead") (1:4) is echoed in the wording the LXX supplied for the shoot of Jesse, ὁ ἀνιστάμενος ("who rises up") to fulfill his messianic role.[61]

Isaiah prophesies that the "root" who is anointed with the Spirit of Yahweh (Is 11:1–2) will execute justice in righteousness (Is 11:3–5). Yet the passage goes on to characterize the Davidic Messiah's reign (ἄρχειν, "rule," LXX Is 11:10, as also in Rom 15:12) over his redeemed people not as a domineering or oppressive one. Rather, in harmony with Paul's depiction of him as a "servant" (Rom 15:8; see "root" and "shoot" for the Suffering Servant in Is 53:2), he will stand as the banner of salvation for all peoples (MT Is 11:10) so that even the Gentile nations are led to "seek" him (MT)[62] and come to "hope" on him (LXX). Paul surely appreciates the LXX's verb "to hope" (ἐλπίζω), which he used for the Christian hope in Rom 8:24–25. The cognate noun ἐλπίς, "hope," appeared in 15:4, and Paul follows up in the next verse with two more uses of the noun in his concluding prayer (15:13).

Scriptural Conclusions

The combined force of these four OT quotations readily discloses itself by the term common to them all. The plural form "Gentiles" or "nations" (ἔθνη) appears in Rom 15:9a for the first time since 11:25. It then occurs in all four OT quotations, including twice in the final citation from Isaiah, and then again in 15:16 (twice) and 15:18. In all the OT passages cited, the underlying Hebrew is the theologically significant גּוֹיִם. This plural generally refers to the non-Israelite "nations" and develops the more pejorative connotations of "Gentiles" (see the first textual note on 15:9). However, the synonymous plural phrases "all the nations" (πάντα τὰ ἔθνη) and "all the peoples" (πάντες οἱ λαοί) from Ps 117:1, cited in Rom 15:11, have an all-inclusive function. Paul reinforces the

---

[60] Dunn, *Romans*, 850, citing Is 11:1–5 (cf. Jer 23:5; 33:15); Sirach 47:22; also Rev 5:5; 22:16.

[61] Jewett, *Romans*, 896; ἀνίστημι is used of Jesus' resurrection (e.g., Lk 24:7, 46; 1 Thess 4:14), and some manuscripts insert it in Rom 14:9 (see the commentary there).

[62] The particular Hebrew verb for "seek" in Is 11:10, דָּרַשׁ, often refers to seeking God in faith and being saved by him (e.g., Deut 4:29; Pss 9:10 [MT 9:11]; 22:26 [MT 22:27]; 34:4, 10 [MT 34:5, 11]; 105:4; 119:2, 10; Is 55:6; 65:1, 10; Hos 10:12; Amos 5:4).

scriptural commonality and continuity by his use of "and again" (καὶ πάλιν) in introducing the final three quotations.

Perhaps most emblematic of Paul's overall thought is the Deuteronomy text (Deut 32:43 in Rom 15:10). There the Gentile nations are summoned to praise God together "with his people" (μετὰ τοῦ λαοῦ αὐτοῦ), Israel. This thought stands at the center of these seven verses (Rom 15:7–13) and reveals its central point. As similarly in the olive-tree analogy in 11:17–24, the plural "you" whom Christ received to himself (15:7) includes believing Jews. Yet "as promised beforehand … in holy writings" (1:2), and *repeatedly* Paul has just proven, Christ the "servant" (15:8) also endeavors to incorporate Gentiles into God's people. This reinforces the two points made in the introduction to this section above. Utilizing 15:7 as a pivot, "Paul has broadened out the whole discussion from the particular issue of 14:1–15:6 to the overall theme of the letter."[63]

Concluding Prayer for You All (15:13)

The plural pronoun "you" in 15:7 (ὑμᾶς) provides the opening frame to this section. Paul employs the identical accusative form twice in the concluding prayer of 15:13. As in 15:5, this prayer-wish has a verb in the aorist optative (πληρώσαι, "*may* God *fill you*"), which provides an added signal that Paul is drawing the section to a close.

"The apostle invokes God as 'the God of hope.' This is an unusual description of God found nowhere else in the NT or the LXX."[64] This opening phrase (ὁ … θεὸς τῆς ἐλπίδος) identifies God as the *source* of the "hope" referenced in 5:4 and, more recently, in 15:4, but he is surely also hope's *object*.[65] As Murray states: "God is the God of hope because he generates hope in us. It is, however, difficult to suppress the thought in this instance that the title points also to God as the object of hope."[66]

Paul's petition is that God would fill his hearers with "joy" (χαρά) and "peace" (εἰρήνη), both of which describe the essence of his kingdom in 14:17. The concluding reference to the "Holy Spirit" also aligns with 14:17. As there, the gifts of "peace" and "joy" both come from God through his Spirit (cf. 5:1–5), but are then *also* to be exercised among the community of believers. The repeated language from chapter 14 implies that "Paul is undoubtedly thinking specifically of the 'weak' and the 'strong' in the Roman community."[67]

---

[63] Dunn, *Romans*, 848.

[64] Kruse, *Romans*, 534.

[65] Wallace, *Greek Grammar*, 119–21, categorizes this double function as a "plenary genitive."

[66] Murray, *Romans*, 2:207.

[67] Moo, *Romans*, 880. For these two parties, see "Who Are the 'Weak' and the 'Strong'? Addressees Again!" in the introduction to 14:1–15:13. Augustine, *Commentary on Statements in Romans*, 82 (Bray, *Romans*, ACCS NT 6:357), applies it in this way:

> If the Gentiles think carefully, they will realize by their own faith, by which they now believe that to the pure all things are pure, that they should not offend those Jewish converts who, perhaps from weakness, dare not touch certain kinds of meat.

At the same time, Jewett observes how the presence of the verb "believe" (πιστεύω) in the clause "while believing" (ἐν τῷ πιστεύειν) "provides a necessary recapitulation of the earlier argument of Romans."[68] It, together with another thematic term utilized prominently in 1:16, the noun for saving "power" (δύναμις), accents the broader themes of the entire letter as discussed in the introduction to this section.[69]

The purpose for and end toward which all of this occurs is introduced with "so that" (εἰς τό followed by an infinitive), the same formula as 15:8b–9a (also 15:16). While the notion of purpose remains, a greater emphasis falls upon result (see the fourth textual note on 15:13). Paul's desire is "so that you might have an abundance in hope."[70] An increase in "hope" stems not from its source or object providing an extra shot of more "joy and peace," but primarily through receiving all three from God "while believing" in Christ and then experiencing each of them more fully in faith. Thus *they increase in our lives*. Paul does not merely pray for this to occur within an individual, but pleads for it to become a communal reality among all of those in Rome who believe, thus the repeated plural "you" (ὑμᾶς). This positive growth occurs only when God's people are "in" the sphere of the Holy Spirit, and it is surely accomplished "by" the Spirit's power (see the last textual note on 15:13).

Due to the service of Christ (15:8) and by the working of that same Spirit through God's Word and Sacraments, Paul's prayer continues to carry the same power as it rings out to all nations and peoples in this day (15:11). To that end, *"now may the God of hope fill you [with] all joy and peace while believing, so that you might have an abundance in hope by [the] power of [the] Holy Spirit"* (15:13).

---

[68] Jewett, *Romans*, 898.

[69] See "Romans 15:7–13 as Paul's Concluding Theological Statement" above.

[70] Paul describes Abraham's "hope" (ἐλπίς) even in his hopeless situation in Rom 4:18; see Middendorf, *Romans 1–8*, 361. Paul elaborates further on Christian "hope" in 5:2–5; 8:24; 12:12; 15:4. Cf. "hope" (ἐλπίς) regarding the whole creation in 8:20.

Paul's Use of the Old Testament in Romans: Reading the Old Testament in, with, and under Romans

Introduction: The Centrality of the Gospel in the Old Testament

Paul's statement about all that "was written previously" (προεγράφη) in 15:4 and the summative theological nature of 15:7–13 with its four culminating scriptural citations combine to make this a good place to assess his overall use of the OT in Romans. Morales contends that "Paul's citation in Rom 15:12 forms a second bookend around the body of the letter, recalling the opening"[1] (see especially 1:2–3). Here, then, the prominent role of the OT reaches its climactic point. Indeed, of more than fifty OT quotations throughout the letter, only one is still forthcoming (Is 52:15 in Rom 15:21). Luther suggests that in writing Romans, Paul sought "to prepare an introduction to the entire Old Testament. For, without doubt, whoever has this epistle well in his heart, has with him the light and power of the Old Testament."[2] What then is its "light and power"?

Silva properly asserts: "It is apparent to virtually all students of Paul that he regarded the Scripture (hē graphē) as proceeding from God himself and therefore as enjoying ultimate authority."[3] Melanchthon conveys this via a rather extraordinary excursus in his Romans commentary. Prior to beginning chapter 15, he devotes almost one-sixth of his commentary to an excursus titled "Excursus on the Authority of Scripture and the Fallibility of the Church Fathers."[4]

As Paul considers the authority of Scripture, he highlights its divine efficacy to, first and foremost, make people wise unto salvation (2 Tim 3:15–17). In the first two verses of Romans Paul speaks about "the Good News of God which

---

[1] Morales, " 'Promised through His Prophets in the Holy Scriptures,' " 123; note the reference to David in 1:3 and to Jesse in 15:12.

[2] Luther, "Preface to the Epistle of St. Paul to the Romans," AE 35:380. Of course, a broader discussion of Paul's use of the OT Scriptures throughout his letters also serves as a topic worthy of careful consideration. While it is beyond the purview of this excursus related solely to Romans, the Society of Biblical Literature conducted a six-year seminar regarding Paul and Scripture. Two monographs resulted with the titles *As It Is Written: Studying Paul's Use of Scripture* (ed. Stanley E. Porter and Christopher D. Stanley) and *Paul and Scripture: Extending the Conversation* (ed. Christopher D. Stanley). For a series of essays covering the influence of the Apocrypha, the Pseudepigrapha, and other noncanonical works on Romans, see Blackwell, Goodrich, and Maston, *Reading Romans in Context*.

[3] M. Silva, "Old Testament in Paul," *DPL*, 638.

[4] Melanchthon, *Romans*, 239–84; in the second English edition, this is 46 pages out of 297.

he promised beforehand through his prophets in holy writings" (εὐαγγέλιον θεοῦ ... διὰ τῶν προφητῶν αὐτοῦ ἐν γραφαῖς ἁγίαις, 1:1b–2). Then, in the second-to-last verse of this lengthy letter, he describes how the mystery of the Gospel was made known "through [the] prophetic writings" (διὰ ... γραφῶν προφητικῶν, 16:26). In the overall context of Romans, both statements refer to the very same OT Scriptures.[5] Not only does this provide a marvelous example of literary framing, but it also affirms a thematic statement Paul makes in the middle of the letter: "But by no means [is it] that God's Word has failed and remains fallen" (9:6a). To be sure, Paul is no Marcionite!

Paul insists that the enduring "light and power"[6] of the OT testifies to the righteousness of God through faith in Jesus Christ (3:21–22; 4:1–25); therefore it contains and conveys an illuminating and saving power. The Good News promised beforehand in the OT (1:1b–2) is, in fact, about God's Son (1:3). The Gospel message of Jesus the Christ (10:17; 15:19; 16:25) was "made known through [the] prophetic writings" (16:26) of old. The "power [δύναμις] of God into salvation for everyone who believes" (1:16), therefore, aligns completely with a clause that Paul uses in 1:17 and fourteen times throughout Romans: "just as it stands written" (καθὼς γέγραπται).[7]

A Variety of Uses of the Old Testament

Ellis asserts the following about Paul (the passages he footnotes as examples come prominently from Romans and are included in brackets):

> Whether he is giving a dogmatic proof [e.g., Rom 3:10–18], an analogy [e.g., Rom 2:24] or an illustration [e.g., Rom 10:6–8], or merely using language with which to clothe his own thoughts [e.g., Rom 12:20; 1 Cor 15:32; 2 Cor 10:17; 13:1], the OT appears frequently throughout the Pauline epistles. The style and vocabulary of the apostle are such that it is often difficult to distinguish between quotation, allusion and language colouring from the OT. This is not only the Word of God but also his mode of thought and speech.[8]

Paul's use of the OT comes out most obviously when he quotes directly from it, something he does more than fifty times in Romans (see below). But *his reliance on the OT should not be limited to this single tactic.* Neither should the categories identified below be viewed as isolated silos. Obviously, OT vocabulary merges into themes. Themes then lead toward allusions to OT accounts or texts. These allusions can then more closely resemble the text and become an echo of a particular passage. Such echoes then have varying degrees of alignment with the foundational text so that, at a certain point, they may be viewed

---

[5] Dunn, *Romans*, 915; Kruse, *Romans*, 588; Moo, *Romans*, 940; against Käsemann, *Romans*, 426, who rejects a connection with the OT and identifies these "prophetic writings" (16:26) as "the apostolic message."

[6] Luther, "Preface to the Epistle of St. Paul to the Romans," AE 35:380, quoted above.

[7] See the fourth textual note on 1:17.

[8] Ellis, *Paul's Use of the Old Testament*, 10.

as a quotation. Of course, some citations clearly provide direct quotes, as Paul's fourteen uses of "just as it stands written" (καθὼς γέγραπται), along with a variety of other introductory formulae, demonstrate.

Vocabulary

Paul relies heavily on the language of the OT. In this regard, it is usually correct to follow the adage of a book title, *Greek Words and Hebrew Meanings*.[9] This approach locates the substantive meaning of NT Greek words, especially theological terms, in underlying contextual meanings of OT Hebrew words. The Greek LXX, translated in the last few centuries before Christ, had already established key links between Hebrew and Greek theological vocabularies.[10] See, for example, the discussion of the OT background of the terms Paul uses for "faith," "righteousness," and "life" in the commentary on 1:16–17.[11]

For a second, more specific illustration, the NT connotations of "hope" (ἐλπίς, e.g., 15:4, 13 [twice]) contrast rather sharply with its meaning in the secular Greek world. The Classical Greek use of ἐλπίς encompasses "good or bad expectations of the future."[12] This can be neutral or deteriorate into a negative resignation to the hand of fate. The NT, however, draws on the more positive sense of corresponding OT terms that have more to do with "trust."[13] In the OT hope stands "closely allied to trust, trustful hope, hope as confidence in God."[14] "Hope" (ἐλπίς), therefore, serves as a good example of a Greek word whose meaning in the NT has been fundamentally transformed by Hebrew counterparts largely via the LXX (see the commentary on 4:18;[15] see ἐλπίς, "hope," also in 5:2, 4, 5; 8:20, 24; 12:12; 15:4, 13).

---

[9] Hill, *Greek Words and Hebrew Meanings*.

[10] The interpreter needs to be aware that there is rarely, if ever, a one-to-one correspondence between words in one language and those in another. The polysemy and contextual usages of each word need to be taken into consideration, as do synonyms that may come from completely different roots. The LXX may translate one Hebrew term by vastly different Greek words depending on their contexts. Likewise, the LXX may use one Greek word to translate a variety of Hebrew terms; for an example, see the footnote below regarding the translation of Hebrew words having to do with "hope."

[11] Middendorf, *Romans 1–8*, 88–90, 92–96, 98–99.

[12] R. Bultmann, "ἐλπίς, ἐλπίζω," *TDNT* 2:518.

[13] OT Hebrew words that have to do with "hope" or trust or confident expectation include the verbs קָוָה, יָחַל, חָסָה, and בָּטַח, as well as various nouns and other forms derived from them, e.g., תִּקְוָה, בֶּטַח, and מִבְטָח. See, e.g., the variety of Hebrew words translated by ἐλπίς, "hope," in LXX Pss 4:9 (MT 4:9; ET 4:8); 13:6 (MT/ET 14:6); 15:9 (MT/ET 16:9); 21:10 (MT 22:10; ET 22:9); 39:5 (MT 40:5; ET 40:4); 60:4 (MT 61:4; ET 61:3); 61:8 (MT 62:8; ET 62:7); 70:5 (MT/ET 71:5); 72:28 (MT/ET 73:28); 77:7, 53 (MT/ET 78:7, 53); 90:9 (MT/ET 91:9); 93:22 (MT/ET 94:22); 107:10 (MT 108:10; ET 108:9); 141:6 (MT 142:6; ET 142:5); 145:5 (MT/ET 146:5).

[14] Dunn, *Romans*, 219.

[15] Middendorf, *Romans 1–8*, 361.

Themes

Another manner in which Paul uses the OT stems from its prevalent themes. Obvious references would be to sin (e.g., 3:9–21; 4:6–8; 5:12, 20–21; 7:7–11) and the Law (see the excursus "Paul and the Law" following the commentary on 13:8–14). The motifs of slavery and freedom throughout Romans 6–8 would likely call to mind those prominent themes in the OT as a whole and particularly the exodus from slavery in Egypt into the freedom of the promised land (e.g., 6:6, 16–22; 7:14; 8:15, 21).[16]

Another more complex example comes from *two* significant theological terms, "righteousness" and "salvation." They interact with one another regularly in the OT and in the thematic verses of Romans, as noted in the first volume of this commentary:

> It may seem odd at first that Paul links the Good News of our *salvation* with God's *righteousness* as he does in Rom 1:16–17. But the OT has already firmly established the connection between those two terms by regularly using them synonymously.[17]

>> The parallel nature of [the terms in] these texts indicates that God's "righteousness" (*dikaiosunē*) is God's "salvation" (*sōtēria*). Righteousness, then, is not a static quality whereby God exercises justice but a dynamic quality whereby God effects salvation.[18]

> Thus already in the OT God's righteousness has been equated with his salvation of his people.[19]

Much the same thing can also be said about terminology for "righteousness" and "justice" in the sense of "justification" through faith.[20] The interaction of these words conveys the theme that God reveals his "righteousness" by saving his people to bring about his "justice," specifically, by "justifying" them through faith and by grace alone, a major theme in Romans (e.g., 1:16–17; 3:21–26; 4:5; 5:18, 21; 10:4). In the OT this theme is especially prominent in Isaiah's prophecies about the saving work of the messianic Davidide, the Suffering Savior.[a]

(a) E.g., Is 4:4; 9:6–7 (MT 9:5–6); 11:4; 26:9; 42:1–6; 49:4–8; 50:8; 52:7, 10; 53:8–11; 56:1; 61:3

---

[16] See Middendorf, *Romans 1–8*, 380.

[17] See, for example, Pss 40:10 (MT 40:11; LXX 39:11); 51:14 (MT 51:16; LXX 50:16); 71:15 (LXX 70:15); 98:2 (LXX 97:2); Is 45:8; 46:13; 51:5, 6, 8; 56:1; 59:16–17; 61:10; 62:1 (cf. Rom 10:10).

[18] Matera, *Romans*, 35–36.

[19] Middendorf, *Romans 1–8*, 93–94.

[20] This commentary generally prefers the translations "righteousness," "righteous," and "declare righteous" for the δικαιόω word group. Unfortunately, the Latin-based noun "justification" literally means "to make [someone] be just" (Latin *justus* + *facio*). This etymological connotation contributed to Luther's struggles. As an Augustinian monk, he was taught Augustine's view of sanative justification in which God is working progressively to cleanse or purify believers so as to "make us just." Luther's discovery of the forensic and declarative sense of the Greek word revealed the Gospel to him. As the Apology of the Augsburg Confession affirms: " 'To be justified' … does not mean that a wicked man is made righteous but that he is pronounced righteous in a forensic way" (Ap IV 252; see also Saarnivaara, *Luther Discovers the Gospel*, 6–9; "The Background and Meaning of 'Righteousness' Words" in Middendorf, *Romans 1–8*, 92–96).

These examples illustrate how Paul consistently relates various OT themes to Jesus Christ and then applies them to the NT community of believers (see the concluding section below).

Allusions

Paul also alludes to OT texts or accounts without offering actual quotations. As will be noted momentarily, and in marked contrast with the rest of Romans, Paul quotes from the OT only twice throughout Romans 5–8 (7:7; 8:36). At the same time, he draws heavily on the OT to make his argument. Rom 5:12–21 provides particularly illustrative material. Paul builds upon the account of Adam's fall and its consequences throughout the section, presuming his hearers can fill in the blanks of the underlying narrative from Genesis 3. His reference to the time between Adam and the revelation of the Mosaic Law (Rom 5:13–14) also assumes that his hearers recognize the general character of that era covered by the book of Genesis (e.g., Gen 6:5–7). Then, in Rom 5:20–21, he draws on the account of the giving of the Law at Sinai (Exodus 20–24) to make further theological points.

In Rom 9:6–18 Paul regularly cites OT passages, but he does so with such brevity that an allusion to the broader biblical narrative must be presumed in order for the hearer to fully grasp the specific points Paul makes. For example, in 9:6–13 he simply mentions Abraham and Sarah, alludes to Hagar and Ishmael, and speaks of Isaac and Rebekah, as well as their sons, Jacob and Esau, without giving details of the narrative which support his argument (Genesis 12–36). The same situation pertains to the interaction between Moses and the Pharaoh in Rom 9:14–18. Texts are quoted, but a fairly deep awareness of the larger context (Exodus 4–14; 33:19) is required, and particularly so in this case, in order to properly interpret them (see the commentary on Rom 9:17–18).

Echoes

Paul also draws from various places in the OT by employing *intertextual echoes*.[21] These are formulations or groupings of words associated with one another in the OT which appear again in Paul's writings. Whether Paul employs them consciously or unconsciously could be debated case by case. But the evidence for these echoes is substantial. Based upon Paul's familiarity with what stands written in the sacred Scriptures (ἐν γραφαῖς ἁγίαις, "in holy writings," 1:2), this should not be at all surprising. "The vocabulary and cadences of Scripture—particularly of the LXX—are imprinted deeply on Paul's mind."[22] When one hears a scriptural echo in Paul's letters, says Hays, it simply "recollects images of God that were in Paul's bones. We, belated rootless readers, can

---

[21] The term comes from Hays. For an explanation of this approach, see Hays, *Echoes of Scripture in the Letters of Paul*, 14–33; his second chapter is titled "Intertextual Echo in Romans" (34–83).

[22] Hays, *Echoes of Scripture in the Letters of Paul*, 16; see further "Assessment of Differences in Application" in "Actual Quotations" below.

learn only through marginalia and concordances—like novice guitarists learning blues riffs from sheet music—what Paul knew by heart."[23]

For example, one of the loudest echoes in Rom 1:16–17 is from LXX Ps 97:2 (MT/ET 98:2). There the psalmist already connects "*salvation* being *made known* in the presence of the *Gentiles* with the *revealing* of the Lord's *righteousness*" (italicized terms are common to both texts).[24] Rom 3:30 provides another illustration with its echo of the *Shemaᶜ*. Paul asserts: "Since God is one" (εἴπερ εἷς ὁ θεός). This clause corresponds closely with the language of Deut 6:4, whose Hebrew may be translated as "hear, O Israel: Yahweh our God, Yahweh is One," while the LXX may be rendered as "hear, O Israel, the Lord our God is one Lord" (ἄκουε, Ισραηλ· κύριος ὁ θεὸς ἡμῶν κύριος εἷς ἐστιν).

A final echo sounds forth at the end of the letter. Even though the LXX translation of Gen 3:15 contains terminology quite different from Paul's, Rom 16:20 echoes the *protoevangelium* quite loudly: "And the God of peace will crush Satan under your feet suddenly" (see the commentary on 16:20a).

Actual Quotations

The Number and Sources

The sheer number of OT quotations in Romans validates the degree to which Paul's theology stands firmly rooted there. However, before presenting statistics, Silva points out: "Unfortunately, there is no unanimity among researchers, particularly as they seek to distinguish between quotations and allusions,"[25] or, one might add, echoes. Hays, for example, surmises that "according to the tabulation provided by Dietrich-Alex Koch in *Die Schrift als Zeuge des Evangeliums*, there are eighty-nine Old Testament quotations in the Pauline letters, fifty-one of which occur in Romans."[26] Ellis, who properly includes Ephesians and the Pastorals in the list of NT letters authored by Paul, then identifies a total of ninety-three citations, with fifty-three in Romans.[27] A third calculation by Silva identifies fifty-nine OT citations in Romans. Silva's count disperses as follows: Romans 1–4 (fifteen); Romans 5–8 (two); Romans 9–11 (thirty); Romans 12–16 (twelve).[28] The radical numerical swing between chapters 5–8 and 9–11 is discussed in the introduction to Romans 5–8 and in the introduction to Romans 9–11.[29]

---

[23] Hays, *Echoes of Scripture in the Letters of Paul*, 43.

[24] Middendorf, *Romans 1–8*, 109.

[25] M. Silva, "Old Testament in Paul," *DPL*, 630.

[26] Hays, *Echoes of Scripture in the Letters of Paul*, 34, citing Koch, *Die Schrift als Zeuge des Evangeliums*, 21–24.

[27] Ellis, *Paul's Use of the Old Testament*, 11, 150–52.

[28] M. Silva, "Old Testament in Paul," *DPL*, 631.

[29] See Middendorf, *Romans 1–8*, 380, and "God's Word" in the introduction to Romans 9–11. In regard to Romans 9–11, Hultgren, *Romans*, 348, including n. 3, observes:

Silva then provides a chart titled "Old Testament Citations in Paul."[30] In it, he assimilates the work of Michel, Ellis, and Koch in order to identify all of Paul's quotations.[31] He then divides them into categories.[32] These groupings attempt to sort out the level of agreement between the Greek text of Romans and that of the LXX and/or the Hebrew Masoretic Text. Here again, he cautions: "It needs to be stressed that a strong subjective element affects some of the decisions reflected in the lists, particularly when one must determine whether a variation is significant enough to be noted as such."[33] Below are slightly adapted portions of Silva's chart representing Romans:[34]

1. Paul represents the LXX and the MT (twenty-three total)

Rom 2:6	Ps 62:12 (MT 62:13; LXX 61:13)
Rom 3:4	Ps 51:4 (MT 51:6; LXX 50:6)
Rom 3:13a	Ps 5:9 (MT/LXX 5:10)
Rom 3:13b	Ps 140:3 (MT 140:4; LXX 139:4)
Rom 3:18	Ps 36:1 (MT 36:2; LXX 35:2)
Rom 4:17	Gen 17:5
Rom 4:18	Gen 15:5
Rom 7:7	Ex 20:17 (‖ Deut 5:21)
Rom 8:36	Ps 44:22 (MT 44:23; LXX 43:23)
Rom 9:7	Gen 21:12
Rom 9:12	Gen 25:23
Rom 9:13	Mal 1:2–3
Rom 9:15	Ex 33:19
Rom 9:26	Hos 1:10 (MT/LXX 2:1)
Rom 10:5	Lev 18:5
Rom 10:13	Joel 2:32 (MT/LXX 3:5)
Rom 10:19	Deut 32:21
Rom 13:9a	Deut 5:17–21 (‖ Ex 20:13–17)
Rom 13:9b	Lev 19:18
Rom 15:3	Ps 69:9 (MT 69:10; LXX 68:10)
Rom 15:9	Ps 18:49 (MT 18:50; LXX 17:50; ‖ 2 Sam 22:50)

Within its 90 verses are 35 direct quotations from the OT (39% of the verses) plus many more allusions and summaries of OT material. ... There are a total of 51 OT quotations in Romans itself [citing Koch, *Die Schrift als Zeuge des Evangeliums*, 21–24]. ... That means that about 69 percent of the OT quotations within Romans are in chapters 9 through 11.

[30] M. Silva, "Old Testament in Paul," *DPL*, 631.

[31] M. Silva, "Old Testament in Paul," *DPL*, 642, citing Ellis, *Paul's Use of the Old Testament*; Koch, *Die Schrift als Zeuge des Evangeliums*; Michel, *Paulus und seine Bibel*.

[32] M. Silva, "Old Testament in Paul," *DPL*, 630–32.

[33] M. Silva, "Old Testament in Paul," *DPL*, 632.

[34] M. Silva, "Old Testament in Paul," *DPL*, 631.

	Rom 15:11	Ps 117:1 (LXX 116:1)
	Rom 15:21	Is 52:15

2. Paul represents the MT but differs from the LXX (four total)

Rom 1:17	Hab 2:4
Rom 11:4	1 Ki 19:18
Rom 11:35	Job 41:11 (MT/LXX 41:3)
Rom 12:19	Deut 32:35

3. Paul represents the LXX but differs from the MT (thirteen total)

Rom 2:24	Is 52:5
Rom 3:14	Ps 10:7 (LXX 9:28)
Rom 4:3 (9, 22)	Gen 15:6
Rom 4:7–8	Ps 32:1–2 (LXX 31:1–2)
Rom 9:29	Is 1:9
Rom 10:16	Is 53:1
Rom 10:18	Ps 19:4 (MT 19:5; LXX 18:5)
Rom 10:20–21	Is 65:1–2
Rom 11:34	Is 40:13
Rom 12:20	Prov 25:21–22
Rom 14:11	Is 45:23 (+ Is 49:18?)
Rom 15:10	Deut 32:43
Rom 15:12	Is 11:10

4. Paul differs from both the LXX and the MT (fifteen total)

Rom 3:10–12	Ps 14:1–3 (LXX 13:1–3; ‖ Ps 53:1–3 [MT 53:2–4; LXX 52:2–4])
Rom 3:15–17	Is 59:7–8
Rom 9:9	Gen 18:10, 14
Rom 9:17	Ex 9:16
Rom 9:25	Hos 2:23 (MT/LXX 2:25)
Rom 9:27–28	Is 10:22–23 (+ Hos 1:10? [MT/LXX 2:1])
Rom 9:33	Is 8:14 + Is 28:16
Rom 10:6–8	Deut 9:4 + Deut 30:12–14 (cf. Ps 107:26 [LXX 106:26])
Rom 10:11	Is 28:16
Rom 10:15	Is 52:7
Rom 11:3	1 Ki 19:10 (cf. 1 Ki 19:14)
Rom 11:8	Deut 29:4 (MT/LXX 29:3) (+ Is 29:10)
Rom 11:9–10	Ps 69:22–23 (MT 69:22–23; LXX 68:22–23)
Rom 11:26–27a	Is 59:20–21
Rom 11:27b	Is 27:9

5. Debated quotations (four total)

Rom 3:20	Ps 143:2
Rom 9:20	Is 29:16 (Is 45:9)
Rom 11:1–2	Ps 94:14 (LXX 93:14)
Rom 12:16–17	Prov 3:7

As Silva readily admits, one might quibble with the categorization of various texts.[35] For example, I would put Rom 1:17 and its Hab 2:4 quotation into category 4 rather than category 2.[36]

The amount of data in the list above becomes almost overwhelming, but it is also impressive and extremely helpful. Silva brings together a number of things this commentary has regularly noted in its treatment of individual texts.

Assessment of Differences in the Texts

First of all, while verbal disparities between Paul's quotations and the underlying OT exist, these should not be exaggerated. Ellis summarizes: "Most often [NT quotations] reproduce the OT passage with occasional variations in conformity with the new context."[37] A more precise evaluation of the underlying sources concludes that "more frequently, Paul follows the LXX over against the Hebrew."[38] However,

> we also find a lack of uniformity with regard to Paul's textual source. His dependence on the current Greek translation of his day is clearly established, but there is good reason to think that he was familiar with the original Hebrew and that the latter, in at least some cases, determined how he used the OT. This general question, unfortunately, becomes tangled in the technical problems of textual transmission.[39]

Commenting specifically on Rom 14:11, Dunn asserts that Paul himself might at times be the source of the variances between Romans and the OT texts he references:

> The following quotation [in Rom 14:11] is a mixed form. Paul either quotes from memory and runs two passages [Is 49:18; 45:23] together without realizing it, or he does so deliberately. Either way it underlines the point that use of (OT) scripture for its authoritative teaching was not simply mechanical: the substance of divine(ly inspired) utterance was more important than a pedantic exactness of form.[40]

This commentary asserts that the best explanation for these differences often resides in a conscious and deliberate alteration made by Paul in order to establish his point most effectively (e.g., Hab 2:4 in Rom 1:17; Is 59:20 in Rom 11:26; see the commentary on those verses).

What does all of this mean? Fortunately, it need not be unnecessarily troubling. Both the OT and Paul's letters are properly identified as the verbally inspired Word of God (2 Tim 3:16). Paul certainly views the original Hebrew text as such (see "Introduction: The Centrality of the Gospel in the Old

---

[35] M. Silva, "Old Testament in Paul," *DPL*, 632.

[36] See Middendorf, *Romans 1–8*, 99–106, 108.

[37] Ellis, *Paul's Use of the Old Testament*, 11.

[38] M. Silva, "Old Testament in Paul," *DPL*, 632.

[39] M. Silva, "Old Testament in Paul," *DPL*, 632.

[40] Dunn, *Romans*, 809.

Testament" above). Before the end of the NT era, Peter indicates that Paul's letters stand on the very same level; they are in the same class as "the other Scriptures" (2 Pet 3:16). In commenting on the statement "just as also our beloved brother Paul wrote to you, according to the wisdom given to him,"[41] in 2 Pet 3:15, Giese recognizes: "With this wording Peter affirms the divine inspiration and authority of Paul's writings."[42] Taken together, 2 Pet 3:15–16 similarly "affirms Peter's high view of Paul's writings as Holy Scripture; they are normative books of the canon, along with the entire OT and the rest of the NT."[43] Thus the form in which Paul presents OT texts comes under the same umbrella of verbal and plenary inspiration which pertains to everything else he writes in Romans. Paul was among those who "spoke from God as they were being moved by the Holy Spirit" (2 Pet 1:21).[44] Pieper, therefore, properly recognizes and affirms the Spirit's role:

> Thus in quoting the Old Testament the Holy Spirit is in a manner quoting Himself. And He has the authority to use His own words as He chooses; in quoting He makes of the Old Testament passage, so to say, a "new text" (Luther's phrase). …
>
> The Holy Ghost is speaking through the Apostles and is "taking liberties" with His own Word.[45]

Assessment of Differences in Application

While affirming this qualitative commonality, a further aspect also comes into play. At times, there seem to be identifiable modifications in Romans of the *meaning or reference* of OT passages. In such cases, the text in its OT contexts applies God's Word in one way; however, Paul sees new meaning in the passage when he cites and applies it in the NT era. For example, consider the following (in each case, see the commentary on the given passage for a more complete explanation):

- The reason for the blaspheming of God's name is different in Is 52:5 than in Rom 2:24.
- The referent of "not my people" in Hos 1:10 (MT 2:1) and Hos 2:23 (MT 2:25)—apostate Israel—changes to that which Paul intends in Rom 9:25–26—Gentiles.
- What is said about the Law's commandment in Deut 30:12–14 applies to the contrasting Word of Christ and of faith in Rom 10:6–8.

---

[41] This is the translation of Giese, *2 Peter and Jude*, 197.

[42] Giese, *2 Peter and Jude*, 205.

[43] Giese, *2 Peter and Jude*, 208.

[44] This is the translation of Giese, *2 Peter and Jude*, 86; see also 94–95.

[45] Pieper, *Christian Dogmatics*, 1:249, 251. In regard to differences in the four accounts of the Words of Institution for the Lord's Supper, Pieper similarly refers to theologians who "ascribe theses variations to the intention of the Holy Ghost, who edited the original words to suit Himself, just as He did in the case of quotations from the Old Testament" (3:349).

- The saving name "Yahweh" (Joel 2:32 [MT 3:5]) upon whom one, and now all, may call for salvation is the name "Jesus" (Rom 10:9, 13), which means "Yahweh saves" (cf. Mt 1:21).[46]

- The relationship between living and the Law differs in Lev 18:5 and Rom 10:5.

- Isaiah's words in Is 65:1–2 are about Israel, but Paul separates the verses and applies Is 65:1 only to Gentiles (Rom 10:20) and then, distinctly, applies Is 65:2 to Israel (Rom 10:21).

- The psalmist David, who bears reviling for God's sake in Ps 69:9 (MT 69:10), has his words fulfilled in a greater way when they are attributed to Jesus in Rom 15:3.

Pieper again properly evaluates this phenomenon, this time by quoting, with agreement, the words of Flacius and then Pfeiffer:

> Flacius writes: "It must be maintained that the Old Testament is usually cited by the holy writers of the New Testament in such a manner that they observed the sense and produced rather the fulfillment of the prophecy than the words of the prophecy."[47]

> A. Pfeiffer remarks: "… Why make much ado about it, since there is here no contradiction? The Holy Spirit has revealed the Old Testament, and He has reserved the right to interpret it in the New."[48]

In response to all this, Silva accurately identifies the cause but then unnecessarily questions the result:

> It is precisely because Paul is never content with merely restating the original, historical meaning of an OT text, but rather applies it to his present situation, that the perennial and troublesome question arises, "Can we use Paul's exegesis today?"[49]

The introduction to this commentary offers the following answer:

> It is not necessary, however, to insist that the meaning of quotations that Paul cites from the OT is always simply equivalent with the intended meaning of the original author. When Paul quotes or alludes to an OT text, he is, at times, revealing more, "extending its meaning in new directions," in order to apply the inspired Word to his own context and time.[50] In so doing, he does *not* deny what the original author meant. Instead, in and through Christ, and by inspiration of the Spirit, Paul sees new or additional meaning in the ancient

---

[46] "Jesus" (Ἰησοῦς) ultimately derives from the Hebrew name יְהוֹשֻׁעַ, *Yehoshua*, "Joshua," which is a compound of the theophoric element -יְהוֹ, *yeho-*, an abbreviation of "Yahweh," and the element -שׁוּעַ, derived from the root יָשַׁע, "to save." See Harstad, *Joshua*, 12–13.

[47] Pieper, *Christian Dogmatics*, 1:249, quoting Matthias Flacius (1520–1575), *Clavis Scripturae Sacrae*, 2:103.

[48] Pieper, *Christian Dogmatics*, 1:249–50, quoting August Pfeiffer (1640–1698), *Critica sacra*, 109–10.

[49] M. Silva, "Old Testament in Paul," *DPL*, 639.

[50] Hays, *Echoes of Scripture in the Letters of Paul*, 5; see his application of this principle on pages 34–83, especially pages 35, 41, 61, 69, 82–83.

words. When this happens, the OT quote then *also* means what Paul intends it to mean as he uses it in the context of Romans.[51]

But Paul is no innovator here.

> Already these Scriptures were awash in what scholars call "intertextuality," fragments of earlier stories echoing in the later chambers of sacred words and promises. Later ... texts and stories ... are told with allusions to earlier stories. ... Paul continues the interpretive practices of his ancestors in faith, extending Scripture beyond their day to his own, finding its fullness in the Lord Jesus Christ.[52]

Paul's exegetical method is comparable to what the technical phrase *sensus plenoir* conveys: the "fuller meaning" of OT texts is revealed in and through NT usage (e.g., Hos 11:1 in Mt 2:15; Jer 31:15 in Mt 2:17–18). Scripture encourages us to read the OT in and through Christ (e.g., Lk 24:25–27, 44–47), yet Fee and Stuart properly caution that "sensus plenior *(fuller meaning) is a function of inspiration, not illumination.*"[53] In other words, the inspired Scriptures interpret one another definitively, and we [believing we have further "illumination"] cannot authoritatively put forth new extended meanings or applications as did Paul and the other NT writers.[54]

Conclusion

An interpretive framework for handling Paul's use of the OT is presented and explained in the excursus "Beyond Typology." It utilizes this diagram:

Figure 6

The Whole Story: The Bow-Tie Diagram

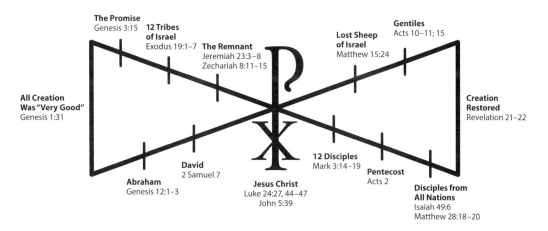

---

[51] See, for example, Hab 2:4 in Rom 1:17; Is 52:5 in Rom 2:24; Deut 30:12–14 in Rom 10:6–8; Is 65:1–2 in Rom 10:20–21.

[52] Capes, Reeves, and Richards, *Rediscovering Paul*, 262.

[53] Fee and Stuart, *How to Read the Bible for All Its Worth*, 202–3 in the third edition quoted in volume 1; 209 in the fourth edition used in this volume.

[54] Middendorf, *Romans 1–8*, 37.

On the *left* side, God spoke his Word to and through the prophets of the OT (e.g., Rom 1:2; 16:26). That Word still stands (9:6), even as its promise now stands fulfilled. Indeed, the righteousness of God is "being testified to by the Law and the Prophets, that is, a righteousness of God through faith of/[in] Jesus Christ into all those who believe" (3:21–22).

For Paul, the OT's "theological function is to testify to the gospel."[55] This means that Jesus' death and resurrection serve as the culmination of God's OT promises.[b] Christ, at the *center* of the diagram, has also become *the focal point and prism through which Paul reads the OT Scriptures.*

(b) E.g., Rom 1:2–4; 3:21–26; 4:24–25; 5:6–11; 9:5, 33; 10:4, 8–9, 11–13, 16–17; 15:8–12; 16:25–27

But Paul's sight is not only retrospective; he also engages his contemporaries and looks forward, all the way to the return of Christ.[56] As he lives on the *right* side, Paul utilizes the OT to describe how the Christ-event is playing itself out, and will in the future, in the ongoing life of God's people on earth, now comprised of both believing Israelites and believing Gentiles.[c] On this basis, Hays supposes that "because Paul sees the fulfillment of prophecy ... in God's gathering of a church composed of Jews and Gentiles together, his hermeneutic is functionally ecclesiocentric rather than christocentric."[57] But that distinction poses a false alternative. Silva responds: "This [ecclesiocentric] concept reflects a view of redemptive history that also functions as an interpretive principle."[58] The Christological and the ecclesiological can be distinguished, but never divided. After all, the church is the body of Christ (Rom 12:4–5). As Paul applies or even extends the meaning of OT passages to and for the church, he does so *only in and through Christ.*

(c) E.g., Rom 1:16; 3:29–30; 4:22–25; 9:24–29; 10:12; 11:17–24, 25–26; 15:8–9

Therefore, one can properly affirm Luther's assertion that Romans provides "an access to the whole of the Old Testament."[59] But it might be even better stated that *Jesus does,* since one must look through him to properly grasp its message.[60] More importantly, access to the *grace* of God now extends to all who believe in him (Rom 3:24; 4:16; 5:2, 21; 10:11–13). This, too, comes just as promised of old to our forefather in the faith: "For what is the Scripture saying? 'And Abraham believed in God, and it was credited to him for righteousness' " (Rom 4:3, quoting Gen 15:6). Paul's use of Gen 15:6 in Romans 4 beautifully illustrates how he extends a passage about Abraham (who had already received

---

[55] Watson, *Paul and the Hermeneutics of Faith,* 24.

[56] See the excursus "Beyond Typology" following the commentary on 12:1–8.

[57] Hays, *Echoes of Scripture in the Letters of Paul,* xiii.

[58] M. Silva, "Old Testament in Paul," *DPL,* 639.

[59] Quoted by Allen, "The Old Testament in Romans I–VIII," 6. The quotation appears to be a somewhat different translation of the German in Luther, "Preface to the Epistle of St. Paul to the Romans," translated farther above as "an introduction to the entire Old Testament" (AE 35:380).

[60] Schreiner, *Romans,* 814, states:

> In light of the fulfillment readers can now perceive that what was hidden in the old is now revealed through the new. What was foreshadowed in the OT is now perceived in its true significance in light of the fulfillment that has arrived.

the promise that "all the families of the earth will be blessed in you" [Gen 12:3]) to all "those who also follow [in] the footsteps of the faith of our father Abraham" (Rom 4:12; cf. also 4:16), and how he does so in and through Jesus:

> [21]And, after being fully convinced that what was promised [by God] and still in effect, he [God] is powerful also to do. [22]Therefore also "it was credited to him for righteousness." [23]But "it was credited to him" was not written on his account only, [24]but also on our account, to whom it is about to be credited, to those who believe upon the one who raised Jesus our Lord from the dead. (4:21–24)

Thus for Paul the Scriptures form a united, inspired, and inspiring story of salvation for the one people of God joined together in a promise fulfilled for one, and for all, in our Lord Jesus Christ.[61]

---

[61] After Rom 4:24, repeated references to "our Lord Jesus Christ" or "Jesus Christ our Lord" function thematically throughout Romans 5–8; see Middendorf, *Romans 1–8*, 377–80.

Wrapping Up the Letter:
Romans 15:14–16:27

Rom 15:7–13 serves to conclude the main theological exposition of the letter (see "Romans 15:7–13 as Paul's Concluding Theological Statement" in the commentary on 15:7–13). After an introduction (1:1–15), Paul states his theme in 1:16–17, which concludes: "The righteous person will live from faith" (1:17b). These key terms are then developed extensively in four chief sections (for further details, see the table of contents):

I.   The righteousness of God (δικαιοσύνη θεοῦ; 1:18–4:25)
II. Life in and through our Lord Jesus Christ (5:1–8:39)
III. The righteousness of God and Israel (9:1–11:36)
IV. Living in response to the mercies of God (12:1–15:13)

In the remainder of chapter 15, Paul turns to describe his mission work. He then ends the letter with numerous personal greetings in Romans 16. Fitzmyer properly observes: "Now that Paul has finished the exposé of his gospel and set forth its implications for upright Christian life, he adds the epistolary conclusion to his letter to the Romans."[1] Two factors verify this assessment of 15:14–16:27.

Framing Parallels between Romans 1:1–17 and Romans 15:14–16:27

The first consists of numerous bracketing *parallels between 1:1–17 and the remainder of Romans*. Moo cites the following connections with the rest of Romans 15:[2]

Commendation of the Romans	15:14	1:8
"Apostle to the Gentiles"	15:15b–21	1:5, 13
Hindrance in visiting Rome	15:22	1:13a
"Indebtedness"	15:27	1:14
Desire to minister for mutual blessing	15:29	1:11–12
Prayer	15:30–32	1:9–10

Matera notes further similarities between these verses: 15:16 and 1:9 (service in the Good News); 15:18 and 1:5b (responsive hearing by Gentiles); 15:19 and 1:1, 3 (the Good News of Christ); 15:24a and 1:11a (Paul's yearning to see the Christians in Rome); and 15:24b and 1:12 (mutual encouragement).[3]

---

[1]   Fitzmyer, *Romans*, 709.

[2]   Moo, *Romans*, 886.

[3]   Matera, *Romans*, 330.

Then Matera establishes the following links between 1:1–17 and the concluding verses of chapter 16 (his translation and emphasis):[4]

16:19   your obedience has become *known to all*
1:8b   your faith has been proclaimed *throughout the world*

16:25a to the one who is able *to strengthen you* in accord with my gospel
1:11b   that I might impart to you some spiritual favor in order *to strengthen you*

16:25b in accordance with *the revelation of the mystery* that was kept secret
1:17   for in it God's righteousness *is revealed*

16:26a but now revealed through the *prophetic writings*
1:2   previously promised *through his prophets in the holy Scriptures*

16:26b that *the obedience that comes from faith* might be made known to *all the Gentiles*
1:5b   *the obedience that comes from faith*, among *all the Gentiles*

These parallel thoughts demonstrate how Paul "employs the letter closing to recall and expand upon motifs found in the letter opening."[5]

Commonalities with Other Pauline Endings

Second, both Dunn and Moo lay out numerous *parallels between features present in the rest of Romans and the (generally) concluding sections of other Pauline letters*. Dunn's less extensive chart identifies these commonalities:[6]

Travel plans	15:14–33	particularly 1 Cor 16:1–12; 1 Thess 2:17–3:13
Request for prayer	15:30–32	Eph 6:18–20; Col 4:3–4; 1 Thess 5:25; 2 Thess 3:1–2; Philem[on] 22
Wish for peace	15:33	2 Cor 13:11; Gal 6:16; Eph 6:23; Phil 4:9; 1 Thess 5:23; 2 Thess 3:16
Additional greetings	16:1–16, 21–23	1 Cor 16:19–20; 2 Cor 13:13 [13:12b in the Greek]; Phil 4:21–22; Col 4:10–15; Philem[on] 23–24
Holy kiss	16:16	1 Cor 16:20; 2 Cor 13:12; 1 Thess 5:26
Concluding grace	16:20b	1 Cor 16:23; 2 Cor 13:13 [ET 13:14]; Gal 6:18; Eph 6:24; Phil 4:23; Col 4:18; 1 Thess 5:28; 2 Thess 3:18; Philem[on] 25

---

[4] Matera, *Romans*, 330.

[5] Matera, *Romans*, 330.

[6] Dunn, *Romans*, 854; comparably, Moo, *Romans*, 884. See also "Paul's Epistolary Conclusions" in Winger, *Ephesians*, 773.

Paul's Ministry: Past and Present

Translation

15 **14**Now I have been persuaded and remain convinced, my brothers, even I myself, concerning you that you yourselves also are full of goodness, having been filled with all knowledge and remaining so, while also being able to admonish one another. **15**But I wrote to you rather boldly in part as repeatedly reminding you on account of the grace which was given to me by God **16**so that I am a minister of Christ Jesus toward the Gentiles, performing priestly service [for] the Good News of God in order that the offering of the Gentiles might be acceptable, having been consecrated and remaining holy by the Holy Spirit. **17**Therefore I have this boast in Christ Jesus with reference to the things pertaining to God.

18Indeed, I will not dare to speak anything of things which Christ Jesus did not accomplish through me toward the responsive hearing of Gentiles, by word and work, **19**by [the] power of signs and wonders, in [the] power of the Spirit of God with the result that I have brought to completion and now finished [proclaiming] the Good News of the Christ from Jerusalem and around as far as Illyricum, **20**and thus while striving eagerly to bring the Good News not where Christ was [already] named in order that I might not build upon another's foundation. **21**But just as it stands written: "[Those] to whom it was not announced about him, they will see, and the ones who have not heard, they will understand." **22**Therefore also I have repeatedly been hindered many times from coming to you.

Textual Notes

15:14 πέπεισμαι δέ—The conjunction δέ has the effect of "linking narrative segments, *now, then, and, so, that is*" (BDAG, 2). Thus rather than a temporal "now" (νῦν), we have a connective conjunction. The identical perfect passive form of the verb πείθω appears in 8:38 and 14:14. Both the past and the present aspects of the perfect are significant: "I have been persuaded and remain convinced."

αὐτὸς ἐγώ—The personal pronoun αὐτός has an intensive function regarding the personal pronoun ἐγώ, thus, "I myself."[1] ἐγώ gives added emphasis to the first person singular verb πέπεισμαι (see the preceding textual note).[2] It is difficult to conceive of how some scholars can hypothesize that this same emphatic form of self-identification in 7:25 could be someone other than Paul referring to himself at the time of writing! See the third textual note and the commentary on 7:25, as well as the excursus "Who Is the 'I' in Romans 7:14–25? Christian or Non-Christian?" following the commentary on 7:14–25.

---

[1] See BDAG, 1; Mounce, *Basics of Biblical Greek*, 102–3; Wallace, *Greek Grammar*, 349.

[2] See Wallace, *Greek Grammar*, 321–23.

αὐτοὶ … ἐστε—For the intensive function of αὐτός, see the previous textual note; here it intensifies the second person plural subject contained in the verb form: "*you yourselves* are."

μεστοί … ἀγαθωσύνης—The adjective μεστός indicates "being thoroughly characterized by someth[ing], *filled w[ith] somet[hing]*." That "something" is defined with a genitive of content:[3] ἀγαθωσύνης, "of goodness." The contrast with 1:29 is marked; see the second textual note on 1:29 and the commentary here.

πεπληρωμένοι πάσης [τῆς] γνώσεως—The perfect tense of this passive participle of πληρόω, "to fill, fulfill," emphasizes both a past event with its present implications:[4] "having been filled and remaining so." The passive functions as a divine or theological passive, which implies being filled by God.[5] See the first textual note on 1:29, and, once again, note the contrast of that verse with 15:14. As in the preceding textual note, a genitive of content indicates that with which the Christians are filled: πάσης [τῆς] γνώσεως, "with all knowledge."

δυνάμενοι … νουθετεῖν—The first term is a present participle of δύναμαι, "be able, capable," used adverbially.[6] The verb δύναμαι regularly takes a complementary infinitive.[7] Here the infinitive is of νουθετέω, "to counsel about avoidance or cessation of an improper course of conduct, *admonish, warn, instruct*" (BDAG).

15:15 τολμηρότερον—This form is the neuter comparative of the adjective τολμηρός, "bold, daring," which functions as an adverb, "*rather boldly*" (BDAG, s.v. τολμηρός). The form of the variant reading τολμηροτέρως (A B 629) is the adverb.

ἀπὸ μέρους—This prepositional phrase appears three times in Romans (11:25; 15:15, 24). While the genitive singular form of μέρος literally means "in part," it conveys a partitive sense here; Paul writes "*very boldly on some points*" (BDAG, 1 c). The same expression has a temporal sense in 15:24 (see the fifth textual note on that verse). See the sixth textual note and the commentary on 11:25 for the significance of interpreting the disputed force of the phrase there.

ὡς ἐπαναμιμνῄσκων ὑμᾶς—The doubly compound ἐπαναμιμνῄσκω (ἐπί + ἀνά + μιμνῄσκομαι), "to cause [someone] to remember, *remind someone*" (BDAG), appears only here in Biblical Greek, but the verb's meaning is clear from Paul's uses of (singly) compound verbs meaning "to remind": ἀναμιμνῄσκω (1 Cor 4:17; 2 Cor 7:15; 2 Tim 1:6) and ὑπομιμνῄσκω (2 Tim 2:14; Titus 3:1). Cranfield suggests that the additional prefixed ἐπί here conveys emphasis: "reminded again and again."[8] The particle ὡς reinforces that the present participle ἐπαναμιμνῄσκων is used adverbially for action concurrent with the main verb,[9] ἔγραψα, thus "I wrote … as repeatedly reminding

---

[3] See Wallace, *Greek Grammar*, 92–94.

[4] See Wallace, *Greek Grammar*, 573.

[5] See Wallace, *Greek Grammar*, 437–38.

[6] See Wallace, *Greek Grammar*, 621–27; Mounce, *Basics of Biblical Greek*, 245–53.

[7] See Wallace, *Greek Grammar*, 598–99; he calls δύναμαι "the most commonly used helper verb."

[8] Cranfield, *Romans*, 754.

[9] See Wallace, *Greek Grammar*, 625–26.

you." Paul also calls to mind the content expressed by the prepositional phrase to follow (see the next textual note).

διὰ τὴν χάριν τὴν δοθεῖσάν μοι—This prepositional phrase is translated as "on account of the grace which was given to me." The passive voice of δοθεῖσαν functions as a divine or theological passive: the grace was given by God.[10] An identical prepositional phrase with διά appears in 12:3 (cf. also 12:6) but with the governed words in the genitive case (τῆς χάριτος τῆς δοθείσης) instead of the accusative case as here.

15:16 εἰς τὸ εἶναί με λειτουργόν—Infinitives take their subject in the accusative case.[11] Here the subject of εἶναι, "to be," is the accusative pronoun με ("me," but translated as "I"), which is followed by λειτουργόν, a second accusative that "makes an assertion about the first" accusative.[12] Articular infinitives with εἰς τό can express purpose,[13] "in order that I might be," but surely the construction here also and even primarily states a result[14] of the grace given to Paul (15:15). The best attempt at combing the two in English becomes "so that I am a minster." For λειτουργός, "one engaged in administrative or cultic service, *servant, minister*" (BDAG, 1), see the third textual note and the commentary on 13:6, its only other occurrence in Romans.

ἱερουργοῦντα—As with the previous term λειτουργός, Paul again employs cultic language. The compound verb ἱερουργέω (ἱερός, "holy," + ἔργον, "work") appears only here in Biblical Greek and means "to act in some cultic or sacred capacity, *perform holy service, act as a priest*" (BDAG). Its present participle is adverbial and expresses attendant circumstance, "used to communicate an action that, in some sense, is coordinate" with the main verb,[15] thus "I am a minister ... performing priestly service" (15:16).

ἵνα γένηται—Here the conjunction ἵνα expresses purpose.[16] The subjunctive of γίνομαι then conveys what the offering might "*be, prove to be, turn out to be*" (BDAG, 7).

ἡ προσφορὰ τῶν ἐθνῶν—Yet another cultic term, προσφορά, also occurs only here in Romans. It denotes "that which is brought as a voluntary expression ... *offering*" (BDAG, 2). The genitive could be read as subjective,[17] referring to "the offering"

---

[10] See Wallace, *Greek Grammar*, 437–38.

[11] See Mounce, *Basics of Biblical Greek*, 302–3.

[12] Wallace, *Greek Grammar*, 190; on 192 he cites Rom 15:16 as an example.

[13] Moo, *Romans*, 889, n. 28, and Cranfield, *Romans*, 754, argue that that is the sense of the construction here.

[14] See Wallace, *Greek Grammar*, 592–93; he notes: That εἰς τό plus the infinitive can indicate result "is disputed in older works, but it is an established idiom in both the NT and extra-biblical literature" (593, n. 10). For the merging of purpose and result, see Wallace's discussion of the matter with respect to ἵνα clauses (471–74), as well as the fourth textual note on 3:8 and the third textual note on 14:9; see also the commentary on 4:16 and 5:20.

[15] Wallace, *Greek Grammar*, 640; see 640–45.

[16] See Wallace, *Greek Grammar*, 472.

[17] See Wallace, *Greek Grammar*, 113–16.

given by "the Gentiles" (see 15:25–26), or objective/appositional,[18] which identifies "the Gentiles" themselves as "the offering" to God resulting from Paul's ministry. The latter is accepted here; see the commentary.

εὐπρόσδεκτος—The adjective εὐπρόσδεκτος "per[tains] to being capable of eliciting favorable acceptance, *acceptable*" (BDAG, 1). The adverb εὖ, "well," is prefixed to a form derived from προσδέχομαι. This verb is used, for example, when Jesus "receives" sinners for table fellowship (Lk 15:2) and in Paul's request that the Roman Christians "receive" Phoebe (Rom 16:2; similarly, Phil 2:29). In LXX Hos 8:13; Amos 5:22; Mal 1:10, the negated verb signifies that God does "not accept" the sacrifices of apostate Israel, but the promises in Ezek 20:40–41; 43:27 are that God will accept his restored people and their offerings. In Romans the adjective εὐπρόσδεκτος appears only here and in 15:31, but compare the synonym εὐάρεστος, "well-pleasing," in the context of sacrificial Christian worship in 12:1–2.

ἡγιασμένη—The perfect tense of the passive participle of ἁγιάζω, "*consecrate*" (BDAG, 2), emphasizes both a past event and its present implications: "having been consecrated and remaining holy." The passive again functions as a divine or theological passive, which Paul makes explicit by adding the prepositional phrase "by the Holy Spirit" (15:16). The verb ἁγιάζω occurs only here in Romans, but note the cognate adjective ἅγιος, "holy," in 1:7 (see the commentary there) and 15:26.

15:17 [τὴν] καύχησιν—See the first textual note on 3:27, the only other use in Romans of this noun, καύχησις, "a boast." The translation accepts the textually disputed definite article τήν, which functions as a demonstrative pronoun referring back to 15:16 as "*this* boast."

τὰ πρὸς τὸν θεόν—BDAG defines τὰ πρὸς τὸν θεόν as "*that which concerns God* or as [an] adverbial acc[usative] *with reference to what concerns God*" (s.v. πρός, 3 e β). It is an adverbial accusative here, but in order to bring out the introductory neuter plural article τά, the phrase is translated as "with reference to the things pertaining to God."

15:18 οὐ γὰρ τολμήσω τι λαλεῖν—For γάρ as "indeed," see BDF, § 452.2; see also BDAG, 1 b. The verb τολμάω, "to be bold or courageous; to dare," occurs only here and in 5:7 (see the fourth textual note there). It is the root of τολμηρότερον; see the first textual note on 15:15. The verb takes a complementary infinitive,[19] λαλεῖν, whose direct object is τι, hence "indeed, I will not dare to speak anything."

ὧν οὐ κατειργάσατο—The genitive plural form ὧν, "of things which," of the relative pronoun ὅς, functions as the direct object of the negated (οὐ) aorist verb κατειργάσατο, "did not accomplish." The expected form of the direct object would be accusative plural, ἅ, "things which." However, an unexpressed genitive plural form (τούτων) of the demonstrative pronoun οὗτος is implied as the antecedent of the relative pronoun, and so the relative pronoun takes on the genitive case of the implied but omitted τούτων. Thus ὧν = τούτων, ἅ (see BDAG, s.v. ὅς, 1 d α). The full expression

---

[18] See Wallace, *Greek Grammar*, 116–19 and 94–100, respectively; Hultgren, *Romans*, 539, identifies it as "an objective genitive; more precisely a genitive of apposition."

[19] See Wallace, *Greek Grammar*, 598–99.

1505

would be translated as "of these things which"; here "of things which" represents the contraction.

The verb κατεργάζομαι, "accomplish," occurs eleven times in Romans. See the textual note on 2:9–10 and the second textual note on 7:15.

εἰς ὑπακοὴν ἐθνῶν—Rather than active obedience or doing (i.e., a "work"), at times ὑπακοή conveys a "responsive hearing" of the Gospel, here by the Gentiles; see the third textual note and the commentary on εἰς ὑπακοὴν πίστεως in 1:5 (similarly, 6:16b; 16:19, 26). See also the commentary on the cognate verb ὑπακούω in 6:17 and, especially, 10:16.

15:19 σημείων καὶ τεράτων—"Signs and wonders"; see the commentary for an explanation of this common biblical combination.

ὥστε με … πεπληρωκέναι—The conjunction ὥστε in dependent clauses expresses "the actual result *so that*" (BDAG, 2 a). In fact, it introduces the "most frequent structure for result infinitive."[20] In this context, the verb πληρόω means "to bring to completion that which was already begun, *complete, finish*" (BDAG, 3). Its perfect active infinitive asserts that the subject in the accusative, με, "I," has "brought to completion and now finished." Cf. the perfect participle of πληρόω in the fifth textual note on 15:14.

κύκλῳ—This form is the "dat[ive] (of κύκλος) of place, fixed as an adv[erb]" (BDAG, s.v. κύκλῳ). Rather than denoting a literal circle, BDAG explains that it pertains "to completion of a circuit, *around*," adding that "this avoids giving the impression that Paul traveled in a straight line, and agrees better w[ith] the comprehensive nature of his activity" (BDAG, 3). For the implications, see the commentary.

15:20 φιλοτιμούμενον—The compound verb φιλοτιμέομαι consists, literally, of "loving honor," which "can easily assume a negative tone."[21] In a positive sense, however, it means to "*have as one's ambition, consider it an honor, aspire*, w[ith] focus on idea of rendering service" (BDAG). Moo notes that "the papyri indicate a weakening in meaning, especially when followed by an infinitive, to no more than 'strive eagerly.' "[22] Paul uses it in this sense here and in its only other NT appearances (2 Cor 5:9; 1 Thess 4:11). The form here is a present participle which functions adverbially:[23] "while striving eagerly."

οὐχ ὅπου ὠνομάσθη Χριστός—The οὐχ negates ὅπου ὠνομάσθη Χριστός, so this literally means "not" in places "where Christ was named," meaning that Paul avoided evangelizing in areas where Christ was already being named. But the sense is virtually equivalent to "where Christ was not [yet] named." According to 10:13–15, "one proclaiming" the "Good News" must be "sent" for people to "believe" and "call on the *name* of [the] Lord" and so "be saved." Regions where Christ was not "named" would be regions to which a proclaimer had not yet been sent.

---

[20] Wallace, *Greek Grammar*, 593; so here, Schreiner, *Romans*, 768.

[21] Dunn, *Romans*, 865.

[22] Moo, *Romans*, 896, n. 80.

[23] See Wallace, *Greek Grammar*, 621–27; Mounce, *Basics of Biblical Greek*, 245–53.

For the passive of ὀνομάζω BDAG suggests " 'be named' in the sense *be known* ... *not where Christ is already known*" (s.v. ὀνομάζω, 3). But "known" seems too weak; people may know of Christ and his name even if they do not believe. The passive of ὀνομάζω functions "with some such solemn sense as 'be named in worship' or 'be acknowledged and confessed' or 'be proclaimed (as Lord)' "[24] (cf. 10:9). This is the force of the verb here. Likewise in the OT קָרָא can mean to "call" on God "as an act of adoration" or "worship"[25] or to invoke the name of Yahweh in faith and with trust in his salvation.[26] Such actions readily stem from Christ's name being placed upon his people in Baptism (Rom 6:1–11), thus "baptized ... in *the name* [τῷ ὀνόματι] of Jesus Christ" (Acts 2:38; 10:48; similarly, Acts 19:5; cf. Acts 8:12, 16; 22:16).

ἐπ᾽ ἀλλότριον θεμέλιον—The adjective ἀλλότριος "pert[ains] to what belongs to another, *not one's own*" (BDAG, 1). The noun θεμέλιος, "foundation," is used metaphorically here to depict "the basis for someth[ing] taking place or coming into being" (BDAG, 2), therefore "upon another's foundation."

15:21 καθὼς γέγραπται—Paul uses this formula to introduce Scripture quotations fourteen times in Romans; see the fourth textual note on 1:17.

οἷς οὐκ ἀνηγγέλη περὶ αὐτοῦ—This clause, quoted verbatim from LXX Is 52:15, is, literally, "to whom it was not announced concerning him." The verb ἀναγγέλλω appears in Romans only here and means "*disclose, announce, proclaim, teach*" (BDAG, 2). The irregular form ἀνηγγέλη is the second aorist passive of this liquid verb.[27]

ἀκηκόασιν—This is the perfect indicative active of ἀκούω, "hear," thus, "they have heard."

15:22 ἐνεκοπτόμην—This imperfect passive form of ἐγκόπτω, "to hinder," has an iterative significance; and it is best translated (as many Greek verbs that refer to the indefinite past) with an English perfect tense (Burton, 28). It comes from the verb ἐγκόπτω, used also in the NT in Acts 24:4; Gal. 5:7; 1 Thess. 2:18; 1 Pet. 3:7. It means the same thing here as the verb κωλύω, which Paul uses in a similar way in 1:13.[28]

τὰ πολλά—The accusative neuter plural of the adjective πολύς, "many," is used adverbially[29] in a temporal sense: "*these many times*" (BDAG, s.v. πολύς, 3 a β, noting that πολλάκις conveys the same sense in 1:13).

---

24 Cranfield, *Romans*, 764, including n. 7, citing in support LXX Is 26:13; Jer 20:9; Amos 6:10; 1 Cor 5:11; 2 Tim 2:19; similarly, Dunn, *Romans*, 865, adding LXX Josh 23:7; Eph 1:21; Moo, *Romans*, 896, n. 82.

25 *DCH*, s.v. קָרָא I, Qal, 2 a.

26 Most relevant for Rom 15:20 is the use of קָרָא with בְּ and שֵׁם, "call on the name" of Yahweh in this sense. BDB, s.v. קָרָא I, Qal, 2 c, and *DCH*, s.v. קרא I, Qal, 2 c, cite a number of verses, including, e.g., Gen 4:26; 12:8; 13:4; 21:33; 1 Ki 18:24; Pss 79:6; 105:1; 116:4, 13, 17; Is 12:4.

27 See Mounce, *Basics of Biblical Greek*, 216.

28 Moo, *Romans*, 899, n. 5, citing Ernest DeWitt Burton, *Syntax of the Moods and Tenses in New Testament Greek* (3d ed.; Edinburgh: T&T Clark, 1898), § 28.

29 For the adverbial accusative, see Wallace, *Greek Grammar*, 200–201, citing πολλά in Mt 9:14, which likewise has a temporal sense.

τοῦ ἐλθεῖν—This articular infinitive of ἔρχομαι, "to come," represents "an epex-egetical (explanatory) infinitive, spelling out what [Paul] was prevented from doing" up until this time.[30]

Commentary

In this section (15:14–22), Paul's overall purpose is to delineate his past missionary conduct leading up to the present. This serves to provide a more detailed explanation of why Paul has not yet been to Rome, something alluded to already in 1:13. The most striking theological feature in 15:14–22 emanates from the numerous cultic terms Paul uses to describe his ministry (see 15:16). He begins, however, by characterizing the previous content of this letter and its intended impact upon his original audience. Now that they have reached this point, Paul hopes to bring the Roman Christians along as partners in his future work (15:23–33). As discussed in the commentary introduction,[31] "the central treatise section [1:18–15:13] was intended in part at least to forward and facil-itate these plans."[32]

Reflections on (the) Romans: The People and the Letter Thus Far (15:14–15)

Assessing the Believers in Rome (15:14)

"Now I have been persuaded and remain convinced, my brothers, even I myself, concerning you that you yourselves also are full of goodness, having been filled with all knowledge and remaining so, while also being able to admon-ish one another" (15:14). The emphatic manner in which Paul speaks of himself is striking. He combines the first person singular perfect form (πέπεισμαι) of the verb "to persuade," a form he utilized identically in 8:38 and 14:14, together with the redundant self-identifier, "I myself" of 7:25 (αὐτὸς ἐγώ, surely also a reference to Paul himself there). Paul addresses his hearers as "my broth-ers" (ἀδελφοί μου; see 1:13) and speaks of them admonishing "one another" (ἀλλήλους). Thus he again includes all the believers in Rome.

His assessment of them as being "full of goodness" (μεστοί ... ἀγαθωσύνης) and "having been filled with all knowledge and remaining so" (πεπληρωμένοι πάσης [τῆς] γνώσεως, 15:14) contains language *strikingly similar to antitheti-cal descriptions* of depraved humanity in 1:29: "having become filled up with every [πεπληρωμένους πάσῃ] unrighteousness, wickedness, greediness, [and] evil; full of [μεστούς] envy, murder, strife, deceit, [and] meanness; [they are] gossipers." Since the opposite now stands true for these Christians, Murray offers the following contextual application regarding both attributes:

> It may not be extraneous to suggest that the reference to these two qualities in particular may have been dictated by their relevance to the subject dealt

---

[30] Kuske, *Romans 9–16*, 333; see also Wallace, *Greek Grammar*, 607.

[31] See Middendorf, *Romans 1–8*, 14–22, especially 18–22.

[32] Dunn, *Romans*, 856.

with in the preceding section (14:1–15:13). Goodness is the quality which will constrain the strong [15:1] to refrain from what will injure the weak [14:1–2; 15:1] and knowledge is the attainment that will correct weakness of faith [14:1].[33]

Paul then adds that the believers in Rome are sufficiently "able to admonish one another" (15:14). Dunn notes: "νουθετέω (constructed from νοῦν τίθημι = 'put on the mind, instruct') denotes basically the well-intentioned attempt to influence mind and disposition by apposite instruction, exhortation, warning, and correction."[34] This ability "to admonish" (15:14), rooted solidly in scriptural instruction (15:4), conveys another sign of spiritual maturity in action within a Christian community.

This extremely positive depiction of the believers in Rome may properly be viewed as reflecting a diplomatic style.[35] But it seems unwarranted to conclude that the language shows Paul "undisguisedly wooing the readers"[36] or suggests that he "walks on eggshells in his desire not to offend the Christians in Rome by assuming an authority over them that they would not recognize."[37] Instead, Ambrosiaster grasps the intended sense of the Greek by recognizing that "these are words of encouragement."[38] Similarly, Pelagius notes: "As a good teacher Paul rouses the people to further progress by praising them."[39] Therefore, "what we have here is Christian courtesy, not flattery, though there is no doubt an element of hyperbole."[40] The same may be said of 1:8, where Paul asserted that their "faith is being announced in the whole world." The fact that, since then, he has written such a long letter to Rome surely reinforces the sense of conscious exaggeration in regard to their knowledge in 15:14; after all, his audience was not omniscient! In a more profound sense, as God sees them in Christ, who is the supreme font of "goodness" and "all knowledge," the descriptions in 15:14 already apply *coram Deo*.[41]

Paul's positive description and emphatic address to them (καὶ αὐτοί, "you yourselves also") in 15:14 do combine to convey his "acknowledgment of the Roman Christians' adulthood as Christians: they themselves—quite independently of him—are already believers."[42] Thus their "knowledge" pertains

---

[33] Murray, *Romans*, 2:209.

[34] Dunn, *Romans*, 858, citing the use of the verb νουθετέω, "admonish," for God's chastening in LXX Job 40:3; Wisdom 11:10; 12:2, 26. Paul uses the verb also in 1 Cor 4:14; Col 1:28; 3:16; 1 Thess 5:12, 14; 2 Thess 3:15.

[35] Dunn, *Romans*, 857.

[36] As does Käsemann, *Romans*, 391.

[37] As Moo, *Romans*, 887, contends.

[38] Ambrosiaster, *Romans* (Bray, *Romans*, ACCS NT 6:359).

[39] Pelagius, *Romans* (Bray, *Romans*, ACCS NT 6:360).

[40] Cranfield, *Romans*, 752.

[41] See Middendorf, *Romans 1–8*, 473–74.

[42] Cranfield, *Romans*, 753.

primarily to having "a firm grasp of the truth of the gospel,"[43] but also includes their maturity in being able to handle tough truths together (e.g., chapters 9–11; 14:1–15:7) and to admonish one another as appropriate.

The Letter Thus Far (15:15)

"But I wrote to you rather boldly in part as repeatedly reminding you on account of the grace which was given to me by God" (15:15). The initial part of this verse refers to the letter up to this point but need not convey any reflective "tentativeness,"[44] e.g., "maybe I was too bold." Instead, the statement exudes the confidence of 1:16, "I am not ashamed of the Good News." Therefore Paul writes powerfully about the Gospel and its implications. The phrase "in part" likely refers to those sections aimed most directly at his Roman audience, but the portions Paul perceives to be particularly bold remain a matter of speculation. They would appear to be chapters 9–11 and, most recently, 14:1–15:13 (see the introductions to Romans 9–16 and 14:1–15:13). Then, as now, the necessity to continually remind believers about the essentials of the faith remains an important part of Christian instruction.

The notion of "repeatedly reminding" (ἐπαναμιμνῄσκων) in 15:15 likely points backward to explain a purpose for that which Paul has written thus far. But this participle also pivots forward as Paul proceeds to direct attention toward himself. One particular element of this "reminding" entails "the grace which was given to me" (15:15).[45] He applies the same phrase to himself earlier in 12:3 (although in a different case; see the commentary there). In this context,

> Paul does not mean that general divine grace that underlies and empowers all of Christian existence. As in 1 Cor. 3:10; Gal. 2:9; Eph. 3:2, 7, 8, Paul refers to that special gift of God's grace which established him as an apostle; cf. 1:5.[46]

This aligns with one of the primary purposes of the letter. "The 'reminder' is Paul's calling card to ensure that the support he hopes for from Rome ([15:]24) will know fully who and what they are supporting."[47] This also leads into and helps explain the upcoming personal references in chapter 16.

An Apostle of Gentiles (15:16–17)

The Greek construction with which Paul begins to elaborate upon his apostolic calling can express purpose or result, though a merging of the two again seems most likely (see the first textual note on 15:16). Primarily, however, he articulates one result of the grace God gave him: "so that I am a minister of Christ Jesus toward the Gentiles, performing priestly service [for] the Good

---

[43] Cranfield, *Romans*, 753; Dunn, *Romans*, 858, comparably speaks of their knowledge as "insight into and understanding of God's saving purpose."

[44] As suggested by Dunn, *Romans*, 858.

[45] See Käsemann, *Romans*, 392; Cranfield, *Romans*, 754; Moo, *Romans*, 889, n. 27.

[46] Moo, *Romans*, 889.

[47] Dunn, *Romans*, 859.

News of God in order that the offering of the Gentiles might be acceptable, having been consecrated and remaining holy by the Holy Spirit" (15:16).

Paul's Priestly Ministry (15:16)

The title "minister" (λειτουργός) is discussed more fully in the commentary on 13:6, its only other appearance in Romans. While it made a "left-hand kingdom" appearance there, referring to a government official, here it reflects the biblical use in the "right-hand kingdom" of God for a minister called to perform divine service, that God may bestow his saving grace upon his people through this ministry.[48] Terms later in the verse ("priestly service," an "offering" that is "acceptable," "consecrated and remaining holy") prove the liturgical connotations of the language. Paul here is a "minister" especially, though by no means exclusively,[49] "toward the Gentiles" (εἰς τὰ ἔθνη, 15:16). Moo expresses this well: "As God indicated in his initial call of him (Acts 9:15; cf. Rom. 1:5; Gal. 1:16), Paul was given a special responsibility for the Gentiles: a call the Jerusalem apostles duly recognized (Gal. 2:1–10)."[50]

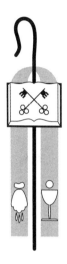

The participle ἱερουργοῦντα comes from a verb (ἱερουργέω) which does not occur elsewhere in Biblical Greek, but since it is a combination of the words for "holy" (ἱερός) and "work" (ἔργον), it readily conveys the sense of doing priestly activity (the cognate noun ἱερεύς means "priest"). While Cranfield advances the more general notion of rendering any kind of "holy service,"[51] that seems less likely in view of the other priestly terms in the verse. Furthermore, "in Philo and Josephus it consistently denotes the priestly offering of sacrifice."[52] Here, however, the specific content which priestly Paul administers to the Gentiles is "the Good News of God" (τὸ εὐαγγέλιον τοῦ θεοῦ, 15:16; cf. 1:16).

---

[48] Besides Rom 13:6; 15:16, λειτουργός, "minister," appears elsewhere in the NT only in Phil 2:25 (Epaphroditus); Heb 1:7 (angels); and Heb 8:2 (Christ himself). In the LXX λειτουργός, "minister," can be used for a priest (LXX Neh 10:40 [MT 10:40; ET 10:39]), a liturgical "servant" in the house of God (LXX Ezra 7:24), or a "servant" of a prophet (Elisha's in LXX 2 Ki 4:43; 6:15). LXX Is 61:6 promises that all of God's people will be called "priests" and "ministers of God" (λειτουργοὶ θεοῦ). The term seems to refer to angels as ministers or servants in LXX Pss 102:21 (MT/ET 103:21); 103:4 (MT/ET 104:4), with the latter verse quoted in Heb 1:7. Cranfield, *Romans*, 755, including n. 2, cites the use of λειτουργέω, "to minister," or λειτουργία, "ministry," in reference to priests in LXX Ex 28:35, 43; 29:30; 30:20; 35:19; 39:12 (MT/ET 39:1); Deut 17:12; Ezek 40:46.

[49] Note that on his missionary journeys Paul regularly begins at the synagogue whenever possible (Acts 13:5, 14; 14:1; 17:1–2; 18:4; 19:8); see Acts 13:46 and " 'To Jew First and Also to Greek' (1:16)" in the commentary on 1:16–17.

[50] Moo, *Romans*, 889; see the commentary on "to Jew first" in 1:16.

[51] Cranfield, *Romans*, 756.

[52] Dunn, *Romans*, 860, citing as examples Philo, *Allegorical Interpretation*, 3.130; *On Planting*, 164; *On Drunkenness*, 138; *On the Confusion of Tongues*, 124; *On the Migration of Abraham*, 67; Josephus, *Antiquities*, 5.263; 6.102; 7.333; 9.43; 14.65; 17.166.

The Gentile Offering (15:16b)

The purpose of the apostle's ministry is "in order that the offering of the Gentiles might be acceptable, having been consecrated and remaining holy by the Holy Spirit" (εὐπρόσδεκτος, 15:16b). The noun προσφορά can denote the act of bringing an offering (BDAG, 1; e.g., Heb 10:10), but it may depict the "offering" itself, as here (BDAG, 2). The manner in which the genitive "of the Gentiles" (τῶν ἐθνῶν) is understood determines how one interprets the verse. It could be subjective, meaning that "the Gentiles" are giving "the offering" soon to be referenced in 15:25–26. Paul's goal, then, is that this monetary "offering" or "service" (ἡ διακονία, 15:31) for the believers in Jerusalem might be "acceptable" (εὐπρόσδεκτος) to the holy ones there (15:31). The repeated use of "acceptable" (15:16, 31) points in that direction.

But the earlier reference to Paul's ministry "toward the Gentiles" (15:16) weighs more strongly in a divergent direction. He envisions "an offering of the nations themselves (an objective genitive; more precisely a genitive of apposition)—'the offering that consists of the nations,' "[53] which would be "acceptable" to God. It also seems more likely that the concluding clause in the verse, "having been consecrated and remaining holy by the Holy Spirit," *describes people rather than a monetary offering.*

(a) E.g., Ex 19:14; 28:36; 31:13; Lev 11:44; 20:8; 21:8; 22:32; Deut 26:19; 33:3; Ezek 37:28; Ezra 8:28; cf. Zech 14:20–21

The OT often describes the people of Israel as "holy" or "sanctified,"[a] that is, having been set apart and consecrated as the people who belong to the thrice-holy holy God (Is 6:3). In the OT theology of the sanctuary and priesthood, as well as in many NT verses,[54] such holiness and sanctification refers, first of all, to salvation itself, to justification with the forgiveness of sins through vicarious atonement, and then also to the holy manner of life of the redeemed.[55]

Now Paul depicts the Gentiles as having been similarly sanctified and remaining holy by the instrumental power of the Holy Spirit. Paul uses the passive form of the verb "to hallow" (ἁγιάζω) similarly elsewhere.[56] The sense, therefore, does not convey an offering dedicated by the Gentiles *to* God.[57] Rather, it is "God himself, by his Holy Spirit, who 'sanctifies' Gentiles, turning them from unclean and sinful creatures to 'holy' offerings fit for the service and praise of a holy God."[58] As Paul tells the Corinthians: "But you were hal-

---

[53] Hultgren, *Romans*, 539.

[54] See 1 Cor 6:11, quoted below. See also the "sanctify" terminology in, e.g., Jn 17:17; Acts 26:18; 1 Cor 1:2, 30; Eph 5:26; Heb 2:11; 10:10, 14; 13:12; 1 Pet 1:2.

[55] See Kleinig, *Leviticus*, 1–13; see also Middendorf, "The New Obedience," 213–15, which discusses both aspects before concluding (215): "On the one hand, the Bible's use of 'holiness' language predominantly expresses the gospel [quoting 1 Cor 1:30; 6:11; referencing Ex 31:13; Lev 20:8; 21:8]. ... At other times, however, believers are in fact called to live holy or sanctified lives" (referencing as examples Lev 19:2; 20:7; 1 Thess 4:7; 1 Pet 1:17; 2 Pet 3:11; cf. Mt 5:48).

[56] Moo, *Romans*, 891, n. 40, citing 1 Cor 1:2; 6:11; 7:14 (twice); 1 Tim 4:5; 2 Tim 2:21.

[57] As Dunn, *Romans*, 861, suggests.

[58] Moo, *Romans*, 891; similarly, Cranfield, *Romans*, 757.

lowed [ἡγιάσθητε], you were declared righteous in the name of the Lord Jesus Christ and by the Spirit of God" (1 Cor 6:11). Augustine understands Rom 15:16 this way: "The Gentiles are offered to God as an acceptable sacrifice when they believe in Christ and are sanctified through the Gospel."[59] The Apology of the Augsburg Confession offers a similar summary:

> The offerings of the sons of Levi (that is, of those who teach in the New Testament) are the proclamation of the Gospel and its good fruits. Thus Paul speaks in Rom. 15:16 of "the priestly service of the gospel of God, so that the offering of the Gentiles may be acceptable, sanctified by the Holy Spirit," that is, so that the Gentiles may become offerings acceptable to God through faith. (Ap XXIV 34)

Cultic Transformations in Romans 15:16

The striking theological feature of 15:16 is that it contains OT priestly terminology ("minister," "priestly service," an "offering" that is "acceptable," "consecrated and remaining holy") which Paul utilizes in a new way. Matera reminds us:

> This is not the first time that Paul has used cultic language. In Rom. 3:25 he employed the ritual background of the Day of Atonement to explain the significance of Christ's death. In 12:1 ... he urged the Roman Christians to offer themselves to God as "a living sacrifice, holy and pleasing to God— your spiritual worship." ... He employs cultic language here and elsewhere to highlight the new creation that God has brought about through the death and resurrection of Christ.[60]

This transformation is discussed in the commentary on the verses he cites and in the excursus "Beyond Typology" following the commentary on 12:1–8. Dunn briefly encapsulates Paul's method and applies the result as follows:

> The cultic language is transformed (not merely spiritualized) by an eschatological fulfillment ... ; that is to say, the division between cultic and secular (together with that between sacred and profane, clean and unclean—14:14, 20) has been broken down and abolished (see also on 12:1) as part of the breaking down of the (in large part cultically determined) distinction between Jew and Gentile.[61]

Paul's Boast (15:17)

Paul concludes: "Therefore I have this boast in Christ Jesus with reference to the things pertaining to God" (15:17). The concluding phrase, literally, "the things toward God," could pertain to all Paul is before God and everything he does in God's name. Here, however, it refers specifically to what Paul describes in 15:16, his ministry to the Gentiles in his priestly role of serving them the Good News of God. The noun for "boast" (καύχησις) appears in Romans only

---

[59] Augustine, *Commentary on Statements in Romans*, 83 (Bray, *Romans*, ACCS NT 6:361).

[60] Matera, *Romans*, 333.

[61] Dunn, *Romans*, 859–60.

here and in 3:27, where such an attitude was excluded.[62] *However, the critical matter does not involve whether one boasts or not, but on what basis.* In regard to the Law of works, boasting is properly shut out (3:27).[63] However, the cognate verb καυχάομαι, "to boast," refers to proper Christian activity in 5:2, 3, 11 (see the commentary on those verses). Here also, on account of the grace given by God (15:15), Paul grounds his boast exclusively "in Christ Jesus" (15:17; cf. 1 Cor 1:31). He proceeds to explain and qualify this even further in Rom 15:18–19a, where "he does all he can to show that the whole thing was God's doing, not his own."[64]

The Power behind the Scenes (15:18–19a)

"Indeed, I will not dare to speak anything of things which Christ Jesus did not accomplish through me toward the responsive hearing of Gentiles, by word and work, by [the] power of signs and wonders, in [the] power of the Spirit of God" (15:18–19a). As noted above, this statement clarifies the previous verse. While Paul "can be proud, he can boast only in Christ, for he is the chosen instrument of Christ (Acts 9:15),"[65] who works through Paul's apostolic ministry.

Responsive Hearing (15:18a)

What is the primary thing Christ sought to accomplish through Paul? "The use of the thematic ὑπακοή ['responsive hearing'] is no accident: it was part of Paul's most basic conviction regarding his mission."[66] In 1:5 he speaks comparably of how he "received grace and an apostleship toward the responsive hearing of faith [εἰς ὑπακοὴν πίστεως] among all the nations in behalf of [Jesus'] name" (see the commentary there). The noun ὑπακοή "will therefore have the same meaning here as in this earlier verse, denoting comprehensively the believers' response to the Lord Jesus Christ, including, but not limited to, faith."[67] Rom 1:5 and 16:26 do, however, single out *faith as the critical response to hearing the Good News of God which Paul proclaimed* (see the third textual note on 1:5 and the commentary on both verses). Rom 10:16 demonstrates this conclusively when Paul utilizes the cognate verb ὑπακούω, "listen responsively," synonymously with πιστεύω, "believe" (see the commentary there). Thus *the proclamation of Christ seeks a responsive hearing.* When this happens, "the Word of Christ" accomplishes its goal, creating receptive faith in the hearer (10:17; see also 10:8–13). Käsemann, therefore, properly contends that

---

[62] Cranfield, *Romans*, 757, dilutes the connection by translating καύχησις as "glorying" here.

[63] Middendorf, *Romans 1–8*, 294–96.

[64] Chrysostom, *Homilies on Romans*, 29 (Bray, *Romans*, ACCS NT 6:362).

[65] Franzmann, *Romans*, 266.

[66] Dunn, *Romans*, 862.

[67] Moo, *Romans*, 892.

"the responsive hearing of Gentiles" (εἰς ὑπακοὴν ἐθνῶν, 15:18) "is identical with acceptance of the gospel."[68]

Five Means to an End (15:18b–19a)

Paul now lists five ways in which Christ accomplished all this through Paul. The first pair of nouns, "by word and work" (15:18), applies to Paul' s ministry in a "wide-ranging and unspecific"[69] manner. One only needs to revisit the book of Acts to grasp numerous examples of each. The latter noun, "work," does not permit any notion of works righteousness, but simply denotes " 'action' as opposed to 'speech.' "[70]

The next two terms, "signs and wonders" (15:19), attest to the miracles which accompanied and, thereby, confirmed the authenticity of Paul's ministry. Elsewhere in the NT, the combination σημεῖα καὶ τέρατα occasionally refers to *deceptive* "signs and wonders" (e.g., Mk 13:22; 2 Thess 2:9),[71] as can the Hebrew equivalents, אוֹת, "sign, miracle," and מוֹפֵת, "wonder, portent," when done by a false prophet (Deut 13:1–2 [MT Deut 13:2–3]; they refer to curses against Israel in Deut 28:46). Furthermore, secular Greek writers viewed "belief in 'signs and wonders' as indicative of naive superstition."[72] Dunn, however, properly concludes that the phrase "is undoubtedly intended to recall its regular OT equivalent," since in most of the OT passages with the word pair אוֹת and מוֹפֵת, the "signs and wonders" are "a traditional way of referring to the miracles of the Exodus."[73] The combination also characterizes the prophetic ministry of Isaiah (Is 8:18; 20:3). Here, then, "Paul's 'signs and wonders' refer to the miracles that attested to the truth of the gospel proclaimed."[74]

> In all of this Paul is declaring that there is a similarity between what transpired at the exodus—and implicitly in the ministries of Jesus and other apostles— and in his own ministry as an apostle. The history of God's saving activity is being carried out as Gentile peoples are being incorporated into the people of the God of Israel, the God of the whole world.[75]

---

[68] Käsemann, *Romans*, 393–94; Dunn, *Romans*, 862, reports that "Lietzmann translates the phrase as 'for the conversion of the Gentiles.' " See Hans Lietzmann, *Einführung in die Textgeschichte der Paulusbriefe: An die Römer* (4th ed.; Handbuch zum Neuen Testament 8; Tübingen: Mohr, 1933), 120.

[69] Dunn, *Romans*, 862.

[70] Cranfield, *Romans*, 759.

[71] Cranfield, *Romans*, 759, n. 4.

[72] Dunn, *Romans*, 863.

[73] Dunn, *Romans*, 862. The two Hebrew terms, אוֹת and מוֹפֵת, appear together in the plural in reference to the exodus deliverance in, e.g., Ex 7:3; Deut 4:34; 6:22; 7:19; 26:8; 34:11; Neh 9:10; Pss 78:43; 105:27; 135:9; Jer 32:20–21. For more details, see G. H. Twelftree, "Signs, Wonders, Miracles," *DPL*, 875–77; Twelftree, *Paul and the Miraculous*.

[74] Schreiner, *Romans*, 768, citing 2 Cor 12:12; also Acts 2:43; 4:30; 5:12; 6:8; 14:3; 15:12; Heb 2:4.

[75] Hultgren, *Romans*, 544.

The final singular phrase, "in [the] power of the Spirit of God" (ἐν δυνάμει πνεύματος [θεοῦ], 15:19), likely encompasses "all the means of ministry that Paul identifies in vv. 18b–19a."[76] As stated similarly at the end of 15:13, all of this happens and is possible only in, with, and by the Gospel power of the Holy Spirit (cf. δύναμις, "power," in 1:16).

The Extent and Emphasis of Paul's Ministry Method (15:19b–22)

Geography (15:19b)

After identifying the means by which he effectively brought the Good News to the Gentiles, Paul now expresses its geographic reach. However, the specific locations he cites, both for its inauguration and current extent, raise intriguing questions. The construction expresses result (see the second textual note on 15:19): "with the result that I have brought to completion and now finished [proclaiming] the Good News of the Christ from Jerusalem and around as far as Illyricum."

In terms of Paul's ministry, the more plausible beginning point might seem to be Antioch in Syria (Acts 11:25–26; 13:1–2). Therefore Bruce contends that Paul "regards Jerusalem as the starting-point and metropolis *of the Christian movement as a whole* (*cf.* Lk. 24:47; Acts 1:4, 8), substance being thus given to the vision of Isaiah 2:3b and Micah 4:2b."[77] Yet the very personal testimony given by Paul throughout 15:16–22 renders that view inadequate. A reference to Paul's early meeting with the apostles in Jerusalem recounted in Gal 2:1–10 seems plausible,[78] but Moo more satisfactorily argues that

> Acts gives plenty of evidence of such ministry [in Jerusalem] ([Acts] 9:26–30; cf. [Acts] 26:20), although Paul's own comments (e.g., Gal. 1:18–19, 22) suggest that it was quite brief. But, however brief, Paul can legitimately claim Jerusalem as the geographical beginning point of his ministry.[79]

Schreiner then references how "the mission to the nations fans out from Jerusalem, the center of the world" (Ezek 5:5; 38:12),[80] and from its salvation history.

Paul says that the Good News of Christ moved out from there "around" (κύκλῳ Rom 15:19). As Dunn correctly maintains, this term need not convey the etymological meaning of a literal circle, as if Paul "presupposed that others were engaged in the bottom sweep (through Egypt, Alexandria, and North

---

[76] Moo, *Romans*, 893.

[77] Bruce, *Romans*, 247 (emphasis added); so also Cranfield, *Romans*, 761.

[78] Dunn, *Romans*, 863; see Das, *Galatians*, 156–95.

[79] Moo, *Romans*, 894; Dunn, *Romans*, 863, contends that "Acts 9:28–29 clashes with Gal 1:17, 18–19, and 2:2." For a thorough discussion of the chronology of Galatians in relation to Acts, see Das, *Galatians*, 31–47, who effectively connects Acts 11–12 with the visit described in Gal 2:1–10.

[80] Schreiner, *Romans*, 769.

Africa)."[81] In fact, a "literal reference to a 'circle' is absent from the word's NT occurrences; it usually means simply 'around,' 'about'" or "'in a circuitous route.'"[82]

Paul then adds that his work currently extends "as far as Illyricum" (15:19). Moo provides this helpful geographical illumination:

> The Illyrians inhabited a region north and west of Macedonia; and the Romans carved out a province in the area, occupied today by northern Albania, much of [the former] Yugoslavia, and Bosnia-Herzegovina. Paul is probably referring to this province.[83]

The immediate question is whether Paul himself actually ventured there. While Cranfield and Dunn find no evidence for such a trip,[84] Moo contends that it quite possibly happened "during his apparently circuitous trip from Ephesus to Corinth on his third journey (Acts 20:1–2)," adding that the famed and heavily traveled Egnatian Way passes through Illyricum.[85] Another possibility is that the Gospel has reached Illyricum as a result of Paul's pattern of evangelization.

> He saw his work very much as the one who laid the foundation ([15:]20); and his strategy seems also to have included the encouraging of fellow workers to go out from the urban centers where he had established the work to the region around (Col 1:6–8; cf. Acts 19:10; 2 Cor 1:1).[86]

This method of "planting strategic churches"[87] in urban centers (e.g., Corinth, Ephesus) then helps explain how Paul can assert that he has already brought to completion and finished evangelizing in those regions (Rom 15:19b). Clearly, not every person or area has heard the Gospel, but this does not mean that Paul simply "thinks in nations."[88] Instead, as 15:20 explains, *the foundation has been laid and a pattern for building upon it has been established*. The existence of the church in Colossae serves as a good illustration. It stems from Paul's work in Ephesus but is not directly the result of his own labors.[89] Yet Paul will not hesitate to send a letter to the Colossians, as he now does to Rome. This scenario fits the focus of his apostolic ministry as described in 1 Corinthians 3 and in the very next verse here (Rom 15:20). It *could* also illuminate how Paul's efforts have impacted Illyricum without Paul himself ever having ventured there. This explanation seems more palatable than characterizing Paul's work

---

[81] Dunn, *Romans*, 864.

[82] Moo, *Romans*, 895, citing (in n. 70) Mk 3:34; 6:6; Rev 4:6; 5:11; 7:11 (see also Mk 6:36; Lk 9:12); similarly, Sanday and Headlam, *Romans*, 407; Cranfield, *Romans*, 761.

[83] Moo, *Romans*, 894; Cranfield, *Romans*, 761, adds that part of Macedonia was also inhabited by the Illyrian race.

[84] Cranfield, *Romans*, 761; Dunn, *Romans*, 864.

[85] Moo, *Romans*, 894–95, n. 64.

[86] Dunn, *Romans*, 864; see also Sanday and Headlam, *Romans*, 409.

[87] Moo, *Romans*, 896.

[88] As Munck, *Paul and the Salvation of Mankind*, 52, contends.

[89] On the background and setting, see Deterding, *Colossians*, 2–3, 12–14.

as a rapid Blitzkrieg-like advance stemming from his conception of "the short period before the *parousia*."[90]

Paul's Modus Operandi (Is 52:15 in Rom 15:20–21)

Paul continues: "and thus while striving eagerly to bring the Good News not where Christ was [already] named in order that I might not build upon another's foundation" (15:20). The initial "thus" (οὕτως) "looks both backward and forward"[91] (as in 11:26). This verse describes the manner in which Paul has "brought to completion and now finished" proclaiming the Gospel in these regions (15:19b). He has gone like a "trail-blazing" pioneer[92] to places where no one has yet acknowledged or confessed the name of Jesus Christ (ὅπου ὠνομάσθη Χριστός; see the second textual note on 15:20) in order to establish "strategic churches in virgin gospel territory."[93] Rather than to avoid "possible rivalry"[94] or out of "antagonism to attempts of others to evangelize where he had already preached,"[95] *Paul simply exhibits the evangelistic fervor of his apostolic calling* (see, e.g., Acts 9:15–16; 26:16–18; Rom 1:1, 16; 1 Cor 9:16–18; 2 Cor 10:15–16). Therefore, Chrysostom reminds us of "how Paul goes to where the labor is more and the toil greater"[96] in order that what he describes in Rom 10:14–15 might become a repeated reality.

To be sure, Paul vociferously defends his apostleship when challenged (e.g., 2 Corinthians 10–12), but he does so primarily for the sake of *the credibility of the message* he proclaims. Furthermore, he was *not* always opposed to working where others had laid a foundation (e.g., a year in Syrian Antioch [Acts 11:25–26], plus an impending visit to Rome), but that was not his particular boast (see 2 Cor 10:16). He was also less concerned with who got the credit so long as Christ was being proclaimed (Rom 15:18; cf. Phil 1:15–18).

At the end of Rom 15:20, Paul briefly employs the imagery of a building (cf. 14:19). 1 Cor 3:9–15 develops the thought further. Paul's role was to lay the foundation upon which others would build when Paul moved on. But he generally sought to lay a deep and stable foundation, as his eighteen months in Corinth and two years in Ephesus demonstrate (Acts 18:11; 19:10). Another metaphor from earlier in 1 Corinthians 3 describes how he planted what others would come along later to water (1 Cor 3:6–8). In both metaphors the field and

---

[90] Contrary to the contention of Barrett, *Romans*, 274; similarly, Munck, *Paul and the Salvation of Mankind*, 49; Käsemann, *Romans*, 395; Dunn, *Romans*, 864. Moo, *Romans*, 893, properly doubts "whether Paul views his role as so narrowly eschatological"; Cranfield, *Romans*, 762, is similarly and appropriately cautious. See the commentary on 11:14, as well as the discussion regarding the imminence of the parousia in the commentary on 13:11–12a.

[91] Moo, *Romans*, 896.

[92] Cranfield, *Romans*, 762.

[93] Moo, *Romans*, 896; for more in-depth studies, see W. P. Bowers, "Mission," *DPL*, 608–19; Burke and Rosner, *Paul as Missionary*; Luckritz Marquis, *Transient Apostle*.

[94] Barrett, *Romans*, 277, affirms that "Paul's motive is not simply to avoid possible rivalry but to cover as wide an area as possible."

[95] As Dunn, *Romans*, 865, maintains.

[96] Chrysostom, *Homilies on Romans*, 29 (Bray, *Romans*, ACCS NT 6:363).

the building belong to God; he alone grants the growth, and Jesus Christ is the sole foundation (1 Cor 3:7, 11).[97]

Paul adds scriptural attestation from Is 52:15 in order to explain his modus operandi: "But just as it stands written: '[Those] to whom it was not announced about him, they will see, and the ones who have not heard, they will understand'" (Rom 15:21). Paul's citation replicates the LXX exactly.

As Paul goes where Christ is not yet named, he fulfills the Isaiah text regarding those who had not yet heard the Gospel message. "That Gentiles are intended by Isaiah is clear, for the same verse says that 'he will sprinkle many nations.'"[98] The quotation comes from the Fourth Suffering Servant Song (Is 52:13–53:12).[99] The "him" concerning whom Paul speaks is the one who has fulfilled that text as the suffering and now glorified Servant of Yahweh[100] (see the commentary on Rom 10:16, which quotes Is 53:1). *After more than fifty quotations from the OT in Romans, this final citation appropriately highlights the one concerning whom Isaiah prophesied, our Lord Jesus Christ* (see the excursus "Paul's Use of the Old Testament in Romans" following the commentary on 15:7–13).

It may, therefore, seem unusual that Paul wants to come to Rome, where a solid foundation has already been laid in order to be with those who have already heard. In so doing, Paul does not in any way imply that the church in Rome remains inadequate or that it lacks an apostolic foundation.[101] Rom 15:14 makes his very favorable assessment of the current status of the Roman Christians abundantly clear. To be sure, Paul will be encouraged by visiting them (1:12). But he explains his primary impetus for doing so in the next section. With their assistance, he hopes to go boldly on to Spain where no evangelist has yet ventured. This leads him and us ahead into 15:23–33.

Past Hindrances (15:22)

All of 15:14–21, however, builds up to and explains the conclusion of 15:22: "therefore also I have repeatedly been hindered many times from coming to you." Paul now clarifies the cause of the hindrance, left ambiguous in 1:13 (see

---

[97] In regard to the varying referents of "foundation," Wright, "Romans," 755, comments: "His [Paul's] use of this metaphor is not uniform"; for its specific meaning in 1 Corinthians, see Lockwood, *1 Corinthians*, 116–17; see also 110–14 regarding the field metaphor.

[98] Schreiner, *Romans*, 770. The Hebrew verb translated as "sprinkle" is, like Paul's terminology in Rom 15:16, associated with priestly sacrifice at the worship sanctuary. It usually refers to the sprinkling of blood from an atoning sacrifice, as on the Day of Atonement (Lev 16:14, 15, 19); see further Mitchell, *Our Suffering Savior*, 101–2, citing also, e.g., Ex 29:21; Lev 4:6, 17; 5:9; 6:27 (MT 6:20); 8:11, 30; 14:7, 16, 27, 51.

[99] For a complete explication, see Lessing, *Isaiah 40–55*, 578–623; Mitchell, *Our Suffering Savior*.

[100] The contention of Dunn, *Romans*, 866, that "Paul *did* evidently see his commission in terms of the commission given to the Servant" may apply elsewhere (e.g., in Acts 13:47 he appropriates "a light for the Gentiles" from the Second Suffering Servant Song, Is 49:6 [cf. Is 42:6], for his own ministry), but it surely does not apply here.

[101] Contrary to the argument of Klein, "Paul's Purpose in Writing the Epistle to the Romans"; for a rebuttal, see Middendorf, *Romans 1–8*, 18; Moo, *Romans*, 897.

the commentary there). It encompasses all the activities described in 15:19–21. "Paul was not hindered by Satan, as some think, but by the fact the he was too busy planting churches in places where nobody had ever preached the gospel before."[102] *Previous mission work in the east* has prevented him from fulfilling his longtime yearning to visit Rome (1:13).[103] However, the emphatic "but now" (νυνὶ δέ) which opens 15:23 heralds an opening for Paul's long anticipated visit to Rome.

Conclusion: Evangelistic Opportunities

This section may seem to dwell on the status of Paul (15:15–17, 19b–20) and the Romans (15:14). However, Paul's key focus resides elsewhere. It is firmly founded upon "the Good News of the Christ" (15:19, cf. 15:18). The noun εὐαγγέλιον, "Good News, Gospel," appears nine times in the letter. Three of these reside emphatically in the first sixteen verses (1:1, 9, 16). Then, after 2:16, it does not occur again until 10:16 and then also in 11:28. But Paul employs it twice here (15:16, 19) and one final time in the third-to-last verse of the letter (16:25). In Romans, Paul elaborates this Good News as "of the Christ" only here in 15:19, but he does so commonly in his other writings.[104] The Good News which stands as the "power of God into salvation for everyone who believes" (1:16) is now *this specific Good News*, the "Word of Christ" which creates and sustains saving faith in the one concerning whom Isaiah prophesied (10:16–17; 15:21, quoting Is 53:1 and 52:15, respectively).

The cognate verb εὐαγγελίζω, "bring the Good News," also shows up in 15:20 as one of only three times in the letter (also 1:15; 10:15). Its evangelistic connotations are readily apparent in all three passages. Here, as dominantly also elsewhere,[105] Paul envisions this action not as taking place among an established gathering of believers, but *in places where Christ has not yet been named* (15:20). Paul devotes himself to go to any and all such locales in order to proclaim "the Good News of Christ" (15:19). After all, this carries out *God's modus operandi* for how people come to believe:

> [14]How, then, might they call [on him] on whom they did not believe? And how might they believe [on him] of whom they did not hear? And how might they hear without one proclaiming? [15]And how might they proclaim if they are not sent? Just as it stands written: "How timely [are] the feet of the ones bringing the Good News [of] the good things." (10:14–15)

---

[102] Origen, *Romans* (Bray, *Romans*, ACCS NT 6:363).

[103] Cranfield, *Romans*, 766; Dunn, *Romans*, 871.

[104] Cranfield, *Romans*, 762, citing 1 Cor 9:12; 2 Cor 2:12; 9:13; 10:14; Gal 1:7; Phil 1:27; 1 Thess 3:2 (cf. 2 Thess 1:8).

[105] See the excursus "The New Testament Connotations and Context of Words Commonly Translated as 'Preach,' 'Teach,' and 'Prophesy'" following the commentary on 10:6–15.

Paul's Future Travel Plans and His Plea for Prayers

Translation

15 ²³But now, while no longer having a place in these regions and having a desire to come to you for many years ²⁴when I journey to Spain—for I hope to see you while passing through and to be sent on there by you, if, first, I might be filled [by being] with you for a time.

²⁵But now I am journeying to Jerusalem while serving the holy ones. ²⁶For Macedonia and Achaia thought it good to do some [sign of] fellowship for the poor of the holy ones in Jerusalem. ²⁷Indeed, they thought it good, and they are their debtors. For if the Gentiles shared in their spiritual [blessings], they are also obligated to offer priestly service to them in the material things. ²⁸Therefore, after completing this and sealing this fruit to them, I will depart through you into Spain. ²⁹And I know that when coming to you, I will come in [the] fullness of Christ's blessing.

³⁰And I urge you, brothers, through our Lord Jesus Christ and through the Spirit's love, to struggle together with me in prayers to God in my behalf ³¹that I might be rescued from those who are unpersuaded in Judea and [that] my service which is for Jerusalem might become acceptable to the holy ones ³²so that, after coming to you in joy through the will of God, I might rest together with you.

³³The God of peace [is] with all of you. Amen.

Textual Notes

15:23 ἐν τοῖς κλίμασι τούτοις—The noun κλίμα (from which we derive "climate") refers to a "*district*" (BDAG). The plural phrase is translated as "*in these regions*" (BDAG). For further clarification, see the commentary on 15:19.

ἐπιποθίαν δὲ ἔχων—The noun ἐπιποθία, a "*longing, desire*" (BDAG), appears only here (and in a variant reading in 2 Cor 7:11) in Biblical Greek. Together with the present adverbial participle[1] ἔχων, the clause means "and having a desire."

15:24 ὡς ἂν πορεύωμαι εἰς τὴν Σπανίαν—The combination ὡς ἂν is used with a "subjunctive of the time of an event in the future *when, as soon as*" (BDAG, s.v. ὡς, 8 c). The verse division disrupts the flow since this clause completes the thought of 15:23: Paul has for some time planned to use Rome as an interim stop "when I journey to Spain."

---

[1] See Wallace, *Greek Grammar*, 621–27; Mounce, *Basics of Biblical Greek*, 245–53.

ἐλπίζω ... θεάσασθαι—"I hope to see." Attached to the main verb ἐλπίζω, "hope," is the aorist infinitive of θεάομαι, "to see," which functions as a complementary infinitive.[2]

ὑφ᾽ ὑμῶν προπεμφθῆναι—The compound verb προπέμπω (πρό + πέμπω) literally means "to send before." However, "in earliest Christianity it becomes almost a technical term for the provision made by a church for missionary support."[3] For what this might entail, see the commentary. The preposition ὑπό with the genitive, here abbreviated and softened to ὑφ᾽ before the pronoun ὑμῶν with a rough breathing mark, expresses agency:[4] "to be sent on by you."

ὑμῶν ... ἐμπλησθῶ—The verb ἐμπί(μ)πλημι means to "*fill*" or "*satisfy*" and usually takes a genitive of content[5] denoting the substance with which a person or thing is filled (BDAG, 1 and 2). The natural meaning, then, is "I might be filled with you." The sense here is metaphorical: the apostle would be filled or satisfied during the time he spent with the Romans, so the clause is translated as "I might be filled [by being] with you." BDAG, 3, cites only this biblical passage as support for extending the notion of the verb to " 'have one's fill of someth[ing],' in the sense *enjoy someth[ing]*" (BDAG, 3). Likewise, Dunn translates the clause as "once I have had the full pleasure of being with you."[6] However, it is better to understand the verb in its usual sense and take its form as a divine passive:[7] "filled" by God. This spiritual gift will come by the work of the Holy Spirit as Paul and the Roman Christians are "mutually encouraged ... through the faith of one another" (1:12; see also 1:11).[8]

ἀπὸ μέρους—For this prepositional phrase, see the sixth textual note on 11:25 and the second textual note on 15:15. The literal meaning, "from a part," appears to have a temporal nuance here, "*for a while*" (BDAG, s.v. μέρος, 1 c). Moo adds that the expression "hints at a fairly short stay."[9]

15:25 διακονῶν τοῖς ἁγίοις—The present participle διακονῶν functions adverbially and expresses an action concurrent with the main verb:[10] "I am journeying ... while serving." Additional interpretive nuances of the participle include purpose, "in order to serve," and/or cause, "because [I am] serving."[11] This represents the only appearance

---

[2] See Wallace, *Greek Grammar*, 598–99.

[3] Dunn, *Romans*, 872, citing Acts 15:3; 20:38; 21:5; 1 Cor 16:6, 11; 2 Cor 1:16; Titus 3:13; 3 Jn 6; similarly, Moo, *Romans*, 901, including n. 26.

[4] See Wallace, *Greek Grammar*, 389.

[5] Since this genitive is used with a verb, ἐμπί(μ)πλημι, it can be specified as a "verbal genitive of content" (Wallace, *Greek Grammar*, 94).

[6] Dunn, *Romans*, 872–73.

[7] See Wallace, *Greek Grammar*, 437–38.

[8] See Middendorf, *Romans 1–8*, 78–79, who concludes that 1:10–12 encapsulates "*what the Holy Spirit always intends to accomplish when those who share the faith are together.*"

[9] Moo, *Romans*, 901.

[10] See Wallace, *Greek Grammar*, 622, 625–26.

[11] See Wallace, *Greek Grammar*, 635–37 and 631–32, respectively. According to Wallace (624) these nuances are to be determined by asking reflective "questions such as, 'Is the author *only* describing when this happened or is he also indicating *why* or *how* it happened?' " Of course,

of the verb διακονέω in Romans. The appearance of the cognate noun διακονία, "service," in 15:31 makes clear that the specific "serving" in this verse refers to a monetary offering (see the commentary). Note the more general use of the noun twice in 12:7. For "holy ones," see the commentary on 1:7.

15:26 εὐδόκησαν ... ποιήσασθαι—The verb εὐδοκέω means "to consider someth[ing] as good and therefore worthy of choice, *consent, determine, resolve*," often followed by an infinitive (BDAG, 1), as here with ποιήσασθαι, "to do." The translation retains the more literal "they thought it good to do," and εὐδόκησαν is rendered the same way at the start of 15:27.

κοινωνίαν τινά—This is the only occurrence of the noun κοινωνία in Romans. Dunn notes that it appears only three times in the LXX and that of the nineteen NT uses, thirteen are by Paul, with four others in 1 John 1.[12] BDAG initially defines κοινωνία as a "close association involving mutual interests and sharing, *association, communion, fellowship, close relationship*" (BDAG, 1). But then, BDAG, 3, observes the use of the abstract for the concrete "*sign of fellowship, proof of brotherly unity,* even *gift, contribution*." The final option, "contribution," is the specific referent of the "[sign of] fellowship" here. Cf. the cognate verb κοινωνέω in the third textual note on 15:27.

15:27 ὀφείλεται—For the noun ὀφειλέτης, "debtor; one who is obligated," see the commentary on 1:14[13] and the third textual note on 8:12. The cognate verb ὀφείλω in the last clause of this verse has the corresponding meaning "to be obligated."

τοῖς πνευματικοῖς ... καὶ ἐν τοῖς σαρκικοῖς—Paul typically portrays the antithetical categories of "Spirit/Spiritual" versus "flesh/fleshly" as theological opposites (e.g., 2:28–29; 7:5–6, 14; 8:4–13). Here and in 1 Cor 9:11, "spiritual" and "fleshly" serve exceptionally to form "a contrast between spiritual blessings and material needs."[14]

ἐκοινώνησαν—In the context here the verb κοινωνέω, "to share in," refers to communion with Jewish Christians in spiritual things (τοῖς πνευματικοῖς). Its only other occurrence in Romans is in 12:13, where it refers to "sharing" by contributing to the material needs of fellow saints.

λειτουργῆσαι—The verb λειτουργέω means "to render special formal service, *serve, render service,* of cultic or ritual responsibilities" (BDAG, 1). This aorist infinitive is translated as "to offer priestly service." As with the cognate noun λειτουργός, "minister," in 15:16 (see the first textual note and the commentary there), the OT cultic connotations have not been eclipsed, but, rather, transformed in Christ.

15:28 τοῦτο οὖν ἐπιτελέσας—The compound verb ἐπιτελέω (ἐπί + τελέω) means "to finish someth[ing] begun, *end, bring to an end, finish*" (BDAG, 1). The adverbial aorist participle ἐπιτελέσας expresses action occurring prior to the future event of the

---

discerning authorial intent in such instances remains speculative; see Middendorf, *Romans 1–8*, 38–40, 51–54.

[12] Dunn, *Romans*, 875.

[13] Middendorf, *Romans 1–8*, 81–82.

[14] Dunn, *Romans*, 876.

main verb,[15] ἀπελεύσομαι (see the third textual note on 15:28): "therefore, after completing this ... *I will depart.*"

σφραγισάμενος αὐτοῖς τὸν καρπὸν τοῦτον—This clause is translated as "after sealing this fruit to them." The aorist participle σφραγισάμενος functions adverbially, as does ἐπιτελέσας in the previous textual note. The verb σφραγίζω, "to seal," literally meant to impress the name of the owner onto something by means of a cylinder seal or signet ring, comparable to the modern practice of signing or affixing one's signature as legal attestation of ownership or authority over something. BDAG fills out the thought contextually as *"when I have placed the sum that was collected safely (sealed) in their hands"* (s.v. σφραγίζω, 5). Elsewhere Paul employs the verb to refer to the baptismal gift of the Holy Spirit, by which God marks us as belonging to him (2 Cor 1:22; Eph 1:13; 4:30).

ἀπελεύσομαι δι' ὑμῶν—The initial word is a future form of the verb ἀπέρχομαι, *"go away, depart"* (BDAG, 1 a). For the prepositional phrase, BDAG then supplies "through your city" (s.v. διά, A 1 a). But in light of 15:25, the specific force of "through you" more likely conveys "through your support."

15:29 ἐρχόμενος—This present participle of ἔρχομαι functions adverbially and expresses an action which takes place at the same time as the main verb (see the first textual note on 15:25). Here the controlling verb, ἐλεύσομαι, is the irregular future indicative form of the same verb, thus "when coming to you, ... I will come."

ἐν πληρώματι εὐλογίας Χριστοῦ—BDAG gives *"with the full blessing"* (s.v. ἐν, 5 a β), but that renders the noun πλήρωμα as an adjective. The noun πλήρωμα, *"fullness"* (BDAG, s.v. πλήρωμα, 3 b), is better conveyed by "in [the] fullness of [the] blessing of Christ." Note the significance of πλήρωμα in its three other occurrences in Romans: 11:12 (see the fifth textual note and the commentary there); 11:25 (see the commentary there); and 13:10 (see the textual note and the commentary there).

15:30 παρακαλῶ—For this verb, "urge," see the first textual note and the commentary on 12:1.

συναγωνίσασθαί μοι—The compound verb συναγωνίζομαι (σύν + ἀγωνίζομαι) occurs only here in the NT. BDAG places a "focus on a supportive role *help, assist*," but the stronger sense of "struggle" better reflects the basic idea of the root ἀγών, "athletic contest, struggle, fight."[16] See Paul's use of the simple verb ἀγωνίζομαι in 1 Cor 9:25; Col 1:29; 4:12; 1 Tim 4:10; 6:12; 2 Tim 4:7.

15:31 ἵνα ῥυσθῶ ἀπὸ τῶν ἀπειθούντων—For the ἵνα purpose/epexegetical clause, see the commentary. For ῥύομαι, "rescue," see the second textual note on 7:24, though the emphasis here is on immediate rescue more than eschatological deliverance. The form ῥυσθῶ is an aorist subjunctive passive, which functions as a divine/theological passive,[17] "rescued" by God. ἀπειθούντων is a present participle, functioning

---

[15] See Wallace, *Greek Grammar*, 624.

[16] Dunn, *Romans*, 878.

[17] See Wallace, *Greek Grammar*, 437–38.

substantively,[18] denoting unbelievers, who are intrinsically hostile toward the truth (2:8) and toward God (10:21; 11:30). For the translation "unpersuaded," rather than "disobedient," see the first textual note on 2:8 and, especially, the commentary on 10:21 and 11:30–32.

ἡ διακονία μου ἡ εἰς Ἰερουσαλήμ—The cognate verb διακονέω in 15:25 described Paul as "serving the holy ones" in Jerusalem. Now the cognate noun διακονία similarly refers to the collection Paul is gathering as "my service which is for Jerusalem." The second definite article, ἡ, functions as a relative pronoun.[19]

εὐπρόσδεκτος—For this adjective, "acceptable," see the fifth textual note on 15:16.

15:32 ἵνα ... συναναπαύσωμαι ὑμῖν—This ἵνα clause with a subjunctive verb conveys result, "so that ... I might rest together with you," though the notion of purpose is not completely absent.[20] Dunn characterizes the doubly compound verb συναναπαύομαι (σύν + ἀνά + παύω) as "a highly unusual formulation: elsewhere in biblical Greek only in Isa 11:6; in secular Greek only in the sense 'sleep with someone.'"[21] The idea in this verse is "to relax in someone's company, *rest with*" (BDAG). Compare its sense in the eschatological promise of LXX Is 11:6: "a leopard shall lie down with a young goat."

15:33 ὁ δὲ θεὸς τῆς εἰρήνης μετὰ πάντων ὑμῶν—For the insertion of the indicative verb "is," "God ... [is] with," rather than "be," see the first textual note on 11:36.

ἀμήν—For "amen," see the third textual note on 9:5.

Commentary

"But Now" (15:23, 25) through Rome to Spain (15:23–29)

The "but now" (νυνὶ δέ) at the beginning of 15:23 and another which opens 15:25 punctuate the initial half of this section. They turn our attention from Paul's past work and present situation, as recounted in 15:14–22, to his *future travel plans*. Rom 15:23–24 repeats Paul's intention to visit Rome, enunciated already in 1:8–15, but also introduces, for the first time, his intent "to be sent on by" the Roman Christians to Spain. The second "but now" (νυνὶ δέ, 15:25) introduces yet another topic, an interim journey to Jerusalem.

Onward to Spain (15:23–24a)

"But now, while no longer having a place in these regions and having a desire to come to you for many years when I journey to Spain" (15:23–24a). The previous section (15:14–22) details how Paul has, up to this point, completed the groundbreaking "pioneer work of evangelism which is his special

---

[18] See Wallace, *Greek Grammar*, 619–21.

[19] See Wallace, *Greek Grammar*, 213–15.

[20] Wallace, *Greek Grammar*, 472–74, first discusses purpose and result separately and then the merging of the two concepts. See the third textual note on 15:4; for other examples, see the commentary on 4:16; 5:20; 14:9.

[21] Dunn, *Romans*, 880.

task"[22] from Jerusalem as far as Illyricum (15:19). While much ongoing work continues in the eastern Mediterranean,[23] the first nineteen chapters of Acts record how churches have been planted in numerous strategic locations "in these regions" (Rom 15:23; e.g., Jerusalem, Syrian Antioch, on Crete, Pisidian Antioch, Iconium, Lystra, Derbe, Thessalonica, Philippi, Berea, Athens, Corinth, Ephesus).

Paul now returns to a thought put forth at the beginning of the letter, his fervent desire to visit the Christians in Rome personally (1:8–15). He has longed to do so for "many years" (15:23). He now implies that he will arrive relatively soon and then, for the *first* time in the letter, he mentions that Rome provides only an interim stop on his journey farther westward "to Spain" (εἰς τὴν Σπανίαν, 15:24). The noun "Spain" appears only twice in the NT, in 15:24 and 15:28. The Iberian peninsula "had been occupied by Rome since about 200 B.C.; but it was only in Paul's lifetime that the Romans had fully organized the entire area."[24] Whether Paul views the area as having some special prophetic significance remains unclear,[25] as does the question of whether a Jewish population lived there.[26] Most likely, Rome and then Spain simply stand next in line on Paul's relentless march westward.

Writing in the late first century AD, Clement strongly suggests that Paul eventually made it to Spain by recapping his ministry in this way:[27]

> After that he had been seven times in bonds, had been driven into exile, had been stoned, had preached in the East and in the West, he won the noble renown which was the reward of his faith, having taught righteousness unto the whole world and having reached the farthest bounds of the West. (*1 Clement* 5:6–7)[28]

Later, Cyril of Jerusalem corroborates that "Paul instructed imperial Rome and extended the zeal of his preaching even to Spain, sustaining countless conflicts

---

[22] Cranfield, *Romans*, 766.

[23] It is not, then, as Munck, *Paul and the Salvation of Mankind*, 53, asserts, that Paul "came to think, among 'all the peoples' to whom salvation was to be preached, not of individuals, but of the nations as a whole," who will stand before God collectively.

[24] Moo, *Romans*, 900.

[25] Schreiner, *Romans*, 769, suggests that the theory "that the table of nations (Gen. 10) formed the map of Paul's day merits serious consideration," as does the proposal that Spain encompassed "the last of the sons of Japheth"; for these ideas Schreiner references the work of James M. Scott, *Paul and the Nations* (Tübingen: Mohr [Siebeck], 1995), 136–47. Moo, *Romans*, 900, n. 19, brings up the theory that Spain "represented for Paul the OT 'Tarshish,' the 'end of the earth' (cf. Isa. 66) to which Paul must travel to complete his task of bringing Gentiles as an offering to Jerusalem and thus usher in the parousia" (citing Roger D. Aus, "Paul's Travel Plans to Spain and the 'Full Number of the Gentiles' of Rom. XI 25," *Novum Testamentum* 21 [1979]: 242–46).

[26] See Moo, *Romans*, 900, nn. 17–18.

[27] See Bruce, *Paul: Apostle of the Heart Set Free*, 447–48.

[28] Quoted from Philip Stafford Moxom, *From Jerusalem to Nicaea: The Church in the First Three Centuries* (Boston: Roberts, 1895), 105.

and performing signs and wonders."[29] If so, the timing of his arrival in Spain hardly took place within the time frame he envisioned when composing Romans. It was postponed significantly by two two-year delays under legal custody in Caesarea and then in Rome itself (Acts 24:27; 28:30). Even Paul's arrival in Rome does not happen in the manner he anticipates (see the commentary on Rom 15:31). Throughout history Christ continues to use his proclaimers mightily, but seldom according to their own anticipated itineraries.

Through and Sponsored by Rome (15:24b)

Rom 15:24b clarifies: "For I hope to see you while passing through and to be sent on there by you, if, first, I might be filled [by being] with you for a time." Now Paul describes his intended visit to Rome with the participle "while passing though" (διαπορευόμενος, 15:24), which sounds relatively brief. This would most readily be explained by the fact that Christ is already being confessed in Rome, and prominently so (see 1:8). Staying there for an extended period of time would stand contrary to Paul's intent just expressed in 15:20–21 as a fulfillment of Is 52:15. There he depicts his evangelistic missionary role as taking the Good News where Christ has not yet been named. Thus Paul already looks *beyond* Rome.

But he does not move past the believers in Rome without a plea for their assistance. He aims "to be sent on" (προπεμφθῆναι, 15:24) to Spain by them. This technical term conveys more than seems possible in any English translation (see the third textual note on 15:24). It implies that they would furnish him with items such as "food, money, [and] letters of introduction" and perhaps assist him by "arranging transport."[30] It might also entail an escort of "companions who would know the country"[31] and could assist in the work (cf. Barnabas, Silas, and Timothy).[32] It might appear somewhat odd to modern ears that Paul brings up his request so late in the letter. By way of contrast, he is not at all timid about financial matters when he writes to the Corinthians about their full participation in the offering for Jerusalem (2 Corinthians 8–9; cf. 1 Cor 16:1–4).

Three factors may help explain this. First, the fact that Paul has not yet been to Rome exerts considerable influence. "Only after he has 'built a relationship' with the community through his letter does he think it appropriate to bring up the matter."[33] Second, Paul's efforts to reconcile the "weak" and the "strong" in 14:1–15:13 also immediately precede his request.[34] This signals his desire for *united support from all the groups of believers in Rome*, rather than only

---

[29] Cyril of Jerusalem, *Catechesis*, 17.26 (Bray, *Romans*, ACCS NT 6:364).

[30] Dunn, *Romans*, 872.

[31] Käsemann, *Romans*, 398.

[32] Moo, *Romans*, 901, n. 26.

[33] Moo, *Romans*, 901–2.

[34] See "Who Are the 'Weak' and the 'Strong'? Addressees Again!" in the introduction to 14:1–15:13.

from certain factions (see 16:1–16). Finally, this tactic emphasizes the importance of laying solid theological groundwork prior to beginning a partnership in mission.[35]

The conclusion of 15:24 is awkward grammatically and communicates an incomplete thought even with the bracketed insertion, but the sense of "if, first, I might be filled [by being] with you for a time" seems clear enough. For whatever time Paul spends with the Roman Christians, he is confident God will use it to fill him with good things (ἐμπλησθῶ, "I might be filled," as a divine passive; see the fourth textual note on 15:24). Here again, these words from the first chapter help fill in the blanks:

> [11]For I yearn to see you so that I might give a spiritual gift over to you with the result that you be strengthened, [12]and this is to be mutually encouraged among you through the faith of one another, yours and also mine. [13]Indeed, I do not want you to be without knowledge, brothers, that many times I placed it before myself to come to you, but was hindered until the present, so that I might have some fruit even among you, just as also among the rest [of the] Gentiles. (1:11–13)

"But Now" to Jerusalem (15:25–29)

Serving the Saints (15:25)

A second "but now" (νυνὶ δέ) opens 15:25 and, also for the first time, introduces Jerusalem: "But now I am journeying to Jerusalem while serving the holy ones" (15:25). This verse assists us in locating the time and provenance of the letter. The introduction to this commentary summarizes:

> On his third missionary journey, Paul left Ephesus after a riot that concluded his extended stay of more than two years (Acts 19:10, 23–41; 20:1). He then traveled through Macedonia and Achaia, revisiting many of the cities of his second journey (Acts 19:21; 20:1–3). Paul was engaged in collecting an offering from the Gentile Christians to be delivered by him, along with delegations from those congregations, to the believers in Jerusalem (Acts 20:4–5; 1 Cor 16:1–4; 2 Corinthians 8–9). …

> Acts records Paul's intent that, after delivering the offering to Jerusalem, he would fulfill his momentous goal of visiting Rome (δεῖ με καὶ Ῥώμην ἰδεῖν, Acts 19:21).[36]

In fact, Paul repeatedly uses the noun "service" (διακονία), which is cognate to the verb "serve" (διακονέω) in Rom 15:25, for this specific collection (διακονία, Rom 15:31; 2 Cor 8:4; 9:1, 12–13; see also διακονέω in 2 Cor 8:19–20).[37]

Reasons for the Offering (15:26–27)

As his correspondence with the Corinthians demonstrates, *Paul himself provides the main impetus for this offering* (1 Cor 16:1–4; 2 Corinthians 8–9).

---

[35] Middendorf, *Romans 1–8*, 17.

[36] Middendorf, *Romans 1–8*, 5.

[37] See Dunn, *Romans*, 873–74; the noun also refers to an earlier offering in Acts 11:29; 12:25.

2 Corinthians 8–9 in particular reveal the fervor and seriousness with which Paul engages in the task, and "each letter he wrote on the [third] journey mentions it."[38] Thus the trip to deliver it can hardly be described as a "detour to Jerusalem."[39] Why does Paul deem it so important? His main motivation reflects an ongoing adherence to the agreement reached in Gal 2:9–10:

> James, Cephas, and John, the ones recognized to be "pillars," gave to me and Barnabas the right hand of fellowship, that we [should evangelize with respect] to the gentiles and they to the circumcised. Only [they asked] that we [continue to] remember the poor, which is the very thing I also had been eager to do.[40]

Acts 11:27–30 tells of an earlier offering delivered to Jerusalem "by the hand of Barnabas and Saul" (Acts 11:30); he now engages in a second.

Another purported explanation draws upon "the widely held Jewish expectation that the wealth of the nations would flow into Jerusalem in the end time."[41] Thus Barrett suggests that the offering "was intended to play a vital part among the events of the last days."[42] Moo, however, properly doubts "whether Paul views his role as so narrowly eschatological."[43]

A more prevalent secondary concern stands evident throughout Romans. It resides in *the equal footing of Jews and Gentiles in Christ*. The offering serves as tangible evidence that they are indeed fully united as one in Christ (e.g., Eph 3:6; see the discussion of μυστήριον, the "mystery," in the commentary on Rom 11:25). As Paul explains in 15:26–27:

> [26]For Macedonia and Achaia thought it good to do some [sign of] fellowship for the poor of the holy ones in Jerusalem. [27]Indeed, they thought it good, and they are their debtors. For if the Gentiles shared in their spiritual [blessings], they are also obligated to offer priestly service to them in the material things.

By speaking of the Roman provinces of Macedonia and Achaia, Paul refers to the believers in cities such as Philippi, Thessalonica, Berea, Athens, and Corinth.

---

[38] Moo, *Romans*, 902.

[39] Käsemann, *Romans*, 396, titles 15:22–29 as "The Motivations for the Journey to Rome and the Detour to Jerusalem."

[40] This is the translation of Das, *Galatians*, 156; for his interpretation, see 188–95.

[41] Dunn, *Romans*, 874, citing Is 45:14; 60:5–17; 61:6; Micah 4:13; Tobit 13:11; 1QM 12:13–15. This expectation is also attested in other OT passages such as Pss 68:29 (MT 68:30); 72:10; Is 18:7; Zeph 3:10; see also 2 Sam 8:2, 6; 1 Ki 4:21 (MT 5:1); 2 Chr 17:11; 26:8; Ezra 6:8. Dunn (864) also attributes Paul's flurry of travel activity to "the pressing imminence of the parousia, leaving all too little time to take the gospel to where it had not so far been heard"; similarly, Munck, *Paul and the Salvation of Mankind*, 303: "They go up to Jerusalem with gifts, as it had been prophesied that the Gentiles would when the last days had come" (citing Is 2:2–3 ‖ Micah 4:1–2; Is 60:5–6); see 303–4. Dunn (874) also considers the notion that the collection is "part of a climactic strategy to stir the Jews to jealousy (11:13–14)," but that seems even more unlikely. See the commentary on 11:14 and 13:11–12a.

[42] Barrett, *Romans*, 278.

[43] Moo, *Romans*, 893; similarly, Cranfield, *Romans*, 770; for a discussion of the imminence of the parousia in Paul's thought, see the commentary on 13:11–12a.

Origen and Pelagius propose that Paul also issues a subtle request for the Romans to participate in the collection as well.[44] That seems *unlikely* as there is no hint of it in the text of Romans. Instead, by repeating the verb "they thought it good" (εὐδόκησαν, 15:26, 27), Paul emphasizes that these *other Christians* who already had extensive interaction with Paul gladly contributed to the offering. The construction in 15:26, as well as Paul's characterizations in 2 Cor 9:5–7, conveys that it was their "free decision."[45]

Paul then articulates the offering idiomatically by describing it as "to do some [sign of] fellowship" (κοινωνίαν τινὰ ποιήσασθαι, Rom 15:26). This is the lone appearance in Romans of the noun κοινωνία, "fellowship, communion," which for Paul denotes particularly significant divine gifts, shared by all baptized and communicant believers.[46] Here *he views the collection as a concrete expression or sign of the fellowship which already exists in Christ* (see the second textual note on 15:26). Wright grasps the ecumenical significance:

> For Gentiles to give money for Jewish Christians was a sign that the Gentiles regarded them as members of the same family; for Jewish Christians to accept it would be a sign that they in turn accepted the Gentiles as part of their family.[47]

Recipients and Delivery of the Offering (15:26b–28a)

The offering is intended "for the poor of the holy ones in Jerusalem" (εἰς τοὺς πτωχοὺς τῶν ἁγίων τῶν ἐν Ἰερουσαλήμ, 15:26). The KJV translates those phrases as "for the poor saints which are at Jerusalem," implying that all the believers in Jerusalem are poor, but that does not make the best sense of the grammar here.[48] Bammel takes "the poor" as an appositional and theological "self-designation or title" of the Jerusalem community itself.[49] However, it seems most plausible that the genitive "of the holy ones" (τῶν ἁγίων) is partitive.[50] While an earlier offering of "service" to the believers in Jerusalem met their needs during a famine (Acts 11:27–30; 12:25), the current collection serves to benefit *the poor who are among the community of believers in Jerusalem.*

---

[44] Origen, *Romans*, and Pelagius, *Romans* (Bray, *Romans*, ACCS NT 6:365).

[45] G. Schrenk, "εὐδοκέω," *TDNT* 2:741, who also observes that when this verb is used with the infinitive or an accusative and the infinitive "there is a clear hint of choice, resolve or decree." So Cranfield, *Romans*, 773; Dunn, *Romans*, 874–75.

[46] The noun κοινωνία pertains to "fellowship" or "communion" through the shared baptismal gift of the Holy Spirit in 2 Cor 13:13 (ET 13:14) and Phil 2:1; through the true body and blood of Christ received in the Lord's Supper in 1 Cor 10:16; through the Gospel in Phil 1:5; through sharing in Christ's sufferings and death in Phil 3:10; and through faith in Philemon 6.

[47] Wright, "Romans," 756.

[48] See Moo, *Romans*, 904.

[49] E. Bammel, "πτωχός," *TDNT* 6:909.

[50] So NASB; ESV; NRSV; Cranfield, *Romans*, 772; Das, *Galatians*, 193; Dunn, *Romans*, 875: "the poor among the saints." For the partitive genitive category, see Wallace, *Greek Grammar*, 84–86.

"Saint" has become the common translation of the substantival adjective ἅγιος, but outside of Lutheran circles that English noun is generally misheard, particularly in light of Roman Catholic use restricted to extraordinary Christians canonized by the church's hierarchy. Here "the saints/holy ones in Jerusalem" (15:26) denotes all those living in that location who match the description Paul just gave of his Gentile converts, "having been consecrated and remaining holy by the Holy Spirit" (ἡγιασμένη ἐν πνεύματι ἁγίῳ, 15:16). Together with all baptized believers they all are "holy ones" in God's sight (see the commentary on 1:7).

In the second half of 15:27, Paul speaks of his Gentile givers and the Jerusalem recipients by using descriptors he typically employs to contrast things of the Spirit versus those of the flesh (see the second textual note on 15:27). But here, as in 1 Cor 9:11, the adjectives serve to distinguish "spiritual" and "material" blessings. "Spiritual" expresses that "the salvation enjoyed by the Gentiles comes only by way of the Jewish Messiah and the fulfillment of promises made to Israel,"[51] for the Christ came from the patriarchs and David "according to the flesh" (Rom 1:3; 9:5). The Gentiles fellowshipped in (ἐκοινώνησαν) and became beneficiaries of "their" (αὐτῶν, 15:27) spiritual blessings as these emanated out from Jerusalem beginning on Pentecost (see Rom 15:19). In *response*, Gentile believers are obliged debtors to the Jerusalem church. Paul views their offering of money to meet "material" needs as a sacred offering of "priestly service" (λειτουργῆσαι, 15:27). He earlier depicted himself as being similarly "obligated" (ὀφειλέτης, 1:14) and, more recently, as a "minister" (λειτουργός, 15:16) in service to the Gospel.

The first half of 15:28 envisions the fulfillment of the immediate task at hand as "completing this and sealing this fruit to them." The noun "fruit" (καρπός) refers to the collection being delivered to Jerusalem. Outside of Romans, Paul always employs the verb "to seal" (σφραγίζω) in reference to the baptismal gift of the Holy Spirit (2 Cor 1:22; Eph 1:13; 4:30). In Romans 4 the cognate noun σφραγίς, "seal," describes the "sign of circumcision" as "a seal of the righteousness of the faith" (4:11), and in Col 2:11–13 Paul declares that the OT rite of circumcision is now fulfilled in Baptism.[52] In Rom 15:28, the term might allude to the baptismal bond of "fellowship" (15:26) which unites all believers with Christ *and* one another (e.g., Rom 6:3–5; 1 Cor 12:13; Gal 3:27–28; Eph 4:4–5).[53] This God-given unity blossoms in a tangible way through the giving and receiving of the offering.

---

[51] Moo, *Romans*, 905, citing 1:16; 4:13–16; 11:17–24; 15:7–8.

[52] In Song 8:6–7 the "seal" is associated with the divine "love" that is the "flame of Yah" (cf. Pentecost) and with "many waters" in a way that is evocative of Baptism, according to Mitchell, *The Song of Songs*, 1210–29.

[53] See the excursus "Baptism in Paul" following the commentary on 6:1–11.

On the other hand, the general word picture may derive from the "commercial sphere" and simply mean completing the task[54] (cf. "sealing the deal"). Moo proceeds to identify a more specific and substantial significance:

> Affixing a seal to something is often an official affirmation of authenticity; perhaps, then, Paul, as the "apostle of the Gentiles," intends to accompany those delivering the collection to Jerusalem in order to affirm its integrity and insure that it is understood rightly.[55]

Pelagius describes the task more relationally and roots the priestly service of the Gentiles in the words of Jesus: "Paul is traveling [to Jerusalem] in order to attend [the saints] in person, and he hopes that his offering will be received by them … thereby showing that it is more blessed to give than to receive."[56]

Again, through Rome to Spain (15:28b–29)

Paul then returns to and completes the thought of 15:24: "I will depart through you into Spain" (15:28b). He yearns to come to Rome (1:11), but, at this point, he intends for his initial visit there to serve as a launching pad for his pioneering evangelistic work in Spain (see 15:20). Thus the notion of "through you" (δι' ὑμῶν, 15:28) is not simply spatial but also conveys agency.[57] *Through their support* Paul hopes to venture on to Spain, a thought which aligns with "to be sent on there by you" in 15:24 (ὑφ' ὑμῶν προπεμφθῆναι ἐκεῖ). This verse then reinforces the interpretation of 15:24 advanced above.

Käsemann characterizes as "a sigh of relief"[58] Paul's added positive thought regarding his visit to Rome in 15:29: "And I know that when coming to you, I will come in [the] fullness of Christ's blessing." In sharp contrast to his "painful visit" to Corinth (2 Cor 2:1), the connotations of "fullness" (πλήρωμα) in Rom 15:29 mean "that Christ's blessing on [Paul's] visit will be pure blessing, without any admixture of something other than blessing, a blessing altogether unambiguous and reliable."[59] Murray takes the direction of blessing as "imparted to the believers at Rome,"[60] but "a mutuality of

---

[54] Dunn, *Romans*, 877.

[55] Moo, *Romans*, 906–7; he cites comparable uses of affixing a seal in Esth 8:8, 10 and Jn 3:33 (906, n. 61), as well as Deissmann's work on papyrus texts that speak of "sealing [sacks] of grain" to certify their contents (907, n. 62, citing Adolf Deissmann, *Bible Studies* [Edinburgh: T&T Clark, 1901], 238–39). However, Jn 3:33 is set in a rich baptismal context. At Jesus' own Baptism (Jn 1:19–34) the Father spoke and the Spirit descended upon him, bearing witness and testifying to his identity, and these themes permeate Jn 3:31–34, which follows Jesus' presentation of the Baptism by which one is born again by water and the Spirit (Jn 3:1–13); see Weinrich, *John 1:1–7:1*, 445–50.

[56] Pelagius, *Romans* (Bray, *Romans*, ACCS NT 6:365), citing Acts 20:35.

[57] See Wallace, *Greek Grammar*, 368; see also the third textual note on 15:28.

[58] Käsemann, *Romans*, 402.

[59] Cranfield, *Romans*, 775; see the second textual note on 15:29 for other significant uses of πλήρωμα, "fullness."

[60] Murray, *Romans*, 2:220.

'blessing' "[61] toward one another more likely conveys Paul's confidence. Here again, the numerous connections between 1:8–15 and 15:14–33 enable the two sections to exegete each other. In 1:11–12 Paul wrote: "For I yearn to see you so that I might give a spiritual gift over to you with the result that you be strengthened, and this is to be *mutually encouraged* among you through the faith of one another, yours and also mine."

A Plea for Fervent Prayer (15:30–31)

The God-Centered Basis of Paul's Appeal (15:30)

"And I urge you, brothers, through our Lord Jesus Christ and through the Spirit's love, to struggle together with me in prayers to God in my behalf " (15:30). Paul's appeal here, "and I urge you, brothers" (παρακαλῶ δὲ ὑμᾶς, [ἀδελφοί]), echoes the opening exhortation of 12:1: "I therefore urge you, brothers" (παρακαλῶ οὖν ὑμᾶς, ἀδελφοί; see the textual notes and the commentary there). While the verb παρακαλῶ exhibits a wide range of meanings from "request" to "command," the force in both passages resides somewhere in between and is translated as "urge."[62]

Paul's appeal in 12:1 was "through the mercies of God." Here it is *twofold.* The first comes "through our Lord Jesus Christ." This phrase, with slight variation, serves thematically throughout Romans 5–8 (5:1, 11, 21; 6:23; 7:25; 8:39; since then only in 15:6).[63] The full explication there resounds with the life God graciously bequeaths to all baptized believers in our Lord Jesus Christ. Thus it is surely wrong to view the phrase here as an assertion of "authority."[64] Instead, it reflects Paul's "strong belief that Christ, including the shared experience of his Lordship ('in Christ'), is a bond between [him and the Roman Christians]."[65]

Second, it comes "through the Spirit's love" (15:30). Again, the emphasis resides less on "the love prompted by the Spirit"[66] (e.g., 12:9) and much more on the love of God which "has been poured out [cf. Baptism] and remains within our hearts through the Holy Spirit, who was given to us" (5:5).[67] As in 12:1, then, Paul's exhortation in 15:30 is based upon and flows "through" *God's merciful and loving actions toward us* through his Son and by his Spirit.

Paul fervently requests that the Roman Christians "struggle together with me in prayers to God in my behalf" (15:30). Earlier, 1:9–10 revealed *Paul's*

---

[61] Moo, *Romans,* 907.

[62] Cranfield, *Romans,* 776, opts for "ask," which is surely too weak. See the first textual note and the commentary on 12:1.

[63] See Middendorf, *Romans 1–8,* 377–80.

[64] As maintained by Cranfield, *Romans,* 776; Moo, *Romans,* 909.

[65] Dunn, *Romans,* 878; Luther elaborates further: "The little word 'Lord' simply means the same as Redeemer, that is, he who has brought us back from the devil to God, from death to life, from sin to righteousness, and now keeps us safe there" (LC II 31).

[66] As Dunn, *Romans,* 878, suggests.

[67] See Middendorf, *Romans 1–8,* 396–97.

ongoing prayers in behalf of those in Rome: "without ceasing, I am making mention of you always upon my prayers." Now he implores *them to engage* in similar agonizing prayers *both* with *and* for him (*agonize* transliterates the basic root ἀγωνίζομαι, "struggle"; see also Christ's "agony," ἀγωνία, in prayer in Lk 22:44). The petitions to come surely reveal the potential peril and significance of Paul's impending trip to Jerusalem, but "it is certainly an exaggeration to think that concern about this enterprise was the motivating factor for his letter to the Romans."[68]

Two Petitions (15:31)

The two clauses governed by ἵνα, "that," in 15:31 express purpose. They describe *why* Paul seeks the prayers of believers in Rome, but they also function epexegetically, explaining or clarifying *what* those prayers should entail.[69] Paul offers these two specific petitions: "that I might be rescued from those who are unpersuaded in Judea and [that] my service which is for Jerusalem might become acceptable to the holy ones" (15:31).

The first request reveals that Paul fears for his safety in Judea. As throughout the letter, ἀπειθέω refers to those who do not believe in Christ and generally should be translated as "be unpersuaded" (or "disbelieving") rather than "be disobedient." The force of the verb does not simply indicate a failure to obey commandments of the Law, but points primarily to the fact that such people are "unpersuaded" by the Good News.[70] Those who "have rejected Christ and the gospel"[71] are "enemies" (11:28) on that account (see the commentary on 10:16, 21; 11:28–32). In other words, " 'the disobedient' refer to unbelievers"[72] who are also often hostile toward the message Paul proclaims.

He has good reason to be wary of them and to request prayers "that I might be rescued" by God from them (ῥυσθῶ, 15:31). Cranfield summarizes:

> For the testimony of Acts to this hostility reference may be made to Acts 9.29; 13.45, 50; 14.19; 17.5–8, 13; 18.12–17; 19.9; 20.3, 23; and (with reference to a time later than the writing of this epistle, when Paul is already on his way to Jerusalem) [Acts] 21.10–14.[73]

Unfortunately, at least from a human perspective, Acts reveals that God does not seem to answer this petition, at least not initially or entirely. Paul is nearly killed in Jerusalem during a riot near the temple (Acts 21:30–31, 35–36; 22:22) and then, soon after, becomes the target of an assassination plot (Acts 23:12–15). Yet, in the midst of all this, *God does, in fact, rescue him* from death in a surprising way, through a Roman officer and his troops (Acts 21:31–34; 22:24; 23:23–24).

---

[68] Moo, *Romans*, 908; argued by Jervell, "The Letter to Jerusalem."
[69] See Wallace, *Greek Grammar*, 472, 476.
[70] See the first textual note on 2:8 and, especially, the commentary on 10:21 and 11:30–32.
[71] Dunn, *Romans*, 878.
[72] Moo, *Romans*, 910.
[73] Cranfield, *Romans*, 778.

Paul's second prayer request implores that "my service which is for Jerusalem might become acceptable to the holy ones" (Rom 15:31). That "my service" (ἡ διακονία μου) refers to the offering seems evident from his use of the cognate verb "serve" to reference it in 15:25: "But now I am journeying to Jerusalem while serving [διακονῶν] the holy ones." Earlier Paul spoke of the Gentiles as an "acceptable" offering to God (εὐπρόσδεκτος, 15:16); now he uses the same adjective in order to plead that their gift to the Jerusalem church might be similarly "acceptable" (15:31).

Was the Offering Received?

Paul surely reckons with the possibility that the offering might *not* be received by the believers in Jerusalem. Cranfield comments:

> Those who still labour in the shadow of the Tübingen school's continuing influence are naturally prone to welcome these words as additional grist for their mill, additional evidence of serious tension between Paul and the Jerusalem church.[74]

On the one hand, any such scholarly perspective which seeks to separate Jewish and Gentile Christianity should surely be evaluated with a healthy dose of skepticism. Paul himself fought fiercely and rather successfully to overcome any such division.[a]

(a) See, e.g., Acts 15; Rom 14:1–15:13; Gal 2:11–14; 3:26–29; Eph 2:11–3:6

At the same time, one should not overlook the difficulties encountered during this transitional time when the ethnic dimension of God's people had been transcended in and through the coming of the Christ (see the excursus "Beyond Typology" following the commentary on 12:1–8). The early church wrestled with the ramifications of this complex and multifaceted situation, which was not without tensions (e.g., Acts 10:1–11:18; 15:1–35; Gal 2:11–14).

Even at this point in Paul's ministry, "the significance of this verse [Rom 15:31] in assessing the relationships between Paul and Jerusalem during his expanding mission through Asia Minor, Macedonia, and Greece should not be discounted."[75] 2 Corinthians 10–13 reveals that Paul continues to experience hostile opposition from rivals who purport to be within the church and even masquerade falsely as "apostles" (2 Cor 11:13; see 2 Cor 10:12; 11:5, 14–15; cf. Rom 16:17–18). Furthermore, while the leaders in Jerusalem receive Paul and his companions gladly when they arrive with the offering (Acts 21:17), they also inform Paul of other sentiments which exist among his fellow Christians:

> There are many thousands of those who believe [τῶν πεπιστευκότων] in Judea, and they are all zealous for the Law. And they were taught concerning you that you teach apostasy [ἀποστασίαν] from Moses [to] all the Jews [living] among the Gentiles, saying that they should not circumcise [their] children nor walk in the customs [of the Law]. (Acts 21:20b–21)

Thus the concern behind Paul's second petition seems to have been well-founded.

---

[74] Cranfield, *Romans*, 778.

[75] Dunn, *Romans*, 879.

Since Acts does not explicitly address the offering itself, we do not know for certain whether it was accepted or not. However, Luke's statement that in Jerusalem "the brothers received us gladly" (ἀσμένως ἀπεδέξαντο ἡμᾶς οἱ ἀδελφοί, Acts 21:17) seems most logically applicable to the offering as well.[76] Kruse also cites Paul's own recounting of the event later in Acts as affirmation "that the offering of the Gentile believers was accepted, and his prayers and those of the Roman believers had been answered."[77] Paul tells Felix: "And after many years, I came to my nation while giving alms and offerings [προσφοράς]" (Acts 24:17). While these statements may not be conclusive, *they strongly imply that the offering was warmly received* and rebut scenarios that postulate a refusal, followed by a resulting divisive conflict.[78]

Conclusion (15:32–33)

An Anticipated Outcome to Prayer (15:32)

Another ἵνα, "that," opens 15:32. Structurally, therefore, it might appear to introduce an added petition to those offered in 15:31. However, it more strongly conveys result: "so that, after coming to you in joy through the will of God, I might rest together with you" (15:32). If the previous two petitions are granted, the outcome will be both joyful relief[79] and mutual refreshment. Chrysostom advises us to "note again Paul's humility. He does not say that he wants to come in order to teach them but in order that he may be refreshed by them!"[80] The sentiments of 15:32 align with the words of 1:11–12 quoted above in the commentary on 15:29.

Sanday and Headlam observe how strongly Paul's words in 15:29 and 15:32, which anticipate an imminent and positive visit to Rome, support "the authenticity and early date of this chapter. No one could possibly write in this manner at a later date, knowing the circumstances under which St. Paul actually did visit Rome."[81]

Their comment prompts two further thoughts. First, it invites practical reflection on how prayer requests, even from the apostle, are not always or even regularly answered in ways we humans think God ought to respond.[82] For example, the violent events in Jerusalem rehearsed above in the commentary on 15:31 are followed by Paul being taken into custody and kept under house arrest in Caesarea for two years while Governor Felix hopes for a bribe

---

[76] Moo, *Romans*, 911.

[77] Kruse, *Romans*, 551.

[78] Contra Dunn, *Romans*, 880, and those of the Tübingen school, referenced in the quote above from Cranfield, *Romans*, 778.

[79] Käsemann, *Romans*, 407, defines ἐν χαρᾷ ("in joy," 15:32) as "with a cheerful, relieved heart."

[80] Chrysostom, *Homilies on Romans*, 30 (Bray, *Romans*, ACCS NT 6:367).

[81] Sanday and Headlam, *Romans*, 414.

[82] See *Theology and Practice of Prayer: A Lutheran View*, a report of the Commission on Theology and Church Relations of The Lutheran Church—Missouri Synod.

(Acts 24:26–27). A treacherous shipwreck journey to Rome, again under Roman guard (Acts 27:1–28:14), finally leads to Paul's arrival in Rome as a prisoner, years later than he anticipated when writing to the Romans.

Second, Sanday and Headlam's observation refutes the notion that chapter 15 did not belong to the original letter Paul sent to Rome. However, it also calls for a brief analysis of the various endings of the letter to the Romans in the textual tradition (see the excursus following this section).

A Peace-Full Affirmation (15:33)

Paul concludes with this blessed reminder: "The God of peace [is] with all of you. Amen" (15:33). The genitive "of peace" (τῆς εἰρήνης) identifies God as the source of this peace (cf. "the God of hope" in 15:13). Rom 5:1 states: "Therefore, after being declared righteous from faith, we have peace with God through our Lord Jesus Christ." As also in 1:7, the Hebrew word *shalom* provides the intended freight of the NT Greek term for "peace" (εἰρήνη). Thus, in the Aaronic Benediction, God's blessing and keeping, the shining of his face and the bestowal of his grace, the lifting up of his countenance and the imposition of his saving name are all encompassed by his giving of *shalom*, "peace" (Num 6:24–27). Rather than a mere cessation of conflict, it conveys *health and wholeness in a reconciled relationship with God* (Rom 5:10–11) and then also "embraces the panoply of blessings God makes available to his people."[83] No wonder, then, that "the God of peace" serves as one of Paul's favorite characterizations of God (also Rom 16:20; 2 Cor 13:11; Phil 4:9; 1 Thess 5:23; see also Heb 13:20; cf. 2 Thess 3:16).

Paul does not merely express a wish that God "be" with those in Rome, as if he were not there otherwise or already. Instead, passages like Mt 1:23; 28:20; and Lk 1:28 illustrate how the Gospel Word of promise assures the Lord's people that he *is* with them, and always (see the first textual note on Rom 11:36; cf. also 9:5; 16:27). To be sure, "judgments over convictions" exist in Rome (14:1), and perilous hostilities lie ahead for Paul (15:31). But God's peace in Christ *remains a present reality* for those in his kingdom (14:17) even, and especially, in the midst of such conflicts. It also calls the believers in Rome to acknowledge how this peace embraces each and every one of them. It *is* "with all of you" (μετὰ πάντων ὑμῶν, 15:33). Therefore, God's ever-present and active peace (Phil 4:7) also influences their relationships with their fellow believers (see Rom 14:19). Ambrosiaster encapsulates both aspects well: "Paul therefore wants [the Roman Christians] to be the kind of people in whom the Lord Jesus Christ dwells, who has shown them that all the discord caused by human sin has been taken away and who has given them what is true, that they may live peacefully in that truth."[84] And so it *is* for us.

---

[83] Moo, *Romans*, 911.

[84] Ambrosiaster, *Romans* (Bray, *Romans*, ACCS NT 6:367).

Excursus

Textual Criticism
and the End of Romans

All Christians should give thanks to God for those who carefully hand-copied and, thereby, preserved the Greek text of Romans, as well as the rest of the NT Scriptures, for future generations over a period of fourteen hundred years prior to the invention of the printing press. While textual variants relating to words and phrases have been discussed throughout this commentary, these are, by and large, isolated instances of relatively minor significance. Kruse, however, observes that the larger "question of the integrity of Romans relates primarily to chapter 16 and its place in the letter."[1]

Challenging Chapter 16

Manson and Moffatt theorize that Romans 16 was originally a series of greetings intended for Ephesus, not Rome.[2] Their Ephesian theory is based on these three factors:

1. Questioning whether Paul could possibly know so many people in Rome by name (he mentions twenty-six in 16:3–16; see the commentary there)

2. The placement of Priscilla and Aquila, whom Paul greets in 16:3–5a, in Ephesus by 1 Cor 16:19

3. The mention of Epaenetus, the first believer in Asia, in Rom 16:5b[3]

Manson then postulates: "Paul prepared a letter (Rom. 1–15) and sent it to Rome. At the same time a copy was prepared to be sent to Ephesus." He supposes that the long list of greetings was originally directed toward and attached *only* to the Ephesian correspondence. Later, however, it inadvertently came to be identified as the final portion of Paul's letter to Rome.[4]

The main textual evidence which lends credence to challenging the originality of chapter 16 (as well as chapter 15; see below) stems from the numerous locations where the doxology of 16:25–27 appears in various manuscripts.[5] Our oldest extant text of (parts of) Romans is Chester Beatty Papyrus II ($\mathfrak{P}^{46}$). Since it "alone has the doxology [16:25–27] between 15:33 and 16:1,"

---

[1] Kruse, *Romans*, 13; for an extensive review, see Guthrie, *New Testament Introduction*, 400–413.

[2] Manson, "St. Paul's Letter to the Romans—And Others"; Moffatt, *An Introduction to the Literature of the New Testament*, 134–39.

[3] Guthrie, *New Testament Introduction*, 400–401.

[4] Manson, "St. Paul's Letter to the Romans—And Others," 13–14.

[5] See Metzger, *A Textual Commentary on the Greek New Testament*, 533–36.

its discovery "raised anew the question about the character of 16:1–23 and especially the question whether Romans ever existed only in the form of 1:1–15:33."[6]

Response

Two initial points should be noted.[7] First, $\mathfrak{P}^{46}$ is the *only* manuscript which places 16:25–27 after 15:33; most other major manuscripts ($\mathfrak{P}^{61\text{vid}}$ ℵ B C D) have 1:1–16:23 followed by the doxology of 16:25–27 (see further below).[8] Second, $\mathfrak{P}^{46}$ actually *retains* 16:1–23; it just places it after the doxology. Along these lines, it should be emphasized that *virtually all known manuscripts* do contain chapter 16.[9] Sumney summarizes as follows:

> Despite these problems, the majority of interpreters think chapter 16 was a part of the original letter. They note that it is present in nearly every ancient manuscript of Romans, and it is not until after the fifth century that it is actually absent from a manuscript—a manuscript that is a Latin translation of the original Greek.[10]

In addition to relying on the solid manuscript evidence, Kruse further defends the place of chapter 16 by summarizing the more expansive work of Lampe as follows:

> (i) Paul never ends his letters with the formulation "the God of peace be with all of you" (15:33); rather, such a formula usually precedes requests to pass on greetings—like those in chapter 16. … (iii) The unique features of chapter 16 with its many greetings coincides with the fact that chapters 1–15 reveal that Paul is writing to a church which he did not found and has never visited, yet from which he seeks support for his mission. (iv) Romans 15:19–29 indicates that chapters 1–15 were written from Greece at the conclusion of Paul's third missionary journey. This coincides with the apostle's situation reflected in chapter 16.[11]

Guthrie then observes how chapter 16 actually fits a Pauline pattern, "for the only other occasion when he appended many personal greetings was when writing to

---

[6] Fitzmyer, *Romans*, 49; he adds that $\mathfrak{P}^{46}$ is "dated usually ca. 200."

[7] Further complicating matters, what was numbered as 16:24 contains a slightly lengthened version of 16:20b which was moved after 16:23 by D and other so-called "Western" texts. It reads: "The grace of our Lord Jesus Christ [is] with all of you. Amen" (ἡ χάρις τοῦ κυρίου ἡμῶν Ἰησοῦ Χριστοῦ μετὰ πάντων ὑμῶν. ἀμήν, 16:24). Jewett, *Romans*, 18, contends that "the original form of Paul's letter … consisted of 1:1–16:16 + 16:21–23 + 16:24." Hultgren, *Romans*, 20, responds that 16:24 "does not, however, appear at this place in earlier, superior texts ($\mathfrak{P}^{61}$, ℵ, A, B, C, and others), and should be omitted." Although retained by the KJV and NKJV as 16:24, most modern English translations properly omit the verse (e.g., ESV, RSV, NRSV). See also Metzger, *A Textual Commentary on the Greek New Testament*, 539–40, and the textual note on 16:24.

[8] See Metzger, *A Textual Commentary on the Greek New Testament*, 534.

[9] See the listing by Metzger, *A Textual Commentary on the Greek New Testament*, 534.

[10] Sumney, "Reading the Letter to the Romans," 8.

[11] Kruse, *Romans*, 14, summarizing the arguments of Lampe, "The Roman Christians of Romans 16," 217–21.

Colossae which he had [also] never visited."[12] Thus the premise (that the many names in Rom 16:1–16 must reflect Paul's extensive familiarity with the letter's recipients) represents the opposite of reality.[13] In other words, "such a list of greetings would be exceptional in a letter written to a church with which Paul was well acquainted."[14]

Could Paul have known the twenty-six people he greets personally in 16:3–16 by name? Franzmann's pithy characterization of them as "a mobile lot"[15] means that this would not have been as extraordinary as it might at first appear. Guthrie references the "extraordinary travel facilities to and from the imperial capital which would make it not so improbable as it seems at first that so many of Paul's acquaintances had migrated to Rome."[16] The Jews in the city had been expelled by Claudius (AD 49 or 50), but his edict was rescinded upon the accession of Nero (AD 54), so the four to eight Jewish believers whom Paul greets may have relocated back to Rome prior to the writing of the letter (AD 55 or 56).[17]

The combined evidence, therefore, supports the authenticity of Romans 16 as the final chapter of Paul's letter to Rome. As originally placed, the doxology of 16:25–27 serves wonderfully as a thematic conclusion (see "Challenges to Authenticity Rebutted" in the commentary on 16:25–27). However, further complexities also need to be considered.

Challenges to Romans 15 *and* 16

Moo observes that "several MSS of the Latin Vulgate omit 15:1–16:23 entirely, an omission for which evidence is also found in another Vulgate codex and in the absence of reference to chaps. 15 and 16 in Tertullian, Irenaeus, and Cyprian."[18] He concludes that this provides "definite evidence of a 14-chapter form of Romans in the early church."[19] How can the absence of both chapters in these diverse and isolated sources be explained?

---

[12] Guthrie, *New Testament Introduction*, 401; see the introductory section of the commentary on 16:1–16 and Deterding, *Colossians*, 183–94.

[13] See "It's Just a Bunch of People—Exactly!" in the commentary on 16:1–16; see also "Christianity in Rome" in Middendorf, *Romans 1–8*, 10–14.

[14] Bruce, *Romans*, 255.

[15] Franzmann, *Romans*, 275.

[16] Guthrie, *New Testament Introduction*, 402.

[17] For further details, see Bruce, *Romans*, 255–56; Middendorf, *Romans 1–8*, 7–12. For the identification of four to eight Jews in 16:3–16, see "What Can We Conclude?" at the end of the commentary on 16:1–16.

[18] Moo, *Romans*, 6–7, where he reports the Latin manuscripts which omit 15:1–16:23 are numbered vg[1648, 1792, 2089]; he adds (n. 16) that the Vulgate codex is called Amiatinus which does, in fact, have "all 16 chapters, but the section summaries corresponding to 15:1–16:24, taken from an earlier Latin version, are not included." Moo further notes (7, n. 17) how "Tertullian refers to 14:10 as being in the last part of the epistle (*Contra Marcion* 5.14)."

[19] Moo, *Romans*, 8; similarly, under the heading "Chapters xv and xvi," Guthrie, *New Testament Introduction*, 406, affirms: "It would seem certain that a shorter recension of the Epistle was in circulation at one time in its textual history."

Origen reports the following:

> Marcion, who interpolated both the Gospels and the Epistles, deleted this passage [16:25–27] from the text, and not only this but everything [after 14:23] as well. In other manuscripts not edited by Marcion we find this passage in different places. Some have it immediately after [14:23], and others have it here, at the end of the epistle.[20]

Guthrie discusses how there is some doubt about the precise meaning of the Latin term *dissecuit*, translated above as "deleted."[21] It may communicate that Marcion received an already existing text without chapters 15 and 16[22] or that he himself cut out everything after 14:23. Guthrie concludes that the latter provides the most natural understanding,[23] and Sanday and Headlam consider it "almost certain."[24] Moo tentatively agrees and offers this speculative explanation: "There is much from 15:1 onward that would have offended Marcion's anti-Jewish sentiments."[25]

Furthermore, some manuscripts have the doxology of 16:25–27 located after 14:23 (e.g., L Ψ 0209[vid] Majority Text).[26] This might seem to call chapters 15 and 16 into question, though it must be noted that these texts retain 15:1–16:24 after the doxology. The Alexandrian text (A) similarly places the doxology after 14:23, but then repeats it again after 15:1–16:23![27] All things considered, it is fair to conclude that the textual evidence raises somewhat more credible concerns regarding *both* chapters 15 and 16, rather than chapter 16 alone.

---

[20] Origen, *Romans* (Bray, *Romans*, ACCS NT 6:379–80). See PG 14:1290 or *CER* 5:280 (the edition translated in ACCS).

[21] Guthrie, *New Testament Introduction*, 406, 409–10, 413, citing (406) the Latin version of Origen's commentary (see PG 14:1290 or *CER* 5:280). That version actually has two verbs that are rendered in the translation above with one occurrence of "deleted." Guthrie explains (406): "Origen states that Marcion removed (*abstulit*) the doxology and cut out (*dissecuit*) chapters xv and xvi."

[22] Capes, Reeves, and Richards, *Rediscovering Paul*, 281, report: "Harry Gamble has demonstrated the fourteen-chapter edition [of Romans] existed in the eastern part of the empire and was used rather than created by Marcion" (citing Gamble, *The Textual History of the Letter to the Romans*). Fitzmyer, *Romans*, 49, adds: "Origen also knew of texts not contaminated by Marcion that had the doxology after 14:23." However, virtually all of these manuscripts then retain 15:1–16:23 afterward; see the remainder of the discussion here and Metzger, *A Textual Commentary on the Greek New Testament*, 533–34.

[23] Guthrie, *New Testament Introduction*, 409.

[24] Sanday and Headlam, *Romans*, xc.

[25] Moo, *Romans*, 8; similarly, Guthrie, *New Testament Introduction*, 409–10.

[26] Metzger, *A Textual Commentary on the Greek New Testament*, 534; Schreiner, *Romans*, 816–17.

[27] For this and other locations of the doxology (16:25–27) in minor texts, see Metzger, *A Textual Commentary on the Greek New Testament*, 534.

Response

While the various locations of the doxology (16:25–27) seem puzzling, challenges to the integrity of Romans 15 and 16 should be regarded as very weak. As noted above, virtually all texts contain all sixteen chapters.[28] Furthermore, the majority of the earliest and best textual witnesses place the doxology of 16:25–27 after 16:23 (e.g., $\mathfrak{P}^{61vid}$ ℵ B C D).[29] Fitzmyer confirms that the traditional "long form of Romans" (1:1–16:27 [or 16:28])

> is found in every extant Greek MS of the letter that contains the full text. Although the quantity of manuscript testimony would support the placing of the doxology after 14:23, the quality of the ancient witnesses supporting the positioning of it at 16:25–27, the geographical spread of their testimony, and the diversity of the textual traditions represented are decisive for reading it after 16:23.[30]

The lack of references to Romans 15 and 16 among the early church fathers pointed out by Moo (see above) also "has little evidential value."[31] It merely recalls an axiom from archaeology: "absence of evidence is not evidence of absence."

Finally, ending the letter after 14:23 seems a very odd place to stop. Moo contends that if Paul had done so, he "would have cut off his epistle in the middle of his argument."[32] Dodd further observes that 14:23

> is a most unlikely close for such a letter, even with the addition of a doxology. It does not bring the argument of chap. xiv. to a conclusion worthy of the level on which it has been conducted; and it makes no attempt to round off the epistle as a whole. As the commentary will show, it is actually the middle of a paragraph, which does not end until xv. 6; and the plan of the epistle demands some such deliberate conclusion as is supplied in xv. 7–13.[33]

What Happened? Three Theories

As a first hypothesis, Metzger speculates "that Paul may have made two copies of the Epistle."[34] He then purportedly sent one to Rome and retained

---

28 See the listing of Metzger, *A Textual Commentary on the Greek New Testament*, 534; he adds (535) that the only evidence indicating the absence of chapter 15 or chapter 16 derives from "headings, or brief summaries of sections, which are prefixed to the epistle in many Vulgate manuscripts," as well as "three Vulgate manuscripts" which contain 1:1–14:23 followed by 16:24 and the doxology (see also 534).

29 Schreiner, *Romans*, 816–17; similarly, Hultgren, *Romans*, 21.

30 Fitzmyer, *Romans*, 50; he further contends (59) that "P^{46} may be witnessing to nothing more than a text form in which the doxology was moved for some reason to the end of chap. 15 from the end of chap. 16."

31 Guthrie, *New Testament Introduction*, 406.

32 Moo, *Romans*, 8.

33 Dodd, *Romans*, xv–xvi; this commentary regards 15:7 as a hinge verse which concludes the discussion of 14:1–15:7 but also provides a segue into 15:7–13 (see the introductory sections of the commentary on those two pericopes).

34 Metzger, *A Textual Commentary on the Greek New Testament*, 533.

the other to be utilized further. If so, the inception of variations in the textual tradition may stem from Paul himself, who "dispatched a longer and a shorter form of the epistle (one form with, and one without, chapter 16)."[35] If so, then Paul *may* have reused the shorter version as something of a circular letter. Capes, Reeves, and Richards devise this scenario:

> Once in prison, Paul decided other churches should read what he wrote to the church in Rome. (Notice that while in a Roman prison, he encouraged the same practice to the Colossians.) When he made another copy of his letter to Rome, there was no need to include the recommendation letter for Phoebe or the greetings (Rom 16). The travel plans in Romans 15 didn't work out as he had hoped and also didn't need to be copied, certainly from verse 14 onward. Rather than claiming a later disciple of Paul took it upon himself to edit Romans, we should consider the possibility that Paul himself did. Ancients loved to share copies of letters with others.[36]

While not impossible, this does not adequately explain the very unsatisfactory proposal that 14:23 could be the conclusion of the letter. As Dodd asserts (see above), the chapter break at 15:1 comes just as Paul wraps up his thoughts to the "weak" and the "strong" (14:1–15:7; see the introduction to 15:1–7). Ending the letter after 14:23 also deletes its climactic theological statement (15:7–13; see the introduction to 15:7–13). In fact, Sanday and Headlam properly argue that nothing in 15:1–13 makes it unfit "for general circulation" and that it is "in fact more suitable for an encyclical than is" chapter 14.[37]

A second theory proposes that adaptations made by *others* produced the variety of endings. The citation from Capes, Reeves, and Richards in the previous paragraph alludes to "a later disciple of Paul."[38] Evidence from Origen is laid out in "Challenges to Romans 15 *and* 16" above. Bruce connects Marcion's lack of appreciation for the OT with the content of 15:4 and 15:9–12 in order to propose that "to Marcion, then, we may assign the edition which ended at 14:23."[39]

A third, more practical theory seems most plausible. Cranfield considers it "more likely … that the variants reflect an omission of the localizing references in liturgical use."[40] In other words, as the letter was used for worship and study, emphasis was placed on the universally relevant content of chapters 1–15. Chapter 16 was not considered to be as pertinent for congregations outside Rome, and so, in the copying process, shortened endings emerged. On this basis, Bruce properly observes:

---

[35] Metzger, *A Textual Commentary on the Greek New Testament*, 536; Dodd, *Romans*, xvi, also mentions this possibility but views it as unlikely.

[36] Capes, Reeves, and Richards, *Rediscovering Paul*, 281.

[37] Sanday and Headlam, *Romans*, xcv.

[38] Capes, Reeves, and Richards, *Rediscovering Paul*, 281.

[39] Bruce, *Romans*, 29; see 28–29.

[40] Cranfield, *Romans*, 9.

There is no difficulty in understanding why an edition should have circulated without chapter 16. If copies of the letter were sent to a number of churches, because of the general interest and relevance of its contents, all but one of these copies would very naturally have lacked chapter 16, which with its many personal messages would have been applicable to one church only.[41]

Aside from the "long and flowing, highly liturgical doxology" of 16:25–27,[42] chapter 16 could have been deemed less helpful for the church's ongoing worship life. Even today it seldom appears in contemporary lectionaries.[43]

Thus the doxology (16:25–27) was retained as a conclusion, but ended up being placed in various locations. Putting it after 14:23, however, raises the thematic problems just cited above. Concluding with the doxology at the end of Romans 15, as $\mathfrak{P}^{46}$ does, surely makes better sense in regard to providing a more logical ending to the letter.

Conclusion

Guthrie submits that "it is not easy to decide which of these theories provides the best solution."[44] However, it seems most likely that Romans 16 was omitted in later copies of the letter; conversely, it is very difficult to comprehend why it would have been added or attached if it were not original. Furthermore, the content of 16:25–27, which "allows the total message of the Epistle to the Romans to pass before our eyes,"[45] recaps the entire letter's themes magnificently.

Therefore, the best evidence, *both in terms of manuscript support and in regard to the summation of Paul's purpose in the letter*, points decisively to the "long form," i.e., 1:1–16:27 (minus 16:24[46]). Since the Spirit-inspired text is properly regarded as the original autograph which Paul sent to Rome, as well as reliable copies stemming from it, all sixteen chapters should be accepted as such.[47]

---

[41] Bruce, *Romans*, 28.

[42] Hultgren, *Romans*, 21.

[43] E.g., the lectionaries in *LSB*, xiv–xxiii, utilize Romans 16 only once, and then only the doxology: 16:25–27 serves as the Series B Epistle reading for Advent 4.

[44] Guthrie, *New Testament Introduction*, 413; he adds: "On the whole that which traces the recensions of the Epistle to Marcion is perhaps least open to objection."

[45] Nygren, *Romans*, 457; similarly, Sanday and Headlam, *Romans*, xcviii.

[46] See the textual note on 16:24.

[47] For a broad presentation of the Reformation view of the inspiration of Scripture in contradistinction to other views, including a discussion of the autographic manuscripts and apographs (copies), see Preus, *The Inspiration of Scripture*, 47–49 and 134–40.

Romans 16:1–16

Greetings to Those in Rome: What's in a Name?

Translation

16 ¹Now I commend to you Phoebe, our sister, who is also a servant of the congregation which is in Cenchreae, ²so that you might receive her to yourselves in [the] Lord [in a manner] worthy of the holy ones and assist her in whatever matter she might have need of you. For she also came to be a benefactor of many, even of me myself.

³Greet Prisca and Aquila, my fellow workers in Christ Jesus, ⁴who placed their own neck (at risk) in behalf of my life, to whom not only I myself am giving thanks, but also all the congregations of the Gentiles, ⁵and [greet] the congregation which [meets] in their home.

Greet Epaenetus, my loved one, who is [the] firstfruits of Asia in Christ. ⁶Greet Mary, who labored earnestly for you. ⁷Greet Andronicus and Junia(s), my kinsmen and my fellow prisoners, who are well-regarded among the apostles, who also came to be in Christ before me. ⁸Greet Ampliatus, my loved one in [the] Lord. ⁹Great Urbanus, our fellow worker in Christ Jesus, and Stachys, my loved one. ¹⁰Greet Apelles, the one tested and approved in Christ. Greet those from the [household] of Aristobulus. ¹¹Greet Herodion, my kinsman. Greet those from the [household] of Narcissus who are in [the] Lord. ¹²Greet Tryphaena and Tryphosa, who labored in [the] Lord. Greet Persis, the loved one, who labored earnestly in [the] Lord. ¹³Greet Rufus, the chosen one in [the] Lord, also his mother and mine. ¹⁴Greet Asyncritus, Phlegon, Hermes, Patrobas, Hermas, and the brothers with them. ¹⁵Greet Philologus and Julia, Nerea and his sister, also Olympus, and all the holy ones with them.

¹⁶Greet one another with a holy kiss. All the congregations of the Christ are greeting you.

Textual Notes

16:1 συνίστημι δὲ ὑμῖν Φοίβην—The verb συνίστημι is used transitively here since it has a direct object (Φοίβην, "Phoebe"), as well as an indirect object (ὑμῖν, "to you"). Its transitive meaning is "to bring together as friends or in a trusting relationship by commending/recommending, *present, introduce/recommend someone to someone else*" (BDAG, A 2).

οὖσαν [καὶ] διάκονον τῆς ἐκκλησίας—For the noun διάκονος, "servant," see the commentary on 13:4; the only other use in Romans besides 13:4 and 16:1 applies to Christ in 15:8. Schreiner contends that this noun in 16:1 is masculine.[1] However, the

---

[1] Schreiner, *Romans*, 787.

masculine-looking forms of a second declension noun such as διάκονος can be either masculine *or* feminine.[2] Here the term may describe Phoebe as the bearer of the letter since διάκονος can mean *"courier"* (BDAG, 1), but more likely, it refers to her role in her congregation. See the commentary.

16:2 ἵνα αὐτὴν προσδέξησθε—For προσδέχομαι BDAG, 1, gives to "receive favorably, *take up, receive, welcome*," which is appropriate, but does not convey the full sense of the middle voice of the subjunctive here. It functions much the same way as does the middle imperative προσλαμβάνεσθε of the essentially synonymous verb προσλαμβάνω in 14:1 and 15:7, "receive *to yourselves*" (see the second textual note on 14:1).

ἐν κυρίῳ—The prepositional phrase "in [the] Lord" occurs seven times in this chapter (16:2, 8, 11, 12 [twice], 13, 22) and only once elsewhere in the letter (14:14; see "Jesus Said So" in the commentary on 14:14).

παραστῆτε αὐτῇ—When in the second aorist tense, as here, παρίστημι functions intransitively and normally means to *"be present"* (BDAG, 2). But here the verb conveys the idea of *"come to the aid of, help, stand by* τινί *someone"* (BDAG, 2 a γ); cf. 2 Tim 4:17. The "someone" is given in the dative, here αὐτῇ, "her."

ἐν ᾧ ἂν ὑμῶν χρῄζῃ πράγματι—The verb χρῄζω means to *"(have) need (of)"* (BDAG) and takes the genitive, here ὑμῶν, "of you." In the prepositional phrase with the dative, ἐν ᾧ ... πράγματι, "in whatever matter," the noun πρᾶγμα refers to a *"deed, thing, event, occurrence, matter"* (BDAG, 1).

προστάτις—This noun appears only here in Biblical Greek and refers to "a woman in a supportive role, *patron, benefactor"* (BDAG).

16:3 ἀσπάσασθε—The deponent verb ἀσπάζομαι, "to greet," occurs twenty-one times in Romans 16. In 16:3–16 this same second person plural imperative form appears sixteen times; for the disputed sense, see the commentary.

16:4 τὸν ἑαυτῶν τράχηλον ὑπέθηκαν—The noun τράχηλος means *"neck, throat"* (BDAG). The verb ὑποτίθημι means to *"lay down"* (BDAG, 1). While the expression "they laid down their neck" is somewhat idiomatic, the picture evoked is clear: *"they put their own necks at risk (in my behalf)"* (BDAG, s.v. ὑποτίθημι, 1 a). The language may recall the ancient custom described in Josh 10:24, where conquerors place their feet upon the necks of their defeated enemies who lie underneath on the ground.[3] Cf. "crush Satan under your feet" in Rom 16:20, recalling Gen 3:15.

16:5 τὴν κατ᾽ οἶκον αὐτῶν ἐκκλησίαν—The literal sense of the preposition κατά is awkward: "the church in accord with their house." While the phrase could possibly identify the congregation as the household of Prisca and Aquila, κατά more likely functions as a "marker of spatial aspect" which here means *"in"* (BDAG, B 1 and B 1 c), thus "which [meets] in their home." ἐκκλησία, which appears for the first time in Romans in 16:1, denotes an *"assembly"* (BDAG, 1) and then "people with shared belief,

---

[2]   In the second declension, the morphology of masculine and feminine nouns is identical; see, e.g., Voelz, *Fundamental Greek Grammar*, 22.

[3]   LXX Josh 10:24 uses ἐπιτίθημι and τράχηλος, "to place (from above) upon the neck": *ἐπίθετε τοὺς πόδας ὑμῶν ἐπὶ τοὺς τραχήλους αὐτῶν. καὶ προσελθόντες ἐπέθηκαν τοὺς πόδας αὐτῶν ἐπὶ τοὺς τραχήλους αὐτῶν.*

community, congregation" (BDAG, 3). The current use of "church" is commonly misunderstood as referring to a building. A more accurate definition for the majority of NT uses is a "congregation," that is, an assembly of believers who gather regularly in a home or other location to hear God's Word and receive the Sacraments and for teaching, prayer, and fellowship (in homes daily in Acts 2:42–47).

τὸν ἀγαπητόν μου—"My loved one" occurs with the masculine adjective, referring to different individuals, in 16:5, 8, 9, and the feminine τὴν ἀγαπητήν, "the loved one," describes Persis in 16:12. Paul used the plural for all the Christians in Rome as "loved ones" in 1:7 and similarly in 12:19.

ἀπαρχὴ τῆς Ἀσίας—For the noun ἀπαρχή, "firstfruits," expressing the OT concept (e.g., Ex 23:16–19; 34:22–26; Lev 2:12–14), see the third textual note on Rom 8:23. Unlike the literal sense in 11:16, here it is used metaphorically of a person, "*first fruits* of Christians" (BDAG, 1 b α) and refers to the first convert "of Asia."

16:6 ἥτις πολλὰ ἐκοπίασεν—The verb κοπιάω means "to exert oneself physically, mentally, or spiritually, *work hard, toil, strive, struggle*" (BDAG, 2). In Romans it appears only in 16:6, 12 (twice). Lampe suggests that it "is a technical term describing the labors of a missionary."[4] This might be suitable in some passages[5] but seems unwarranted here and is excluded by the context in, e.g., Eph 4:28; 2 Tim 2:6. The accusative neuter (plural) of the adjective πολύς functions adverbially:[6] "*greatly, earnestly, strictly, loudly, often*" (BDAG, 3 a β). Thus Mary is identified as one "who labored earnestly." The same clause recurs in 16:12.

16:7 Ἰουνίαν—The form, derivation, and gender of this name are hotly debated. It is unaccented in early manuscripts: Ιουνιαν (ℵ A B* C D* F G P). The form Ἰουνίαν, given at the beginning of this textual note, is the reading of NA²⁸, whose apparatus lists these manuscripts with that reading: B² D² L Ψᵛⁱᵈ 33 81 104 365 630 1175 1241 1505 1739 1881 𝔐.[7] This form is usually understood to be a *feminine name*, although it could theoretically be a masculine name (see below). The form printed in most recent prior editions of the Nestle(-Aland) text is Ἰουνιᾶν,[8] a *masculine name* (see below).

---

4. Lampe, "The Roman Christians of Romans 16," 223.

5. Paul uses the verb for his own apostolic labors in, e.g., 1 Cor 15:10; Phil 2:16; Col 1:29 and for that of other church leaders in 1 Cor 16:16; 1 Thess 5:12; 1 Tim 5:17.

6. For the adverbial use of accusative neuter adjectives, see Wallace, *Greek Grammar*, 293.

7. See also the extensive list of manuscripts with that reading in Swanson, *New Testament Greek Manuscripts: Romans*, 256.

8. The first edition of the Nestle text (*Novum Testamentum Graece*) was published in 1898 by Eberhard Nestle (1851–1913). The introduction to NA²⁸ (p. 46*) explains Nestle's methodology:

    Nestle took the three leading scholarly editions of the Greek New Testament at that time by Tischendorf, Westcott/Hort and Weymouth as a basis. (After 1901 he replaced the latter with Bernhard Weiß's 1894/1900 edition.) Where their textual decisions differed from each other Nestle chose for his own text the variant which was preferred by two of the editions included, while the variant of the third was put into the apparatus.

    This first edition of the Nestle text has the reading Ἰουνίαν in Rom 16:7, as do subsequent editions through the 12th (1923). (The 1st, 5th, 6th, 7th, 9th, and 12th editions were consulted and have that reading; presumably the other editions up to that point do as well.)

According to BDAG (s.v. Ἰουνιᾶς), "the accented form Ἰουνιᾶν has no support as such in the m[anuscript] tradition," but Swanson lists manuscript 1837 as having that reading.[9]

Relevant also is the testimony of the church fathers. From the patristic era through the twelfth century, the name commonly was interpreted as feminine. See further the commentary.

As with other names in this section, this name, whether accented as Ἰουνίαν or Ἰουνιᾶν, is a direct object of the imperative ἀσπάσασθε ("greet") and thus is accusative. The form Ἰουνίαν is accented like a Greek noun in the first declension. Most nouns in the first declension are feminine, but a few are masculine. If Ἰουνίαν is the accusative of a *feminine name*, the nominative form would be Ἰουνία, "Junia." While "Junia" is rarely found as a Greek name,[10] it is a widely attested Latin name. Lampe notes over 250 occurrences of that feminine name in Rome from various sources.[11] If the name in 16:7 does derive from the feminine Latin "Junia," as accepted with some hesitation in this commentary, Andronicus and Junia may represent another married couple (see the commentary), as do "Prisca and Aquila" in 16:3 and perhaps "Philologus and Julia" in 16:15.

If, on the other hand, Ἰουνίαν is the accusative of a *masculine name*, following the less-common first-declension pattern for masculine Greek nouns, the hypothetical

Eberhard Nestle's son Erwin (1883–1972) "provided the 13th edition of 1927 with a consistent critical apparatus showing evidence from manuscripts, early translations and patristic citations" (NA[28], 46*). Although Erwin Nestle was not working with primary sources (NA[28], 46*), given that edition's emphasis on "evidence from manuscripts," it seems ironic and irrational that it has the reading Ἰουνιᾶν (see the text above for its textual support). And nothing is listed in the apparatus about the reading. The apparatus of the 14th edition (1930) notes that HTW (Hort and Westcott, Tischendorf, and Weiß) have the reading Ἰουνίαν. The apparatus of the 17th edition (1941) includes for the first time the variant reading found in 𝔓[46] (Ἰουλιαν).

Kurt Aland (1915–1994) began working on the project in the 1950s (NA[28], 46*). But the 25th edition (1963) has the same reading (Ἰουνιᾶν) with the same information given in the apparatus (the note about HTW and the variant reading of 𝔓[46]). The 26th edition, seventh printing (1979), no longer has the note about HTW, but is otherwise the same. The first printing of the 27th edition (1993) has the reading Ἰουνιᾶν, but its apparatus lists manuscripts that have the reading Ἰουνίαν. The fifth printing of the 27th edition (1998; the 100-year Jubilee edition) has the reading Ἰουνίαν in the text, as does the 28th edition (2012), as noted above.

The editions of the Nestle(-Aland) text that have the reading Ἰουνιᾶν with no indication in the apparatus that nearly all accented manuscripts have the reading Ἰουνίαν are misleading and prone to cause confusion. Note, for example, the erroneous conclusion of Lampe, "The Roman Christians of Romans 16," 223 (whose 1991 article predates NA[27]): "According to Aland's textual critical apparatus, the feminine 'Junia' does not appear in the manuscripts"; similarly, Moo, *Romans*, 922, n. 30; Fitzmyer, *Romans*, 738; Wallace, "Junia among the Apostles: The Double Identification Problem in Romans 16:7."

9 Swanson, *New Testament Greek Manuscripts: Romans*, 256.

10 Moo, *Romans*, 922, n. 34, notes that three occurrences outside of Rom 16:7 have been found.

11 Lampe, *Die stadtrömischen Christen in den ersten beiden Jahrhunderten* (Tübingen: Mohr [Siebeck], 1987), 139, 147; similarly, Metzger, *A Textual Commentary on the Greek New Testament* (2d ed.; New York: United Bible Societies, 1994; elsewhere in this commentary, the 1st ed. is cited), 475: "The female Latin name Junia occurs more than 250 times in Greek and Latin inscriptions found in Rome alone." See also "Additional Note: Junia or Junias?" in Kruse, *Romans*, 563–65.

nominative form would be Ἰουνίας, "Junias." This would make "Junias a name in its own right and not a contracted name [see the next paragraph]. This possibility is put forward by Sanday and Headlam."[12] See also the proposal of Wolters, discussed below, that Ἰουνίας is derived from a masculine Hebrew name.

The form Ἰουνιᾶν, with a circumflex on the *alpha* in the ultima, is accented like a contracted form of a longer name.[13] The hypothetical nominative form of the contracted name would be Ἰουνιᾶς, "Junias." Robertson gives Ἰουνιανός as the Greek spelling of the uncontracted name,[14] which would be equivalent to the common masculine Latin name "Junianus."[15] However, as Schulz points out: "The difficulty with the name Junias, whether uncontracted or contracted … is that the name is otherwise entirely unknown."[16]

Wolters, however, postulates that the Greek name in 16:7, which he accents as Ἰουνίας, derives from the masculine Hebrew name יְחֻנִּי, *yĕḥunnī*. This attested name is a short form; the longer form would be יְחֻנִּיָה, *yĕḥunniah*, and the longest would be יְחֻנִּיָהוּ, *yĕḥunniahu*, although those two longer forms are unattested at the present time. All three forms mean "may Yahweh be gracious" and are derived from the verb חָנַן, *ḥanan*, "be gracious," with a theophoric ending (ִי-, "*ī*," or יָה-, "Yah," or יָהוּ-, "Yahu") that is short for יהוה, "Yahweh."[17] In summary, Wolters argues:

(1) A Hebrew name *yḥwny* [יחוני], meaning "may he be gracious," is attested in Paul's own day. (2) This name would most likely have been pronounced *yĕḥunnī*. (3) In biblical Greek, the name *yĕḥunnī* would have been hellenized as the first declension masculine noun Ἰουνίας.[18]

This proposal also "at least partially accounts for the fact that [almost] all accented manuscripts of Rom 16:7 have the reading Ἰουνίαν (with acute accent)."[19] While the Greek Ἰουνίας as a transliteration of a Hebrew name would be a hapax legomenon, the phenomenon of transliterating Hebrew names in this way occurs repeatedly in the NT (Ῥησά in Lk 3:27; Ἐλμαδάμ in Lk 3:28; Χουζᾶς in Lk 8:3; Κλωπᾶς in Jn 19:25) and dozens of times in the LXX.[20] Thus, as Wolters states: "It is not unreasonable, from a

---

[12] Schulz, "Romans 16:7: Junia or Junias?" 109. See Sanday and Headlam, *Romans*, 422.

[13] Robertson, *A Grammar of the Greek New Testament*, 172, lists other contracted names, including Λουκᾶς (Col 4:14; 2 Tim 4:11; Philemon 24), a contracted form of Λουκανός and of Λούκιος, and Θευδᾶς (Acts 5:36), possibly a contracted form of Θεόδωρος.

[14] Robertson, *A Grammar of the Greek New Testament*, 172, followed by Lenski, *Romans*, 905.

[15] That Ἰουνιᾶς, "Junias," is a contracted form of "Junianus" is given as a possibility by, e.g., BDAG, s.v. Ἰουνιᾶς; BDF, § 125.2; Sanday and Headlam, *Romans*, 422.

[16] Schulz, "Romans 16:7: Junia or Junias?" 109; similarly, Jewett, *Romans*, 961: elsewhere "not a single example of a masculine name 'Junias' has been found"; Dunn, *Romans*, 894; see also Bruce, *Romans*, 258.

[17] Wolters, "ΙΟΥΝΙΑΝ (Romans 16:7) and the Hebrew Name *Yĕḥunnī*," 400–401.

[18] Wolters, "ΙΟΥΝΙΑΝ (Romans 16:7) and the Hebrew Name *Yĕḥunnī*," 407.

[19] Wolters, "ΙΟΥΝΙΑΝ (Romans 16:7) and the Hebrew Name *Yĕḥunnī*," 399.

[20] Wolters, "ΙΟΥΝΙΑΝ (Romans 16:7) and the Hebrew Name *Yĕḥunnī*," 407–8.

philological point of view," to conclude that the name Ἰουνίας in Rom 16:7 belongs to a Jewish male.[21]

A variant reading in 𝔓⁴⁶ is Ιουλιαν.[22] This variant may have been influenced by the preferred reading in 16:15, Ἰουλίαν, "Julia." The reverse process seems to have happened in 16:15, where a few scribes wrote Ιουνιαν, "Junia(s)," apparently under the influence of Ιουνιαν in 16:7, instead of Ιουλιαν.[23] However, in 16:7 the variant Ιουλιαν is easily dismissed due to its inferior attestation. Metzger attributes it to "a clerical error."[24]

In conclusion, then, the linguistic derivation and the gender of Ἰουνίαν remain open questions. However, neither issue rises to the level of importance for interpreting the passage as does the meaning of the later phrase ἐπίσημοι ἐν τοῖς ἀποστόλοις (see the fourth textual note on 16:7, and see further the commentary).

συγγενεῖς—For the adjective συγγενής, "kinsman," a compound with the prefixed preposition σύν, "with," see the fifth textual note on 9:3. It recurs in the singular in 16:11 and the plural in 16:21.

συναιχμαλώτους—Another compound with the prefixed preposition σύν, "with," the noun συναιχμάλωτος means "*fellow-prisoner*" (BDAG) but can be understood in various ways (see the commentary).

ἐπίσημοι ἐν τοῖς ἀποστόλοις—The adjective ἐπίσημος basically means "well-known." This can be in a negative sense, "*notorious*" (BDAG, 2), as in its only other NT use for Barabbas (Mt 27:16). But here, in a positive sense, ἐπίσημος describes someone known to be "of exceptional quality, *splendid, prominent, outstanding*" (BDAG, 1). The controverted issue, then, is the sense of the prepositional phrase with ἐν and the dative τοῖς ἀποστόλοις. See the commentary.

16:10 τὸν δόκιμον—For the adjective δόκιμος, translated with two English terms, "tested and approved," see the fourth textual note on 14:18. The definite article τόν is used with it because Ἀπελλῆν is definite by virtue of being a proper name.

16:12 τὰς κοπιώσας—For the verb κοπιάω, see the textual note on 16:6. This form is a present active participle used adjectivally[25] with the article and translated as a relative clause: "who labored."

ἥτις πολλὰ ἐκοπίασεν—For the identical expression, referring to a woman "who labored earnestly," see the textual note on 16:6.

16:13 τὸν ἐκλεκτόν—The adjective ἐκλεκτός means "chosen." It appears twice in Romans, here in the singular and in the plural in 8:33 (see the commentary there).

---

[21] Wolters, "ΙΟΥΝΙΑΝ (Romans 16:7) and the Hebrew Name *Yĕḥunnī*," 407; for the matter of gender, see 408.

[22] The apparatus of NA²⁸ lists these later manuscripts that also have that reading: 6 606 1718 2685.

[23] See the notes on both 16:7 and 16:15 in Metzger, *A Textual Commentary on the Greek New Testament*, 539.

[24] Metzger, *A Textual Commentary on the Greek New Testament*, 539.

[25] See Wallace, *Greek Grammar*, 617–19.

16:16 ἐν φιλήματι ἁγίῳ—The noun φίλημα denotes a "kiss" and is modified by the adjective ἅγιος, "holy." The preposition ἐν has an instrumental sense: "with."[26] This clause should not be weakened to "*greet one another w[ith] a kiss of esteem*" (BDAG, s.v. φίλημα), but it bears the literal sense "greet one another with a holy kiss."

Commentary

It's Just a Bunch of People—Exactly!

Those wishing to plumb the depths of Paul's theology can find no better place to do so than the first fifteen chapters of Romans. But what of Romans 16? It seems like just a list of names. Paul follows his commendation of Phoebe, likely the courier of the letter, in 16:1–2 with greetings to twenty-six named people in Rome, at times together with their households and those who worship with them. Later, in 16:21–23, eight more people send their greetings to the believers in Rome (see the commentary there). While the latter grouping reflects a typical Pauline practice, "in no other letter does Paul even come close to the number of personal greetings he asks to be conveyed in vv. 3–15."[27] The primary explanation resides in the fact that Paul has not yet been to Rome. The vast majority of his hearers have not heard Paul and do not know him personally. Those who are acquainted with him, therefore, serve something like his personal references to the whole community of believers. For the sound probability that Paul would in fact know this many people in Rome by name, see the excursus "Textual Criticism and the End of Romans" following the commentary on 15:23–33.[28]

Colossians reflects a comparable situation since Paul had not yet visited Colossae, and he concludes a much shorter letter to the believers there similarly. He commends the bearer of the letter, Tychicus, and his companion, Onesimus (Col 4:7–9). This is followed by greetings from Paul's companions to the Colossians (Col 4:10–14) and then by more specific greetings from Paul to people there (Col 4:15–17).[29] By way of marked contrast, "when Paul writes to churches he knows well there is a remarkable absence of named greetings (1 and 2 Corinthians, Galatians, Philippians, 1 and 2 Thessalonians)."[30]

A common tendency is to overlook the entire chapter, or at least 16:1–16, as lacking any meaningful content. As an extreme example, Nygren's 457-page commentary dispenses with 16:1–27 in merely two pages.[31] Chrysostom responds:

---

[26] See Wallace, *Greek Grammar*, 372.

[27] Moo, *Romans*, 912.

[28] For a broader study, see Porter and Land, *Paul and His Social Relations*.

[29] See Deterding, *Colossians*, 183–94, who titles the commentary on Col 4:7–18 "Concluding Matters."

[30] Wright, "Romans," 761.

[31] Nygren, *Romans*, 456–57.

I think there are many, even some apparently good commentators, who hurry over this part of the epistle because they think it is superfluous and of little importance. They probably think much the same about the genealogies in the Gospels. Because it is a catalog of names, they think they can get nothing good out of it. People who mine gold are careful even about the smallest fragments, but these commentators ignore even huge bars of gold![32]

His admonition should be heeded for at least a couple of reasons. First of all, to neglect this section ignores the main purpose of all Christian theology. It never ought to exist in the abstract or remain isolated in the library or study. *God intends for his message to communicate and interact with people.* This chapter emphasizes the point.

Second, the names in this section reveal some things about the believers in Rome, at least those whom Paul knows personally. It does not seem possible to determine whether or not this section gives us a roster that is proportionally representative of all the believers in Rome. But with that caveat, for those "interested in the socioeconomic composition of the early church, it is a gold mine. For there was a tendency in the ancient world to give certain names to certain kinds of people."[33] Therefore, various studies of these names have been conducted and conclusions about them will be drawn at the end of this commentary section.

Commendation of Phoebe (16:1–2)

"Now I commend to you Phoebe, our sister, who is also a servant of the congregation which is in Cenchreae" (16:1). In 16:1 the postpositive δέ, translated as "now," indicates the attachment of this section with what precedes. Thus despite the theory of Manson and others,[34] this chapter should not be regarded as a stand-alone piece. Paul commends Phoebe "to you" plural (ὑμῖν), encompassing all the believers in Rome. Paul calls her "our sister" (τὴν ἀδελφὴν ἡμῶν), thus identifying her as a fellow believer. Her name indicates that she is a Gentile since "a Jewess would scarcely have had a name deriving from pagan mythology."[35]

Paul's commendation implies that it is she who delivers the letter to Rome.[36] "It is a natural deduction from the fact that she is named first (cf. 2 Cor 8:16–24; Phil 2:25–30; Philem[on] 8–20; ...)."[37] But it may also be explicit, since Paul calls her a διάκονος, "servant." The Greek term can denote an "*intermediary,*

---

[32] Chrysostom, *Homilies on Romans*, 30 (Bray, *Romans*, ACCS NT 6:369).

[33] Moo, *Romans*, 918.

[34] For example, Manson, "St. Paul's Letter to the Romans—And Others"; Moffatt, *An Introduction to the Literature of the New Testament*, 134–39; see the excursus "Textual Criticism and the End of Romans" following the commentary on 15:23–33.

[35] Cranfield, *Romans*, 780.

[36] Cranfield, *Romans*, 780; (Pseudo-)Constantius, *Romans* (Bray, *Romans*, ACCS NT 6:369) states: "He sends his letter to Rome by the hand of a woman."

[37] Dunn, *Romans*, 886.

courier" (BDAG, 1), and that definition would seem applicable in this context (see the second textual note on 16:1). Paul uses the identical term for Tychicus as the carrier of his letter to the Colossians: "brother … servant" (ἀδελφὸς … διάκονος, Col 4:7) is comparable to "sister … servant" (ἀδελφὴν … διάκονον, Rom 16:1).

However, in light of the added qualification, "of the congregation which is in Cenchreae" (16:1), the term "servant" (διάκονος) more likely describes her role there.[38] Interestingly, this phrase contains Paul's *first use* of "congregation, church" (ἐκκλησία) in the entire letter. Its connotations "drew heavily on the LXX use of ἐκκλησία to denote the assembly of Yahweh."[39] The word "church" can be misleading here if taken as a reference to a building. This can be clarified by translating ἐκκλησία as "house church." Paul is referring to "a gathering (not a building) of persons within someone's home, whether it be a villa or an apartment, that was ordinarily used for domestic purposes."[40] The translation *"congregation"* (BDAG, 3) is used here in order to depict the local, worshiping community of believers in Cenchreae (for various congregations in Rome, see 16:5a and the conclusion to 16:1–16 below). Cenchreae was a port city eight miles east of Corinth.

How, then, should διάκονος, *diakonos*, be understood in the context "a servant of the congregation which is in Cenchreae" in 16:1? Almost every rendering seems problematic. Wright contends:

> "Minister" (REB) is imprecise, because that word is used for several pastoral offices in today's church; "deaconess" (RSV, JB, NJB) is inaccurate, because it implies that Phoebe belonged to a specific order, of female church workers quite different from "deacons," which would not be invented for another three hundred years.[41]

He concedes that "servant" "does indeed offer a valid translation of the word,"[42] and it is utilized here. The group of words related to διάκονος can depict Christian service in a general manner. As the commentary on "serving in the service" (διακονίαν ἐν τῇ διακονίᾳ) in 12:7 discusses, this could entail tasks such as visiting the sick, caring for the poor and needy, and managing finances. These would likely have been exercised in behalf of the Christian community in order to benefit those both within and outside of it. These types of "service" are supported by the attribution of the title for a "patron" or "benefactor"

---

[38] Schreiner, *Romans*, 787, points out that "this is the only occasion in which the term διάκονος ['servant'] is linked with a particular local church."

[39] Dunn, *Romans*, 887, citing as examples Deut 23:1–2 (MT/LXX 23:2–3); 1 Chr 28:8; Neh 13:1; Micah 2:5; see also Barclay, *The Mind of St Paul*, 236–37; P. T. O'Brien, "Church," *DPL*, 124.

[40] Hultgren, *Romans*, 701.

[41] Wright, "Romans," 762.

[42] Wright, "Romans," 761–62.

(προστάτις) to Phoebe in 16:2 (see the fifth textual note on that verse and the commentary below).

Moo points out how "people who regularly ministered in a certain way were gradually recognized officially by the congregation and given a regular title."[43] Therefore taking the term as a *title* would seem to be appropriate, especially in light of the comparable use of διάκονος, "servant," for Paul and Timothy in Phil 1:1 and for deacons in 1 Tim 3:8, 12.[44] Dunn argues that in Rom 16:1 the use of διάκονος, *diakonos*, together with the participle "who is" (οὖσαν), indicates that she should be viewed as a "minister" having some "position of responsibility in the congregation."[45] Schreiner contends that "she held the office of deacon."[46] While this may well be appropriate, two words of caution also seem advisable. First, as Dunn recognizes, at this point in the early church "it would be premature to speak of an established office of diaconate."[47] Whatever "office" she might have held is to be defined by the NT depiction of it, not by later ecclesiastical terminology. Second, while Paul praises Phoebe with the term "servant" (διάκονος), she is not given one of the three interchangeable terms which the NT applies to the pastoral ministry. These are "shepherd" (ποιμήν, e.g., Eph 4:11), "elder" (πρεσβύτερος, e.g., Acts 14:23; 1 Tim 5:17, 19; Titus 1:5; 1 Pet 5:1), and "overseer" (ἐπίσκοπος, Acts 20:28; Phil 1:1; 1 Tim 3:2; Titus 1:7; 1 Pet 2:25).

In Rom 16:2, Paul merges purpose[48] and result with this ἵνα clause:[49] "so that you might receive her to yourselves in [the] Lord [in a manner] worthy of the holy ones and assist her in whatever matter she might have need of you. For she also came to be a benefactor of many, even of me myself." The believers in Rome should receive Phoebe to themselves "in [the] Lord" (ἐν κυρίῳ; the phrase occurs seven times in 16:1–22) and in a manner worthy of those who are "holy" (τῶν ἁγίων) by faith in him (see the commentary on 1:7 and 15:26). The sense of "receive" (προσδέχομαι, 16:2) surely goes beyond "welcome" (ESV, NRSV) and includes also providing food, shelter, and, most importantly, reception into the worshiping fellowship (see, e.g., Phil 2:29; cf. Lk 15:2).[50] This coincides with the practice of hospitality toward fellow believers praised earlier in the letter (Rom 12:13). The thematic use of a comparable verb for

---

43 Moo, *Romans*, 914.

44 Cranfield, *Romans*, 781.

45 Dunn, *Romans*, 886–87; so also Wright, "Romans," 762, quoted above.

46 Schreiner, *Romans*, 787.

47 Dunn, *Romans*, 887; so also Moo, *Romans*, 914, n. 11.

48 Cranfield, *Romans*, 781; Moo, *Romans*, 915, including n. 12.

49 For the merging of purpose and result, see Wallace, *Greek Grammar*, 473–74; see also BDAG, s.v. ἵνα, 3, which states: "In many cases purpose and result cannot be clearly differentiated, and hence ἵνα is used for the result that follows according to the purpose of the subj[ect] or of God." For other examples, see 4:16; 5:20; 14:9; 15:4, 32.

50 Käsemann, *Romans*, 411, includes "offering lodging and help," but reduces this to a "secular sense."

"receiving" (προσλαμβάνω) in 14:1 and 15:7 may have some influence here as well. In any case, Paul gives general instructions to aid her in whatever "matter" (πρᾶγμα, 16:2) she might have need.[51]

Paul then offers an explanation. The term προστάτις in 16:2 has been translated as "helper" (NASB, RSV); on the other hand, Paul occasionally uses the cognate verb to mean *"direct, be at the head (of)"* (BDAG, s.v. προΐστημι, 1; e.g., 1 Tim 3:12; 5:17), which might point to a leadership role here (see the second textual note and the commentary on 12:8). "But it is difficult to conceive how Phoebe would have had the opportunity to be a 'leader' of Paul"[52] ("even of me myself," 16:2). Therefore the "most natural and obvious sense of 'patron' "[53] seems contextually appropriate (so ESV), though "benefactor" (NRSV) also serves well. It "implies that Phoebe was possessed of some social position, wealth and independence."[54] More importantly, she uses those means for the sake of the church in Cenchreae (cf. Lk 8:3; cf. also Lydia in Acts 16:14–15). And, Paul emphatically adds, she has done so for his own sake as well.

Greetings to Those in Rome (16:3–16)

Paul uses the second person plural imperative "greet" (ἀσπάσασθε) sixteen times in 16:3–16 in order to greet various people in Rome. Other forms of the same verb (ἀσπάζομαι) occur an additional five times in 16:16 and 16:21–23. The verb's repeated use, then, stands most comparable to the much shorter ending of Philippians:

> [21]Greet [ἀσπάσασθε] all the holy ones in Christ Jesus. The brothers with me are greeting [ἀσπάζονται] you. [22]All the holy ones are greeting [ἀσπάζονται] you, and especially the ones of the household of Caesar. (Phil 4:21–22)

The imperative may sound like a command calling the divided believers to greet one another[55] or even to extend greetings to others outside the audience of the letter.[56] However, Gamble notes that "the imperative form of the greeting verb functions here as a surrogate for the first person indicative form, and so represents a direct personal greeting of the writer himself to the addressees."[57] Thus BDAG (s.v. ἀσπάζομαι, 1 a) states that the imperative may be translated as

---

[51] The term πρᾶγμα is used for a "lawsuit" in 1 Cor 6:1, but there is no hint of that specialized sense here. According to Käsemann, *Romans*, 411, "it is going too far to try to deduce from πρᾶγμα … that Phoebe was involved in some kind of legal action"; so also Cranfield, *Romans*, 782.

[52] Moo, *Romans*, 916.

[53] Dunn, *Romans*, 888.

[54] Cranfield, *Romans*, 783.

[55] Watson, "The Two Roman Congregations," 211: "Paul is in effect requesting his readers in both groups to introduce themselves to one another."

[56] Das, "The Gentile-Encoded Audience of Romans," 38: "The named people would be *outside* the Roman congregations or perhaps newcomers into their midst."

[57] Gamble, *The Textual History of the Letter to the Romans*, 93; cf. Dunn, *Romans*, 891.

"*greetings to (someone)* or *remember me to (someone)*."[58] "By using this imperative, Paul invites the Romans, who belong to different house and tenement churches, to greet one another in his name."[59] Hultgren identifies a comparable "modern usage. A person might say at the conclusion of a conversation, or in a letter, 'be sure to greet' so-and-so, whereby it is understood that the greetings being conveyed are those of the sender."[60]

The most critical factor which explains the extensive list to follow is the fact that Paul has not yet been to Rome. Yet he has just sought the support of the Christians there, financial and otherwise, for carrying out mission work in Spain (15:24). Thus these acquaintances serve as personal references, both for Paul himself and for the character of the ministry in which he is engaged, something he has also just described in some detail (15:16–21).

Prisca and Aquila (16:3–5a)

There seems to be a progression in the names listed in 16:3–15, from those with whom Paul is most familiar to those with whom he is least acquainted. Paul begins with those who know him best and whom he describes most extensively. Acts 18:2 introduces us to the first couple: "Aquila," a Jew from Pontus, and his wife, "Prisca" (Luke favors the diminutive form "Priscilla"). Interestingly, Prisca is mentioned first in four of the six times the couple is named in the NT, including Rom 16:3 (also Acts 18:18, 26; 2 Tim 4:19; Aquila comes first only in Acts 18:2 and 1 Cor 16:19). This ascribes some sense of prominence to her, but exactly what kind of importance remains unclear (family, business, or faith?).

The couple fled from Rome due to the decree of Claudius[61] and met Paul in Corinth during his second journey. Both worked together with Paul in tentmaking (Acts 18:2–3) and may have served within the newly formed Corinthian congregation. When Paul left Corinth after eighteen months (Acts 18:11), Prisca and Aquila accompanied him (Acts 18:18). Paul then left them in Ephesus (Acts 18:19), where they "established Apollos in the faith"[62] (Acts 18:24–26). He rejoined them there during his two-year stay on his third journey (Acts 19:1, 10; see also 1 Cor 16:19). Then they "returned to Rome once the severity of the decree was relaxed,"[63] most likely upon the death of Claudius in AD 54.[64]

---

[58] The aorist middle imperative of ἀσπάζομαι, "greet," is used in the plural, ἀσπάσασθε, in Rom 16:3, 5–16; 1 Cor 16:20; 2 Cor 13:12; Phil 4:21; Col 4:15; 1 Thess 5:26; Heb 13:24; 1 Pet 5:14 (see also Mt 10:12), and in the singular, ἄσπασαι, in 2 Tim 4:19; Titus 3:15. The present middle imperative in the singular, ἀσπάζου, appears in 3 Jn 15.

[59] Matera, *Romans*, 339; see also Jewett, *Romans*, 951–52; Moo, *Romans*, 919, who concludes: "It is clear that Paul is asking the Roman Christians to convey his own greetings to the respective individuals and groups" in Rome.

[60] Hultgren, *Romans*, 579–80.

[61] See Middendorf, *Romans 1–8*, 10.

[62] Pelagius, *Romans* (Bray, *Romans*, ACCS NT 6:370).

[63] Origen, *Romans* (Bray, *Romans*, ACCS NT 6:370).

[64] See Middendorf, *Romans 1–8*, 12.

Lampe considers the possibility that "their return to Rome had been 'strategically' planned by Paul."[65] Interestingly, 2 Tim 4:19 later has them back in Ephesus. Such travels were not extraordinary in NT times; consider those of Paul himself! However, the assemblage of these varied locations implies that Prisca and Aquila were fairly wealthy business people who had spent extensive time together with Paul. Thus he begins with them:

> [3]Greet Prisca and Aquila, my fellow workers in Christ Jesus, [4]who placed their own neck (at risk) in behalf of my life, to whom not only I myself am giving thanks, but also all the congregations of the Gentiles, [5]and [greet] the congregation which [meets] in their home. (16:3–5)

Paul calls Prisca and Aquila "fellow workers." "Fellow worker" (συνεργός) is a term he regularly uses for those who labor for Christ together with him.[a] While Paul is often viewed as a stand-alone apostle, one should correct the misperception that he regularly worked alone. On the contrary, he almost always traveled with partners and worked to establish a team ministry (see "What Can We Conclude?" below and the commentary on 16:21–23).

Jesus said: "No one has greater love that this, that someone might place (down) his life in behalf of his friends" (Jn 15:13). Prisca and Aquila seem to have dedicated their lives to the work of the Gospel and, apparently, almost laid down their lives in behalf of Paul. Perhaps Paul refers to a literal near loss of life, for example, at the riot in Ephesus (Acts 19:23–41).[66] It also seems plausible to take the reference more broadly since "there is no lack of situations where the influence of Prisca and Aquila at considerable risk to themselves may have been decisive."[67] The thanks they are due comes not only from Paul but from "all the congregations of the Gentiles" as well (Rom 16:4). This certainly includes those in Corinth and Ephesus.

Finally, Paul references "the congregation which [meets] in their home" (τὴν κατ᾽ οἶκον αὐτῶν ἐκκλησίαν, 16:5a). As in Ephesus (1 Cor 16:19), Prisca and Aquila hosted a congregation of believers in Rome. The fact that they could afford such a sizable residence corroborates the presumption that they had financial means. It further illustrates the often overlooked point that "there were … no buildings specially appropriated to church purposes at this time."[68] Instead, Meeks points out: "The local structure of the early Christian groups was … linked with what was commonly regarded as the basic unit of society,"[69] the home (see the commentary on 16:1).

The term ἐκκλησία, "congregation" or "church," is surprisingly absent from Romans 1–15, but 16:5 marks its third of five appearances in this chapter

(a) Also Rom 16:9, 21; 1 Cor 3:9; 2 Cor 1:24; 8:23; Phil 2:25; 4:3; Col 4:11; 1 Thess 3:2; Philemon 1, 24

---

[65] Lampe, "The Roman Christians of Romans 16," 220.

[66] Moo, *Romans*, 920.

[67] Dunn, *Romans*, 892, citing Acts 18:12–17; 19:23–41; 1 Cor 15:32; 2 Cor 1:8–10; 6:5; 8:2; 11:23.

[68] Cranfield, *Romans*, 786.

[69] Meeks, *The First Urban Christians*, 75.

(also 16:1, 4, 16, 23). On the one hand, this singular noun "is never used in Romans with reference to the Christian community in Rome as a whole"[70] or for the church universal. Paul does, however, clearly use ἐκκλησία in the latter sense elsewhere.[71] This proves that he apprehends and acknowledges the over-arching existence of the "one holy catholic and apostolic church" (μίαν ἀγίαν καθολικὴν καὶ ἀποστολικὴν ἐκκλησίαν, Niceno-Constantinopolitan Creed).[72]

In this regard, however, a congregation does not merely represent a small portion of what it means to be the church (e.g., an isolated, incomplete segment like the foot or ear of 1 Cor 12:12–27). "Each community, however small, represents the total community, the Church."[73] Therefore Paul more commonly uses ἐκκλησία to refer to one or more "congregations," as his regular use of plural forms attests (e.g., "all the congregations," πᾶσαι αἱ ἐκκλησίαι, 16:4).[74]

Further Personal Greetings (16:5b–15)

As Paul continues he utilizes a variety of different descriptors for those he names. These indicate his desire "to add a personal note to each of his greetings."[75] But he *repeats* a number of them regularly throughout 16:3–15: "in [the] Lord" (16:8, 11, 12 [twice], 13; also 16:2, 22); "in Christ" (16:3, 5, 7, 9, 10); "loved one" (16:5, 8, 9, 12); "labored" (16:6, 12 [twice]); "fellow worker" (16:3, 9; also 16:21); "kinsman" (16:7, 11; also 16:21); "tested and approved" (16:10); "chosen" (16:13). This probably means these descriptors serve as representative characterizations that apply—in varying degrees, to be sure—to other, or even all, believers. Thus they do not generally single out a specific individual or action which goes beyond the applicable trait(s).

Epaenetus (16:5b)

"Greet Epaenetus, my loved one, who is [the] firstfruits of Asia in Christ" (16:5b). Epaenetus is not mentioned elsewhere. However, since Ephesus is in the province of Asia, it is feasible that Epaenetus had previously been associated with Prisca and Aquila there. This would explain why he comes next, right after them.[76] Paul uses ἀπαρχή to speak of the Holy Spirit as the "firstfruits" in 8:23 (cf. 11:16), but here the noun has the sense of the "first convert" in a region.

---

[70] Cranfield, *Romans*, 22.

[71] 1 Cor 10:32; 15:9; Gal 1:13; Eph 1:22; 3:10, 21; 5:23–32; Phil 3:6; Col 1:24. Barclay, *The Mind of St Paul*, 232–33, describes the ways in which Paul uses ἐκκλησία, "church," and concludes: "Lastly, Paul uses *ekklēsia* to describe the Church as a whole, the whole company of believers in Jesus Christ in every place and in every nation." See also P. T. O'Brien, "Church," *DPL*, 125–26, under the heading "A Heavenly Gathering."

[72] Kelly, *Early Christian Creeds*, 298.

[73] K. L. Schmidt, "ἐκκλησία," *TDNT* 3:506.

[74] See the plural of ἐκκλησία also in, e.g., Rom 16:16; 1 Cor 7:17; 16:1, 19; 2 Cor 8:18–19, 23–24; 11:28; 12:13; Gal 1:2, 22; 1 Thess 2:14; 2 Thess 1:4.

[75] Dunn, *Romans*, 893.

[76] Moo, *Romans*, 921.

Paul speaks similarly of Stephanus as the "firstfruits of Achaia" (ἀπαρχὴ τῆς Ἀχαΐας) in 1 Cor 16:15.

Mary (16:6)

"Greet Mary, who labored earnestly for you" (Rom 16:6). Μαρία is the Greek form of the Hebrew name "Miriam." As the NT illustrates with its six or seven Marys, the name was quite common among Jewish people of the time. Although not specifically stated, it seems most probable that this "Mary" is Jewish.[77] Note that Aquila, a Jew (Acts 18:2), is not identified as such in Rom 16:3. Paul praises Mary highly for her hard work. Interestingly, however, he adds that it was done "for you" (εἰς ὑμᾶς) rather than "me" or "us" (cf. 16:2, 4). This implies that Mary was not a co-worker or direct associate of Paul.

Issues Surrounding Andronicus and Junia(s) (16:7)

"Greet Andronicus and Junia(s), my kinsmen and my fellow prisoners, who are well-regarded among the apostles, who also came to be in Christ before me" (16:7). One fundamental issue here concerns whether the second name refers to a man or a woman. The first textual note on 16:7 discusses the matter in detail, but does not resolve it decisively.[78] The possibility of a masculine name derived from Latin or Hebrew must be seriously considered.[79] But, if forced to choose, a feminine Latin name appears more plausible. Moo summarizes the intriguing history of interpretation as follows:

> Interpreters from the thirteenth to the middle of the twentieth century gener-
> ally favored the masculine identification. But it appears that commentators
> before the thirteenth century were unanimous in favor of the feminine
> identification;[80] and scholars have recently again inclined decisively to this
> same view.[81]

If the name is feminine, Andronicus and Junia "are man and woman, perhaps husband and wife or possibly brother and sister."[82] Early church tradition gen-erally viewed them as a married couple, as were Prisca and Aquila (16:3)[83] and perhaps "Philologus and Julia" in 16:15.

The *first descriptor*, "kinsmen" (the plural of συγγενής, 16:7), indicates that they are fellow Jews (see 9:3). The *second*, "fellow prisoners" (the plural of

---

[77] Käsemann, *Romans*, 413, who adds: "It is open to question … whether the name occurred outside the Jewish world."

[78] See also "Additional Note: Junia or Junias?" in Kruse, *Romans*, 563–65.

[79] The Latin possibility and the proposal of Wolters, "ΙΟΥΝΙΑΝ (Romans 16:7) and the Hebrew Name *Yĕḥunnī*," are laid out in the first textual note on 16:7; others who espouse the male view include Lenski, *Romans*, 905–6, and Franzmann, *Romans*, 276.

[80] The only possible exception appears to be Origen, *Romans*; see Moo, *Romans*, 922, n. 32.

[81] Moo, *Romans*, 922.

[82] Wright, "Romans," 762.

[83] So Morris, *Romans*, 533, including n. 28, quoting BDF, § 125.2, which states: "The ancients understood a married couple like Aquila and Priscilla."

συναιχμάλωτος), if taken literally, asserts that they were imprisoned with Paul at some point. He also uses the term for Aristarchus (Col 4:10) and Epaphras (Philemon 23). Murray explains by simply claiming that Paul's "imprisonments were frequent (*cf.* II Cor. 6:5; 11:23)."[84] But locating the referent of such a joint incarceration is a bit more complicated than Murray suggests. From what we are told thus far in Acts, we only know of one overnight stay in jail at Philippi (Acts 16:22–34). The Corinthians passages that Murray cites point toward possible, but otherwise uncorroborated, times of imprisonment in Ephesus, which we would then have to assume included Andronicus and Junia. On the other hand, Paul may mean that they have also endured imprisonment for the sake of Christ, though *separately from him.* Less likely would be a metaphorical reference to "sharing the special hardships incident to Paul's warfare in behalf of the gospel."[85]

The *third* description, "well-regarded among the apostles" (ἐπίσημοι ἐν τοῖς ἀποστόλοις, 16:7), continues to cause much controversy. Many scholars properly insist on translating ἐν as "among" or "to" rather than "by."[86] But that decision alone is by no means decisive in regard to how the phrase should be understood. For example, in an academic context, one could readily speak of exceptional students who were "well-regarded among" the faculty, without implying in any way that they were also among the professors and thus part of the faculty. Kruse articulates the disputed force of the prepositional phrase more precisely: should it be taken "inclusively," that is, "well known" and also included as members "among the apostles," or "exclusively," that is, "well known to the apostles" but excluded from membership among them?[87]

Many modern scholars read the phrase inclusively and thereby hypothesize that both Andronicus and Junia were apostles.[88] Jewett, for example, contends that "the adjective ἐπίσημος lifts up a person or thing as distinguished or marked in comparison with other representatives of the same class, in this instance with

---

[84] Murray, *Romans*, 2:229.

[85] Lenski, *Romans*, 906.

[86] Lampe, "The Roman Christians of Romans 16," 224, says that "*en* has to be translated as 'among'"; similarly, Dunn, *Romans*, 894: "among" is "almost certainly" the meaning; also Schreiner, *Romans*, 796; even Lenski, *Romans*, 907, concludes that "'by' is incorrect." Wallace, "Junia among the Apostles: The Double Identification Problem in Romans 16:7," also disallows "by" when he says that "ἐν plus a personal dative does not indicate agency," but then observes that "in collocation with words of perception, (ἐν plus) dative personal nouns are often used to show the recipients. In this instance, the idea would then be 'well known *to* the apostles.'"

[87] Kruse, *Romans*, 565; see his full treatment of the topic in "Additional Note: 'Well Known among,' or 'Well Known to,' the Apostles?" (565–67).

[88] This hypothesis then becomes part of the argument by some in favor of the ordination of women to the pastoral office. However, that practice is contrary to Paul's apostolic teaching elsewhere, e.g., 1 Cor 14:33–35; 1 Tim 2:8–15, as well as other Scripture passages.

other apostles."[89] Even if that were so, they were surely *not* among the Twelve[90] nor to be included in a group that Dunn labels as "premier" or "foundation apostles of Christianity."[91] Instead, Moo claims: "Paul often uses the title 'apostle' in a 'looser' sense: sometimes simply to denote a 'messenger' or 'emissary' and sometimes to denote a 'commissioned missionary.'"[92] But his use of "often" is a bit of a stretch. For the first two examples, he offers only 2 Cor 8:3 and Phil 2:25.[93] By the first reference he means 2 Cor 8:23, which speaks of "brothers" accompanying Titus whom Paul describes as ἀπόστολοι ἐκκλησιῶν. Rather than the titular "apostles," most translations render ἀπόστολοι in 2 Cor 8:23 with "messengers," a fitting term for those in the delegation accompanying the collection for Jerusalem (e.g., ESV, KJV, NASB, NRSV). Phil 2:25 refers singularly to Epaphroditus as ὑμῶν ... ἀπόστολον, again commonly understood as "your messenger" to Paul.

Moo's last suggestion, that of a "commissioned missionary," stands comparable to Cranfield's "itinerant missionaries."[94] Moo supports this definition of ἀπόστολος somewhat tenuously with "the probable distinction in 1 Cor. 15 between 'the twelve' ([1 Cor 15:]5) and 'all the apostles' ([τοῖς ἀποστόλοις πᾶσιν, 1 Cor 15:]7)"; for the latter category, Moo also cites passages which suggest that Paul's co-worker Barnabas was called an ἀπόστολος (Acts 14:4, 14; 1 Cor 9:5–6; Gal 2:9).[95] However, once again in 1 Cor 15:7, the specific referent of the plural term remains uncertain. Wright, for example, defines "Paul's meaning of 'apostle' as 'witness of the resurrection,' see 1 Cor 9:1 (cf. Acts 1:22)."[96] Das helpfully adds to the list Paul's use of "the term 'apostle' for itinerant missionaries such as Silvanus and Timothy (1 Thess 1:1 [Paul, Silvanus, Timothy]; 1 Thess 2:7 [ET 2:6b; 'we' 'apostles of Christ']; cf. *Did[ache]* 11.3–6)."[97] To be sure, "false apostles" also exist (ψευδαπόστολοι, 2 Cor 11:13). Thus, while there is warrant for a broader or nontechnical use of the term ἀπόστολος (see the commentary on ἀποσταλῶσιν in Rom 10:15), the components of its applicability to Andronicus and Junia in 16:7 seem nebulous at best.

---

[89] Jewett, *Romans*, 963; similarly, Bruce, *Romans*, 258: They "were apostles themselves ... and eminent ones at that."

[90] Schreiner, *Romans*, 796: "Paul is certainly not placing them in the ranks of the Twelve."

[91] Dunn, *Romans*, 895; for the former, he cites Eph 2:20.

[92] Moo, *Romans*, 923–24.

[93] Moo, *Romans*, 924, n. 41; see also Das, *Galatians*, 74, who affirms that Paul "recognizes 'apostles' who are messengers or emissaries of particular churches (e.g., Phil 2:25: 'your' apostle; 2 Cor 8:23)."

[94] Cranfield, *Romans*, 789; similarly, Käsemann, *Romans*, 414: "Jewish-Christian missionaries"; Matera, *Romans*, 341: "commissioned for special work."

[95] Moo, *Romans*, 924, n. 42.

[96] Wright, "Romans," 762; considered by Käsemann, *Romans*, 414; Franzmann, *Romans*, 276–77; Matera, *Romans*, 341.

[97] Das, *Galatians*, 74.

Ellis offers some proper qualifications when he speaks of Andronicus and Junia as "commissioned missionaries" under a section titled "Apostles of the Churches," a category he distinguishes from "Apostles of Jesus Christ":[98]

> (1) This otherwise unknown couple could hardly be described, in comparison with Peter, James or even Paul himself, as "outstanding among the apostles of Christ." (2) Also, if they were "apostles of Christ," the phrase "who were in Christ before me" would be a meaningless redundancy (cf. 1 Cor 15:8).[99]

Also worthy of consideration is an extrabiblical passage that may be the closest Greek grammatical parallel to ἐπίσημοι ἐν τοῖς ἀποστόλοις in Rom 16:7. Wallace has called attention to Ps Sol 2:6, which uses the same adjective translated as "well-regarded" in Rom 16:7, ἐπίσημος, with the same construction (ἐν plus a definite dative plural noun) to describe Jewish captives: they were ἐπισήμῳ ἐν τοῖς ἔθνεσιν, "a spectacle among the Gentiles." Since they are Jewish, these captives obviously are not to be included "among the Gentiles" who so regarded them.[100]

In context, Paul's *fourth and final description* of Andronicus and Junia, "who also came to be in Christ before me" (οἳ καὶ πρὸ ἐμοῦ γέγοναν ἐν Χριστῷ, 16:7), provides an important clue regarding the third. This dependent relative clause follows after "well-regarded among the apostles" (16:7). It thereby provides substantial, clarifying evidence which *tilts the scales toward an exclusive reading of the third description*.[101] The fact that Andronicus and Junia were in Christ before Paul identifies them as early Jewish converts, which almost certainly places them in Jerusalem during the early chapters of Acts. It may also imply that they were, in fact, witnesses of the resurrection (cf. the five hundred referenced in 1 Cor 15:6). This extraordinary statement aligns well with and explains how "these persons were well known to the apostles and were distinguished for their faith and service."[102] Thus the preposition "ἐν" states *where* these two were considered illustrious: 'in the circle of' the Twelve

---

[98] E. E. Ellis, "Coworkers, Paul and His," *DPL*, 185–86.

[99] E. E. Ellis, "Coworkers, Paul and His," *DPL*, 186.

[100] Wallace, "Junia among the Apostles: The Double Identification Problem in Romans 16:7," who goes on to point out the precise grammatical parallels between Rom 16:7 and Ps Sol 2:6 in Greek. They include

> (a) people as the referent of the adjective ἐπίσημος, (b) followed by ἐν plus the dative plural, (c) the dative plural referring to people as well. All the key elements are here. Semantically, what is significant is that (a) the first group is *not* a part of the second— that is, the Jewish captives were not gentiles; and (b) what was "among" the gentiles was the Jews' notoriety. This is precisely how we are suggesting Rom 16:7 should be taken. That the parallels discovered so far conform to our working hypothesis at least gives warrant to seeing Andronicus' and Junia's *fame* as that which was among the apostles.

[101] See Wallace, *Greek Grammar*, 335–36 and 659, who states that the "regular" function of the relative pronoun (here, οἳ) "describes, clarifies, or restricts the meaning" (336).

[102] Murray, *Romans*, 2:230.

at Jerusalem."[103] As the apostles guided the infant church in its earliest days, these two believers were "well known *to* the apostles"[104] and had a great reputation "among" them (16:7).

Further Names; Fewer Details (16:8–15)

After the more descriptive greetings in 16:3–7, we get increasingly simpler ones in 16:8–13, with only one or two noteworthy characteristics stated. This probably indicates a lesser degree of familiarity between Paul and those listed. In 16:14–15, Paul merely grants greetings by giving the names or references without further ado.

> [8]Greet Ampliatus my loved one in [the] Lord. [9]Great Urbanus, our fellow worker in Christ Jesus, and Stachys, my loved one. [10]Greet Apelles, the one tested and approved in Christ. Greet those from the [household] of Aristobulus. [11]Greet Herodion, my kinsman. Greet those from the [household] of Narcissus who are in [the] Lord. [12]Greet Tryphaena and Tryphosa, who labored in [the] Lord. Greet Persis, the loved one, who labored earnestly in [the] Lord. [13]Greet Rufus, the chosen one in [the] Lord, also his mother and mine. [14]Greet Asyncritus, Phlegon, Hermes, Patrobas, Hermas, and the brothers with them. [15]Greet Philologus and Julia, Nerea and his sister, also Olympus, and all the holy ones with them. (16:8–15)

Both "Ampliatus" and "Urbanus" (16:8–9a) served commonly as names for slaves, though one or both of these individuals may now be freedmen.[105] Paul describes Ampliatus as "my loved one" (16:8), as he does Epaenetus in 16:5, and as being "in [the] Lord," like Phoebe in 16:2. He calls Urbanus "our fellow worker [τὸν συνεργὸν ἡμῶν] in Christ Jesus" (16:9), using a term which he uses to describe Prisca and Aquila more personally as "my fellow workers" (16:3; also Timothy, 16:21). Perhaps this signals that Paul knows Urbanus "only by reputation."[106]

Paul then uses "my loved one" for a third time (16:9b; also 16:5, 8) in reference to Stachys, who is otherwise unknown. Also otherwise anonymous is Apelles, referred to uniquely in this list as "the one tested and approved in Christ" (τὸν δόκιμον ἐν Χριστῷ, 16:10a). Whether this alludes to trials Apelles has endured is impossible to know. In a general manner, it may simply reflect a characteristic of all believers who have kept the faith (cf. 14:18), as does the cognate noun "tested character" (δοκιμή) in 5:4.

Paul's greeting to "those from the [household] of Aristobulus" (16:10b) piques a bit more interest. In contrast with the pattern thus far, Paul does not extend a personal greeting directly to Aristobulus (i.e., "greet Aristobulus").

---

[103] Lenski, *Romans*, 907; this would be the category "spatial/sphere" in Wallace, *Greek Grammar*, 372. The applicability of "among" would seem to fit under "association."

[104] Wallace, "Junia among the Apostles: The Double Identification Problem in Romans 16:7."

[105] Cf. Dunn, *Romans*, 895; Moo, *Romans*, 924; Lampe, "The Roman Christians of Romans 16," 228.

[106] Moo, *Romans*, 924; see also Murray, *Romans*, 2:230.

Instead, Paul literally greets "those from the ones of Aristobulus" (τοὺς ἐκ τῶν Ἀριστοβούλου).[107] This implies that Aristobulus himself is one or more of these three: (1) not known by Paul personally, (2) not a believer, and/or (3) no longer living. While the name was common, Dunn contends that there is "a strong plausibility in the suggestion that the Aristobulus here mentioned was the grandson of Herod the Great" who came to Rome with his brother Agrippa I.[108] If so, at least some of the members of his household, likely including slaves, *would have been Jewish*. This certainly applies to the next name on the list, Herodion, both by virtue of the origin of the name and explicitly so via Paul's description of him as "my kinsman" (τὸν συγγενῆ μου, 16:11a), as with "Andronicus and Junia(s), my kinsmen" (16:7).

Next, greetings are literally given to "the ones from the ones of Narcissus," that is, those of his household (16:11b). This phrase, in place of a direct personal greeting to Narcissus himself, parallels the phrase involving Aristobulus in 16:10b. As with Aristobulus, this wording implies that Narcissus is (1) not known by Paul personally, (2) not a believer, and/or (3) no longer living. While the name was common for slaves, this Narcissus must be a freedman since he has or had a household. Here, again, Paul may refer to a well-known person in Rome, "a freedman who maintained a substantial household in the early 50s"[109] until he "committed suicide just before Paul wrote Romans" at the instigation of Agrippina.[110] While those of Aristobulus are otherwise undefined in 16:10b, Paul speaks of the ones of Narcissus as being "in [the] Lord" (16:11).

Paul earlier described Mary as one "who labored earnestly for you" (16:6b). Now he greets three more women whom he commends for similar hard work. "Tryphaena and Tryphosa" may be sisters whose Greek names derive from a Greek verb (τρυφάω) that involves being "delicate" or "dainty."[111] But this did not prohibit them from receiving the vigorous appellation "who labored in [the] Lord" (16:12a). The same applies to Persis to an even greater degree. She, like Mary (16:6), "labored earnestly" (πολλὰ ἐκοπίασεν, 16:12) and, like Tryphaena and Tryphosa, did so "in [the] Lord" (ἐν κυρίῳ, twice in 16:12). Persis is also the fourth person described with the adjective "loved" (16:12b; also 16:5, 8, 9).

Paul then greets a son and mother: "Rufus, the chosen one in [the] Lord, also his mother and mine" (16:13). Mark's Gospel alone records that Simon of Cyrene was the father of Alexander and Rufus (Mk 15:21). The Roman

---

[107] Note the contrast with 16:3–5, where Paul greets Prisca and Aquila by name first (16:3) and then those who meet "in their home" separately (16:5).

[108] Dunn, *Romans*, 896, citing Josephus, *War*, 2.221; Josephus, *Antiquities*, 20.12; similarly, Moo, *Romans*, 925.

[109] Dunn, *Romans*, 896.

[110] Moo, *Romans*, 925, including n. 52, citing Tacitus, *Annals*, 13.1.

[111] Moo, *Romans*, 925, n. 54, observes that children (in the same family) were often given different names from the same Greek root.

provenance of that Gospel,[112] together with the inclusion of the names of two of his sons, strongly suggests that one or both are known to the believers in Rome. Thus Paul likely greets the son of Simon of Cyrene. If so, the son of the one forcibly *chosen* to carry Jesus' cross would be able to provide a powerful witness to the crucifixion. Perhaps it is not without reason, then, that in this catalog Paul describes only him as "the chosen one in [the] Lord" (τὸν ἐκλεκτὸν ἐν κυρίῳ, 16:13; cf. 16:10a). This may subtly link him with his father or suggest "a certain prominence."[113] But it could also simply be a general description applicable to all believers as "chosen" (the plural of ἐκλεκτός in Rom 8:33, the only other use of the adjective in Romans). Paul not only knows Rufus but also expands the greeting to include "also his mother and mine" (καὶ τὴν μητέρα αὐτοῦ καὶ ἐμοῦ, 16:13). Although not providing her name, this would imply that, at some point obscure to us, she provided "mothering" care for Paul.[114]

The brevity of greetings to follow even more starkly reflects the generally decreasing length of Paul's descriptions. Paul continues: "Greet Asyncritus, Phlegon, Hermes, Patrobas, Hermas, and the brothers with them" (16:14). Here we have a series of stand-alone names followed by the more encompassing expression "brothers" for the "other Christians who met in the same house church as they did."[115] Ambrosiaster describes them as a group of men who "agreed with one another in Christ and were loyal friends."[116]

The specific names of those receiving greetings concludes in 16:15: "Greet Philologus and Julia, Nerea and his sister, also Olympus, and all the holy ones with them." The wording suggests that Paul speaks initially of "Philologus and Julia" as another married couple[117] (like "Prisca and Aquila" in 16:3 and, if the second name is feminine, "Andronicus and Junia" in 16:7) that, together with their family and/or servants, hosts yet another congregation.[118] If so, Paul knows Philologus and Julia by name, as well as Nerea, who may be their son or servant, but not Nerea's unnamed "sister." Due to the manner in which the sentence ends, it would appear that Paul knows another participant in their house church by name, Olympus. The concluding phrase, "and all the holy ones with

---

[112] See Voelz, *Mark 1:1–8:26*, 78–79; Middendorf and Schuler, *Called by the Gospel*, 267.

[113] Matera, *Romans*, 342.

[114] What such "mothering" implies remains speculative, but provides an interesting thought to ponder. Perhaps she supplied Paul with provisions for his ministry, hosted him in her home, or personally nurtured him in the faith when he was discouraged. Note how Jesus goes so far as to call believers his "mother" (Mt 12:48–50 and parallels). It also seems plausible that Paul might call her his "mother" because of her relationship to the person presumed to be her husband, Simon of Cyrene, who met Christ and carried his cross. If so, she may have become a Christian before Paul and then "mothered" the infant church by nurturing him, Rufus, and others in the faith.

[115] Moo, *Romans*, 926.

[116] Ambrosiaster, *Romans* (Bray, *Romans*, ACCS NT 6:374).

[117] Origen, *Romans* (Bray, *Romans*, ACCS NT 6:374), states: "It is possible that Philologus and Julia were married and that the others named here were their domestic servants."

[118] Moo, *Romans*, 926.

them" (καὶ τοὺς σὺν αὐτοῖς πάντας ἁγίους, 16:15) would then encompass the remainder of the congregation, as Paul deems all the Christians in the Roman churches to be "holy ones" (1:7; cf. 12:1, 13; 15:16, 25–26, 31; 16:2).

Mutual Greetings (16:16)

Paul wraps up his greetings and signals the end of the list in an all-encompassing manner. The first half of 16:16 addresses the intracongregational life of each of the various churches in Rome. Paul calls the members to "greet one another with a holy kiss." He "uses the same formula regularly with only minor variations (1 Cor 16:20; 2 Cor 13:12; 1 Thess 5:26); also 1 Pet 5:14."[119] Stählin broadens the sense by discussing the widespread secular background where "occasions of kissing are greeting, parting, making contracts, reconciliation, games etc."[120] In the OT, however, the kiss often serves as a more profound demonstration of kinship, loyalty, and unity in the faith.[121] It could even be an act of worship, as for idolaters who kissed Baal (1 Ki 19:18; cf. Hos 13:2) or those who would heed the call to kiss God's Son (Ps 2:12; cf. "righteousness and peace kiss," Ps 85:10 [MT 85:11]). The practice is also reflected in Jesus' ministry and words. In Luke's Gospel, kisses of greeting come at a Pharisee's house, from the waiting father to his prodigal son, and in the betrayal by Judas (Lk 7:45; 15:20; 22:48).

In the early church, the holy kiss seems to have been shared as a sacred act during the time of worship and prayer.[122] But one should not limit it to a specific liturgical role in the service.[123] This is especially true in this case; even

---

[119] Dunn, *Romans*, 898.

[120] G. Stählin, "φιλέω κτλ.," *TDNT* 9:121.

[121] See נָשַׁק, "to kiss," in the anointing of King Saul (1 Sam 10:1) and among (God's) people on other occasions, e.g., Gen 27:26–27; 29:11, 13; 31:28; 31:55 (MT 32:1); 33:4; 45:15; 48:10; 50:1; Ex 4:27; 18:7; 1 Sam 20:41; 2 Sam 14:33; 15:5; 19:39 (MT 19:40); 20:9; 1 Ki 19:20; cf. Song 1:2; 8:1. See also "Additional Note: Kissing" in Kruse, *Romans*, 573–74.

[122] Origen, *Romans* (Bray, *Romans*, ACCS NT 6:375), comments that "it was the custom to greet one another with a kiss after the prayers"; Ambrosiaster, *Romans* (Bray, *Romans*, ACCS NT 6:375), equates it with "the peace of Christ"; see also Cranfield, *Romans*, 796.

[123] Franzmann, *Romans*, 277–78, may be anachronistic in assuming that rites attested in later centuries were already in place in Paul's day as he wrote to the Romans in AD 55 or 56:

> The picture of an early Christian service of worship shimmers through vv. 16–20. The assembled congregation has heard Paul's apostolic Word; the service of the Word is concluded, and the solemn celebration of the Lord's Supper is about to begin. The church marks and expresses its solidarity in the Lord by the exchange of the holy kiss (cf. 1 Thess. 5:26; 2 Cor. 13:12; and especially 1 Cor. 16:20–22), which is found as a fixed part of the liturgy in 2d-century sources. Having spoken a corporate yea to the Lord, whose body and blood, given and shed for them, they are about to receive, the members of the church speak the inevitable nay to all who will not call Him Lord and exclude them from their communion. In 1 Cor. 16:22 we hear such an anathema: … Here, in the Letter to the Romans, the anathema takes the form of a stern warning against those who serve not our Lord Christ but their own appetites. (Vv. 17–20)

Cf. Winger, *Ephesians*, 10–12. This level of liturgical specificity remains speculative for the apostle's lifetime; as Maschke, *Gathered Guests*, 72, observes: "During the time of the

though these various congregations were not physically able to worship together as one, Paul certainly wants the greeting to be shared *among all the believers throughout Rome*, whenever and wherever they might come into contact with one another. Fortunately, the cultural milieu of first-century Rome allowed for this holy kiss to function appropriately and meaningfully across a much broader spectrum of contexts.[124]

After sixteen consecutive uses of the second person plural imperative form of the verb "to greet" (ἀσπάσασθε) in 16:3–16a, Paul concludes with an indicative: "All the congregations of the Christ are greeting you" (ἀσπάζονται, 16:16b). This reinforces the force of the imperatives adopted above (see the commentary on 16:3): they function as a command for those who hear them to pass on *Paul's greetings* to the people and groups listed. This final greeting goes out to all those in Rome and it comes, fittingly, from numerous other congregations of believers. The "all" probably refers inclusively to "the sphere of churches that know and support" Paul,[125] e.g., those in Corinth, Thessalonica, Berea, Philippi, and Ephesus.

What Can We Conclude?

Before drawing some conclusions about the varied recipients of this string of greetings, it also reveals an important aspect of Paul's ministry.

> Paul's reference to coworkers (vv. 3, 9; cf. v. 7) reminds us that Paul was not a "lone ranger" kind of missionary. At every point in in his ministry, Paul depended on a significant number of others who were working along with him. And if Paul needed such help, how much more do we.[126]

One can easily assemble a list of "fellow workers" (συνεργοί, 16:3; see also 16:9, 21) which would include Barnabas, John Mark, Silas, Timothy (see 16:21), Prisca and Aquila (see 16:3–5a), Luke, and numerous others.

The most exhaustive study of the Christians listed in Romans 16 comes from an article by Peter Lampe titled "The Roman Christians of Romans 16." The caveat noted at the beginning of the commentary on this section should be

---

New Testament, Christians worshiped in various ways, though little is actually recorded in Scripture."

[124] The practice prompts a number of questions. On what basis are Scripture's repeated injunctions for believers to greet one another with a holy kiss (Rom 16:16; 1 Cor 16:20; 2 Cor 13:12; 1 Thess 5:26; 1 Pet 5:14) generally dismissed without much thought? What would happen if contemporary churches took the language literally? At the very least, it seems appropriate to ponder what a comparable expression would be within one's current social norms, both in and outside of worship. The wide variety of cultures and contexts within global Christianity means a "one size fits all" answer, other than returning to the biblical practice, probably does not exist. Nevertheless, an equivalent physical sign of fellowship surely extends beyond a stiff and uncomfortable handshake combined with the rote recitation of a greeting. While it might take some time and teaching, the goal of finding and actually expressing the significance of our oneness in Christ in appropriate, relevant, and meaningful ways seems well worth the effort.

[125] Moo, *Romans*, 927.

[126] Moo, *Romans*, 927.

reinforced. We do not know whether the names listed here provide a proportional representation of the entire community of believers in Rome. But we have what we have and can at least benefit from a study of those who are named or referenced by Paul.

Jews and Gentiles

(b) E.g.,
Rom 1:16;
2:9, 10; 3:9,
29; 9:24;
10:12;
15:8–9

Based on significant references throughout the letter,[b] the most relevant grouping to analyze is that of Jew and Gentile/Greek. Paul refers explicitly to Andronicus, Junia(s), and Herodion as his Jewish "kinsmen" (16:7, 11). They, along with Aquila, as verified by Acts 18:2, form what Lampe identifies as the *only* four Jews in the list of twenty-six.[127]

Lampe does point to Jewish inscriptions in Rome bearing the names Maria (Μαρία, "Mary," 16:6, from the Hebrew "Miriam") and Rufus.[128] But he then argues that Mary must be a Gentile because Paul does not specifically identify her as Jewish.[129] Moo responds: "Lampe assumes, however, that Paul specifically identifies all the Jewish Christians that he can. ... But this is not true, since Paul does nothing to identify Prisca and Aquila; and the latter, at least, was certainly Jewish"[130] (see Acts 18:2). Thus the exclusion of Mary is unwarranted and probably incorrect. In regard to Rufus, Pelagius and Jewett identify both him and his mother as Jewish,[131] which seems very probable (see the commentary on 16:13). Additionally, BDAG, s.v. Ἀπελλῆς, indicates that the Greek name "Apelles" (16:10) was "common among Jews."[132] *This would essentially result in a doubling of Lampe's four Jews to eight.* In Paul's list of twenty-six names, Jews would then represent nearly *a third of the total.* Furthermore, if Aristobulus is correctly identified above, it seems likely that Jews were also included in the household Paul greets in 16:10.

Whether four or eight or, in all likelihood, somewhere in between, the number of Jews listed by name coincides with the depiction of the Roman believers throughout this commentary as consisting of a majority of Gentiles together with a sizable minority of Jewish Christians.[133]

House Churches

A second category of significance seeks to determine the number of congregations mentioned by Paul. "During the first two centuries the Christians of

---

[127] Lampe, "The Roman Christians of Romans 16," 224–25.

[128] Lampe, "The Roman Christians of Romans 16," 225.

[129] Lampe, "The Roman Christians of Romans 16," 225.

[130] Moo, *Romans*, 918, n. 7.

[131] Pelagius, *Romans* (Bray, *Romans*, ACCS NT 6:374), says of Rufus and his mother: "These were Jews"; see also Jewett, *Romans*, 953.

[132] This is supported by Ἀπελλῆς, "Apelles," as a variant reading in Acts 18:24; 19:1. The man is "Jewish" (Ἰουδαῖος, Acts 18:24), but in both verses the best manuscript support is for the name "Apollos."

[133] See Middendorf, *Romans 1–8*, 10–14, 17–18; in this volume, see "Who Are the 'Weak' and the 'Strong'? Addressees Again!" in the introduction to 14:1–15:13.

the city of Rome met separately in privately owned locations scattered around the capital city."[134] These different gatherings inevitably caused some unavoidable *physical separation* of the congregations from one another. But a mirror reading of the letter also points to a division in fellowship within congregations and, perhaps more prominently, between various house churches. This seems particularly evident based on the lengthy discussion of "judgments over convictions" (14:1) in 14:1–15:13. These deal with OT stipulations for clean and unclean foods, as well as the observance of holy days. Paul's climactic plea, "receive one another to yourselves, just as the Christ also received you to himself" (15:7), reinforces the notion of a rift based on a theological issue (whether the OT food and festival laws apply to the NT church) which he ardently seeks to overcome. Paul speaks to the "weak" (14:1–2; 15:1) and the "strong" (15:1) while addressing these matters, but the controverted issues involved indicate that the divisions fell generally between those adopting a Jewish perspective versus a Gentile one.[135] Thus other related topics which Paul deals with in the letter (e.g., the role of the Law, a proper definition of "Israel") may also have been disruptive and caused separations along the same general lines.

Lampe aptly titles his section on this topic "Divided Nature of the Roman Christianity—House Congregations."[136] At least three congregations are specifically identified as such in the text:

1. The congregation in the house of Prisca and Aquila (16:5)
2. Those of the household of Aristobulus (16:10)
3. Those of the household of Narcissus (16:11)

Based upon the final phrases in 16:14 and 16:15, Lampe identifies two other congregations as follows:[137]

4. The Christians around Asyncritus, Phlegon, Hermes, Patrobas, and Hermas (16:14)
5. The Christians around Philologus, Julia, Olympus, Nerea, and his sister (16:15)

Then Lampe draws this further reasonable conclusion:

> If we assume that the other fourteen individuals in the Romans 16 list belonged to none of these five crystallization points, and that they hardly [would] have belonged to only *one* further circle, the result is at least seven separate groups.[138]

---

[134] Lampe, "The Roman Christians of Romans 16," 229.

[135] Paul uses the dual description of Jew and Gentile/Greek eight times in the letter (1:16; 2:9, 10; 3:9, 29; 9:24; 10:12; 15:8–9); see also "Who Are the 'Weak' and the 'Strong'? Addressees Again!" in the introduction to 14:1–15:13.

[136] Lampe, "The Roman Christians of Romans 16," 229.

[137] Lampe, "The Roman Christians of Romans 16," 230; Hultgren, *Romans*, 699–700; and Schreiner, *Romans*, 797, also identify these first five groups.

[138] Lampe, "The Roman Christians of Romans 16," 230; Hultgren, *Romans*, 701, counters that to consider these groups " 'house churches' requires that the term be used rather broadly, if at all." But he concludes: "Insofar as they were identifiable groups that would have gathered for Christian worship at all, they can be considered house churches in a broad sense."

Again, this coincides with the identification throughout this commentary of the conflicted context Paul addresses.[139] More importantly, this seemingly insignificant and drawn-out listing of names reveals yet another tactic by which the apostle seeks to overcome all such divisions in order to bring together "all the congregations of the Christ" (16:16) in Rome.

> Reading between the lines, we can see Paul taking care to greet several Christian gatherings in Rome that may have taken different positions on the issues he discusses in chaps. 14–15. Being a bridge builder between different Christian groups and opinions is hard and painstaking work. … Today's church badly needs a new generation of bridge builders.[140]

Women and Men

If "Junia(s)" (Ιουνιαν) in 16:7 denotes a female,[141] Paul's list contains seventeen men and nine women. But the manner in which he characterizes the women in the list[142] reveals some distinction in quality over against quantity. Among the eleven people who receive explicit recognition for their service to Christ and his church beyond Paul's greeting, seven are women. These include Prisca (also mentioned before her husband [16:3–4]), Junia (well-regarded [16:7]), and then Mary, Tryphaena, Tryphosa, and Persis (all four of whom labored for the Lord [16:6, 12]). Additionally, Rufus' mother (16:13) acted as a mother to Paul.[143] He also gives a glowing recommendation regarding Phoebe's service in 16:1–2: "a servant of the congregation which is in Cenchreae" (διάκονον τῆς ἐκκλησίας τῆς ἐν Κεγχρεαῖς) and "benefactor." On the other hand, Paul adds a direct word of commendation for service to only four men: Aquila (16:3–4), Andronicus (16:7), Urbanus (16:9), and Apelles (16:10).

This surely sends a twofold message. First, Origen recognizes that "Paul is teaching here that women too ought to work for the churches of God."[144] These women were not ordained pastors, nor was Junia(s) an apostle (see the commentary on 16:7). As Moo explains: "Nothing Paul says in this passage (even in v. 7) conflicts with limitations" on the service of women required by passages such as 1 Tim 2:8–15.[145] While Scripture prohibits the ordination of women and their service in the pastoral office, it does recognize the significance of their labors in other appropriate roles. Schreiner strikes a good balance in this regard:

---

[139] Middendorf, *Romans 1–8*, 17–18; in this volume, see "Universal Application Has Contextual Implications" in the introduction to Romans 9–16 and "Who Are the 'Weak' and the 'Strong'? Addressees Again!" in the introduction to 14:1–15:13.

[140] Wright, "Romans," 766.

[141] Ambiguity remains on the matter of gender; see the first textual note and the commentary on 16:7.

[142] While this author does not agree with all the conclusions, a comprehensive study is conducted by Mathew, *Women in the Greetings of Romans 16.1–16*.

[143] Lampe, "The Roman Christians of Romans 16," 222.

[144] Origen, *Romans* (Bray, *Romans*, ACCS NT 6:371).

[145] Moo, *Romans*, 927.

One should scarcely conclude from the reference to Junia [reading the name in 16:7 as feminine] and the other women coworkers named here that women exercised authority over men contrary to the Pauline admonition in 1 Tim. 2:12. We see evidence that women functioned as early Christian missionaries, and it may have been the case that they concentrated especially on other women.[146]

Second, as Rom 16:1–16 exemplifies, such women are then to be recognized and commended for their dedicated labors. In contrast to men who may not have labored so industriously, Chrysostom poses the following profound thoughts while commenting on Mary in 16:6:

How can it be that yet another woman is honored and proclaimed victorious! We men are put to shame yet again. Or rather, we are not merely put to shame; we have a different honor conferred on us. For it is an honor to have such women as these among us, though we are put to shame in that we are left so far behind them.[147]

Status in Society

Lampe's study of the names in Romans 16 leads to two further assertions. While these seem less theologically relevant, they are significant for sociological studies and for ascertaining trends in the church of the first century and, perhaps, throughout time.[148] A comparison with exhaustive lists covering the entire city of Rome leads to the conjectural assertion that approximately fourteen out of the twenty-six people in 16:3–15 were "presumably not born in Rome itself."[149] Thus *over half were immigrants* to the city.

Second, based upon the typical usage of names in first-century Rome, Lampe contends that "more than two-thirds of the people for whom we can make a probability statement have an affinity to slave origins."[150] In comparison to a study of the population of the city as a whole at the time, "the social profile of the church indeed seems to mirror the profile of the entire society."[151]

---

[146] Schreiner, *Romans*, 797; Käsemann, *Romans*, 413, speaks of the advantages of husband-and-wife "missionary couples" ("Prisca and Aquila," 16:3, and perhaps "Philologus and Julia," 16:15): "The wife can have access to the women's areas, which would not be generally accessible to the husband."

[147] Chrysostom, *Homilies on Romans*, 31 (Bray, *Romans*, ACCS NT 6:371–72).

[148] See Porter and Land, *Paul and His Social Relations*.

[149] Lampe, "The Roman Christians of Romans 16," 227.

[150] Lampe, "The Roman Christians of Romans 16," 228.

[151] Lampe, "The Roman Christians of Romans 16," 229; Moo, *Romans*, 918, concurs that a majority are Gentiles and slaves or freedmen.

A Word of Warning
and Greetings from Corinth

Translation

16 **¹⁷But I urge you, brothers, to watch out for those who cause the dissensions and the stumblings contrary to the teaching which you yourselves learned, and keep away from them. ¹⁸For such ones are not serving as slaves to our Lord Christ, but to their own belly, and through their smooth speech and eloquence they are deceiving the hearts of the naïve. ¹⁹For your responsive hearing has reached to all. Therefore I rejoice over you, but I desire you to be wise toward the good and innocent toward the evil. ²⁰And the God of peace will crush Satan under your feet suddenly. The grace of our Lord Jesus [is] with you.**

²¹Timothy, my fellow worker, greets you. Also Lucius and Jason and Sosipater, my kinsmen [greet you]. ²²I, Tertius, the one who wrote this letter, greets you in [the] Lord. ²³Gaius, my host and [the host] of the whole church, greets you. Erastus, the treasurer of the city, and Quartus, the brother, greet you.

[²⁴The grace of our Lord Jesus Christ (is) with all of you. Amen.]

Textual Notes

16:17 παρακαλῶ δὲ ὑμᾶς, ἀδελφοί, σκοπεῖν—For the verb παρακαλέω, "urge," see the first textual note and the commentary on 12:1. It takes the complementary infinitive[1] σκοπεῖν, "to watch out for." The verb σκοπέω means "to pay careful attention to, *look (out) for*" (BDAG). Outside the NT, it carries the negative nuance of "to look at critically."[2] "Apart from Luke 11:35 it occurs only in Paul in the NT (and only twice in the LXX)—2 Cor 4:18; Gal 6:1; Phil 2:4; and 3:17."[3]

τοὺς … ποιοῦντας—This definite participle serves as the object of the infinitive σκοπεῖν, indicating the people of whom the Roman Christians are to beware. The common verb ποιέω normally means "to make" or "do" (see the second textual note on 7:15). The specific nuance in this context (with the objects discussed in the next two textual notes) is rendered in English by "*create*" (BDAG, 2 c) or "cause."[4] Though somewhat distant, the accusative plural definite article τούς earlier in the verse goes with ποιοῦντας, rendering it a substantival participle:[5] "those who cause."

---

[1] See Wallace, *Greek Grammar*, 598–99.

[2] E. Fuchs, "σκοπέω," *TDNT* 7:414–15.

[3] Dunn, *Romans*, 902.

[4] Moo, *Romans*, 930; Dunn, *Romans*, 902.

[5] See Wallace, *Greek Grammar*, 619–21.

τὰς διχοστασίας—The noun διχοστασία refers to "the state of being in factious opposition, *dissension*" (BDAG). Elsewhere in Scripture, it appears only in the list of the works of the flesh in Gal 5:20. The form here is accusative plural.

τὰ σκάνδαλα—For σκάνδαλον as "stumbling," see the third textual note on 9:33 (see also 11:9; 14:13). For its use here BDAG suggests "an action or circumstance that leads one to act contrary to a proper course of action or set of beliefs, *temptation to sin, enticement* to apostasy, false belief" (BDAG, 2). Lenski contends that the word "always designates what is fatal" and translates the plural here as "deathtraps."[6] However, he references only 9:33 and 11:9, overlooking 14:13, where that is not the case. The general sense of "stumblings" better represents all the uses in the letter.

παρὰ τὴν διδαχὴν ἣν ὑμεῖς ἐμάθετε—The preposition παρά with the accusative occasionally serves as a "marker of that which does not correspond to what is expected, *against, contrary to*" (BDAG, C 6). In the Gospels the noun διδαχή often refers to the "teaching" of Jesus (e.g., Mt 7:28; 22:33; Mk 1:22, 27). Paul uses it to denote the Christian faith in Rom 6:17; Titus 1:9 (see also 2 Jn 9–10). The pronoun ὑμεῖς is emphatic with the second person plural verb ἐμάθετε, the aorist of μανθάνω, "to learn," hence "you yourselves learned."

ἐκκλίνετε ἀπ᾽ αὐτῶν—For the verb ἐκκλίνω, see the first textual note on 3:12, where it means "turn away" from God. Here the idea is "to keep away from, *steer clear of*" certain persons (BDAG, 1). The notion of avoidance is reinforced by the prepositional phrase ἀπ᾽ αὐτῶν, "from them."

16:18 οἱ γὰρ τοιοῦτοι—The correlative adjective τοιοῦτος used substantivally can denote "*such a person*; ... a definite individual with special characteristics ... or ... any bearer of certain definite qualities" (BDAG, c α ‭ℵ‬) and then, in the plural, "such persons."

τῷ κυρίῳ ἡμῶν Χριστῷ οὐ δουλεύουσιν—Earlier Paul used δουλεύω, "serve as a slave," for formerly being an unbaptized slave to sin (6:6), and in the positive sense of the baptized believer serving "in [the] renewal of the Spirit" (7:6), serving the Law of God (7:25), and serving Christ (12:11; 14:18). Here the service would have been "to our Lord Christ" if the verb had not been negated (οὐ).

ἀλλὰ τῇ ἑαυτῶν κοιλίᾳ—The noun κοιλία means "*belly, stomach*" (BDAG, 1 b), thus "but to their own belly." Numerous self-centered appetites may be included; see the commentary.

διὰ τῆς χρηστολογίας καὶ εὐλογίας—The noun χρηστολογία, which occurs only here in the Greek Bible, refers to "*smooth, plausible speech*" (BDAG). The second noun, εὐλογία, normally communicates positive notions of "*praise*" or "*blessing*" (BDAG, 1 and 3). However, εὐλογία can also carry "an extended sense of 'fine speaking'" in order to describe "words that are well chosen but untrue, *false eloquence, flattery*" (BDAG, 2). The notion of "false" is not in the word itself. Both terms, in and of themselves, depict oral skills which can be used for good or evil, but the context here indicates sinister

---

[6] Lenski, *Romans*, 915.

intent. The definite article τῆς functions as a personal possessive pronoun.[7] Thus the translation here is "through their smooth speech and eloquence."

ἐξαπατῶσιν—The verb ἐξαπατάω means "to cause someone to accept false ideas about someth[ing], *deceive*" (BDAG). In Paul's usage the subject who deceives can be "sin" (Rom 7:11), "the serpent" (2 Cor 11:3; similarly, 1 Tim 2:14), oneself (1 Cor 3:18), or another (2 Thess 2:3).

τὰς καρδίας τῶν ἀκάκων—The plural of the adjective ἄκακος (an *alpha* privative [α-] prefixed to κακός, literally, "not bad"), denotes those who are "*innocent, guileless*" (BDAG). The possessive genitive τῶν ἀκάκων indicates that "the hearts" (τὰς καρδίας) being deceived are theirs. The warning may be directed toward the "unsuspecting," but "naïve" seems to capture the overall sense best.

16:19 ἡ γὰρ ὑμῶν ὑπακοή—For the noun ὑπακοή here, as in 1:5; 15:18; and 16:26, as similarly with the cognate verb ὑπακούω in 6:17 and 10:16, the translation "obedience" is inadequate since it pertains to the Law and a response to the Gospel is in view. See the commentary on 1:5 and 6:17 and, especially, the extended discussion in the commentary on 10:16–17. "Responsive hearing" works well as it allows the context to determine the specific content and response; see the commentary.

εἰς πάντας ἀφίκετο—The verb ἀφίκετο is an aorist indicative of the deponent ἀφικνέομαι, "to reach," which appears only here in the NT. The statement "your responsive hearing has reached to all" means that "all" have heard that the Roman Christians responded to the Good News by believing it (cf. 10:10, 14–17). While "all" is something of a hyperbole (as is "all the world" in 10:18), Rome was the capital of the empire; due to its central location and influence, a very large portion of the civilized world would have heard of their response of faith.

ἐφ᾽ ὑμῖν οὖν χαίρω—The only other instances of the verb χαίρω, "rejoice," in Romans are in 12:12, 15. The verb can take the preposition ἐπί with the dative (here ὑμῖν, "over you") to indicate the cause or basis of rejoicing (also, e.g., Lk 1:14; Acts 15:31; 1 Cor 16:17). ἐφ᾽ is the abbreviated and softened form of the preposition ἐπί before a vowel with a rough breathing mark, ὑμῖν.

εἰς τὸ ἀγαθόν ... εἰς τὸ κακόν—Both uses of the preposition εἰς here convey the same meaning but in regard to antithetical terms (ἀγαθόν ... κακόν). Moo suggests with "respect to,"[8] but better is Cranfield: "in the direction of, for the purpose of."[9] The article in both phrases "is equivalent to a relative pronoun in *force*":[10] "toward *that which is* ..." The more literal translation is retained: "toward the good ... toward the evil."

ἀκεραίους—The literal sense of the adjective ἀκέραιος (an *alpha* privative [α-] prefixed to a word derived from κεράννυμι, "to mix, mingle") is "unmixed," but in the

---

[7] See Wallace, *Greek Grammar*, 211–12.

[8] Moo, *Romans*, 932, n. 36.

[9] Cranfield, *Romans*, 802.

[10] Wallace, *Greek Grammar*, 213, speaking in general about the use of the article as equivalent to a relative pronoun.

NT (elsewhere only Mt 10:16; Phil 2:15) it always has a figurative sense: "*pure, inno-cent*" (BDAG).

16:20 συντρίψει—This is the future indicative of the verb συντρίβω, which here means "to overcome by subduing completely, *annihilate, crush* enemies" (BDAG, 3). Elsewhere in the NT it refers to breaking earthenware vessels (Mk 14:3; Rev 2:27), shackles (Mk 5:4), bones (Jn 19:36), and a reed (Mt 12:20), and to a demon beating the one whom he possesses (Lk 9:39).

ἐν τάχει—Here the preposition ἐν serves as a "marker denoting kind and man-ner, esp[ecially] functioning as an auxiliary in periphrasis for adverbs" (BDAG, 11), so the phrase is best rendered adverbially. In regard to the noun τάχος, BDAG places this verse under "a relatively brief time subsequent to another point of time, ... *soon, in a short time*" (BDAG, 2). But it belongs better with the initial definition that puts the "focus on speed of an activity or event, *speed, quickness, swiftness, haste*" (BDAG, 1). A comparable instance of ἐν τάχει in the LXX is in the warning of Deut 11:17, where it likely means "perish *quickly.*" Moo gives the meaning "quickly" for the phrase here,[11] but translates it with the conventional "soon"[12] (also ESV, NASB). Literally the phrase means "with suddenness," but the adverbial use of ἐν suggests "suddenly" or "swiftly."[13]

ἡ χάρις τοῦ κυρίου ἡμῶν Ἰησοῦ μεθ᾽ ὑμῶν—The verb to be supplied is the indic-ative "is," rather than the imperative "be," as also in 11:36; 15:33; 16:24. See the first textual note on 11:36 and the commentary on 16:20.

16:21 ἀσπάζεται—For ἀσπάζομαι, "greet," also in 16:22–23, see the textual note and the commentary on 16:3.

ὁ συνεργός—For "*fellow-worker*" (BDAG), see also 16:3, 9.

οἱ συγγενεῖς—For "kinsman," meaning "a Jewish person" when spoken by Paul, see the fifth textual note on 9:3; see also in 16:7, 11.

16:22 ὁ γράψας τὴν ἐπιστολήν—For the sense of this aorist participle of γράφω, "write," see the commentary. The definite article τήν has the deictic force of a demonstrative:[14] "*this* letter."

16:23 ὁ ξένος μου καὶ ὅλης τῆς ἐκκλησίας—The noun ξένος normally describes a "*stranger, alien*" (BDAG, 2 a), but then by extension can depict a "*host, one who extends hospitality and thus treats the stranger as a guest*" (BDAG, 2 c). Two objective genitive constructions follow (μου and ὅλης τῆς ἐκκλησίας), literally, "the host of me and of the whole church," but the statement is best rendered in English by "my host and [the host] of the whole church."

ὁ οἰκονόμος τῆς πόλεως—The noun οἰκονόμος by itself commonly refers to a "manager of a household or estate, *(house) steward, manager*" (BDAG, 1, citing Lk 12:42; 16:1, 3, 8; 1 Cor 4:2; Gal 4:2). Since the manager here is τῆς πόλεως, "of the

---

[11] Moo, *Romans*, 933, n. 41.

[12] Moo, *Romans*, 928.

[13] Lenski, *Romans*, 923.

[14] Wallace, *Greek Grammar*, 221.

city," BDAG gives "public treasurer, *treasurer*" (BDAG, 2; also ESV, NASB, NRSV). See the commentary.

16:24 ἡ χάρις τοῦ κυρίου ἡμῶν Ἰησοῦ μετὰ πάντων ὑμῶν. ἀμήν—This verse, with the indicative "is" supplied (see the third textual note on 16:20), reads: "The grace of our Lord Jesus Christ [is] with all of you. Amen." Moo concludes that this blessing "is omitted in the earliest and most important MSS (P[46], ℵ, B, the secondary Alexandrian uncial C, P[61], 0150, and a few minuscules) and is clearly a later addition to the text."[15] How did it come to be added? First, most of "the authorities which include the grace [i.e., the benediction] as 16.24 are those which have the doxology [16:25–27] at the end of chapter 14 or else omit it altogether."[16] Metzger speculates that several so-called "Western" texts (e.g., D, G) then "transfer the benediction" of 16:20b to after 16:23 (where it is later numbered as 16:24), thus preventing the greetings of 16:21–23 "from having the appearance of being an afterthought."[17] The conclusion that 16:24 "is secondary may be regarded as certain."[18] See also the excursus "Textual Criticism and the End of Romans" following the commentary on 15:23–33.

Commentary

A Word of Warning and a Prevailing Promise (16:17–20)

In contrast to the many seamless connections throughout Romans, the warning contained in 16:17–20 "abruptly separates the greetings in vv. 3–16 and those in vv. 21–23," and some interpreters find "nothing in the context or in the preceding epistle to explain its sharpness."[19] A number of suggestions attempt to explain this. The simplest, knee-jerk reaction by critics is to omit 16:17–20 entirely. Jewett, for example, titles this passage "The Church's Campaign against Heretics" and (as he doubts the genuineness of other Pauline epistles) he asserts that it was added later by "the group that produced the Pastoral Epistles toward the end of the first century."[20] However, the parallel warnings evident in other epistles by this apostle, including the Pastorals, support the authenticity of Rom 16:17–20. Moreover, "there is no textual basis for omitting the verses"[21] or for postulating that they are a later addition.

Two other observations lend further credibility to this brief section. First, "structurally it is most closely parallel to Paul's practice of appending a final paragraph in his own hand."[22] Thus it seems most likely that the apostle

---

[15] Moo, *Romans*, 933, n. 1.

[16] Cranfield, *Romans*, 6.

[17] Metzger, *A Textual Commentary on the Greek New Testament*, 540.

[18] Cranfield, *Romans*, 808.

[19] Käsemann, *Romans*, 416–17.

[20] Jewett, *Romans*, 985, 988.

[21] Moo, *Romans*, 928; see also Matera, *Romans*, 343.

[22] Dunn, *Romans*, 901, citing 1 Cor 16:21–24; Gal 6:11–18; Col 4:18; 2 Thess 3:17; see also Cranfield, *Romans*, 797. Lenski, *Romans*, 914, shows "how naturally this admonition flows from the preceding salutations" and disagrees with the rather dramatic suppositions of others

authenticated the letter in that way, after which Tertius resumed his task as an amanuensis and recorded Paul's final words (16:21–27; see 16:22).[23] Capes, Reeves, and Richards observe that an "abrupt or stern" tone appears regularly "whenever Paul personally picked up the pen (1 Cor 16:21–24; Gal 6:11–18; Col 4:18)."[24] Second, Paul often concludes his letters with similar "exhortations and warnings (cf. 1 Cor. 16:13–14; 2 Cor. 13:11b; Col. 4:17; cf. also Gal. 6:12–15; Eph. 6:10–17)."[25]

The Warning (16:17–18)

Context (or Lack Thereof)

What prompts the specific warning to the Romans in 16:17–18? In the immediate context, perhaps "the greetings Paul conveys from 'all the churches' (v. 16b) sparked his concern about the potential of the false teachers who plagued those churches to disrupt the Roman community also."[26] The crushing of Satan under their feet (16:20) alludes to the eschatological end of such deceivers who, knowingly or not, would carry out the devil's schemes in the congregations. But does Paul target it against any person or group in particular?

Since the warning appears to come out of the blue, this poses a difficult question to answer. It seems unwise to look for its basis in the disagreements discussed in 14:1–15:13. There, as Paul strives for unity (e.g., 14:1, 7–8, 19; 15:2, 6–7), a conciliatory tone dominates. Much earlier, 3:8 briefly references those who are slandering Paul's teaching (see the commentary there), but that seems quite remote from chapter 16. Dodd points to those "who practised and defended immoral license in the name of Christian liberty" (cf. 1 Corinthians 5–6).[27] Dunn similarly refers to "the morally dangerous social conditions in Rome (cf. 13:12–14)."[28] Käsemann offers a related contention "that we have here an early battle against heresy which, as in 2 Corinthians 10–13 and Philippians 3, is directed against libertinizing and gnosticizing Jewish-Christians,"[29] but narrowing the focus to such a precise group is speculative. Sanday and Headlam,

---

that it resulted from " 'a sudden flaming impulse breaking through the reticence hitherto maintained' (L[ietzmann]). Paul suddenly took the pen from the hand of Tertius, to whom he was dictating, dashed down these admonitions, then handed the pen back and again dictated with calmness. Paul becomes a rather erratic, impulsive person." See Hans Lietzmann, *Einführung in die Textgeschichte der Paulusbriefe: An die Römer* (4th ed.; Handbuch zum Neuen Testament 8; Tübingen: Mohr, 1933), 127.

[23] Cranfield, *Romans*, 797, n. 5, observes: "That the secretary should take the pen again and add a postscript, after the sender had authenticated the letter by writing the subscriptio in his own hand, was quite a normal practice in the composition of ancient Greek letters."

[24] Capes, Reeves, and Richards, *Rediscovering Paul*, 73.

[25] Moo, *Romans*, 928. See further parallels cited below in "Concluding Reflections on Romans 16:17–18."

[26] Moo, *Romans*, 933; see also Cranfield, *Romans*, 798.

[27] Dodd, *Romans*, 243.

[28] Dunn, *Romans*, 904.

[29] Käsemann, *Romans*, 418.

following a number of church fathers, suggest that Paul opposes "the teaching of the Judaizers"[30] (cf. Galatians), a party on the other theological extreme, but again, such an identification may be too limited, and it is an inappropriate label in any case.[31]

All of these theories remain hypothetical and without any solid basis in Romans. Therefore it seems best to leave the answer unspecified and open-ended. Paul's warning stands applicable to whatever self-serving and misleading teachers might be on the horizon. Franzmann expands upon this view as follows:

> Apparently they have not yet appeared in Rome; the fact that the warning appears so late in the letter is evidence of that. If they were an immediate threat, we should expect that Paul would have dealt with them in the body of his letter. The language of the warning is, moreover, quite general; Paul is forewarning against a possible attack, not meeting a specific attack as in his Letter to the Galatians.[32]

False Content (16:17)

"But I urge you, brothers, to watch out for those who cause the dissensions and the stumblings contrary to the teaching which you yourselves learned, and keep away from them" (16:17). The verb "urge" (παρακαλῶ) serves to introduce an authoritative plea (as also in 12:1; 15:30). Paul issues this warning regarding false teachers whom he defines as schismatics who cause offense; their dissensions fracture the church's unity and cause some Christians to fall from faith. Both of the abstract nouns, "the dissensions" and "the stumblings" (τὰς διχοστασίας καὶ τὰ σκάνδαλα), have the definite article (so they might refer to particular errors and downfalls), but they are also both plural. Thus Paul's words are not limited to a specific cause at a certain time.

One could feasibly take the entire statement "contrary to the teaching which you yourselves learned" (παρὰ τὴν διδαχὴν ἣν ὑμεῖς ἐμάθετε) as asserting that causing dissensions and stumblings, in and of itself, stands contrary to the Christian faith the Romans had learned. That would certainly be an appropriate Pauline thought; earlier he had admonished: "Judge this: not to place a [cause for] stumbling [πρόσκομμα] or offense [σκάνδαλον] to [your] brother" (14:13). But in this context, the divisions and offenses are being caused by doctrines promulgated by *false teachers*. Therefore Christians who respond by separating

---

[30] Sanday and Headlam, *Romans*, 430; so also Ambrosiaster, *Romans*; Chrysostom, *Homilies on Romans*, 32; Theodoret of Cyrus, *Romans*; Pelagius, *Romans* (Bray ACCS NT 6:376–77).

[31] The central concern of the Jewish apostle Paul is right belief (by Jews and Gentiles) in the Christ. Das, *Galatians*, 16, properly argues:

> The term "Judaizers" must also be abandoned. "Judaizers" wrongly gives the impression that Paul's struggle was somehow with Judaism. The letter to the Galatians is a testimony to a struggle between two different (and ultimately incompatible) Jewish understandings of *Christ's* Gospel.

[32] Franzmann, *Romans*, 278–79; similarly, Cranfield, *Romans*, 802.

from them are not acting "contrary to the teaching"; instead, they do so in order to remain faithful to the Good News they received.

Hoerber's exhaustive study of the grammar of 16:17 concludes that the phrase "contrary to the teaching" (παρὰ τὴν διδαχήν) goes with "the divisions and offenses."[33] Thus

> St. Paul is admonishing the Christians at Rome to avoid, not all who cause divisions and offenses, but those who cause the divisions and offenses contrary to the teaching—not contrary to any teaching, but to the teaching which they learned from him and the other apostles.[34]

What, then, is "the teaching" (τὴν διδαχήν)? Note that since Paul includes the definite article, he does not refer to "a/any teaching"; neither does he use plural forms to speak of "the teachings." Hoerber points out the parallelism between this statement and 6:17:[35] "But thanks [be] to God, because you were slaves of sin, but you responded from [the] heart to [the] form of *teaching* [τύπον διδαχῆς] into which you were handed over." The statement "contrary to the teaching which you yourselves learned" (παρὰ τὴν διδαχὴν ἣν ὑμεῖς ἐμάθετε) in 16:17, with the definite article and singular noun τὴν διδαχήν, "the teaching," is parallel to the phrase "[the] form of teaching" (τύπον διδαχῆς) in 6:17.[36] Furthermore, the clause "into which you were handed over" (εἰς ὃν παρεδόθητε) in 6:17 stands equivalent to the clause "which you yourselves learned" (ἣν ὑμεῖς ἐμάθετε) in 16:17. A number of other commonalities with the latter portion of Romans 6 identified below solidify the close connection between the passages.[37]

The singular "teaching" (διδαχή) in 6:17 refers to the "impartation of the Good News" from God, which is passively received in faith by those whom God, working through the "power" of the Gospel itself (1:16), enables to believe it.[38] In parallel fashion, the singular "the teaching" (τὴν διδαχήν) in 16:17 similarly *refers to the saving message of Jesus Christ*. It encompasses "the divine realities and facts concerned with our salvation,"[39] which Paul himself has expounded upon so profoundly thus far in the letter (see "Concluding

---

[33] Hoerber, *A Grammatical Study of Romans 16, 17*, 31.

[34] Hoerber, *A Grammatical Study of Romans 16, 17*, 31.

[35] Hoerber, *A Grammatical Study of Romans 16, 17*, 31.

[36] Moo, *Romans*, 930, n. 21; Bruce, *Romans*, 263, also recognizes the connection with 6:17, but unfortunately obscures it in translation: "The same word, *didachē*, is translated 'teaching' there and 'doctrine' here."

[37] See "Improper Motivation and Deceptive Tactics (16:18)" below.

[38] Middendorf, *Romans 1–8*, 500; see 499–502; Franzmann, *Romans*, 279, describes "that 'standard of teaching'" in 6:17 similarly as "that Gospel which set them free from sin."

[39] Lenski, *Romans*, 916; later (917–18) he adds: "Paul's injunction is not to keep away only from total rejecters of the gospel—what Christians ever needed such a warning?" Unfortunately, those who reject the Gospel often are "deceiving" (16:18) and can be identified as false teachers only by carefully comparing their teaching to the Scriptures. Therefore Paul's admonishment was needed by the first-century Christians in Rome and Galatia, as well as in the Reformation era, and is equally incumbent today.

Reflections on Romans 16:17–18" below). Therefore, "it is those who cause divisions and occasions of stumbling contrary to the truth of the gospel against whom Paul warns."[40] Here one need think only of the context of Galatians years earlier and the furor with which Paul opens that letter (Gal 1:6–10).[41]

If divisive pseudo-teachers arise in Rome or elsewhere, Paul's imperative ἐκκλίνετε (Rom 16:17) means that Christians are to "turn away" or "keep away" from them. "The language is characteristic of wisdom exhortation,"[42] but not limited to that genre.[43] The present tense of the imperative ἐκκλίνετε need not imply that the activity of "turning away" is currently going on in Rome, but it certainly calls for an ongoing readiness to "keep away."[44]

Improper Motivation and Deceptive Tactics (16:18)

Then Paul explains why: "For such ones are not serving as slaves [δουλεύουσιν] to our Lord Christ, but to their own belly, and through their smooth speech and eloquence they are deceiving the hearts of the naïve" (16:18). The notion of serving as a slave either to sin or to righteousness was also taken up repeatedly in the latter half of Romans 6 (see the commentary on 6:15–19). The positive sense of slavery to God/Christ has also been expressed repeatedly elsewhere (e.g., δοῦλος, "slave," 1:1; δουλεύω, "serve as a slave," 7:6, 25; 12:11; 14:18).

With such teachers, however, another master is in charge (cf. "Satan" in 16:20). Utilizing "standard polemical language in the Jewish world of Paul's day,"[45] Paul accuses such false teachers of serving as slaves "to their own belly" (τῇ ἑαυτῶν κοιλίᾳ, 16:18). While the expression could apply literally to gluttony, that particular sin surely does not fit the discussion of quarrels over convictions about foods in 14:1–15:13.[46] This provides further evidence for treating the matters addressed in the two sections separately. Instead, Paul's comparable description in Phil 3:19, "whose God [is] the[ir] belly" (ὧν ὁ θεὸς ἡ κοιλία), indicates this broader concept:

---

[40] Cranfield, *Romans*, 798.

[41] See Das, *Galatians*, 97–114. Galatians likely dates to AD 48 (Das, *Galatians*, 47), whereas Romans was written seven or eight years later, in AD 55 or 56 (Middendorf, *Romans 1–8*, 5–7).

[42] Dunn, *Romans*, 902, citing, e.g., Pss 34:14 (MT 34:15; LXX 33:15); 37:27 (LXX 36:27); Prov 1:15; 3:7; 4:15; 14:16.

[43] Other biblical parallels may include Num 16:26; 1 Sam 15:6; Job 1:1; 28:28; Ps 119:115; 139:19; Is 52:11; 2 Thess 3:6; 2 Tim 3:2–5; Titus 3:2, 9; 1 Pet 3:11.

[44] Wallace, *Greek Grammar*, 721, summarizes that the present imperative "is used for the most part for general precepts—i.e., for habits that should characterize one's attitudes and behavior—rather than in specific situations."

[45] Wright, "Romans," 764.

[46] Against Barrett, *Romans*, 285; apparently also Pelagius, *Romans* (Bray, *Romans*, ACCS NT 6:377).

"Serve one's own belly" is used in the sense of serving oneself, of being the willing slave of one's egotism, of that walking according to the flesh and having one's life determined by the flesh, to which 8.4 and 5 refer.[47]

On the one hand, Paul tells the Philippians that personal motivations do not really matter to him, so long as Christ is being proclaimed (Phil 1:15–18). But when the *content* of what is taught is "contrary to the teaching" of the Gospel (Rom 16:17), it will inevitably "create disunity in the Christian community."[48] Thus such teachers attempt to operate *within* the churches. They may view themselves as belonging there and even as saving or restoring the true faith. But Paul vehemently opposes them whenever they advocate positions contrary to the Good News of Christ. Biblical examples include the teachers from Judea in the intrachurch dispute laid out in Acts 15:1–5; the teachers of "a different gospel" (ἕτερον εὐαγγέλιον, Gal 1:6) in Galatia;[49] but also Peter, who was not acting in line with the Gospel in Antioch (Gal 2:11–14);[50] and the false apostles in 2 Corinthians 10–12.

Paul then describes how such teachers misuse the gift of language. Neither Greek term that he uses in the phrase "through their smooth speech and eloquence" (διὰ τῆς χρηστολογίας καὶ εὐλογίας, 16:18) is negative in and of itself (see the fourth textual note on 16:18). But contextually God's good gift of verbal proficiency has been perverted by the desire and ability to "deceive" (ἐξαπατάω). In 7:11, Paul uses the same verb to describe how sin "deceived" him through the commandment, which, like the gift of speech, is "good" (ἀγαθή, 7:12), but through it sin was able to deceive and kill him (7:11). Since Paul was still "fleshly, having been sold and still under sin" even as a believer (7:14), he remained susceptible to similar deceptions, and so do we.[51] While human belly-servers are the ones who "are deceiving" (16:18), the verb may suggest a demonic origin of their teaching, since Paul names "the serpent" (ὁ ὄφις) as the one who originally "deceived" Eve (ἐξηπάτησεν) in 2 Cor 11:3 (similarly, 1 Tim 2:14), and Paul cites that primordial event to warn the church in Corinth similarly to beware of anyone who "proclaims another Jesus [ἄλλον Ἰησοῦν] whom we did not proclaim" or "another gospel" (εὐαγγέλιον ἕτερον, 2 Cor 11:4). During the church age this is an ever-present danger, but it will end when the deceiver is vanquished forever (Rom 16:20).

---

[47] Cranfield, *Romans*, 800.

[48] Moo, *Romans*, 930.

[49] Das, *Galatians*, 16, describes the Galatian context well:

The letter to the Galatians is a testimony to a struggle between two different (and ultimately incompatible) Jewish understandings of *Christ's* Gospel. Of course, Paul would ultimately deny the label "Christian" to the outsiders at Galatia (1:8–9). They nevertheless understood their message as the "Gospel" of Jesus Christ."

[50] See Das, *Galatians*, 196–215.

[51] Throughout 7:14–25 Paul is speaking about his condition after his conversion to faith in Christ, and thus we Christians today live in the same situation; see the excursus "Who Is the 'I' in Romans 7:14–25? Christian or Non-Christian?" following the commentary on 7:14–25.

Dunn connects "the naïve" (the plural of ἄκακος) who are being deceived here in 16:18 with "the simple" in wisdom literature (e.g., ἄκακος in LXX Prov 1:4, 22; 8:5; 14:15; 21:11, translating the Hebrew פֶּתִי), but the more derogatory nuance in Proverbs ("gullible") does not apply.[52] While "the innocent" provides a possible translation of τῶν ἀκάκων in Rom 16:18, the apostle's point here does not emphasize theological innocence.[53] Rather, "the naïve" (ESV) captures the overall sense well. As Bruce describes it, Paul warns the Roman believers not to be "so 'simple-minded' as to swallow whatever is offered."[54] He will elaborate this in the next verse ("wise toward the good and innocent toward the evil"); see "Paul's Positive Desire (16:19)" below.

Concluding Reflections on Romans 16:17–18

We lack further evidence from within or outside the letter about any specific historical context in Paul's day that may have warranted this admonition. Wright summarizes its role in this way:

> This short interjection, coming between the greetings to friends in Rome and the greetings from friends with Paul, functions rhetorically like the sudden reminder that breaks into a family farewell scene: … It is clearly heartfelt; Paul knows that troublemakers will surface in any church. … His concern is to warn against any attempt to pull church members away from the central tenets of the faith.[55]

Consequently 16:17–18 may be compared to similar broad warnings for the church that may appear before a departure, such as that of Jesus when he sends out the seventy-two (Lk 10:3; cf. Mt 7:15) and Paul's farewell to the Ephesian elders in Acts 20:29–31. Analogous admonitions to stand firm in the apostolic faith and thwart those who would divide and mislead believers appear commonly near the end of many NT letters.[a] Elsewhere in his writings, Paul also vigorously and vehemently opposes those who teach contrary to the Gospel, typically excoriating them with language that is quite harsh.[b] Even though such spiritually destructive challenges have not yet arisen in Rome, Paul warns the believers how to respond when (not if) false teachers arrive among them.

The general, timeless, open-ended nature of Paul's admonition here suggests its ongoing relevance for the church in all times and places. That said, a

(a) E.g., 1 Cor 16:13, 22; Eph 6:11–12; 2 Thess 3:14; 1 Tim 6:3–5; 2 Tim 4:3–4, 15; Titus 3:10–11; Heb 13:9; 1 Pet 5:8; 2 Pet 2:1; 3:1–3, 17; 1 Jn 5:21; 2 Jn 10–11; Jude 18–19

(b) E.g., Gal 1:6–9; Phil 3:2–3; 1 Tim 1:3–11; 2 Tim 2:16–18, 23–26; 3:1–9; Titus 1:10–16; 3:9–11

---

[52] In some passages "the simple" may receive divine wisdom (Prov 1:4; 8:5), but in others they are in the same category as mockers who delight in mocking and fools who hate divine knowledge (Prov 1:22). See "פֶּתִי, 'Gullible Person' " in Steinmann, *Proverbs*, 30.

[53] Cf. Rom 14:14–15. The innocence of Eden was lost in the fall but is regained in Christ. In 2 Cor 11:2–3 Paul portrays the church which was in danger of being deceived as "a pure virgin" (παρθένον ἀγνήν) with a "sincere and pure devotion to Christ" (τῆς ἁπλότητος [καὶ τῆς ἁγνότητος] τῆς εἰς τὸν Χριστόν), but that is not a description of the believers' innate human nature; rather, it is a declaration of who they are in Christ through his baptismal washing of regeneration. See the bride in Eph 5:26–27 (cf. Titus 3:5 and the "bride" [νύμφη] who becomes the "wife" [γυνή] of the Lamb in Rev 21:2, 9).

[54] Bruce, *Romans*, 264.

[55] Wright, "Romans," 765.

full and proper comprehension of "the teaching which you yourselves learned" (16:17) is crucial if the passage is to be applied rightly and not wrongly. Paul does not uniformly urge the Roman Christians to "keep away from" (16:17) those with different convictions about any and every issue that might spark controversy among churches. His resolute striving for unity throughout the lengthy discussion of controverted issues conducted in 14:1–15:7 demonstrates this (see further below). Instead, his language here warns against those who advocate positions "contrary to the teaching" of the Gospel (see the commentary on 16:17 above).

At times, it may be difficult to determine which issues strike at "the divine realities and facts concerned with our salvation."[56] But Paul's apostolic exposition of the Good News (1:16), articulated with universal implications throughout chapters 1–8,[57] provides the Roman believers and us with helpful parameters. In addition to whatever else they had learned regarding the Gospel prior to the arrival of this letter (see 6:17), Paul has expounded the following essential doctrines (see the referenced sections in volume 1 of this commentary):

- The apostolic witness to the Gospel stands as foundational and authoritative (1:1–6).
- The OT Scriptures have been fulfilled in the incarnation, death, and resurrection of "Jesus Christ our Lord" (1:2–4; the quote is from 1:4).
- The Good News is the power of God into salvation for everyone who believes (1:16).
- The righteousness of God is "from faith[fulness] into faith" so that those righteous from faith shall live (1:17).
- God shows no partiality between Jew and Greek or regarding those having the Law or not having it (2:1–16).
- All have sinned and rightly deserve God's wrath (1:18–3:20); therefore under the Law no one is righteous and all stand condemned (3:1–20).
- The righteousness of God is received through faith in Jesus Christ in a manner fully consistent with Abraham's faith in God's promise (3:21–4:25).
- The first Adam brought sin and death, while Christ brings righteousness and life (5:12–21).
- Baptism incorporates the baptized into the death and resurrection of Christ, which ends their slavery to sin and enables them to walk in life's renewal (6:1–23).
- Even though believers continue to struggle to fulfill the Law, "nothing [is] condemnation for the ones in Christ Jesus" (7:1–8:4; the quote is from 8:1).
- Believers remain in mortal bodies amid a fallen creation; yet nothing can separate them from God's love in Christ Jesus (8:5–39).

---

[56] Lenski, *Romans*, 916; in the quotation above, Wright, "Romans," 765, speaks similarly of "the central tenets of the faith."

[57] See "Conclusion: A Contextual Letter with Universal Application" in Middendorf, *Romans 1–8*, 49–51.

Applying the statement "the teaching which you yourselves learned" (16:17) to the essential contours of the Gospel aligns well with the Augsburg Confession, which affirms:

> For it is sufficient for the true unity of the Christian church that the Gospel be preached in conformity with a pure understanding of it and that the sacraments be administered in accordance with the divine Word. It is not necessary for the true unity of the Christian church that ceremonies, instituted by men, should be observed uniformly in all places. It is as Paul says in Eph. 4:4, 5, "There is one body and one Spirit, just as you were called to the one hope that belongs to your call, one Lord, one faith, one baptism." (AC VII 2–4)

The Formula of Concord offers similar, though somewhat more expansive, counsel:

> We believe, teach, and confess that no church should condemn another because it has fewer or more external ceremonies not commanded by God, as long as there is mutual agreement in doctrine and in all its articles as well as in the right use of the holy sacraments, according to the familiar axiom, "Disagreement in fasting does not destroy agreement in faith."[58]

When situations do arise which challenge the essentials of the Gospel, and those who are serving our Lord Christ (16:18), that is, true teachers or believers, are "walking according to love" (14:15; cf. 13:8–10), then the fault lies with those who oppose them. As Lenski observes:

> Note well that the apostolic doctrine never causes either inward or outward rents in the church, either division of mind or schism in communion and fellowship. How can it when it is ever one and the same? Being one, it unifies, holds in unity.[59]

Instead, those advocating positions contrary to the Gospel (16:17a) are to blame for the destructive dissensions and tragic stumblings. While such teachers should initially be confronted with fraternal church discipline, it might eventually be necessary to remove them from teaching positions and even expel them from the fellowship. Paul and other apostles also warn even faithful Christian ministers to continue to scrutinize their own teaching, lest they themselves fall into error and judgment: "Keep a close watch on yourself and on the teaching. Persist in them, for doing this you will save both yourself and your hearers" (1 Tim 4:16; see also James 3:1; 1 Pet 4:17–5:4).

In Rom 16:17–18 Paul calls the Roman Christians to be on guard against pernicious *teachers*, but he does *not* generally speak in the same terms about them separating from *fellow believers*. The members of various house churches in Rome were engaged in "judgments over convictions" (14:1) regarding OT regulations about foods, the Sabbath, and festival days. In Paul's eyes, the

---

[58] FC Ep X 7, quoting Irenaeus, *Epistle to Victor*, quoted in Eusebius, *Ecclesiastical History*, 5.24.13.

[59] Lenski, *Romans*, 916.

Gospel is not at stake in such disputes (14:3, 14, 17, 20); these are adiapho-ra.[60] He advises the Roman believers to handle such matters within the body of Christ (12:4–5) by exercising the self-sacrificial, authentic love described in 12:9–13:10. Paul demonstrates how such love refrains from judging and despising (14:3–4, 10, 13, 15). Instead, as he counsels the "strong" (15:1) most directly in 14:13–15:3, he calls them to willingly relinquish their own Christian freedoms and graciously accommodate the traditions and idiosyncrasies of the "weak" (14:1–2; 15:1) with whom they disagree (e.g., 14:15–19). Furthermore, all believers are summoned to "receive" to themselves those whom God has "received to himself" (14:1, 3; 15:7). They are to embrace fellow believers whose understandings and practices in such matters differ; they are not to allow adiaphora to cause a severance in fellowship. Yet, as the discussion in 14:1–15:7 also shows, even "convictions" (14:1) about seemingly inconsequential mat-ters such as food and the observance of holy days, which certainly are not foundational for the kingdom of God (14:17), may, *if elevated to be necessi-ties*, jeopardize the salvation of individuals and the preservation of the Gospel (14:13–15, 20–23).

Looking beyond Romans, numerous others differences threatened to divide the early church. Yet, whenever possible, the NT consistently seeks to maintain unity based on the integrity of the Gospel. Consider the following:

- The divine revelation to Peter and his experiences in Acts 10–11 lead him to the conclusion that ethnicity (i.e., Jew versus Gentile) and restrictive rules for table fellowship ought not be allowed to separate those within the family of faith (see the commentary on Rom 2:11).

- Paul deals with the matter of eating meat offered to idols in 1 Corinthians 8–10 with striking similarities to his counsel to the Romans in Rom 14:1–15:7 (see the introduction to 14:1–15:13).

- In 1 Corinthians 15, some in the church were skeptical of or did not adequately comprehend the resurrection of the dead (1 Cor 15:12). Paul's response reaffirms the basic tenets of the Gospel, including the historical witnesses to Christ's resur-rection (1 Cor 15:1–11), spells out the disastrous situation the Corinthians would be in if Christ had not been raised from the dead (1 Cor 15:12–19), and winsomely presents the truth of his resurrection and its implications for their own resurrection to eternal life (1 Cor 15:20–28, 35–57). Thus he exhorts the Corinthians to accept and adhere to the apostolic message.

- Circumcision provides a most intriguing illustration.[61] When prescribed as a necessity for righteousness before God, Paul declares: "If you let yourselves be circumcised, Christ will benefit you nothing" (Gal 5:2). Succumbing to such legalism has tragic consequences (Gal 5:3–4). Therefore *teachers* who contend that circumcision is necessary for membership in the people of God advocate what stands contrary to the teaching of the Gospel (Rom 16:17); they must be

---

[60] For this term, see the commentary on 14:14, 20b–21; 15:5b–6; and "Application of Paul's Instruction in the Lutheran Confessions" in the commentary on 15:1–7.

[61] For a more complete discussion, see Middendorf, *Romans 1–8*, 207–10; see also Das, *Galatians*, 522–23; 637–44.

actively opposed, even anathematized, as Paul himself resoundingly articulates (Gal 1:6–9; 2:4–14). But he also contends: "Neither circumcision nor uncircumcision is anything, but a new creation [is]" (Gal 6:15; similarly also, Gal 5:6). In and of itself, he insists that the matter of whether a baptized believer is circumcised or not *should not be allowed to disrupt the fellowship* (cf. 1 Cor 7:17–19).

Similar misapprehensions, misconceptions, and misunderstandings have existed ever since the NT era and still persist within the family of faith today. These may involve overly sensitive consciences, legalisms, pietisms, or flagrant floutings of freedom. Paul's counsel in 14:1–15:7 advises us how to handle quarrels over permissible differences. Believers are to seek reconciliation first; only if there is a denial of a basic tenet of the Christian faith is the communion to be severed.[62] Then the faithful are indeed called to draw back and stay away from those who advocate false doctrines which compromise the Gospel (16:17). However, in the earlier section, Paul strives for an outcome far more edifying than keeping away from one another, demanding uniformity, or even resigning oneself to separation. He, like Jesus (Jn 17:11), prays for God-given unity:

> [5]And may the God of patient endurance and of encouragement give to you the same mindset among one another in accord with Christ Jesus [6]so that with the same purpose you might with one mouth glorify the God and Father of our Lord Jesus Christ. [7]Therefore, receive one another to yourselves, just as the Christ also received you to himself to [the] glory of God. (Rom 15:6–7)

Paul's Positive Desire (16:19)

"For your responsive hearing has reached to all. Therefore I rejoice over you, but I desire you to be wise toward the good and innocent toward the evil" (16:19). The noun ὑπακοή depicts listening and responding appropriately, hence "responsive hearing." The context determines the meaning more specifically. "Toward the responsive hearing of faith" (εἰς ὑπακοὴν πίστεως) is discussed in the commentary on 1:5, and the same phrase recurs almost immediately in 16:26 (cf. also 15:18). The cognate verb ὑπακούω has the same receptive sense in 6:17, "you responded from [the] heart to [the] form of teaching," which marks yet another connection between 16:17–19 and that section.[63] In these passages, Paul rejoices in the responsive hearing of the believers in Rome for they have listened and responded appropriately to the Gospel in faith, and the news of it is widely known.[64] Elsewhere, the noun ὑπακοή can express active "obedience" toward instruction and the Law. In the context of Paul's admonition in 16:17–18,

---

[62] Thus Paul is following the pattern set by Jesus himself in, e.g., Mt 18:15–18. Dialogue with the opportunity for repentance from sin and the pardoning of offense are of the first order. Only after repeated attempts to restore the offender have been refused is the person to be excluded from the church. See also Paul's prescriptions for the conflicts in 1 Corinthians 5–6.

[63] The unbelief of some is expressed by the negation of the verb ὑπακούω in 10:16: "they did not all listen responsively to the Good News."

[64] For "reached to all," see the second textual note on 16:19.

the Roman Christians' "responsive hearing" in 16:19 should result in avoiding teachers who spew divisive content contrary to the teaching of the Gospel.

By way of contrast, Paul desires that his hearers remain wise toward, or in regard to, that which is good, but innocent toward/in regard to that which is evil. This thought typifies wisdom in the OT.[65] Although Paul uses an adjective (σοφός, 16:19) from the more common word group for "wise," his statement sounds very "reminiscent"[66] of what Jesus says in Mt 10:16: "Therefore become wise [φρόνιμοι] as the serpents and innocent [ἀκέραιοι] as the doves."[67] Another significant intertextual echo follows in the next verse.

The Promise (16:20)

"And the God of peace will crush Satan under your feet suddenly" (16:20a). "The God of peace" repeats an expression from 15:33 (see the commentary there). In the remainder of 16:20a, Paul echoes Gen 3:15 rather loudly, even though the LXX translation of Gen 3:15 contains terminology quite different from Paul's. MT/LXX Gen 3:15b and Rom 16:20a read as follows:

הוּא יְשׁוּפְךָ רֹאשׁ,
וְאַתָּה תְּשׁוּפֶנּוּ עָקֵב:

He [זַרְעָהּ, "her (Eve's) Seed," Gen 3:15a] will crush you
[with respect to your] head,
and you [הַנָּחָשׁ, "the serpent," Gen 3:14] will crush him
[with respect to his] heel. (MT Gen 3:15b)[68]

αὐτός σου τηρήσει κεφαλήν,
καὶ σὺ τηρήσεις αὐτοῦ πτέρναν.
He himself will keep your head,
and you yourself will keep his foot. (LXX Gen 3:15b)

συντρίψει τὸν σατανᾶν ὑπὸ τοὺς πόδας ὑμῶν ἐν τάχει.
He [the God of peace] will crush the Satan under your feet suddenly.
(Rom 16:20a)

In eternity past, before the foundation of the world, God had already formulated his plan to send his Son for our salvation (Rom 8:29; Eph 1:4; 1 Pet 1:20; Rev 13:8). Ever since the fall, God has been working to establish a restored relationship with humanity through the promised seed of the woman, culminating in the incarnation of Christ in the womb of the Virgin Mary. On the one hand, already

[65]   See especially Proverbs; see also, e.g., Job 1:1; 28:28. Cf. Dunn, *Romans*, 904.

[66]   Cranfield, *Romans*, 802.

[67]   For a contextual analysis of the meaning in Matthew, see Gibbs, *Matthew 1:1–11:1*, 518–21.

[68]   The best linguistic evidence for the meaning of the Qal imperfect of שׁוּף, repeated in each clause, supports "crush, break" (*DCH*, s.v. שׁוּף I, Qal, 1). Each of the body parts, רֹאשׁ, "head," and עָקֵב, "heel," is an accusative of specification ("accusative of limitation" according to Joüon, § 126 g), signifying which part of each one's body will be crushed. The Hebrew pronouns "you" and "him" are each suffixed to the verb "crush," as indicated in the translation above. However, the meaning of the (literal) "will crush you (with respect to the) head" is conveyed appropriately in English by "will crush your head."

now, through the suffering, death, and resurrection of Christ, "being declared righteous from faith, we have peace with God through our Lord Jesus Christ" (Rom 5:1). Therefore Satan can no longer accuse us for our sins in the presence of God. But in order to *fully* restore eternal peace, God must crush "the Satan" (τὸν σατανᾶν, Rom 16:20) forever (Rev 20:10). Paul uses the name "Satan" only here in Romans, but nine times elsewhere.[c] The cognate Hebrew verb (probably denominative) is שָׂטַן, *satan*, which means "to accuse."[69] Literally, then, "the Satan" is "the Accuser" or "the Adversary"[70] who had access to operate within the council of God in the OT (Job 1–2; Zech 3:1–2; cf. 1 Chr 21:1). The retention of the definite article in "the Satan" (τὸν σατανᾶν, Rom 16:20) "probably reflects the functional significance which still attached to the name."[71] Stemming from the *protoevangelium* in Gen 3:15 and expanded in such OT passages as Job 26:12; Pss 74:13; 89:10 (MT 89:11); 91:13; Is 27:1; 51:9, "the hope of Satan being 'crushed under foot' is part of a larger eschatological hope for the final binding or defeat of the angelic power hostile to God."[72] He was cast out from heaven through the earthly ministry of Jesus (Lk 10:18; Rev 12:7–13). Therefore during the present church age (the millennium) Satan is bound (Rev 20:2) so that he cannot "deceive [πλανάω] the nations" in the sense of completely stopping the proclamation of the Gospel (Rev 20:3). Nevertheless, he does succeed in "deceiving" many and is given more leeway to do so as history marches toward the second advent of Christ (πλανάω, Rev 20:8, 10).

Here and elsewhere, the translation of ἐν τάχει as "soon" may be misleading in English (see the second textual note on 16:20). Lenski properly recognizes that

> ἐν τάχει is not "shortly" (our versions), soon, as though soon after Paul's writing Satan would invade the Roman congregation; the phrase means "swiftly."
> As with a swift stamping of the feet one crushes a snake's head.[73]

It is erroneous to regard this verse as evidence that Paul was historically incorrect in his expectation that the parousia would take place "soon" (see the commentary on Rom 13:11–12a). The identical Greek phrase (ἐν τάχει) in Rev 1:1; 22:6 refers to the full span of history from the NT era to the second coming of Christ as a series of events that will take place "soon" or "quickly." All believers at all times are called to regard the Lord's return as imminent, regardless of when it

---

[69] See both his Hebrew name הַשָּׂטָן, "the Satan," and the Hebrew verb שָׂטַן, "accuse," as he accuses the high priest (Zech 3:1). He accuses Job in the presence of God (Job 1:9–11; 2:4–5). He accuses Christians ("our brothers") day and night before God until he is cast out from heaven (Rev 12:10).

[70] Origen, *Romans* (Bray, *Romans*, ACCS NT 6:377) states: "It seems to me that *Satan* here refers to any spirit which is opposed to God. For in our language, *Satan* means *adversary*."

[71] Dunn, *Romans*, 905.

[72] Dunn, *Romans*, 905, citing as examples *Jubilees* 5:6; 10:7, 11; 23:29; *1 Enoch* 10:4, 11–12; 13:1–2; *2 Enoch* 7:1; *Testament of Moses* 10:1; 1QM 17:5–6; 18:1; Rev 20:10.

[73] Lenski, *Romans*, 923.

may actually take place, as it will come suddenly and unexpectedly, as a thief in the night, as Paul says elsewhere (1 Thess 5:1–8).[d]

(d) See also
Mk 13:32–37;
Lk 12:35–40;
21:34–36;
2 Pet 3:3–10;
Rev 3:3, 11;
16:15; 22:7,
12, 20

While the ultimate eschatological fulfillment properly draws our dominant attention, lesser fulfillments relevant to the context of the preceding verses should not thereby be totally excluded. It is best to "view the promise as a general one, similar to others that occur in Paul's letter endings, but with obvious relevance to the false teachers that Paul has just warned the church about [16:17–18]."[74] At the same time, the personal language, "your feet," should not be taken as a promise that believers themselves will be able to vanquish Satan and his assaults on the Gospel using their own power.[75] Rather, it is Christ's victory over the devil, through his cross and empty tomb, and the power of his proclaimed Gospel (1:16) that will cause their ancient foe to lie dead underfoot, as Christ told the seventy-two proclaimers before sending them out: "Behold, I have given you authority to tread upon serpents and scorpions and upon all the power of the enemy, and nothing shall harm you" (Lk 10:19).

Every one of Paul's letters begins and ends with a reference to "grace" (χάρις).[76] It has been a keynote throughout this letter, appearing twenty-four times. In 16:20b, it comes in what was likely Paul's final handwritten clause.[77] Before giving the pen back to Tertius, he signs off with "the grace of our Lord Jesus [is] with you." Where no verb is present, the norm is to assume the present indicative "is" (as in 11:36; 15:33; 16:24).[78] Rather than merely expressing a wish that God's grace "be" with them, Paul conveys a foundational Gospel truth. Whenever baptized believers (note ὑμῶν, "you" *plural*, 16:20) face the divisiveness of false teachers promulgating alternative gospels (16:17–18), as they hold fast to the good amidst evil (16:19), and as long as they await the eschatological and complete crushing of Satan's power (16:20), they do so *together confidently*, knowing that God's grace, which comes in and through our Lord Jesus, *is* with them always.

---

[74] Moo, *Romans*, 932.

[75] Ambrosiaster, *Romans* (Bray, *Romans*, ACCS NT 6:378), asserts: "Paul says this about his own coming to them, for then he will crush the devil so that they will be able to receive spiritual grace"; so also Cranfield, *Romans*, 803; apparently Origen, *Romans* (Bray, *Romans*, ACCS NT 6:377–78); and Lenski, *Romans*, 923: "The moment the snake's head of false teaching would raise itself among them, the Romans will by God's help stamp it to death."

[76] See especially the commentary on 1:5, 7; 3:24. See also Barclay, *The Mind of St Paul*, 157–59.

[77] See "A Word of Warning and a Prevailing Promise (16:17–20)" above. See also Cranfield, *Romans*, 804.

[78] Note the conventional translation of ὁ κύριος μετὰ σοῦ in Lk 1:28 as "the Lord is with you" (ESV, NASB, NRSV; similarly, KJV). Similar translations are preferable for μεθ᾽ ἡμῶν ὁ θεός, "God is with us" (Mt 1:23); ἐξ ὧν ὁ Χριστός, "from whom is the Christ" (Rom 9:5); and ᾧ ἡ δόξα, "to whom is the glory" (Rom 16:27). A Greek present indicative verb is explicit in ἰδοὺ ἐγὼ μεθ᾽ ὑμῶν εἰμι, "behold, I am with you" (Mt 28:20). Dunn, *Romans*, 906, notes that "Schmidt follows Schlatter in reading the verb (understood) as indicative: 'the grace of our Lord is with you.'" See Hans Wilhelm Schmidt, *Der Brief des Paulus an die Römer* (Berlin: Evangelische Verlagsanstalt, 1962), 256, 259; Adolf Schlatter, *Erläuterungen zum Neuen Testament* (Stuttgart: Calwer Verlag, 1962), 5:241.

Greetings from Those in Corinth (16:21–23)

These verses contain a group of greetings from eight individuals who are with Paul in Corinth.[79] In contrast to the exceptional inclusion in 16:3–16 of twenty-six names of people who are among his addressees, the listing in 16:21–23 of colleagues present with him reflects a more conventional Pauline practice. In keeping with the dominance of ἀσπάζομαι, "to greet," in 16:3–16, the verb regains prominence here, occurring four additional times. Rather than the second person imperative form (ἀσπάσασθε) used in sixteen of the seventeen instances in 16:3–16, however, all four forms in 16:21–23 are indicatives, three in the third person singular (ἀσπάζεται, 16:21, 23 [twice]) and one in the first person singular (ἀσπάζομαι, 16:22).

Timothy and Others (16:21)

"Timothy, my fellow worker, greets you" (16:21a). Timothy's credentials certainly warrant him coming first in the list. After meeting Paul in Lystra (Acts 16:1–4), he accompanied the apostle on the rest of his second missionary journey and then also on his third. Timothy appears as coauthor of six of Paul's letters (2 Corinthians, 1 and 2 Thessalonians, Philippians, Colossians, and Philemon) and is himself the addressee of two of them (1 and 2 Timothy). In fact, he "is the person who is most frequently mentioned elsewhere in Paul's letters."[80] Therefore Käsemann rightly describes him "as a constant companion and delegate of the apostle [who] has a matchless claim to the predicate ὁ συνεργός μου"[81] ("my fellow worker," 16:21; cf. 16:3, 9).

Paul then adds greetings from "Lucius and Jason and Sosipater, my kinsmen" (16:21b). The adjective "kinsman" (συγγενής, which also occurs in 16:7, 11) implies that all three are fellow Jews. This makes the identification of "Lucius" (Λούκιος) as the similarly named "Luke" (Λουκᾶς), the author of Luke-Acts, mentioned in Col 4:14; 2 Tim 4:11; and Philemon 24,[82] problematic, though not entirely impossible.[83] Acts 13:1 mentions an actual "Lucius" (Λούκιος) in Antioch, but whether this is the same "Lucius" as in Rom 16:21 seems unknowable and unlikely.[84] It seems more plausible that the "Jason" in Rom 16:21b is the same "Jason" who met and then hosted Paul in Thessalonica on his second journey (Acts 17:5–9). Even more probable is the identification of the third person, "Sosipater" (Σωσίπατρος), with the "Sopater" (Σώπατρος)

---

[79] See Middendorf, *Romans 1–8*, 5–7.

[80] Dunn, *Romans*, 908–9. See 1 Cor 4:17; 16:10; 2 Cor 1:19; Phil 2:19; 1 Thess 3:2, 6; see also Acts 16:1; 17:14–15; 18:5; 19:22; 20:4.

[81] Käsemann, *Romans*, 420.

[82] Lenski, *Romans*, 924: "This is, of course, not Luke (= Lukas = Lucanus) who was a Gentile Christian."

[83] Juel, *Luke-Acts*, 7: "Tradition pictures Luke as a Gentile. I am presently inclined to view him as a Jew, or at least as a proselyte to Judaism."

[84] Sanday and Headlam, *Romans*, 432, make the connection but conclude that it "might be" the same person.

from Berea in Acts 20:4.[85] Based upon the setting of the letter's composition in both time and place,[86] *these three Jews probably formed part of the delegation accompanying Paul as he delivers their offering to Jerusalem* (see the commentary on Rom 15:25–27).

Tertius, the Scribe (16:22)

Paul is the author of Romans, but it appears that he wrote only 16:17–20 in his own hand.[87] Who recorded the rest? "I, Tertius, the one who wrote this letter, greets you in [the] Lord" (16:22). Grammatically, "in [the] Lord" (ἐν κυρίῳ) at the very end of the verse seems to go best with the very first word, "I greet" (ἀσπάζομαι).[88] However, Morris counters:

> In this chapter "in Christ" or "in the Lord" occurs repeatedly in verses which convey greetings (vv. 3, 7, 8, 9, 10, 11, 12 [twice], and 13), and not once is it connected with the greeting. It may well be that Tertius meant that he wrote the letter "in the Lord," which, of course, immediately raises the question of what it means to "write in the Lord." If this is the way to take it, we should see the writing of the letter, not as a mechanical project, but as something Tertius undertook as a piece of service to his Lord.[89]

If so, perhaps Tertius was a professional scribe who donated his services gratis. But in either case, "in [the] Lord" indicates that Tertius is a fellow believer. We know nothing more about him.

The verb "to write" (γράφω) can literally refer to the action of inscribing or penning the words with one's own hand (cf. BDAG, 1), but the notion of producing a written record "of pronouncements and solemn proceedings" (BDAG, 2 b) fits this context as well. The use of a scribe or amanuensis was common in the OT era and in Paul's day,[90] and Tertius here indicates that he actually penned the vast majority of the letter as Paul dictated it to him. Whatever influence Tertius might have exerted on the grammar, vocabulary, or perhaps even the content of the composition remains unknowable, but such factors in no way diminish the verbal inspiration of the letter or its apostolic authority.[91]

---

[85] According to BDAG, s.v. Σωσίπατρος, "linguistically this is prob[able]."

[86] See Middendorf, *Romans 1–8*, 5–7.

[87] See "A Word of Warning and a Prevailing Promise (16:17–20)" above.

[88] Cranfield, *Romans*, 806.

[89] Morris, *Romans*, 543.

[90] See Capes, Reeves, and Richards, *Rediscovering Paul*, 68–78; see also Cranfield, *Romans*, 2–5.

[91] The example of Jeremiah illustrates the kind of writing process that might have produced other biblical books too, including Romans. Jer 1:1–2 states that the book consists of "the words of Jeremiah" which resulted from "the Word of Yahweh" coming to him. Later, however, we learn more about the process of composition: Yahweh instructed Jeremiah to dictate Yahweh's words to the scribe Baruch (Jer 36:1–18). Yet Baruch still could assert that he "wrote" the words (the verb כָּתַב, Jer 36:17–18). After King Jehoiakim burned the original scroll penned by Baruch, Jeremiah repeated the dictation of the same words of Yahweh to Baruch to produce another scroll, to which further divine oracles were added (Jer 36:27–32). Jeremiah thus obeyed the divine command for him to "write" (כָּתַב, Jer 36:28) the second scroll even

Many imagine an unmediated Paul (the individual) is the closest to the inspired word. Yet the letter is what is inspired. … For Paul, the letter was not finished until he agreed with all of its content, because Paul was accountable for it.[92]

Gaius and Erastus (16:23a–b)

Finally, Paul conveys greetings from three more men: "Gaius, my host and [the host] of the whole church, greets you. Erastus, the treasurer of the city, and Quartus, the brother, greet you" (16:23). This verse introduces us to an intriguing mix of characters, two of whom were discussed in the commentary introduction in order to establish Corinth as the place from which Paul writes.[93]

First,

"Gaius" was a common name; and at least three different men in the NT bore it: Gaius "of Derbe" (Acts 20:4; cf. [Acts] 19:29); a Gaius from Corinth (1 Cor. 1:14); and a Gaius who was a church leader in Asia Minor (3 John 1). The Gaius … here was almost certainly Gaius of Corinth.[94]

Origen recognizes this "Gaius" as the second Gaius above, the one "whom Paul mentioned as having baptized at Corinth" (1 Cor 1:14).[95] Bruce argues that he should also be identified with the Titius Justus who welcomed Paul when he first came to Corinth on his second missionary journey (Acts 18:7),[96] but that seems less certain.

Gaius currently hosts Paul,[97] providing him with food and lodging during his three-month stay in Corinth (Acts 20:2–3). The respected practice of providing hospitality to travelers like Paul extends beyond the familiar. The basic and normal meaning of the word translated here as "host" (ξένος) more commonly denotes a "stranger." One characteristic of the authentic love detailed in 12:9–21 involves "pursing the love of strangers" (τὴν φιλοξενίαν διώκοντες, 12:13; see the commentary there). The fact that Gaius also provides hospitality for "the whole church" (16:23) signals an economic status and a large house capable of hosting the regular meetings of the Corinthian community.[98] Dunn restricts the meaning to accommodating united gatherings of the Corinthian congregation, which he projects as "meetings of 30–40, at best 50."[99] But his argument

---

though it was Baruch who actually "wrote" it (כָּתַב, Jer 36:32). In all these verses (Jer 36:17, 18, 28, 32), the LXX (LXX Jer 43:17, 18, 28, 32) translates the Hebrew verb כָּתַב with the same Greek verb γράφω, "to write," as used in Rom 16:22.

[92] Capes, Reeves, and Richards, *Rediscovering Paul*, 73; see also Middendorf, *Romans 1–8*, 4–5.

[93] Middendorf, *Romans 1–8*, 5–7.

[94] Moo, *Romans*, 935.

[95] Origen, *Romans* (Bray, *Romans*, ACCS NT 6:379).

[96] Bruce, *Romans*, 265–66; see Middendorf, *Romans 1–8*, 6.

[97] So Chrysostom, *Homilies on Romans*, 32 (Bray, *Romans*, ACCS NT 6:379).

[98] Käsemann, *Romans*, 421, disagrees, contending that the phrase "involves hospitality, and not providing a place for assembly"; similarly, Moo, *Romans*, 935.

[99] Dunn, *Romans*, 911.

stems from the unwarranted contention that "nowhere else in the undisputed letters does Paul use ἐκκλησία of the universal church"[100] (see the commentary on 16:5a). It also poses a false alternative. There seems to be no valid reason to dismiss either component from Paul's phrasing in 16:23. Gaius hosts the gatherings of the entire local Christian community and also provides accommodations for visitors from the church at large, as exemplified by Paul himself.

The name "Erastus" also shows up elsewhere in the NT. In Acts 19:22, Paul sends an Erastus from Ephesus to Macedonia. In 2 Tim 4:20, Paul says an Erastus "remained" (ἔμεινεν) in Corinth. It seems reasonable to ask whether all of these passages, including Rom 16:23, refer to the same person. Could one Erastus have ventured from Corinth to Ephesus and then Macedonia? This degree of travel may have been difficult in light of his duties in Corinth, which Paul references with the title ὁ οἰκονόμος τῆς πόλεως (16:23). BDAG defines this as the lofty position of city *treasurer* (BDAG, s.v. οἰκονόμος, 2). Bruce argues that it, rather, reflects a "much humbler" role, which he titles "clerk of works."[101] In either case, Erastus was a city official who should likely be identified as the person whose name is inscribed on a Latin inscription found in 1929 near the theatre in Corinth. It reads: *ERASTVS. PRO. AED. S. P. STRAVIT*, "Erastus, during/in return for his aedileship, laid this pavement at his own expense."[102] The Greek title ὁ οἰκονόμος may be equivalent to the Latin *aedile*,[103] but, if not, it seems likely that the same person occupied both roles at different times. As Morris suggests: "There seems no reason why we should not think that our Erastus was the city treasurer at the time Paul wrote and that he later was honored with the office of aedile."[104]

Concluding with Quartus (16:23c)

The introduction to 16:1–16 began with the observation that scholars and lectionaries alike often ignore this chapter because it consists largely of a long listing of names. In those earlier verses, Paul sends greetings to twenty-six named individuals in Rome. Rom 16:21–23 then consists of greetings from eight named persons in Corinth. While listed in Scripture, to modern-day readers they generally seem to have lived long ago and far away. In other words, with the exception of Timothy and some brief descriptions of the others, they, by and large, remain unknown to us.

---

[100] Dunn, *Romans*, 910.

[101] Bruce, *Romans*, 266.

[102] See Bruce, *Romans*, 266; Cranfield, *Romans*, 807; Maier, *In the Fullness of Time*, 289; "Additional Note: The Erastus of 16:23 and the Erastus of the Inscription" in Kruse, *Romans*, 585–87.

[103] Maier, *In the Fullness of Time*, 289, says that the Latin title "is easily the equivalent" of the Greek one.

[104] Morris, *Romans*, 544, also noting the aedile "held office for a year only, and he normally had held other offices previously"; similarly, Moo, *Romans*, 935–36, who adds: "The aedile was appointed for one year and was responsible for the city streets and buildings" (935, n. 21).

Appropriately, then, Quartus comes as the final named greeter in the chapter. Although his name (Κούαρτος, 16:23) was common among slaves and freedmen,[105] he otherwise rests in obscurity. Even Paul simply calls him "the brother" (ὁ ἀδελφός). Bruce speculates that this indicates he may be "the brother" of the previous man in the list, Erastus.[106] Alternatively, since Tertius means "third" and Quartus "fourth," Bruce wonders whether those two could be consecutive brothers in the same family.[107] More likely, and in keeping with the general descriptors utilized throughout the chapter (e.g., "in [the] Lord/ Christ," "loved one," "fellow worker," "kinsman"[108]), the term "brother" has its common religious sense. Thus Paul identifies Quartus as a fellow Christian.

This means, however, that while all else about Quartus remains a mystery to us, he is not anonymous at all to the One who really matters. He belongs in the family of the triune God, who relationally knows each one of his own by name.[e] Quartus is acknowledged as a brother of Jesus (Mt 12:49; Jn 20:17), the Good Shepherd, who also calls his sheep by name (Jn 10:3). Therefore Quartus lives as an eternal brother to all those "in Christ Jesus our Lord" (Rom 6:23). For physical death cannot separate us from God's love (Rom 8:38–39), which comes to us in the name of him who remains "the same yesterday and today and into the ages" (Heb 13:8).

(e) Cf. Gen 17:5, 15, 19; 35:10; Ex 31:2; 33:12, 17; 35:30; Eccl 6:10; Is 40:26; 43:1–7; 45:3–4

---

[105] Dunn, *Romans*, 911.

[106] Bruce, *Romans*, 266.

[107] Bruce, *Romans*, 266.

[108] See "Further Personal Greetings (16:5b–15)" in the commentary on 16:1–16.

Final Restatement
of the Theme and Doxology

Translation

16 **25Now to the one who is powerfully able to establish you according to my Gospel, namely, the proclamation of Jesus Christ, in accord with the revelation of the mystery having been concealed for long ages, 26but now revealed, and made known through [the] prophetic writings in accord with the decree of the eternal God toward the responsive hearing of faith into all the nations, 27to [the] only, wise God, through Jesus Christ—to him [is] the glory into the ages. Amen.**

Textual Notes

16:25 τῷ δὲ δυναμένῳ ὑμᾶς στηρίξαι—The aorist infinitive of στηρίζω, "to establish," functions here as a complementary infinitive with the participle δυναμένῳ, "who is powerfully able," from δύναμαι (see the commentary).[1] The verb στηρίζω means "to cause to be inwardly firm or committed, *confirm, establish, strengthen*" (BDAG, 2). Its only other appearance in Romans is in 1:11. There Paul's visit would strengthen the Roman Christians in their faith; now he speaks of the Gospel through which God is powerfully able "to establish" them.

κατὰ τὸ εὐαγγέλιόν μου—The preposition κατά serves primarily as a marker of norm:[2] "according to my Gospel." Wallace describes this use of κατά as indicating a "standard: *in accordance with, corresponding to*."[3] At the same time, a causal sense ("because of my Gospel"), seem applicable to the divine "establishing" under consideration as well (see the previous textual note). As BDAG observes: "Oft[en] the norm is at the same time the reason, so that *in accordance with* and *because of* are merged" (s.v. κατά, B 5 a δ). "Since κατά can have both senses, … there is no reason the writer should not have had both senses in mind."[4] One can further recognize how the element of cause leads toward and also conveys *means* ("by means of my Gospel"). In situations like this, the interpreter should acknowledge that these imposed grammatical categories are somewhat artificial and need not be viewed as completely isolated from one another.[5]

---

[1] For the complementary infinitive construction, see Wallace, *Greek Grammar*, 598–99.

[2] BDAG, B 5; Käsemann, *Romans*, 424; Murray, *Romans*, 2:241.

[3] Wallace, *Greek Grammar*, 377.

[4] Dunn, *Romans*, 914; similarly, Schreiner, *Romans*, 811.

[5] See Middendorf, *Romans 1–8*, 53–54.

καὶ τὸ κήρυγμα—The conjunction καί here is translated as "namely" because it is explicative or epexegetical.[6] In the phrase discussed in the preceding textual note, the preposition κατά governed the accusative phrase τὸ εὐαγγέλιόν, and it also governs the second accusative phrase τὸ κήρυγμα here. The preposition's force, therefore, continues to emphasize norm, though elements of cause and, particularly, means also remain in play (see the previous textual note). This is the only appearance of the noun κήρυγμα in Romans. It denotes "a public declaration, *someth[ing] proclaimed aloud, proclamation,* by a herald sent by God" (BDAG, 2). It is the cognate noun of the verb κηρύσσω; see the fourth textual note on 10:8.

κατὰ ἀποκάλυψιν μυστηρίου—This phrase is translated as "in accord with the revelation of the mystery." For the preposition κατά, see the second textual note on this verse; the normative sense seems dominant here. For the noun ἀποκάλυψις, "revelation," see the fourth textual note on 2:5 (it also occurs in 8:19); for the cognate verb, ἀποκαλύπτω, see the second textual note on 1:17. For μυστήριον, "mystery," see the second textual note and the commentary on 11:25, as well as the commentary below.

χρόνοις αἰωνίοις σεσιγημένου—The clause means "having been concealed for long ages." The verb σιγάω normally means to "be silent" (BDAG, 1), but it can have the transitive meaning "to keep someth[ing] from becoming known, *keep secret, conceal*" (BDAG, 2), and the perfect passive participle σεσιγημένου (genitive singular to agree with the word that it modifies, μυστηρίου) has the passive meaning of that transitive sense. BDAG defines the plural χρόνοι as "a rather long period of time composed of several shorter ones" (s.v. χρόνος, 1). As modified by the adjective αἰώνιος, we have "a long period of time, *long ago* χρόνοις αἰ[ωνίοις] *long ages ago*" (BDAG, s.v. αἰώνιος, 1). Thus in the dative χρόνοις αἰωνίοις means "for long ages" and refers to past time (contrast εἰς τοὺς αἰῶνας in the second textual note on 16:27).

16:26 φανερωθέντος δὲ νῦν ... γνωρισθέντος—While the two genitive singular aorist passive participles are at the opposite ends of the verse, they, like σεσιγημένου ("having been concealed") in the previous verse, both modify μυστηρίου, the "mystery" in 16:25. The verbs ("revealed" and "made known") are synonyms. For φανερόω, "to reveal," see the fourth textual note on 3:21, where the "righteousness of God ... through faith" (3:21–22) is revealed. Here too it functions as a divine/theological passive: "revealed" by God.[7] For the second verb, γνωρίζω, "to make known," see the second textual note on 9:22. It also functions as a divine/theological passive: "made known" by God. The four prepositional phrases in the rest of the verse all precede the participle γνωρισθέντος ("made known") but go with it semantically (see the next textual note), so the participle is translated first for clarity in English.

διά τε γραφῶν προφητικῶν—The enclitic and postpositive τε, "and," embedded in "through [the] prophetic writings" means that this prepositional phrase along with the

---

[6] See BDAG, 1 c; BDF, § 442.9; so Moo, *Romans*, 938, n. 13; Schreiner, *Romans*, 811; and Dunn, *Romans*, 914, who labels it as "epexegetic = 'that is to say.'"

[7] See Wallace, *Greek Grammar*, 437–38.

three that follow all go with the aorist passive participle γνωρισθέντος, "made known," at the end of the verse.[8] (For that verb's meaning, see the preceding textual note.)

κατ᾽ ἐπιταγήν—This is the only use of the noun ἐπιταγή in Romans. It refers to an "authoritative directive, *command, order, injunction*" (BDAG, 1). To avoid the nuance of a commandment (i.e., ἐντολή), it is translated as "decree." The preposition κατά here indicates norm, "in accord with," although a causal sense may also be present (see the second and fourth textual notes on 16:25). God's "decree" caused the revelation through the writing of the prophetic Scriptures (cf. Ps 68:11 [MT 68:12]).

εἰς ὑπακοὴν πίστεως—For the identical phrase, see the third textual note and the commentary on 1:5; it means "toward the responsive hearing of faith." The noun ὑπακοή also appears in this sense in 6:16 and 15:18. For the word group, see also the commentary on the cognate verb ὑπακούω, "listen responsively to," in 10:16.

16:27 ᾧ—The concluding clause of the letter begins with this dative relative pronoun, literally, "to whom." However, if that rendition is used ("to whom [is] the glory") the English translation of 16:25–27 is not a complete sentence. To solve that problem most English versions omit any rendition of ᾧ, e.g., "to the only wise God, through Jesus Christ, be the glory forever" (NASB). The translation above renders the pronoun as "to him," which enables the passage to be a complete English sentence.

Grammatically it would be possible for the antecedent of the dative pronoun ᾧ to be the genitive Ἰησοῦ Χριστοῦ, "Jesus Christ,"[9] but in all likelihood it refers back to the dative "only, wise God" (μόνῳ σοφῷ θεῷ).[10] This is a "resumptive use" of the pronoun, "for it intends to resume all that has been said about God"[11] in a letter that is, first and foremost, all about God himself (see the commentary on 16:25a).

ἡ δόξα εἰς τοὺς αἰῶνας—The verb to be supplied is the indicative "is" (see the first textual note on 11:36; see also 15:33; 16:20), thus "to him [is] the glory." The prepositional phrase εἰς τοὺς αἰῶνας, "into the ages," commonly refers to future time, into and throughout eternity, as also in 1:25; 9:5; 11:36 (contrast χρόνοις αἰωνίοις in reference to past time in the fifth textual note on 16:25).

ἀμήν—See the third textual note on 9:5.

---

8   Recognized by Cranfield, *Romans*, 811; Dunn, *Romans*, 915; Moo, *Romans*, 939; Schreiner, *Romans*, 813; see BDAG, s.v. τέ, 2; BDF, § 443. Against Barrett, *Romans*, 286, and Käsemann, *Romans*, 421, 426, who ignore or misinterpret τε and take "through [the] prophetic writings" with "but now revealed."

9   The relative pronoun "agrees with its antecedent in gender and number," but not necessarily in case; "its case is determined by the function it has in its own clause" (Wallace, *Greek Grammar*, 336; emphasis removed).

10   Moo, *Romans*, 941, n. 34; Dunn, *Romans*, 916; contra Barrett, *Romans*, 287, who contends: "The author now forgets the datives he has already set down, and ascribes glory to Christ." However, the sense of the passage as discussed here speaks against taking "Jesus Christ" as the referent.

11   Lenski, *Romans*, 933, quoting Robertson, *A Grammar of the Greek New Testament*, 437.

Commentary

Challenges to Authenticity Rebutted

As discussed in the excursus "Textual Criticism and the End of Romans" following the commentary on 15:23–33, the doxology of 16:25–27 appears in numerous locations within the textual tradition. $\mathfrak{P}^{46}$ places it after 15:33. The Alexandrian text (A) places it both after 14:23 and again at the end of the letter. However, "the strength of impressive manuscript evidence" (e.g., $\mathfrak{P}^{61}$ ℵ B C D)[12] indicates that it was almost certainly here originally. In other words, it serves as the conclusion to the letter Paul sent to Rome. The reasons why it would have been moved elsewhere strongly outweigh those ushered forth to explain why it would have been relocated here.[13]

The Pauline authorship of the doxology which concludes Romans has also been widely challenged. Hultgren, for example, considers it "a deutero-Pauline addition to the Letter to the Romans."[14] He points out that this "one long sentence of 53 words in the Greek NT … contain[s] phrases not found elsewhere in the undisputed letters of Paul."[15] Furthermore,

> to have a doxology at the end of a letter by Paul is unusual, for although doxologies appear *within* Paul's undisputed letters (e.g., at Rom 11:36; Gal 1:5; Phil 4:20), they do not occur at the *end* of any of them. Instead they end with a benediction.[16]

Cranfield agrees that 16:25–27 gives "a rather un-Pauline impression"[17] and also regards it as a "non-Pauline … doxological appendix."[18] Käsemann goes so far as to title his treatment of the verses "Inauthentic Concluding Doxology (16:25–27)."[19]

While this seems to be the majority opinion among scholars currently,[20] their arguments against Pauline authorship reveal a number of serious weaknesses. First, the fact that Romans alone ends with a doxology, rather than

---

[12] Metzger, *A Textual Commentary on the Greek New Testament*, 540; see also 534.

[13] See further the excursus "Textual Criticism and the End of Romans" following the commentary on 15:23–33.

[14] Hultgren, *Romans*, 601.

[15] Hultgren, *Romans*, 601.

[16] Hultgren, *Romans*, 601. For Paul's use of a benediction at the close of a letter, see 1 Cor 16:23; 2 Cor 13:13 (ET 13:14); Gal 6:18; Eph 6:24; Phil 4:23; Col 4:18; 1 Thess 5:28; 2 Thess 3:18; 1 Tim 6:21; 2 Tim 4:22; Titus 3:15; Philemon 25.

[17] Cranfield, *Romans*, 7.

[18] Cranfield, *Romans*, 809, though he also regards it as "a not unworthy … appendix to Paul's most weighty epistle."

[19] Käsemann, *Romans*, 421 (see also 423, 427). He attributes it to "a community at the beginning of the second century which was under Pauline influence" (428).

[20] Also, for example, Barrett, *Romans*, 286; Dodd, *Romans*, 245–46; Dunn, *Romans*, 913; Fitzmyer, *Romans*, 753. Jewett, *Romans*, 1002, contends that "the doxology is lumbering, redundant, and somewhat contradictory in its theological impulses," and he accepts "a three-step creation and redaction of the doxology, two of which occurred before the Marcionite mutilation of Romans" (1003).

Paul's typical concluding blessing, does not, by itself, provide sufficient reason to question its authenticity. On the contrary, it actually provides a strong argument for its authenticity: a pseudonymous author trying to impersonate the apostle convincingly would have imitated his practice elsewhere. In regard to vocabulary, Hultgren concedes that "there actually are no *hapax legomena*" in 16:25–27.[21] Other factors, such as the sheer length of the letter addressed to a location Paul has not yet visited,[22] may well explain why he chooses to close with these words of praise.

Second, the best manuscript evidence retains the doxology here (see above) and in its full form. In regard to the latter point, Bruce discusses the theory of Harnack that our current text "represents an orthodox expansion of a shorter Marcionite doxology" before pointing out that "we have, indeed, no MS or other objective evidence for such a shorter text of the doxology."[23]

Moo marshals these further decisive arguments in favor of the doxology's acceptance as fully genuine, a position adopted by numerous others as well:

- "Differences from Paul's own style are largely eliminated if we maintain the Pauline authorship of Ephesians and Colossians."
- "It does not seem credible that Paul would end his letter with 'Quartus, the fellow Christian'" (16:23; for 16:24, see the textual note on it in the commentary on Rom 16:17–24).
- "The language of the doxology demonstrates remarkable parallels to the language of Romans, and especially its opening."[24]

The latter point provides an appropriate lead into the text itself. Moo demonstrates how the doxology

> deliberately echoes … the language and themes of the letter, and particularly its opening section:

"who is able" (power) [16:25]	cf. 1:4, 16
"strengthen you" [16:25]	1:11
"[my] gospel" [16:25]	1:1, 9, 16; cf. 2:16
"revelation"/"manifested" [16:25–26]	1:17; 3:21
"prophetical writings" [16:26]	1:2; 3:21
"obedience of faith" [16:26]	1:5
"all the nations (Gentiles)" [16:26]	1:5; passim
"only God" [16:27]	3:29–30
"wise God" [16:27]	11:33–36

---

[21] Hultgren, *Romans*, 601.

[22] See Middendorf, *Romans 1–8*, 4, 14–15.

[23] Bruce, *Romans*, 267, citing Adolf von Harnack, "Über I. Korr. 14, 23 ff. und Röm. 16, 25 ff. nach der ältesten Überlieferung und der Marcionitischen Bibel," in *Studien zur Geschichte des Neuen Testaments und der Alten Kirche* (Berlin: De Gruyter, 1931), 184–90.

[24] Moo, *Romans*, 937, n. 2; see also Murray, *Romans*, 2:262–68; Sanday and Headlam, *Romans*, 433; Schreiner, *Romans*, 810, 816–17; Nygren, *Romans*, 457; Lenski, *Romans*, 926–27.

Prominent here again is the theme of the revelation of the gospel as the pinnacle of salvation history and as a message of universal applicability.[25]

Schreiner, with some qualification, similarly contends: "[The final sentence of the letter] is authentic, and it matches the opening (1:1–7) of the letter in a remarkable way."[26] However, the parameters of Paul's opening section should be extended all the way through 1:16–17, where he gives the letter its theme: "the righteous person will live from faith."[27]

Furthermore, the parallels cited above, together with others detailed below, validate that key connections exist among *yet another* section. This commentary titles 3:21–31 "Restatement and Expansion of the Theme."[28] Based upon 1:1–17 and drawing upon 3:21–31, Paul's ending in 16:25–27 serves appropriately *both* as a final restatement of the theme *and* a resounding doxology.

Christ as the Culmination of the Good News (16:25–26)

Powerfully Established (16:25a)

Paul frames his final words by beginning and concluding with a phrase in the dative ("now to the one … to him … ," 16:25, 27). Both of them draw together what this commentary has demonstrated throughout—Romans is primarily and dominantly a book about God.[29] Paul therefore ends the letter most appropriately by articulating further truths about God in 16:25 and 16:27.

He begins: "Now to the one who is powerfully able to establish you" (16:25a). God is characterized with an articular substantival participle[30] of the verb δύναμαι, "be able" (τῷ … δυναμένῳ, as also in Eph 3:20; Jude 24[31]). This verb carries the connotations of its cognate noun δύναμις, "power," in Rom 1:16. There Paul declares that "the Good News" is the "power [δύναμις] of God into salvation for everyone who believes." The dominant force of this noun (δύναμις) throughout Romans conveys God's *saving power* (also 1:4; 9:17; 15:13, 19).[32] Paul also uses the cognate adjective "powerful" (δυνατός) to describe the

---

[25] Moo, *Romans*, 937–38.

[26] Schreiner, *Romans*, 810.

[27] See the commentary on 1:16–17; this is also recognized by Matera, *Romans*, 330; see "Wrapping Up the Letter: Romans 15:14–16:27" before the commentary on 15:14–22.

[28] Middendorf, *Romans 1–8*, 270 (see also 277), following Melanchthon, *Romans*, 98; similarly, Witherington, *Romans*, 21.

[29] See Middendorf, *Romans 1–8*, 21–22, 27, 49–51; in this volume, see "Romans 1–4: The Righteousness of God" in the introduction to Romans 9–16, as well as "God" in "The Three Foci of Romans 9–11" in the introduction to Romans 9–11. See also the commentary on 1:17, 32; 2:11, 16, 29; 3:1–8, 19–20, 26, 29–30; 4:5, 17, 21; 9:5, 11b–12a, 16, 22–24, 29; 10:21; 11:1–2, 33–36; 12:19; 13:1–2; 14:10–12; 15:5, 8, 13. See, similarly, Hultgren, *Romans*, 26; Morris, "The Theme of Romans," 263; Hays, *Echoes of Scripture in the Letters of Paul*, 34–83, especially 52; Matera, *Romans*, 21, who declares: "From start to finish, Romans is about God."

[30] See Wallace, *Greek Grammar*, 619–21.

[31] See Giese, *2 Peter and Jude*, 360, who states: "Although Jude's reference to God's ability pertains to his omnipotence, it is his power pressed into service of his mercy."

[32] See Middendorf, *Romans 1–8*, 86–87, 364–65.

content of Abraham's faith: he believed that "what was promised [by God] and still in effect, he [God] is powerful [δυνατός] also to do" (4:21; see also 11:23). Thus Abraham "was empowered in the faith" (ἐνεδυναμώθη τῇ πίστει, 4:20), as are all of his offspring, by the God "who is powerfully able" (16:25).

In 1:11 Paul expresses his hope that his impending visit to Rome will result in the Roman Christians being "strengthened" (aorist passive infinitive στηριχθῆναι). Here he uses the same verb (στηρίζω), but in a different infinitive form (aorist active, στηρίξαι, 16:25). In this context, the translation "to establish" better conveys the meaning. As Paul proceeds to state, "the Good News" (τὸ εὐαγγέλιον, 16:25) stands as the foundational power which establishes believers in faith as God's people (see 1:16); Paul's visit to Rome, then, will strengthen the Christians there in that faith (1:11). Both the divine passive in 1:11 ("strengthened" by God) and the active form here with God as the implied subject ("able to establish you") depict God acting powerfully to accomplish these gracious blessings. There is no room for synergism, only divine monergism.[33] As Paul proceeds to explain, God works through the means of the "prophetic writings" of the OT (16:26; cf. 1:2; 15:4), through the oral proclamation of Jesus Christ (16:25; cf. 10:14–17), and now through his Word being delivered to the believers in Rome via this lengthy apostolic letter which here draws to its conclusion.

Good News—the Proclamation of Jesus Christ (16:25b)

The remainder of 16:25 and 16:26 consists of an intricate and lengthy incomplete Greek sentence which is, at the same time, compact and full of meaning. The structure of the Greek sentence can be illustrated as follows:

> ... according to my Gospel, namely, the proclamation of Jesus Christ
> in accord with the revelation of the mystery
> > having been concealed for long ages
> > but now revealed
> > and made known
> > > through [the] prophetic writings
> > > in accord with the decree of the eternal God
> > > > toward the responsive hearing of faith
> > > > into all the nations (16:25b–26)

Paul explains how God establishes the Romans within his plan of salvation with two phrases that both begin with the preposition κατά ("according to ... in accord with ... ," 16:25). First, he describes *how* God is powerfully able to establish them: it is "according to my Gospel" (κατὰ τὸ εὐαγγέλιόν μου). Paul also speaks of "my Gospel" in 2:16. In both places, the phrase refers to "the

---

[33] God alone does all the work for our salvation, including the gift of faith and preservation in the faith, which is wrought by the Holy Spirit through the power of the Word. Neither human works nor free will contributes anything. See further Article IV, "Justification," and Article XVIII, "Freedom of the Will," in both the Augsburg Confession and the Apology of the Augsburg Confession. See also the commentary on 10:16–17, 21.

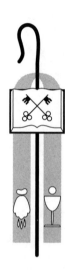

Gospel message which Paul proclaims (e.g., 1:1, 16–17)."[34] He expounded upon numerous facets of his ministry recently in 15:14–23. He sees himself as "performing priestly service [for] the Good News of God" and will not dare to speak anything except the things which Christ Jesus accomplished, particularly those Christ accomplished through him (15:16, 18).

Second, Paul appropriately restates this norm in a manner which also expresses the means by which God establishes us. He does so appositionally with an explicative (or epexegetical) καί, "namely, the proclamation of Jesus Christ" (καὶ τὸ κήρυγμα Ἰησοῦ Χριστοῦ; see the third textual note on 16:25). The objective genitive "of Jesus Christ" conveys the one being proclaimed (cf. 10:17).[35] While the noun for "proclamation" (κήρυγμα) occurs only here in Romans, the cognate verb κηρύσσω, "to proclaim," functions comparably and prominently in 10:8, 14, 15. There Paul describes how God sends the Word of the Christ out to be proclaimed to those who have not yet heard it (cf. 15:20–21). He then concludes: "Consequently, faith [comes] from hearing, and the hearing through [the] Word of Christ/[the] Messiah" (10:17: cf. 15:20–21). The noun "proclamation" (κήρυγμα) carries the same connotations of public and evangelistic preaching (see the third textual note on 16:25; see also the excursus "The New Testament Connotations and Context of Words Commonly Translated as 'Preach,' 'Teach,' and 'Prophesy' " following the commentary on 10:6–15).

Together these two synonymous phrases, "my Gospel, namely, the proclamation of Jesus Christ," encapsulate the content of Paul's message, mission, and apostolic ministry as just laid out in 15:14–22. He has also just invited the believers in Rome to participate in that very mission by supporting it (15:23–33).

A Mystery Concealed, but Now Revealed (16:25c–26a)

Paul uses the preposition κατά again, as in 16:25b with a focus on norm, in order to assert that his preaching conforms to the revealed Gospel of Christ. He declares that "my Gospel," which is "the proclamation of Jesus Christ," stands "in accord with the revelation of the mystery" (κατὰ ἀποκάλυψιν μυστηρίου, 16:25).[36] As in 2:5 and 8:19, the noun "revelation" (ἀποκάλυψις) "has its full force of the unveiling of a heavenly secret in the end time."[37] In 1:17, Paul uses the present tense of the cognate verb ἀποκαλύπτω, "reveal," to declare how this long-promised eschatological time has now arrived; the righteousness of God "is being revealed" (ἀποκαλύπτεται) in the Good News.

---

[34] Middendorf, *Romans 1–8*, 189.

[35] Those who rightly take the genitive as objective include Cranfield, *Romans*, 810; Dunn, *Romans*, 914; Lenski, *Romans*, 928; Sanday and Headlam, *Romans*, 433; and Schreiner, *Romans*, 812. Chrysostom, *Homilies on Romans*, 27 (Bray, *Romans*, ACCS NT 6:380), takes it as subjective: "In order to back up what [Paul] says, he bases it all on *the preaching of Jesus Christ*, by which he means the things that Jesus himself preached."

[36] Murray, *Romans*, 2:241, says it this way: "The 'gospel' and 'preaching' are in accordance with the revelation of the mystery."

[37] Dunn, *Romans*, 914.

This phrase ("in accord with the revelation of the mystery," 16:25) and 11:25 contain the only appearances of the noun μυστήριον, "mystery," in Romans. One can, therefore, presume a comparable content in both places, and context supports this assumption.[38] Based on 16:25 and what will soon be spelled out in 16:26, the revelation of this mystery entails the proclamation of the Good News of Christ going out to all nations so that they might hear and believe. Its disclosure, therefore, reveals how the Gentiles can also now be incorporated into the family of God simply through faith in the Gospel message of Israel's Messiah, Jesus the Christ. Paul clearly illustrates this with his olive-tree analogy in 11:16–24. That picture, along with his explanation of "mystery" (μυστήριον) in 16:25–26, should be allowed to influence and reinforce the understanding that Paul intends his hearers to grasp in 11:25–26a. *The "mystery"* which asserts that "all Israel will be saved" (11:26a) *applies to those Jews who remain in, or are regrafted into, God's one Israel through faith in the OT promises now fulfilled in Jesus Christ (11:16; the "among them" in 11:17; 11:23; cf. 15:8), together with those believing Gentiles who stand grafted into the same people of God (11:17, 25c; cf. 15:9) through that same faith (11:20; cf. 3:30).* This common understanding of both uses of "mystery" (μυστήριον) in Romans also aligns with the dominant content of the term throughout Paul's writings.[39]

On the one hand, Paul depicts this mystery as "having been concealed for long ages" (χρόνοις αἰωνίοις σεσιγημένου, 16:25). This clause conveys yet another common Pauline thought. For example, both Eph 3:9 and Col 1:26 speak of "the mystery having been hidden from the ages" (τοῦ μυστηρίου τοῦ ἀποκεκρυμμένου ἀπὸ τῶν αἰώνων, Eph 3:9; similarly, Col 1:26; cf. also 2 Tim 1:9–10; Titus 1:2–3; 1 Pet 1:20).[40] The perfect tense of "having been concealed" (σεσιγημένου) reaches back to encompass the entire OT era ever since the fall and leads up to the incarnation. It conveys what was unknown to humanity, but does not, of course, include any ignorance of the plan within the eternal will of God (see "the decree of the eternal God" in 16:26). Even here on earth, there were hints of God's intention to fulfill the promise he inaugurated in Gen 3:15 and reiterated in many and various ways numerous times afterward.[41] But exactly *how* it would come to pass was not yet revealed by God (cf. 1 Pet 1:10–11).

---

[38] So Murray, *Romans*, 2:241: "The term 'mystery' has the same connotation as in 11:25"; however, Moo, *Romans*, 939, attempts to draw a contrast.

[39] E.g., Eph 1:9; 3:3–9; 6:19; Col 1:26–27; 2:2; 4:3; 1 Tim 3:16; for a full discussion, see the commentary on Rom 11:25–26a.

[40] Cf. Dunn, *Romans*, 915.

[41] See Rom 16:20; see also Rom 1:1–2; 16:26; Heb 1:1; as well as the excursuses "Beyond Typology" following the commentary on 12:1–8 and "Paul's Use of the Old Testament in Romans" following the commentary on 15:7–13. See also Romans 4, which expounds the Abraham narrative along with the patriarchal blessing promises that build on Gen 3:15 (Gen 12:1–3; 15:1–6; 18:18; 22:15–18; 26:1–5; 28:13–15).

This situation has been *dramatically altered* by the eschatological "but now" (δὲ νῦν) which opens 16:26. It echoes the same form of expression as in 3:21 (νυνὶ δέ; see also 6:22; 7:6; cf. Col 1:26; 2 Tim 1:10). There Paul declares that the "righteousness of God has been revealed and is now out in the open" (πεφανέρωται, perfect passive indicative, Rom 3:21). Now he uses a participle of the same verb (φανερόω), "revealed" (φανερωθέντος, aorist passive, 16:26). "It was in the gospel events, the life, death, resurrection and ascension of Jesus Christ, that the mystery was manifested decisively, but there is a continuing manifestation … in the on-going proclamation of that once for all manifestation."[42]

The Mystery Made Known—Four Prepositional Propositions (16:26b)

All four of the prepositional phrases in 16:26 go with the participle "made known."[43] These phrases, in order, explain (1) one way in which the mystery was divulged and (2) then express its source/norm. These are followed by (3) a statement of the mystery's purpose and goal and, finally, (4) the direction of its outward and ongoing movement.

"Through [the] Prophetic Writings" (16:26)

The mystery was disclosed "through [the] prophetic writings" (διά … γραφῶν προφητικῶν, 16:26). In a fine example of literary framing, this phrase in the second-to-last verse of Romans coincides with what Paul wrote in the second verse of the letter. There he spoke about "the Good News of God which he promised beforehand *through his prophets in holy writings*" (διὰ τῶν προφητῶν αὐτοῦ ἐν γραφαῖς ἁγίαις, 1:1b–2). In the overall context of Romans, both phrases refer to the very same OT Scriptures.[44]

Schreiner provocatively asks: "How can the gospel be both hidden and prophesied, concealed beforehand [16:25] and anticipated in the Scriptures?"[45] Cranfield answers that question as follows:

> It is when the manifestation of the mystery is understood as the fulfilment of God's promises made in the OT (cf. 1.2), as attested, interpreted, clarified, by the OT (cf., e.g., 3.21; 9.33; 10.4–9, 11, 13, 16, 18–21; 11.2, 26[–27]), that it is truly understood as the gospel of God for all mankind.[46]

Schreiner later articulates his own answer in this way:

> The most satisfactory solution, therefore, is to acknowledge the tension. … For instance, the equal status of Jews and Gentiles in the people of God was not clearly communicated [in the OT] (cf. Eph. 3:3–6). On the other hand,

---

[42] Cranfield, *Romans*, 811.

[43] See the first and second textual notes on 16:26.

[44] Dunn, *Romans*, 915; Kruse, *Romans*, 588; Moo, *Romans*, 940; against Käsemann, *Romans*, 426, who rejects a connection with the OT and identifies these "prophetic writings" (16:26) as "the apostolic message."

[45] Schreiner, *Romans*, 812.

[46] Cranfield, *Romans*, 812.

the Pauline gospel fulfills what was prophesied in the OT. ... In light of the fulfillment readers can now perceive that what was hidden in the old is now revealed through the new. What was foreshadowed in the OT is now perceived in its true significance in light of the fulfillment that has arrived.[47]

"In Accord with the Decree of the Eternal God" (16:26)

The mystery was also made known "in accord with the decree of the eternal God" (16:26). The noun translated as "decree," ἐπιταγή, should not be viewed as consisting of a "commandment" of Law, i.e., equivalent to ἐντολή.[48] Neither does ἐπιταγή denote a "specific historical divine command, but refers [instead] to the expression of God's will."[49]

Interestingly, the Greek phrase "the eternal God" (τοῦ αἰωνίου θεοῦ) appears only here in the NT, but equivalents are attested in the OT (θεὸς αἰώνιος, LXX Gen 21:33; Is 40:28; ὁ θεὸς ... ὁ αἰώνιος, LXX Is 26:4).[50] It then extends from there to become "a familiar phrase across the spectrum of Jewish literature."[51] Thus what was hidden for a long time from humanity (16:25) nevertheless resided from eternity in the will of "the eternal God" (16:26). He is the source, and his decree is the norm by which the mystery was made known.

"Toward the Responsive Hearing of Faith" (16:26)

Paul then uses the preposition εἰς, "toward," to expresses the purpose or goal for which the Gospel mystery was made known.[52] It aims "toward the responsive hearing of faith" (εἰς ὑπακοὴν πίστεως, 16:26). For the noun ὑπακοή, "responsive hearing," as also in 1:5 and 15:18, as well as for the cognate verb ὑπακούω, "listen responsively to," in 6:17 and 10:16, a translation with "obedience" or "obey" is inadequate at best (see the commentary on 1:5; 6:17; and, especially, the extended discussion on 10:16–17). The implications of "doing" in the sense of attempting to comply with requirements, which is inherent in the English word "obedience," stand in direct contradiction to the Gospel, the Good News Paul proclaims. The basic concept of the ὑπακοή word group throughout Scripture involves "hearing under," that is, hearing and responding appropriately by believing. Thus in 16:19 "your responsive hearing" (ἡ ... ὑμῶν ὑπακοή) refers to the Christian faith of the believers in Rome. If a law or the Law is given, "obedience" involves doing it as prescribed or not doing it

---

[47] Schreiner, *Romans*, 814; see the discussion of the continuity and discontinuity between the OT and the NT presented in terms of seven "thematic polarities" by G. Goldsworthy, "Relationship of Old Testament and New Testament," *NDBT*, 86–89.

[48] As Murray, *Romans*, 2:242–43, maintains. Paul used ἐντολή to refer to the "commandment" of the divine Law, particularly a commandment in the Decalogue, in 7:8–13; 13:9.

[49] As Moo, *Romans*, 940, rightly asserts.

[50] Cf. Moo, *Romans*, 940, n. 28.

[51] Dunn, *Romans*, 916, citing, e.g., Baruch 4:8, 10, 14, 20, 22, 35; 5:2; 2 Macc 1:25; 3 Macc 6:12; *Jubilees* 12:29; 13:8; 25:15; *Sibylline Oracles* 3:698; *Testament of Moses* 10:7; Philo, *On Planting*, 8, 74, 89.

[52] Schreiner, *Romans*, 815; Cranfield, *Romans*, 812.

as proscribed. However, such a response to commandments, with the result of doing "works of the Law," is repeatedly precluded and excluded as a possible path to righteousness (3:19–20, 28; 4:4–5; 9:30–10:5). Neither is "obedience" the way of the Gospel, the Good News that God bestows his righteousness by his grace alone and that it is received through faith alone. And "my Gospel" (τὸ εὐαγγέλιόν μου, 16:25) is the context in which "the responsive hearing [ὑπακοή] of faith" is to be heard here in 16:26.

Paul explains this most fully from 9:30–10:17. After excluding the way of works (9:30–10:5), he powerfully articulates the righteousness from faith extensively in 10:6–17. When the Good News of Christ is proclaimed, the appropriate and divinely intended desire is that people "listen responsively to" (ὑπακούω), that is, "believe" (πιστεύω), the Gospel message (10:16).[53] For Paul, faith stands antithetical to works (e.g., Rom 3:28; 4:4–5; Gal 2:16; 3:2). Thus the Word of Christ, when heard, creates and establishes faith in the heart ("faith [comes] from hearing … through [the] Word of Christ/[the] Messiah," 10:17), and this faith passively receives the righteousness of God in Jesus Christ ("the righteousness from faith," 10:6; "with the heart it is being believed into righteousness," 10:10). Therefore in 16:26, as with the identical phrase in 1:5, Paul depicts the purpose for which God decrees that the Gospel be made known. It aims "toward the responsive hearing of faith" (εἰς ὑπακοὴν πίστεως, 16:26). Kruse maintains the confusing use of "obedience," but properly grasps that it "consists in faith in the gospel."[54] Similarly, he correctly concludes that in 1:5 "obedience appears to be acceptance of the gospel call to believe in Christ, that is, the obedience that consists in faith."[55] As 10:16–17 makes clear, this "responsive hearing of faith" (1:5; 16:26) comes from hearing the Word of Christ (10:17) and stands equivalent to believing it (10:16).[56]

"Into All the Nations" (16:26)

Finally, the outward and ongoing movement of the mystery extends "into all the nations" (εἰς πάντα τὰ ἔθνη, 16:26). The mystery now made known is the Good News of Christ *for all*. As 10:14–15 and 10:18 describe, God sends out his messengers into all the world to herald that news. Through their "proclamation of Jesus Christ" (16:25), God delivers his salvation and righteousness to all who hear and believe (10:8–11), that is, to all who receive it with "the responsive hearing of faith" (16:26).

---

[53] Theodoret of Cyrus, *Romans* (Bray, *Romans*, ACCS NT 6:381), puts it this way: "The obedience of faith is the result of the preaching of the gospel."

[54] Kruse, *Romans*, 589.

[55] Kruse, *Romans*, 51.

[56] Lenski, *Romans*, 931: "The obedience lies in the act of believing." However, one might quibble with his use of "act." For interpreting the phrase εἰς ὑπακοὴν πίστεως in 1:5 and 16:26, he references the German "compound term: *Glaubensgehorsam*." It combines the noun "faith" (*Glaube*) with a cognate of the verb "to hear" (*hören*; cf. the noun *Hören*, "hearing").

The neuter plural noun ἔθνη is translated as "nations" in 16:26 rather than "Gentiles" (as also in 15:11; see the commentary there). This translation emphasizes that the Gospel reaches out and seeks to encompass all people, Jews as well as Gentiles.[57] "For there is not a difference [between] a Jew and a Greek, for the same Lord [is] of all, being rich to all the ones who are calling on him. For 'everyone who ever might call on the name of [the] Lord will be saved' " (10:12–13). This also stands consistent with words Paul cites from Isaiah at the end of Romans 10, applying them sequentially to the Gentiles and then to Israel:

> [20]But Isaiah is bold and says: "I was found among the ones not seeking me; I became visible to the ones not inquiring after me." [21]But to Israel he says: "The whole day I stretched out my hands to an unpersuaded and contradicting people." (Rom 10:20–21, quoting Is 65:1, 2)

And his hands still remain stretched out to those in Israel who do not now believe (see Rom 11:1–2, 5–6, 14–15); "for God is powerful [δυνατός] to graft them in again," if only "they do not remain in unbelief" (11:23). In fact, the Good News is the "power of God into salvation for everyone who believes, to Jew first and also to Greek" (1:16). Such was the movement of Jesus' ministry, first to the lost sheep of Israel and then to all nations (Mt 15:24; 28:19), and so it is with Paul's (see the excursus "Beyond Typology" following the commentary on 12:1–8). Pelagius summarizes it all this way:

> The mystery of the calling of all the Gentiles, which through Paul's gospel, using the testimonies of the prophets, had now been plainly disclosed in Christ, had long been hidden in the law. Although the prophets had said many things about the Gentiles, none had recognized as clearly as Paul how Gentiles and Jews would become one in Christ.[58]

To God Is the Glory! Amen! (16:27)

The final statement of the letter utters a doxology with the same type of God-centered dative expression with which Paul began this brief section. Rom 16:25 opens with "to the one who is powerfully able" (τῷ δὲ δυναμένῳ, see the commentary on 16:25). Now 16:27 concludes comparably: "To [the] only, wise God, through Jesus Christ—to him [is] the glory into the ages. Amen" (μόνῳ σοφῷ θεῷ, διὰ Ἰησοῦ Χριστοῦ, ᾧ ἡ δόξα εἰς τοὺς αἰῶνας, ἀμήν).[59]

In this appellation to God, the two Greek adjectives (μόνῳ σοφῷ) translated as "only, wise," both describe the God to whom all glory belongs. In English

---

[57] Moo, *Romans*, 940, speaks of its "universal applicability," though universal *availability* might be more accurate.

[58] Pelagius, *Romans* (Bray, *Romans*, ACCS NT 6:381).

[59] Interestingly, Jude 24–25 provides further parallels with Rom 16:25 and 16:27. Giese, *2 Peter and Jude*, 361–62, observes that in Jude 25,

> Jude attributes all praise μόνῳ θεῷ σωτῆρι ἡμῶν διὰ Ἰησοῦ Χριστοῦ τοῦ κυρίου ἡμῶν, "to the only God, our Savior, through Jesus Christ our Lord," which stands in apposition to τῷ δὲ δυναμένῳ, "to him who is able" (Jude 24).

they may appear to conflate into a single reference to the "only wise God."[60] However, Paul declares two truths. First, 3:30 asserts: "God is one" (εἷς ὁ θεός); now this phrase similarly states that he is the "only" (μόνῳ) God. Second, this one, true God is defined as "wise" (σοφῷ). Instead of understanding the assertion purely in terms of intelligence, Moo reminds us that "God's 'wisdom,' as in 11:33, has to do with his 'wise' plan for salvation history."[61] This salvific thought echoes resoundingly throughout the doxology of 11:33–36 (see the commentary on 11:33). Paul speaks comparably of how God's saving wisdom is centered in Christ in 1 Cor 1:20–25 and 3:18–20.

The next phrase, "through Jesus Christ" (διὰ Ἰησοῦ Χριστοῦ, Rom 16:27), then flows logically from "wise." The second and third phrases at the beginning of the doxology state: "according to my Gospel, namely, the proclamation of Jesus Christ" (16:25b). Thus a reference to Christ appropriately belongs in the second-to-last phrase as well. Paul can speak of Christ himself as "the wisdom of God" (1 Cor 1:24) and as the one "in whom all the treasures of the wisdom and knowledge [τῆς σοφίας καὶ γνώσεως] are hidden [ἀπόκρυφοι]" (Col 2:3).[62] But, *just as with the mystery (11:25; 16:25), those once concealed treasures are now revealed and made known in the very same Christ*, "who became wisdom [σοφία] for us from God, also righteousness and holiness and redemption" (1 Cor 1:30). Franzmann describes how Paul's hearers then and now

> bow in adoration before the God whose wisdom guides all history toward His goal, to the glory of His grace. Faith sees that goal and glory even now and gives God glory through Him in whom God's glory has appeared, through Jesus Christ.[63]

The concluding clause of the letter literally begins "to whom" (ᾧ, 16:27b) but is rendered as "to him." Although it could refer to "Jesus Christ," it more likely refers to the "only, wise God" (see the first textual note on 16:27). Yet, as Paul has also just stated, Jesus "is our only Mediator even for this approach to God."[64] Therefore, all those in Christ are able to confidently join in granting God the Father the acclaim which surely *all, and already, belongs to him*.[65] As Morris puts it: "To this God is ascribed glory forever through Jesus Christ."[66]

---

[60] That rendering might be open to the misinterpretation that there could be other gods who are not (as) wise. To prevent such a misunderstanding the GNT translates with "to the only God, who alone is all-wise."

[61] Moo, *Romans*, 940.

[62] Theodoret of Cyrus, *Romans* (Bray, *Romans*, ACCS NT 6:381), points this out by stating: "If the heretics try to use this [verse] to prove that Christ is not God, it should be remembered that Christ not only is called wise, he is even called *Wisdom*."

[63] Franzmann, *Romans*, 282.

[64] Lenski, *Romans*, 933.

[65] Lenski, *Romans*, 933, properly suggests assuming a present indicative verb: "he to whom through Jesus Christ the glory (belongs) to the eons." For this commentary's use of the bracketed "is" in the translation, see the second textual note on 16:27.

[66] Morris, *Romans*, 547.

Thus we do *not* make God any more glorious than he already is. Instead, when we join in Paul's affirmation "to him [is] the glory into the ages" (16:27b), we simply and profoundly acknowledge that our righteous God (3:26; cf. 1:17) rightly possesses all glory, both now and forever.[67]

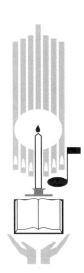

As with Johann Sebastian Bach's custom of writing at the end of each piece of his magnificent music *S.D.G.* (*soli Deo gloria*, "to God alone the glory"), so this acclamation provides a most fitting conclusion to Paul's most influential letter. For in it

> he speaks of Abraham giving glory to God by his unwavering faith (4:20). He urges his Roman audience to bring praise to God by accepting one another (15:7). He [similarly] encourages the Corinthian believers to glorify God in whatever they do (1 Cor 10:31), and reminds them that when they add their "Amen" to the promises of God it brings glory to God (2 Cor 1:20).[68]

So here, the final Greek word of Romans, ἀμήν, *amen*, simply transliterates the Hebrew word אָמֵן, from the root whose forms can mean "believe," "faith," and "be faithful, trustworthy" (see the third textual note and the commentary on 9:5). Faith receives the saving righteousness of the only, wise God and affirms that he remains powerfully and eternally able to accomplish all that he promises in and through the Good News of "Jesus Christ our Lord."[69] He is utterly trustworthy and forever faithful.[70] Upon that sure and solid foundation, "the righteous person will live from faith" (Rom 1:17b, quoting Hab 2:4).

The voice of faith then responds, as it did from within Paul and as it has from believers throughout the ages, by adding its own ongoing "amen!"[71]

---

[67] Lenski, *Romans*, 933, comparably concludes: " 'He is the one *to whom* the glory,' etc. And we need not supply εἴη or ἔστω, 'be' the glory, for the Greek uses the dative with ἐστί to indicate possession."

[68] Kruse, *Romans*, 589.

[69] Rom 1:4; 5:21; 7:25; cf. 5:1, 11; 6:23; 8:39; 15:6, 30; 16:18, 20, 25. For the thematic use of this phrase, particularly in Romans 5–8, see Middendorf, *Romans 1–8*, 377–79.

[70] When Jesus speaks, he often begins his trustworthy and true words with "amen" (e.g., Mt 5:18, 26), and in the Gospel of John it is always the double "amen, amen" (e.g., Jn 1:51; 3:3, 5, 11; 6:53; 10:1; 21:18). Indeed, Jesus himself is "the Amen, the faithful and true witness/ martyr" (Rev 3:14).

[71] The continual prayer of the church on earth is "Amen. Come, Lord Jesus" (Rev 22:20). The simultaneous worship in heaven also utters the "amen" (Rev 5:14). After Christ's return, the eternal praise of the saints in the church triumphant will be bracketed with it: "*Amen*! The blessing and the glory and the wisdom and the thanksgiving and the honor and the power and the strength [belong] to our God forever and ever! *Amen*!" (Rev 7:12).

Index of Subjects

Index of Passages

Galatians